THE ENCYCLOPEDIA OF SURFING

The Encyclopedia of Surfing

MATT WARSHAW

HARCOURT, INC.
Orlando Austin New York San Diego Toronto London

Copyright © 2003 by Matt Warshaw
Foreword copyright © 2003 by William Finnegan

All rights reserved. No part of this publication may be
reproduced or transmitted in any form or by any means,
electronic or mechanical, including photocopy, recording,
or any information storage and retrieval system, without
permission in writing from the publisher.

Requests for permission to make copies of any part of
the work should be mailed to the following address:
Permissions Department, Harcourt, Inc.,
6277 Sea Harbor Drive, Orlando, Florida 32887-6777.

Photo credits appear on page 773.

www.HarcourtBooks.com

Library of Congress Cataloging-in-Publication Data
Warshaw, Matt, 1960–
The encyclopedia of surfing/Matt Warshaw.—1st ed.
p.   cm.
Includes bibliographical references.
ISBN 0-15-100579-6
1. Surfing—Encyclopedias.   I. Title.
GV840.S8W3476 2003
797.3'2—dc21   2003005274

Text set in ITC Stone Serif
Designed by Kaelin Chappell

Printed in the United States of America

First Edition
K J I H G F E D C

INTRODUCTION

When does a subject become a candidate for its own encyclopedia? There isn't a formula or set of guidelines, but at some point the thing in question takes on enough history, depth, and color, expands beyond some invisible mark, and is ready to be disassembled and reconstituted as an A-to-Z reference book. Surfing has reached that point. I've been reminded of this at regular intervals since 1996, when the idea for a surfing encyclopedia first crossed my mind. Many recent surf-related events and milestones are plainly, prodigiously, quantitative: $4.5 billion in aggregate surf industry sales for 2002, or the October 1999 issue of *Surfer* magazine coming in at a hefty 340 pages. Other markers, smaller but no less compelling, include a PBS-aired documentary on big-wave riding, commemorative U.S. Postal Service stamps honoring surfing patriarch Duke Kahanamoku and the board-carrying woody station wagon, and obituary notices for well-known surfers in *Time, Newsweek,* and the *New York Times.* Add to this the introduction of women-only surf magazines, the antique surfboard sold at auction for $18,500, and the campaign poster for Hawaiian gubernatorial candidate Fred Hemmings showing the former world champion leaning into a back-arched bottom turn, with the slogan: "Hemmings: He Doesn't Golf."

Time for an encyclopedia.

Database software was installed on my home computer, followed by a long, slow, sometimes groping formatting process. Fifteen hundred A through Z entries were eventually assigned to one of four primary categories—people, place, culture, science/technology—further sorted by secondary classifications, and finally given an assigned word length between 100 and 1,000, for a book-length total of roughly 500,000 words. The idea, before the first entry was researched or written, was to throw a light, evenly distributed framework across the entire length and breadth of the sport. Each entry candidate was a negotiation. Ratios were struck between men and women; between surf breaks, surf regions, and surf countries; between surfboard-related design and wave-related oceanography. The shortboard revolution had to square with the longboard renaissance. The New Era wanted parity with the New School. Quotas were filled for surfing photographers, writers, editors, moviemakers, videographers, businessmen, and organization leaders. Relative word lengths were calculated for essays on television and surfing, sharks and surfing, racism and surfing, war and surfing, nudity and surfing, cars and surfing.

Nearly half of the 1,500 entry slots were taken up by people and, not surprisingly, this is where the in or out decisions were hardest. A surfer's contest results and rankings were often used as a starting point, but rarely as a decider. Barry Kanaiaupuni's ninth-place finish on the 1976 world pro tour for example, his best year-end result, barely hints at his exalted position in the surf world pantheon. Author subjectivity, meanwhile, had a magnetic pull on the whole project and had to be checked continuously. (And indulged occasionally—Kanaiaupuni's mention here surely comes from my flash-indoctrination to the cult of power surfing, at age 13, during a sequence in the 1974 surf movie *Fluid Drive* set to Jimi Hendrix's "Voodoo Chile," where the dark-haired Hawaiian rides like Thor up and down the giant faces at Sunset Beach.)

With all entries named, ranked, and classified, it was on to researching and writing 1,500 separate blocks of text, each of which needed to be factual but not dry, compact but not cramped, surfy but not flippant. Print sources included roughly 250 surf-related books, primarily histories, biographies, and autobiographies, along with more than 500 articles from mainstream newspapers and magazines, including *Time, Outside, Sports Illustrated, Life, Newsweek,* the *New York Times,* the *Los Angeles Times, USA Today,* and the *San Francisco Chronicle.* Past and present English-language surf magazines were consulted almost by the minute, with most queries resolved by searches in *Surfer, Surfing, The Surfer's Journal, Surf Guide, Wahine, Eastern Surf Magazine, Australia's Surfing Life, Tracks, Petersen's Surfing,* and *Longboard.* The annual *Association of Surfing Professionals Media Guide* was invaluable for world pro tour statistics.

Nearly every living surfer in the *Encyclopedia* was contacted and asked a series of biographic questions; for the deceased, information was gathered from print sources, or friends and family. Fact sheets were created for all entries on breaks, regions, and countries worldwide, plus U.S. states; much of the wave- and weather-related information for these was gleaned from the *Surf Report* and the *Stormrider Guide* books, while regional surf history (first surfers, surf shops, and local surf organizations) was gathered with the assistance of longtime resident surfers. Research assistants Nathan Myers and Marcus Sanders set up DSL-equipped workstations here in my home office; e-mails were sent and received by the thousands, the phone lines were in near-constant use, megabytes of raw information were cut, pasted, and entered into the *Encyclopedia* database, and 1,500 entries were first-drafted at a rate of about three a day. A few dozen entries were eliminated as the project progressed; about the same number were added. Then a final change of gears for fact-checking and editing, an opening essay on the sport's history, and the creation of a set of appendices on surf-related books, magazines, movies, contest results, and music albums. My folly to think the whole enterprise, start to finish, would take 18 months. We clocked out instead at just over three years.

In many ways, and despite a pretty large outlay of time, energy, and money, the finished book, for me, retains an air of improbability. Printed and bound, held at arm's length, it appears to have the required encyclopedic heft and scope. The details are vetted and checked. The anecdotes and quotes seem to break up the book's requisite neutral voice. *The Encyclopedia of Surfing,* I believe, delivers on its promise of being a definitive single-volume book on the sport.

But "definitive" doesn't seem entirely right. Surfing, in fact, as it exists in these pages, is only sketched, not defined. I took on this project in part because it seemed as if I already had the sport's measure; that I knew its basic shape and contours the way I know the rooms of my own home. But the boundaries only expanded and the terrain grew more complex and interesting as the book progressed. This is a daunting notion, on one hand, because I intend to write, revise, and expand a second edition of *The Encyclopedia of Surfing* before 2010, and it plainly won't be a mail-in job. But it's a satisfying notion as well. Surfing itself has proven up to the task of filling out a comprehensive reference book. I've come to the end of the *Encyclopedia,* in fact, knowing that the subject is so big and rich that only a highly distilled version can fit into 800 pages—and that some vital matter has likely slipped by altogether and continues to roll on, as indefinable as it is beautiful.

Matt Warshaw
San Francisco, CA
—2003

Surfing as a subject really has no edges. It's not like baseball or aviation or beekeeping, where the relevant information—box scores, airports, honey produced—is more or less identifiable. Organized competition, for instance, takes up only a small corner of the surfing world. There is a loose set of enterprises known as the surf industry, which surfers depend on for equipment (though it seems geared mainly to selling sunglasses by wrapping them in the mystique of surfing), but if it were to vanish tomorrow nearly all surfers would somehow carry on with their wave-riding lives. So surfing, in a way, has no center, no institutional structure—no obvious place to start or finish the kind of monumental project of intellectual organization represented by the book you hold in your hands.

There are, of course, great and famous surfers, whose influence and inspiration are widely felt, and great and famous waves that every surfer dreams about riding. These are some of the shoo-in entries for an encyclopedia of surfing. But it is in the nature of the sport, somehow, that there are even more great surfers who are not famous, and an unknowable number of great spots that still break unridden, or are ridden by only a few discreet devotees. ("Lo pro bro" is the term of art here.) It's sometimes said that surfing is a religious practice more than it is a sport, and there is certainly something deeply private about it for many of us—not just the untranslatably personal experience of riding waves, but the fact that most surf sessions take place in utter obscurity, leaving no public record, no tangible mark on the world.

Matt Warshaw knows all this. He lives and surfs at Ocean Beach, San Francisco, which is one of the lonelier, more humbling and capricious spots around. He is also surfing's foremost scholar and scribe. As editor, author, screenwriter, journalist, and consummate niche savant, he's spent decades sifting through historical memorabilia and the riprap of daily surf life for the scattered gold of the newsworthy, the meaningful, the amusing, the lore that's worth preserving. He is definitely the only person I know, or know of, who could have tackled with any hope of success the job of sorting and distilling the whole, hopelessly diffuse body of surf-related knowledge into a useful, authoritative encyclopedia. Even so, this is a totally idiosyncratic magnum opus. I know that Matt and his research team built a database full of primary and secondary classifications, arcane ratios and quotas, and that they consulted thousands of sources, all toward creating an "evenly distributed framework across the entire length and breadth of the sport." Still, the project as a whole is at least half mad, which helps give it, to my mind, a glittering vitality that precious few reference works attain. Matt acknowledges his own subjectivity, and he battled it, by his own testimony, with exhaustive peer review and extra research in sensitive cases, all of which did not succeed, fortunately, in purging the finished work of innumerable quirks.

Leafing idly, one passes from a blow-by-blow description of an epic swell-producing cyclone off the coast of Queensland in 1982 to an entry on Angola, featuring oil-field workers who surf only under armed guard, and then on to a fine short essay on ding repair. I'm sure that each of these anecdotes and disquisitions, along with ten thousand others, belong somewhere on an evenly distributed framework. But that careful framework stretches, I would argue, not across a vast, edgeless field of tangentially related phenomena—certain reefs, minor celebrities, hydrodynamic discoveries—that, taken all together, constitute "surfing." The true framework instead delineates the capacious, discriminating mind and archives—the manic curiosity and Talmudic diligence—of Matt Warshaw. And that is simply much more interesting country than the data world of conventional sports almanacs. It's rock-solid on the facts, of course, but quietly funny and consistently original in their selection and expression.

A magazine article, published while he was somewhere in the middle of this massive task, called Warshaw "the Madame Winchester of surf writing." Madame Winchester was a nutty nineteenth-century heiress to a gun-making fortune. She was reportedly told by a psychic that she wouldn't die as long as she kept adding on to her California mansion, and so she kept a brigade of carpenters busy for decades, building and unbuilding hundreds of rooms. It was an ominous simile, you could say, but Matt, with the publication of this book, has lived it down. This is his mansion, complete (at least until the next edition) and extraordinarily well furnished.

For the initiated, it's full of things that you feel you should have already known. It's a sour sort of pleasure to learn, say, that Mark Richards used to shill for Kentucky Fried Chicken, but I'm still glad to know that. The introduction of surfing to France, through a California screenwriter working in Biarritz on a film of *The Sun Also Rises*, makes a neat little story, and it's especially good to have it from such a reliable source. There are, inevitably, countless choices and considered omissions for the cognoscenti to stew over and debate. (Why "dogs and surfing" but no Dogtown? Is that some kind of self-censoring South Bay reverse bias at work?)

For non-surfers, this book will provide a terrific peephole into an elaborate and esoteric world. Its built-in emphasis on the public sphere may seem to belie my contention above about the essentially solitary quality of most surfers' experience. But there is actually a powerful paradox at the heart of the sport. One pursues a kind of satori, an electrifying asocial bliss, through years of hard effort and ocean study. At the same time, almost all surfers love to be watched (at least when they're ripping). They're performing, they're competing, and they love to surf better—and to be *seen* to surf better—than their friends.

So part of surfing takes place inside society, in sanctioned spots, even in commercialized zones, and an encyclopedia naturally highlights this visible and conventional side of the story. But surfing's vitality, I want to say, flows largely from elsewhere—from its consuming relationship with the wildness and violence of the ocean, from the obsessiveness that is required to get any good at it, and from its outlaw roots as an idle, barbarous pastime abhorred by the prim and industrious. Surfing has a scruffy, even avant-garde, side that has always attracted free spirits. It privileges, as an academic might say, personal satisfaction over social production, animal joy over a steady job. Although fundamentally apolitical, the simple fact of its popularity carries, in most places and contexts, a whiff of dissent, a faintly anarchistic suggestion about what really matters.

Becoming a competent surfer actually does bear a resemblance to joining some rigorous cult. And this book will, I believe, become one of the sect's principal texts. It's a grand compendium of the tribe's arcana. And, in an odd way, a surfing encyclopedia seems to me to come along just in time. Part of learning to surf has always been absorbing the lore. I started surfing in the sixties, and there was already much to absorb then—the names of the elders and their exploits, the fabled breaks, the fabled sessions, the reigning hotshots. There were a few books around, and there were always the surf mags, but there was nothing comprehensive. The closest thing to a bible we had was the *Surfing Guide to Southern California,* which was a wonderful spot-by-spot guidebook, compiled and written by David Stern and William Cleary. My friends and I practically memorized the book, and we certainly knew all the pithy, clever picture captions by heart. There is something in surfing that craves a literature that rings true. But then surfing's popularity boomed. And boomed again. What had been the eccentric pursuit of a few zealots became a mass phenomenon. Worldwide, the number of surfers today is said to approach twenty million. A subculture so immense is a contradiction in terms and breeds a kind of internal frenzy. Nothing can be allowed to stay the same. Board designs change constantly. High-performance surfing mutates endlessly. New heroes, a new aesthetics, seem to scream across the sky every month. New spots are discovered, new frontiers crossed. Aerials, tow-ins, giant Tasmanian death barrels. Somebody has to go surf Antarctica. The lore of surfing, in other words, has been expanding relentlessly and alarmingly for a long time now. It's like the universe, as cosmologists have come to understand it. But no one knows what to do about the universe. Surfing, blessedly, has Matt Warshaw.

William Finnegan

"The Most Supreme Pleasure": Premodern Surfing

Inca fishermen in what is now northern Peru may have been riding waves on their streamlined bundled-reed *cabillitos* as far back as 3000 B.C., and chances are that other temperate-zone premoderns also discovered the singular thrill of riding an incoming swell—if not on a watercraft of some kind, then by simply bodysurfing. But surfing as it exists today is a Polynesian invention, with most of the development taking place in the Hawaiian Islands. Stand-up surfing (as opposed to bellyboarding or kneeboarding) likely began around A.D. 1000 and was soon deeply integrated into Hawaiian culture, practiced by commoners and royalty, young and old, men, women, and children. Villages were nearly deserted when a good swell arrived, as everyone took to the waves; top surfers met in competitions that drew hundreds of spectators and featured wagering at all levels—from fishing nets and pigs to servitude or even life itself. Myths, legends, and chants passed from generation to generation, dramatizing surfers and surfing feats of the past. Surfboards were made from felled hardwood tree trunks, either koa, breadfruit, or wiliwili wood. They were rough-shaped with an ax, smoothed with a handheld piece of coral, sanded with stones, then rubbed to a finish with tree roots or bark. Boards came in three types: the *paipo* was ridden on the belly and used mainly by children; the *alaia,* between seven and 12 feet long, was ridden prone, kneeling, or standing; and the imposing *olo,* up to 17 feet, was used by royalty only. The Big Island of Hawaii had the greatest concentration of surfers, followed by Oahu.

Eighteenth-century British sea captain and explorer James Cook, during his third and final transpacific voyage, came upon a canoe surfer in Tahiti in 1777. "I could not help concluding," Cook noted appreciatively in his ship's log, "that this man felt the most supreme pleasure while he was driven on so fast and smoothly by the sea." One of Cook's officers wrote a few months afterward about the "great art" of stand-up surfing, as seen in Hawaii. A few decades later, engravings made by European visitors afforded a romantic glimpse of the still-atavistic Hawaiian surfing life. In one, a ranking Big Island native stands proudly in front of his house, holding a spear, with his *olo* board laid out in prominent display in the foreground. In another, a pair of barebreasted native women lounge seductively in the surf zone atop their wooden boards. American Calvinist missionaries founded their first Hawaiian settlements in 1820, and took a much sterner view of local culture. As the visitors established a de facto theocracy, surfing was disparaged as nonproductive, licentious, and dangerous. It wasn't banned outright, but left to wither as surf-related festivals were canceled, while gambling and coed recreation—even leisure itself—were denounced as immoral. By 1892, as a missionary's son noted with a touch of bitterness, surfing had all but vanished under "the touch of civilization," and surfboards were rarely seen outside of local museums. Meanwhile, without natural immunity to European- and American-borne diseases, natives died by the thousands; it was later estimated that the Hawaiian population was reduced by 90 percent between Cook's arrival and the close of the 19th century.

Revival and Expansion (1900–45)

Surfing revived and flourished in the opening years of the 20th century, as religious authority in Hawaii was replaced by the secular interests of tourism and agriculture. The broad wave field at Waikiki was all but synonymous with the newly invigorated sport; Duke Kahanamoku, George Freeth, and Alexander Hume Ford were the period's leading figures. The Irish-Hawaiian Freeth is often credited as the first of the revivalists to ride standing up (others remained on their bellies or knees) and the first to angle across the wave instead of heading straight for shore. The energetic Ford, born in South Carolina, took to the surf immediately upon his arrival in Hawaii in 1907, became the sport's greatest proselytizer, and the following year formed the Outrigger Canoe Club in Waikiki—surfing's first organization. Ford also introduced Freeth to visiting American writer Jack London, who published a feature article on surfing in a 1907 issue of *Woman's Home Companion,* giving Americans their first detailed account of the sport. It was, London wrote, "a royal sport for the natural kings of earth." (Mark Twain had visited Hawaii 50 years earlier and, as part of an article dispatched to the *Sacramento Union,* recalled his failed attempt at surfing. "The board struck the shore in three-quarters of a second, without any cargo, and I struck the bottom about the same time, with a couple of barrels of water in me.") Freeth had by that time sailed to the mainland and introduced surfing to Southern California with a series of demonstrations at Los Angeles and Orange County beaches in 1907 and 1908, first at Venice, then Redondo, Huntington, and elsewhere. For decades, it was believed that Freeth was mainland America's first surfer. It was later revealed that Hawaiian siblings Jonah, David, and Edward Kawananakoa, while attending boarding school near Santa Cruz in 1885, took to the surf at the San Lorenzo rivermouth using redwood boards of their own design. Locals may have followed, but the sport didn't catch on, almost certainly because the northern California water was too cold.

Ford's promotion of the new sport continued with his 1909 article in *Collier's,* where he noted that among Waikiki's "surfboard enthusiasts" were "judges of the Supreme Court in Hawaii, their wives and daughters, ex-Governors and their families, and the greater portion of the prominent businessmen." By this time the teenage Duke Kahanamoku was recognized as Waikiki's finest surfer. He became internationally famous as a gold medal swimmer in the 1912 Olympics, held in Stockholm; while traveling to and from Europe he surfed with Freeth in California, and introduced the sport to the American East Coast, at Atlantic City, New Jersey. In late 1914 and early 1915, he gave well-attended surfing demonstrations in Australia and New Zealand. Along with being a peerless boardrider, graceful and athletic, Kahanamoku put a friendly, gracious, even regal face on the sport; it also helped that the broad-shouldered Hawaiian was, as a female sculptor put it, "the most magnificent human male that God ever put on this earth."

Surfers at the time generally used redwood plank boards measuring 10 feet long and weighing 65 pounds, and wave-riding style was dictated by the heavy equipment: a narrow, straight-backed stance, with head and chin up. Angling was a part of the advanced surfer's repertoire, but the finless boards had to be coaxed slowly into any kind of change in direction, straight-off rides were common, and surfers often demonstrated their command by simply posing with arms bowed and flexed. Waikiki was by then becoming an international vacation spot of choice for the wealthy and glamorous, and surfing's image was in large part defined by photographs of handsome, glistening men and women racing for shore on wind-burnished walls of water, with Diamond Head in the background; Amelia Earhart, Babe Ruth, and Prince Albert were among the celebrities who took to the surf at Waikiki, and wave-riding was briefly featured in Hollywood movies like *Bird of Paradise* and *Waikiki Wedding*. A loose confederation of professional beachboys worked as tourist guides along the Waikiki beaches, spending their off-hours surfing, making music, and "talking story," and helping to give the sport a relaxed demeanor.

Small surf communities formed in California during this period, from the San Francisco Bay Area to San Diego. Regional surf clubs were organized, and the 1928-founded Pacific Coast Surf Riding Championships—first held in Corona del Mar, then San Onofre—brought together dozens of the best surfers from up and down the coast. (George Freeth had died in the 1919 flu epidemic, but not before he'd become the country's first professional beach lifeguard, and made dozens of celebrated rescues, allowing the surfer to be presented as gallant beachfront protector.) Wisconsin-born Tom Blake took first in the debut Pacific Coast event, riding a hollow board of his own design. Blake's "cigar-box" hollows—longer, lighter, and more tippy than the planks—were being made commercially in Los Angeles by the early '30s, and helped introduce the sport to hundreds of newcomers. Blake was also the era's original surf photographer (a portfolio of his work was published in a 1935 issue of *National Geographic*), innovator of the surfboard fin (in 1935), and author of the first surfing book (*Hawaiian Surfboard*, also in 1935) as well as build-it-yourself surfboard articles in *Popular Mechanics* and *Popular Science.*

Things developed along similar lines in Australia, where surfers were regarded as a subset of the Australian Surf Life Saving Association. Sydney was the national wave-riding hub, but by the early '40s lifeguard clubs, filled with surfers, were established in the states of Queensland, Victoria, South Australia, and Western Australia. Surfers here favored hollow boards over planks, in large part because the hollows were used by lifeguards as rescue vehicles.

Surfboard design took an important step forward in 1937, when a group of Honolulu teenagers, including John Kelly and Wally Froiseth, developed the narrow-tailed hot curl board, which allowed the rider to maintain a tighter angle across the wave. With their new boards, Kelly, Froiseth, and a few others began searching out bigger and more challenging waves at places like Makaha on the west side of Oahu. Plank-riding surfers generally were unable to ride waves over six feet; the hot curl surfers were soon challenging waves up to 12 or even 15 feet.

World War II brought an end to modern surfing's pioneering phase as surfers enlisted and shipped out, and many popular beaches—including Waikiki—were requisitioned by the military and lined in barbed wire to guard against a feared Japanese submarine attack. Surfing colonies had been established in Durban, South Africa, and Lima, Peru, and up and down the American eastern seaboard; the sport was exported the following decade to France, England, and Spain, with Brazil, Canada, Ireland, and other countries soon to follow.

From the Malibu Headwaters (1945–66)

Malibu replaced Waikiki after World War II as the clearinghouse for nearly all surf-related matters. The beautifully foiled point waves at Malibu became the standard against which all other breaks were measured, and the war-weary surfers drawn to this temperate corner of the coast began to develop a set of characteristics particular to their sport—relaxed and easygoing, but also insolent and elitist—that would later provide a framework for baby boomer surfer rebelliousness. A small group of Los Angeles–area surfboard builders, including Bob Simmons, Joe Quigg, Matt Kivlin, and Dale Velzy, used Malibu as a test track when they retooled the heavy, finless, cumbersome plank board. (Neither the hot curl board nor the Blake-designed fin had become popular on the mainland.) Lightweight balsa replaced redwood as the primary board-building material, dropping the board's weight to less than 30 pounds; a fin was added, and the entire board was covered with a protective skin of resin-saturated fiberglass. The front was scooped up to help prevent the nose from "pearling," or digging into the water; the edges were thinned and tapered for added maneuverability. On their new Malibu chips, surfers by the late '40s were able to perform rudimentary turns and cutbacks, and were soon stepping forward to ride the nose. In 1956, a group of California lifeguard/surfers introduced the chip to Australian beaches, where hollow boards were still the rule. Australian surfers converted almost overnight to the new boards, and in doing so drove a wedge into the traditional Aussie lifeguard-surfer alliance, as the guards dismissed the chip as having no use for rescue work.

Three surf shops had meanwhile opened in California—Hobie Surfboards and Velzy Surfboards in Southern California, and Jack O'Neill's Surf Shop in San Francisco—and the first surfing wetsuits were being sold. Polyurethane began to replace balsa as the board's core material in 1956, and by the end of the decade the balsa board was all but obsolete.

But none of these growth indicators could have predicted the success of *Gidget,* Frederick Kohner's 1957 novel based on his teenage daughter's introduction to surfing and romance at Malibu. A few months after the book's release *Life* magazine followed with "Gidget Makes the Grade," a photo feature showing Kathy "Gidget" Kohner riding waves and hanging out on the beach, and the surfer's ongoing shift from noble sportsman to bleached-blond rebel continued as *Life* quoted an anonymous Malibu regular as scorning the very idea of a surfing novel. "If I had a couple of bucks to buy a book," he said, "I wouldn't. I'd buy some beer." Hollywood's version of *Gidget,* released in 1959, was even more popular, and teenage surfing neophytes took to the California beaches by the thousands. Smaller but equally energetic surf booms followed on the East Coast and in Australia, and beachfront municipalities—worried about the danger posed by mixing surfers and swimmers, but also looking to maintain control over a lively new breed of teenager whose ranks were known to be filled with "gremmies," "hodads," and "surf hooligans"—began to pass surf-restrictive legislation. Sydney surfers had to buy registration stickers for their boards; surfing was banned outright in Palm Beach, Florida; the city council in Newport Beach, California, voted to tax local surfers three dollars a year. Nearly all punitive measures were lifted before decade's end, while safety laws remained in place.

At least three Southern California–based surf magazines were founded in 1960, with *Surfer* quickly emerging as the industry leader. Santa Monica schoolteacher Bud Browne, having invented the surf movie genre in the mid-'50s, was soon joined by other moviemakers such as big-wave rider and surfboard manufacturer Greg Noll, John Severson (founder of *Surfer*), and Bruce Brown. Surfing's first media-generation stars were all Californian, and included original hotdogger Dewey Weber, the articulate and powerful Phil Edwards, and the subversive Mickey Dora. Hawaiians George Downing and Wally Froiseth, along with Buzzy Trent and Walter Hoffman of California, had already led the push into bigger waves; by the late '50s they'd ridden 25-footers at Makaha, and had begun to master the ferocious surf along the North Shore of Oahu. Big-wave surfing was in fact often looked upon as a separate and higher form of the sport; few surfers understood this better than bull-necked Californian Noll, who tackled giant waves at North Shore breaks like Waimea Bay and Pipeline while wearing his trademark black-and-white–striped "jailhouse jams," and emerged as the era's most popular big-wave rider. (Noll and Dora were among the stunt surfers in Columbia Picture's 1964 big-wave film *Ride the Wild Surf.*)

Dozens of regional, national, and even international competition-based surfing organizations were founded in the early and mid-'60s, including the United States Surfing Association, the Australian Surfriders Association, and the International Surfing Federation; among the most prestigious surfing events were the Makaha International, the Peru International, the United States Surfing Championships, the Australian National Titles, and the Duke Kahanamoku Invitational. Results from these contests gave an indication of surfing's global reach, as Australian Midget Farrelly won the debut World Championships in 1964, while Felipe Pomar of Peru took the event in 1965. The 1966 Championships featured riders from England, France, New Zealand, South Africa, India, Ireland, and Mexico. (If competition demonstrated the sport's growing internationalism, it also verified a fast-growing gender inequity; *Surfer* magazine didn't even bother to publish the women's division results for the 1965 Championships.)

The Beach Boys, Jan and Dean, and frothy Hollywood beach movies like *Beach Party* and *Beach Blanket Bingo* all contributed to the surf craze of the early and mid-'60s. Hang Ten, Kanvas by Katin, Sand Comber, and Birdwell Beach Britches were among the founding surfwear manufacturers, while surfing T-shirts sold by the tens of thousands, and surf fashion spreads were featured in *Sports Illustrated* and *Playboy.* Hamm's Beer used a photo of American surfer Rusty Miller charging down a huge wave at Sunset Beach for a national billboard ad campaign; Triumph featured world champion Joyce Hoffman in full-page magazine ads for the 1966 Spitfire convertible. Australian teens danced to Little Pattie's hit single, "He's My Blond-Headed Stompy Wompy Real Gone Surfer Boy," while in Southern California—then and now the runaway surf industry and entertainment leader—there were surfing trade shows, surfing TV shows, surf music battle of the bands, and surf-related promo giveaways at fast-food restaurants.

The sport at times seemed to be awash in marketing hype, competition results, signature model surfboards, and surfing organizations, and maybe this explains why Bruce Brown's 1966 film *The Endless Summer,* an easygoing travelogue featuring a pair of surfers who leave it all behind to seek out the perfect wave, struck such a deep chord among both surfers and nonsurfers. Brown's movie was nothing but cheerful and celebratory. It was also set almost completely outside the confines of the surf industry and ignored surf competition altogether, making the point that the sport's water-born soul would always exist well beyond the mercantile clang and clamor.

Revolution's Children: Locals, Pros, Merchants, and Soul Monsters (1967–91)

Noseriding in the mid-'60s was sometimes called the "sport within the sport," and hanging ten was generally regarded as the last word in small-wave performance surfing. But Australian surfer Nat Young, the talented and brusque winner of the 1966 World Championships, was correct in noting that "if you just stand on the nose from start to finish, you've defeated creativity and individualism, the very essence of surfing!" Young was part of a small group of Australian-based surfers, including Bob McTavish of Queensland and California expatriate George Greenough, spearheading the New Era movement. Greenough, a kneeboarder, cameraman, and board designer, was able to direct his "spoon" kneeboard into radical turns and cutbacks that stand-up surfers wouldn't match for nearly 10 years. The effervescent McTavish, a first-rate surfer and board-maker, set out just a few weeks after Young's win in the 1966 Championships to create a stand-up surfboard that would allow surfers at to least begin to approximate the Greenough style. Surfboards at the time were generally 10 feet long, weighed 25 pounds, and had a wide, blunt nose. Handling characteristics had gradually but steadily improved since the development of the Malibu chip, but the boards still didn't fit easily into the steep part of the wave, and surfers tended to avoid the curl. McTavish made his first Plastic Machine vee-bottom in March 1967—a nine-foot board with a distinctive two-panel rear planing surface. Six months later McTavish and a few other Aussies were making vee-bottom boards as small as 7′6″; by December, as word of the new boards finally reached America, the blunt-nosed 10-footer was on its way to obsolescence (for a few years, anyway), and the shortboard revolution was under way. New board designs popped up month to month, some reasonable, some absurd, with the main trajectory always toward the smaller and lighter; six-foot, seven-pound boards were available by late 1969.

In the early '70s, the sport was further changed by the introduction of the surf leash, a tethering device that allowed surfers to spend more time riding waves and less time swimming after lost boards, but also permitted the less-qualified into lineups at rock-lined or offshore breaks that had previously been open to advanced riders only. Overcrowding had been the rule at many breaks since the early '60s; the leash made the problem worse. Product development in other areas continued apace. The full-length surfing wetsuit was offered for the first time in 1970 by O'Neill, and was a boon to cold-water surfers everywhere. Three years later brought the introduction of the Morey Boogie bodyboard—a small, soft, easy-to-use bellyboard—which over the decades would introduce the joys of wave-riding to hundreds of thousands of people.

Surfing enthusiastically joined up with the counterculture in the late '60s: surfers let their hair grow, drug use was common, surfing competition was disparaged (although never abandoned) as being part of "the system," and newly psychedelicized surf magazines published articles on yoga, health foods, and the environment. Surf movies were more popular than ever, with films like *Five Summer Stories* (1972), *Morning of the Earth* (1972), and *Free Ride* (1977) barnstorming up and down coastlines in surfing nations around the world and playing to full houses at high school auditoriums and art-house theaters. (The genre was running out of steam as the decade ended, however, and by the mid-'80s surf movies had been all but replaced by surf videos. Hollywood, meanwhile, produced a small number of banal movies set in the surf world, including *Big Wednesday, Point Break,* and *North Shore.*)

Exotic surf travel—in large part a ripple effect from *The Endless Summer*—had become a surfing specialty unto itself, as thousands of low- or no-budget surfers fanned out across the world during the late '60s and '70s to ride waves in places like Morocco, the Philippines, and Sri Lanka. (American soldiers during the Vietnam War held small surfing contests and made their own boards from an army-subsidized beachfront shack in Da Nang.) Reports of perfect surf in Bali began to spread in the early '70s, and Indonesia would soon prove to be the world's richest wave field. Localism was the period's ugliest development, as surfers in a given region tried to keep nonresidents away by methods ranging from cold stares to verbal harassment, theft, vandalism, and physical violence.

High-performance surfing, memorably described by four-time world champion Mark Richards as the "rip, tear and lacerate" method, continued to be a dominant surf world theme in the '70s, led by energetic riders like Larry Bertlemann, Michael Peterson, and Dane Kealoha. Jeff Hakman and Barry Kanaiaupuni had meanwhile become power surfing icons in the bigger waves at places like Sunset Beach, with able support from more than a dozen contemporaries, including Terry Fitzgerald and Reno Abellira. (Old school favorite Greg Noll left the sport following a crash-and-burn 30-footer at Makaha in 1969; Eddie Aikau and James Jones were among a small number of surfers who remained dedicated to riding giant waves, but big-wave surfing was much less fashionable than it had been in the '60s.) Tuberiding had replaced noseriding as the sport's greatest high-performance achievement, and the cyclonic wave at Pipeline on the North Shore of Oahu was universally recognized as the ultimate tube. Hawaiian goofyfooter Gerry Lopez single-handedly defined tuberiding elegance in the early '70s, riding with quiet panache through the exploding Pipeline interior; Shaun Tomson then made a big performance leap in the winter of 1975–76 by turning his board from inside the tube, allowing him to ride deeper and extending the amount of time spent behind the curl.

Professional surf contests had been introduced in the mid-'60s, but "professionalism" didn't really catch on until the early '70s. Fourteen prize-money events were linked together in 1976 under the auspices of the just-formed International Professional Surfers (IPS) group, founded by 1968 world champion Fred Hemmings, to create the first global pro tour. Australian Peter Townend was named that year's world champion, but his contest earnings for the season—about $7,500—barely covered travel expenses. A women's division was added to the pro circuit the following year, with Margo Oberg of Hawaii taking the title. The tour grew steadily from season to season (the Association of Surfing Professionals took over administrative duties from the IPS in 1982; the average per-event prize purse for a men's event in 1990 was just under $100,000), but never achieved the kind of success organizers hoped for—not just with general audience sports fans, but among rank-and-file surfers, who, for the most part, had little or no interest in the latest pro results. Still, events like the Pipeline Masters, the Billabong Pro, and the Op Pro dependably showcased the world's most progressive surfing. Amateur competition meanwhile received a boost in 1978 with the return of the World Surfing Championships (in hiatus since 1972) and the formation in California of the National Scholastic Surfing Association.

Australians continued to make the most significant breakthroughs in board design. Newcastle's Mark Richards, reinterpreting the double-finned "fish" design introduced nearly 10 years earlier by Californian Steve Lis, came up with his stubby twin-fin board in 1977—which he rode to four consecutive world pro championships, beginning in 1978. The twin-fin was fast and maneuverable, but also quirky and hard to control. Simon Anderson of Sydney, looking for a compromise between the twin-fin and the stable but less-responsive single-fin, developed his tri-fin Thruster in 1981. The tri-fin had a narrow nose, a fairly wide tail, and worked in virtually all wave conditions; by 1983 it was the standard choice on high-performance boards, virtually eliminating both the single-fin and twin-fin. (Other noteworthy board design and construction advances in the '70s and '80s include the swallowtail, the bonzer, the four-fin, the stinger, the no-nose, and the epoxy board.)

Tom Curren of California and Tom Carroll of Australia, both early proponents of the tri-fin, won five world titles between them from 1983 to 1990, and together set the new wave-riding standard—Curren with his flawless technique and Carroll with his gouging turns and dead-eye calm in the tube. Aerial surfing began to take on a life of its own, led by 1989 world champion Martin Potter, originally from South Africa, and California's Christian Fletcher.

Big-wave surfing returned to prominence during the storm-filled El Niño winter of 1982–83, and 1986 brought the debut of the Quiksilver in Memory of Eddie Aikau contest at Waimea Bay, held in honor of the Hawaiian big-wave master who had drowned in a 1978 boating accident. A professional corps of big-wave riders soon developed, led by Hawaiians Brock Little, Mark Foo, Darrick Doerner, and Ken Bradshaw. But it was quiet Keone Downing, son of big-wave pioneer George Downing, who won the 1990 Quiksilver/Aikau, a benchmark competition held in breathtaking 25-foot surf at Waimea. (Australian surfwear giant Quiksilver would continue to be the grand patron of big-wave surfing, and was among the leaders in a surf business surge that saw annual industrywide profits go from tens of millions in the early '80s to nearly $2 billion by the end of the decade. In 1987, Quiksilver became the first publicly traded surf company.)

But surfing's most significant trend during this period was the return of the longboard. Seemingly banished forever in the late '60s, the smooth-riding 10-footers in fact began returning to lineups in the mid-'70s—especially when the waves were small—and longboarding made steady gains through the '80s and into the '90s. A longboard world championship was first held in 1986 (won by original shortboard proponent Nat Young); longboard clubs, magazines, surf shops, movies, and videos soon followed. The shortboard revolution would remain surfing's evolutionary high point. But a comfortable, practical, dependably graceful aspect of the sport had been left behind in the rush toward the latest and usually smallest equipment, and many surfers felt a sense of restoration as longer boards made their way back into the lineup. Shortboard architect Bob McTavish himself admitted that he'd been riding longboards, at least in small waves, since the early '70s.

Planet Surf (1992–2003)

A new era in surfing began in the early '90s. Kelly Slater's win on the 1992 world tour marked the ascendancy of the New School—a group of kinetic teenagers, including Shane Dorian and Rob Machado, who rode knife-thin boards and favored acrobatic tailslide and aerial maneuvers. Slater, the handsome Floridian, dominated the sport like no surfer before him, winning another five world titles before taking a break from full-time competition after the 1998 season, and resetting the limits in virtually every category of high-performance riding. Slater's annual salary from primary sponsor Quiksilver was kept secret, but by the mid-'90s he likely became the first surfer to earn $1 million a year.

Even more spectacular was the development of tow-in surfing. Big-wave surfers had for decades been frustrated in their attempts to ride waves over 30 feet, as they were unable to generate enough takeoff speed to overcome the sweep of water up the wave face. A mechanical solution arrived in 1992, as Hawaii's Buzzy Kerbox, Laird Hamilton, and Darrick Doerner began towing each other into waves, first using an inflatable boat, then switching to personal watercraft. The new method not only allowed big-wave riders to break the 30-foot barrier (50-foot-plus waves were ridden before the end of the decade), it completely reordered big-wave board design. Paddle-in big-wave surfers continued to use unwieldy 10-foot, 20-inch-wide boards known as "guns," which forced a simple, direct, no-frills riding style. Tow-in surfers were soon using boards measuring just seven-feet by 15-inches, taking advantage of the reduced area to carve magnificent turns up and down the wave face. The new method had its critics. Personal watercraft, it was argued, not only pollute the air and water in the surf zone, but destroy the sport's elemental man-in-nature simplicity.

Hawaii's Waimea Bay, the ultimate big-wave break for more than 35 years, was overshadowed during this time by two newly revealed breaks: Maverick's in northern California, and Jaws on the island of Maui. Maverick's made international news in late

1994 when veteran Hawaiian big-wave surfer Mark Foo, during his first visit, drowned following what appeared to be a routine wipeout. Big-wave contests were regularly scheduled, big-wave movies, videos, and books were produced; and expeditions to seek out and ride new big-wave breaks were launched, including a one-day voyage in 2001 to Cortes Banks, an open-ocean reef located 100 miles off the coast of San Diego, where a small group of tow-in surfers rode enormous 50-foot-plus waves.

The rise of women's surfing, the era's third significant change, got under way quietly in 1991 with the founding of Roxy, Quiksilver's young women's clothing line. With a few exceptions, the history of 20th-century women's surfing up to that point could be told as a series of dismissals and insults: females were ignored by surf magazines and surf moviemakers, women pros earned less than 1/10th that of their male counterparts, and newcomers had to contend with people like world champion Nat Young, who told *Surfing* magazine that "girls shouldn't surf; they make fools of themselves." A new generation of surfwear executives recognized both a moral and economic void, and rushed to fill it. Roxy introduced the functional but stylish female "boardshort" in 1993, one year before team rider and surfing glamour girl Lisa Andersen won the first of four consecutive pro world titles. Key markets were saturated with fun-in-the-sun Roxy ads; other companies launched young women's lines, and the women's surfing movement (criticized by some as a girls' fashion movement) was on. *Wahine,* the first women's surf magazine, launched in 1995, and was followed shortly by all-women surf shops, surfboard-makers, and surf schools, as well as surf videos and movies—including Universal's hypermarketed 2002 effort, *Blue Crush.* Females accounted for less than five percent of the surf population in the early '90s, but the numbers had gone up by 2002 to an estimated 10 to 15 percent. Surf business analysts predicted that by 2004 women would generate half of all surfwear sales.

World tour pros, men and women alike, had meanwhile demanded and received a schedule that took them to high-quality surf breaks like Grajagan, Tavarua, Jeffreys Bay, Mundaka, and Trestles instead of breaks conveniently located next to crowd-accommodating parking lots. Career spans were lengthening as well. Pre–New School power surfer Mark Occhilupo of Australia won the 1999 world title at age 33, and Hawaii's Sunny Garcia won the following year at age 30. Layne Beachley of Australia was 30 in 2002 when she won her fifth consecutive world title.

Longboarding continued its rise in popularity, due in part to a general aging trend among surfers, and by 2002 it was estimated that longboarders made up as much as 40 percent of all surfers worldwide. Aside from tow-in boards, surfboard design changed little during the '90s and early '00s. The manufacturing process, however, began to shift in the middle of the decade as leading board-makers like California's Al Merrick started using computer-programmed shaping machines. A smaller number of molded boards also began to make their way into the market.

Growth and expansion, for better and worse, has been the driving force in surfing over the past few years. Ad sales for the established surf magazines hit record highs, despite competition from dozens of new titles. Surf videos were released by the hundreds. Industrywide sales in 2002 (surfwear, boards, wetsuits, videos, and accessories) soared to $4.5 billion. New surf break discoveries were made in Norway, Iceland, Russia, Oman, and Mozambique, as well as northwest Indonesia and across the tropical Pacific. Discovery of a good wave, in even the most remote locations, often led to the founding of a nearby surf resort or surf charter tour. Waves in general became less mysterious, as surf forecasters (led by California's Sean Collins) began to accurately predict incoming swells days in advance, and companies like Surfline took to the Internet with a widening network of image-streaming surf cams. (The jet-propelled FlowRider machine meanwhile introduced a strange, open-loop, freshwater version of the sport, as riders on specialized boards were able to carve back and forth on the stationary wave for minutes at a time.) Crowds grew thicker, and often surlier, as a new wave of beginners took to the sport; Manly Surf School in Sydney claimed in 2002 to have given surf lessons to 25,000 people. Surfing was also co-opted by a seemingly endless array of faction groups: environmentalists formed the Surfrider Foundation; gerontologists helped make *Surfing for Life,* a PBS documentary on senior surfers; fashion designers sent runway models down the catwalk with surfboards during the Spring 2003 shows in Paris; venture capitalists spent more than $50 million to fund three Internet-boom surf sites; collectors bought and sold antique surfboards for up to $18,000; academics taught courses in surf culture at colleges and universities; museum and gallery curators staged surf-themed exhibitions in New York, San Francisco, and Los Angeles; gamers developed at least four surf titles in the early '00s; and big-money agencies created surf-flavored ads for Kodak, American Airlines, Target, Ford, Merrill Lynch, and Sony.

The sport's frenetic rate of change in the '90s caused some surfers to look back, often wistfully, to bygone eras. A meditative 1915 black-and-white portrait of Duke Kahanamoku was used on the cover of *Surfer* magazine's 40th anniversary issue, published in 1999; inside, a feature article titled "When We Were Kings," written by editor Sam George, identified the first six decades of the century as the sport's Romantic Period, while the decades to follow are blandly designated as Post-Romantic. Indeed, it's difficult to look at the gyre of crowds and commercialism in surfing and not see a growing stain. Then again, it isn't hard to do what surfers have always done, and move to the fringe, even if just for a few hours at a time, where the sport remains pure. Or pure enough. George himself is optimistic about the future, noting in his "Kings" article that the ride itself is still worth being passionate about and that the sport's iconoclastic legacy, if stretched a bit thin, is nonetheless intact. "I see no reason why being a surfer in the coming century," George concludes, "will be any less fulfilling than having been one during the last."

A

A-frame Peak-shaped wave, generally short, hollow, and powerful; ridable in either direction—left or right—and often well-suited to tuberiding. Viewed front on, the A-frame wave has a symmetrical outline resembling that of an A-frame building.

Aaberg, Denny Good-natured surfer/writer/musician from Pacific Palisades, California; best known as cowriter of Warner Brothers' 1978 surfing film *Big Wednesday.* Aaberg was born (1947) in Boston, Massachusetts, and moved with his family at age two to the west Los Angeles town of Pacific Palisades. By the time Denny Aaberg began surfing in 1959 as a 12-year-old, his older brother Kemp was regarded as one of California's top surfers. Aaberg's involvement in the sport branched out as he played guitar on *Innermost Limits of Pure Fun,* a 1970 surf film, and contributed a song to *Big Wednesday*—a movie inspired by a 1974 *Surfer* magazine short story written by Aaberg titled "No-Pants Mance" that looked back at his wave- and beer-soaked salad days at Malibu in the early '60s. The sandy-haired Aaberg continued to serve as keeper of the Malibu flame, appearing in the 1987 documentary *The Legends of Malibu,* and describing in detail Malibu's characters, scene, and rituals in "Tres Amigos," a 1994 *Longboard* magazine feature. "Malibu was rough theater," Aaberg wrote. "In ancient Greece, plays lasted all day, beginning at dawn and not ending until dusk. Malibu was the same way." *See also* Big Wednesday.

Aaberg, Kemp Lean, blond, smooth-surfing regularfooter from Santa Barbara, California; a *Gidget*-era Malibu icon and costar of filmmaker Bruce Brown's 1958 surf movie, *Slippery When Wet.* Aaberg was born (1940) in Peoria, Illinois, spent his early childhood in Boston, Massachusetts, and moved with his family in 1948 to Pacific Palisades, in west Los Angeles. Eight years later he began surfing, at Malibu, first using a right-foot-forward goofyfoot stance, then switching to a left-foot-leading regularfoot stance so as to be facing the long right-breaking Malibu waves. Although Aaberg had been surfing for less than three years when he was picked to go to Hawaii with Brown to film *Slippery When Wet,* he was already regarded as one of California's premier surf stylists. A black-and-white photo of him back-arching in perfect trim at Rincon appeared in the second issue of *Surfer* in 1961; a duotone version of the shot became the magazine's first logo later that year, and was reprinted on the magazine's 25th anniversary issue cover in 1985. The *Surfer's Journal* later described the Aaberg back-arch shot as "one of the most instantly identifiable surf images of all time, and an enduring statement about the joy of surfing." Australian Peter Townend, the 1976 world champion, reintroduced Aaberg's move in the mid-'70s as the soul arch. Congenial and easygoing, Aaberg could nonetheless be obsessive: he avoided surf competition, but won the grueling 32-mile Catalina-to–Manhattan Pier paddleboard race in 1961; he studied flamenco guitar in Spain for six months in 1972; he placed highly in triathlons in the mid-'80s.

Aaberg wrote articles for *Surfer, Surf Guide,* and *H2O* magazines, and his monthly "Surf Scrolls" column appeared in the *Santa Barbara News Press* from 1989 to 1992. He appeared in a number of '60s surf movies, including *Surfing Hollow Days* (1962) and *A Cool Wave of Color* (1964). The Jack Barlow character in Warner Brothers' 1978 surf movie *Big Wednesday* was loosely based on Aaberg; the *Big Wednesday* screenplay was cowritten by Denny Aaberg, Kemp's younger brother. Aaberg received a B.A. in social sciences from University of California, Santa Barbara, in 1966; in 1991 he was nominated to the International Surfing Hall of Fame. Aaberg is married and has no children.

Abellira, Reno Stylish, enigmatic regularfooter from Honolulu, Hawaii; world-ranked #4 in 1977, and a central figure throughout the first decade of shortboard surfing. Abellira was born (1950) and raised in

Reno Abellira

Honolulu, the son of a middleweight boxer who was shot and killed in a barroom fight. Abellira began surfing at age four in Waikiki, but didn't get his first board until 11. He won the juniors division of the Makaha International in 1966 and 1967, and earned $200 for winning the 1966 Hawaiian Noseriding Contest, the state's first professional surfing event. Abellira was Hawaii's juniors division champion in 1968, and made his international debut later that year in the World Surfing Championships, held in Puerto Rico. Although he placed sixth, many observers thought the small-framed (5'7", 135 pounds) 18-year-old was the event's most exciting surfer, as he consistently rode just beneath the curl on a stiletto-like purple surfboard. "It was a skateboard," California surf publisher Dick Graham wrote, marveling at Abellira's radical new equipment, "and he rode it like a god, because he is one."

Abellira's style developed over the next three years. He rode in a low crouch, chin tucked into his left shoulder, arms extended, wrists cocked, each part of his body precisely arranged. Whether or not the streamlined stance added speed to Abellira's surfing is impossible to say, but nobody in the '70s—except for Australia's Terry Fitzgerald—*looked* faster on a surfboard. Abellira also proved to be one of the sport's most mysterious figures: he kept to himself for the most part, rarely smiled, and countered the scruffy surfer image with Italian-made leather loafers, pressed linen pants, and neatly coiffed hair. "He's a bit of a dandy," Australian surf journalist Phil Jarratt wrote of the dark-eyed Hawaiian, "and

could teach most surfers a thing or two about color coordination."

Abellira competed regularly throughout the '70s, winning state titles in 1970 and 1972, placing fourth in the '70 World Championships, second in the 1973 Duke Kahanamoku Classic, and making the finals in more than a dozen professional events on the North Shore of Oahu. He was also an Expression Session invitee in 1970 and 1971. In what many still regard as surfing's most thrilling big-wave contest, Abellira beat fellow Hawaiian Jeff Hakman by a fraction of a point to win the 1974 Smirnoff Pro, held in cataclysmic 30-foot surf at Waimea Bay. Among the first Hawaiians to set out on the pro circuit, Abellira was world-ranked #4 in 1977, #8 in 1978, and #13 in 1979.

Abellira was also a first-rate surfboard shaper, learning the craft from board-making guru Dick Brewer in the late '60s and early '70s, then going on to work for the Lightning Bolt label; Abellira and Brewer together experimented with an early version of the tri-fin design in 1970 and 1971. Mark Richards of Australia later became an international surf hero while riding Abellira-shaped boards, and it was Abellira's stubby double-keeled "fish" that inspired Richards to produce in 1977 the twin-fin design that swept through the surf world in the late '70s and early '80s.

While Abellira was for the most part removed from the surf scene beginning in the early '80s, he occasionally produced thoughtful and eloquent articles for the American surf press. He made headlines in 1993 when he disappeared for several months after being indicted on cocaine distribution charges; he was later convicted and spent several months in prison.

Abellira appeared in more than 15 surf movies, including *Hot Generation* (1968), *Sea of Joy* (1971), *Going Surfin'* (1973), and *Tales of the Seven Seas* (1981). In the late '70s, he lent his name to a short-lived surfwear company called Reno Hawaii. He competed in the 1990 Quiksilver in Memory of Eddie Aikau big-wave contest at Waimea Bay at age 40, finishing 24th in a field of 33. Abellira has been married once, and has one child; in 2002 he was living in Santa Monica, California.

Abubo, Megan   Determined pro surfer from Haleiwa, Hawaii; world-ranked #2 in 2000. "Abubo looks soft but surfs hard," *Surfer* magazine said in 2000, noting that the Hawaiian regularfooter, then 22, was likely five or six years from her prime. Abubo was born (1978) in Connecticut, moved with her family to Hawaii, began surfing at age 10 in Waikiki, and won seven national titles as an amateur. She was the pro tour's rookie of the year in 1996, and in 2000 won two of nine world circuit events to finish runner-up to Australian Layne Beachley. Abubo had by that time developed a reputation as both friendly and feisty. "What man-made object best represents your personality?" *Surfer* asked her in 1998. "What a stupid question," she answered. Abudo faltered competitively after her second-place finish in 2000, placing 8th in 2001 and 9th in 2001. Abubo has been featured in a number of surf videos, including *Triple C* (1996) and *Peaches* (2000); she also stunt-doubled in the 2002 Universal film *Blue Crush.* Abubo posed in the nude (covering herself with a surfboard) for *Rolling Stone*'s 2001 Sports Hall of Fame issue.

academia and surfing   Although tens of thousands of recreational surfers have enrolled in colleges and universities over the decades, and coastal-area college surf teams and clubs have been around since the mid-1960s, surfing and the academy have had little effect on each other, and connections between the two are still for the most part regarded as novel, quirky, or gently amusing. Just a small number of well-known surfers have earned graduate degrees of one kind or another, the best known being a pair of California big-wave riders: Ricky Grigg (Ph.D., oceanography, Scripps Institution, 1970) and Peter Cole (M.S., informational sciences, University of Hawaii, 1971). The number of first-rate academics who also surf is proportionally small, and includes Kary Mullis, a San Diego longboarder and 1994 Nobel Prize winner in chemistry, and Donald Cram, another San Diego surfer, who earned his chemistry Nobel in 1987. (It is estimated, meanwhile, that between one-third and one-half of the world pro tour's top 44 surfers in any given season are high school dropouts.)

Colleges and universities have produced more than 500 surf-related thesis papers, and a much smaller number of journal articles, with titles including "A Study of the Growth of a Deviant Subculture" (1962), "Legends of the Surfer Subculture" (1976), "Waves of Semiosis: Surfing Iconic Progression" (1987), and "Ambiguities in Pleasure and Discipline: The Development of Competitive Surfing" (1995). "Surfing Subcultures of Australia and New Zealand," a doctoral thesis by University of Queensland sociology professor Kent Pearson, became a minor surf

world curiosity when it was published as a 213-page hardcover book in 1979. "[Surfboard] design development," Pearson writes in the desiccated academic prose style familiar to all grad students, "took place in accord with objectives of maneuverability and wave-riding performance by persons primarily interested in surfing pleasure."

Surfing: American Culture or Subculture?, a 2000-founded honors course taught by assistant professor Patrick Moser at Missouri's Drury University, explored through readings and film "the positive side of surfing as an idealistic escape from modern-industrialized society, and its darker residence squarely within American imperialistic practices." One year earlier, Plymouth University in southwest England began offering a three-year B.S. in surf science and technology—designed primarily as a surf industry vocational program—with course requirements including Meteorology and Waves, Competitive Surfing and Event Management, Biology and Human Performance, Advanced Surf Dynamics, and Contemporary Issues in Surfing. In 2001, Edith Cowan University in Western Australia began offering a degree similar to that at Plymouth; The Endless Summer Revisited: Surfing in American Culture and Thought was offered for the first time at the University of California Santa Cruz in 2003.

The first annual Surfing, Arts, Science and Issues Conference (better known as SASIC I), organized by the Oxnard-based Groundswell Society and formatted on the lines of an academic seminar, was held on October 27, 2001, in Ventura, California. SASIC I featured 14 symposiums and seminars, led by surfing environmentalists, artists, lawyers, writer/publishers, and others. *See also* Kary Mullis, Western Intercollegiate Surfing Council.

Action Sports Retailer Trade Expo (ASR)   Frenetic three-day surf industry trade show held twice yearly in Southern California, one at the Long Beach Convention Center and the other at the San Diego Convention Center; the most widely attended event of its kind in the United States; long known by its ASR acronym. The ASR show is where surf companies display their newest wares—everything from surfboards and surf trunks to water slingshots and sparkling tanning lotion—for surf industry retailers and the surf industry at large; ASR is not open to the public. Other action sports represented at ASR include skateboarding, snowboarding, climbing, BMX, wakeboarding, kiteboarding, and sailboarding. The cacophonous hivelike convention hall atmosphere is filled with rows of surf company booths, hundreds of TV screens showing repeat-loop DVD and video presentations, pro surfers in search of sponsors, roving bikini models in thongs and high-heels, and legions of retail buyers. Although ASR was created in part to put some business rigor into a notoriously lax industry, the social whirl surrounding the show is nonstop. *Surfing* magazine's report on the 1997 show was titled "ASR You Hungover?"

ASR was preceded by the Los Angeles Surf Fair, held from 1962 to 1964 in Santa Monica, California; the 1976-founded Surf Expo show in Florida; and the one-off Surfing Expo '77, held in Costa Mesa, California. ASR has its origins in the 1979-founded *Action Sports Retailer* magazine, published by Southern California surfers Jeff Wetmore and Steve Lewis. Wetmore was inspired to create a surfing trade show after noticing that virtually all surf shops had pushed surfboards to the back of the store, and were giving over more display space to a fast-multiplying assortment of beachwear items and surfing accessories. The first Action Sports Retailer show was held at the Long Beach Convention Center in February 1981, drawing 150 companies and perhaps 500 registered buyers. The show grew in popularity as the surf industry itself took a sharp turn up in the second half of the decade; the San Diego show was added in 1989. Fashion shows, book signings, meet-and-greet celebrity appearances, surfboard auctions, and after-hours concerts all became part of ASR as the shows grew bigger and more complex. The 2002 Long Beach ASR booked 500 companies and drew 17,000 attendees.

While America has always been by far the biggest force in the international surf marketplace (the U.S. surf industry generated sales of $4.5 billion in 2002), overseas surf industries have also done well. As of 2002, there were surfing or surf-related trade shows in France (Glisse Expo), Germany (IPSO), Brazil (Surf and Beach), Australia (Action Retail Surf Expo), and Japan (Action Sports Retailer). *See also* Los Angeles Surf Fair, Surf Expo, Surf Industry Manufacturers Association.

advertising and surfing   Surfing has been used as an advertising tool for over 100 years. The sport's revival in Hawaii during the early 20th century was in fact greatly encouraged by Waikiki hotel owners and other regional boosters who recognized "surf-riding"

as a romantic tourist-trade marketing device. Surfing was introduced to Southern California in 1907 when Waikiki surfer George Freeth, arriving on the mainland with a letter of introduction from the Hawaii Promotion Committee, was hired as a beachside attraction at the Redondo Plunge in southwest Los Angeles County and billed as "The Hawaiian Wonder." Surfing's attractiveness to advertisers was and remains obvious: it's healthy and exciting, sexy but not lewd, and performed in a beautiful and photogenic natural setting. Most surf-themed print ads between the '20s and '50s had to do with travel promotion for companies like Matson Line cruises, or tropical-grown foods and beverages like Dole Pineapple.

As surfing boomed in the late '50s and '60s, slipstreaming in large part behind the consumer-powerful teenage baby boomers, advertisers began putting the sport to use for an expanding range of products and services, including obvious youth market items like Coca-Cola and the inexpensive Buick Opel sedan, as well as more imaginative wares like Cutex's "Hang Ten" nail polish (available in "Shoot the Curl Coral" and "Wipe Out Pink"), Canadian Club Whiskey, Salem cigarettes, and Clairol Sudden Summer hair lightener. Niche advertising also exploded during the '60s, as surf companies booked ad pages in dozens of regional, national, and international surf magazines.

The story of surf-themed advertising over the past three decades has been little more than a constant broadening of product application, and by the '90s surfing was being used to promote toothpaste (Crest), allergy pills (Allegra), camcorders (Sony), wireless phone service (AT&T), credit cards (Visa), and department stores (Macy's), along with dozens of car models and alcohol brands. A Café de Colombia ad superimposed fictitious coffee grower Juan Valdez, along with his donkey, atop a surfboard inside a thundering Hawaiian tube. Baby boomers, now approaching retirement age, returned as a surf-ad target demographic, with companies like Kodak, Aetna, Kellogg's, and Wilmington Trust creating print and TV campaigns using gray-haired surfer/models. In a 2000 print ad for Springmaid Bed and Bath, legendary Hawaiian surfer Albert "Rabbit" Kekai, 80, posed on the beach wrapped in a seafoam-green sheet, a small wave rushing around his feet, with text reading simply, "I dream of the next wave." (A partial list of famous surfers who have done advertising work includes Duke Kahanamoku for Sears and Roebuck,

Tom Blake for Matson Line, Mickey Dora for Oldsmobile, Nat Young for White Stag, Joyce Hoffman for Triumph, Corky Carroll and Rob Machado for Miller Lite, Mark Richards for Kentucky Fried Chicken, Wayne Bartholomew for Smirnoff, Cheyne Horan for Sunkist, and Laird Hamilton for Nike.)

A 1986 TV ad for California Coolers, a sugary wine-based drink, featured the old Trashmen hit "Surfin' Bird," used vintage clips of Terry "Tubesteak" Tracy at Malibu, and was a hit with rank-and-file surfers. Most surf-themed ads, however, are met with resignation or irritation, as companies put the sport to use in ways that surfers deem inappropriate or insulting. Occasionally those feelings are stronger. In 1999, longboard-era surfers George Downing, Paul Strauch, and Ben Aipa brought a $5.5 million defamation suit against clothing giant Abercrombie & Fitch after a 1965 photo of them was used in the middle of a four-page A&F ad spread (shot by fashion legend Bruce Weber) featuring nude surfers. The suit was pending as of 2003, but surf journalist Gary Taylor spoke for the sport at large when he described the A&F ad as "a high-profile example of corporate America's attempt to cash in on surfing mystique and getting it wrong yet again."

Aeder, Erik Levelheaded surf photographer from Hawaii; best known for his evocative travel photography and his mid-'90s images of the Hawaiian big-wave break known as Jaws. Aeder was born in Seattle (1955), grew up in La Jolla, California, began surfing and photography in his early teens, and with no formal training had several photos published in *Surfer* and *Surfing* magazines before his senior year of high school. Aeder moved to Maui in 1975, and three years later he and his younger brother Kirk were listed as contributing photographers on the *Surfer* masthead; in 1987 Erik was promoted to senior photographer. Aeder often traveled to exotic surf locations, and developed a knack for the pulled-back angle: his 1978 lineup shots of Nias helped alert surfers to Indonesia's vast wave potential, and an image from Easter Island—included in his 1982 *Surfer* feature, "The Most Remote Surf Spot in the World"—showed a lone surfer walking across a grass-covered plateau, framed by ancient lava-stone *moai* statues, with a perfect wave breaking in the background. In 1994, at Jaws, Aeder began shooting the small group of Hawaiian surfers who had recently invented the personal watercraft–assisted tow-in method, which reconfigured

big-wave riding. Aeder has contributed to a number of illustrated surfing books, including *Stoked: A History of Surf Culture* (1997), *Maverick's: The Story of Big-Wave Surfing* (2000), and *The Perfect Day* (2001).

aerial Skateboard-influenced surfing maneuver where the rider launches off the wave crest into one of an ever-growing number of board- and body-torquing airborne variations, then lands back on the wave face. Aerials are performed almost exclusively in waves under six feet. Along with the tow-in method of big-wave riding, aerial surfing split off into something close to its own distinct branch of the sport during the 1990s, with aerial specialists and aerial-only competitions. Skateboarders riding the banked walls of empty swimming pools began doing aerials above the rim in about 1977; surfers—including Florida's Matt Kechele and Kevin Reed of California—initiated their version of aerials in the late '70s. Progress was slow. Surfboards couldn't be gripped and handled in the air as easily as skateboards, and waves, unlike pools, change shape constantly. The "chop-hop," an early and rightfully maligned aerial variant, was enough to keep most progressive surfers working on deep turns and tuberides. But some continued to push forward with the aerial, including Davey Smith, John McClure, and Bud Llamas of California, along with Australia's

Frontside aerial by Hawaii's Bruce Irons

Cheyne Horan, Hawaii's Larry Bertlemann, and most notably Martin Potter of South Africa. But it was the tattooed and punkish Christian Fletcher of San Clemente, California, along with neighbor Matt Arch-bold, who gave aerial surfing much of its present-day shape and character; both surfers were not only lifting four or five feet above the crest by the late '80s (and regularly completing their lower-flying attempts), but establishing the aerialist as a kind of surf guerrilla. Fletcher also introduced the surfing world to the colorful skateboard-invented aerial lexicon, including "mute air," "indy air," "air-to-reverse," "slob air," "madonna," and "stalefish."

Future world champion Kelly Slater of Florida brought the aerial into the surfing mainstream in 1990, as the leader of the teenage New School group—including Shane Dorian, Rob Machado, Shane Beschen, and Ross Williams, all of whom were first-rate aerialists. Above-the-curl surfing also got a push from the footstrap-wearing tow-in surfers, who were able to fly higher and in more complex patterns than any unstrapped paddle-in rider. Not everybody was thrilled by the new direction. *Surfer* journalist and former world tour pro Dave Parmenter described the aerial crew as "flying squirrels," and correctly noted that the success rate on the towering air moves shown in the magazines was virtually nil. Fabled power surfers Gary Elkerton and Sunny Garcia were also dismissive of aerials. "Good surfing," Elkerton said, "is all about power, speed and flow. The other stuff isn't real surfing."

Aerials are categorized according to four factors: 1) The rider's position during lift-off; either frontside or backside. 2) The positioning of the rider's hands as he flies; either hands-free or with one or both hands gripping the edges of the board. 3) The flight pattern of the board; usually a simple arc, a 180-degree spin, or a 360-degree spin. 4) The board position on landing; either nose-forward or "reverse" (tail first). "Air" is synonymous with "aerial," and surfers generally say they "boost," "launch," or "bust" airs. Specialized aerial-only airshow contests were introduced in 1996 in Santa Cruz, California, and by 2002 the combined prize money for the small but entrenched airshow circuits worldwide was more than $250,000. While virtually all young pro surfers by the turn of the century were expert aerialists, some of the most inventive moves were being performed by a small group of air specialists, including Oscar "Ozzie" Wright, Josh Kerr, Dave Reardon-Smith, Jason "Ratboy" Collins, Eric McHenry, Randy "Goose" Welch, and Aaron

Cormican. Some of the top aerialists discuss their moves in *Flight Academy*, a 2002 surf video. *See also* Airshow.

Aguerre, Fernando   Kinetic surf-world industrialist and contest organizer; owner of Reef Footwear. Aguerre was born (1958) in Mar del Plata, Argentina, began surfing at age 11, immigrated to Southern California in 1984 after earning a law degree, and the following year launched Reef Brazil with younger brother Santiago. Based in San Diego, Reef soon gained international notice for a relentless advertising campaign featuring a series of back-arched, thong-bikini models; a second marketing coup was the 1998 Reef Big-Wave Team World Championships, held at Todos Santos, Mexico, in 30-foot surf. By 2002, Reef sandals were sold in more than 100 countries. Aguerre had meanwhile earned a reputation as a tireless organizer: in 1978 he led the charge to get a citywide surfing ban lifted from his hometown, then founded the National Surfing Association of Argentina; in 1992 he was cofounder (and first elected president) of the Pan American Surfing Association; in 1994 he was elected chairman of the International Surfing Association, amateur surfing's umbrella organization (Aguerre was the first Latin American to hold the chairmanship, and was reelected in 1996, 1998, and 2000); in 1996 he organized the first biannual World Surfing Games (replacing the 32-year-old World Surfing Championships) as a strategic move to get surfing accepted into the Sydney-held 2000 Olympic Games. The Olympic move failed, but not for lack of effort on Aguerre's part, and he vowed to keep trying. *Surfer* magazine wasn't entirely convinced the effort was worthwhile, noting that many surfers were ambivalent, even hostile, to the idea of surfing being reformatted to the Olympic standard. "Fernando Aguerre is Going for the Gold," a 1996 *Surfer* headline read. "Is Anyone Going With Him?" *See also* Argentina, International Surfing Association, Olympics and Surfing, World Surfing Games.

Aichner, Scott   Innovative freelance surf photographer from Ventura, California. Aichner was born (1970) in Long Beach, California, raised in Ventura, began bodyboarding at age seven, and had a career in the '80s as a professional bodyboarder. He shot and produced local surf videos while working as a bellhop in his early and mid-20s (including 1994's *Ventura: The Surf Movie*), and continued to do so after moving to the North Shore of Oahu in 1996. Two years later he switched to still photography, electing—against the advice of every working surf photographer he consulted—to use a manual-advance, large-transparency-format camera, which produced razor-sharp images. Within four months, the self-taught Aichner produced his first *Surfer* magazine cover, and was able to quit his hotel job and work full-time on photography. His work has appeared in surf magazines worldwide including the *Surfer's Journal, Tracks, Waves, Surfer's Path, Trip Surf, Fluir,* and *Surfing Life*; in 2001, he published 16 surf magazine covers. Aichner also shoots 16-millimeter film of waves and surfers, some of which has been used in nationally aired TV commercials.

Aikau, Clyde Graceful regularfoot surfer from Haleiwa, Hawaii; winner of the 1986 Quiksilver in Memory of Eddie Aikau contest at Waimea Bay. Clyde Aikau began surfing in 1964 at age 15, in Waikiki, and before the year was out had become the Hawaii's juniors division champion. For years he was somewhat overshadowed by older brother Eddie, who made a spectacular debut at Waimea in 1966, and was regarded as the finest big-wave rider of his generation. In 1967, Clyde later recalled, "I said to my brother, 'Hey, Eddie, can you take me out there and show me how to surf the Bay?' So we went out and he showed me exactly where to go and where not to go, and what to watch for." Clyde and Eddie rode well at all the North Shore breaks; in 1971 they both made the finals of the Smirnoff Pro and the Duke Kahanamoku Classic; two years later Clyde won the Duke, the first contest ever held at Waimea. In 1977, Eddie also won the Duke; three months later he was killed in a boating accident. Clyde and Hawaiian surfer Mark Foo were tied at the end of the 1986 Quiksilver/Eddie Aikau contest, but Clyde won after each surfer's next-highest wave was scored. He continued to perform well in the Quiksilver/Aikau event, placing fifth in 1990 and 10th in 2001. In the 2002 Quiksilver, the 52-year-old Aikau placed eighth.

Aikau, Eddie Iconic big-wave rider from Honolulu, Hawaii; winner of the 1977 Duke Kahanamoku Classic surf contest, just three months before dying in a boating accident; regarded as the greatest Waimea surfer of his time, and namesake to the Quiksilver in Memory of Eddie Aikau big-wave surf contest. "He had the ultimate Hawaiian style," next-generation big-wave surfer Darrick Doerner said in 1990. "Take off and drop in, big bottom turn, disappear into a mountain of whitewater, pop out, throw his hair back; that was Eddie. Bully style." Aikau was born (1946) and raised in Kahului, Maui, the son of a truck driver, began surfing at age 11, and moved with his family to Honolulu in 1959. His debut at Waimea in late 1966 was astounding: "he rode giant waves for over six hours without a break," *Surfing* magazine reported, "and when he finally left the water, he was judged by most to have been one of the finest riders of the day." The impression Aikau left was strengthened by his dark and rugged good looks, his fire-engine red board, and his white surf trunks decorated with a single red horizontal stripe.

Aikau was a steady performer during the early years of professional surfing on the North Shore of Oahu. He was a six-time finalist in the prestigious Duke Kahanamoku Classic between 1966 and 1974; in the Smirnoff he placed fifth in 1971, fourth in 1972, and third in 1976; he also finished third in the 1976 Lancers World Cup, and was invited to the 1971 and 1973 Expression Sessions. When Aikau won the 1977 Duke, he beat future world champions Mark Richards and Wayne Bartholomew, as well as world tour standouts Dane Kealoha, Bobby Owens, and Rory Russell. He finished the season world-rated #12. (Younger brother Clyde Aikau also made a name for himself in the big Hawaiian surf.) Aikau's distinctive bowlegged stance was widely imitated in the late '60s and early '70s, and photos of him at Waimea were published in *Life* magazine in 1966, three years before Bank of America used an Aikau shot in a nationwide billboard ad campaign. A career low point came in 1972, when he visited Durban, South Africa, for a pro contest,

Eddie Aikau

and was turned away from his hotel for being dark-skinned. It was further required that he get a special permit to surf Durban's whites-only beaches.

In 1978, Aikau gained a berth on the *Hokule'a*, a replica of the double-hulled canoe used by ancient Polynesians to sail between Hawaii and Tahiti. On March 16, Aikau and 15 other *Hokule'a* crew members left Honolulu for a 2,400-mile voyage that would reenact the midocean crossing; five hours into the trip, the starboard hull developed a leak and the boat capsized, leaving the crew hanging on to the port hull. At 10:30 the following morning, Aikau took a life vest, rain slicker, knife, and strobe light, and set out on a 10-foot surfboard for the island of Lanai, 12 miles to the east. Later that day the *Hokule'a* crew was picked up by a rescue team. Coast Guard rescuers searched for a week, but Aikau's body wasn't found.

A few weeks later, the governor of Hawaii declared April 1 to be Eddie Aikau Day, and in 1980 a commemorative plaque was installed in Aikau's honor at Waimea, not far from the lifeguard tower where he worked. A pro surf contest in Aikau's name was held at Sunset Beach in 1984; the event soon evolved into the Quiksilver in Memory of Eddie Aikau big-wave contest, held at Waimea Bay. The 1986 edition of the contest was won by Clyde Aikau, who used a 10-year-old board that had belonged to his brother.

Eddie Aikau appeared in about 10 surf movies, including *Golden Breed* (1968), *Waves of Change* (1970), and *Fluid Drive* (1974). In 2000 he was inducted into the Huntington Beach Surfing Walk of Fame; a biography, *Eddie Would Go: The Story of Eddie Aikau, Hawaiian Hero* was published in 2002. Aikau was married once and had no children. *See also* Quiksilver in Memory of Eddie Aikau.

Aipa, Ben   Innovative surfer/board-maker/coach from Honolulu, Hawaii; a top competitor in the 1960s and early '70s, and innovator of the swallowtail and stinger surfboard designs. Aipa was born (1942) in Honolulu, the son of a sugar plantation worker, and didn't begin riding waves until his early 20s, after an ankle injury ended his semipro football career. He trained for surfing with the single-mindedness he'd developed as a linebacker, not missing a day in the water for all of 1965, and the following year he was a finalist in the Duke Kahanamoku Classic at Sunset Beach. Aipa also finished fourth in both the 1967 Makaha International and the 1975 Lightning Bolt Pro, and competed in the World Championships in 1968 and 1970. It was expected that Aipa, at 250

Ben Aipa

pounds, would put more power into his turns than virtually any of his surfing contemporaries, but he augmented strength with agility, balance, and finesse. He was also one of the era's fiercest-looking surfers, helping him to get virtually any wave he wanted, even in the most crowded Hawaiian lineups. "There's a kind of silently powerful presence about him," *Surfer* magazine said of Aipa in 1972, understating the case. Pipeline virtuoso Gerry Lopez put it better: "When you see Ben coming, don't think, just get out of the way."

Aipa began shaping surfboards in 1966, and two years later made the board that fellow Hawaiian Fred Hemmings used to win the World Championships. Aipa Surfboards was founded in 1970, and Aipa soon came into his greatest influence as a designer, first inventing the double-point swallowtail in 1972, followed two years later by the split-rail stinger; both designs were ridden to electrifying effect by a group of Aipa-led Hawaiian test pilots including Larry Bertlemann, Michael Ho, Montgomery "Buttons" Kaluhiokalani, and Mark Liddell. Aipa served as an informal trainer/coach for these surfers, all of whom competed during the early years of the pro world tour, and he continued to coach in the decades to come, working with pro standouts Sunny Garcia, Brad Gerlach, Kalani Robb, and the Irons brothers, Andy and Bruce. Aipa himself continued to enter contests, winning the grandmasters division of the 1989 United States Surfing Championships and the legends division of the 2000 U.S. Championships.

In the early '80s, Aipa began producing a slightly smaller updated version of the longboards he and the rest of the sport had left behind 15 years earlier. "I was targeting the guys who were getting married and had less time to surf and weren't in the best of shape," Aipa told *Longboard* magazine in 1999. "They needed a board that could catch waves." Aipa himself was riding a 7'6" hybrid in 1998 when *Surfer* called him "the hottest 56-year-old surfer in the world." Akila Aipa, Ben's oldest son, was runner-up in the 1989 U.S. Championships, and has himself become a popular surfboard shaper.

Ben Aipa appeared in more than a dozen surf movies, including *The Natural Art* (1969), *Tracks* (1970), and *Fluid Drive* (1974); he was nominated to the International Surfing Hall of Fame in 1991. Aipa has been married three times and has three children. *See also* stinger, swallowtail.

air *See* aerial.

air surfing, airboarding *See* foilboarding.

air-drop Controlled maneuver where rider and surfboard, as a unit, momentarily lift off the water as they drop down a steep or concave wave face. An air-drop is usually performed immediately after the surfer stands and begins the ride. For decades, surfers mistakenly became airborne on takeoffs, almost always as a prelude to wiping out. Not until the late '80s was it discovered that by shifting the weight to the back foot while remaining centered and low over the board, the surfer could improve his chances of making a steep drop by intentionally going airborne. *See also* late takeoff.

airbrush Surfboard-coloring method using water-soluble acrylic paints sprayed in a mist through a handheld, air-pressurized nozzle. Airbrushing—also known as airspraying—is usually done directly onto the board's polyurethane foam core, prior to fiber-glassing; it can also be applied in between the sanding coat of resin and the gloss coat. Airbrush designs range from clean and simple to wildly extravagant; the process adds between $20 and $200 to the board's retail cost. Some airbrush work is done freehand, but generally it begins by marking off the to-be-colored areas with masking tape. Airbrushed surfboards were introduced in the late '60s; by the early '80s airbrushing had become the most popular form of board decoration—ahead of resin-based tints, opaques, and pinlines—partly because the colors were more vivid, and could be faded, blended, and otherwise played with, and partly because airbrushing added virtually no extra weight to the board. Early surf-world airbrush masters included California's Jim Phillips and Martyn Worthington of Australia. Airbrush designs have always served as a cultural barometer for surfing, with the galactic interplanetary space scenes of the mid-'70s giving way to New Wave checkerboard designs in the early '80s, followed by the streamlined single-color accent of the mid- and late '80s, then the neopunk anarchy and Pacific Islander tattoo-pattern styles of the '90s.

Airshow Specialized surfing event where competitors are judged solely on aerial maneuvers; conceived in 1996 by aerialist Shawn "Barney" Barron of Santa Cruz, California, and developed by *Surfing* magazine senior editor Skip Snead. Aerials—a constantly evolving set of through-the-air maneuvers invented in the late '70s, and popularized by the Kelly Slater–led New School surfers in the early '90s—are too difficult to perform regularly in traditional-format surf contests. The first all-aerial contest ran as an adjunct to the 1996 Cold Water Classic event in Santa Cruz, and was won by Shawn Barron. Over the next 16 months, six aerial contests were linked together as the original Surfing Magazine Airshow (SMAS) tour, worth a total of $10,000, with aerial pioneer Christian Fletcher topping the ratings at the end of the season. SMAS events over the years have occasionally featured some of the world's best-known mainstream surfers—including Kelly Slater, Matt Archbold, Andy Irons, Kalani Robb, and Darryl "Flea" Virostko—but the top slots invariably go to a small, dedicated group of aerial specialists, like Eric McHenry, Jason "Ratboy" Collins, and Randy "Goose" Welch.

The crowd-pleasing SMAS series grew quickly, and in 1999 the tour was underwritten by Vans shoes. Copycat airshow events and tours soon followed, including the National Scholastic Surfing Association O'Neill Airshow Series (an amateur version of the SMAS) and Surfing Australia's Quiksilver Airshow Series. The 2002 Quiksilver Airshow World Championships, a $64,000 one-off event held at Manly Beach, Australia, was won by Hawaiian Randy "Goose" Welch, who earned $20,000.

Competitors in the Vans/SMAS are judged on the combined scores of their two best aerials; the nine-contest 2002 Vans/SMAS tour, with events in Hawaii and Costa Rica, was worth $100,000 in total prize money. None of the airshow tours has a women's division.

Vans/SMAS year-end winners: Christian Fletcher (1996–97), Jason "Ratboy" Collins (1998, 1999), Randy "Goose" Welch (2000), Eric McHenry (2001, 2002).

Quiksilver Airshow Series winners: Oscar "Ozzie" Wright (2000–01), Dave Reardon-Smith (2001–02). *See also* aerial.

Ala Moana   Long, fast, left-breaking wave in Honolulu, Hawaii, located next to the Ala Wai Yacht Harbor; "the agony and the ecstasy of the South Shore," as described by *Surfing* magazine; a high-performance haven for local surfers, nearly as famous for its mashing crowds as for its tubing Bowl section. While Ala Moana breaks from two to 10 foot and is ridable almost daily from midspring to midfall, it rarely gets over eight feet, and hits peak form just a few times each season. The dependable northeast tradewinds blow offshore at Ala Moana, so that the afternoon surf is often better groomed than the morning surf.

Ala Moana (Hawaiian for "Ocean Street") was dynamite-blasted into existence when the Ala Wai Harbor entrance was rerouted from nearby Kewalo Basin in 1952, producing a deep-water channel for waves to spill into. Still, most surfers thought the new break was too fast to ride. Not until the early '60s did local surfers, including Sammy Lee, Paul Gebauer, Conrad Canha, Paul Strauch, and Donald Takayama, transform Ala Moana into Hawaii's premier summer surfing hot spot. Lee was particularly gifted at threading his way through the Bowl section, placing himself and his 10-foot board behind the curl with such regularity that he's been noted as the original tuberider.

Ala Moana has hosted dozens of state championship surf contests, along with the 1976, 1992, and 1996 editions of the United States Surfing Championships. But its greatest moments have traditionally taken place during unscheduled free-surf sessions. Larry Bertlemann, Ben Aipa, and Gerry Lopez were among the top performers at Ala Moana in the early '70s—the break's golden decade—followed shortly by Montgomery "Buttons" Kaluhiokalani, Mark Liddell, and Dane Kealoha. Ala Moana has been featured in more than 30 surf movies and videos, including *Barefoot Adventure* (1960), *The Endless Summer* (1966), *Super Session* (1975), *We Got Surf* (1981), and *Aloha Bowls* (1994). A sequence from *Tales of the Seven Seas* (1981) perfectly captures the superheated thrills and chaos of a big day at Ala Moana, with deep tuberides, flying boards, gurgling wipeouts, and merciless drop-ins, all building to a climax as a baby-blue catamaran exiting the nearby harbor is pulled into the vortex of a 10-foot closeout set. *See also* Waikiki.

Alabama   With 53 miles of coastline along the frequently waveless Gulf of Mexico, bayou-filled Alabama is home to just a small number of dedicated and often frustrated surfers. Erratic three- to four-foot waves hit the Alabama shore in fall and early winter, as hurricanes cross the Gulf of Mexico. Alabama Point, a long, diagonally laid seawall, is the state's best break, and can maintain form during the heaviest hurricane swells. Several other clean white-sand beachbreaks—including West End and the Stumps—are found on bridge-accessed Dauphin Island, the largest of Alabama's several offshore islands. Waves across the state tend to be windblown and choppy. Average air and water temperatures in Alabama both range from the low 80s in summer to the low 50s in winter. "Alabama's good surfers travel frequently," Swell.com noted in 2001. "In some cases, permanently."

Surfing was likely introduced to Alabama in the early '60s by navy servicemen stationed in the Florida Panhandle town of Pensacola, about 10 miles from the Alabama state line. Alabama was included in the 1968-formed Gulf Coast Surfing Association, and was given its own Eastern Surfing Association (ESA) district in 1987; membership in 2003 was about 40. Gulf Coast surfing godfather Yancy Spencer claimed in a 1973 article that Alabama had on occasion provided him with "some of the best small waves" he'd ever ridden, and Hurricane Andrew created excellent six-foot tubes at the Stumps, but wave-riding here has otherwise passed by with little or no notice from the outside surf world. In 2002, Alabama had no surf shops and fewer than two dozen full-time surfers, including ESA Alabama director Chuck Barnes. The ESA hosts two events each year in Alabama.

alaia board   A thin, round-nosed, square-tailed surfboard, used by commoners and royalty alike in pre-20th-century Hawaii. The *alaia* was generally made of koa wood (sometimes breadfruit or wiliwili), and was the most suitable type of board for riding the steep, fast-breaking waves common to the Islands. Of the 13 premodern boards housed in Honolulu's Bishop Museum, 10 are of the *alaia* type, ranging from seven to 12 feet in length, with an average width of 18 inches, and an average thickness of one inch. It's believed that most *alaia*-riding surfers used the *lala* technique of sliding at an angle along the wave face ahead of the white water. By comparison, the longer, thicker, heavier *olo* boards—thought to have been reserved for use by royalty only—were likely used to ride straight to shore on waves that were either unbroken or barely cresting. *See also* olo board, plank surfboard.

Alaia board; late nineteenth-century Waikiki, Hawaii

Alaska   The largest of America's 50 states, twice the size of runner-up Texas, Alaska has the smallest population of any state save Wyoming. While it's unclear just when Alaska was initially surfed, Daniel Brandel wrote to *Surfer* magazine in 1967 to announce the formation of the Kodiak Island Surfing Association, the state's first surf club. "As of this date," Brandel reported, "we have 57 active members and 38 inactive members, [as] not everybody has their own board." Washington surfer Greg Wheaton further explored dozens of southeast Alaskan lineups in the late '70s and '80s. The American surf press began getting packages of photographs of the Alaskan surf in the early '80s from bodyboarder Robert Kemp, along with detailed handwritten notes on local wave and weather conditions. "The main difficulty here is access," Kemp wrote in 1988. "You have to either fly in or take a boat. Both are expensive. Backpacking is an option, but it's a two day hike and there's the problem of the notorious Alaskan bears, both black and grizzly. Not surprisingly, everyone here carries a gun."

California surfer/board-maker/journalist Dave Parmenter, along with pro surfers Brock Little and Josh Mulcoy and photographer Bob Barbour, spent two weeks surfing along the jagged coastline of Alaska's Tongass Park in 1992, riding desolate but beautiful point surf, while trying their best to adapt to a tidal range that gets up to 30 foot. "A lot of the times the tide changed so quickly," Parmenter wrote later, "that by the time you returned to the same spot in the lineup [after a ride], the wave-focus had shifted elsewhere along the point." In 1998, following in Kemp's footsteps, California big-wave riders Mark

Renneker, Peter Mel, and Jay Moriarity, along with surf journalist Steve Hawk and photographer Tom Servais, explored Unalaska in the Aleutian Islands—the chain extending southwest between the Pacific Ocean and the Bering Sea, terminating a few hundred miles from Russia—and found near-permanent cloudy skies, frequent high winds, predictably cold air and water temperatures, and a number of high-quality albeit temperamental surf breaks.

As of 2003, Alaska has less then 100 resident surfers, all part-timers, and most of them doing their wave-riding along the fjord-filled southeast coastline. Yakutat is the state's most popular surfing area; Cannon Beach provides sand-bottom peaks in the summer; the rock-lined surf at Graveyards requires a big winter swell. Air and water temperatures in this part of the state are relatively mild, due to the Alaska Current. Water temperatures here range from the upper 30s in January to the mid-50s in August; air temperatures range from the mid-20s to the mid-50s. Although the Alaskan surf often gets huge, the best waves—from two to eight foot—are generally found in the state's wave- and wind-protected coves and inlets; the number of undiscovered high-quality surf breaks along Alaska's 2,800-mile Pacific coastline is probably in the dozens. Autumn is the best time to surf here, as the days are still long, the weather tolerable, and the surf fairly consistent as storm systems begin to form in the North Pacific. Summer waves are often small and fogged in; winter surfing is all but impossible, as nights last for 18 hours or more, and violent weather frequently forces everyone into gloomy hibernation. "Ninety-nine percent of the people up here drink," a guide told surf journalist Dave Parmenter in 1992, explaining how the natives survive the cold and dark winter months. "The other one percent are court-ordered not to." Alaska was featured in Bruce Brown's 1994 movie *Endless Summer II,* and in the 1995 surf video *Feral Kingdom.* Icey Waves Surf Shop, the first retail outlet of its kind in the state, opened in Yakutat in the summer of 1999. A small number of Alaskan surf breaks are detailed in *The Stormrider Guide North America* (2002).

alcohol and surfing   The surf world's relationship to alcohol isn't much different from that of other sporting or recreational cultures. For a small percentage of surfers, drinking is addictive, hazardous, and occasionally deadly, but for a huge majority it's a safe and enjoyable part of their après-surf lives. "We thought that our last pints were being pulled at 11:30," American surf nomad Kevin Naughton wrote in a 1978 *Surfer* magazine article, describing his first visit to an Irish countryside pub, not long after a cold water wave-riding session in the North Atlantic. "At three in the morning, I just managed to squeeze my way through the chattering, musical crowd, and nonchalantly asked the barman, 'When does the pub close?' He answered with a deadpan voice, 'In October.'"

Alcoholic beverage companies have long recognized the marketing value of surfing: Smirnoff Vodka sponsored a popular pro surfing contest from 1969 to 1978, and other pro events have been sponsored by Bundaberg Rum, José Cuervo Tequila, Kahlúa, Coors, Fosters, and Michelob. Budweiser was the primary backer of the Professional Surfing Association of America tour from 1987 to 1993. Primo Beer sponsored Hawaiian pro surfer Hans Hedemann in the '90s. California's Zele Breweries produced a line of beers in 1990 named after famous surf breaks, including Rincon Dry, Trestles Lager, and Zuma Light, while Napa Valley's Random Ridge Vineyard has produced since the late '90s Old Wave zinfandel and Cloudbreak chardonnay. The link between drinking and surfing was more immediate in events like the annual Stone Steps Surf Contest in San Diego, California, held in the '70s and '80s, where entrants all had to down a one-quart bucket of beer before each heat.

There have been no studies on surfers' drinking habits, but they're generally thought of as a beer-drinking group—although rum-based tropical drinks were popular with mainland American surfers in the '30s and '40s, in homage to the sport's Polynesian roots, and surfers in the '50s and early '60s sometimes warmed themselves with cheap red wine before hitting the waves during the cold winter months. In the late '60s and early '70s, a generational gap opened up between older surfers, who were drinkers, and younger surfers, who also drank, but usually as an adjunct to their drug use.

Alcoholism rates among surfers may likely be slightly less than that of the population at large. Surfers by nature are health conscious, mildly optimistic, and forward looking ("We're happy people because we always know what we want," big-wave rider Mark Foo pointed out in 1985), each of which acts as a deterrent to hard drinking. Nonetheless, alcoholics have regularly and sometimes tragically passed through the sport, most notably '60s surf headliners Dewey Weber and Butch Van Artsdalen, both of Cali-

fornia. Weber, the prototype hotdogger and surfboard manufacturing kingpin—who later noted that his first taste of beer, at age 11, "really lit my life on fire"—died of alcohol-related heart failure at 53. Pipeline tuberiding ace Van Artsdalen died of liver failure at 38.

Surf culture reflects the culture at large in the way it chooses not to deal with the ambivalence between approved, or glorified, drinking and problem drinking. A rare exception came in the form of a reader response to a 1998 *Australia's Surfing Life* magazine article that cheerfully examined how heavy off-hours drinking helped a group of Aussie pros improve their competitive performances. "So, Matt Hoy is a hot surfer who drinks heaps of beer?" noted an anonymous surfer from the Sydney beachside town of Maroubra. "Big deal! So was I and now I am a fat, bloated, red-faced has-been with nothing to look forward to in life." *See also* drugs and surfing.

Aleutian Islands   *See* Alaska.

Allen, Chuck   Education-minded surf contest administrator from Southern California by way of the American south; cofounder in 1978 of the National Scholastic Surfing Association (NSSA), and cofounder shortly thereafter of the United States Surfing Federation (USSF). Allen was born (1936) and raised in Oklahoma, trained racehorses and competed in rodeos as a young man, moved to Southern California in 1960 to work in banking, and became interested in surfing in 1977 when he decided to help organize a surf team at his sons' high school. The following year, working with teacher/coaches John Rothrock and Tom Gibbons, Allen formed the NSSA, an organization first noted for its link to education (members were required to stay in school and maintain a 2.0 GPA), and later for producing top world pro tour competitors such as Tom Curren, Kim Mearig, Rob Machado, and Andy Irons. Allen also cofounded the USSF, which, in keeping with the convoluted feud-prone nature of amateur competitive surfing, soon became an NSSA adversary.

Allen coached the Huntington Beach High School surf team from 1981 to 1988, taking them to seven consecutive national titles, and in 1984 he helped coach the American national team to victory in the World Surfing Championships. Allen served as NSSA president from 1978 to 1988. Turning his attention to mountain sports, he founded the United States of America Snowboard Association in 1989 and the All-Terrain Boarding Association in 1999. Allen was inducted in 1999 into the Huntington Beach Surfing Walk of Fame. *See also* National Scholastic Surfing Association.

aloha shirt   Casual short-sleeve print shirt, originally made in Hawaii; a colorful fashion item that through the decades has bounced all over the fashion spectrum, from practical to casually elegant; tacky and garish to collectible. Native Hawaiians for years had been hand-painting island motifs onto the drab tapa-bark *palaka* shirts favored by Chinese immigrant workers, when, in 1931, Honolulu tailor Ellery Chun began putting the same brightly colored pattern onto silk. Five years later, Kamehameha Garment Company in Honolulu brought the newly named "aloha shirt" to mass market for the first time, and it instantly became a must-have fashion accouterment for mainland American tourists who were now pouring into Hawaii by the tens of thousands. Popular prints included hula dancers, palm trees, surfers, flowers, pineapples, tikis, tropical fish, leis, and ukeleles. Celebrities like Montgomery Clift, Bing Crosby, Elvis Presley and Frank Sinatra helped popularize the aloha shirt; President Harry Truman wore one in a photograph used on a 1951 *Life* magazine cover; surfer and Olympic swimming champion Duke Kahanamoku virtually lived in aloha shirts from the '30s until his death in 1968. Silk and rayon were the favorite materials in the early decades of the aloha shirt, followed by cotton. California surfers visiting Hawaii just before and after World War II, meanwhile, were enthusiastic about exporting native culture back to the mainland, and loaded their steamer trunks with aloha shirts, along with ukuleles, palm-frond hats, and tiki torches.

Aloha shirt quality began to decline in the mid-'50s as polyester photolithograph knockoffs were stacked high in department stores like Sears and Roebuck; through the '60s and early '70s the aloha shirt was so associated with tourists and waiters in Polynesian-theme restaurants that owners of genuine "silkies" purged the items en masse from their wardrobes as hopelessly out of fashion. By the mid-'70s, however, vintage aloha shirts, purchased at thrift shops or flea markets, were not only coming back into fashion as retro-chic, but were starting to be collected and traded. Prices went up dramatically in the '80s and '90s. Aloha shirt specialty shops were founded, books were written on the subject, and by 2000 it was

possible to spend more than $5,000 on a well-preserved rayon or silk. "Condition, rarity, coconut buttons, print, and fabrication are all factors to be considered when assessing a shirt," authority Dale Hope wrote in the *Surfer's Journal* in 2000, noting that most aloha shirt collectors keep their shirts in use. "Aficionados of the rayon silkies say that there is no better feeling than that cool, smooth fabric against the skin." Hawaii governor Ben Cayean declared 2000 as "The Year of the Aloha Shirt," in honor of originator Ellery Chun, who had just died at age 91. Books on the aloha shirt include *The Hawaiian Shirt* (1984), *Hawaiian Shirt Designs* (1997), and *The Aloha Shirt: Spirit of the Islands* (2000). *See also* fashion and surfing.

Alter, Hobart "Hobie"   Ocean-sports industrialist from Orange County, California; founder of Hobie Surfboards in 1954 and the Hobie Cat sailboat company in 1967. "Perhaps more than anyone else," surf journalist Drew Kampion wrote in 1988, "including Gidget, Dora, Frankie and Annette, even the Duke,

Hobie Alter

Hobie Alter has been responsible for the growth and development of surfing." Alter was born (1933) in Ontario, California, the son of an orange farmer, and began surfing at age 16 in Laguna Beach, near his family's summer home; he made the finals of the Makaha International surfing contest in 1958 and 1959. Alter made balsa boards out of his garage from 1950 to 1953; the following year he opened Hobie Surfboards in Dana Point; in 1958, after teaming up with board laminator Gordon "Grubby" Clark to develop a commercially viable polyurethane foam surfboard blank, he began using foam instead of balsa on all Hobie surfboards. Alter's company was the industry leader for the next 12 years, selling up to 6,500 boards annually during the mid-'60s.

The sturdy, broad-shouldered, plainspoken Alter had meanwhile developed into one of the world's best tandem surfers; with partner Laurie Hoover, he won the 1961 West Coast Surfing Championships, as well as the Pacific Coast Tandem Championship in 1962 and 1963. Hoping to link surfing and recreational boat use, Alter became the leading advocate in the mid-'60s for wake surfing, in which the surfer rides the wave created by a boat wake (an early version of wakeboarding, but with conventional surfboards instead of specially designed wakeboards), and in 1965 he wake-surfed 30 miles from Long Beach to Catalina Island. Hobie Skateboards was meanwhile launched in 1964. Alter was also a key figure in the creation of the United States Surfing Association in 1961, and served as the group's vice president for four years.

In 1967, Alter began marketing the Hobie Cat, an easy-to-use 14-foot catamaran designed to launch from the beach and ride over the surf. "The Cat That Flies," a *Life* magazine photo feature on the Hobie Cat, was published in 1968, and sales for Alter's new creation soared. More than 110,000 Hobie 16s—the most popular Hobie Cat model, released in 1969—have been manufactured worldwide since the late '60s. Alter sold Hobie Cat to the Coleman outdoor supply company in 1976, but continued to design and commercially build catamarans and boats.

Alter received a Waterman Achievement Award from the Surf Industry Manufacturers Association in 1993; in 1997 he was inducted into the Huntington Beach Surfing Walk of Fame. Alter has been married five times and has three children. He lives in Macal, Idaho. *See also* Hobie Surfboards.

Alvarez, José "Pepe"   Efficient surfing organizer from San Juan, Puerto Rico; president of the International Surfing Association (ISA) from 1988 to 1990. Alvarez was born (1957) in Miami, Florida, moved with his family to San Juan in 1965, and began surfing two years later. He competed for Puerto Rico in the 1978 World Championships in South Africa. In Australia for the 1982 Championships he lobbied the ISA on behalf of Puerto Rico to the rights to host the 1988 Championships. Alvarez founded the Puerto Rico Surfing Federation (PRSF) in 1984, and later that year led the national team to a fourth-place finish at the World Championships in California. Four years later, the Puerto Rico–held Championships were a huge success, due in part to Alvarez's fund-raising prowess, as he gathered nearly $1 million from the government and private businesses. Alvarez was elected president of the ISA shortly after the 1988 event; two years later he retired from both the ISA and PRSF. *See also* International Surfing Association.

American Surfing Association (ASA)   Controversial amateur surfing organization founded by Gary Filosa in 1976, based in Huntington Beach, California. The Vermont-born Filosa, described by surf journalist Rus Calisch in 1977 as "clever, ruthless and vindictive," claimed to have started the American Surfing Association (ASA) in order to guide surfing into the Olympic Games, and Filosa did manage to open lines of communication to both the Amateur Athletic Union and the International Olympic Committee. But not long after Filosa had set up the five-region ASA—complete with a detailed constitution and set of bylaws—*Surfing* magazine reported that "some members of the organization's board of directors had never consented to be directors," and that Filosa had threatened ASA dissenters "with investigation by everyone from political figures to the FBI." As American amateur surfing was at the time all but moribund, the ASA did manage to attract some of the country's best amateur surfers to its one and only All-American Surfing Championships, held from December 28–30, 1977, at Huntington Pier. The following year the ASA was superseded by the formation of the National Scholastic Surfing Association—which largely based its constitution and bylaws on those used by the ASA. *See also* Dr. Gary Filosa.

Ancell, Kevin   Burly California artist best known for his rich, layered, allegorical, and often satirical surfing-themed oil paintings, produced in the style of Rembrandt and Caravaggio. Ancell was born (1963) and raised in Santa Monica, and began surfing at age

Kevin Ancell

nine. He moved to China in 1985 and briefly taught Western culture at the Beijing Institute of Science and Technology; two years later, after the Chinese government expelled him as a "cultural pollutant," he moved to San Francisco and began drinking heavily. "When I cleaned up," he told *Longboarder* magazine in 1998, "the taverns in San Francisco flew their flags at half mast." *Better Living Through Medication* (1996) is typical of Ancell's work, showing a nude surfer floating between a skeleton and a tiny Prozac-bearing angel. For *Surf Trip*, a 2000 surf-art exhibition at the Yerba Buena Center for the Arts in San Francisco, Ancell grouped together 25 full-size polyurethane hula dancer automatons, some of them wielding assault rifles and hand grenades. "Here's the dashboard hula doll," Ancell told the *San Francisco Chronicle,* gesturing to the slowly gyrating assemblage, "except now she's got guns and she's been drinking and she's pissed off." As a scenery painter in Hollywood, Ancell worked on *Sphere* (1997), *What Dreams May Come* (1998), and *The Phantom Menace* (1999), among other movies. His work was also featured in the 2002 Laguna Art Museum show, *The Art History of Surfing. See also* surf art.

Andaman Islands   Lightly populated tropical island chain, governed by India and located in the Bay of Bengal, about 200 miles off the coast of Myanmar; described by Sinbad in the *Arabian Nights* as a "string of pearls." While small groups of Australian surfers began visiting the Andamans in the early 1980s, the islands weren't revealed to the surf public at large until 1998, when a *Surfer* magazine expedition (including pro surfer Chris Malloy, musician/photographer Jack Johnson, and writer Sam George) landed in the capital city of Port Blair, with permits to sail the coasts of nearby islands. Access to the 204-island Andaman chain is tightly restricted or prohibited outright, as the hilly and densely forested region is home to a number of antediluvian native tribes having little or no contact with the outside world. The *Surfer* group, over the course of two weeks, found some high-quality reef waves, but chose not to publish the spots' exact locations. A right-breaking wave called Kumari Point proved to be the great discovery, as it raced evenly down the reef for more than 300 yards. "Faster than G-land, faster than J-Bay," as the *Surfer's Journal* later reported, citing two of the most famous high-velocity waves. "Quite possibly the best coral-reef point on the planet." But a follow-up trip in 1999 produced no surf whatsoever. April and May are thought to be the two best months for surfing in the Andamans, as Indian Ocean swells are strong enough by that time to reach into the Bay of Bengal, while the seasonal southwest monsoons haven't yet started in earnest. Since 1998 a Thailand-based charter company has run 10- to 14-day surf tours into the Andamans. The Andaman surf is featured in the 1999 surf video *Thicker Than Water.*

Andersen, Lisa   Masterful and enigmatic pro surfer from Ormond Beach, Florida; four-time world champion (1994–97), and the omnipresent public face for the female surfing movement in the mid-'90s. "She's the first woman to cross over into surfing celebrity-hood," *Outside* magazine wrote about Andersen in 1996, "and achieve a dominance that made the pig dudes shut up and take notice." Andersen was born (1969) in New York, raised in Maryland and Virginia, and began surfing at age 13, after moving with her family to Ormond Beach. Two years later, her father destroyed her surfboard while Andersen watched; at 16, with money saved from summer jobs, she bought a one-way plane ticket to Los Angeles and ran away from home, leaving a note saying that she was going to California to become the women's world surfing champion. (Andersen later admitted she "didn't even know if there was such a thing as a surfing world

Lisa Andersen

championship.") She landed in Huntington Beach, worked part-time as a waitress, and slept where she could, sometimes on the beach. A year later the 17-year-old won the girls' division of the United States Surfing Championships, placed third in the World Surfing Championships, and turned professional, winning the world pro tour's rookie-of-the-year honors in 1987. Although Andersen was touted as a future world champion, her surfing talent was consistently undermined by a fragile self-confidence. She was ranked 10th in the world in 1988, seventh in 1989, fourth in 1990, seventh in 1991, and fourth in 1992. While inspired by fellow Floridian Frieda Zamba (four-time world champion between 1984 and 1988), Andersen often said she wanted to "surf like a guy," and to a degree she did. She directed and focused her speed better than any woman before her, and was therefore able to put maximum power into her turns; she also maintained a balletic line through her head and body. "When you surf with Lisa," Hawaiian tuberiding ace Rochelle Ballard said, "you find yourself smoothing out your own surfing. Her technique is so refined that it rubs off on everybody around her."

Andersen married Brazilian surfer and world pro tour head judge Renato Hickel in March 1993, and five months later gave birth to a daughter, Erica. Andersen competed while pregnant, missing just the final contest of the year, and finished the season ranked ninth. Motherhood, she later noted, turned her career around. Childbirth had been "the worst, most painful thing ever; everything's easy after having a baby." Andersen made a competition final just five weeks after giving birth; she then won three of eleven world tour events in 1994 to earn her first

championship, and continued on a similar pace to win an additional three titles. A low point came in 1995, when she herniated a disk in her back near the end of the season and barely held off Australian Pauline Menczer to retain the championship. While a much steadier competitor than she had been, Andersen still lost routine matches to second-stringers and wild cards, and seemed to ride at full strength only against her primary foes.

Personally and professionally, 1996 was the busiest and most chaotic of Andersen's life. She left Hickel, saying she "just wasn't interested in him after Erica was born." *Surfer* put Andersen on the cover (the first female-surfer cover shot in 15 years), with a sly blurb directed at an overwhelmingly male readership: "Lisa Andersen Surfs Better Than You." She was meanwhile profiled in newspapers and general-interest magazines around the world. In *Outside*'s "Gidget Kicks Ass" feature, Andersen was lauded for her surfing talent, good looks, and determination, but described as "oddly impenetrable [and] closed down, as if the personality of a 17-year-old linebacker had been grafted onto her feminine psyche." Three years into her contract with Roxy, a women's spinoff line from surfwear giant Quiksilver, Andersen helped design a new function-over-fashion women's boardshort (which immediately became fashionable), and was the star of a massive promotional campaign that nearly defined the decade's boom in women's surfing. The trim (5'7", 125 pounds), blond, smiling Andersen was seen in full-page magazine ads, on posters, and in promo videos. As former world champion Pauline Menczer noted in 1996, in an understandably bitter tone, "Women's surfing right now is Lisa Andersen. The rest of us might as well not even be here." The Andersen juggernaut came to a sudden halt in July 1998, when her back seized up, forcing her to miss the second half of the season; she was virtually unseen in 1999. In 2000, at age 30, she returned to competition and finished the year ranked fifth; in 2001 she skipped the tour and gave birth to a son; she was granted a wild-card seed into all world tour events for 2002, but failed to qualify for the 2003 tour.

Andersen is a six-time winner of the *Surfer* Magazine Readers Poll Award (1992, 1994, 1996–99); in 1998 she was voted "Female Athlete of the Year" by Condé Nast's *Sports for Women* magazine; in 1999 she was the only female surfer, along with Kathy "Gidget" Kohner, to be listed in *Surfer*'s "25 Most Influential Surfers of the Century" article; in 2000 she was ranked #76 in *Sports Illustrated for Women*'s "Greatest Sportswomen of the Century." She's been featured in dozens of surf movies and videos, including *Atlantic Crossing* (1989), *Surfers: The Movie* (1990), *Triple C* (1996), *Performers III* (1999), and *Tropical Madness* (2001). Andersen lives in Ormond Beach, Florida, with her two children.

Anderson, Simon   Lantern-jawed Australian surfer/board designer from Narrabeen, New South Wales; world-ranked #3 in 1977, and the inventor, three years later, of the tri-fin surfboard design. "With that one startling innovation," surf journalist Sam George later wrote, "Simon reshaped the surfing style of an entire generation—and the next couple of generations to follow, for good measure." Anderson was born (1954) in Sydney, and spent his first five years in the suburb of Balgowlah, before his father won the lottery and moved the family to a beach-front house at Collaroy, near Narrabeen. Mark Anderson, Simon's older brother, swam for Australia in the 1968 Olympics, and Simon himself swam regularly until his 13th birthday, when he received his first new surfboard. In 1971, as a gangly 6'3" 17-year-old, he won the juniors division in both the Australian National Titles and the Bells Beach contest; in 1972 he successfully defended both titles and made the Australian team for the World Surfing Championships. Although not yet filled out to his midcareer weight of 200 pounds, Anderson had already gained a reputation as one of the country's best power surfers, connecting his forceful turns with a graceful and easygoing style. With little or no training ("he likes his snooker, the pub and his mates," surf journalist Phil Jarratt noted, "and can watch television for three or four days at a stretch"), Anderson's natural talent took him to the forefront of national and international competitive surfing. In 1973 he placed third at Bells and sixth in the Coca-Cola Surfabout (held at Narrabeen, Anderson's home break); in 1975 he placed fourth in the Coke; in 1976 he was a finalist in the Australian National Titles; in 1977 he won Bells and the Coke, placed fourth in the Pipeline Masters, and finished the world tour ranked third. Anderson also became known as one of the world's best in larger surf, particularly at Hawaii's Sunset Beach.

In late 1977, Australian pro Mark Richards introduced his version of the twin-fin, a pivoting small-wave board that helped Richards win four world titles, which in turn made the twin-fin the hottest

Simon Anderson

board of the late '70s and early '80s. While Anderson maintained a high position in the world rankings, finishing 15th in 1979 and sixth in 1980, he struggled with the hard-to-control twin-fin, and in 1979 began thinking of ways to modify the design. He'd been shaping surfboards since 1972, had founded his own Energy Surfboards label in 1975, and had developed into one of Australia's most highly respected board designers. In October 1980, he noticed that fellow Narrabeen surfer/shaper Frank Williams had placed a small half-moon fin near the tail of his twin-fin as a stabilizer. Inspired, Anderson immediately made himself a square-tailed board with three like-sized fins, all smaller than those used on a twin-fin. He called his new design the "Thruster," as a slightly racy play on words and because the third fin in fact added thrust to the board's turning capabilities; he then set out to convince the surf world that the tri-fin was superior to the twin-fin. Anderson scored back-to-back wins at Bells and the Surfabout in 1981, then finished the season by winning the Pipeline Masters. Mark Richards again won the championship—Anderson chose not to compete in about one-third of the scheduled events for 1981, and finished #6—but the shambling, straw-haired surfer from Narrabeen was clearly the breakthrough performer of the year, and twin-fin surfers the world over began converting to tri-fins. He finished 11th in the world in 1982, 19th in 1983, then quit the circuit.

Throughout, Anderson remained a plain Aussie bloke, never veering, as Phil Jarratt phrased it, from "the pursuit of ordinariness." Aside from his wave-riding, Anderson called no attention to himself whatsoever, with the notable exception of his alcohol-fueled postcontest banquet speeches, which consisted mainly of cutting deadpan gibes toward the surf industry, other surfers, and mainly himself. He later joked somewhat bitterly about his failure to patent the tri-fin design, thus missing out on perhaps millions of dollars in licensing fees. Anderson was named the "Surfer of the Year" by *Surfing* magazine in 1981, and inducted into the Australian Hall of Fame in 1989. *Surfer* magazine listed him as the eighth most influential surfer of the 20th century; he was inducted into the Huntington Beach Surfing Walk of Fame in 2001. Anderson regularly appeared in surf movies between the mid-'70s and mid-'80s, including *A Winter's Tale* (1974), *Fantasea* (1978), *Wizards of the Water* (1982), and *Totally Committed* (1984). Now living in Newport, Sydney, Anderson is married and has two children. *See also* Thruster, tri-fin.

Angel, Jose   Fearless surfer from Haleiwa, Hawaii, described by fellow big-wave pioneer Greg Noll as "the gutsiest surfer there ever was." Angel was born (1934) and raised in San Francisco, California, and became a casual surfer while attending San Francisco State College. He took to the ocean in part because he had severe skin allergies, and seawater provided quick and easy relief. In 1955 he followed wife-to-be Mozelle Gooch to Hawaii; she was at that point the more accomplished surfer of the two. But Angel, a brawny goofyfooter, immersed himself in the powerful waves along the North Shore of Oahu, and by the end of the decade he'd earned a singular reputation as a thrill-seeker who loved a thumping wipeout just as much—perhaps more—as a successfully completed ride. "He'd take an unbelievably hairy drop," fellow California transplant Ricky Grigg recalled in 1993, "make the hard part of the ride, and then just step off the board and let the wave blast him; just *destroy* him." Angel was also one of Hawaii's best free divers; without scuba tanks, he was able to descend more than 300 feet below the surface. When Angel was separated from his boat following a long dive off Maui, he swam 13 miles to the island of Molokai, then hiked four miles to the nearest phone. In 1974, however, while diving for black coral near Kauai, he came up too fast and suffered a case of the bends (nitrogen bubbles in the body tissues caused by rapid decompression), which left his right leg partially paralyzed and slowed down his wave-riding. On July 24,

1976, Angel and Grigg went diving at a place called Shark Ridge, off Maui. Angel dropped below 300 feet, and never came up. Grigg later said that Angel probably misgauged the dive and blacked out. Shelly Angel, Jose's oldest daughter, thought her father took his own life. "My dad was never going to grow old gracefully," she said in 1993. "He needed to go out with a bang."

On land, Angel had been easygoing, gentle, polite, and helpful; he began working as a teacher at Haleiwa Elementary School on the North Shore in the late '50s, and became the school's principal in 1974. Angel appeared in more than a dozen surf movies, including *Surf Safari* (1959), *Barefoot Adventure* (1960), *Cavalcade of Surf* (1962), and *Waves of Change* (1970). He was featured on the cover of the first issue of *Surfer* magazine in 1960, dropping into a giant wave at Sunset Beach. Angel was married twice and had four children.

angle   The veering path a surfer takes across the smooth, unbroken face of the wave, ahead of the whitewater; to follow diagonally along the wave's sloping shoulder, as opposed to riding on a line perpendicular to the beach. After learning how to stand on a board, a beginning surfer next learns to angle—either to the left or right, as the wave dictates. Angling, in turn, is the basis for all surfing maneuvers, from cutbacks to noseriding, tuberiding, and aerials. Ancient Polynesian surfers may have veered their boards to one degree or another, but angling really came into its own around 1910. Waikiki was at that time the crucible for high-performance surfing, and by 1915, writer Jack London noted that surfers were riding at "astonishing slant angles," instead of heading beeline for shore as they had during his previous visit seven years earlier. "Slide," "trim," and "cut" are used synonymously with "angle." *See also* trim.

Angola   War-torn country in southwest Africa, sandy and dry to the south, tropical to the north, with a 950-mile coastline facing the South Atlantic Ocean. "The waves are there, and if you're a goofy-footer, it's paradise," Hawaiian surfer Randy Rarick wrote in 1975 after spending six weeks in Angola. "So far as we could tell, there's only been a handful of surfers in the south, and no one in the north." As of 2003, surfing remains a lightly practiced sport in Angola, due primarily to an enduring civil war, which, over the decades, has drawn in Portugal, the former

Soviet Union, Cuba, and South Africa, among other nations. A 2000 U.S. State Department travel advisory warned against any visits to Angola, citing "bandit attacks, undisciplined police and military personnel, high-intensity military actions in the interior provinces and unexploded land mines in rural areas." A 1998 issue of *Australia's Surfing Life* went into greater detail, listing "cholera, malaria, dengue fever, typhoid, HIV, Ebola, sharks, barracudas, hippos, crocs, snakes, revolutionaries and terrorists."

Southern Angola is geographicaly defined by the Namib, the world's oldest desert, and the surf spots here—mostly beachbreaks—are virtually inaccessible for lack of roads. Northern Angola is tropical, and both the central and northern regions feature dozens of left-breaking points; in the 300 miles of coast between Benguela and the capital city of Luanda there are more than 30 good-to-excellent pointbreaks, many producing 100-yard-long rides. Angola's climate is mild, with air and water temperatures both ranging from 60s to the low 70s. May through September is the best time to surf, as the waves are consistently five to eight foot, and sometimes bigger. Angola's wave-riding community is made up primarily of a handful of American expatriates working in the oil industry who usually hit the surf with at least two heavily armed guards.

Angourie   Gemlike pointbreak in rural North Coast New South Wales, Australia, three miles from the fishing town of Yamba, and 140 miles south of the NSW/Queensland border; listed by *Surfing* magazine in 1989 as one of the world's 25 best waves. Angourie was probably first ridden in the late '50s or early '60s by fisherman/surfers of the Yamba lifesaving club; it was presented to the Australian surf world at large in the debut issue of *Surfing World Monthly* magazine in 1962. Angourie breaks best from February to May, on an east swell with a light south wind. Its semiremote location—and proximity to Yuraygir National Park— has kept real estate developers more or less at bay, and the natural beauty of the small boulder- and tree-lined beach at Angourie is largely intact. As the wave wraps into the lee of the Angourie point, it seems to be continuously bending in toward the rider, a quality that helps make the break, as *Surfing* magazine described it, a "high-performance heaven." The shortboard revolution was in part conceived and launched at Angourie, as evidenced in a number of surf films, including *Splashdown* (1969), *The Innermost*

Limits of Pure Fun (1970), and *Morning of the Earth* (1972). David "Baddy" Treloar, one of the top riders of the shortboard revolution, has been regarded as Angourie's master surfer for more than 30 years. Angourie has also appeared in a number of surf videos, including *Water Slaughter* (1988), *Sultans II* (1989), *Soul Patrol* (1997), and *Quiver* (2001). *See also* North Coast, New South Wales.

Antarctica   Icebound continent covering and surrounding the South Pole; site of the coldest recorded temperature, –128, on July 21, 1983, at Vostok Station. Porter Turnbull, a chiropractor from Hawaii, joined a chartered Antarctica wildlife expedition in early 1999, and brought along his portable two-piece surfboard. Midway down the Antarctic Peninsula he assembled the board, was ferried to shore, hiked over a headland wearing a hooded six-millimeter wetsuit, gloves, and booties, and rode what he later described as "head-high walling lefts . . . alone with 30,000 penguins." A more ambitious Antarctica surf voyage was undertaken in February 2000 by eight Californians, including big-wave riders Chris Malloy and Mark Renneker, former *Surfer* magazine editor Steve Hawk, and surf photographer Art Brewer. "The first time we lowered a thermometer into the water to measure the sea temperature," Renneker wrote in a *Surfer* feature article, "it was eaten by some creature; maybe a leopard seal." The group rode more than a dozen breaks during their monthlong voyage—all located off islands rather than the Antarctic mainland—and the waves were generally small with average shape. Water temperatures ranged from the low to mid-30s, and the surfers wore custom-made dry suits with full-body fleece undersuits. At one point, while the surfers were riding in a glacier-lined bay, a nearshore wall of ice collapsed and sent a wave racing out toward them. "We were awestruck," Malloy remembered, "as it hit deeper water, flattened out, then passed under and through us like a specter." Using a portable satellite dish, Hawk posted daily entries from his Antarctica log, along with digital photographs, to Quokka.com, an outdoor sports/adventure Web site.

Apocalypse Now   Sprawling 1979 Vietnam War epic, directed by Francis Ford Coppola for 20th Century Fox, based on Joseph Conrad's 1902 novella "Heart of Darkness." Captain Benjamin Willard (Martin Sheen), while sailing upriver into the depths of the Cambodia jungle to assassinate the psychotic Colonel

Kurtz (Marlon Brando), spends a night with an army outfit headed by Colonel Kilgore (Robert Duvall), a swaggering and utterly fearless surfer/soldier. Willard looks on as Kilgore is introduced to newly arrived corporal Lance Johnson, a famous surfer from California. Mortar shells are exploding nearby. "It's an honor to meet you, Lance," Kilgore says, his surf obsession blocking out the swirling noise and danger. "I've admired your noseriding for years. I like your cutback, too." The surfers in Kilgore's unit have a few surfboards in camp, and the following morning they load up the helicopters and fly off to "Charlie's Point," deep in Vietcong-held territory. Willard and Johnson are both stunned when a coastal village is destroyed so that Kilgore's men can ride a few waves. "I love the smell of napalm in the morning," Kilgore says, idly running his fingers through the sand as he takes in the burning jungle as well as the nicely shaped point surf in the distance. "Smells like . . . victory." Kilgore is a surfing lunatic, but it's a lunacy that most surfers at some level understand and identify with.

The R-rated *Apocalypse Now* was cowritten by John Milius, who wrote and directed Warner Brothers' 1978 surf movie *Big Wednesday.* Duvall received an Academy Award nomination for his performance, which was described by *Surfing* magazine as "the sport's greatest cinematic moment," and cited by the *New York Times* as the ultimate example of the "power [of] the California surfer as existential cowboy." *See also* Hollywood and surfing.

Arabian Sea   Part of the Indian Ocean, bordered by Iran, Pakistan, Oman, Yemen, India, and Somalia, located between the Arabian Peninsula to the west and India to the east; the Red Sea, Persian Gulf, Gulf of Aden, and the Gulf of Oman are arms of the Arabian Sea. Indian Ocean monsoons from May to October will push small- to medium-sized surf into the Arabian Sea's south-facing shores—virtually all of which rolls into dozens, if not hundreds, of as-yet-uncharted surf breaks. From November to April the warm Arabian Sea surf is generally small to nonexistent, although waves sometimes arrive from distant storms in the Southern Ocean. India has a small number of native wave-riders; surf ventures have been launched in Oman and Pakistan. *See also* India, Oman, Persian Gulf, Red Sea.

Aragon, Janice   Headstrong, hardworking surfer/ organizer from Huntington Beach, California; 1984

world amateur surfing champion, and executive director, since 1989, of the National Scholastic Surfing Association (NSSA). Aragon was born (1955) in Fresno, California, raised in Downey, and began surfing at age 16. She entered and won her first surfing contest in 1983, at age 29, and was thus a near-total unknown—as well as the mother of a two-year-old daughter—when she won the Southern California–staged 1984 World Championships. Aragon had a second child in 1985, and the following year won the NSSA Nationals, one of amateur surfing's most prestigious events. She became an NSSA competition judge in 1986, and the following year she became the first woman to judge a world pro tour event, working the Op Pro in Huntington. She was hired as the NSSA's executive director in 1989; four years later she dropped a bomb onto the already rubble-strewn field of American amateur surfing by splintering the NSSA away from the United States Surfing Federation, thus barring NSSA-only competitors from competing in the World Surfing Games. Aragon was inducted into Huntington Beach Surfing Walk of Fame in 2001. *See also* National Scholastic Surfing Association.

Arakawa, Eric   Unobtrusive surfboard shaper from Oahu, Hawaii, best known for his elegant thin-railed Pipeline guns. Arakawa was born (1960) in Honolulu, raised in nearby Pearl City, began surfing at age 10 and shaping at 14. He's produced boards for a number of companies, including Town & Country, Lightning Bolt, Brewer, and Surfing Hawaii, but is best known for the work he did with Hawaiian Island Creations. Arakawa has made boards for many of the world's best surfers, including Michael and Derek Ho, Damien Hardman, Shane Beschen, and Andy Irons. In 1986, Arakawa helped develop the Nose Guard, a small and inexpensive soft-rubber bumper that glues to the tip of the board to prevent injury. *See also* noseguard.

arch   *See* soul arch.

Archbold, Matt   Regularfoot surfer from San Clemente, California; one of the sport's great natural talents, introduced in the mid-1980s as a bashful child prodigy, then evolving into a heavily tattooed and periodically self-destructive cult figure. The son of a banker, Archbold was born (1968) in Fontana, California, and raised in San Clemente. He began bodyboarding at age five; six years later, when he got his first surfboard, he proved to be a natural, able to

Matt Archbold

do full turns and 360s in less than a month. He entered his first surf contest at 13 and finished second in the boys' division to future world pro tour star Brad Gerlach; in 1984, the 16-year-old Archbold won the juniors division of the United States Surfing Championships. He turned pro after dropping out of the ninth grade and had some minor placings on the world tour in the mid- and late '80s, but lacking the aptitude and interest for formal competition, he turned his attention completely to free-surfing. By 1988 he'd earned a reputation as one of the world's best aerialists, along with fellow San Clemente surfer Christian Fletcher—both were greatly influenced by aerial pioneer and world tour champion Martin Potter—but to categorize him as such was a disservice: in small- and medium-sized waves Archbold was simply one of the best surfers in the world—fast, fluid, limber, and innovative, with near-perfect balance and the quickest reflexes in the sport. It was often said that his raw talent was second only to that of three-time world champion Tom Curren.

The monosyllabic Archbold was reserved by nature, but also insatiably attracted to heavy metal rock-and-roll excess. Dozens of top surfers began getting tattoos in the late '80s; Archbold started and didn't stop, and by the late '90s his torso, arms, legs, and neck were covered in inky flames, crowns, spiderwebs, and angels. Archbold made surf world headlines in 1993, when he was given a six-month "work farm" prison sentence following a drunk driving arrest, his second such conviction, on top of a number of similar arrests. "I have a problem with drinking,

and it gets me in trouble," Archbold told a surf journalist while serving his term at a state-run minimum security facility in El Toro, California. A childhood friend of Archbold's, interviewed for the 1998 surf video documentary *Addiction: The Archy Story,* agreed. "He's on the wagon, he's off the wagon. He doesn't care about the wagon. He'd break the wagon and put it on your tab if he could." One of the sport's most photogenic surfers, Archbold has appeared in more than 40 surf movies and videos, including *Amazing Surf Stories* (1986), *Surfers: The Movie* (1990), *Panama Red* (1994), *What's Really Goin' Wrong* (1995), *Voluptuous* (1996), and *Aloha from Hell* (2000). Archbold has been married twice and has two children.

Arena, Eduardo   Baronial surf contest organizer from Lima, Peru; founder, in 1964, of the International Surfing Federation, and director of the World Surfing Championships in 1965, 1966, 1968, 1970, and 1972. Arena was born (1928) and raised in Lima, and began riding waves in 1946 in front of Club Waikiki in Miraflores, the birthplace and longtime hub of Peruvian surfing. He earned an engineering degree from Lima's National University in Lima in 1950, and three years later took a master's in engineering from UCLA. He won the debut Peru International contest in 1956, and in 1964 traveled to Sydney, Australia, to represent Peru in the first World Surfing Championships. While in Sydney, Arena laid the groundwork for the formation of the International Surfing Federation (ISF), to consolidate the surf world's quickly multiplying organizations, and to provide an overseeing body for future World Championship events. A few weeks later the group was chartered, with Arena elected chairman. The ISF produced the 1965 World Championships, held in Lima, with Arena serving admirably as contest director; "a dapper Peruvian gentleman," Australian contestant Nat Young later recalled, "with a warm smile and a distinguished mane of gray hair." It was Arena, more than anyone else, who first codified the rules and regulations of international competitive surfing. Arena also helped convince ABC to cover the 1966 World Championships in San Diego, California, as well as the 1968 Championships in Puerto Rico. The 1970 and 1972 Championships (held in Victoria, Australia, and San Diego, respectively) didn't go nearly as well as the previous three, and in late 1972 Arena and the ISF both quietly withdrew from the surf scene. *See also* International Surfing Federation, World Surfing Championships.

Argentina   Argentina covers much of the southern portion of South America and has nearly 1,500 miles of Atlantic-facing coastline. Most surfing in Argentina is practiced along a 40-mile stretch between the northern cities of Mar del Plata and Miramar, an area containing over 30 beach- and pointbreaks. A continental shelf reduces both the size and the power of Argentina's waves, but head-high surf is common all year, with the best and biggest waves—occasionally up to 10 foot—arriving between April and October. The winds during this period are generally offshore in the morning and onshore in the afternoon. Mar del Plata is the country's top beach resort town as well as the Argentinean surf capital, and is inundated with tourists during the summer months. Yath, a long, tubular right-breaking point next to the city harbor, is one of the area's best breaks; Paradise, another right point, just south of town, can also produce first-rate waves. While the northern coastal regions of Argentina are subtropical, the southern areas can be bitterly cold and windy. It is thought that dozens of good surf breaks remain to be discovered in the south. Air and water temperatures vary widely, depending on season and location. Surfing in Argentina presents few hazards, and most breaks in the north are easily accessible. Stand-up surfing, however, is banned along popular beaches for much of the day during summer months.

Surfing was introduced to Argentina in 1963, when native teenager Daniel Gil traveled with his father's soccer team to Peru and returned with a surfboard. Gil first rode a beachbreak he named Kikiwai (a play on Waikiki), near Mar del Plata; he eventually built a house at Kikiwai and opened a small surf school. California's Mark Martinson, draft dodger and reigning U.S. men's division surfing champion, arrived in Mar del Plata in June 1966, after a two-month drive, and rode some "beautiful walls, sandy and perfect, six and seven feet, with the hollow rights a little better than the lefts." Infamous California surfer renegade Mickey Dora, also on the run from the law, visited Argentina in 1971. A military-installed government banned surfing in Mar del Plata in 1977, but the sport continued nonetheless; in 1978, when local surfing brothers Fernando and Santiago Aguerre, along with Luis Villaverde, formed the National Surfing Association of Argentina (NSAA), the country had about 150 surfers. Just two years later—thanks largely to NSAA's successful lobbying effort to lift the Mar del Plata surfing ban, along with the pop-ularity of the NSAA-published "Argentina Surf and Skate Magazine," as well as the NSAA-operated Ala Moana surf shop—there were more than 2,000 surfers in Argentina. The Aguerre brothers later moved to La Jolla, California, and founded the Reef Brazil sandal company. Surf industry in Argentina, meanwhile, continued to grow at a steady rate, and Reef sponsored Argentina's first international pro contest at Playa Grande in 1996, near Mar del Plata. As of 2003, Argentina is home to about 30 surf shops, and an estimated 30,000 surfers, along with 20,000 bodyboarders. *Surfista, Rad,* and *MDQ* are the three most popular domestic surf magazines.

artificial reefs   Artificial surfing reefs were thought about, talked about, written about, and occasionally blueprinted as far back as the early 1960s, but not until the late '90s were such reefs producing ridable waves. Artificial reefs have been proposed as a crowd-reduction measure in heavily surfed areas, and as a way to channel and shape incoming wave energy along beaches that otherwise produce lousy surf. In a remark typical of the sport's early enthusiasm for artificial reefs, *Surfer* magazine noted in 1967 that "thousands of new surfing spots" might be created, that an early review of surfer-designed reef plans by the Army Corps of Engineers was "encouraging," and that U.S. Senator George Murphy of California was said to be reviewing a proposal for a "nationwide artificial reef program." There was precedent of sorts in that man-made fishing reefs had been created as far back as the 1700s. Reef design itself had never been much of a problem, as natural reefs around the world provided engineers with the necessary dimensions. But construction costs generally proved too high, while cities and counties were frightened off by potential surfer-injury liability suits. None of which kept surf magazines from publishing artificial reef plans, diagrams, and layouts, from the crude (dumping old cars into the surf zone) to the prosaic (crane-dropped sandbags) to the futuristic (a submersible and adjustable Y-shaped structure made of polyethylene pipe).

At least three pre-'90s American artificial surfing reef projects were carried out. The Army Corps of Engineers in 1970, with input from California canoe surfer Ron Drummond, dropped mud and sand offshore at Doheny, in south Orange County, which predictably washed away before creating any ridable waves. The following year, a consortium of regional government agencies sponsored a project that placed

55 reinforced industrial-grade nylon sandbags, each weighing 7,000 pounds, just to the north of the Hermosa Beach Pier—to no wave-producing effect whatsoever. In late 1988, the Surfrider Foundation convinced the U.S. Navy to dump 150,000 cubic yards of dredged sand off San Diego's Silver Strand State Beach, which temporarily produced a good peak wave. (A pair of 200-foot-long precast concrete reefs were positioned 350 feet off the mean high-tide line in Sea Isle City, New Jersey, in 1989, but they were designed only to reduce the energy of incoming swells, not create a surfing wave.)

Unplanned man-made surf breaks have been part of the sport since the 1920s, when first-generation California surfers discovered well-shaped waves on sandbars adjacent to the south seawall at Corona del Mar in Newport Beach. All surf breaks created by jetties, breakwaters, seawalls, and piers are in fact man-made waves.

America's most determined effort at building an artificial surfing reef took place in El Segundo, an industrial beachfront town in southwest Los Angeles County. The 2,000-ton, V-shaped, sandbag-constructed "Pratte's Reef" (named after popular surfing environmentalist Tom Pratte) cost $300,000 and was created in 2000. Whether the reef was too small, or positioned too close to shore, or in too deep of water (all after-the-fact explanations), Pratte's Reef in its first season was a spectacular failure, having virtually no effect on the surf. A $200,000 renovation in 2001 did nothing to improve the reef's performance.

Australia had meanwhile produced two viable artificial surfing reefs. Cable Station reef was planned, funded, and built by the Western Australia government. Made from 10,000 tons of granite, at a cost of nearly $1 million, Cable Station was operational by mid-1998, and produced fast, shapely waves that sometimes broke for up to 150 yards. A less-ambitious sandbag reef was installed at Narrowneck, Queensland, the following year. It was designed to slow down beach erosion, but the reef on occasion produced a well-utilized surfing wave. In both Perth and Narrowneck, local surfers complained that media interest in the reefs had brought more people into the water than ever before. "There may be a fantastic wave created out of all this," a Narrowneck surfer told *Australia's Surfing Life* magazine, "but a lovely beach has been destroyed in the process." The new reefs, the magazine went on to note, "could be causing as many problems as they solve." More Australian artifi-

cial surfing reefs were in the planning stages as of 2003, while America seemed to have lost interest in the whole concept. *See also* FlowRider, Tom Pratte, wavepools.

Ashton, Juan   Regularfoot surfer from San Juan, Puerto Rico; ninth-place finisher in the 1988 world amateur championships, and winner, the following year, of the Natural Art/Carib Pro-Am. Ashton began surfing in 1982 at age nine. He was the third Puerto Rican surfer to catch the attention of the international surf media, following Jorge Machuca and Edwin Santos, and turned pro in 1987. In the 1989 Natural Art/Carib Pro-Am, Ashton narrowly defeated 16-year-old Kelly Slater—future six-time world champion. Ashton appears in *Surf NRG*, vol. 2, a 1991 surf video.

ASR trade show   *See* Action Sports Retailer Trade Expo.

Association of Surfing Professionals (ASP)
Governing body of the world professional surfing tour, founded in 1982 by former world tour runner-up Ian Cairns of Australia as a replacement for International Professional Surfers (IPS). The IPS brought together a disparate group of contests in 1976 to form the original international pro circuit, and over the next five years the tour made modest but steady gains as measured by prize money, media coverage, and sports-world stature. But competing surfers as well as contest sponsors were unhappy with the tour's rate of progress, and at the end of the 1982 season Cairns convinced virtually every key player on the circuit to jump over to the Association of Surfing Professionals (ASP), the organization he'd just created with financial backing from surfwear giant Ocean Pacific. World tour headquarters moved from the North Shore of Oahu to Huntington Beach, California. More contests were added to the tour: the 1982 IPS men's division season featured 12 events worth a total of $338,100, while the debut ASP men's season in 1983 had 16 contests, plus four "specialty events" in Australia, for a combined worth of $487,900. Contestants were glad for the additional prize money, but the extra contests made for an exhausting travel schedule. Meanwhile, a disagreement between Hawaiian contest promoters and the ASP led Cairns to break a seven-year pro tour tradition and drop Hawaii as the circuit's season-ending location, finishing up instead in Australia—a decision that greatly subtracted from

the drama of the tour, pushed the schedule into the next calendar year, and taxed the ASP's credibility.

Over the next 20 years the ASP stayed the course of slow progress interrupted by setbacks—many of them self-inflicted. A number of top-rated surfers, including three-time world champion Tom Curren, left the tour during the '80s and early '90s, burned out by a schedule that crammed up to 25 events into a season. The ASP also insisted on holding events in South Africa in the '80s, when virtually all other sports groups had boycotted the country due to its race-segregating apartheid policies. The ASP's insistence on transforming its events into huge, added-attraction, beach-carnival surf extravaganzas blew up in the organization's face in 1986, when spectators at the Op Pro in Huntington Beach rioted. Franchise-making TV deals came and went over the years. Ocean Pacific pulled out as ASP sponsor in 1984; Coca-Cola signed on as the tour's umbrella sponsor in 1993, then quit in 1997; sports-watch giant G-Shock sponsored the 1999 tour but didn't sign up for 2000. The ASP dream of turning pro surfing into a mainstream sport had all but died by the early '00s. "We've rarely been able to convince anyone from outside the sport that competitive surfing is worth watching," California surf journalist Sam George noted in 2002, "because we don't believe in it ourselves."

The ASP has nonetheless produced an excellent set of world champions, including Tom Carroll, Frieda Zamba, Martin Potter, Kelly Slater, Mark Occhilupo, Lisa Andersen, Sunny Garcia, and Layne Beachley. The number of events per season was scaled back in 1992, and not long afterward the balance of contests began to shift from spectator-accommodating beachbreak sites (which invariably led to undistinguished small-wave competition) to prime high-performance locations in places like Grajagan, Teahupoo, and Cloudbreak. Except for the 1994 season, the season finale has been staged in Hawaii since 1988. The ASP added a longboard world title in 1986, a masters division title in 1997 (for surfers 36 and older), and a juniors division title in 1998 (for surfers 19 and under). In 1992, the ASP introduced a two-tiered schedule consisting of the premier-level World Championship Tour (WCT) and the World Qualifying Series (WQS). The WCT is made up of 48 male surfers and 18 women, competing for their respective world titles over a fairly short series of international contests (11 for the men in 2002, six for the women). The WQS tour has 50 events per year,

composed of an interconnected series of domestic ASP-affiliate circuits, through which aspiring pro surfers qualify for the WCT. Each men's division WCT contest is worth a minimum $250,000 in prize money; women's events are worth $60,000.

Graham Cassidy of Australia served as ASP executive director from 1987 to 1994, followed by South Africa's Graham Stapelberg (1995 to 1998) and former world champion Wayne Bartholomew of Australia (1999 to present day). The ASP offices moved to Queensland, Australia, in 1999. ASP membership in 2002 was just over 1,000. *See also* Ian Cairns, competitive surfing, International Professional Surfers, professional surfing.

Atlantic Ocean   The world's second-largest ocean, after the Pacific, covering 51 million square miles (about 25 percent of the global sea area), including the Baltic Sea, the Caribbean Sea, the Gulf of Mexico, the Mediterranean Sea, the North Sea, and other tributary bodies of water. The Atlantic is bordered by the eastern coasts of North and South America on one side, and by Western Europe and western Africa on the other. Geographers disagree about the Atlantic's northern and southern edges, some drawing boundaries at the Arctic and Antarctic Oceans, others viewing both as Atlantic adjuncts. While the Atlantic produces waves along roughly 70,000 miles of coastline, it has proportionally fewer first-rate surf breaks than either the Pacific or the Indian Oceans. Some of best waves in the Atlantic are located in Europe (in the French/Spanish Bay of Biscay), and along the west and northwest Irish and Scottish coastlines. Tropical reefs in the Caribbean, meanwhile, can produce excellent waves, but not with anywhere near the frequency or power of the Pacific islands.

The equator divides the Atlantic into two halves, each with a distinctive character. The world's roughest and windiest seas are found in the upper reaches of the North Atlantic, between Nova Scotia and the United Kingdom, where the average wind speed is 35 mph, and huge, cold, unridable winter waves pound the coastlines of Iceland and Newfoundland. In late summer and early fall, North Atlantic tropical storms often form off the coast of west Africa and travel west, toward the Caribbean and the American eastern seaboard. In the South Atlantic, wave-producing storms, the majority of which are formed between June and September, tend to be much smaller and weaker. The entire ocean is cleaved by the Mid-

Atlantic Ridge, a deep, curving, underwater north-to-south mountain range that juts above the surface to form the Azores island chain in the North Atlantic and the Ascension group in the South Atlantic. Major currents run clockwise in the North Atlantic and counterclockwise in the South Atlantic. Water temperatures range from 84 degrees near the equator to 28 degrees near the poles. While the Caribbean and Mediterranean contain hundreds of islands, there are fewer than 100 islands in the main body of the Atlantic. The greatest depth in the Atlantic is about 28,500 feet, in Puerto Rico Trench, just north of Puerto Rico. A broad, wave-reducing continental shelf—up to 300 miles across—is found along most Atlantic-facing coastlines.

August, Robert   Agreeable, clean-cut goofyfooter from Orange County, California; costar of Bruce Brown's 1966 crossover hit surf movie *The Endless Summer,* and longtime surfboard shaper/manufacturer. August was born (1948) in Hermosa Beach, California, and raised primarily in Seal Beach, just north of Huntington Beach. He began surfing at age six, under the guidance of his father, Orral "Blackie" August, a one-time Redondo Beach lifeguard who surfed with Duke Kahanamoku during the famous Hawaiian's frequent visits to California. Robert August developed a smooth and relaxed wave-riding style, and later became a dependable if not spectacular competitive surfer, placing fourth in the men's division of the 1963 West Coast Championships, third in the 1964 United States Invitational, and third in the 1965 United States Surfing Championships. He was also invited to the 1965 Duke Kahanamoku Invitational. In his early teens, August was featured in two of Bruce Brown's surf movies, and a few months after high school graduation (he was senior class president), the 18-year-old flew with Brown and San Diego surfer Mike Hynson to Senegal to begin filming *The Endless Summer.* Over the next few months they traveled through Africa, India, Australia, New Zealand, and Tahiti. A live-narration version of *The Endless Summer* debuted on the beach-city surf circuit in 1964; the slightly modified final edition came out in 1966 to glowing reviews in *Time, Newsweek,* and the *New Yorker.* August and Hynson had no speaking lines (Brown's narration is heard throughout), but both became minor pop culture stars.

August worked in 1965 as a salesman at Jacobs Surfboards in Hermosa Beach. He began shaping boards in 1966, first for Jacobs, then as a Huntington-area freelancer. August opened the Endless Summer restaurant in Huntington in 1971, a venture, he later told *Longboard* magazine, that "set a world record for losing money." In 1974 he opened Robert August Surf Shop in Fullerton, and two years later relocated to Huntington. The longboard renaissance, beginning in the early '80s, was a boon to August's business; he closed the retail store in 1998, but by 2000 his board-making factory was producing about 4,000 boards a year—almost exclusively longboards and longboard hybrids—and distributing them to dozens of outlets worldwide.

August had a cameo in 1994's *Endless Summer II,* Bruce Brown's long-awaited sequel, and he was inducted that year into the Huntington Beach Surfing Walk of Fame. In 2001, he was featured in *Biographies,* an Outdoor Life Network documentary series. August was married once and has one child. *See also* The Endless Summer.

Aurness, Rolf   Gentle-natured goofyfoot surfer from Pacific Palisades, California; winner of the 1970 World Surfing Championships, at age 18, just months before dropping off the surf scene entirely. Aurness was born (1952) in Santa Monica, California, the son of Hollywood actor James Arness, who played Marshal Matt Dillon on *Gunsmoke,* CBS-TV's long-running western drama series. ("Aurness" is the original family name; James used the shortened version once he began acting.) The elder Arness began surfing after World War II, had his son on a board at age eight, and was soon ferrying Rolf up and down the coast for competitions. Aurness was the top-rated boys' division surfer in California in 1967; the following year, at 16, he competed in the World Championships in Puerto Rico; in 1969 he won three consecutive events on the Western Surfing Association's elite AAAA circuit on his way to becoming the nation's top-ranked surfer for the year. James Arness provided his son with near-fantasy surf environment, regularly filming Rolf with a Super-8 camera for post-surf analysis, taking the family to Hawaii three times a year, and piloting his Cessna for father-son weekend surf getaways to Baja, Mexico. Aurness developed a smooth but aggressive surfing style. "He rode the back half of his board," 1969 Makaha International winner Paul Strauch remembered, "and was constantly turning, climbing and dropping, cutting back and reversing direction."

Rolf Aurness

Aurness was the first overseas competitor to arrive in Victoria, Australia, for the 1970 World Championships. Nearly all of the heavily favored Australian surfers, including Wayne Lynch and 1966 world champion Nat Young, were using experimental sub-six-foot boards. Aurness, riding a streamlined 6'10", stood out immediately as the contest's fastest and most precise surfer, and in the six-man final, held in beautiful overhead waves at a rural surf break called Johanna, he won easily. "Rolf was going twice as fast as we were," finalist Nat Young recalled, "and covering twice the ground."

The soft-spoken, curly-haired Aurness was interviewed by the surf press after the contest, appeared in a few surfboard and wetsuit ads, and was a guest on the *Merv Griffin Show.* But he never again competed, and soon removed himself completely from the spotlight. "I didn't know how to be famous," he later said. "I think growing up just became a personal battle." As detailed in a lengthy *Surfer's Journal* profile in 2001, Aurness's adult life has been full of hardship

and tragedy. His sister overdosed and died in 1975, his mother drank herself to death a few months later, and Aurness's first wife died of cancer in 1978. Aurness meanwhile had drug problems, spent time in a psychiatric ward in 1972, was in drug rehab in 1976, entered and dropped out of college, and spent the early and mid-'80s as more or less a recluse on his father's property in the Hollister Ranch, just north of Santa Barbara. He was working as a volunteer at a mental health clinic in Santa Monica in 2001, and surfing just once a year at San Onofre. "People say, 'Well, if you'd kept going you could have kept on top of the game for many years,'" Aurness said with a shrug when surf journalist Drew Kampion asked if he regretted not carrying on as a surfing front-runner. "But I couldn't see trying to keep up that level of performance forever. I'd done my best, I was maxed out." Aurness appeared in a small number of surf movies, including *Cosmic Children, Pacific Vibrations,* and *Freeform,* all released in 1970.

Auster, Ken   Artist from Laguna Beach, California, best known for his soothing, vaguely impressionistic, often sentimental paintings of surfing and beach scenes. Auster was born (1949) in Los Angeles, and began surfing in 1963. While working on an M.F.A. at Long Beach State College, he began screen-printing T-shirts for LBSC fraternities. The beachwear line he produced for his 1969-founded California T-shirt company—usually a high-contrast surfing image framed in a horizontal floral band—was an integral part of the American surfer's wardrobe in the early and mid-'70s. In 1984 he opened Auster Design Gallery in Laguna Beach, and in 1987 he began doing graphic work for the Chart House restaurant chain. The *Surfer's Journal* magazine published an eight-page portfolio of Auster's work in 1994. *See also* surf art.

Australia   The wave-lined Australian continent is bordered by the Indian Ocean to the west, the Southern Ocean to the south, the Tasman Sea to the southeast, the Coral Sea to the northeast, and the virtually waveless Gulf of Carpentaria to the north. The country's 20,000-mile coastline can be divided by state: 1) Queensland, featuring nearly a dozen subtropical right-breaking point waves and an assortment of beachbreaks in the southernmost 200 miles of the state. The Gold Coast is Queensland's best-known surfing area; the Great Barrier Reef is the state's most exotic surfing area. 2) New South Wales, including the bucolic North Coast pointbreaks, as well as the teeming urban- and suburban-lined beaches of the greater Sydney area. 3) Victoria's serrated coast has an array of frequently wet and chilly surf breaks. 4) South Australia has a limited number of high-quality reef- and beachbreak waves, most of them cold, isolated, and powerful. 5) Tasmania, the remote island state located off Australia's southern tip, is colder still, with fewer surfing options. 6) Western Australia, with its vast desert coastline, is home to dozens of wild frontier-style reefbreaks. 7) The Northern Territory's shallow offshore waters are for the most part cut off from incoming swells by New Guinea, although the far northeast coast of Arnhem Land will occasionally produce small, choppy waves. Australia's best-known waves include Noosa, Burleigh Heads, and Kirra (Queensland); Lennox Head, Narrabeen, and Manly Beach (New South Wales); Bells Beach (Victoria); Cactus (South Australia); and Margaret River (Western Australia). Australia receives surf all year, but the waves are generally best from March to September, as Southern Hemisphere winter storms deliver swells to virtually all east-, west-, and south-facing beaches.

Australian waves were bodysurfed as far back as the early 1900s, and boardsurfed in Sydney as early as the 1910s by members of the local Surf Lifesaving Clubs. But the sport didn't really catch on until surfer and Olympic gold medal swimmer Duke Kahanamoku of Hawaii gave a pair of wave-riding demonstrations in Sydney in 1914 and early 1915. The sport evolved slowly here, and remained closely allied to the Surf Lifesaving Clubs, until a group of visiting American surfers introduced the lightweight balsa Malibu boards to Sydney and Victoria wave-riders in 1956. Sydney's Gordon Woods also opened Australia's first surf shop that year, in Bondi Beach.

By the early '60s, Australian surfers had almost completely split off from the lifesaving organizations. Between 1961 and 1963, Sydney surfer Bob Evans premiered the first Australian-made surf film, launched *Surfing World* magazine, and formed the Australian Surfriders Association (now Surfing Australia). Across the country, local "boardrider" clubs formed by the dozens. The first Australian National Titles were held at Sydney's Bondi Beach in 1963, and won by Doug Andrews and Pearl Turton; Australians Bernard "Midget" Farrelly and Phyllis O'Donell won the inaugural World Surfing Championships, held at Manly in 1964. The country's surf-world presence continued

to grow as Sydney's Nat Young won the 1966 World Surfing Championships in San Diego, California; the following year Queensland-born surfboard shaper Bob McTavish made the single most influential contribution to surfboard design when he built the first vee-bottom surfboard and launched the shortboard revolution. (Other major Australian surfboard design contributions include Mark Richards's revamped twin-fin board in 1977, Geoff McCoy's "no-nose" outline in 1980, and Simon Anderson's tri-fin in 1981.)

Australia became a major surf industry power in the 1970s, as companies like Rip Curl and Quiksilver (established in 1969 and 1973, respectively) built international reputations, greatly helped by American surf culture's growing obsession with all things Australian—including the aggressive but matey Down Under attitude. Australian words like "grommet" and "boardshorts" soon found their way into popular usage on surf beaches worldwide. Surfers from New South Wales and Queensland, meanwhile, have dominated the international pro tour, led by world champions Peter Townend (1976), Wayne Bartholomew (1978), Mark Richards (1979–82), Tom Carroll (1983, 1984), Damien Hardman (1987, 1991), Barton Lynch (1988), Pam Burridge (1990), Pauline Menczer (1993), Layne Beachley (1998–2001), and Mark Occhilupo (1999). Nat Young returned to win longboard world championships in 1986, 1988, 1989, and 1990, while Newcastle's Stuart Entwistle took the title in 1987. Sydney kneeboarders Mike Novakov and Simon Farrer between them won five consecutive world titles in the '80s and early '90s.

As of 2003, Australia was home to more than 800 surf shops, with estimates of the Australian surfing population ranging from 250,000 (*The World Stormrider Guide*) to nearly two million (the Australian Sports Commission). *Surfing World, Tracks* (founded in 1970), *Australia's Surfing Life* (1985), *Waves* (1985), and *Pacific Longboarder* (1997) are among the leading Australian-published surf magazines. Surfworld, the world's biggest surfing museum, opened in Torquay, Victoria, in 1994 and houses the Australian Surfing Hall of Fame. The Association of Surfing Professionals moved to Coolangatta, Queensland, in 1999. Each year, Australia stages dozens of regional, national, and international pro competitions, including two world circuit events (the Quiksilver/Roxy Pro on the Gold Coast and the Bells Rip Curl Easter Classic), along with hundreds of amateur contests. Victoria hosted the 1970 World Surfing Championships;

Queensland hosted the 1982 World Surfing Championships.

The Australian surf is detailed in a number of books, including *The Surfing and Sailboarding Guide to Australia* (1993), *Atlas of Australian Surfing* (1998), *Surfing Australia* (1998), and *The World Stormrider Guide* (2001). Australian surfing documentaries include Nat Young's *History of Australian Surfing* (1985) and *Legends: An Australian Surfing Perspective* (1994). *See also* New South Wales, Queensland, South Australia, Tasmania, Victoria, Western Australia.

Australia's Surfing Life magazine   Loud, impudent, well-crafted glossy surf magazine, founded in 1985 by New Zealander Peter Morrison, published monthly out of Burleigh Heads, Queensland. For its first five years, under the editorial reign of California-born Mike Perry, *Australia's Surfing Life* (*ASL*) was colorful but predictable; it didn't really find its footing until 1991, when it lured editor Tim Baker away from rival surf magazine *Tracks,* hired cheeky Derek Rielly as associate editor, and began publishing columns and articles by international surf press veteran Nick Carroll. Art director Graeme Murdoch, responding to the new editorial team, gave ASL a confident but playful new look. ASL's photography was first-rate thanks primarily to homegrown talent Ted Grambeau, Sean Davey, Bill Alexander, and Peter Wilson. While feature articles were at times distinctive (a mix of profiles, interviews, travel pieces, board design articles, contest coverage), the magazine's character was for the most part developed in columns: "Backwash" contained the surf world's best gossip; the purple-caped "ASL Man" (created by surfer/artist Paul Collins) was the sharpest and best-drawn cartoon; "What's Hot/What's Not," like many of the magazine's columns, was built on reader input. In "The ASL Bravery Test" (sometimes titled "The ASL Dare"), magazine staffers in bright orange jumpsuits would turn up unannounced at the home of a famous surfer and offer a $50 or $100 check if the surfer would agree to perform an embarrassing or semidangerous task: big-wave rider Ken Bradshaw took the dare and had his chest and back waxed; pro surfer Dave MacAulay, a devout born-again Christian, refused the dare by not setting foot inside a notorious Honolulu strip bar. Many of *ASL*'s best moments came in the second half of the '90s, after Rielly was promoted to editor. While freely indulging his schoolboy obsession with breasts and bowel movements, and too

often playing the surf-nationalism card, Rielly also wrote eloquently and pointedly on a range of surf world topics, including the shortcomings of the international pro tour and the monopolizing of some exotic first-rate surf breaks by expensive surf resorts. "The whole notion," Rielly wrote in 1996, "that waves can be bought and turned into enclaves for those able to afford a weighty daily tariff, is reminiscent of a money-bloated, right-wing country club." While the magazine is still plush and well-produced, it lost focus with Rielly's departure in 1999.

ASL is distributed worldwide, and in 2003 its monthly circulation was 38,500. *ASL* published *Visions of the Australian Coast,* a photo book, in 2001. *See also* Peter Morrison, Derek Rielly.

Australian Championship Circuit (ACC)   Domestic competition circuit formed in 1993 by the Australian Surfriders Association (ASA) to replace the collapsing Australian Professional Surfing Association (APSA) tour. Until 2002, the Australian Championship Circuit (ACC) served as an intermediary step between the amateur ranks and the world pro tour. In 1989, during a national recession, the APSA raised its minimum per-contest prize money requirement. Sponsors balked, the circuit withered, and in 1991 the APSA was absorbed into the regional division of the world-circuit-managing Association of Surfing Professionals (ASP). The Australian Championship Circuit was developed in mid-1992 and launched early the next year, fusing together six events from the Queensland Professional Surfing Circuit (managed by 1978 world champion Wayne "Rabbit" Bartholomew, and better known as the "Rabbit Circuit"), with a series of Quiksilver-sponsored contests. Administrators reduced production costs and cut the average prize purse down to about $7,000 per contest in order to attract sponsorship for the 24-event circuit. Domestic pros grumbled about the low prize money, but had no alternative except to try their luck on the expensive and talent-heavy world pro tour. But the ACC, as future world tour star Jake Paterson said in 1994, was "more of a stepping-stone than a money-making thing." Amateur surfers were allowed to compete on the ACC, but any money they won was put into a personal ACC-administered travel fund.

After the 2001 season, the ACC split into a number of statewide circuits administered by the Association of Surfing Professionals Australasia. Australian Championship Circuit division champions for men's, juniors (under 20), and girls' (under 20) are as follows:

1993: Richie Lovett, Jake Paterson, Trudy Todd
1994: Grant Frost, Nathan Webster, Trudy Todd
1995: Jye Gofton, Beau Emerton, Trudy Todd
1996: Sasha Stocker, Taj Burrow, Jenny Boggis
1997: Paul Ward, Trent Munro, Stacey Emerton
1998: Jeremy Walters, Darren O'Rafferty, Crystal Vail
1999: Jeremy Cohen, Joel Parkinson, Amee Donohoe
2000: Drew Courtney, Adrian Buchan, Chelsea Georgeson
2001: Dave Reardon-Smith, Adrian Buchan, Chelsea Georgeson

Australian National Titles Organized primarily by surf impresario Bob Evans of Sydney, the first "Australian Interstate Surf Meet" was a two-day, five-division contest held in May 1963 at Sydney's Avalon Beach before nearly 1,000 spectators. Winners included Doug Andrews (men's), Pearl Turton (women's), and future world champion Nat Young (juniors). The similarly titled Australian Surfing Championships event was held in December of that year, and is sometimes confused with the national titles. At some point in the '80s, the Evans-founded contest became known as the original Australian National Titles.

The Nationals have been held in every Australian state except the Northern Territory. Surfers must first perform well in regional events to qualify for their state titles, where they can qualify for the Nationals. During the contest's early years, the Nationals were a bellwether event for high-performance surfing. Internationally known surfers who won the contest between 1964 and 1975 include Midget Farrelly, Nat Young, Phyllis O'Donell, Wayne Lynch, Simon Anderson, Mark Richards, Michael Peterson, and Terry Fitzgerald. With the formation in the mid-'70s of domestic and international professional circuits, many of Australia's top surfers began concentrating on cash-prize events and didn't bother trying to qualify for the National Titles. The contest's prestige continued to suffer after amateur surfers were allowed to compete on the Australian Championship Circuit and the Association of Surfing Professionals World Qualifying Circuit—both of which allowed top-placing amateurs to put their prize money into an easily accessed "travel fund." The Nationals offered no money whatsoever. In 1995, *Australia's Surfing Life* magazine called the National Titles "a joke" and "the carcass of a pointless surfing event." Top surfers, nonetheless, continued to vie for National Title honors, and the post-1975 winners list includes future pro tour world champions Tom Carroll, Pam Burridge, and Damien Hardman. The Australian National Titles are held under the auspices of Surfing Australia and the host state's governing surf association. Beginning in 2002, the national juniors division title was awarded at a separate event called the Australian Grommet Titles.

Men's, women's, and juniors division winners of the Australian National Titles, along with host state and surf break, are as follows:

1963: Doug Andrews, Pearl Turton, Nat Young (Avalon Beach, NSW)
1964: Midget Farrelly, Phyllis O'Donell, Robert Conneeley (Manly Beach, NSW)
1965: Midget Farrelly, Phyllis O'Donell, Peter Drouyn (Manly Beach, NSW)
1966: Nat Young, Gail Couper, Peter Drouyn (Coolangatta, QLD)
1967: Nat Young, Gail Couper, Wayne Lynch (Bells Beach, VIC)
1968: Keith Paull, Judy Trim, Wayne Lynch (Long Reef, NSW)
1969: Nat Young, Josette Lagardere, Wayne Lynch (Margaret River, WA)
1970: Peter Drouyn, Judy Trim, Wayne Lynch (Coolangatta, QLD)
1971: Paul Neilsen, Gail Couper, Simon Anderson (Bells Beach, Johanna, VIC)
1972: Michael Peterson, Gail Couper, Simon Anderson (Narrabeen, NSW)
1973: Richard Harvey, Kim MacKenzie, Mark Richards (Margaret River, WA)
1974: Michael Peterson, Kim MacKenzie, Steve Jones (Burleigh Heads, QLD)
1975: Terry Fitzgerald, Gail Couper, Steve Jones (Middleton, SA)
1976: Mark Warren, Jill Patti, Dave McDonald (Mornington Peninsula, VIC)
1977: Col Smith, Leigth Goebell, Chris Byrne (Sydney, NSW)
1978: Col Smith, Leigth Goebell, Tom Carroll (Margaret River, WA)
1979: Nick Carroll, Leith Temple, Richard Cram (Gold Coast, QLD)
1980: Terry Richardson, Angela Zorica, Wayne McEwen (Victor Harbour, SA)

1981: Nick Carroll, Pam Burridge, Warren Powell (Bells Beach, Johanna, VIC)

1982: Dougall Walker, Jenny Gill, Bryce Ellis (Narrabeen, NSW)

1983: Bill Sedunary, Jenny Gill, Greg McCann (Margaret River, WA)

1984: Gary Elkerton, Jenny Gill, Damien Hardman (Gold Coast, QLD)

1985: Mark Sainsbury, Connie Nixon, Matt Branson (Victor Harbour, SA)

1986: Richard Marsh, Cathy Ryan, Nicky Wood (Phillip Island, VIC)

1987: Darren Magee, Cathy Ryan, Ben Webber (Sydney, NSW)

1988: Mick McAuliffe, Kathy Newman, Rob Brumms (Margaret River, WA)

1989: Darren Landers, Kathy Newman, Peter Boyd (Margaret River, WA)

1990: John Mills, Sandra Dryden, Mark Bannister (Sunshine Coast, QLD)

1991: Jason Frost, Sandra Dryden, Jake Spooner (Victor Harbour, SA)

1992: Grant Frost, Lynette MacKenzie, Beau Emerton (Bells Beach, VIC)

1993: Tony Seddon, Lynette MacKenzie, Chris Davidson (Central Coast, NSW)

1994: Tony Seddon, Hayley Tasker, Mick Lowe (Margaret River, WA)

1995: Glenn Pringle, Hayley Tasker, Taj Burrow (Gold Coast, QLD)

1996: Peter Hayes, Michelle Hewitt, Tom Whittaker (Geraldton, WA)

1997: Simon Massey, Holly Monkman, Zane Harrison (Geraldton, WA)

1998: Rob Bain, Yvonne Rogencamp, Dean Morrison (Cronulla, NSW)

1999: Glenn Pringle, Sandra English, Jock Barnes (Cronulla, NSW)

2000: Mark Richardson, Dara Penfold, Leigh Sedley (Tasmania)

2001: Joel Jones, Brooke Farris, Tevita Gukilau (Rottnest Island, WA)

2002: Brett Hardy, Amy Johnson, Ben Dunn (Rottnest Island, WA)

Australian Professional Surfing Association (APSA)

The world's first professional surfing association, formed in Coolangatta, Queensland, in 1975, by contest promoter Graham Cassidy, Rip Curl wetsuits cofounder Doug Warbrick, and Australian pro surfers Ian Cairns, Peter Townend, Mark Warren, and Terry Fitzgerald. The Australian Professional Surfing Association (APSA) was designed primarily to standardize, organize, and manage a domestic pro circuit, and later served as Australia's organizational link to the International Professional Surfers (IPS) world tour. Professional surfing in Australia began with the $1,500 Rip Curl Pro at Bells Beach in 1973; by the middle of the decade there were more than a half-dozen Australian pro events. The first order of business for the APSA—founded in a sidewalk burger café in Coolangatta, with Warbrick elected president—was to create a standardized points system in order to crown a year-end national pro champion. Public image was important as well, as Townend expressed that surfing, through the APSA, could "project an image of authenticity and responsibility."

The APSA was anathema to thousands of Australian surfers, who felt it was wrong to try and transform their freewheeling activity into a points-and-ratings sporting contest; Cassidy himself said he was "racked with these fears that what I'm doing is going to take away from surfing the virtues that first attracted me." Six APSA events were, nonetheless, held in 1976, with the $12,000 Coca-Cola Surfabout in Sydney lauded as a model pro surfing contest. By the time Cassidy took over the APSA presidency in 1981, there were 18 events on the schedule, some of them making headlines in the Australian mainstream sports pages. (Hawaiians Fred Hemmings and Randy Rarick, with input from Townend and Cairns, had meanwhile formed the IPS world tour in 1976, using the APSA points system.) While some APSA events had juniors and women's events, most of the contests were men's division only. In 1983, the APSA created Surf League to help reinvigorate Australia's long-neglected surfing clubs. Along with overseeing contests, the APSA also petitioned state and local governments on surfers-rights issues, organized environmental gatherings, and served as a surfing-information conduit to the mainstream media.

The APSA raised contest sanctioning fees and the minimum prize money requirements during a national recession in 1989, which helped drive sponsors away. Two years later the APSA was brought into the regional branch of the Association of Surfing Professionals; in 1993 the APSA events were run under the auspices of the newly formed Australian Championship Circuit. *See also* professional surfing.

Australian Surf Board Association (ASBA)

Surfing organization founded in 1945, led by Sydney board-builder Ken Adler. Australian surfing had up to that point been regarded as an auxiliary to the popular and somewhat autocratic Surf Life Saving Association of Australia (SLSAA). The breakaway Australian Surf Board Association (ASBA) wanted to focus on wave-riding only, instead of lifeguarding. Further, the new group had little or no interest in military-style beach-side pomp and pageantry, as exhibited in the traditional SLSAA surf festival. The ASBA's first group outing at Bondi Beach was documented in a 1945 newsreel, "Surf Board Association Holds First Meeting," shown in movie theaters around Australia. Although there was a large overlap in membership between the ASBA and the SLSAA, there was a strong rivalry—even dislike—between the two, and in 1946 Australia surfboard champion Keith Hurst was suspended from the SLSAA after winning a marathon paddling race organized by the ASBA. *See also* lifeguarding and surfing.

Australian Surfing Hall of Fame

Memorial hall honoring Australian surfing legends, located in Surfworld, a museum in the surf industry town of Torquay, Victoria. The Australian Surfing Hall of Fame was developed by Surfing Australia, a national umbrella group for wave-riding sports. One or two surfers are added to the Hall of Fame each year during a semiformal induction ceremony held in conjunction with the Rip Curl Pro contest. The Hall of Fame's first awards ceremony took place in 1985—long before the hall itself was built—and honored surfing pioneer Charles "Snow" McAlister and four-time world circuit champion Mark Richards. Nominees for the Hall of Fame are chosen by Surfing Australia, and approved by a panel of contest administrators, distinguished surfers, and surf industry executives. In 1994, the Hall of Fame finally gained a home in the just-completed Surfworld museum; in an exhibit hall, each inductee has a board shaped in his or her honor by Torquay surfboard-maker Russell Graham, which is placed next to a glass-topped tablet describing the surfer's achievements. Along with the Hall of Fame inductees, awards are given out each year in six additional categories: administration, innovation, pioneering, media, special overseas surfer, and service. Australian Surfing Hall of Fame members:

1985:	Charles "Snow" McAlister, Mark Richards
1986:	Bernard "Midget" Farrelly, Robert "Nat" Young
1987:	Bob Evans, Wayne "Rabbit" Bartholomew
1988:	Wayne Lynch
1989:	Simon Anderson
1990:	Tom Carroll
1991:	Peter Drouyn
1992:	Michael Peterson
1993:	Ian Cairns, Isabel Letham
1994:	(no inductees)
1995:	Terry Fitzgerald
1996:	Bob McTavish, Phyllis O'Donell
1997:	Pam Burridge
1998:	Barton Lynch
1999:	Damien Hardman
2000:	Gail Couper, Rob Brooks
2001:	Peter Townend
2002:	Peter Troy

See also Huntington Beach Surfing Walk of Fame, East Coast Surf Legends Hall of Fame, International Surfing Hall of Fame.

Australian Surfing World magazine

Enduring Sydney-based Australian surf magazine, founded in 1962 as the *Surfing World Monthly* by surf impresario Bob Evans; second only to *Surfer* as the world's longest continuously published surf magazine. Two issues of the *Australian Surfer* had been published the year before, and the debut issue of *Surfabout* magazine came out a few weeks prior to *Surfing World,* but Evans has nonetheless been credited as Australia's first surf publisher. The early issues of *Surfing World* were conventionally designed and written, and the magazine at times seemed to be obsessed with surf competition—not surprising, as Evans was also founder of the Australian Surfriders Association, and was responsible for bringing the debut World Surfing Championships to Sydney's Manly Beach in 1964. *Surfing World* changed direction somewhat in mid-1966, with the publication of the "New Era" issue that dismissed 1964 world champion Midget Farrelly, while heaping praise on Bob McTavish, Nat Young, and George Greenough—the three surfers who would soon launch the shortboard revolution. *Surfing World* maintained a fairly progressive voice in the late '60s, but was rendered stodgy in 1970 with the founding of the genuinely counterculture *Tracks* magazine.

Surfing World photographers Hugh McLeod and Bruce Channon bought the magazine in 1979, turned it into a two-man operation, scaled back production to roughly four issues a year, added "Australian" as a

Surfing World magazine cover, 1972

title prefix, and transformed Evans's magazine into what amounted to a luxurious photo book. Graphic designer McLeod gave *Surfing World* a highly textured look that was at once soulful and New Wave. Portraiture and candid photographs ran in near-equal proportion to action surf shots; featured surfers were almost exclusively Australian. Some issues were given over entirely to a single article, as was the case in mid-1983, when McLeod and Channon focused on a road trip to Red Bluff, Western Australia.

Readers in the '90s began to leave *Surfing World* for younger, brasher magazines like *Australia's Surfing Life* and *Waves*; Channon and McLeod sold *Surfing World* to Breaker Publications in 1997. The quarterly magazine's circulation in 2003 was about 15,000. *See also* Bruce Channon, Bob Evans, Hugh McLeod.

Australian Surfriders Association (ASA)   National government-supported administrative body for competitive surfing in Australia from 1963 to 1993; originally formed by Sydney surfers to protect local beach access rights. Australian surfers in the early

'60s had been branded (not without some justification) as loudmouth hedonist rowdies, and municipal courts in Sydney had restricted beach access for surfers and imposed mandatory surfboard registration. Pioneering Australian surf filmmaker and publisher Bob Evans, backed by a group of prominent surfers including Midget Farrelly, John Witzig, Stan Couper, Ross Kelly, and Ray Young, formed the loose-knit Australian Surfriders Association (ASA) in 1963, to unify individual surf clubs into a single representative coalition. With help from the ASA, beach access rights were restored and surfboard registration was repealed. By 1964, each Australian state had formed its own surfing association, all of which were ASA-affiliated. Evans and the ASA also convinced Australian oil giant Ampol Petroleum Limited to underwrite the first World Surfing Championships, held in May 1964 and won by Farrelly. (The ASA would also host the 1970 World Championships, in Victoria, and the 1982 World Championships in Queensland.)

The ASA survived two membership revolts in the '70s: dozens of elite surfers left to join the newly founded Australian Professional Surfing Association (APSA) in 1973, and virtually all of the country's top female surfers came together in 1978 to form the Australian Women Surfriders Association. The women rejoined the ASA in 1983, and in 1993 the ASA took over operations of the APSA's dwindling pro-am circuit to form the Australian Championship Circuit. Throughout the '80s and early '90s, the ASA sanctioned national and club competitions, established coaching and judging credential programs, and supported surfing-related events throughout the country. In 1993, the 6,000-member ASA reformed and incorporated as Surfing Australia. *See also* Bob Evans, Surfing Australia, World Surfing Championships 1964.

Australian Women Surfriders Association (AWSA)   First Australian women's competitive surfing association, founded in 1978 by Queensland surf shop owner Gail Austin. The Australian Women Surfriders Association (AWSA) was a breakaway group from the Australian Surfriders Association (ASA). "We were tired of being given the run of the surf when conditions were poor," AWSA organizer Robyn Burgess later said. "So we decided to set up our own association." Phyllis O'Donell, 1964 world champion, was one of the first AWSA members; 78-year-old Isabel Letham, Australian surf icon, was an AWSA honorary member and supporter. Regional AWSA branches were set up in each state, and in 1980 the group hosted its first national championship, won by 14-year-old sensation and future world champion Pam Burridge. Austin retired from the AWSA in 1981, not long after Burridge successfully defended her national title, and in 1982 the 300-member AWSA voted to merge with the ASA, who in turn created a women's director position with voting power equal to each of the Australian states.

Avalon, Frankie Sweet-faced American teen idol, paired with Annette Funicello in more than a half-dozen Hollywood beach movies of the early and mid-'60s, including *Muscle Beach Party* (1964), *Beach Blanket Bingo* (1965), and *How to Stuff a Wild Bikini* (1965). Born Francis Avallone, in Philadelphia, Pennsylvania, in 1939, Avalon was one of the original *American Bandstand* stars, and in 1959 had a national #1 hit with "Venus." In the beach movies, Avalon was cast as Funicello's fun-loving and often jealous boyfriend. For his brief but obligatory surfing scenes, Avalon either had a stunt double (usually Malibu surfer Mickey Dora who, like Avalon, had thick black hair), or was filmed in close-up, sprayed down with water and teetering back and forth with a breaking wave superimposed behind him. Avalon and the silly-but-fun beach films were a hit with young audiences—1963's *Beach Party* cost $400,000 and earned $4 million—and uniformly dismissed by the critics. Avalon, as noted in a caustic 1965 *Saturday Evening Post* feature that brought up "the acne that once dotted Avalon's forehead," as well as a two-year-old paternity suit, was paid "roughly $35,000 a film to sing a couple of songs, to function as Miss Funicello's boyfriend, and to simulate the form of a champion surfer." Avalon played himself in the 1978 blockbuster *Grease,* and was reunited with Funicello in 1987's *Back to the Beach. See also* Hollywood and surfing.

Azores Mountainous and well-forested Portuguese archipelago located in the North Atlantic Ocean, about 800 miles west of Lisbon. Although waves can strike the Azores from any direction, and most of the islands' 360-mile coastline is open to surf, swells here tend to be short-lived. The Azores's biggest and best surf comes from the North Atlantic during fall and winter; because the island chain has no swell-reducing continental shelf, waves are generally thick and hard-breaking. Wind and rain are common during the surf season, but midday temperatures are usually mild, ranging from the upper 50s to the mid-70s, with water temperatures ranging from the low 60s to the low 70s. More than 40 breaks have been mapped in the Azores—mostly on São Miguel and Terceira Islands—and dozens more are either uncharted or being kept secret. Nearly all breaks here are shallow, rock- or cliff-lined points and reefs; many spots are difficult to access.

Azores natives have been bellyboarding and bodysurfing since the 1920s, but stand-up surfing wasn't introduced here until the mid-'60s, by American military personnel stationed on Terceira Island. "The main handicap," one GI wrote at the time, on behalf of a group of fellow surfers, "is lack of boards. In fact, at present we have only one." As of 2003, there were first-generation surfers on all nine Azores islands, but very little commercial surf culture. The Azores' surf is detailed in *The Stormrider Guide Europe* (1998).

B

back arch   *See* soul arch.

backdoor   To begin a tuberide from behind an already-dropping tube section, that is, a section breaking ahead of the curl line, but not so far ahead as to render the wave unmakable. The surfer enters the "back door" to what, in the late '60s and '70s, was often referred to as the "green room." An advanced maneuver, not especially difficult, but requiring nerves, a steady hand, and a detailed store of tube-riding knowledge. Surfers will often backdoor a tube by paddling to the far side of a wedge-shaped wave, then crosscutting through the hollow section at the wave's apex directly after standing up. The backdoor route can be spectacular if the tube is already fully formed prior to the surfer's entrance.

Backdoor   *See* Pipeline.

Backdoor Shootout   *See* Da Hui's Backdoor Shootout.

backside   Riding so the heels, butt, and back are facing the wave. After standing, the surfer angles into either a backside or frontside ride; frontside means the face, chest, and toes are facing toward the wave. Regularfoot surfers (those using a left-foot-forward stance) ride backside when they angle to the left; goofyfooters (right foot forward) ride backside on right-breaking waves. Backside maneuvering, like backhand tennis strokes, tends to be more difficult—the wave is harder to see; the heel-weighted bottom turn is harder to control—and most surfers prefer riding frontside, particularly in bigger waves. Ian Cairns, 1976 world title runner-up, once described backside surfing as "doing the unspeakable." Wayne Lynch, Tom Carroll, Kelly Slater, Bruce Irons, and a number of other groundbreaking surfers, however, have ridden backside with a flair and enthusiasm that matched, and at times even surpassed, their frontside surfing. "The true test of a man," 1977 world cham-

pion Shaun Tomson said, "is dropping down a 12-foot beast of a wave, backside, coming off the bottom and just standing there in the tube." Australian surfers say "backhand" instead of "backside." *See also* backside attack, frontside, pigdog, rail grab.

backside attack, Pipeline   The notoriously steep and hollow surf at Pipeline, in Hawaii, has always been more difficult for regularfoot (left-foot-led) surfers, who take on the left-breaking waves backside—with their backs to the wave. Right-foot-led goofyfooters have an advantage here as they face the wave while riding frontside. In the winter of 1975–76, a small group of regularfooters led by Shaun Tomson, Michael Tomson, and Wayne Bartholomew made a sudden leap in progress at Pipeline, and closed the performance gap with the goofyfooters; *Surfer* magazine soon labeled the movement as the "backside attack." Much of the groundwork, Pipeline guru Gerry Lopez later recalled, came during a memorable period in late December 1975, when the usually fickle Pipeline surf broke with near-mechanical repetition for more than two weeks. "Just one swell after another," Lopez said, "and it gave those guys enough time to really figure the place out." Regularfooters began to consistently ride inside the tube at Pipeline, and the new backside venture was crowned as Shaun Tomson won the 1975 Pipeline Masters, beating five goofyfooters, including Lopez, in the final.

backwash   A short-lived counterdirectional wave, generally produced as an expiring line of white water rushes up a canted beach, turns, and flows back into the surf zone. The resulting backwash—which can appear as a small unbroken swell or a small foam-fringed wave—can then ruffle or explode across the next incoming wave. Surfers at Makaha, on Oahu's west side, have for decades made a game of facing off against the break's famous backwash, which is often big and strong enough to be ridden. But backwash for the most part is regarded as either a nuisance or a

Backwash at Makaha, Hawaii

danger, and for the unprepared surfer it usually means a blind-side wipeout.

baggies   Surf world expression, popular from the late 1950s to the late '60s, used to describe a type of loose-fitting men's bathing suit that rides low on the hips and is cut long and full in the leg. Baggies were developed as a more comfortable and practical alternative to the typical midcentury swim trunk; the loose fit prevented water from filling in while surfing and allowed air to circulate freely while on land, while the added length protected the surfer's inner thighs from chafing while straddling the deck of a surfboard. Some of the first commercially made baggies were produced by M. Kii's in Hawaii and Sandcomber in Southern California. ("One Size—Huge," reads a 1962 Sandcomber ad.) As the Beach Boys described the "newest" Southern California sport in their 1963 hit "Surfin' USA," baggies were an essential component of early surf fashion, along with huarache sandals and a "bushy-bushy blond hairdo." Surf trunks became smaller and tighter in the '70s and '80s, then once again ballooned in the '90s, at which point women began wearing a slightly less full version of the surf trunk instead of bikini bottoms. While the term "baggies" has all but dropped out of use, nearly all surf trunks are now cut in the baggie style. *See also* fashion and surfing, surf trunks.

Bahamas   Subtropical West Indies nation composed of nearly 700 islands and 2,300 rocky islets and reefs; the Bahamas chain begins just 50 miles east of West Palm Beach, Florida, and runs 500 miles to the southeast. Florida surfers began visiting Eleuthera Island—a popular Bahamas tourist destination famous for its pink-sand beaches and translucent water—in the early 1960s, when an easygoing reefbreak soon known as Surfer's Beach was discovered just south of Gregory Town. By the early '70s, Eleuthera had become a regular stop for East Coast surfers looking for a temperate wintertime getaway; those with boat access soon began a more thorough exploration of the outlying Bahamian islands and reefs.

There are essentially two seasons in the Bahamas: the warm months from May to October and the slightly less warm months from November to April. Average daytime air temperatures range from the high 60s to the low 80s; water temperatures range from the low 70s to the low 80s. Winter generally brings the best waves, as four- to eight-foot swells drop down with some regularity from the North Atlantic and meet up with the north- and east-facing Bahamian reefs; infrequent hurricane swells in late summer and fall, however, can produce surf up to 15 feet. June and July are often waveless. The best surf in the Bahamas breaks on coral reefs or rocky points, and the lack of outlying continental shelf means the waves here can be powerful. Shallow reefs and relentless sun are the main surfing hazards. While Surfer's Beach remains the most popular break in the Bahamas, the premier spots—like the gin-clear tubing left at Garbonzo's, a reef on Elbow Cay in the Abaco chain—are located further afield. The island chain holds dozens of semisecret or hard-to-access breaks.

By 2003, there were two Bahamian surf shops and roughly 80 resident surfers. A national team competed in the 1993 Pan American Surfing Games; newer versions of the team have since been part of the biannual World Surfing Games. The Bahamian surf is featured in a small number of surf movies and videos, including *Atlantic Crossing* (1989).

bail out   Abandoning the surfboard in one of two way. 1) Jumping from the board during a ride; almost always performed as a last-second alternative to wiping out. This type of bail out is in fact a controlled wipeout. 2) Diving off one side of the board after getting "caught inside"; that is, trapped while paddling out toward a nonnegotiable breaking wave. The bail out—either kind—is common procedure for beginning surfers and a fairly regular occurrence for intermediates and even experts. While practical, the bail out is often frustrating and time-consuming, as it often means getting tumbled and pushed shoreward. Before the development of the surf leash in the early 70s, a bail out was almost always followed by a board-retrieving swim to the beach. Surfing's stringent code of cool has meanwhile seen to it that the surfer who bails out, rather than iron-grip his board come what may, should be made to feel a sense of shame. In 1995 surf journalist Sam George likened the bail out to masturbation. "The key here—as with that other embarrassing urge we seldom talk about—is to do it seldom, get it over with quick, and don't let anybody catch you doing it."

"Bail out," or "bail," is also surf jargon synonym for "leave" or "go," as in "let's bail to that peak down the beach."

See also caught inside.

Bain, Rob   Droll but friendly Australian goofyfooter from Queenscliff, New South Wales; world-ranked #5 in 1990. Bain was born (1962) in Sydney, began surfing at age 10, then all but quit at 13, not long after his father died. He left home at 16, worked a series of laborer jobs, then picked up surfing again in his late teens. Bain finished third in the 1984 Australian National Titles, turned pro, and steadily worked his way up the ratings, finishing in the top 10 from 1988 to 1991, and winning four events in his career, then retired from the international pro tour. He continued to enter lower-level competitions midway through the 1995 season. Bain's wide-stanced, lateral-driving surf style was functional rather than graceful, but earned a reputation as one of the world's best in bigger, hollower waves. His dry wit made him a favorite with the surf media as well as his peers. "There's the druggies, the beer guys and the yuppies," Bain explained in a 1988 profile. "Suppose I'm a bit of each." In June 1993, Bain made a $500 bet with a friend that he could stop drinking for the rest of the year; on New Year's Eve he bought a keg with his winnings, and later described the first swallow as feeling like "a thousand angels crying on my tongue." A few weeks earlier, Bain finished third in the 1993 longboard world championship. In 1998 he won his second Australian Titles (becoming, at 35, the oldest Australian men's division champion ever), and placed fourth in the World Surfing Games. Bain was featured in a small number of surf movies and videos, including *Just Surfing* (1989), *Rad Movz* (1993), and *Overdrive* (1994).

Baja California   The lightly populated Baja Peninsula extends for 780 cactus-filled miles below California, is made up of two states (Baja California and Baja California Sur), and has been long regarded by American surfers as a vast, adventurous, often frustrating, and occasionally frightening surf destination. With the exception of Baja's southernmost tip, and the 65-mile north coast between Ensenada and the California border, Baja surf breaks are for the most remote and widely dispersed. As much of the Trans-Baja California Highway is located miles from the coast, getting to a beach often means a long drive on rutted and sometimes washed-out dirt roads, with no emergency services. "South of Ensenada," the *Surf Report* newsletter said in 1997, "you enter a refuge in which time has stopped and you can be left entirely to your own devices. This means both freedom and danger. It is vital that you plan a Baja trip carefully and take all essentials with you." That said, surfers have always viewed the area as a place to slow down and relax, and a typical Baja jaunt will often consist of equal parts beer drinking, fishing, napping, reading, and surfing.

North Baja was probably first ridden in the late '40s or early '50s by visiting San Diego surfers. Mike Hynson and Bill Fury rode waves about 75 miles south of Ensenada in 1963; two years later the Windansea Surf Club boated out from Ensenada to ride Todos Santos Island; in 1967, Steve Bigler visited San Jose del Cabo, at the tip of Baja. San Miguel, a point-break just north of Ensenada, was the most popular Baja wave in the '60s, and the Baja Surf Club Invitational—held at San Miguel from 1966 to 1969, directed by local surfer and 1966 World Surfing Championships competitor Ignacio "Nacho" Cota—was attended by most of the top California surfers. After the two-lane Trans-Baja California Highway opened in late 1973, California surfers began making longer, more in-depth forays down the narrow peninsula; new discoveries included Scorpion Bay and Abreojos, both first-rate pointbreaks. Isla Natividad, a tubing beachbreak located on a small island off Punta Eugenia, became popular in the '80s, as did Killers, the ferocious big-wave break on Todos Santos Island. The warm, easy-to-ride surf breaks in and around the resort towns of Cabo San Lucas and San Jose del Cabo also became popular in the '80s.

The Cabo-area surf breaks from May to October, and is otherwise all but dormant; portions of Pacific-facing Baja are open to waves all year, although summer waves are often small to nonexistent for days or even weeks at a time, and spring winds can be relentless. Cabo can be unbearably hot in summer; the Pacific coast is cooler, with strong, dusty offshore winds in winter, and an average water temperature five to 10 degrees below that found in Southern California. As of 2003, Baja was home to an estimated 1,000 native surfers and 10 surf shops, most catering to visiting surfers near the California border, and around the Cabo San Lucas area. The Baja surf is detailed in *The Surfer's Travel Guide* (1995), *The Surfer's Guide to Baja* (2001), and *The Stormrider Guide North America* (2002). "Baja" was the title of the Astronauts' 1963 reverb-heavy instrumental hit; the Con Surfboards Baja Model was introduced in 1966; part one of Allan Weisbecker's 2001 surfing/drug smuggling memoir *In Search of Captain Zero* is set in Baja. *See also* Cabo San Lucas, Mexico, Todos Santos.

Baker, Bernie   Effervescent surf photographer/journalist/contest director from Sunset Beach, Hawaii; a *Surfer* magazine masthead-listed contributor since 1977; contest director for the Triple Crown of Surfing since 1983. Baker was born (1949) in Toledo, Ohio, and began surfing in 1965, after his family settled near Santa Barbara, California. That same year, the 16-year-old published his first articles and photographs in *Surfing* magazine. Baker moved to Hawaii in 1970, and in 1976 won the men's division of the state surfing championships; in 1975 he'd become the director of the Pro Class Trials, an international surfing contest held directly in front of his house at Sunset Beach. At the end of 1976, Baker—hypersocial and already connected to virtually everyone of note in the surf industry—helped create International Professional Surfers, producers of the first world circuit. Seven years later he was picked to direct the three events that made up the Triple Crown, the prestigious minicircuit that overlaps with the world pro tour. Baker has also worked as a judge for national and international amateur contests, including the World Championships, the United States Surfing Championships, and the National Scholastic Surfing Association National Championships. He continued to write surf features and columns, and by 2003 had published more than 75 pieces in *Surfer* alone, to go with his several hundred published photographs, including two *Surfer* covers and a best-selling poster. From 1974 to 1982 Baker and fellow Hawaiian surf photographer/journalist Leonard Brady worked together as a two-man surf media team under the name Island Style. Baker's articles and photos have appeared in more than a dozen other surf magazines around the world; his photographs have been published in *Sports Illustrated, GQ,* and *Outside* magazines. Baker has also contributed to a number of illustrated surfing books, including *Stoked: A History of Surf Culture* (1997), *Maverick's: The Story of Big-Wave Surfing* (2000), and *The Perfect Day* (2001). Baker is married and has no children.

Bali   Enchanting temple-filled island located in south-central Indonesia, home to more than a dozen good-to-excellent reef waves, including Uluwatu and Padang Padang; the first island in the Indonesian chain to be explored for surf. Bali is the lone Hindu enclave in an overwhelmingly Islamic nation, and its uniquely gentle and artistic culture for decades has had an exotic pull on traveling westerners. "This is Bali," surf journalist Laurie McGinness wrote in 1978, "island of the gods, land of harmony. Travel no further in search of your goal, it is under your feet."

Bali's surf-lined southern coast (the north shore is virtually waveless) can be divided into four main surfing areas: 1) The teeming resort town of Kuta, which includes the sand-bottomed peaks of Kuta Beach and well-shaped left walls of Kuta Reef. 2) The southwest Bukit Peninsula reefbreaks, home to the winding lefts of Uluwatu, as well as the perfect blue tubes of Padang Padang. 3) The southeast Bukit Peninsula reefbreaks, including Nusa Dua's powerful right-breaking barrels, and the tapering right tubes of Sanur. 4) The small offshore island of Nusa Lembongan, home to the high-tide-only right tubes of Shipwrecks. Bali has reasonably consistent surf all year, but the June-to-September dry season is considered the best time for surf, as Indian Ocean storms often generate four- to eight-foot surf, with bigger swells reaching to 12 feet. Waves along Kuta and southwest Bukit Peninsula are improved by a light and dependable offshore breeze during the dry season. Average daytime air and water temperatures both range from the mid-70s to the mid-80s. The December-to-March wet season brings fewer waves, rain, and southwest winds, which blow offshore at the southeast Bukit Peninsula breaks. Sea snakes and sharks are occasionally spotted at Balinese breaks, but sharp reefs and crowded lineups are the island's main surf hazards. While malaria is a concern throughout the rest of Indonesia, Bali is malaria-free.

Bali was first surfed in the late 1930s by American-born Kuta Beach hotel owner Robert Koke, who fled the country just prior to the Japanese occupation during World War II. The sport was reintroduced, again at Kuta Beach, by visiting Australian and American flight attendants in the late '60s. Sydney surf moviemaker Bob Evans filmed Nat Young, Mark Warren, and Col Smith riding Kuta in 1971; a few weeks later Australian filmmaker Alby Falzon, along with surfers Steve Cooney and Rusty Miller, were among the first to ride the gorgeous transparent-blue surf at Uluwatu. Falzon showed the break in his memorable 1972 film *Morning of the Earth,* and Bali quickly became the surf world's new dream destination. A handful of Balinese took to the water on surfboards in the mid-'70s (native children had in years prior ridden waves on rough-shaped pieces of wood), and local surfers Ketut Menda, Made Kasim, Bobby Radiasa, and Gede Narmada joined well-known surf travelers Gerry Lopez, Rory Russell, and Peter McCabe in lineups around the island. Joe's Surfshop, the first store of its kind on Bali, opened in 1974; the first Balinese Surfing Championships (won by Wayan Sudirka) were also held that year, at Kuta's Legian Beach. The Bali Surfing Club, Indonesia's first surfing association, was formed in 1979, and later that year staged the inaugural Indonesian Championships (also at Legian), attended by the governor of Bali and the Indonesian minister of sports—greatly raising the status of surfing on Bali. The OM Bali Pro, an international pro surf contest, was held at Uluwatu from 1980 to 1982.

As of 2003, Bali was home to nearly 50 shops, most in Kuta, and nearly 1,000 native surfers, the best known being goofyfoot tube-stylist Rizal Tanjung. Tens of thousands of surfers from around the world visit Bali annually. (Dozens of surfers—mostly Australian—were among the nearly 200 dead in the 2002 terrorist attacks or a pair of Kuta Beach nightclubs.) The 1999-founded *Surf Time* magazine, focusing on Indonesia, is published in Bali; the Bali Surfing Association organizes about 20 amateur surf contests annually. Guidebooks with information on the Balinese surf include *Indo Surf and Lingo* (1992), *Surfing Indonesia* (1999), and *The World Stormrider Guide* (2001). *See also* Indonesia, Padang Padang, Uluwatu.

Ball, John "Doc"   Prototype surf photographer and surf club organizer from Los Angeles, California; founder of the Palos Verdes Surf Club in 1935; author of the seminal 1946-published *California Surfriders.* While Ball and Wisconsin-born Tom Blake are both credited as the forebears of surf photography, it was Ball who had the greater influence on the next generation of photographers, including fellow California surf world icons Leroy Grannis and Don James. "The quality of his shots was superb," James later said of Ball's work. "I always wanted to try and get photos as good as Doc's, and I never quite made it." Ball was born (1907) in Los Angeles, raised in the nearby agricultural suburb of Redlands, and began surfing in 1929, just after enrolling in dental school at the University of Southern California. Three years earlier he'd begun shooting photos with a Kodak Autographic folding camera; in 1931, after seeing a Tom Blake surf photo published in the *Los Angeles Times,* the stocky, round-faced Ball began studiously framing and shooting the nascent Southern California surf culture. Over the next 10 years he took about 900

John "Doc" Ball

black-and-white exposures showing all aspects of the sport: surfers riding waves, watching the surf from a nearby cliff or pier, relaxing in the sand, making surfboards, or loading boards into a trailer. Ball purchased a Graflex camera in 1937, constructed a pine-box waterproof housing, and began taking photos from the water. His images appeared in *Life, Look, Popular Mechanics,* and a half-dozen other nationally distributed magazines, as well as the *Los Angeles Times. National Geographic* published "Surf-Boarders Capture California," an eight-page Ball portfolio, in September 1944. Meanwhile, weekly meetings for the Palos Verdes Surf Club—the second organization of its kind in America, established two years after Ball graduated from dentist school—were held at Ball's apartment/dentist office in south Los Angeles; members often adjourned to the nearby Zamboanga Club, a popular L.A. nightspot, where a four-foot by five-foot Ball surfing print was hung on the wall. Ball himself neither drank nor smoked, and was one of surfing's first health food advocates.

Ball served as a Coast Guard dentist during World War II, then returned home and put together a book of his photos, titled *California Surfriders.* Along with more than 150 photographs, it featured dozens of fervid Ball-written captions: "These giant storm peaks broke in monstrous wedges," he wrote about a 1938 photo of Hermosa Beach, "spilling tons of brine into a grinding, churning 'soup,' [and] an experienced surfer trapped in a series of these behemoths can have a serious time of it." Just over 500 first-edition copies of *California Surfriders* were printed in 1946. Virtually all photo negatives used for the book, along with hundreds of other negatives and prints, were damaged or destroyed when Ball's house was flooded in 1964. Later editions of Ball's book were made using reproductions shot from the original; first-edition copies of *California Surfriders,* as of 2003, were being sold by collectors for as much as $2,500.

Ball, along with his wife and two children, moved from Los Angeles to the Northern California town of Garberville in 1952; nearly 20 years later, Ball and his wife moved further north, to Eureka, where Ball continued to surf on occasion at nearby Shelter Cove. He died of heart failure in late 2001 at age 94. Ball was inducted into the International Surfing Hall of Fame in 1991; at age 89 he was filmed riding a skateboard near his home for a PBS documentary titled *Surfing For Life,* which aired in 2000. Ball's work has appeared in more than a dozen illustrated surfing books, including *Surf's Up! An Anthology of Surfing* (1966), *A Pictorial History of Surfing* (1970), *Surfing: The Ultimate Pleasure* (1984), and *Maverick's: The Story of Big-Wave Surfing* (2000). *See also* California Surfriders, Palos Verdes Surf Club, surf photography.

Ballard, Bill   Amiable surf videographer from Kauai, Hawaii; best known for filming the top women pro surfers in the '90s and '00s. Ballard was born (1967) on Edwards Air Force Base, in Kern County, California, and began surfing at age 18. In 1993, one year after marrying up-and-coming Hawaiian pro Rochelle Gordines and moving to Kauai, Ballard bought a Canon video camera, and while traveling with Rochelle as she competed on the world tour, began to film both the men's and women's pros. *Insanity,* his first commercial video, came out in 1995. His next work, *Voluptuous,* made with Jason Kenworthy, Ryan Ray, and Ryan Dival, earned five *Surfer* magazine Video Award nominations in 1996, including video of the year. Ballard went on to make at least two videos a year, including *Triple C* (1997), *The Moment* (1998), *Iratica* (2001), and *Because* (2002). *Blue Crush* (1998) and *Peaches* (2000) were Ballard's first all-women projects. In 1994, Ballard founded Billygoat Productions, a surf video production/distribution company. When Universal decided to make a surfing romance movie, they bought the *Blue Crush* title from Ballard and hired him as a cameraman; Universal's like-titled film came out in 2002.

Ballard, Rochelle   Dynamic regularfoot surfer originally from the Hawaiian island of Kauai, world-ranked #4 in 1998 and 2001, and generally regarded as the first great female tuberider. Born Rochelle Gordines in 1971, in the Los Angeles suburb of Montebello, she moved to Kauai with her family at age six months, and began surfing at 11, encouraged by neighbor and four-time world champion Margo Oberg. The tomboyish Gordines placed fourth in both the 1988 and 1990 World Amateur Surfing Championships, and finished 15th as a world tour rookie pro in 1991. The following year she married California-born surfer and videographer Bill Ballard. In 1997 she won the World Qualifying Series tour, and the following year finished #4 on the world tour circuit. From 1993 to 2001 she won eight circuit events, plus the nonrated '00 Op Boat Trip Challenge, held in flawless six-foot surf in Indonesia's Mentawai Islands. Each year from 1996 to 1999 she

Rochelle Ballard

finished runner-up to four-time world champion Lisa Andersen in the annual *Surfer* Magazine Readers Poll Awards.

Ballard's surf world stature, however, has little to do with contest results and everything to do with her groundbreaking performances in the hollow, hard-breaking waves at places like Backdoor Pipeline in Hawaii and Lance's Rights in the Mentawais. The small but well-muscled Ballard (5′1″, 105 pounds) wasn't the first woman surfer to ride inside the tube, but she was the first to do so habitually. Always a gutsy surfer, by the late '90s she'd added finesse and style to her repertoire, and was able to adjust her speed from behind the curl, weaving from one hollow section to the next. It was rare to see a woman riding the tube in 1995; five years later the top females were all competent, and in some cases first-rate, tuberiders. As surf journalist Gina Mackin wrote in 2000, "Ballard was the spark that touched off the women's tube revolution." She won the Surfer Poll Award in 2000, 2001, and 2002.

Ballard has appeared in more than two dozen surf videos (more than half made by her husband),

including *Triple C* (1996), *Peaches* (2000), and *Poetic Silence* (2001); she also stunt-surfed for lead actress Kate Bosworth in Universal's 2002 surfer girl movie *Blue Crush*. Bill and Rochelle Ballard moved to the North Shore of Oahu in 1995. Four years later she became cofounder of International Women Surfers, a small public relations/lobbying group that in 2000 helped raise the minimum mandatory prize money for women's world tour pro events.

balsa   Smooth, porous blond wood, lighter than cork, grown mainly in Central and South America; the most popular core material for surfboards in the 1940s and 1950s. Surfers first used balsa in combination with redwood; the all-balsa board became standard in Southern California after World War II, when board-makers Bob Simmons, Matt Kivlin, and Joe Quigg developed the "Malibu chip," which weighed as little as 25 pounds—40 pounds less than the average redwood plank boards popular just a few years earlier. By 1956, molded polyurethane foam blanks began to replace balsa. While foam was lighter, less expensive, and easier to find than balsa, not everybody was happy with the change. "The stuff just felt wrong," recalls board-maker and big-wave pioneer Greg Noll. "Foam was gritty and it didn't have a good smell. It had no life to it. It was just . . . available." Original California power surfer Phil Edwards actually preferred the wood boards; he continued to use "Baby," his favorite balsa board, long after most surfers had switched to foam. "We used to have a saying," Edwards said in 1992. "Spastic on plastic, good on wood." Balsa is still used for a tiny percentage of new boards—mostly custom longboards. Original balsa boards are now valued as both historical artifacts and objects of beauty, and sell to collectors for up to $9,000. *See also* polyurethane foam.

Baltic Sea   Long, cold, narrow body of water separating the Scandinavian Peninsula from the northern coast of Europe, and linking Sweden, Finland, Russia, Germany, Estonia, Latvia, Lithuania, and Poland with the North Sea and the North Atlantic Ocean. The Baltic Sea is about 950 miles long and 400 miles wide at its widest point. Water temperatures range from the low 30s in January to the upper 50s in July. Winds over the Baltic Sea can generate swells in nearly any direction, but only the Swedes, Germans, and Danes regularly take advantage of the generally small and easy-breaking Baltic Sea surf. Toro, a beach-break located just south of Stockholm, is the Baltic

Sea's most popular surf break. *See also* Denmark, Germany, Sweden.

Banks, Jim   Soulful Australian surfer and surfboard shaper from the Sydney suburb of Cronulla; world-ranked #14 in 1980, and regarded for years afterward as one of the sport's premier tuberiders, as well as a comprehensive master of the surfing life. "Nearly everything he does suggests an easy flow and serene focus," surf journalist Tim Baker wrote of Banks in 1996. "You just don't see him fumbling with his boardbag, or getting tangled in his legrope, or hollering out for wax or sunscreen." Banks was born (1959) in Sydney, and began surfing at age 11, after his family moved to Cronulla. He turned pro in 1978, won that year's Pro Class Trials, and finished the season world-ranked #18. He spent the next four years on the pro circuit, finishing 18th in 1979, 14th in 1980, 16th in 1981, and 16th in 1982. His first and only world tour win came at the 1981 OM Bali Pro in Indonesia; later that year, while competing in the Pipeline Masters contest, Banks was hit by his board and needed 150 stitches to close the gash in his forehead. In late 1978, the straw-haired Banks somewhat improbably became a member of the hard-sell Bronzed Aussies promotional group, led by 1976 world champion Peter Townend and 1976 runner-up Ian Cairns; two years later he resigned, saying he was tired "of always being considered a Bronzed Aussie rather than Jim Banks."

From 1981 to 1988 Banks owned and operated his own Cronulla surfboard shop. He'd taught himself how to shape at age 12, and by his early 20s had a reputation for producing sleek, fast boards designed for tuberiding. He meanwhile made long forays to the South Pacific, Indonesia, and Western Australia in search of empty waves. By the mid-'90s, when Banks was in his mid-30s, he was a better tuberider than he'd been as a touring pro, able to casually disappear behind the curtain for seconds at a time. Banks quit making surfboards in 1996, worried that his health was being affected by the toxicity of the board-building process. In the late '90s he helped develop a hemp-laminate surfboard, but was unable to turn the innovation into a business. In 1999 he began designing boards by computer, and shaping with the help of a computer-driven machine, and thus reentered commercial board manufacturing.

Banks appeared in several surf movies, including *Bali High* (1981), *Wizards of the Water* (1982), and *Totally Committed* (1984), and was the featured surfer in

Jim Banks

the 1992 surf video *Can't Step Twice on the Same Piece of Water*. He's also written more than two dozen articles for surf magazines, mostly on travel. Banks has been married once and has five children. In 2003 he was living in the New South Wales town of Byron Bay where, aside from building surfboards, he was conducting 10-day surf retreats involving yoga and meditation, as well as wave forecasting, board design, and surfing technique.

Barbados   Small pear-shaped tropical island nation located about 250 miles northeast of Venezuela; the easternmost island in the West Indies, and thought to be the second-most popular Caribbean surfing destination, after Puerto Rico. Barbados has been described as having the world's best beach weather, with average daytime temperatures ranging from the low 70s to the upper 80s, and water temperatures ranging from the mid-70s to the low 80s. The Barbados surf for the most part breaks over flat coral reefs or along pristine white-sand beaches; waves on the Caribbean side of the island are best during winter, with consistent offshore winds grooming the surf; the east and north coasts receive dependable head-high surf all year, with bigger waves hitting the north coast during winter. Barbados has about 30 charted breaks and a dozen more semisecret spots. Soup Bowls—a first-rate performance wave with a wedging takeoff, usually compromised by onshore winds—is the island's best-known and most crowded break, and is estimated to have head-high or bigger waves 300 days a year. No two surf breaks along Barbados's 166-square-mile island are more than 45 minutes apart by car. Coral and sea urchins are the island's main surfing hazards.

Malibu surfers Butch Linden and Johnny Fain introduced surfing to Barbados in 1965; they left their boards behind and the sport was picked up by a handful of Bajans (natives) including David Allen, Scaul Worme, and the Knowls brothers Val and Allen. The Barbados Surfing Association was formed three years later, and the country sent teams to the 1968 and 1972 World Surfing Championships, as well as every major international amateur surfing event from 1984 on. Lazy Days and Islands Waves, Barbados's first surf shop, opened in 1978. Since the mid-'80s, Barbados has hosted dozens of international surf contests, amateur and professional, including the Caribbean Cup and the Independence Pro. Steel-drum bands often play calypso music on the beach during contests.

In 2003, Barbados was home to two surf shops and about 200 local surfers. Thousands of visiting surfers fly in each year, mainly from America's East Coast. The Barbados surf has been featured in a small number of surf movies and videos, including *Atlantic Crossing* (1989), *Factory Seconds* (1995), and *Arc* (2002).

Barbour, Bob Durable and meticulous surf photographer from Santa Cruz, California; a *Surfing* magazine masthead photographer from 1975 to 1991, before switching to *Surfer.* Barbour was born (1950) in Santa Monica, California, grew up in San Diego, moved to Santa Cruz in 1974—two years after he began shooting photos—and was soon producing richly colored, all-angles-covered images taken at the reefs and points near his house. By the late '70s, the bearded and sometimes prickly Barbour had developed into a well-traveled, first-rank surf photographer. His most famous image was taken in 1994, and shows 16-year-old Santa Cruz surfer Jay Moriarity suspended in midair, just ahead of the crest on a huge wave at Maverick's, the deadly big wave located a half-hour south of San Francisco. Barbour's shot of Moriarity made the cover of the May 1995 issue of *Surfer,* and was featured in the *New York Times Magazine,* under the title "Really Big Wave, Really Bad Wipeout." Barbour's work is also featured in a number of surfing books, including *The History of Surfing* (1983), *Maverick's: The Story of Big-Wave Surfing* (2000), and *The Perfect Day* (2001).

Barland, Michel Pioneering surfer and surfboard manufacturer from Bayonne, France; inventor, in the late 1970s, of the computerized board-making machine. Barland was born (1929) in Bayonne, grew up in the nearby beach resort town of Biarritz, became one of France's original surfers in 1957, and won the 1962 French Surfing Championships. Barland built his first surfboard in 1957 out of plywood, and the following year constructed the first European-made polyurethane foam board. In 1959, he and wealthy Peruvian surfer Carlos Dogny founded the Biarritz-based Waikiki Surf Club, France's first surfing organization. Barland graduated from the University of Paris in 1954 with a degree in mechanical engineering, and returned to Bayonne to work in the family-owned machine shop. In 1968 he became the European licensee for Clark Foam—then and now the leading manufacturer of polyurethane foam surfing blanks—and the company, over the years, regularly incorporated Barland's design and equipment advances. He also worked on injection-molded boards and boards made from Styrofoam and epoxy resin.

Barland began to design a computerized shaping machine in 1979, and five years later he was able to key in 50 variables, hit a button, and 13 minutes later have a mechanically shaped surfboard blank that required just a few minutes of additional fine sanding. Fifteen years later, most major board manufacturers around the world would be using an updated version of Barland's shaping machine. A quiet, intense, sometimes congenial man, Barland disliked long journeys away from home, and visited America just once during his lifetime. He died of a stroke in 1992 at age 63. *See also* shaping machine.

Barnfield, Bill Analytical and meticulous surfboard shaper from Oahu, Hawaii, best known for his North Shore guns in the 1970s and early 1980s. Barnfield was born (1948) in Cherry Valley, California, began surfing at age 12, moved to Southern California in 1967, and shaped his first board early the following year. Over the next four years Barnfield spent time in Oregon (founding Evergreen Surfboards), Hawaii (establishing himself as a first-rate surfer at Pipeline), and Santa Barbara (where he helped nascent boardmaker Al Merrick get his company up and running). In 1973 he signed on at Lightning Bolt Surfboards in Hawaii. As a Bolt shaper, and later under his own Bill Barnfield Performance label, he made boards for dozens of top surfers, including world champions

Shaun Tomson, Margo Oberg, Tom Carroll, and Tom Curren. Barnfield kept detailed measurements for all the boards he shaped, and was the first American shaper, beginning in 1983, to log board information into a computer. Although he was sometimes presented as a salty-haired board-making oracle—a favorite surf media archetype for shapers—surfboards in fact appeared to Barnfield as manifestations of applied formulae. "A surfboard's rocker," he said in 1980, "is like a section of a spiral which, mathematically, should be adjustable to fit various needs. I work to give my boards coherency." From 1983 to 1985, Barnfield wrote "Builder's Emporium," a monthly column for *Surfing* magazine on board materials and board-building technique. In 1987, he opened Proglass, the North Shore's first city-approved surfboard factory, and in so doing became something of a pariah to dozens of local under-the-table, cash-and-carry board-makers.

Barreda, Sergio "Gordo"   Burly regularfoot surfer from Lima, Peru; national champion in 1968, 1969, 1970, and 1974. Barreda was born (1951) and raised in Lima, the son of Sonia Barreda, Peru's first woman surfer. He began riding waves in 1959, and was celebrated as a 15-year-old phenomenon when he placed second in the 1966 Peru International, finishing ahead of surf world luminaries such as Midget Farrelly, Fred Hemmings, and Paul Strauch. The dark-haired, smooth-turning Barreda—better known by his nickname "Gordo"—continued to have an international surf scene presence through the rest of the '60s and into the '70s, making the finals of the 1969 Duke Kahanamoku Invitational, and earning Duke invites in 1970 and 1972. In the Peru International he placed second in 1968 and 1970, then won in 1971 and 1973. He also competed in the World Surfing Championships in 1966, 1968, and 1970. Carlos Barreda, Sergio's older brother, was one of Peru's best small-wave surfers in the '60s. Sergio Barreda opened Lima's first surf shop in 1975, working out of his father's garage, and continued to make boards for more than 25 years. Barreda suffered a heart attack while surfing near his Miraflores home in 2002, and died a few days later, at age 50.

barrel   *See* tube.

barrel roll   Corkscrewing maneuver usually performed in tubing waves, where the rider angles up the face, goes upside down on the underside of the crest, then completes the loop either attached to or alongside the curl as it drops into the trough. The barrel roll has for years been the stuff of fantasy for stand-up surfers. *Petersen's Surfing* magazine published a full-page illustration of the barrel roll in a 1970 article titled "What's Next for the Revolution?" while four years later, *Surfer* ran a mock how-to article, also illustrated, on the "Three-dimensional 360." In 1984 Hawaiian stand-up surfer Johnny-Boy Gomes developed what was called the "pivot roll," turning up into the curl, grabbing the rails of his board as it flew nose-first and upside down toward shore, and wresting it beneath his chest and stomach as he reconnected to the wave face, riding prone. Gomes's novelty move wasn't quite a barrel roll, and soon fell out of use. By 2003, surfers were nearly able to perform a standing-up version of the pivot roll, but an in-the-tube barrel roll remained elusive, as nobody was able to manage the exploding area where the curl meets the trough. Bodyboarders such as Hawaii's Mike Stewart, with their lower center of gravity and easier-to-control boards, began successfully performing barrel rolls in the late 1970s. *See also* aerial.

Barry, Michael   Easygoing regularfoot pro surfer from south Queensland, Australia; world-ranked #14 in 1993 and 1996, but better known as a globe-trotting and perpetually tubed free-surfer. Barry was born (1969) in Sydney, moved to Queensland's Gold Coast as a child, began surfing at 13, and traveled extensively through Indonesia as a teenager. He won Australia's prestigious Pro Junior contest in 1989, and had two world tour victories: the 1993 Miyazaki Pro, in Japan, and the 1996 Billabong Pro, at Jeffreys Bay, South Africa. Australian surf journalist Derek Rielly described 5'7", 145-pound Barry as a "fiercely determined little creature, eyes almost popping from the sockets as he powers through cutbacks and reentries," but he was celebrated as a purebred tuberider, and images of Barry racing smoothly through exotic and perfectly shaped barrels were the highlight of many early and mid-'90s surf videos, including *Bunyip Dreaming* (1991), *The Green Iguana* (1992), and *Sik Joy* (1994).

Bartholomew, Wayne "Rabbit"   Kinetic Australian pro surfer and contest organizer from Queensland's Gold Coast; 1978 world champion and president, beginning in 1999, of the Association of

Wayne Bartholomew

Surfing Professionals. Born (1954) and raised on the Gold Coast, the son of a high school science teacher/fisherman father and a dance instructor mother, Bartholomew was a grade school honors student and a nimble soccer player (nicknamed "Rabbit" for his speed) before he began surfing at age 11. His family was poor, and when his parents split in 1966, Bartholomew helped support his mother and four sisters by stealing wallets from beachgoing tourists. Not a great natural surfing talent, Bartholomew became a top rider through endless hours of practice, and by making a study of the entire sport, including wave conditions, surfboards, other surfers, and competition tactics. He also developed a great sense of style and flair. (As seen in a clip from a 1977 surf movie, Bartholomew emerges from a huge tube at Pipeline, casually examines the fingernails of his right hand while gliding into deep water, then buffs the digits on his chest in a quick gesture of self-congratulation.)

As a juniors division surfer in 1972, Bartholomew was Queensland state champion and second runner-up in the Australian National Titles; in the men's division he was Queensland champion in 1973, 1974, and 1976; fourth in the 1974 nationals, and third in the 1976 nationals. Bartholomew's two greatest rivals throughout the period were both from the Gold Coast: Peter Townend (1976 world champion) and Michael Peterson (national champion in 1972 and 1974). Professional contests in Hawaii, Australia, and South Africa in the mid-'70s offered enough money to keep a dozen or so surfers traveling from country to country over much of the year, Bartholomew included; the International Professional Surfers (IPS) world tour was formed in 1976, with the scruffy Gold Coast regularfooter as one of the tour's most enthusiastic supporters. "To actually make a living from what we were doing," pro surfer Shaun Tomson of South Africa later recalled, "I didn't think it was possible. Rabbit did. And a lot of us were carried along by his momentum." Bartholomew's contest results in 1976 were poor, but in 1977 he finished runner-up to Tomson for the world title. The following year he won the season's first contest and held the ratings lead throughout the 11-event schedule to take the championship—earning an underwhelming $7,650 in total prize money.

Meanwhile, as presented in surf movies like *Free Ride* ('77) and *Tubular Swells* (1977), and in surf magazine interviews and profiles, Bartholomew had become one of the sport's most compelling figures. Slender (5'10", 150 pounds), pale, and plain-looking, Bartholomew dazzled with the force of his personality. Inspired by a range of pop culture figures including J. R. R. Tolkien, Muhammad Ali, and David Bowie, he viewed the surfing experience as an opportunity for grand theater, surfing in the nude for a *Tracks* magazine cover in 1975 and dressing in a silk boxing robe and aviator shades for a *Surfer* magazine portrait shot. Pipeline, he said, was Mordor. Rival Mark Richards was Joe Frazier to his Ali. "I am the legacy of ancient warriors and kings," Bartholomew later wrote in his autobiography, gleefully going over the top. "I've passed through the dark caverns of fear, I've overcome the pain barrier and now fully acknowledge my ability to fly through cliffs and shoulder the mountains themselves." He was a hell-bent driver, once picking up three speeding tickets in three states while travelling from Victoria to Queensland. He was also an unbeatable competitive eater, tucking away seven pounds of food in one hour during a 1976 all-surfers event in Sydney. It was all an act, but a heartfelt and much appreciated one. While on the road in the late '70s and '80s, according to four-time world champion Mark Richards, pro surfers would "go into a mad scramble" to see who got to sit next to Bartholomew at dinner.

Bartholomew finished third at the end of the 1979 tour, fourth in 1980, fourth in 1981, fifth in 1982, and second in 1983, then fell steadily down the ratings before retiring at the end of 1988. He won a total of eight world tour contests, and was a finalist in the Pipeline Masters in 1981, 1984, and 1985. (Riding Pipeline regularly in the winter of 1975–76, Bartholomew contributed greatly to what was soon known as the "backside attack," a sudden performance leap by Pipeline's left-foot-forward surfers.) Future three-time world champion Tom Curren would later cite Bartholomew as his greatest stylistic influence.

In the late '80s and '90s, Bartholomew was hired as a surf contest announcer by the Association of Surfing Professionals (ASP; the replacement group for the IPS), ran a surf school, and became a part-time environmental crusader, helping stop a harbor development at Kirra, the Gold Coast's premier surf break. He continued to write columns and features for surf magazines, as he'd done regularly since the mid-'70s. ("Bustin' Down the Door," his aggressive 1976 article for *Surfer* magazine, was misread by some Hawaiian surfers as an insult; he was jumped later that year while visiting the North Shore and had two front teeth broken out.) Bartholomew also coached the Australian amateur national team to wins in the 1992, 1994, and 1998 world contests. He began organizing local surf contests in 1989; three years later he was directing ASP contests, and from 1995 to 1998 he ran a series of high-profile (though non-world-rated) Billabong Challenge events. He succeeded Graham Stapelberg as ASP president in 1999, and in 2002 helped engineer the ASP's TV partnership with marketing giant International Management Group.

Bartholomew was elected to the Australian Surfing Hall of Fame in 1987 and to the Huntington Beach Surfing Walk of Fame in 2001. *Bustin' Down the Door,* his autobiography, was published in 1996 by HarperCollins and revised in 2002. In 1999 he won the over-40 division of the Quiksilver Masters World Championships; in 2001 he finished 2nd, and in 2003 he again won. Bartholomew has been married twice and has one child. *See also* Association of Surfing Professionals, backside attack, Billabong Pro (Queensland), International Professional Surfers, nudity and surfing.

Baxter, Jackie Spontaneous do-or-die regularfoot surfer from Huntington Beach, California. Baxter began surfing in 1959 at age 11, near his home in Venice Beach, and moved to Hawaii at 20, during the first phase of the shortboard revolution. He was invited to the Expression Sessions events in 1970 and 1971, as well as the 1971 Duke Kahanamoku Classic,

but earned his reputation by regularly throwing himself into the steepest and hairiest places on the wave during free-surf sessions at Pipeline and Sunset Beach. Vardeman Surfboards introduced the Jackie Baxter signature model surfboard in 1967; Baxter appeared in a small number of surf movies, including *The Natural Art* (1969) and *A Sea For Yourself* (1972). He returned to California in 1974. Josh Baxter, Jackie's son, became a professional longboarder in the mid-'90s.

Bay of Bengal Large and relatively shallow bay in the northeast Indian Ocean, bordering India, Bangladesh, and Myanmar, and containing the Andaman and Nicobar Islands. Southwest monsoons between May and October regularly deliver small- to medium-sized surf to the Bay of Bengal's north and east shores, and often-perfect surf to the Andaman and Nicobar groups. The monsoon system reverses from November to April, which generally means poor surf in the Bay of Bengal—although long-distance waves will occasionally arrive from storms in the Southern Ocean. Air and water temperatures in the Bay of Bengal are tropical to subtropical. Because the Ganges, Brahmaputra, and Irrawaddy Rivers all empty into the Bay of Bengal, salinity here is lower than in the rest of the Indian Ocean. *See also* Andaman Islands, India, Myanmar.

Bay of Plenty *See* Durban.

Baywatch Hugely popular and frequently mocked television series, airing from 1989 to 2001, about the loves and adventures of a skin-baring crew of Los Angeles County lifeguards stationed in Malibu. *Baywatch* starred David Hasselhoff as Lt. Mitch Bucannon, with a supporting cast that included sexpot pinup girl Pamela Anderson. *Baywatch* debuted on NBC, was canceled after its first full season, then revived in 1991 for the first-run syndication market. It went on to become the world's most popular TV show, with nearly 2.5 billion weekly viewers in 140 countries tuning in by the late 1990s. The show's surfing connections were slight (the son of the lead character is named Hobie, presumably after pioneering surfboard manufacturer Hobie Alter; Hollywood tough guy and longtime Malibu surfer Richard Jaeckel played an aging lifeguard during the show's early years) with one notable exception: Jimmy Slade, the Malibu High surfer character introduced in 1992, was played by just-crowned world champion Kelly

Slater from Florida. In his debut, Slater takes on a rowdy gang of surfers called the Tequila Shooters, who temporarily slow him down by running a submerged length of barbed wire in the surf zone and pulling it tight as he rides past. Slater's *Baywatch* participation didn't go over well with most surfers, including Hawaiian big-wave rider Brock Little, who said it was "an embarrassment to the sport." Slater left *Baywatch* in late 1993, after appearing in 10 episodes over two seasons. A few months later he was romantically linked with Pamela Anderson, then still married to Mötley Crüe drummer Tommy Lee, the father to her two children. *Baywatch Nights,* with Hasselhoff's Bucannon moonlighting as a private detective, aired from 1995 to 1997. *Baywatch Hawaii* aired in 2000 and 2001. *See also* Kelly Slater, television and surfing.

Beach Boys, The   Hugely popular vocal-rock group from Los Angeles, California, led by songwriting savant Brian Wilson; acclaimed for their soaring melodies and lush, intricately harmonized vocals, and best known for a string of early and mid-1960s hits about surfing and the sun-filled Southern California beach life. "The Beach Boys," *Rolling Stone* magazine wrote, "virtually invented California rock." The band's original lineup consisted of the three Wilson brothers, Brian, Carl, and Dennis, their cousin Mike Love, and friend Al Jardine. Influenced primarily by Chuck Berry and the Four Freshmen, Brian wrote "Surfin'" in 1959 for his 12th-grade Piano and Harmony class (earning a C for the semester); "Surfin'" became a regional hit in 1961, just a few

The Beach Boys

months after the Beach Boys formed. Signed to Capitol Records, the Beach Boys hit the national charts in 1962 and 1963 with "Surfin' Safari" (#14), "Surfin' USA" (#3), "Catch a Wave" (#7), and "Surfer Girl" (#7). Brian produced and arranged the group's music in the mid-'60s, and added layers of melancholy and complexity to songs like "In My Room," "Don't Worry Baby," "God Only Knows," and "Caroline, No." Paul McCartney later said that Wilson and the Beach Boys helped inspire the Beatles' *Rubber Soul* and *Sgt. Pepper's* albums, and lauded the Beach Boys' 1966 release *Pet Sounds* as "perhaps the album of the century."

While the Beach Boys wrote songs about surfing, by strict definition they aren't part of the nonvocal, heavy-reverb-guitar surf music genre. But along with *Gidget* (the book and the movie), the Beach Boys helped introduce surfing to America and the rest of the world, with join-in lyrics like "Let's go surfing now, everybody's learning how, come on a surfari with me." Most early and mid-'60s surfers, meanwhile, didn't care for the often-sentimental Beach Boys music. "I remember the first time we heard 'Surfer Girl,'" California 1960s surf icon Mike Doyle said in 1993, "we started hissing and hooting because we thought it was so dumb." Surf filmmakers Greg MacGillivray and Jim Freeman used new Beach Boys music on the soundtrack to their 1972 hit surf movie *Five Summer Stories*; Beach Boys' songs were also used in David Sumpter's 1974 surf movie *On Any Morning.* As the years passed, even die-hard detractors came around. "None of us much liked the Beach Boys when they first came out," *Surfer* magazine founder John Severson said in 1997. "Now I think their music is wonderful; now I understand it, and know why everyone thought they were so incredible."

Misfortune and tragedy have plagued The Beach Boys: Murray Wilson, father of the three Wilson brothers and the band's first manager, beat Brian hard enough to deafen the boy's right ear, and Brian has suffered throughout his life from drug addiction and mental illness. Dennis Wilson—the only band member who actually surfed—befriended convicted murderer Charles Manson in the late '60s, was an alcoholic, and died in 1983 after diving off his marina-anchored boat. Carl Wilson died in 1998 of lung cancer. Mike Love sued Brian Wilson for defamation of character in 1992, after reading Wilson's autobiography, *Wouldn't It Be Nice*; they settled out of court two years later, but Love soon prevailed against Wilson in a royalties dispute. The Beach Boys continued to release albums in the '80s and '90s; Brian Wilson released five solo albums between 1988 and 2000. The Beach Boys were inducted into the Rock and Roll Hall of Fame in 1988, and by 2000 they'd sold nearly 70 million albums worldwide. Books on the group include *The Surf's Up: The Beach Boys on Record, 1961–1981* (1982), *Beach Boys* (1985), *Heroes and Villains: The True Story of the Beach Boys* (1986), and *The Nearest Faraway Place* (1996). *See also* surf music.

beach bunny   *See* surf bunny.

beach movies   *See* Hollywood and surfing.

beach, the   Geologically defined as a sandy intertidal buffer between land and sea, the beach has long represented a kind of relaxed pleasure zone for surfers and non-surfers alike. The sport of surfing is in some respects defined as much by behavior on the beach as by performance in the water. Most of the stories about Malibu in the '50s and early '60s, for example, have to do with the social interplay around the Pit, a sandy area near the base of Malibu Point that served as a kind of outdoor theater for surfers like Terry "Tubesteak" Tracy, Mickey Dora, Lance Carson, and Kemp Aaberg. Similarly, the 1959 Malibu-based movie *Gidget* features dozens of beach scenes and just a passing few moments of wave-riding.

Most surfers, particularly in temperate suburban areas like Southern California and much of the east coast of Australia, have not only an affinity for the beach in general, but allegiance to a particular beach; two-time world champion Tom Carroll, for example, speaks lovingly of the Sydney community of Newport Beach, where he grew up and learned to surf. Two beaches that have been all but defined by surfers are San Onofre in north San Diego County, where senior wave-riders meet almost daily to barbecue and play music on ukuleles and guitars, and Makaha, on the west side of Oahu, where local surfers of all ages gather on weekends to form what amounts to a temporary beach village. Contests can also create transient—although sometimes massive—beach scenes: world pro tour contests in Huntington, Rio, Sydney, and Biarritz, for example, can draw up to 10,000 spectators.

While surfers generally view the beach as a place to fraternize, nonsurfers see it as a giant recreation area, ideal for volleyball, football, soccer, Frisbee, sunbathing, and sandcastle building. Surfers and non-

surfers alike recognize the beach as a transcendent background for love and romance; all are drawn to the constantly changing vista of land, sea, wind, and sky. (There are exceptions. "The beach," acerbic California surf icon Phil Edwards noted, "is just something you cross to get to the surf.")

The beach, and its attendant sociology, has been the subject of dozens of pop songs; the setting for *Baywatch,* the world's most popular TV show, as well as a number of '60s-era Hollywood beach movies; and inspiration for hundreds of poems, essays, and paintings, a few books, and a small number of highbrow literary critiques. "Legally, socially and morally," the *New York Review of Books* wrote in 1994, "the beach is a marginal zone to which marginal people tend to gravitate, and where respectable folk tend to behave in marginal and eccentric ways."

Beacham, Debbie   Resolute pro surfer and organizer from La Jolla, California; professional world champion in 1982, and president of the Women's Professional Surfing Association from 1982 to 1986. Born Debbie Melville in 1953 in Corpus Christi, Texas, the daughter of a navy pilot, she spent her early years living on or near a series of naval bases around the country. At 13 she moved with her family to La Jolla, and soon took up surfing. Melville had become one of California's best female surfers by 1971, winning two of the Western Surfing Association's elite AAAA events, and placing third in the United States Surfing Championships; the following year she was runner-up in the U.S. Championships, and placed fifth in the World Championships. The women's pro world tour debuted in 1977, and Melville finished the year ranked eighth. She married real estate developer Louis Beacham in 1979. After three desultory years on the world tour, Beacham opened the 1982 season with a win at Bells Beach, Australia—her first and only world tour victory—and placed highly enough in the remaining four events to take the championship. Beacham used a functional, straight-backed stance, and performed best in larger surf. By 1983, she was facing a group of hot young teenage surfers—including Kim Mearig and Frieda Zamba from the U.S., as well as Australians Jodie Cooper and Pam Burridge—and dropped to fourth in the rankings. The following year she finished sixth, and retired from full-time competition.

Beacham's focus had by that time shifted to organizing and promoting women's surfing. In 1977 she'd been a founding member of the Golden Girls, a short-lived group of six Californians remembered primarily for their color-coordinated wetsuits. In 1982, Beacham became president of the Women's Professional Surfing Association—an organization founded in 1979, but at that point not yet activated—and put together a five-contest pro circuit as an alternative to the world tour. She served from 1983 to 1992 as the women's representative to the Association of Surfing Professionals. In 1994 Beacham coproduced *Surfer Girl,* a beautifully photographed documentary about women's surfing.

Beacham won the 1983 *Surfer* Magazine Readers Poll Awards, and from 1985 to 1991 she worked in *Surfer*'s advertising department. She appeared in *Going Surfin'* (1973) and a small number of other surf movies and videos. Beacham lives in La Jolla with her husband and three children. *See also* The Golden Girls.

beachboys   Lionized and partially mythologized band of easygoing Hawaiian surfer/waterman/hustlers who worked and lounged on the beach at Waikiki in the early and middle 20th century. The beachboy was both a cause and by-product of the booming Hawaiian tourist trade; he earned a living primarily by lifeguarding and giving surf lessons and canoe rides, and spent his free time surfing, swimming, fishing, and playing music. Beachboys first appeared on Waikiki not long after the 1901 completion of the Moana, the area's first hotel. Surfing and outrigger canoeing—nearly wiped out in the 19th century, as Calvinist missionaries frowned on such native recreations—were recast by tourist boosters as romantic symbols of tropical Hawaiian paradise. By 1911, two surfing/canoeing clubs, the Outrigger and Hui Nalu, had beachfront quarters in Waikiki. The clubs brought a level of organization to the collection of locals who were already freelancing their surf lessons and canoe ride services to tourists, and when Hui Nalu captain Edward "Dude" Miller made an arrangement in 1916 with the Moana Hotel to officially provide their concession on Waikiki, most of the beachboys came from his club. Miller's clean-cut uniform-wearing beachboys, known as the Moana Bathhouse Gang, weren't allowed to drink, gamble, or touch female visitors while working. Turning a pastime into a tip-making operation, a group of guitar- and ukulele-playing beachboys meanwhile performed nightly on the Moana pier. They found

Bing Crosby, with beachboys (left to right) Pua Kealoha, Chick Daniels, and Joe Minor

other ways to entertain as well. "In their leisure moments," *Good Housekeeping* magazine reported in 1926, "the beachboys array themselves in outlandish costumes and parade along the beach indulging in all sorts of pranks and buffoonery, their own childlike enjoyment in these pastimes quite as great as the amusement they afford to others." Others weren't so charmed. The beachboys, according to one newspaper-quoted Honolulu businessman, were "a bunch of lazy male prostitutes who made their living off mainland divorcees." The California surfers who began coming to Waikiki in the '20s were perhaps more enamored of the beachboys than anybody, and after returning home went to great lengths to reproduce their laughing, easy-does-it style.

With the opening of the grand pink-stucco Royal Hawaiian Hotel in 1927, Waikiki became one of America's premier vacation destinations, especially for the rich and famous, and beachboys were soon tending to the likes of Carole Lombard, Charlie Chaplin, Cary Grant, and Bing Crosby. The number of beachboys shot up to keep pace with the growing number of tourists, and in 1934 the Outrigger Canoe Club formed the Waikiki Beach Patrol to bring individual beachboy entrepreneurs into a single concession. The unsalaried Beach Patrol was a success, with beachboys taking care of wealthy tourists, who, in turn, presented them with envelopes of cash upon their departure for the mainland. "Panama Dave" Baptiste, William "Chick" Daniels, Joseph "Scooter Boy" Kaopuiki, and Sam "Steamboat" Mokuahi were among the period's best-known beachboys. While Olympic gold medal swimmer and surfing patriarch

Duke Kahanamoku was never a wage-earning beachboy, he was, in many respects, as 1968 world surfing champion Fred Hemmings put it, the "ultimate beachboy."

As World War II disabled the Hawaiian tourist industry, the beachboys took other jobs or joined the war effort. Afterward, "wildcatter" beachboys who often hustled the less-wealthy visitors north of the Royal Hawaiian—renting defective surfboards, for example, then charging to bring the sinking boards back to shore—quickly earned the animosity of the more genteel old guard beachboys. By 1959, as Hawaii became America's 50th state, beachboys were being licensed; but overdevelopment, along with jet travel that brought more tourists but shortened the average length of visits, soon marginalized the entire group. Beachboys of one kind or another have continued to work in Waikiki, but when Duke Kahanamoku died in 1968, the beachboy lifestyle in a sense died with him. Albert "Rabbit" Kekai, 83 in 2003, has sometimes been called the last beachboy. "The aloha spirit that was once authentic has become commercialized," Grady Timmons wrote in his richly detailed 1989 book *Waikiki Beachboy.* "But the ocean remains. For a beachboy, it is the one constant, the one thing he knows he can go back to." *See also* Duke Kahanamoku, Albert "Rabbit" Kekai, Waikiki.

beachbreak   Type of surf break that takes shape over a sandy beach. Because beachbreak surf is dependent on sandbars, it's far more mutable and unpredictable than the surf found at pointbreaks or reefbreaks. A poststorm beachbreak sandbar might last for months, or might be removed entirely by the next storm. This ephemeral quality is alternately wonderful and frustrating. "Beachbreak waves are anything and everything," surf journalist Nick Carroll wrote. "One minute they're Pipeline, the next Indonesia, the next they're gone." While beachbreaks run the gamut in terms of power, and can indeed impersonate some of the world's best point- and reefbreaks, for the most part they generate short, quick waves, frequently breaking in both directions, and often without a set takeoff area or lineup. Beachbreak surf is thought of as categorically inferior to that of pointbreaks and reefbreaks, but beachbreaks have nonetheless produced a majority of the world's best surfers—in part because beachbreaks greatly outnumber point- and reefbreaks in the world's coastal population centers, and in part because beachbreak waves demand quick reflexes, as well as a try-again-and-try-harder attitude.

Because beachbreaks tend to be the least hazardous form of surf break, they are favored among beginning surfers. On the other hand, because beachbreaks are often crowded, and because beginning surfers may not be aware of the dangers of riptides and currents, they account for a disproportionate number of surfing mishaps, injuries, and even drownings. With very few exceptions—Mexico's Puerto Escondido in particular—beachbreaks are best when the surf is small- or medium-sized. Bigger waves tend to overpower most sandbars and dump over as shapeless closeout waves; when the shape does hold, the absence of deep-water channels at most beachbreaks makes paddling through the nearshore surf difficult or impossible. Puerto Escondido, Hossegor (France), and Duranbah (Australia) are some of the world's premier beachbreaks. On the eastern seaboard, virtually all surfing from New York to Florida is done in beachbreaks. In the reef-fringed tropics, beachbreaks are almost nonexistent. *See also* pointbreak, reefbreak.

Beachcomber Bills Grand Prix   Short-lived world tour pro circuit ratings system, founded in late 1976, almost simultaneously with the International Professional Surfers (IPS) tour. Beachcomber Bills was a central California–based sandal manufacturer; the Grand Prix structure and format were developed primarily by Australian pro surfer Ian Cairns. The Grand Prix and the IPS started off as friendly rivals and officially launched their tours at the same kickoff party, at the Kuilima Hyatt hotel on the North Shore, on October 13, 1976; but whereas the IPS retroactively tabulated contests from the previous 10 months in order to determine a 1976 world champion (Peter Townend of Australia), the Grand Prix launched in early 1977 simultaneously with the second IPS tour. At year's end, South Africa's Shaun Tomson won both the IPS and Beachcomber Bills titles. Because of slightly different scoring systems, many of the pros had two distinct rankings; Australian Peter Drouyn, for example, finished sixth in the IPS and fifth in the Grand Prix. Beachcomber Bills threw a black-tie formal awards ceremony at the end of the season, but the Grand Prix didn't return in 1978, and the company itself soon folded. *See also* Ian Cairns, International Professional Surfers, professional surfing.

Beachley, Layne   Lively and charismatic Australian regularfoot surfer from Dee Why, Sydney; winner of five consecutive pro world championship titles from 1998, and generally regarded as the sport's greatest female big-wave rider. "She trains, focuses, paddles out with a pleasant smile and fillets the opposition with roughly the compassion of a shark," surf journalist Nick Carroll said of Beachley in 1999. "And the best thing about her is that she'd laugh her guts out at this description and then cheerfully agree with it." Beachley's life got off to a rough start. She was born (1972) Tania Maris Gardner in Sydney; as an infant she was adopted and renamed by Neil and Valerie Beachley; Valerie died when Layne was six. Beachley began surfing at age four, but wasn't fervent about it until 16. "I was the only girl that hung around at the beach," she later said. "I had to be one of the guys. I had to surf as good as the guys, give as much shit as the guys, and to take as much as they could give me."

Beachley had no amateur contest to speak of when she turned pro in 1989. She didn't win a world tour event until 1993, then placed herself firmly near the top of the ratings, finishing fourth in 1994, second in 1995, third in 1996, and second in 1997. Beachley began the 1998 circuit accompanied by veteran Hawaiian big-wave surfer Ken Bradshaw, 19 years her senior, who had recently become her boyfriend, coach, board-maker, and big-wave mentor. She dominated the schedule, winning five of 11 events, on her way to an easy world title victory. Hobbled somewhat by a knee injury in 1999 season, she nonetheless won four of the season's 14 events, and after winning her

Layne Beachley

second title was described by *Surfer* magazine as "simply the most powerful woman in surfing today." For her 2000 title she won four of nine contests, then won one of the three events in the abbreviated 2001 season. She won just one of six contests in 2002 but it was enough to earn the title and make her the only five-time women's tour champion.

Beachley's competitive success was paralleled by her development as a big-wave rider. She'd performed well in the powerful Hawaiian surf through the early and mid-'90s, but in late 1997, as her relationship with Bradshaw took off, she surpassed all the female big-wave benchmarks set years earlier by Hawaii's Margo Oberg and Australian Jodie Cooper. On December 22, 1997, with Bradshaw driving the personal watercraft, Beachley was catapulted into three 15- to 18-foot waves at a North Shore break called Phantoms. Sarah Gerhardt of California had earlier become the first woman tow-in surfer, but Beachley (5′5″, 125 pounds) was the first woman to master the art. She later towed in to 25-footers at Hawaii's Outside Log Cabins in Hawaii and Todos Santos in Baja California.

Beachley won Hawaii's Triple Crown of Surfing in 1997 and 1998. As of early-2003, she was the all-time women's surfing prize money leader, having won just over $400,000. Beachley has appeared in a number of surfing videos, including *Empress* (1999), *Tropical Madness* (2001), and *7 Girls* (2002). She also was the top vote-getter in *Australia's Surfing Life* magazine's Peer Poll in 1998, 1999, 2000, and 2001. *Outside* magazine in 1998 published a profile on Beachley titled "I'm Going Big. Anyone Care to Follow?" She was also profiled in *Girl in the Curl: A Century of Women in Surfing,* an illustrated history published in 2000. Beachley is unmarried.

beachwear   *See* surfing and fashion.

beavertail   Front-zip wetsuit jacket, usually long sleeve; originally developed for skin divers, appropriated by surfers in the late 1950s, and popular until the mid-'70s. The "beavertail" referred to a vertical flap of neoprene, about 16 inches long and six inches wide, that hung down from the back of the suit and was designed to loop over the crotch and snap to the front hem, at waist level. Fastened, the beavertail looked like a rubber codpiece, and surfers, more beach-fashion conscious than divers, chose to leave the rubber appendage unsnapped, where it would dangle, twist, flutter and snap during a ride. Why surfers didn't simply cut the beavertail off remains a mystery. The beavertail was the most popular surfing wetsuit of the late '50s and '60s, when it was alternately known as a "rubber jacket." *See also* wetsuit.

Becker, Phil   Hardworking surfboard shaper from Hermosa Beach, California; best known for his longboards and easy-to-ride funboards; thought to have shaped more boards than anyone in the world. Becker learned his craft as a young teenager in the early '50s from California board-building pioneers Dale Velzy and Hap Jacobs, and became the primary shaper for Rick Surfboards in Hermosa from 1958 to 1979. He and fellow Californian Mike Eaton are thought to be the only two full-time shapers who made longboards throughout the '70s. In 1980, at age 40, he founded Becker Surfboards in Hermosa Beach. Working at a rate of roughly 10 boards a day, Becker likely passed the 100,000-board mark sometime around the year 2000—putting him about 25,000 boards ahead of anyone else in the world. Becker continues to use the Rockwell planer he bought in 1965, rebuilding it when necessary.

Bedford-Brown, Stuart   Hot-tempered surfer/ model from Perth, Western Australia; world-ranked #12 in 1993, at age 27, one year before the end of a pro career that began in 1984. Bedford-Brown is best remembered for his contentious relationship with the surf press. He was described as "a brat" in *Surfer* magazine, and surf journalist Derek Hynd said in 1990 that "his surfing is not as flawless as his looks. Actually, his surfing can be ugly as sin." In early 1990, the always-cheeky *Australia's Surfing Life* magazine published a short article titled "The Very Last Stuart Bedford-Brown Interview," in which the handsome, dark-haired surfer, who worked as a model in Europe between pro contests, opens by asking the editors to "do something on me," and a short while later concludes by complaining that "no surf magazines support me, and when the TV show comes out [Bedford-Brown was set to cohost an Australian surfing variety show], everyone's going to want to interview me, and I'm going to tell them all to fuck off." Bedford-Brown appeared in a small number of surf videos, including *La Scene* ('94) and *Cyclone Fever* ('94).

Belgium   Summer surf along Belgium's 100-mile-long coastline is virtually nonexistent, while autumn and winter swells funnel down through the North Sea and produce cold, crumbling, but serviceable waves. Surfer's Paradise, the wryly named beach area in the northwest, is Belgium's premier wave-riding area, with a breakwater helping to create shapely beachbreak peaks. Further south, in Blankenberge and Oostende, there are several beachbreaks and two surf shops. Surfing is limited to designated areas during the summer months, when the water temperatures reach the high 50s and vacationers take over the beach; from late fall to spring, as the water temperature drops to the low 40s, the entire coast is open to surfers.

Surfing was introduced to Belgium in 1983 after a small group of locals returned from a visit to Morocco with surfboards. The Belgium Surfing Association was formed in 1993; the group petitions local government agencies on surf restrictions, publishes a surf magazine, and sponsors surf competitions. The Belguim surf is detailed in *The Stormrider Guide Europe* (1998).

Bells Beach   Right-breaking Australian reef wave located three miles southwest of Torquay, Victoria. Facing the chilly and powerful Southern Ocean, and flanked by limestone cliffs, Bells Beach—named after the Bell farming family—has for decades been a venerated surf break. The wave at Bells is for the most part sloping and wide-based, strong but rarely hollow; tuberides at Bells are rare. The break consists of three main sections: 1) Little Rincon, located to the south, needs a higher tide and a sub-six-foot swell. 2) Outside Bells, the main break, is a long, fast, evenly formed wall that begins to take form when the surf is about six foot. 3) The Bowl is the steep final section of the Outside Bells wave. Centerside, located 150 yards outside of Little Rincon, is an inconsistent right that eventually closes out. Southside, located further around the Bells Beach headland, is a left-breaking wave that spills into a nearby bay. Winkipop, the reef just east of Bells, is a spectacularly fast and hollow right-breaking wave, and generally regarded as superior to Bells proper. (Four-time world champion Mark Richards once called Bells "a dud; the most overrated wave in the world.") Bells is at its best from March to October, as Southern Ocean storms frequently produce six- to eight-foot surf, with waves sometimes topping 15 feet. Rain and wind are common at this time of year. Air temperatures range from the mid-50s to the high 70s; water temperatures range from the mid-50s to the mid-60s.

Bells was first ridden in the late 1940s by Torquay natives Vic Tantau and Owen Yateman, but it remained a surfing backwater until 1956, when a group of visiting American surfer/lifeguards introduced the area to the lighter, more maneuverable balsa-core Malibu longboards, which were much easier to carry down the long dirt track leading to Bells than the heavy plywood surf skis popular at the time. Early Bells standouts included Peter Troy, Joe Sweeny, Charles "China" Gilbert, and George "Ming" Smith, all members of the 1958-founded Bells Boardriders Club. The annual Bells Beach Easter contest, inaugurated in 1962, became the Rip Curl Pro in 1973, after Torquay-based Rip Curl Wetsuits signed on as event sponsor. Bells event winners over the years have included world champions Nat Young, Margo Oberg, Mark Richards, Tom Curren, Barton Lynch, Tom Carroll, Kelly Slater, Mark Occhilupo, Lisa Andersen, Sunny Garcia, and Layne Beachley. Torquay-area local and five-time national champion Gail Couper holds the record for most Bells victories, with 10. Favorite son Wayne Lynch, from the nearby town of Lorne, won four consecutive Bells juniors division titles, from 1966 to 1969. Bells also hosted the early rounds of the 1970 World Surfing Championships.

Australian surfers in decades past often used Bells as a test track for new board designs: Nat Young, Bob McTavish, and Midget Farrelly rode first-generation vee-bottom shortboards here during the 1967 Easter contest; Mark Richards unveiled his new twin-fin design during the 1978 Rip Curl Pro; and Simon Anderson proved the worth of his new tri-fin Thruster by winning the 1981 Rip Curl Pro, the middle rounds of which were held in 15-foot-plus surf. Bells was featured in *Great Waves,* an Outdoor Life Network documentary series; it's also appeared in more than 40 surf films and videos over the years, including *The Endless Summer* (1966), *Evolution* (1969), *Free Ride* (1977), *Storm Riders* (1982), *Beyond the Boundaries* (1994), and *Bells 2 Burleigh* (2001). *See also* Rip Curl Pro, Bells Beach; Torquay, Victoria.

belly   Gently rounded rail-to-rail convexity on the bottom of a surfboard, almost always located in the board's middle or front section. The longer ancient Hawaiian boards had belly from tip to tail, and post–World War II board-makers Bob Simmons and Renolds Yater of California both put belly into their boards' nose sections. While belly provides an easy and more forgiving planing surface, it also slows the board down, as water "sticks" to the curve. For this reason, the bottom surfaces on virtually all modern shortboards are made up of speedier flats and con-

caves, with little or no belly. Modern longboards, as with the pre–shortboard revolution counterparts, employ belly to one degree or another. Also known as "roll." *See also* bottom, concave, spoon nose.

bellyboarding   Prone method of wave-riding using a small, thin, rigid board. Bellyboarding was almost certainly the original form of board-surfing, and is thought to date back as far as 2,000 B.C. The oldest extant bellyboards—owned by Honolulu's Bishop Museum, and probably built in the early 18th century— are flat and blunt-nosed, between four and four and a half feet long, made of either breadfruit or koa wood, and are believed to have been used by children as an intermediary step to stand-up surfing. Hawaiian-styled wooden bellyboards are known as *paipo* boards; bellyboarding itself is sometimes referred to as *paipo* boarding. While bellyboard design and construction evolved along with stand-up boards during the first half of the 1900s, slapdash models remained popular. "One guy might be using a board made of beautiful balsa wood with redwood stringers, covered in fiberglass and rubbed out to a dazzling finish," *Surf Guide* magazine wrote in 1965, "while riding the same wave, and having just as much fun, might be a guy on a board carved from an old signboard." Most midcentury bellyboards—some with stabilizing fins, others without—were simply made of water-sealed plywood. Bellyboarding was often done at breaks regarded as unsuitable for stand-up surfing: the Wedge in Southern California, for example, or Makapu and Sandy Beach on Oahu. Bellyboarders were by then using swim fins to power themselves into waves.

Bellyboarding

American and Australian board-making companies like Dextra and Newport Paipo made lines of foam-and-fiberglass bellyboards in the early and mid-'60s, with the idea that this form of surfing—much easier to learn than stand-up riding—was set to become the next big thing in beachside recreation. The market was all but cornered instead by the inflatable rubber-and-canvas surf mat, and later by the soft-skinned bodyboard, both of which were for the most part ridden prone. Bellyboarding was all but forgotten by the mid-'70s. Modern surfing techniques as well as the modern stand-up board, nonetheless, were influenced by the bellyboard. Compared to the unwieldy stand-up boards used until the late '60s, the bellyboard—as well as the kneeboard, and even the surf mat—allowed the rider to get close to the curl, and to dig out from hard-to-make positions. "If there's one thing the bellyboard has over the surfboard, it is intimacy," California bellyboarder Gary Crandall wrote in 1970. "[It's] a more visceral, close-to-the-gut type of surfing." The late-'60s shortboard revolution came about in large part as stand-up surfers looked to get closer to the breaking wave. Bellyboarding is featured in a small number of surf movies from the late '50s and '60s, including *Angry Sea* (1963), *Golden Breed* (1968), and *Waves of Change* (1969). *See also* bodyboarding, kneeboarding.

Bennett, Barry   Mid-1950s Australian surfboard industry pioneer from Sydney, New South Wales; founder of Bennett Surfboards, the country's longest-surviving board manufacturer. Bennett was born (1931) in Sydney, raised in the coastal suburb of Bronte, began surfing at age 15, and made his first board—a 15-foot plywood "toothpick"—the following year. In 1956, a group of visiting California surfer/lifeguards including Greg Noll and Tom Zahn introduced Australia to the easy-to-turn balsa-core Malibu board. Bennett Surfboards opened almost immediately thereafter, and soon became one of the country's leading board-makers. Bennett founded Dion Chemicals in 1962, and began manufacturing polyurethane foam surfboard blanks, as well as importing high-quality resins for use in board construction. In 1970, Bennett and Sydney businessman John Arnold formed Golden Breed, Australia's first international surfwear company. In the meantime, as former pro surfer and Hot Buttered Surfboards founder Terry Fitzgerald later recalled, Bennett became "a financially-abused creditor for almost every Aus-

tralian surfboard manufacturer. We—the collective industry—could not have survived without him." Bennett was listed as one of Australia's "50 Most Influential Surfers" by *Australia's Surfing Life* magazine in 1992; Bennett Surfboards and Dion Chemicals were both still operating as of 2003.

Benson, Becky   Pioneering Hawaiian pro surfer, state champion in 1973, and world-ranked #3 in 1977. Becky and her sister Blanche—daughters of Albert Benson, a cameraman whose work was featured in more than a dozen surf movies—were fixtures on Oahu's North Shore in the mid- and late '70s. Becky Benson had a long if not entirely consistent run as a surfing competitor, winning the Makaha International in '71 and the Op Pro in 1982. She finished sixth on the world tour in 1978 and eighth in 1982. A tiny surfer (98 pounds when she won her state title), Benson was nonetheless a cool hand in bigger Hawaiian waves, and in top form during a short appearance in the 1973 surf movie *A Sea For Yourself,* carving beautiful lines across double overhead waves at Haleiwa.

Benson, Linda   Flashy goofyfoot surfer from Encinitas, California; the 15-year-old winner of the 1959 Makaha International. "Linda was the hotdogger of the women," California ironman surfer Mike Doyle once said. "She had incredible wave judgment and just ripped the waves apart." Benson was born (1944) and raised in Encinitas; her father had been a drummer in the Tommy Dorsey Orchestra. She began surfing at age 11, and was greatly influenced by Dewey Weber, the zippy blond small-wave ace from Hermosa Beach; the diminutive Benson (5′2″ as an adult) quickly learned how to walk the board, do multiple spinners, and hang five. She made her competition debut in the 1959 West Coast Surfing Championships, won the event, then went on a few weeks later to win Makaha, during her first visit to Hawaii. Just days later, the pageboy-coiffed Benson became the first woman to ride the fabled big surf at Waimea Bay, on the North Shore of Oahu.

Benson competed on and off for 10 years, winning the West Coast Championships in 1960 and 1961, and the United States Championships in 1964 and 1968. She also won the United States Invitational in 1964, and was the top female vote-getter in the 1965 *Surfing Illustrated* magazine reader's poll. *Surf Guide* magazine published a 1963 cover shot of Benson

Linda Benson

exiting the water, with a coverline reading: "Linda Benson: World's Greatest!" It was the first time a woman had appeared on the cover of a surf magazine. In the mid- and late '60s, Benson often jousted with two-time world champion Joyce Hoffman of California, and in the late '60s she came up against four-time world champion Margo Oberg, also from California. Benson never won a world title. She quit competing in 1969, then left surfing entirely. She was an alcoholic for a number of years, and stopped drinking in 1977. Two years later she began to surf again, and continues to surf today.

Benson was featured in a number of surf movies, including *Cavalcade of Surf* (1962) and *Gun Ho!* (1963). She occasionally worked as a surfing stunt double in films like *Gidget Goes Hawaiian* (1961), *Muscle Beach Party* (1964), and *Beach Blanket Bingo* (1965). Benson was inducted into the Huntington Beach Surfing Walk of Fame in 1997. "The Making of a Champion" is the title of the Linda Benson chapter in Andrea Gabbard's 2000 book on women's surfing, *Girl in the Curl: A Century of Women in Surfing*. Benson never married.

Bermuda   Cluster of 300 humid, densely populated subtropical islands and tiny islets, with a total aggregate area of just 20 square miles; located in the North Atlantic Ocean, about 900 miles due east of Charleston, South Carolina. Bermuda is a British dependency and a longtime popular resort center (home of the perennially popular Bermuda shorts), and the world's most northerly group of coral islands. While Bermuda is perfectly situated to receive all manner of Atlantic-generated surf, the waves are generally small and sloppy as incoming waves get filtered

through barrier reefs, and the wind often blows onshore at the better breaks. Tuckers, also known as Windsor Beach, located to the north on the perimeter of Castle Harbor, is Bermuda's premier surf spot—a long, winding, left-breaking point that is best during winter. Bermuda's average annual temperature is 70 degrees; water temperatures range from the mid-60s in winter to the mid-70s in summer. Bermuda was first surfed in the mid-'60s by visiting Americans. Today, there are fewer than 50 resident surfers in Bermuda, and just one small surf shop.

Bertlemann, Larry   Dynamic regularfoot surfer from Honolulu, Hawaii; winner of the 1973 United States Surfing Championships, and often cited as progenitor for today's high-performance shortboard surfing. "A truly gifted surfer," as described by Australian journalist Phil Jarratt in 1979, "with an outrageously overblown ego." Bertlemann was born (1955) in Hilo, Hawaii, the son of an auto mechanic, and began surfing at age 11, just after moving with his family to Honolulu. Three years later he placed fourth in the boys' division of the Hawaii state championships, beginning a successful amateur career that included a win in the juniors division of the 1971 Makaha International and a fourth in the 1972 World Surfing Championships. In 1973 he won both the state and national titles. As a professional—the line between amateur and professional surfing was virtually nonexistent until the mid-'70s—he placed third in the 1972 Pipeline Masters, third in the 1973 Smirnoff Pro, first in the 1974 Duke Classic, second in the 1975 Lightning Bolt Pro, and first in the 1978 Katin Team Challenge. He was world-ranked #13 in 1976 and #12 in 1979.

Nicknamed "Rubberman," the kinetic and hyperflexible Bertlemann surfed in a low, springy, open-knee crouch. He worked his board constantly, but the motion was blended and synched, and he brought a smoothness to even the most explosive turns. Some of Bertlemann's best surfing was done on the Ben Aipa–designed split-railed stinger boards of the mid-'70s. An avid skateboarder, the 5'9", 160-pound Hawaiian regularly practiced his high-torque turns on asphalt and concrete. Bertlemann permanently altered the body dynamics of surfing, which in turn opened up the range of on-wave lines, angles, and arcs; his style was imprinted directly on a slightly younger group of Hawaiian surfers, including Dane Kealoha, Buttons Kaluhiokalani, and Mark Liddell. In the late '70s, borrowing a move from the skateboard world, Bertlemann began working on aerials—what he immodestly called "Larryials"—and became a forerunner to high-flying Kelly Slater and the rest of the early '90s New School surfers.

Bertlemann's obsession with image and commercialism, meanwhile, put him on the wrong side of surfing purists. Always fashion conscious, instantly recognizable by his neatly tended afro hairstyle, Bertlemann frequently surfed and skateboarded in color-coordinated outfits, and at one point took to the waves at Pipeline wearing a customized blue-and-red bell-bottom wetsuit. A pioneer in surf world corporate sponsorship, Bertlemann by the late '70s was plastering his boards with oversize stickers from Pepsi, United Airlines, and Toyota, and even adopted the Pepsi swirl emblem for his board's design motif. "I get off on promoting things," the easy-smiling eighth-grade dropout once said. "I keep my sponsors happy, and they keep me in business." Bertlemann, who also worked as a surfboard shaper, was featured eight times on the cover of *Surfer* and *Surfing* magazines in the 1970s. (Gerry Lopez had five covers; Shaun Tomson and Mark Richards each had four.) As crass as he was popular, Bertlemann at one point was "signing" autographs with a rubber stamp.

Bertlemann dropped off the surf scene from 1985 to 2000; he resurfaced in 2001, featured in the *Surfer's Journal*/Outdoor Life Network cable TV series *Biographies,* and profiled at length in the *Surfer's Journal,* where it was revealed that he'd been unable to surf since the late '90s due to a series of back injuries and

surgeries. Long associated with the Honolulu underworld, Bertlemann himself was arrested on robbery and firearm charges in the summer of 2001.

Bertlemann appeared in more than 25 surf movies, including *Going Surfin'* (1973), *Fluid Drive* (1974), *Super Session* (1975), *Free Ride* (1977), and *Tales from the Seven Seas* (1981). He's been married twice and has three children.

Beschen, Shane   Dour regularfoot pro surfer from San Clemente, California; world-ranked #2 in 1996, and the only pro surfer in history to score a perfect 30 during a heat. Beschen was born (1972) and raised in San Clemente, the son of a general contractor, began surfing at age 10, and was soon a leading light among a neighborhood group of surfers that including Matt Archbold, Dino Andino, and Christian Fletcher. A rivalry with Kelly Slater of Florida began in 1985, when Beschen finished second to the future six-time world champion in the menehune division (12 and under) of the United States Surfing Championships. The following year Beschen finished second to Slater in the boy's division, and in 1987 Beschen placed fourth in boys' while Slater again won. Beschen capped his amateur career with a second in the juniors division of the 1988 U.S. Championships. He turned pro at 17, and three years later, without backing from any major sponsors, won the 1992 Professional Surfing Association of America tour; in 1993 he finished 11th on the world tour. Beschen remained in the top 10 for five years, placing fourth in 1994 and 1998, and finishing second to Slater in 1996. Blond and long-limbed (6'0", 165 pounds), Beschen was a quick, loose, moderately experimental surfer. He rode in a slightly different fashion than the rest of the New School teenagers who came to prominence in the early '90s, holding his arms away from his body, in a way reminiscent of '70s surf hero Michael Ho of Hawaii. By 1998 Beschen had four world tour victories, including a breathtaking win in the 1996 Quiksilver Pro at Grajagan, Indonesia, and a satisfying win over Slater in front of 40,000 spectators at the 1994 U.S. Open in Huntington Beach, a victory made all the more impressive by Beschen's refusal to wear a surf leash. At the 1996 Billabong Pro at Kirra, Queensland, Beschen scored 10s on three consecutive waves for a perfect total score of 30. He'd also become known as a world tour loner and malcontent. During a short losing streak in 1998, Beschen complained to a surf journalist that he felt "like a black person in South

Larry Bertlemann

Africa 50 years ago, and all the judges are white." At the time he was making more than $100,000 a year and owned houses in San Clemente and Oahu; he finished the season ranked #4. The following year he purposely missed contests, was fined $10,000 by world tour organizers, and saw his rating drop to #24. In 2000 he finished 26th; the following year he dropped to 37th and didn't make the cut for the 2002 circuit.

Beschen has appeared in more than 25 surf videos, including *The Search II* (1993), *Cyclone Fever* (1994), *Metaphysical* (1997), and *The Experience* (1999). In 2000 he produced his own surf video, *Box of Blues.* He is married and has one child. Gavin Beschen, Shane's younger brother, also a lanky blond regular-foot, became a minor surf media sensation in the mid-'90s; in 2000 he earned $30,000 for winning the Red Bull Tube Ride contest in Brazil, then followed up a few weeks later with a victory in the Xcel Pro, at Sunset Beach, netting another $4,000.

beveled rail   *See* chine rail.

Biarritz   Elegant beachfront holiday town in south-west France, 20 miles north of the Spanish border, facing west into the Atlantic Ocean's Bay of Biscay; the birthplace of French surfing. The surf along the two-mile-long Biarritz beachfront—Côte de Basques and le Grande Plage are separated by a small, craggy headland—is generally mediocre beachbreak. But the adjacent town of Anglet, located just to the north and regarded by most surfers as an extension of Biar-ritz, has nearly two miles of high-quality beachbreak waves, including Les Cavaliers, site of many world pro tour surf contests. The rivermouth-formed La Barre, one of France's premier surf breaks, located at the north end of Anglet, was destroyed by a break-water project in the early '70s. As with the rest of Atlantic-facing France, the surf here is best in fall and early winter.

Surfing was introduced to France in 1956 when Hollywood screenwriter Peter Viertel, on location in Biarritz to film *The Sun Also Rises,* took note of the local waves and sent back to Malibu for his balsa surf-board. Locals Georges Hennebutte, Michel Barland, and Parisian-born Joel de Rosnay later took turns rid-ing Viertel's board, and shortly after began making their own equipment. The 1959-formed Waikiki Surf Club Biarritz hosted the first French surf contest at Côte de Basques in 1960, with de Rosnay as the win-

ner. Cultivated but lightly bohemian, Biarritz by the late '60s had become a popular jumping-off point for surfers traveling through France, Spain, and Portugal, with detours into Morocco.

The World Amateur Surfing Championships were held in Biarritz in 1980, with future three-time world champion Tom Curren winning the juniors division. The world pro circuit scheduled an annual event in Biarritz from 1987 to 1996. The 1992-founded Biarritz Surf Festival has become one of the premier events in the longboarding world.

Commerce and industry have been an integral part of the Biarritz surf scene since the late '50s, with the opening of Barland Surfboards. By 2003, the town's narrow cobblestoned streets contained 12 surf shops, another dozen fashion-conscious surf "bou-tiques," and the offices for two French surfing magazines. Biarritz is also home to the European headquarters for surfwear giant Quiksilver. About 300 year-round surfers live in Biarritz (the best known being Christian "Che" Guevara), with thou-sands of surf tourists visiting during the summer and early fall months. Beaches throughout southwest France, Biarritz included, were closed in 2003 a few weeks after the oil tanker *Prestige* broke apart and sank off Spain, spilling more than 50,000 tons of heavy fuel oil. The surf in Biarritz and Anglet has been featured in more than a dozen surf movies and videos, including *A Life in the Sun* (1966), *Evolution* (1969), *Waves of Change* (1970), *A Sea for Yourself* (1973), *110/240* (1992), and *Endless Summer II* (1994). The area's waves are detailed in *The Stormrider Guide Europe* (1995). *See also* Biarritz Surf Festival, France.

Biarritz Surf Festival   Annual Polynesian-flavored surfing festival/competition held in early summer in Biarritz, a French Basque country resort town located near the Spanish border; created in 1993 by local events promoter Robert Rabagny. The International Longboard Classic, a qualifying event for the profes-sional World Longboard Tour, is the main attraction of the weeklong Biarritz Surf Festival; other surf-related festival attractions include tandem exhibitions, paddleboard races, outrigger canoe demonstrations, surf movies and videos, and live music (Toots and the Maytals performed in 2000; the Beach Boys in 2001). Juniors division long- and shortboard contests are also held, along with a European-only longboard contest. In 2000, former world champion Nat Young introduced an event in which 16 of the world's best longboarders competed on identical 10-foot molded boards. Equal parts competition and social event, the Biarritz Surf Festival attracts tens of thousands of spectators, and attendees over the years have included surf world icons like Rell Sunn, Greg Noll, and Peter Cole, along with longboard pros like Joel Tudor, Beau Young, Colin McPhillips, and Bonga Perkins. *See also* Biarritz.

Big Wave Dave's   Short-lived 1993 CBS-TV sitcom about three 30-something friends from Chicago who abandon their urban lives, fly to Hawaii, and open a surf shop on the North Shore of Oahu. *Big Wave Dave's* aired Mondays at 9:30, and starred David Morse (*The Green Mile*), Adam Arkin (*Chicago Hope, Northern Exposure*), and Patrick Breen (*Men in Black*). Creator and executive producer David Issacs described *Big Wave Dave's* as "a metaphor for freedom." Critics and audiences thought it was a metaphor for banality. The show debuted August 9 and was canceled September 13. *See also* television and surfing.

Big Wednesday   Warner Brothers' 1978 coming-of-age surfing movie directed by John Milius, starring Gary Busey, Jan-Michael Vincent, and William Katt; initially a critical and box-office disappointment, but rehabilitated over the years into a cult favorite. While Hollywood made about two dozen beach movies in the '60s, including the cartoonish *Beach Party* and *Beach Blanket Bingo* (along with *Ride the Wild Surf,* a fairly straightforward drama), the $11 million PG-rated *Big Wednesday* was the only movie of its kind in the '70s. Milius and Denny Aaberg, *Big Wednesday* cowriters, were both Malibu regulars in the early and mid-'60s; "No-Pants Mance," Aaberg's lightly fictionalized account of his salad days at Malibu, published in *Surfer* magazine in 1974, became a thumbnail sketch for *Big Wednesday.* The story takes place over 12 years, from 1962 to 1974, and follows three friends—the straight-shooting Jack Barlow (Katt), the raunchy but amiable Leroy "The Masochist" Smith (Busey), and hot-shot surfer/alcoholic Matt Johnson (Vincent)—as they evolve from party-loving local surf heroes into young adults dealing with friendship, love, marriage, war, and death. After drifting apart during the counterculture years, the three surfers reunite at the film's climax to face an afternoon of huge, dangerous, metaphorically cleansing surf, "a day like no other," as the sagacious boardbuilder known as Bear forecasts early in the film.

Gary Busey in *Big Wednesday*

Warner Brothers hired a top crew of surf world cameramen, including Greg MacGillivray, George Greenough, Dan Merkel, and Bud Browne, to film the *Big Wednesday* action sequences. Stunt-double surfers included Peter Townend and Ian Cairns, the 1976 world champion and runner-up, respectively, along with Jackie Dunn, Bill Hamilton, J Riddle, and Bruce Raymond. Pipeline maestro Gerry Lopez plays himself in a cameo. The surfing sequences in *Big Wednesday* are exciting, well-paced, and beautifully photographed. But the movie itself was panned by both the mainstream and the surf press. "The dialogue is embarrassing," *Surfer* magazine wrote, "the fight scenes are ridiculously overdone, the soap opera scenes are too long, and the surfing scenes are too short."

Big Wednesday was pulled from theaters after taking in a disappointing $4.5 million at the box office, then it slowly but steadily found new life as a video rental. By 1998 the turnaround seemed complete. *Big Wednesday* was shown at the Newport Film Festival, a 20th-anniversary party reunited the cast and creators, and the *Los Angeles Times* reported that the film was "one of the very few to really capture the surfing life." *Surfer* magazine also changed its view, saying that "*Big Wednesday* makes you proud to be a surfer."

The *Surfer's Journal,* however, felt that time had done nothing to improve the film, calling *Big Wednesday* as "flat and mawkish" as it had been when it debuted, and crediting its newly elevated status as "another triumph in Baby Boomer nostalgia marketing." *See also* Hollywood and surfing.

big-wave surfboard   Type of surfboard designed for waves roughly 10 feet or larger, although "big-wave board" often refers to equipment used for huge outer-limits surf. Until the early 1990s brought the development of tow-in surfing—where the rider gets pulled into the wave from behind a personal watercraft—big-wave boards were essentially longer and more streamlined versions of regular surfboards. The finless hot curl design, invented in 1937, is sometimes noted as the first big-wave surfboard. Teenage surfer John Kelly of Hawaii made the first hot curl by paring down the back end of his redwood plank from 18 inches to 11 inches (as measured one foot up from the tail), thus reducing the board's tendency to "slide ass"—lose traction—and instead track on a tighter angle on the wave. While the hot curl wasn't designed just for big waves, it was by default the era's best big-wave board, as planks were nearly uncontrollable in surf over four foot. California surfer Joe Quigg and Hawaii's George Downing, working separately, both developed 10-foot single-finned balsa-core boards in the early '50s, each designed specifically for big waves. By the middle of the decade, at Point Surf Makaha, Downing and a handful of other surfers were able to race across 15- to 18-foot waves. Longer boards used in big waves were nicknamed "guns." Paddle speed, then and today, was the big-wave board's most important design consideration, followed by control and maneuverability. As bigger waves are more difficult to catch, board size goes up along with wave size. Preference varies slightly from rider to rider, but seven-foot boards are commonly used in eight-foot waves; nine-foot boards are used in 15-foot waves; and 10-foot 6" to 11-foot boards are used in 25-foot waves.

While Mike Diffenderfer, Bob Shepherd, Tom Parrish, Bill Barnfield, Pat Rawson, Glenn Minami, and perhaps a dozen more surfboard shapers from the mid-'50s to the present day have earned a reputation for crafting superior big-wave paddle-in surfboards, Pat Curren and Dick Brewer in large part defined the form. The finely crafted 40-pound balsa guns made by Curren in the late '50s and early '60s, most of them around 11 foot, were described by *Surfer's Jour-*

nal editor Steve Pezman as "the Ferrari of surf craft," and contributed greatly to Curren's reign as the top big-wave rider of his era. Brewer's polyurethane foam guns picked up where Curren's boards left off, were then refined and slimmed down during the late '60s and mid-'70s, then copied by virtually every big-wave shaper for the next 10 years. Big-wave boards, unlike regular boards, weren't drastically redesigned during the late '60s shortboard revolution. By the early '70s, however, the average Brewer gun was about a foot smaller and three inches narrower in the nose (as measured one foot down from the tip) than a vintage Curren gun, with more rocker and a deeper fin. Brewer had also cut the weight down to less than 20 pounds. "Semi-guns"—boards for medium-big waves—were quicker to take on design advances first used on small-wave boards. So it was that the tri-fin design, a standard feature on small-wave boards and semi-guns by 1982, was still a hotly debated topic among big-wave shapers in the late '80s. Paddle-in big-wave boards by the turn of the century, however, were nearly all tri-fin, with the weight further reduced to about 15 pounds.

The use of personal watercraft reconfigured big-wave surfing entirely. Up to that point the game had been based more on paddling—on stalking and catching the wave—than riding. With paddling taken out of the equation by the tow-in launch, the new boards could be designed solely for on-wave performance, for doing turns and cutback waves up to 50 feet or bigger. Board speed, as it turned out, had less to do with the momentum carried by a long board and more to do with being able to hold position in the wave's energy-rich "pocket" area adjacent to the curl. Small tow-in boards, if designed properly, allowed the surfer to remain in the pocket. In 1993, master tow-in surfer Laird Hamilton of Hawaii began dropping the size on his boards (while adding lead plates for stability, along with leverage-aiding footstraps), and by the end of the decade the average tow-in board measured about seven feet by 15 inches, and weighed 25 pounds; most were tri-fins, some were twin-fins. Top tow-in shapers include Gerry Lopez, John Carper, Jeff Timpone, and Maurice Cole. *See also* Bill Barnfield, Dick Brewer, Pat Curren, Mike Diffenderfer, gun, Glenn Minami, Tom Parrish, Pat Rawson, Bob Shepherd.

big-wave surfing   While premodern and early modern surfers were thrilled and in some cases attracted to riding bigger waves, big-wave surfing as a specialized branch of the sport is often said to have begun in the late 1930s. Honolulu teenagers John Kelly, Wally Froiseth, and Fran Heath invented the streamlined hot curl surfboard in mid-1937, which allowed them to hold a higher, more controlled line across the wave; a few months later the same group ventured to the west side of Oahu and discovered the beautifully formed waves of Makaha. A right-breaking wave, best in winter and easy riding up to 12 feet, Makaha turns into a fast, roaring, challenging wall at 15 feet or bigger. A 1953 Associated Press photograph of George Downing, Woodbridge "Woody" Brown, and Buzzy Trent angling across a sparkly

Big-wave surfing at Waimea Bay, Hawaii

15-footer at Makaha was published in newspapers across America, and inspired a group of California surfers—including Fred Van Dyke and Peter Cole—to move to Hawaii and take up big-wave riding in earnest. Two years earlier, Downing had made himself a racy 10-foot balsa-core surfboard, with a raked stabilizing fin (the hot curl boards were finless and made primarily of redwood), and the control afforded by this new board allowed surfers like Downing and Californian Walter Hoffman to ride waves half again as big as those ridden in the late '40s. This type of long, narrow board, designed to provide enough paddling speed to catch bigger waves, was later nicknamed an "elephant gun" by Trent; surfers still call a paddle-driven big-wave board a gun. (Pat Curren of California would later become surfing's premier gun maker, followed by Hawaii's Dick Brewer.)

A new era in big-wave riding began in the mid-'50s, as surfers started making regular visits to Oahu's North Shore, a seven-mile rural stretch of coast filled with more than a dozen breaks offering consistently large winter surf; the shifty A-frame waves at Sunset Beach in particular became a big-wave mainstay. In 1957, California surfer Greg Noll led a group of riders out to Waimea Bay for the first time. Fourteen years earlier, high school surfer Dickie Cross of Waikiki had paddled out at Sunset, got caught outside on a fast-rising swell, and drowned while trying to paddle through the huge waves at Waimea; after the Noll-led breakthrough in 1957, the photogenic and centrally located Waimea quickly became the last word in big-wave riding, and remained so for nearly 35 years.

Big-wave surfing was a media sensation in the 1960s. Virtually all surf movies ended with a Waimea

sequence—Hollywood chipped in with *Ride the Wild Surf,* also featuring a Waimea climax—and big-wave articles appeared in *Life, Reader's Digest,* and the *Saturday Evening Post,* with Waimea challengers likened to astronauts and bullfighters. Wave height measurement had meanwhile become somewhat arbitrary, as play-it-cool big-wave surfers nonchalantly identified 40-foot waves, as measured from trough to crest, as 25 or 30 feet. (There is no demarcation line between big-wave surfing and regular surfing, but it might be said that the former begins at about 15 or 18 feet. Big-wave riders, furthermore, spend most of their surfing time in waves under six feet, as suitable giant waves are rare; in a good season, a big-wave surfer might find about 20 days of 18-foot-or-bigger waves.) The '60s era of big-wave surfing peaked in 1969, as Noll dropped into a 35-footer at Makaha, and soon after gave the sport up. Giant waves never went entirely out of fashion, but the specialty fell out of style as the focus shifted to small-wave riding and the nascent professional competition scene.

Big-wave surfing returned to the fore during the winter of 1982–83, as Waimea had its most consistent season in more than 10 years. *Surfer* magazine encouraged the renaissance with articles like "Whatever Happened to Big-Wave Riding?" and three years later the Waimea-hosted Quiksilver in Memory of Eddie Aikau event—named after the bowlegged Hawaiian big-wave master who died in a 1978 boating accident—became the first contest designed specifically for big-wave surfing. The west coast of North America soon revealed itself as a big-wave source equal to that of Hawaii, first with the rediscovery of Todos Santos in Baja Mexico in the mid-'80s, a break that had been surfed as far back as the early '60s, followed in the early '90s by the exposure of a San Francisco–area spot called Maverick's. Both are right-breaking waves; both hit the 20-foot mark with equal or greater frequency than Waimea. Maverick's made international headlines in late 1994, when Hawaiian big-wave pro Mark Foo drowned there on his first visit. Many of the era's most famous big-wave riders had come to Maverick's that week, including Brock Little and Ken Bradshaw of Hawaii, and California's Mike Parsons, Peter Mel, Darryl "Flea" Virostko, and Richard Schmidt. Foo was the first big-wave specialist to die in the water; two years later fellow Hawaiian Todd Chesser died after getting caught inside a set of 25-footers on the North Shore.

Big-wave performance improved slowly but steadily from the '40s to the early '90s, with riders occasionally able to ease into a long, attenuated turn, and on rare occasion ride inside the tube. But the big-wave ceiling had been stuck at 30 feet since the late '50s, as a paddling takeoff, even under ideal conditions, couldn't gain enough speed to overcome the rapid trough-to-crest current generated by the moving swell. Big-wave surfing's quantum leap took place in the early '90s, as Hawaiian surfers Laird Hamilton, Buzzy Kerbox, and Darrick Doerner began using a motor-assisted tow entry—first from behind an inflatable boat, then a personal watercraft—to give them a running start. Tow-in surfing allowed surfers to easily break the 30-foot barrier, and 50-footers were being ridden by the end of the decade. The miniaturized tow-in boards, moreover, allowed surfers to perform on huge waves in similar fashion to the way they rode eight- or 10-foot waves—tube-riding included. Jaws, a wind-whipped break on Maui used exclusively by tow-in surfers, was added to the big-wave register, while Jaws regular Laird Hamilton became the sport's dominant figure. Once again big-wave riding caught the eye of the mainstream media, generating articles in *Rolling Stone, Outside, National Geographic,* and the *New York Times,* and featured in documentaries on MTV and PBS. *In God's Hands,* another Hollywood big-wave movie, was released in 1998; *Maverick's: The Story of Big-Wave Surfing* was published in 2000. Big-wave surf videos were produced by the dozens, including *Wake Up Call* (1995), *Condition Black* (1998), *Monstrosity* (1999), and *Whipped!* (2001). Big-wave contests were held at Maverick's, Waimea, and Todos Santos, as well as in Peru (at a Sunset-like break in Lima called Pico Alto) and South Africa (at a Maverick's-like Cape Town break called Dungeons). The 1998 K2 Big-Wave Challenge initiated a different kind of competition in which the riders submit a photograph of themselves to a panel of judges, who then measure the wave height and declare a winner. The Tow-In World Cup, the first tow-in big-wave contest, was held at Jaws in early 2002. The Billabong Odyssey, a three-year big-wave project launched in 2001, billed itself as "the search for the 100-foot wave." Odyssey team member and four-time world champion Layne Beachley of Australia had meanwhile been recognized as the first hardcore female big-wave surfer. *See also* Eddie Aikau, big-wave surfboard, death and surfing, George Downing, Laird Hamilton, Jaws, Makaha, Maverick's, Greg Noll, North Shore, Quiksilver in Memory of Eddie Aikau, Todos Santos, tow-in surfing, Waimea Bay.

Biggest Wednesday, 1998 Tremendous winter storm swell resulting in smooth 35-foot-plus surf on the North Shore of Oahu on Wednesday, January 28, 1998, before striking the mainland at a slightly reduced size two days later. "The Pacific Ocean put on a once-in-a-lifetime show," surf journalist Bruce Jenkins wrote. "The North Shore was giant and perfect . . . Maverick's [in California] was surreal . . . Northern Baja was a shocking array of mysto cloudbreaks." The surf was produced by an El Niño–amplified winter storm located between Japan and Hawaii; data from a buoy located 200 miles northwest of Maui reported a wave height of 27 feet and a swell period of 20 seconds. Fifteen feet at 20 seconds is usually enough to produce large waves at places like Waimea Bay or Maverick's.

On Wednesday morning in Hawaii, under cloudless skies with a faint offshore breeze, professional big-wave surfers who gathered at Waimea Bay for the Quiksilver in Memory of Eddie Aikau big-wave contest found unridable 30-foot waves closing out across the bay, and the event was called off. The Hawaiian Civil Defense declared a Condition Black, meaning the ocean was closed to everybody. Local surfer Jason Majors nonetheless ran a gauntlet of police and lifeguards at Waimea, paddled out to try and ride something, and was beaten back to shore exhausted and near death about 30 minutes later; he was taken away in handcuffs. Shortly afterward, a half-dozen tow-in teams—including Ken Bradshaw and Dan Moore, Ross Clarke-Jones and Tony Ray, Noah Johnson and Aaron Lambert, Cheyne Horan and Sam Hawk—

began riding at Outside Log Cabins, a rarely surfed break located about one mile east of Waimea. At about 10:00 A.M. Moore pulled Bradshaw into the biggest wave ever ridden up to that point, estimated to be 40 or 45 feet, which translates wave-face height of about 60 or 70 feet. Meanwhile, at Jaws, a big-wave break located on Maui, Laird Hamilton and Dave Kalama, along with a group of fellow tow-in surfers including Buzzy Kerbox, Mike Waltze, Pete Cabrinha, and Rush Randle, rode a near-endless procession of 30-foot-plus waves. "How big was it?" Kalama asked rhetorically a few days later. "You can't even say at that size. After 25 feet it's all just ridiculous anyway."

By the time the swell hit Maverick's, the big-wave break located just south of San Francisco, it was at least five feet smaller than it had been in Hawaii, not as well groomed, and ridden for the most part by paddle-surfers rather than tow-in surfers. Darryl "Flea" Virostko of Santa Cruz almost drowned after being pushed into the nearshore rocks, and surfer/journalist Ken Collins described the bigger waves at Maverick's as "tubing death wishes." Most West Coast breaks were too big to ride; a small number, however, were in peak form.

The huge Log Cabins surf was featured in the IMAX film *Extreme* (1999) and a small number of surf videos, including *The Moment* and *Biggest Wednesday,* both released in 1998. Maverick's footage from January 30 is seen in *Twenty Feet Under* (1998). In early 2002, PBS aired *Condition Black,* a one-hour documentary on big-wave surfing and the giant surf of January 28. *See also* big-wave surfing, Maverick's, Outside Log Cabins, Swell of 1969.

Bigler, Steve   Slippery regularfooter from Santa Barbara, California; fourth-place finisher in the 1966 World Surfing Championships. Bigler was born (1946) and raised in Santa Barbara, began surfing in 1958, and three years later moved with his family to Honolulu, Hawaii. He returned to California after graduating high school and became one of the nation's top competitive surfers: in 1966 he won the Malibu Invitational, finished second in the United States Surfing Association's final ratings, and placed fourth in world titles. The following year he won the East Coast Surfing Championships and finished fourth in the United States Surfing Championships. Bigler also competed in the 1965 and 1968 World Surfing Championships, and in 1966 he designed and promoted the Harbour Surfboards Cheater model.

Just before the turn of the decade, Bigler set out on a 20-year drug-financed surfing odyssey, basing himself in California and Hawaii, but spending weeks or months at a time in France, Spain, Portugal, Afghanistan, Indonesia, and the Philippines. In 1996 he was arrested in Santa Barbara on smuggling charges and served 27 months in federal prison, getting out in early 2001. Bigler appeared in a small number of surf movies from the mid-'60s to early '70s, including *Inside Out* (1965), *Fantastic Plastic Machine* (1968), and *Waves of Change* (1970).

Billabong   Australia-based surfwear and wetsuit company founded in 1973 by former surfboard shaper Gordon Merchant; one of the world's largest international board-sports clothing manufacturers. Merchant and his wife produced the first Billabong surf trunks in the basement of their home at Burleigh Heads, Queensland, and drove from one surfing area to the next selling the "boardshorts" from the back of Merchant's station wagon. After 10 years of steady growth, Billabong, by the early '80s, had become a hip alternative to surfwear powerhouse Quiksilver, and had an expanding number of successful overseas licensing agreements. The company's line of durable and unpretentious surfwear was augmented in the early '90s by a wetsuit division that soon proved equally popular.

Billabong's popularity is due in large part to Merchant's unerring talent for marketing and promotions. Team members over the years have included world champions Wayne Bartholomew, Layne Beachley, Sunny Garcia, and Mark Occhilupo (the company's premier rider since 1983), and pro circuit standouts like Shane Dorian, Michael Barry, Luke Egan, Keala Kennelly, Joel Parkinson, and Taj Burrow. Billabong has also sponsored some of the most innovative and successful pro surfing competitions, including the Billabong Pro in Hawaii, the final event on the world tour from 1988 to 1990; and the Billabong Challenge, a series of nonrated showcase events held in the mid-'90s, in which a small group of top surfers were taken to an exotic location for a documentary-filmed surf-off. Billabong's longstanding relationship with surf movie auteur Jack McCoy has meanwhile produced a series of excellent surf videos, including *The Green Iguana* (1992), *Sik Joy* (1995), *The Billabong Challenge* (1996), and *The Occumentary* (1999). The Billabong Odyssey, a three-year big-wave exploration project initiated in 2001, was launched with the idea that Odyssey crew members would find and ride a 100-foot wave.

Billabong made business media headlines in 1999 when California's Bob Hurley, president and license holder of the wildly successful Billabong USA, left the company to form his own self-named surfwear and wetsuit operation—a move the *L.A. Times* called "equivalent to Lee Iacocca leaving Ford to join rival Chrysler." (Hurley International was bought by the Nike shoe company three years later for an estimated $120 million.) Billabong Australia then sold 49 percent of the company to former Qantas Airlines chairman Gary Pemberton (Merchant retained 23 percent), who was instrumental in seeing the enterprise listed on the Australian Stock Exchange in 2000. Billabong shocked investors the following year by nearly doubling both its share price and profits.

While company policy prohibits Billabong products from being sold in department stores as a way to maintain on-the-beach credibility, Billabong is nonetheless retailed in more than 60 countries worldwide, with clothes and accessories designed also for skateboarders, snowboarders, and in-line skaters. Sales in 2001 were estimated to be $216 million.

Billabong Odyssey   Three-year adventure and marketing project, launched in 2001, billed as "the search for the 100-foot wave." Sponsored by surfwear and wetsuit giant Billabong, the Odyssey was developed by California surf impresario Bill Sharp who, in January 2001, led a group of tow-in surfers out to ride 50-foot-plus waves at Cortes Bank, an open-ocean break located 100 miles west of San Diego. "We've scoured the world looking for the perfect 6-foot wave," Sharp said while introducing the Odyssey concept to the surf press, "but nobody's gone looking for the best 60-foot wave, because until now, with the advent of tow-in technology, nobody would know what to do with it." Initiated in October 2001 with an orientation and safety course near the Oregon/Washington border, the Billabong Odyssey calls for teams of professional big-wave surfers, along with photographers, television crew, and support staff, to be on alert for three quick-strike expeditions each year to virtually any break in the world.

The four primary tow-in teams were Shane Dorian/Ken Bradshaw (Hawaii), Ken Collins/Josh Loya (California), Darryl Virostko/Shawn Barron (California), and Mike Parsons/Brad Gerlach (California),

along with Hawaiian water-safety experts and big-wave riders Brock Little and Brian Keaulana. As the Odyssey project aims to be somewhat improvisational, however, new teams may qualify as needed. The surfer to ride the biggest wave of each Odyssey session is awarded $1,000 per foot of wave height, so that the mythical 100-foot wave would pay out $100,000. How the wave would be measured—whether or not such a wave even exists—was unclear as of late 2002. The Odyssey's first official foray came in January 2002, as members of the group chased a large North Atlantic swell to Hossegor, a French beachbreak located just north of Biarritz, and were met with disappointing 15-foot surf.

Billabong Pro (Jeffreys Bay)   World tour competition held in the magnificent point surf at Jeffreys Bay, South Africa; a favorite "prime venue" contest, with the emphasis on quality waves, as distinguished from the sideshow-filled beachbreak events held at places like Huntington Beach, California, and Rio de Janeiro, Brazil. The Jeffreys Bay Country Feeling Surf Classic was founded in 1983, with beachwear giant Billabong taking over as primary sponsor in 1987. The contest was included on the world tour championship schedule in 1984 and 1996, and from 1998 forward. A women's division was added in 1996, 1998, 1999, and 2000; prize money for the 2002 Billabong Pro was $250,000.

1983:	David Barr
1984:	Mark Occhilupo
1985:	(not held)
1986:	(not held)
1987:	Grant Myrdal
1988:	Michael Burness
1989:	Justin Strong
1990:	Marcus Brabant
1991:	Pierre Tostee
1992:	Seth Hulley
1993:	Michael Barry
1994:	Justin Strong
1995:	Seth Hulley
1996:	Kelly Slater, Lisa Andersen
1997:	Jevon le Roux
1998:	Michael Barry, Trudy Todd
1999:	Joel Parkinson, Melanie Redman
2000:	Jake Paterson, Megan Abubo
2001:	Jake Paterson
2002:	Mick Fanning

Billabong Pro (North Shore) Men's-only world pro tour contest sponsored by Billabong surfwear, held annually at various locations on the North Shore of Oahu from 1985 to 1990; generally regarded as the era's premier event, along with the Pipeline Masters. The 1988, 1989, and 1990 versions of the Billabong Pro were also the season-ending contests, as well as the richest stops on the tour schedule. Early rounds of the 1985 and 1986 Billabong events were held at Waimea Bay; both contests then finished at Sunset, with semi-retired four-time world champion Mark Richards winning each time. The 1986 Billabong was especially dramatic, as the Waimea heats were staged in heaving 25-foot surf, allowing Richards to shine—he later called it "the most memorable contest of my career"—while forcing two terrified competitors to withdraw rather than paddle out. Australian Gary Elkerton, just days after he won the World Cup, defeated Shaun Tomson to win the 1987 Billabong. Both events were held at Sunset. The following year, the Billabong Pro became the world tour's first $100,000 contest, and the final day was held in superb 10-foot waves at Pipeline, with Australian Barton Lynch, third in the ratings going in, charging past Tom Carroll and Damien Hardman to win the world championship in what was long regarded as the most thrilling day of competition in world tour history. The following year was also dramatic, as 29-year-old pro circuit warhorse Cheyne Horan of Australia, winless for more than five years and reduced earlier in the season to selling his boards one by one for food money, picked up his final pro circuit win at Sunset and a $50,000 prize check. The sixth and final Billabong Pro, worth $200,000, also held at Sunset, was won by Australian Nicky Wood.

Results of the Billabong Pro:

1985: Mark Richards
1986: Mark Richards
1987: Gary Elkerton
1988: Barton Lynch
1989: Cheyne Horan
1990: Nicky Wood

Billabong Pro (Queensland) Professional surfing contest held on the Gold Coast of Queensland, Australia, from 1992 to 2000; often in the bullet-fast tubes of Kirra Point. Gold Coaster and 1978 world champion Wayne "Rabbit" Bartholomew inaugurated a regional pro contest at Kirra in 1992, with pri-

mary sponsor Billabong putting up $5,000 in prize money. On the opening day of competition, as Bartholomew later recalled, the fabled pointbreak was producing tubes that were "six feet by six feet, with corduroy swell lines stacked to the horizon... the most perfect Kirra I'd seen for years." World tour standouts Mark Occhilupo and Luke Egan competed, but first place went to local surfer Michael Barry. The Billabong Pro became a world tour event in 1996. Because Kirra is notoriously fickle, the six-day contest was designated as "mobile," meaning it would be staged wherever the surf was best in the immediate area. The Billabong Pro was held at a number of breaks over the next five years, including Kirra, Burleigh Heads, Duranbah, and Stradbroke Island. A Billabong Pro highlight came in 1996, at Kirra, when California pro Shane Beschen had three 10-point rides during a heat to post the world tour's first and only perfect 30.

A women's division was added to the Billabong Pro in 1996; in 1998, 1999, and 2000, it was the season-opening event; the 2000 event had a combined men's and women's prize purse of $167,000. Billabong Pro highlights are featured in more than a dozen surf videos, including *Sons of Fun* (1993), *Cyclone Fever* (1994), *Sik Joy* (1995), and *Sabotaj* (1999). The event was canceled after 2000, but Quiksilver began sponsoring a similar world pro tour contest on the Gold Coast in 2002. Results of the Billabong Pro in Queensland are as follows:

1992: Michael Barry
1993: Martin Potter
1994: Sunny Garcia
1995: Jake Paterson
1996: Kaipo Jaquias, Pam Burridge
1997: Kelly Slater, Rochelle Ballard
1998: Kelly Slater, Trudy Todd
1999: Beau Emerton, Serena Brooke
2000: Sunny Garcia, Layne Beachley

Billabong Pro Teahupoo *See* Tahiti Pro.

Biolos, Matt Reticent New School surfboard shaper from San Clemente, California; cofounder of Lost Enterprises, a punk-tinged surfboard and surfwear manufacturing company. Biolos was born (1969) in Anaheim, California, raised in Chino, and began surfing in 1983 during a family vacation to Orange County's Dana Point. After high school he moved to

Dana Point and took a job sanding and hand-painting boards at Herbie Fletcher Surfboards in nearby San Clemente, where he also learned the basics of shaping. Biolos was making boards out of his garage under his own Mayhem label in 1992 when he founded Lost Enterprises in San Clemente with partner Mike Reola; Biolos made the boards, while Reola ran the business and produced ribald surf videos, including *What's Really Goin' Wrong* (1995) and *Lost Across America* (1999). *Lost* was an instant success among "defiant" Southern California suburban surfers, while Biolos's growing skills as a shaper had him making boards for top American riders like Shane Beschen, Cory Lopez, Christian Fletcher, and Chris Ward. Biolos and surfer Dean Randazzo won the 2000 "Anything But Three" surfer/shaper challenge at San Diego's Black's Beach; by 2002, Biolos estimated that he'd shaped more than 12,000 surfboards.

Birk, Sandow   Soft-spoken artist from Seal Beach, California, best known to surfers for his wickedly funny and beautifully rendered versions of famous 18th- and 19th-century marine paintings. Birk's work, as summarized by the *Surfer's Journal* in 1992, "hotwires art history and surfing." Birk graduated in 1988 from the Otis College of Art and Design; in 1990

Sandow Birk's *Et in Arcadia Ego,* 1989

he produced *Outside Set at Malibu,* an eight- by 10-foot acrylic-on-canvas update of Théodore Géricault's *The Raft of the Medusa,* with panicking French sailors transformed into a pack of hostile, wetsuit-wearing surfers. He similarly converted John Singleton Copley's *Watson and the Shark* into *Aggro Crowd at Lower Trestles.* Birk has received a National Endowment of the Arts grant, a Guggenheim Fellowship, a Fulbright grant, and a J. Paul Getty Fellowship for the Visual Arts. His mock-historical book *In Smog and Thunder: Historical Works from the Great Wars of the Californias* was published in 2001; his illustrated and updated version of Dante's Inferno, co-translated by surf journalist Marcus Sanders, came out in 2003. Birk has also written a half-dozen articles for surf magazines, including a 2000 essay for *Surfing* titled "Surfing Sucks: One Man's Opinion," in which he pilloried "the surfing lifestyle" and its numbing effect on some people, including "40-year-old men who should be in the prime of their careers vacuuming under clothes racks in surf shops." *See also* surf art.

Bishop Museum   Museum of natural and cultural history located in Honolulu, Hawaii, featuring the world's best collection of early Polynesian surfboards; the first museum to house surfing artifacts. The Bishop Museum was founded in 1889 by Charles Reed Bishop in honor of his late wife, Princess Bernice Pauahi Bishop; it was originally intended to house and display the princess' collection of Hawaiian artifacts and royal heirlooms. The museum has 43 surfboards, including four traditional *olo* boards, six *alaia* boards, and four *paipo* boards—all from the early 19th century—along with 14 koa wood boards, 11 redwoods, three of surf pioneer Duke Kahanamoku's personal boards, and a Tom Blake "cigar-box" hollow board. The Bishop's archives also contain hundreds of surfing and surf-related photographs.

The Hawaiian Sports Hall of Fame, which opened in 1997 as one of the museum's permanent exhibits, featured four surfers as of 2003: Duke Kahanamoku, 1968 world surfing champion Fred Hemmings, "Queen of Makaha" Rell Sunn, and four-time world champion Margo Oberg. *See also* California Surf Museum, Huntington Beach International Surfing Museum, Santa Cruz Surfing Museum, Surfworld Museum.

black ball flag   Distinctive rectangular flag featuring a solid-black circle set against a bright-yellow background; raised over Southern California lifeguard towers during the beachgoing months to signify a ban on surfing—or, more specifically, surfing on hard, fiberglass-covered boards—as a safety measure to protect swimmers and bodysurfers. The black ball flag was introduced in Santa Monica, probably in the summer of 1960, and over the next few years it was installed on high-use beaches from San Diego to Santa Barbara. Orange County's Newport Beach instituted the state's most restrictive black ball ordinance in 1966, prohibiting surfing on all city beaches daily from noon to 4:00 P.M. between June 10 and September 15. Black balled beaches in other communities were broken up with "surfing only" areas. (No-surfing beaches along America's East Coast were often designated by checkered flags, or red and yellow triangular flags.) Black ball skirmishes between surfers and local authorities—on the beach, in the surf, even in the town halls and courts—have been a small but colorful part of Southern California beach culture for generations. In a locally publicized battle off Newport Point in 1974, a group of surfers, holding position in the water long after the black ball flag went up, were eventually flushed out with helicopters and lifeguard boats. Stealing a black ball flag from a manned lifeguard tower (a team effort usually involving a "drowning swimmer" decoy, a runner/pole-climber, and a sharp pair of scissors) has traditionally been a supreme challenge for teenage layabout surfers during the torpid and often waveless summer months. In 2002, California surfboard company INT introduced the Black Ball Beater, a 4′11″ stand-up surfboard made from bodyboard material with fiberglass stringers. *See also* Newport Beach, politics and surfing.

Black Sea Large inland sea located in southeast Europe, eight times bigger than Lake Michigan, bordered by Ukraine, Russia, Georgia, Turkey, Bulgaria, and Romania; connected to the Atlantic via the Bosporus, Sea of Marmara, and the Mediterranean Sea. Named after the heavy winter fog that makes it appear dark, the Black Sea is lined with pleasant sandy beaches and upscale summer vacation resorts, particularly in the north; sailing and sailboarding are popular, and rental surfboards are available—probably for paddling. "I could have been the first man to surf the Black Sea," author/surfer William Finnegan wrote in his 1999 "Black Sea Blues" article for the *New Yorker,* going on to describe "brown, misty, mediocre, blown-out waves dribbling in from the general direc-

tion of Odessa." It was 1970; Finnegan was a heartbroken 17-year-old bumming through Europe, and instead of surfing he "turned and trudged inland and had a little nervous breakdown." Little is known about surf conditions in the Black Sea. Powerful storms are common here during the winter, however, and with 700-mile east-to-west fetch, it's easy to imagine ridable waves as big as six feet moving into dozens of cold and dimly lit Black Sea beaches and points.

Black Shorts, The *See* The Hui.

black surfers *See* race and surfing.

Blair, Larry Australian goofyfooter from Sydney's Coogee beach, world-ranked #10 in 1979, and back-to-back winner of the Pipeline Masters contest in 1978 and 1979. Blair was born (1958) in Sydney, began surfing at age 11, and was a surprise winner in the 1978 Coca-Cola Surfabout, after scoring an eight-second tuberide in the finals to defeat Australian surf icon Wayne Lynch. Blair enrolled in acting school the same year he turned pro, and between Pipeline Masters wins played Sir Andrew Aguecheek in Shakespeare's *Twelfth Night* for a Sydney theater company. He also had a regular role—as an injured surfer—on *The Young Doctors,* an Australian soap opera. Blair appeared in a small number of surf movies, including *Bali High* (1981), *Tales of the Seven Seas* (1981), and *Wizards of the Water* (1982).

Blake, Tom While Tom Blake can't be placed ahead of Duke Kahanamoku as the world's most influential surfer, his contributions to the sport—in terms of board design, wave-riding technique, competition, surf photography, and literature—are in many ways more tangible. "Blake altered everything," surf journalist Drew Kampion wrote in 2001. "He almost single-handedly transformed surfing from a primitive Polynesian curiosity into a 20th century lifestyle." Blake was born (1902) in Milwaukee, Wisconsin, the son of a club steward and former bar owner. His mother died of tuberculosis when Blake was an infant, and his father left him to be raised by a series of Milwaukee-based relatives; isolated as a child, Blake grew up to become a quiet and detached adult. At age nine or 10, he saw a newsreel featuring a short clip of surfing in Hawaii; at 18, as a high school dropout living in Detroit, Michigan, he met Hawaiian surfer and

Olympic gold medal swimmer Duke Kahanamoku in a movie theater lobby. Blake moved to Los Angeles the following year where he began swimming competitively, and was soon one of the nation's best all-around swimmers, winning a 10-mile AAU race in 1922, and later defeating Kahanamoku himself in a 220-yard sprint.

Blake first surfed in 1921 in Santa Monica, but wiped out badly and waited three years to try again, after becoming a lifeguard at the Santa Monica Swim Club. In 1924, just a few months after he began surfing regularly, Blake visited Hawaii for the first time; Kahanamoku wasn't there, but his brothers took Blake to the best breaks in Waikiki, and introduced him to the local surfers. Blake also visited the Bishop Museum and studied the long, streamlined *olo* surfboards, similar to those once used by Hawaiian royalty. (Two years later, Bishop curators hired Blake to restore the wooden boards.) Blake was back in Santa Monica in early 1925, where he lifeguarded alongside Kahanamoku, and for the next 30 years he divided his time between Hawaii and Southern California. He was the first American-born *haole* (Caucasian) surfer to live in Hawaii, and one of a very few nonnatives to gain admittance to Waikiki's Hui Nalu surf club.

Nearly all of Blake's great surfing accomplishments were made between 1926 and 1935. In September 1926, Blake and New Jersey–born surfer Sam Reid were the first to ride Malibu, after driving north from Santa Monica on the newly paved two-lane road that would later be called Highway 1. That same year in Hawaii, Blake built himself a 15-foot replica *olo* board, which he lightened by drilling hundreds of holes through the deck, sealing the openings with a thin layer of wood. Paddleboard racing had become almost as much a passion for Blake as wave-riding; lighter paddleboards and surfboards would remain his primary design concern. He made a 16-foot chambered-hull paddleboard in 1929, which he used to set paddling records, then developed a hollow surfboard far lighter than the average 55-pound plank board popular at the time. The 1931-patented Blake hollow surfboard (used for decades internationally as a lifeguard rescue device) weighed as little as 40 pounds, and opened the sport up to hundreds of people who weren't able to muscle the heavy plank boards down the beach and into the water. Blake became one of the first commercial board-builders in 1932, as the Thomas Rogers Company of Venice, Cali-

Tom Blake

fornia, introduced a line of Tom Blake Hawaiian Paddleboards. Other manufacturers, including the Los Angeles Ladder Company and the Catalina Equipment Company, would later produce Blake boards. Blake made his most significant design breakthrough in 1935, by attaching a stabilizing fin—a four-inch-deep by one-foot-long keel scavenged from an old speedboat—to the tail of his surfboard. The fin allowed Blake to ride on a tighter angle across the wave. In the early '30s he also created a sailboard prototype, as well as a waist-secured surf leash.

Blake entered and won the inaugural Pacific Coast Surf Riding Championships in 1928, the first major American surfing contest, held at Corona del Mar. The competition format and rules were in large part drafted by Blake, and the event combined paddleboard racing and wave-riding. In 1932, Blake became the first person to paddle the 26 miles between Catalina and San Pedro. Blake also helped develop surf photography and journalism. A few months after buying a Graflex camera from Duke Kahanamoku in 1929, he crafted a first-of-its-kind camera housing for use in the surf, and in 1931 one of his from-the-water Waikiki surf photos was published as a full-page image in the *Los Angeles Times*. In 1935, *National Geographic* published "Waves and Thrills at Waikiki," an eight-page portfolio of Blake's surfing photography; Blake's *Hawaiian Surfboard,* the first book on surfing, was also published that year, with sections on history, board construction, competition, and wave-riding technique. Blake also wrote a soft-cover *Manual of Surfboard Technique* (1935), as well as surfboard-construction articles for *Popular Mechanics* (1936) and *Popular Science* (1939). Blake himself, as handsome as he was innovative, was often written about and photographed for newspaper and magazine articles.

Blake traveled to Florida, New York, and the Bahamas, continued to license his board designs, and worked as a lifeguard when necessary. He was hired on occasion as a Hollywood bit actor and stunt double. During World War II he served as an older-than-average enlisted man in the Coast Guard. By 1955, living in Waikiki, Blake was disillusioned with the crowds on the beach, and somewhat frustrated with his still-fit but nonetheless aging body. He was an admired figure, but an oddity as well, living by himself on a homemade boat in the Ala Wai Yacht Harbor. "Late in the evening," the *Honolulu Star-Bulletin* reported the day after Blake took his leave of both Hawaii and surfing, in September 1955, "he would seek his way back to the tiny boat, carrying a brown paper sack containing carrots, celery, a loaf of bread, some cheese (and) ice cream for his lonely evening meal." In 1961 Blake published his second book, *Hawaiian Surfriding: The Ancient and Royal Pastime.*

Blake continued to work as a lifeguard into his early 60s, mainly in Florida; in 1967 he returned to his childhood home in Wisconsin, where he wrote "Voice of the Wave," a religious-themed essay on surfing, published in a 1969 issue of *Surfing* magazine and later reworked into "Voice of the Atom." The essential Blake philosophy, one that he carved into stone in Wisconsin, came to be: Nature = God. Blake, a vegetarian from early adulthood, died in 1994 at age 92. He was married once, for less than a month, in 1925, and had no children.

Blake was inducted into International *Surfing* Magazine's Hall of Fame in 1967, to the International Swimming Hall of Fame in 1992, and to the Huntington Beach Surfing Walk of Fame in 1994. *Tom Blake: Surfing 1922–1932,* a book of photographs of and by Blake, was published in 1999. *Tom Blake: The Uncommon Journey of a Pioneer Waterman,* a richly detailed biography by Gary Lynch and Malcolm Gault-Williams, was published in 2001. Portions of a 1990 videotaped interview with Blake were used in *Great Waves,* an Outdoor Life Network TV documentary series. Some of the luster came off the Blake legend when *H2O* magazine in 2001 reported that he "fa-vored certain now-scientifically discredited and controversial beliefs regarding race and ethnicity." *See also* fin, Hawaiian Surfriders, hollow surfboard, Malibu, Pacific Coast Surf Riding Championships, paddleboarding, surf leash, surf photographer, swallowtail.

blank Molded surfboard-shaped core material, usually made of polyurethane foam bisected by a thin wood strip, from which a board shaper or board-shaping machine produces a ready-to-fiberglass surfboard. Today, Clark Foam, the world's largest blank manufacturer, offers 70 blank models in seven densities, ranging in size from 5′9″ to 12′8″. The 6′6″ blank used for a high-performance shortboard weighs just over five pounds. Several well-known shapers, including Al Merrick, Dick Brewer, Rusty Preisendorfer, and Pat Rawson, have designed signature model blanks. *See also* Clark Foam, polyurethane foam.

Blears, Jim Wide-stanced goofyfooter from Honolulu, Hawaii; winner of the 1972 World Surfing Championships. Blears was born (1947) in Santa Monica, California, and moved with his family to Hawaii at age 11. He was the Hawaiian Surfing Association ratings leader in 1969 and 1970 and a four-time Duke Kahanamoku Classic invitee between 1968 and 1971. He also placed third in the 1970 Smirnoff. Blears's 1972 world contest victory was controversial. "David surfed the best," wrote *Surfing* magazine journalist Drew Kampion, speaking of precontest favorite David Nuuhiwa, who placed 2nd "while Blears got the good waves towards the end, when the judges tend to score higher." Other members of Blears's immediate family were also surf world notables. Lord James "Tallyho" Blears, British-born family patron and midcentury wrestling star, was featured in the surf movie classic *The Endless Summer* (1966), and was Hawaii's favorite on-site surf contest announcer during the '70s, '80s, and '90s. Clinton Blears, younger brother to Jim, was a pro surfer in the '80s; sister Laura was a top amateur in the early '70s, and one of the original female pro surfers. Jim Blears appeared in a small number of surf movies, including 1973's *Going Surfin'. See also* World Surfing Championships 1972.

Blears, Laura Agile surf vixen of the early and mid-1970s, from Honolulu, Hawaii; one of the first women professional surfers, and younger sister of 1972 world champion Jimmy Blears. Laura Blears was born (1951) in Buffalo, New York, moved with her family to Hawaii as a child, and began surfing at Waikiki at age seven. She was Hawaii's top-rated woman surfer in 1970, a World Surfing Championship finalist in 1972, and women's division winner in the 1974 Smirnoff Pro—the first women's professional surf contest. Blears became a minor pop culture celebrity the following year, when she was invited to ABC-TV's multievent Superstars competition, where she vied against the likes of Olympic gymnast Cathy Rigby and Wimbledon champion Billie Jean King. Blears also surfed in the nude for "Here's Why the Lady is a Super Surfer!," a six-page layout in the July 1975 issue of *Playboy.* A photo of her surfing topless was later turned into a best-selling poster. *See also* nudity and surfing.

blown out   Ocean surface condition created by a moderate-to-strong onshore wind, which, by degrees, produces chopped-up, crumbly, messy surf. Blown out waves are a regular feature in many of the world's best-known surfing areas. In Southern California, the surf generally blows out by late morning, and in northern California during the spring and summer months the surf often remains blown out for days, even weeks, at a time. *See also* wind chop.

Blue Crush   Amiable teenage action/romance movie released by Universal in 2002, directed by John Stockwell (*crazy/beautiful*), and produced by Academy Award winner Brian Grazer (*A Beautiful Mind*), starring Kate Bosworth as Anne Marie, an attractive surf-stoked hotel maid living in Hawaii with her younger sister and two friends. Anne Marie spends nearly all her free time preparing for the big surf contest at Pipeline, but her routine is interrupted when she falls in love with pro football quarterback Matt Tollman. The *Blue Crush* reviews were mixed; praised by the *Orange County Register* as "an energetic exercise in grrrrl power wish fulfillment," but dismissed by the *San Francisco Chronicle,* calling it "one big wipeout." A number of pro surfers were involved with the making of *Blue Crush,* including Keala Kennelly, Rochelle Ballard, Megan Abubo, Kate Skarratt, and Mike Stewart; big-wave rider Noah Johnson wore a bikini and blond wig to stunt-surf for Bosworth during her Pipeline scenes. Surf photographer/filmmakers Don King, Sonny Miller, and Bill Ballard also worked on the film. *Blue Crush,* rated PG-13, was the first Hollywood-made movie featuring women surfers since 1959's

Gidget; budgeted at $35 million, and marketed heavily, *Blue Crush* was and remains the most expensive surf movie ever made. *See also* Hollywood and surfing.

bluebirds   Expression used by pre–World War II surfers, mainly in Hawaii, to describe an exceptionally big set of waves taking shape on the horizon. As the incoming swells first show themselves on distant reefs, they appear as dark blue bands.

boardbag   Catchall description for a variety of surfboard-protecting sheaths, generally divided into two categories: the soft bag and the travel bag. Soft bags protect against nicks and scratches, shield the board from the sun, and keep surfboard wax from rubbing off onto clothes, car roofs and interiors, and furniture. Originally made of canvas, corduroy, denim, or vinyl, commercially produced soft bags were available as far back as the early 1960s, but didn't catch on as an accessory until the early '80s, about five years after the introduction of the stretch-cotton bag. This tight-fitting "board sock," featuring a nylon nose piece and a drawstring opening at the tail, has become the soft bag standard. Some are made with a zipper along one side, instead of a drawstring. The Pro-Lite company in California introduced the travel boardbag in 1982, made of dense but bendable polypropylene material about one-half-inch thick. The travel bag, designed mainly for air travel and featuring a removable shoulder strap and heavy-duty zipper running from one side of the bag to the other, wasn't a guarantee against cargo-hold damage, but was nonetheless a huge improvement on the sleeping bags and the do-it-yourself duct-taped cardboard boxes that surfers had long been using. Larger travel bags, holding up to eight boards, were later introduced, and are sometimes referred to as "coffins." Hard plastic board cases, used exclusively for travel, are also available.

boardshorts   *See* baggies, surf trunks.

Body Glove   *See* Meistrell brothers.

bodyboarding   Type of surfing performed on a soft, square-nosed, semiflexible board, usually in a prone position; invented and developed in the early 1970s by Southern California surfboard designer Tom Morey. Bodyboarding is sometimes described as the most popular form of surfing, as body-boards outsell surfboards by a ratio of four to one. While bellyboarding (prone riding) is the original form of board-surfing, dating back hundreds of years, it was all but moribund by the late '60s, as the vast majority of surfers rode standing up, while a small percentage used knee-boards. Morey gave new life to prone surfing in 1973 by marketing his two-year-old invention called the Morey Boo-gie, a 4'6" by 23" bellyboard made primarily of closed-cell polyethylene packing foam. Easier, cheaper, and safer to ride than a surfboard, Boogie boards soon became popular, especially with children and tourists: 80,000 units were sold in 1977, just before Morey was bought out by American toy giant Kransco. Sales figures more than quadru-

Bodyboarding

pled by the end of the decade, and body-boards were soon available in thousands of coastal American drugstores and sporting goods stores, as well as surf shops. By the early '80s bodyboarding had taken on its own identity, separate from stand-up surfing, with its own evolving high-performance standards and homegrown heroes—most notably Jack Lindholm of Hawaii, inventor of the drop-knee stance and the first bodyboarder to ride Pipeline.

The first professional bodyboarding contest was the 1979 Morey/Gap Pro, held in Huntington Beach, California; six years later a bodyboarding division was added to the United States Surfing Champi-onship, and in 1990 it became part of the World Am-ateur Surfing Championships. The Morey Boogie International Bodyboarding Championship, held at Pipeline and long considered the sport's unofficial world title, was founded in 1982, with Hawaiian sen-sation Mike Stewart winning the event 10 out of its first 15 years. (Stewart's reputation was so high in 1991 that his *Surfer* magazine profile was titled, "Is Mike Stewart the Best Surfer in the World?" The Pipeline contest itself was later renamed the Mike Stewart International Pipeline Pro.) *Bodyboarding* magazine, a spin-off of *Surfing* magazine, began pub-lishing in 1985; more than 15 bodyboarding publica-tions have been founded worldwide since then. The Hawaii-based Global Organization of Bodyboarders was launched in 1995 to oversee and unify interna-tional professional competitions. While the number

of dedicated bodyboarders in America is thought to have dropped slightly since the late '80s, its popular-ity remains on a steep increase in other parts of the world, particularly in Latin American countries like Chile and Brazil.

Although millions of low-end bodyboards are still made from single-foam molds (using poly-styrene, polyethylene, or EVA foam), today's high-performance bodyboards are laminates, usually made of EVA foam on the rails and deck, a polyethylene core, an internal carbon-fiber nose-to-tail stringer for added strength, and a slick hard-plastic bottom. Bodyboards are virtually indestructible. A high-quality bodyboard is generally about four feet long, two feet wide, two inches thick, and costs about $200. Nearly 50 companies worldwide manufacture high-performance bodyboards; more than 100 others produce inexpensive single-foam models. About 750,000 bodyboards were sold in the United States in 2002, compared to an estimated 200,000 surfboards. Intermediate and advanced bodyboarders use swim fins to aid in catching waves; riders of all levels use a leash attached to the wrist or ankle.

The key to bodyboarding's popularity is that it's easy and immediately enjoyable for the beginner, but also an open-ended performance challenge to the ex-pert. Small numbers of bodyboards are seen at most surf spots around the world; at a few dozen breaks generally regarded as too dangerous (or too shape-less) for board-surfing—Sandy Beach in Hawaii, the

Wedge in California, Shark Island in Australia—bodyboards are the preferred wave-riding craft. Top bodyboarders can ride as deeply inside the tube as surfers; popular bodyboard maneuvers include 360-degree spinners, barrel rolls, and aerials. Some bodyboarders still use the drop-knee stance, placing one foot on the forward-area deck of the board; a smaller number rise all the way to their feet.

Stand-up surfers have traditionally viewed bodyboarders with ambivalence, or outright malice; their learning curve is too fast, their numbers are too large, and their sense of cool is less developed. "They're just incredibly easy to hate," Australian surf journalist Nick Carroll wrote of bodyboarders in 1997. "Clinging on to their brightly-colored mass-produced plastic things like life-rafts in a storm, then riding the wave prone like a turtle, or half-raised on one knee like some brave competitor in the Special Olympics." ("Sponger," "booger," "lid-rider," and "speed-bump" are oft-used nicknames for bodyboarders.) A 1990 *Tracks* magazine article titled "Will the Next Generation of Surfers Please Stand Up" suggested that bodyboarding was compromising Australia's ability to produce world-class surfers. But bodyboarding has in fact been used as a stepping stone for many of the world's top surfers—Matt Archbold, Ross Williams, and Kelly Slater all rode bodyboards before graduating to surfboards—as well as providing a simple means for just about anyone to experience the power and thrill of riding a wave. *See also* bodysurfing, kneeboarding, Tom Morey, Morey Boogie, Mike Stewart.

bodysurfing   Riding a wave using only the body as a planing surface; bodysurfing is the original and purest form of surfing. Prior to the invention of the surf leash in the early 1970s, virtually all dedicated surfers were forced to become adept bodysurfers, as nearly every wipeout was followed by a bodysurfing ride to the beach to retrieve the lost board. By the mid-'90s, bodysurfing was often described as "the forgotten art." While nothing is known about the origins of bodysurfing, it's possible that humans were inspired to emulate wave-riding sea animals such as dolphins and seals. Bodysurfing almost certainly predates board-surfing, which itself, University of Hawaii anthropologist Ben Finney suggests, may date as far back as 2000 B.C. Recorded bodysurfing history, however, begins after that of board-surfing. In 1899, Australian Fred Williams was taught to bodysurf by Tommy Tanna, a Polynesian islander brought to Syd-

ney to work as a gardener; Williams in turn taught local "surf-bathers" how to ride waves. Bodysurfing was first popularized in the United States during the mid-'20s by Olympic swimmer Wally O'Conner of Los Angeles, who would visit local beaches and draw an audience by diving underwater while facing an incoming wave, do a push-turn off the sand, then burst out of the shore-bound white water. (USC football player Marion Morrison, an early California bodysurfer, tore ligaments in his shoulder while riding the surf near Balboa Pier in 1926; finished with organized sports, he went to Hollywood and was eventually renamed John Wayne.)

In 1931, Los Angeles bodysurfer Ron Drummond published *The Art of Wave-Riding,* a 26-page primer on bodysurfing basics, and the first book of any kind on surfing. California surfer Owen Churchill visited Hawaii the following year and noticed that locals were able to increase the power of their kick stroke—and thus catch waves easier—after fixing palm fronds to their feet with tar. Churchill kept the idea in the back of his mind, and in 1940 introduced what would become a bodysurfing equipment standard: the Churchill "Duck Feet" swim fin. Lifeguard Cal Porter of Santa Monica had meanwhile taught himself how to ride at an angle across the wave face rather than straight to the beach. Tens of thousands of coast-dwelling Americans had by that time taken to waves. A bodysurfing article published in 1940 by *Life* magazine, "Surf-Riding is a Favorite Summertime Sport," noted that "almost every boy and girl [in California] is an expert surf-rider." Board-surfing, mat-riding, and bodyboarding would all become popular in the years and decades to come—and gain far more attention—but bodysurfing, practiced almost entirely by tourists and day visitors during the warmer months, has quietly remained the most popular form of wave-riding.

Beginning bodysurfers ride near the shore, in water shallow enough to allow them to catch an incoming wave—sometimes already broken—with a jumping push-start, followed by a straight-for-the-beach ride either with their arms tight against their sides or extended out before them. Intermediate and advanced bodysurfers catch unbroken waves and angle in one direction or another across the wave face, usually extending the wave-side arm and using the palm of the hand as an added planing surface. (A variety of handheld planing aids, ranging from a simple plywood rectangle to plastic-molded devices

Bodysurfing

board-dominated Pipeline, was unanimously regarded as the world's premier bodysurfer from the mid-1970s to the early '90s; nine-time bodyboarding world champion Mike Stewart has since become the sport's dominant presence, and was the first to do a full barrel roll at Pipeline.

Bodysurfing has no organized contest circuits or leagues, or a definitive world championship. A limited number of individual contests, however, have long been attended by a small international cadre of full-time bodysurfers. Two of the biggest events, both founded in 1977, are the Oceanside World Bodysurfing Championship, held in midsummer, and the Pipeline Bodysurfing Classic, usually held in January. The Pipeline Classic, long regarded as the sport's most prestigious contest, became the first professional bodysurfing contest in 1980, but soon returned to amateur status after organizers were unable to find sponsors. Record-keeping for the Pipeline Classic has been spotty; available results are as follows:

1981:   Mark Cunningham
1982:   (no results available)
1983:   (no results available)
1984:   Mark Cunningham
1985:   (no results available)
1986:   Bob Thomas
1987:   Jame Jonsson
1988:   (no results available)
1989:   Mark Cunningham
1990:   Mark Kalaugher
1991:   Mike Stewart
1992:   Don King
1993:   Mike Stewart
1994:   Mike Stewart
1995:   John Fink
1996:   Larry Russo
1997:   Mike Stewart
1998:   Mike Stewart
1999:   Mike Stewart
2000:   Mark Cunningham
2001:   Mike Stewart
2002:   Mike Stewart

Included among the small number of bodysurfing video titles are *Primal Surf* (2000) and *Pure Blue* (2001). Bodysurfing has also been featured in more than a dozen surf movies and videos, including *Barefoot Adventure* (1960), *Gun Ho!* (1963), *The Endless Summer* (1966), *Going Surfin'* (1973), and *We Got Surf* (1981). *The Art of Bodysurfing,* a paperback book offering both history and instruction, was published in

with straps and minifins, have been used and typically discarded over the decades.) Swim fins are an essential piece of bodysurfing equipment, as they allow the bodysurfer to catch waves in deeper water, and can also provide a burst of speed while riding. While bodysurfing for the most part involves "trimming" along the wave face and riding inside the tube whenever possible, maneuvers such as spinners and barrel rolls are fairly common among advanced riders. The best waves for bodysurfing are steep, fast, tubing beachbreak waves that are often unsuitable for boardsurfing; two of the best known are Sandy Beach and Makapuu on the east shore of Oahu in Hawaii. The Wedge, in Newport Beach, California, a ferocious sand-pounding peak wave aptly described by *Sports Illustrated* in 1971 as "a great big screaming shorebreak," has for decades been bodysurfing's most fearsome, and famous, break. The Wedge is responsible for a dozen or more neck and back injuries each year; some are permanent.

Bodysurfing has always been the least-publicized form of surfing, in part because it offers little to promoters and marketers and also because the act doesn't have the same visceral impact as boardriding. Several bodysurfers have nonetheless distinguished themselves through the years, including Richard "Buffalo" Keaulana and Barry Holt of Hawaii; Californians Bud Browne, Candy Calhoun, Larry Lunbeck, and Mickey Muñoz; Wedge riders Fred Simpson, Terry Wade, and Mark McDonald; and Australians Don McCredie, Tony Hubbard, Max Watt, and Michael Fay. Hawaiian lifeguard Mark Cunningham, a sublimely smooth master at the

1972. *See also* bodyboarding, Mark Cunningham, kneeboarding, Sandy Beach, Mike Stewart, the Wedge.

boil   A circular pattern on the water surface, usually between three and 15 feet in diameter, formed as a wave passes over a raised area on the bottom—usually a large rock or cluster of rocks. Boils are generally a red flag, as they indicate shallow water. They can also be difficult to traverse, as the boil's perimeter can "grab" the rail of a surfboard, and because the water within can be unstable. Boils are greatly affected by tides, and a churning gyre at low tide might vanish altogether at high tide. In between rides, surfers often use a boil as a lineup marker, and position themselves accordingly for the next good wave. Surfers often have to negotiate the boils at Hawaii's Waimea Bay and Todos Santos in Mexico. Waimea Bay in Hawaii and Mexico's Todos Santos are both marred somewhat by a boil near the take-off zone.

Bold, Harry   Pioneering South African surfer and surfing promoter. Bold was born in Durban (1938), the son of a former lifeguard; he started bodysurfing in 1950, got his first board—a 12′6″ hollow wooden paddleboard—two years later, and in 1961 imported the first polyurethane foam board to South Africa from California. He was the country's *Surfer* magazine distributor from 1960 to 1965, at which point he became cofounder of *South African Surfer,* the first domestically produced surf magazine. Bold moonlighted by barnstorming American- and Australian-made 16-millimeter surf films up and down the South African coast. "In the mid-'60s," he later recalled, "I was passing through Cape St. Francis and there were a bunch of surfers camped out at Seal Point. There was no electricity, so we asked the lighthouse keeper for power and I showed Bud Browne's *Locked In* on the side of the lighthouse under the stars." Bold owned and operated a Durban surf shop from 1984 to 1994. He is married and has two children.

Bolster, Warren   Protean self-taught American surf photographer from Oahu, Hawaii; a top name in the field from the 1970s to the present day, best known for his water-shot images. Bolster was born (1947) in Washington, D.C., the son of a ranking American Foreign Service diplomat, and spent much of his childhood overseas. His family moved to Sydney,

Australia, in 1963, and Bolster began surfing at Bondi Beach; in 1967 he moved to Cocoa Beach, Florida, and soon earned a reputation as one of the state's top competitive surfers. Bolster moved to San Diego, California, in 1970, and two years later—using a new waterproof camera housing for the first time and shooting his first roll of color film—he produced a *Surfing* magazine cover shot; later that year he was listed on the *Surfing* masthead. Bolster switched to *Surfer* in 1975, where he remained a staff photographer until 1992. In 1976 and 1977 he also worked as *Surfer's* associate editor; from 1975 to 1978 he was the editor of *Skateboarder;* by 2000 he'd written more than 30 articles for the American surf press. Bolster was constantly on the lookout for new angles, shooting from helicopters and often using a surfboard-deck-mounted camera to get spectacular in-the-tube photos from behind the surfer, or noseriding photos from in front of the surfer. In 2000, the *Surfer's Journal* published "The 50% Solution," a 10-page portfolio of Bolster's recent work, with each color-saturated wide-angle image shot half above and half below the ocean surface; *Masters of Photography: Warren Bolster,* a lavish 250-page retrospective photo book, was published by the *Journal* in 2002. Portfolios of Bolster's work have been published in *Sports Illustrated* (1977) and *Oceans* (1981), among other magazines. His photos have also been used in a number of illustrated surfing books, including *The History of Surfing* (1983), *Surfing: The Ultimate Pleasure* (1984), and *The Perfect Day* (2001). Bolster was elected to the East Coast Surf Legends Hall of Fame in 2000. He's been married twice, has three children, and has lived in Hawaii since 1979.

bomb   A bigger-than-average set wave; usually only applied when the surf is well overhead. "Bring on the Bombs" was the title of a 1999 *Surfing* magazine article looking ahead to the winter season at Maverick's in northern California. Also used by surfers in the hip-hop sense, as a designation for anything impressive.

bombora   Australian surf slang for a big-wave reef or sandbar located well past the normal surfing lineup; an Aborigine expression, synonymous to the American-coined "cloudbreak." As with many Australian nouns, "bombora" is usually shortened to "bombie." Sydney surfer Dave Jackman made national headlines in 1961 when he became the first surfer to ride the dreaded Queenscliff Bombora; two years later the Surfaris, an American surf band, released an instrumental single titled "Bombora." *See also* cloudbreak.

boneyard   General description for the turbulent area between where a wave initially breaks and where the shore-bound white water dissipates. Almost exclusively used for surf breaks that are either dangerous, or for lineups that are hard to access. The "boneyard" is similar to the "impact zone." Hawaii's Sunset Beach and Maverick's in northern California both have notorious boneyard areas. "Boneyard" is also used to describe a more specific—and more hazardous—area of reef that is barely (or partially) covered by water.

Bonyhton, Tim   Indefatigable surf video-maker from Sydney, Australia. Bonyhton was born (1958) in Adelaide, South Australia, and moved with his family at age 13 to Sydney's Bondi Beach, where he began surfing. He worked his way into surf moviemaking in the late 1970s and early '80s by showing home-edited Super-8 films at local pubs. Bonyhton was hired by surfwear manufacturer Billabong to film *Surf Into Summer,* their 1987 promotional video. He also shot promos for Piping Hot (*Strike Force*), Gorilla Grip (*Gripping Stuff*), and Morey Boogie (*Raw*). In 1998, Bonyhton filmed Ken Bradshaw, Cheyne Horan, Ross Clarke-Jones, Tony Ray, and others surfing 35-foot-plus waves at Outside Log Cabins—the largest ridden surf in history at the time. The result was a cult favorite video called *Biggest Wednesday.* Bonyhton founded the annual Australian Surfing Photography Awards in 1999, with a ceremony held in conjunction with the Rip Curl Pro at Bells Beach; prizes and small cash awards are given to winners in categories such as Best Water Shot, Best Empty Barrel, and Best Sequence.

bonzer   Surfboard design introduced in 1972 by Malcolm and Duncan Campbell of Oxnard, California. The bonzer was one of the first boards to use three fins: a pair of toed-in, keel-like side fins, located in front of a standard center fin. The board also had two parallel concaves down the bottom rear half of the board. The bonzer (period Australian slang for "bitchin'") was a hot surf media topic in 1973 and 1974, and pro surfers Ian Cairns and Jeff Hakman were among the design's proponents, saying the board was both faster and more maneuverable than the standard single-fin boards in use at the time; Bing

Bonzer

Surfboards in California licensed the Campbell brothers' idea and put out a trademarked Bonzer model in 1973, but the design never really caught on and by 1976 it had all but disappeared. In 1975 Duncan and Malcolm founded a small commercial board-making interest, which later became Campbell Brothers Surfboards. An updated five-fin version of the bonzer was first developed by the Campbell brothers in 1982 and later gained a small measure of popularity. Variations on the double concave and the tri-fin board, meanwhile, had become all but universal on high-performance shortboards. *See also* Campbell brothers, concave, reverse vee, tri-fin.

books and surfing   Film, video, magazines, television, and the Internet have proven to be the most popular media outlets for surfing, but the sport has also been consistently well served by books. Surfing was first brought to the attention of the English-speaking world in Volume II of *A Voyage to the Pacific Ocean,* the serialized and wildly popular accounts of Captain James Cook's exploratory voyages across the Pacific Ocean, from Tasmania to the Arctic. Upon seeing a native canoe surfer riding waves in Tahiti, Cook wrote, "I could not help concluding that this man felt the most supreme pleasure while he was driven on so fast and smoothly by the sea." In Volume III, one of Cook's lieutenants writes about board-surfing in Hawaii. Surfing was described in 19th-century books by American Henry Wise (*Los Gringos,* 1850) and Isabella Lucy Bird of Great Britain (*The Hawaiian Archipelago,* 1875). A dispatch sent by Mark Twain in 1866 to the *Sacramento Union* newspaper included an account of Twain's failed attempt at surfing, and was later reprinted in his 1872 book *Roughing It.* "The board struck the bottom in three-quarters of a second without any cargo," Twain wrote, "and I struck the bottom about the same time, with a couple of barrels of water in me." Jack London had better luck with his attempt at surfing during his first visit to Hawaii, and his account was published in a 1911 travelogue titled *The Cruise of the Snark.* London's dramatic presentation, with its descriptions of "bull-mouth monsters" (waves) and "Kanakas" (surfers), was a great boon to surfing's popularity in America.

The Art of Wave Riding (1931), lifeguard Ron Drummond's 26-page instructional pamphlet on bodysurfing, has been called the first surfing book. The 95-page *Hawaiian Surfboard,* published four years later by Wisconsin-born surfing icon Tom Blake, offers a far more detailed look at the sport, with sections on history, board design, and riding technique, along with dozens of black-and-white surfing photographs. *California Surfriders,* a 108-page photo book published by Los Angeles surfer/photographer John "Doc" Ball in 1946, was the first hardbound work to examine the sport in California. *California Surfriders* and *Hawaiian Surfboard* (renamed *Hawaiian Surfriders*) have both been reprinted.

The large-format, photo-heavy coffee-table surfing book, a perennial favorite, got its start in 1964 with *Modern Surfing Around the World,* written by *Surfer* magazine founder and publisher John Severson. These kinds of surf books can be divided into a number of categories, including history (*The History of Surfing,* 1983; *Surfing: The Ultimate Pleasure,* 1984; and *Girl in the Curl: A Century of Women in Surfing,* 2000), photography (*The Book of Waves,* 1989; *Photo: Grannis,* 1998), and surfing breaks/surfing areas (*Aloha Blue,* 1997; *Maverick's: The Story of Big-Wave Surfing,* 2000).

This Surfing Life (1965), by 1964 world champion Bernard "Midget" Farrelly of Australia, had some biographic information, but *You Should Have Been Here an Hour Ago* (1967), by California surf stylist Phil Edwards, is rightly considered to be surfing's first real biography. As of 2003, more than three dozen surf world biographies or autobiographies had been written, including titles on Duke Kahanamoku, Fred Hemmings, Nat Young, Wayne Bartholomew, Tom Blake, Mark Richards, Tom Carroll, Pam Burridge, Greg Noll, Rick Grigg, Mike Doyle, and Mark Occhilupo. Daniel Duane's 1996 book *Caught Inside,* the first surfing memoir, was excerpted in the *New York Times Sunday Magazine.* Other semibiographic first-

person books featuring surfing include *Walking on Water* (Andy Martin, 1991) and *In Search of Captain Zero* (Allan Weisbecker, 2001).

Surfing Guide to Southern California (1963), by Bill Cleary and David Stern, was the sport's first guidebook. Other popular titles in the genre include *Where the Surfers Are* (1968), *Surfing California* (1973) and *Surfing Indonesia* (1999), and *The Surfer's Travel Guide* (1995). More than two dozen surfing instruction books and how-to manuals have been published since the mid-'60s, along with a smaller number of books on surf forecasting/wave formation, and how-to books on surfboard construction and repair.

Frederick Kohner's *Gidget* (1957) is the best-known title in the small and highly uneven canon of surf fiction. While Columbia Pictures' movie version of *Gidget* was maligned as frivolous and inauthentic, Kohner's book is smart, funny, lively, and full of neatly sketched characters. *The Ninth Wave* (Eugene Burdick, 1956), *A Native Son of the Golden West* (James Houston, 1971), *Tapping the Source* (Kem Nunn, 1984), *The Tribes of Palos Verdes* (Joy Nicholson, 1997), and *Dogs of Winter* (Nunn, 1997) were all critically acclaimed works of fiction set at least partially in the surfing world. Not as well received, but hot sellers nonetheless, were the "pulp" surfing books of the mid-'60s and early '70s, including *Surf Broad* (1965), *Hang Dead Hawaiian Style* (1969) and *Scarlet Surf at Makaha* (1970). Children's surfing books have meanwhile been dependably ignored by the surf press, but are often charming and well-crafted. *Broderick* (Edward Ormondropy, 1969), tells the story of an intrepid mouse who runs away from home and becomes a world-famous surfer; *Mrs. Armitage and the Big Wave* (Quentin Blake, 1997) is about a cheerfully acquisitive woman who glides across a 15-foot swell towing her dog, a beach umbrella, a wind sock, and a horn, and performs "a California slither, a Bali serve [and] a Waikiki flip" while heading for the beach.

The 1990s and early '00s brought a small explosion of new surf books, with a broadening of subjects and formats. Some books were available in bookstores, though most were sold in surf shops or by mail order, or on the Internet; categories included interviews and profiles (*The North Shore Chronicles,* 1990), health, diet, and fitness (*Sick Surfers,* 1993), reference (*The Surfin'ary,* 1991), and essays/stories (*Good Things Love Water,* 1994).

Peter Dixon's *The Complete Book of Surfing* (1965), originally published by Coward-McCann and released in paperback by Ballantine, sold more than 300,000 copies worldwide, making it by far the best-selling book on the sport. *The Water Log,* an online surf-book bibliography, has about 380 titles; other surfing bibliophiles, using an expanded definition of "surf book," claim that the total number of surf-related books is closer to 600. By the early '90s, early surfing books were being actively collected, traded, auctioned, and sold. First-edition copies of Blake's *Hawaiian Surfboard* and Ball's *California Surfriders,* by the end of the decade, sold for between $2,000 and $4,000. *Surf's Up: Collecting the Longboard Era* (2001) includes a section on books. *See also* California Surfriders, Peter Dixon, Gidget, Hawaiian Surfriders, The Ninth Wave, Kem Nunn, The Pump House Gang, Surfing: The Ultimate Pleasure, Surfing California, You Should Have Been Here an Hour Ago.

Booth, Jeff   Hard-turning goofyfoot pro surfer from Laguna Beach, California; world-ranked #4 in 1995. Booth was born (1969) in Los Angeles, moved with his family to Laguna the following year, and began surfing at age eight. He was runner-up in the juniors division of the 1984 World Amateur Surfing Championships, runner-up in the men's division in 1986, and was the 1988 world tour rookie of the year. American surf journalist Ben Marcus described Booth's wave-riding technique in 1991 as both powerful and predictable ("more workman than showman"), and noted that Booth was especially adept at leveraging his six-foot, 185-pound frame at big, hollow, left-breaking waves like Pipeline or Cloudbreak. Booth maintained a fairly low profile, with two exceptions. In 1989, he wrote a letter to *Surfer* complaining that the magazine was publishing too many photos of "lesser-known surfers" at the expense of "high-ranked professionals." *Surfer* received more than 300 letters from readers, virtually all of them denouncing Booth as elitist. The second instance took place during a 1994 Pipeline Masters heat, in front of a beach full of spectators, when Booth punched local surfer Liam McNamara in the head after the widely disliked Hawaiian purposely rode up Booth's back and shoulders while paddling for a wave.

After finishing ninth in the 1996 ratings, the 28-year-old Booth gracefully retired, saying he was "fulfilled with my career, and wanted to leave on my own terms." He appeared in more than two dozen surf movies and videos, including *All Down the Line* (1989), *110/240* (1992), and *Endless Summer II* (1994).

booties   Wetsuit socks, generally made with three-millimeter neoprene uppers and a treaded hard-rubber sole; named for their resemblance to baby booties; almost always worn in conjunction with a fullsuit—a one-piece wetsuit that covers everything but a surfer's hands, feet, and head. Booties come in round-toe or split-toe designs, and often have a cinch-down Velcro strap around the opening to prevent water from flushing in. Early versions of the booty had vertical zippers up the back seam, over the Achilles tendon. Surfers generally begin to wear booties when the ocean temperature drops below 60 degrees; virtually all surfers wear booties once the water hits the low 50s. As with most items in the wetsuit wardrobe, booties were originally made for skin and scuba diving. *See also* reef walkers, wetsuit.

Botha, Wendy   Resolute pro surfer originally from East London, South Africa; four-time world champion (1987, 1989, 1991, 1992), and the only surfer to twice regain the title. Botha was born (1965) and raised in East London, began surfing at age 13, and won four consecutive South African National Championship titles from 1981 to 1984. She turned pro and finished the 1985 world tour season ranked seventh, earning rookie-of-the-year honors. Two years later she won the first three events of the year and cruised to her first world title. Botha became an Australian citizen in 1989, moving to the Sydney beachfront suburb of Avalon, partly to avoid sanctions placed on South African athletes and also because there were virtually no women sparring partners in her home country. The change suited her, as she won seven of 12 events on the 1989 tour and cruised easily to her second world title. Botha, a regularfooter, was slight (5'4", 115 pounds) but strong, and known for throwing her board and body into risky maneuvers, a habit that led to four knee surgeries during the course of her pro career.

As Botha settled into her reign as the world's best female surfer, her natural self-confidence began shading into arrogance. Asked in early 1988 who her toughest challengers might be that year, she offhandedly replied that "no one even comes to mind." She often said she wanted to surf like a man, and in 1989 told *Surfer* magazine that "on any given day I can surf as good as a lot of the guys on the world tour"— a piece of verbal showmanship that earned Botha a fusillade of scornful reader-reply mail, including a note from the "Anti-Big-Headed-Women Club." She

Wendy Botha

was nonetheless voted women's division winner in the annual *Surfer* Poll awards in 1990, 1991, and 1993.

Botha's boldest PR gambit came in September 1992, when she posed nude for Australian *Playboy,* earning the Down Under version of the magazine its first sold-out issue. "The girls on the tour were a little shocked," Botha reported. "The guys all think it's unreal." Later that year she won her fourth and final world title, and after the 1993 season she retired and moved to New Zealand with her new husband. Two years later she was featured, along with four other champion women surfers, in a well-crafted documentary called *Surfer Girl.* "Just that little bit of aggression," the stylish blond-haired Botha said on camera, describing her rise to the top of her profession. Somebody would say to me, 'Hey, off my wave!' and I'd go, 'Yeah? Up yours!' and off I'd go. As shy as I was at times, once I hit the surf it was just—get out of my way." Botha's seven wins in 1989 remain a single-season record. Botha appeared in a small number of surf movies and videos, including *Gripping Stuff* (1987) and *Oz on Fire* (1991). *See also* nudity and surfing.

bottom   "Bottom" has three primary surf-world meanings: 1) The underside of a surfboard; the board's planing surface. Bottom design is hugely important to performance, and board-makers spend much of their time blending, refining, and reconfiguring the four basic bottom design elements—flatness, concavity, convexity, and rocker—always with an eye toward increasing speed, control, and maneuverability. Bottom design characteristics can be amplified, mitigated, or nearly canceled outright when used in combination with other design features (board outline, thickness, foil, etc.), and virtually all modern shortboards feature combination bottoms. In general, a flat surface is fast and relatively stable, concavity improves speed but reduces control, convexity improves maneuverability but reduces speed. 2) The base or trough of a wave, where the surfer does a bottom turn. 3) The topographic surface over which a wave breaks; "bottom" in this context generally doesn't refer specifically to the type of break (e.g., reefbreak, pointbreak, beachbreak), but to the geologic composition itself, such as sand bottom or coral bottom.

bottom turn   The fundamental surfing turn, performed along the wave's trough or "bottom"; a cornering maneuver thought of as both a discrete entity—particularly in bigger surf—as well as a preface to tuberiding or any of a variety of off-the-top maneuvers. "Without a good bottom turn," 2000 world champion Sunny Garcia said, "you have nothing." Bottom turning was invented in the mid-1940s, as direction-stabilizing surfboard fins were popularized and boards were lightened and made more maneuverable. California's Les Williams and Hawaii's George Downing were two early proponents of the bottom turn, but Phil Edwards, California's best surfer in the late '50s and early '60s, is thought of as the first real master of the art. Bottom turning's golden era took place in the years during and just after the late-'60s shortboard revolution, as boards were redesigned from blunt-nosed "logs" to sleek, narrow, high-traction "pocket rockets." Along with the ability to ride inside the tube, a good bottom turn became surfing's ultimate mark of distinction. Hawaii's Jeff Hakman used a perfectly grooved bottom turn to become the era's most successful competitive surfer; Ben Aipa and Nat Young, from Hawaii and Australia, respectively, were also renowned for their powerful bottom turns. All were overshadowed, however, by Hawaii's Barry Kanaiaupuni, whose best turns at Sunset Beach set a standard for velocity, power, and style that has yet to be matched. "The consummate bottom turn," Pipeline master Gerry Lopez said about Kanaiaupuni, "where the speed going in is whiplashed into even more speed coming out. No one does it better. In fact, no one else can even do it—not like this."

Other surfers known for their powerful bottom turns include Australians Tom Carroll, Gary Elkerton, Simon Anderson, and Mark Occhilupo, and Hawaiians Laird Hamilton and Johnny-Boy Gomes. In the mid-'80s, California surfer and three-time world champion Tom Curren developed the "double-pump" bottom turn, where the arc of the turn is briefly interrupted as the rider begins riding back up the wave face, then reset, allowing him to rebound off the curl on a sharper, more critical angle.

Bottom turning lost some of its cachet and much of its style beginning in the early '90s, as high-performance surfboards became thinner, narrower, lighter, and "twitchier" than ever before. The new boards allowed surfers to ride deeper inside the tube, and create spectacular new off-the-top moves, but reduced the board's capacity to maintain speed and drive through a bottom turn.

bowl A type of wave, or portion of wave, that bends in on itself as it breaks; as viewed from above, a bowl section is crescent-shaped. Bowl waves are generally caused by a raised area of reef or sandbar; they can also be formed as a wave bounces off a jetty or headland and intersects with the following wave. A bowl section tends to be bigger than the rest of the wave— hard-breaking, hollow, and good for tuberiding. The Makaha Bowl—the final section of wave at Makaha, on the west side of Oahu—is the most famous big-wave bowl. Ala Moana, a small- to medium-sized wave on the south side of Oahu, is often referred to simply as "Bowls." *See also* wedge.

Boyd, Duke Never-say-die entrepreneur from Southern California; cofounder of prototype surfwear company Hang Ten. Boyd was born (1934) in Kansas City, Kansas, grew up in Los Angeles, Hawaii, and Panama, began surfing at age 12 in Waikiki, and graduated in 1963 with a B.A. in education from Long Beach State College. He formed Hang Ten in 1960, helped design the company's trademark horizontal stripe–design trunks and T-shirts, and drafted virtually every famous surf personality of the decade into a long-running ad campaign. From 1968 to 1970,

Boyd moonlighted as managing editor for Petersen's *Surfing* magazine. Boyd sold Hang Ten in 1970 and immediately founded Golden Breed surfwear; Golden Breed sponsored as a promotional device the first Expression Session showcase event, held in Hawaii in late 1970, featuring the world's best surfers in what was called a "noncontest." In 1975, after Golden Breed failed to catch on, Boyd became a partner and licensing agent for Lightning Bolt Surfboards, which he helped turn into a surf accessories giant. In 1996 he founded Duke Boyd America surfwear, targeting the same baby boomer surfers who were wearing Hang Ten three decades earlier. The Duke Boyd America ad campaign, moreover, featured many of the surfers—silver-haired and jowly in most cases—from the original Hang Ten ads. Boyd was elected to the International Surfing Hall of Fame in 1991, and the East Coast Surf Legends Hall of Fame in 2000. *See also* Expression Session, fashion and surfing, Hang Ten.

Boyer, Lynne Quiet but hypercompetitive surfer from Haleiwa, Hawaii; world champion in 1978 and 1979; a cool hand in the big Hawaiian surf, but lauded for her aggressive and tight-cornering approach in smaller waves. "You could say she was a more radical surfer than I was," rival and four-time world champion Margo Oberg of Hawaii recalled. "She was pretty, she had wild red hair, she painted her boards up . . . she sure *looked* radical." Boyer was born (1956) in Allentown, Pennsylvania, the daughter of an army oncologist, raised in Maryland, and was 11 in 1968 when she moved with her family to Hawaii, where she began surfing. She placed third in the 1973 state championships, won in 1975, and turned pro the following year, just out of high school, flying to California to win the Hang Ten Pro Championships at Malibu, earning $1,500. Margo Oberg, the 1968 world champion and long the dominant figure in women's surfing, finally had a worthy rival. Whereas Oberg was a classicist, using a fairly upright stance and connecting turns with quiet precision, Boyer (5'7", 125 pounds) rode in a low attacking crouch and worked her board constantly. She was often described as the female Larry Bertlemann—the electrifying Hawaiian who reinvented hotdog surfing in the early 1970s. Boyer meanwhile accoutered herself with a set of brightly airbrushed boards, most of them bearing her trademark ribbon pattern across the deck.

The women's world tour made its debut in 1977, and for the next few years it was essentially a

Lynne Boyer

two-surfer showcase. Boyer won three of nine events in 1977, but Oberg won four and took the title. In 1978 they each took two, but Boyer had the higher result in the fifth and final contest, and won the championship. Oberg took the following year off, and Boyer won three of the four scheduled contests to easily take her second title. She also won the 1979 *Surfer* Magazine Readers Poll Award. Just two contests were held in 1980; Oberg won both and reclaimed the championship, with Boyer runner-up.

Boyer's rating slipped over the next three years, from fourth to fifth to eighth. In 1984 she won the World Cup at Haleiwa, but had otherwise all but vanished from the surf scene, revealing years later that she was addicted to cocaine and alcohol, and that her reticence as a pro had been determined in large part because she'd been a closeted lesbian. "It was lonely at the top," she told the *Honolulu Star-Bulletin* in 1997. "You have all these secrets, and you can't let everyone know who you are because they might get an edge on you." Boyer worked as a stock clerk in a Honolulu surf shop after quitting the pro tour; in 1985 she moved back to her parents' house while she got sober; through the '90s she worked as a housecleaner and did tropical-landscape oil paintings for the tourist-supported Haleiwa Art Gallery. She continued to surf, but as she said in 1997, "It took 13 years of being sober to make it fun again."

Boyer was the most photographed female surfer of her era, and appeared regularly in surf films, including *Playgrounds in Paradise* (1976), *Five Summer Stories Plus Four* (1977), and *Ocean Fever* (1983). She was also profiled in writer Andrea Gabbard's book *Girl in the Curl: A Century of Women in Surfing,* published in 2000.

Boyum, Mike and Bill   Adventurous and enterprising American brothers best known for their discovery and commercialization of Grajagan, the exotic world-class wave located at the southeast tip of Java, Indonesia. Mike Boyum was born in 1946 in Key West, Florida, the son of a career navy pilot; Bill was born in 1951 in Philadelphia, Pennsylvania; the Boyum family moved often, from one American naval station to another. Both boys started surfing in 1962, but Mike soon quit. Mike, the more restless of the two, dropped out of George Washington University in the mid-'60s, traveled to Aspen, Tahiti, Fiji, New Zealand, and Australia, then moved to Bali in 1969. Bill flew over the following year and brought a surfboard; he decided to stay there as well, and convinced Mike to begin surfing again. The brothers, along with a small group of other expatriate Australians and Americans, including California surfer Bob Laverty, rode Uluwatu—Bali's best-known break—for months at a time with nobody else in the water. By 1972, however, Bali had caught the attention of the larger surf world, and visitors were beginning to stream in. Laverty convinced Bill to join him on a search for waves on the edge of a jungle reserve in southeast Java, where they found flawless eight-foot left-breaking tubes a few miles up the beach from a fishing village named Grajagan. They surfed for three days, sleeping on the beach and conserving their small reserves of food and water, then returned to Bali, where, days later, Laverty drowned while surfing Uluwatu.

Mike Boyum joined Bill and a few others for the next few Grajagan trips, and it was Mike who conceived and developed the G-land Surf Camp, building a small row of wooden-stilt huts along the perimeter of the jungle in 1974 and hassling endlessly with the Indonesian bureaucracy to maintain a Grajagan surf resort exclusive. The camp became a commercial interest in 1978. By allowing 10 surfers in at a time, and charging $200 a day per surfer over the course of a four-month surf season, Mike Boyum was grossing roughly $250,000 per year by the mid-'80s. He had meanwhile branched into cocaine trafficking, and in

1985 was arrested and jailed on drug charges while passing through the South Pacific islands of Vanuatu. Released after serving two years in prison, Boyum spent another two years on the run from drug dealers. In 1989, while living in the Philippines under an alias, he discovered the perfectly shaped right-breaking wave that would later be called Cloud Nine. Boyum had recently taken to fasting, believing it to be the path to improved health and spirituality; on June 14, he died on the 45th day of a fast at Cloud Nine. He was buried overlooking the break.

Bill Boyum had meanwhile moved to Hawaii to raise a family, but continued to make regular visits to Grajagan; Cyrus, his youngest son, began to help run the G-land camp in 2002. *See also* Grajagan, surfing resorts.

Bradbury, John   Tall, leathery, plainspoken surfboard builder from Santa Barbara, California; an early proponent of Styrofoam/epoxy resin boards. Bradbury was born in 1944, began surfing in the mid-'50s, worked in the Yater Surfboards factory in the early '60s, and started shaping boards on his own in 1965. He was virtually unheard of outside of the Santa Barbara area until 1985, when he made an ultralight Styrofoam/epoxy resin board for future world champion Martin Potter—virtually all boards at the time consisted of polyurethane foam and polyester resin—who immediately rode it to victory in a world pro tour event. Top pros Brad Gerlach and Cheyne Horan, among others, also began riding Bradbury epoxies. The shaper had by that time earned a reputation as the definitive laid-back surfing artisan, making each board himself start to finish in his one-man backyard factory. He died of leukemia in 1999 at age 55, almost certainly contracted from decades' worth of exposure to toxic board-making materials. Josh Bradbury, 26 at the time of his father's death, was, and remains, one of Santa Barbara's best surfers. *See also* epoxy surfboard.

Bradshaw, Ken   Iron-willed big-wave surfer from Sunset Beach, Hawaii; winner of the 1982 Duke Kahanamoku Classic; often credited as the first surfer to ride a 40-foot wave. Bradshaw was born (1952) in Houston, Texas, the son of powerful steel industrialist. An All-City linebacker in high school, Bradshaw nonetheless had thought of himself as a surfer since riding his first wave at age 14 at Surfside Beach on the Texas Gulf Coast. He immersed himself in surfing

after moving to California in 1969; three years later he relocated to Oahu's North Shore, a raw but game big-wave hopeful, and in 1974 he rode his first 20-foot wave at Waimea Bay.

Because Waimea breaks just a few times each season, Bradshaw generally rode Sunset Beach, the North Shore's most dependable big-wave break. By the late '70s the bearded and slightly manic Bradshaw was patrolling the Sunset lineup like a hair-trigger sheriff; anyone who interfered with his rides was ordered to leave the water, or told to dismount so that the six-foot, 185-pound Texan could disable the surfer's board by smashing off a fin with the heel of his hand. Bradshaw worked as a surfboard shaper—creating the Bradshaw Hawaii label in 1978, after working two years for Lightning Bolt Surfboards—but spent uncountable hours in the water in all conditions, and throughout the mid- and late '70s, his surfing improved dramatically. He rode in a taut crouch, and was slighted by big-wave peers as a surfer of average technical ability ("He's a little off in his timing sometimes," Darrick Doerner noted; "He doesn't

Ken Bradshaw

really connect his moves too well," Mark Foo said), but by the turn of the decade he was in fact an accomplished North Shore surfer, and at Sunset Beach he rode with knowledge, precision, and power. He finished second in the 1982 Pro Class Trials, first in the 1982 Duke (beating world tour stalwarts Peter Townend and Dane Kealoha in the finals), and third in the 1983 Duke.

Bradshaw rode yellow and orange surfboards covered in sponsors' stickers, and was a leading figure in the 1983-launched big-wave surfing revival in part because he brought brightly packaged professionalism to a surfing specialty that for years had been regarded as a nonmarketable backwater. Darrick Doerner, Roger Erickson, and a few others were equal or superior to Bradshaw in giant surf, but nobody trained harder (vegetarian diet, no alcohol or drugs, running, swimming, and weight training), surfed more often, or was more accessible to the media. A rivalry was born in 1985 when Bradshaw was joined in the Waimea lineup by Mark Foo, a younger, even brasher big-wave rider; their feud was the subject of "The Divided Rulers of Waimea Bay," a 1988 *Outside* magazine feature story. The two surfers eventually became friends, and flew to San Francisco together in late 1994 to ride Maverick's. Near midday, both paddled for a 15-foot wave; Bradshaw missed it, Foo wiped out, went over the falls, and drowned.

Tow-in surfing, introduced two years earlier, had already reconfigured big-wave surfing, and for the next few years Bradshaw focused on this new mechanized version of the sport. Regarded as long past his big-wave prime, the 45-year-old Bradshaw surprised everyone on January 28, 1998, when he was towed into a wave at Outside Log Cabins on the North Shore estimated to be between 40 and 45 feet (or about 65 feet from trough to crest), bigger by far than any wave ridden to that point, and unmatched until 2001. Bradshaw fell into an existential depression after his giant wave, wondering out loud, "How can I ever get that high again?" Changing gears, he became an adviser/coach for his Australian girlfriend Layne Beachley, and helped her to win the first of five consecutive pro world championships in 1998.

Bradshaw has been featured in more than 20 surf movies and videos, including *Adventures in Paradise* (1982), *Journey to the Impact Zone* (1987), and *The Moment* (1998), as well as the IMAX film *Extreme* (1999). Bradshaw placed third in the 1986 Quiksilver in Memory of Eddie Aikau big-wave event at Waimea;

along with tow-in partner Dan Moore, Bradshaw competed in the 2002 Tow-In World Cup, the first tow-in contest held in Maui. Since the late '90s he's been an advocate for tow-surfing safety and training, and lobbied against those in local and state government who would legislate against the use of personal watercraft in nearshore waters. "The Nation of Ken," a 35-page *Surfer's Journal* profile, was published in 2001, in which writer Bruce Jenkins described the never-married Bradshaw as "the most driven individual the sport has ever known." *See also* Outside Log Cabins.

Brady, Leonard   Trenchant, often caustic surf photographer/journalist from Honolulu, Hawaii; author of "Whatever Happened to Big-Wave Riding?," a 1983 *Surfer* magazine article that marked a resurgence in big-wave surfing. Brady was born (1949) in Honolulu, and began surfing in 1963 at Waikiki; he received a B.A. in art from Maui's Mauna Olu College in 1971, had his first *Surfer* article published in 1974, and his first photographs published in 1975. One year earlier, Brady and fellow surf photographer/writer Bernie Baker formed Island Style, a two-man surf media team. Hawaiian big-wave surfing was Brady's primary focus. "Have surfers turned into candyasses?" he asks in the introduction to "Whatever Happened to Big-Wave Riding?," using the mocking high-handed tone that became his signature style. Subsequent Brady-written big-wave articles included "Waimea: A Short Paddle into Oblivion" (1980) and "The Return of Big-Wave Competition" (1986). The article "20 at 36" (1987) described Brady's personal quest to ride a 20-foot Waimea wave, something he accomplished at age 36. Brady moved to Hollywood in 1988 to work for screenwriter/director John Milius.

Brazil   This vast South American nation is home to a near-endless string of sand-bottom surf breaks and a colorful, hypercompetitive, fast-growing surf culture. Brazil's sun-warmed 5,000-mile Atlantic coastline runs in a sawtooth pattern from the subtropical south to the equatorial northeast, and can be divided into four main surfing areas: 1) The southern states, most notably Santa Catarina, home to Brazil's most consistent surf, including the well-shaped beachbreak waves of Imbituba and Joaquina, as well as the right-breaking point surf—one of the few such breaks in Brazil—at Silviera. 2) The frenetic and urban central coast, which includes the crowded lefts of Arpoador and the shifty beachbreak peaks of Ipanema, both in Rio; Saquerema's wave-rich Ituana; and the punchy São Paulo beachbreaks, including Guaruja, Maresias, and Itamambuca. 3) The hot and sprawling north and northeast coasts, where a broad continental shelf filters out much of the size and power of incoming swells. The beachbreak at Maracaipe (site of the 2000 World Surfing Games), near Recife, can produce well-shaped peaks. 4) Fernando de Noronha, the volcanic offshore island located about 220 miles from the mainland near the country's easternmost tip, is often described as Brazil's Hawaii due to its powerful wintertime surf, including the consistent waves at Praia do Italcabe and the perfect-but-fickle lefts of Abras. (It might be said that Brazil's most famous break, featured in general-interest media sources around the world, is the Pororoca, a tidal bore wave that occasionally runs up the Amazon River.) The surf on Brazil's central and south coasts is best from April to October, as South Atlantic storms generate fairly consistent three- to six-foot waves; breaks on the north and northeast coasts, as well Fernando de Noronha, are best from November to March, in response to North Atlantic storms. Rarely does the Brazilian surf get over 10 foot. Average daytime air temperatures in the far south range from the high 50s to the low 80s, with water temperatures between 62 and 75; air temperatures in the sweltering north range from 75 to 90, with year-round water temperatures in the low 80s. Shark sightings in Brazil are fairly common, especially in the north (the threat of shark attacks since 1998 has kept 40 miles of Recife coastline off-limits to swimmers and surfers), and water in urban areas can be highly polluted; many of the urban surf lineups are also crowded and aggressive.

Surfing was introduced to Brazil at Rio's Copacabana Beach in 1928, when an unknown American took to the warm blue waves on a redwood board; Rio native Paulo Preguica rode a hollow paddleboard at the same beach in the early '30s, and in 1939 a pair of Rio teenagers constructed the first Brazilian-made surfboard by following a do-it-yourself *Popular Mechanics* magazine article. Skin diver Arduino Colassanti imported the first foam-core board to Brazil in 1960, just as Rio craftsman Irencir Beltrao started mass-producing plywood paddleboards called "Madeirites." Australian surf traveler Peter Troy arrived in Rio in 1964 and showed the locals how to build foam boards, and Brazil's first board-making factory opened the following year, in the Rio suburb of São Conrado. (Troy also introduced local surfers to the latest high-performance turns and maneuvers.) The Carioca Surfing Federation, Brazil's first surf club, was founded in 1965, by Rio locals Ylen Kerr, Walter Guerra, Fernanda Guerra, and Maria Helena Beltrao; the following year, with help from visiting American surfers Mark Martinson and Dale Struble, along with filmmakers Greg MacGillivray and Jim Freeman, the club organized the Brazilian Surfing Championships, the country's first surf contest, won by Jorge Bailley and Fernanda Guerra.

Surfing's popularity in Brazil skyrocketed during the '70s. The first official Brazilian National Championships were held at Ubatuba in 1972, the first international pro event was held in Rio three years later, and Rio surfer Pepe Lopez—the country's first surf star—was a finalist in the 1976 Pipeline Masters, and won the 1976 Waimea 5000, a world pro circuit event held in Arpoador. *Brasil Surf,* the country's first surf magazine, began publishing in 1975; *Realce,* Brazil's first surfing TV show, premiered in 1982. Competition became a defining element of Brazilian surfing, and 1986 saw the founding of the Association of Brazilian Surfing Professionals, as well as Hang Loose Pro, an international pro event in Florianópolis. (The Waimea 5000 contest ran intermittently until 1982; other Rio-based international events included the Alternativa Surfmasters and the Rio Surf Pro. Brazil also hosted the 1994 World Amateur Surfing Championships and the 2000 World Surfing Games.) Brazilian pro surfers Flavio Padaratz and Fabio Gouveia had by the late '80s given Brazil a formidable presence on the pro circuit. The domestic surf industry, meanwhile, led by Hang Loose surfwear, Mormaii wetsuits, and Redley beachwear, was versatile and competitive enough to obviate almost completely the need for imported goods.

Brazilian surfers flourished on the pro circuit throughout the '90s and '00s, with Padaratz, Gouveia, Peterson Rosa, Victor Ribas, Maria Tavares, and Jaqueline Silva all, at one time or another, finishing in the year-end top 10. Carlos Burle of Recife became the country's top big-wave rider, winning the 1998 Reef Brazil Big-Wave World Championships, as well as the 2002 Nissan Xterra XXL Big Surf Awards. Meanwhile, Brazilian surfers in general were often derided by surfers from other countries as loud, pushy, and rude. "It's a cultural thing," Rio pro Renan Rocha explained in 2000. "In Brazil, the only rule is survival of the fittest. So we've got to be aggressive in the water, and we learn to fight for waves."

As of 2003, Brazil was home to approximately one million surfers, nearly 1,000 surf shops (mainly in the urban centers of Rio, São Paulo, Florianópolis, and Recife), four major surf magazines (*Fluir, Hardcore, Alma Surf,* and *Trip Surf*), one world pro tour contest (the Rio Surf International), 10 lesser international pro contests, and countless local pro and amateur events (most held under the auspices of the 2000-founded Confederation of Brazilian Surfing). *Surf TV* and *Surf Adventures* are two of Brazil's roughly half-dozen cable TV surfing shows. The Brazilian surf is detailed in *The World Stormrider Guide* (2001). *See also* Pororoca, Rio de Janeiro.

breakwater Good surf is occasionally found adjacent to breakwaters. The rebounding "wedge" is the most common type of breakwater wave, in which an incoming swell pushes up against the breakwater boulders or seawall and forms a rebound swell, then angles across the following wave to form a wedging peak. Florida's Sebastian Inlet and the Wedge in Newport Beach, California, both break in this manner. Breakwaters have erased surfing spots as well, most famously at Dana Point in Orange County, California, and breakwater projects have long threatened to destroy the surf at Kirra, Australia, and at Maalaea, Hawaii. *See also* jetty.

Brennan, Kevin Australian teenage surfing genius from Bondi Beach; the 15-year-old winner of both the juniors and men's divisions of the 1965 New South Wales State Titles. Brennan stood 4'9" and weighed 94 pounds when he entered the 1965 NSW state titles, and on his way to a double victory beat the cream of Australian surfing, including Midget Farrelly, Nat Young, and Robert Conneeley. Brennan also rode beautifully at Noosa and Burleigh in Paul Witzig's 1967 surf film *Hot Generation,* snap-turning where other riders maintained trim, and switching stance at will. Early adulthood found Brennan addicted to heroin, and he died of an overdose in 1975 at age 25. *Australia's Surfing Life* magazine in 1992 named Brennan as one of the country's "Fifty Most Influential Surfers"; Brennan's memory was honored with a small surf art show at the Bondi Pavilion in October 1997. *See also* drugs and surfing.

Brewer, Art Creative and temperamental photographer from Dana Point, California; a surf media

Art Brewer

mainstay since 1968, best known for his portraiture and land-based action shots, and sometimes referred to as the sport's most naturally gifted surf photographer. Brewer was born (1951) and raised in Laguna Beach, California, began surfing in 1963 at age 12, took up photography in 1967, and produced his first *Surfer* cover shot in 1968. He took two photography courses at the Art Center College of Design in Pasadena, California, but is largely self-taught.

Brewer gained a spot on the *Surfer* masthead in late 1968, and was the magazine's dominant photographer in 1970 and early 1971, at one point shooting six out of nine covers. In 1971 he jumped to *Surfing* magazine; in 1975 he was back with *Surfer;* from late 1978 through 1981 he was *Surfer's* photo editor; from 1981 on he's been the magazine's ranking contributor. Brewer's eye for color and framing is unmatched in the surf world, and much of his best work has been done as a portraitist, when he has unfettered control over light, texture, and mood. Brewer's size (he once weighed nearly 300 pounds) and flaring temper, meanwhile, further suggested the idea of grand, even explosive creative talent. At times Brewer played on his aggression. Asked to supply a self-portrait for a 1997 portfolio, "this big elephant seal of a man," as described by surf journalist Evan Slater, provided a green-tinged face shot negative, jaggedly cut in two, then taped and stapled back together, with the handwritten caption: "Surf photography constipates me!"

Brewer has published photos in dozens of mainstream magazines, including *Rolling Stone, Sports Illustrated, Men's Journal, Outside, Esquire* (shooting the July 1992 cover), *Seventeen, Playboy, Spin, Us, American Photographer, Communication Arts,* and the *New York Times Magazine. Masters of Surf Photography: Art Brewer,* a luxurious 250-page hardcover retrospective of Brewer's work, was published by the *Surfer's Journal* in 2001; he's also contributed to a number of illustrated surfing books, including *The History of Surfing* (1983), *Stoked: A History of Surf Culture* (1997), and *The Perfect Day* (2001). In 2002, Brewer made his first surf video, titled *The Misfits.* Brewer is married and has one child.

Brewer, Dick   Brilliant but moody surfboard designer/shaper from Hanalei, Kauai, Hawaii, generally regarded as the sport's most influential board-maker; creator of the popular Bing Pipeliner model longboard in 1967, and venerated in the late '60s and early '70s as the first master of shortboard design. "He's got the magic eye," Hawaiian surfer Jeff Hakman said. "Outlines, fins, edges, contours; he knew how to put everything together." Brewer was born (1936) near Duluth, Minnesota, the son of an aircraft machinist, moved with his family to Long Beach, California, in 1939, and began surfing in 1953. In the mid-'50s he worked as a toolmaker and machinist; in 1959 he shaped his first surfboard, and the following year he moved to Oahu where he was informally mentored by California-born shapers Mike Diffenderfer and Bob Shepherd. Brewer opened Surfboards Hawaii in Haleiwa in 1961, the first retail surf shop on the North Shore of Oahu, surfing's big-wave capital.

Brewer returned to California in 1964 to open a mainland branch of Surfboards Hawaii, but legal problems with royalties and licensing soon forced him out of the company altogether. He worked for manufacturing giant Hobie Surfboards in 1965 as a big-wave board specialist, and produced the Dick Brewer Model; Jeff Hakman, Eddie Aikau, and Buzzy Trent were among the big-wave aces who rode Brewer boards that winter in Hawaii. Brewer himself was an enthusiastic big-wave rider in the late '50s and '60s, and was featured riding Waimea Bay in the surf movie classic *The Endless Summer.* Brewer switched from Hobie to Harbour Surfboards in 1966, then to

Dick Brewer

Bing Surfboards, where in 1967 he produced a series of models that are collectively regarded as the last word in original-era longboards, including the Pipeliner, the Lotus, the Pintail, and the Nuuhiwa Lightweight. But after Australian Nat Young won the 1966 World Championships on a self-made board that was thinner and lighter than anything in use at the time, the seeds were planted for a drastic change in board design.

The origins of the 1967-launched shortboard revolution are still debated. Brewer claims he began making shorter, more streamlined boards in the spring of 1967, and the radical new designs got him fired from Bing. Australian surfer/board-maker Bob McTavish, influenced by California-born kneeboarder and designer George Greenough, had meanwhile developed the short, wide-tailed vee-bottom design, and the generally accepted view is that McTavish and Greenough are responsible for getting the shortboard revolution started. It was Brewer, however, in the months and years to come, who did the most to bring the shortboard revolution into focus.

After getting fired from Bing, Brewer moved to Maui and started Lahaina Surf Designs, which lasted one year; he worked briefly for Plastic Fantastic Surfboards and Inter-Island Surfboards, then moved to Kauai in 1969 and founded the Dick Brewer Surfboards label. More legal problems followed, and Brewer eventually lost control of Brewer Surfboards. Whatever label they were shaped for, Brewer's boards continued to be popular among the world's best surfers, and his team roster from the late '60s to the early '70s included David Nuuhiwa, Reno Abellira, Gerry Lopez, Jock Sutherland, Jeff Hakman, Barry Kanaiaupuni, Sam Hawk, and Michael Ho. Design refinement, rather than breakthrough, was Brewer's biggest contribution; year after year his big-wave guns were synthesized and polished versions of all that was known in board design at that point. Brewer influenced virtually every shaper of the late '60s and '70s, and was mentor to Gerry Lopez, Reno Abellira, Terry Fitzgerald, Mark Richards, and other notable surfer/shapers. He also became one of surfing's outsized characters, as a beatific surf mystic; for a 1968 portrait he sat gurulike in a full lotus position, flanked by headstanding team riders Gerry Lopez and Reno Abellira. He was highly intolerant of criticism as well. When Jeff Hakman remarked that the tail of a new gun looked perhaps a bit too pulled in, Brewer quickly sawed off the back 12 inches and let the board drop to the floor, then turned to Hakman and asked, "How's that? Is that better for you?"

Brewer was a heroin addict when he all but dropped off the surf scene in the mid-'70s. He came back in the late '80s to make longboards, sailboards, and big-wave guns, and in the mid-'90s he made tow-in boards for a small group of Maui big-wave riders, including Laird Hamilton. In 2001, Brewer cofounded Plumeria Surfboards in Encinitas, California. Brewer lives in Hanalei, Kauai. He's been married twice, and has two children. *See also* big-wave surfboard, shortboard revolution, tucked-under rail, wings.

Briley, Shawn   Heavyset thrill-seeking goofyfoot surfer from Sunset Beach, Hawaii; a top surfer at Pipeline for most of the 1990s, and winner of the 1995 Tavarua Tube Classic. Briley was born (1974) in Oceanside, California, spent his early childhood in Montana and Honolulu, began surfing at age four, and moved with his family to Sunset Beach in 1981. He began riding Pipeline at age 12; by 17 he'd earned a reputation as one of Hawaii's hardest-charging young tuberiders, and as a surfer uniquely dedicated to high-risk excitement of any kind. He surfed the notorious Waimea

Bay shorebreak; rode left at right-breaking Waimea Bay; and frequently placed himself in the maw of hopeless Pipeline closeouts. On land he enjoyed shooting firearms, and had a long record of vehicular accidents; less than four months after breaking his back in a dirt-bike pileup in late 1997, Briley rolled his truck down a cliff face. "Crazy people in general are stupid," Hawaiian big-wave surfer Brock Little said in 1994. "Briley is relatively intelligent and yet he knows what he's getting into, which in a way is even crazier." Not interested for the most part in surfing competition, Briley nonetheless cruised to a win in the 1995 Tavarua Tube Classic, a novelty event in which surfers were scored solely on the amount of time spent inside the tube. He was also invited to the Quiksilver in Memory of Eddie Aikau big-wave contests at Waimea Bay in 1995 and 1999. Briley was featured in more than two dozen surf videos in the '90s, including *The Kill* (1994), *Fluid Combustion* (1995), *Voluptuous* (1996), and *The Bomb* (1998).

British Columbia   *See* Canada, Vancouver Island.

British Surfing Association (BSA)   National governing body for competitive surfing in Great Britain, founded in 1966, originally to fight municipal anti-surfing rules and regulations imposed at several English beaches. The British Surfing Association (BSA) today runs instructional clinics, coaching and judging programs, and annually stages approximately 10 surf competitions, including the British Nationals, the British University Championships, and the British Inter-Club Championships. BSA members—about 2,500 in 2003—receive £2 million of third-party collision insurance, should they injure somebody else while surfing. Members also get a newsletter, yearbook, surf shop discounts, and free e-mail on the BSA's Web site. Government officials have consulted the BSA on surfing-related issues.

Bronzed Aussies   Talented, highly elitist surfing troupe led by 1976 world champion Peter Townend and 1976 runner-up Ian Cairns; ostensibly created to further the cause of professional surfing and thus improve the lot of surfers everywhere, but essentially a promotional vehicle for the Bronzed Aussies themselves, who are best remembered for arriving at surf contests and postevent banquets in matching velvet jumpsuits. As a media phenomenon, the group was a success. "The Bronzed Aussies have made it impossible

The Bronzed Aussies (top to bottom) Ian Cairns, Mark Warren, Peter Townend

for us to ignore them," surf journalist Michael Tomson wrote in 1979. "Never before has any group in the sport been so scorned, so trodden, so insulted, and very occasionally praised, as the Bronzed Aussies."

The group was formed in 1976 by Townend, Cairns, Sydney surfer Mark Warren, and Sydney newspaper journalist/manager Mike Hurst. (Future four-time world champion Mark Richards declined an invitation to join.) The Bronzed Aussies' timing seemed good, as surfing's back-to-nature "country soul" period had run its course. Pro contest prize money and surf industry sponsorships were meanwhile on the rise, but still negligible, and the Bronzed Aussies—modeling themselves in part on the 1960s Australian pro tennis triumvirate of Rod Laver, Roy Emerson, and John Newcombe—hoped to sell their clean, brushed-back, prepackaged "glam-surf" image to corporate sponsors. As Hurst put it, the immediate goal was to make enough money so that Cairns, Townend, and Warren could comfortably get from event to event on the world tour, while the long-term

plan was nothing less than the establishment of "a global industry, franchising ideas and products into every country in the world." Australia's mainstream media initially showed interest in the Bronzed Aussies, but the surf media was less than enthusiastic, and international big-money sponsorship never materialized. In his coverage of the 1976 Smirnoff Pro-Am, *Sports Illustrated* writer Richard Johnston mockingly referred to the Bronzed Aussies as the "corporate kings of Australia," then played up the incongruity between surfers and corporate underwriting. "One begins to wonder if the endless summer is about to fade into the fiduciary fall." In a backfiring promotional gambit, the Bronzed Aussies in 1976 rented a mansion in the wealthy landlocked Sydney suburb of Pymble. The average surfer on the beach, taking it as an article of faith that the sport was best left noncorporate, nonconformist, and nonglamorous, meanwhile dismissed the Bronzed Aussies as ostentatious at best, and rank sellouts at worst. When Bronzed Aussie surfwear and a line of Bronzed Aussie surfboards were later introduced, both met with swift commercial failure.

Cheyne Horan became a Bronzed Aussie in 1977, just a few months before Warren quit the group; Jim Banks joined in 1978, not long before Horan left and was replaced briefly by Steve Jones; Banks quit in 1980, saying that the group's dictatorial rules and strictures "slowed down my surfing." Townend and Cairns kept a quieter and less-ambitious version of the Bronzed Aussies alive into the early '80s. Townend later claimed that he invested and lost nearly $100,000 in the Bronzed Aussies. Sounding for better or worse just as he did in 1976, he also resolutely claims that the Bronzed Aussies had a "huge impact" in transforming surfers into "legitimate sportsmen." *See also* Ian Cairns, Peter Townend, Mark Warren.

Brooke, Serena Levelheaded, media-friendly regularfoot pro surfer from Coolangatta, Australia; world-ranked #2 in 1998 and 1999. Brooke was born (1976) in Nambour, Queensland, began surfing at Caloundra in 1989 at age 14, and was the world tour rookie of the year in 1995. "If there's a formula for creating a successful pro surfer," *Australia's Surfing Life* magazine said of Brooke in a 1997 profile, "then it's come together here: strong, fit, gutsy, somewhat reckless and destructive without being self-destructive, common sense, blonde, and attractively packaged for marketing." Brooke is a punchy, low-centered surfer, and performs best in overhead beachbreak waves. She's appeared in more than a dozen surf videos, including *Triple C* (1996), *Peaches* (2000), and *Poetic Silence* (2001).

Brooks Street Surf Classic   The world's longest continuously running surfing competition, held each summer since 1955 at Brooks Street, Laguna Beach, California. Developed by the Laguna Beach Recreation Department, and originally titled the Laguna Beach Surfing Tournament, the contest is open only to Laguna residents. Larry Brixley and Mike Sagar won the men's and juniors division, respectively, in 1955; bodysurfing, paddleboard, and skimboard divisions were added in the early '60s. Brooks Street contest winners have included surfboard manufacturing magnate Hobie Alter, bodyboard inventor Tom Morey, three-time Makaha International winner Joey Cabell, and world tour standouts Jeff Booth and Alisa Schwarzstein. There were 12 divisions as of 2003, including a special category open only to artists.

Brown, Bobby   Small-framed Australian regular-foot surfer from the Sydney beachfront suburb of Cronulla. Brown defeated Midget Farrelly to win the 1964 New South Wales state titles, and a few weeks later placed sixth in the debut World Surfing Championships, held in Manly Beach; at 18, he was the youngest finalist. Brown's aggressive but ultrasmooth style of surfing was a highlight in Paul Witzig's 1968 film, *The Hot Generation,* most of which was shot in the months just before the shortboard revolution. On August 19, 1967, the 22-year-old Brown was killed in a bar fight at the Taren Point Hotel, near his Cronulla home. "Bobby Brown," 1966 world champion Nat Young wrote in his *History of Surfing* book, first published in 1983, "played a significant part in the inside-the-curl style which was to take Australia to the front in world surfing." Brown was also featured in *The Young Wave Hunters* (1964) and *A Life in the Sun* (1966).

Brown, Bruce   Oscar-nominated surf moviemaker from Dana Point, California; producer of 1966's *The Endless Summer,* the sport's best and best-known movie. Brown was born (1937) in San Francisco, California, spent his first nine years in Oakland, then moved with his family to Long Beach, in southwest Los Angeles County, where he began surfing. Along with hundreds of other young surfing fanatics, Brown went to the local Elks Club auditorium when-

ever original surf filmmaker Bud Browne barnstormed into town to screen his latest movie. Brown himself made his first surf movie, an 8-millimeter short, while stationed on a navy submarine in Honolulu in 1955; two years later, back in California, surfboard-maker Dale Velzy bought Brown a new 16-millimeter movie camera and paid his way to Hawaii to shoot *Slippery When Wet,* his first feature-length surf film. *Slippery* was easygoing, colorful, neatly edited, and scored by West Coast jazz favorite Bud Shank—but the movie was in large part defined by Brown's smooth and casual narration. Brown, Browne, Greg Noll, and John Severson were the only surf filmmakers at the time.

Surf Crazy (1959) and *Barefoot Adventure* (1960), Brown's next two movies, resembled *Slippery When Wet,* and were filmed exclusively in California, Hawaii, and Mexico. *Surfing Hollow Days* (1961), Brown's fourth movie, spotlighting California power surfer Phil Edwards, branches out to Australia and New Zealand, and also shows Edwards on the first documented rides at the Pipeline in Hawaii. Brown's fifth movie, *Waterlogged,* was a rush-job compilation film that gave Brown something to put on the market in 1963. That year he set out with California surfers Mike Hynson and Robert August to film *The Endless Summer,* a semidocumentary on "the search for the perfect wave." The $50,000 film debuted in the summer of 1964 and was shown in the same manner as Brown's previous films, on the beach-city circuit, with Brown himself driving from auditorium to auditorium to do live-narration screenings. He added a recorded narration in 1965 and showed the movie in Wichita, Kansas, where for two weeks it outsold *My Fair Lady.* The following year, *Endless Summer* was blown up to 35-millimeter, re-edited slightly, and put into movie houses across the country to rave reviews: *Newsweek* named it one of the 10 best films of 1966; *Time* magazine called Brown the "Bergman of the boards." Writer Tom Wolfe, meanwhile, in his otherwise acerbic 1966 essay "The Pump House Gang," had nothing but nice things to say about the young California surf moviemaker. "Bruce Brown has the money and *The Life.* He has a great house on a cliff about 60 feet above the beach, [and] a rain-barrel old-apple-tree Tom Sawyer little-boy roughneck look about him, like Bobby Kennedy."

Brown provided footage for ABC and CBS surfing specials in the mid-'60s, and won two Cleo Awards in 1964 for his work on a Kodak Instamatic ad campaign.

Bruce Brown

On Any Sunday, Brown's 1971 motorcycling movie, co-produced by actor Steve McQueen, earned Brown an Academy Award nomination for Best Documentary. Brown then retired and spent 20 years restoring and racing cars, playing the stock market, and deep-sea fishing. In 1992 he came out of retirement to begin work on *Endless Summer II.* Unlike the original, the sequel was backed by a studio (New Line), and had a Hollywood budget ($3.5 million) as well as a film crew. But the new movie, while beautifully photographed, didn't have the magic of the original. "Brown isn't as well-versed as he once was," *Surfer* magazine wrote in its review, "and his narration, so effortless and warm in the late '50s and early '60s, now sounds a little forced." Brown had in a way become the victim of his own success; virtually every post-1964 surf movie had borrowed from *Endless Summer,* and the genre itself seemed to be played out. Brown, meanwhile, claimed his experience with New Line had been awful, and that his moviemaking days were through.

Brown was the top vote-getter in the Motion Picture/Photography category of the 1966 *International Surfing* Magazine's Hall of Fame Awards; in 1994 he received the Waterman Achievement Award from the Surf Industry Manufacturers Association. In 1997 he was presented with a lifetime achievement award at the *Surfer* Magazine Video Awards banquet, and was profiled in *50 Years of Surfing on Film,* an Outdoor Life Network television series. Two years later, *Surfer* named Brown the sport's fifth most influential surfer of all time. Brown is married and has three children; oldest son Dana Brown was cowriter of *Endless Sum-*

mer II and director of *Step Into Liquid,* a 2003 surf movie. Bruce Brown has lived in Gaviota, California, near Santa Barbara, since 1981. *See also* Endless Summer, Endless Summer II, surf movies.

Brown, Chris Mild-mannered pro surfer from Santa Barbara; described as a preadolescent "surfing genius," and winner of the juniors division in the 1988 World Amateur Surfing Championships. Brown was born (1970) in Los Angeles, raised in Santa Barbara, and began surfing at age 10, taught by his father, a Santa Barbara–area surfer since the late '50s. The smooth and flowing surf style Brown developed resembled that of Tom Curren, a three-time world champion who also grew up in Santa Barbara. Raised in what *Surfer* magazine described as a "fervently born-again family," Brown was unhappy as a world tour rookie in 1988, and went into semiretirement at the end of the following season. He returned to the circuit in 1992 and finished the 1993 season ranked 23rd, then drifted down in the ratings and off the world tour in 1995. Meanwhile, he won the Professional Surfing Association of America tour in 1994, and took individual honors in the 1996 Katin Team Challenge, held at the Huntington Pier, California. Brown was featured in more than two dozen surf videos, including *In the Wind* (1990), *Cyclone Fever* (1994), and *Bliss* (1996).

Brown, Woodbridge "Woody" Unsinkable regularfoot surfer from Kahului, Maui, Hawaii; pioneering big-wave rider in the early 1940s. Brown was born (1912) in New York City, the only son of a prosperous Wall Street brokerage firm owner. At 15, Brown worked for aviator Charles Lindbergh, just before Lindbergh made his historic transatlantic flight in 1927; Brown then dropped out of high school, ran away from home, and became obsessed with glider flying. He moved to Southern California in 1936, towing his glider, settled in La Jolla, built himself a surfboard, and a few months later became the first person to ride Windansea, which soon became the hub of La Jolla surfing. At a 1939 gliding competition in Texas, Brown set world records for altitude, distance, and time aloft, earning a congratulatory telegram from former President Herbert Hoover; one day after he returned home, his pregnant wife went into labor and died in childbirth. Grief-stricken, Brown abandoned his son at the hospital, left all his possessions in La Jolla, and moved to Hawaii.

In the early '40s, befriended by Honolulu surfers Wally Froiseth, John Kelly, and Fran Heath—all using the new hot curl board, which enabled them to ride much bigger waves—Brown began surfing Makaha, as well as the North Shore. A pacifist (as well as a vegetarian and an atheist), he refused to fight in World War II. Brown meanwhile met and married a Hawaiian hula dancer, and fathered two more children.

On the afternoon of December 22, 1943, Brown drove from Honolulu to the North Shore with teenage surfer Dickie Cross, and the two decided to ride Sunset Beach, where the surf looked to be 10 feet. The waves came up quickly, and a half-hour later the two surfers found themselves paddling out, more than a half-mile from the beach, with 25-foot waves exploding in their wake. The North Shore was then lightly inhabited, and nobody had seen the two surfers enter the water. The sun was getting low and the surf was still building when Brown told Cross they'd have to paddle three miles down the coast to Waimea Bay, where they might be able to get in through a deep-water channel. But the Waimea channel was impassable. Cross made a break for the beach, was caught by a set of 40-foot waves, and never seen again. Brown, meanwhile, lost his board, but was unharmed; a few minutes later he also made a break for shore, was rolled by a dozen or more breaking waves, then washed up into shallow water, and was dragged to safety by a group of soldiers who happened to be on the beach. Brown never again surfed the North Shore, and the harrowing Brown/Cross tale kept surfers away from the area for a few years.

In the mid-'40s, working from designs used by ancient Polynesian sailors, Brown built a pair of twin-hull sailboats that were generally regarded as the fastest nonmotorized boats in the world. These were the first two modern catamarans, and for the next 40 years Brown earned a living as a boatbuilder. He continued to surf, usually at Makaha, and in 1953 he was photographed, alongside George Downing and Buzzy Trent, racing across a beautiful 15-foot Makaha wall. Associated Press bought the photo, and it was published in newspapers across the nation, giving the country its first real look at big-wave riding and triggering a small but influential migration of surfers from California to Hawaii.

Brown returned to gliding in 1971, and age 59 set a world altitude record by soaring more than 12,500 feet about Maui. His second wife died in 1986. Brown married for the third time in 1987, to a 20-year-old Filipina, and the following year, at age 76, he again became a father. Brown has been featured in two PBS-aired documentaries: *Liquid Stage: The Lure of Surfing* (1995) and *Surfing for Life* (1999). In the latter, the thin-shouldered octogenarian drops into a six-foot wave and angles smartly along the trough on his way to calm water. A portrait of Brown holding his surfboard was used on the cover of *Growing Old Is Not for Sissies II: Portraits of Senior Athletes* (1995), a photo book. *See also* big-wave surfing, Dickie Cross, Waimea Bay.

Browne, Bud   The original surf moviemaker, from Southern California; producer of 13 full-length movies from 1953 to 1973. Browne was born (1912) in Newtonville, Massachusetts, near Boston, and moved to Los Angeles in 1931 to attend the University of Southern California. He was captain of the top-ranked USC swim team in 1934, learned to surf at Venice Beach five years later, and was a Los Angeles County lifeguard before and after serving in the navy during World War II. Nicknamed "Barracuda" for his tall, angular build and because he spent so much time in the ocean, Browne was long regarded as one of the world's best bodysurfers. In the early '50s, Browne worked as a schoolteacher while attending film school at USC; in 1953 he began editing together the 16-millimeter surfing footage he'd shot during his annual summer visits to Waikiki. The result was the first commercial surf film—a simple but energetic 45-minute film titled *Hawaiian Surfing Movies*. It debuted to a full house that fall at John Adams Junior High School in Santa Monica, with Browne sitting in the projection booth doing narration over the school's PA system, playing his own reel-to-reel music soundtrack at the appropriate times, and trying not to panic as the take-up reel malfunctioned and the film piled onto the floor behind the projector. Browne produced one movie annually for the next 11 years, including *Cat on a Hot Foam Board* (1959), *Spinning Boards* (1961), and *Cavalcade of Surf* (1962), all made for less than $3,000 and all following the same format: lots of surfing action from California and Hawaii, interrupted now and then with short comedy bits. Browne at first barnstormed his movies from San Diego to San Francisco, renting out school auditoriums and Rotary Club halls for live-narration screenings. Beginning in 1961, he hired radio disc jockeys to do taped narration, and was then able to ship copies of his films out to the East Coast and to the growing surf markets in Australia, New Zealand, France, and South Africa. Browne made his own waterproof camera housings, and developed his own dry suit that allowed him to shoot film from the water for hours at a time without getting cold.

The 60-year-old Browne came out of retirement in 1971 to begin work on his last and best surf movie, *Going Surfin',* which debuted in 1973. Browne was then still regarded as the finest water photographer in the business—a few years earlier he was the first person to take a movie camera out at Pipeline—and he also filmed the breathtaking water sequences for MacGillivray-Freeman's 1972 hit *Five Summer Stories.* Browne retired for good in 1977, after working on Warner Brothers' *Big Wednesday.* A dry, reticent, undemonstrative man, the never-married Browne kept his own company for the most part, and always seemed a step removed from the generally loud and raucous profession he invented. Surf moviemaking covered his living expenses, and nothing more. "But it was always worthwhile for me," Browne said in 1995, "because I got such a big hoot out of everyone enjoying the films."

In 1987, *Surfer* magazine selected Browne's *Locked In* (1964) as one of the best three surf movies ever made, along with *The Endless Summer* (1966) and *Five Summer Stories. Surfing the '50s,* a video compilation of Browne's early work, was released in 1994, and some of his midcareer titles have also been released on video. Browne was inducted into the International Surfing Hall of Fame in 1991 and the Huntington Beach Surfing Walk of Fame in 1996. He was profiled in *50 Years of Surfing on Film,* a 1997 Outdoor Life Network TV series; the following year he received the Lifetime Achievement Award at the *Surfer* Magazine Surf Video Award show; in 2001, at age 89, he won the Waterman Achievement Award from the Surf Industry Manufacturers Association. *Bud Browne: Works from 1955–1975,* an exhibition of Browne's still photography, was held at the Surf Gallery in Laguna Beach in 2002. *See also* surf movies.

Buchanan, Ian   Leather-wearing mid-1980s pro surfer from Christchurch, New Zealand; five-time national champion from 1983 to 1987; later a surfboard shaper, and a coach for the New Zealand national team. Buchanan was born (1961) and raised in Christchurch, began surfing in 1972, and six years later moved to Sydney, Australia. His five-year world tour career, launched in 1983, never really got off the

ground, but he was virtually unstoppable in his home country. From 1981 to 1989, Buchanan shaped for Hot Buttered Surfboards in Sydney; from 1989 to 1999 he worked as a Hot Buttered product manager; from 1990 to 2000, he was a coach to the New Zealand national amateur team, which, during this period, competed in six world contests. Buchanan appears in a small number of surf videos and movies, including 1989's *Sultans 2: The Force Strikes Back.*

Budweiser U.S. Pro Tour of Surfing   *See* Professional Surfing Association of America.

Bunger, Charlie   New York surfboard manufacturer and surf museum owner/curator from Gilgo Beach. Bunger was born (1941) and raised in Brooklyn, New York, began surfing at age 20, and shaped his first board in 1962, working out of his garage in Gilgo Beach, on the south shore of Long Island. He opened East Coast Surfboards later that year (the name was soon changed to Bunger Surf Shop), and by 1965 was selling 1,500 boards a season. Bunger helped organize and run the 1962-founded East Coast Surfing Championships, which began in Gilgo. In 1990, Bunger opened the Long Island Surfing Museum next door to his surf shop, and filled the space with a collection of historical photos, trophies, contest programs, and surfboards from every phase of East Coast surf history. Bunger was elected to the East Coast Surf Legends Hall of Fame in 1996.

buoy reports   Meteorological information gathered from at-sea devices—generally referred to as "buoys," whether buoy-shaped or not—and relayed by satellite to data-processing centers, where the data is translated and made available to weather services, shipping concerns, fishermen, surfers, and others. About 150 weather-data buoys are scattered throughout the world's oceans. While some are government property (those launched by the Army Corps of Engineers, for example), others are owned by oil companies or other private interests; nearly all are overseen by the National Data Buoy Center. About two-thirds of the buoys are tethered to the ocean floor; others drift in predetermined ocean currents, while still others are attached directly to the ocean floor. A surface buoy can be as small as a beach ball or as large as a camper van, and come in a variety of shapes, with instruments rising as high as 30 feet out of the ocean; they measure and transmit barometric pressure, wind direction, average wind speed, gusting wind speed, air and sea temperatures, and wave energy spectra from which wave height and period are determined.

Although meteorological buoys were first launched in the early '60s, it wasn't until the late '70s that a few data-minded surfers began tracking the information with an eye toward predicting incoming swells. Open-ocean wave size and period (the interval between two consecutive waves) are the two most important figures in surf forecasting. But raw height and period data—available to anyone with a weather radio—can be hard to interpret, as there will often be two or more swells moving through the same area of ocean. A buoy device measuring two separate, dovetailing four-foot swells, for example, might give an exaggerated reading of six feet. Data for swell period can be equally hard to translate. Deciphering and distributing buoy report information became a hot surf world industry in the mid-'80s, and several swell forecasting agencies—including Surfline, Wavetrak, and 976-SURF, all based in Southern California—appeared almost overnight. While professional surf forecasters vied for prominence in the years ahead, growing numbers of armchair forecasters began taking advantage of the data-rich buoy report sites on the Internet. *See also* Internet and surfing, surf forecasting, swell period, wave height and measurement.

Buran, Joey High-voltage pro surfer from Carlsbad, California; world-ranked #7 in 1983 and winner of the 1984 Pipeline Masters; founder of the Professional Surfing Association of America. Buran was born (1961) in Cleveland, Ohio, the son of a career marine sergeant father, grew up on military bases in Virginia and Guam, and moved with his family to Carlsbad in 1972, where he began surfing the following year. He was California's top-rated boys' division surfer in 1976 and 1977, and the top junior in 1978. After finishing sixth in the 1978 World Surfing Championships, the raspy-voiced 17-year-old goofyfooter dropped out of high school, gave up his amateur status, and quickly won the California Pro—a big achievement, marred slightly by the fact that his $3,000 first-prize check, as surf journalist Steve Pezman wrote, "bounced higher than his off-the-lip." Two months later Buran flew to Hawaii and placed fifth in the Pipeline Masters, finishing the year ranked #27. In 1980, Buran placed fourth in the Masters and won the Waimea 5000 in Brazil—becoming the first California male surfer to win a world pro tour event—and his year-end rating jumped to #13. A small number of other West Coast surfers were on the circuit, but none had anywhere near Buran's success; he was known as the "California Kid," and remained the state's pro circuit standard bearer until Tom Curren turned pro in 1982.

The white-blonde Buran (5'8", 155 pounds) was a perpetual motion surfer, riding out of a low, bandy-legged stance, his legs, arms, shoulders, head, and torso almost blurry with expansion and contraction. Depending on Buran's performance (or the viewer's preferences), his method was either exhilarating or tiring. His peak moments were at Pipeline, where his line was smoother, his energy focused, and he was able to make full use of his considerable tuberiding skills. In 1981 he again finished 13th in the world, in 1982 he dropped to 14th, then in 1983, spurred by the fast-rising Curren, Buran put in one last sustained effort and finished the year ranked seventh—one place ahead of Curren. He quit touring the following year, but nonetheless won the Katin Pro-Am in Huntington Beach. That December he rode to a stirring victory in the Pipeline Masters. (Rob Machado, 2000 Masters champion, is the only other California surfer to win at Pipeline.)

By the end of 1984, Buran had developed and launched the Professional Surfing Association of America, the country's first domestic pro tour, but the effort was exhausting, and Buran had what he later called "a full emotional breakdown" while directing the circuit in 1986. He sold the tour later that year. In 1991, three years after getting married and more than 10 years after becoming a born-again Christian, Buran and his new family moved to the East Coast where he spent nearly six nonsurfing years working as a pastor in a series of Calvary Chapel churches. The Burans moved back to California in 1996, Buran began surfing again, and in 1998 he won the Masters World Championships (for ex-pro surfers 36 and older), held in thumping Pipeline-style waves at Puerto Escondido, Mexico. After a brief work stint with surfwear giant Billabong, he returned in 2000 to full-time ministry work.

Buran appeared in a small number of surf movies, including *We Got Surf* (1981) and *Ocean Fever* (1983), as well as the religious-themed surf videos *Son Riders* (1987) and *A Wave of Life* (1990). He is married with four children, and lives in Costa Mesa, California. *See also* Professional Surfing Association of America.

Burle, Carlos Gritty big-wave surfer from Recife, Pernambuco, in northeast Brazil; winner of the 1998 Reef Brazil Big-Wave World Championship, and the

2002 Nissan Xterra XXL Big Surf Awards. Burle was born (1967) and raised in Recife, the son of a chicken farmer, and began surfing at age 13. Four years later he was the third-ranked juniors division amateur surfer in the country, and in 1987 he turned professional, finishing fifth that year on the Brazilian domestic pro tour. Burle developed a taste for big surf during a 1989 visit to Easter Island, where he used a stable, low-squat stance to good effect in 12-foot-plus reef waves. Highly regarded in Brazil, Burle was a virtual unknown to the rest of the surf world when he won the 1998 Reef event, held in 20- to 30-foot surf at Mexico's Todos Santos, coming out ahead of Brock Little, Ross Clarke-Jones, and other celebrated big-wave riders. Burle was justifiably upset the following year when he was left off the invite list for the season's two major big-wave events—the Quiksilver in Memory of Eddie Aikau contest at Waimea and the Quiksilver Maverick's Men Who Ride Mountains event—claiming he'd been overlooked because of the international surf industry's bias against Brazilians. Undaunted, the slender-framed Burle (5′8″, 140 pounds) turned in a magnificent series of performances in 1999 and 2000, made the invite list for the 2001 Maverick's contest, and finished third in the 2002 Tow-In World Cup, held at Jaws, in Maui. In April 2002, Burle was announced as the winner of the Nissan Xterra XXL Big Surf Awards for having ridden the largest photographed wave of the winter season—a Maverick's behemoth measuring 68 feet from trough to crest. He received $50,000 and a new Nissan truck. In early 2003, Burle broke his hip while tow-surfing Jaws, on Maui. Burle has appeared in a small number of surf videos, including *Players* (1995), *The Reef at Todos Santos* (1998), and *Whipped* (2001). He's married and has one child, and has lived in Rio de Janeiro since 1990.

Burleigh Heads   Gleaming right-breaking Australian point wave located on the subtropical Gold Coast of Queensland, set against a picturesque lava-rock headland; a high-performance wonder, famous for its long, spinning tubes, with a reputation for producing some of the world's best surfers. Burleigh Heads is generally best during the Coral Sea cyclone season (December–March), but the Down Under winter months (May–August) can produce bigger waves along with steady offshore winds. Average daytime air temperatures at Burleigh range from 80 in summer to 60 in winter; water temperatures range from the high 60s to the high 70s. The wave at Burleigh is

Burleigh Heads

dependent on sand flowing out of the nearby Talle-budgera River, which is then sculpted by prevailing south swells into what is often a long and perfectly tapered sandbar in the lee of the headland. Burleigh is generally better on lower tides. The wave has two primary sections that can link together: the Cove is a long, tubing, often segmented wall that runs into the Point, which is equally hollow and slightly better defined. (Sharkies, a third Burleigh break located beyond the Cove, offers a shorter and less organized right; Rockbreak, inside of the Point, can show form when the surf is smaller.) The aquamarine Burleigh barrels, as Australian journalist Laurie McGinness noted, will sometimes allow a surfer to "spend so much time in the tube that it becomes hard to separate the memory into individual waves." The surf here can be taxing, however, as the rider has to first navigate a boulder-lined entry point, then battle a fierce north-running current, and vie for waves with an aggressive local crowd that can number up to 150. Burleigh is often spoken of in tandem with Kirra, the faster, hollower, less-consistent point located eight miles to the south.

Gold Coast lifeguards were riding the nearby beachbreaks as early as the 1920s, but Burleigh's advanced-level surf remained empty until 1958, when brothers Hugh and John McMaster visited from Brisbane and were able to handle the fast point waves. Ten years later Burleigh was home break to some of Australia's best surfers, including national champions Keith Paull, Peter Drouyn, and Paul Neilsen, and the standard only improved in the '70s, as Burleigh riders Peter Townend and Wayne Bartholomew both went on to win world championships. Other international-caliber Burleigh surfers from the period included two-time national champion Michael Peterson, Peter Harris, Richard Harvey, Tony Eltherington, Joe Engel, Guy Omerod, and Thorton Fallander.

The Burleigh Festival of Boards, a single-day club competition held in 1965—the same year the Burleigh Heads Boardriders Club was formed—was the break's first surfing event. Burleigh hosted the Australian National Titles in 1974 and the World Amateur Surfing Championships in 1982. The Stubbies Pro, however, would be the contest most closely associated with Burleigh. Conceived by local pro surfer Peter Drouyn and making its debut in 1977, the Stubbies was the first contest to use a man-on-man format, and is regarded as the prototype event for today's international pro circuit. Surf for the debut Stubbies was five foot and perfect, and local ace Michael Peterson emerged from an early retirement to beat a hot international field. The Stubbies ran continuously until 1986; winners included world champions Tom Curren, Margo Oberg, Tom Carroll, and Damien Hardman.

As of 2003, Burleigh was home to five surf shops, the Burleigh Heads Boardriders Club, Surfing Queensland (the state-wide governing body for amateur surfing), and the popular *Australia's Surfing Life* magazine. Dozens of amateur and pro contests are held at Burleigh each year, including—conditions permitting—a world circuit event. Top Burleigh riders in the '90s and '00s include pro tour standouts Michael Barry, Dean Morrison, and David Rastovich, and world title contenders Mick Fanning and Joel Parkinson. Burleigh was cited as one of the 25 best waves in the world by *Surfing* magazine in 1989, and has been featured in dozens of films and videos over the decades, including *The Hot Generation* (1967), *Fluid Drive* (1974), *Storm Riders* (1982), *Cyclone Fever* (1994), and *Bells 2 Burleigh* (2001). *See also* Gold Coast, Queensland.

Burma   *See* Myanmar.

Burness, Michael   Quiet, ectomorphic goofyfooter from Durban, South Africa; world-ranked #7 in 1985. Michael Burness, the soon of contest organizer Peter Burness, began surfing at Durban's Bay of Plenty in 1970 at age eight. His pro career was put on hold in 1981, as he completed his mandatory two-year army service, which Burness claimed helped him on the

world tour. "Kids start out on the circuit, and think they're a big deal. The army will wake you up from that, quickly." Burness was a light (6', 140 pounds), fast, flowing surfer; he never won a world tour contest, but consistently made the quarterfinals. He was nonetheless a virtually invisible pro. Not once did he appear in an American- or Australian-made surf movie or video, and at the end of the 1986 season, surf journalist Derek Hynd, in his annual review of the ratings leaders, could say little about Burness's season except to note that "he holds the current pro circuit record for a steady, faithful relationship while touring this defiled, AIDS-infested globe with a circus of marauding, sexual animals. Future world title: No chance." Fearful of big waves, Burness pulled out of the 1986 Hawaiian Triple Crown, the only top-rated surfer to do so that year.

Burness, Peter   Contest director and organizer; sometimes referred to as "the father of South African surfing." Burness was born (1928) in Cape Town, and began riding waves in Durban at age 20 on a wooden surf-ski. His father owned a timber company, which Burness eventually took over, but surfing—along with surfing competitions and organizations—was the main focus of his life. He became secretary of the Natal Surfriders Association in 1966, and four years later was named director of the Gunston 500 pro competition—a post he held until his death in 1999. Burness also helped create the International Professional Surfers circuit in the mid-'70s. John Burness, Peter's older son, was South Africa's juniors champion in 1977; Michael Burness, his younger son, was world-ranked #7 in 1985. *See also* Gunston 500.

Burridge, Pam   Warm and articulate Australian pro surfer originally from Sydney's Manly Beach; world champion in 1990; described by *Surfer* magazine in 1999 as the "Mother Superior of women's surfing." Burridge was born (1965) and raised in Sydney, the daughter of a computer programmer father who became a competitive marathoner; Donella Burridge, Pam's older sister, swam in the 1984 Olympics. Pam began surfing at age 10, and turned pro at 15, just after winning the Australian National Titles, and finished her world tour rookie season rated fifth. She dropped out of high school the following year to concentrate on the circuit and finished runner-up to California's Debbie Beacham. Her basic surfing style wouldn't change much over the years: smooth,

Pam Burridge

wrote. Burridge in fact went on to her worst showing of her career, finishing seventh in 1987, then bounced back to runner-up for the next two seasons.

By the end of 1989, Burridge was living with surfboard shaper Mark Rabbidge, 15 years her senior and the #3-rated longboarder in the world. Going into the 1990 season, Rabbidge helped Burridge with her boards, technique, and strategy. He also served as agent–manager, screening phone calls and booking plane tickets, car rentals, and hotel reservations. Burridge had lost her major sponsors, and at one point Rabbidge sold his car to pay for her airfare to a contest in California. But the effort paid off. Burridge was runner-up in the season opener, won two events during the middle of the schedule, and had a slim lead going into the final event, at Sunset Beach in Hawaii—just as she had in 1986. But this time she seemed inspired by the challenge, rather than cowed, and in powerful 12-foot surf she convincingly won both the contest and the world title. Burridge finished runner-up twice over the next three seasons, retired for three years, came back to finish third in 1997, then retired for good at the end of 1998, with 20 total world tour contest wins. She'd been ranked in the top eight for 15 seasons, a pro circuit record.

Burridge's place in surfing had meanwhile become bigger than her contest results. She'd played with her image over the years, first coming into public view as a teenage surfing tomboy, then going from a spiky tangerine-haired punker to sultry diamond-wearing sex kitten to rural country gal. She caused a minor national sensation in 1984 after singing lead on "Summertime All 'Round the World," a song recorded, Burridge said, "as a bit of a joke" with her rock musician boyfriend. "Summertime" earned Burridge mainstream press coverage in *People* and *Count Down* magazines—even through it sold fewer than 500 copies, and she never once performed the song in public.

Burridge had also developed problems with drinking and anorexia, and in 1985, according to her 1992 biography, was "suicidally depressed for about six months." Rabbidge, himself a former alcoholic, steered her into a 12-step program. Surfing itself was part of the problem. "It's so conducive to self-centeredness," Burridge said, "which is essential to addiction."

Burridge and Rabbidge were married in 1993, and the following year they moved to Bendalong, a semi-rural town 100 miles south of Sydney. Burridge was

strong, deliberate turns, performed out of an easy, almost laconic stance.

Australian men had won six of seven world titles since the formation of the world tour in 1976, but Australian women had so far come up empty-handed, and Burridge was designated by the national magazines and newspapers, along with the surf press, as the champion-in-waiting. But year after year she came up short, and from 1983 to 1986 she finished, in order, third, third, third, and second—the last result was a heartbreaker, as she led the ratings going into the final event of the season, but was eliminated in the first round. The contest-obsessed Australian surf press had by this time grown impatient, even surly, with Burridge. "She's never been as fit as she should and always crumbles under pressure," reporter John Elliss wrote in a 1987 *Tracks* magazine cover story. Burridge said she was ready for the next season—she'd finished runner-up the year before, after all—but Elliss wasn't buying. "It's hard not to be skeptical when she says she's going to do it properly this time," he

inducted into the Sport Australia Hall of Fame in 1996 and the Australian Surfing Hall of Fame in 1997. Burridge and Rabbidge today run Feisty Girl Surfboards and Mark Rabbidge Shapes and Designs. They have two children. Burridge has appeared in more than a dozen surf movies, videos, and documentaries, including *Gripping Stuff* (1987) *Oz on Fire* (1991), and *Surfer Girl* (1994). *Pam Burridge: A Biography* was published in 1992.

Burrow, Taj   Lightning-fast regularfoot pro surfer from Yallingup, Western Australia; world-ranked #2 in 2000, and reportedly one of Australia's top-paid athletes as of 2002. Burrow was born (1978) and raised in Busselton, Western Australia, the only child of two New Age surfers originally from San Diego, California, and began surfing at age seven. At nine he entered and won a local contest for surfers 18 and under; at 16 he was the national juniors division champion; at 17 he won the prestigious Pro Junior. Burrow earned a coveted slot on the 1997 world pro circuit, which he turned down—the first and only surfer to do so—claiming that at 17, he was "too young to do the tour full-on." The slender (5'9", 140-pound) white-blond Australian had by that time distinguished himself as one of the world's most exciting surfers, matching an electrifying aerial repertoire with impossibly cool-handed tuberiding skills, and directing all maneuvers out of a smooth, low, pleasingly aerodynamic stance.

Taj Burrow

Burrow easily qualified for the 1998 world tour, and earned rookie-of-the-year honors on his way to a #12 year-end finish. The following season he won his first two world tour events (the Coke Surf Classic in Sydney and the Rio Marathon in Brazil) and finished the year runner-up to fellow Australian Mark Occhilupo. Burrow dropped to sixth in 2000, then faltered badly in 2001, finishing 35th in a contest season reduced to five events after the 9/11 terrorist attacks. "At 23," surf journalist Matt George wrote, "he's bone tired. His surfing is still electric, but the current is irregular, and fuses blow all the time." In November 2001, however, Burrow signed a six-year contract with surfwear giant Billabong thought to be worth $650,000 a year. Added to his other sponsorship deals—along with sales from a Taj Burrow surfing action figure, a diary-style book, and surf contest prize money—Burrow had become one of Australia's best-paid athletes, bringing in an estimated $1 million a year. He made a return to competitive form in 2002, winning a world tour event in Brazil, and finishing #4 in the final standings.

Burrow is the subject of two sponsor-financed video documentaries, *Sabataj* (2000) and *Montaj* (2001), and has been featured in more than two dozen other surf videos, including *The Show* (1996), *Hit and Run* (2000), and *Pickled: The Movie* (2001). Burrow is unmarried, and lives in a house across the street from his parents.

Byrne, Allan   Mustachioed surfer and surfboard shaper originally from New Zealand; an eight-time national champion in the 1960s and '70s; later described as "the guru of the channel bottom" for his mastery of the difficult-to-make water-directing surfboard design. Byrne was born (1950) in Hamilton, New Zealand, began surfing at age 10, and shaping at 18. He won the New Zealand juniors division national title in 1966, and both the men's and juniors in 1967, and went on to take five more national titles. He competed in the World Surfing Championships in 1966, 1968, and 1970; in 1981, at age 31, the goofy-footed Byrne finished runner-up to fellow board-maker Simon Anderson in Hawaii's Pipeline Masters contest. Byrne moved in 1977 to the Gold Coast of Queensland, Australia, and later founded his Byrning Spears surfboard label. Australian surf icons Wayne Bartholomew and Gary Elkerton were devoted to Byrne's big-wave boards, which featured a wicked-looking, deeply hewn, six-channel bottom feature, designed to increase speed and traction. *See also* channel bottom.

Byrne, Chris "Critta"   Rambunctious Australian pro surfer, world-ranked #8 in 1980. Byrne was born (1960) and raised in Wollongong, New South Wales; by the time he turned pro in 1977—just after winning the juniors division of the Australian National Titles— his older brother Phil had become one of Australia's best-known surfboard shapers. Surf magazines labeled Byrne and future two-time world champion Tom Carroll the "Australian Aggronauts," for their aggressive, even pushy, mode of attack, on land and water. Byrne was originally the more photogenic of the two, zapping across waves in a low, streamlined, widespread stance. He was world-ranked #15 after the 1978 tour, then finished ninth and eighth over the next two seasons. In early 1981, Byrne discovered that he had a cracked vertebra from a horse-riding accident eight years earlier, and after surgery was put in a full-body fiberglass cast for several months. Byrne would surf again, but not as a potential world-beater. He appeared in a few surf movies, including *Free Ride* (1977), *Fantasea* (1978), and *Storm Riders* (1982).

Byrne, Phil   Accomplished and persevering surfboard shaper from Wollongong, New South Wales, Australia; best known as the main board supplier for two-time world champion Tom Carroll. Byrne was born (1952) and raised in Wollongong, began surfing at age 12 and shaping surfboards five years later. After receiving a B.A. in commerce from the University of New South Wales, Byrne began working as a professional shaper, and in 1975 opened Byrne Surfboards with younger brother Dave. The new label was immediately popular, and soon supported by a red-hot stable of team riders including Chris "Critta" Byrne (youngest of the three siblings, national juniors division champion in 1977) and most notably Tom Carroll (world champion in 1983 and 1984), as well as surf icons Shaun Tomson and Larry Bertlemann. Byrne was one of the first Australian shapers to make refinements on the tri-fin surfboard, not long after its introduction in 1981 by surfer/shaper Simon Anderson, also of Australia. Byrne's boards, like Anderson's, were favored by power surfers who required steady, wave-gripping equipment.

Byron Bay   Bucolic Australian resort town located 500 miles north of Sydney on the wave-rich North Coast of New South Wales; home to several first-rate sand-bottomed surf breaks, and a proving ground for the late-'60s shortboard revolution. Cape Byron is the easternmost point on the Australian continent and divides the town's eight-mile coast into two distinct surf zones. The north-facing beaches include the Wreck, a two-way peak just steps away from downtown Byron, and the Pass, a beautifully tapered right wave that can spin along for up to 300 yards. The southeast-facing beaches include the dependable aquamarine peaks of Tallows, the only Byron break protected from the dreaded summertime northeast winds, and the beautifully transparent right-breaking tubes of Broken Head. While Byron has surf all year, the best waves generally arrive between April and October, as South Pacific storms broadcast dependable three- to four-foot swells, along with the occasional six- to eight-footer. December-to-March cyclone storms can produce good waves as well. Average daytime air temperatures in Byron range from the upper 60s in winter to the mid-80s in summer. Water temperatures range from the low 60s to the low 70s. Hazards include sharks—local surfer Marty Ford was killed by a bronze whale shark at Tallows in 1982— and bluebottle jellyfish.

The Byron Bay surf was first ridden in the late '20s by local surf lifesaving club members, and was rediscovered in the late '50s by locals Semi Gilmore, Max von Pendergast, and Keith Anderson. American surf filmmaker Bruce Brown gave Byron its first international exposure by filming Phil Edwards and Paul Witzig at the Pass for his 1962 release *Surfing Hollow Days*. In the late '60s, Queensland shaper Bob McTavish and 1966 world champion Nat Young of Sydney were among a small group of Australians who used the Pass—and other nearby waves, including Broken Head and Lennox Head—as a test track for the new shorter/lighter board designs. By the early '70s, Byron had become the hub of Australian surfing's short but influential back-to-nature "country soul" movement, an era beautifully captured in Alby Falzon's 1972 surf movie classic *Morning of the Earth*.

The Byron Bay Surfing Championships debuted in 1963, the Bay Area Surf Shop opened the following year, and the Bay Area Boardriders Club was founded in 1972. The Byron Bay Easter Classic surf contest debuted in 1976 (with the juniors division won by local soon-to-be-pro ace Gary Timperley), and remains a cherished local event. The Byron surf, and the area's lush rustic ambience, continued to attract surfers, many of whom took up residence, and by 1988 it had become, as Australian surf journalist Terry Willcocks noted, "a veritable little surf city. By nine in the morning, just about every shopkeeper in town will know where the waves are happening." As of 2003, Byron Bay (population 24,000) was home to 18 surf shops, 12 learn-to-surf camps, and two surf clubs. Top Byron surfers include pros Danny Wills, Kieren Perrow, and Brenden Margieson. The Byron-area surf is detailed in a number of books, including *The Surfing and Sailboarding Guide to Australia* (1993) and Mark Warren's *Atlas of Australian Surfing* (1998), and is featured in more than two dozen surf films and videos, including *The Hot Generation* (1967), *Sultans of Speed* (1987), and *Gestation* (2000), an all-Byron video. *See also* North Coast, New South Wales.

Bystrom, Chris Prolific surf movie- and video-maker from Queensland, Australia. Bystrom grew up in Redondo Beach, California, began surfing in 1968, at age 18, and released his first surf movie in 1977, the 8-millimeter *Room to Move.* He would eventually have 29 movie or video titles to his credit, a surf world record, including *Blazing Boards* (1984), *Madmen, Saints and Sinners* (1992), and *Longboarding Is Not a Crime* (1996). Bystrom moved to Australia in 1985, and much of his work in the '90s focused on longboarding. He founded the quarterly *Pacific Longboarder* magazine in 1996, and three years later edited and published a coffee-table book titled *The Glide: Longboarding and the Renaissance of Modern Surfing.* In 2000 he opened the Retro Groove surf shop/museum/art gallery in Queensland's Gold Coast. Bystrom had a long history of feuding with surf magazine editors, and in 1993, following a negative review for his latest video, he sent a letter to *Australia's Surfing Life* describing the reviewer as a "purse-carrying nancy boy," and labeling the review itself as "the slimiest piece of yellow journalism ever published in an Australian surf magazine." Bystrom was killed in a car accident near his home in May 2001; he was 51.

C

Cabell, Joey   Cool-handed regularfooter from Honolulu, Hawaii; arguably the finest all-around surfer of the '60s, and certainly the decade's best in international competition; cofounder of the Chart House steak and seafood restaurant chain. "He's Mr. Perfect," California surfer Mickey Muñoz said of Cabell. "Everything he does, he does well." Cabell was born (1938) and raised in Honolulu, and began surfing at age seven. By the late '50s he'd become a surfer of unmatched range and polish, able to ride with great panache in waves from two to 25 feet. He studied the moves and countermoves of surfing competition as if it were chess, and won easily, unemotionally. In 1963 he placed first in both the Makaha International, held in booming 15-footers, as well as the Malibu Invitational, where the waves were barely waist-high. The following year he was runner-up in the United States Surfing Association final standings and also finished third in the World Surfing Championships—denied the win because he ignored a newly installed "sportsmanship" rule by riding in front of other competitors. Cabell then spent two years in Colorado. In 1967 he returned to surf competition and won at Makaha; in 1968 he won the Peru International, and defended his Makaha title; in 1969 he won the Duke Kahanamoku Invitational; in 1970 and 1971 he was invited to the Expression Session contests.

Cabell and partner Buzzy Bent opened the first Chart House restaurant in 1962 in Aspen, and it was an instant success. Branches soon appeared in Redondo Beach, Newport Beach, and Honolulu. Cabell created the Chart House ambience, selecting the menu items, designing the wood-paneled decor, and dressing the staff in brightly colored aloha shirts. The Chart House became a kind of surfing institution, as generations of Californian and Hawaiian surfers took jobs there as waiters or bartenders, so as to free up daylight hours for surfing. A sequence of Redondo Breakwater in John Severson's 1970 surf movie *Pacific Vibrations* is shot from the low-lit interior of the beachfront Redondo Chart House. Cabell sold his interest in the chain—but retained ownership of the Honolulu Chart House—in the early '70s.

Cabell's interest in the restaurant business faded in part because of his involvement with the late-'60s shortboard revolution, as boards were transformed from bulky 10-footers to sleek seven-footers. In 1968, at the relatively advanced age of 30, Cabell became one of the shortboard movement's key figures, putting forth his "speed surfing" theory, wherein the surfer rides in a crouch with his feet and knees together, seeking out the fastest line across the wave. Cabell himself, riding a pointy 8′3″ homemade board called the White Ghost, seemed to be riding faster than any surfer alive. Speed surfing was a forgotten concept by 1971—surfers opened their stance and simply ran the new equipment all over the place on the wave—and Cabell didn't have any direct heirs to his style of riding. But he'd done his part for the shortboard movement, and for a time established himself as a kind of surfing demigod. "He is a leader," Pipeline surfer Gerry Lopez said in 1970, by which time Cabell had grown a full Moses-like beard, "whose followers seldom realize they're being led."

Cabell appeared in more than a dozen surf movies, including *Surf Safari* (1959), *Strictly Hot*

Joey Cabell

(1964), *Evolution* (1969), and *Forgotten Island of Santosha* (1974). He was named to *Surf Guide* magazine's First All-American Surfing Team in 1963; the following year the California state legislature drew a one-page resolution congratulating Cabell following his 1963 Makaha win. In 1985, *Surfer* magazine named him as one of "25 Surfers Whose Surfing Changed the Sport." Cabell has been married twice and has three children. His oldest daughter, Raina, is married to 2000 world professional surfing champion Sunny Garcia.

Cabo San Lucas   Dry, hilly, cactus-filled region located at the tip of Baja California, Mexico; packed on one end with hotels, resorts, and restaurants; fringed throughout with a generous assortment of warm-water surf breaks. As it appears on a map, the overdeveloped resort town of Cabo San Lucas is found on Baja's southwest corner; as defined in the surf world, "Cabo" refers to a roughly 50-mile, 20-surf-break stretch of coastline beginning at Cabo San Lucas and extending northeast, past the town of San Jose del Cabo and into the mouth of the Gulf of California. Cabo receives its best waves—generally ranging from three to six feet—during the June-to-October North Pacific hurricane season; long-distance swells also roll in occasionally from South Pacific storms. With the notable exception of the Estuary, a tubing San Jose del Cabo beachbreak, Cabo surf spots are almost exclusively beginner- and intermediate-level pointbreaks and reefbreaks. Zippers and Shipwrecks are the area's best-known surf spots (Zippers, located just off the highway in San Jose del Cabo, is also far and away the most crowded, with territorial locals sometimes harassing visiting Americans); while Boca del Tule and Punta Perfecto, to the northeast, on rare occasions produce exquisite high-performance waves. The daytime summer air temperature is often in the upper 90s or low 100s; the water temperature can reach 80.

California surfer Steve Bigler flew into San Jose del Cabo to shoot footage for *Golden Breed,* a 1968 surf film, but it was years before the area became popular with surfers. In "The Tip," a 1980 *Surfer* magazine photo feature, Cabo is presented as a near-virgin surf destination. By the mid-'80s, however, it had earned a reputation among American surfers for consistently fun waves and for the consistently raucous Cabo San Lucas *tourista* nightlife. Representatives from the California-based Surf Industry Manufacturers Associ-

ation have traveled to Cabo since 1998 for an annual weekend-long seminar and booze-up. Regional and American-sponsored surf contests have been held here as well, most notably the 1991 Fletcher Los Cabos Classic, won by six-time world champion Kelly Slater, and the 2002 World Longboard Championships, won by Colin McPhillips. Cabo is featured in a small number of surf films, including *Surf Hits,* vol. 1 (1989), *Surfers: The Movie* (1990), and *Powerglide* (1995). A few notable American surfers have retired in Cabo, including big-wave pioneer Pat Curren and 1968 Duke Kahanamoku Invitational winner Mike Doyle. *See also* Baja California, Mexico.

Cairns, Ian   Commanding surfer and surf contest organizer/promoter from Perth, Western Australia; world-ranked #2 in 1976; founder of the Association of Surfing Professionals. "He's a strong-minded son of a bitch," fellow Australian and 1978 world champion Wayne Bartholomew once said of Cairns, "a brilliant politician, and an absolute monster in big surf." Cairns was born (1952) in Kew, Victoria, the son of a mechanical engineer. He was raised in Melbourne and Sydney, and began surfing at age 12, a few months before moving with his family to Perth, where he soon earned a reputation for charging fearlessly into the powerful reef waves in and around Margaret River. Cairns won six Western Australia state titles, three in the juniors division (1967–69), three in the men's (1970–72); in 1970 and 1972 he competed in the World Surfing Championships.

Cairns was Australia's most successful first-generation international pro surfer, and did especially well in Hawaii: he won the 1973 Smirnoff Pro and placed third in the Hang Ten American Pro; in 1974 he was runner-up in the Duke Kahanamoku Classic; in 1975 he won the Duke (held in 25-foot surf at Waimea Bay) and placed second in the Smirnoff. Cairns was cofounder of the Australian Professional Surfing Association (APSA) in 1975, which consolidated the nascent Australian pro events into a domestic circuit; the following year he won the APSA tour and finished runner-up to fellow Aussie Peter Townend in the International Professional Surfers (IPS) circuit—the newly formed world tour created by Hawaiians Fred Hemmings and Randy Rarick, with input from Cairns and Townend. By the end of 1976, the two Australian surf champions had become cofounders and business partners in the Bronzed Aussies, a swaggering and often-ridiculed surfing

Ian Cairns

promotions group best remembered for the matching black velvet jumpsuits Cairns and Townend wore to contest banquets in 1977 and 1978.

Cairns was regarded, along with Hawaii's Barry Kanaiaupuni, as the world's premier power surfer. Riding from the tail of his board in a plain upright stance, the rangy and well-muscled Australian regularfooter (6'2", 190 pounds) carved trenchlike turns at favorite breaks such as Sunset Beach and Haleiwa in Hawaii. "I've got such a powerful bottom turn it's berserk," the steely-eyed surfer once said. "It even surprises *me* sometimes." He competed on the pro tour into the early '80s, never again finishing in the year-end top 10, but winning the 1977 World Cup, the 1978 Pro Class Trials, and the 1980 World Cup, all held in Hawaii. He meanwhile gained a reputation as an articulate and passionate supporter of professional surfing, contributing as much as anybody to the form's original structure, while sometimes alienating himself to rank-and-file surfers with quotes like "Competition is the essence of surfing." Cairns was also considered a turncoat by flag-waving Australians following his move to Huntington Beach, California, in 1979. Along with Peter Townend, who also moved to Huntington Beach, Cairns further aligned himself with American surfing by signing on as the head coach for the National Scholastic Surfing Associa-

tion, and helping the group's top surfers to victory in both the 1980 and 1984 World Amateur Surfing Championships.

Backed by California-based surfwear giant Ocean Pacific, Cairns led a successful revolt in 1982 to overthrow the IPS and replace it with the Association of Surfing Professionals (ASP), with Cairns serving as executive director. Cairns and Ocean Pacific had one year earlier debuted the Op Pro, America's biggest and richest surf contest, in Huntington Beach. Cairns resigned from the ASP in 1986 and moved back to Western Australia after spectators rioted and looted during the final day of that year's Op Pro. He returned to Southern California in 1991 and again worked as a contest organizer, first as executive director of the Professional Surfing Association of America and of ASP North America, then as founder of the U.S. Open of Surfing in Huntington, and owner of U.S. Surfing. He also branched out into surf media (as executive producer of *Surf the Planet,* a 26-part Fox TV cable series, and as founding shareholder in Broadband Interactive Group, or BIG) and sports promotions (as founder of Beach Games). Cairns became president of BIG in 2002, overseeing the Gotcha surfwear label, as well as the teen-oriented Bluetorch media company.

Cairns was inducted into the Western Australian Sporting Hall of Fame in 1985 and the Australian Surfing Hall of Fame in 1993. He appeared in more than two dozen surf movies, including *Splashdown* (1969), *Fluid Drive* (1974), *Free Ride* (1977), and *Wizards of the Water* (1982); he also worked as a stunt surfer for Gary Busey in Warner Brothers' 1978 surf epic *Big Wednesday.* Cairns has lived in Laguna Beach, California, since 1991. He's been married twice—the second time to Alisa Schwarzstein, a member of the Cairns-led NSSA National Team, and women's world amateur champion in 1980—and has four children. *See also* Association of Surfing Professionals, Australian Professional Surfing Association, Beachcomber Bills Grand Prix, Bronzed Aussies, International Professional Surfers, National Scholastic Surfing Association, professional surfing.

Calhoun, Marge Cheerful, robust regularfooter from Laguna Beach, California; winner of the Makaha International in 1958, and matriarch of the surfing Calhoun family. Marge Booth was born (1926) and raised in Hollywood, California, the daughter of a film set designer. She gave birth to her first daughter, Candy, in 1945, married her high school sweetheart Tom Calhoun in 1946, had second daughter Robin in 1947, and began surfing at Malibu in 1955, with instruction from Darrylin Zanuck, daughter of Hollywood mogul Darryl Zanuck. Calhoun visited Hawaii for the first time in 1958, where she lived for a month out of a panel van with surfing friend Eve Fletcher, and earned a reputation for charging into larger waves. "I was a big, strong woman," she later recalled, "and I was always good in big surf." While in Hawaii, the 32-year-old Calhoun won the Makaha International, then the surf world's most prestigious event.

Calhoun and her two daughters were beaming surf world fixtures in California and Hawaii during the early and mid-'60s. Marge was the first secretary of the 1961-formed United States Surfing Association, and was the organization's first and only female surf contest judge; Marge and Candy finished second and fourth, respectively, in the 1962 Makaha contest; the following year Robin placed third in the annual Brooks Street Surf Classic surfing contest in Laguna Beach, while Candy won the West Coast Surfing Championships; Candy and Marge were both selected for *Surf Guide* magazine's All-American Surfing Team in 1963; Candy placed third in the 1965 World Championships. Candy also became a top bodysurfer, and was the first woman to ride both the Newport Wedge and Pipeline. The Calhouns were all beautiful and athletic, with sun-streaked hair and radiant smiles, and were often celebrated as the feminine surfing ideal: the debut issue of *Petersen's Surfing* magazine in 1963 featured a centerspread photo of Marge, Candy, and Robin, walking merrily down the beach at Makaha with surfboards; the cover of the December 1964 issue of *Surf Guide* shows the Calhouns shoulder-to-shoulder in the ready area of the U.S. Championships at Huntington Beach. "They were like Greek goddesses," California surf icon Mike Doyle recalled. "Each one beautiful. And together, they were just . . . overwhelming."

Marge Calhoun worked part-time as a stuntwoman in the '50s and early '60s, appearing in Frank Capra's *Hole in the Head* (1959), among other movies. In 1967, she was married for the second time, to popular surf event master of ceremonies Brennan "Hevs" McClelland. Calhoun was featured in surf moviemaker Bud Browne's films from the late '50s, as well as his 1994 compilation video *Surfing the '50s*. She also appeared in the PBS-aired documentary *Surf-ing for Life* (1999), and was profiled in *Girl in the Curl: A Century of Women in Surfing,* published in 2000.

California   While Hawaii is the birthplace of surfing, California has for better and worse been the center of the surfing world since the mid-20th century. It is the design and manufacturing headquarters for surfboards, wetsuits, beachwear, surf entertainment/media, and surf forecasting; it has been home to generations of influential surfers, including George Freeth, Tom Blake, Mickey Dora, and Tom Curren. California's 840-mile coastline alternates from urban to suburban to rural, and is visited regularly by sharks, fog, fire, flood, heat waves, and earthquakes, as well as the much-lauded sunshine. Among California's 750,000 surfers (out of two million nationwide) are dedicated competitors, reclusive soul surfers, and dangerous turf-protecting locals; the surfing ambience ranges from the manic commercialization of the Action Sports Retailer trade show in Long Beach to the serene cliff-lined beauty of Big Sur; the surf itself ranges from deadly 40-foot tubes at Maverick's to finely tapered six-foot walls at Malibu to gently sloped two-foot rollers at San Onofre.

Point Conception marks the geographic and cultural dividing point between the state's two main surfing regions. (Conception itself, home to the wave-rich and privately owned Hollister Ranch, is often said to constitute a third California surfing region.) Southern California is warm, crowded, and topographically rounded, with a surf scene that, to a degree beyond that of anywhere else in the world, is commercially driven. North of Conception the shoreline is colder and more rugged, and far less populated. Bank Wright's 1973 guidebook *Surfing California* lists just over 400 point-, reef-, and beachbreaks from border to border, but a more detailed survey would likely triple that number. (Wright lists two breaks in Marin County, for example; the actual number is closer to 12.) Open to a full range of swell-producing storms in the North and South Pacific, waves are found all year in most regions of California. Malibu and Lower Trestles are among the better-known California spots during south swells, which generally arrive in late summer and early fall; Maverick's and Rincon are among the spots that require north or west swells, which generally arrive from late fall to early spring. Summer coastal air temperatures in the south can reach into the mid-90s; winter air temperatures in the north can drop into the low 30s.

Water temperature, thanks to the North Pacific current, is relatively stable, ranging from the mid-40s to the low 70s.

Surfing was introduced to California in 1885, in Santa Cruz, by three Hawaiian brothers who were attending a nearby boarding school; small numbers of Santa Cruz natives continued to ride waves over the next few years. But the sport didn't really take root in the state until 1907, when Hawaiian-Irishman George Freeth began riding waves at Los Angeles's Venice Beach. Surfer and Olympic gold medal swimmer Duke Kahanamoku, also from Hawaii, helped popularize the sport here beginning in 1915, with the first of a half-dozen visits that included surf stops at a number of Southern California beaches. The annual Pacific Coast Surf Riding Championships, America's first major surfing competition, debuted in 1928, and was won by Tom Blake—the first surfer to ride Malibu (in 1926) and the inventor of the hollow surfboard (1929), as well as the surfboard fin (1935). The Corona del Mar Surfboard Club, the first club of its kind, was formed in the late '20s; the Pacific System Homes company, located in Los Angeles, introduced the mass-produced surfboard in 1930; surfer photographer/dentist John "Doc" Ball published the sport's first photo book, *California Surfriders,* in 1946. Paddleboard Cove, Corona del Mar, and San Onofre were among the favorite surf breaks in California prior to World War II.

After the war, Los Angeles–area board-builders Bob Simmons, Matt Kivlin, and Joe Quigg all contributed to the development of the "Malibu chip," forerunner of today's longboard. In 1950, board-maker Dale Velzy opened in Venice Beach what many regard as the world's first surf shop; the production-line board-making industry was founded three years later with the opening of Hobie Surfboards, a custom-built surfboard factory/showroom located in Dana Point. In San Francisco, Jack O'Neill opened a surf shop in 1952 that carried neoprene wetsuit vests, and by the end of the decade O'Neill, along with the Meistrell brothers at Dive n' Surf in Redondo Beach, had established the fast-growing surfing wetsuit trade. Santa Monica school teacher and former lifeguard Bud Browne debuted the first surf film in 1953, screening his homemade *Hawaiian Surfing Movies* in a local junior high school auditorium; three years later, UC Berkeley professor Eugene Burdick released *The Ninth Wave,* the first surfing novel, and Brentwood screenplay writer Frederick Kohner followed the next

year with his best-seller *Gidget.* By the late '50s, Phil Edwards from north San Diego County and Mickey Dora of Los Angeles were the two best surfers in America, and possibly the world; both were smart, funny, and iconoclastic, and embodied perfectly the still-cherished idea that surfing is less a sport and more a grand pursuit and passion. California-born surfers Greg Noll, Rick Grigg, Peter Cole, Fred Van Dyke, and Buzzy Trent were meanwhile doing much of the big-wave pioneering work on the North Shore of Oahu.

Los Angeles, as home to Hollywood-made surf-themed movies (*Gidget, Ride the Wild Surf*), as well as surf music acts like the Beach Boys and Jan and Dean, was the font of surf culture in the late '50s and '60s. Former Laguna Beach High School art teacher John Severson founded *Surfer* magazine in 1960, establishing the surf magazine genre; more than a half-dozen other California-based surf magazines debuted over the next five years. In 1964, Dana Point filmmaker Bruce Brown barnstormed his new 16-millimeter surf movie *The Endless Summer* up and down the California coast; two years later he took a 35-millimeter version of the movie into theaters and had a critical and box-office smash hit. Surf music was largely a spent force by 1965, but Hollywood continued with varying degrees of authenticity and success to try its hand at surfing, most notably with *Big Wednesday* (1978), *North Shore* (1987), *In God's Hands* (1998), and *Blue Crush* (2002).

With companies like Hobie Surfboards and Clark Foam leading the way, the California board-making industry exploded during the early and mid-60s, as Jacobs, Weber, Bing, Gordon & Smith, Greg Noll, and other companies sold thousands of boards locally, and shipped thousands more to the East Coast, Gulf Coast, and Hawaii. Meanwhile, the Hang Ten clothing company, formed in 1960 and headquartered in Long Beach, almost single-handedly launched the surfwear industry.

The United States Surfing Association, formed in 1961 and based in Laguna Beach, was the first nationwide surf organization, and helped turn Southern California into the world hub of competitive surfing. California surfers throughout the decade were equal to the best from Australia and Hawaii—the other two surfing power centers—with top riders including Mike Doyle, Joyce Hoffman, Skip Frye, David Nuuhiwa, Linda Benson, Margo Godfrey, Corky Carroll, and Rolf Aurness. Professional surfing was born in

1965 with the KHJ Hermosa contest (winner Denny Tompkins received an MG sedan), and the $1,500 Tom Morey Invitational, held in Ventura. The World Surfing Championships (later renamed the World Surfing Games) were held in California in 1966, 1972, 1984, and 1996.

The late-'60s shortboard revolution badly damaged the state's board-building industry and all but wiped out its competition structure, and the California surf scene as a whole was bleak during the first few years of the '70s. Ocean Pacific nonetheless became the world's largest surfwear company, and California surf filmmakers continued to make popular movies—including MacGillivray/Freeman's *Five Summer Stories* (1972), Bud Browne's *Going Surfin'* (1973), and Bill Delaney's *Free Ride* (1977)—but none of the state's surfers (save Mike Purpus) figured on the international stage, and a sometimes-violent strain of localism flourished from San Diego to Santa Cruz. In 1977, with the first annual Katin Pro-Am Team Challenge, a $10,000 contest held in Huntington Beach, California, began to reintegrate with not only the larger surf community, but with itself.

California surfing boomed in the '80s. The 1981 Instinct Pro at Malibu put the state on the world pro tour schedule for the first time, and in 1982 the debut Op Pro at Huntington Beach introduced the sport to big-market hype and spectacle. Seal Beach surfer Sean Collins, cofounder of Surfline, a pay-per-call phone service, meanwhile helped transform surf forecasting from voodoo magic to a commercially viable art/science. Hugely successful Orange County–based surfwear companies—founded in California, or licensed from Australia or Hawaii—included Quiksilver, Gotcha, Stussy, Billabong, and Maui and Sons; wetsuit companies also thrived; and the 1981-founded Action Sports Retailer trade show in Long Beach became surfing's biggest international wares exhibition and market bazaar, with a second annual event added in San Diego in 1987. The San Clemente–based Surfrider Foundation, launched in 1984, became surfing's first environmental group, and in 1991 Surfrider made national headlines by winning a $6.3 million case against two Humboldt County paper mills.

Graceful Santa Barbara surfer Tom Curren not only won the world title in 1985, 1986, and 1991, but did so in a way that endeared him to both competitive and noncompetitive surfers. (Santa Barbara's Al Merrick, Curren's board-maker, attained a similarly high rank in his field.) Californians Joey Buran, Brad

Gerlach, and Richie Collins all won world tour events during the '80s; Christian Fletcher, by the end of the decade, was the world's premier aerialist; California old school longboard aces Herbie Fletcher, Dale Dobson, and David Nuuhiwa helped spark a renewed interest in longboarding that soon led to a full-scale international revival.

California surf businesses suffered during the nationwide recession in the early '90s, but bounced back stronger than ever by the end of the decade, led by most of the '80s companies, along with newcomers like Reef Brazil, Hurley, Volcom, Oakley, and Black Flies. "Killer Profits in Velcro Valley," a 1999 *Time* magazine article, reported that sales for the Quiksilver company were up to $316 million annually; two years later the publicly traded Quiksilver went over the half-billion-dollar mark. Much of the upswing was attributed to a long overdue rise in women's surfing; California was home to Quiksilver spinoff Roxy, as well as Surf Diva, the first women's surf school, and *Wahine*, the first women's surf magazine. Perhaps the most spectacular surf business development of the period was the creation and implosion of Hardcloud.com and Bluetorch.com, the venture capital–funded surfing Web sites that each spent tens of millions of dollars in 1999 and 2000, before folding. A third site, Swell.com, spent nearly as much, and survived only by hastily transforming itself into a surfing mail-order house. Meanwhile, the post-Curren generation of surfers, including Rob Machado, Tim Curran, Jeff Booth, Shane Beschen, and Taylor Knox, were among the world's best, but had nothing like Curren's influence. By the early '90s, video had helped finish off the already-weak surf movie industry, leaving room for San Diego videographer Taylor Steele to rise as the new king of surf cinema, with his rough-hewn works such as *Momentum* (1992) and *Focus* (1994), which served as templates for hundreds of video titles to follow.

Northern California also began making its presence felt. "Playing Doc's Games," writer William Finnegan's 40,000-word *New Yorker* article on surfer/physician Mark Renneker, was set in San Francisco; Daniel Duane's critically acclaimed memoir *Caught Inside* (1996) took place in Santa Cruz; novelist Kem Nunn's surfing psychodrama *The Dogs of Winter* (1997) was set near the California/Oregon border. Maverick's, the big-wave break located between Santa Cruz and San Francisco, was introduced to the surfing world in 1992, and to the public at large in 1994, when Hawaiian surfer Mark Foo died there during his first visit. More attention was given to Maverick's in 1999, with the debut of the Quiksilver-sponsored Maverick's Men Who Ride Mountains big-wave contest. A group of aggressive young Santa Cruz surfers, having already gained a reputation as first-rate aerialists, were now among with the world's best big-wave riders as well—particularly Peter Mel, Darryl "Flea" Virostko, and Kenny Collins, all of whom made an easy transition from paddle-in surfing at Maverick's to mechanized tow-in surfing. Mel and Collins were both part of a January 19, 2001, expedition to Cortes Banks, a big-wave reefbreak located 100 miles off San Diego, where Mike Parsons rode a wave described as between 40 and 65 feet high. Hawaii had always been the big-wave surfing crucible; attention would now be split between Hawaii and California.

As of 2003, it was estimated that California was home to about 350 surf shops. The California surf is outlined in a number of books, including *Surfing Guide to Southern California* (1963), *Surfing California* (1973), *Southern California's Best Surf* (1989), and *The Stormrider Guide North America* (2002). *See also* Los Angeles, Orange County, the Ranch, San Diego, Santa Cruz.

California Surf Museum   Twelve-hundred-square-foot museum, located on Pacific Coast Highway, directly east of the pier in Oceanside, California. The California Surf Museum was founded in 1987 by librarian Jane Schmauss and architect Stuart Resor, and opened in an Encinitas, California, shopping plaza. An early exhibit was *Iron Men and Wooden Boards,* documenting with period photographs and surfboards the contributions of surfing pioneers Duke Kahanamoku, Tom Blake, and Bob Simmons. The museum moved to San Diego's Pacific Beach in 1988, then to Oceanside in 1991. Six years later the city of Oceanside gave the museum a free 10-year lease. In 2003, the museum had one full-time employee, a volunteer staff, a gift shop, and a Web site; items on display are divided into standing exhibits and one feature exhibit—*It Takes Two to Tandem* and *The Golden Age of Big-Wave Guns* were presented in 2000—which changes every six months. *See also* Bishop Museum, Huntington Beach International Surfing Museum, Santa Cruz Surfing Museum, Surfworld Museum.

California Surfriders   The original surfing photo book, John Heath "Doc" Ball's 108-page *California Surfriders* was first published in 1946, and was made up of Ball's black-and-white photographs accompanied by short captions. "The purpose of this volume," Ball wrote in the book's foreword, "is to present pictorially some of the thrills, spills, personalities and places pertinent to surfriding, which, since its importation from Hawaii in 1907, is now becoming California's favorite saltwater sport." The original press run for *California Surfriders* was 510, and copies of the red-leather-bound book sold for the fairly exorbitant price of $7.25. Ball's photographs—action shots, portraits, and candids, augmented by a few images from other photographers—are grouped by location and presented in geographic order, beginning with Pedro Point, just south of San Francisco, and ending with Windansea in San Diego County. At least a dozen of Ball's *California Surfriders* photographs had already been published, in *Life* magazine or the *Los Angeles Times;* eight of his *Surfriders* photos were featured in "Surf-Boarders Capture California," a 1944 *National Geographic* article. Mountain and Sea Books republished Ball's book in 1978 as *California Surfriders 1946,* and a third edition, *Early California Surfriders,* was released in 1995 by Pacific Publishers. In early 2001, a first edition of *California Surfriders* was sold on an Internet auction site for $2,500. *See also* John "Doc" Ball, books and surfing, surf photography.

Calisch, Rus   Systematic writer/photographer/competition organizer from San Clemente, California; original editor of the 1980-founded *Surf Report,* a subscription-only newsletter published monthly by *Surfer* magazine that carefully mapped out, area by area, most of the world's known breaks. Calisch was born (1945) in Toledo, Ohio, moved to Southern California in 1961, and began surfing two years later in Newport Beach. He was cofounder of the Western Intercollegiate Surfing Council in 1966, president of the UCLA Surf Club in 1967, advertising director for *Surfing* magazine in the early '70s, and an occasional contributing writer/photographer for *Surfer* in the mid-'70s, when he also worked as general manager for surfwear manufacturer Kanvas by Katin. It was Calisch who developed the popular Katin Team Challenge surf contest, held annually in Huntington Beach beginning in 1977; from 1977 to 1979 Calisch was the executive director of the United States Surfing Association; in 1979 he was a founding member of the United States Surfing Federation. Calisch's surfing novel, *Paumalu: A Story of Modern Hawaii,* was published in 1979; the *Surf Report* debuted the following year. In 1992, he started the *Orange County Blade,* a gay and lesbian newsmagazine. A navy officer during the Vietnam War, Calisch was awarded the Bronze Star.

Campbell brothers, Malcolm and Duncan   Low-key surfboard shaper/designers from Southern California; creators of the bonzer design in the early 1970s. Brothers Malcolm and Duncan Campbell were born (1952 and 1955, respectively) in Santa Monica, and began surfing in 1965; the following year they moved with their family to Oxnard, just south of Ventura. In 1968, their father encouraged them to build their own surfboards, and later suggested that they experiment with a three-fin configuration (virtually all boards at the time had one fin); in 1970, the teenagers produced their first tri-fin board, which quickly developed into the bonzer. The Campbells' strange-looking new board made its public debut in 1972: it featured a double-concave bottom, and had two long-base, low-profile keel fins near the rails, set just ahead of a standard single fin. The bonzer didn't catch on, but tri-fins would eventually become a near-universal choice for shortboards, as would bottom concaves. Malcolm, in 1990, recalled the morning he tried the bonzer for the first time, in 1970: "After one wave, I knew we were on to something, and an hour later I knew the single-fin was obsolete as a high-performance vehicle." Malcolm noted also that the "bonzer" name—period Australian slang for "bitchin'"—was their father's idea. Duncan had by that time moved to the North Shore of Oahu and opened a popular café; Malcolm continued making boards in Ventura County. In 1982 they began to develop a five-fin version of the bonzer; updated versions found a niche market in the late '90s and early '00s. *See also* bonzer.

Campbell, Mick   Blunt-talking, freckle-faced pro surfer from Port Macquarie, Australia; world-ranked #2 in 1998. Campbell was born (1974) and raised in the New South Wales town of Port Macquaire, began surfing at age nine, placed fifth in the 1993 Pro Junior contest, and in 1997 was the world pro circuit's rookie of the year. Campbell and good friend Danny Wills were the most physically fit surfers of the late '90s, as both were trained by Sydney rugby drillmaster Rob Rowland-Smith; Campbell used fitness and consistency, rather than inborn surfing genius, to, as surf journalist Derek Hynd put it, "rip every pro off the ladder, one by one." Campbell led the world tour ratings going into the 1998 Pipeline Masters, the final

Mick Campbell

contest of the season, but faltered badly in the second round, scoring a total of 1.9 points and allowing reigning world champion Kelly Slater to pass him for the title. Campbell's temper was on display in the fall of 2000, when an Internet-circulated video clip showed the redhead punching Hawaiian surfer Andy Irons in the face after a man-on-man heat during a competition in France. Earlier, Campbell had signed off on a short questionnaire with *Australia's Surfing Life* magazine by writing, "To all the people who said I wouldn't be anything, teachers, and so-called friends: FUCK YOU! The End." Campbell has appeared in more than a dozen surf videos, including *Sacred Water* (1999), *The Theory* (1999), and *Performers III* (1999). He won the men's division of the 1998 World Surfing Games, held in Portugal.

Canada   Canada, the second-largest country in the world after Russia, in terms of landmass, is fringed with temperamental and isolated surf spots on both the Atlantic and the Pacific, as well as dozens of freshwater breaks in the Great Lakes. Air temperatures along the Canadian east coast and around the Great Lakes drop to 30 degrees below zero during winter and can exceed 70 in summer; water temperatures range from the mid-30s to the upper 60s. Due to the Gulf Stream current, the ocean is warmer along much of the Canadian east coast than it is in New England. West coast air temperatures range from 20 to 70; water temperatures range from the low 40s to the low 60s.

The diverse Canadian surf ranges from minuscule summer beachbreak waves to burly 12-foot rock-reef pounders. Three- to four-foot waves are common throughout the year. Much of the convoluted island- and river-filled Canadian west coast is virtually inaccessible, with dense rainforest extending nearly to the water's edge, and just a few sandy areas. British Columbia's Vancouver Island is the center of Canadian west coast surfing, and Long Beach, located near the town of Tofino, is Vancouver Island's best-known break—not so much for its gentle sand-bottom waves, but for its accessibility and easy parking. Jordan River, a hollow right-breaking wave located inside the Juan de Fuca Strait and favored by territorial local surfers ("slippery black leprechauns," as described by native surf journalist Kevin Brooker), is often cited as Canada's best break. Dozens of other spots along Vancouver Island are accessible only by boat. August through December is the best time to surf on the west coast, as the weather is still relatively warm and the North Pacific begins to regularly produce swell-generating storms.

While the Newfoundland province has an assortment of high-quality but fickle and remote breaks, and is home to a small cadre of dedicated local surfers, central Nova Scotia has long been the hub of east coast Canadian surfing. Prime surf season here lasts from late August to November, as the area pulls in waves created by central Atlantic hurricanes and North Atlantic storms. The Lawrencetown Beach area, located just outside of Halifax, is Nova Scotia's best-known surf zone—which leaves it well short of famous. "Ask your average Bluenoser about surfing here," former Canadian surfing champion Lesley Choyce wrote in a 2000 issue of the *Surfer's Journal,* "and they will tell you with great confidence that nobody surfs in Nova Scotia." Canadian surf hazards include rock reefs and extreme cold on both coasts, and aggressive sea lions and sharks on the west coast. Nova Scotia's Bay of Fundy has the world's largest tidal range, with water levels sometimes changing by as much as 50 feet in less than seven hours.

Surfing in Canada started in 1965 on Vancouver Island's Wreck Bay (later renamed Florencia Bay), after a small group of locals (including Tofino's Jim Sadler) and American expatriates took to the waves using crude homemade boards and scuba wetsuits. Vancouver Island became a semicommunal refuge for draft dodgers and hippies in the late '60s and early '70s, with a few dozen surfers included. Jordan River surfer Jim Van Dame was among the first native board-makers, setting up a backyard operation in the mid-'70s. The Canadian east coast was first surfed in the mid-'70s by American surfers tracking hurricane swells across the border. A small number of surfers eventually settled in the Lawrencetown area. Surfing was introduced to the Canadian side of the Great Lakes in 1966, at Wyldewood Beach, Ontario. The surf press all but ignored Canada until 1988, when *Surfer* magazine published an article on Nova Scotia; the first Canadian west coast feature was published in 1994. The Canadian Surfing Contest debuted in 1966, at Long Beach, but competition wasn't really part of the surf scene here until the late '80s. Westbeach, Canada's first surf shop, opened in Vancouver in 1979.

By 2003, there were roughly 15 surf shops in Vancouver and eight in Nova Scotia, surf schools on both coasts, and about 10,000 surfers (less than 1,000 of them all-year riders) across the country. The all-Canadian *Island Swell* magazine was founded in 1992, changed its name to *Northern Swell* in 1994, and became an Internet-only publication the following year. Top Canadian surfers include the Bruhwiler brothers, Raph and Sepp, of Vancouver, and Nova Scotia's Stevie Marsh. Regional and/or national surf contests are organized by the Canadian Surfing Association and the Surfing Association of Nova Scotia, both founded in 1989, along with the 1992-founded British Columbia Surfing Association and the 1966-founded Great Lakes Surfing Association. *5mm Canada* (2000) and *Numb* (2002) were the first two internationally distributed surf videos to feature Canadian waves and surfers exclusively. The Canadian surf is detailed in *The Stormrider Guide North America* (2002). *See also* Great Lakes, Vancouver Island.

Canary Islands   String of 13 Spanish-held volcanic islands located in the Atlantic Ocean about 60 miles west of Morocco; sometimes called "the Hawaii of the Atlantic." While the western Canary islands have some vegetation and cultivation, the geologically younger eastern islands of Lanzarote and Fuerteventura—the region's best surf destinations—are nearly lunar in appearance, with just a few gray-green shrubs dotting the cracked fields of dried lava. The eastern Canaries produce consistent, frequently hollow waves of all sizes, and the easternmost island of Lanzarote has become a favorite destination for European surfers, particularly the British. Summertime brings surf to the south and east coasts, while bigger winter swells hit the north- and west-facing coasts. Though not as consistent as the eastern islands, especially during the summer months, the western islands of Gran Canaria and Tenerife also receive high-quality surf. Poor road access across the Canaries means that dozens of breaks go unridden, but surf spots in well-populated Gran Canaria, as well as Lanzarote, often get crowded, and local surfers now sometimes gang up to prevent visitors from catching waves. Daytime coastal temperatures in the Canaries average between 75 and 85; water temperatures range from 65 to 72. Sirocco winds from the African mainland sometimes dust the Canaries with powdery sand from the Sahara.

Surfer magazine travel correspondent Ian Harwood wrote in 1969 about the cheap living and the powerful, well-shaped, empty waves he'd discovered on Gran Canaria Island. More surfers followed, including Raul Dordal, one of the first wave-riders from the Basque region of Spain, who moved to the Canaries in the early '70s and became an integral part of the budding Tenerife surf scene. Aloha Surf, the islands' first surf shop, opened on Tenerife in 1980. By 2003, the Canaries were home to about 12 surf shops, five surf camps or schools, and 15,000 surfers. The 1999 World Longboard Championships, won by California surfer Joel Tudor, were held on Fuerteventura. World Qualifying Tour pro events have been held in the Canaries since 2001. The Canary Islands' surf is featured in a small number of surf videos, including *The Seedling* (1999), *Atlantic Moon* (1999), and *Imagine: Surfing to Sadhama* (2000), and detailed in the *Stormrider Guide Europe* (1998).

Canha, Conrad   Bandy-legged surfer from Hawaii; winner of the 1956 Makaha International; an original hotdogger in the mid- and late '50s, and sometimes additionally credited as the sport's first tuberider. Canha was born (1932) and raised in Puunene, Maui, moved with his family to Oahu, and began surfing at age 15 in Waikiki. He became a regular at Makaha in the early '50s, riding an all-black balsa surfboard. After winning the 1956 Makaha International, he

traveled to South America and won the 1957 Peru International, taking out both the small- and big-wave events.

Canha was the most influential Hawaiian performance surfer of the period. With his low center of gravity, the prematurely bald goofyfooter was rock solid on his board, and his turns were as well-placed as they were powerful. In 1962 he began surfing the fast-breaking waves at Ala Moana, at the west end of Waikiki, and by using a unique rear-weighted stance that would years later become a standard for tuberiding, Canha was able to position himself behind the curtain with some frequency. Progressive as he was, Canha was nonetheless one of the last balsaboard holdouts, and was still riding one as late as 1963, four years after most surfers switched over to polyurethane foam boards. Meanwhile, Canha was unapologetic about his life as a good-time surfer—what the sport's blue bloods disdainfully called a "surf bum"—and seemed pleased with himself while describing his union-protected truck driving job during an *International Surfing* magazine interview in 1967. "It's bitchin'. I work three months, then draw unemployment for the rest of the year and have a great time." Canha appeared in a small number of surf movies in the '60s, including *Surfing Hollow Days* (1962), *Cavalcade of Surf* (1962), and *The Endless Summer* (1966).

canoe surfing   Ancient Polynesian form of wave-riding, still practiced in most Pacific Ocean islands, and along a small number of North American and European beaches. Anthropologists regard the canoe as a defining item in Polynesian culture, with dozens of models and variations used for transport, fishing, racing, war, and burial, as well as recreation. With the exception to the great double-hulled canoes used for lengthy interisland voyages, all ancient Hawaiian canoes followed a similar blueprint: a long and narrow koa wood main hull—just wide enough for a single person and ranging in length from 20 to 80 feet—with a parallel-running *wiliwili* wood outrigger attached by two booms of *hua* wood, and all connecting points fastened by braided coconut sennit. Ancient Polynesians almost certainly knew how to catch and ride unbroken open-ocean swells as they traveled from island to island; at what point canoes were put to use for recreation in nearshore surf is unknown. The English-speaking world's first contact with surfing came in 1777, as British explorer Captain

Canoe surfing at Avalanche, Hawaii

James Cook watched a Tahitian canoe surfer. "I could not help concluding," Cook wrote in his daily log, "that this man felt the most supreme pleasure while he was driven so fast and so smoothly by the sea." Canoe surfing faded during the 1800s, along with many other Hawaiian traditions—board-surfing included—then was revived in the early 1900s, in large part due to the efforts of the 1908-founded Outrigger Canoe Club, as well as the Hui Nalu organization. Waikiki beachboy Edward "Dude" Miller began taking tourists out for canoe surfing rides in 1906, and the practice caught on immediately. Babe Ruth, Amelia Earhart, and Bing Crosby were among the hundreds of celebrity tourists who thrilled to long, smooth, fast beachboy-led canoe rides, framed by Diamond Head and the hotel-lined beaches of Waikiki. Prince Albert, after canoe surfing with Olympic swim champion and surfing patriarch Duke Kahanamoku in 1920, insisted on spending the next three days riding waves.

Modern outrigger canoes, made primarily of fiberglass, are nearly exact copies of the ancient Polynesian outriggers. For wave-riding, one to five oarsmen, paddling on alternate sides of the canoe, gain position beyond the surf zone, select a wave, then paddle in synchronization until the wave is caught. A steersman then guides the craft down the face of the wave, either straight for shore or on an angle just ahead of the white water. In 1980, Hawaiian canoeist Tommy Holmes organized Project Avalanche, an attempt by three veteran canoe surfers (Holmes included) to paddle into a 20-foot wave at a Hawaiian break called Avalanche, on the North Shore of Oahu. The team caught two 20-foot waves, wiped out spec-

tacularly on both, but earned coverage in both *Surfer* and *Surfing* magazines.

While canoe surfing remains popular among tourists as well as dedicated canoeists in Hawaii, the expense and bulkiness of the craft, along with the fact that most breaks are already dangerously overcrowded, have limited the canoe's wave-riding appeal elsewhere. Don Golden and Ron Drummond both rode one-man, single-hull canoes—in a variation of the sport later called Canadian canoe surfing—in California during the '50s and '60s. As of 2003, Canadian canoe surfing clubs had been founded in California, England, and Ireland.

Cape Hatteras   *See* North Carolina.

Cape St. Francis   Hypnotic right-breaking point wave located on the southeast coast of South Africa, about 60 miles from Port Elizabeth; the fabled "perfect wave" as featured in Californian Bruce Brown's 1966 hit movie *The Endless Summer*. Cape St. Francis is in fact the name of a sandy three-mile-long triangular point that features at least six distinct breaks; since the late '60s, the surf spot featured in *Endless Summer* has been known among South African surfers as Bruce's Beauties—or just Bruce's—in honor of Brown. Filming in South Africa in November 1963, Brown, along with *Endless Summer* costars Mike Hynson and Robert August, checked into a pair of thatched-roof rondavel holiday cottages near the base of Cape St. Francis. While riding a mediocre beachbreak in front of their rooms the following morning, Hynson spied a likely-looking wave about a mile up the point, and convinced Brown and August to follow him up for a look. The flawless waves Brown filmed—crisp, hollow, fast, and even, with rides lasting more than 30 seconds—became the high point of *Endless Summer*. "It was so good it was almost unbelievable," Brown later wrote about Cape St. Francis. "It was the kind of wave that at first you'd start giggling, then you'd start laughing, then you'd start screaming at the top of your lungs, until you felt like you were about to snap your twig."

Cape St. Francis requires a powerful east or northeast swell, which has to bend around the tip of the cape, greatly reducing the wave size; rarely does the surf here get over six foot. The best waves generally arrive from May to September, when water temperature can drop to the low 60s and offshore winds blow up to 30 knots. Mussel-covered boulders along Cape

St. Francis can be hazardous, as can the great white and Zambezi sharks that patrol this part of the coast. The beautifully desolate sand dunes that fronted the break when Brown and company visited were parceled off and sold in 1967, and have long since been covered by rows of condominiums and town-houses. *Endless Summer* viewers were told that Cape St. Francis produces good surf roughly 300 days a year, but in truth the waves usually hit peak form less than a dozen days a year. *Surfer* magazine introduced the break to the surf world in a 1964 article titled "Africa: The Perfect Wave"; *Surfing*'s better-informed 1968 feature was titled "Cape St. Francis: Not so Hot." But by that time, word was out about Jeffreys Bay, a pointbreak located 12 miles north of Cape St. Francis that offered bigger, far more consistent waves that were just as perfectly formed. Cape St. Francis has been featured in a small number of surf movies and videos, including *Oceans* (1972), *Playgrounds in Paradise* (1978), *Endless Summer II* (1994), and *Wave Spotting* (1998). *See also* The Endless Summer, Jeffreys Bay, perfect wave.

Cape Verde Islands Rugged, isolated, rarely surfed African nation composed of 10 main islands and five islets, located 400 miles west of Senegal, in the Atlantic Ocean. "This one is as down and dirty as they come," reported *Eastern Surf Magazine* after a 1993 visit to the Cape Verde Islands, in an article that described some of the world's most depressed living conditions, as well as surf breaking up to 15 to 18 feet. Cape Verde's volcanic origins are all too obvious, as the islands are almost completely without beaches, and virtually every surf spot breaks over a lava-rock bottom. From November to April, low-pressure storm systems in the North Atlantic funnel waves directly into the subtropical and frequently windy Cape Verde waters; Sal Island, in the northeast, has a number of temperamental but world-class pointbreaks, including Ponto Grande and Ponto Alcol. The islands have no surf industry and no native surfers; little is known about when these notoriously powerful waves were first ridden or by whom. Sailboarders and kite-boarders, along with a small number of surfers, have begun visiting the Cape Verde Islands.

Captain Goodvibes Vulgar but intrepid Australian surfing cartoon character created by Sydney artist Tony Edwards; the satirically named Captain Good-vibes—a hard-drinking, drug-taking, straight-talking pig with a tunnel-shaped snout—was a big hit among Australian surfers in the 1970s and early '80s. The "Pig of Steel" debuted in *Tracks* magazine in 1972; he spoke in broad Aussie surf brogue, and the multi-panel strips often ended with Goodvibes archly commenting on some man-made apocalyptic disaster. "Maybe if I study hard and do me homework," he once noted, watching as a nuclear blast sends forth an enormous wave, "I might one day get a chance to press the button meself!" (Edwards later admitted that he lifted the idea for Captain Goodvibes directly from American underground comic hero Wonder Warthog, the "Hog of Steel.")

Goodvibes was arguably the most popular surfer in Australia during the mid- and late '70s, appearing in comic books, calendars, and records. Edwards himself provided the gravelly Goodvibes voice for the radio version of the cartoon, heard on Sydney-based station 2JJ; *Hot to Trot,* a 35-millimeter Goodvibes ani-mated short, was released in 1977 and toured with Australian-produced surf movies. *Tracks* published the final Goodvibes cartoon strip in 1982. A Good-vibes panel was the main attraction of 2001's *Tubular Cels: A Wild and Wet Exhibition of Loons, Goons and Surfin' Toons,* a Sydney-hosted Australian surfing car-toon retrospective. Edwards went on to do cartoon work for the *Sydney Morning Herald*; in 1992 he was named by *Australia's Surfing Life* magazine as one of "Australia's 50 Most Influential Surfers." *See also* surf cartoons and comics, *Tracks* magazine.

Caribbean Sea The Caribbean measures about 1,700 miles from west to east and between 500 and 800 miles from north to south; it's bordered to the south and west by South America and Central Amer-ica, and is separated from the Atlantic by the 2,000-mile-long West Indies island chain, which includes Cuba, Haiti, the Dominican Republic, Jamaica, Puerto Rico, Barbados, Trinidad and Tobago, and the Grand Cayman Islands. The Caribbean coastline is generally warm and balmy. Average daytime air tem-peratures range from 75 to 80; water temperatures range from 70 to 80. Most of the islands are of vol-canic origin, and surf spots include coral reefs, rocky points, and white-sand beachbreaks. Winter gener-ally brings the best surf to the Caribbean, although autumn hurricane swells can also produce good waves. Summer is often waveless for weeks at a time. Caribbean swells tend to be short-lived, and don't often produce waves over eight foot; many of the best breaks, furthermore—including the sublime aquamarine rights of Cane Garden Bay in Tortola and the scalloping tubes of Soup Bowls in Barbados—are notoriously fickle. Dozens of high-quality surf breaks across the Caribbean meanwhile remain secret or uncharted.

Surfing was introduced to the Caribbean in Puerto Rico in the late 1950s, with Costa Rica following in the mid-'60s, and the sport gradually spread from one end of the sea to the other. Famous for its slow-rolling, rum-tinged, tropical paradise ambience, the West Indies—especially Puerto Rico—have long been a cherished travel destination for American East Coast and European surfers. Parts of Central America's Caribbean coastline—especially Costa Rica—meanwhile are popular with surfers from North and South America. *See also* Colombia, Costa Rica, Cuba, El Salvador, Jamaica, Nicaragua, Panama, and Venezuela.

Carper, John   Surfboard shaper/manufacturer from the North Shore of Oahu, Hawaii; founder of JC Hawaii Surfboards. Carper was born (1947) in Los Angeles, California, raised in the beach cities of south Santa Monica Bay, and began surfing at age nine. He moved to Maui not long after graduating from high school, and began shaping boards in 1968, during the early stages of the shortboard revolution. Carper over the years worked for Surfboards Hawaii, Lightning Bolt, and Rusty. He introduced the JC Hawaii label in 1990 as a subsidiary of Hawaiian Island Creations; in 1996 he made JC Hawaii an independent company. Carper specializes in high-performance shortboards and tow-in boards, and he's equipped some of the world's best surfers, including Shane Dorian, Rochelle Ballard, Peter Mel, and Mike Parsons. Carper is featured in *Shaping 101* and *Glassing 101,* a pair of instructional videos released in 1997 and 1998, respectively.

Carroll, Charles "Corky"   Flamboyant goofyfooter from Surfside, California; winner of the United States Surfing Championships in 1966, 1967, and 1969, and the sport's chirruping master of media in the '60s, '70s, and '80s. "He's been cheered and booed," surf journalist Jim Kempton wrote in 1998, "reviled, honored, laughed at, accused and credited with everything from defiling the name of surfing to inventing the career of 'pro surfer.'" Carroll was born (1947) in Alhambra, California, the son of an electrician, raised

Corky Carroll

in the southwest Los Angeles County town of Surfside, and got his first surfboard at age nine. He developed into a razzle-dazzle hotdogger who viewed the sport as an opportunity to entertain. "Corky Carroll: The Clown," a 1964 *Surf Guide* magazine interview, introduced the "controversial" gap-toothed 16-year-old as a surfer who "does so much so fast that spectators have trouble keeping up with him." Although not a great natural talent, like silky-smooth rival David Nuuhiwa, Carroll was the most dedicated competitor of his generation, and won more surf events than anybody during the '60s and early '70s. Aside from his three U.S. titles, he won the juniors division of the 1963 West Coast Championships, placed third in the 1966 World Championships, won the 1967 Peru International, and was the United States Surfing Association season points leader in 1966 and 1967. (He competed in the 1968, 1970, and 1972 World Championships without making the finals; in the 1970 event, held in Victoria, Australia, it was front-page news when he was temporarily suspended from the meet after allegedly starting a food fight during a precontest banquet.) Well-muscled at 5′10″, 160 pounds, Carroll was also among the world's top paddleboard racers, winning the pier race in the 1964 U.S. Surfing Championships.

Carroll's claim to being the first professional surfer is valid, as he won a TV set for his juniors victory in the 1965 Laguna Swimwear Masters contest in Redondo Beach, and placed first in the goofyfoot division of the 1965 Tom Morey Invitational in Ventura, winning $250 in the first-ever cash-prize surfing event. But it was endorsement money that paid the bills; a 1969 *Sports Illustrated* article on the Smirnoff Pro-Am, held in Santa Cruz, noted that Carroll made $29,000 in 1968—all but $400 from an array of sponsors, including Hobie Surfboards, who carried an ever-changing line of Corky Carroll signature model boards. Carroll retired from competition surfing at the end of 1972, at age 25, but kept up his bantering surf scene presence. "Cowabunga, it was good," he wrote in a 1973 *Surfing* magazine article, describing a big summer swell at Newport Beach. "Utter bliss and all those super-great adjectives that describe hot waves!"

Carroll appeared in more than two dozen surf movies, including *Gun Ho!* (1963), *The Endless Summer* (1966), *Golden Breed* (1968), *Pacific Vibrations* (1970), and *Five Summer Stories* (1972); in the '60s he was a guest on the *Tonight Show,* the *Merv Griffin Show,* and *What's My Line?* In 1972, Carroll recorded *Laid Back,* an album of earnest folk and blues songs; in 1977 he recorded the novelty single "Skateboard Bill" (with cover art by *Surfer* magazine cartoonist Rick Griffin); in 1978 he performed "I Wanna Be a Surf Freak, Daddy" on the nationally syndicated *Gong Show* (he was gonged); in 1979 he recorded the album *A Surfer for President,* which included the single "Tan Punks on Boards." In 1983, the high-voiced Carroll presented himself as the happy but perpetually jobless surfer in a nationally aired Miller Lite beer commercial; from 1987 to 1989, he had an Andy Rooney–like segment on *Surfer* magazine's ESPN television show. He wrote more than 25 articles and columns for surf magazines from 1964 to 2000; since 1994 he's written a weekly surf column for the *Orange County Register. Surf-Dog Days and Bitchin' Nights,* Carroll's bawdy autobiography, was published in 1989. Meanwhile, he was *Surfer* magazine's advertising director from 1977 to 1986, a Honda car salesman in 1989, and a tennis instructor from 1990 to 1996. He founded the Huntington Beach–based Corky Carroll Surf School in

1996, the same year he released *Learn to Surf the Fast, Easy Way,* an instructional video. He also founded or cofounded Corky Carroll Spacestix (1970 to 1972), Corky Carroll Coolstix (1986–90), and Corky Surfwear (1986–90).

In 1967, Carroll won the *Surfer* Magazine Readers Poll Award and was California's top vote-getter in *Surfing* magazine's Hall of Fame balloting. He was inducted into the Huntington Beach Surfing Walk of Fame in 1996. Carroll has been married twice, has three children, and lives in Huntington Beach.

Carroll, Nick High-output Australian surf journalist and editor from Newport, New South Wales; *Surfing* magazine editor from 1993 to 1996; *Deep* magazine editor from 1997 to 2000; regarded since the mid-'80s as the sport's most popular and knowledgeable writer. Carroll was born (1959) in Brisbane, Queensland, moved with his family to Newport in 1961, and began surfing at age 11. As a juniors division surfer he placed fifth in the 1976 Australia National Titles, and was runner-up in 1977; he was the men's division national champion in 1979 and 1981. (Tom Carroll, Nick's younger brother, was world pro tour champion in 1983 and 1984.) After freelancing articles to the Australian surf press in the late '70s, Carroll was hired as an associate editor at *Tracks* magazine in 1981, then promoted to editor in 1983. He returned to freelancing in 1986, and for three years contributed sports and feature articles to the *National Times* and the *Sydney Morning-Herald* newspapers, while continuing to work for Australian and American surf magazines. In 1990 he moved to Capistrano Beach, California, and for seven years was a staff member at *Surfing* magazine, becoming editor in 1993. Three years later Carroll returned to Australia, where he remained *Surfing*'s "global correspondent," edited *Deep* magazine, and contributed regularly to *Australia's Surfing Life* and Swell.com.

Carroll writes in the italicized and exclamatory style of American New Journalism innovator Tom Wolfe, but his enthusiasm for surfing makes for a less cynical, less ironic voice. Although he once said he "didn't want to intellectualize surfing," Carroll—an expert in virtually every surfing-related subject, but returning often to board design, contest reportage, profiles, and wave-related meteorology—has in fact been one of surfing's smartest and most analytical writers. "It can hardly have escaped anyone's notice by now that the '90s have been the decade of Selling Youth," Carroll noted in "Reborn," a 1999 article for *Surfing*.

> *The world is now completely chock full of people who want to sell stuff to kids via other kids, and in doing so, to somehow convince everyone else that they have some unbreakable hold on what's Cool. And the surfing world, being about as Cool as it apparently gets, is no exception. If you're in a certain frame of mind, this relentless pursuit of Youth can look to be a truly frightening thing. The speed with which it's been incorporated! The brainpower exerted on the subject! The sheer ferocity with which the old go about making money from the young!*

Carroll was named by *Australia's Surfing Life* in 1992 as one of the country's 50 most influential surfers. He's written, edited, or contributed to a number of surfing books, including *How to Surf: The Complete Guide to Surfing* (1986), *The Next Wave* (1991), and *Surf Rage* (2000); he's also published articles in *Rolling Stone, Playboy, Village Voice, Men's Journal,* and *Outside.* Carroll is married and has two children. *See also* Australia's Surfing Life magazine, Deep magazine, Surfing magazine, Tracks magazine.

Carroll, Tom   Dynamic and durable power surfer from Sydney, Australia; world champion in 1983 and 1984, and one of the sport's premier tuberiders. Carroll was born (1961) in Sydney, the son of a newspaper editor, was raised in the beachfront suburb of Newport, and began surfing at age eight, a few months after his mother died of pancreatic cancer. Hawaiian style master Gerry Lopez was an early influence on Carroll, as was hard-turning local surfer Col Smith. He was a two-time juniors division winner in the Australian National Titles (1977 and 1978) and a two-time winner of the Pro Junior (1977 and 1980). As a world pro tour rookie in 1979, he made the finals in the Pipeline Masters, and finished the year ranked #24. After making a steady climb up the ratings over the next three seasons—from 17th to 10th to third— Carroll earned his first world title in 1983, winning six of 13 events, and becoming the first goofyfooter to take the championship. The following year he won just two of 24 events and was pushed to the wire by 1977 world champion Shaun Tomson, but came out on top; in 1985 he lost the title to Californian Tom Curren. For the rest of the decade, it would be Carroll

Tom Carroll

and Curren, more than any other two surfers, who aesthetically as well as competitively defined the sport.

Small and well-muscled (5′6″, 145 pounds), with huge energy-storing thighs, Carroll was a power surfer with uncommon finesse. Naturally gifted, but not to the degree of world champions Tom Curren or Mark Occhilupo, Carroll steadily and willfully improved his craft, one facet at a time. The effort sometimes showed in small, weak surf, but in waves from four to 20 feet Carroll was a marvel: planting his back foot squarely over the tail section of his board and assuming a fencer's stance, he adapted perfectly to the given surf break, drawing long and sinewy lines across the bottom-heavy rollers at Sunset Beach, or hooking fiercely under the curl at Bells Beach, or flying arrowlike through the tube at Pipeline. "I've always thought that's where you see the true TC," older brother and top surfing journalist Nick Carroll wrote in 1994, "alone in that utterly silent moment of freefall down the face of the wave, the impossibly accurate first turn, the perfect stillness and control in the midst of chaos." While the sport was to a large degree recast in the image of Tom Curren in the '80s and '90s, Carroll's effect was nearly as great, and he was the primary influence on surfers like Mark Oc-chilupo and Luke Egan. Carroll's disposition amplified his popularity. He was confident but not arrogant, emotional but not volatile, dignified but still matey. He projected a sense of gratitude—not just for a career that afforded him prestige and a handsome living, but for the good luck of having been born a surfer.

Carroll retired from the world tour at the end of the 1993 season. He'd placed second in the final standings in 1986, finished third in 1985, 1988, and 1991, and was the 1991 Triple Crown champion. He had 26 career pro tour event victories (second only to Curren's 33), including Pipeline Masters wins in 1987, 1990, and 1991. He detoured neatly into politics in 1985, boycotting the South African events on the world tour as a protest against apartheid, saying he'd taken "a basic humanitarian stand" and that he wouldn't return "until black surfers are allowed on all beaches." In 1988 he became the first million-dollar surfer, signing an exclusive five-year contract with Quiksilver. Australian prime minister Bob Hawke, along with world champions Kelly Slater, Wayne Bartholomew, and Mark Richards, spoke at a mid-1993 testimonial dinner in Carroll's honor. Some speakers got a laugh while making reference to Carroll's career-long assortment of injuries, including a surfboard-inflicted stomach rupture, a concussion, two knee injuries requiring major surgery, and, most famously, a perforated rectum suffered after being speared by the nose of his board. The hardest blow of Carroll's life came the afternoon before the finals of the 1987 Pipeline Masters, when he found out his older sister had just been killed in a car accident. A smaller trial was met in 1989, when Carroll had an ac-rimonious public split with Peter Mansted, his effective but abrasive manager.

Carroll won the *Surfer* Magazine Readers Poll Award in 1984. He was inducted into the Australian Surfing Hall of Fame in 1990, won the *Australia's Surfing Life* Peer Poll in 1991, and was inducted into the Huntington Beach Surfing Walk of Fame in 1999. *Tom Carroll: The Wave Within,* an autobiography cowritten with Australian surf journalist Kirk Willcox, was published in 1994; Carroll also wrote *Surfing the World* (1990), a book on the pro circuit, as well as roughly

40 surf magazine articles in the '90s and early '00s. Carroll has appeared in more than 60 surf movies and videos, including *Bali High* (1981), *Ocean Fever* (1983), *Amazing Surf Stories* (1986), *All Down the Line* (1989), *Rolling Thunder* (1991), *Endless Summer II* (1994), *The Hole* (1997), and *The Path* (2000); he was also featured on *Biographies,* a 2001 Outdoor Life Network series. Carroll lives in Newport, Australia. He's married and has two children. *See also* Pipeline Masters.

cars and surfing   Surfers traditionally have had a function-first attitude toward cars. Surfboard transportation all but demands a big, roomy, essentially nonstylish vehicle, while the by-products of a surfing life—damp towels, sand, surfboard wax, moldering wetsuits, and salt air—ensure that the surf car, unless looked after with the kind of obsessive care and concern that generally doesn't sit well with the surfing obsession itself, operates as a rolling model of disorder and decay. A few surfers have broken the mold. California board-maker Dale Velzy recalled that he "stayed out of the water for two weeks" not long after World War II to work on his chopped and bored-out 1940 Ford Mercury, and four-time world pro tour champion Mark Richards of Australia bought a new silver 911SC Porsche after winning his second title in 1980. But surfers, while respecting the car as essential to their surfing pursuit, for the most part keep their automotive investment to a minimum. As vocal duo Jan and Dean phrased it in "Surf City," their 1963 chart-topper: "Well, it ain't got a backseat or a rear window / But it still gets me where I want to go."

The American-made woody station wagon was the first real surfing car, and the only one with any lasting cultural significance. The wood-paneled wagons, built mostly in the '30s and '40s and bought secondhand by surfers for as little as $75 in the '50s and early '60s, had room enough for a half-dozen 10-foot boards (with tails sticking out over the tailgate), and provided shelter during overnight surf trips. Originally regarded by surfers as all but disposable, wood-ies were being restored, shown, and collected by the early '70s. Woodies aside, dilapidated older cars of any shape or form have always been popular with surfers; cultural statements of a kind were made in the '50s as surfers often hand-painted slogans on the doors, hood, and trunk; pioneering big-wave rider Greg Noll decorated his 1948 Oldsmobile with swastikas, "just to piss people off."

While American-made vans like the Ford Econo-line were popular to a degree among surfers in the '60s and '70s, the inexpensive and easy-to-fix Volks-wagen was far and away the car of choice. The VW bus, just prior to the late-'60s shortboard revolution, was omnipresent at surfing areas in America, Europe, and South Africa; when boards got smaller, the VW Bug became, as the *Surfer's Journal* wrote in 2001, "the official staff car of 20th century surfing." (The Holden Wagon and Plymouth Valiant Wagon were the pre-ferred surfers' cars in Australia, while the Hawaiians came to favor jacked-up, open-bed pickup trucks.)

No surf-car consensus emerged in the early '80s, as coastal parking lots were filled with wagons, pick-ups, post-Bug VWs, vans, and first-generation mini-vans. As surfing itself became more mainstream, surfers began making more predictable car choices, leading inevitably to board-carrying fleets of Ford Ex-plorers, Isuzu Troopers, and sundry other sport utility vehicles.

Car manufacturers, meanwhile, have for decades viewed surfing as an ideal marketing tool. Surf-themed print or television ads have been used to sell dozens of models, from the 1960 Buick Opel to the 1975 Dodge Dart (a "Hang Ten" package was offered) to the 2001 Acura MDX. Renegade Malibu surfer Mickey Dora was featured in nationally aired TV com-mercial for the 1964 Oldsmobile F-85. Cars have also been used as a grand prize in surfing competitions, starting with the 1965 KHJ contest in Hermosa Beach, California, with winner Denny Tompkins receiving a new MG sedan, followed shortly by Nat Young win-ning the keys to a new Chevy Camaro for his 1966 world contest victory. In 2003, surfwear giant Bill-abong and French automaker Renault released the limited-edition, Europe-only Clio Billabong, backed with an ad campaign featuring top European pro surfers Tiogo Pires and Antoine Cardonnet. Cars and trucks were regularly given away to world tour pro event winners in the '80s—three-time world cham-pion Tom Curren won no less than six automobiles in the early and mid-'80s. *See also* woody.

Carson, David Audacious graphic designer from Southern California, best known in the surf world for his jarring but innovative 1991 redesign of *Surfer* mag-azine. Carson was born (1956) in Corpus Christi, Texas, began surfing after moving with his family in 1965 to Cocoa Beach, Florida. In 1973, four years after relocating to Rolling Hills, California, Carson was a

David Carson's 1991 work for *Surfer* magazine

top-rated competitor in the Western Surfing Associa-tion's prestigious AAAA division, and in 1976 he ap-peared in the surf film *Playgrounds in Paradise*. Carson earned a B.A. in sociology from San Diego State Uni-versity in 1977; in the early '80s he enrolled in a series of graphic design workshops. Carson then became the art director for a series of magazines, including *Transworld Skateboarding* (1983–87), *Musician* (1988), *Beach Culture* (1989–91), *Surfer* (1991–92), and *Ray Gun* (1992). By the time he arrived at *Surfer* his dark-palette, industrial meltdown style—featuring compressed text; mismatched font size; chopped, scratched, cut, and mixed type; and radically cropped photos—was fully developed. Some *Surfer* readers ap-proved of Carson's redesign, but a majority felt, as one Pasadena subscriber put it, that the new look was "jumbled, ugly, chaotic and hard to read." Carson co-founded *Blue,* an outdoor sports magazine, in 1998. From his Del Mar, California, design studio (and later from his studios in New York and Tortola), he also did work for Pepsi, Nike, MCI, and Sega, and the Carson style was widely copied through the '90s and early '00s. Carson and his work have been the subject of three books: *The End of Print: The Graphic Design of David Carson* (1996), *David Carson, 2nd Sight: Grafik Design after the End of Print* (1997), and *Fotograficks: David Carson* (1999). Carson's own book, *Surf Culture: The Art History of Surfing,* was published in 2002. *See also* surf art.

Carson, Lance Boisterous pointbreak specialist from Pacific Palisades, California; best known for his noseriding and deep-set turns at Malibu in the late '50s and '60s. "He was the best surfer there," Hollywood director/screenwriter and former Malibu surfer John Milius said in 1999. "He read the waves better, never made a mistake, and only fell off deliberately at the end of a ride . . . or if he was drunk." Lance Carson was born (1943) in Santa Monica, California, and raised in nearby Pacific Palisades. He was a spina bifida baby, and his parents were told that water exercise might promote bone growth, so Carson took to the surf at age four, at Malibu, on a four-foot-long balsa bellyboard made by his father. In 1956, Carson was the youngest of a new generation of Malibu surfers that included Mickey Dora, Mike Doyle, and Mickey Muñoz. By the turn of the decade, Malibu had become the world's best-known surf break, and Carson and Dora all but defined Malibu surfing: the dark-haired Dora with his jazzy, theoretical style, Carson with his forceful cutbacks and perfectly composed noseriding. Both were featured in Bruce Brown's 1966 surf movie classic *The Endless Summer,* with narrator Brown commenting during a long Carson noseride that "he's so relaxed up there you get the feeling he could have a ham sandwich while he's waiting around." Although Carson had no interest in surfing contests, he was ranked #2, behind David Nuuhiwa, on a 1965 *Surfer* magazine list of the world's 10 best noseriders. He worked at Jacobs Surfboards in Hermosa Beach, first as a salesman, then as a board-shaper, and in 1965 Jacobs introduced the popular Lance Carson signature model surfboard.

Carson's reputation for beer-soaked capers and stunts, meanwhile, nearly matched his standing as a wave-rider. "Every time I went to a party," he recalled in 1984, "I seemed to think of something new and crazy to do." An oft-told tale in the Carson canon, perhaps apocryphal, has Carson perched on the hood of a friend's station wagon while being ferried across a Winchell's Donut shop parking lot dressed in nothing but a strategically placed honey-glazed donut. He continued to drink heavily through the '60s and into the '70s, then quit in 1979. Carson later expressed regret for his "wild and radical" years, saying it made him "a second-rate person."

Carson was all but left behind as a relic during and after the late 60s shortboard revolution. In 1976, however, anticipating the longboard revival, he founded the Lance Carson Surfboards label and began selling longboards to Santa Monica–area surf shops. Carson himself had never stopped longboard-

ing, and continued to surf Malibu on a 9′6″ noserider. He became an early surfing environmentalist in 1984, spearheaded a local effort to clean up the polluted Malibu Lagoon, and was a cofounder of the Surfrider Foundation.

Carson appeared in a small number of surf films in the early and mid-'60s, including *Walk on the Wet Side* (1963), *A Cool Wave of Color* (1964), and *Strictly Hot* (1964), and is featured in *Legends of Malibu,* a 1987 documentary. Carson was the model for the talented but alcoholic surfer Matt Johnson, played by Jan-Michael Vincent, in Warner Brothers' 1978 surf movie *Big Wednesday.* In 1991, Carson was nominated to the International Surfing Hall of Fame. Carson has been married twice and has one child. *See also* Malibu, noseriding.

Cassidy, Graham   Pleasant, well-spoken, hardworking competition official and promoter from Sydney, Australia; the executive director for the Association of Surfing Professionals from 1987 to 1994. Cassidy was born (1947) and raised in Sydney, and began surfing at age 15. In 1969 he earned a B.A. in communications from Sydney College of Journalism. He'd meanwhile begun to work as a surfing competition judge, and was selected for the 1970 World Surfing Championships judging panel. Cassidy had his first big organizational success in 1974, when he produced the debut 2SM/Coca-Cola Surfabout, Australia's richest pro contest at the time, convincing a radio station and a soft-drink bottler to put up $7,000 in prize money. In 1981, Cassidy, by then a journalist for the *Sydney Sun* newspaper, was made president of the Australian Professional Surfing Association. Five years later he was named executive director of the Association of Surfing Professionals (ASP), the governing body of the international pro circuit—a part-time job at first, but eventually paying a full-time annual salary of $70,000. Cassidy was instrumental in the ASP securing a million-dollar sponsorship from Coke for the 1994 season. But in December of that year, he was ousted by the ASP board of directors in a swift and unexpected 13–0 vote, partly because the pro surfers felt he wasn't doing enough to attract more prize money, and partly because Cassidy had moved the season-ending contests from Hawaii to Australia—a business move that vastly reduced the tour's finish-line drama.

In 1983, Cassidy published *Greats of the Australian Surf,* a compilation of his profiles on Australian surfing champions. Cassidy is married and has two children. *See also* Association of Surfing Professionals, Australian Professional Surfing Association, Coke Classic, professional surfing.

catalyst A liquid chemical consisting primarily of methyl ethyl ketone peroxide, added in small amounts to resin as a hardening agent. Once the catalyst and resin are mixed, a board-builder (or ding repairman) has to complete his task before the resin "goes off" and becomes gelatinous and unworkable. Temperature and humidity affect the timing of this reaction, but usually an ounce of resin mixed with 10 drops of catalyst remains in a liquid state for about 20 minutes. Overcatalyzed resin produces a noxious smoke and a too-brittle, yellowish final product. *See also* resin.

Catri, Dick Swashbuckling surfer/organizer/board manufacturer from Miami Beach, Florida; described by Swell.com in 2000 as "the godfather of East Coast surfing." Catri was born (1938) in Carteret, New Jersey, moved with his family to south Florida at age seven, and was a state championship high jumper in high school. He worked in a Miami Beach high-dive comedy act in 1957, along with California transplant Jack Murphy, who a few years later became internationally known as the diamond-stealing "Murph the Surf." It was Murphy who showed Catri how to ride waves in early 1958, and not long afterward the two traveled north to introduce surfing to the Indialantic/Cocoa Beach area. Catri and Murphy drove to California in 1959, ending their visit by stealing two boards from a Carlsbad surfing school; Catri then moved to Hawaii where, over the next five years, he worked as a lifeguard at the Pearl Harbor Officers' Club, fixed dings and swept the floors at Surfboards Hawaii on the North Shore of Oahu (where he learned how to build surfboards), and became the first East Coast surfer to ride Pipeline and Waimea Bay. He also appeared in Bruce Brown's movie *Surfing Hollow Days* (1962), as well as Dale Davis's *Inside Out* (1965), and was hired as the "aquatics director" and extra during the filming of Columbia Pictures' 1964 film *Ride the Wild Surf.* Returning to Florida in 1964, Catri opened the Satellite Beach Surf Shop; the following year he and his stellar East Coast surf team—including Bruce Valluzzi, Mimi Munro, Mike Tabeling, and Gary Propper—became part of the Hobie Surfboards empire. In 1966 Catri opened Shagg's

Surf Shop on the Cocoa Beach Pier, with another outlet in Indialantic. One year earlier he'd founded the precursor to today's Cocoa Beach Easter Surfing Festival.

Catri Surfboards opened in Cocoa Beach, Florida, in 1968, and a few years later Catri got involved with the nascent East Coast pro scene as a way to promote his business. He founded the Florida Pro contest in 1972, along with the American Professional Surfing tour, which, by 1975, had a 14-event schedule. The 1976 Florida Pro was the first East Coast contest to be part of the world pro tour. Catri also had a hand in local surfing politics; in 1970 he played a crucial role in resolving the wars between surfers and fishermen at Sebastian Inlet, Florida's premier surf break, lobbying local and state politicians until the property next to the Sebastian jetty was designated a state park and surfing area. Catri turned his attention to East Coast amateur surfing in the early '80s, and coached a number of preteen surfers, including Todd Holland and Kelly Slater. Catri himself had been competing all along, winning the senior men's division of the 1969 East Coast Surfing Championships, and finishing runner-up in the seniors division of the 1978 United States Surfing Championships. He also competed in the 1967 Duke Kahanamoku Invitational at Sunset Beach, Hawaii. Catri was the top East Coast vote-getter in the 1966 International Surfing Hall of Fame Awards; exactly 30 years later he was among the first group of surfers inducted into the East Coast Surf Legends Hall of Fame.

Catri was convicted in 1972 for selling 200 pounds of marijuana to an undercover agent, and served 13 months in jail. He's been married three times, and has four daughters.

caught inside Being trapped on the shoreward side of an incoming wave, or set of waves. Many surfers feel that being caught inside is the worst-case scenario during a heavy swell, in part because it forces the surfer to contemplate, sometimes for a minute or longer, the approaching wave as it gathers and looms. A big-wave wipeout, by comparison, is nearly instantaneous. California surfer Donnie Solomon died after getting caught inside at Hawaii's Waimea Bay in 1995, and Hawaii's Todd Chesser died two years later after getting caught inside at Outside Alligator Rock, just west of Waimea. A less-threatening variation on being caught inside—a regular occurrence for beginners and intermediates at surf breaks lacking a deep-water paddling channel—has the rider stuck in the broken-wave zone, unable to punch through to the lineup, where waves are initially picked up. *Caught Inside: A Surfer's Year on the California Coast* is the title of a critically acclaimed 1996 memoir by San Francisco writer Daniel Duane. *See also* bail out.

Cazenave, Sylvain   Well-rounded and well-traveled surf photographer from Biarritz, France; best known for his 1990s helicopter-angle shots of big-wave surfing in Hawaii. Cazenave was born (1954) in Lille, France, spent his first five years in the African nation of Chad, then moved with his family to Biarritz. He began surfing in 1968, and competed in the European Surfing Championships in 1971 and 1972. He took up photography in 1975, and was first published two years later in a French sailboarding magazine. Cazenave's crisp, neatly composed shots have been used internationally since the late 1970s in surf magazines (including *Surfer,* the *Surfer's Journal,* and *Australia's Surfing Life*), as well as mainstream magazines (including *Sports Illustrated, Playboy, Geo,* and *Paris Match*), and a small number of French-produced surfing books. In 1994, Cazenave went up in a helicopter to take the first aerial photographs of Jaws, a big-wave break on Maui where a small group of surfers using the newly developed motorized tow-in method began setting new height and performance standards for big-wave surfing.

Center, George "Dad"   Versatile water sportsman and early surfing booster from Honolulu, Hawaii; the "Captain of the Outriggers" for Waikiki's Outrigger Canoe Club from 1910 to 1932; once celebrated as Hawaii's unofficial record holder for the longest surfing ride, after catching a big summer wave in 1917 from outside Castles Break off Waikiki to the inner waters past Cunha Break—a distance of about three-quarters of a mile. Center was born (1886) and raised in Honolulu; he excelled at all sports, but was primarily a canoeist and swimmer. When he began surfing in 1908, he was one of the only *haole* (Caucasian) practitioners, and helped convince others that the sport—nearly moribund just a few years earlier—wasn't just for those of Hawaiian blood. In 1911, Center finished runner-up to local surfer/swimmer Duke Kahanamoku in a 220-yard freestyle race in which Kahanamoku set a world record. Nine years later Center was the swim coach for the Hawaiian members of

America's 1920 Olympic team, including double gold medal winner Kahanamoku. He later became the swim coach at Oahu's elite Punahou school. Center died in 1962 at age 76, and his ashes were scattered into the ocean at Waikiki. Center was inducted into the International Swimming Hall of Fame in 1991. *See also* Outrigger Canoe Club.

Chang, Aaron   Soft-voiced photographer from San Diego, California; a longtime senior contributor to *Surfing* magazine; generally regarded as surfing's premier all-around lensman in the 1980s and early '90s. "People always ask me who the best surf photographer is," *Surfer* magazine photo editor Jeff Divine said in 1994, "and I've always said Aaron Chang." Born (1956) in Tucson, Arizona, Chang began surfing not long after moving with his family to San Diego at age nine, and took up photography and filmmaking at 16. Four years later, while living in Hawaii, Chang made a full-length Super-8 surf movie titled *Out of the Blue* (1976), but was soon concentrating on still photography. He began contributing to *Surfing* magazine, was hired as a senior staffer in 1979, and for the next 10 years was regularly dispatched on travel assignments to exotic surf world locations. *American Photographer* magazine named Chang as one of the top five emerging American sports photographers in 1980, and in 1985 Chang was the subject of an *American Photographer* cover story. He was by then expert in all aspects of surf photography: action shots (taken from water or land), portraiture, candids, landscapes, and lifestyle. His composition was masterful; the color palette he worked from was broader than that of any of his surf-world peers. Over the years Chang's work has been published in *Newsweek, Esquire, Sports Illustrated, GQ, Elle,* and dozens of other mainstream magazines; he's contributed to a number of illustrated surfing books, including *Pure Stoke* (1982), *The History of Surfing* (1983), and *Surfing: The Ultimate Pleasure* (1984). Chang also produced a line of top-selling romance posters and, in the 1980s, contributed to the Day in the Life photo books.

Chang is quiet, aloof, intense, and keenly business-minded, branching out to do high-paying work for Nike, among other accounts. In 1994 he launched Aaron Chang Clothing, a successful beachwear line, and in 2001 he was featured in "Loaded: Ten Surfing Millionaires," an *Australia's Surfing Life* article. Chang was part of a 12-man expedition in January 2001 to ride and photograph the huge deep-water surf at Cortes Banks, 100 miles west of San Diego; three months later his photo of California big-wave surfer Mike Parsons riding a 60-foot wave was named the winner in the Swell XXL Big-Wave contest. Chang is married and has one child.

channel   An area of deep water adjacent to a surf break, usually running perpendicular to the beach. Channels are fundamental to many of the world's best surf breaks, as they help create the underlying high-to-low bathymetric profile that allows waves to break with consistent and predictable form. Channels also provide a safe and quick route into the surf zone, as well as a stand-by area. Surf photographers often shoot from the channel. Most waves in the tropics spill into reef channels created by freshwater river runoff; at beachbreaks, temporary channels are frequently carved in the sand by riptides and littoral currents; channels can also form next to piers and jetties. The expression "closeout set" is often used to describe a set of waves large enough to break in the channel.

channel bottom   Surfboard design feature, generally manifested as four or six longitudinal slotlike channels in the back half of the board's underside, thought to increase board speed by directing water rearward. Jim Pollard, Australian surfboard shaper from the Sunshine Coast of Queensland, produced the first channel bottom boards in 1974; Pollard's "beetail" featured four elliptical sets of channels—eight channels total, four on either side of the board's

Channel bottom

centerline. New South Wales surfer Col Smith introduced a modified version of the channel bottom in 1977, optimistically calling his six-channel boards "as significant a breakthrough as shortboards and lightweight materials were a few years ago." But it was New Zealand–born shaper Allan Byrne who really brought the channel bottom to the attention of the surf world, shaping them for top Australian pros like Wayne Bartholomew and Gary Elkerton, and adapting the design to the tri-fin in 1982.

On "soft" channel bottoms, the slot edges are rounded and the channels blended into the flat bottom surface near the tail. "Hard" channel bottoms, as developed by Byrne, cut up to a half-inch into the bottom of the board, forming table-edge ridges that run all the way to the end of the tail. Both versions are time-consuming and expensive to build, and neither caught on with the surfing public at large. Channel bottom boards for the most part are used in larger surf, although a four-channel design, introduced in 2000 to critical praise (but low sales), has been used in smaller waves as well. Concave bottom boards, on the other hand, while similar in theory to the channel bottom, met with far greater success, and became a standard design on most shortboards by the mid-'90s. *See also* Allan Byrne.

Channon, Bruce   Versatile surf photographer and magazine editor from Sydney, Australia; coowner from 1979 to 1997 of *Australian Surfing World* magazine. Channon was born (1950) and raised in Sydney, began surfing in 1959, and was a juniors division finalist in the 1966 and 1968 Australian National Titles. Channon taught himself how to take surf photographs in 1972 (eventually publishing his work in *Tracks, Surfing,* and the *Surfer's Journal*), worked as a surf movie cameraman for *A Winter's Tale* and *Drouyn* (both released in 1974), and became the editor of *Surfing World* in 1975. In 1979, Channon and photographer/graphic designer Hugh McLeod bought *Surfing World,* changed the name to *Australian Surfing World,* and transformed what had been a somewhat ordinary periodical into a decorative and richly colored showcase magazine. Channon and McLeod also published two popular coffee-table books, *Surfing Wild Australia* (1984) and *Surfing the Chain of Fire* (1986). In 1998, Channon founded Surfinfo.com, an Australia surfing industry database; in 2001, he became the editor for *Australian Longboarder* magazine. Channon also works as exhibition manager for the Action

Retail Surf Expo, an annual trade show that debuted in March 2002 in Sydney. *See also* Australian Surfing World.

Chantays   Instrumental surf band from Santa Ana, California, whose guitar-driven "Pipeline" single went to #4 on the national charts in 1963. The five members of the Chantays were between 13 and 17 years old when the band formed in 1961. In July of the following year they recorded "Pipeline" for Downey Records, a tiny Los Angeles label; the song was originally titled "Liberty's Whip"—inspired by the John Wayne western, *The Man Who Shot Liberty Valance*—but the name changed after two band members saw a surfing movie featuring the guillotine-like waves at Pipeline. After a slow start, "Pipeline" began moving up the charts in the spring of 1963, peaking at #4 in May. It was the first surf song to chart in England, hitting #16 in June, and was voted Record of the Year in Australia. While none of the Chantays' follow-up singles made the charts, the turbocharged "Pipeline" ranks just behind the Surfaris' drum-heavy "Wipeout" as the best-known instrumental surf song. *See also* surf music.

Chapin, Gard   Innovative but prickly surfer from Hollywood, California; stepfather to surfing icon Mickey Dora. Little is known about Chapin other than he was one of the most talented and least-liked surfers of the prewar era. He was born in Hollywood, probably in 1916, and began surfing in the early '30s. The heavy solid-wood boards in use during the '30s and '40s allowed for very little maneuvering, but Chapin, after developing a drop-knee stance in order to lower his center of gravity, had greater command over his board than virtually anyone on the coast. He preferred to ride "deep" (close to the breaking part of the wave), and when others rode in front of him he shouted or pushed them out of the way or simply ran them over. Surfboard design genius Bob Simmons is said to have bought his first board from Chapin; the two surfers later built boards together. Chapin married Mickey Dora's mother in the early '40s; he brought his stepson to the beach fairly regularly when the boy was in his preteens, introduced him to surfing, and had a great influence on Dora's personality. Chapin died under mysterious circumstances in Baja, Mexico, in the mid-50s. Dora later told *Surfer* magazine that his stepfather had been murdered. John "Doc" Ball's book *California Surfriders,* originally

published in 1946, features a half-dozen photos of Chapin. *See also* Mickey Dora.

Chapman, Craig "Owl"   Frizzy-haired regularfoot surfer from the North Shore of Oahu, Hawaii; famous in the early and mid-'70s for his tuberiding at Sunset Beach and Maalaea, and for his flamboyant "hood ornament" stance at Pipeline, where he'd race through the tube with arms spread and his right knee dropped to the deck of his board. Chapman was born (1950) in Detroit, Michigan, moved with his family at age nine to Newport Beach, California, and soon began surfing with his older brother, Gary. Both the Chapman boys moved to Hawaii in 1967, and Gary, while living on Maui, became one of the first shortboard test pilots. Craig—nicknamed "Owl" as a play on his woeful nearsightedness—soon became one of the most dedicated surfers on the North Shore, and was featured in a number of period surf movies, including *Cosmic Children* (1970), *A Sea for Yourself* (1973), and *Super Session* (1975). He was also invited to both the 1970 and 1971 Expression Session events. Chapman remained a part of the North Shore surf scene long after most all his contemporaries moved on, and became known for

Owl Chapman

his zoned-out but epigrammatic phrasing. "When I was 22," he said in 1985, "I had a Cadillac, ten surfboards and ten girlfriends. Man, I thought it would be like that forever." As journalist Mike Latronic later described it, Chapman "walks the fine line between profound philosopher and space-cadet."

cheater five   Noseriding maneuver invented and popularized by Hawaii's Paul Strauch in the early 1960s, where the surfer moves to the front third of the surfboard, crouches, and extends the leading foot to the board's tip. "Cheater" refers to the fact the surfer's weight is virtually all on the rear foot, a yard or more away from the nose of the board; "five" means that five toes are lined up on the front end. The cheater five is the only type of noseride that can be performed in bigger surf. In 1965, 17-year-old Jeff Hakman of Hawaii clinched the inaugural Duke Kahanamoku Surfing Classic after racing through a hot Sunset Beach section in full cheater five stance; Paul Strauch was runner-up. The cheater five is performed almost exclusively on longboards. Also known as a "Strauch crouch" or a "stretch five." *See also* noseriding, Paul Strauch.

Chesser, Todd   Garrulous and sharp-witted professional surfer from Oahu, Hawaii; described by *Surfing* magazine in 1995 as "the greatest non-rated surfer in the world"; a big-wave virtuoso by the early '90s, and a big-wave fatality in 1997. Chesser was born (1968) in Florida, and moved to Hawaii with his mother, Jeannie, at age three, after his surfer father was killed in a car accident. Jeannie became one of Hawaii's top-rated amateur surfers, finishing fourth in the 1973 United States Championships, fourth in the 1980 World Championships, and fourth again in the 1984 Championships. Chesser finished fourth in the final ratings for the 1990 Professional Surfing Association of America tour, but didn't have the temperament for competition, and decided instead to make a career as a big-wave rider and a globe-trotting "photo surfer." He also wrote surf magazine articles, and in a 1994 issue of *Surfer* described his recent near drowning after getting caught inside by a 20-foot set at Himalayas, an outer reefbreak on the North Shore of Oahu. But for another *Surfer* article on big-wave danger, Chesser nonetheless said that "if you know the basics, the danger is minimal."

On February 13, 1997, Chesser was scheduled to fly to Maui to stunt-surf a death scene for TriStar's big-wave movie, *In God's Hands.* But the surf was good in Oahu, so he stayed home, and at 9:00 A.M. paddled with two friends into the lineup at Outside Alligator Rock, another outer reefbreak. Chesser drowned two hours later, after getting caught inside by a 25-foot set. He was the third notable surfer to die in big waves in just over two years: in late 1994 Hawaiian surfer Mark Foo was killed at Maverick's in California, and Donnie Soloman of California died at Waimea Bay in 1995. Chesser was remembered as fun-loving and cynical, with a penchant for streaking. He died, engaged to be married, three days before his 29th birthday. Chesser appeared in more than 20 surf movies and videos, including *Just Surfing* (1989), *Momentum* (1992), and *Under the Same Sun* (1994). *See also* death and surfing.

Chew, Rich   Disciplined regularfooter from Seal Beach, California; overall ratings leader for the United States Surfing Association's 1964 season. Chew began surfing in 1957 at age 13, and his career hit a peak in 1965, directly after his USSA win, as he appeared in two surf movies (*The Performers* and *Inside Out*), made the cover of *Surfer* magazine, was chosen to compete in the inaugural Duke Kahanamoku Invitational, and reached the semifinals of the World Surfing Championships, held in Lima, Peru. Chew became a lifeguard in San Clemente, California, in 1972, and by 2000 had more than 2,200 rescues to his credit.

Chicama   Sand-bottom pointbreak located near a small fishing port in northern Peru, about 400 miles north of Lima; generally regarded as the world's longest wave. Half-mile rides are common at Chicama, and rides up to a mile or more are possible. May to August is the best time for surf here, and even then the waves tend to be small—only a few times a year does the surf get above four foot. The two-and-a-half-mile point at Chicama is usually divided into three separate breaks. When the surf hits six foot, the breaks begin to link together, with the fastest and most powerful section of wave found near the base of the point. A Chicama wave is a joy to ride, as it changes speed often, and mixes hollow sections with softer-breaking ones, allowing the surfer to easily go through an entire repertoire of moves, tuberiding included, on a single wave. Surfers usually paddle out at the top of the point, generally ride three, four, or five waves down the length of the point, then exit the water and walk back to the top. Water temperatures during the surf season average in the low 60s, air temperatures in the upper 60s, the prevailing wind is offshore, and the surf is good on all tides. Rarely are there more than 20 surfers riding Chicama at one time; a majority of waves, no matter the size of the crowd, go unridden. Another half-dozen first-rate surf breaks are located nearby. The landscape, however, is dreary, made up entirely of sand, dirt, and rocks, and accommodations are spartan.

The Chicama waves were spotted from the air by Hawaiian surfer Chuck Shipman in 1966. Upon arrival at Honolulu, Shipman phoned the news back to Lima; in September of that year, a group of top Peruvian surfers, including Carlos Barreda, Oscar Malpartida, and Ivo Hunza, drove north to Chicama and became the first surfers to ride the break. Chicama was listed as one of the 10 best waves in the world in a 1981 *Surfing* magazine article; the Chicama surf is featured in *Lunar Road,* a 2002 surf video.

Chile Chile occupies roughly the bottom two-thirds of South America's west coast, and its 4,000-mile shoreline pulses with a diverse, consistent, and largely uncrowded array of surf breaks. There are two popular surfing areas in Chile: 1) The arid north coast surrounding the cities of Iquique and Arica, filled with hard-breaking rock reefs like El Gringo, a vicious peak often described as the "Chilean Pipeline." 2) The milder south-central coast around the town of Pichilemu, home to the world's largest collection of left-breaking points. Dozens of excellent breaks are located outside these areas—Chile has been described as a "cold-water Indonesia" for its abundance of surf spots—but many are inaccessible by car. (The surf-lashed Chilean province of Rapa Nui, or Easter Island, is located 1,800 miles off the mainland; the Juan Fernández Islands, 400 miles off the coast—once the makeshift home to Scotsman Alexander Selkirk, the real-life Robinson Crusoe—are moderately stocked with waves.) Chile's dependable surf is largely a product of the Humboldt Current, which consistently pushes storms up from Antarctica. The coast is also fronted by a wave-amplifying offshore trench. The Chilean surf is often four to six foot, and 12-foot-plus swells are not uncommon during the winter season. Waves arrive all year, but are generally best during the milder months between November and May. Water temperatures are affected by the chilly Humboldt, dropping down to the upper 40s in winter, and rising

only to the mid-60s in summer. Daytime air temperatures on the central coast range from 40 to 70; temperatures in the north range from 50 to 90. Sharp, shallow, urchin-lined reefs are the main surfing hazard.

Chilean surfing began in 1969, when native marine biologist Sergio Santa Cruz built a surfboard that doubled as a flotation device for studying marine life. In the early '70s, professional divers Luis "Lucho" Tello and Isaac "Icha" Tapia took to the surf at Ritoque, near Santiago, and in 1972, Claudio Castro built and sold 60 boards on the central Chilean coast. Santiago's Ricardo Gomez opened Tropicana Surf Shop, the first retail outlet of its kind in the country, in 1985. Chile held its first national surf contest in 1986, at Pichilemu, with Ricardo Tompson of Iquique winning the event. American surf magazines began publishing feature articles on Chile in the early '80s, but for reasons that remain unclear the sport was slow to catch on; northern neighbor Peru had taken to surfing with gusto decades earlier, and Brazil was on its way to becoming a world surfing power. By 2003, Chile was home to about 20 surf shops, two surf magazines (*Marejada* and *Demolicion*) and 2,500 surfers, with several thousand more bodyboarders. The vast majority of surfers and surf industry is located in the northern half of the country. Diego Medina and Eduardo Panat are often cited as the country's top surfers. Domestic surf companies include Salerno (surfboards), Flashback (beachwear), Bomb (wax and sunglasses), and Dreamstyle (board covers). Small-operation overland surf tours cover the remote coastline around Pichilemu. The Chilean surf has been featured in a small number of surf and bodyboard videos, including *Boogie Knights* (1999).

China China is the world's most populous nation, with its 1.2 billion inhabitants making up one-fifth of the world's total; it is also the third largest nation in terms of landmass, behind Russia and Canada. China's eastern border is marked by the Yellow Sea, the East China Sea, and the South China Sea. Australian expatriate Rod Payne tried to become the first surfer in China by paddling out at Hong Kong's Big Wave Bay in 1979, but was removed from the water by police. Former Australian national surfing champion Peter Drouyn contracted with the national government in 1985 to form a Chinese surf school, and began giving lessons to a group of Chinese student/gymnasts in the gentle waves off Hainan Island, located in the South China Sea between mainland China and Vietnam. Drouyn's project was terminated two months later, without explanation, and he returned to Australia. In November 1986, a group of visiting surfers from California and Hawaii—Rell Sunn, Jon Damm, Willy Morris, Matt George, and Warren Bolster—were feted in the capital city, then transported to Hainan, where they rode small but warm three-foot waves. "The huge bay was hugged in between two rocky headlands," George wrote in the subsequent *Surfer* article. "We were hell and gone from the official receptions and banquets of Beijing now. We were just surfers again."

Surfing had meanwhile taken root in Hong Kong, 300 miles to the northeast. In the spring of 1997, American-born surfer Francesco Suarez, a 15-year local at Big Wave Bay, founded the Hong Kong Surfing Association, along with Australians Simon Chau and Grant Robinson. China also hosted its first surf competition in 1997, the Hong Kong Cup, with more than 60 native-born and visiting surfers vying in the small, crumbly surf typical of the ill-named Big Wave Bay; winners were invited to an international competition in Bali. By 2003 there were six surf shops and a surf school in Hong Kong; the Hong Kong Surfing Association had more than 500 members; and the field for the annual Hong Kong Cup included surfers from Australia, France, Japan, England, and China. Hainan Island is now home to perhaps two dozen native surfers. *Action Asia,* an outdoor sports magazine that includes surfing, began publishing in 1998.

While virtually the entire Chinese coastline remains unexplored for surf, the known areas—Hainan and Big Wave Bay—contain mostly beachbreaks. Autumn and winter monsoons produce waist- to chest-high wind swell waves with some regularity; spring and summer typhoon surf is bigger, but shiftier and more difficult to ride. The weather in Hainan and Hong Kong is subtropical, with water temperatures usually in the upper 60s and low 70s.

chine rail Surfboard design where the lower half of the rail—the curve that connects the perimeter of the board to the bottom surface—is sheared off and flattened. The chine rail is usually placed in the middle and nose sections of the board, and was popularized in the mid-'70s as a design feature on the stinger surfboard, and to a lesser degree with the mid-'80s hydro-hull tri-fin. Proponents claimed that water would break more quickly from the chine rail as the board moved through the water, as compared to a conventional rounded rail, and thus increase speed. Also known as a beveled rail. *See also* stinger.

chip board Type of balsa-core surfboard designed after World War II by California board-maker Bob Simmons, and refined primarily by Joe Quigg and Matt Kivlin, also from California, with most of the field testing done at Malibu. "Chip" was short for "potato chip," as the new boards were so much lighter than those used in the '30s; they were also called "Malibu chips." Surfers in the prewar years either rode blunt-nosed redwood or redwood-balsa "plank" boards that weighed anywhere from 45 to 100 pounds, or tippy, streamlined, and somewhat lighter "cigar-box" hollow boards. Simmons's fiberglass-sealed balsa boards ('30s boards were finished in varnish) had scooped-up noses, wider and curvier outlines, and weighed about 30 pounds. Subsequent boards by Quigg and Kivlin were lighter still. The rear-anchored stabilizing fin, introduced in the mid-'30s but not popularized until the mid-'40s, was standard on the chip. All these features combined to make an easier-turning board that also rode tighter to the curl. The chip, Quigg said in 1984, "busted the whole surfing thing right open," with bottom- and top-turns coming about as a direct result of the new boards. The beginning of the end for the chip board came in the mid-'50s, with the introduction of the wide-backed "pig" model, and by the end of the decade, with polyurethane foam taking over as the near-universal core material for surfboards, the chip was all but extinct. By the end of the century, collectors were paying up to $18,000 for an original Simmons chip. *See also* Matt Kivlin, Malibu board, Joe Quigg, Bob Simmons.

chop *See* wind chop.

Chouinard, Yvon Innovative businessman and environmentalist from Ventura, California; founder of Patagonia, the hugely successful "green" sportswear and sporting goods company. Chouinard was born (1938) in Lewiston, Maine, and was nine when he moved with his family to Burbank, California. He started surfing in high school, became a legendary rock climber in the '60s, began selling handmade climbing hardware in 1964, and founded Patagonia in 1974. Chouinard remained an avid surfer, and long after Patagonia's warm and soft polar fleece jackets became a fashion favorite for urbanites as well as hardcore climbers, he began putting more time and money into what he called his "favorite sport." In 1988 he spent $25,000 on a feasibility study for building an artificial reef at Emma Wood State Beach in Ventura (construction costs prevented the reef from being built). In 1997 Patagonia brought out a strong, light, expensive ($500 to $780) line of surfboards. Chouinard had meanwhile put Patagonia on a "no growth" business plan, as a way to balance environmental sustainability with profits, and his company donated millions to environmental groups. The philanthropy, Chouinard told the *Los Angeles Times* in 1994, was liberating. "I'm not finished [with charity], but I'm doing enough. And because of that, it's a lot easier to say, 'Screw it, I'm going surfing.'" Chouinard's surfing adventures in the Pacific have been featured in *Surfer* and the *Surfer's Journal* magazines.

Christian Surfing Association   *See* Western Surfing Association.

Christmas Island   Low-lying coral atoll, 35 miles long and 15 miles wide, located in the Pacific Ocean, 2,200 miles south of Hawaii and 120 miles north of the equator; the largest of 33 atolls that make up the Republic of Kiribati. The island was named when Captain James Cook anchored here on Christmas Eve, 1777. The same North Pacific swells that produce big waves in Hawaii in winter and early spring generally hit Christmas Island three or four days later at about half the size; a small number of north-facing reefbreaks offer fast, warm, relatively easy-to-ride surf, the vast majority of which goes unridden, thanks to the island's remote location. Strong tradewinds often reduce the quality of the waves. Christmas Island (also known as Kiritimati) is a world-renowned bird preserve, and its inner waters are loaded with famously high-spirited bonefish, making it a dream destination for fly fishermen. Nearby atolls were the site of 26 American and British hydrogen bomb test explosions in the late '50s and '60s, and not until 1975 was Christmas Island declared free of radioactivity; in 2003 there were about 1,300 people living there. Surfing was introduced to Christmas Island in the early 1980s by American marine surveyor Ward Graessle.

cigar box   *See* hollow surfboard.

Clark, Calvin "Tulie"   Indefatigable surfer from Palos Verdes, California; an original member of the Palos Verdes Surfing Club, and the original financial backer, in 1964, of *International Surfing* magazine. Clark was born (1917) in Azusa, California, and began surfing in 1927, using a wooden ironing board liberated from the family laundry room. Ten years later, at age 20, Clark became the first surfer to beat legendary waterman Pete Peterson in a paddling contest; he was also featured in John "Doc" Ball's seminal 1946 photo book *California Surfriders*. Clark later became a successful home builder, and in 1964 became the main investor for *International Surfing* magazine—known today as *Surfing*. Interviewed in 1995, the 78-year-old Clark said he still rode his 11-foot Bob Simmons balsa board at San Onofre. *See also* Palos Verdes Surfing Club.

Clark Foam   World's leading producer of the polyurethane foam blanks that are used as the surfboard's core material; founded in 1961 by Gordon "Grubby" Clark and located in Laguna Niguel, California; suppliers for an estimated 90 percent of all surfboard blanks internationally. Board-makers had been experimenting with foam since the late '40s, but balsa remained the industry's primary material until 1958, when leading Southern California manufacturer Hobie Surfboards switched its entire stock from balsa to foam. Shop owner Hobie Alter had for the previous three years been partners with Clark (the Hobie Surfboards laminator) on a secret foam-manufacturing project in Laguna Canyon, hoping to get an edge on the competition. As their foam-making production grew, Clark bought Alter's share in 1961 and founded Clark Foam, in order to sell blanks to other board-makers. The business moved to its current Laguna Niguel location in 1964, and by the end of the decade Clark Foam had all but monopolized the world surfboard blank market.

A Clark Foam production flaw in the early '90s resulted in blanks erupting in hundreds of tiny but board-ruining gaseous emissions ("blowthrough") during the laminating process. The company sent out industry memos blaming a newly formulated resin (although the problem didn't occur when the resins were used on non-Clark blanks), and Clark himself later threatened to close his factory and quit the business altogether, which likely would have resulted in dozens of surfboard company bankruptcies. It took Clark more than three years to solve the blowthrough

Clark Foam surfboard blanks

problem—no explanation was ever given as to how the problem started or how it was resolved—and board manufacturers had to absorb the cost of the faulty blanks.

As of 2003, there were 70 blanks in the Clark Foam line, ranging in size from 5′9″ to 12′8″, along with seven different foam densities and a number of rocker and center-cut wood stringer options. Many of the Clark Foam molds were designed by the world's top surfboard shapers, including Rusty Preisendorfer, Dale Velzy, Pat Rawson, and Dick Brewer. Blanks generally wholesale for about $50 to $80 each; larger blanks can cost up to $150. It was estimated that Clark sold about 300,000 blanks in 2002, distributing through warehouses in Florida, Hawaii, England, and France. Walker Foam, Clark's only current American competitor, is thought to produce about 50,000 blanks annually. *See also* Gordon Clark, polyurethane foam.

Clark, Gordon "Grubby"   Powerful and reclusive behind-the-scenes surf industrialist from Orange County, California; an innovator of the polyurethane foam blank used since the late 1950s as the core material for virtually all surfboards; founder of Clark Foam. Clark has always refused to talk about himself on record, but it is believed that he was born in 1931 in Los Angeles, raised in Whittier, and learned to surf while attending Pomona College in the late '40s and early '50s, where he earned a B.S. in engineering. In 1955, after spending two years in the

army, Clark was working as a laminator for Hobie Surfboards, the soon-to-be world's largest board manufacturer. Clark began to develop polyurethane foam molds in the mid-'50s, along with shop owner Hobie Alter, looking for a replacement material for balsa wood, which was costly and often hard to find; three years later Hobie Surfboards switched entirely from balsa to foam. Clark made an amicable split from Hobie in 1961 to form Clark Foam in Laguna Canyon—later relocated to Laguna Niguel—and by the mid-'60s Clark had become the runaway leader in blank production. He later attributed his success to the fact that nobody else wanted to do the job. "There's nothing romantic about foam," he said in 1972. "It's dirty, messy and smelly, and nothing you'd dream of doing for a career."

Alter later said that Clark became the blank king because he's "unbelievably efficient." Others have described him as aggressive and ruthless, and *Surfing* magazine said he had put a "hammerlock" on the board-making industry. Clark constantly updated and refined his product, and remained in contact with the surf world in large part by sending out long, detailed, well-written memos (sometimes referred to as the Clark Foam Pamphlets), with titles like "Analysis of Future Trends in Surfboard Construction." Holding a near monopoly on blanks, he was the most powerful man in surfboard manufacturing, and feared as such. "Nobody has ever wanted to do anything to upset Clark," *Surfing* magazine noted in 1992. "They don't want to lose their shipping seniority or have their invoices start to get 'misplaced.'" *Surfer* magazine named Clark as the 10th most influential surfer of the 20th century. A longtime resident of Laguna Beach, Clark was married once and has two children. *See also* Clark Foam, polyurethane foam.

Clark, Jeff   Flinty big-wave rider from Half Moon Bay, California; the first surfer to ride Maverick's, the beautiful but malevolent reefbreak known today as the big-wave capital of the continental United States. Clark was born (1957) in Redwood City, California, the son of a carpenter, moved with his family to Half Moon Bay in 1966, and began surfing the following year, at age 11. Maverick's was located about two miles north of his house, and as a high school sophomore he began watching the break from the nearby headland; on a warm February afternoon in 1975, 17-year-old Clark paddled out alone and rode five left-breaking Maverick's waves, each about 10 or 12 feet.

In the weeks to come he tried to get some of the local surfers to join him for a return visit, but nobody was interested. For 15 years Clark rode Maverick's by himself. None of the board manufacturers in the area knew how to make a board for 15- to 25-foot waves, so Clark, a trained carpenter and a board shaper since he was 16, taught himself how to make a serviceable 10-foot big-wave gun. A born goofyfoot, he also learned how to ride in a left-foot-forward stance, making it easier to ride the long and more intricate Maverick's rights.

Clark developed over the years into a solid big-wave rider: his stance was inflexible and straight-backed, but his line across the wave was smooth and knowledgeable. In early 1990, he finally brought Maverick's to the attention of surfers outside of Half Moon Bay, in part because he wanted company and to help promote his new Maverick's-named line of surfboards. *Surfer* magazine introduced the break to the surf world at large in early 1992, describing the dark-haired, strong-jawed Clark as a "hellman," and the "unofficial guardian of a true secret spot." As Maverick's popularity skyrocketed over the next two years, Clark remained the break's unofficial spokesman, and as such was featured in *Rolling Stone, Spin,* the *New York Times, Outside,* NBC Nightly News, and MTV Sports. Using a soft, drawling voice, Clark described Maverick's as "the most radical wave on the planet" to the *Los Angeles Times,* and remembered back to when he'd been "the Lone Ranger out there."

As of 2003, Maverick's has been featured in more than 50 surf videos and documentaries, and Clark appears in nearly all of them, including *Gravity Sucks* (1994), *Maverick's* (1997), *Monstrosity* (1999), and *Year of the Drag-In* (2000). Clark was also featured in *Adventures in Wild California* (2000), an IMAX movie, and in *Maverick's: The Story of Big-Wave Surfing* (Chronicle Books, 2000). Clark was hired as the contest director for the debut Quiksilver Maverick's Men Who Ride Mountains contest in 1999, and served again in 2000. He competed in the 2002 Tow-In World Cup, held at Jaws, Maui. He's been married twice and has three children; his second wife opened the Maverick's Roadhouse Cafe in 1995. *See also* Maverick's, Quiksilver Maverick's Men Who Ride Mountains.

Clarke-Jones, Ross   Sleepy-eyed Australian big-wave rider from Avoca, New South Wales; winner of the 2001 Quiksilver in Memory of Eddie Aikau con-

test at Waimea Bay. Clarke-Jones was born in Sydney on June 6, 1966 (or 6/6/66, as surf journalist Derek Rielly gleefully pointed out in a *Surfer* magazine profile titled "The Devil's Playground"), and began surfing at age 10. He finished third in the men's division of the 1986 World Amateur Surfing Championships, and three months later, as a pro tour rookie competing in the Billabong Pro at Waimea Bay, he casually dropped into a half-dozen 20-foot waves on a 7'10" surfboard—the smallest board in the event by more than a foot. Clarke-Jones went as high as #24 on the world rankings (in 1989), but was never regarded as anything more than an average pro competitor; his reputation was instead made as a surfer who never seemed to be more than a few months removed from a near-death experience. On his third visit to Hawaii, in 1987, he broke his ribs and was unconscious underwater after being hit by a loose board. He nearly drowned in Sumatra in 1992, and six months later was driven tailbone first into the reef at Hawaii's Off the Wall, cracking four vertebra and temporarily losing feeling in his legs. In 1998, he and tow-in partner Tony Ray were rolled by a 30-footer at Outside Log Cabins, also in Hawaii, and along with their flooded personal watercraft drifted four miles west through enormous seas, before getting picked up outside of Haleiwa Harbor. Clarke-Jones has competed in every big-wave event held since the late '80s (finishing seventh in the 1990 Aikau contest at Waimea, and third in the 1999 Quiksilver Men Who Ride Mountains event at Maverick's), and was 34 years old when he picked up the $50,000 winner's check for the 2001 Quiksilver/Aikau. He finished fifth in the 2002 Quiksilver/Aikau. Clarke-Jones has been featured in more than two dozen surf movies and videos, including *Mad Wax* (1987), *All Down the Line* (1989), *110/240* (1992), and *The Moment* (1998). He's been married twice and has two children.

clean-up set   A set of waves much bigger than the going standard; a fairly regular occurrence when a swell is on the rise. A clean-up set should break far enough beyond the prevailing surf zone that it will "clean up" the area of surfers by sweeping them toward the beach. The phrase is generally used only when the surf is medium-sized or bigger. Hawaiian big-wave rider Todd Chesser drowned at Oahu's Outside Alligator Rock in 1997 after being rolled by a 25-foot clean-up set. *See also* caught inside.

Clean-up set at Hawaii's Sunset Beach

Cleary, Bill Soulful and articulate writer/editor from Ventura, California; coauthor of 1963's *Surfing Guide to Southern California,* and the mid-'60s editor of *Surf Guide* magazine. Cleary was born (1938) in Los Angeles, raised near Pasadena, began surfing in 1953 at age 15, and received a premed B.A. from UCLA in 1962. During and after college, Cleary wrote a first draft for *Surfing Guide,* a detailed spot-by-spot guidebook, and the first publication of its kind for surfers. Cleary then handed the project off to coauthor David Stern, and left for France; returning home, he was surprised to find that letters he'd mailed back to friends in the L.A. area had been gathered and printed as an article in the recently founded *Surf Guide* magazine, published in Santa Monica. Cleary wrote more *Surf Guide* articles in 1963, and near the end of the year became the editor, a post he held until the magazine's demise in 1965. While never more than gently subversive, Cleary was the first ranking surf magazine writer to downplay competition and instead view surfing as something of a counterculture pursuit. "We're interested," Cleary wrote, "in the surfing mood, as well as surfing action; not just what's on the surface of the wave, but what lies beneath it." Cleary was hired by *Surfer* magazine in late 1965, where he spent three years as associate editor, while freelancing youth culture articles to *Time* and *Life* magazines. *Surfing: All the Young Wave Hunters,* his surf history book, was published in 1967 by New American Library.

Cleary continued to surf in the '70s, but quit surf publishing and wrote for *Playboy* and other adult magazines. He was married three times and had three children. Cleary died of Parkinson's disease in 2002, at age 64. *See also* Surf Guide magazine.

climb and drop A sustained, winding, up-and-down, trough-to-crest series of turns performed as the surfer rides across a long and evenly tapered wave. Generally, no single turn within a climb-and-drop sequence is flashy or radical; the object is to gain speed and establish rhythm.

closeout A wave that folds over all at once, without a "shoulder," or declining crest line, that allows a rider to angle across the wave face; avoided by boardriders as a rule, although beginners usually learn on soft-breaking closeouts. Better surfers are often forced into closeouts due to crowds, or lured into closeouts that at first appear to have a shoulder. Bodysurfers and bodyboarders have made an art of riding closeout tubes at places like Sandy Beach and Makapuu in Hawaii.

closeout tube A nonnegotiable, no-possible-exit tuberide, often performed to impress onlookers; dangerous for beginners and intermediates, as the rider can easily be hit by his board, or bounced off the bottom. Advanced surfers will avoid injury by either jabbing their board and body sharply through the tubing wave face, or by ejecting off the tail as the tube implodes. "A moment of simultaneous disappointment and joy, of victory and defeat," *Surfing* magazine wrote of the closeout tube in 1998, "a glorious stand in the face of certain destruction." Sometimes called a "suicide tube."

Closeout at Redondo Beach, California

cloth   *See* fiberglass.

Cloud Nine   Warm, tubing, right-breaking reef wave located on the island of Siargao, near Mindanao, in the Philippines. "Cloud Nine," *Australia's Surfing Life* magazine said in 1995, "is as perfect a reef as you could conjure in your most fantastic dream; fast, easy-to-surf barrels." Also known as "Boyums," after American surf explorer and convicted drug smuggler Mike Boyum, who discovered Cloud Nine in 1989 and died two months later in a nearby grass shack after a 45-day fast. Cloud Nine, named after a locally produced candy bar, was introduced to the surf world in a 1993 *Surfer* magazine article. Two surf resorts had been built on the beach in front of the break by mid-1995, and the following year, according to the *Surf Report* newsletter, a good day at Cloud Nine could draw up to 100 surfers. Visitors meanwhile discovered that the Philippine surf, even during the height of the wave season, can go flat or near flat for weeks at a time.

The best time for waves at Cloud Nine is between September and November, as typhoons arc in a northerly direction across the Philippine Sea. Daytime temperatures here average in the low 80s, with water in the mid-70s. Cloud Nine is featured in more than a half-dozen surf videos, including *Overdrive* (1993) and *Surf Adventures* (2000).

Cloudbreak   See Tavarua.

cloudbreak   Big-wave break, usually a reef, located well beyond the normal surf zone. Cloudbreaks come into full form only during the biggest storms, and more often than not go unridden—although tow-in surfing, developed in the early 1990s, has slowly brought more cloudbreak locations into play. Outside Log Cabins on the North Shore of Oahu is one of the best-known cloudbreak waves. "Outer reef" is often used synonymously with "cloudbreak"; a distant big-wave break in Australia and New Zealand is usually referred to as a "bombora." *See also* bombora.

Clough, Greg   Low-key Australian surfboard shaper, originally from the Gold Coast of Queensland. Clough began shaping in 1969 at age 21. In 1974 he started working for Midget Farrelly Surfboards in Sydney, and four years later he founded Aloha Surfboards, also located in Sydney. In the early and mid-'80s, Clough helped refine the newly introduced

tri-fin board. At one time or another, he made boards for world champions Damien Hardman, Barton Lynch, Pam Burridge, Tom Curren, and Shaun Tomson, as well as Brad Gerlach, Shane Powell, Johnny-Boy Gomes, and Luke Egan. Clough finished fourth in an *Australia's Surfing Life* magazine shaper's poll in 1992, the highest of any Australian.

Club Waikiki   Elegant, class-conscious Peruvian beachfront surfing club located in Miraflores, the wealthiest suburb of Lima. Club Waikiki was founded in 1942 by Peru's original gentleman surfer Carlos Dogny, after he visited Waikiki and was introduced to surfing by Duke Kahanamoku. Surfing in Peru was (and in large part remains) a pastime for the wealthy, and the sport here evolved in and around the hushed and expensively accoutered rooms and patios of Club Waikiki. California surfers visiting for the 1965 World Championships were impressed by the building's split-level size and grandeur. "It's built into the side of a cliff," Long Beach Surf Club president Jim Graham wrote. "The entrance lobby is used to display surfboards and club trophies; the outside terrace has a bar, and a spacious, beautifully-kept pool surrounded by deck chairs and lounging pads." Graham was thrilled by the black-tied waiters and hired "beachboys" who applied surf wax to the boards of club members and their visitors, carried the boards to water's edge, and retrieved lost boards from the rock-lined beach. Club Waikiki was remodeled in 1956 and again in 1962. The joining fee in the mid-'60s was $25,000. More than just a surf society club, Club Waikiki was (and to a large degree remains) a power spot for those at the highest levels of Peruvian business, entertainment, and government. Dogny himself gave a surf lesson to the queen of Denmark in the soft, rolling breakers outside the club, and the Peruvian president often hosted visiting dignitaries in the club dining room. Not all surfers liked the posh Club Waikiki atmosphere. "The whole scene seemed unnatural," said California surfer Mike Doyle, winner of the 1969 Peru International surf contest, "and made me uncomfortable." Australian and 1966 world champion Nat Young, approached once too often by a beachboy intent on ferrying Young's board to the shore, shouted, "Goddamnit, leave me alone! I'll carry my own board!" *See also* Carlos Dogny.

Coalition of Surfing Clubs   Loose-knit, California-based nonprofit umbrella organization, created in

1992 to oversee interclub competition and do grass-roots beach-related environmental work. The California surf club scene was lively in the 1930s and '40s, and again in the '60s, then was wiped out entirely during the shortboard revolution. Surf clubs began to return in the early '80s, as the longboard made its comeback. The seven charter members of the Coalition of Surfing Clubs were the Santa Cruz Longboard Union, the Doheny Longboard Club, the Malibu Boardriders Club, the Malibu Surfing Association, the Windansea Surf Club, the Pedro Point Surf Club, and the Swami's Surfing Association. The coalition was formed in San Luis Obispo, but had no mailing address and virtually no infrastructure; club representatives nonetheless managed to organize an interclub competition every other month, at which time club presidents met to address and form positions on water-quality issues, coastal development, and beach access, thus allowing the coalition to speak with one voice. Individual clubs in turn lobbied local, state, and federal politicians, and held fund-raising events for favorite causes.

By 2003, the Coalition of Surfing Clubs represented 30 clubs from California, the East Coast, and Hawaii with affiliate members in Europe. The environmental work continued apace, while the group's annual California contest circuit, according to *Longboard* magazine, had become "quite prestigious, and often features the best underground talent in the United States." The club issues a biannual newsletter, and compiles year-end club standings. *See also* surf clubs.

Cocoa Beach   Central Florida barrier island resort town, located just south of Cape Canaveral; filled for the most part with nondescript sand-bottom waves, yet home to a wildly disproportionate number of first-rate surfers, including six-time world champion Kelly Slater. While Cocoa Beach itself has just 12 miles of coast (and only 15,000 residents), the city name is often used as shorthand for a 72-mile stretch of Brevard County that includes Satellite Beach, Indialantic, and Melbourne, ending to the south at Sebastian Inlet, the state's best-known surf break.

The American space program brought thousands of engineers, scientists, technicians, builders, and support staff to the Cape Canaveral area in the late '50s, '60s, and '70s, and while they worked on the Gemini and Apollo missions, their sons—and to a far lesser degree, daughters—crossed the powder-sand beaches and began riding the warm central Florida surf. Many of them went on to become national or international figures in surfing, including Gary Propper, Bruce Valluzzi, Mike Tabeling, Claude Codgen, Greg Loehr, Jeff Crawford, Greg Mungall, Matt Kechele, Todd Holland, and Kelly Slater. Four-time world champion Lisa Andersen lives in Ormond Beach, just a few miles north of Cocoa, as does 1966 World Championship runner-up Mimi Munro; four-time world champion Frieda Zamba lives in Flagler Beach, one town north of Ormond. *Surfing* magazine posed the question in a 1991 feature article, "Why are the Cocoa Beach Guys so Good When the Waves are so Bad?" Greg Loehr thought it was because local surfers were competitive among themselves, but united in wanting to prove something to the rest of the surf world. "We surfed for fun, of course," Loehr said, "but we also surfed to be better than the Californians." Claude Codgen's view was slightly different. "These little waves here are just enough to get you stoked, but not quite enough to get you spoiled."

Ron Jon's, the world's biggest (52,000 square feet) and gaudiest surf shop, is located in central Cocoa Beach. The Cocoa Beach Easter Surfing Festival (originally called the Easter Surfing Classic) was founded in 1965. In honor of Kelly Slater, 3rd Street North was renamed Slater Way in 2002.

Codgen, Claude   Smooth, cheerful goofyfooter from Cocoa Beach; regarded by many as the best East Coast surfer of the mid- and late 1960s. Codgen was born (1949) and raised in Florida's Cape Canaveral area, and began surfing at age 11. He was the East Coast's juniors division ratings leader in 1966, and topped the men's division in 1967 and 1969. He also competed in the World Surfing Championships in 1966, 1968, and 1970. Gary Propper became the East Coast's first real star surfer in 1965, but the blond-haired, baby-faced Codgen was hot on his heels, signing a deal for his own signature model board—the CC Rider, made by Con Surfboards—in late 1966. A fluid and graceful small-wave specialist, Codgen was sometimes compared to Hawaiian-born style master David Nuuhiwa. Codgen appeared in a small number of surf movies, including *Follow Me* (1968) and *Tales from the Tube* (1975). He founded Sunshine Surfboards in 1970, which he still owns and operates; in 1996 he was inducted into the East Coast Surfing Hall of Fame.

coffin   Hotdogging maneuver introduced in the late 1950s, where a longboard-riding surfer drops to his back while angling across the wave, and lies feet forward, with hands folded corpselike upon the chest. In a slight variation, hands are templed together in the "pray for surf" position.

Coke Classic; Coca-Cola Surfabout   Australian professional surfing contest held in Sydney from 1974 to 1999, usually in April at North Narrabeen or Manly Beach; conceived and developed by Sydney newspaper journalist and future world pro tour executive director Graham Cassidy; sponsored by soft-drink giant Coca-Cola. Described by 1979 world champion Wayne Bartholomew as the original forum of "slick surfing professionalism," the Coke was by far the richest contest on the world pro tour from 1976 to 1982. Unfortunately, because it was scheduled two or three months before prime surf season, the Coke was often forced to run in poor waves. The $7,000 debut contest, however, was helped in spectacular surf at Fairy Bower, Narrabeen, and other Sydney beaches, with Queensland surfer Michael Peterson overtaking Peter Townend at the wire to win the $3,000 first prize. Other memorable Coke matchups include the Larry Blair/Wayne Lynch tube-duel final in 1978 (listed by *Surfer* magazine in 1999 as one of the "Top Five Greatest Surf Contests"); the air-lift event in 1979, when meet director Paul Holmes chartered two planes to fly the 11 remaining contestants, plus judges and reporters, from Sydney to Bells Beach in Victoria; the Gary Elkerton/Damien Hardman semifinal match in 1988 to decide the world title (won by

Hardman); and the Shane Herring/Kelly Slater "New School" final in 1992. At different times in its history, the Coke served as either the season-opening or season-ending event. From 1974 to 1976 the Coke used an objective "points-per-maneuver" judging system; from 1974 to 1983 the event was cosponsored by radio station 2SM, and the event's official title was the 2SM/Coca-Cola Surfabout. Australian surf filmmaker Alby Falzon was commissioned by Coca-Cola to produce *Surfabout '74*, a short documentary; six more Surfabout films were made between 1975 and 1983. Men's and women's combined prize money for the 1999 Coke was $150,600.

Winners of the Coke/2SM Surfabout and the Coke Classic (no women's division winners in 1974–76, 1979–83, and 1986):

1974:   Michael Peterson
1975:   Wayne Lynch
1976:   Mark Richards
1977:   Simon Anderson, Margo Oberg
1978:   Larry Blair, Lynne Boyer
1979:   Cheyne Horan
1980:   Buzzy Kerbox
1981:   Simon Anderson
1982:   Wayne Bartholomew
1983:   Tom Carroll
1984:   (not held)
1985:   (not held)
1986:   Barton Lynch
1987:   Tom Carroll, Frieda Zamba
1988:   Damien Hardman, Toni Sawyer
1989:   Martin Potter, Wendy Botha
1990:   Rob Bain, Wendy Botha
1991:   Brad Gerlach, Wendy Botha
1992:   Shane Herring, Pam Burridge
1993:   Todd Holland, Layne Beachley
1994:   Shane Powell, Pauline Menczer
1995:   Vetea David (nonrated men's event), Michelle Donoghoe
1996:   Kelly Slater, Kylie Webb
1997:   Kelly Slater, Kylie Webb
1998:   Shane Beschen, Layne Beachley
1999:   Taj Burrow, Layne Beachley

Colbert, Peter   *See* Peter Mansted.

Colburn, Con   Southern California surfboard and surf product manufacturer, and founder of Con Surfboards; "a wily but likable businessman," as described by *Surfing* magazine in the mid-1960s. Although Col-

Mark Richards, 1976 Coke Classic winner

burn didn't begin surfing until 1956 when he was 22, he quickly recognized that the surf market was about to expand, and in 1958 opened the Surf House in Santa Monica. He soon changed the business name to Con Surfboards. By 1965 he had three retail stores, and by late 1966 he had two of the more popular surfboard models on the market: a blunt-ended noserider appropriately called "The Ugly" and the "C.C. Rider," an East Coast–marketed signature board designed by Claude Codgen of Florida. The circular Con Surfboards logo was by that time nearly as recognizable as the Hobie and Weber marks. In 1970, Colburn produced the first commercially manufactured surf leash, the Power Cord, and the following year he invented the leash plug, a half-dollar-sized plastic cup that set flush to the deck of a board as a leash-anchoring device. In 1988, Colburn moved to Bishop, just below the Sierra Nevada mountains in California; he died four years later of lung cancer, at age 57. *See also* leash plug, surf leash.

Cole, Maurice Bearish surfer and surfboard shaper from Victoria, Australia; three-time finalist in the Australian National Titles from 1979 to 1981; board-maker to some of the world's best surfers in the '90s and '00s. The part-Aboriginal Cole was born (1954) in Ballarat, Victoria, moved with his adopted family to nearby Port Campbell at age four, and began surfing at 13. Chubby, strong, and determined, Cole won the 1972 Victoria state titles, one year before he started dealing drugs. In 1974 he was arrested for possession of hash oil, and in 1976 he was convicted and served just over two years in prison, with part of the time spent in a maximum security cell. Released in February 1978, Cole returned to Torquay, his home since 1972, and the capital of Victoria surfing. The following year he again won the Victoria state title. Competing in the nationals, he placed fifth in 1979, third in 1980, and fifth in 1981; he also finished sixth in the 1980 World Surfing Championships.

Cole had been shaping surfboards since 1974, and by 1976 was one of his country's best-paid boardmakers. He became a partner in Watercooled Surfboards in Victoria in 1978; two years later he sold his interest in Watercooled and moved to Hossegor, France, to build surfboards under his own name and to work as a surf accessories distributor. Cole gained an international reputation as a shaper in 1990, as California surfer Tom Curren won his third world pro championship while using Cole-made boards; the following year, Cole made Curren a board with reverse vee—putting a slight vee-panel concavity in the tail of the board, instead of the usual convexity—and the design feature soon became a shortboard standard. The bearded and frequently scowling Cole went on to build boards for world champions Barton Lynch, Kelly Slater, Tom Carroll, and Mark Occhilupo, as well as pro tour standouts Kalani Robb, Taj Burrow, and Jake Paterson, and big-wave rider Noah Johnson. His French-based surfing business, meanwhile, put him deeply into debt by the early '90s.

Cole moved to Margaret River, Western Australia, in 1995, and two years later founded MC Surfboards. He was soon making news as a vocal critic of arch-conservative politician Pauline Hanson, leader of the anti-immigrant One Nation party. "Are we on course to become the South Africa of the new millennium?" Cole asked in an *Australia's Surfing Life* magazine opinion piece before going on to describe Hanson and her followers as "short-sighted, power-hungry lunatics." Cole also lampooned Hanson in full-page color MC Surfboards advertisements.

In 1999, Cole, along with pro surfers Ross Clarke-Jones, and Brenden Margieson, introduced tow-in surfing to Western Australia. Cole has appeared in a small number of surf movies and videos, including *A Day in the Life of Wayne Lynch* (1978), *Wizards of the Water* (1982), and *Storm Riders* (1982). He is married and has two children. *See also* reverse vee.

Cole, Peter Bright, gracious, persevering big-wave surfer from the North Shore of Oahu, Hawaii; winner of the 1958 Makaha International contest, and one of the original California-born surfers who helped shape big-wave riding in the late '50s and early '60s. "He'd wait with the patience of Job for the biggest wave of the day," fellow California transplant Rick Grigg said. "And when it came he usually caught it." Cole was born (1930) in Los Angeles, the son of a stockbroker, raised in Highland Park and San Marino, and began surfing at age 14 when he moved with his family to Santa Monica.

Cole graduated in 1953 with a B.A. in fine arts from Stanford University, where he played water polo and was a nationally ranked middle-distance freestyle swimmer. While at Stanford he often drove to nearby Santa Cruz to ride Steamer Lane, developing a taste for large waves. Cole taught high school and served in the army, then moved to Honolulu in 1958 to teach math at Punahou School, and to test his mettle on the North Shore of Oahu, which had just eclipsed the west side's Makaha as the center of big-wave surfing. George Downing, Wally Froiseth, and a few other Hawaiians were riding the North Shore, but much of the groundbreaking work at places like Waimea Bay and Sunset Beach was being done by California-born surfers like Buzzy Trent, Pat Curren, Fred Van Dyke, and Greg Noll; Cole and fellow Stanford grad Rick Grigg joined the group in 1958. At 6′4″, Cole was the tallest of the big-wave surfers, and perhaps the least nimble. But because of his tremendous swimming ability, along with an inborn calmness and an analytic mind that told him big-wave danger was overstated, he soon gained a reputation as one of the sport's boldest riders. In 1972, however, Cole was struck by his surfboard and blinded in his right eye.

Cole received an M.S. in information sciences from the University of Hawaii in 1971. He had left Punahou School (where he'd taught Gerry Lopez and Jeff Hakman, among other well-known '70s surfers), and was then working as an operations research analyst for the Navy Civil Service. Decades passed, and Cole continued to ride big waves on the North Shore, attributing his longevity in part to the fact that he had a rich life outside of surfing. "Those of my generation who dedicated all their time to surfing aren't in the lineup anymore. For a surfer to ride into old age, it's important that surfing be nothing more than a recreational activity. It should never be a person's entire life." Although he won the 1958 Makaha International and rode in the 1965 Duke Kahanamoku Invitational, Cole generally took a dim view of surfing contests, saying that they worked against the main purpose of the sport, which is to have a good time.

Cole rode Waimea for the last time in 1995 at age 65, but was still riding Sunset Beach as of 2002. "When Peter paddles out at Sunset," Rick Grigg said in 1998, "everyone cheers." Cole appeared in a half-dozen surf movies including *Surf Safari* (1959), *Barefoot Adventure* (1960), and *Cavalcade of Surf* (1962); he was also featured in *Surfing for Life*, a 1999 PBS-aired documentary about aging surfers. Cole wrote articles for *Surf Guide* magazine in the mid-'60s, mainly on big-wave riding, and narrated Bud Browne's *Surfing the '50s* compilation video in 1994. He's been married twice and has three children.

Collins, Richie Emotional and eccentric regular-foot pro surfer from Newport Beach, California;

world-ranked #8 in 1989 and 1990; as famous in surf circles for his oversize, trash-talking personality as for his inventive high-speed floater maneuvers. Collins was born (1969) and raised in Newport Beach, the son of surfboard-maker Lance Collins, founder of Wave Tools Surfboards. Lance took Richie out surfing as a toddler; at age eight, Collins entered and won his first contest; at 14 he turned professional, and four years later finished his debut year on the world tour ranked #30. He won the 1988 O'Neill Coldwater Classic in Santa Cruz, the 1989 Op Pro in Huntington Beach (beating three-time world champion Tom Curren in the final), and the 1992 Rip Curl Pro at Bells Beach; in a four-year stretch from 1988 to 1991, he finished the year rated 14th, eighth, eighth, and 10th. Collins dropped off the tour in 1993, then returned in 1995 for a brief and unsuccessful comeback attempt.

The lanky Collins (6′, 150 pounds) was never a great stylist, appearing at times to be all knees, elbows, and bony size-13 feet, but in the late '80s he put more variations and twists into his off-the-top maneuvers than anybody in the world, and was able to stretch his floaters out for yards at a time. He rarely kept anything in reserve, and would launch one move after the other until either the wave ended or he fell off. Collins began shaping at age 15, and was the only top-rated surfer of the period to make his own surfboards. He was also known as confrontational, self-abusive, wickedly funny, and apocalyptic. Collins would smash his head against his board during a losing streak; he said that "soul surfing" was foreign to him and that he surfed "only for competition"; he went on record noting that masturbation was key to maintaining the celibacy demanded by his born-again Christian faith.

Collins appeared in nearly two dozen surf movies and videos including *Filthy Habits* (1987), *No Limits* (1988), *Pump!* (1990), and *Session Impossible* (1991). From 1992 to 1995 he owned and operated Contra Surfboards; from 1996 to 1999 he owned and operated California Hot Shapes. Collins is married and has one child.

Collins, Sean Soft-spoken, data-crunching surf forecaster from Long Beach, California; owner and cofounder of Surfline wave-information service. Collins was born (1952) in Pasadena, the son of a navy navigator, grew up in Long Beach, and began surfing in the mid-60s. He was interested, as all serious surfers are, in the mechanics of wave-producing storms. But where others ended their information search with the weather page in the local newspaper or prerecorded lifeguard reports, Collins was eventually synthesizing data from at-sea ships, National Oceanic and Atmospheric Administration (NOAA) millibar charts, and satellite photos into his own customized—and, at first, personal-use only—surf forecasts. Driving through Baja on surf junkets in the early '80s with a first-generation fax machine, Collins would pull off the road, plug the device into his car battery, toss a 100-foot antenna wire over the tallest available cactus, and wait for satellite images of the Pacific Ocean to scroll out. He would then decide what beach to shoot for. Back in Orange County he waited tables and worked as a freelance photographer to earn money.

Although Collins was a junior college dropout with no formal meteorological training, he had nonetheless earned a local reputation as a wave-predicting genius by 1984 when he became a founding partner of Surfline, a new Huntington Beach–based pay-per-call phone service. Surfline launched in March 1985, utilizing the just-approved 976 customer toll numbers; for 55 cents, callers got a recorded description of the surf, updated twice daily, plus a 72-hour Collins-formulated wave forecast. Less than two years later Collins left Surfline and founded Wavetrak, a competing phone service. The two companies merged in 1991; together they received more than a million calls that year, and by 1993 Surfline/Wavetrak was covering 11 U.S. coastal states, Mexico, the Caribbean, and much of Central America. Surfline went online in 1995; three years later Collins bought the entire Surfline/Wavetrak operation. In 2000 he sold the company to Swell.com, but stayed on as Surfline's president and Chief Weather Officer, overseeing 10 full-time employees. (Surfline ownership changed hands again in 2001; Collins's position was unchanged.) By that time Collins had been profiled in *Newsweek,* the *Los Angeles Times,* and *Sports Illustrated.* He was also moonlighting as a consultant to lifeguard chiefs, harbormasters, and Hollywood filmmakers looking for dramatic camera-ready surf.

Not everybody was happy with Collins's ever-more accurate wave predictions. Many of California's surf breaks were already filled to capacity by the time Surfline launched, and Collins's service had almost certainly made the crowds worse. "If you live by the beach," as a *Kema News* surf magazine reader put it in 1993, "you know what's happening with the surf. If

you live in Kookamonga or some inland valley, you don't have a clue, unless some capitalistic scumbag sells the information to every wannabe this side of Bakersfield." Collins admitted that Surfline/Wavetrak and the rest of the surf-forecasting services had not only put more bodies in the lineup on good days, but that the new science had to some degree reduced the sport's mystique. "Some of the magic is gone," he said in 1998, recalling a bygone era of the unannounced and seemingly miraculous arrival of good waves. But he also pointed out that surfers were no longer wasting time on fruitless wave hunts. Time management, Collins said in 1999, was what counted. "If I wanted to surf into my old age and share it with my kids, I was going to have to do a better job of getting waves when it counted and going to work when it didn't count." In a 1999 article, *Surfer* magazine named Collins as one of the "25 Most Influential Surfers of the 20th Century." The *New York Times,* in a 2002 profile, described him as "the ultimate web surfer" and "the new kahuna." Collins is married, has two children, and lives in Seal Beach. *See also* Surfline, surf forecasting.

Colombia Warm and moist South American country adjoining the continent to Central America via Panama; the only South American country with coastlines on both the Atlantic (by way of the Caribbean Sea) and Pacific Oceans. Surfing is virtually unheard of in Colombia; wave-riders number in the dozens, and the country's civil war and reputation for drug-trade violence has for the most part kept tourists at bay—surfers included. Colombia's 580-mile Pacific Ocean coastline is one of the country's least-inhabited areas, roadless in places, and surfing here often requires a boat or plane. Waves arrive all year, but are best and biggest—often 10 feet or larger—during the November-to-February dry season. Temperatures along the coast are typically equatorial, ranging from warm and pleasant to insufferably hot. The water temperature is generally around 80. Playa Boca Grande, a road-accessible beachbreak near Tumaco, close to the Ecuadorian border, is Colombia's most popular surf break. Colombia's 710-mile Caribbean shore has more roads than the Pacific coast. The surf is dependent almost exclusively on short-fetch wind swell, and rarely gets over six foot. Nearly all of Colombia's Caribbean surf breaks, however, are fronted by deep-water offshore canyons, which help produce faster, more powerful waves than might be expected. Cabo La Vela, near Colombia's northeast tip, has aquamarine water and white-sand beaches, and some of the country's finest surf. It's also been used as an exit port for drug traffickers, as have many dozens of other beaches across the Colombian coast, both Pacific and Caribbean. Many of the coastal roads were in fact made by drug cartels as transportation links, and are patrolled regularly; visiting surfers have been advised not to get too ambitious in their search for waves.

competitive surfing   Ancient Hawaiian chiefs competed against one another in surfing matches often accompanied by high-stakes wagering; stakes included canoes, fishing nets, tapa cloth, or swine; servitude, even life itself, was occasionally put on the line. Both contestants rode a wave together, and a point was awarded to the surfer who first reached a marker floating near shore. Several such rides constituted a match. Surfing was checked and suppressed by missionaries in the 19th century in large part because of the gambling associated with competition; surf matches came back not long after the sport's revival in the early 20th century, with contests held in Australia and Hawaii during the late 1910s. "On one occasion," American surf icon Tom Blake wrote in 1935, sounding a prescient note of ambivalence with regard to surfing competition, "about 1918, a riding contest [in Hawaii] was held, the winner being judged on form, etc. Everybody disagreed and that led them to believe surfriding contests were impractical." To remove subjectivity, surfing events were then based on the old Hawaiian format, with riders lining up beyond the surf line, then catching a wave at the sound of a starting gun and racing in together, often all on the same wave, with everyone aiming for an inshore buoy. Ten points were awarded to the first surfer to cross the buoy, the next rider got nine, and so on. Events often consisted of five so-called races. The first of roughly a dozen Australian Championship contests took place in 1919; California's first events were held in 1918; the Pacific Coast Surf Riding Championships—the most prestigious American event—ran from 1928 to 1941; the first of a small number of Hawaiian championship contests was held in 1935. Paddleboard races were almost always held in conjunction with surf contests.

The Makaha International Surfing Championships event debuted in 1954, and is often cited as the first modern surfing contest; from the late '50s to

Competitive surfing; California's Chris Brown (third from right) wins the 1994 Wyland Pro

early '60s it was regarded as the unofficial world championship and drew up to 500 entrants. The contest was held at Makaha, on the west side of Oahu, and the format was changed to include a panel of judges, with each ride scored on a 1–30 point scale, with roughly equal weight given to three criteria: wave size, length of ride, and the surfer's performance. As many as 20 surfers were sent out in a heat, usually lasting between 30 and 90 minutes, and surfers often rode in bunches, with a tactical advantage going to those who were able to "fade" their competitors into a low-scoring whitewater ride. The Makaha International was the first surfing contest to have a women's division. Paddling races were also held, and would continue to be a part of most surfing contests until the mid-'60s. The Peru International, held in Lima, debuted in 1956 and became the second major international surf contest.

The next shift in surfing competition took place in the early '60s, with the founding of administrative groups such as the United States Surfing Association, the Australian Surfriders Association, and the International Surfing Federation. Competition rule changes included an increased emphasis on performance, and the introduction of a "one rider per wave" standard that penalized any surfer who "dropped in" on a surfer who already had "wave possession." The first World Surfing Championships were held in Sydney, Australia, in 1964. Surf industrialists throughout the '60s viewed competition as the primary method by which the sport could bury its prevailing "surf bum" image. "It's your duty," publisher John Severson told *Surfer* magazine readers in a 1961 editorial, "to 'clean up' the sport through a membership in the United States Surfing Association!" Most top surfers competed, but some—including Phil Edwards of California, generally regarded as the world's best in the late '50s and early '60s—felt that competition violated the sport's basic man-meets-nature code and opted out.

Competition surfing continued to grow and evolve. The 1965 Tom Morey Invitational, with a $1,500 purse, introduced cash prizes to the sport, although professional surfing is often said to have begun in 1976 with the formation of the International Professional Surfers, an umbrella organization linking together a series of contests into a world championship pro tour. The circuit grew steadily through the years, from $218,400 in aggregate prize money in 1980 to just over $3.5 million in 2003. Since 1983, the international pro tour has been run by the Association of Professional Surfers. Smaller pro circuits were also founded, including the Professional Surfing Tour of America and Australian Championship Circuit; the number of amateur competition associations expanded as well, with groups in virtually every surfing country running a series of regional and national contests (the Eastern Surfing Association and the National Scholastic Surfing Association have long been the most stable and best-known American amateur groups).

The line between pros and amateurs began to dissolve in the '90s, however, as amateurs were allowed to accept money from contests and sponsors, usually as nominally regulated contributions to their "travel fund." Longboard competitions became popular in the early '80s, and a world pro longboarding championship was established in 1986; bodyboarders also developed their own events, tours, and championships.

Contests were occasionally held in big surf in the '60s and '70s, but not until 1986 were events designed specifically for big waves. Contests judged solely on photographs of surfers riding big waves first appeared in 1997, and the first tow-in big-wave contest took place in 2002. Dozens of other types of events have been staged over the years, including tuberiding contests, exotic-surf contests, single-board-design contests, combined surf-and-snowboard contests; bodysurfing, kneeboarding, wave-ski contests; nude surfing contests; contests that require entrants to drink a bucket of beer before each heat; contests limited to older surfers, teenagers, military personnel; as

well as high school, college, and club contests. But surfers in general remain for the most part indifferent, and in some cases hostile, toward competition. Surf magazines published feature articles in the late '90s and early '00s with titles like "What if They Held a Surf Contest and Nobody Cared?" and "Pro Surfing: Is it Dead, or Does it just Smell Funny?" Events such as the Pipeline Masters in Hawaii or the Tahiti Pro at Teahupoo have served as brilliant showcases for the sport, and competition has likely been a spur to developments in both wave-riding technique and surfboard equipment. But competition surfing has a built-in limitation, as California surf journalist Sam George wrote in 1999, not just because the sport doesn't fit easily into a winner/loser competitive format, but "because very few of us want to sit around and watch someone else play." In 2003, it was estimated that fewer than 9,000 American surfers, out of 2.5 million total, regularly entered surf contests. *Competitive Surfing: A Dedicated Approach,* a how-to book, was published in 1988. *See also* professional surfing.

concave   A depressed area on the bottom of the surfboard. California board designer Bob Simmons experimented with longitudinal concave in the 1950s, on the premise that the indented section would trap air and "lift" the board, increasing speed. But concave didn't really catch on as a design feature until the mid-'60s, when it was put into the board's nose section as an aid to noseriding. The Ego-Builder Concave by Del Cannon Surfboards was one such model. The bonzer design, introduced in 1972, had twin concaves down the board's middle and tail sections; the concave was reinvented yet again in the mid-'90s as the "single-to-double" (a shallow but wide indentation in the middle of the board leading to a pair of lateral concaves in the tail area), generally thought to be one of the decade's most significant design advances, improving both speed and turning characteristics. *See also* reverse vee.

Congo   Tropical French-speaking country located on the west coast of Africa, bisected by the equator. Much of Congo's 100-mile coastline remains uncharted for surfing breaks; most of the half-dozen known spots are located to the south, near the city of Pointe-Noire. Côte Savage is the most popular break, a rock reef that consistently produces long, well-formed rights and lefts, and is conveniently located near a bar and restaurant where local wave-riders can cool off après surf.

Congo receives head-high surf all year, with bigger waves in winter, but because of the continental shelf—a shallow, submerged apron of land just offshore—the surf tends to be soft and easy-breaking. The wind is generally calm in the morning and evening, with a light onshore breeze in the afternoon. Average daytime air temperatures range from the upper 70s to the low 90s; water temperatures range from the low 70s to the mid 80s. Congo has no surf industry, and the roughly 300 local wave-riders, many of them French expatriates, depend largely on donated or cheaply bought gear from visiting surfers. The Congolese are friendly, although thievery is common on the beaches as well as in the cities—even though thieves are often stoned to death by local vigilantes.

Connecticut   Connecticut can hardly be thought of as a surfing state, as all but the easternmost edge of its 220-mile harbor- and bay-studded coastline is blocked by New York's Long Island. Giant hurricane-generated swells, however, will sometimes enter the mouth of Long Island Sound in late summer or early fall and produce small, easygoing sandbar waves near the towns of Groton, New London, and Mystic.

John and Bill Spicer opened Spicer's Surf Shop in Stonington, Connecticut, near the Rhode Island border, in 1964, and went on to open additional shops in Rhode Island and Massachusetts. In 2003 a half-dozen Connecticut sporting goods stores carried boards and wetsuits. The Connecticut chapter of the Surfrider Foundation environmental group was founded in 1999. Rudy Huber, cofounder of the Eastern Surfing Association in 1967, is from Connecticut.

Conneeley, Robert   Sure-footed Australian regular-footer from Sydney's Bondi Beach; one of the country's best teenage competitors in the mid-1960s. Conneeley was born (1948) in Sydney and raised in Bondi; he placed second in the juniors division of the 1963 and 1964 National Titles, and won the all-Australian juniors division of the 1964 World Surfing Championships. At age 17, Conneeley won the 1965 Bells Beach contest, held in massive 15-foot-plus surf. "The final went on for two-and-a-half hours," he later recalled. "It took me 20 minutes just to get through the shorebreak." Conneeley beat rival and former teammate Nat Young in the Bells final; the next year Young went on to win the world title.

Cook Islands   Group of 15 small, widely scattered South Pacific tropical islands, a self-governed protec-

torate of New Zealand, located roughly 1,800 miles northeast of New Zealand's North Island. While the two furthermost Cook Islands are separated by more than 1,000 miles, the total Cook Islands landmass is just 93 square miles. The seven islands to the north are primarily coral atolls, with reef passes that can produce smooth, hollow, beautifully shaped waves from December through March. The eight southern islands are volcanic in origin, and positioned to catch South Pacific swells, which usually arrive between April and October. Although dozens of first-rate breaks have been mapped throughout the Cook Islands (and dozens more have been ridden and kept secret), the entire chain is subject to stinging tradewinds, and waveless spells lasting two weeks or longer. The Cooks have been surfed since the mid-1970s, but have never become a popular spot for the traveling surfer. Locals picked up the sport in the early '90s, and the area's first surf shop opened in 1995 on Rarotonga, the biggest and most-surfed island of the Cook group. A Cook Islands surf team competed in the 2000 Quiksilver Oceania Cup, held in Tonga.

Cook, James   Eighteenth-century English sea captain and Pacific Ocean explorer whose voyages led to European colonization throughout the Pacific; Cook and his crew were the first English-speaking people to witness and write about surfing. Cook was 48 in 1776 when he launched his third and final Pacific expedition, piloting the *Resolution* and the *Discovery* to Tasmania, New Zealand, Hawaii (named the Sandwich Islands by Cook, honoring the Earl of Sandwich, chief of the British navy), and the west coast of North America, then up through the Bering Strait and into the Arctic Ocean. On the return voyage, Cook stopped at Kealakekua Bay, on the Big Island of Hawaii; after going ashore to recover a stolen launch, he was clubbed to death by a group of natives.

Cook's first-person ship logs were published and republished in London for decades. In a 1777 entry, appearing in chapter 9, volume II, of *A Voyage to the Pacific Ocean*, Cook describes his first encounter with canoe surfing, at Tahiti's Matavai Point:

He went out from the shore till he was near the place where the swell begins to take its rise; and, watching its first motion very attentively, paddled before it with great quickness, till [it] had acquired sufficient force to carry his canoe before it without passing underneath. He sat motionless, and was carried along at the same swift rate as the wave, till it landed him upon the beach. Then he started out . . . and went in search of another swell. I could not help concluding that this man felt the most supreme pleasure while he was driven on so fast and smoothly by the sea.

Cook went on to note that this particular "amusement" seemed "to allay any perturbation of mind with as much success as music." Volume III of the *Voyage* series includes a 1778 entry on board-surfing in Hawaii, written by Lieutenant James King, the officer who commanded the *Discovery* after Cook's death.

A diversion the most common is upon the water, there is a very great sea, and surf breaking on the shore. The men, sometimes 20 or 30 . . . lay themselves flat upon an oval piece of plank about their size and breadth. [Keeping] their legs close on top of it, and their arms are used to guide the plank, they wait [until] the time of the greatest swell . . . and push forward with their arms to keep on its top, [and] it sends them in with a most astonishing velocity, and the great art is to guide the plank so as always to keep it in a proper direction on the top of the swell. On first seeing this very dangerous diversion I did not conceive it possible but that some of them must be dashed to mummy against the sharp rocks, but just before they reach the shore, they quit their plank and dive under. By such exercises, these men may be said to be almost amphibious.

Cooke, Alec Showboating big-wave surfer from Hawaii, also known as "Ace Cool"; best remembered for his heavily promoted venture into the big surf at Oahu's Kaena Point in 1984, and at Outside Pipeline the following year. Cooke, a descendent of Captain James Cook, was born (1956) in Boston, Massachusetts, raised in Kauai and Oahu, and started surfing at age six. He earned a reputation in the early '80s as a raw but gutsy Waimea Bay surfer, and was interviewed, along with big-wave stalwarts Ken Bradshaw, James Jones, and Peter Cole, in *Surfer* magazine's 1983 feature "Whatever Happened to Big-Wave Riding?"—an article that helped bring giant surf back in fashion. Cooke had already shattered the taciturn big-wave-rider archetype with his self-awarded "Ace Cool" title, and the brawny blond regularfooter further estranged himself from his peers by saying "I don't want to be a member of the big-wave club, I want to be chairman of the board." On January 5, 1985, Cooke was dropped by helicopter into the lineup at Outside Pipeline—one of the first surfers to take on what are known as Oahu's "outer reefs"—and

rode three waves, including what Cooke later described as a 35-footer (other estimates put it at 25 feet). Video footage of Cooke's Outside Pipeline wave was shown on Hawaii's CBS-TV affiliate, and a photograph of the ride was made into one of Hawaii's best-selling postcards, titled "The Biggest Wave."

Cooke received a B.A. in liberal arts from Hawaii Loa College in 1979. He did radio-broadcast surf reports from 1978 to 1988, owned and operated Country Surf Shop on Oahu from 1980 to 1984, was an invitee to the 1986 Quiksilver in Memory of Eddie Aikau big-wave contest at Waimea Bay, wrote a weekly surfing column for the *North Shore News* from 1982 to 1985, and again from 1995 until the present. "Ace Cool refuses to go away," he said in 1991. "I'm a legend and I'll continue to be a legend." But five years later his fame was such that *Australia's Surfing Life* magazine published a short article titled "Anyone Remember Ace Cool?"

Cool, Ace *See* Alec Cooke.

coolite Generic Australian term for any one of a number of small, inexpensive polystyrene beaded-foam surfboards; the introductory board for thousands of Aussie preteen surfers in the 1970s, including future world champions Tom Carroll, Damien Hardman, and Pam Burridge. Early versions of the coolite (similar to the $10 Styrofoam boards sold in Thrifty and other American drugstore chain outlets in the '60s and '70s) were being used in 1962, but the board really took off in the early '70s. Australian surfboard manufacturer Shane Stedman produced thousands of blunt-nosed, brightly colored

Surfing on a coolite

coolites, while Kentucky Fried Chicken sold more than 100,000 coolites during two six-week promotions in 1973 and 1975—each board going for $5 with the purchase of a bucket of chicken. The average coolite was about five feet long and 20 inches wide, with one or two long, narrow finlike runners along the bottom. They were allowed inside the lifeguard-patrolled "no surfboard" zones, which was a relief to parents. "If you were a kid in Sydney during the '70s," Australian surf journalist and two-time national champion Nick Carroll later recalled, "you bodysurfed until you were 11 or 12, got a coolite and rode it for a year or two, then graduated to a second-hand surfboard." Bodyboards replaced coolites as the young surfer's start-up vehicle in the late '70s, but Sydney board manufacturer Hot Buttered introduced the Hot Grommet coolite model in 1998. *See also* bodyboarding, mat surfing.

Cooper, Bob Cheerful, freethinking regularfoot surfer originally from Southern California; popular throughout the 1960s, and regarded of as the original surfing beatnik. Cooper was born (1937) in Santa Monica, California, the son of a milkman who died around the time of his birth. He was raised in the Los Angeles–area suburbs of Culver City and Mar Vista, and began surfing in 1952 at age 15, at Malibu; eight years later he was one of the first American surfers to visit Australia. Cooper earned a reputation not as a contest champion or a big-wave hero or even a small-wave performer—although he had an appealing, loose-limbed style, and a fine sense of trim—but as an articulate and slightly eccentric surfing character. In "Bob Cooper: Prophet on a Wave," a glowing 1964 *Surf Guide* magazine profile, he's lauded for his "Mount Everest beard, radical sandals, spectacular shirts and tunics of a thousand colors," as well as his ability to "remain composed and totally unaffected even at the most radical parties." The Bob Cooper Blue Machine signature model, produced in 1967 and early 1968 by Morey-Pope Surfboards, was the only board of the era to feature an asymmetrical fin setup.

Cooper lived in Australia from 1964 to 1966, returned to California, traveled to the U.K. in 1968, and won the European Surfing Championships, then moved permanently to Australia in 1969. After living for almost 25 years in Coffs Harbor, New South Wales, where he owned and operated Cooper Surf Shop, he moved in 1993 to Marcus Beach, Queensland. Cooper is married and has five children. While never a proselytizer, Cooper has often said that Mormonism, not surfing, has been the unifying and driving force in his life.

Cooper appeared in a small number of surf movies in the late '50s and '60s, including *Slippery When Wet* (1958), *Surfing Hollow Days* (1962), and *Strictly Hot* (1964); he also wrote about 10 articles for the American surf press in the '60s and early '70s. Cooper allowed that he "hung a pretty mean ten in the early '60s," but said that he was "famous in surfing for being famous; for having been around a long time; for having a beard." The celebrated Cooper beard, as noted in a lavish 37-page *Surfer's Journal* profile in 1999, originated as part of a ruse to stay out of the army.

Cooper, Jodie Candid and intrepid Australian pro surfer originally from Albany, Western Australia; world-ranked #2 in 1985, and remembered as her generation's best female big-wave rider. Cooper was born (1964) and raised in the small whaling town of Albany, and didn't begin surfing until age 16. Making her pro debut just three years later, she placed runner-up in the 1983 Rip Curl Pro at Bells Beach, and finished the year world-ranked #6. Over the next nine years the dependably cheerful Cooper won seven world tour events and never finished lower than fourth on the year-end ratings. Raised on the powerful reefbreaks of Western Australia and employing a functional straight-backed style, Cooper was completely at ease in the big Hawaiian surf; in 1985 she became the first woman to regularly venture into the tube at Off the Wall and Backdoor Pipeline, and in 1992 she won back-to-back events at Sunset Beach

Jodie Cooper

and Haleiwa. (Vivaciously attractive, with high cheekbones and a perfect smile, she also did a small amount of modeling work in France and Australia in the late '80s.) Cooper retired from the circuit in early 1993, but continued to make her presence felt in the surf world. "Don't Think With Your Dick," her treatise on sexism and basic civility, was published in 1994 by *Australia's Surfing Life* magazine; three years later Cooper came out publicly as a lesbian, the first well-known surfer to do so. She appeared in a small number of surf movies and videos, including *Ticket to Ride* (1986), *Shock Waves* (1987), and *Surfer Girl* (1994). Cooper lives in Sydney's Newport Beach.

Copeland, "Bing" Herbert   Market-wise surfboard manufacturer from Hermosa Beach, California; founder of Bing Surfboards, one of the sport's best-known brands in the 1960s. Copeland was born (1936) in the Los Angeles County oceanfront suburb of Torrance, raised in nearby Manhattan Beach, and began surfing at age 13, with future big-wave virtuoso Greg Noll. Copeland and Noll both learned how to make surfboards from American board-manufacturing pioneer Dale Velzy. Copeland joined the Coast Guard and was stationed in Hawaii from 1955 to 1957; the following year he and surfing friend Rick Stoner set out on a six-month oceangoing surf cruise across the Pacific, with stops in Hawaii, Tahiti, Moorea, Bora Bora, and Fiji. They ended their journey with a two-month stay in New Zealand, where they introduced the Malibu surfing style to the wave-ski-riding locals, and together built about 10 boards to leave behind as gifts. In September 1959, a few months after returning home, Copeland opened Bing Surfboards on the Hermosa beachfront (Stoner opened Rick Surfboards shortly after); in 1963 he moved the shop to Pacific Coast Highway and went on to become one of the most popular board-makers of the decade. Surfer/shaper Donald Takayama was an early Bing team rider; shaper Dick Brewer produced the Bing Pipeliner model in 1967 (a board, as surf historian Mark Fragale later noted, that "forever changed the parameters for big-wave guns and speed designs"); California surfer Rolf Aurness won the 1970 World Surfing Championships on a Bing surfboard. The company's most famous surfer by far was Hawaiian-born David Nuuhiwa, who fixed his name to two hot-selling Bing models, the Noserider and the Lightweight. In 1965, while negotiating with the teenaged Nuuhiwa to ride for his company, Copeland

is said to have closed the deal by buying the young smooth-riding goofyfooter a purple Porsche 912.

The late '60s shortboard revolution was disastrous for all established board manufacturers, as surfers by the thousands flocked to small label "backyard" builders, who were quicker to pick up on the newest designs. Bing Surfboards survived, and in 1973 began to market the bonzer, a futuristic board invented by Malcolm and Duncan Campbell, with a double-concave bottom and three fins—design features that would later become standard. But Copeland had by that time grown tired of the business, and was feeling estranged from the longhaired surf scene; in 1974 he licensed the shop name and moved with his wife and three children to Ketchum, Idaho, where he became a partner in a moving and storage business.

cord   *See* surf leash.

Corona del Mar   *See* Newport Beach, Pacific Coast Surf Riding Championships.

Cortes Banks   Big-wave break located 100 miles west of San Diego, California; part of a 25-mile-long underwater mountain range named after vicious Spanish conquistador and explorer Hernando Cortés; a navigational hazard for centuries. Cortes Banks was first spied as a potential surfing location in the late 1960s by California big-wave pioneers Walter and Flippy Hoffman; photographer Larry Moore and pilot Mike Castillo reconnoitered the break by air in 1990. The ridable portion of Cortes Banks—a tilting, shifting peak, resembling Sunset Beach in Hawaii—is a few hundred yards southeast of a nightmarish swirl of white water later described by surf journalist Evan Slater as "a half-mile chunk of reef forever doomed to 360-degree confusion."

Moore boated back to Cortes in 1990, accompanied by three surfers who rode a handful of eight-foot waves. But Cortes's real debut was on January 19, 2001, during an expensive and intricately planned one-day excursion dubbed "Project Neptune," engineered by Moore with assistance from former *Surfing* editor Bill Sharp, involving two boats, a single-engine plane, three personal watercraft, six cameramen, and six surfers. The ocean was glassy smooth, and an enormous swell rolled in from the northwest. Following a nighttime boat trip, two tow-in teams set out to ride Cortes Banks not long after dawn: Mike Parsons and Brad Gerlach, both from Southern California, and Kenny Collins and Peter Mel of Santa Cruz. About three hours later, Parsons was towed in to a wave that measured roughly 65 feet on the face—by far the biggest wave ridden off the continental United States up to that point, and perhaps the biggest wave ever ridden. Two months later Parsons's wave earned him the $60,000 first-place check in the Swell XXL Big-Wave Contest. The Cortes Bank surf adventure was featured in the *Los Angeles Times* and *Newsweek,* as well as all the network news stations, and two surf videos, *XXL: Biggest Waves Wins* (2001), and *Step Into Liquid* (2003).

Costa Rica   Warm, fertile, wave-rich Central American country, bordered by Nicaragua to the north and Panama to the south, often called the "Switzerland of Central America" for its economic and political stability. Costa Rica's combined 510 miles of coast (380 miles facing the Pacific Ocean, 130 along the Caribbean Sea) can be divided into four main surfing areas: 1) The wet and jungle-lined Caribbean shore, home to more than a dozen shallow-water coral reefbreaks including Salsa Brava, a powerful right-breaking tube. 2) The popular northwest coast, filled with a variety of beach-, reef-, and pointbreaks, including the beautifully sculpted waves of Ollie's Point and the translucent beachbreak tubes of Witch's Rock. 3) The accessible beachbreak-lined central coast, featuring the long rivermouth lefts of Boca Barranca. 4) The remote southwest coast, home to nearly a dozen fast but relatively easy-to-ride pointbreaks, including Pavones, one of the world's longest lefts.

The best surf along Costa Rica's west coast is generated by South Pacific storms, and arrives during the April-to-November rainy season. Four-foot waves are common during this time of year; eight- to ten-foot surf is not unheard of. The December-to-March dry season brings less consistent west and northwest swells to the Pacific coast, but the smaller waves are improved by a steady offshore breeze, while dry and sunny weather makes traveling easier. Hurricanes in the Caribbean Sea, despite its limited fetch, can deliver powerful Hawaiian-style surf to the northeast-facing Costa Rican shore, from December through February, with waves reaching 12 feet. September and October can also produce impressive surf on the Caribbean side. Coastal temperatures in Costa Rica range from the low 70s to the low 90s; water temperatures range from the mid-70s to the low 80s. Crocodiles and sharks have been spotted in the estuaries

and rivermouths on the Pacific side, but there have been no reported attacks on surfers; primary surfing hazards in Costa Rica are the shallow coral reefs on the Caribbean coast, and a few shallow rock reefs along the Pacific.

Visiting Americans rode the Pacific side of Costa Rica in the mid-60s, and the Caribbean side a few years later, but the sport didn't really catch on among residents—there were said to be just 20 native Costa Rican wave-riders in 1974—and traveling surfers of the period thought of the area as too remote. Costa Rica was "discovered" as a surfing area in the early '80s, as the American surf press ran a series of colorful features on what was often described as a "Central American paradise." By the early '90s, Costa Rica was home to about 500 native surfers, 100 resident American expatriates, and a few dozen foreign landowners (including *Endless Summer* star Robert August, surfboard shaper Mike Diffenderfer, and surf magazine publisher Steve Pezman) who took extended surfing vacations two or three times each year. In 1992, retired American big-wave hero Greg Noll ran the first of his five old-timer "Legends" events at Boca Barranca, a muddy rivermouth break near the resort town of Puntarenas; Boca Barranca has also hosted the annual Women's Longboard World Championships since 1999. A Quiksilver-sponsored pro-am event in 2001 was held at a central coast break called Playa Hermosa, and matched surfers from America, Brazil, Puerto Rico, Venezuela, El Salvador, Panama, and Italy against the rapidly improving natives.

By 2003, there were about 30 surf shops in Costa Rica (clustered mainly around the capital city of San José and the resort towns of Jaco and Tamarindo), 5,000 resident surfers, and a thriving surf-tourism trade (more than 100,000 visitors annually) including more than a dozen surf tour operations, the first of which opened in 1985. Drinkable tap water, excellent medical facilities, and safe roads are part of the attraction for amenity-loving surf travelers. *Surfos,* the country's first domestic surf magazine, began publishing in 1997; other publications include *Surf Guide* and *Global Surf.* A small domestic competition circuit is run by the 1999-founded Costa Rica Surfing Association; top Costa Rican surfers as of 2003 include Federico Pilurzu, Gilbert Brown, and Diego Naranjo. Costa Rica has been featured in more than two dozen surf movies and videos, including Scott Dittrich's *Follow the Sun* (1983), *Overdrive* (1993), and *Lost in Costa Rica* (1998); Ollie's Point and Witch's

Rock were both shown off beautifully in Bruce Brown's 1994 movie *Endless Summer II*. Guidebooks to the country include *Surfer's Guide to Costa Rica* (1996) and *Costa Rica: Land of Waves* (2001).

Couper, Gail   Invincible Australian surfing competitor of the 1960s and '70s from Lorne, Victoria; five-time national champion, and ten-time winner of the prestigious Bells Beach event. Couper was born (1947) in Melbourne, the daughter of Australian Surfriders Association president Stan Couper, and began surfing at age 14, two years after moving with her family to Lorne, not far from Bells. Three years later, in 1964, the shy but surefooted Couper won the first of 14 Victoria state titles (losing only in 1965), and in 1966 she took her first of ten Bells events, winning every year up until 1977 with the exception of 1969; she won the Australian National Titles in 1966, 1967, 1971, 1972, and 1975. Lorne neighbor and fellow surf prodigy Wayne Lynch, Couper later said, was a great inspiration during her early years. Couper also surfed in the World Championships, making the semifinals in 1964, placing fourth in 1966, and making the semifinals again in 1968. Couper was the top Australian women's division vote-getter in the 1967 *International Surfing* Magazine Hall of Fame Awards, and was inducted into the Australian Surfing Hall of Fame in 2000.

Couper, Stan   Systematic competition organizer and administrator from Lorne, Victoria, Australia; co-founder of the Australian Surfriders Association (ASA) in 1963, and the group's first president. Couper was born (1923) and raised in Sydney, and began surfing in the mid-'40s. While surf filmmaker and magazine publisher Bob Evans was the key figure in the formation of the ASA, Couper contributed to virtually all facets of operation, and was ASA president in 1964 when the group hosted the debut World Surfing Championships. Couper's no-nonsense reputation was burnished during the 1970 Australian National Titles, held in Queensland, when he confronted former world champion and living legend Nat Young on the beach, after the 22-year-old surfer began shouting complaints about the choice of venue. "Couper was a small, very straight kind of Victorian administrator," Australian pro surfer Wayne Bartholomew later recalled, "and he marched Nat up the hill, virtually by the ear, and just gave him an incredible dressing down. And Nat pulled his head in." Couper resigned as ASA president in 1976; he died in 1985, at age 63. Five-time national champion Gail Couper is Stan Couper's daughter. *Australia's Surfing Life* magazine, in 1992, named Couper as one of "Australia's 50 Most Influential Surfers."

Couture, Colin "Doc"   Surf contest organizer from Rhode Island; executive director of the Eastern Surfing Association (ESA) as well as president of the United States Surfing Federation (USSF) for most of the 1970s and '80s; described by *Surfing* magazine as "the political guru of amateur surfing competition." Couture was born (1943) and raised in Rhode Island; he received a doctorate in clinical psychology from Boston University, and became director for a health and human services agency. He began working for the ESA in 1969, and two years later was named the group's executive director. Overweight, shambling, and gracious, Couture wore aloha shirts, cord shorts, and sneakers, no matter what the occasion. Under his direction (1971 to 1989), ESA membership went from 1,000 to 6,000, making it the sport's largest amateur body. He launched an ESA college scholarship program, steered the organization into the political arena by taking on beach access issues, and helped get surfing accepted into the Amateur Athletic Union. As head of the USSF, American amateur surfing's umbrella organization, Couture worked mightily to bring some measure of order to the internecine warfare that has long been the hallmark of American amateur surfing. Couture himself quit riding waves after an ankle injury in 1970, and he was occasionally accused of having lost touch with the noncompetitive aspects of surfing. "A lot of resistance to progress is actually coming from within the sport," he said in 1984, "from people who think surfing should remain an art form. These are the people holding the sport back, in my opinion." But a majority of surfers, East Coasters in particular, felt Couture was always looking out for their best interests. Couture never married, but adopted two sons. He died of a brain aneurysm in 1989, at age 46. He was inducted into the International Surfing Hall of Fame in 1991 and into the East Coast Surf Legends Hall of Fame in 1996. *See also* Eastern Surfing Association, United States Surfing Federation.

cover-up   A full or partial disappearance behind the curl; generally regarded as better than a head dip but not quite a full tuberide. The cover-up is most often performed in small surf.

cowabunga   All-purpose declaration of stoke and enthusiasm, popular in the '50s and early '60s. Chief Thunderthud, a character on NBC's popular children's program *The Howdy Doody Show,* used the made-up expression "Kawabonga" to voice frustration and surprise; surfers borrowed it, changed the spelling and pronunciation slightly, and made it their own. The entertainment world later took the word back: Snoopy of "Peanuts" fame shouts "Cowabunga!" to himself as he shoots the curl in a 1965 panel, trying to impress an unseen "beach-beagle"; the word was also used by Bart Simpson, the Teenage Mutant Ninja Turtles, and as a tag line for *Lilo and Stitch,* a 2002 Disney animated movie. Sometimes spelled "kowabunga."

Cram, Richard   Good-natured Australian pro surfer of the early and mid-'80s from Sydney's Bondi Beach; world-ranked #10 in 1984; remembered for his starring role in *The Performers* surf video (1984), and for his scything forehand cutback. Cram was born (1961) in Sydney, and began surfing at age 10, at Bondi. He won the juniors division of the 1979 Australian National Titles, and two years later, during his rookie year on the world tour, won the Pro Class Trails at Sunset Beach. In early 1985, the curly-haired 23-year-old surprised his peers by retiring from competitive surfing, in large part to stay home and raise a family. Full-time surfing competition, he said, required a kind of focus that he regarded as unhealthy. "The guys who are way up there in the ratings get really weird sometimes." Cram appeared in a small number of surf movies and videos, including *Wizards of the Water* (1982) and *Ticket to Ride* (1986).

Crawford, Jeff   Brusque, hard-charging goofyfooter from Melbourne, Florida; Pipeline Masters winner in 1974, and the dominant surfer at Florida's Sebastian Inlet throughout the '70s and early '80s. Crawford was born (1952) in Melbourne, the son of an army colonel, grew up on or near military bases in Florida, Hawaii, Oklahoma, and Virginia, and began surfing at age 16, at New Smyrna Beach, Florida, after his father became the commander of nearby Patrick Air Force Base. Just three years later he won the men's division of the 1971 Florida State Championships, and had become the alpha male in the often-vicious Sebastian Inlet lineup. He finished runner-up in the 1972 United States Championships, and was a semifinalist in the 1972 World Championships. Although

Jeff Crawford

the blond-haired Crawford was badly beaten up by local surfers during his first visit to Oahu's North Shore in the winter of 1972–73—in part because he surfed in Hawaii with the same voluble aggression he used at Sebastian—he jumped directly to the front rank at Pipeline. Two years later he received his first invitation to the Pipeline Masters, and beat former Masters winners Gerry Lopez and Rory Russell in the finals to become the first East Coast surfer to win the prestigious event. Crawford placed fifth in the Lightning Bolt Pro and the Duke Kahanamoku Invitational in 1975, both held on the North Shore. In 1976 he was world-ranked 16th, and in 1978 he finished 12th; he won the Florida Pro, a world pro tour event, in 1977 and 1978, and remained a part-time competitor on the world tour until the end of the 1987 season.

Crawford learned how to shape surfboards in the early '70s, began selling Jeff Crawford Surfboards out of his house in 1974, opened Inlet Surf and Sport in 1979 (later renamed Crawford Surf and Wear), and opened two more retail outlets in the mid-'80s. Crawford fled the country for Indonesia in 1991 to avoid prosecution on what he later referred to as "some illegal business transactions." Two years later he moved to South Africa, and in 1994 he returned to Florida, resolved his problems, settled in Melbourne, and began to breed and sell exotic animals, including zebras, rhinos, and leopards. Crawford appeared in more than a dozen surf films in the 1970s, including *Going Surfin'* (1973), *Fluid Drive* (1974), and *Tales from the Tube* (1975). He was inducted into the East Coast

Surf Legends Hall of Fame in 2002. Crawford is married and has two children.

Crawford, Peter Quirky Australian photographer from Sydney, New South Wales; regarded by many as his country's best all-around surf lensman from the late 1970s through the '80s. Crawford was born (1952) in Sydney, raised in the beach suburbs of Bondi and Dee Why, and began kneeriding in 1963. He was the Australian national kneeboard champion in 1976, 1977, and 1978, a *Surfer* masthead photographer from 1977 to 1994, cofounder of *Waves* magazine in 1980, and a regular contributor to virtually all Australian surf magazines from the mid-'70s until his sudden death in 1999. Small, thin, garrulous and profane, Crawford was fond of popping up unexpectedly—in both work and social settings—rushing about in a blur of manic energy, then vanishing just as fast. He shot with equal skill from land and water, and was one of the first surfing photographers to explore the Indonesian island chain beyond Bali and eastern Java. His work was featured in a number of illustrated surfing books, including *The History of Surfing* (1983), *Surfing: The Ultimate Pleasure* (1984), *The Next Wave* (1991), and *The Perfect Day* (2001). Crawford died in Bali on Christmas Day 1999 at age 48, from complications arising from a snakebite. In 2001, he was posthumously inducted into the Australian Surfing Hall of Fame. Crawford was married and had three children. *See also* Waves magazine.

crest In general, the top portion of a wave; more specifically, the top portion of the wave just as it's about to break or beginning to break. "Crest" is similar to "curl" or "lip." The word "crest" is used more often by nonsurfers than surfers.

Cross, Dickie Teenage surfer from Honolulu, Hawaii, who drowned at Waimea Bay in 1943. On December 22 of that year, Cross and 31-year-old Woody Brown, a New York–born surfer, drove from Honolulu to the North Shore of Oahu and set out to ride some eight-foot waves at Sunset Beach. Cross, a quiet blond 17-year-old, was regarded as one of Waikiki's best young surfers and paddleboard racers, and was eager to learn how to ride bigger waves. A larger-than-average set arrived just as the two surfers paddled into the lineup at Sunset, and each successive group of waves continued to build, forcing Cross and Brown to paddle further and further outside in order to remain beyond

the surf line. Realizing their route back to the beach had been cut off, they decided to paddle three miles down the coast to Waimea, where they hoped to make it to shore through the bay's deep-water channel. But Waimea was also washed out. As Brown later told the story, Cross panicked and bolted toward the beach, quickly lost his board, and disappeared under the next set of waves, never to be seen again. Brown timed his approach with more care, but was nonetheless unconscious by the time he washed ashore. Cross's death contributed greatly to what California big-wave rider Greg Noll later described as the "Waimea taboo"— a general fear that kept surfers from riding there until 1957. *See also* death and surfing, Waimea Bay.

cross-step The class method for getting to the front end of a surfboard, where the back foot crosses the front foot, is planted so the legs form an X, and is in turn crossed as the other foot swings past. The cross-step is distinct from the much-easier "shuffle," in which both feet advance to the nose without crossing. After two or three cross-steps, the surfer will be in position to hang five or ten toes off the nose of the board. Cross-stepping is performed almost exclusively on a longboard. *See also* noseriding.

Cuba Communist-ruled island nation located 90 miles south of Florida, flanked by the Atlantic Ocean to the north and the Caribbean Sea to the south. Cuba's 2,320-mile tropical coastline is home to a small number of charted and infrequently surfed breaks;

Cross-step by California's Joel Tudor

dozens more will likely be discovered in the years ahead. Cuba is the largest island nation in the Caribbean and has a balmy tradewind-moderated climate, with a dry season lasting from November to April. Cold fronts in the Gulf of Mexico during this time often create waves along the northwest coast, including beaches in and around the capital city of Havana; North Atlantic storms produce waves along the central north coast. Small and sporadic waves are the rule during the May-through-October rainy season, although Caribbean hurricanes can on occasion produce big swells between September and October. Air and water temperatures both range from the low 70s to the low 80s. Cuban surf generally breaks over sharp, shallow coral reefs, and the form can be excellent; the best and most consistent waves are found on the small offshore islands near the north-central coast between Havana and Sagua la Grande, accessible only by boat.

Despite Cuba's proximity to the United States, more than 40 years' worth of unrelenting political enmity with America (including a near-complete ban on tourism) has left the island nation a near-virginal surfing area. While a few Europeans and Canadians tested Cuba's waves in the '90s, the country wasn't revealed to the surf world at large until 1999, in a *Surfer* magazine article featuring Floridian pros Shea and Cory Lopez, their father Pete, and California pro Dino Andino, all of Cuban ancestry. As of 2003, roughly 50 natives had taken to the surf, some of them fashioning boards from insulating foam ripped out of old refrigerators.

Cunningham, Mark   Amphibious bodysurfer from Honolulu, Hawaii; winner of the first professional bodysurfing contest, and unchallenged as the world's best bodysurfer from the mid-1970s to the early '90s. "If Charles Darwin were alive today," two-time Pipeline Masters winner Rory Russell said in 1994, describing Cunningham's half-man/half-fish physiology, "Mark would have blown his mind and sent him back to the drawing board." Cunningham was born (1955) in Milton, Massachusetts, the son of an air traffic controller, and moved with his family to Honolulu while still an infant. He began riding waves at age nine, quickly progressed to Makapuu and Sandy Beach—Oahu's world-renowned bodysurfing breaks, both located on the island's east side—then traveled across the island to the North Shore where he learned how to ride the big, spinning tubes at Pipeline. As a high school senior in 1974, Cunningham won the annual North Shore Bodysurfing and Paipo Contest,

held at Pipeline, and for the next 15 years he won contests almost at will, including the first two pro events, held at Pipeline in 1980 and 1982, each paying $1,000 to the winner. "If you picked up the paper and saw that Mark didn't win," fellow bodysurfer Fred Asmus later said, "you figure he either didn't show or the waves were so shitty it didn't matter." In 1990, North Shore surfer and veteran pro contest organizer Randy Rarick listed Cunningham as one of the 10 best Pipeline surfers, along with Derek Ho, Tom Carroll, Gerry Lopez, and a half-dozen other stand-up riders. Cunningham became a lifeguard in 1974 in Santa Barbara; since 1976 he's been a guard for the city and county of Honolulu; working at Ehukai Beach Park, adjacent to Pipeline, from 1980 to 1990.

The eel-shaped Cunningham (6'4", 170 pounds) chose bodysurfing over stand-up surfing, he said in 1994, because he prefers to be "totally immersed in water." Unlike most top bodysurfers, Cunningham rarely does spins, "bellyrolls," or tricks of any kind, preferring instead to draw uncluttered lines and arcs across the wave face, keeping himself near or behind the curl at all times. In the '90s, Cunningham was twice defeated in the annual Pipeline Bodysurfing Classic by nine-time bodyboarding world champion Mike Stewart of Hawaii. Cunningham came back to win the Pipeline contest for the last time in 2000, at age 44.

Waves to Freedom, a 23-minute video documentary on Cunningham, was released in 1988; he also appeared in two bodysurfing videos, *Primal Surf* (2000) and *Pure Blue* (2001). Cunningham was featured in an 18-page *Surfer's Journal* profile in 1994—the only bodysurfer ever profiled by a surf magazine. Cunningham is married to Linny Morris-Cunningham, a photographer who often does surf magazine portraiture. *See also* bodysurfing.

cure   A new surfboard's final drying phase, when the board's resin-and-fiberglass skin hardens and strengthens. The curing process follows the polymerization (or "gel") stage, where resin transforms from liquid to gelatinous, then to solid. While boards can be ridden just hours after the final coat of resin is applied, California master shaper Al Merrick has recommended they be set aside to cure for three weeks. *See also* resin.

curl   The crest of the wave as it loops over and drops toward the trough. The surfer positioned beneath a just-forming curl is in the "pocket"; the surfer in the hollow area between the wave face and the plunging curl is in the "tube." Soft, crumbly waves have a crest, but no curl. "Lip" is often used as a synonym for "curl."

Curran, Tim Limber and innovative goofyfoot pro surfer from Ventura, California; world-ranked #6 in 1999. Curran was born (1977) and raised in Temecula, California, and began surfing at age 11, after moving with his family to a beachfront house in Ventura's Silver Strand. He shot to prominence in early 1995, when surf video mogul Taylor Steele opened *Focus,* his new video, with a shot of the slender 17-year-old landing an aerial 360; later in the video Curran burned through an advanced repertoire of tailslides and aerials. Quiksilver signed Curran to a six-figure contract, and he was touted as a threat—maybe the primary threat—to world champion Kelly Slater. Curran, a longtime born-again Christian, seemed to take it all in humble stride, but was in fact destabilized by the attention, and admitted to having "a nervous breakdown" at age 18 after doing poorly in a contest. "I just lost it," he told *Surf News* magazine. "I didn't even want to surf anymore, and the feeling lasted about four months." Curran went on to win two world tour events in 1999, but lacked the killer instinct required to win consistently, and lost his world tour seed at the end of the 2000 season. He requalified two years later, and was back on the tour in 2003. "A strange bird," *Surfer* magazine said of Curran in 1999. "Outside the inner circle." Curran has been featured in more than three dozen surf videos, including the family-made biography *Here and Now* (1995) and the *Surfing Techniques with Tim Curran* series (beginning in 2001), as well as *Good Times* (1996), *Speechless* (1998), and *Surf 365* (2000).

Curren, Pat Impenetrable surfer and surfboard shaper from La Jolla, California; generally regarded as the best big-wave rider of the late 1950s and early '60s, as well as the era's finest big-wave surfboard craftsman; father of three-time world champion Tom Curren. Pat Curren was born (1932) in Carlsbad, California, the son of a surveyor, and grew up in San Diego's Mission Beach. At 18, two years after dropping out of high school, he moved to La Jolla and began surfing; he later became an original member of the La Jolla–based Windansea Surf Club, the loudest and rowdiest group of its kind in the nation.

Curren first visited Hawaii in 1955, and two years later was among the first group of surfers to ride Waimea Bay; the slim regularfooter wiped out on nearly all his rides, as did the rest of the half-dozen surfers out that day, largely because their surfboards were unsuited to the conditions. Curren had been shaping boards for less than two years at that time; he returned to La Jolla and dedicated himself to making specialized big-wave equipment, and before the end of the decade he'd become the acknowledged master of the big-wave board. "Pat was the first guy to produce the ultimate gun," California-born surfer Fred Van Dyke later said. "Others were making nice all-around boards, but Pat made the stiletto, specifically for Waimea, where all you want to do is make it alive from Point A to B." Curren had meanwhile become the most patient of the big-wave surfers, and would often sit quietly for two hours or longer waiting for the right wave. He took off on fewer Waimea waves than any of his companions, but invariably got the one that everybody remembered. Once up and riding, Curren kept his feet and legs fairly close together and used a medium crouch, with a ramrod-straight back, his arms swept out like wings.

Nearly mute at times, Curren nonetheless had a fully developed sense of humor. In the winter of 1958, inspired by the Anglo-Saxon legend of Beowulf, he rented a three-bedroom house on the North Shore along with eight other La Jolla surfers, gutted the interior so that it was essentially one high-ceilinged room with a surfboard rack along the wall, and built a giant communal table down the center. Curren called it Meade Hall, and presided over dinners with a Viking helmet jammed down over his close-cropped

Pat Curren

black hair. He meanwhile showed little or no interest in the surf media, and responded as follows to a 1963 *Surfer* magazine questionnaire:

What do you like about surfing? no answer
Club affiliation: none
Personal surfing history: no answer
Hobbies: no answer
Other sports of interest to you: diving
Future plans: no answer
Outlook for surfing: no answer

Curren had a midday wedding in Hawaii, in 1961, and surfed Waimea that afternoon. He and his wife, Jeanine, moved to California the following year, where Curren worked mainly as a diver and board-builder. Tom Curren, the couple's first son, was born in 1964; second son Joe was born in 1974. Pat left the family in 1981 and moved to Costa Rica; he and Jeanine were soon divorced. Curren moved to the southern tip of Baja in 1988, near San Jose del Cabo. Pat and Tom surfed together in Costa Rica in 1985, while Joe joined his father and older brother for a surf trip to Ireland and France in 2000, but Curren family members have for the most part gone their own ways.

While Pat Curren has had almost nothing to do with the nostalgia-tinged "surf legends" revival of the '90s and '00s, he returned to California to produce six full-size replica balsa guns in 1994 and 10 more in 1996, selling them for an average price of $3,500; in 2000 he announced that he would start making two or three $10,000 boards per year. The 68-year-old Curren also had a baby daughter in 2000. Curren is featured in many first-generation surf movies, including *Surf Crazy* (1959), *Barefoot Adventure* (1960), *Cavalcade of Surf* (1962), and *Gun Ho!* (1963). *See also* big-wave surfboard.

Curren, Tom   Enigmatic professional surfer from Santa Barbara, California; three-time world champion (1985, 1986, 1990), and incomparable surfing stylist; one of the sport's most revered and influential figures. Curren was born (1964) in Newport Beach, California, the son of pioneering big-wave surfer and board-maker Pat Curren, and raised in Santa Barbara. Pat first put Tom on a surfboard at age two, but Curren didn't start surfing regularly until age six; at 14 he began a remarkable four-year streak as an amateur competitor, winning the boys' division of the United States Surfing Championships in 1978 and 1979, and the juniors title in 1980; he also won the juniors title of the 1980 World Championships, and followed up two years later with a victory in the men's division. In 1981 he

Tom Curren

finished runner-up to former world pro champion Shaun Tomson in the Katin Pro-Am, then won the following year. He turned pro just before his 18th birthday and signed contracts with Rip Curl wetsuits and Ocean Pacific beachwear worth $40,000 a year—a record at the time for a first-year pro. Curren won the Trestles-hosted Stubbies Pro, his debut event; entering just four of 12 world tour events in 1982 (including the Marui Pro in Japan, which he won) Curren finished the year rated #19. His rating jumped from eighth to fourth over the next two years, helped by consecutive wins in the Op Pro at Huntington Beach.

By mid-decade, the handsome and reclusive teenager had become an international surfing phenomenon. Apart from his contest record, Curren developed an original wave-riding style—influenced to a degree by 1978 world champion Wayne Bartholomew—that was both functional and poetic. Using Al Merrick–shaped tri-fin surfboards, Curren planted his front foot at a 90-degree angle upon standing up, tucked his back knee in, and rarely moved his feet as he rode. The lines he drew across the wave face were alternately sinuous and explosive, each turn blending perfectly into the next. Although relatively slender at 5'8", 150 pounds, Curren was able to synchronize his limbs, head, and torso so as to leverage maneuvers with a deceptive power. He invented the "double-pump" bottom turn by adding a quick booster second turn while climbing toward the crest, resulting in greater torque and rotation during the following off-the-top maneuver. Curren's style became the pattern for virtually every hot young surfer in the world during the 1980s and early '90s.

Curren's first two world titles seemed predestined. He won five of the season's 21 events in 1985, and took the championship by defeating Australian Mark Occhilupo in the semifinals of the Rip Curl Pro at Bells Beach—still regarded as one of the greatest matches in world tour history. He was the first American male surfer to win a world tour title since the circuit had been founded in 1976. The following year Curren, 21, won five of the first 10 events, faltered over the last eight contests, but held on to win a second title. By that time he'd been canonized by the surf press, and was featured in virtually every contemporary surf movie. Details of Curren's personal life—that he was drinking premixed cocktails in sixth grade and getting stoned in seventh grade; that his always-distant father had left home for good when Curren was 17, by which time his mother was a devout and proselytizing born-again Christian; that the 18-year-old Curren had in 1983 married a French teenager—were revealed in a lengthy *Sports Illustrated* profile. *Rolling Stone* also published a full-length Curren profile that included a seductive black-and-white portrait by fashion photographer Herb Ritts. Curren himself, while exquisitely uncomfortable in the spotlight, mumbling his way through interviews and awards presentations, proved to be both intelligent and self-deprecating, and eager to deflate the Currenmania. "There's a lot more to life than winning a championship," he told surf journalist Matt George in early 1986. "All it signifies is who's best at getting four waves to the beach, and when you look at it in that form, it's really insignificant." Along with pro tour standouts Martin Potter and Tom Carroll, Curren also helped introduce world politics to surfing, boycotting the 1985 world circuit events in South Africa as a protest against apartheid.

Curren seemed to lose interest in competing in 1987 and 1988, dropping from fifth to 15th in the ratings, then virtually quit the tour altogether in 1989, choosing instead to spend time with his wife and two young children in Anglet, his newly adopted coastal hometown in southwest France. Returning to competition in 1990, the 26-year-old won a record-tying seven events for the season and cruised to his third and final world title. He then spent much of the early and mid-'90s traveling the world as the star of the Rip Curl's "The Search" marketing campaign. A longtime drummer and guitar player, Curren recorded his *Ocean Surf Aces* album in 1993, and went on a one-month, 23-show tour of the East and West coasts with his semithrash band, the Skipping Urchins. (It was never determined if Curren was displaying his chronic absentmindedness or making a quiet but ef-

fective anticorporate statement in 1992 when he won a world tour surf contest in Hawaii on a board conspicuously free of logos and trademarks; longtime sponsor Ocean Pacific, however, was angry enough to drop Curren from its roster. A few weeks later Curren signed the richest contract in surfing at the time: a five-year, $2 million deal with Rip Curl.)

Curren and his first wife divorced in 1993; the following year he married Makeira Caicedo of Panama, returned to Santa Barbara, and by 1996 had fathered two more children. He remained as enigmatic as ever, riding strange homemade surfboards, appearing on MTV's *Alternative Nation* in 1995 to promote the Ocean Aid environmental group, and telling 40,000 people at a religious rally in Anaheim Stadium that "the ocean is a sign of God's power, [and] it's really good to live for Jesus Christ." He made two or three halfhearted returns to competition, but never again traveled on the world tour. He continues to hold the world tour record for career victories, with 33. (Younger brother Joe Curren had meanwhile launched his low-key pro career in the early 90s.)

Filmmaker Sonny Miller's *Search For Tom Curren* documentary won *Surfer* magazine's Video of the Year Award in 1997; *Follow the Leader,* another Curren documentary, was also released that year. Curren was featured in *Biographies,* a 2001 Outdoor Life Network TV series. All told, Curren appeared in more than 100 surf movies and videos, including *Tales of the Seven Seas* (1981), *Amazing Surf Stories* (1986), *Surfers: The Movie* (1990), *Momentum* (1992), *The Search* (1992), *Endless Summer II* (1994), *Litmus* (1997), and *Nine Lives* (1999). He was inducted into the Huntington Beach Surfing Walk of Fame in 1995, and won the *Surfer* Magazine Readers Poll award for eight consecutive years, from 1985 to 1992. Curren finished second to Australian Gary Elkerton in the 2000 Quiksilver Masters World Championships.

current   Directed water flow, used to describe everything from near-perpetual transoceanic streams, to temporary local eddies. Circulatory ocean currents are often hundreds of miles wide and thousands of miles long, and can stretch from continent to continent; they keep some coastlines chillier than would be expected (the California Current keeps Baja colder than San Diego) and others warmer (Icelandic surf breaks remain unfrozen in winter due to the Gulf Stream current), and play a key role in the formation of wave-generating storms. Local currents are often fleeting, short in length (from a few miles long to 50 yards or less), often run parallel to the shore, and are usually caused by tidal movement, a heavy swell, strong winds, or water flowing off a raised section of underwater topography, such as a reef or sandbar. A current running from the beach out toward the open sea is commonly called a riptide; spent waves rushing back down a steep beach will form a brief but intense current known as undertow. While local currents can be hazardous, even deadly, to unpracticed swimmers and surfers, they also help produce high-quality waves by sculpting the bottom surface, particularly at sand-bottom breaks. *See also* riptide.

cut off   *See* drop-in.

cutback   Maneuver that takes a surfer from the wave's shoulder—the noncresting area ahead of the curl—back to the steeper, more critical, and powerful part of the wave. The cutback is one of the sport's three fundamental turns, along with the bottom turn and top turn. "It's the purest power move in the book," Australian surf journalist Nick Carroll wrote in 2000. "In the hands of a master, it becomes a slashing, elegant work of art." Surfers began doing cutbacks of a sort in the early 1900s, after they began angling along the wave face, instead of riding straight for shore. But the cutback as it exists today depended on the post–World War II popularization of the fin, which allowed a surfer to lean the board over and apply pressure to a turn without having the back end of the board lose traction and spin out. By 1950, Malibu's Les Williams had become an early master of the cutback; Hawaii's Conrad Canha, and especially California's Phil Edwards, took cutting back to a higher level before decade's end. Australian Nat Young used the cutback to devastating effect to win the 1966 World Surfing Championships. The late-'60s shortboard revolution, when boards were reduced from 25-pound 10-footers to streamlined seven-footers, introduced a new era of cutting back. California's Mike Purpus, Hawaii's Larry Bertlemann, Australian Michael Peterson, and Shaun Tomson of South Africa had each worked out their own deeply set, watershifting cutback by 1975; virtually all notable surfers since have developed a first-rate cutback.

The cutback has a number of variations, the most basic being the "roundhouse"—a long, smooth, arcing turn that usually finishes with the surfer rebounding high off the oncoming white water. A '90s-developed variation is the "cutback 360," where the surfer either extends the cutback into a full circle or

uses the white-water rebound as the starting point for a sliding 360. Other variations include the double-pump cutback, the tail-slide cutback, and, for longboarders, the drop-knee cutback.

Cyclone Abigail   Long-duration South Pacific tropical cyclone that produced more than two weeks of high-quality surf off the east coast of Australia—particularly south Queensland's Gold Coast—in late January and early February 1982. Cyclone Abigail was a meteorological oddity in that it tracked south, parallel to the Queensland coast, faded briefly, strengthened, looped back out to sea, and made a second pass virtually identical to the first. The Queensland surf season that year was already above average, with a six-day swell arriving around Christmas, and a nine-day swell lasting from early to mid-January. The national weather service identified Cyclone Abigail on January 20, and two days later the surf at bellwether Gold Coast pointbreak Burleigh Heads was four foot and tubing. By the 27th, Abigail had moved closer and was bombarding the Gold Coast with nonstop overhead surf, accompanied by clear blue skies and brisk offshore winds. As native Queenslander and 1978 world champion Wayne Bartholomew noted, surfers from across Australia's east coast were now funneling into the Gold Coast. "The jockeying and jostling bordered on comical," Bartholomew reported in a surf magazine article. "You had to ride like greased lightning with a permanent scowl on your face, and often you'd expend so much energy intimidating the hundred-or-so shoulder hoppers that you'd outrun the wave and miss the tube altogether."

By the 30th, Abigail had moved still closer to the Gold Coast, increasing the wave size but also bringing torrential rains and mixed-up seas; by normal cyclone standards, the storm should have fizzled out at this point. Abigail instead moved back out to sea, dropped to the southeast, intensified, turned once again, and made a second, even stronger run toward the Gold Coast. This time around Kirra was the focus of attention, and the storied Gold Coast pointbreak delivered hundreds of high-speed tuberides over a four-day period, before Abigail finally unwound on February 7.

Standout performers during the Abigail swell included Wayne Bartholomew, Wayne Deane, Tony Eltherington, Joe Engel, Peter Harris, Wayne McEwan, and Dominic Wybrow. Abigail was featured in three surf movies: *Storm Riders* (1982), *Blazing Boards* (1983), and *Kong's Island* (1983).

D

Da Hui's Backdoor Shootout Nonrated midwinter professional surfing contest held at Pipeline in 1996, 1997, 1999, and 2000, with the 1999 event offering a $200,000 prize purse, including a first-place prize of $56,000—at the time, the biggest prize ever awarded. The Backdoor Shootout (named after contest site Backdoor Pipeline) was developed by Hawaiian surfer Eddie Rothman, cofounder in 1975 of the informal but intimidating Hui surfing group, also known as the Black Shorts, from which the Da Hui surfwear line was formed in 1995. Thirty-six male surfers were invited to the inaugural Backdoor Shootout, with each paying an entry fee of nearly $4,000—also a record. The event format was unique, as all surfers rode three times over the course of three days, and each rider's three highest-scoring rides were added for a final score. No colored jerseys were used, as contest judges were able to recognize each surfer by style and form. Held in smooth six- to 10-foot surf, with riders occasionally going left at Pipeline but mainly riding Backdoor, the contest was won by six-time world champion Kelly Slater of Florida, who came out just ahead of Hawaii's Johnny-Boy Gomes, to take the $35,000 first-place check, with the four-man Hui squad earning team honors.

In the 1997 Shootout, held in excellent 10-foot-plus Second Reef surf, Hawaiian pro Kalani Robb won his first major pro event and was awarded $30,000. The 1999 Shootout was supposed to give $50,000 to the winner, but as the contest was immediately preceded by the Quiksilver in Memory of Eddie Aikau big-wave contest at Waimea Bay, where Hawaiian surfer Noah Johnson won $55,000, the Hui decided at the last minute to raise the grand prize to $56,000. Once again, the surf for the Backdoor Shootout was superb, and the powerful Johnny-Boy Gomes barely outpointed Robb to win the giant check. In keeping with Da Hui's beach-thug reputation, advertising for the 1999 Shootout included guns, holsters, bandoliers, barbed wire, and flying bullets over the aggressive slogan, "The Core of Surfing is Gonna Rumble Again!" The 2000 Shootout was pulled from Backdoor and instead held at Sunset Beach, and was won by just-crowned world champion Sunny Garcia.

Dale, Dick Lightning-fast instrumental rock guitarist; surf music innovator in the early 1960s, and known still as the "King of Surf Guitar." Born Richard Monsour (1937) in Boston, Massachusetts, the son of a Lebanese machinist, Dale as a child taught himself how to play Hank Williams songs on ukulele and guitar. He began surfing as a teenager in the mid-'50s, after his family moved west to the Los Angeles County beachfront suburb of El Segundo; he was also writing instrumental country-western tunes. In 1956, not long after changing his name, Dale won an Elvis Presley soundalike contest, and while he began changing his style from country to rock and roll, the band name on his debut single in 1958 was Dick Dale and the Rhythm Wranglers. In late 1959, backed by his new rock band the Del-Tones, Dale played his first concert at the Rendezvous Ballroom, a Newport Beach concert hall. Local surfers went wild over Dale's hard-driving sound; Dale and his band soon became the Rendezvous house band, and their 1961 single "Let's Go Trippin'" is considered the first true surf record. "Surfer's Choice," Dale's debut album, with Dale shown surfing on the album cover, sold more than 80,000 copies. As Dale later noted, the heavy-reverb "wet" guitar sound that became his trademark was absent from "Surfer's Choice." It was only after dozens of trial-and-error design sessions with guitar- and amplifier-maker Leo Fender that Dale was able to achieve the sonic power and thrust that came to define his music—most famously on "Misirlou," the Greek standard that Dale transformed into the quintessential surf song in 1962. ("Misirlou" was used as the opening song in the 1994 hit movie *Pulp Fiction*.) Genre purists regard Dale-type instrumentals—as distinct from the richly layered vocal songs produced by groups like the Beach Boys and Jan and Dean—as the true form of surf music. Dale later said he was trying through his music to "match the feeling I had while surfing; [the] vibration and

Dick Dale

pulsification, and the tremendous power." The best way to cast surfing in aural form, Dale discovered, was a hammering guitar-pick attack on a single string while sliding his fret hand high to low down the neck of his battle-scarred Fender Stratocaster. (Although left-handed, Dale played a right-handed guitar flipped upside down, leaving the heavier-gauge strings on the bottom, a style copied by Jimi Hendrix.)

Dale appeared on the *Ed Sullivan Show* in 1963, released four albums in quick succession (*King of the Surf Guitar* and *Checkered Flag* in 1963, *Mr. Eliminator* and *Summer Surf* in 1964), and performed in Hollywood beach movies (*Beach Party* in 1963, *Muscle Beach Party* in 1964). Because he refused to tour outside of Southern California, however, he remained something of a regional phenomenon. He retired in 1965, then reformed the Del-Tones five years later and has been performing on and off ever since. Dale and guitar legend Stevie Ray Vaughan together earned a Best Instrumental Grammy nomination in 1987 for their recording of the Chantays' 1963 hit "Pipeline." Four years later Dale was nominated to the International Surfing Hall of Fame. He recorded two new albums in the mid-'90s (*Tribal Thunder* and *Unknown Territory*), launched his first nationwide tour, and even made an MTV video. In 1996 he was elected to the Hollywood Rock Walk of Fame, and in 2000 the U.S. House of Representatives inducted Dale into the Library of Congress Hall of Records for outstanding achievements in music. *Surf Beat: The Dick Dale Story* was published in 2000. *See also* surf music.

Damm, Jon   Cosmopolitan goofyfoot surfer from Hawaii, best known as a Pipeline specialist in the mid- and late-'80s. Damm was born in Chicago (1957), but his father, an executive with Sherwin-Williams Paints, moved his family to prerevolution Cuba, then El Salvador, Venezuela, Ohio, and finally Puerto Rico, where Damm began surfing at age 13. He was a three-time Puerto Rican national champion (1973–75); in 1976 he enrolled at the University of Hawaii, moved to Oahu, and was soon riding Pipeline. He received his first Pipeline Masters invitation in 1984, and in 1985 was twice featured on the cover of *Surfer* magazine—both photos taken at Pipeline. Damm appeared in a small number of surf movies, including *Amazing Surf Stories* (1986) and *Gone Surfin'* (1987).

Dana Point   Town and surf break in south Orange County, California, named after 19th-century American author and sailor Richard Henry Dana, who described the area in his 1840 book *Two Years Before the Mast;* a popular wave from the 1930s to the mid-'60s. Although surfers had mapped out five different breaks at Dana Point by the late '50s, the main spot—a right-breaking wave, sometimes called "Killer Dana"—was located just off the headland, and was famous for producing bigger surf than anywhere in Southern California during a south swell; waves here occasionally hit 10 or 12 feet. Some of state's most celebrated pre–World War II–era surfers (including Lorrin Harrison, George "Peanuts" Larson, and Ron Drummond) were Killer Dana regulars, and the adolescent Phil Edwards, soon recognized as the world's best surfer, made his first big impression here during a 10-foot south swell in 1953, hotdogging the sloping walls while the older surfers aimed carefully for deep water. Construction on Dana Point Harbor began in 1966, and was completed two years later, destroying the Dana Point surf (with the exception of the soft-breaking waves of nearby Doheny) and giving the not-yet-formed surfing environmental movement its first martyred break. *Surfer* magazine and Hobie Surfboards were both founded in Dana Point. *See also* Dana Point Mafia.

Dana Point Mafia   Surfboard manufacturer Hobie Alter, *Endless Summer* filmmaker Bruce Brown, and *Surfer* publisher John Severson, all based within a two-mile radius in south Orange County's Dana Point in the early and mid-'60s, formed the core of a group known as the Dana Point Mafia for the collective power they held over the surf industry. In 1966, when Hermosa Beach board-maker Greg Noll threw a party for the opening of his new 20,000-square-foot surfboard factory, Severson, Brown, and Alter arrived together dressed to the nines as Prohibition-era gangsters, complete with molls, fedoras, and firearms.

David, Vetea "Poto" Square-jawed power surfer from Papeete, Tahiti; world-ranked #17 in 1992 and 1993; known for his big-wave cool and his easygoing Polynesian charm. David was born (1968) and raised in Papeete, and began surfing at age 10. He won nearly every contest he entered in the mid-'80s—including the juniors division of the 1984 French Championships and 1985 European Championships—but was nevertheless a dark horse going into the 1986 World Amateur Surfing Championships, in Newquay, England, where he defeated Kelly Slater and Nicky Wood, among others, for his final juniors. David was the first Tahitian sportsman to win a world title of any kind. He joined the international pro tour, and by 1989—with a runner-up placing in the Pipeline Masters and a #22 year-end ranking—he'd earned praise as one of the world's best young surfers. "Five years ago he was a kook," surf journalist Derek Hynd wrote. "Four years ago, junior world champion. Last year, 'learning.' Now Vetea David is the biggest all-around talent in his age group." The regularfooted David had a unique surfing style: blocky and functional, knees apart, chest puffed out, head tilted upward. There was nothing smooth or subtle about his method, but it contained

Vetea David

finesse of a kind and was loaded with power, as he leveraged his 6′2″, 185-pound frame through deeply set turns.

David had his best run on the world tour during the early '90s, placing 19th in 1990, 22nd in 1991, and 17th in 1992 and 1993. He won a nonworld tour contest at Pipeline in 1992, beating Derek Ho and Johnny-Boy Gomes in the finals. He finished runner-up to Kelly Slater in the 1994 Pipeline Masters, and competed in the 1995 Quiksilver in Memory of Eddie Aikau big-wave event at Waimea Bay. David retired from the world tour at the end of the 1997 season, but continued to enter contests on occasion: he finished runner-up in the 1999 Reef Big-Wave World Championships, and won the 2000 ISA Big Wave World Championships (held in not-so-big eight- to 10-foot surf on Portugal's Madeira Island). In the mid-'90s he introduced the tow-in method in Tahiti, eventually launching into some deadly powerful waves at a break called Teahupoo.

David appeared in more than 20 surf movies and videos, including *Amazing Surf Stories* (1986), *Sultans of Speed* (1987), *Sultans II: The Force Strikes Back* (1989), and *Beyond the Boundaries* (1994). He's unmarried, and has two children. David has been known throughout his career as "Poto," Tahitian slang for young surfer, similar to "gremmie" or "grommet."

Davis, Dale Capable and eager surf filmmaker of the 1960s and early '70s from Santa Monica, California. Davis was born (1940) and raised in Santa Monica, began surfing in his early teens, graduated in 1963 from the Brooks Institute of Photography, and later that year released *Walk on the Wet Side,* his first surf movie. *Strictly Hot,* his 1964 follow-up, was one of the first surf films to use a prerecorded narration. Davis continued with *Inside Out* (1965), and a pair of short subjects: *A Place Called Malibu* (1966) and *War at Malibu* (1967). While filming the big surf at Hawaii's Waimea Bay for his next movie, 1968's *Golden Breed,* the small-boned Davis—always afraid of big waves—slipped from an open helicopter cockpit and dropped 40 feet into the water, breaking his back. *Liquid Space,* his 1973 comeback film, was a critical and financial disappointment. Davis wasn't a particularly original filmmaker, but his camerawork, framing, and editing were better than most of his '60s surf movie peers, and in 1967 he was voted runner-up to Greg MacGillivray in the filmmaker division of the *International Surfing* Magazine Hall of

Fame Awards. Davis went on to make soft-core pornography. He died of a stroke in 2001 at age 61.

Davoli, Linda Regularfoot surfer from Brigantine, New Jersey; world-ranked #3 in 1980; described by *Surfer* magazine in 1981 as "very possibly the finest women's surfer in the world." Davoli began surfing in 1967 at age 11, and in 1973 she won the girls' division of the United States Surfing Championships—the first East Coast surfer to take a national title. She moved to Hawaii in 1975, and two years later competed in the debut women's world circuit, finishing fifth for the season. While filming an episode of ABC's *American Sportsman* in 1980, along with former U.S. champion Rick Rasmussen and surfer/actor Gregory Harrison (Dr. Gonzo on CBS-TV's *Trapper John, M.D.*), Davoli became the first woman to ride the exotic left-breaking waves of Grajagan in Java. She was featured in a small number of surf movies, including *Super Session* (1975) and *Bali High* (1981). Davoli was inducted into the East Coast Surf Legends Hall of Fame in 2002.

dawn patrol To be on the beach or in the water at sunrise. The phrase "dawn patrol" originated in the military, to describe early morning maneuvers. In surfing, the dawn patrol is used primarily as a tactical move to beat the crowds. Many surfers also value the quiet, contemplative beauty of surfing at daybreak.

Day, Greg Neatly groomed Australian regularfoot pro surfer from Sydney's Coogee Beach; world-ranked #10 in 1983, and a pro surfing manager/trainer after his retirement from the circuit. Day dropped out of school at age 16 and five years later fell into a pro surfing career—his amateur results had been mostly unimpressive—after losing his job as an advertising agency computer operator. Day and 19 contemporaries were featured on the cover of *Surfing* magazine in 1984, next to a caption reading: "20 Who Rip: A Tribute to the World's Greatest Surfers." Terry Day, Greg's younger brother, was a world tour judge for three years in the mid-'80s, and also became a pro surfing manager/trainer. The likable and highly fitness-conscious Day brothers worked with world champions Damien Hardman and Wendy Botha, among others. Greg Day was featured in a small number of surf movies, including *Totally Committed* (1984).

de la Rosa, Luis Miguel "Magoo" Sturdy goofy-foot surfer from Lima, Peru; seven-time national champion between 1983 and 2001. De la Rosa was born (1965) and raised in Miraflores, a wealthy Lima suburb, and began surfing at age 12. He took his first national title in 1983 at age 18, and won again in 1990, 1992, 1993, 1997, 1999, and 2001. From 1987 to 1991 he traveled with little success on the world pro circuit. He also explored much of the coast between northern Peru and central Chile, and served in the mid- and late '90s as guide and travel liaison on a number of high-profile visits by American and Australian surfers. A thunderous left-breaking reef wave in Arica, Chile, was dubbed "Magoo's Left" by *Australia's Surfing Life* magazine, and the bandy-legged English-speaking Peruvian rode the terrifying break the way world champion Tom Carroll rode the Pipeline in Hawaii—with clean, efficient lines, matching power with power. In 1987, de la Rosa helped rediscover Pico Alto, the fabled big-wave break near Lima that had been ridden from the mid-'60s to the mid-'70s, then fallen out of fashion. In 1983, de la Rosa took a degree in production and communication from the Charles Chaplin Institute in Lima; in 1993 he began producing and hosting *Free Ride,* a cable TV surfing show.

de Rosnay, Arnaud Dashing French surf photographer/journalist and sailboarder. De Rosnay was born (1946) in Paris, the younger brother of pioneering French surfer Joel de Rosnay. He was raised in Mauritius as well as Paris, and began surfing in the early '60s in the French resort town of Biarritz. In early 1966, the teenage de Rosnay shot the first French covers for both *Surfer* and *Surfing* magazines; in 1968, while on assignment for *Paris Match,* de Rosnay wrote "Diamond Waves" for *Surfer,* an article about the empty, perfectly shaped, highly guarded surf in southern Namibia, adjacent to the de Beers beachfront diamond mines. De Rosnay crossed the Sahara desert in 1979 on a "speedsail," a device of his own invention, resembling an oversized skateboard with rubber tires and a sail. Later that year he crossed the Bering Strait on a sailboard, then went on to cross the Strait of Gibraltar (Morocco to Spain), the Straits of Florida (Florida to Cuba), and the English Channel. De Rosnay vanished in 1984 trying to sail across the Taiwan Strait; his body was never recovered. He was married to Jenna Severson, daughter of *Surfer* magazine founder John Severson.

de Rosnay, Joel Worldly, well-educated French surfing pioneer. De Rosnay was born (1937) in Mauritius, moved with his family to the coastal resort town

Joel de Rosnay

of Biarritz, France, at age two, and to Paris at seven. He began bellyboarding at 10, during family vacations in Biarritz. In the summer of 1957, American screenwriter Peter Viertel, while in France to shoot *The Sun Also Rises* for 20th Century Fox, wired to California and had his Hobie balsa surfboard freighted over. Viertel rode the warm beachbreak waves in Biarritz, then gave de Rosnay a surfing lesson; the teenage Frenchman, a former member of the Paris University ski team, thus became the country's first native surfer. Two years later he cofounded the Waikiki Surf Club of Biarritz; in 1960 he won the first French Surfing Championships; in 1964 he regained the national title and became France's sole representative in the first World Surfing Championships, held in Sydney, Australia. Later that year, the dark-haired Frenchman became the first and only surfer from his country to be profiled in *Surfer* magazine. De Rosnay also competed in the 1965 and 1966 World Championships. He was *Surfer*'s first French-based photographer and a masthead-listed "foreign representative" from 1962 to 1966; he was also the top French vote-getter in the 1966 International Surfing Hall of Fame Awards.

De Rosnay received an M.S. in organic chemistry from the University of Paris in 1962 and a Ph.D. from the Louis Pasteur Institute in 1966, and worked as a research associate at the Massachusetts Institute of Technology from 1967 to 1971. He returned to the Pasteur Institute and served as director of applied re-

search from 1976 to 1985, by which time he'd published six science books. De Rosnay is married and has three children; he remains an active surfer.

Deane, Wayne   Smooth-riding Australian regular-foot surfer/shaper from Queensland's Gold Coast; domineering presence at Kirra beginning in the late '60s; Australian seniors division national champion in 1982 and 1984; Australian professional longboard champion in 1994, 1995, and 1996. Deane was born (1952) in south Queensland, and began surfing in 1960. By the end of the decade he was a pace-setter at Kirra, the long, hollow, sand-bottom point wave that would soon be recognized as one of the world's premier surf breaks; he was also an informal mentor to 1978 world champion and fellow Queenslander Wayne Bartholomew. Deane won the longboard division of the 1990 World Amateur Surfing Championships, held in Chiba, Japan; in 1995, at age 43, he finished fifth in the Longboard World Championships; in 2000 he won the longboard division of the Australian National Titles. Deane-shaped surfboards have been popular among Gold Coast surfers since the '70s. Inducted into the Australian Surfing Hall of Fame in 2003, Deane has appeared in a small number of surf movies including *Sultans of Speed* (1987) and *Longboarding Is Not a Crime* (1995).

death and surfing   There are reasons why surfing has a reputation as a somewhat deadly sport. Surfers die in movies (*Point Break, In God's Hands*) and novels (*The Ninth Wave, Dogs of Winter*), and when Hawaiian big-wave rider Mark Foo drowned while surfing Maverick's in 1994, the story was covered at length in the *New York Times,* the *Los Angeles Times, Outside,* and *Rolling Stone,* and featured on network news shows and MTV. Plus, people who live away from the coast are often afraid of the ocean in general, and breaking waves in particular. Surfers themselves, will sometimes use the notion surfing mortality to dramatic effect. "There were three sure ways to get killed out there," surf journalist Drew Kampion wrote, looking out at the huge morning surf at Makaha in late 1969. "If you got caught inside, you were dead. If you took off too late, you were dead. Or if you tried to turn at the bottom of the wave, you were dead." A dozen surfers rode Makaha that morning; none died.

In the world of sport and recreation, surfing mortality rates are in fact at the low end of the spectrum. "Deaths from surfing are so rare," Dr. Mark Renneker, founder of the Surfer's Medical Association, wrote after Foo's drowning, "that each one becomes newsworthy." Renneker went on to estimate that the annual death rate from surfing is one per 100,000 surfers, less by far than for skateboarders, skiers, and snowboarders. A majority of surfing deaths occur after the surfer is knocked unconscious, either by hitting his board (or someone else's board), or from striking the bottom. The surf leash, introduced in the early '70s, is responsible for some small number of deaths as surfers have been held underwater and drowned after their leash snagged on a rock or coral outcropping. Foo almost certainly died this way at Maverick's. But leashes have almost without question saved a greater number of lives, as there are fewer loose boards in the lineup. Big-wave surfers, furthermore, have also on occasion saved themselves after a long wipeout only by climbing their leash to the surface.

Simple drowning, with no other primary cause, is rare but not unheard of in surfing. Hawaiian Todd Chesser drowned at Outside Alligator Rock on the North Shore of Oahu in 1997 after he was held beneath at least three 20-foot waves. Fatal shark attacks make up a small but notorious percentage of surfing deaths. Other surfing deaths have little or nothing to do with the sport itself: 1986 world amateur champion Mark Sainsbury of Australia suffered a fatal brain aneurysm while paddling through small waves at his home break in 1992. Hawaii's Pipeline is thought to be the world's most deadly surf break, in part because the wave breaks in shallow water and is enormously powerful and also because of the crowds. As estimated five surfers die each decade at Pipeline.

Just a handful of well-known (or even slightly known) surfers have died while surfing, including Hawaiian Dickie Cross at Waimea Bay in 1943, Peru's Joaquin Miroquesada at Pipeline in 1967, and California's Donnie Soloman at Waimea in 1995. Wave-riding has proven to be less lethal to notable surfers than drug or alcohol abuse (Butch Van Artsdalen, Dewey Weber, Eric Diaz, Rusty Starr, Bunker Spreckles, Ted Deerhurst), vehicular accidents (Jim Freeman, Greg Tucker, Ronnie Burns, Chris Bystrom), suicide (Bob Pike, Angus Chater, Jose Angel), even murder (Bobby Brown, Rick Rasmussen, Randall Kim).

The surfer's memorial service often takes place at the deceased's favorite surf break, where friends and family will paddle out and form a circle, then sprinkle the ashes into the water. When Hawaiian surfer Jonah Binkley died in a traffic accident in late 1992, friend Shawn Briley paddled out at Pipeline with Binkley's ashes tied in a pouch around his waist.

Briley, then one of the world's best Pipeline riders, released the ashes while riding inside the tube on a 10-foot wave.

Sometime in the 1940s, California bodysurfer and canoe surfer Ron Drummond wrote a poem titled "Death at San Onofre," which begins as follows:

Oh, place me not on a high hillside
With a sweeping view of the country wide,
But bury me close to the clear green sea
Where the crashing waves will spray over me;
Where my soul will rise with the rising sun,
And be surfing still when the day is done.

See also injuries and surfing.

deck   The top surface of a surfboard, gently convex as a rule; the area upon which the rider stands. While bottom design has always been a hot topic among board-makers, the deck's design has generally been a matter of increasing or decreasing a board's flotation: greater convexity (or "dome") to increase buoyancy, near-flat or flat to reduce buoyancy. Concave decks and split-level "step decks" have been made on occasion. For traction, the deck of an in-use surfboard is usually covered by a layer of wax, or by molded soft rubber stick-on strips or mats. *See also* bottom, rails, surfboard.

deck grip   *See* traction pad.

deck patch   An area-specific layer of fiberglass placed on the deck of a surfboard during the construction process for added strength. Knees, ribs, heels, and toes can all dent a board during normal use, and dents can eventually create a board-ruining delamination, where the fiberglass separates from the board's foam core. Deck patches became popular in the mid-'60s, as thinner fiberglass was used to make lighter, quicker, more responsive boards. The original deck patch was placed in the center of the board to reinforce the area used while knee-paddling, and was sometimes called a butterfly patch. During the shortboard revolution, as boards became yet smaller and lighter, a two-thirds patch was often used, covering the back two-thirds of the board, to fortify the sections beneath the rider's feet. A tail patch covers only the back-foot area.

Deep magazine   Well-designed and well-written Australian surf magazine published out of Sydney from 1995 to 2000. The editor's note in the first issue of *Deep* declared that the new magazine would "draw no boundaries between generations, geographical areas and special interest groups," but this text-heavy newsprint tabloid (converted in 1998 to regular-format color glossy) was plainly a magazine for older Australian surfers. *Deep* was smart and even sagacious, thanks to veteran surf editors John Elliss and Nick Carroll. It could also be fun, opinionated, and impudent, but was somber as a textbook compared to the frothing surf/beer/boobs format of Australian magazines like *Waves* and *Australia's Surfing Life*. *Deep* began as a bimonthly, faltered in 1997 (only three issues were published that year), returned as a quarterly in 1998, and folded in 2000. Its peak circulation was 9,000. *See also* Nick Carroll.

Deerhurst, Ted   English-born viscount, the son of the 11th Earl of Coventry, who engineered what *Australia's Surfing Life* magazine called "a strangely beautiful surfing career." Deerhurst was a handsome, likable, modestly talented surfer who wanted more than anything to be a success on the world pro tour. His fifth-place finish in the juniors division of the 1973 English National Championships, however, more or less set a standard for the rest of his competitive career. Deerhurst was good enough to get invited to pro circuit events in the '70s and early '80s—and for years was the only touring British pro—but also seemed to be doomed to failure, and never once advanced to the final day of competition. Deerhurst came to the attention of the surfing world in 1982, when he was featured on the cover of *Surfer* magazine, posed with five custom surfboards and two hunting hounds on the rolling lawn before the family manor. Deerhurst made brief appearances in two surfer movies, *Storm Riders* (1982) and *Rolling Thunder* (1991). Over the years, he organized charity surfing events, including the 1986-founded Excaliber Cup, which raised money for Easter Seals. Deerhurst died of sudden heart failure in 1997, in a Honolulu hotel room. He was 42, and a law student at the University of Hawaii.

delamination   A spreading and degenerative surfboard condition, where the board's resin-bonded fiberglass skin pulls apart, or "delaminates," from the underlying foam core. Most delaminations are found on the board's deck, in the areas beneath the surfer's feet—particularly the rear foot—and are caused when an area of fiberglass, repeatedly dented by heels, knees, and toes, finally pops back to more or less its original shape. A delamination can also form around an unfixed crack or ding. Delaminations can be repaired, but the process is costly and adds weight to the board; usually they're left to spread until the board is thrown out. Finally, a board left in a superheated environment—usually inside a sealed car on a hot summer afternoon—can be ruined by a spectacular nose-to-tail set of delaminations. *See also* ding, ding repair.

Delaney, Bill   Reserved and meticulous filmmaker from Ventura, California; producer of *Free Ride* (1977) and *Surfers: The Movie* (1990). Delaney was born (1946) in Santa Barbara, began surfing in 1962, and started shooting surf photos three years later. He attended the Brooks Institute of Photography in Santa Barbara in 1969, served in the army, worked as a *Cycle* magazine freelance photographer, then returned to surfing. *Free Ride* was his first film, and the most memorable footage showed a hot new generation of surfers, including future world champions Shaun Tomson, Wayne Bartholomew, and Mark Richards, riding the North Shore of Oahu during the wave-rich season of 1975–76, a surfing epoch long referred to as the "Free Ride" winter. Delaney's nonnarrative $70,000 film wasn't a milestone in creativity, but it was nonetheless a testimony to his skill as a cameraman, editor, and sound scorer. *Surfing* magazine called *Free Ride* "a finely cut and polished diamond," and *Surfer* said it "conveyed the essence of the surfing experience." Updated versions of *Free Ride* followed in 1978 and 1983, each a critical and box-office success.

Delaney worked as an automotive freelance photographer in the mid-'80s. He made a promo short for the Gotcha surfwear company in 1987 called *Waterborn,* and the following year he began shooting the Gotcha-funded *Surfers: The Movie,* a more ambitious but less-focused effort than *Free Ride,* combining new footage with vintage clips from the '50s, '60s, and '70s. *Surfers* cost $400,000; *Surfers: Take Two,* a revised edition, was released in 1991. The surf video had by that time replaced the surf movie as the sport's primary cinematic form, and Delaney, satisfied with his two-and-a-half film oeuvre, returned to the car industry. He was profiled in *50 Years of Surfing on Film,* a 1997 Outdoor Life Network TV series. *See also* Free Ride.

Delaware   The second-smallest state in America after Rhode Island, with the second-smallest coastline (28 miles) and a minuscule surfer population (about 300), Delaware has understandably been over-looked by the larger surf world since the sport was in-troduced here in the early '60s. Wedged between Maryland and Pennsylvania, as surf journalist Peter Interland put it, "Delaware is just a blip on the hori-zon," even for East Coast surfers. Fewer than six surf magazine features have been published on the state over the past 40 years; article titles include "Delaware: Where's That?," "Unaware of Delaware," and "Delaware?" Fall and winter produce the best surf in this area of the country, and the twin jetties of the Indian River Inlet, located within the Delaware Seashore State Park, produce the state's best waves. The easy-breaking rights on the north side of the inlet are surfed almost exclusively by longboarders, and the harder-breaking peaks on the south side are favored by shortboarders. Indian River Inlet waves, as with the other half-dozen Delaware surf spots—in-cluding Naval Jetties and Bethany Beach—break over a sand bottom. Winter water temperatures can drop to the mid-30s; in summer, as thousands of vacation-ers from the northeast settle in, the water tempera-ture rises to the mid-70s. The oldest state in the union (constituted in 1787), Delaware is home to a uniquely diverse and relatively peaceable set of cul-tures. South Bethany, located in the southern part of the state, was founded as a religious retreat town and is still alcohol-free; centrally located Dewey Beach is a popular hangout for the young and straight; remote Gordon's Pond, to the north, has long been a favorite gay/lesbian beach.

Delaware residents Bill Wise, George Pittman, and Bill Pike, along with visiting California wave-rider Don Graham, were the first to surf Delaware, in early 1962. Wise and Pittman soon opened Eastern Surfer, the state's first shop, in landlocked Harring-ton, with merchandise often loaded into the back of the company panel truck so that business could be conducted beachside. Eastern Surfer relocated to Re-hoboth Beach in 1966, the same year Delaware-born surfer Thurman "Skip" Savage opened Surf Shop East, also in Rehoboth.

Delaware was featured in Bill Yerkes's *Summer of '67* surf video. The Eastern Surfing Association (ESA) has been staging regional surf contests on the north side of the Indian River Inlet since the late '60s; Delaware mainstay and longtime top-rated ESA com-petitor Skip Savage was inducted into the East Coast Surf Legends Hall of Fame in 1996. "But other than the fact that everybody in the state literally knows

everybody else," as longtime Delaware surfer Wally "Which Way" Abrams said in 1999, "it's hard to think of anything really unique about surfing here."

Denmark   Denmark takes up much of the Jutland Peninsula and extends out to nearly 500 surround-ing islands. Native-born Rolf Erikson began surfing Denmark's frigid North Sea waters in 1986, and was joined the following year by Reimer Hansen; they rode the north shore of Sjælland Island alone for two years before anyone else followed them into the lineup. The Danish Surfing Association was formed in 1995, and the first Danish Surfing Championships were held the next year at Klitmoller, now known as one of Europe's premier reefbreaks. Later that year, a team of Danes attended the World Surfing Games in Huntington Beach, California. April through Novem-ber is generally the best time for surf in Denmark, as North Sea wind swells often fan across the country's rocky points and reefs. Water temperatures in sum-mer go as high as the mid-60s; winter conditions are far less pleasant. A typical Danish winter surf sce-nario, according to the *Stormrider Guide,* a directory of European surf spots, "is overhead swell, offshore winds, subzero temperatures and powder snow on the beach." Water temperatures drop as low as 35 de-grees. As of 2003, Denmark was home to four surf shops and an estimated 250 surfers. The Denmark surf is detailed in *The Stormrider Guide Europe* (1998).

Dent, Chuck   Sharp-tongued surfboard manufac-turer and gadfly from Huntington Beach, California. Dent was born (1943) in Bellflower, California, began surfing at age 16, and by the early '60s was working as a salesman for Jack Haley Surfboards in Seal Beach, where he built an impressive customer base, as he later put it, out of local "dropouts, lowriders, grem-mies, dopers, juicers, radicals, dirtbags and general riffraff." Dent opened his own shop in 1964 in Hunt-ington, and his all-star surf team included Bill Hamil-ton, Barry Kanaiaupuni, and Mark Martinson. Dent's inflammatory anti-surf-industry monologues in *Pa-cific Vibrations* (1970) and *Five Summer Stories* (1972), two popular surf movies, were whining, cynical, and funny. In a 1974 surf magazine article, he applied his jive-talking invective to himself, as well as others. "So there I was," he wrote describing his early years on the Orange County surf scene, "a flatland ho-daddy transplant, no rating, no nickname, no Clearasil, no money, a semi-kook who hardly knew how to make a surfboard. What does a poor boy do who's too fat to play in a rock and roll band?" Dent closed his shop in the mid-'70s, made a half-hearted return to business in 1978 with the Chuck Dent Surf Center, then died in 1980, age 37, of drug- and alcohol-related heart failure. Dent was inducted into the Huntington Beach Surfing Walk of Fame in 1998.

Diffenderfer, Mike   Grinning surfboard builder from La Jolla, California, once described as the "Michelangelo of shapers"; best known in the 1960s and '70s for his exquisitely crafted big-wave guns. Diffenderfer was born (1937) in Beverly Hills, California, raised in La Jolla, began surfing in 1949, and two years later shaped his first surfboard, out of balsa. In 1955, after graduating from high school—where he played for the golf and football teams, and dated classmate Raquel Welch—Diffenderfer made the first of several annual trips to Hawaii; the following year he began shaping boards commercially in La Jolla, mentored by Pat Curren and influenced by the hydrodynamically advanced designs of board-maker Joe Quigg. Diffenderfer was one of the first shapers with a full understanding of "rocker"—the board's nose-to-tail curve, as viewed from the side; now recognized as one of the most important design characteristics. Diffenderfer had meanwhile become an accomplished surfer, and was featured in Bruce Brown's 1958 movie *Slippery When Wet*. (It was Diffenderfer who later suggested to Brown that the explosive left-breaking wave just west of Ehukai Beach Park, on the North Shore of Oahu, should be called "Pipeline.") The glib and handsome Diffenderfer moved to Hawaii in 1959, where his streamlined big-wave boards quickly earned him a devoted following; in 1960 he shaped for both Inter-Island Surf Shop and Hobie Surfboards; in 1968 he became partners with laminator Tony Channin to form Channin-Diffenderfer; in the early 1970s he lived and worked in Kauai, and made boards for some of the era's best Hawaiian surfers, including Jeff Hakman, Joey Cabell, and Jimmy Lucas. Many regarded a Diffenderfer gun (big-wave board) as equal to those made by shaping guru Dick Brewer. Returning to his roots, Diffenderfer also began making a limited number of boards out of balsa wood. By the early '80s, Diffenderfer estimated he'd shaped roughly 25,000 boards.

Diffenderfer was inducted into the International Surfing Hall of Fame in 1991; by then he was putting much of his time and energy into golf, and made sev-

eral attempts, none successful, at qualifying for the PGA Seniors Tour. He spent the first half of the '90s in Tamarindo, Costa Rica, where he designed a resort golf course and continued to shape surfboards. Diffenderfer never married, and died of brain cancer in 2002, at age 64. *See also* big-wave surfboard.

dig a rail   When the surfboard's rail (edge) unexpectedly catches or "digs" into the water during a ride, abruptly slowing the board down and making it temporarily impossible to control. The surfer, after digging a rail, is either put off balance or tossed off altogether. Digging a rail is most likely to happen when the water surface is choppy, if there's backwash or any kind of secondary "lump" running across the surf zone, if the surfer miscalculates a turn or turns from the wrong place on the board (too far forward, usually), or if the board itself is badly designed. Similar to catching an edge while skiing.

Dillon, Scott   Australian surfboard manufacturer from Sydney's Bondi Beach; cofounder of the Australian board-building industry in the late 1950s, along with Gordon Woods, Barry Bennett, and Bill Wallace. Dillon was born (1928) and raised in Bondi, and was tandem bodysurfing with his father, the treasurer of the Bondi Beach Surf Club, before he could walk. He began stand-up surfing at age six. Dillon trained as a boxer after World War II, was twice national bantamweight champion, and just missed qualifying for the 1952 Australian Olympic team. Later that year he traveled to North America, where he worked as a logger in Canada, and surfed in California and Mexico. He returned home and decided to make a career in surfboard building, and in 1957, with partner Noel Wood, he cofounded Wood and Dillon Surfboards. Wood left the business in early 1959, and Dillon Surfboards moved into a new factory/showroom in the northern Sydney suburb Brookvale, which quickly became the hub of Australian board commerce. In the early '60s, Dillon was one of the first in his country to make polyurethane foam surfboard blanks. He also made boards for future world champion Nat Young, and gave shaping instruction to Queenslander Bob McTavish, who would soon create the first short surfboards. Dillon's big-wave boards were especially prized. By the early '70s, the shortboard revolution, along with its new generation of board manufacturers, had all but pushed Dillon and the rest of the Brookvale originals out of business.

Dillon then moved to the mid–New South Wales town of Coffs Harbor. He opened the Legend Surf Museum in 2001, at which time the 73-year-old was still surfing regularly and making a limited number of boards.

DiMenna, Ron (Ron Jon)   *See* Ron Jon Surfboards.

ding, ding repair   A crack, gouge, fracture, puncture, or cleft in the surfboard's fiberglass skin, often accompanied by damage to the board's polyurethane foam core. Most unrepaired dings will absorb seawater, which corrupts the foam/fiberglass bond, adds weight to the board, and causes yellowing. The serrated edges on a ding can also cause scratches or cuts. Although brought on by mishaps of every description—flying off car roof racks, swung into a doorjamb—the vast majority of dings come from the board striking an inanimate surf-zone object (rock, jetty, pier piling), or hitting another board. The solid-wood boards in use before and just after World War II were often fixed by excavating the area around the ding, gluing in a rough-shaped piece of wood, sanding the wood flush to the surface, and overlaying the area with a coat of varnish. The bow-tie-shaped "butterfly" repair was commonly seen on prewar Hawaiian-made boards. Splits and punctures in the hollow wooden boards used in the '30s and '40s had to be taken care of immediately, as the board would otherwise take on water and begin to sink. Ding repair changed in the late '50s, when foam and fiberglass surfboards became popular, but the basic idea was the same: patch the area with the same type of materials used in the board's original construction. The per capita number of dings was greatly lowered in the early '70s after the introduction of the surf leash, which kept loose boards from washing into rocks, jetties, breakwaters, piers, and other boards.

Surfboard dings are fixed either as an inexpensive but often messy and laborious do-it-yourself project, or by dropping the board off for a fairly expensive and sometimes lengthy professional job. Many surf shops offer ding repair services; all well-populated surfing areas have at least one full-time ding repair pro who usually works out of a garage or backyard shed. Basic ding repair components include fiberglass, at least two types of resin, catalyst, masking tape, and sandpaper. Q-cel, a resin thickening agent, is often used; bigger dings can be filled with a pre-shaped piece of foam. A simplified version of the ding repair process is as follows:

1) Remove damaged fiberglass; allow foam to dry completely; clean and sand the area.
2) Isolate the repair area with masking tape.
3) Fill the ding with unadulterated catalyzed resin (for small, shallow dings) or resin mixed with Q-cel (medium-sized dings) or resin-bonded foam (large dings); let dry; sand to a level just below that of the surrounding area.
4) Apply a precut resin-saturated swatch of fiberglass over the ding and the surrounding area; let dry.
5) Add sanding coat of resin, let partially dry, trim excess fiberglass, dry fully, and sand the ding flush to the rest of the board. Pros often use a power sander. A gloss coat of resin may be added; color pigments and airbrushing can be used to match the ding repair to the rest of the board.

The ding repair process is also used to repair loose or broken fins, foam/fiberglass delaminations, and completely broken boards. A professional ding repairman might charge $20 for a small crack, and $100 to restore a broken board. Because of the time, expense, and hassle involved with ding repair, many surfers will often leave a ding unrepaired—particularly if it's small—or apply a makeshift patch using either duct tape, surfboard wax, or a sticker. Commercially made ding tape is also available. (A small but growing percentage of boards are made from epoxy resin, or are molded, both of which require a slightly different ding-repair process.)

Books on ding repair include *The Ding Repair Scriptures: The Complete Guide to Surfboard Repair* (1986) and *Fiberglass Ding Repair* (1993). Ding repair videos include *The Original Surfboard Repair Video* (1995), *Backyard Ding Repair* (1996), *Surfer's Guide to Ding Repair* (1997), and *Glassing 101* (1998).

Dittrich, Scott   Industrious surf moviemaker of the 1970s and '80s, from Topanga, California; best known for his hard-driving 1974 debut *Fluid Drive*. Dittrich was born (1945) in Detroit, Michigan, learned to surf in Florida at age 10, and moved in 1966 to Hollywood, California. He received a B.A. in economics from UCLA in 1969, went on to take a master's in the same field from the University of Florida, then returned to California where he soon began making his first movie. *Fluid Drive* didn't break any new ground, but the surfing action was first-rate, and the soundtrack, bootlegged from Dittrich's personal record collection, included songs from Led Zeppelin, the

Rolling Stones, Jimi Hendrix, and Lou Reed. Dittrich went on to make *Tales of the Seven Seas* (1981), *Adventures in Paradise* (1982), *Follow the Sun* (1984), *Amazing Surf Stories* (1987), *Gone Surfin'* (1987), and *Rolling Thunder* (1991). He was profiled in *50 Years of Surfing on Film,* a 1997 Outdoor Life Network cable television series produced by the Opper Sports and the *Surfer's Journal.*

Divine, Jeff   Good-natured surf photographer and photo editor from San Clemente, California; a steady surf world presence since the early 1970s, and long regarded as one of the genre's most versatile and dependable talents. Divine was born (1950) in San Diego, raised in the wealthy beach town of La Jolla, started surfing in 1964 and bought his first camera the following year; he soon began selling prints to his high school surfing friends for a dollar apiece. *Surfer* magazine published Divine's work for the first time in 1968; three years later, the 21-year-old was pulled aside by *Surfer* photo editor Brad Barrett and told that he was about to become "the new Ron Stoner," in reference to the brilliant *Surfer* lensman who had rede-

fined surf photography in the mid- and late '60s, and was then rendered virtually housebound by mental illness. If Divine never burned quite as brightly as Stoner, he nonetheless became one of the sport's great all-arounders, shooting both land and water action shots, along with portraiture, landscapes, and candids. In the early and mid-'70s, Divine was often described as the best photographer in surfing, along with Steve Wilkings and Art Brewer.

Although well-traveled, Divine is best known for the work he's done in Hawaii, California, and Baja California, Mexico. He's been a photo editor for most of his career, with *Surfer* from 1981 to 1998, then the *Surfer's Journal.* He also wrote nearly 40 feature and column articles for *Surfer* between 1973 and 1997. *Masters of Surf Photography: Jeff Divine,* a luxurious 236-page hardcover retrospective of his work, with extended captions written by the photographer, was published by the *Journal* in 2000; Divine has also contributed to more than a dozen illustrated surfing books, including *The History of Surfing* (1983), *Surfing: The Ultimate Pleasure* (1984), *The Next Wave* (1991), *Girl in the Curl* (2000), and *The Perfect Day* (2001). Divine has been married twice and has one child.

Dixon, Peter   Surf writer from Malibu, California; best known for his four surfing books published in the 1960s: *The Complete Book of Surfing* (1965), *Men and Waves: A Treasury of Surfing* (1966), *Where the Surfers Are* (1967), and *Men Who Ride Mountains* (1969). Dixon was born (1931) in New York City, moved with his family to Southern California at age seven, and began surfing in 1948 in Palos Verdes. He graduated from UCLA in 1960 with an M.A. in education, began publishing articles in American surf magazines in 1964, and edited *Surfing Illustrated* in 1966 and 1967. Dixon's books are straightforward and authoritative (Dixon himself was an avid surfer), and well researched. *The Complete Book of Surfing* includes chapters on surf history, wave formation, surfing for beginners, competition, and board-building. Sales figures for the paperback version of *The Complete Book of Surfing,* published by Ballentine Books in New York, topped 300,000, more than double the number for the next-highest-selling surfing book. Dixon also wrote books on hang gliding, ocean diving, and skiing, and did television scripts for *Flipper, The Waltons, Little House on the Prairie,* and *Paper Chase. Wipe Out,* Dixon's surfing novel, was published in 1971. His latest surfing book, *The Complete Guide to Surfing,* was published in 2001.

Jeff Divine

Dobson, Dale Enduring and disciplined switchfoot surfer from San Diego, California; winner of the 1972 United States Surfing Championships; the last top-drawer California surfer to give up longboarding, in 1968, and one of the first to take it back up full-time, in the late '70s. Dobson was born (1947) and raised in San Diego, and began surfing at age 10. Influenced in the early '60s by ace switchfooter Butch Van Artsdalen of La Jolla, Dobson, a born goofyfoot, soon became a nearly ambidextrous wave-rider, able to ride nearly as well in a regularfoot stance. Dobson was something of a surf world curiosity when he notched his first big competition win, in an early 1968 Santa Cruz event. The shortboard revolution was in full swing, and surfers had taken to the counterculture, with long hair, beads, and bell-bottoms; the strong-jawed Dobson had a crew cut and rode a 9′6″ longboard. All but ignored by the surf media, Dobson over the next few years was one of California's most dependable competitors, placing highly in the elite AAAA-rated Western Surfing Association events between 1969 and 1972, and winning the 1972 U.S. Championships. In 1973 he won the U.S. kneeboarding title, and in the 1975 U.S. Championships he placed third in men's stand-up division, second in longboarding, and third in kneeboard. As longboarding began to return to West Coast surf breaks in the late '70s, the perennially fit Dobson came out of semiretirement, perfected the noseride 360 (where the hanging-five surfer spins the board around in a full circle), and proved nearly unbeatable in longboard competition. He placed first in the 1981 Peff Eick/Dewey Weber Invitational Longboard Classic in Manhattan Beach, and six times won the prestigious Oceanside Longboard Contest during the late '80s and early '90s. Dobson has appeared in more than a dozen surf films and videos over the decades, including *Tracks* (1970), *Five Summer Stories* (1972), *A Matter of Style* (1975), *Gone Surfin'* (1987), and *Powerglide* (1995).

Doerner, Darrick Terse big-wave surfer from Hawaii; a top performer at Waimea Bay from the early '80s to the early '90s, and one of the original tow-in surfers. Doerner was born (1957) in Fresno, California, the son of a French-born mother and a former Santa Barbara County lifeguard, and began surfing at age five. Moving often after his parents divorced, Doerner lived in Texas, Maine, North Carolina, France, and Los Angeles, before settling on the North Shore of Oahu in 1975 at age 18; the following year he be-

came a career North Shore lifeguard. Doerner was attracted to big waves from the moment he arrived on Oahu, and took his style cues—a slightly bowlegged stance, a smooth, composed line—from respected North Shore surfers Tiger Espere and Eddie Aikau. In 1982, after guru board-maker Dick Brewer made him a 9′6″ big-wave gun, Doerner began focusing on Waimea Bay. He was small (5′6″, 140 pounds), but fast, focused, and well-trained, and on January 31, 1988, Doerner caught a 30-foot wave at Waimea Bay that big-wave veteran Peter Cole described as the "most impressive ride I've seen in the past ten years." Doerner tied with fellow Hawaiian Brock Little as the "best Waimea surfer" in a 1990 *Surfer* magazine peer poll; the two also tied in a similar *Australia's Surfing Life* magazine poll in 1993.

In 1992, along with Laird Hamilton and Buzzy Kerbox, the quiet-voiced Doerner became a cofounder of tow-in surfing, the revolutionary approach to big-wave riding where the surfer holds on to a towline attached to a personal watercraft and is pulled into waves that are too big to catch by paddling. In early 1996, at a Maui big-wave break named Jaws, Doerner slotted himself in the hollows of a 35-footer, setting a new standard for big-wave tuberiding. Doerner placed sixth in both the 1986 and 1990 Quiksilver in Memory of Eddie Aikau contests at Waimea Bay, but was ambivalent about competitive surfing. "It brings out the wrong feelings," he once said. "People get aggressive, they get upset, they get into fights. It's like, try another sport if it comes to that."

Doerner, unmarried and the father of one child, has lived for decades in near-monastic seclusion at Sunset Beach, Hawaii. Indifferent to surf media, he was nonetheless profiled in both *Surfer* and *Surfing* magazines in 1990; the following year he did stunt work for 20th Century Fox's surf-caper picture *Point Break*, and in 1998 he had a cameo in TriStar's big-wave melodrama *In God's Hands*.

Dogny, Carlos Wealthy gentleman surfer and socialite from Lima, Peru; the founder of Club Waikiki, and often referred to as the father of Peruvian surfing. Dogny was born (1909) in Barranco, the only son of a French army colonel and a Peruvian sugarcane heiress, and grew up in both Lima and the beachside resort town of Biarritz, France. In 1938, the 29-year-old Dogny traveled with a French polo team to Honolulu, where he learned to surf in the gentle waves at Waikiki. Hawaiian surf legend Duke Kahanamoku gave Dogny a heavy wooden board to take back to Peru; on the beach at Miraflores, on the outskirts of Lima, Dogny passed the board around to a group of similarly wealthy friends. Surfing had been practiced off the beaches of Lima as far back as 1923, but had died out by the mid-'30s; Dogny and his small band of wave-riders have long been thought of as the original Peruvian surfers.

The surf world's original aristocrat organization, and the long time hub of Peruvian surfing Club Waikiki was founded and built in 1942, with Dogny serving as club president. In 1959, Dogny and French surfer Michel Barland cofounded the Waikiki Surf Club, France's first surfing organization, in Biarritz. Dogny died in 1997, age 87; his ashes were spread in the ocean in front of Club Waikiki. *See also* Club Waikiki.

dogs and surfing   A time-honored surf world novelty, where the surfing dog owner trains his pet to ride waves, usually on the nose of the board with the owner standing behind, but sometimes riding solo. *National Geographic* published a full-page photograph in 1944 of the "World-champion Dog Surfer, Rusty," and over the decades the surf media has featured bodysurfing dogs, dogs on bodyboards, and a Labrador from Honolulu named Kam who surfed in a semi-prone position while drinking beer from a bottle. Threats were occasionally made to alert the Society for the Prevention of Cruelty to Animals, but surf-dog owners claimed the animals enjoyed riding. "Every time I pick up my board," one surfer said, "he's running back and forth across the yard, jumping up and down; he can't wait."

There were two celebrated 20th-century surfing dogs. Sandy, a "poi dog" mongrel from Waikiki, began surfing with noted beachboy Joseph "Scooter Boy" Kaopuiki in 1950. The two appeared in a UPI photograph published in newspapers across the country, and were featured on ABC's *You Asked For It!* as well as in California surf moviemaker Bud Browne's early films. As Grady Timmons wrote in his 1989 book *Waikiki Beachboys,* Sandy "could go anywhere in Hawaii, scratch on any door and get a place to sleep, go into any restaurant and be served." When Sandy died in 1958, the Waikiki beachboys bore his ashes to sea in a flotilla of canoes.

Max, a terrier mix belonging to Dave Chalmers of San Diego, first appeared in *Surfer* magazine in 1977. Three years earlier, Chalmers trained his pet by tap-

Californian Jim Bailey and his cocker spaniel, Rusty; late 1930s

ing dog biscuits to the nose of his longboard. Max surfed dozens of breaks between Santa Barbara and the southern tip of Baja California, Mexico; he appeared in surf movies, and was featured on the syndicated TV show *Amazing Animals. Surfer* published "Max's Last Ride," a two-page article about the 15-year-old dog's final surf session, in 1989. "It was a beautiful sight," the magazine reported. "Chalmers and Max gliding along for 60 yards, in perfect trim, with Max rocking back and forth on the nose."

Domenech, Thierry   Smooth-surfing regularfooter from Biscarrosse, France; runner-up in the French Surfing Championships in 1986, 1988, 1989, and 1990, and runner-up in the 1987 European Surfing Championships. Domenech was born (1964) in Arcachon, France, and began surfing at nearby Biscarrosse at age 11. He won the 1982 juniors division national title, and traveled that year to Australia to compete in the World Surfing Championships. While many French surfers have little interest in visiting other countries in search of waves, Domenech has made regular and lengthy overseas forays. He moved to Hawaii in 1985 and for 12 years laminated surfboards for Hawaiian Island Creations, Barry Kanaiaupuni, Dick Brewer, and Jack Reeves. He moved to the French Polynesian island of Moorea in 1997. Domenech appeared in a small number of surf movies and videos, including *All Down the Line* (1989) and *The Mondo X-treme X-periment* (1992).

Dooley, Mick   Bantamweight Australian regular-footer from Sydney; one of the country's best competitive surfers in the early and mid-'60s. Dooley began riding waves in 1957 under the guidance of Aussie surf legend Jack "Bluey" Mayes. In 1963 he was runner-up to Nat Young in Australia's first national titles, and in 1964 he won the annual Bells Beach contest, again finished runner-up in the national titles, and placed fifth in the World Surfing Championships. Dooley was small (5′6″, 135 pounds), but quick and strong. He had an "easy-going, controlled style," as described by *Surfing World* magazine, but was also a "temperamental performer" who may have lost the world championship due to nerves. Dooley was briefly seen in Bruce Brown's 1962 film, *Surfing Hollow Days.*

Dooley, Pete   Energetic surf shop owner and surf contest organizer/judge from Satellite Beach, Florida; cofounder in 1971 of Natural Art Surfboards, and a longtime head judge at national and international professional surfing events. Dooley was born (1949) in Lakewood, Ohio, and began surfing at age 13 after his family moved to Tampa, Florida. In 1971 he launched Natural Art in Cocoa Beach, Florida, with soon-to-be East Coast Surfing Championships winner Greg Loehr; by the early '80s the shop was building and selling up to 4,000 boards a year. Additional Natural Art shops later opened in North Carolina, South Carolina, Georgia, as well as other Florida locations. Dooley had meanwhile become a contest judge and a judge trainer, and helped to organize pro events on both American coasts, as well as France, Puerto Rico, Barbados, and Panama. He served as head judge for a number of world pro tour events, including the Op Pro and the California Stubbies Pro.

Dora, Mickey   Irresistible American surf rogue, originally from Hollywood, California; the light-footed master of Malibu during the 1950s and '60s, and surfing's definitive outlaw figure. Dora was born (1934) in Budapest, Hungary, the son of a wine merchant. His parents divorced when Dora was six, and his mother soon married Gard Chapin, regarded at the time as California's best surfer, as well as the angriest and most disliked. Chapin sent his stepson to boarding school, which Dora hated, but also intro-

Mickey Dora

duced him to surfing in the late '40s; Dora later said he didn't get a board of his own until 1950, at age 15, just before he began riding Malibu. By 1956, Malibu had become the hot spot of the surfing world, with riders like Dewey Weber, Mike Doyle, Mickey Muñoz, and young Lance Carson setting new performance standards in the water, while Terry "Tubesteak" Tracy and Billy "Moondoggie" Bengston invented an easy-going but elitist surfer-nomad way of living. Dora interacted with the regulars at Malibu, Windansea, Santa Monica, and elsewhere, but the surf scene was never a big part of his social life. "Living at the beach isn't the answer," he once said. "Guys who live at the beach get waterlogged. I'm there for the waves, nothing else." Through the decades he remained something of a loner.

Dora initially patterned his surfing style on that of postwar Malibu ace Matt Kivlin, riding with a slight haunch to his upper back, his back knee tucked inward, hands held palm-down at waist level. Dora's turns and cutbacks, taken individually, were similar to those of Phil Edwards, Mike Doyle, and the rest of the era's top riders. Dora set himself apart with the near-constant adjustments he made between moves—hands, head, shoulders, and feet bebopping to a complex rhythm no other surfer heard—and by the elegant trim line he drew across the wave face. Strong and broad-shouldered, with a mat of black hair across his chest, Dora was nonetheless light on his feet, earning himself the nickname "Da Cat."

Head-high California point waves matched his riding style perfectly, but he also performed well in small beachbreak surf. Dora called himself a "four-foot-and-under man," and tended to stay away from big surf, but turned in some of the year's best performances at Sunset Beach and Waimea Bay during his only extended visit to the North Shore of Oahu, in the winter of 1962–63.

Dora meanwhile earned a reputation as a prankster, shooting army surplus rockets off the end of Malibu pier, painting swastikas on his board, and releasing a jar full of moths into a theater during the screening of a surf movie. Some of his ploys were more intricate. "Mickey loved fraud," filmmaker and '50s Malibu surfer John Milius once said. "He'd turn up at some function with a couple of young guys and word would pass around that Dora is gay. Three days later he'd show up with the most extraordinary girl on his arm." At the 1967 Malibu Invitational (one of perhaps a half-dozen surf contests Dora entered in his life), he advanced to the semifinals, where he paddled into a wave, stood and trimmed, dropped his trunks to moon the judging panel, and left the beach. Dora skirmished constantly with the ever-growing number of surfers at Malibu, threading his way past other riders, or shoving them off their boards, or sometimes using his own board to knock them down. Darkly handsome, with a mischievous grin and a low, somewhat affected manner of speech, Dora was labeled by the surf press as "the angry young man of surfing." He railed against the thronging Malibu crowd in a 1967 *Surfer* magazine article, saying the break had been all but ruined by the influx of "kooks of all colors, fags, finks, ego heroes, Amen groupies and football-punchy Valley swingers." Never afraid to be self-contradicting, Dora fumed against surfing's commercialization even as he hired out as an extra or stunt double in a series of Hollywood surf-themed movies, including *Gidget* (1959), *Beach Party* (1963), and *Ride the Wild Surf* (1964). He also posed for Hang Ten surfwear ads, and promoted his signature Greg Noll Surfboards Da Cat model with full-page ads in surf magazines in 1966 and 1967—including one with Dora crucified on a cross made of two surfboards. Dora's act struck a nerve with surf magazine readers, many writing letters to the editor in praise, while others described him as a "sick and ignorant" person who should be "banned from the beach."

The late-'60s shortboard revolution pushed Dora out of the wave-riding vanguard, but he continued to have a strong presence. He wrote a lengthy article for *Surfer* in early 1969, was interviewed by the magazine a few months later, then gave a short but articulate on-screen harangue in the 1970 surf movie *Pacific Vibrations*. A warrant for credit card and check fraud charges had meanwhile been issued in Dora's name, and he was forced to leave the country, at age 36, to avoid arrest. He traveled constantly over the next three decades, spending much of his time in France and South Africa, but also visiting Argentina, Brazil, Namibia, Angola, and Australia. He was arrested in 1973 after returning to California, and sentenced to three years' probation, which he broke; he was again arrested, in France, where he spent three months in jail in 1981, then returned to stand trial in California and Colorado, and was incarcerated for most of 1982. The Dora mystique only grew during this period, and in 1983 he was featured in a *California* magazine cover story titled "Endless Summer: From Surfing Legend to International Fugitive, the Wild Ride of Mickey Dora." *Surfer* magazine paid Dora $10,000—still the highest figure ever paid by a surf magazine—to write an article, the long and discursive first-person "Million Days to Darkness," published in 1987. Three years later, Dora gave one last grand public performance, with a bitter-funny soliloquy in *Surfers: The Movie* (1990). He remained on the fringes of surf society, but turned up occasionally at old-timers' events. He continued to surf often and well: "Dora Still the King" was the title of a short article by surf journalist Derek Hynd, published in *Australia's Surfing Life* magazine in 1997, describing Dora's magnificent two-minute-long ride at Jeffreys Bay, South Africa. Dora never had a profession, and lived for the most part by staying for weeks at a time with various friends and admirers. He raised money in the late '90s and early '00s by selling personal effects, including an ID bracelet and signed family photos. In the early '90s, Dora asked that he be referred to as "Miki," the correct diminutive spelling of Miklos, rather than Mickey.

Dora died of pancreatic cancer in early 2002, at age 67, after spending his last few months at his birth-father's home in Montecito, California. He never married and had no children. Newspapers around the world noted his death; a *London Times* obituary described him as a "West Coast archetype and antihero . . . the siren voice of a nonconformist surfing lifestyle." Dora was inducted into the International Surfing Hall of Fame in 1966; in 1999 he was cited as one of the "25 Most Influential Surfers of the

Century" by *Surfer* magazine. A documentary titled *In Search of Da Cat* was released in 1998. Dora was featured in about 40 other surf movies, videos, and documentaries, including *Search for Surf* (1958), *Surfing Hollow Days* (1962), *Gun Ho!* (1963), *Inside Out* (1965), *The Endless Summer* (1966), *Golden Breed* (1968), *A Sea for Yourself* (1973), *Legends of Malibu* (1987), and *Great Waves* (1999). Dora was inducted into the Huntington Beach Surfing Walk of Fame in 2002. *See also* Gard Chapin, Malibu, Malibu Invitational.

Dorian, Shane   Fearless, fashion-conscious pro surfer from Hawaii's Big Island; world-ranked #4 in 2000, and costar in the 1998 big-wave melodrama *In God's Hands*. Dorian was born (1972) and raised in Kona, Hawaii, the son of a restaurateur and former Hollywood stunt double, and began surfing at age five. He was a menehune division finalist in the 1984 and 1985 U.S. Championships, competed in the 1986 and 1988 World Amateur Surfing Championships, turned professional at 17, and beginning in 1992 made a long, slow climb up the world tour standings to peak at #4 in 2000. He won the 1998 Billabong Challenge, the 1999 Rip Curl Bells, and the 2000 Billabong Pro Europe. Competition has always been a chore for Dorian—he freely admits to lacking a killer instinct, and didn't win his first major world tour event until 1999—and his ratings have little or nothing to do with his longstanding reputation as one of the world's premier all-around surfers. The wiry (5′8″, 150 pounds) Dorian was a leading New School aerialist in the early '90s, was and remains a tuberider of phenomenal agility and precision, and since the mid-'90s has been one of the world's best big-wave riders. Dorian further distinguished himself as one of the few surfers of his generation not to pattern his style after three-time world champion Tom Curren, developing instead his own curious-but-pleasing form, marked by a raised chin, down-turned wrists and hands, and splayed fingers.

Dorian took a critical thrashing for his *In God's Hands* performance as Shane, the monosyllabic surfing genius who can't decide if he should join the world tour ("he has the onscreen presence of Melba toast," one reviewer noted), and for a few months after the movie debuted he was presented as surfing's answer to Brad Pitt. "Suave Surfer Stokes New Style," a *Los Angeles Times* feature article about Dorian's fashion sense, described the Kona surfer as having "Adonis looks that surfer girls' dreams are made of," and a

wardrobe holding a "Versace lambskin boot-cut pants and an ankle-length Gucci peacoat." Media attention had no effect on Dorian's surfing skills, and by the end of the decade he'd lifted his performance to an even higher level. "Shane has the best reputation on the world tour," *Surfer* magazine wrote in 2000. "Hot, progressive, utterly fearless." The glam accolades kept rolling in as well, and Dorian was named as the sixth sexiest male athlete in the world in an 2002 ESPN Internet poll.

Dorian finished 2nd in the 2001 Quiksilver in Memory of Eddie Aikau big-wave contest at Waimea Bay in Oahu. He also finished runner-up to Kelly Slater in the 2000 *Surfer* Magazine Readers Poll Awards. *The Blueprint*, Dorian's video biography, was released in 2002; he had by that time been featured in more than 60 surf videos, including *Momentum* (1992), *Focus* (1994), *Psychedelic Desert Groove* (1997), *Nine Lives* (1999), and *September Sessions* (2000). Since 1995 Dorian, along with friend and fellow pro surfer Conan Hayes, has directed the Shane Dorian/Conan Hayes Keiki Classic for surfers 17 and under. Dorian is married.

dory surfing   *See* surf boat.

double-up   Two separate waves merged into one; distinguished, as it breaks, by a midface step or terrace. Double-up waves are stronger and more dangerous than regular waves, and can be completely unridable. They also create some of the biggest, widest, and most thrilling tubes. Double-ups occur most often when wave trains from two different swells crosshatch as they move toward shore.

Downing, George   Magisterial regularfoot surfer from Honolulu, Hawaii, often thought of as the original "complete" big-wave rider; winner of the Makaha International in 1954, 1961, and 1965; longtime competition director of the Quiksilver in Memory of Eddie Aikau event at Waimea Bay. Downing was born (1930) and raised in Honolulu, the son of a marine machinist, and began surfing Waikiki at age nine. In the latter years of World War II, as a young teenager, Downing lived with Wally Froiseth, one of the sport's original big-wave riders and a cocreator of the racy hot curl surfboard. Froiseth taught Downing how to make boards, and introduced him to the big surf at Makaha, on the west side of Oahu; along with fellow Honolulu surfer Russ Takaki, they became the first to

George Downing

Brown and Californian-born surfers Walter Hoffman and Buzzy Trent, had cracked the 20-foot barrier at Makaha. Downing, Trent, and Froiseth were the standout riders on a glassy Makaha afternoon on January 13, 1958, when the waves were roaring in at 30 foot.

Waimea Bay on the North Shore was regarded by then as the new capital of big-wave surfing; because Downing preferred the long walls of Makaha to the short but explosive drops at Waimea—where the cameras were—his profile in the big-wave world was lower than it might have been. But insiders recognized him as a master. Downing's line across the wave was precise, even conservative, but he invariably rode the biggest and best waves of the day, and rarely fell off his board. (He also invented a cannonball dismount off the back of his board that allowed him to sink beneath the whitewater explosion.) Downing was the last of the great upright surfers, dropping to a modified crouch when necessary, but preferring to ride in a straight-backed, low-shoulder, palms-down stance. He was the stylistic link between the pose-and-go Waikiki surfers of the prewar era and the kinetic high-performance riders of the '60s. Downing's encyclopedic knowledge of the sport was meanwhile looked upon with awe. He was referred to by the world's most knowledgeable surfers as "the teacher"; '60s big-wave rider Ricky Grigg called him "the guru." Downing mentored dozens of top Hawaiian surfers over the decades, including Joey Cabell, Reno Abellira, and Michael Ho. He worked as a Waikiki beachboy from the early '40s to the late '70s, giving surf lessons, coaching outrigger canoe teams, and running a beach concession stand. Generous and giving for the most part, Downing also proved to be congenitally private—he's never been profiled or interviewed at length in the surf media—and occasionally aloof and argumentative. A note on the final page of Australian Nat Young's 1983 surf history book notes that "George Downing has been omitted from *The History of Surfing* at his request, although he has played a significant part in the sport."

Downing won his first Makaha International in 1954, but didn't really hit stride as a competitor until the '60s—a remarkable feat given that he was consistently matched against riders 10 or 15 years his junior. Aside from his run at Makaha (winning again in 1961 and 1965; placing second in 1966 and fourth in 1968), Downing finished seventh in the 1965 World Championships, second in the 1967 Duke, and third

ride Laniakea on the North Shore, in 1946, as well as Maui's Honolua Bay, in 1947. The following year the three men sailed to Southern California and spent two months surfing up and down the coast, a rarity at the time, as virtually all cross-Pacific surf travel involved California surfers visiting Hawaii. While in the Los Angeles area, Downing met with surfer/board designer Bob Simmons and learned how to fiberglass surfboards.

The wiry, dark-haired Downing made a study of surfing, analyzing weather maps to better understand swell formation, snorkeling over reefs on waveless days to learn how their topography affected the surf, calculating wave intervals, observing wind patterns and ocean currents, and absorbing all there was to know about surfboard theory and construction. In 1950, Downing produced the first in a new generation of big-wave surfboards. The hot curl had been finless, made primarily from redwood, and finished with varnish; "Rocket," Downing's new 10-footer, was narrow-tailed like the hot curls, but constructed from balsa, fiberglass, and resin; it also had the first removable fin. On this new board, Downing was able to ride bigger waves than anybody before him, and by the mid-'50s he and Froiseth, along with Woody

in the 1968 Peru International. At 40, he competed one last time in Peru, finishing fourth. He coached the Hawaiian team to victory in the 1968 World Surfing Championships. (He had also set a number of paddling records—from 100 yards to one mile—that as of 2003 were still standing.) Downing was named as contest director for the Quiksilver in Memory of Eddie Aikau contest in 1985, and it's his decision each year as to whether or not the Waimea surf is big and well-formed enough for competition. He gave the go-ahead in 1986, 1990, 1995, 1999, 2001, and 2002. Downing opened the Wavecrest Hawaii surf shop in 1979 and Downing Hawaii in 1989.

Downing appeared in a small number of surf movies from the '50s and '60s, including *Surf* (1958), *Cat on a Hot Foam Board* (1959), *Cavalcade of Surf* (1962), and *Gun Ho!* (1963). He was also featured on Duke Kahanamoku's *World of Surfing,* a 1968 CBS special. He was the top Hawaiian vote-getter in the 1966 *International Surfing* Magazine Hall of Fame Awards; in 1998 he was inducted into the Huntington Beach Surfing Walk of Fame. Downing is married and has three children. Oldest son Keone Downing won the 1990 Quiksilver/Aikau event; younger son Kainoa Downing was a finalist in the 1980 Pipeline Masters and the 1982 Duke. *See also* big-wave surfboard, big-wave surfing, Quiksilver in Memory of Eddie Aikau.

Downing, Keone   Smooth and steady regularfoot surfer from Hawaii; winner of the 1990 Quiksilver in Memory of Eddie Aikau big-wave contest at Waimea Bay; son of big-wave pioneer George Downing. Keone Downing was born (1953) and raised in Honolulu, and began surfing at age five in Waikiki. He won the juniors division of the Makaha International in 1968 and 1969, placed fifth in the 1970 World Surfing Championships, and was runner-up in the 1980 Duke Kahanamoku Classic. He was one of Hawaii's most decorated outrigger-canoe paddlers in the '80s, helping his team to five victories in the Molokai-to-Oahu championship between 1980 and 1988, and winning the World Canoe Surfing Championships in 1988. Downing graduated in 1975 with a degree in commercial art from California College of Arts and Crafts, and went on to design logos for surf industry giants Quiksilver and O'Neill. In the 1990 Quiksilver/Aikau event, still considered by many to be the most exciting big-wave contest ever seen, Downing was re-garded as a longshot contender. But he selected waves perfectly, went through the one-day event without so

much as a slip or bobble, and led from start to finish. He rode a beautifully streamlined board shaped by his father. Downing's $55,000 winner's check was the sport's biggest-ever cash prize at the time. He competed in other Quiksilver/Aikau events, placing seventh in 1986, 11th in 1999, 13th in 2001, and 18th in 2002.

downrail   *See* tucked-under edge.

Doyle, Mike   Hawk-nosed regularfoot surfer from Leucadia, California; runner-up in the 1964 World Surfing Championships; a champion paddleboard racer, tandem rider, and big-wave rider, and arguably the 1960s' best all-around surfer. "Everybody wanted to be like Mike Doyle," 1966 East Coast champion Gary Propper said. "He had style; everyone wanted to surf like him, look like him, dress like him." Doyle was born (1941) in Los Angeles, raised in the southwest Los Angeles suburbs of Inglewood and Westchester, and began surfing at age 13 at the Manhattan Beach Pier. He rode as a goofyfooter for nearly three years, then relearned as a regularfooter in 1956, once he began riding Malibu. Two years later he was good enough to work as a surfing stunt double on *Gidget,* the 1959 film that helped spark a national surf craze. (Doyle had sold Kathy Kohner, the real-life Gidget, her first surfboard in 1956.) The easy-smiling Doyle himself was in many ways the archetypal California teenage surfer: deeply tanned with peroxide-blond hair, rowdy and prank-happy but not malicious. But at 6'2", 190 pounds, Doyle was bigger than most surfers, and vastly more athletic. He excelled at paddleboard racing, an adjunct sport for most surfers in the preshortboard era, winning the West Coast Championships pier race in 1959, 1960, and 1962, and anchoring California's World Contest–winning relay team in 1968. As a tandem surfer, Doyle was second only to the great Pete Person. Often riding with Linda Merrill of San Clemente, Doyle won the 1962 Pacific Coast Championships, the 1963 West Coast Championships, the 1965 United States Surfing Championships, and the 1965 World Surfing Championships. He also won the tandem division at the Makaha International in 1963, 1964, and 1965.

Doyle had fewer wins as a nontandem surfer, but his results spanned the decade. He finished third in the 1961 West Coast Championships, second in the 1964 World Championships, second in the 1966

Duke Kahanamoku Invitational, first in the 1968 Duke, and first in the 1969 Peru International. He also won the *Surfer* Magazine Readers Poll Award in 1964 and 1965, and was voted the top international surfer in *Surfing* magazine's 1966 Hall of Fame Awards. The Mike Doyle signature model, by Hansen Surfboards, was introduced in 1967.

Doyle's presence in the surf world came partly from his reputation as a competitor, but just as much from his powerful and slightly theatrical free-surfing style. It also helped that he was friendly, articulate, and had good beach-fashion sense. "He was riding a mauve board with white competition stripes, and I was totally and utterly infatuated," Australian surfer Nat Young wrote about Doyle's appearance in Sydney for the 1964 World Championships. "We couldn't believe it when he actually showed up at our local beach [and] brought with him a handmade, embroidered Mexican shirt as a present for me. It was a perfect fit and became my all-time favorite shirt, worn only on special occasions." Young borrowed liberally from Doyle's surfing style, went on to win the 1966 World Championships, and in turn became the most copied surfer in history.

Doyle was also innovative and, to a lesser degree, entrepreneurial. In the mid-'60s he cofounded Surf Research and developed the first surfing-specific board wax; in 1970 he invented the Single Ski, a forerunner to the snowboard; in 1974 he helped create the Morey-Doyle soft surfboard, featuring the same spongy covering as the Morey Boogie bodyboard, and the prototype for today's soft-exterior surfboards used by beginners. Profits from Doyle's innovations, however, were small or temporary.

Doyle is featured in more than two dozen surf movies of the late '50s and '60s, including *Surf Safari* (1959), *Barefoot Adventure* (1960), *Cavalcade of Surf* (1962), *Strictly Hot* (1964), and *Golden Breed* (1968). *Morning Glass: The Adventures of Legendary Waterman Mike Doyle,* a self-published autobiography, was released in 1993. Doyle moved to San Jose del Cabo, at the southern tip of Baja California, in 1980. He's been married three times and has no children. *See also* soft surfboard, tandem surfing.

drag-foot turn Discarded method of turning a surfboard by dipping the back foot into the water along the board's tail section; a right dip to turn right, left dip to turn left. The long wooden surfboard used in the first half of the 20th century was not only heavy—generally 50 pounds or more—but rudderless, so that anything but the gentlest turning motion on the part of the surfer did nothing but throw the board's tail into a ride-ending slide. Origins of the drag-foot turn are unknown, although it was likely developed in Waikiki sometime before World War I. By the late 1940s, after surfers began using a stabilizing fin on the back of their boards, the drag-foot turn was obsolete. *See also* hollow surfboard, plank surfboard.

drop The beginning of a ride, when the surfer "drops" down the wave face; frequently the most thrilling part of the ride, and potentially the most dangerous, as the drop is often engaged where the wave is biggest and strongest. Asked about the attraction of riding giant surf, California big-wave pioneer Flippy Hoffman shrugged and replied, "I like the drop." *See also* air-drop, late takeoff.

drop-in The act of taking off on a wave in front of another surfer who is closer to the curl, and thus thought of as having first claim to the wave; an intentional drop-in is generally regarded as nothing less than wave theft, and can lead to argument, retaliatory drop-ins, even violence. Surfers in bygone eras often rode happily side by side on the same wave, and until the early 1950s—when turning became the new criterion of high-performance surfing, and the one surfer/one wave standard was adopted—surfers at popular breaks like Waikiki and San Onofre frequently rode together by the half-dozen. (In preChristian Hawaii, men and women rode waves together as a form of courtship.) By the late '50s, however, not dropping in on your fellow surfer had become, as surf journalist Nick Carroll later wrote, surfing's "First Commandment," albeit one that is broken freely and often, especially when the waves get crowded. Malibu, Sunset Beach, and Kirra are nearly as famous for repetitive, multiparty drop-in violations as for their perfectly shaped waves. In competition, a drop-in surfer is virtually assured of elimination. In a 1970 Huntington Beach small-claims court case, a drop-in surfer was found liable for $100 in damages after causing the right-of-way surfer to lose his board into the pier. A drop-in is sometimes justified, particularly if the already-riding surfer is taking more than his or her fair share of waves. Also known as "snaking," "burning," "cutting off," "fading," or "shoulder-hopping."

Drop-knee bottom turn by California's Henry Ford

drop-knee turn   A longboard-only variation on
the frontside cutback or backside bottom turn, where
the trailing knee is bent inward and lowered throughout the turn, with the kneecap sometimes dropping
all the way to the deck of the board, just behind the
front foot. The drop-knee turn was invented by California surfer Gard Chapin in the late 1930s or early
1940s as a way to leverage turns out of the heavy
wooden boards of the period. Not a particularly functional maneuver as practiced today, but showy in
the best sense of the word. In bodyboarding, riding
"drop-knee" is to assume a half-standing position,
with the front foot planted on the deck while the rear
leg remains kneeling; popular in the late '70s and
'80s.

Drouyn, Peter   Innovative and dramatic Australian
surfer from the Gold Coast of Queensland; winner of
the Australian National Titles in 1970 and world-
ranked #6 in 1977; inventor of the man-on-man surf
contest format. Drouyn, surf journalist Phil Jarratt
wrote in 1978, is "an immensely likable bundle of
neurotic nervous energy." Drouyn was born (1949) in
Surfer's Paradise, Queensland, the son of a clothing
store owner/jazz saxophonist, and began surfing at
age nine. The sad-eyed, scruffy-haired regularfooter
had an excellent run in the Australian National
Titles, winning the juniors division in 1965 and 1966,
placing second to Nat Young in the men's division
in 1967 and 1969, winning in 1970 (the first Queenslander to do so in men's), placing second in 1971, and
finishing fourth in 1974 and 1976. In 1970 he also
placed fourth in the Smirnoff, second in the Duke
Kahanamoku Classic and third in the World Champi-

onships. He finished second at the annual Bells
Beach event in 1971, 1974, and 1977.

Drouyn made the late '60s transition from longboards to shortboards with ease. He rode aggressively,
but with consummate control, and was one of the period's great stylists, using an open-knee stance, keeping a slight curve to his back, and combining elegant
periods of trim with swooping arms-extended power
turns. The theatrical Drouyn style was expressed just
as strongly on land. "He showed me what show business was all about," fellow Queenslander and 1978
world champion Wayne Bartholomew said. "He had
a caddie who would carry his boards around everywhere, while Drouyn walked around supreme, like
Marlon Brando."

Drouyn was hired as contest director for the inaugural Stubbies Pro in 1977, held at his home break
of Burleigh Heads, Queensland. Surf contest heats
had up to that point been filled with anywhere from
four to eight surfers; to put the spotlight more on
the individual, Drouyn introduced a man-on-man
format, which proved an instant success and was
adopted for virtually all world tour events thereafter.
(Drouyn's attempt to incorporate what he called "effective cheating"—to broaden the sport's audience
appeal by allowing full contact between riders—was
a failure.) Drouyn himself retired from competitive
surfing in 1978, but he called out four-time world
champion Mark Richards to a man-on-man "World
Masters Super Challenge" in 1984, and promoted the
event with full-page surf magazine advertisements
of himself splayed out, wearing only underwear and
splattered in ketchup, next to copy reading "I'm
going to kill or be killed." Drouyn quit near the end
of the event and declared the contest a tie (though
Richards was well ahead on points), claiming he'd
been struck by lightning.

In 1985, just after receiving a B.A. in Asian studies
from Brisbane's Griffith University, Drouyn introduced surfing to China, on Hainan Island in the
South China Sea. He hoped to become China's national surfing coach, but was instead asked to leave
the country four months after his arrival. Drouyn
also studied acting (and briefly ran his own drama
school), oceanography, and engineering. He sold life
insurance door-to-door, owned three surf shops,
drove a cab, worked as a surf coach, received a patent
for the "Drouyn Wave Stadium," helped develop a
Philippine surf resort, and made an unsuccessful bid
to open a surf resort on an island off Yemen. Mean-

while, he also claimed (and not without some justification) that the surfing "power structure" had ignored or spurned him through the decades, viewing him as a grandiose troublemaker. "Drouyn was a good-looking kid," he later said in a typically mischievous half-ironic comment, "and that was a real problem for them. I'm sure there was some jealousy." Drouyn starred in the 1974 surf movie *Drouyn and Friends,* and was featured in more than a dozen others, including *A Life in the Sun* (1966), *The Hot Generation* (1968), *Oceans* (1972), and *On Any Morning* (1974). Drouyn was married once and has one child. *See also* China, Stubbies Surf Classic.

drugs and surfing Surfing allied itself with the mid-1960s-launched youth movement, more so than any other sport or recreation, so it's not surprising that drug use quickly became a popular and often celebrated part of surf culture. *Surfer* magazine cartoonist Rick Griffin embroidered a two-page illustration with marijuana leaves in 1967; surf movies of the late 1960s often featured processing effects that allowed the on-screen surfers to leave "acid tracks" as they rode; Wilkins Surfboards introduced the Meth Model in 1970 with the slogan "For Those Who Like Speed"; and surf journalist Drew Kampion, in his *Surfing* magazine coverage of the 1972 World Surfing Championships in San Diego, wrote of "the occasional snow-flurry" passing through the contestants' hotel rooms—an in-crowd (at the time) reference to cocaine use.

Heroin, psychedelics, and amphetamines have gone in and out of fashion in the surf world, but marijuana has always been the sport's most popular drug—influenced perhaps by surfing's fundamental Hawaii-based easy-does-it outlook. Surfers in the '60s and '70s, meanwhile, seemed to be more inclined than their peers toward drug dealing and trafficking, in part because they were already members of a mildly outlaw society, and for the more practical reason that flexible work hours allowed the surfer/dealer to spend as much time as possible in the water. That said, drug use and abuse among surfers has for the most part been similar to that of any other young, entitled, leisure-class group.

The surf world's register of drug-related mishaps and tragedies has long been a source of anguish, sadness, fear, and prurient interest. Mid-'60s surfing prodigy Kevin Brennan of Australia died in 1975 of a heroin overdose; 1974 U.S. champion Rick Rasmussen

was shot and killed during a 1981 drug deal in Harlem, New York. Hawaiian surfers Tommy Winkler, Rusty Starr, Tim Fretz, and Eric Diaz; California photographer Ron Stoner; Florida surfer/writer Bruce Valluzzi—all died of drug-related causes. Dozens of well-known famous surfers have meanwhile been convicted on drug charges, including Steve Bigler, Donald Takayama, Les Potts, Robbie Page, Nick Wood, Maurice Cole, and Montgomery "Buttons" Kaluhiokalani.

The surf industry's intermittent and often self-contradictory response to drug use within the sport began with a 1967 *Surfer* magazine editorial noting that "no real athlete uses stimulants to improve performance," and that "the fad of pot smoking will pass from the scene." Other surf-world antidrug gestures over the years have included opinion pieces from famous surfers (including world champions Midget Farrelly and Fred Hemmings), world pro tour surf contests (the Drug Offensive Surfmasters in Australia), print ad campaigns (most notably by the Chart House restaurant chain in the early '90s), and even antidrug clubs (surf journalist Derek Hynd formed On the NOD—Not on Drugs—in 1986). By the mid-'80s, as the surfing industry began to grow into what would soon be a multibillion-dollar interest, celebratory drug references were all but excised from the surf media; if drug use was mentioned at all, as surf journalist Steve Barilotti pointed out, it was with "a muffled puritanical tone." World pro tour organizers in 1990 voted for drug testing, at the discretion of individual event directors, but no tests were ever performed, in part because competitors insisted that tour officials and judges be tested as well.

Occupying a vast middle ground between drug-related catastrophes and pieties is the generally unacknowledged majority of surfers for whom drug use is—or was—in some way valuable. In 1994, not long after kicking a 15-year heroin addiction, Hawaiian surf legend Jeff Hakman allowed that "the best memories of my surfing career" had come while riding Honolua Bay with his friend Jock Sutherland when both were high on LSD. In 1990, Australian pro Cheyne Horan came out in favor of legalizing drugs altogether, while 1998 longboard world champion Joel Tudor supported legalizing marijuana. California stylist Rob Machado, 1995 world pro tour runner-up, allowed that "down on the beach, you're in the most beautiful environment, relaxing, surfing, having a great time, [and] if someone was going to break out a joint, you're in the best place to do it." When *Surfer* magazine did a quick online poll in 2002, asking readers to respond to the question, "Surf and weed . . . who likes it?" five were against, 11 were neutral, and 20 were enthusiastically supportive. *See also* alcohol and surfing, death and surfing.

Drummond, Ron   Lanky, durable bodysurfer and canoe surfer from Capistrano Beach, California. Drummond was born (1907) in Los Angeles, raised in Hollywood, and traveled with his family each summer to Hermosa Beach, where he learned to bodysurf and surf. He bought his first canoe at age 14, which he dragged into the Hermosa surf on a dare from his brother, and watched helplessly as a wave broke it in two. Drummond persevered, and eventually rode a canoe in waves as big as 15 feet. The bearded Drummond was featured in a 1967 issue of *Surfer* magazine using his open-shelled "Canadian canoe" (as compared to the enclosed kayak); he also appeared in two surf movies, *Big Wednesday* (1961) and *Pacific Vibrations* (1970).

Drummond published 500 copies of his 1931 book *The Art of Wave Riding,* a 26-page primer on bodysurfing, and regarded by some as the first book on surfing. "One feels sorry for those who have not learned to enjoy surf swimming," Drummond wrote in the introduction, before going on to define "glide waves" and "sand busters," then offering step-by-step bodysurfing instructions. "To spend a day in the sand developing a 'beautiful tan' is pleasant; but the real pleasure of a trip to the beach is derived from playing in the breakers." *Wave Riding* has become prized among surfing "ephemera" collectors, and copies have sold for up to $1,200.

The 6'6" Drummond was a track star at UCLA in the mid-'20s, specializing in discus and the shot, and continued to swim, canoe, and bodysurf into his mid-80s. In 1990, he appeared in a nationally aired Nike ad featuring senior surfers. Drummond died in 1996, at age 89. *See also* bodysurfing, canoe surfing.

dry suit   Air- and watertight suit for use in extremely cold water, marketed to surfers for the first time in 1972 as an alternative to the wetsuit. Dry suits are made of thin, nonporous rubber, similar in thickness and consistency to the material used for an innertube (wetsuits are made of a thicker closed-cell neoprene rubber); they were developed by the U.S. Navy during World War II, and navy divers were orig-inally called "frogmen" because of their olive-green dry suits. Unlike the wetsuit, which lets in water, the dry suit is designed to keep water out entirely. Surfers buying a dry suit in the early '70s were instructed to wear clothes as needed (thermal underwear was recommended) to keep warm. The Shultz Dri-Duk company in Los Angeles offered a zipperless two-piece dry suit with built-in booties and gloves; Aquala, based in Louisiana, made a one-piece dry suit—booties, no gloves—with a shoulder-to-shoulder zip. Why the dry suit never caught on with surfers is something of a mystery. Dry suits cost more than wetsuits, but last longer and are more easily repaired. The most likely explanation is that dry suits were by necessity wrinkly and baggy—the extra room is needed for mobility—while wetsuits are nicely formfitting. Dry suits are still available, although the cost has gone up enormously: Aquala's 2002 surfing suit cost $795. *See also* wetsuit.

dry tube   A tuberide where the surfer is completely untouched by water. A wave needs to be exceptionally hollow and well-formed to allow for a dry tube. The stand-up dry tube—where the rider comes up out of a crouch and stands at full height while inside the wave—is generally regarded as the ultimate tuberide.

Duane, Daniel   Contemplative writer from the San Francisco Bay Area, best known to surfers for his 1996 memoir *Caught Inside: A Surfer's Year on the California Coast.* Duane was born (1967) in Washington, D.C., raised in Berkeley, California, and began surfing in 1989. As described in *Caught Inside,* Duane found thrills, beauty, and identity as he came to surfing maturity in Santa Cruz:

> *Unless you're a strolling naturalist by nature, or a farmer or commercial fisherman or ranger, you need a medium, a game, a pleasure principle that turns knowing your home into passionate scholarship. . . . I didn't move to the beach to perfect my backside aerial attack (or even just to learn what the hell a backside aerial attack is, for that matter); I moved because my need to be in the clear, alive water of my California's Pacific, on a real, honest-to-God surfboard, on a daily basis, had been a source of nagging angst since the first time I'd ridden a wave.*

Caught Inside, published by North Point Press, a division of Farrar, Straus and Giroux, was favorably reviewed in the *Los Angeles Times,* the *New Yorker,* and

Sports Illustrated. Duane was 29 when the book was released, and had just completed a Ph.D. in American literature from UC Santa Cruz. In the late '90s and early '00s he wrote surf-related articles for the *New York Times, Outside,* the *Village Voice, Men's Journal, Surfer,* and the *Surfer's Journal;* he also wrote the forewords for *Surfer: Photographs by Patrick Cariou* (1997) and *Maverick's: The Story of Big-Wave Surfing* (2000).

Duane, Gordon   Plainspoken California surfboard manufacturer from southwest Los Angeles County; founder in 1956 of Gordie Surfboards, in Huntington Beach. Duane was born (1930) in Los Angeles, and began surfing in 1951 in Hawaii, while stationed on a Pearl Harbor naval base. Two years later he shaped his first board. Duane began building boards commercially in the mid-'50s, working out of his parents' garage in Lynwood. In 1956 he opened Gordie Surfboards, a beachfront shop at the foot of the Huntington Beach Pier; dozens of other surfers were making and selling boards, but only Hobie Alter and Dale Velzy had similar storefront retail operations. In early 1958, Duane was one of the first manufacturers to put a wooden stringer down the center of the just-developed polyurethane foam-core surfboards, for added strength and rigidity. Gordie Surfboards burned to the ground in late 1958, destroying more than 100 stock boards, along with the rest of the store's inventory. Duane reopened a few hundred yards to the northeast, on Pacific Coast Highway, where he stayed in business until 1988. In the late '50s and '60s, Gordie Surfboards were noted for their abstract resin designs and their curving, intersecting, multilaminate stringers. Duane was inducted into the Huntington Beach Surfing Walk of Fame in 1997. *See also* stringer.

duck dive   Method of burrowing through or beneath an incoming wave that is either cresting or already broken. The surfer paddles toward the wave, grips the rails as he jackknifes his body, sinks the nose of the board, then pushes the tail down with one foot while kicking up with the other to help leverage board and body into a submarine arc as the wave rolls over. Duck-diving becomes progressively more difficult as the surf gets larger and more powerful. Bigger, wider boards are harder to duck-dive than small, thin boards; duck-diving is virtually impossible in waves of any size on a longboard. The exact origins of the duck dive are unknown, but 1977 world champion Shaun Tomson, of Durban, South Africa, along with his cousin Michael Tomson, invented what they called "pushing under" in 1970, after watching local kneerider Leighton Alcock dive his thin "spoon" board beneath broken waves at Durban's Bay of Plenty. *Surfer* magazine introduced the maneuver to its readers in a 1980 "Tips" column, calling it "the porpoise technique"—although by that time most surfers were referring to the maneuver as a duck dive.

Duke Kahanamoku Invitational   Annual surfing meet held on Oahu's North Shore, usually at Sunset Beach, from 1965 to 1984; named in honor of Hawaiian surfing pioneer and Olympic gold medal swimmer Duke Kahanamoku; regarded until the mid-'70s as surfing's premier competition. The Duke event was developed by Kimo McVay, Honolulu entrepreneur and Kahanamoku's manager, partly as a marketing device for the just-opened Duke Kahanamoku's restaurant and nightclub in Waikiki. Newspaperman Leonard Lueras and big-wave surfer Fred Van Dyke also helped organize the contest. Although Oahu's North Shore had long been recognized as the richest big-wave area, with Sunset Beach known as the best oversize high-performance break, the Duke was the first major surf event held in this part of Hawaii. As selected primarily by Van Dyke, 24 surfers received red-velvet gold-embossed invitations to the first Duke Kahanamoku Invitational Surfing Championships (the suffix was changed to Surfing Classic in 1968), including Jeff Hakman, Mickey Dora, Mike Doyle, Joey Cabell, Paul Strauch, Mickey Muñoz, and Corky Carroll. The exclusions of 1964 world champion Midget Farrelly and 1965 world champion runner-up Nat Young, both from Sydney, were generally regarded as a tactical low blow by American partisans against the surging Australians; reigning world champion Felipe Pomar of Peru was the only non-American Duke invitee. Contest organizers paid the airfare for all non-Hawaiian entrants; competitors were given a $50 appearance fee and lodged in Waikiki's upscale Surfrider Hotel. CBS was on hand to shoot a one-hour Duke Invitational sports special. The contest took place on December 14, in big, rough, challenging surf, and high school senior Jeff Hakman, was a surprise winner. Comparisons were immediately made between the Duke contest and the venerable Makaha International Championships, with the Duke event coming up a unanimous winner: "A marvel of organization and planning," as

Surfer magazine reported, "featuring the greatest surfing ever seen in competition."

The Duke became a professional event in 1968, with Mike Doyle earning the $1,000 winner-take-all purse. With the formation of a world pro tour in 1976, the Duke became the second-to-last event on the contest schedule. Two years later, however, the Duke was dropped from the world tour schedule "for not meeting IPS [International Professional Surfers] sanctioning requirements"—although what exactly this meant has long since been forgotten.

Sixteen of the 20 Duke contests were held at Sunset Beach. The 1978 event took place at Laniakea, and the 1973, 1975, and 1980 events were held at Waimea Bay. CBS produced Duke sports specials from 1965 to 1967, and the network's 1966 coverage was nominated for an Emmy. ABC's *Wide World of Sports* intermittently covered the event from 1968 to 1982. Results of the Duke Kahanamoku Surfing Classic:

1965:	Jeff Hakman
1966:	Ricky Grigg
1967:	Jock Sutherland
1968:	Mike Doyle
1969:	Joey Cabell
1970:	Jeff Hakman
1971:	Jeff Hakman
1972:	James Jones
1973:	Clyde Aikau
1974:	Larry Bertlemann
1975:	Ian Cairns
1976:	James Jones
1977:	Eddie Aikau
1978:	Michael Ho
1979:	Mark Richards
1980:	Mark Warren
1981:	Michael Ho
1982:	Ken Bradshaw
1983:	Dane Kealoha
1984:	Derek Ho

Dungeons   Thunderous big-wave break located off Hout Bay, Cape Town, South Africa; often called the Southern Hemisphere's version of Maverick's. Dungeons, a right-breaking wave, reportedly was given its name by a local surfer who was trapped underwater for two consecutive 25-foot waves. Dungeons begins to break when the surf hits 10 feet, but doesn't come into peak form until 18 feet, and can hold waves up to 40 feet or bigger. Dungeons-sized waves are generated with some frequency between May and October from

storms tracking along the infamous Roaring 40s; the chilly Cape Town water temperature at this time is usually in the low 50s. Like Maverick's, Dungeons offers a harrowing near-vertical takeoff, followed by one or more churning bowl sections; rides last for up to 300 yards before tapering off into a deep-water channel. The Dungeons reef is located relatively close to a hilly shoreline (part of the Cape Peninsula National Park) and adjacent boat harbor; surfers can paddle to the break, but generally approach by boat. Great white sharks frequently cruise this portion of coastline.

Dungeons was first ridden in 1984 by Cape Town surfers Pierre de Villiers and Peter Button, but it was another 10 years before a small group of locals—including Jonathan Paarman, Justin Strong, Ian Armstrong, Cass Collier, Chris Bertish, and Mickey Duffus—began riding the break with any regularity. Dungeons is the host site for the 2000-founded international Red Bull Big Wave Africa contest. The break is the subject of a small book, *Dungeons* (2001), and appears in a locally made video, *African Sensimilia 2: Big Buddy* (2002).

Dunn, Jackie   Fearless 1970s Pipeline specialist from Hawaii. Dunn was born (1957) in Newport Beach, California, won the 11-year-old division of the 1967 Menehune contest in La Jolla, and two years later moved with his mother to Maui, Hawaii. He was featured in a 1970 *Petersen's Surfing* magazine article titled "Jack is Nimble, Jack is Quick," which showed the white-blond 13-year-old goofyfooter dropping into a double-overhead wave at Honolua Bay. The '70s would be Gerry Lopez's decade as reigning king of Pipeline, but Dunn, along with Rory Russell, was in the vanguard. He competed at times, finished third in the 1975 Pipeline Masters, but is best remembered for his arms-spread do-or-die approach to free-surf sessions. Dunn appeared five times on the cover of *Surfer* and *Surfing* magazine between 1971 and 1980, and was featured in nearly a dozen surf movies, including *Cosmic Children* (1970), *Going Surfin'* (1973), *Super Session* (1975), and *In Search of Tubular Swells* (1977). He also did stunt-double surfing for Warner Brothers' 1978 surf movie *Big Wednesday.*

Durban   Bustling port city and resort center located on the east coast of South Africa, near the center of the KwaZulu-Natal coast; the birthplace and hub of South African surfing. Durban can be divided into two main surfing regions: the urbanized area to the north, home to the Golden Mile beaches, including the Bay of Plenty, North Beach, and New Pier; and the suburban coast to the south, home to an explosive and notoriously shallow reefbreak known as Cave Rock. "I remember doing a turn at the Rock and feeling the tip of my fin scrape the reef," Durban-born pro surfer and beachwear magnate Michael Tomson once said, going on to describe the break as "a playground for masochists." Durban receives surf all year, but often shows best form between February and May, as Indian Ocean hurricanes often push three- to eight-foot surf directly onto the KwaZulu-Natal coast. Durban is subtropical, with average daytime air temperatures ranging from the high 70s in summer to the low 60s in winter, and water temperatures ranging from the high 70s to the high 60s. While the majority of Durban's city beaches are protected by shark nets, the greater KwaZulu-Natal coast saw 100 shark attacks (29 fatal) on swimmers and surfers between 1920 and 2000.

Durbanite beachgoers were riding wooden bellyboards as early as the 1920s, with stand-up surfing introduced just prior to a visit by Australian surfing champion Charles "Snow" McAlister in 1928. The South Beach Surfboard Riders Club was founded in 1948, but the sport was practiced by just two or three dozen people up until the mid-'50s. Durban residents Baron Stander, Harry Bold, and Max Wetteland opened Safari Surfboards, the country's first surf shop, in 1963, the same year California moviemaker Bruce Brown passed through while filming *The Endless Summer*—which gave America its first look at the Durban surf. The Gunston 500 pro surfing contest, held at the Bay of Plenty, was up and running by the end of the decade, and would soon become a major stop on the burgeoning world pro circuit. Durbanite Shaun Tomson—tuberiding gentleman and six-time

winner of the Gunston 500—became the toast of South Africa in 1977 when he won the world pro title. Other well-known Durban surfers over the years include top '60s competitor George Thomopolous; Gotcha surfwear founder Michael Tomson; world tour pros Mike Burness, Marc Price, and Paul Canning; Billabong surfwear executive Paul Naude; surfboard manufacturer Mike Larmont (cofounder of the Durban-based *Zigzag* surf magazine in 1976); and surf contest organizer Peter Burness. British-born surfer Martin Potter became a teenage surfing phenomenon in the early '80s while living in Durban, but had moved to Australia by the time he won the 1989 world championship. Surfing ran up against South Africa's race-segregating apartheid policies in 1972, when dark-skinned Hawaiian surfer Eddie Aikau, having arrived to compete in the Gunston 500, was turned away from a whites-only Durban hotel, and was told he couldn't surf on Durban's whites-only beaches. Top pro tour surfers Tom Curren, Tom Carroll, and Martin Potter refused to compete in the Gunston event from the mid-'80s to the early '90s as a protest against apartheid.

By 2003, the postapartheid surf scene in the greater Durban area was bustling, with about 10,000 resident surfers, 25 surf shops, and more than a dozen annual surf contests. Durban surfer Travis Logie led South Africa to victory in the 2002 World Surfing Games, held at Durban's North Beach. The Durban surf has been featured in dozens of surf movies and videos, including *Freeform* (1970), *Fantasea* (1978), *The Search* (1992), *Jacked* (1995), and the locally produced *Zagland* (2000). Durban surf breaks are detailed in *The World Stormrider Guide* (2001) and *Surfing in South Africa* (2002). The Timewarp Surfing museum, located in Durban's Dairy Beach, the first museum of its kind in South Africa, opened in 1993.

E

East Coast of America Surfing was introduced to the East Coast in 1912, when Virginia Beach resident James Jordon returned from a world cruise with a nine-foot Waikiki-made redwood surfboard; over the next several decades the sport developed a cult following in a few areas, helped along by occasional visits from surf world luminaries Duke Kahanamoku and Tom Blake, and proselytizing surf crusades from people like Bob Holland of Virginia and Bill and Dudley Whitman of Florida. But the East Coast surf scene didn't boom until the early and mid-'60s, when surf shops, clubs, and competition groups were founded by the dozens from New England to Florida. The 2,100-mile-long East Coast is often divided into three basic geographic surfing zones: the diverse and often rocky coast north of Long Island, New York; the beachbreak-lined areas of the mid-Atlantic, and the Southeast. The East Coast generally breaks best during fall, as Atlantic Ocean hurricanes track to the northwest; most areas have surf of one kind or another in winter and spring. Summer is often flat from New England to Florida.

Although surfing on the East Coast is split into hundreds of divisions and subdivisions according to region, age, equipment preference, and skill level, the entire region is nonetheless allied to a far-greater degree than the American West Coast. Surfing in mainland America got its start in California, and California surfers, board-makers, photographers, filmmakers, and writers largely remade the sport in their image after World War II. Thus East Coast surf culture, as it took shape in the early 1960s, was essentially flattened by the weight of California surfing history and surf enterprise. It didn't seem to matter that the East Coast was capable of producing first-rate surfers (Gary Propper, Claude Codgen, Mimi Munro, and Mike Tabeling all had national reputations by 1968), along with first-rate surf; the entire region was treated by the California-dominated surf industry/media as little more than an American surfing annex, filled with barely differentiated surf breaks and hundreds of thousands of surf plebe consumers. Treated as a minority group, East Coast surfers to some degree pulled together. There have been factions, and even internecine fighting—most famously the north-south rift following the 1970 Eastern Surfing Association Championships. But East Coast surfers for the most part have used collective identity as a strength, drawn together by their own surf magazines (*Atlantic Surfing* and *Surfing East* in the '60s, *Surf* and *Wave Rider* in the '70s, *Swell* and *U.S. Surf* in the '80s, *Eastern Surf Magazine* in the '90s and '00s), along with their own surf movies and videos, including *How the East Was Won* (1967), *Directions* (1972), *Atlantic Crossing* (1989), the *Liquid NRG* series (beginning in 1995), *Flail* (1996), and *Proj. X* (1999). The 1967-founded Eastern Surfing Association has for decades been the world's premier amateur surfing group. The East Coast Surf Legends Hall of Fame—an institution with no West Coast equivalent—was founded in 1996.

While the East Coast surf is weaker and less consistent than that found on the West Coast, it seems to produce a more enthusiastic wave-rider, and this may be the greatest difference between surfers from the East and West coasts. The jaded and enervated surfers sprinkled throughout California are nearly impossible to find on the East Coast, where waist-high waves are often treated as a gift, not an insult. From the '60s through the '90s, meanwhile, East Coast surfers were united by their desire to prove themselves equal to or better than West Coasters in competition. "We surf for fun, of course," world tour surfer Wes Laine of Virginia Beach said in 1991. "But we surf mainly to be better than the Californians." Laine and Charlie Kuhn of Florida were the first East Coast surfers, after Florida's Jeff Crawford, to perform well on the world pro tour, inaugurating a trend. The East Coast surf industry would remain insignificant compared to that of California, but East Coast pros, led by Kelly Slater, Frieda Zamba, Lisa Andersen, and CJ Hobgood, have long been dominant over their West Coast counterparts. As of 2002, East Coasters had won a combined 15 world pro tour championship titles, to just five for California. *See also* Connecticut, Delaware, Florida, Georgia, Maine, Maryland, Massachusetts, New Hampshire, New Jersey, New York, North Carolina, Rhode Island, South Carolina, Virginia.

East Coast Surf Legends Hall of Fame   Honor roll for American East Coast surfers, surf industrialists, and surf organizers, formed in 1996 by California big-wave rider and board manufacturer Greg Noll. The initial 23 East Coast Surf Legends Hall of Fame (ECSLHF) inductees, according to *Eastern Surf* magazine, were picked by "an ad hoc committee of both East and West coast surfers, industry heads and organization presidents." Subsequent inductees have been chosen by those already selected. According to ECSLHF member Bill Yerkes there is no official criteria for induction: "We just know." Furthermore, as of 2003 there is no actual hall for the East Coast Surfing Hall of Fame. Inductees are instead featured in a booth at the annual Surf Expo trade show in Orlando, Florida. Induction ceremonies are also held at the expo. The four groups of ECSLHF inductees are as follows:

1996:   Charlie Bunger, Dick Catri, Claude Codgen, Colin Couture, George Gerlach, Jack Hannon, Dan Heritage, Rudy Huber, Bob Holland, Cecil Lear, Mimi Munro, Jack Murphy, Pat O'Hare, Peter Pan, Gary Propper, David Reese, Thurman "Skip" Savage, Pete Smith, Yancy Spencer, Mike Tabeling, Bruce Valluzzi, Bob White, Bill Wise

1998:   David Aaron, Joey Rohrer Adric, Kathy Anderson, Ron DiMenna, Eddie Fawess, Fred Grosskreutz, Charlie Keller, Bette Marsh, Jim Phillips, Gauldin Reed, Joe Roland, Fletcher Sharp, Bill "Flea" Shaw, Reuben Snodgrass, Bill Whitman, Dudley Whitman, Bill Yerkes

2000:   Charlie Baldwin, Tom Blake, Warren Bolster, Duke Boyd, Babe Braithwaite, John Carey, Bruce Clelland, Janice Domorski, Renee Eissler, Sam Gornto, Bob Hawkins, Graham Hinnant, Mike Howes, Greg Loehr, Tommy McRoberts, Greg Noll, Buddy Pelletier, Henry Pohl, Ricky Rasmussen, Rick Salick, John Smith, Joe Twombly

2002:   Jeff Crawford, Linda Davoli, Bill Frierson, Dick Lyon, Howie Lyond, John Chummer McCranels, Mike Oppenheimer, Lisa Muir-Wakley, Bruce Walker

East Coast Surfing Championships   Midsummer pro-am surfing contest and beach festival held annually since 1963 at Virginia Beach, Virginia; America's second-longest continuously running surf event. The East Coast Surfing Championships (ECSC)—unaffiliated with the annual Eastern Surfing Association (ESA) East Coast Championships—is open to surfers of all ages, regions, and skill levels. In the summer of 1961, a group of blue-blood New York teenagers returned home with surfboards after visiting California and Hawaii, went to Gilgo Beach, a nascent East Coast surfing hot spot on Long Island, and had a private surf-themed party that included an impromptu surfing contest. Gilgo surf shop owner John Hannon organized the second version of the contest and ambitiously titled it the East Coast Surfing Championships; locals George Fisher and Donna Snodgrass won their divisions. Attending Virginia Beach surfers Bob Holland, Pete Smith, and Butch Maloney then decided, with the support of the Virginia Beach Chamber of Commerce and local surfboard dealers, to host a similar event in 1963, calling it the Virginia Beach Surfing Festival. By 1965, the Virginia Beach contest was renamed the East Coast Surfing Championships, and the Long Island contest was in its second year as the Gilgo Beach Surfing Championships; the 1963 Virginia Beach event has come to be known as the first ECSC. To further complicate matters, in 1971 the ESA staged its first East Coast Championships. (The 1955-founded Brooks Street Surf Classic in California is the only surf contest in America older than the ECSC.) Ranking California surfers often entered the ECSC in the '60s and early '70s; East Coast winners from those early years included Florida's Gary Propper, Mike Tabeling, Claude Codgen, and Mimi Munro; California winners included Steve Bigler, Joey Hamasaki, Margo Godfrey, and Corky Carroll.

As the ECSC grew and expanded over the years to include a skimboard contest, skateboard and BMX demonstrations, a bikini contest, a 5K run, volleyball and golf tournaments, and live entertainment, the event's title was again changed, to the East Coast Surfing Championships and Beach Sport Festival.

Held on the last weekend of August, in the middle of the Atlantic hurricane season, the ECSC, with a few exceptions, has nonetheless been plagued by small, windblown surf. The ECSC has continued to draw international talent, including Tom Curren, Joel Tudor, Nick Wood, and Bruce Irons. The 2001 ECSC, with a $20,000 prize purse, featured over 600 competitors and attracted more than 10,000 spectators; a 2000 *U.S. News and World Report* sidebar listed the ECSC as one of "America's Best Festivals."

Easter Island   Rugged 47-square-mile island in the South Pacific, located 2,300 miles west of Chile, its governing nation; best known for its eternally impassive lava-stone head statues, called *moai,* the largest of which stand 40 feet tall and weigh more than 90 tons. Easter Island, or Rapa Nui as it's known to its 2,000 residents, is the most remote inhabited spot on earth. Wave-riding has been part of its history since it was settled, probably around A.D. 400, by either Polynesians or South American Indians. Both *haka honu* (bodysurfing) and *haka nini* (surfing on a long craft made of bundled reeds) have been practiced on Easter Island for centuries, possibly even before the Tahitians and Hawaiians began riding waves. The island's first modern surfboard is said to have mysteriously floated into the east shore in the mid-1960s, where it was picked up by a fisherman who intuited the board's purpose, rode it, and shared it with family and friends. *Surf* photographer Bev Morgan had by that time already had a look at the subtropical Easter Island surf. "Morgan raves about perfect Malibu-type waves coming off a point," *Surfer* magazine wrote in 1962, "with the left slide equally as good as the right." Twenty years later *Surfer* published photos of two Chilean surfers, Luis Tello and Isaac Tapia, riding steely-blue overhead waves along a rocky, *moai*-lined coast, in what the magazine called "the most mysterious surf location in the world." Hawaiian big-wave riders Laird Hamilton and Brock Little arrived in 1994 with a camera crew to film an episode of *Expedition Earth,* an ESPN documentary series. For two weeks Hamilton and Little shared waves with a few dozen local surfers at a playful break near the island's only town, Hanga Roa—almost certainly the spot that Bev Morgan had seen more than 30 years earlier. Two days before Hamilton and Little departed, the surf jumped to 12 feet, and the Hawaiians reveled in the thick, hollow, dangerously powerful waves. More than 20 surf breaks are scattered around the rocky

Easter Island coast. Waves break here throughout the year, with the biggest surf arriving from July to September. Average midday air temperatures range from the mid-60s (winter) to the low 80s (summer). Water temperatures range from 68 to 72. Dozens of native surfers have taken up surfing, riding for the most part at breaks in and around Hanga Roa.

Eastern Surf Magazine   Energetic youth-oriented tabloid newsprint magazine, published eight times a year out of Indialantic, Florida, devoted for the most part to East Coast surfers and surf breaks. The sometimes-lewd *Eastern Surf Magazine* was founded in 1991 by photographers Dick Meseroll and Tom Dugan, along with Lally Collins. Popular features include "ESM Girl" (bikini cheesecake), "Eargasm" (CD reviews), "Who Da Guy?" (hot but not-yet-famous East Coast surfers), and "Blah Blahs" (short, often gossipy items from across the eastern seaboard). The American surf media has always been dominated by West Coast–based magazines—led by *Surfer* and *Surfing*—who for decades tended to either ignore or condescend to East Coast surfers. A half-dozen East Coast–based magazines tried and failed in the '60s, '70s, and '80s to balance the equation to a degree; *ESM* succeeded—in large part due to its insolent and sometimes self-abusing sense of humor. The cover for the 2001 *ESM* Comedy Issue featured a cartoon of porn star Ron Jeremy sitting on the toilet reading the "1st Annual ESM Girl Swimsuit Issue." *ESM* circulation in 2003 was 25,000. *See also* Dick Meseroll.

Eastern Surfing Association (ESA)   Durable and well-organized amateur competitive association governing the American East Coast, as well as the eastern shores of the Gulf Coast. The Eastern Surfing Association (ESA) was formed in 1967 by New Yorker Rudy Huber and Cecil Lear of New Jersey, partly as a way to demobilize several regional competition groups, each of whom were directing their own version of the East Coast Championships, and partly as a way to select the best possible East Coast team for the United States Surfing Championships. The ESA later went on to conduct surf clinics, organize beach cleanups, and act as a lobbying group for surfing-related issues. Distinguished ESA alumni include Mike Tabeling, Gary Propper, Claude Codgen, Matt Kechele, Wes Laine, Charlie Kuhn, Todd Holland, Ben Bourgeois, and CJ and Damien Hobgood, as well as six-time world champion Kelly Slater and four-time world champion Frieda Zamba.

The ESA was originally divided into seven districts, with Huber serving as executive director and Lear as competition director. "The primary purpose of this organization," Lear wrote in early 1968, as the ESA looked forward to its first year, "is to produce standard rules and regulations for surfing competition and a feeling of *esprit de corps* from Maine to Florida and the Gulf Coast." (The Gulf Coast states were reassigned to the Gulf Coast Surfing Association in late 1968; west coast Florida returned to the ESA in 1975.) The ESA Championships have long been measured against the 1963-established East Coast Surfing Championships; the ESA had a setback in 1970 when in-house political squabbling resulted in the championships being canceled midevent, setting off a long feud between Florida and the rest of the East Coast. In 1971, the ESA Championships—better known as "the Easterns"—gained a permanent home in Cape Hatteras, North Carolina, and found a stabilizing influence in newly hired executive director Colin Couture, a Boston University–trained clinical psychologist who piloted the ESA until his death in 1989.

In 1974, with membership just over 1,800, the ESA expanded to 14 districts, opened a permanent headquarters in Rhode Island (the home office had up to that point been the mailing address of the presiding executive director), and for the first time hosted the U.S. Championships. (The U.S. Championships were subsequently held on the East Coast in 1978, 1982, 1986, 1990, and 1994.) The ESA continued to grow, in large part due to Couture's steady leadership, and was virtually untouched by the infighting that characterized nearly all other American amateur surfing groups, including the Western Surfing Association, the National Scholastic Surfing Association, and even the Couture-led United States Surfing Federation.

The ESA split into three regions in 1984, requiring district championships to qualify surfers to the ESA championships; in 1991, new executive director Kathy Phillips moved ESA headquarters to Ocean City, Maryland; in 2001, ESA membership was up to nearly 8,000, making it far and away the world's largest competition-based surfing group. *See also* Colin Couture, Eastern Surfing Association Championships, Rudy Huber, Cecil Lear.

Eastern Surfing Association Championships

Popular amateur surfing competition organized and managed by the Eastern Surfing Association (ESA),

held annually since 1971 at Cape Hatteras, North Carolina; unaffiliated with the annual pro-am East Coast Surfing Championships held in Virginia Beach. The ESA Championships (or "Easterns") debuted after a lengthy and somewhat complicated phase in East Coast competitive surfing. In 1966, *Atlantic Surfing* magazine consolidated a number of independent statewide surfing championships into a 10-event United States Surfing Association–sanctioned Grand Prix series, the winner of which was crowned as the East Coast champion. The ESA replaced the USSA the following year, and from 1967 to 1969 competing East Coast surfers were ranked according to their aggregate point scores over a six-event ESA series held from Rhode Island to Florida. The first ESA Championships got under way at Sebastian Inlet, Florida, in the summer of 1970, but were scrapped midevent after the Floridian contingent tried to wrest control of the contest from ESA competition director Cecil Lear, resulting in what was later described in the surf press as "a Civil Surf War."

On September 11 and 12, 1971, the ESA Championships were held in well-shaped three- to four-foot beachbreak waves at a relatively unknown surfing area called Cape Hatteras, located on the southeast elbow of North Carolina's bucolic Outer Banks. About 100 surfers competed in four categories, with Florida's Charlie Baldwin winning the men's division, and Linda Davoli of New Jersey winning the women's. By the mid-'70s, the Easterns at Hatteras had become an East Coast surfing institution, with the contest absorbing and reflecting the tranquil Outer Banks atmosphere. Longtime ESA Championship participants often become rapturous when describing the event. "There's something in the air here that just galvanizes everybody," New Jersey–based surf journalist Lisa Roselli wrote about the '89 ESA Championships, "and makes them feel extremely fortunate to be in the best place in the world with the best people in the world."

The number of ESA Championship competitors and divisions have both increased steadily through the years, with the massive 2001 event heldover seven days, featuring nearly 600 surfers, ages seven to 71, in 20 separate divisions. ESA Championship winners over the years include 1975 U.S. amateur champion Rick Rasmussen, and world tour standouts Wes Laine, Todd Holland, Kelly Slater, CJ and Damien Hobgood, and Cory and Shea Lopez. *See also* Eastern Surfing Association, North Carolina.

Eaton, Mike   Tireless and unobtrusive surfboard shaper from San Diego, California; best known as a leader of the longboard renaissance in the '70s and early '80s. Eaton was born (1934) in New York, New York, raised in Palos Verdes, California, and began surfing at age 14, helped along by seminal surf figure Tom Blake; Eaton used to transport his heavy wooden board to the Palos Verdes Cove using an army stretcher customized with a pair of rear-mounted wagon wheels. He began shaping surfboards in 1955 for wetsuit magnate-to-be Jack O'Neill, out of O'Neill's San Francisco garage/surf shop. In the late '50s and early '60s, Eaton worked as a whale trainer at Marineland, a Palos Verdes ocean animal theme park, and not until 1965 did he become a full-time shaper, working simultaneously for Bing Surfboard and Rick Surfboards, both located in nearby Hermosa Beach. By 1968, Eaton had left Rick and was shaping as many as 20 boards a day for Bing; in 1970 he introduced a wide-backed square-tail version of the twin-fin, which had a burst of popularity in 1971 and 1972; in 1973 he produced a ballyhooed but unsuccessful version of the bonzer, the first three-fin board. Bing Surfboards by that time had been purchased by San Diego–based Gordon and Smith Surfboards (G&S); Eaton was meanwhile having second thoughts about the late-'60s shortboard revolution—a 1974 G&S ad shows an 8'2" Eaton-made "Fun Shape," and asserts that "80% of all surfers would be better off with an eight-foot board." Although the longboard renaissance wouldn't begin in earnest for another few years, and Eaton continued to make shortboards—he crafted some of the finest big-wave guns of the '70s—Eaton-produced longboards sold in ever-higher numbers from 1975 on. Eaton Surfboards was founded in 1978, and by 2002 Eaton estimated he'd made more than 50,000 boards. Paddleboards were added to the Eaton line in 1989, and Eaton himself competed four times in the grueling 32-mile Catalina Classic paddleboard race, entering for the last time in 1998, at age 65. Eaton has been married once and has three children. He lives in San Diego.

Eberle, Jackie   Soft-spoken goofyfoot surfer from Hawaii. Eberle won the 1965 state championships, and placed fourth in the inaugural Duke Kahanamoku Classic, held the same year. He was a World Surfing Championships invitee the following year; in 1967 he wowed the surf world during the Duke contest by twice riding left into no-man's-land

at Sunset Beach during the finals—he wiped out both times, and finished seventh. Lithe and quick on his feet, Eberle was also one of the best first-generation surfers at Pipeline. He appeared in a small number of surf films, including *Gun Ho!* (1963) and *Golden Breed* (1968).

Eberly, Tom   Surfboard shaper from Carlsbad, California; one of the 1970s most in-demand board craftsmen. Eberly was born (1950) in Bend, Oregon, and moved with his family at age two to Torrance Beach, in southwest Los Angeles. He began surfing at nine, and shaping boards at 17. After high school he moved to the North Shore of Oahu, Hawaii; in 1970 he began working for the newly founded Lightning Bolt Surfboards. Eberly's neatly foiled semi-guns (boards used for medium-big waves) were popular throughout the '70s, and he equipped 1978 world champion Wayne Bartholomew and big-wave master Darrick Doerner, among others. Eberly moved to Carlsbad in 1980 and opened a Lightning Bolt outlet, which he ran for five years. In 1987 he founded Eberly Surf Designs, a factory/retail outlet in nearby Encinitas.

Eckert, Ned (JJ Moon)   Round-faced surfer from Newport Beach, California, who became a surf world comedy phenomenon in the mid-1960s as "JJ Moon," the self-proclaimed "number-one surfer in the world." Eckert was born (1937) in St. Louis, Missouri, moved with his family at age two to Beverly Hills, California, began surfing at 18, and in 1961 received an M.A. in physical education from Chapman College. The affable and sociable Eckert became friends with some of California's top riders while surfing at Malibu and Huntington, and often introduced himself as JJ Moon, the nom de plume he used for a horse-race handicapping column he wrote for the Newport Beach *Daily Pilot.* California surfer Rick Steer secretly entered JJ Moon into the 1964 Makaha International contest in Hawaii, billing him as the Lake Michigan wake-surfing champion. Prior to the contest, a radio interviewer asked top California surfer and Eckert friend Mickey Muñoz who he thought would be the toughest competition at Makaha. Muñoz said that there were a lot of hot surfers, but the one he feared most was "the fabulous JJ Moon." A surf legend was born. For a 1966 *Surfer* magazine interview, the paunchy and slightly cross-eyed Moon said he'd never in his life wiped out or lost his board; that he'd recently won the "Natchez to Mobile Invita-

Ned Eckert; better known as JJ Moon

tional" as well as the "Memphis to St. Joe Wake Surf-ing Championships"; and that his favorite breaks were the "Cincinnati Pipeline" and "tornado surf in Kansas." The magazine also reported that because Moon had six toes on his right foot, he was the only surfer in the world who could hang 11. That summer, *Life* magazine published a two-page article asking "Is JJ Really King of the Surf?" and noted that Moon "holds more titles than there are surfing competi-tions." The fad continued with JJ Moon fan clubs, JJ Moon Competition Surf Team stickers and T-shirts, and "JJ Moonshot" cocktails served at a bar near Moon's Newport Beach home. Moon answered read-ers' questions in *Surfing* magazine's "Dear JJ" column in 1967, then disappeared the following year. Ned Eckert meanwhile became a stock investor as well as the basketball and football coach at Beverly Hills High School.

Ecuador Geographically diverse country located on the west coast of South America between Colom-bia and Peru, bisected by the equator, featuring 1,400 miles of Pacific Ocean coastline. The Galápagos Is-lands, located 600 miles to the west, are a province of Ecuador. (*See* Galápagos Islands.) Although Ecuador

receives surf from the northwest, west, and south-west, waves here are rarely over six feet. Most of the best breaks are located on the dusty-brown alluvial plain of the central coast, between the city of Manta in the north and Salinas to the south. Manta is Ecuador's primary surf area. Salinas, a busy tourist zone, features a series of rock reefs that produce well-shaped waves, but many of its best breaks are located in a military zone, and access is by governmental per-mission only; Costa Surf Club, a local organization, can sometimes make the arrangements. Montanita, a hard-breaking right located north of Salinas, occa-sionally shows world-class form; Rio Chico, Punta Mala, and Cayo Pipeline, all north of Montanita, offer well-shaped lefts. Ecuador has surf all year, but the biggest and best-shaped waves generally arrive during the November-to-March rainy season, when windless conditions prevail. Water temperatures range from 70 to 75 degrees, but air temperatures can be harsh. "There were moments," surf photographer Aaron Chang wrote in 1982, after returning from one of the first American-launched surf expeditions through Ecuador, "when a blast of hot air would rush through the car and it felt as if your eyeballs would burst." Ecuador was likely first surfed in the early 1960s; it was featured in *The Long Way Round,* Aus-tralian Bob Evans's 1965 surf movie.

Aside from the health dangers typical of most tropical destinations—malaria, dysentery, hepatitis, and cholera—Ecuador is a relatively safe, and rela-tively underutilized, surfing area. As of 2003, Ecuador was home to five surf shops and about 2,000 surfers. *Olas de Mar,* the country's first and only surf maga-zine, was published in 1999. The wood used in balsa-core surfboards—standard in the '40s and '50s and still occasionally used today—is grown mainly in Ecuador.

edge In surfboard design, "edge" refers not to the board's outer perimeter, but to the angled point where the elliptical line of the rail meets the flat bot-tom surface. Longboards tend to have little or no edge, while most shortboards have pronounced ("hard") edge in the tail section, softer edge in the middle, and mild or nonexistent ("rolled") edge in the nose. Edge is also used in various ways to describe the rail's traction, or lack thereof, to the wave face. To "lose an edge" means the board has come untracked and gone into a sideways drift. To "catch an edge" means the rail, usually in the nose section, digs in and checks the board's progress—or halts it altogether. In either case, the rider is put off balance or thrown off altogether. To "set an edge" means to bring the board out of a drift, and save the ride. *See also* rail, tucked-under rail.

Edwards, Phil   Groundbreaking regularfooter from Dana Point, California; often described as the original power surfer for his water-gouging turns, and credited as the first person to ride Hawaii's Pipeline. It was Edwards, along with friend and part-time rival Mickey Dora, who created the technique, image, and language for surfing in America—and the rest of the surf world—from the mid-'50s to the mid-'60s. Edwards was born (1938) and raised in Long Beach, California, moved with his family to Oceanside in 1946, and began surfing at age 12. He wasn't the first surfer to turn consistently on the wave; by the time he was 20, however, he was turning harder, and with more authority, than anybody else, and was a consensus pick as the world's best surfer. Edwards often began his rides by assuming a straight-backed, bowlegged trim stance. Hitting a likely spot on the wave, he'd quickly move his back foot to the tail of the board and stomp into a turn, leveraging with bent arms, knees, ankles, and hips, often pushing the move a little too far before letting up and recovering with a series of improvisational nods, feints, and shimmies. "It all seemed too radical, or too deep, or too much on edge," surf magazine publisher Steve Pezman said of Edwards's surfing. "But it was totally controlled. And it was like he understood something that no one else did."

Although Edwards's claim to being the first to ride Pipeline has been challenged (by 1968 world champion Fred Hemmings, among others), he was almost certainly the first to *complete* a ride at Pipeline (Hemmings admits he wiped out), and was without question the surfer who proved that the notoriously dangerous break could in fact be survived. Edwards's second ride at Pipeline was memorably captured in *Surfing Hollow Days,* Bruce Brown's 1962 surf film, with Edwards dropping into an eight-foot wave and angling at high speed in the shadow of the curl. "Now it hunkered high up over me," Edwards later wrote of his ride, "hissing and singing, white and boiling, moving faster than anything I had ever seen."

In 1964 Edwards finished fourth in the United States Surfing Association final standings and second in the Peru International, and served as a judge in the World Surfing Championships. For the most part,

Phil Edwards

however, he avoided surfing competition. His reputation was first earned through word of mouth, then from surf movies—he starred in *Cat on a Hot Foam Board* (1959) and *Gun Ho!* (1963), among others—and surf magazines. Good-looking and articulate, Edwards was surfing's first media star, winning the inaugural *Surfer* Magazine Readers Poll Award in 1963, as well as the sport's first professional surfer, as Hobie Surfboards introduced the Phil Edwards signature model surfboard in 1963, and Hang Ten sportswear produced a Phil Edwards line of beachwear in 1964. Edwards's fame continued to grow. He was introduced as "the amazing Mr. Phil Edwards" in Bruce Brown's 1966 surf movie classic *The Endless Summer,* and the following year he was featured in a *Sports Illustrated* cover story. *You Should Have Been Here an Hour Ago,* Edwards's Harper and Row autobiography—the first book of its type—was published in 1967, and was excerpted for a six-page *Saturday Evening Post* feature. The "power surfing" mantle had by that time passed from Edwards to Australian Nat Young, 1966 world champion, who in turn became the most influential surfer of his generation. Edwards dropped off the surf scene during the late '60s shortboard revolution, and was all but unheard from until 1988, when the longboard revival prompted him to reissue his Hobie signature model.

Edwards was inducted into the International Surfing Hall of Fame in 1966, and to the Huntington Beach Surfing Walk of Fame in 1995. *Surfer* magazine in 1999 named him as one of the "25 Most Influential Surfers of the Century." Edwards has been married twice and has one child. *See also* Pipeline, power surfing, You Should Have Been Here an Hour Ago.

Edwards, Tony   *See* Captain Goodvibes.

Egan, Luke   Drawling goofyfoot pro surfer originally from Newcastle, New South Wales, Australia; world-ranked #2 in 2000, and described at that time by surf journalist Steve Barilotti as "possibly the best all-around surfer in the world after [six-time world champion] Kelly Slater." Egan was born (1969) and raised in Newcastle, the son of Sam Egan, one of the area's first surfers and a nationally respected boardmaker. On the day Luke was born, Sam made him a 4′3″ surfboard, inscribed with the words "World Champion 2000." Egan began surfing at age seven; at 13 he gained admission to Merewether Boardriders, and was soon joined by up-and-coming local surfers Matt Hoy, Nick Wood, and Shane Powell, all of whom would compete successfully on the world tour.

Egan won Australia's prestigious Pro Junior event in 1988, two years after turning pro, and it was predicted that he'd cruise to the top of the world ratings. He became instead a perennial underachiever who year after year seemed out of focus or out of sync during competition. Egan himself didn't seem overly concerned, in part because his peers, along with the surf media, all recognized the thick-chested Australian (5′11″, 185 pounds) as a markedly gifted surfer, regardless of his contest record. While expert in all facets of high-performance shortboard surfing, the Nordic-looking Egan is best known for power and understated flow. Riding in an easy, relaxed stance, his size-12 feet seemingly molded to the deck of his board, Egan regularly punctuates his line of motion with deeply inscribed turns. As a teenager he was often described as "the next Mark Occhilupo," and if Egan lacked the brilliance of the 1999 world champion, he nonetheless rode with the same force and control. He was seen at his best in surf videos like *Bunyip Dreaming* (1991) and *Green Iguana* (1992).

Egan cracked the top five for the first time in 1996, finishing the season ranked #4; in 1997, after 11 full years on the world tour, he at last won his first major event, the Quiksilver Grajagan Pro in Indonesia; in 2000 he won Quiksilver Pro Fiji, and finished runner-up to Hawaii's Sunny Garcia for the world title. The unmarried Egan was the top vote-getter in

Australia's Surfing Life 2001 Peer Poll. He lives on the Gold Coast of Queensland.

egg   Wide, thin, midlength surfboard design; a slightly racier version of the "funboard" or "hybrid." Australian surfer Wayne Lynch rode an egglike board in 1968, the first full year of the shortboard revolution, but credit for the prototype egg is generally given to Southern California surfer/designers Skip Frye and Steve Krajewski who, working independently, were producing refined egg boards by 1970. San Diego surfer Tony Staples also contributed to the design, and the dimensions of his favorite board in 1977, a nine-pounder, are similar to today's eggs: 7′6″ by 22.5″, with a 16.5″ nose and 15″ tail. On the surfboard design spectrum, the egg is located in the broad middle ground between the twitchy modern shortboard and the easy-gliding, slow-turning longboard, and performs best in small- to medium-sized waves. *See also* hybrid.

egg rail   *See* 50/50 rail.

Eggers, David   Hyperactive child surf star from San Diego, California; a nearly unbeatable amateur competitor in the early and mid-'80s. Eggers was born (1970) in Mountain View, California, raised in Clairemont, and began surfing at age seven. He was introduced to the surf world in a short 1984 *Surfer* magazine profile as a family-loving, antidrug 14-year-old, with two United States Amateur Championship titles to his credit, a B+ average, and a selfless attitude. "It's important to stay down to earth," the towheaded goofyfoot told *Surfer*. "Being a nice guy will get you a lot further in life." In December 1985—after amassing 225 trophies as an amateur, 150 of them for first place, including four U.S. titles—Eggers dropped out of 10th grade, signed pro contracts worth an estimated $30,000, set out on the world tour, and in 1986 was world-ranked #34. His spectacular rise was followed by an equally spectacular descent. Eggers quit the tour in 1987, began freebasing cocaine, was reported in a local newspaper article to have been disowned by his father, and was in drug rehab by early 1989. Eggers later said, recalling his days as an amateur competitor, saying "There's nothing better than looking into somebody's eyes and seeing the agony of defeat. Yeah, I ate that shit up." Eggers was featured in a small number of surf movies and videos, including *Gone Surfin'* (1987).

Ekstrom, Carl   Innovative surfboard shaper/designer from La Jolla, California; creator of the asymmetrical surfboard. Ekstrom was born (1941) and raised in La Jolla, began surfing at age 11, and built his first board at 15. In the early '60s he shaped for Wardy, Ole, Jacobs, Bing, and Con, among other surfboard companies; in 1963 he opened his own shop with fellow La Jolla surfer Al Nelson. Ekstrom developed the first asymmetrical tail design in 1965 (patenting it in 1968), based on the idea that the board should better match the rider's own nonlinear stance. While the idea never became popular, asymmetrical boards have turned up now and then over the decades, and sailboarders have long used asymmetrical designs. In 1988, Ekstrom and Tom Lochtefeld, a real estate developer and Windansea regular, began working on a machine to produce a stationary wave; their FlowRider device made its public debut in a Texas waterpark in the summer of 1991. Ekstrom continued to work with Lochtefeld, helping with the design of the wave itself, as well as the specialized FlowRider-compatible surfboard, which is small, blunt, finless, and made of hard porous rubber. He quit the whole project in 2000 when, by his reckoning, the FlowRider wave became too big and dangerous. Ekstrom has also designed plastic benches for Jack in the Box restaurants, military training helmets, and Reebok shoes. *See also* FlowRider.

El Niño   Ocean-related meteorological phenomenon thought to amplify storm and wave activity in the Pacific Ocean. An El Niño condition begins with a slackening of the east-to-west tradewinds across the equatorial regions of the Pacific, which triggers a globally felt weather imbalance thought to contribute to flooding, drought, fires, and giant waves. An El Niño generally occurs once every three to six years, and lasts from six to 12 months. It was first identified in the late 19th century by Peruvian fishermen who noted the change seemed to arrive around Christmas; El Niño means "little boy" or "Christ child."

The effect of tropical-latitude tradewinds on the earth's oceans is so persistent that water actually piles up in the west-central Pacific. Sea level in the Philippines, for example, is nearly two feet higher than it is in Ecuador. This displacement contributes to cold-water upwelling along South America's west coast, particularly near the equator. When the trade winds

die off—the beginning of an El Niño—the "piled-up" water quickly begins to level out, warming the central Pacific by anywhere from two to six degrees. Scientists have yet to figure out exactly how the process works, or what triggers it in the first place, but the widespread effect of El Niño comes from the symbiotic relationship between the ocean and the atmosphere, and because atmospheric change in the Western Hemisphere will produce change in the Eastern Hemisphere as well. El Niño's most immediate effect is a change in the ocean-borne food chain off the northwest coast of South America, and increased rainfall—often catastrophic—in nations like Peru and Ecuador. Warmer waters in the northern Pacific tend to make a more combustible atmosphere when mixed with cold arctic air, which in turn creates bigger storms. It also causes the storm track to drop further south, further amplifying wave height along the North American west coast. Meanwhile, Brazil, Australia, and eastern Asia typically experience drought and drought-affiliated famines and brush fires, while the number of Atlantic Ocean hurricanes is reduced.

Although the phrase "El Niño" was unheard of in North America in the winter of 1939–40, surfers in California and Hawaii were certainly aware that the waves were significantly bigger than they had been over the previous few years, and meteorologists have since identified that season—as well as the infamous big-wave winter of 1969–70—as an El Niño. *Surfer* magazine introduced El Niño into the surf world lexicon in 1977, and by 1982–83, during the second-strongest El Niño on record, many surfers understood that the equatorial warm-water phenomenon was responsible. It's been estimated that storms and waves from the 1982–83 El Niño caused 2,000 deaths and $13 billion in damages worldwide. The 1997–98 El Niño was preceded by weeks of media fanfare, and the waves that season were in fact spectacular. On January 28, 1998, at Outside Log Cabins, on Oahu's North Shore, Hawaiian surfer Ken Bradshaw was towed in to what was then the biggest wave ever ridden, measuring somewhere between 60 and 70 feet from trough to crest. The 1997–98 El Niño was the strongest on record.

The most severe El Niño systems seem to come in an alternating pattern, occurring roughly once every eight to 15 years. Between most El Niños there will be a counterbalancing La Niña, a reverse set of meteorological effects with far less severe consequences. El

Niño prediction, as of 2003, was still an inexact science. *See also* surf forecasting.

El Salvador   Small, tropical, densely populated Central American country located between Honduras and Guatemala, featuring 150 miles of wave-rich south-facing Pacific Ocean coastline. El Salvador regularly produces three- to six-foot waves between March and October, with 10-foot-plus surf sometimes hitting in late summer and early fall. About two-dozen breaks have been mapped in El Salvador; more than half are located near the coastal town of La Libertad, just south of the national capital of San Salvador. Because incoming swells hit the coast at an angle, most spots—pointbreaks, beachbreaks, and rivermouths—break to the right. The Point at La Libertad is the country's most popular spot, and its long, powerful, well-foiled waves are often compared to Rincon in California. Rarely surfed pointbreaks to the north, some accessible only by boat, are just as good. Ocean and daytime air temperatures in El Salvador both remain near 80 degrees from month to month; the dry season lasts from November to April; the rainy season from May to October.

El Salvador was probably first surfed in the mid-1960s by Peace Corps volunteers; when surf journalist Bernie Baker arrived in 1970, he reported back to California that he was one of three surfers in the entire country, all visiting Americans. Florida surfer Bob Rotherman moved to La Libertad in 1974 and opened a restaurant catering primarily to the small but growing number of peripatetic surfers from California, Florida, and Texas who had heard of the Point's world-class waves. In 1977, filmmaker John Milius and a group of famous surfers and surf photographers, including Peter Townend, Ian Cairns, Bill Hamilton, Gerry Lopez, George Greenough, and Dan Merkel, spent a month in La Libertad shooting for Warner Brothers' surf-nostalgia film *Big Wednesday.* Two years later, just as crowds were beginning to become a problem at La Libertad, civil war broke out in El Salvador and surf tourism all but vanished. Adding to the country's woes, an earthquake in 1986 leveled portions of San Salvador, killing more than 1,000 and leaving tens of thousands homeless.

By 2003, there were fewer than 150 native El Salvadorian surfers, most living in or around La Libertad, virtually no domestic surf industry, and a steady but not-overwhelming stream of visiting surfers.

Crime was a problem, but the civil war had ended 10 years earlier, the international surf press was producing articles about El Salvador's high-quality waves, and the country's popularity as a surf destination was rising.

elephant gun   *See* big-wave surfboard, gun.

Elfick, David   Enterprising 1970s surf journalist and film producer from Sydney, Australia; best known as cofounder of *Tracks* magazine. Elfick was born (1944) and raised in Sydney's Maroubra Beach, and began surfing at age eight; in 1968 he received a B.A. in history from the University of New South Wales, and was soon hired as an editor of the popular teen-directed *Go-Set* music magazine. Elfick, along with surf journalist John Witzig and filmmaker Alby Falzon, founded the counterculture tabloid-size *Tracks* in 1970; "the magazine attacked polluters," surf scholar Albie Thoms later wrote, "promoted hippie diets and country lifestyles, and ignored surfing competition in favor of surfing for the love of it. It was right on the pulse and proved an instant success." Elfick produced Falzon's 1972 hit surf movie *Morning of the Earth,* which introduced the surfing world at large to Bali's perfect tropical reef surf. In 1974 he teamed up with Falzon and California-born kneeboarder George Greenough to produce *Crystal Voyager,* and the following year he produced *Captain Goodvibes,* an animated film, as well as *Surfabout '75,* a documentary on Sydney's Coca-Cola/Surfabout pro contest. Elfick sold his interest in *Tracks* in 1973. For a few months in 1974, Elfick, Witzig, and Falzon owned and operated the Silver Screen, an all-surf movie theater, in Sydney's Manly Beach. Elfick went on to produce and direct Australian-made movies and TV miniseries, including 1993's *Love in Limbo,* starring future Oscar winner Russell Crowe. Elfick's movie *Blackrock* premiered at the 1997 Sundance Film Festival. *See also* Morning of the Earth, Tracks magazine.

Elkerton, Gary   Blunt, brawny, hot-headed Australian power surfer from Queensland's Sunshine Coast; world title runner-up in 1987, 1990, and 1993; Triple Crown winner in 1987 and 1989. Elkerton was born in 1964, and spent much of his childhood at sea on his father's Queensland-based shrimp trawler, gaining a measure of formal education through correspondence courses. He began surfing at age 13, after

Gary Elkerton

his family settled in the resort town of Mooloolaba, a few miles north of Brisbane. The Australian surf press began raving about Elkerton after the pudgy 17-year-old (5′9″, 180 pounds) won the Pro Junior competition in Sydney in 1982. But when surfwear company Quiksilver signed Elkerton and began an all-out marketing campaign for "Kong"—his new nickname—it was based less on contest performance and more on Elkerton's explosive free-surfing, as well as a growling and intimidating public image built in large part on gross alcohol consumption, public nudity, and smashed rental cars. "If You Can't Rock and Roll, Don't Fuckin Come," read a tag line from one of Elkerton's early Quiksilver ads. *Surfer* described him as the "Lord of Mayhem," and asked if he'd really once done a handstand on an eighth-floor balcony rail to psyche up for a competition. "Nah," Elkerton said. "It was the 15th floor." By the time he moved into the pro ranks, in late 1984, he was one of the world's most exciting surfers, using a wide no-nonsense stance and pushing his board into one chunky turn after another. His hands meanwhile worked independently of the rest of his body, sometimes chopping the air and other times moving in little circles—a trait he picked up from fellow Queenslander Michael Peterson. Elkerton's style often looked clumsy in small waves, but in surf ranging from six to 20 feet, he was a wonder—and he knew it. "I'm gifted with something," he once said. "When I get the speed, no one can touch me."

Elkerton married a French woman in 1986, moved to the French resort town of Lacanau, and issued a press release disavowing the name of Kong,

saying that he was now, at age 24, remodeling himself as a dedicated professional sportsman. He lost the world title by the narrowest of margins in the final event of the 1987 season, and his two subsequent runner-up finishes were nearly as close. While Elkerton carried on for the most part as a responsible and sober-minded pro, he remained outspoken (calling American surfers "a bunch of softcocks" for not attacking big waves with enough vigor), and by the mid-'90s he was in a near-constant state of anger about the pro tour and what he saw as a conspiracy to keep him from the championship. "In my mind I've won the world title; last year was my world title," he told *Surfing* in early 1994. "They just put a knife in my chest and opened it up," he said a few months later, after a close loss in France. "I should quit the whole thing right now; they've broken my balls." Elkerton went on to compete full-time for two more seasons, but in 1998 allowed that he'd overplayed his competitive career. "I went on five years too long," he told *Deep* magazine.

Elkerton starred in *Kong's Island,* a 16-minute surf movie short made in 1983, and *The Performers,* released the following year, but his big-wave animal essence is best viewed in *Filthy Habits* (1988), showing Elkerton riding to victory at Sunset in the 1987 Billabong Pro. Elkerton won the Quiksilver Silver Edition World Masters Championship, for surfers over 35 in 2000, 2001, and 2003. He was voted "Best at Sunset Beach" by his peers in a 1992 *Australia's Surfing Life* poll. *See also* power surfing.

Ellis, Bryce   Easygoing Australian regularfoot pro surfer from Avoca Beach, New South Wales; world-ranked #10 in 1989. Ellis was born (1965) in Sydney, raised in nearby Avoca, and began surfing at age 10, when a congenital kidney defect (later surgically corrected) kept him from playing football. He was the juniors division winner in both the 1982 Australian National Titles and the World Surfing Championships. He turned pro in 1984, after completing a two-year plumber apprenticeship, and was named the world tour's rookie of the year. A smooth, fast, stylish surfer, Ellis won the 1988 Gunston 500 in Durban, South Africa; he's also remembered for his decision to withdraw from the 1986 Billabong Pro competition at Hawaii's Waimea Bay because the surf was too big. The ginger-haired Ellis appeared in a small number of surf movies and videos, including *The Performers* (1984) and *Water Slaughter* (1988).

Emerson, Nancy   Vivacious blond pro surfer and surfing instructor from Hawaii. Born (1952) in Los Angeles, California, raised in Hollywood, Emerson began surfing at age nine, and at 17 moved to Hawaii. She received a B.A. in social science from the University of Hawaii in 1975, two years after opening the first Nancy Emerson School of Surfing in Maui. She was world-ranked #8 in '78, and finished #6 the following year, then left the pro tour to concentrate on surf instruction. Nancy Emerson surf schools opened in Malibu, Honolulu, Fiji, Queensland, and Japan—with a money-back guarantee that students would stand and ride before the end of their first lesson—and chief instructor Emerson appeared in feature articles for the *New York Times,* the *Los Angeles Times,* and *Outside* magazine. Island Vision Productions, Emerson's 1983-founded film company, worked on commercials for Coke, Honda, and Sony, and Emerson did stuntwork for *Eye of the Tiger* (1986), *North Shore* (1987), and *Waterworld* (1995). *See also* surf schools.

Endless Summer, The   Long-celebrated surf movie made by California filmmaker Bruce Brown; originally screened on the beach city surf circuit in 1964, two years before it was put into general release, where it became a surprise critical and commercial hit. "A brilliant documentary," a *New Yorker* review said of Brown's deceptively simple $50,000 film, "perfectly expressing the surfing spirit. Great background music. Great movie. Out of sight." Just a half-dozen surf movies are thought of as first-rate; *Endless Summer* alone is regarded as a surfing masterpiece.

Brown was 26 when he made *Endless Summer,* and had already produced five well-received movies for surfers. *Endless Summer* was different from the others in that it had a plot of sorts, as it followed two surfers—Californians Robert August and Mike Hynson—as they traveled the world for three months in search of the perfect wave. The dark-haired and easygoing August, a nimble goofyfooter, was just out of high school when he signed up to make *Endless Summer.* Hynson, a sauntering 21-year-old regularfooter with slicked-back blond hair, was regarded as one of the sport's top stylists. Brown carried a single 20-pound box of camera equipment during the *Endless Summer* shoot that took the group to Africa, Australia, New Zealand, Tahiti, and Hawaii; he shot virtually all the travel footage himself. The highlight of the trip came with the discovery of a remote pointbreak

Handbill for *The Endless Summer*

along Cape St. Francis in South Africa, where four-foot swells arranged themselves into long, fast, beautifully groomed walls. "On Mike's first ride," Brown says in a climactic bit of *Endless Summer* voice-over narration, "he knew he'd finally found that perfect wave."

Editing his film in early 1964, Brown masterfully split the difference between his core surfing audience and a hoped-for mainstream audience. *Endless Summer* had far less actual wave-riding than any surf film yet produced, and Brown, while never once sounding pedantic to surfers, narrates the movie as a primer to nonsurfers. His definitively casual Southern California voice is in fact the star of the film—more so than the seen-but-not-heard August and Hynson—and imitation Brown voice-overs would be the norm in surf movies for the next 20 years. (The Sandals' soundtrack is another enduring Endless Summer legacy, along with the John Van Hamersveld–designed poster, featuring Brown, August, and Hynson in silhouette against a Day-Glo orange, pink, and yellow background.)

Brown toured a 16-millimeter version of *Endless Summer* across the East and West coasts in 1964; the following year he screen-tested the movie in Wichita, Kansas, in the dead of winter, and it was a smash hit; in 1966 the film was re-edited slightly, blown up to 35-millimeter, and put into general release by Columbia Pictures, where it eventually earned $30 million. Critics loaded praise on the earnest, nonpoliticized, nonsexualized film. *Time* magazine called Brown a "Bergman of the boards," and his movie was "an ode to sun, sand, skin and surf." *Newsweek* named *Endless Summer* as one the 10 best films of 1966. (Robert August, who went on to become a successful surfboard manufacturer, later said that *Endless Summer* was a hit in large part because it served as "a big time-out" from the Vietnam War.)

Endless Summer quickly became dated, as the late-'60s shortboard revolution dovetailed with the counterculture movement, changing the sport forever. But if '70s wave-riders got a chuckle watching the movie on television, as August and Hynson walk across the Los Angeles International Airport parking lot wearing suits and ties, *Endless Summer* remained near and dear to surfers everywhere. The feelings *Endless Summer* evoked, if not the surfing performances themselves, were timeless.

Brown dropped off the commercial surf scene entirely for nearly 25 years; *On Any Sunday,* his popular 1971-released *Endless Summer* follow-up, was about motorcycle racing, and he resisted making *Endless Summer II* until the early '90s. Brown and August meanwhile remained close friends, while the irascible Hynson, after distancing himself from anything having to do with *The Endless Summer*—including Brown and August—became a first-rate board-maker in the late '60s and early '70s, then fell into drug addiction, served time in jail, and lived for a while on the streets. He unsuccessfully sued Brown in 1995 for breach of contract (Brown paid the surfers' expenses during *Endless Summer,* but didn't give them a salary), and later called Brown "a kook who doesn't surf [and who's] made millions off surfers like me." All three surfers showed up for a terse but cordial *Endless Summer* reunion at the 2001 San Diego County Fair.

Endless Summer was released on video in 1986 and on DVD in 2001. In a 2000 poll conducted by Real-Surf, an Australian online site, *Endless Summer* not only came out on top, but nearly doubled the vote tally of the second-place finisher—which was Brown's 1994 sequel, *Endless Summer II. See also* Robert August, Bruce Brown, Cape St. Francis, Endless Summer II, Mike Hynson, perfect wave, surf movies.

Endless Summer II   California filmmaker Bruce Brown's long-awaited and much-hyped *Endless Summer* sequel, produced by New Line pictures and released in 1994, was a critical and box-office disappointment—but it was far from a total washout. Reprising the original film by taking a pair of surfers on a worldwide hunt for the perfect wave, *Endless Summer II* follows 26-year-old longboarder Robert "Wingnut" Weaver and 20-year-old shortboarder Pat O'Connell, both from California, as they visit Costa Rica, France, Fiji, South Africa, Hawaii, and Indonesia. Whereas the first *Endless Summer* was an inexpensive one-man project (filmed, edited, narrated, and scored by Brown for $50,000), the sequel cost $3.5 million, was filmed by a team of cameramen (including surf world stalwarts Jack McCoy, Dan Merkel, and Don King), and was fraught with conflict between director/editor Brown and New Line.

Video had by that time wiped surfing off the big screen, where it had been a surf culture mainstay from the late '50s to the mid-'80s. Because *Endless Summer II* was beautifully filmed and expertly edited, with high-performance guest appearances by world champions Tom Curren, Kelly Slater, and Tom Carroll—and because it was the first time that surfing had been given a full display in theaters since 1990's *Surfer: The Movie*—it was a huge improvement over the previous few years' worth of VCR surf cinema. Brown, furthermore, hadn't lost his sense of proportion, neatly balancing his surfing and nonsurfing footage; and a midfilm sequence featuring tow-in surfing innovator Laird Hamilton was spellbinding. But *Endless Summer II* lacked both the confidence and the charm of the original. Brown's narration, which played over the original like a relaxed jazz line, is weary, even creaky—not surprising, given his age (53), the time he'd spent away from the surf scene (more than 25 years), as well as the nonstop creative turf wars fought against New Line executives. The surf world's reaction to *Endless Summer II* was mixed, while mainstream film critics, overjoyed at Brown's work in 1966, were for the most part savage. Roger Ebert's review said, "The operative word is endless, not summer," while the *Washington Post,* after crediting the *Endless Summer II* photography as "ravishing" in places, described the film overall as an "endless bummer . . . flat and corny . . . redundant and hackneyed."

Step Into Liquid, a $2.5 million film coproduced by Dana Brown (Bruce's son) and released in 2003, has been referred to as *Endless Summer III. See also* Bruce Brown, The Endless Summer, Pat O'Connell, surf movies, Robert "Wingnut" Weaver.

Engel, Joe   Stocky regularfoot surfer from Sydney, Australia; Pro Junior winner in 1978 and 1979. Engel was born (1960) in Sydney, began surfing in the early '70s, but didn't flourish until moving to Queensland's Gold Coast in 1975. He was runner-up to future two-time world champion Tom Carroll in the juniors division of the 1978 Australian National Titles. As *Deep* magazine later noted, Engel was a "frightening ball of energy, with a short thick neck, and broad shoulders that seemed to fall straight down to his waist." He was featured the 1982 surf movie *Storm Riders,* riding the exotic and then-unknown waves of Nias in Indonesia. Engel won a world tour contest at Bells Beach in 1983, at age 22, but never really regained the competitive form he'd shown as a teenager, and in 1985 he quit the circuit. A *Deep* magazine feature in 2000 described Engel's subsequent troubles with drugs and mental illness.

England   England's 1,100-mile coastline is bordered by the Celtic Sea, the Irish Sea, the North Sea, and the English Channel, and features an assortment of temperamental surf breaks, some of them first-rate on occasion, and all greatly affected by the tides, which can rise or drop as much as 30 feet in six hours. While surfing is an all-year activity in England, the best waves generally arrive between September and April, when storms in the mid-Atlantic as well as the North Sea often produce clean four- to six-foot waves, along with the occasional 10-foot-plus sweeper swell. Most of the premier breaks are found in the country's more temperate southwestern corner, where the coast has the broadest exposure to the Atlantic. Newquay's Fistral Beach (sometimes called "Surf City U.K."), with its cluster of breaks including North Fistral, South Fistral, and Little Fistral, has long been the capital of English surfing, and the site of vir-

tually all major professional and amateur British surfing competitions. Top breaks in other parts of the country include the variegated surf of East Runton in East Anglia; Porthleven, a barreling reef-bottom wave in South Devon; and the sandbar-filled beach at Croyde Bay in North Devon. Surging tides often produce a ridable wave several miles up the Severn Bore River, located 100 miles west of London. Good surf is also found on Guernsey and Jersey, the two biggest of the Channel Islands. Summer water temperatures in Newquay (to the south) and Newcastle (to the north) peak at about 68 and 62 degrees, respectively; Newquay drops to 45 in winter, while Newcastle dips to the low 40s. England's climate is mild, windy, and wet, with average midday air temperatures in Cornwall ranging from the mid-40s to the mid-60s. Rocks and polluted water are the only real surfing hazards.

A small number of Englishmen, including Edward, Prince of Wales, learned to surf while visiting Waikiki in the early decades of the twentieth century. Bellyboarding was practiced along a few English beaches prior to World War II, and American servicemen stationed in Cornwall during the war reportedly brought boards and rode stand-up at Newquay's Watergate Bay. But British surfing is often said to have began in 1959, not long after Newquay staffed the local beaches with full-time lifeguards, who sometimes used their hollow wooden paddleboards to ride waves. In 1962, four visiting Australian surfer/lifeguards—Bob Head, Ian Tilley, John Campbell, and Warren Mitchell, all from the Avalon Surf Lifesaving Club in Sydney—surfed in Newquay on their foam and fiberglass Malibus, the first such boards brought to England. Newquay remained the hub of a fast-expanding English surf scene. In 1963, Head, along with local shaper Bill Bailey and two other English partners, started Newquay's successful Bilbo Surfboards, the country's first homegrown surf retailer. Local surfing communities across England began hosting regional surfing competitions, and the first Great Britain National Championships were held in 1965 in Jersey, with natives competing against a small number of overseas surfers. The well-organized British Surfing Association (BSA) was formed in 1966 and remains the governing body for amateur competitive surfing in England. In 1970, Jersey hosted the first European Surfing Championships.

Watford-born Rodney Sumpter was all but synonymous with English surfing from the mid-'60s to the early '70s. Sumpter grew up in Australia and returned to England in mid-1966 having won the juniors division in both the 1963 Australian Championships and the 1964 United States Championships, and the men's division in the 1965 European Championships. Sumpter flew from London to San Diego, California, for the 1966 World Surfing Championships, where he unsheathed his Britannia signature model Bilbo surfboard, decorated with a nose-to-tail Union Jack flag, and finished fifth. Sumpter produced *British Surfer,* the area's first surf magazine, in 1969, and also made England's first commercial surf films.

Following a commercial slump in the early '70s, English surfing was reinvigorated beginning in the late '70s, influenced in part by natives Nigel Semmens (Europe's first professional surfer) and Tigger Newling, and later by Spencer Hargraves. The Foster's Pro, a world pro tour event, was held at Fistral Beach from 1983 to 1986 (winners included world champions Tom Carroll, Martin Potter, and Tom Curren); the Foster's was replaced by the Hot Tuna/UK Surf Masters, which ran from 1987 to 1989; the Alder Surf Pro ran in 1991. Fistral also hosted the 1986 World Amateur Surfing Championships. In 1997, Newquay surfer Russell Winter became the first English surfer to qualify for the world pro tour.

In 2003, England was home to about 30,000 surfers and 35 surf shops. *You Should Have Been Here Yesterday: The Roots of British Surfing* was published in 1994; English surfing has been featured in dozens of domestic surf movies and videos, and a lesser number of international releases, including *Come Surf With Me* (1967), *Playground in Paradise* (1976), *Sarge's Scrapbook, Take Three* (1991), and *Made in Britain* (2001). The English surf scene was the background for *Blue Juice,* a 1995 movie starring Ewan McGregor and Catherine Zeta-Jones. The English surf is detailed in *Surfing in Great Britain* (1972), *Surfing: A Modern Guide* (1972), *The British Surfing Association Guide to Surfing in Britain* (1993), *Surf UK* (2000), and *The Stormrider Guide Europe* (third edition, 1998). *Wavelength, Carve,* and the *Surfer's Path* were the leading English surf publications in 2003. *See also* Ireland, Scotland, Wales.

Entwistle, Stuart Nimble and likable Australian longboarder from Manly Beach, New South Wales; winner of the 1987 World Longboard Championships. Entwistle was born (1949) in Brisbane, Queensland, moved with his family to Manly at age six, began kneeriding as a preadolescent, then changed to stand-up surfing at 17. A fine shortboarder through the '70s and early '80s, the goofyfooted Entwistle was one of Australia's early converts to new-era longboarding— although he continued to ride a variety of equipment and won the masters division of the 1985 Australian National Titles on a shortboard. Entwistle, a handyman by trade and known for his crowd-pleasing hang heels noserides, defeated Australian surfing icon Nat Young to win the 1987 longboard title at his home break in Manly, and remained a championship contender for the next four years, finishing third in 1988, second in 1989, and third in 1990. Entwistle died of skin cancer in 2002, age 52.

environmentalism and surfing Surfing and environmental activism were joined at the national level for the first time in early 1969, after a Union Oil platform off Santa Barbara, California, ruptured and spilled more than 230,000 gallons of oil, much of it washing up on a 30-mile stretch of nearby coastline. Surf magazine editorials urged surfers everywhere to join GOO! (Get Oil Out), a grassroots Santa Barbara group founded in opposition to offshore drilling. "So many good days of surfing were ruined for me by the oil," four-time world champion Margo Godfrey said after the spill. "The sea, my playground and my temple, was destroyed by a few people trying to make some money." The surfing-environmental cause was furthered in 1970, as Hawaii's John Kelly organized more than 2,000 demonstrators—mostly surfers and their friends—for a rally at the state capitol building in Honolulu, to protest a development plan for Waikiki. *Surfer* magazine that same year began publishing "Our Mother Ocean" (OMO), an environmental column that continues to this day, focusing attention and promoting activism on surf-specific environmental issues including development-threatened surf breaks, beach access, and water quality. (OMO scored a coup in the late '70s by hiring beloved oceanographer/environmentalist Jacques Cousteau to write a short series of articles.) The vast majority of surfers have since proven to be dormant environmentalists at best, supporting the movement in abstract, but for the most part roused to action only for a pressing local concern that might despoil their beach.

The Surfrider Foundation, surfing's biggest and most successful environmental group, was formed in 1984 by California surfers Glenn Hening, Tom Pratte, and Lance Carson, in response to the badly polluted water at world-famous Malibu Beach. Surfrider had some important early victories—shutting down a breakwater project in San Diego, for example—and lots of glowing press, but individual memberships initially remained fairly low (fewer than 15,000 by 1990), and corporate interest, with a few exceptions, was even lower (a late-'90s survey showed that surf companies donated a far lower percentage of profits to environmental groups than did oil companies). Surfing environmentalism made national headlines in 1991 when *Surfrider* won a $5.8 million lawsuit against two Humboldt County paper mills whose toxic runoff was fouling nearby surf spots. The victory remains the second-largest Clean Water Act suit in U.S. history, and it spawned a decade of growth for Surfrider, as well as the formation of other surf environmental groups. Meanwhile, dozens more surf-related environmental problems were making headlines around the world, including sewage and industrial hospital waste (including hypodermic needles) washing up on the Jersey Shore; a heavily publicized 1990 oil spill in Huntington Beach; the loss of Akatei, one of Japan's best pointbreaks, to a harbor in 1993; a condo/golf course proposal for the North Shore of Oahu; ongoing sewage outfall problems across Great Britain; a proposed nuclear reactor near Jeffreys Bay in South Africa; and a proposed harbor for Kirra in Australia. Groups formed in response to these or other issues included Surfers Against Sewage (created in 1990), the Save Sunset Beach Coalition (1991), Surfer's Environmental Alliance (1993), the Groundswell Society (1994), and Save the Waves (2001). Surfrider Foundation chapters were also formed in Europe, Australia, Japan, and Brazil in the early and mid-'90s.

Surfrider scored another victory in 2000 with the passage of the Beaches Environmental Assessment and Coastal Health (BEACH) Act of 2000, a landmark federal law coauthored by the group, requiring stringent water-quality testing statewide. Coupled with other programs such as Respect the Beach, which teaches high school students about coastal stewardship, and the annual State of the Beach Report, which gives water-quality letter grades to beaches across the nation, Surfrider—and surfing environmentalism in general—continued to grow and mature. Surf industry contributions to environmental causes was also up; as of 2002, the Surf Industry Manufacturers Association's Environmental Fund had do-

nated more than $1.75 million to various surf-related causes. That said, only 35,000 American surfers, out of an estimated 2.5 million total nationwide, are members of Surfrider. Furthermore, the surfing environment was dealt a serious blow in late 2002, when the oil tanker *Prestige* broke apart off Spain, dumping 70,000 tons of heavy fuel into the Atlantic and causing entire Bay of Biscay coastline to be closed to surfing. *See also* Yvon Chouinard, Glenn Hening, John Kelly, Mark Massara, politics and surfing, Tom Pratte, Surfrider Foundation.

epoxy surfboard   A type of surfboard that uses epoxy resin during the lamination process, rather than the industry-standard polyester resin. Epoxy-built boards are lighter, stronger, more buoyant, and more environmentally sound than standard boards. But up until 2001, they were also more difficult to make, more expensive, and much harder to find. Virtually all surfboards since the late '50s have been made from a polyurethane foam core wrapped in a skin of fiberglass saturated in polyester resin. Since the late '60s, when board weight was drastically reduced, fragility has been a problem; pro surfers by the early '90s might break in half 10 or more boards each year. Epoxy-built surfboards were introduced in the early '80s—developed separately by American designers Greg Loehr, Clyde Beatty, and John Bradbury—primarily as a way to improve board strength. Epoxy resin, aside from being stronger and more durable than polyester resin, also allowed board-makers to use alternate types of foam; Bradbury's mid-'80s epoxy boards, the first to attract any real attention, were made from Styrofoam, which is both stronger and lighter than polyurethane foam. But Styrofoam was difficult to shape, the epoxy resin turned a sickly yellow upon drying, and the cost of an epoxy board—when one could be found at all—was as much as $150 more than a standard board. Also, a ding or crack on a Styrofoam/epoxy board quickly soaked up water, meaning it had to be decommissioned for at least a week to dry out before it could be fixed. New Styrofoam-like blanks developed in the early '90s didn't soak up water, and were recyclable. Greg Loehr's Florida-based Resin Research company was by then already developing a new generation of nonyellowing, toxin-reduced epoxy resins.

The surfboard industry has been slow to adapt to the new materials, accustomed after nearly four decades to working only with polyurethane foam and polyester resin. By 2003, it was estimated that about 8 percent of all new boards were epoxy-made, and the price gap between epoxies and standards had dropped to about $50; the popular Surftech line of molded epoxy boards were in fact sold for the same price as standard boards. *See also* John Bradbury, Greg Loehr, surfboard construction.

Erickson, Roger   Shell-shocked big-wave surfer from Virginia Beach, Virginia; among the first to ride Hawaii's Kaena Point in 1976, and a competitor in the 1986 and 1990 Quiksilver in Memory of Eddie Aikau contests at Waimea Bay. Erickson was born (1948) and raised in West Los Angeles, and began surfing at 15. He joined the marines in 1966 and was sent to Vietnam, where he served at Khe Sanh during the deadly Tet Offensive and caught malaria. Back in Los Angeles in 1968, he served 10 months in prison for assaulting a police officer, then suffered a fractured skull after brawling with a group of bikers. Erickson moved to the North Shore of Oahu in the early '70s

Roger Erickson

and soon began riding Sunset Beach, Waimea Bay, and the rest of the area's fabled big-wave breaks. Kaena Point was then regarded as the next frontier in big-wave surfing, and Erickson was the newcomer in a small group of big-wave veterans—including Jeff Johnson and Flippy Hoffman—who, on January 19, 1976, rode Kaena for the first time. The brawny, bearded Erickson later became a North Shore lifeguard. In 1990, *Surfer* magazine named him as one of the 10 best Waimea surfers, along with better-known riders like Brock Little, Darrick Doerner, Mark Foo, and Ken Bradshaw.

Esposito, Mike   Unheralded but richly talented goofyfoot surfer from Durban, South Africa; runner-up in the 1975 Gunston 500, and third-place finisher in the 1991 Longboard World Championships. Esposito was born (1953) in Pietermaritzburg, in South Africa's Kwazulu-Natal province, and raised in Durban. He began surfing at 12, and just a few months later placed second in the boys' division of the South African Championships. Esposito's flashy but coherent surfing style prompted Durbanite and 1977 world champion Shaun Tomson to label him as the "South African Wayne Lynch," in reference to the preternaturally talented Australian. Esposito competed in the 1972 World Championships, and was a six-time finalist in the Gunston 500. He was featured in the 1974 surf movie *A Winter's Tale*. Esposito moved to Sydney, Australia, in 1993, and competes regularly in longboard events.

Evans, Bob   Protean surf world impresario from Sydney, Australia; surf filmmaker throughout the 1960s and early '70s; founder of the Australian Surfriders Association, and founder/publisher of *Surfing World* magazine; often called the "father of modern Australian surfing." Evans was born (1928) and raised in Sydney's Manly Beach, began surfing as a young teenager, and by 1950 was one of the country's best waveriders. In 1956, the Sydney beaches were visited by a group California surfer/lifeguards who introduced the paddleboard-riding Australians to the easy-to-turn balsa-core Malibu boards; Evans's local prestige shot up when he took possession of Greg Noll's 10'6" Malibu when the Americans departed. The following year Evans met California surf filmmaker Bud Browne, and agreed to promote and tour Browne's movies in Australia. Evans was tireless in the early and mid-'60s, channeling his energy into an endless number of surf-related projects. In late 1961 he organized a trip to Hawaii for a group of 20 Australians, including Midget Farrelly, Bob Pike, and Dave Jackman; Evans filmed the group and sold some of the footage to ABC to help finance *Surf Trek to Hawaii* (1962), his first surf movie and the first produced out of Australia. The dark-haired, solemn-faced Evans also debuted his *Surfing World Monthly* magazine in 1962. Evans's movies and magazines weren't particularly bold or creative, but they were embraced nonetheless as a homegrown alternative to American imports. Evans had meanwhile taken up still photography, and became the first Australian radio surf reporter, giving daily descriptions of the Sydney-area surf. "Whenever something is happening in the sport," 1964 world surfing champion Midget Farrelly said at the time, "Evans is sure to be mixed in with it somewhere."

An organizer of local boardriding clubs and competitions for years, Evans in 1963 created the Australian Surfriders Association, the country's first nationwide surf group; in what remains as one of the greatest promotional and organizational efforts in the sport's history, Evans then convinced oil giant Ampol to underwrite the first World Surfing Championships, held at Manly Beach in 1964. Evans's projects were all tied together: his magazine ran articles about his movies and covered his contests; his movies were shown at "surf stomp" events he staged at Sydney dance halls and clubs; and the surf trips he organized provided still photos or movie footage for his magazines and films. Meanwhile, as 1966 world champion and surrogate son Nat Young later noted, Evans "religiously adhered to the cocktail hour" and earned a reputation as an insatiable womanizer.

Surfing World was the voice of Australian surfing through the '60s (and is still published out of Sydney), while Evans's surf movie output continued apace, with *Midget Goes Hawaiian* (1963) followed by another 16 full-length or short features, including *The Young Wave Hunters* (1964), *The Long Way 'Round* (1966), *The Way We Like It* (1968), *Tracks* (1970), and *Family Free* (1971). He mentored dozens of Australian surfers, photographers, surf journalists, and moviemakers, most notably Alby Falzon, who went on to produce the 1972 surf film classic *Morning of the Earth. Drouyn and Friends,* Evans's last movie, a documentary on former Australian national champion Peter Drouyn, was released in 1974; two years later, while touring *Drouyn* in Florida, Evans died suddenly of a brain hemorrhage. He was 47.

Evans was inducted into the Australian Surfing Hall of Fame in 1987, and was featured in *50 Years of Surfing on Film* (1997), an Outdoor Life Network documentary series. The Bob Evans Memorial professional surfing contest was held in Cronulla, NSW, in 1982 and 1983. Evans was married once and had three children. *See also* Australian Surfriders Association, Australian Surfing World magazine, World Surfing Championships 1964.

Evolution   Crude but influential 1969 Australian-made surf movie made by Paul Witzig of Sydney; cherished as a document of the opening year of the shortboard revolution, as well as a showcase for teenage sensation Wayne Lynch and 1966 world champion Nat Young. *Evolution* was Witzig's second feature-length movie, following *The Hot Generation,* which bridged the longboard and shortboard eras. All aspects of the surfing life were changing, along with the boards themselves, and *Evolution* captured the shift. Where *Hot Generation* was narrated and featured a straight-ahead rock soundtrack, *Evolution* used only terse subtitles—usually just to identify a surfer or surf break—and a free-flowing jazz rock score by underground bands Tamam Shud and Tully. "For music," one surf magazine reviewer noted, "an Aussie group got stoned out of their minds and made it up as they watched the film." *Evolution,* as with virtually all surf films, is little more than a montage of surf clips. But its impact was felt across the surf world, mostly in response to the 16-year-old Lynch, who pushed his new sub-seven-foot board up and down the wave face, bounced off the crest, and tucked himself inside the tube; just 18 months earlier the focus in surfing had been on trimming and noseriding. "We couldn't get a seat in the theater, so we had to lay on the floor," world champion Peter Townend said years later, recalling his first viewing of *Evolution.* "And suddenly here's Wayne Lynch doing stuff that we never even thought was possible, coming off the bottom and going vertical through the lip, while we were all just going straight." About one-third of the 65-minute-long *Evolution* follows Lynch, Young, and 1968 New South Wales champion Ted Spencer as they surf through France, Spain, and Morocco. Another notable section covers the 1968 World Championships, held in Puerto Rico.

Evolution works well as a time capsule for one of surfing's most interesting periods. But Witzig's camerawork and editing are flat, the music often drones, and the action gets repetitive. The principals understand this as well as anybody. Lynch once said he'd never actually managed to sit through an entire screening of *Evolution,* and Witzig himself admitted in 1997 that he'd watched the film recently and "it gave me a headache." Nat Young recalled the moviemaking process: "We were all just hanging out and smoking dope, then going surfing, then coming back and Paul would do some editing. It's a miracle the thing came out as well as it did." *Evolution* was featured in *50 Years of Surfing on Film* (1997), an Outdoor Life Network documentary series. *See also* shortboard revolution, surf movies, Paul Witzig.

exostosis   *See* surfer's ear.

Expression Session   Surfing showcase event without judges, scores, winners, or losers, held in 1970, 1971, and 1973, primarily on the North Shore of Oahu, featuring a select group of the world's best surfers. The Expression Session was presented as a soulful "anticontest" alternative to the standard surf meet. In his 1970 "Death of all Contests" article for *Surfer* magazine, Drew Kampion proposed a "new system" in which the challenge, rather than being surfer against surfer, would be "between the individual and himself, to do the thing he does best as well as he can." Duke Boyd, owner of the California-based Golden Breed beachwear company, along with pro surfer Jeff Hakman and surf magazine publisher Dick Graham, brought Kampion's idea to life with the Golden Breed Expression Session, a 24-man event (women were excluded from all three Expression Sessions), with each entrant getting a $200 appearance fee. For the first time, the surfers would be given full control over when and where their event would be staged. The inaugural Expression Session got off to a rocky start as the invitees, selected by Hakman, brawled with an irate group of noninvitees who crashed the event-opening "Good Karma Party" barbecue. The waves, furthermore, didn't cooperate: the first round of Expression Session surfing was held in desultory five-foot waves at Rocky Point (four "sessions" made up a round, each session featured six riders); a second round was held in slightly better surf the following week on Maui at a break called Rainbows, with nine of the invited surfers not bothering to fly over from Oahu. Standouts in the first Expression Session included Jock Sutherland, Nat Young, and David Nuuhiwa.

The 1971 Expression Session fared much better: The opening party was fight-free, the first round was held in beautiful 10-foot surf at Pipeline, and the second round was held at Sunset Beach. Gerry Lopez, Owl Chapman, and Jeff Hakman set the standard. A third and virtually forgotten Expression Session took place in February 1973, with an opening round at Off the Wall/Backdoor, and a second round beginning at Haleiwa, then switching to Pipeline, with "some surfers getting lost along the way," as one entrant later recalled. This final Expression Session event went all but unreported in the surf media; the entry list itself has been lost to time. Invitees to the first two Expression Session events included:

1970:   Reno Abellira, Ben Aipa, Jim Blears, Gary Chapman, Owl Chapman, Ryan Dotson, Tiger Espere, Herbie Fletcher, Bill Hamilton, Jeff Hakman, Sam Hawk, James Jones, Barry Kanaiaupuni, Gerry Lopez, Brad McCaul, David Nuuhiwa, Keith Paull, Les Potts, Tom Stone, Jock Sutherland, Mike Tabeling, Greg Tucker, Butch Van Artsdalen, Nat Young

1971:   Reno Abellira, Eddie Aikau, Ben Aipa, Rolf Aurness, Jackie Baxter, Jim Blears, Joey Cabell, Corky Carroll, Owl Chapman, Ryan Dotson, Peter Drouyn, Tiger Espere, Jeff Hakman, Bill Hamilton, Sam Hawk, James Jones, Barry Kanaiaupuni, Gerry Lopez, Brad McCaul, David Nuuhiwa, Rory Russell, Tom Stone, Paul Strauch, Mike Tabeling, Herbie Torrens, Nat Young

California surf moviemakers Greg MacGillivray and Jim Freeman produced a short-subject film on the first Expression Session, with a few shots making it into their blockbuster move *Five Summer Stories*; the 1971 Expression Session was documented in a Hal Jepsen short, and was also featured in *Oceans* (1972) and *Super Session* (1975).

Impromptu Expression Session–style matches were fairly common in the '80s and '90s, usually when contest organizers, looking to fill time between semifinal and final heats, would send six or more already-eliminated surfers into the water as a way to hold the attention of the beach audience. When the surf at Waimea Bay wasn't quite big enough to run the 1988 Quiksilver in Memory of Eddie Aikau contest, meet director George Downing quickly organized a three-hour, no-prize-money Expression Session.

F

50/50 rail   Surfboard rail design where the deck-to-edge curve, in cutaway, is more or less symmetrical with the bottom-to-edge curve. As compared to the dropped-profile "hard edge" rail, the 50/50 is forgiving and easy turning, but tends to allow a board to fall out of its forward-moving track into a spin-out. The 50/50 rail—also known as an egg rail—for the most part is used on longboards or funboards, and works best in smaller waves. *See also* egg rail, rail, tucked-under rail.

face   The smooth, unbroken portion of a wave, bordered by the curl, trough, and whitewater. Aerials, floaters, and white-water ricochets aside, surfing for the most part is performed on the face.

fade   An angled descent down the wave face, usually performed just after takeoff, where the surfer "fades" toward the steeper and more critical portion of the wave, then turns and rides in the opposite direction, away from the whitewater and across the unbroken wall. A simple, elegant, confident move when done well. The fade is sometimes used as a stalling move to set up a tuberide; similar to the "S-turn." Also, one surfer can "fade" another by riding in front and delaying a turn to the point where the back surfer can't make the wave; similar to a "drop-in."

Fain, Johnny   Fast-talking, whip-turning regular-foot surfer from Malibu, California; described by the *Surfer's Journal* magazine as "one of the four aces of Malibu"—along with Mickey Dora, Lance Carson, and Dewey Weber—during the late '50s and early '60s. Fain was born (1943) to a wealthy Hollywood family, grew up among producers, directors, and film stars in the Malibu Colony, one mile north of Malibu Pier, and began surfing at age 13. Just three years later, the diminutive Fain (5′5″) had developed into an agile, quick, flamboyant surfer—a near replica of Weber. He often surfed to please the Malibu beach crowds, and an early '60s black-and-white photo

shows him pressed up into a handstand while angling his board across a glassy three-foot wall. A media-amplified feud between Fain and Dora began in the summer of 1965, as the two surfers pushed and shoved one another during the finals of the annual Malibu Invitational; Fain placed second in the event, Dora third. Unlike most of his Malibu contemporaries, Fain made the transition to the short surfboard in 1968, and the Fain Formula model, produced by Greg Noll Surfboards, sold well in the late '60s. Fain competed in the 1965 and 1968 World Championships, and appeared in surf movies throughout the '60s, including *Gun Ho!* (1963), *Strictly Hot* (1964), and *Golden Breed* (1968). Blond and boyishly handsome, he also worked as a stunt double and extra in *Gidget* (1959), *Beach Blanket Bingo* (1965), and other Hollywood beach movies, and had a small speaking part in *Big Wednesday* (1978). *See also* Malibu.

Falconer, Neridah   Steady and unassuming goofy-foot pro surfer from Scotts Head, New South Wales; world-ranked #3 in 1993, 1995, and 2001; described by

Johnny Fain

Australian surf journalist Alison Smith as "a simple country girl with huge talent." Falconer was born (1970) and raised in Macksville, a northern NSW town of 800. She began surfing at age 16, became a full-time world tour pro at 20, and quietly won 11 events through the 2001 season. In 2000, midway through her 11th season as a world tour pro—six of those rated #5 or better—Falconer was suddenly being noticed, in large part for *not* being noticed. "She's been around," *Surfing Girl* magazine wrote, "you just weren't paying attention." *Surfer,* however, was just plain snide. "Despite having one of the best names in surfing, she's a blank. She's just . . . *here.*" Falconer drew some attention in 2001, at a contest in Durban, South Africa, when she and fellow Australian pro Lynette MacKenzie got into a postmatch brawl on the beach. She also won the 1996 World Surfing Games, and the 2002 Triple Crown. Falconer has appeared in a small number of surf videos, including *Tropical Madness* (2001).

Falzon, Alby   Soulful Australian surf filmmaker, best known for his lush and beautifully crafted 1972 movie *Morning of the Earth.* Falzon was born (1945) in Sydney and raised in the beachfront suburb of Maroubra, but didn't begin surfing until age 14, after moving with his family two hours north to the New South Wales central coast. By 1966 he was working for Sydney-based surf impresario Bob Evans, shooting still photographs for Evans's *Surfing World* magazine and film sequences for his surf movies. Along with surf journalist John Witzig and editor David Elfick, Falzon co-founded *Tracks* magazine in 1970, a counterculture newsprint surf tabloid where surf features were published alongside articles on organic gardening, treehouse building, and the environment. Falzon and Elfick also applied for and received a $20,000 grant from the Australian Film Development Corporation, and began planning *Morning of the Earth,* which featured Nat Young, Michael Peterson, and Terry Fitzgerald, among others. A memorable sequence shows Rusty Miller and Stephen Cooney riding the long, aquamarine lefts at Bali's Uluwatu—a break Falzon spotted during a sight-seeing excursion. The flowing, unnarrated *Morning of the Earth* has long been regarded as the high point in Australian surf cinema.

In 1973, Falzon and California surfer/designer/filmmaker George Greenough made *Crystal Voyager,* a documentary on Greenough, with Pink Floyd on the soundtrack. *Voyager* earned rave reviews in the mainstream press, was picked up by a British distributor,

and played for a record-breaking six months in London's West End. Falzon made a few additional surf movies, short subjects, and videos, including *Surfabout '74, Can't Step Twice on the Same Piece of Water* (1992), and *Metaphysical* (1997), but has always maintained that *Morning of the Earth* was his one true surf movie. "I put everything into that one, and did it right. I said what I wanted to say in that film." Falzon was profiled in *50 Years of Surfing on Film* (1997), an Outdoor Life Network cable TV documentary series. His still photography has also been featured in a number of illustrated surfing books, including *Where the Surfers Are* (1968), *A Pictorial History of Surfing* (1970), and *The History of Surfing* (1983). *See also* Morning of the Earth, Tracks magazine.

Fanning, Mick   Electrifying regularfoot pro surfer from Tweed Heads, New South Wales, Australia; world-ranked #5 in 2002. Fanning was born (1981) in the landlocked Sydney suburb of Penrith, raised in various parts of North Coast New South Wales, first surfed at age five, but didn't do it regularly until age 12, after his family moved to Tweed Heads, on the Queensland/New South Wales border. He placed third in the juniors division of the 1997 Australian National Titles, and two years later won the prestigious Pro Junior. In 2001 the white-blond Fanning earned a wild-card entry into the Rip Curl Pro at Bells Beach and won the event; he also won the World Qualifying Series to earn a slot on the 2002 world pro circuit. Fanning dedicated his Rip Curl Pro victory to

Mick Fanning

his older brother Sean, also a top Queensland surfer, who was killed in an auto accident in 1998.

Lanky and flexible (5′10″, 150 pounds), Fanning rides by touch as much as he does rehearsed athleticism, charging into critical positions—a vertical takeoff, a deep tube, a lofty aerial—and trusting his reflexes and intuition to bring him back to center. "Good surfing," he said in 1999, "is all about feelings." *Australia's Surfing Life* magazine described Fanning in mid-2001 as "the most in-form surfer in the world right now"; a few months later, *TransWorld Surf* called him the "fastest surfer on earth." Fanning and fellow regularfooters Joel Parkinson and Dean Morrison—often labeled the "Coolangatta Kids" after the area all three call home—have been regarded as Australia's hottest young surf trio since Michael Peterson, Peter Townend, and Wayne Bartholomew shot forward as a unit in the early '70s. On the 2002 tour, Fanning won the Billabong Pro at Jeffreys Bay, finished the year ranked #5, and was named rookie-of-the-year.

Fanning the Fire, a sponsor-funded documentary surf video, was released in 2002. He's appeared in more than a dozen other videos, including *Enjoy the Ride* (1998), *The Ritual* (2000), and *Momentum: Under the Influence* (2001). Fanning was named *Surfer* magazine's Breakthrough Performer of the Year in 2001, just before he signed sponsorship deals thought to be worth $1 million per year over three years, making him one of the world's best-paid surfers.

Fantastic Plastic Machine, The   Schizophrenic 1969 surf movie produced by Californians Eric and Lowell Blum for 20th Century Fox, narrated by *Dennis the Menace* television star Jay North. *The Fantastic Plastic Machine* starts off as a travelogue, following La Jolla's Windansea Surf Club members, including Skip Frye, Steve Bigler, Joey Hamasaki, and Mike Purpus, from Los Angeles to Sydney for an October 1967 team competition against Australia. The first half of the movie, with surf stopovers in Fiji and New Zealand, is a well-filmed but otherwise insipid copy of Bruce Brown's 1966 classic *Endless Summer.* Once in Australia, the longboard-riding Windansea surfers lose badly to the vee-bottom-riding Australians, at which point the Blum brothers submissively turn their film over to Nat Young, Bob McTavish, and George Greenough—the three titans of the just-launched shortboard revolution. ("Plastic Machine" was the name McTavish had written across the bottom of his first short surfboard a few months earlier.) Jay North's narration drops out of the film completely, as does the Windansea Surf Club. The second half of the film is a nonlinear ode to the new shortboard surfing and its concomitant philosophy, with Young, McTavish, and Greenough getting virtually all the screen time. Young, in a stentorian voice-over that is by turns indulgent and insightful, celebrates the period's peace-and-love ethos, but is candid enough to admit that "anger always seems to bring out the best in my surfing." As reported in the film's companion book, *The Fantastic Plastic Voyage,* written by Brian St. Pierre, the film's producers knew something about anger themselves. "I was bothered," 28-year-old Eric Blum said, "with the lack of redeeming features in most of the surfers who surrounded me." *Fantastic Plastic Machine* opened to poor reviews, and was pulled from theaters after a short run. A soundtrack album was released on Epic Records. *See also* Hollywood and surfing, shortboard revolution.

Farrelly, Bernard "Midget"   Smooth, tightly drawn regularfoot surfer from Sydney, Australia; winner of the 1964 World Surfing Championships, and runner-up in 1968 and 1970; long regarded as the brilliant but bitter patriarch of modern Australian surfing. Farrelly was born (1944) in Sydney, the son of a taxi driver, and spent the first nine years of his life living in Australia, Canada, and New Zealand. He began surfing at age six, on an 18-foot hollow plywood paddleboard, and from 1962 to 1970 he was arguably the best competitive surfer in the world. He won the 1962 Makaha International, then regarded as the unofficial world championship, and upon his return to Australia the 17-year-old Farrelly became a nationwide sports hero; he responded by dyeing his white-blond hair black in order to regain a measure of anonymity. The diminutive Farrelly (5′8″, 145 pounds) rode in a slightly bowlegged stance, and as *Australia's Surfing Life* magazine would later describe it, was already possessed of "superhuman elegance." He was predictable from one move to the next, but so refined and graceful that his performances never seemed rote. After winning the Australian National Titles in 1964, Farrelly went on to take the inaugural World Championships, held in small but well-shaped waves at Sydney's Manly Beach. Farrelly later discredited his performance, saying he "just felt sick of it all," and that he "more or less took it easy and was probably a little lazy."

Midget Farrelly

Farrelly was by then more comfortable with his role as a surfing leader. He'd been instrumental in the formation of the Australian Surfriders Association, and in 1964 helped launch the International Surfing Federation, to oversee subsequent World Championship events. Farrelly repeated as national champion in 1965, but failed to make the finals in the 1965 World Championships, held in Peru, and watched from the beach as his 17-year-old protégé Nat Young, also from Sydney, finished runner-up. Young went on to win both the national and world titles in 1966; Farrelly—regarded by many in the Australian surf media, and probably by Young as well, as yesterday's news—was generally made unwelcome in what was being billed as the "New Era."

While the exact origins of the Farrelly/Young feud are unclear, and the details of its escalation are all but forgotten, by 1967 the onetime friends had cultivated a near hatred for each other, with Farrelly eventually calling Young a "brazen, conniving, ruthless megalomaniac," and Young describing Farrelly as "a whinging Pom." Farrelly had cause for grievance as he defeated Young in both the 1968 and 1970 World Championships (and won the 1970 Gunston 500 in South Africa) but was nonetheless viewed as Australia's champion of the past. Furthermore, his signif-

icant contribution to late-'60s surfboard design was almost completely overshadowed by the work of Bob McTavish, the Australian designer who, along with Young and Californian George Greenough, is generally credited with inventing the short surfboard. Farrelly Surfboards was founded in 1965 in Palm Beach, and the following year saw the release of the lightweight, easy-turning Midget Farrelly Stringerless model (sold in America by Gordon and Smith Surfboards); Farrelly continued over the next few years to produce some of the sport's most progressive boards.

Farrelly meanwhile seemed to go out of his way to present himself as the grim outsider: the epigraph to *The Surfing Life,* his 1964 book, reads, "When you're comfortable, you're dead." In 1969 he put himself in a tiny minority within surfing by speaking out publicly against drug use. While Farrelly stayed active in the sport—in 1972 he founded the Sydney-based Surfblanks manufacturing company, an ongoing business—he seemed to do so in a bubble. By the early '90s, he was convinced that the late-'60s surfing era was nothing less than "the beginning of the end of sanity" as well as "a waste of time," and that Nat Young and a compliant surf media had "thrown vinegar" into what had been a pure sport.

Farrelly appeared in more than a dozen surf movies including *Cavalcade of Surf* (1962), *Midget Goes Hawaiian* (1963), *The Young Wave Hunters* (1964), *To Ride a White Horse* (1968), and *Pacific Vibrations* (1970). He was Australia's top vote-getter in *International Surfing* Magazine's 1966 Hall of Fame Awards. *The Midget Farrelly Surf Show,* a 10-part series made by ABC in Australia, aired in 1967; *How to Surf,* his second book, was published in 1968. Farrelly was inducted, along with Nat Young, into the Australian Surfing Hall of Fame in 1986. Making a rare venture into surf society in 1999, Farrelly agreed to participate in a novelty contest featuring the five surviving finalists from the 1964 World Championships. He placed first. Farrelly is married and has three children. *See also* World Surfing Championships 1964.

Farrer, Simon   Friendly but fervently competitive kneeboarder from Sydney, Australia; nearly unbeatable from the early 1980s to the mid-'90s; kneeboard division winner in 1988 and 1990 World Championships. Farrer was born (1968) in Carlisle, England, grew up in Sydney's northern beaches, and began stand-up surfing in 1978. Two years later he switched to kneeboarding, believing that he could ride deeper inside the tube from a kneeling position. From 1982 to 1986, while competing in the juniors division, Farrer won four national amateur titles; as a men's division competitor, from 1986 to 1996, aside from his two world titles, Farrer won four national amateur titles, five national pro titles, and was runner-up in the 1986 World Championships. No Australian surfer has more national championships to his or her credit. Farrer was unique among kneeboarders for not wearing swim fins, which allow a rider to catch waves earlier and with more speed. On occasion, he would hop to his feet and ride his kneeboard standing up. Farrer coproduced the full-length kneeboarding video *The Sparrow Has Landed and Friends* in 1998. Farrer himself appeared in a small number of surf movies and videos, including 1988's *Water Slaughter. See also* kneeboarding.

fashion and surfing   While trunks were designed for surfing as far back as the 1930s, the basic precepts of surf fashion—a look based mainly on soft, loose-fitting, comfortable clothes—took shape not long after World War II. Surf style developed mostly out of function (long, loose surf trunks wouldn't fill up with water, and kept the rider's thighs from abrasive rubbing against the surfboard's deck), and partly from a desire to break away from button-down and corseted mainstream fashions. "We wanted to stand out," recalled American big-wave pioneer Greg Noll, who made a surfing fashion statement of sorts in 1952 by entering his eighth-grade homeroom class wearing a trench coat with a rotting anchovy in the pocket. "We had the teachers and the parents a little worried, and we made a game of it." A tropical influence was felt as well, as surfers favored straw hats and flower-print fabrics. But jeans, T-shirts, and sneakers were surfing fashion staples in the '50s, and remain so today.

As the sport's popularity skyrocketed in the late '50s and '60s, the "surfer look" took on new elements, including peroxide-treated hair (the "bushy-bushy blond hairdo," as the Beach Boys put it in their 1963 hit "Surfin' USA"), woolen Pendleton shirts, Mexican-made huarache sandals with tire-tread soles, snap-fly nylon trunks, and zip-up nylon competition-stripe jackets. The surfing T-shirt was introduced in 1961—each white cotton short-sleeve shirt emblazoned with the logotype for Weber Surfboards, or Hobie Surfboards, or Jacobs Surfboards, or dozens of other board-making companies—and within five

Former world champion Nat Young featured in 1989 issue of *Vogue* Australia

years had become the sport's most recognizable and durable fashion item. In 2002, it was estimated that 300 million surf-themed T-shirts were produced worldwide.

While beach-city tailors and seamstresses had been custom-making trunks for surfers for more than 20 years, the surfwear industry began in California in 1959, when boat-cover manufacturers Kanvas by Katin, located in the north Orange County town of Surfside, began making a line of indestructible lace-fly canvas surf trunks. Another half-dozen surfwear companies were founded in the early and mid-'60s, including industry leader Hang Ten. As the initial surf boom faded, surf fashion nearly disappeared into the counterculture fashion swirl; attendees at the 1968 *Surfer* Magazine Readers Poll Awards wore buckskin jackets, bell-bottoms, fringed vests, paisley-print shirts, scarves, ascots, beads, headbands, and body paint. Surf styles returned in the early and mid-'70s, defined for the most part by a series of fashion missteps, including airbrushed shirts, muslin drawstring pants, oval "mat slaps," and the snug short-inseam surf trunk. Ocean Pacific's corduroy "walkshort" was by far surfing's biggest contribution to the larger world of fashion, with puka-shell necklaces a distant second.

Australia-based Quiksilver, founded as a surf trunk company in 1973, was a surf world hit by the end of the decade, on its way to becoming the international beachwear industry kingpin. The mid- and late '80s brought a second surf boom: Hobie Sportswear and Ocean Pacific were among the profit leaders, and as reported in *Time* magazine, total retail surfwear sales in 1986 for the first time hit the $1 billion mark (with a high percentage of items, the magazine noted, going to "beach potatoes who are nonetheless attracted to the image of eternal youth and endless summers"). Other top labels of the period included Gotcha, Billabong, Maui & Sons, Mossimo, and Stussy. Loose, full-cut trunks returned, but the industry detoured into a garish neon-hued new wave phase. By 1990, surfwear designs were on their way to being thoroughly co-opted by the fashion mainstream. Baggy "boardshorts" (Australian for surf trunks) were available at Sears and Macy's, and surf logo T-shirts were ubiquitous summer attire in every state in the nation, and at vacation areas worldwide. Casual Fridays, the relaxed dress-code policy adopted by hundreds of American corporations in the early '90s and beyond, might even be seen as a move toward the surfer fashion ethos. Quiksilver meanwhile became the first surf company to go mainstream and not lose its surfer base. (It was also the first surf company to go public, with an initial public stock offering in 1986.)

After a flat period in the early '90s, the beachwear market once again exploded, with global retail sales in 2002 thought to be as high as $8 billion. Women's surfwear for the first time was driving the industry, with Quiksilver spinoff Roxy leading the way; surfwear insiders predicted that women's lines would account for half of all surfwear sales by 2003. (Roxy introduced female boardshorts and nonslip bikini tops not long after its founding in 1991; the line grew to include beachwear of every description, plus shoes, bed linens, luggage, jewelry boxes, and steering wheel covers.) An aggressive surfer skateboarder hybrid fashion sense was meanwhile brought to bear on sunglasses (Black Flys) and shoes (Vans, Globe, Airwalk). Since the late '90s, business-related surfwear articles have appeared in *Time,* the *Wall Street Journal,* the *New York Times,* and the *Los Angeles Times; Vogue, Details, Outside,* and the *New York Times Sunday Magazine* have all published surf fashion photo spreads. Gucci introduced a line of $1,900 Italian-made surfboards in 2001; runway models for the spring 2003 fashion shows in Paris were accoutered with longboards. California's Orange County, sometimes called "Velcro Valley," remains the center of surf fashion and industry. *See also* aloha shirt, baggies, slaps, surf trunks, surfing T-shirt, ugg boots.

Fast Times at Ridgemont High   First a 1981 bestselling book about life in a Southern California beach-area high school, written by 23-year-old Cameron Crowe and published by Simon and Schuster, then an even bigger hit as a Universal movie; "the quintessential high school film," as *Premier* magazine called it. Although *Fast Times* has virtually no surfing, Jeff Spicoli, one of the ensemble characters, is a composite of some of the surfers Crowe met during his two-semester undercover "senior" year at Clairemont High in San Diego. "Most every morning," Crowe wrote, "Spicoli awoke before dawn, smoked three bowls of marijuana from a small steel bong, put on his wetsuit, and surfed before school." While Spicoli was a funny presence in the book, 21-year-old actor Sean Penn, in his second film role, played the surfer to drawling and zoned-out comic perfection. "All I need," Spicoli points out in his most famous line, "are some tasty waves, a cool buzz, and I'm fine." Surf industry bluenoses were upset at what they perceived to be a gross injustice done to the sport's image. But most surfers reveled in Spicoli's daft genius—or at least recognized him as a completely familiar surf world archetype. Director Amy Heckerling (*Clueless, Look Who's Talking*) made her film debut with the R-rated *Fast Times,* and the cast included Jennifer Jason Leigh, Judge Reinhold, Eric Stoltz, and Forest Whitaker. *See also* books Hollywood and surfing, Jeff Spicoli.

fetch   Distance traveled by a band of wind along the curved, usually oblong perimeter of an open-ocean storm. Wind creates ripples, which combine into wavelets, which in turn combine to form ever-bigger waves, depending on fetch length. Fetch, wind speed, and wind duration are the three primary factors in wave height and power; given an equal wind speed and duration, and an equal distance from storm center to shoreline, a longer fetch will produce a larger wave. The fetch on a prime big-wave-producing North Pacific storm might be 1,000 miles.

fiberglass   Thin, pliable, silica-based fabric that, when saturated in resin, forms the brittle skin on a surfboard. The raw materials in fiberglass are primarily sand, limestone, and clay, which are mixed and melted, strained into filaments, twisted into strands, and woven into a fabric that is chemically treated to bond with resin. Fiberglass was invented in Germany during World War I as a substitute for asbestos, but wasn't commercially available in the United States until the 1930s; surfers at the time were sealing their wooden boards with multiple coats of varnish. In 1946, Southern California surfer/designer Bob Simmons fortified the nose and tail sections of his new board with strips of Owens-Corning fiberglass, and within five years virtually all new boards made in California and Hawaii were being completely wrapped in the new material. Surfers often refer to fiberglass as "cloth."

Fiberglass comes in many composites, weaves, and weights. High-performance shortboards are almost exclusively covered in four-ounce cloth (as measured per square yard of material), while heavier, stronger, six-ounce cloth is generally used on longboards. All varieties are smooth, almost silky to the touch, but microscopic shards can easily lodge into skin pores, producing a short-term but irritating condition known as "fiberglass itch." Inhaled fiberglass dust during the sanding process is a more serious problem; in 1987, the World Health Organization's International Agency for Research on Cancer listed fiberglass as a "probable [human] carcinogen." *See also* resin, surfboard construction.

fiberglass rope   Rope-shaped type of fiberglass. During the laminating process, resin-saturated lengths of fiberglass rope are laid on either side of "glass-on" fins, along with oval-shaped patches of cloth fiberglass, to attach the fin to the bottom of a surfboard.

Fiji   Tropical South Pacific island nation made up of roughly 330 wave-fringed volcanic islands (100 inhabited) and 500 atolls covering 120,000 square miles; home to Restaurants and Cloudbreak, both premier left-breaking reef waves located off Tavarua Island. Fiji can be divided into three areas: 1) The Mananuca Island group, just west of Viti Levu, in-

Cloudbreak, Tavarua Island, Fiji

cludes Tavarua and the popular Tavarua Island Resort; and nearby Namotu Island, featuring the high-performance tubes of Namotu Lefts, Swimming Pools, and Wilkes Pass. 2) The south shore of Viti Levu, Fiji's biggest island, home to the temperamental sand-bottom peaks of Sigatoka Rivermouth, and the hollow rights at Hideaway. 3) The scattered islands south of Viti Levu, including Beqa Island's open-ocean waves at Frigates Pass and Nagigia Island, home to the quick tubes of King Kong Lefts. Fiji gets its best surf between May and October, as Southern Hemisphere storms regularly generate four- to six-foot swells, along with the occasional 12-footer. Many of the breaks are improved by offshore or side-offshore tradewinds. The surf from February to April is less consistent, but passing Coral Sea cyclones will occasionally create excellent waves. Access to most Fijian surf breaks is by boat. Average daytime air temperatures vary from 70 to 90 degrees, with water temperatures ranging from the low 70s to the low 80s; the Fijian people themselves are famously warm and welcoming. Sharks and sea snakes are plentiful, but shallow reefs are by far Fiji's biggest surf hazard.

Although Fiji was visited by surfers as far back as the early '60s, it didn't become popular until 1984, not long after the opening of Tavarua Island Resort—the first all-amenities surf camp—with Cloudbreak and Restaurants immediately touted in surf magazines as two of the world's best breaks. Additional resorts opened on Viti Levu and Namotu in 1992. The Fiji Surfing Association formed in 1995, and began holding contests at the beachbreak peaks of Sigatoka

Rivermouth; Viti Surf, Fiji's first surf shop, opened in 1995 in the main port city of Suva. Tavarua has been the site of more than dozen major international pro contests since the late '80s. By 2003, Fiji was home to two surf shops (both on Viti Levu), about 1,000 native surfers, and nearly a dozen surf camps and resorts scattered across the island cluster, with per-day prices (not including airfare) ranging from $20 to $800. *See also* Tavarua.

Filosa, Gary, Dr.   Erratic but efficient competition promoter and organizer; founder in 1976 of both the American Surfing Association (ASA) and the International Amateur Surfing Federation (IASF); author of the error-riddled *Surfer's Almanac.* Filosa was born (1931) and raised in Vermont; in the '50s and '60s he worked as a writer and editor for various magazines in New York and Los Angeles. He came to the attention of the surfing world in 1975, after writing a letter to *Surfer* magazine complaining about the editors using the female gender ("our mother ocean") when describing the sea and surf. When *Surfer* replied by publishing a curvaceous photo of a breaking wave, Filosa threatened a lawsuit, and for nearly 10 years he continued to feud with the surf media, along with many of surfing's most respected figures. As reported by *Surfer,* Filosa launched a defamatory letter campaign against surfing matriarch Nancy Katin in 1976 after she refused to sell Filosa her Kanvas by Katin surfwear business; in 1983, contest promoter and former world surfing champion Fred Hemmings won a $36,000 judgment against Filosa after Filosa sent a vilifying letter about Hemmings to the Federal Communications Commission.

Filosa hoped to get surfing accepted as an Olympic sport, and while the ASA was viable for just a short period in the mid- and late '70s (the IASF was little more than a shell organization), he was nonetheless able to establish communication with both the Amateur Athletic Union and the International Olympic Committee, and temporarily position himself as the head of world amateur surfing. While the surf industry had unified against Filosa by 1977, successfully refuting his claims to the AAU and IOC, he remained an active presence in the sport until the early '80s. Filosa's *Surfer's Almanac,* published in 1977 by E. P. Dutton, was described by one reviewer as "a cornucopia of misinformation and inaccuracies." *See also* American Surfing Association.

fin   Rudderlike device attached to the surfboard's rear bottom surface, singly or in a multifin cluster, to give directional stability, control, and maneuverability. Before the development of the fin, surfers gained a small amount of traction and control through the use of convex hull shapes, and were able to make slight directional changes by dipping a foot in the water alongside the board's tail section. "Sliding ass" was the expression used to describe the way the tail section of a finless board often slipped out of its track and swung to the fore, almost always causing a wipeout. In 1935, Wisconsin-born surfing innovator Tom Blake, while living in Waikiki, removed the metal keel off an abandoned speedboat and bolted it to the bottom of his surfboard. The fin was about one foot long and four inches deep. "My first wave revealed the truth," Blake later said. "Never before had I experienced such control and stability." For reasons not entirely clear (although some thought the new addition was dangerous), the fin didn't catch on until the mid-'40s, when Southern California surfers began gluing (and then fiberglassing) crescent-shaped wooden fins onto the tails of their balsa-core boards. A few surfers—most notably California surfer/designer Bob Simmons—experimented briefly with two-fin designs, setting a pair of fins near the board's edges, equidistant from the tail.

The slightly swept-back fixed-in-place glass-on fin was a universal surfboard design feature by the mid-'50s, with most fins measuring about nine inches tall and nine inches along the base. The all-fiberglass fin, followed shortly by the injection-molded hard plastic fin, began to replace the wood-and-fiberglass models in the mid-'60s, while the fin's silhouette began to resemble the dorsal fin of a dolphin—a shape that made turning easier. Surfers in general paid little attention to the shape of their fin until Australian Nat Young won the 1966 World Surfing Championships title using a narrow-based "high-aspect ratio" fin created by California kneeboarder/ designer George Greenough. Young's fin gave him an advantage over the competition in the 1966 championships, increasing both the sharpness and strength of his turns, and Young later credited his world title victory to fin-maker Greenough.

Although big-wave surfing pioneer George Downing of Hawaii invented a removable fin system in 1951, the idea didn't become popular until 1967, with the introduction of the Water Apparatus and

Vehicular Engineering Interchangeable Fin System (or W.A.V.E. Set), developed primarily by California surfer/designer Tom Morey. The original W.A.V.E. Set line was composed of six different molded polypropylene fins, each of which could be bolted into a slotted hard-plastic "box" installed flush to the board's bottom surface. Fin experimentation, amplified by the late-'60s shortboard revolution, went off on the number of interesting but for the most part dead-end tangents in the '70s and early '80s, including the attenuated keel fin, the V-shaped butterfly fin, the wide-based fin, an assortment of flexible fins, the boomerang fin, the slotted jet-ducting fins, the tri-fin bonzer design, hollow fins, and more. The twin-fin was reintroduced for a brief period in the early '70s, then returned in 1977 to become a hugely popular small-wave board; 1981 saw the introduction of the Thruster Model tri-fin, featuring two side-mounted fins and a trailing fin, each about five inches in height. The tri-fin soon became standard on virtually every high-performance shortboard and big-wave board. (The quad-fin found a small number of adherents; not so for the five- and six-fin designs.) The mid-'90s brought a new generation of lighter, stronger, more convenient removable fins, most notably by Fin Control Systems (FCS) who, by 2002, had a line of 26 different fiberglass or foam-core/carbon fins. FCS uses a pair of circular board-mounted "plugs" to anchor each fin; other companies use slotted boxes.

Professional surfers occasionally give instructions as to where their fins (or fin boxes/plugs) are set on the board, but the vast majority of fins are set according to the specifications of the surfboard shaper. In the standard tri-fin setup, fins grouped closely together allow for sharper turns, while a more spread-out configuration increases stability. Surfers choose their fins according to wave type, board type, and personal preference. Increasing or decreasing a single aspect of fin design can amplify or mitigate the performance characteristics of other design aspects. Basic fin design definitions are as follows:

Template: the fin's outline or silhouette.

Depth: The fin's maximum height as measured from the bottom surface of the board; the distance the fin penetrates the water. More depth increases the board's hold on the wave, but can also make the board harder to turn. Average depth for a shortboard tri-fin is between four and five inches. Average depth on a longboard single fin is about nine inches.

Base: The length of the fin where it meets the surfboard; increased base length adds forward drive, but can stiffen the board's turning characteristics. Average base measurement for a shortboard tri-fin is between three and a half and four and a half inches; base on a longboard single fin is about six inches.

Rake: the amount of distance between the fin tip and the trailing edge of the fin base; defines to what degree a fin is "swept back." Increased rake adds traction; less rake allows for tighter turning arcs.

Foil: The fin's horizontal curve as measured from front edge to trailing edge.

Tip: The upper third of a fin; more tip area provides better hold in turns; less makes the board more pivotal.

Flex: The fin's pliability; rigid fins are faster; more pliable fins give a softer and more forgiving ride.

Fin lacerations account for nearly half of all surfing-related injuries; rubber-lined safety fins are available but not widely used. A small number of seminovelty fins remain on the market, including the winged-keel fin (a single fin with flared-out wings at the tip) and the Turbo Tunnel Fin (a traditional fin with a pipe-shaped cylinder running in the middle, parallel to the base). In 2001, an estimated 80 percent of shortboard surfers in the United States used the FCS fin system, 5 percent used other removable fin systems, and 15 percent used glass-ons. From the mid-'40s to the late '60s, fins were often called "skegs." *See also* fin box, fin hum, four-fin, single fin, tri-fin, twin-fin, twinzer.

fin box Slotted, rectangular plastic box set flush into the tail section of a surfboard to hold a fin. The fin box, as opposed to the fixed glass-on fin, allows the fin to be removed, adjusted, or exchanged, and also makes surfboard transportation easier. George Downing of Hawaii installed a handmade redwood-lined fin box into his big-wave balsa board in 1951, and Hobie Surfboards had an "exclusive removable fin system" as early as 1966. But the fin box didn't become popular until 1967, with the introduction of the Water Apparatus and Vehicular Engineering Interchangeable Fin System (W.A.V.E. Set), developed by

Fin box

California surf design guru Tom Morey, and a similar product by Fins Unlimited. The original W.A.V.E. Set line had six molded polypropylene fins, all of which fit into the same box and were locked in place with a pair of flathead screws. Later fin box models allowed the fin to be moved forward or back, allowing the surfer to fine-tune the board's turning radius. By the mid-'80s, after the tri-fin design had become standard, fin boxes were all but phased out as heavy, difficult to install, and easily damaged. While almost all of the newly popularized longboards came equipped with fin boxes, virtually all high-performance shortboards had glass-on fins. A new, lighter, stronger, easier-to-set generation of boxes was introduced in the mid-'90s, with Fin Control Systems (FCS) soon becoming the popular favorite. FCS used a pair of spherical "plugs," rather than a box, to hold each fin in place, and offered a wide selection of fin shapes and models; industry leader Rusty Surfboards was installing FCS plugs and fins into 80 percent of new boards by 1997. *See also* fin.

fin hum   High, piercing sound made by a rapidly vibrating surfboard fin as it moves through water, usually caused by a thin bead of resin along the fin's perimeter, or by a nick or dent near the fin's tip. Fin hum is annoying and can marginally reduce board speed. Repairing a humming fin isn't difficult, and can usually be done with sandpaper, but it can be hard to pinpoint the hum source, especially with multifinned boards. Also known as fin whistle.

fin-first takeoff   Hotdog version of the takeoff, almost always performed in small surf, where the rider paddles into the wave fin-first, stands, and immediately slides the board in a half-revolution to get into a standard nose-first position. Also known as a reverse takeoff, or skeg-first takeoff. *Endless Summer* star Mike Hynson did a prone version of the fin-first takeoff in the early '60s; California surfer David Nuuhiwa popularized the move in the mid-'60s. Rarely done on a shortboard.

Finney, Ben   California-born professor emeritus of anthropology at the University of Hawaii; coauthor of 1966's *Surfing: A History of the Ancient Hawaiian Sport,* a comprehensive study of the origins of surfing. Finney was born (1933) and raised in San Diego, California, and learned to surf as a teenager. He earned an M.A. in anthropology from the University of Hawaii in 1959, a Ph.D. in anthropology from Harvard in 1964, and was awarded a Fulbright Scholarship. He worked with novelist James D. Houston on *Surfing* before going on to his primary area of research concerning ancient Polynesian voyaging techniques. Finney returned to the University of Hawaii as a professor in 1970, and later became a research assistant at Honolulu's Bishop Museum, home to the world's finest collection of pre–20th-century surfboards. His other published works include the *A Pictorial History of Surfing* (1970) and *Voyage of Rediscovery: A Cultural Odyssey through Polynesia* (1994). A revised edition of *Surfing* was produced in 1996. Finney helped curate *Surf Culture: The Art History of Surfing,* a 2002 exhibit at the Laguna Art Museum in Laguna Beach, California.

fish   Stumpy, blunt-nosed, two-finned surfboard design invented by San Diego kneeboarder Steve Lis in 1967, featuring low rocker and a split tail, and later adapted for stand-up surfing. The fish was recognized as a small-wave speed machine—Jim Blears of Hawaii used a 5'10" fish to win the 1972 World Championships, held in sloppy waist-high surf in San Diego—but because the stand-up versions of the boards were nearly impossible to control in waves over four feet, they never gained widespread popularity. In 1976, however, Hawaii's Reno Abellira took a fish to Australia, where it was closely inspected by future world champion Mark Richards, who modified the design the following year to produce a version of the twin-fin that became a surf world best-seller. Clyde Beatty and Steve Brom of Southern California meanwhile developed the Rocket Fish, a longer, curvier version of the original Lis fish. A three-fin,

Fish surfboard

small-wave board design from the mid-'90s—shorter, wider, and thicker than the average tri-fin—was also labeled a "fish," although it had little in common with the Lis design. *See also* kneeboarding, Steve Lis, twin-fin.

fitness and surfing   "Surfing is a whole body exercise," the Surfer's Medical Association wrote in 1993, "utilizing most of the body's 600 or so muscles, particularly the heart." A study conducted by Australian fitness expert Rudi Meir found that a typical one-hour beachbreak surf session—with 44 percent of the time spent paddling, 35 percent waiting for waves, and 5 percent spent riding waves—burned nearly 500 calories. By comparison, a one-hour six-mile run burns 750 calories, while a four-mile walk burns 420 calories. The average heart rate for a one-hour surfing session is about 135 beats per minute, with peaks up to the 170s. As determined by the American College of Sports Medicine, requirements for proper cardiovascular training are three to five workouts per week, at 20 to 30 minutes per session, at an intensity of 70 to 80 percent of maximum heart rate—all numbers that fall well within the range of the dedicated surfer's routine. Further evidence for the beneficial effect of surfing is found in the surfer's typically lean and muscular physique, despite the fact that surfers are on the whole indifferent, if not opposed outright, to nonsurfing workouts. Surfing is one of the few sports where even professional-level riders choose not to train. Mark

Richards of Australia, world champion from 1979 to 1982, confessed that the only training he ever did during his four-year title reign was a single lap around the local sports track on his way home from surfing one afternoon. "If you went down and did stretches on the beach," Richards later recalled, "people would throw rocks at you." By the late '80s, however, a small but growing number of professionals—including world champions Tom Carroll, Damien Hardman, and Wendy Botha—were developing extracurricular programs to help their surfing, under the auspices of personal trainers such as Greg Day and Rob Rowland-Smith, both of Australia. Big-wave rider Brian Keaulana of Hawaii, meanwhile, trained in part by holding his breath and running sprints along the ocean floor while holding an 80-pound boulder. Cross-training has been limited for the most part to older pros, or those recovering from an injury. Top pros in 2002 who cited "surfing only" as their training regimen (stretching and yoga aside) included Andy Irons, Taj Burrow, and Shea Lopez.

At least two training devices have been designed specifically for surfers: the balance-enhancing Indo Board and the Vasa Trainer paddling machine. Books on surfing and fitness include *Surf Flex, Fit to Surf,* and *A Surfer's Guide to Flexibility and Conditioning,* all published in 2001. *See also* injuries and surfing.

Fitzgerald, Joel   Photogenic Australian goofyfooter from Narrabeen, New South Wales; best known as a fearless tuberider. The younger son of '70s surf icon Terry Fitzgerald, Joel was born (1973) in Sydney, and began surfing at age eight. He placed third in the 1992 Pro Junior event, held at his home break in Narrabeen, but had little interest in competition. He made a name for himself three years later as a guest at the 1995 Quiksilver Pro at Grajagan, Java, when he all but stole the show with some impossibly deep free-surf tuberiding. "Golden Child," a 1996 *Australia's Surfing Life* profile on Fitzgerald, described the 22-year-old as "a pure surfer in an age when hype and tricks and fashion have infiltrated the once-simple world of surfing." But in a 1999 follow-up article, titled "Dreams Lost," Fitzgerald, now a born-again Christian, admitted he'd never really lived up to his surfing potential. "I was a yobbo, getting drunk, doing drugs, and mucking around." Fitzgerald is seen riding big, powerful surf in Ireland in *Litmus,* a 1997 surf video. Kye Fitzgerald, Joel's older brother, also a goofyfoot, was regarded in the mid- and late '90s as one of Australia's premier surf stylists.

Fitzgerald, Terry   Frizzy-haired Australian surfer and entrepreneur from Narrabeen, Sydney, New South Wales; one of the sport's premier stylists; winner of the 1975 Australian National Titles and founder of Hot Buttered Surfboards. Fitzgerald was born (1950) in Sydney, the son of a Royal Australian Navy diver, and raised in the suburbs of Helensburgh, Maroubra, and Collaroy. At age 10 he contracted osteomyelitis, a degenerative bone disease, and nearly had his left leg amputated below the knee; a series of bone grafts saved the limb. He began surfing in 1964 at 14; six years later, at the 1970 World Surfing Championships, held in Victoria, Australia, the flamboyant and well-muscled Fitzgerald made the semifinals, and was the buzz surfer of the event. "Electroshock on a surfboard," surf journalist Drew Kampion wrote. "He seemed to defy or ignore all previous surfing styles, traditions and mannerisms, and took the still-new short surfboard to its limit." The 5′9″, 165-pound Fitzgerald had by that time developed an entirely unique surfing form, riding in a bowlegged stance, arms extended symmetrically from the shoulders and hands cupped; he initiated turns through his hips and pelvis, with shoulders, knees, and head following in perfect synchronization. He was nicknamed the Sultan of Speed, and at any given moment his board seemed to be a divining rod in search of the fastest section of the wave. Whether he was in fact going faster than the rest of the world's best surfers is uncertain. But the odd and beautiful poses he struck suggested speed, and few surfers have ever drawn the spectator's eye the way Fitzgerald did—particularly at expansive breaks like Jeffreys Bay and Sunset Beach.

Fitzgerald visited Hawaii for the first time in 1971, and became an instant surf media sensation. Master

Terry Fitzgerald

board shaper Dick Brewer invited him to his home in Kauai, and gave the cocksure Australian informal shaping lessons; at the end of the year Fitzgerald opened his own surfboard factory/retail store in the Sydney town of Brookvale, lifting the Hot Buttered Surfboards name from the title of Isaac Hayes's 1969 album *Hot Buttered Soul.* Fitzgerald specialized in narrow, racy, semiexperimental surfboards that were often airbrushed nose to tail in bright swirling colors. He served as the company's model and pitchman; for a magazine ad shoot he once laid out an array of vibrant Hot Buttered boards across the lawn, then put himself in the center of the frame, seated in full lotus position, wearing aviator sunglasses and a blue work shirt unbuttoned to the waist, with a cigar wedged between the fingers of his right hand.

His business up and running, Fitzgerald turned his attention to national and international surf contests. In 1971 he'd been a finalist in the Australian National Titles, the Duke Kahanamoku Classic, and the Bells Beach contest. In 1972 he won Bells; in 1974 he was a finalist in the Duke, Bells, and at the Coca-Cola Surfabout, held at his home break of Narrabeen; in 1975 he became the Australian national champion, placed third in the Coke, and won the $5,000 Lightning Bolt Pro contest at Velzyland, Hawaii. He finished #9 on the 1977 world tour final ratings; in 1980 he won the OM Bali Pro in Indonesia. Hot Buttered, meanwhile, adding a popular clothes and accessories line in the early '80s, grew steadily through the years, and by 2001 had retail outlets in New Zealand, Brazil, Bali, and Italy. Since 1980, Hot Buttered has cosponsored the Pro Junior contest, an international showcase for teenage surfers, with Fitzgerald serving as competition director.

One of the most photogenic surfers of his era, Fitzgerald appeared in more than two dozen surf movies, including *Tracks* (1970), *Morning of the Earth* (1972), *Five Summer Stories* (1972), *A Winter's Tale* (1974), *Fantasea* (1978), and *Adventures in Paradise* (1982). He was a cofounder in 1975 of the Australian Professional Surfing Association, which put together the first domestic pro tour. In 1995 he was inducted into the Australian Surfing Hall of Fame; in 2001 he was featured in *Biographies,* an Outdoor Life Network surfing documentary series. Fitzgerald is married and has three children. Kye and Joel Fitzgerald, the oldest two, are both well-known surfers in Australia. *See also* Australian Professional Surfing Association, Pro Junior.

Handbill for *Five Summer Stories*

Five Summer Stories   Well-crafted and hugely popular 1972 surf film made by Californians Greg MacGillivray and Jim Freeman. Although the MacGillivray-Freeman team had been making surf films together for more than five years and were regarded as tops in the field, their previous movie, *Waves of Change* (1968), was somewhat lost in the swirl of the early shortboard revolution and had been a box-office disappointment. It was agreed that *Five Summer Stories* would be their last surfing film, as both MacGillivray and Freeman were being courted by Hollywood studios. *Five Summer Stories* didn't break any new ground conceptually, but its production values were outstanding across the board: the film was well-composed and color-saturated (including water photography by original surf moviemaker Bud Browne), the editing was smooth (with some perspective-lending black-and-white clips from past decades), and the soundtrack was excellent (featuring the Beach Boys and Laguna Beach country rockers Honk, among other artists). Revered surf artist and cartoonist Rick Griffin was commissioned to do the film's poster.

Five Summer Stories debuted to a full house at the 3,000-seat Santa Monica Civic Auditorium on March 24, 1972, compelling a *Rolling Stone* film critic to note that the audience was "dazzled [and] stunned." Hawaiian surfer Gerry Lopez was the star of *Five Summer Stories,* supported by Jeff Hakman, David Nuuhiwa, Margo Oberg, Terry Fitzgerald, Bill Hamilton, Angie Reno, Corky Carroll, and dozens of others. Updated versions of the movie came out each year until 1978, and ticket volume remained high season after season.

After *Five Summer Stories,* Freeman worked on a small number of Hollywood-made movies, including *Jonathan Livingston Seagull* (1973) and *The Towering Inferno* (1974), then was killed in a 1976 helicopter accident. MacGillivray contributed to *Big Wednesday* (1978) and *The Shining* (1980), then went on to great success working in the IMAX big-screen format.

Surfer magazine in 1987 picked *Five Summer Stories, Locked In* (1964), and *The Endless Summer* (1966) as the three best surf movies of all time. *Five Summer Stories* was released on home video in 1995. *See* Beach Boys, Jim Freeman, Honk, Greg MacGillivray, surf movies.

Flame   *See* Larry Moore.

flat   A complete or near-complete absence of surf. "Dead flat" is used for added emphasis. A "flat spell" is when the surf is down for some lengthy but indefinite period of time, usually at least a few days. As applied to a wave, a "flat spot" or "flat section" occurs when the wave moves into deeper water, slows down, levels out, and becomes less powerful.

Flaxman, Vicki   Malibu surfer from the 1950s; part of a small group of teenagers who rode "girl boards"—thinner, lighter, easier-turning balsa boards, the immediate forerunners to the Malibu chip, which led to the development of the high-performance climb-and-drop style of surfing. The regularfooted Flaxman learned to ride at Malibu in the summer of 1950 on a custom-made Joe Quigg balsa. "Vicki was athletic and aggressive," Quigg later recalled. "In a couple of months, she learned to surf better than most men." Flaxman's board was 9′6″ long and weighed just 24 pounds, about 10 pounds lighter than most boards at the time, and it immediately became a popular loaner board for the Malibu men. Aggie Bane, Claire Cassidy, Robin Grigg (sister of big-wave pioneer Rick Grigg), Darrylin Zanuck (daughter of Hollywood mogul Darryl Zanuck), and other female Malibu surfers were also regularly lending out their new boards. While Kathy "Gidget" Kohner is regarded as the prototypical American female surfer, Flaxman and her contemporaries had already created an admirable female presence in what was soon to become an oppressively sexist sport.

Flecky, Dan Quiet, mustachioed surfer from Newport Beach, California; one of the state's few international-caliber surfers in the early and mid-'70s. Flecky was born (1952) in Newport Beach, began surfing in 1965, was California's top-rated amateur in 1974, and competed sporadically on the pro tour in the late '70s and early '80s. He cofounded the Black Flys sunglasses company in 1991, which soon earned a reputation for its lurid marketing campaigns, including an ad blitz featuring large-breasted strippers wearing nothing but strategically placed Black Flys stickers, and a 1999 surf video titled *Rat F@#ed*. Flecky appeared in the 1975 surf movie *A Matter of Style*.

Fletcher, Christian Innovative and theatrical goofyfooter from San Clemente, California; an aerial surfing icon since the late 1980s. Fletcher was born (1970) in Kahuku, Oahu, Hawaii, the son of long-boarder and surf impresario Herbie Fletcher, grandson of big-wave pioneer Walter Hoffman, and nephew of two-time world champion Joyce Hoffman. He began surfing with his father as a toddler, and moved with his family to Capistrano Beach in 1974. Fletcher had some good contest results as a preteen, finishing second in the menehune division of the 1983 United States Surfing Championships and second in the open-age longboard division of the 1985 U.S. Championships. He also earned $31,725—surfing's biggest-ever cash prize at the time—for his win in the 1989 Body Glove Surf Bout. But Fletcher later had nothing but scorn for competition. "I could give a fuck about being world champion," the ninth-grade dropout told *Surfing* magazine in 1991, in the linguistic style that helped make him a surf rebel icon. "But I like to go out and fuck with people during the heats."

Matt Kechele, Kevin Reed, and Larry Bertlemann more or less simultaneously invented aerial surfing in the late '70s, and the new form continued to slowly develop in the early and mid-'80s. But it was Fletcher, in the late '80s, who transformed the aerial from novelty to high-performance mainstay, and introduced the surf world to a new sub-lexicon that included "mute air," "indy air," air-to-reverse," "slob air," and "stalefish." He also defined the aerial as the move of

choice for surf rebels. In 1990, a few weeks after a group of world tour pros signed a letter to *Surfer* complaining about the amount of media coverage Fletcher was getting, the drawling aerialist shot back in a *Surfer* interview, saying "it was stupid" that former world champion Damien Hardman didn't ride bigger waves, that top-rated Richie Collins was "the biggest kook there is," and that former world champion Barton Lynch was "conservative to the max." Magazine readers liked Fletcher's aggressive approach, and voted him #7 in the 1990 *Surfer* Poll Awards.

Throughout the early '90s, the heavily tattooed and pierced Fletcher launched ever-higher aerials, and regularly added to his on-record litany of scandalous and often spiteful quotes. He told *Australia's Surfing Life* magazine in 1993 that he was probably an alcoholic, that he smoked "maybe 10 joints a day," and that he'd let his three-year-old son smoke "if he wanted to do it at home, off the streets." At night, he played bass in several local death-metal bands, including Bloodshot, Mutilage, and Axefukk. Six-time world champion Kelly Slater, meanwhile, along with dozens of surfers including Kalani Robb, Tim Curran, and Jason Collins, had followed Fletcher's lead and become master aerialists by the mid-'90s. Fletcher himself developed a drug problem, was divorced, lost his home, and began living in a warehouse. His 1991-

Christian Fletcher

founded line of punk-decorated surfboards and beachwear had also failed. Off drugs by 1996, he announced that he was landing "the biggest airs of my life; huge ones, like five feet," and the following year he won the inaugural *Surfing* Magazine Airshow tour. Fletcher has been featured in more than 50 surf movies and videos, including all of the Herbie Fletcher–produced *Wave Warrior* and *Adrenaline Surf* series videos, along with *Runman 69* (1989), *Surfers: The Movie* (1990), *Rolling Thunder* (1991), *Mental Surfing* (1993), and *Digital Daze* (1999).

Nathan Fletcher, Christian's younger brother, born in 1975, earned a reputation by the late '90s as a first-rate aerialist and tuberider, as well as a hard-charging snowboarder, skateboarder, and dirt bike rider. *See also* aerial.

Fletcher, Herbie   Hustling, media-obsessed surfer/manufacturer/impresario from San Clemente, California; semifinalist in the 1966 World Surfing Championships; leader of the longboard renaissance in the 1970s; owner of Astrodeck traction pads and producer of the *Wave Warrior* video series; father of aerial specialists Christian and Nathan Fletcher. "In rock and roll we've got Iggy Pop and Mick Jagger," surf journalist Jamie Brisick wrote in 1996, "in surfing we've got Herbie Fletcher." Born in Pasadena in 1948, Fletcher began surfing at age nine. In 1966, the brown-haired 17-year-old won the juniors division of the Laguna Swimwear Masters contest at Redondo Beach, finished second to David Nuuhiwa in the United States Surfing Association juniors division final ratings, and placed seventh in the World Championships. Fletcher kept a fairly low profile during the shortboard revolution, then suddenly reappeared on the cover of *Surfer* magazine in 1976, noseriding on a bright red longboard—it was *Surfer*'s first longboard cover since 1968 (and the last until 1997) and an early and unmistakable sign of the nascent longboard resurgence. Herbie Fletcher Surfboards was founded the same year, with a Dana Point showroom stocked full of Fletcher-shaped longboards, and an advertising campaign built around images of Fletcher hanging ten and a slogan proclaiming "The Thrill is Back." With the exception of Gordon & Smith Surfboards in San Diego, Fletcher was the only person keeping longboards in stock.

In 1975, Orange County surfer Jim Van Vleck developed Astrodeck, a spray-on urethane nonslip coating for surfboards; Fletcher bought the company the following year, created a peel-and-stick version, and turned Astrodeck into the sport's best-known accessory, largely due to the fact that he personally distributed the product to nearly every top surfer in the world during the late '70s and '80s.

Fletcher positioned himself in the vanguard of the surf video movement in 1985 with the release of *Wave Warriors,* a no-frills 45-minute promo for Astrodeck. Four *Wave Warrior* sequels followed, each as energetic and mindless as the original, followed by *The Best of Wave Warriors* in 1991. Next came the Fletcher-produced *Adrenaline Surf* series, released at about twice the rate of the *Wave Warrior* videos, as well as a steady supply of longboard-only videos. "I've made so many movies," Fletcher declared in 1996, "I don't know how many I've made." Fletcher himself continued to surf at a furious pace, accoutered in the brightest possible colors (lime-green surfboards and flaming red wetsuits in the mid- and late '80s), and in 1995 he again made the cover of *Surfer.* While Fletcher appeared in *Free and Easy* (1967) and *Five Summer Stories* (1972), he didn't become a surf cinema regular until the '80s, first in surf movies like *Ocean Fever* (1983) and *Amazing Surf Stories* (1986), and then in dozens of his own videos. Fletcher was also a tow-in surfing forerunner: in 1985 he rode 25-foot waves at Waimea Bay on his Kawasaki 550 Jet Ski, and in 1987—four years before Laird Hamilton helped popularize the technique—he towed Martin Potter, Tom Carroll, and Michael Ho in to 12-foot waves at Pipeline.

Fletcher is married to Dibi Hoffman, sister of two-time world champion Joyce Hoffman and daughter of big-wave pioneer and surfwear textile giant Walter Hoffman. Christian Fletcher, Herbie's oldest son, became a trailblazing aerial surfer in the late '90s; second-born Nathan Fletcher, also a first-rate surfer and aerialist, branched out into motocross, snowboarding, and skateboarding. Both were shamelessly promoted in their father's videos, and the entire Fletcher clan was described as "The First Family of Surfing" in a 1992 *Esquire* magazine cover feature that was by turns impressed by their wealth and surf world fame and mocking of their near-complete ignorance of anything in the nonsurfing world. Herbie Fletcher was inducted into the Huntington Beach Surfing Walk of Fame in 1995. *See also* traction pad.

flip-flops   *See* slaps.

Backside floater by Kelly Slater, Pipeline, Hawaii

floater   Hovering, neutral-edged maneuver, where the surfer distributes his weight evenly across the center of the board and "floats" laterally across the crown of whitewater—or on top of the curl as it pitches over—before dropping back down the wave face. Australia's Mark Sainsbury, 1986 world amateur champion, is often credited as the first to master the floater, but it was Cheyne Horan, also from Australia, and Davey Smith of Santa Barbara, California, who more or less simultaneously invented the move in the late 1970s. "Whitewater Ripping," a short 1982 *Surfing* magazine article, noted that Horan could "gain an extra 10 feet [of lateral ground] by coasting over the foam, where he might be fighting with small bottom turns to go around it." The term "floater" was introduced later that year. Floaters—performed almost exclusively by shortboarders—would in turn lead to tailslides, reverses, and other moves popularized by the teenage New School surfers of the early '90s. As of 2003, floaters were still a rarity in waves eight feet or bigger, although they'd been attempted in surf up to 12 or 15 feet.

Florida   Although Florida's low-lying subtropical coastlines, on both the Gulf of Mexico and the Atlantic Ocean, tend to produce nothing more than mediocre surf, the state is home nonetheless to an astonishing number of first-quality surfers. Composed of a long and nearly unbroken string of beachbreaks (580 miles long on the Atlantic side, 770 miles in the Gulf) punctuated by jetties, inlets, and piers, Florida

can be divided into three main surfing regions: 1) The Gulf Coast hooks down from the Alabama border southeast to Key West, and is filled with erratic, here-and-gone beachbreak waves. The best-known breaks include Picken's Point in Pensacola, 12th Avenue in Indian Rocks, and Naples Pier. 2) The southern Atlantic coast, Florida's most popular surfing area, extends south from Cape Canaveral and is home to the ferociously crowded peaks of Sebastian Inlet, the sloping semireef waves at RC's (which holds the biggest surf in the state), and the inconsistent but well-shaped lefts of Reef Road. 3) The northern Atlantic coast from Cape Canaveral to the Georgia border contains more than 50 breaks, including the crowded but dependable peaks at Jax Beach Pier and the sometimes-tubing waves of New Smyrna Beach. The Florida Keys, a 150-mile chain of islands extending southwest from Florida, generally has poor surf. Florida's entire coast is bordered by a wide continental shelf that filters out much of the power of incoming swells. The fall hurricane season is the best time to surf, although winter and spring produce plenty of small but ridable wind swells and a few larger ground swells. Summer can be flat for weeks at a time. Average daytime air temperatures in Florida range from the low 90s in summer to the upper 50s in winter; water temperatures range from the high 70s to the low 60s. More than half of America's total reported shark attacks took place in Florida, although a majority were nonfatal strikes by spinner or black tip sharks.

Stand-up surfing was introduced to Florida at Miami Beach in the early '30s by a small group of local bodysurfers and bellyboarders—including Bill and Dudley Whitman, Paul Hart, and Gauldin Reid—who built their own solid-wood surfboards after watching a pair of visiting Virginia surfers ride Miami's easy-rolling waves. Wisconsin-born surfing pioneer Tom Blake befriended the Whitman brothers in 1933 and showed them how to build hollow paddleboards for surfing. Daytona Beach then became the main surfing area, and in 1939 was the site of the East Coast's first surf competition. Florida surfing died out during World War II, then reemerged in the mid-'50s, largely due to the efforts of the original surfing pioneers, who later formed the Daytona Beach Surfing Association in 1960, and taught hundreds of interested beachgoers how to ride. Dudley Whitman was the first Hobie Surfboards dealer on the East Coast, and began selling boards from his Daytona home in the late '50s; Daytona Beach Surf

Shop, the first retail store of its kind in the state, opened in 1961. Soldiers stationed at the Pensacola Naval Air Station meanwhile brought surfing to Florida's Gulf Coast in the early '60s, making their own boards under the "Hutson" label—the name of the local hardware store.

The Florida Surfing Association was formed in 1962, and the first annual Daytona Beach Surfing Championships were won that year by Cocoa Beach surfer and soon-to-be-infamous jewel thief Jack Murphy. The Eastern Surfing Association held its first annual Championships event at Sebastian Inlet in 1970, before moving the contest to its permanent location on North Carolina's Outer Banks. Surfing grew rapidly in Florida throughout the '60s and '70s, and the state's organized and highly competitive surf scene was immediately recognized for producing the best riders on the East Coast. Top Floridian surfers from the '60s and early '70s included Mimi Munro, Gary Propper, Mike Tabeling, Claude Codgen, and Yancy Spencer; high performers from the next generation included Greg Loehr, Jeff Crawford, Jim Cartland, Isabel McLaughlin, and Greg Mungall. The Wave Rider Magazine Florida Pro, mainland America's first world pro tour event, took place at Sebastian Inlet in 1976, and carried on through 1979; Sebastian was also the location of the United States Surfing Championships, held in 1986, 1990, and 1994. Another seven world tour events—including the Wave Wizards Pro, the Tropix Pro, and the Aloe Up Cup—were held in the state between 1983 and 1989. Pro tour competitors Matt Kechele, Charlie Kuhn, Todd Holland, and Frieda Zamba were among the top Florida riders in the '80s. "Florida waves have half the juice of California waves, and one-quarter the form," local boardmaking guru Dick Catri said in 1976, explaining why the state produces such talented surfers. "So these guys push that much harder to compensate . . . and when they finally get the good stuff, man, they're crying for it." Florida surfers continued to be a force on the pro tour in the '90s and early '00s, led by six-time world champion Kelly Slater, four-time world champion Lisa Andersen, and 2001 world champion CJ Hobgood, with support from Damien Hobgood and Cory and Shea Lopez.

Wave Rider magazine was published out of Cocoa Beach from 1975 to 1982; *Surf* magazine was headquartered in Melbourne from 1977 to 1979; *Eastern Surf Magazine* has been publishing out of Indialantic since 1991. Ron Jon Surf Shop, which opened in

Cocoa Beach in 1963, was remodeled in the early '90s into a mind-boggling 52,000-square-foot, 24-hours-a-day retail emporium, making it by far the largest shop of its kind in the world. By 2003, Florida was home to an estimated 250,000 surfers and 120 surf shops. The Floridian surf has been featured in dozens of surf movies and videos, including *The Performers* (1965), *Gone Surfin'* (1987), *Atlantic Crossing* (1989), *Kelly Slater in Black and White* (1991), and *The Green Room* (2000). *The Surfer's Guide to Florida,* by surf journalist Amy Vansant, was published in 1995. *See also* Cocoa Beach, Sebastian Inlet.

FlowRider   Brand name for a 1990-patented wave machine developed by San Diego surfer/designer Tom Lochtefeld, with help from Carl Ekstrom and Jeff Clark. The FlowRider shoots a thin sheet of water over a hard rubber hump, which directs the water up and over into a stationary wave with a riding surface, as described in a 1999 *Los Angeles Times* article, "about as big as a two-car garage." The first FlowRider opened in the Shilitterbahn Water Park in New Braunfels, Texas, in 1991. At full capacity, it cycled through 100,000 gallons of water a minute, with the resulting wave—up to six foot high—breaking into about six inches of water. The Shilitterbahn machine was at first limited to bodysurfing and bodyboarding. Small, thin, finless stand-up boards with footstraps were later designed specifically for the FlowRider by Ekstrom. By 2000 there were 25 FlowRiders in operation around the world, in Mexico, Japan, South Korea, Norway, Germany, Guam, and across the United States, mostly at waterparks, hotels, and resorts. Each FlowRider machine has adjustable rates of water flow and pressure,

FlowRider at Shilitterbahn Water Park, New Braunfels, Texas

allowing the wave to be customized. An installed FlowRider costs about $350,000; the more powerful Wave Loch model costs about $3 million.

The 1999 Swatch Wave Tour, using a semi-portable FlowRider, made stops in Munich, Germany; Florence, Italy; and Long Beach, California. It featured Kelly Slater, Rob Machado, Bruce Irons, Tom Curren, and other surf world luminaries, along with top skateboarders, snowboarders, skimboarders, and wakeboarders, all taking turns performing tricks on the transparent blue wave through which a giant Swatch logo could be read. Opinion on the FlowRider has varied. A writer for the *Surfer's Journal* magazine described it as "the most intense, 100% fun surfing binge of all time," while *Australia's Surfing Life* declared the machine to be "gimmicky, cheap, nasty [and] unfit for real surfers." The shallow water depth beneath the FlowRider's breaking wave, as well as its 30 mile per hour water flow—ocean waves travel at about 17 miles per hour—also make for punishing wipeouts. "Whenever you fall, which was often," said Bill Bryan of Laguna Beach, winner of the 1999 Swatch Wave Tour event in Munich, "you'd get sucked into the lip, fall 12 feet down into an inch of water, refract off a wall and then get sucked into a metal grill with thin rubber padding. It was brutal. I've got golf-ball-size bruises all over me." *See also* Carl Ekstrom, Tom Lochtefeld.

flying kickout   A showy and sometimes dangerous type of pullout during which the surfer aims toward the curl and ejects off the tail section while kicking the board skyward over the top of the wave; given a stiff offshore wind, the board might then fly and spin for 75 feet or more. The flying kickout was most popular during and just after the late-'60s shortboard revolution, before the introduction of the board-tethering surf leash rendered the move all but obsolete. There was a practical aspect to the flying kickout, as a surfer could get out of a tight spot that otherwise wouldn't allow an exit. But often it was performed on a macho whim, with nearby surfers diving for the bottom to avoid being impaled. In an updated version of the flying kickout, the rider remains planted to the board, rides briefly through the air, then kicks it away just before splashdown. The flying kickout is also known as a "flyaway."

foam   *See* polyurethane foam.

foam   *See* whitewater.

foil   The distribution of thickness in a surfboard from nose to tail, as viewed from the board's side. The thickest point is almost always located just forward of center, under the surfer's chest while paddling. From this area, the board usually becomes thinner in all directions—toward the nose, tail, and rails—primarily to make the board lighter and easier to turn. "Trust your eye," Australian shaper Al Byrne once said, "because good foil should look like a natural thing. If it looks good, it goes good." The term "foil" also refers to the thickness of a surfboard fin from its leading to trailing edge. *See also* rocker, volume.

foilboarding   Alternative form of surfing using a small, thin, egg-shaped foilboard (also known as an airboard) fitted on the rear underside with a narrow two-foot-long vertical aluminum column, which splits at the bottom into two sets of horizontal wings. The boot-wearing surfer clips into deck bindings and is towed in to an unbroken swell from behind a personal watercraft; at about six miles per hour, foilboard and surfer both elevate, at which point the surfer drops the tow rope and rides the swell or breaking wave virtually drag- and friction-free, connected to the surface only by the foil wings.

Foilboarding is a variation on a 1988 invention called the AirChair, a seated hydrofoil device that allows the user to float above the water while being towed from behind a boat. Hawaiian tow-surfing pioneers Laird Hamilton, Dave Kalama, Rush Randle,

Foilboarding; Laird Hamilton in Maui

and Brett Likkle began experimenting with the Air-Chair in 1997 in Maui. "Right away," Hamilton recalled, "we knew we wanted to stand up on the thing." It was Hamilton who assembled the first working model for wave-riding. He started the early prototypes (wakeboards fitted with ski boots) from the beach, using a kiteboarding harness and sail. The foilboarders quickly switched to a water start from behind a personal watercraft. In 2000, the *Surfer's Journal* magazine published an exciting and bizarre photograph spread of Hamilton levitating two feet above the water, connected to the surface only by a thin aluminum stem, with barely a ripple across the wave face behind him. Hamilton said the ultimate objective of foilboarding is to ride huge, unbroken swells in the middle of the ocean. "Can you imagine," he asked, "riding from Molokai to Oahu on one wave?" Foilboarding is seen in *Laird,* a 2001 surf video. The first commercially made foilboards came out in 2002, with a complete package—foil, boards, boots, and bindings—costing about $1,400.

Foo, Mark   High-profile big-wave rider from the North Shore of Oahu, Hawaii, whose 1994 death at Maverick's became surfing's biggest national and international news story. Foo was born (1958) in Singapore, the son of a Chinese-American photojournalist who worked for the U.S. Foreign Service. He moved with his family to Honolulu at age four, didn't learn to swim until 10, began surfing the following year, then moved to Rockville, Maryland. Foo later spent two years living with a friend in Pensacola, Florida, then reunited with his family in Honolulu; he moved to the North Shore in 1975, after graduating from high school, looking for a career as a professional surfer. Frustrated on the world pro tour—his best year-end rating was 66th in 1979—Foo diversified: he wrote articles for surf magazines, opened a North Shore bed-and-breakfast catering to surfers, and did voice-overs for surf movies and on-site announcing at surf contests. He hosted a surfing radio show, then teamed up with fellow North Shore surfer/journalist Mike Latronic to cohost a surfing cable television show called *H2O.* Meanwhile, Foo's wave-riding improved steadily. He tucked his compact 5'8", 135-pound frame into a low crouch, and dissected the powerful Hawaiian surf with tidy, efficient lines. He also worked closely with the top surf photographers, and became one of the sport's most visible figures; he made the cover of *Surfer* and *Surfing* magazines in 1978, and was often featured in surf movies, includ-

Mark Foo

ing *Fantasea* (1978), *Follow the Sun* (1982), and *Totally Committed* (1984). All of it contributed to what Foo, in his four-color glossy-stock résumé, called a "multifaceted professional profile." (In the same résumé, Foo immodestly referred to himself as "surfing's consummate living legend.") Intelligent, driven, and dependable, well versed in the language of marketing, Foo became one of the first surfers to be sponsored by a nonsurfing corporation, signing a modest deal with the Anheuser-Busch brewery in mid-1981. If Foo was at times opportunistic, even crass, he also had a great appreciation of surfing's mystery, power, and beauty. "How can you describe the feeling of looking into a 30-foot tube, like a hole in the ocean?" Foo rhetorically asked in a surf magazine article. "How do I convey the sights, sounds and sensations that just a handful of humans out of the billions of humans past, present and future will ever experience? What's it like to walk on the moon, Mr. Armstrong?"

Foo gained notice as a big-wave rider on January 18, 1985, when he paddled into the teeth of a 50-foot Waimea closeout set, and shortly after, with hundreds of people on the beach looking on, tried to ride a 30-footer. He didn't make the wave, but wrote about the experience for the surf press, and would later memorably describe the waves he'd seen that day at Waimea as belonging to "the unridden realm." A feud had meanwhile developed between Foo and Texas-born big-wave rider Ken Bradshaw, and in 1988 the two were profiled in an *Outside* magazine feature titled "The Divided Rulers of Waimea Bay." In that article, and in dozens of private and public conversations, Foo talked about the possibility of dying in big surf, telling one TV interviewer that "it would be a glamorous way to go, a great way to go; I mean, that's how I'd like to go out." Foo also acknowledged that he was an unlikely big-wave rider, as he was afraid of heights and speed, and didn't think of himself as athletically inclined. Foo was the first to ride a tri-fin surfboard at Waimea, and was the first to use a leash in big surf. In 1986, he finished runner-up to Clyde Aikau in the Quiksilver in Memory of Eddie Aikau contest at Waimea; he also competed in the 1990 Quiksilver/Aikau event.

Foo visited Maverick's for the first time on December 23, 1994, flying over from Hawaii with rival-turned-friend Ken Bradshaw, and died after wiping out on a 15-foot wave; the evidence wasn't conclusive, but he was probably driven to the bottom, where his leash or surfboard snagged on an outcrop of rock, and he drowned. Along with lengthy write-ups in the surf press, Foo's death was covered by the network news, MTV, the *New York Times* (who described him in a detailed obituary as "the Joe Montana of big waves"), the *Los Angeles Times, Outside, Rolling Stone, Spin,* and *Paris Match* magazines. Foo is the central character in the 2000-published *Maverick's: The Story of Big-Wave Surfing.* He was engaged at the time of his death. *See also* death and surfing, Maverick's.

Ford, Alexander Hume   Relentlessly energetic promoter of the Hawaiian Islands and "the art of surf-riding" in the early 20th century; founder of the Outrigger Canoe Club, surfing's first organized group. Alexander Hume Ford, born into a wealthy South Carolina plantation family, wrote for the New York daily newspapers and magazines, produced children's theater, and traveled extensively through Russia and China before settling in the newly acquired American territory of Hawaii in 1907. Ford, 39, fell in love with the islands and quickly became one of the territory's most ardent political and cultural boosters. Nothing

thrilled Ford more than the ancient Hawaiian sport of surfing, which had all but vanished during the previous century under the influence of Calvinist missionaries. Ford made himself a wooden plank board and took to the surf at Waikiki virtually the moment he arrived in Hawaii, practiced every day for four hours, and was riding alongside the native surfers three months later. When Jack London visited Honolulu in May 1907, Ford—a slight, quick-moving man, with a pointy goatee and enormous whisk-broom mustache—marched over and introduced himself, and convinced the athletically inclined writer that he had to try surfing. London's account of the experience was published a few months later in *Woman's Home Companion.* He never got to his feet and picked up a blistering sunburn for his troubles, but nonetheless experienced "ecstatic bliss at having caught [a] wave." Ford himself wrote an article on surfing for *Colliers* two years later, noting that the sport was already being exported to the mainland. "It has been done at Atlantic City, and is being taught by a Hawaiian youth [George Freeth] in southern California."

Ford helped organize the Outrigger Canoe Club in the spring of 1908, for the purpose of "reviving and preserving the ancient Hawaiian sport of surfing on boards and in outrigger canoes." The Waikiki beachfront club and its two grass-covered houses immediately became the hub of Hawaiian surfing. Its mostly white membership, however, led to the formation of a second club in 1911, Hui Nalu, consisting mainly of native-born wave-riders, including surfer and Olympic swimmer Duke Kahanamoku.

Ford never married, and died in 1945. His memorial service was held at the Outrigger Canoe Club, and he was eulogized in the *Honolulu Advertiser* as "the livest live wire of all the Pacific commonwealth." *Hawaiian Prophet,* Ford's biography, was published in 1980. *See also* Hui Nalu Club, Jack London, and Outrigger Canoe Club.

forecasting   *See* surf forecasting.

Foster, Marvin   Fearsome Hawaiian goofyfooter ace Pipeline rider and an early proponent of the lay-forward tube stance. Foster was born (1962) in Honolulu, raised in Waialua, and began surfing at age 14. He was one of the top tuberiders at Pipeline by 18, and at nearby Backdoor his compressed, square-shouldered, lay-forward body positioning allowed him to ride nearly as deep inside the tube backside as he did frontside. Foster turned pro in 1980 and was the world tour's rookie of the year; in 1983 he was runner-up in the Pro Class Trials and placed third in the Duke Kahanamoku Classic, both held at Oahu's Sunset Beach; he also won the 1984 Peru International. The heavily tattooed surfer then joined the local underworld, and in 1993 was convicted on a weapons charge and sentenced to 18 months in prison. In one of the surf world's strangest ads, beachwear giant Quiksilver bought space in *Surfer* and *Surfing* magazines to print a handwritten "message from Marvin Foster, Haleiwa State Prison," with the former pro telling young surfers that "prison's too crowded for newcomers [and] it ain't easy to do time." Foster was released in 1994, broke parole the following year, and was put on a statewide 10 MOST WANTED poster before he was caught and sent back to prison for an additional six months. Foster appeared in about 10 surf movies and videos, including *Ocean Fever* (1983), *The Performers* (1984), *Wave Warriors* (1985), and *Shock Waves* (1987).

Foster's Pro Surfing Tour   American pro surfing circuit, founded in 2002, run under the auspices of Surfing America and sponsored by Foster's brewery. Foster's Pro Surfing Tour (FPST) events are all part of the international World Qualifying Series circuit, which is the stepping stone to the World Championship Tour. The FPST was, in part, created as an alternative to the 1999-founded Professional Surfing Tour of America, which by 2001 didn't seem to be growing fast enough to attract top sponsors and surfers. The 2002 FPST consisted of fourteen events—eight in California; others in New Jersey, New York, and North Carolina, as well as Panama, Costa Rica, and Mexico—worth an aggregate of $410,000. Jesse Merle-Jones of Kauai won the men's division of the 2002 FPST; the women's division was won by 1993 world champion Pauline Menczer of Australia. Total prize money for the 2003 FPST is just over $500,000, with a minimum per-event purse of $25,000; the U.S. Open at Huntington Beach is worth $125,000.

four-fin   Surfboard design first popularized by Australian pro surfer Glen Winton in 1982, just as the tri-fin was becoming a near-universal board design standard. The four-fin (or quad) was essentially a reworked version of the twin-fin, with an additional small set of fins added just behind the standard fins. It was said to combine the maneuverability of the

twin-fin with the power and traction of the tri-fin, and a few hundred four-fin boards were sold in 1982 and 1983. But the quad, like the twin-fin, proved skittish in medium- and large-sized surf and by the mid-80s it was all but forgotten. Four-fin boards reappeared in the early '90s, as California shaper Will Jobson introduced the "twinzer"—this time with the smaller fins set ahead of the larger fins—and again in 1996 with Australian Bruce McKee's "quattro." Five-fin boards were briefly experimented with as well in 1982 and 1983. *See also* fin, single-fin, tri-fin, twin-fin.

France   The rolling and sublime French coastline is home to dozens of first-rate surf breaks, as well as Europe's oldest and most diverse surf culture. While surfing has taken root on the French Mediterranean, as well as the northwest-facing beaches along the English Channel, the majority of worthwhile French surf breaks—and virtually the entire French surf industry—is located along a 400-mile coastline in the Bay of Biscay that can be divided into three main surfing areas: 1) The long and rocky shoreline north of the Gironde River, including Brittany and the Côte de Lumiere, characterized by extreme tides and a range of temperamental reef- and beachbreaks, all of them compromised to some degree by a wave-reducing offshore continental shelf. 2) The Aquitaine coast, south of the Gironde, consisting primarily of 125 miles of sandy beaches terminating at the southern end at Hossegor, which is often cited as the world's best beachbreak. 3) The reef- and beachbreak-studded French Basque coast, just north of the Spanish border, home to the celebrated reefbreaks of Guethary and Lafitenia, as well as Biarritz, the birthplace of European surfing.

September, October, and early November are the best months for surfing on the west coast of France, as offshore winds are common, water and air temperatures are still comfortable, and North Atlantic storms—France's primary source of waves—regularly produce three- to eight-foot waves. The surf at Hossegor and the Basque coast is always bigger than that found to the north, due to an offshore trench that allows incoming swells to advance at full strength. Enormous tidal changes (up to 23 feet along the Basque coast and up to 50 feet in the northwest) make French Atlantic coast surfing a hit-or-miss proposition; excellent sandbar waves can disintegrate within the hour into a morass of riptides. Winter surfing in France is marked by dramatic weather changes

France; reef waves at Guethary

("with four seasons packed into one day," as described by California surf journalist Kevin Naughton), and waves can hit 15 feet or bigger. Summer beach conditions in the Bay of Biscay are generally hot and waveless. Average daytime air temperatures in the Basque area range from the low 50s (winter) to the mid-70s (summer); water temperatures range from the upper 40s to the low 70s. Temperatures around Brittany are a few degrees colder. French surfing hazards include a few shallow rock reefs in the north and far south, and pollution near many of the rivermouths.

The French were riding bellyboards as far back as the 1930s, but stand-up surfing wasn't introduced here until 1956, when Hollywood screenwriter Peter Viertel flew into Biarritz for the filming of *The Sun Also Rises,* spotted some likely-looking waves, and sent back to California for his Velzy-Jacobs pig model. Viertel lent his board to a few local bodysurfers, including 18-year-old Paris-born ski racer Joel de Rosnay (who became the first national French surfing champion in 1960), Jacques Rott, Georges Hennebutte, Jo Moraiz, and Bruno Reinhardt. They were soon joined by engineer Michel Barland. Hollywood actress Deborah Kerr, Viertel's wife, became the patroness of France's first surfing organization, the 1962-established Waikiki Surf Club, cofounded by Moraiz and Peruvian surfing godfather Carlos Dogny. Barland was by that time making and selling surfboards out of a machine shop in nearby Bayonne (he would later invent the computer-driven shaping machine).

The sport steadily gained popularity in the early and mid-'60s. *Surf Atlantique,* the first French-language surfing magazine, debuted in 1964, the same year de Rosnay was France's sole representative in the first World Surfing Championships, held in Sydney, Australia. Jo Moraiz Surf Shop, the first shop of its kind in France, opened in 1965.

The surf world at large paid little attention to France until the late 1960s, when two popular surf movies, *Evolution* and *Waves of Change,* both featured perfect beachbreak waves at Hossegor and La Barre, near Biarritz. (To the great dismay of locals and visiting surfers, La Barre was destroyed by a river dredging project in the early '70s.) The French International Open, the country's first major surf contest, was held at La Barre in 1968, and won by Australian teenage phenomenon Wayne Lynch. Hundreds of surfers made extended visits to France over the next few years, including surfboard shaper Mike Diffenderfer, Malibu icon Mickey Dora, and Hawaiian powerhouse Jeff Hakman. "I read all the Henry Miller novels while in France one year," British-born surf journalist Paul Holmes wistfully recalled in 1987, and defined his "romance" with France in terms of perfect empty beachbreak waves, steaming bowls of *soupe de poissons,* and cups of pitch-black coffee served at sidewalk bistros. World tour mainstays Tom Curren and Gary Elkerton both married French women in the '80s and moved to the southern Bay of Biscay. French-born surfers, despite a steady flow of high-quality waves, have meanwhile showed little interest in surfing as a career. Gerard Dabbadie, 1975 European surfing champion, was the top French surfer of his generation; handsome blond-haired Thierry Domenech was the country's best, and best-known, rider from the mid-'80s to the mid-'90s. Top present-day French surfers include Didier Piter, Mikael Picon, Frederik Robin, and Christian "Che" Guevara. Biarritz-based Sylvain Cazenave has meanwhile been one of international surfing's top photographers since the late '80s.

As of 2003, France was home to about 200 surf shops, 100 surf schools, 50 surf clubs, 80,000 surfers (most of whom only surf in the warmer months of summer and fall), four French-language surf magazines (*Surf Session, Surf Trip, Surf Europe,* and a licensed version of the *Surfer's Journal*), and six international contests, including the popular Biarritz Surf Festival (a longboard event) and a World Championship Tour event. The World Amateur Surfing Championships were held in France in 1980 and 1992. Quiksilver, Rip

Curl, Billabong, and O'Neill are among the international surf companies with regional headquarters in or near Biarritz, along with domestic beachwear giant Oxbow. In early 2003, the oil tanker *Prestige* broke apart and sank off the Spanish coast, spilling 70,000 tons of heavy fuel. Most of the Atlantic-facing French coast was closed to surfing. *Guidebook on the French Coast: Surf and Beaches* was published in 1979; the French surf is also featured in both *The Stormrider Guide Europe* (1998) and *The World Stormrider Guide* (2001). *See also* Biarritz, Hossegor.

Frankenreiter, Donavan   Image-conscious regular-footer from San Juan Capistrano, California; one of the world's busiest "photo-trip" surfers in the 1990s. Frankenreiter was born (1972) in Downey, California, raised in Mission Viejo, and began surfing in 1982 in San Clemente. He won the juniors division of the 1988 National Scholastic Surfing Association Nationals, then turned pro at age 16, at which point he was regarded as one of America's fastest and most style-conscious young surfers. As a pro he chose to travel rather than compete, and surf magazines featured Frankenreiter riding in Chile, Iceland, and Fiji, among other exotic destinations. He became obsessed with '70s fashion and culture, dressing in beads and bell-bottoms, and riding cast-off single-fin surfboards. He also played guitar in Sunchild, a 1992-formed retro rock band that opened for aging '70s acts like Peter Frampton, the Doobie Brothers, and Ted Nugent. The lanky and likable Frankenreiter has appeared in more than two dozen surf videos, including *In the Wind* (1990), *Focus* (1994), *Sik Joy* (1995), and *Pickled* (2001).

freak set   *See* clean-up set.

Free Ride   Handsome era-defining surf movie, first released in 1977, produced by California filmmaker Bill Delaney; a showcase for pro surfers Shaun Tomson, Mark Richards, and Wayne Bartholomew, as well as water photographer Dan Merkel; often referred to as the "last great surf movie." *Free Ride* has long been regarded as the marker for a surf world generational change that saw a young, aggressive group of Australians and South Africans forge ahead of the long-established Hawaiians.

Delaney, a 27-year-old Brooks Institute of Photography dropout, began making *Free Ride* in early 1975, filming in Australia, Indonesia, and California. It was his first movie. Delaney wisely hired Dan Merkel,

Surfing magazine's top photographer, to film slow-motion action footage from the water during the Hawaiian winter of 1975–76. Merkel had never before shot movie film, but was known as an obsessively hard worker and had great rapport with the surfers. Using a cumbersome 21-pound high-speed camera, capable of shooting at 200 frames per second, Merkel positioned himself deep inside the tube as surfers rode past, and the footage he produced was crystalline, well-framed, and tighter on the action than anything yet seen in a surf movie. Delaney meanwhile shot from land, and focused on the right surfers: Tomson, Richards, and Bartholomew all went on to win world titles before the decade ended. Special attention was given to Bartholomew, as Delaney showed the frenetic but likable Australian on the soccer field, as well as playing pinball, skateboarding, and relaxing in the squalor of his Hawaiian rental unit between surf sessions. Tomson and Richards, however, are *Free Ride*'s standout surfers, Tomson with his newly developed serpentine tuberiding style and Richards with his acrobatic turns. The often-fickle Hawaiian surf was big, smooth, and sunny for days at a time during the *Free Ride* shoot.

In postproduction throughout 1976, Delaney assembled a versatile and largely bootlegged soundtrack that included Pablo Cruise and Joan Armatrading, then hired Hollywood actor Jan-Michael Vincent to do the narration—which unfortunately came out terse and humorless and is the film's weakest point. *Free Ride* cost $70,000, costly for a surf film of the period; it debuted in Honolulu in early 1977. *Surfing* magazine called it "a finely cut and polished diamond," and for the next few months it played to full houses in surf cities worldwide. Revised and updated versions of the film came out in 1978 (*Free Ride: Take Two*) and 1983 (*Free Ride: The Final Edition*). A conventional surf movie in most respects—no plot, lots of Hawaiian footage—*Free Ride* nonetheless beautifully captured a transforming era in the sport's history.

Free Ride has never been released on video, in part because the music rights were never cleared and also because Delaney believes the film should be seen in a theater and not on a television screen. The film title itself has long been part of the surfing lexicon, as surfers make reference to the "Free Ride era" with the film's stars and costars grouped together as the "Free Ride generation." *See also* Bill Delaney, surf movies.

freeboarding   *See* wake surfing.

Freefall

freefall   Thrilling and sometimes dangerous wave-riding situation, sometimes controlled, often not, where surfer and surfboard both disconnect from the upper reaches of a steep wave and drop vertically toward the trough. Freefalls happen often during last-second takeoffs, particularly at tubing breaks like Pipeline in Hawaii. Professional surfers can freefall by design, even in huge surf; beginning and intermediate surfers freefall by mistake for the most part, and invariably wipe out. *See also* air-drop, late takeoff.

Freeman, Jim   Surf filmmaker from Santa Ana, California; cocreator along with Greg MacGillivray of the 1972 surf movie classic *Five Summer Stories.* Freeman was born (1944) and raised in Santa Ana. *Let There Be Surf,* his debut film, was released in 1963; over the next two years he produced *Outside the Third Dimension* (surfing's only 3-D movie) and *The Glass Wall.* He was also cohost for the 1964 Los Angeles–based *Surf's Up* TV show. Freeman was 22 in 1966 when he met Greg MacGillivray, another Orange County surf filmmaker, and formed what would be one of surfing's best-matched and most successful partnerships. While both were meticulous and hardworking, the easygoing Freeman generally served as the team's technical expert, while MacGillivray was the creative force. They made three full-length surf films—*Free and Easy* (1967), *Waves of Change* (1970; rereleased in 35-millimeter the following year as *The Sunshine Sea*), and *Five Summer Stories*—along with a number of shorts, including *Moods of Surfing* (1967),

The Loser (1968), and *Who's Best?* (1969). They also filmed the 1967 and 1968 Duke Kahanamoku Invitational contests for ABC-TV.

The MacGillivray-Freeman team began working in Hollywood in the early '70s, with Freeman establishing himself as an aerial-shot expert in movies such as *Jonathan Livingston Seagull* (1973) and *The Towering Inferno* (1974). *To Fly!,* MacGillivray-Freeman's 1976 IMAX film, was the first movie shown in the just-opened National Air and Space Museum in Washington, D.C. On the day *To Fly!* debuted, Freeman, 32, was killed in a helicopter crash in the Sierra Nevada, near Bishop, California. Film critic Charles Champlin, in a eulogy for the *Los Angeles Times,* wrote, "It is hard to imagine anyone cramming more excitement and achievement into 32 years." MacGillivray continued to make movies under the MacGillivray-Freeman imprimatur. Freeman was inducted into the Huntington Beach Surfing Walk of Fame in 2000. *See also* Five Summer Stories.

Freeth, George   Colonizing surfer from Honolulu, Hawaii; referred to in his time as the first expert Caucasian surfer, and long regarded as the first surfer in mainland America after his 1907 wave-riding demonstrations in Southern California. Although it was later proven that the California surf had been ridden as far back as 1885, it was Freeth, with help from fellow Hawaiian surfer Duke Kahanamoku, who established the sport in the continental United States. Freeth was born (1883) in Honolulu to an Irish sea captain father and a half-Polynesian mother. Although one-quarter Hawaiian, Freeth was blue-eyed and relatively fair-skinned, and regarded as *haole,* or white. He probably began surfing just before the turn of the century, after a decades-long period of repressive Calvinist missionary influence in Hawaii that had nearly extinguished the sport. Freeth's contribution to surfing's revival began early, as he was one of the first of the new generation to ride in a standing position rather than prone. Around 1905, Freeth was the first—or among the first—to angle across the wave rather than head straight for shore.

In the summer of 1907, Freeth gave a surfing lesson to American novelist Jack London, who was visiting Hawaii for the first time. Writing for *Woman's Home Companion* magazine, London described his surf instructor as a "sea-god . . . calm and superb." The near-silent Freeth packed up his eight-foot redwood board and sailed to San Francisco later that year, with the idea of popularizing the sport on the mainland. (It was

George Freeth, Redondo Beach, circa 1912

long believed that Freeth was brought to California by hotelier/railroad executive Henry Huntington and hired to ride waves at Redondo Beach as an attraction for Huntington's new southbound Red Car trolley line. Recent studies suggest that Freeth sailed to the mainland on his own accord.) The earliest printed reference to Freeth surfing in California came in October 1907, when he took to the waves at Venice Beach. In July of the following year he gave a well-attended surfing demonstration at the Venice breakwater; in the summer of 1909 he gave demonstrations at Redondo Beach for the opening of the Henry Huntington–owned Redondo Plunge. Freeth's performances often drew hundreds of spectators. More important for American surfing, he taught dozens of school-age boys how to ride waves and make solid-wood plank surfboards, and charted new surf breaks in Ventura, Palos Verdes, Huntington Beach, and San Diego. He also helped bring the Hawaiian swim team to California for the first time; one of the visiting swimmers was surfing patriarch Duke Kahanamoku, who was likely introduced to California surfing by Freeth.

Freeth became the state's first professional lifeguard in 1907, and was lauded in the *Los Angeles Times* the following year for helping to rescue 11 Japanese fishermen in Venice Beach during heavy surf; at one point he climbed aboard a small fishing boat and, as the *Times* reported, "guided the boat as if it was a surf-board through the giant breakers." Freeth later trained Olympic-bound swimmers and divers.

Little is known about Freeth's character or personality, but he seemed to have lived a somewhat quiet and isolated existence, and in 1919—unmar-

ried, rooming in a San Diego hotel—he died in the great flu epidemic that swept across much of the world. He was 35. Freeth was nominated to the International Surfing Hall of Fame in 1991; a bronze bust of Freeth is located at the foot of the Redondo Pier.

French Polynesia   French-held territory in the balmy South Pacific Ocean, located north of the Tropic of Capricorn and roughly midway between Australia and South America, composed of more than 120 islands scattered across an area about the size of Western Europe. Islands in French Polynesia are divided into five main groups: the Society Islands (including Tahiti) and the Marquesas to the northeast, the Tuamotus to the east, the Australs to the south, and the Gambier Islands to the southeast. The same North Pacific–generated swells that produce giant waves in Hawaii arrive in French Polynesia three or four days later, at about half the size. April through October sees bigger, more consistent surf, as storms off New Zealand and Antarctica frequently push swell up from the south and southwest. Waves in French Polynesia are typically hollow and powerful, and break in shallow water over coral reefs. Water and air temperatures are sublimely tropical.

French, Randy   Surfboard shaper and manufacturer from Santa Cruz, California; founder in 1992 of Surftech, a company specializing in replicable molded/composite-laminate boards. French was born (1952) and raised in San Diego, California, began surfing at age 10, not long after moving with his family to Santa Cruz, and in the late '60s started making boards for himself and a few friends. In 1978, he launched SeaTrend, originally to produce the AquaToy, a molded Styrofoam beginner board that went nowhere in the marketplace. SeaTrend became a production center for a number of Santa Cruz board-makers, then in 1984 branched into sailboard construction. The surfing industry had dabbled with molded boards over the previous twenty-five years, but stuck almost exclusively with a board-making process developed in the late '50s: hand-shaped polyurethane foam wrapped in a layer of resin-saturated fiberglass. Not so with sailboard manufacturers, who profited greatly from molding technology and new materials. French sold SeaTrend in 1988 and four years later founded Surftech, with the idea that the latest molding systems—which could now make a board both lighter and stronger than the traditional foam-and-resin process—would lead to commercial success. He enlisted the help of top board-shapers such as Dale Velzy, Donald Takayama, Renolds Yater, and Glenn Minami, slowly built a line of both longboards and shortboards, moved his production facilities to Thailand (a first for the surfboard industry), and, by the turn of the decade, had established Surftech as one of the industry's strongest and richest companies. Meanwhile, fairly or not, French has been lambasted by some in the board-making industry for using Third World production facilities and for producing boards that will almost certainly bring about a decline in business for the local corner-store shaper. *See also* molded surfboards

Froiseth, Wally   Prototype big-wave rider from Honolulu, Hawaii; an original hot curl surfer of the late 1930s, and one of the early surf explorers on the west and north shores of Oahu. Froiseth was born (1919) in Los Angeles, spent his early years living with his grandmother in Del Paso Heights, Sacramento, and moved with his family to Honolulu in 1925. He began surfing at age eight, renting a board for 25 cents a day from a beachfront vendor in Waikiki; he was later informally mentored by master surf innovator Tom Blake. Soon Froiseth was riding with John Kelly and Fran Heath, two other local *haole* (Caucasian) surfers. In 1937, after a frustrating morning when their finless redwood plank surfboards kept "sliding ass"—the rear section refusing to hold traction on the wave face—the three surfers returned to Kelly's house where Kelly, using an ax and drawknife, streamlined the tail section of Heath's board. The new design allowed them to hold a tighter angle across the wave face, which in turn enabled them to ride larger waves. It was Froiseth who noted that the narrow-tailed board could "really get you in the hot curl," and the name stuck. The outline of the hot curl was the basis for the big-wave gun board.

Froiseth, Kelly, and a few other surfers drove out to the west side of the island in the fall of 1937 and discovered waves at the mouth of Makaha Valley; for almost 20 years, Makaha would be the big-wave surfing crucible, while the quiet and methodical Froiseth earned a reputation as the island's most dedicated big-wave rider. (Froiseth, Kelly, and Heath began making occasional day trips to the North Shore in the late '30s, but all of them preferred Makaha.) In 1942, Froiseth married Pearl Downing, aunt to future big-wave great George Downing; the following summer, the 13-year-old Downing came to live with Froiseth, who became the boy's surrogate father.

Froiseth and Downing became the first to ride Laniakea on the North Shore in 1946; the following year they pioneered Honolua Bay on Maui; in 1948, along with Russ Takaki, they sailed to the mainland and toured through Southern California with their hot curls. Froiseth worked as a tugboat operator during World War II, became a fireman after the war (eventually rising to chief of the Pearl Harbor Fire Department), then worked as a pilot boat operator.

The Makaha International surf contest, founded in 1954 and originally cosponsored by the Waikiki Surf Club, of which Froiseth was a member, was the sport's most prestigious event in the '50s and early '60s; Froiseth won the 1959 Makaha at age 39. The following year he became the Makaha contest director, and ran the event until its demise in 1971. He was also the head judge for the Duke Kahanamoku Invitational in 1965 and 1966 and a judge for the 1966 World Surfing Championships. Throughout his adult life, Froiseth built, sailed, and paddled all manner of canoes and catamarans. Froiseth has been married twice and has six children. *See also* hot curl board, Makaha International Surfing Championships.

frontside   A riding stance where the toes, kneecaps, chest, and face—the surfer's front side—are facing the wave. After standing, the surfer will either angle into a frontside or backside ride; backside means the heels, butt, and back are facing the wave. Surfers are generally more comfortable riding frontside, just as tennis players are more comfortable hitting forehand. "Forehand" is also a surf world synonym for "frontside." *See also* backside.

Frye, Harry "Skip"   Smooth, quiet, refined surfer and surfboard shaper from San Diego, California; competitor in the World Surfing Championships in 1966 and 1968; leader of the late-'60s shortboard revolution in California; and a master of the undervalued art of trim—finding and holding a pure angle in the fastest part of the wave. "He's something of a minimalist," surf journalist Chris Ahrens wrote in 1992, "all function, flow and speed." Frye was born (1941) in San Diego, the son of a navy aircraft mechanic, raised in East Mission Bay, and began surfing at age 16 after moving with his family to the north San Diego suburb of Pacific Beach. By the mid-'60s the shy but focused Frye had become one of California's best competitors. He finished third in the 1965 Tom Morey Invitational, and was runner-up in both the 1965 and 1967 United States Surfing Association's

Skip Frye

year-end standings; he placed second in the 1966 U.S. Pro Championships, won the 1967 Laguna Masters, and placed third in the United States Surfing Championships. Frye was in many respects the model California surfer, with combed-back white-blond hair, a friendly grin, and a pair of black Ray-Ban sunglasses.

Frye began shaping surfboards in 1962, and within two years was working for San Diego's Gordon & Smith Surfboards. In 1966, G&S introduced the Skip Frye signature model. Frye was riding a 9′6″ board in late 1967 when he traveled to Australia with the Windansea Surf Club—a group based in nearby La Jolla, whose membership included most of the top California surfers of the day—for an American versus Australia team contest. Once in Sydney, Frye and the rest of the Americans were astounded to find the Australian surfers riding wide-backed eight-foot boards ("like something out of *Star Wars*," Frye later recalled) that literally turned circles around the longboard-riding California surfers. It was the beginning of the shortboard revolution, and back in California a few weeks later, Frye was the first West Coast shaper to build the new Australian-invented vee-bottom design. Frye began working under his own label in 1976, specializing in boards that were slightly longer, wider,

and thinner than those in use across the state, and in 1990 he opened a surfing factory-retail outlet called Harry's. Frye has shaped boards for 1995 world champion runner-up Rob Machado and 1991 world champion runner-up Brad Gerlach, among other surfers. Frye himself, in the early '90s, began to use a 12-foot surfboard as he invented a kind of cross-country form of surfing, riding each wave as long as possible, then paddling to an adjacent surf break, riding, and moving on to another spot—often stringing together as many as seven different breaks, and once riding a dozen in a single go.

Though Frye was seen on ABC's *Wide World of Sports* in 1965, when he finished runner-up in the slalom division of the International Skateboard Championships, he was missing almost completely from '60s-era surf movies, apart from a lengthy appearance in 1969's *The Fantastic Plastic Machine*. He was later featured in a number of longboard surf videos, including *On Safari to Stay* (1992), *Blazing Longboards* (1994), and *The Seedling* (2000), as well as *Liquid Stage: The Lure of Surfing* (1995), a PBS-aired documentary. Frye was nominated to the International Surfing Hall of Fame in 1991, and in 2000 he won the masters division of the 2000 *Longboard* Magazine Readers Poll. Frye's wife, the former Donna Sarbis, won the 2001 Surf Industry Manufacturers Association Environmentalist of the Year Award, and that same year was elected to a San Diego city council seat. Frye has been married twice and has three children.

fullsuit   Single-piece wetsuit covering everything except the head, feet, and hands. Surfers in the early 1960s began to guard against cold water by layering a front-zip wetsuit jacket over a torso-and-legs-covering "long john"; by 1969 many surfers instead used a zipperless long-sleeve top worn underneath the long john. These two-piece solutions were warm, but restrictive. The O'Neill Supersuit, introduced in 1970, was the first marketed fullsuit. First-generation fullsuits had either a front zipper or shoulder-to-shoulder zipper; by the mid-'70s, most fullsuits had a back zipper; the zipperless fullsuit became popular in the mid-'90s, as did the back-located "short zip." Nearly all fullsuits feature a combination of neoprene thickness—usually two, three, or four millimeters—with the thicker rubber used for the torso. The cold-water hooded fullsuit has an attached neoprene head piece. *See also* wetsuit.

funboard   *See* egg, hybrid.

G

Gabaldon, Nick America's first African American surfer, Gabaldon taught himself how to ride waves in the late 1940s from inside a demarcated shoreline area of Santa Monica, California, informally known as "Negro Beach." One morning, probably in the summer of 1949, Gabaldon arrived at Malibu for the first time after paddling 12 miles up the coast from Santa Monica. That afternoon he paddled back. He followed the same route almost daily for the next few weeks—he didn't own a car—before some of the local surfers began driving him to and from the break. On June 9, 1951, at Malibu, during an eight-foot south swell, the 20-year-old Gabaldon rode a wave long past the normal kick-out zone and was killed after running into the Pier. He was a second-year student at Santa Monica City College, and one week before his death had submitted to the college literary magazine a poem titled "Lost Lives," which included the lines: "The sea vindictive, with waves so high / For men to battle and still they die." *See also* racism and surfing.

Gabon Humid and heavily forested oil-rich country straddling the equator on the west coast of Africa; filled with rolling, easy-to-ride surf. Although Gabon has 600 miles of tropical coastline, most of its dozen-or-so charted surf breaks are located between the capital city of Libreville, just a few miles north of the equator, and the Cap Lopez peninsula, 100 miles to the south. Because the peninsula juts into deeper water, the surf here is more powerful then anywhere else on the Gabonese coast, and the rights at Cap Lopez, Gabon's most popular break, can tube and spit. Prime surf season here is brief, lasting from July to August, when regular three- to four-foot surf is sometimes broken up by an eight-foot swell. The long off-season has smaller waves. Daytime temperatures range from 75 to 95 degrees, with humidity at 90 to 100 percent for eight months of the year. Water temperatures are constantly in the low 80s. Sharks are plentiful, but no attacks have yet been reported; malaria is a far greater danger for visiting surfers,

along with a shortage of medical facilities. Gabon is a French-speaking country, and many of its roughly 100 surfers are French expatriates.

Galápagos Islands Volcanic island chain, a province of Ecuador, composed of 15 main islands and hundreds of tiny islets; located roughly 600 miles west of Ecuador. While the Galápagos' wildly diverse flora and fauna have for centuries been a source of wonder to naturalists, scientists, botanists, and tourists, surfers have found the island-fringing surf to be less interesting—good on occasion, but generally small to midsize, inconsistent, and nothing like the world-class waves of Tahiti, Fiji, Hawaii, and nearly all other tropical Pacific island groups. The Galápagos receive surf from the south, west, and northwest, but swells generally have to travel more than 3,000 miles to reach this equatorial corner of the world, and are often depleted upon arrival. Flat spells are common, but three- to six-foot surf hits the Galápagos with some regularity throughout the year. The islands are geologicaly new and thus still rough-edged; swirls and eddies are common in the wave zone, as the reefs have yet to be smoothed out by a few millennia of crashing surf. Ocean temperatures here are affected by the Antarctica-fed Humboldt Current, and colder than anywhere else on the equator, ranging from 64 to 75 degrees. Air temperatures are also reasonably cool, between the mid-60s and mid-80s, and rainfall is light. The prevailing wind is from the south-southeast, which means most of the best breaks are found on north-facing shores. Some of the prime surf spots in the Galápagos—including the left-breaking El Canyon and the hollow rights of Carola—are located in and around the administrative capital city of Puerto Baquerizo on the island of San Cristóbal.

California surfer Jim Kalseth rode waves off Santa Cruz Island in 1962, while on a semester at sea with the California Maritime Academy, and traveling surfers trickled in throughout the '60s and '70s. But the Galápagos didn't come to the attention of the surfing world until 1981, when *Surfer* magazine published an eight-page color article featuring two Florida surfers riding lovely transparent waves off Santa Cruz and San Cristóbal Islands. Surfers, like all visitors to the Galápagos, are frequently awestruck by the islands' animal population, which includes penguins, 500-pound turtles ("Galápagos" is Spanish for turtles), four-foot-long iguanas, blue-footed boobies, and scarlet crabs.

A few dozen Galápagos natives were surfing by 2003, but crowds have never been a problem, and the island chain as yet has no surf industry. Territorial sea lions can be a worry, along with sun exposure and craggy reefs. Visiting surfers generally stay in Baquerizo, or hire one of a small number of surf charter boats. Virtually the entire Galápagos chain is a marine refuge, and access to many breaks—by land or water—is either restricted or prohibited. The Galápagos surf is featured in a small number of surf videos, including *Surf Addicts* (1997) and *Contours* (2002).

games/toys and surfing   Surfing games and toys have been a small, sometimes fun, and generally unprofitable part of the sport since 1962, with the introduction of Ride the Surf, a dice-and-board game illustrated by "Murphy" cartoon-strip creator Rick Griffin. Board games to follow included Surf's Up (introduced in 1979), Surf Trip (1989), and Tubular Pursuit (1998). Perhaps the best of the group was 1982's The Game of Surfing, where each player begins as a bewildered Iowa tourist at Goonlight Beach, then races to become the first Super Kahuna, dodging sharks, closeout waves, and unruly locals, and advancing with TV appearances, tuberides, and competition wins. Nonboard surfing games include the marble-based Shoot the Curl (1989); Mattel's Wipe-Out (1993), with each player racing his "awesome surfin' dude" statuette down a plastic tower just ahead of a slow-moving "wave" of viscous green slime; and Surf Bored (1998), a cheekily illustrated Australian-produced card game based on the pro surfing tour, with contestants trying to steal sponsorships from each other and rack up contest wins.

The Japanese-produced Surferboy (1982) was the first video surfing game, a handheld two-button device, with points scored as the player maneuvers an LCD-screen surfer past sharks, rocks, and other surfers. The joystick-controlled Surfer Video Game (1985), made in California, sold as a diskette for the Commodore 64 PC, and featured 16 different wave conditions and 10 levels of difficulty. The Waterless Surfing Machine (1986) used the same programming and graphics as Surfer Video, but the player controlled the on-screen rider by actually maneuvering a surfboard bolted to a floor-mounted sensor device. (A Queensland surfer developed a mechanical surfboard two years later, similar to the mechanical bull made popular in the 1980 film *Urban Cowboy*; world pro tour champion Tom Curren was unable to stay atop the board for more than 18 seconds.) SurfRiders (1998), made for Sony PlayStation and Nintendo 64, was the first modern surf video game; five more were released in the early '00s: Surfing H30 (for Sony PlayStation 2), Championship Surfer (by Mattel, for Sega Dreamcast, Sony PlayStation, and Windows), TransWorld Surf 2001 (for Microsoft's X-Box, PlayStation 2, and Nintendo GameCube), Kelly Slater's Pro Surfer (PlayStation 2 and an X-Box version developed by the same company that produced the best-selling Tony Hawk's Pro Skater series), and Sunny Garcia Surfing (PlayStation 2). In TransWorld Surf 2001, described in a *Los Angeles Times* review as "the first surfing game that is actually fun to play," each contestant not only has to complete a virtual photo shoot before going surfing, but has to monitor his or her "karma" gauge—if it gets too low, the surfer becomes unwelcome at new beaches. Meanwhile, the Topological Slide, the first virtual reality "surfing experience," was introduced in Canada in 1993: an art exhibit of sorts rather than a game, the "surfer" wore an enclosed wire-connected helmet and stood on a motion-sensor disk, then "rode" across an endless wave-shaped field made up of color-shaded polygons.

Kuta Brown, the first scale-model remote-control surfer, was introduced in 1991. "Recommended for use in waves from one inch to two feet," the packaging text instructed. "In four-foot-or-bigger surf, Kuta Brown doesn't carve as well, and you should be out surfing anyway." At least three other remote-control surfers were manufactured over the next 10 years, including Radio Shack's Surf Monster, released in 2001.

Surf magazines have over the years occasionally published surfing crossword puzzles and surf trivia quizzes. "Doctor Dume's Annual Trivia Quiz," a *Surfer* feature from 1986 to 1990, rewarded surf knowledge—but only to a point. In the answer box at the end of the 1989 Dr. Dume quiz, a 75 score is "Right where you want to be. You surf and you know a little trivia." A perfect 100 is rated as "Disgusting. Trivia is your life; your life is trivial."

Garcia, Vincent "Sunny"   Surly Hawaiian power surfer from Waianae, Oahu; 2000 world champion and five-time winner of the Triple Crown; described by surf journalist Derek Hynd as "a modern-day Cassius Clay . . . a slick, black nightmare come to whup some ass." Garcia was born (1970) in Honolulu, the son of an auto mechanic father and housekeeper mother, and raised in the rough-and-tumble westside town of Waianae. He began surfing at age seven, won the boys' division of the 1984 United States Surfing Championships, then dropped out of ninth grade to turn pro. Two years later, at age 17, he was the 17th-ranked surfer in the world, and already regarded as one of the sport's great stylists—influenced primarily by Hawaiian great Dane Kealoha—as well as an instant contender for the pro tour title. The following year Garcia developed a cocaine habit, lost 20 pounds, and rolled his brand-new Pontiac Trans Am. "In one year," *Surfer* magazine wrote, "Garcia has self-destructed. The gift he once had is a strewn memory."

Garcia quit drugs just prior to the 1989 competition season, and began a slow but steady march up the ratings, finishing 10th in 1990, sixth in 1991, and third in 1992, by which time he was being described as the last of the old school power surfers. Floridian Kelly Slater had just won the first of his six world titles, and was heading up a group of young surfers who were reinventing the high-performance standard aerials and tailslides. Garcia continued to rely on a simple but devastatingly effective set of power turns. He also became the world's most elegant tuberider, using a longer and thicker board at places like Backdoor Pipeline in Hawaii, where he often assumed a tranquil parade-rest stance as the wave whirled and exploded around him. Slater was justly regarded as the best all-around surfer in the world, but Garcia was nearly untouchable in the powerful Hawaiian waves, winning the Triple Crown a record five times (1992, 1993, 1994, 1999, and 2000), and in 1993 he finished ahead of Slater to win the *Australia's Surfing Life* Magazine Peer Poll Awards. He meanwhile continued to be a force on the pro tour, finishing third from 1994 to 1996, seventh in 1997, and sixth in 1998 and 1999.

Garcia also developed a reputation for being outspoken and difficult. In 1993 he got into a fistfight with fellow Hawaiian pro and world champion Derek Ho; in 1995 he threw a muffin at a panel of contest judges in response to a decision that went against him. He didn't like the French leg of the world tour

Sunny Garcia

because "I hate the food and the waves suck," and responded to a nonenthusiastic notice in the surf press by calling the journalist "a fag." In *The Billabong Challenge,* a video documentary of the 1995 contest of the same name, Garcia gazes out to a lineup of beautiful waves in Western Australia, and says, "I don't care how good this looks, it's shit."

An extra-fit Garcia (5'10", 180 pounds) won the first two contests on the 2000 tour, and held on to the ratings lead through the remaining nine events to easily win the championship, an achievement only slightly compromised by the fact that Kelly Slater had taken the year off. The 30-year-old Garcia was by then the world tour's aggregate prize-money leader, having earned $826,330 over his 15-year pro career, and was the only male pro surfer to finish in the top 10 for 11 consecutive years. He was also elected president of the World Professional Surfers, a 2000-formed union group for pro tour competitors; threatening a "surf stoppage," Garcia was able to help raise the minimum per-event men's division prize-money purse, beginning in 2001, from $135,600 to $250,000. His year-end rating began to slip in the early '00s, as he finished #13 in 2001, and #23 in 2002.

One of the sport's most filmed and photographed surfers, Garcia has appeared in more than 75 surf movies and videos, including *Filthy Habits* (1987), *Rolling Thunder* (1991), *Focus* (1994), and *Nine Lives* (1999). *Sunny Daze: A West Side Story,* a sponsor-funded surf video documentary, was released in 2000. Sunny Garcia Surfing, a video game for Sony's PlayStation 2, was released in 2001. Garcia has been married twice, and has three children. His second wife is Raina Cabell, daughter of 1960s surf hero Joey Cabell. Garcia has lived in Kauai since 1999.

George, Matt Grandiloquent California-based surf journalist/screenwriter/actor; a longtime contributor to both *Surfer* and *Surfing* magazines; coauthor and costar in the 1998 big-wave drama *In God's Hands.* George was born (1958) in Bath, Maine, the son of a navy fighter pilot, and was raised on military bases in France, Hawaii, and the San Francisco Bay Area. He began surfing in Waikiki in 1967, competed professionally in the late '70s and early '80s, and was first published in 1983 in *Surfer* magazine. Matt and older brother Sam (also a loquacious pro surfer/writer) were often presented in tandem: "The Brothers George: Vocal Talent," was the title of a short 1981 *Surfing* magazine profile.

Although George wrote for *Surfing* magazine from late 1995 to mid-1997, the vast majority of his surfing work has been published in *Surfer,* where he's specialized in dramatically rendered profiles, including "The Private World of Tom Curren" (1985), "Cheyne Horan's Rainbow Bridge" (1988), and "The Seduction of Kelly Slater" (1989). George's portraiture photography often accompanied his articles. He also hosted *Surfer* magazine's ESPN cable television series in 1986 and 1987, and narrated more than a half-dozen surf movies and videos, including *Amazing Surf Stories* (1986) and *Gone Surfin'* (1987). *In God's Hands,* produced by TriStar, cost $10 million and featured some riveting surf sequences, but was lambasted by critics and surfers alike, and pulled from its limited-theater run after two weeks. George was also creator, cowriter, and supporting actor for NBC's *Wind on Water,* a one-hour drama series starring Bo Derek as the matriarch of a Big Island ranch and the mother of two surfing sons; *Water* debuted in 1998 and was canceled after just two episodes; "dreadful, tedious and humorless" was the Primetime.com online review summary.

George's nonsurfing life has been every bit as dramatic as his scripts and articles: he worked as a Karl Lagerfeld model, trained as a Navy SEAL, fought in Golden Gloves boxing tournaments, and twice climbed Mount Kilimanjaro. *See also* In God's Hands.

George, Sam Passionate, prolix surf journalist from San Clemente, California; a ranking surf magazine editor since the mid-1980s. George was born (1956) in Bethesda, Maryland, the son of a naval offi-

cer; he moved often as a child, began surfing at Waikiki in 1967, was California's top-ranked men's division amateur surfer in 1978, and surfed as a professional—along with younger brother Matt—in the early 1980s. He began publishing articles in *Surfing* magazine in 1982, and later that year was listed on the masthead as a contributing editor; from 1985 to 1993 he was a senior editor. George did dozens of interviews for the magazine's "Conversations" column, but was better known for his short, funny, well-crafted, and often lightly exasperated first-person articles on virtually any surf-related topic, from tandem surfing to surf art to localism to the surfwear industry.

George began writing longer feature articles after becoming associate editor at *Surfer* magazine in 1995 (he was promoted to editor in 2000), including "Soul Search," a nuanced critique of the theory and practice of soul surfing, and "Is Surfing Hip?", a limber essay in which George affirms surfing's prominence in the trendy new world of "extreme" sports. "Hip is where you live," he noted. "It's something you do, someone you are. It's got to make someone else want to be like you, to wonder about what you know, and why they don't know." As commodified as it's become, George finished, surfing nonetheless remains "hipper than hip." He had meanwhile earned a reputation as one of the world's best-traveled surfers, having ridden waves in Ghana, the Andaman Islands, Rapa Nui (Easter Island), Mozambique, El Salvador, Scotland, Guam, and dozens of other exotic locations.

George has contributed articles to *Outside* and *Men's Health,* and worked on more than a half-dozen books (as primary writer, contributing writer, or editor), including *Surfing: A Way of Life* (1992), *Surfing* (1994), *Tom Blake: Surfing 1922–1932* (1999), and *The Perfect Day: 40 Years of Surfer Magazine* (2001). George has narrated dozens of surf movies, videos, and documentaries, including *Shock Waves* (1987), and was himself featured in the PBS-aired documentary *Liquid Stage: The Lure of Surfing* (1995). He moonlighted in 2000 and 2001 as editor for *Surf News* magazine, a tabloid-style monthly, often publishing articles under the names Rod Cox and Gina Makin. George has been married three times.

Georgia Most of Georgia's 100-mile island- and marsh-lined coast is protected as a National Wildlife Refuge, meaning the beaches here are quiet, peaceful, and undeveloped. The surf for the most part doesn't disturb the tranquillity, as it tends to be small and inconsistent. Because the state is fronted by a continental shelf extending about 60 miles out to sea, incoming waves lose much of their power before hitting the beach. Swells tend to arrive and depart quickly, and an above-average tidal range allows for the outgoing tide to further suck the life out of whatever surf is available. The North Atlantic tropical hurricane season, from late summer to early fall, provides Georgia with its most dependable waves; winter and spring storms can also produce surf. Six-foot waves here are rare; eight-foot waves are almost unheard of. Daytime winter air temperatures average about 65, while the water drops down to the low 50s; by May the water hits 70, and in August it can go beyond 80. Summers on the Georgia coast are for the most part intolerably hot, humid, waveless, and bug-filled. Tybee Island and adjacent Little Tybee Island, just east of Savannah, near the South Carolina border, are by far Georgia's best-known and most-visited surfing areas. Popular breaks include Tybee Island Pier and nearby 17th Street. Virtually all surf spots in Georgia are beachbreaks, with the best sandbars forming near piers and jetties. Many of the islands are accessible only by boat or ferry; some can be reached by wading or paddling. Jekyll Island, to the south, was once a winter retreat for the Morgans, Rockefellers, and Pulitzers, and their mansions remain as beautifully preserved state-owned museums. St. Catherines Island, near Savannah, off-limits to visitors except by special permit, is a zoological preserve inhabited by lemurs, macaques, giraffes, gazelles, and zebras.

The Kaiser brothers—Dale, Billy, and Bobby, ages seven to 10—brought a 14-foot wooden surfboard with them from California when they moved to Tybee Island in 1942, and occasionally dragged it into the ocean to ride waves on their bellies. Three years later, the Kaiser family returned to California, but left their board with neighbor Jim Burke, who became the state's first full-time surfer. But not until the early '60s did the sport gain any kind of toehold in Georgia. Burke and business partner Barney Paderewski founded the Tybee Island Surf Club in 1960 (with members often traveling to Nags Head and Cape Hatteras in North Carolina), as well as the Tybee Island Surf Shop; the Tybee Island Open, the state's first surf contest, was held the following year. The first Georgia State Surfing Championships took place in 1967.

In 2003, Georgia was home to roughly 800 surfers and two surf shops. The Eastern Surfing Association holds five events in Georgia each year.

Gerhardt, Sarah Big-wave rider from Santa Cruz, California; the first woman tow-in surfer, and the first female stand-up surfer to ride Maverick's. Born Sarah Livermore in 1974 in Port Townsend, Washington, she learned to surf in the late 80s at Pismo Beach, California, and started riding bigger waves during her freshman year at Cal Poly San Luis Obispo. During her second visit to Oahu's North Shore, in the winter of 1995–96, Livermore dated big-wave veteran Ken Bradshaw, who also served as her board-maker and coach, and took her out to ride 20-foot waves at Waimea Bay on Thanksgiving. She became the first women's tow-in surfer when Bradshaw launched her into some 15-foot North Shore outer-reef waves in early 1996. Livermore and Bradshaw split later that year, and she married Malibu surfer Mike Gerhardt in 1998; the newlyweds moved to Santa Cruz, where she began a doctoral program in physical chemistry at University of California, Santa Cruz. Gerhardt paddled out twice at Maverick's without taking a wave (bodyboarder Sarah Lucas broke the Maverick's gender barrier in 1994, catching a single left-breaking 15-footer) then finally caught one on February 26, 1999. "I love it all," she told *Wahine* magazine afterward. "I love the smallest, junkiest days; I love head-high waves, I love big waves. I'd surf in my toilet bowl if I could." *One Winter Story*, a documentary on Gerhardt, came out in 2003. She was also featured in *Game Face: What Does a Female Athlete Look Like?*, a photo book published in 2001. She was included as an alternate on the invite list for the 2000 Quiksilver Maverick's Men Who Ride Mountains competition.

Gerlach, Brad Witty pro surfer from Leucadia, California; world-ranked #2 in 1991, and one of the state's top tow-in big-wave riders in the early '00s. Gerlach was born (1966) in Miami, Florida, the son of a stuntman and former Olympic high-diver, and began surfing in 1976, after his family moved to the north San Diego County suburb of Encinitas. From 1982 to 1984, Gerlach lived with his father in Huntington Beach, where he became the top-rated juniors division competitor in the National Scholastic Surfing Association, and was selected to compete on the national team. He turned pro after a so-so performance in the 1984 World Amateur Surfing Champi-

Brad Gerlach

onships, joined the world tour, and was proudly introduced in a *Surfing* magazine profile as a "class clown, cut-up, rebel and miscreant." Gerlach rode with a refinement and power beyond his years, always on the attack but never at the expense of form or style; he won the 1985 Stubbies Pro, beating reigning world champion Tom Carroll in the final, in large part by deploying a new "double-pump" bottom turn that allowed him to ricochet off the curl with added speed and torque. A diehard party-goer, celebrated as a rambunctious wit and first-rate mimic, Gerlach's athleticism didn't suffer from all the late nights out: tested by the Australian Sports Fitness Institute in 1989, the 5'11", 165-pound surfer had the best muscle-to-body-fat ratio on record.

Gerlach finished his rookie year rated #27, then spent five seasons hovering at the lower edge of the world tour elite, always finishing between 10th and 20th. In 1991 he won two events (the Gunston 500 in South Africa, and the Coke Classic in Australia), led the standings for much of the year, then faltered near the end and placed runner-up to Australian Damien

Hardman. A few months later, halfway through the 1992 season, the 25-year-old Gerlach made a surprise announcement that he was quitting the world tour, saying he wanted to rediscover "the artistic side of surfing." The smashed-nosed regularfooter pursued the artistic muse in his own fashion, riding in the nude for a *Surfer* magazine feature, traveling to exotic surf breaks, and experimenting with alternative board designs. More significantly, he turned his attention to big-wave riding and eventually became a first-rate tow-in surfer. In 2001 Gerlach was among the first surfers to ride the giant open-ocean reef waves of Cortes Bank, located 100 miles west of San Diego; the following year he and tow-in partner Mike Parsons finished second in the inaugural Tow-In World Cup, held at Jaws, Maui. He was also selected as a member of the 2001-launched Billabong Odyssey, a three-year big-wave exploration project.

Gerlach has appeared in nearly 50 surf movies and videos, including *Gone Surfin'* (1987), *Surfers: The Movie* (1990), *Fluid Combustion* (1995), *Thicker Than Water* (1999), and *All Aboard* (2002). In 1998 he and his father launched Carveboard, a skateboard-manufacturing company. The never-married Gerlach was inducted into the Huntington Beach Walk of Fame in 2002.

Germany   Germany has roughly 600 miles of coastline on the North Sea and 800 on the Baltic Sea. Summer surf here is virtually nonexistent, and the beaches are crowded with weekend vacationers; small- to medium-sized waves arrive from September to April after traveling southeast across the North Sea. Winter air temperatures often drop below freezing, and the ocean temperatures can dip into the high 30s. There are several breaks on the northeast coast of Germany, facing the Baltic Sea, but the surf is weaker, less consistent, and colder. The small island of Sylt—actually connected to the northwest mainland by a narrow isthmus—is the capital of German surfing, and features a half-dozen beachbreaks along its 24 miles of coast facing the North Sea.

Resident lifeguard Uwe Drath introduced surfing to Germany in the mid-1950s, riding waves off Sylt on a paddleboard, and was soon joined by fellow lifeguards Dieter Behrens and Walter Viereck, all of them wearing thick dive suits. A group of Sylt surfers imported a small number of up-to-date boards from France in the early '60s, and in 1966 they formed Surfing Club Sylt, meeting weekly in a local pig stable to watch 8-millimeter surf films from America. Germany sent a 12-man team to Puerto Rico for the 1988 World Amateur Surfing Championships; the German Surfing Federation was formed in 1991.

Germany's most consistent surf is found inland, at a waterpark in Bad Tolz, where a FlowRider stationary-wave machine opened in 2000. Meanwhile, in the center of Munich, a swift-flowing River Isar tributary forms a natural standing wave as it meets a cluster of underwater rocks, and urban surfers ride the break constantly. German surfers tend to be well-traveled, and many spend their winters seeking waves in other parts of the world. As of 2003, Germany had an estimated 25,000 surfers, along with dozens of watersports retail shops selling boards and wetsuits, and three surfing publications: *Line Up, Surfers,* and *Blue.* Germany's surf is detailed in *The Stormrider Guide Europe* (1998).

Ghana   English-speaking west African country, located about 300 miles north of the equator on the Gulf of Guinea; full of warm, empty, easy-to-ride surf. California surf filmmaker Bruce Brown, along with surfers Mike Hynson and Robert August, arrived in Ghana in 1963 to shoot a sequence for Brown's *Endless Summer,* and *Surfer* magazine's nomadic wave-hunters Kevin Naughton and Craig Peterson, also from California, spent time here in 1975. The 335-mile Ghanaian coastline is for the most part made up of gently sloping tropical beaches, interspersed with a few dozen point- and rivermouth breaks, some charted, others still unsurfed. Labadi Beach, a sand-bottom break near the capital city of Accra, is Ghana's most popular surf spot, and is conveniently located in front of the country's only luxury hotel. Prime surf season runs from May to October, as Atlantic Ocean swells arrive from the south and southwest, daytime air temperatures cool down to about 80 degrees, and water temperatures dip to the low 70s. Ghana is one of Africa's healthiest countries, but malaria and hepatitis remain a threat. Visiting surfers must bring all necessary equipment with them, as Ghana has no surf industry and just a handful of native surfers. "Even at the beach nobody seemed to have any idea what a surfboard was," surf journalist Sam George wrote in 1997, describing his journey through Ghana, towing a surfboard behind his mountain bike. "'Where you go, white man?' they'd ask. 'And why do you bring a bed?'"

Gidget   Nickname for Kathy Kohner of Brentwood, California, whose lightly fictionalized life as a teenage surfing neophyte at Malibu in the mid-1950s became a durable pop culture phenomenon, branching into books, movies, comics, television, and theater. "It was Gidget," *Los Angeles* magazine wrote in 1994, "along with the Beach Boys, who gave surfing its most memorable turn in the great American youth culture parade." Kohner was born (1941) in Los Angeles and raised in the fashionable west Los Angeles suburb of Brentwood; her parents were well-to-do Czechoslovakian Jews who had fled the Holocaust. Frederick Kohner, her father, with a Ph.D. in psychology from the University of Vienna, became an Academy Award–nominated screenplay writer and Broadway playwright, and occasionally taught classes at University of California, Los Angeles.

Kohner, a five-foot, 95-pound 10th grader, began surfing at Malibu in the summer of 1956 and became, in her words, the "group mascot" to Mickey Dora, Terry "Tubesteak" Tracy, Kemp Aaberg, and another half-dozen Malibu regulars who in large part set the tone for California surfing. It was Tracy who said that Kohner looked like a girl-midget—a "Gidget." Kohner spent her summer days learning to surf and trying her best to fit in with the Malibu crew (in part by distributing a bottomless supply of homemade sandwiches), then went home and relayed all to her parents in long, gushing soliloquies. It was her idea to do a book about her new Malibu beach life; her father took on the project in early 1957, and in just six weeks wrote *Gidget,* his first novel. New York's G. P. Putnam published the hardcover edition of *Gidget* in September; *Life* magazine followed up with "Gidget Makes the Grade," a photo feature showing Kohner surfing at Malibu, and hanging out on the sand with Tracy and the rest of the crew. "Among surfers themselves," *Life* reported, "the novel [*Gidget*] made hardly a ripple. 'If I had a couple of bucks to buy a book,' said one, 'I wouldn't. I'd buy some beer.'"

Francine Lawrence is the whip-smart, slightly manic heroine of *Gidget,* in love equally with surfing and surfer-boy Moondoggie. The book is both funnier and darker than the like-titled movies and television shows that followed. The surfers talk dirtier, and the tedium and peril of '50s suburban living are rendered as vividly as the easygoing good times. Author Frederick Kohner, a 51-year-old nonsurfer who didn't learn English until his 20s, does an excellent job at

Gidget; first edition, 1957

tures movie version—Hollywood's first surf film—which became a nationwide hit starring Sandra Dee and James Darren. Surfing fact and fiction began to blur. Mickey Dora, Johnny Fain, and Mike Doyle were among the top Californian surfers who stunt-surfed in *Gidget,* with bantamweight Mickey Muñoz in a blond wig and bikini doubling for Sandra Dee. The "Malibu" surfing clips in the movie were shot at Leo Carillo, about 20 miles north of Malibu; the real Malibu was by that time overrun with teenage gremmies and hodads. "To the chagrin of surfers suddenly having to share waves with the hordes," surf writer Andrea Gabbard wrote in 2001, "and to the delight of those who would create business out of surfing, Gidget lured inland America to the beach." Kathy Kohner had meanwhile enrolled at Oregon State College and quit surfing altogether. "My ego was never tied into being Gidget," she later said. "I was just a girl who surfed, and the guys named me Gidget, then I left and everything kind of went crazy."

Surf culture continued its rapid growth over the next few years: *Surfer* magazine was founded in 1960; the Beach Boys had their first hit in 1962; and *Beach Party,* the first in a series of bubbly Frankie Avalon/Annette Funicello beach movies, was released in 1963. *Gidget Goes Hawaiian,* Frederick Kohner's sequel, was published in 1961, and almost simultaneously made into a movie, with Deborah Walley replacing Sandra Dee in the title role. Kohner also wrote *Gidget Goes to Rome* (1962, also made into a movie), *The Affairs of Gidget* (1963), *Gidget in Love* (1965), *Gidget Goes Parisian* (1966), and *Gidget Goes New York* (1969). In 1965, ABC-TV debuted *Gidget,* a short-lived half-hour comedy series starring 18-year-old Sally Field; the following year brought the debut issue of the Dell-produced *Gidget* comic book. *The New Gidget,* a syndicated TV series with Gidget and Moondoggie married and living with their rambunctious Gidget-like niece, ran from 1986 to 1988. Other small-screen adaptations include the animated *Gidget Makes the Wrong Connection,* and a pair of made-for-television movies, *Gidget Gets Married* (1972) and *Gidget's Summer Reunion* (1985). Fred Reiss's *Gidget Must Die: A Killer Surf Novel,* a black-comedy harangue about Southern California's overcrowded surf breaks, was published in 1995. Hollywood producer/director Francis Ford Coppola cowrote *Gidget: The Musical,* which in 2000 had a brief but sold-out run in Los Alamitos, California.

describing the thrill of learning to surf. "I felt so jazzed about this ride," Gidget says after her first wave, "I could have yelled."

> *Every day, someone else let me have a board to practice. On Don Pepe's board I learned how to keep in the center and paddle evenly—on Hot Shot Harrison's how to control the direction you're taking with your feet—on Malibu Mac's how to get out of a "boneyard" when you're caught in the middle of a set of breakers—and on Scooterboy Miller's hot rod I learned how to avoid a pearl dive. The great Kahoona showed me how to push the shoulders up and slide the body back—to spring to your feet quickly, putting them under you in one motion. That's quite tricky. But then, surf-riding is not playing Monopoly and the more I got the knack of it, the more I was crazy about it and the more I was crazy about it, the harder I worked at it.*

Gidget sold a half million copies, and Kohner was hired to write the script for the 1959 Columbia Pic-

After college Kathy Kohner returned to California, married a Yiddish scholar, and had two children; she worked as a bookstore clerk, travel agent, and restaurant hostess. With surf world nostalgia on the rise in the late '90s (first edition copies of *Gidget* have been sold for up to $1,000), Kohner finally embraced her surfing alter ego, began selling black-and-white reproductions of her Malibu scrapbook photographs, and in 1999 founded a "Gidget" line of postcards. She was featured on the cover of the March 1999 issue of *Wahine* magazine, and later that year *Surfer* named her as the seventh most influential surfer in history. "If not for that pervasive Gidget myth, however homogenized," *Surfer* wrote, "American youth would have missed one of the most potent archetypes available in the early '60s—a rebellion based not on angst or anger, but on joy." *Gidget* was reprinted in the summer of 2001, with Kathy Kohner-Zuckerman writing a new foreword. *Cowabunga! Gidget Goes Encyclopedia,* a 248-page reference book, was published in 2001. *See also* books and surfing, Hollywood and surfing, Malibu.

Gilovich, Dave   Even-tempered surf magazine editor from Laguna Beach, California; a mainstay at *Surfing* magazine from the mid-1970s to the mid-1990s. Gilovich was born (1952) in San Jose, California, began surfing in Santa Cruz in 1962, and published his first surfing article in 1975. He was hired as an associate editor at *Surfing* in 1975, served as editor from 1979 to 1985, then as editorial director from 1985 to 1991. Gilovich himself didn't write often, but worked closely with some of the most popular surf journalists of the period, including Sam George, Bill Sharp, Dave Parmenter, and Nick Carroll. He was vice president of sales for Gotcha surfwear from 1996 to 2000, then became executive vice president at Surfline, the hugely popular Huntington-based surf forecasting company founded by Sean Collins. *See also* Surfing magazine, Surfline.

glass-off   When the wind calms and the water surface becomes smooth and glassy. The expression "glass-off" almost always refers to a dying onshore wind. While the surf might get glassy at any time throughout the day, "glass-off" is most often used to describe a semiregular late-afternoon condition; the longer version of the phrase is "evening glass-off."

glass-on fin   *See* fin.

glassing, glasser   *See* laminate, surfboard construction.

glassy   Windless condition, allowing the ocean surface to become as smooth as glass. Some surfers believe that waves are improved with the addition of a light offshore breeze; others prefer the quietude and serenity of glass. Glassy surf can happen at any time, but in many parts of the world it's most common during the morning hours. California surfer Mike Doyle, winner of the 1968 Duke Kahanamoku Classic, titled his autobiography *Morning Glass,* and California surf moviemaker Jim Freeman's 1965 film was called *The Glass Wall.*

Glazner, Elizabeth   Buoyant editor of *Wahine,* the first women's surf magazine, published from 1995 to 2001. Glazner was born (1963) in Upland, California, raised in Illinois, spent three years at the New York School of Visual Arts, and in 1989 received a B.A. in communications from California State University, Fullerton. She was introduced to surfing in 1993 by speech therapist and triathlete Marilyn Edwards, and a few months later the two women began talking about a women's-only surf magazine—a logical response to both the unbearably macho surf print media and the fast-growing ranks of female surfers. "That [Marilyn and I] are both Libras makes coming together naturally an ordeal," Glazner wrote in the debut issue of *Wahine,* striking a touch-feely tone that would to a large extent define the magazine, "but we just accepted the job." Apart from her editing duties, Glazner wrote *Wahine* profiles on 1990 world champion Pam Burridge, Hawaiian surf icon Rell Sunn, and Kathy "Gidget" Kohner. *See also* Wahine magazine.

gloss coat   The third, final, optional coat of resin brushed onto a surfboard. After being machine-polished, a gloss coat brings up a high, lustrous, showroom shine; it also adds marginally to the board's strength. Longboards almost always have a gloss coat, while high-performance shortboards almost always go without, as the extra resin adds a few ounces of weight. *See also* pinstripe, resin, surfboard construction.

gnarly   Any kind of intense or dangerous thing, person, or situation; most often applied to waves. Pipeline, Teahupoo, and Shipstern Bluff are among the world's gnarliest breaks. "Gnarly by Nature" was the title of a 1997 *Surfing* magazine profile on Hawaiian power surfer Sunny Garcia. Also used as a derogatory expression; greasy food at a breakfast café can be described as "gnarly."

go-behind   Weaving maneuver during which two surfers on the same wave, one ahead of the other, exchange positions and continue riding. Usually the trailing surfer will angle high across the wave, aiming for the shoulder, while the lead surfer cuts back from the shoulder to the whitewater. A go-behind can happen inadvertently, especially at a crowded surf break, but more often it occurs when two friendly surfers find themselves on what amounts to a throwaway wave and decide to have some fun. Good surfers might string together a half-dozen or more go-behinds on a single ride.

Godfrey, Margo   *See* Margo Oberg.

Gold Coast, The   Teeming subtropical Australian vacation metropolis, located on the far south coast of Queensland, facing the South Pacific Ocean; home to a celebrated lineup of right-breaking point waves, including Kirra and Burleigh Heads. The Gold Coast's narrow 26-mile coastal plain can be divided into two main surfing areas: 1) The glittery hotel-lined north, beginning with the sandy beachbreak tubes of South Stradbroke Island, moving through the resort area incongruously known as Surfer's Paradise, and extending south to Burleigh. 2) The residential south, which includes the point waves at Greenmount and Snapper Rocks, the bullet-fast tubes of Kirra, and the consistent beachbreak peaks at Duranbah. The Gold Coast has reasonable beachbreak surf all year, but is best during the December-to-March cyclone season, as each month brings an average of two or three swells big enough to turn the points on, with some swells lasting up to a week or more. A few south-facing Gold Coast breaks—most notably Burleigh Heads and Duranbah—can also show good form between March and July. Average Gold Coast wave height is three to four feet; eight-foot-or-bigger surf is rare but not unheard of. Average daytime air temperatures range from 90 (summer) to the mid-60s (winter); water temperatures range from the low 80s to the mid-60s. Hazards include sharks, bluebottle jellyfish, manic crowds of surfers, and shallow sandbars. Portions of the Gold Coast's lush backcountry hills

are nature preserves, veined with waterfalls and filled with chattering, brightly colored birds.

Kirra Surf Lifesaving Club members Sid Chapman, Bill Davies, Eric Lane, Lance Powell, and Laurie Powell were the first to surf the Gold Coast in the early '20s, riding the easy-rolling breakers near the base of Kirra point. The sport here grew slowly but steadily over the years, and 1963 saw the formation of the Queensland branch of the Australian Surfriders Association (later renamed Surfing Queensland), as well as the Kirra Surfriders Club. The first Queensland State Titles were held on the Gold Coast in 1964; the Australian National Titles came to the Gold Coast in 1966, and returned roughly every five years thereafter. Although Sydney remained the hub of Australian surfing, Gold Coast surfers of the late '60s and early '70s began proving themselves equal to Sydney's best, with Keith Paull, Josette Lagardere, Peter Drouyn, and Paul Neilsen all winning national titles. This led to a peak era for Gold Coast surfers, as the supercharged triumvirate of Michael Peterson (national champ in 1972 and 1974), Peter Townend (1976 world champion), and Wayne Bartholomew (1978 world champion) set a standard not just for Australia, but for the world.

The Gold Coast surf didn't fully catch the attention of the international surf community until 1977, with the debut Stubbies Pro, held in flawless sapphire-blue tubes at Burleigh Heads. "These are not just three or four wave sets," American surf photographer Jeff Divine reported, after seeing Burleigh during a cyclone swell. "These are nonstop lines, all barreling down the point at once, sometimes stacked eight deep." The Gold Coast replaced Hawaii in the eyes of many as the new ultimate surfing destination. As with Hawaii, however, this area of Queensland soon fell victim to its own popularity, and by the 1980s crowds of more than 100 surfers were often wedged into the lineup at Burleigh and Kirra.

But the Gold Coast continued to be one of the sport's most vital areas, serving as home base to first-rate surfboard shapers (Dick Van Straalen, Al Byrne, Gil Glover, and Nev Hyman), photographers (Lee Pegus, Ted Grambeau, Dick Hoole, Martin Tullemans, and Andrew Shield), and surf industrialists (Peter Morrison, and Rick and Paul Neilsen). A short list of past or present Gold Coast world tour pros includes Joe Engel, Peter Harris, Michael "Munga" Barry, Mick Fanning, Joel Parkinson, Trudy Todd, Serena Brooke, and Dean Morrison. As of 2003, the Gold Coast was home to more than 10,000 surfers, roughly 75 surf shops, a dozen surf clubs, and three surf magazines—*Australia's Surfing Life, Australian Longboarder,* and *Pacific Longboarder.* Dozens of amateur surf contests are held yearly on the Gold Coast (the World Amateur Surfing Championships were held here in 1982), along with a small number of pro events, including the world circuit's Quiksilver Pro (formerly the Billabong Pro). The Association of Surfing Professionals, the governing group for the world pro tour, moved its offices to the Gold Coast in 1999. Burleigh, Kirra, Duranbah, and other Gold Coast surf breaks have been featured in hundreds of surf movies and videos over the decades, and the area is detailed in more than a half-dozen specialty guidebooks, including *The Surfing and Sailboarding Guide to Australia* (1993), *Surfing Australia* (1998), Mark Warren's *Atlas of Australian Surfing* (1998), and *The World Stormrider Guide* (2001). *See also* Burleigh Heads, Kirra, Queensland.

Golden, Don   Daring San Francisco Bay Area kayak surfer of the 1960s, best known for paddling into the big ones at Steamer Lane in Santa Cruz. Golden was born (1917) in Great Falls, Montana, grew up in Washington state, moved to California in 1934, and didn't take up surf kayaking until 1957, at age 39. He was seen trimming his streamlined 13-foot, 65-pound homemade kayak in early '60s surf movies like *Barefoot Adventure* (1960) and *Angry Sea* (1963). "He turns well, plays his waves tight, and employs a driving pull-out for dangerous situations," John Severson wrote in his 1964 book *Modern Surfing Around the World.* In 1968, Golden, 51, finished third in the first annual Steamer Lane-hosted United States Kayak Surfing Championships, behind two surf-ski riders. He remains the only kayaker to be profiled in *Surfer* magazine. Golden said in 2001 that he was glad he'd given up kayaking before the popularization of Maverick's, the notorious big-wave break located between San Francisco and Santa Cruz. "Otherwise I'd have probably been out there, getting all smashed up." *See also* canoe surfing.

Golden Girls, The   Attractive, media-savvy group of California women surfers, formed in 1977 by Jericho Poppler. Other members included Shannon Aikman, 1982 world title winner Debbie Beacham, Brenda Scott, Lisa Tomb, and Candy Woodward. The Golden Girls had no real agenda except, as they announced, to promote themselves "collectively and in-

dividually as pro women athletes." ABC's *Eyewitness News* did a feature on the Golden Girls in 1979, with lots of shots of the Girls in their matching customized wetsuits, but the group drifted apart in the early '80s. The Golden Girls' position relative to both surfing and feminism was later questioned. "The problem was," *Wahine* magazine wrote in 1998, "not every girl was a Golden Girl. In retrospect, the public relations ploy didn't really jibe with the larger women's movement." *See also* Debbie Beacham, Jericho Poppler, women and surfing, Women's International Surfing Association.

Gomes, Johnny-Boy   Snarling Hawaiian regular-footer from Makaha, Oahu; winner of the 1997 Pipeline Masters, and a power surfer for the ages. "He's outrageously talented," Australian surf journalist Tim Baker wrote of Johnny-Boy Gomes in 1993, before noting that the menacing and heavily muscled Hawaiian had also "soured more surf sessions for more people than any surfer alive." Gomes was born (1965) and raised in Makaha, the son of a roofer father and waitress mother, and began surfing at age six. At 12 he was sent to a juvenile detention facility on theft charges; two years later, after his mother and father had both died (of breast cancer and diabetes, respectively), the teenage Gomes was adopted by Israel Kamakawiwo'ole, a 700-pound angel-voiced Hawaiian who became famous as the lead singer for the Makaha Sons. Gomes served a 14-month sen-

Johnny-Boy Gomes

tence following a second theft conviction, was released on his 18th birthday, and pledged a new life dedicated to surfing. Two years later, with help from friend and mentor Dane Kealoha, he'd worked his way up to the top of the pecking order on the North Shore of Oahu, and by the end of the '80s he'd earned a reputation as a surfer of near-superhuman strength. The keglike Gomes (5'9", 200 pounds) rode in a tightly clenched weightlifter's squat, with a ramrod straight back, leveraging his board into one massive turn after the other, and often riding deep inside the tube. His small-wave skills were limited and early in his pro career made a smart decision to not follow the world pro circuit and instead concentrate on the bigger Hawaiian surf. "It's among the grunt and fury of the North Shore," *Australia's Surfing Life* magazine wrote, "that Johnny-Boy is in his element."

Gomes was a brilliant if inconsistent competitor in Hawaii, winning the 1993 World Cup at Sunset Beach and the 1997 Pipeline Masters. The 34-year-old Gomes earned $56,000—still the biggest prize check in pro surfing history—by winning the 1999 Backdoor Shootout, held at Pipeline. He placed third in the 1999 Quiksilver in Memory of Eddie Aikau big-wave contest at Waimea Bay; in 2002 he finished sixth. Meanwhile, he'd done nothing to ameliorate his reputation as a thug. In 1991 he was fined $1,000 by world tour officials for punching a fellow competitor during a match; in 1993 he slapped female pro surfer Jodie Cooper off her board after she interfered with one of his rides ("Mike Tyson," Gomes stated two years earlier, "is my biggest inspiration"); and in 1999 he was convicted of assault and fined $6,300 after breaking a surfer's nose during a punchout at Chun's Reef on the North Shore.

Gomes has appeared in more than 50 surf movies and videos, including *Ticket to Ride* (1986), *Momentum* (1992), *Surfers: The Movie* (1990), and *Voluptuous* (1996). He's married and has one child.

Gonad Man *See* Mark Sutherland.

goofyfoot A right-foot-forward stance on a surfboard. Goofyfooters were sometimes regarded as inferior to left-foot-forward regularfoot surfers until the late '60s, when Australian teenage sensation Wayne Lynch is said to have "liberated" the goofyfooter—never mind that goofies had already been on surf magazine covers and won international competi-

tions. About 35 percent of surfers are goofyfoot. Famous goofyfooters include David Nuuhiwa, Gerry Lopez, Tom Carroll, Pam Burridge, and Mark Occhilupo. Also called "screwfoot" in Australia and New Zealand. *See also* regularfoot, switchfoot.

Gordon, Larry Persevering surfboard and surf-accessories manufacturer from San Diego's Pacific Beach, California. Gordon's family moved from Illinois to Southern California in 1943 when Gordon was three, and he began surfing during high school. In the summer of 1959, he and Floyd Smith, another San Diego teenage surfer, began building surfboards in Smith's garage; within two years, Gordon & Smith Surfboards (usually called G&S) became the board of choice in San Diego. Smith had taken a silk-screening class in high school, and in 1961, as a promo effort, he invited young surfers to bring in white T-shirts, upon which he screened the G&S logo, free of charge. He's thus been credited as inventing the surfer T-shirt.

Some of America's best surfers in the '60s and '70s were affiliated with G&S, most noticeably Mike Hynson and Skip Frye, as well as Barry Kanaiaupuni, Butch Van Artsdalen, Dale Dobson, Tony Staples, and Charlie Kuhn. Hynson's G&S Red Fin model was one of the most advanced boards of the preshortboard era; the full-templated, soft-railed G&S Modern Machine, introduced in 1974, was the "fun board" prototype. Under Gordon's guidance (Smith sold his interest in the company in 1971), G&S flourished from era to era, and by the late '80s the company was one of the world's biggest surfboard/accessories/surfwear manufacturers. Following the early-'90s recession, however, Gordon reduced the operation to boards only. *See also* surfing T-shirt.

Gotcha Aggressively marketed surfwear company based in Costa Mesa, California; founded in 1978 by former pro surfer Michael Tomson. A native of Durban, South Africa, Tomson took the company name from a popular Gillette razor television ad, where "Gotcha!" popped up suddenly on screen. Tomson himself, along with top Australian pro surfer Cheyne Horan, modeled the new line of surfwear in advertisements, and the company quickly earned a reputation as hip and audacious. Bold marketing was a Gotcha trademark, with many of their promo efforts criticized as sexist or elitist. The Gotcha Pro in Hawaii, featuring a bikini contest entered mainly by

Honolulu strippers, was regarded as the gaudiest event on the world pro tour during its 1986 to 1989 run. Critics spoke out against a 1986 punk-inspired print ad featuring three famous surfers hovering over an unconscious spread-eagled model, while another Gotcha ad from the same period showed a man rolling up his sleeve, fist balled up, before a cowering woman. A 1988 campaign based on the slogan "If You Don't Surf, Don't Start" was also denounced. Gotcha was the first and only company to produce a 3-D print ad, complete with cardboard-framed cellophane glasses. U.S. sales of $65 million in 1987 placed Gotcha third among surfwear companies, behind Ocean Pacific and Hobie, and ahead of Quiksilver. The company was lauded for single-handedly sponsoring 1990's *Surfers: The Movie,* one of the last big-budget surf films. It also sponsored the world's most thrilling pro surf contest, the Gotcha Tahiti Pro, held in the predatory left-breaking tubes of Teahupoo. Gotcha team riders over the years have included world champions Martin Potter and Derek Ho, big-wave standout Brock Little, free-surf specialist Matt Archbold, bodyboarding icon Mike Stewart, and world tour leaders Brad Gerlach, Rob Machado, and Shea Lopez.

MCD (More Core Division), Gotcha's first spin-off company, was launched in 1989; the GirlStar line debuted in 1995. Tomson sold the company to Marvin Winkler in 1996, who then sold it to Broadband Interactive Group in 1999. *See also* fashion and surfing, Michael Tomson.

Gouveia, Fabio   Quiet and serene Brazilian regular-footer from João Pessoa, in the state of Paraíba; one of Brazil's most successful competition surfers; world amateur champion in 1988, and ranked #5 on the 1992 international pro circuit. Gouveia was born (1969) in the northeast town of Bananeiras, Paraíba, the son of an agricultural engineer, raised in João Pessoa, and began surfing at age 13. Five years later he was the Brazilian amateur champion, and in 1988 he was the surprise winner of the World Amateur Surfing Championships—the first Brazilian surfer to win a world title of any kind, pro or amateur.

Gouveia turned pro along with Flavio Padaratz, another highly regarded Brazilian. Although close friends, the two surfers were an odd couple: the blond-haired Padaratz was an extroverted goofyfoot from a moneyed family who spoke near-perfect English. The shy, dark-haired Gouveia spoke only Por-

Fabio Gouveia

tuguese and avoided the surf media spotlight. It was expected that Padaratz would be the one to crack the top of the ratings—and eventually he did, finishing #8 in 1994. But the small-framed Gouveia (5′3″, 140 pounds) quickly developed into an easygoing but often deadly efficient pro surfer, placing third in his first world tour event outside of Brazil, and finishing the 1989 season ranked 35th, with rookie-of-the-year honors. After winning his first world tour event in 1990, Gouveia became, as surf journalist Derek Hynd noted, "a god in Brazil, [and] the vanguard of his nation's long promise in surfing." Gouveia had by then developed a refined closed-knee style, grooved but not rote, expertly blending his turns and often finding a sinuous line over flat spots where other surfers had to hop and bounce; his technique was sometimes compared to that of California surf icon Tom Curren. And like Curren, Gouveia had a childlike tendency to become distracted. Having reached the semifinals of a big event early in his career, he nearly missed the match as he'd wandered off to a grassy area behind the contest site and was feeding the pigeons.

Gouveia rose steadily up the pro tour ratings over the next three years, finishing 25th in 1990, 13th in 1991, and fifth in 1992—each mark a new high for a Brazilian surfer—winning four events during the period, including the season-ending 1991 World Cup at Sunset Beach, Hawaii. By 1996 he slipped down to 37th, and dropped off the tour. Two years later he won the World Qualifying Series tour and again earned a spot on the world tour, where he's been steady if unspectacular, usually finishing in the mid- to high 20s. While Gouveia is seen briefly in *Sarge's Scrapbook: Take Three* (1991), *Gripping Stuff* (1991), *La Scene* (1994), and a small number of other surf videos, he has been without question the least-photographed and -filmed pro surfer of his generation. Gouveia is married and has three children.

Graham, Dick   Well-organized surfwear executive and surf magazine editor/publisher from Orange County, California; *Surfing* magazine cofounder in 1964. Graham was born (1937) in Los Angeles, California, raised in Hollywood, and began surfing at age 18, while attending Chapman College on a basketball scholarship. In 1961, following a three-year tour in the marines, Graham was hired as a data processor for the Petersen Publishing magazine conglomerate; the following year Graham and surfboard manufac- turing titan Hobie Alter wrote *Surfing Made Easy,* an instructional handbook for beginners; in 1963, Gra- ham served as coordinator on *Petersen's Surfing Year- book,* the publishing group's debut surfing magazine. Later that year he became the "technical editor" of *Petersen's Surfing* magazine, and in 1964 he was pro- moted to editor. Graham and California-based photographer Leroy Grannis founded *International Surfing* at the end of 1964 (the name was later short- ened to *Surfing*), which soon established itself as the top rival to powerhouse *Surfer.* A photographer as well as a writer/editor/publisher, Graham had cover shots on four of six *Surfing* issues in 1967. In October of that year, the short-haired, barrel-chested Graham trav- eled with the Windansea Surf Club to Australia, and was among the first Americans to see the new stubby vee-bottom boards that would mark the first phase of the shortboard revolution. Returning to California, Graham left *International Surfing* and went back to Pe- tersen's to convince them to try another surfing mag- azine. The second run of *Petersen's Surfing*—identified by its "Surfing Action Around the World" subhead— debuted in April 1968, with publisher/editor Graham breaking the shortboard news to the Americans. (*Surfer* wouldn't report on the shortboard until September.) Graham's magazine performed well throughout 1968. But *Surfer* reasserted itself the fol- lowing year, and *International Surfing* made a come- back in 1970 after briefly dropping off the scene in 1968; *Petersen's Surfing* once again folded. In 1969, Graham wrote *Kings of the Surf,* a book of profiles on

top wave-riders; then quit surf publishing altogether. From 1968 to 1975 he worked as vice president of mar- keting for Hang Ten beachwear, and from 1977 to 1987 he was coowner of surf industry giant Lightning Bolt Incorporated. *See also* Surfing magazine.

Grajagan   Panoramic left-breaking wave located on the jungle-lined southeast tip of Java, Indonesia; one of the world's longest and most challenging reef- breaks, and site of the original surfing camp. Graja- gan (or G-land) breaks best from May to October, as winter storms in the Indian Ocean frequently gener- ate four- to eight-foot swells—with the occasional 10- to 12-footer—which are groomed as they reach shore by Java's reliable southeast offshore tradewinds. The waves along Grajagan's enormous coral-studded lava reef are more shifty and powerful than those found nearly anywhere else in Indonesia. Grajagan has three main sections: 1) Kong's, uppermost on the point and most exposed to incoming swells, is some- times erratic and hard to read, but can produce rides up to 300 yards. 2) Moneytrees, the most-surfed sec- tion, is a long, dependable, frequently tubing wave that breaks up to eight foot. 3) Speed Reef, Grajagan's funneling inside break, and by far the premier sec- tion—as well as the most fickle—is best at six to eight feet; waves here can tube flawlessly for 200 yards, al- lowing surfers to ride inside the tube for as long as fifteen seconds. Other waves in the area include the soft-breaking lefts at Chicken's and 20-20's, just down from Speed Reef; and Tiger Trails, an agreeable right-breaking wave located nearly two miles to the west. The area is tropical and humid, with water tem- peratures consistently in the upper 70s. Despite

Grajagan

Grajagan's enormous lineup and consistent surf, crowds are often a problem, with up to 200 surfers visiting at a time during peak season. Other hazards include the shallow reef and malaria. A hut-leveling tsunami roared through the Grajagan camps in 1994, resulting in a few minor injuries.

Grajagan was first surfed in 1972 by Americans Bob Laverty (who had spotted the break a few months earlier during a plane ride from Jakarta to Bali) and Bill Boyum. The two surfers motorcycled from Bali to the beachside Javanese fishing village of Grajagan, their backpacks full of supplies, ferried across the bay, then followed the shorefront edge of the enormous Plengkung National Forest. For three days they surfed perfect six- to eight-foot waves at Grajagan, camping on the beach near the jungle. Laverty died in a surfing accident just a few days after returning to Bali. Mike Boyum (Bill's brother) opened the G-land Surf Camp two years later, housing fewer than a dozen guests at a time in three wooden huts. Although the break appeared in magazines and films over the next few years, it wasn't named, and thus didn't become well known until 1980. In 1981 it was listed by *Surfing* magazine as one of the "Ten Best Breaks in the World," and by 1985 Mike Boyum was grossing $250,000 annually from his newly expanded surf camp.

Grajagan has been featured in more than three dozen surf movies and videos, including *In Search of Tubular Swells* (1977), *Storm Riders* (1982), *Filthy Habits* (1987), *The Search* (1992), *Endless Summer II* (1994), and *Metaphysical* (1997). Long Island surfer and former U.S. champion Rick Rasmussen was featured surfing Grajagan on an 1980 ABC *American Sportsman* special; the break was also featured in *Great Waves,* an Outdoor Life Network documentary series. The inaugural Quiksilver Grajagan Pro in 1995 met with transcendental four- to eight-foot surf for the entire week of the event, and was won by world champion Kelly Slater. Similar Quiksilver meets were held at Grajagan the following two years, before the event was canceled due to Indonesia's growing social and political unrest. As of 2003, there were three surf camps operating at Grajagan, with an average one-week rate of about $350. *See also* Quiksilver Pro (Grajagan), surfing resorts.

Grambeau, Ted   Versatile and peripatetic Australian photographer, originally from Victoria. Grambeau was born (1954) in Melbourne, and raised in the small west Victoria town of Wonthaggi; a football injury in 1973 forced him to take a break from surfing, and to pass the time he began to photograph friends riding waves at in the local breaks. Grambeau completed a three-year commercial photography course at the Royal Melbourne Institute of Technology, did apprentice work in Melbourne (fashion photography) and New York (photojournalism), then became a full-time surf photographer in the mid-'80s, traveling from one exotic location to another and selling his images mainly to *Australia's Surfing Life* and *Surfer* magazines. Grambeau's versatile work is color-rich and neatly composed, and has been used in more than a half-dozen surfing books, including *The Next Wave* (1991), *SurfRiders* (1997), and *The Perfect Day* (2001). In 1994, the *Surfer's Journal* published a lavish 23-page retrospective of his photographs.

Grannis, Leroy   Gruff-voiced photographer from Hermosa Beach, California; best known for the lucid, unadorned, well-composed surfing images he took during the 1960s; also a cofounder in 1964 of *Surfing* magazine. Grannis was born (1917) and raised in Hermosa, began surfing in 1931, and was one of the state's top wave-riders in the '30s and '40s; more than a half-dozen photographs of Grannis are featured in John "Doc" Ball's 1946 book *California Surfriders.* (Grannis and Ball were both charter members in 1935 of the Palos Verdes Surf Club.) Grannis was working as a Pacific Bell switchboard installer in 1959 when he was diagnosed with stress-related ulcers, and advised by his doctor to take up a relaxing hobby. He bought a 35-millimeter camera and a 400-millimeter lens, spent two months learning how to use the equipment, built a darkroom in his garage, and in September of that year had eight black-and-white images published in *Reef* surf magazine. The tall, hawk-faced photographer went on to contribute shots to *Surfer* and *Surf Guide,* became the general manager and head photographer of *Surfing Illustrated* in 1962, then cofounded *International Surfing* (today's *Surfing*) in 1964, along with editor Dick Graham. Grannis had little to do with the day-to-day mechanics of publishing, and for the most part remained behind the camera. He shot from the water at times, but preferred a straight-on angle from the beach; his best work—much of it in black and white, often shot at Malibu—seemed to have a unique blending of light and shadow. "There was a texture about Grannis' shots," fellow photographer Brad Barrett later wrote, "that for me took them into another realm." Others felt the same way. Grannis polled ahead of Californians Don James and Ron Stoner to win the still photography division of 1966 International Surfing Hall of Fame award; in 1967 he finished runner-up to James. Grannis worked almost exclusively in Southern California and Hawaii, and quit shooting professionally in 1971. Apart from his photography, he wrote surf articles throughout the '60s, was a charter member of the 1961-formed United States Surfing Association, and was a top competitor in the seniors division of the United States Surfing Championships, placing fourth in 1968 and second in 1971.

Grannis was featured in a *Life* magazine article about older surfers in 1990, and also appeared that year in a Nike television ad. In 1991 he was inducted into the International Surfing Hall of Fame; in 1999 he was featured in the PBS-aired documentary *Surfing for Life* about senior surfers, and was inducted into the Huntington Beach Surfing Walk of Fame. *Photo: Grannis—Surfing's Golden Age, 1960–1969,* a lavish 224-page photo book, was published by the *Surfer's Journal* in 1998. Grannis also contributed to more than a dozen other illustrated books, including *Where the Surfers Are* (1968), *A Pictorial History of Surfing* (1970), *The History of Surfing* (1983), *The Next Wave* (1991), *Stoked: A History of Surf Culture* (1997), and *The Perfect Day* (2001). Grannis is married, has four children, and lives in Carlsbad, California. As of 2002 he was still surfing regularly. *See also* Surfing magazine.

Great Barrier Reef   World's largest coral reef, extending for 1,250 miles along the northeast coast of Queensland, Australia, between 10 and 100 miles from shore. The Great Barrier Reef is formed from the skeletons of more than 400 species of red, yellow, green, purple, or blue sea animals called polyps, and is home to roughly 1,500 species of fish, as well as some as-yet-undetermined number of high-quality surf breaks. Between November and April, cyclone storms can create waves ranging from four to 12 feet along the Great Barrier Reef; smaller but more predictable surf arrives from May to October. Wind is the great impediment to surfing here, as both wind direction and speed are unpredictable. Air temperatures in the area range from 50 to 80 degrees, while the water remains in the mid-'70s.

Queensland surfer and shark-net tender Jody Perry began exploring the Great Barrier Reef for waves in the early '80s; soon after he set up a surf charter service, which he shut down voluntarily after realizing the area was perhaps better served by not being marketed and promoted. But the word was out, and a small number of Queensland boat owners were willing to take surfers on the 12-hour journey to the known breaks. In the early '90s, articles on the Great Barrier Reef were published in *Australia's Surfing Life* and *Surfer* magazines, and a 1993 issue of the *Surf Report* newsletter mapped out 21 Great Barrier Reef breaks.

The vibrantly colored Great Barrier Reef is known as one of the Seven Natural Wonders of the World, along with the Grand Canyon, Mount Everest, Ayers Rock, the Matterhorn, Victoria Falls, and Meteor Crater. Most of the Great Barrier Reef is protected as an Australian national park.

Great Britain   *See* England, Ireland, Scotland, Wales.

Great Lakes   World's largest group of freshwater lakes, located in North America on the border between the United States and Canada. Each of the Great Lakes—Michigan, Superior, Huron, Erie, and Ontario—has distinguishing surf features. Michigan, the only Great Lake located entirely in the United States, is the most surfed and the birthplace of freshwater surfing; Superior has the largest surface area of any lake in the world, and the biggest, roughest, coldest waves in the Great Lakes; Huron, with its numerous inlets and nearly 30,000 islands, has the most coastline, is the least surfed, and has the most secret breaks; Erie is the smallest, shallowest, and warmest of the Great Lakes, with popular surf breaks in Pennsylvania, Ohio, Ontario, and New York. Ontario, though smaller on the surface than Lake Erie, in fact, contains more water and often produces the Great Lakes' largest waves.

Surfing came to the region in 1945, when an unidentified army serviceman, after being stationed in Hawaii, returned home to Grand Haven, Michigan, with a wooden surfboard and began riding the local wind swells. By 1964, the local surf scene had developed enough for Grand Haven local Rick Sapinski to form the Great Lakes Surfing Association; Ontario's Wyldewood Surf Club was formed the following year; and in 1966 the Dunes Beach Surf Club (Waukegan, Illinois) and the Lake Shore Surf Club (Sheboygan, Wisconsin) were established. Forty-four Great Lakes surfers met in Grand Haven in the fall of 1966 to compete in the first Great Lakes Surfing Championships.

Great Lakes waves are created by local storms, and generally require a durable (five hours or more) and steady breeze over at least a 50-mile stretch of water. Fall and winter bring the biggest and most consistent surf to the lakes. While temperatures vary from region to region, summer air and water readings generally range from 60 to 70 degrees. Winter air temperatures are often below freezing, with the water usually just above the freezing mark. (Lake Erie often freezes completely.) There are hundreds of surf spots along the lakes' 11,000-mile coast, nearly all soft-breaking sandbar breaks formed next to piers, jetties, rock piles, or rivermouths. Occasionally the wind backs off to create smooth and glassy conditions, but Great Lakes surfers for the most part ride small, choppy waves. Longboards are popular. P. L. Strazz, in his 2000 book *Surfing the Great Lakes,* estimates there are 750 surfers in the Great Lakes region, with Lakes Michigan and Erie being the most popular, followed, in order, by Ontario, Huron, and Superior. A *Surfer* magazine editor visited the lakes in 2001 and found a surf competition taking place without judges. "The swells only last a few hours," a local explained, "and nobody's going to miss them sitting on the beach scoring rides. We just go surfing and agree on a winner later, at the bar." A 20-minute video titled *Surf Michigan: Vol. 1* was released in 2000. The Eastern Surfing Association introduced the Great Lakes competition district in 1984; as of 2002, the Great Lakes area was home to an estimated 20 surf/skate/snow shops.

Greece   *See* Mediterranean Sea.

Green, Alan   Low-profile cofounder of Quiksilver, the world's leading surfwear company, from Torquay, Western Australia. Green was born (1947) in Melbourne, Victoria, began surfing in 1960, and in 1969, along with partner John Law, founded a small wetsuit-making operation in the coastal town of Torquay. Green and Law began making surfing trunks under the Quiksilver label in 1973; three years later their scalloped-leg "boardshorts" became a hot-selling item in America, and by the middle of the following decade the company was among the biggest in the surf industry. Green proved to be a masterful behind-the-scenes administrator, with a special talent for hiring people who were both surf- and business-savvy, like Australians Bruce Raymond and Harry Hodge, and Bob McKnight from California. *See also* Quiksilver.

Green, Gary   Sardonic Australian pro surfer from Cronulla, New South Wales; world-ranked #14 in 1986. Green, born in 1963 and raised in a $30-a-week flat in land-locked western Sydney, began surfing in Cronulla at age 10. His parents divorced when he was 14, and two years later his mother married a wealthy man, who moved the family to the upscale beach suburb of Newport, where the goofyfooted Green was taken in by the local surfers, including future world tour pros Tom Carroll and Derek Hynd. Green joined the pro tour circuit in 1984, the same year he moved to Cronulla, and in three years his rating went from 31st to 20th to 14th. He was fast and nimble in the water, best in smaller waves; on land he was full of banter and quips. Asked by an interviewer to list his greatest achievements, he said, "reaching puberty, and getting free drinks." Midway through the 1987 season, while holding the #6 position in the ratings, Green abruptly quit the tour and returned to Cronulla, saying he was "just sort of jacked off with the whole lot of it," and that his world circuit peers for the most part had become too serious, "checking the wax on their boards all the time, counting their contest points again and again." Green then became one of the first surfers to draw a salary as a globe-trotting "photo pro"—paid to get himself, and his sponsors' logos, into surf magazines and videos. He appeared in a number of surf videos, including *Surf Into Summer* (1987), *Sultans 2* (1988), and *The Search* (1992).

green room   *See* tube.

Greenough, George   Eccentric and innovative kneeboarder/designer/filmmaker from Montecito, California; known as the "barefoot genius," and regarded by many as the most influential surfer of his generation. Greenough was the mid-1960s originator of full-speed, banked-turn, high-performance surfing, a leading figure in the shortboard revolution, and the producer of 1969's *The Innermost Limits of Pure Fun,* with its groundbreaking in-the-tube photography. Greenough was born (1941) into a wealthy Santa Barbara railroad family, a direct descendant to 19th-century American sculptor Horatio Greenough, and he grew up in a sprawling Spanish hacienda in nearby Montecito. Open-heart surgery at age 10 made Greenough something of an outsider among his peers, and helped direct his attention to the ocean; he rode briefly as a stand-up surfer in the mid-'50s,

George Greenough

then switched to kneeboarding and mat-riding, in part because he liked being closer to the water surface. Greenough made balsa kneeboards in his high school wood-shop classes—soon adding a narrow-based, swept-back fin that he patterned after a tuna tail fin—and also began shooting film with his father's movie camera. He started making regular visits to Australia in 1964, where he was befriended by a group of top surfers including Bob McTavish and Nat Young. Greenough had by then developed his sub-five-foot flexible "spoon" kneeboard (consisting of an all-fiberglass kneeling area edged in foam on the nose and rails), upon which he was able to perform water-gouging turns and cutbacks; direction changes made by stand-up surfers, on their bulky 10-foot boards, were slow and tedious by comparison. Greenough's riding was a revelation to McTavish. "Look at that thrust!" he later wrote, recalling the first time he watched the round-shouldered, straw-haired Californian surf. "Carve off the top, drive back down the face, repeat. That's it!" Young won the 1966 World Surfing Championships using a Greenough-made fin,

and in early 1967 McTavish developed the vee-bottom surfboard—the opening move in what would soon be called the shortboard revolution—in order to try and made a stand-up board that performed similarly to Greenough's kneeboard. A clip of Greenough surfing was included in Bruce Brown's 1966 crossover hit *The Endless Summer*; jaw-dropping footage of him was included in *The Hot Generation* (1968), *Evolution* (1969), *Splashdown* (1969), and *Fantastic Plastic Machine* (1969). Greenough was single-handedly responsible for the kneeboarding boom in the late '60s and '70s; Nat Young, in 1968, flatly declared Greenough to be "the greatest surfer in the world today." (Greenough meanwhile continued to ride an inflatable mat—his favorite wave-riding vehicle—and a long sequence of him mat-surfing was used in the 1978 surf film *Fantasea*.)

Greenough had also developed as a photographer. His 1966 photograph of Australian Russell Hughes was billed as the first water-shot image to show a surfer completely inside the tube. Two years later Greenough began work on *The Innermost Limits of Pure Fun*, his only full-length surf movie, which built up to a spectacular sequence—shot with a shoulder-mounted waterproof camera rig weighing 28 pounds—that took the viewer deeply and hypnotically inside the tube. Nothing like it had been seen before. Members of British rock band Pink Floyd were so impressed with Greenough's movie that they donated music to his next work, *Echoes* (1972), a 23-minute short, filmed at 300 frames per second, that further explored the textures and patterns of the breaking wave from deep inside the tube and below the water surface. Greenough worked on a small number of big-budget surf movies or TV movies, including *Big Wednesday* (1978) and *Rip Girls* (2000). Greenough himself was the subject of 1973's *Crystal Voyager*, a surf movie/documentary.

The slightly built Greenough (5'9", 150 pounds), regarded for decades as the surf world's most beloved eccentric, will go for months without wearing shoes, and sometimes uses a length of rope for a belt. Often monosyllabic, Greenough can also launch into droning and highly technical one-sided conversations. He's also earned a reputation for being guileless and altruistic. "George will spend months finding the solution to a design problem," surf journalist and fellow mat-rider Paul Gross wrote in 1994, "then share it with whoever happens to be on the phone the next morning."

Greenough and his surfboards were the subjects of a 1969 feature article in *Popular Science*; in 1997 he was profiled in *50 Years of Surfing in Film,* a TV series produced by the Outdoor Life Network. His short-subject films include *Rincon '71* (on kneeboarding) and *Rubber Duck Rider* (on mat-riding, also released in 1971); in 2003 he was set to release the long-awaited *Dolphin Glide,* a 35-millimeter short that gives a dolphin's-eye view of water travel. The never-married Greenough lives in Byron Bay, New South Wales, Australia. *See also* fin, kneeboarding, mat-surfing, short-board revolution, spoon kneeboard.

gremmie   Mildly derogatory term used to describe an inexperienced but enthusiastic young surfer; popular during the late '50s and '60s; derived from "gremlin," the invisible beings said to be responsible for mechanical failure, particularly in airplanes, when no other explanation is available. While "gremmie" can be used as a term of affection, in the early '60s it was also used to label a nonsurfing poser—similar to hodad. "Gremmie" is one of the few words defined in the *Oxford English Dictionary* as "surfing slang." Also spelled "gremmy," and often shortened to "grem." Precursor to the Australian expression "grommet."

Griffin, Rick   Richly talented artist and cartoonist originally from Palos Verdes, California; best known to surfers as the creator of Murphy, the cheerful cartoon gremmie who debuted in *Surfer* magazine in 1961; also celebrated as one of the San Francisco psychedelia movement's "Big Five" artists. Griffin was born (1944) and raised in Palos Verdes, began surfing at age 12, and learned to draw by copying *Mad* magazine cartoons. As a high school freshman he charged 50 cents to sketch wave-riding surf characters onto T-shirts; at 16 he illustrated a price list for Greg Noll Surfboards in exchange for a new board; in late 1960 he met John Severson, who had just published the first issue of *Surfer* magazine, and agreed to produce a cartoon strip: "The Gremmies" was published in the second issue of *Surfer;* "Murphy and the Surfing Contest," the first in the Murphy series, appeared in the following issue. With his beaming smile and mop of sun-bleached hair, Murphy was quickly accepted as a favorite surf world mascot; he made the cover of *Surfer* in 1962, and he was featured in each issue of the magazine until late 1964.

A 1964 car accident left Griffin with a damaged left eye and long scars on the side of his face. Murphy

vanished for five years, then turned up occasionally between 1969 and 1987, first as a kind of guide to a hallucinatory fantasy world, then as a chirpy born-again Christian, and finally as a somewhat muted surfing philosopher. All told, *Surfer* published 28 Murphy strips.

Griffin moved to San Francisco in 1966, after attending Chouniard Arts Institute (now California Institute of the Arts) in Valencia, California. In 1965 he'd begun illustrating the zany Griffin-Stoner adventures for *Surfer,* with cartoon versions of himself as the cunning beatnik and *Surfer* photographer Ron Stoner as the gee-whiz innocent. Griffin's cartoons, while still fun and jovial, had become denser, and were occasionally populated with stoic Native Americans, as well as sly references to the counterculture scene he'd become a part of in San Francisco. A close inspection of the Griffin-Stoner strips reveals a Grateful Dead poster, a cluster of magic mushrooms, and background characters pulling on joints or hookah pipes. Eleven Griffin-Stoner strips appeared between 1965 and 1967.

Earning notice for the poster he made announcing the 1967 Human Be-In at San Francisco's Golden Gate Park—later regarded as the Summer of Love's inaugural event—Griffin was hired to make coming-attractions posters for acts at the Avalon Ballroom and the Fillmore Auditorium, including Jimi Hendrix and the Jefferson Airplane. He also created the original logo for *Rolling Stone* magazine, and did album cover artwork for the Grateful Dead (*Aoxomoxoa*), The Eagles (*On the Border*), Jackson Browne (*Late for the Sky*), and Quicksilver Messenger Service (*Sons of Mercury*). Griffin's cartoons were also published in *Zap Comix,* the seminal underground magazine founded in 1967 by cartoonist R. Crumb. He returned now and again to the surf world, producing the artwork for three surf movies: *Pacific Vibrations* (1969), *Five Summer Stories* (1972), and *Blazing Boards* (1983).

Griffin died in a motorcycle accident in 1991. His wake was attended by Jerry Garcia and other members of the late-'60s San Francisco art and music scene, as well as a number of his old *Surfer* magazine associates. Griffin was married and had five children. *Rick Griffin,* a biography and retrospective written by Gordon McClelland, was published in 1980; his work is also featured in 2003's *Rebel Visions: The Underground Comix Revolution, 1963–1975.* Griffin was inducted into the Huntington Beach Surfing Walk of Fame in 1997. A show of Griffin's poster art was staged at San Francisco's Artrock Gallery in 2001. *See also*

Murphy, surf cartoons and comics, Tales from the Tube.

Grigg, Rick   Supremely confident surfer from Honolulu, Hawaii; winner of the 1966 Duke Kahanamoku Invitational, and sometimes referred to as the first big-wave hotdogger. Grigg was born (1937) in Los Angeles, raised in Santa Monica, began surfing at age nine, and by the early '50s was one of the hottest young surfers at Malibu. In 1955 Grigg won the first annual Catalina–to–Manhattan Beach paddleboard race, a 32-miler that would come to stand as paddleboarding's supreme test. Older sister Robin Grigg had meanwhile become California's best female surfer and bodysurfer.

Grigg often rode waves in Santa Cruz while attending Stanford University. After receiving a B.S. in biology in 1958, he went directly to the North Shore of Oahu, Hawaii, and joined a half-dozen of his California-born friends and acquaintances who were pioneering the big surf at places like Sunset Beach and Waimea Bay. Grigg adapted quickly to the tropics, and applied his small-wave maneuvers into the bigger surf, climbing and dropping across the wave face, riding closer to the curl, and often throwing his arms up for dramatic embellishment during a bottom turn. "A lot of us had a real barroom-brawl attitude, almost vicious, about catching the biggest wave," Waimea trailblazer Greg Noll said years later. "With Ricky, it was more of a playful thing. He had a real love affair with the ocean." Other big-wave surfers from Grigg's era admired his riding, but were put off by his air of superiority. "Ricky is an intellectual," fellow California transplant Fred Van Dyke once said. "But he's an arrogant intellectual." Grigg spent three years surfing and working nights as a stevedore on the Honolulu docks. He then returned to school, earning a master's in zoology from the University of Hawaii in 1964 and a Ph.D. in oceanography from the Scripps Institution in La Jolla in 1970. In 1965 he was selected as a crew member for Sealab II, a NASA/U.S. Navy project designed to test the effects of underwater immersion: Grigg and nine others lived off the coast of La Jolla for 15 days in a 12- by 60-foot cylindrical steel chamber.

Grigg's win in the 1966 Duke contest was something of a surprise, as he'd been away from the North Shore for two years, and at 29, was one of the event's oldest surfers. But he rode masterfully, and won going away. He was a finalist in the next two Duke events, placing fifth in 1967 and second in 1968. Grigg mean-

Rick Grigg

while appeared in more than a dozen surf movies of the late '50s and '60s, including *Slippery When Wet* (1958), *Gun Ho!* (1963), and *Golden Breed* (1968). He also starred in *Surfari,* a 1967 Hollywood-made beach movie that debuted in New York City but quickly disappeared. In 1963 he finished runner-up to California surfer Phil Edwards in the first annual *Surfer* Magazine Readers Poll Awards, and in 1967 he was the top vote-getter in the big-wave category of *International Surfing* Magazine's Hall of Fame Awards. *Big Surf, Deep Dives and the Islands: My Life in the Ocean,* Grigg's autobiography, was published in 1998. A *Surfer* magazine review noted the author's accomplishments and erudition—he quotes Einstein, Dostoyevsky, Newton, and Shakespeare—as well as the book's "continuous hum of self-congratulation." Grigg was also the coauthor of 1963's *Surfer in Hawaii: A Guide to Surfing in the Hawaiian Islands.* Grigg has been married three times and has three children; he's been a professor in the University of Hawaii's Oceanography Department since 1970.

Grigg, Robin   Pre-*Gidget* surfer originally from Santa Monica, California; tandem event winner in the 1960 Makaha International, and older sister of big-wave rider Rick Grigg. Robin Grigg was born (1934) in Los Angeles, California, and began surfing at age eight, one year before moving with her family to Santa Monica. She started riding Malibu in the late '40s, and soon took delivery on a Joe Quigg–shaped balsa board, one of the first of what were soon known as the "girl boards" (Grigg's friends Claire Cassidy and Vicki Flaxman, among others, got similar boards around the same time), which were thinner, lighter, and far more maneuverable than what was currently in use, and prototypes for the soon-to-be popular Malibu chip design. Grigg moved to Hawaii after graduating from Stanford and became a physical therapist. She won the 1960 Makaha International tandem event with partner Mud Werner. Grigg is featured bodysurfing in John Severson's 1963 surf movie, *Angry Sea.*

Grissim, John   San Francisco–born, U.C. Berkeley–educated surf journalist; editor of Australia's *Tracks* magazine in 1974 and 1975, and author of *Pure Stoke,* published in 1982 by Harper & Row. Grissim became a freelance journalist in 1968, and contributed articles *to Rolling Stone, Sports Illustrated,* and *Playboy,* as well as *Surfer* and *Surfing. Pure Stoke* is made up of 11 well-written and frequently humorous essays that collectively, as Grissim says in the book's preface, present surfing as "a consuming passion, a lifestyle, a great teacher, a doorway to the world, a kick-ass good time, and generally cheaper than drugs." In 1995, Grissim founded *Marine Watch,* a short-lived quarterly newsletter dedicated to ocean-related adventures and oddities, surfing included.

grommet   Broadly defined as any young surfer; more specifically, an insolent, hyperenthusiastic and frequently underfoot young surfer. While the Australian-coined "grommet" came into the American surf lexicon in the mid-1970s, it's derived from "gremmie," a popular American surf word from the '50s and '60s used to identify either a young surfer or a surf poser of any age. The grommet experience is defined in large part by hazing rituals. At Sydney's North Narrabeen, young surfers have for decades been ritualistically stripped nude and lashed securely to a tall metal "grommet pole" for public viewing and/or abuse. A 2001 *Surfer* magazine article noted that the developing grommet can expect to be "punched, kicked, spit on, Dutch-rubbed, pantsed, pink-bellied, head-shaved, tampon-nosed or otherwise humiliated by older surfers." As with frat house plebes, however, grommets will be protected if harassed by anyone from outside their own beach clan.

As the surf magazine's target audience grew younger during the '90s and early '00s, editors with increasing frequency began to publish grommet-

Grommet; Hawaii's Jon-Jon Florence

specific articles and columns, with titles such as "Know Your Grom," "A Grom's Guide to Life," "Great Moments in Grom History," and "A Deep, Penetrating Look into the Mind of the Grommet." By 2000, "Gromfest" was a suffix to a number of kids-only competitions worldwide, led by the popular and well-attended Rusty Gromfest series, sponsored by California-based surfboard and surfwear giant Rusty. (While Australia's 1977-founded Pro Junior competition has been called the original grommet event, surf history buffs will cite the 12- and-under Windansea Menehune Contest, held in La Jolla, California, from 1965 to 1970.) Grommets have often occasionally been able to match skills with the world's best surfers, as was the case with young teenage phenomenons Jeff Hakman, Margo Godfrey, Wayne Lynch, Martin Potter, and Kelly Slater. "Grom" is the universally used short version of "grommet," while "grub" (Australia) and "helgie" (Santa Cruz, California) are synonymous with "grom."

Grondin, Kevin   Ironman regularfoot surfer from Hampton, New Hampshire, three-time senior men's division winner of the United States Surfing Championships (1992–94), and holder of 10 East Coast titles. Grondin was born (1956) in Peabody, Massachusetts, began surfing at age 11, and won his first East Coast title in 1982. He served as head coach for the 1996 United States national team, and led the group to victory in the World Surfing Games in Huntington Beach, California. In 2000, *Sports Illustrated* named Grondin as one of New Hampshire's "50 Greatest Sports Figures of the Century," although as cheeky

Eastern Surf Magazine was quick to point out in an interview with Grondin, "When you think of sports, New Hampshire really isn't a state that pops to mind." Grondin's reply: "I went out surfing on Sunday in 33 degree water, and every single person who was out there deserves to be in *Sports Illustrated.*"

ground swell Swell originating from a distant open-ocean storm. The standards aren't exact, but a fully developed (or "significant") ground swell requires about 2,000 miles between the wave-generating storm and the coast. Ground swell is sometimes defined as having a period (the average time between the crests of two consecutive waves) of more than 15 seconds, while a locally generated wind swell can be defined as having a period of 11 seconds or less. Swells with a 12- to 15-second period originate from midrange storms. A ground swell, as compared to a wind swell, produces faster, stronger, more durable, and better-defined waves. Beachbreaks excepted, ground swells generally produce high-quality surf.

The term "ground swell" is used because the energy gyre of a long-period wave has a much larger diameter than that of a wind swell, and thus comes into contact with the ground—the ocean floor—much earlier. A 10-foot wave with a 20-second period begins to touch the ocean floor at a depth of about 1,200 feet, while a 10-second wind swell touches ground at about 40 or 50 feet. *See also* wind waves.

groyne *See* jetty.

Guam Tropical island in the western North Pacific, about 32 miles long and six miles wide, located 1,300 miles east of the Philippines and 800 miles north of the equator; an unincorporated territory of the United States and the largest of the Mariana Islands. In 1962, local surfers took turns riding the island's only surfboard (almost certainly left by a visiting U.S. Marine); by the end of the decade, Guam had an estimated 200 surfers. The island is ringed by powerful, tubing, shallow-water reefbreaks, virtually all of which are ridable only on higher tides. The surf is first-rate when conditions are right, but days or weeks can pass without any decent waves. The best surf generally arrives during the July-to-November rainy season. A 1993 issue of the *Surf Report* charts 24 surf breaks on Guam, with unnerving spot-by-spot descriptions such as "Long, grinding, super-hollow

right," "insanely hollow right with protruding coral heads," "shallow tube with no channel; guaranteed reef beatings," "great wave, but deadly over eight-foot." While local surfers are known to be protective of their increasingly crowded breaks, the island's tourist economy and the long-standing presence of a U.S. military base has accustomed them to the comings and goings of visitors—surfers included. By 2003, Guam had about six boutique-style surf shops. Nearby Cocos Island also has excellent surf.

Guatemala Mountainous coffee-producing country in Central America, bordered by Mexico, El Salvador, Honduras, and Belize, with 250 miles of southwest-facing Pacific Ocean coastline. The 50-mile stretch of Caribbean coast on the east side of Guatemala is in a waveless bay. "Guatemala is not a surfer's destination by itself," a 1986 *Surf Report* newsletter states. "But it's a nice stop on the way from Mexico to El Salvador." Guatemala's undefiled and lightly populated Pacific shoreline has no points or reefs, and is made up entirely of tropical sandy beaches, most of them steep-faced and better suited for bodyboarding, bodysurfing, or skimboarding. The best surf breaks are almost all located near rivermouths, and are in a constant state of flux as sandbars arrange and rearrange themselves. Winter surf in Guatemala is usually under four foot, but hard-breaking. In late summer and fall, during the Pacific hurricane season, waves can get up to 15 feet or bigger, but the absence of points and reefs makes for unridable conditions. The prevailing wind is offshore. Midsummer air temperatures along the coast will often top 100 degrees; winter temperatures rarely drop below 70; water temperatures are usually in the low 80s. The Guatemalan dry season begins in November and lasts until April; the rainy season extends from May through October. As of 2003, Guatemala had no surf industry and no more than a few dozen native surfers.

Guethary Shifty, long-rolling French reefbreak, located adjacent to the charming Basque village of Guethary, between Biarritz and the French/Spanish border. Guethary breaks best in fall and early winter, with a north-northwest swell and a light east wind. It holds form up to 15 feet—at which point it begins to break more than a half mile offshore—and is often compared to Hawaii's Sunset Beach. Guethary is for the most part a right-breaking wave, with rides lasting up to 400 yards, but lefts can be ridden at higher tides. Local surfers Michel Barland, Jo Moraiz, and Andrew Plumcocq were among the first to ride Guethary in the early '60s; famous California expatriate surfer Mickey Dora often rode here in the '70s, as did Quiksilver executive and first-generation pro surfer Jeff Hakman in the '80s and '90s. The 1996 World Longboard Championships were held at Guethary in wild 10-foot surf, with Bonga Perkins of Hawaii winning the event. Guethary has been featured in a small number of surf movies and videos, including *Oceans* (1972) and *Legends in Southern France* (1997).

Gulf Coast   *See* Gulf of Mexico.

Gulf Coast Surfing Association   *See* Texas Gulf Surfing Association.

Gulf of Mexico   Subtropical sea all but encircled by eastern Mexico, Cuba, and the southeast United States, including Florida, Alabama, Mississippi, Louisiana, and Texas. The Gulf of Mexico's 3,000-mile coastline is primarily low and level, filled with estuaries and salt marshes. Except for the southern coast of Mexico, near the Bay of Campeche, and Cuba's northwest coast, the entire Gulf Coast is fronted by a long and shallow wave-depleting continental shelf formed by rivermouth silt deposits. Long-distance ground swells can only enter the Gulf through the Yucatán Channel, the 100-mile-wide gap between the western tip of Cuba and the eastern tip of Mexico that separates the Gulf from the Caribbean Sea. Gulf surfers rely almost entirely on locally spawned, short-period, soft-breaking wind swell. The best waves here arrive between late fall and early spring, as wind-generating cold fronts traverse the Gulf. Swells are brief and choppy for the most part, and rarely over four feet, although storm waves of up to 10 feet are not unheard of. The off-season tends to be nearly waveless, aside from the occasional tropical storm or hurricane. Gulf of Mexico water temperatures range from the mid-50s in winter to the low 80s in summer.

Eastern Mexico and the Yucatán Peninsula remain largely unexplored for waves, and the Louisiana and Mississippi coasts are fringed with swampy wave-sucking bayous, but surfing is well established in Florida, Alabama, and Texas, and is also being prac-

ticed in Cuba. Surfing was introduced to the Gulf sometime in the early 1930s in Galveston, Texas, by a pair of local lifeguards. Yancy Spencer, the 1975 U.S. Surfing Championships runner-up from Pensacola, Florida, is the Gulf's best-known surfer. Big-wave rider Ken Bradshaw of Hawaii was born and raised in Houston, and learned to surf in Galveston; present-day world tour pros Cory and Shea Lopez were raised in Indian Rocks, Florida, not far from Tampa Bay. *See also* Alabama, Cuba, Florida, Mexico, Texas.

Gulf Surfing Association   *See* Texas Gulf Surfing Association.

gun   Short for "big-wave gun," which in turn is a variation of "elephant gun." As reported in the February 1964 issue of *Petersen's Surfing* magazine, California-born big-wave leatherneck Buzzy Trent

Gun; Hawaii's Owl Chapman with his 12-foot pintail

came up with the phrase in 1956 while working on a new streamlined 12-foot board with shaper Joe Quigg. "You don't hunt elephants [big waves] with a b.b. gun or a pistol," Trent told Quigg, trying to explain how he wanted the new board to perform. "You use an elephant gun." The modifier was later dropped; "gun" remained. A board used for medium-big surf is often called a semi-gun. *See also* big-wave surfboard.

Gunston 500   Professional surf contest held in South Africa from 1969 to 1999, originally called the Durban 500; a world pro circuit mainstay in the '70s, '80s, and part of the '90s. The inaugural Durban 500 was South African surfing's first pro event, and was billed as a team match between South Africa and Australia. Sponsor Gunston Cigarettes put up a 500 rand first-place prize; other prizes included a motorcycle and hi-fi set. The two-day event was organized by Durbanites Ernie Tomson, Ian McDonald, and Max Wetteland, was held in good six-foot surf at North Beach, and won by 16-year-old Gavin Rudolph of Port Elizabeth. The contest was renamed the Gunston 500 in 1971. By the time the world pro tour made its debut in 1976, the Gunston was attracting surfers from Australia, California, Hawaii, Brazil, France, and Great Britain. In 1973, local surfer and future world champion Shaun Tomson won the first of six consecutive Gunstons—no other pro surfer has so dominated a single event. The Gunston 500 was occasionally held at Nahoon Reef in East London, 400 miles south of Durban, but most of the events were staged in Durban's Bay of Plenty. It was a men's division championship-rated tour event until 1993, and a championship-rated women's event from 1992 to 1997. Gunston 500 winners:

1969:	Gavin Rudolph
1970:	Midget Farrelly
1971:	Brad McCaul
1972:	Jeff Hakman
1973:	Shaun Tomson
1974:	Shaun Tomson
1975:	Shaun Tomson
1976:	Shaun Tomson
1977:	Shaun Tomson
1978:	Shaun Tomson
1979:	Dane Kealoha
1980:	Mark Richards
1981:	Cheyne Horan
1982:	Mark Richards
1983:	Hans Hedemann
1984:	Tom Carroll
1985:	Mark Occhilupo
1986:	Gary Green
1987:	Damien Hardman
1988:	Bryce Ellis
1989:	Brad Gerlach
1990:	Damien Hardman
1991:	Brad Gerlach
1992:	Sunny Garcia, Neridah Falconer
1993:	Gary Elkerton, Rochelle Ballard
1994:	Richie Collins, Pauline Menczer
1995:	Shane Powell, Lynette MacKenzie
1996:	Todd Prestage, Pauline Menczer
1997:	Simon Law, Rochelle Ballard
1998:	Shane Bevan, Lynette MacKenzie
1999:	Luke Hitchings, Layne Beachley

H

H₂O magazine   Eclectic surf art magazine founded in 1979 in Malibu, California, and published by Martin Sugarman, a photojournalist who once called himself "the John Cassavetes of the surf world." Subtitled the "Magazine of Waterfront Culture," *H2O* is a slender, glossy black-and-white amalgam of interviews, poetry, fiction, T&A, fine-art photography, and topical articles such as "Why Blacks Don't Surf," along with a small number of surf photos, mostly of Malibu. "I always thought surfing magazines didn't paint a truthful picture of surfing," Sugarman said, "because 90% of the time there are no waves. Moreover, they never portrayed the surfer as having problems in his life." Sugarman published eight issues of *H2O* between 1979 and 1989, and though the magazine had a low circulation, it became a Southern California cult favorite. Sugarman spent most of the '90s taking photographs in Kashmir, Tibet, Afghanistan, Iraq, Bosnia, and other war-torn regions. In 1999, at age 52, he moved onto a sailboat in Marina del Rey and once again began producing *H2O*, at which point the *Los Angeles Times* proclaimed that Sugarman's magazine was something that could be "waved in the face of anyone who ever sneered at LA as a cultural wasteland." He produced five issues of *H2O* between 1999 and 2001.

Hakman, Jeff   Smiling power surfer from Oahu, Hawaii; the sport's most successful pro during the early and mid-'70s, and cofounder of Quiksilver USA. Hakman was born (1948) in Redondo Beach, in southwest Los Angeles County, the son of an aeronautical engineer, and raised in nearby Palos Verdes. His early years in the sport were marked by a dazzling combination of talent and good fortune: his surfing father bought him a beautiful new 7'11" balsa Velzy-Jacobs board when he was eight, taught him how to ride, and later insisted that Jeff cut school to join him for day trips up and down the coast. In 1960, when Hakman was 12, the family moved to Oahu; he was soon getting free boards from master shaper Dick

Brewer, and the following year, at age 13, he rode Waimea Bay for the first time and had a movie-stealing cameo in the John Severson surf movie *Angry Sea*. During his high school years, Hakman had Peter Cole for algebra and Fred Van Dyke for science—both were pioneering big-wave surfers on Oahu's North Shore and remained lineup fixtures at Sunset Beach and Waimea. Hakman was the youngest (17) and smallest (5'4", 125 pounds) invitee to the inaugural Duke Kahanamoku Invitational in 1965, held at Sunset; he nonetheless won the event going away, beating surfers like Mike Doyle, Paul Strauch, Fred Hemmings, and Mickey Dora.

Hakman had no big contest wins over the next four years, but his surfing continued to progress during the late-'60s shortboard revolution, and by 1970 he'd developed the ultimate form-follows-function riding style: feet cemented to the deck of his board, knees open, weight low and shifted back slightly onto an overdeveloped rear thigh (he was nicknamed "Surf Muscle"), back and shoulders slightly hunched, chin tucked down toward his left shoulder. Hakman's outstretched hands waved slightly to some inner rhythm as he rode, and a smile often played over his features; few surfers have ever looked so joyous in the water. The lines he drew were more precise than innovative, but his mastery was complete, and he could ride for hours—sometimes days—without falling off his board.

International surf competitions began offering modest but encouraging cash prizes in the early '70s, and while Hakman, Gerry Lopez, Barry Kanaiaupuni, and Reno Abellira, all from Hawaii, were more or less held in equal esteem as the period's top riders, Hakman's consistency brought him the lion's share of first-place checks. He won the Duke contest in 1970 and 1971 and the inaugural Pipeline Masters in 1971; in 1972 he won the Hang Ten American Pro and the Gunston 500; in 1973 he again won the American Pro. In the 1974 Smirnoff—held in 30-foot surf at Waimea Bay and regarded still as a benchmark in big-

Jeff Hakman

in a high-end rehab clinic outside of London, and as of 2003 remained drug-free. Long-term drug use seemed to have little or no effect on Hakman's health and fitness, and in his 50s he remained one of the most dynamic surfers of his age group.

Hakman was the top vote-getter in the Big Wave category of the 1966 *International Surfing* Magazine Hall of Fame Awards. He appeared in more than two dozen surf movies in the '60s and '70s, including *Inside Out* (1965), *Golden Breed* (1968), *Cosmic Children* (1970), *Five Summer Stories* (1972), *A Sea for Yourself* (1973), and *Super Session* (1975). He was also featured on *Biographies,* a 2001 Outdoor Life Network cable TV series. *Mr. Sunset: The Jeff Hakman Story,* a biography written by surf journalist Phil Jarratt, was published in 1997; in 2000 Hakman was featured in a lengthy *Outside* magazine profile titled "Mr. Sunset Rides Again." Hakman is married and has two children, and works as marketing director for Quiksilver Europe. *See also* drugs and surfing, power surfing.

wave competition—he finished second by a fraction of a point to Abellira. In 1976, at age 26, in what amounted to his professional surfing farewell, he became the first non-Australian to win the prestigious Bells Beach event in Victoria.

Hakman had by that time developed a drug problem. He'd traveled to Australia with three ounces of cocaine glassed inside the hollowed-out fin of his contest board, with the idea that he'd barter coke for heroin once he arrived, heroin at the time being far less expensive in Australia than America. Hakman was in fact loaded when he won the 1976 Bells event. Nevertheless, he recognized a business opportunity in the form of a new, well-fitting Australian-made brand of trunks called Quiksilver, and before the contest was over he had secured the Quiksilver USA manufacturing license. Hakman made a small fortune with Quiksilver, sold company shares to buy drugs, lost his money and the company license, and was reduced to working as a surf shop clerk. He was high during the birth of his son in 1982, and not long afterward contracted hepatitis from sharing a needle with another surfer. Quiksilver, surprisingly, gave him another chance as a founding partner in their new French-based European office in 1984, but Hakman was demoted to special projects manager after spending company money on drugs. In 1990 he spent six weeks

Haleiwa   Harbor town located at the western end of the seven-mile-long North Shore of Oahu, Hawaii, fronted by a temperamental right-breaking surf spot. Haleiwa breaks best during the winter season, and requires a west swell. From three to eight feet it's a lively high-performance wave, with tube sections. At 10 to 15 feet it's a thrilling but punishing wave that invariably winds down to a closeout finish in what is called the "toilet bowl." A steady eastbound current generally gets stronger as the waves get bigger, and often pulls unwary or incautious surfers into the "pit," to get rolled by incoming set waves. Haleiwa is often the North Shore's most active and crowded break. It's a full-amenity area, with a parking lot, showers, lifeguard, barbecue pits, a popular nearshore beginner's surfing area, and the beachfront Haleiwa Surf Center.

The town of Haleiwa was originally populated almost exclusively by plantation workers, who worked the nearby sugarcane and pineapple fields. Soloman Kukea, a full-blooded Hawaiian whose brother was a Waikiki beachboy, started riding the nearshore waves at Haleiwa sometime in the early '20s, and was later joined by a small number of Haleiwa residents. But the break long remained unknown to the rest of Oahu's surfers, as well as visiting mainlanders. Hawaii's Henry Preece began riding Haleiwa in the mid-'50s, and was soon joined by California big-wave pioneer Greg Noll, who filmed Preece at Haleiwa for his 1957 surf movie *Search for Surf*. By that time, surfers were migrating in ever-larger numbers each winter to the North Shore, usually renting houses a few miles to the east; they used Haleiwa as a supply stop and mail depot, and occasionally dined at the town's cafés.

Haleiwa has been the site of hundreds of amateur surfing contests over the years, beginning with the 1964 Dick Brewer Championships, the first surfing event held on the North Shore. The pro tour's World Cup was the best-known money contest held at Haleiwa, and from 1976 to 1982 it was the international circuit's final event. World Cup winners included Mark Richards, Shaun Tomson, and Margo Oberg. Other pro contests staged at Haleiwa included the 1977 WISA Cup (won by Lynne Boyer), the 1991 Wyland Pro (Tom Curren), the 1992 Marui Women's Masters (Pauline Menczer), and the 1993 Oxbow World Longboarding Championships (Rusty Keaulana).

Haleiwa, with a population just below 2,500, has long been a minor tourist attraction and its two-lane main thoroughfare is lined with kitschy art galleries and gift stores. It also remains the commercial and social hub of North Shore surfing, and is home to a dozen surf shops, a major board-making factory, and a surfing museum, as well as a number of surfer-frequented cafés and restaurants. Haleiwa is featured in Columbia Pictures' 1964 movie *Ride the Wild Surf*, as well as dozens of surf movies and videos, including *Barefoot Adventure* (1960), *The Endless Summer* (1966), *Cosmic Children* (1970), *Wizards of the Water* (1982), *For the Sea* (1994), and *Harvest* (2002). *See also* North Shore.

Haley, Jack   Charismatic surfer from Seal Beach, California; winner of the first West Coast Surfing Championships, held at the Huntington Beach Pier in 1959. Mike Haley, Jack's younger brother, won the event the following year. Jack Haley Surfboards opened in Seal Beach in 1961, and four years later the lean (6'6") and loud regularfooter, nicknamed "Mr. Excitement," opened the still-popular Captain Jack's restaurant on Pacific Coast Highway in nearby Sunset Beach. When Haley died of cancer in 2000 at age 65, a *Los Angeles Times* obituary noted that he "had planned his own beach party memorial bash, with mariachi music and Hawaiian shirts." Haley appeared in a small number of surf movies in the late '50s and early '60s, including *Surf Safari* (1959). He was inducted into the Huntington Beach Surfing Walk of

Fame in 1999. His son, Jack, Jr., played two seasons of basketball with the Los Angeles Lakers.

Halloween Storm, 1991   On October 29, 1991, a North Atlantic storm named Hurricane Grace met a tropical cyclone tracking along a Canadian-born cold front off Nova Scotia, and the two systems combined into what would soon be known as the Halloween Storm, or, as renamed by Sebastian Junger's hugely popular 1997 book, the Perfect Storm. While it killed 10 and produced an estimated half-billion dollars' worth of damage along the eastern seaboard (mostly in New England), the Halloween Storm also created some of the biggest and cleanest waves ever seen by East Coast surfers.

Florida and North Carolina got the best of it, with some areas receiving beautifully groomed eight-foot-plus waves from November 27 to December 2, with the biggest surf—up to 15 foot—hitting on Halloween. The sun was out, the wind was lightly offshore, and the water warm enough that most surfers didn't wear wetsuits. Scott Bouchard and Adam Chatteroff tried something new by using a personal watercraft to tow each other in to waves; a year later, surfers in Hawaii would use the same method to remake big-wave riding. The surf in the northeast was for the most part too big and stormy to ride, with wind gusts up to 75 miles per hour, although excellent smaller waves were found on the lee side of a few New England headlands and coves. Record high tides combined with the enormous incoming waves to destroy hundreds of beachfront homes and businesses. Seven Massachusetts counties were declared federal disaster areas, as were five in Maine and one in New Hampshire, with the bulk of the damage occurring on Halloween. All six men aboard the swordfishing boat *Andrea Gail* were killed; a fisherman in New York and another in Rhode Island both died after being swept from the beach, and two New Yorkers drowned when their boat capsized off Staten Island.

In his book *The Perfect Storm*, a semifictitious reconstruction of what happened to fisherman Billy Tyne and the rest of the crew of the *Andrea Gail*, Junger imagines the comprehensive horror of being trapped at sea in the middle of a violent North Atlantic storm.

Statistically, a 40-knot wind generates a 30- or 40-foot breaking sea every six minutes or so; greenwater over the bow and whitewater over the house. Every hour, perhaps, Billy might get hit by a breaking 50-

footer. That's probably the kind of wave that blew out the windows. And every 100 hours, Billy can expect to run into a nonnegotiable wave; a breaking 70-footer that could flip the boat end over end. He's got to figure the storm's going to blow out before his hundred hours are up.

Hamasaki, Joanne "Joey" Small, shy, whisper-voiced regularfooter from Honolulu, Hawaii; runner-up in the 1966 World Surfing Championships, and remembered for her subtle but beautiful technique. Hamasaki was born (1946) and raised in Honolulu, and began surfing at age 10 in Waikiki. In 1963 she moved to Dana Point, California, where she lived for 10 years. Had it not been for Capistrano Beach surfer and two-time world champion Joyce Hoffman, Hamasaki would have been the dominant woman surfer of the era. As it was, the dark-haired Honolulu transplant finished second to Hoffman in the 1964 Makaha International, the 1965 United States Surfing Association (USSA) final ratings, the 1966 World Championships and the 1967 USSA final ratings, as well as the 1965, 1966, and 1967 *Surfer* Magazine Readers Poll Awards. Hoffman was the more aggressive and creative surfer, but the 5′2″ Hamasaki was grace personified on a wave, with a hip-cocked, back-arch bottom turn that helped define the mid-'60s surfing style. She won the 1966 Malibu Invitational (Hoffman placed third), just before Wardy Surfboards in Laguna Beach introduced the Joey Hamasaki signature model in 1966, one of the very few models endorsed by a woman. A career highlight came in 1967, when she won the East Coast Surfing Championships, beating both Hoffman and soon-to-be world champion Margo Godfrey in the final. The reserved Hamasaki was never interviewed or profiled by the surf press, and appeared in just a small number of surf films, including *Barefoot Adventure* (1960) and *Fantastic Plastic Machine* (1969).

Hamilton, Bill Fluid regularfooter from Hanalei, Kauai; regarded by many as surfing's definitive stylist from the mid-1960s to the mid-'70s; father of big-wave rider Laird Hamilton. Bill Hamilton was born (1948) in Long Beach, California, the son of a former big-band orchestra leader father and a commercial artist mother. He was raised in Laguna Beach, began surfing at age 11, and at 15 was invited to join the prestigious Windansea Surf Club. In 1966, after graduating high school, Hamilton moved to the North Shore of Oahu, was featured on the cover of *Surfer*

Bill Hamilton

magazine, and had a star-making turn in the surf movie *Free and Easy.* Surfboards Hawaii introduced the Stylist, Hamilton's signature model, in 1967. Hamilton rode with a toreador's poise and refinement, his body moving quietly, almost formally, from one position to the next, panache radiating from his hands and fingers. He later said that his trademark frontside cutback, executed with symmetrically extended arms, elbows bent slightly, was based on an illustration of Jesus' Sermon on the Mount.

The broad-shouldered Hamilton (5′11″, 190 pounds) adapted smoothly to the new short surfboards introduced in late '60s, and was a model for the turn-of-the-decade surfer who chose to de-emphasize competition surfing. Hamilton did in fact compete—in 1971 he placed fifth in the Pipeline Masters and finished runner-up in both the Duke Kahanamoku Classic and the Smirnoff Pro—but gave the appearance of being above the fray. He consolidated his position as soul-surfing guru with two or three popular if sophistic surf magazine articles. "Life to me is a constant movement," he noted in a 1974 essay, "an ever-changing, swirling mass of variables interconnecting with each other to create a whole, [and] if you're willing to compare them to riding a wave, then comprehension of the totalness of here and now is at least partially attained."

Hamilton began shaping surfboards in 1967; over the years he made boards for Surfboards Hawaii, Country Surfboards, Chuck Dent Surfboards, Lightning Bolt, Bear Surfboards, and—from 1972 to present day—Bill Hamilton Custom Designs. He has also worked in construction and as a commercial fisherman. He stunt-doubled Jan-Michael Vincent's surfing scenes in the 1978 Warner Brothers' film *Big Wednesday,* and producers paid him an additional $5,000 to pilot a jerry-rigged "Malibu lifeguard boat" into the jaws of a 15-foot wave at Sunset Beach. Hamilton also appeared in more than a dozen surf movies, including *Golden Breed* (1968), *Waves of Change* (1970), *Pacific Vibrations* (1970), and *Five Summer Stories* (1972). He was cited in a 1985 *Surfer* magazine article as one of "25 Surfers Whose Surfing Changed the Sport." "Up a Lazy River with Bill Hamilton," a 39-page profile written by surf journalist Drew Kampion, was published in the *Surfer's Journal* in 2000. Hamilton has been married twice, has lived in Kauai since 1972, and has two children. Laird Hamilton, his adopted oldest son, helped invent tow-in surfing in the early '90s, and is generally regarded as the world's premier big-wave rider.

Hamilton, Laird Brawny blond master of tow-in surfing from Maui, Hawaii; the near-unanimous choice as the best big-wave rider of the 1990s and '00s, and one of the four or five surfers throughout the sport's history to significantly change the way waves are ridden. Hamilton was born (1964) in San Francisco, California, the son of surfing parents. Laird is Scottish for "lord." His father left the family and joined the Merchant Marines when Laird was five months old; at age two Laird moved to the North Shore of Oahu with his mother, who soon married revered California-born surfer Bill Hamilton. The new family lived first on the North Shore, then Kauai, and Hamilton began surfing as a toddler. At 16 he dropped out of high school and worked as a mason, carpenter, and plumber; at 17 he moved to California and found part-time work as a model. Hamilton lived on the North Shore of Oahu in the late '80s and early '90s, and was a noncompetitive professional surfer, paid by sponsors to be part of the surf-media-saturated North Shore scene. He rode in the disciplined neoclassic style used by his stepfather, keeping his head, arms, hips, torso, even fingers all perfectly aligned, and blending each maneuver seamlessly into the next. But where the medium-sized Bill was

Laird Hamilton

smooth and subtle, Laird, at 6'3" and a ripped 220 pounds, was smooth and brutally powerful.

In 1992, former world tour pro Buzzy Kerbox convinced Hamilton to try towing in to waves from behind Kerbox's inflatable boat. Tow-in surfing was Kerbox's idea, but by 1994 Hamilton had such command of the new sport that it was his to define. Personal watercraft had by then replaced the inflatable boat, footstraps had been added to the new small-dimension tow-in boards, and headquarters for the tow-in project had moved from the North Shore to Jaws, a big-wave break located not far from Hamilton's new home on Maui. As seen in Bruce Brown's 1994 surf film *Endless Summer II*—a movie debut for tow-in, with Hamilton starring in the Jaws sequence—it was obvious that mechanization not only allowed surfers to ride much bigger waves than ever before, but opened up a new performance frontier, with banked turns, cutbacks, and even tuberides. Hamilton's performance in *Endless Summer II* was a revelation. "He can actually challenge the wave," as

Hawaiian surfer Brock Little noted said, "whereas the rest of us are forced to just ride it." Peter Mel, Darrick Doerner, Dave Kalama, and Ken Bradshaw all helped make tow-in surfing the sport's most compelling facet through the '90s and early '00s. Hamilton meanwhile seemed to make a game of letting everyone get close, before suddenly and spectacularly moving forward. On August 17, 2000, at Teahupoo in Tahiti, he was towed in to the thickest, hardest-breaking wave ever ridden, making it clear once again that he was operating alone on a different, higher plane.

Usually described as "focused" and "intense," Hamilton was less generously labeled as an "egomaniac" by a number of surfing acquaintances and as "smug" by the surf press. Billy Hamilton said his son was at times "mean, arrogant and gnarly." When not surfing, the talkative and frequently hyperactive Hamilton was indiscriminate in his pursuit of thrills, making his debut bungee jump off a 700-foot-tall bridge, riding a street luge headfirst at 50 miles per hour (most ride feet-first), and breaking a rib after jumping off a 125-foot cliff in Hawaii. He entered a sailboard competition in France in 1986 and set a European speed record at 36 knots per hour. He made headlines in 1990 after crossing the English Channel with Buzzy Kerbox on paddleboards, landing at Dover, England, five and a half hours after leaving Calais, France. He invented foilboarding (sometimes called "airboarding") in 1997 after attaching a three-foot-long, split-bottom aluminum hydrofoil to the back of a wakeboard. Pulled into an open-ocean swell, the foilboard rises until just the bottom few inches of foil are connected to the water surface; Hamilton, levitating above the water, can ride this way for minutes at a time.

Hamilton has also become one of surfing's greatest crossover media personalities. He and fellow Hawaiian big-wave rider Brock Little starred in *Easter Island: Forbidden Surf,* a one-hour ESPN documentary that aired in 1994; in June of that year, he was featured in an *Outside* magazine cover story; in 1996 he was named as one of the "50 Most Beautiful People" by *People* magazine. He played a snarling pro surfer in *North Shore* (1987), and did stunts in *Waterworld* (1995), and *Die Another Day* (2002). Hamilton has also appeared in more than 40 surf movies, videos, and documentaries, including *Totally Committed* (1984), *Gone Surfin'* (1987), *Surfers: The Movie* (1990), *Wake-Up Call* (1995), and *Biggest Wednesday* (1998).

Laird, a biographic video and DVD, was released in 2001. A photo of Hamilton riding a 35-foot wave was selected for the cover of *Jaws,* a 1997 surf photography book; the same photo was used the following year for a *National Geographic* cover story on Jaws. *Outside* named him in 2000 as one of 25 "Outside Super Heroes," along with athletes like cyclist Lance Armstrong and mountaineer Ed Viesturs. Hamilton was again featured on the cover of *Outside* in 2002, while *Sports Illustrated Women* named him as one of the "Sexiest Men in Sports." Hamilton's spectacular ride at Teahupoo was featured on the front page of the *Los Angeles Times,* and earned him the Action Sport Feat of the Year at the 2001 ESPN Action Sports and Music Awards. Hamilton seemed a bit disoriented as he accepted his statuette; he thanked Jesus Christ 12 times, then finished by saying, "We're all equal before the wave." In 2003, Hamilton won the Surf Industry Manufacturers' Association's Waterman of the Year award. Hamilton has a daughter by his first wife; his second wife is model and professional volleyball player Gabrielle Reece. *See also* big-wave surfing, foilboarding, Jaws, kiteboarding, power surfing, tow-in surfing.

Hamrock, Kim   Hyperfit competitive surfer from Huntington Beach, California; winner of six United States Surfing Championship titles in the 1990s, and winner of the 2002 Women's World Longboard Championship. Hamrock was born (1960) in Whittier, California, and began surfing at age 16. Married three years later and the mother of three by 28, Hamrock didn't start competing until 1990 at age 30. Entering both shortboard and longboard divisions (and occasionally kneeboard and bodyboard as well), the diminutive blond goofyfoot won her first U.S. shortboard title in 1993, repeated in 1994, then won both longboard and shortboard titles in 1995 and 1996. Hamrock became a professional longboarder in 1998; the following year she placed third in the Women's World Longboard Championships, and in 2000 she took fifth. She earned $3,000 for her win in the 2002 Championships. Hamrock has been the owner and chief instructor of Surf City Surf Lessons in Huntington since 1995; from 1996 to 1999 she wrote the instructional "Water Wisdom" column for *Wahine* magazine, and in 1996 she produced the instructional video *Safe Surfing with Danger Woman.* Hamrock was profiled in the 2000-published women's surfing book, *Girl in the Curl: A Century of Women in*

Surfing. Her drive and motivation, she says in *Curl,* comes from the fact that she didn't begin surfing until the relatively late age of 16. "That's why I'm such an animal. I don't think I'll ever ride enough waves to catch up."

hang five   Type of noseride where the in-trim surfer, having already "walked" the board, moves the leading foot forward until the toes hang off the tip; not impossible on a shortboard, but generally regarded as a longboard maneuver. Hanging five is the first on-the-tip noseride mastered by the intermediate long-boarder; the rider's stance remains in line with the board's longitudinal stringer, and the weight is mostly on the back foot—about 18 inches behind the front foot—which makes it fairly easy to retreat back to a middle-of-the-board trim stance. Hanging ten is far more difficult than hanging five. *See also* noseriding.

hang heels   *See* heels over.

hang ten   Longboarding maneuver during which the rider hangs all 10 toes off the front end of the surfboard—the most celebrated form of noseriding. "Getting ten," Florida surf journalist Jim MacLaren wrote in 1995, "separates the good noseriders from everybody else." Surfers generally prepare to hang ten by trimming (angling) the board across the wave face and cross-stepping to the front. One of the sport's most difficult and delicate maneuvers, hanging ten is possible for the most part only on smaller waves; few surfers can hang ten in surf over four feet.

California surfer and surfboard manufacturer Dale Velzy is occasionally cited as the first surfer to hang ten, in 1951; it's possible that noseriding surfers in Waikiki, especially Albert "Rabbit" Kekai, were hanging ten in the late '40s on their finless hot curl boards—although it's unlikely they were able to backpedal and return to a trimming position. While Californians Mickey Dora, Mickey Muñoz, and Dewey Weber were among the first to consistently hang ten in the mid-'50s, Malibu specialist Lance Carson is sometimes named as the first real master of the art, having all but perfected the maneuver in the early '60s. Hawaiian-born David Nuuhiwa made further refinements in the mid-'60s. Hanging ten, and noseriding in general, fell out of fashion after the late-'60s shortboard revolution; longboarding and noseriding regained popularity beginning in the late '70s, and by the early '90s California teenage long-

Hanging ten; Duane DeSoto of Hawaii

board phenomenon Joel Tudor was hanging ten with a style and consistency that surpassed anyone from the original longboard era—Carson and Nuuhiwa included. "Hang ten" has for decades been the sport's most famous phrase (along with "wipeout"), familiar even to nonsurfers across the English-speaking world. *See also* noseriding.

Hang Ten   Beachwear company founded in 1960 by surf fashion entrepreneur Duke Boyd, based in San Diego, California. By the mid-'60s, the chubby Hang Ten feet—stitched in gold thread near the hem of tens of thousands of nylon surf trunks, and over the left breast of hundreds of thousands of cotton T-shirts—had become one of the first nationally recognized surfing logos, along with the marks for Hobie and Weber. Top surfers including Phil Edwards, Dewey Weber, Mike Doyle, Greg Noll, Hobie Alter, Joey Cabell, and David Nuuhiwa were featured in full-page Hang Ten print ads. Hang Ten's fashion cachet then plummeted during the late-'60s hippy-influenced fashion shift. Boyd sold the company in 1970, and it changed owners a few times in decades to come. In the early '90s the label became popular among thrift-store habitués, pursuing what Altculture.com called "street fashion's growing infantilization." The still-viable Hang Ten company meanwhile introduced a "new" line of retro-designed beachwear virtually indistinguishable from the original, with an ad campaign tag line reading "Hang Ten: Bitchin' When Your Mom was a Babe." *See also* Duke Boyd, fashion and surfing, surf trunks.

Hannon, John   Vigorous surfer/manufacturer/organizer from Long Island, New York; founder of Hannon Surfboards, the first shop of its kind in New York. Hannon was born (1927) in Bellmore, New York, raised on Jones Beach, and began surfing at age 11. He served in the Marine Corps during World War II, earned a B.A. in social science from Niagara University, worked in corporate finance in Long Beach, California, then returned to New York in 1959, and soon began making boards out of his mother's garage on Long Island. Hannon Surfboards opened in Great Neck in 1961, moved a few years later to Garden City, then to Farmingdale. Hannon helped organize a surf contest at Lido Beach in 1960 that evolved into the East Coast Surfing Championships (throughout the '60s, Hannon was often runner-up to Virginia Beach surfer Bob Holland in the seniors division of the ECSC). Hannon also ran a beach concession at Gilgo Beach, where he rented boards and gave surf lessons. After closing his surfboard shop in 1969, Hannon owned a ski store, taught at a community college, and was the recreation direction for Nassau County. Often described as the "father of New York Surfing," Hannon was inducted into the East Coast Surf Legends Hall of Fame in 1996.

Hansen, Don   Surfboard shaper and manufacturer from San Diego County, California; founder of Hansen Surfboards, and a leader of the signature-model era in the mid-1960s. Hansen was born (1937) and raised in South Dakota, lettered in boxing, track, and football, and earned up to $600 a week as a mink trapper. He began surfing at age 18, after graduating high school and moving to San Diego. In 1958, while stationed at Fort Ord army base, he began shaping surfboards in nearby Santa Cruz. Hansen was back in Southern California by 1961, working for industry leader Hobie Surfboards, and in June of that year he opened Hansen Surfboards in the San Diego County beachside town of Cardiff. Four years later, the company was grossing more than $500,000 a year. Hansen sponsored some of California's best riders, including Mike Doyle, Rusty Miller, Linda Benson, and Margo Godfrey, and produced some of the most popular surfboard models, like the Master, the Hustler, the Powerflex, and the 50/50. Hansen was also good with the media: his advertisements were well-designed and clever, Hansen himself made the cover of *Surfer* magazine in 1962, and he was one of 10 board manufacturers featured on a 1965 *Surfing* por-

trait cover. But Hansen Surfboards, along with the rest of the old guard surf retailers, fell into decline during the late-'60s shortboard revolution, when quicker-moving backyard board-makers were better able to respond to a whipsawing market. Hansen meanwhile seemed uncomfortable with the era's cultural changes. "More than a year has passed since surfdom was hit by a psychedelic tidal wave," he wrote in a 1969 surf magazine article. "There is certainly nothing wrong with this, [but] the last thing a kid needs are six strings of beads to weight him down as he tries to catch a wave."

haole   Hawaiian term for Caucasian; generally, but not always, derogatory. *Haole* is a compound of *ha*, for "breath," and *ole*, for "no" or "without." Ancient Hawaiians prepared for religious ceremonies with deep-breathing rituals; American and European missionaries, who began arriving in the Islands in the early 19th century, placed no emphasis on breathing, and thus became known as *haoles*. "Haole rot" refers to the peeling, flaking, postsunburn skin often found on the shoulders, backs, and faces of light-skinned visitors to the tropics.

Harbour, Rich   Enduring surfboard manufacturer from Seal Beach, California. Harbour (born in 1943) began surfing near his Seal Beach home after getting a board for his 16th birthday. Two months later the board was stolen, and Harbour, broke, was forced to make one from scratch. In 1962 he dropped out of college and opened Harbour Surfboards in Seal Beach (just south of Huntington Beach), and soon put together one of the West Coast's hottest surf teams, headed by 1966 world contest runner-up Jock Sutherland, 1965 U.S. champion Mark Martinson, and 1966 Malibu Invitational winner Steve Bigler. Harbour Surfboards also produced some of the period's best-selling models, including the Banana, the Trestle Special, and the Cheater. In 1998, *Longboard* magazine noted that Harbour was about to enter his 40th continuous year as a working surfboard shaper. His shop, furthermore, remained at its original Seal Beach location. Asked how the business got started, Harbour said, "I got booted out of my parents' garage when they got a new yellow Camaro and I dripped resin on it."

Hardman, Damien   Steely Australian pro surfer from Narrabeen, New South Wales; world champion

Damien Hardman

in 1987 and 1991; described by fellow Australian title-holder Pam Burridge as "the ice-man, [and] the world's toughest competitor." Hardman was born (1966) in Sydney, the son of financier Brian Hardman, who later became the world pro tour's media director. He was raised in the beachfront suburb of Warriewood, began surfing at age 10, and moved with his family in 1984 to Narrabeen, another Sydney coastal suburb, famous for producing gruff, hard-drinking, high-performance surfers such as Col Smith and Simon Anderson. Hardman placed third in the juniors division of the 1982 Australian National Titles; two years later he won the juniors in both the National Titles and World Championships, turned pro, competed in less than one-third of the season's events, and finished the circuit ranked #36. In 1985, his first full season on the world tour, the plain-looking curly-haired goofyfooter finished #17 and was named rookie of the year; the following year he jumped all the way to #6.

Few surfers have ever gone as far as Hardman has in removing all stylistic hitches and flaws; his back-

side turns, in particular, were models of precision and could be linked together in endlessly replicated sequences at places like Bells Beach in Australia. Hardman's technical mastery was of such a high order that it was sometimes held against him, as critics said he was automated and predictable. A more legitimate criticism was that he was gun-shy in big waves.

Hardman, then 21, won the 1987 world title in a thrilling showdown against fellow Australian Gary Elkerton in the season's final contest at Sydney's Manly Beach. In the weeks and months ahead, he was finally given a measure of recognition by the American surf press, who had up to this point ignored him. California surf journalist Bill Sharp pointed out Hardman's "humility and lack of showmanship," but went on to call him "a killer who has pretty much nailed everyone to the wall." Hardman, citing tennis champion Ivan Lendl as his favorite sports figure, was the tour's best competitor over the next six years, finishing #2 in 1988, #4 in 1989 and 1990, #1 in 1991, #2 in 1992, and #4 in 1993. He dropped to #13 the next year and nearly vanished from sight over the next two years, then came back for an all-out final season in 1997, at age 31, finishing #6. Hardman announced his retirement, then changed his mind, finishing the 1998 season rated #14. He rose to #9 in 1999, dropped to 25th in 2000, then finally retired in 2001—when he was described by Swell.com as "the ultimate professional surfer." He finished with a total of 19 pro tour wins, including the 1986 Stubbies Classic, the Rip Curl Pro in 1988 and 1993, and the Rip Curl Hossegor Pro in 1998. In 1988 he became the first male surfer to win seven events in one season (equaled later only by world champions Tom Curren and Kelly Slater).

Hardman had little or no interest in surfing for the cameras but was nonetheless featured in more than two dozen surf movies and videos, including *Gripping Stuff* (1987), *Madmen, Saints and Sinners* (1992), *Beyond the Boundaries* (1994), and *Feral Kingdom* (1995). He remained a largely uncelebrated figure outside of Australia, never rising above fifth in the annual *Surfer* Magazine Readers Poll. If the lack of recognition bothered Hardman he didn't let it show, saying in 1998 that he preferred to "blend into the crowd." He was inducted into the Australian Surfing Hall of Fame in 1999; the following year he founded Instyle Enterprises, a surf accessories distribution company. Hardman is married and has three children.

Harehoe, Arsene   Wiry regularfoot surfer from Tahiti; a perennial national and French champion in the 1970s and '80s, and a first-rate tuberider described by California surf journalist Steve Hawk in 1995 as "the Gerry Lopez of Tahiti." Harehoe was born (1959) and raised in Papeete, and began surfing in 1971; two years later he won the first of 15 Tahitian national titles, the last coming in 1989. His record in the French nationals was similar, with seven wins between 1974 and 1989. Harehoe did well in the World Amateur Surfing Championships, finishing fifth in 1980, ninth in 1986, and fifth in 1990. He also mentored 1986 Juniors division amateur world champion and fellow Papeete surfer Vetea "Poto" David. A masterful tuberider, backside or frontside, Harehoe was featured in nearly a dozen surf movies and videos of the '80s and early '90s, including *Amazing Surf Stories* (1986), *Mad Wax* (1987), and *Gen X* (1990). He began working as a shaper since 1980, and two years later opened Arsene Harehoe Surfboards in Papeete.

Hargraves, Spencer   Well-traveled regularfoot surfer from Newquay, England; European pro champion in 1990, 1991, and 1992. Hargraves was born (1973) and raised in Newquay, the son of a first-generation British surfer, and began riding waves at Fistral Beach at age five. He won both the British juniors and men's titles in 1989, again won the men's in 1990, then turned pro and began his three-year domination of the European circuit. He later competed without much success on the World Qualifying Series tour. Hargraves became manager of the Quiksilver European Surf Team in 2000, and since then has spent half of each year living on the Gold Coast of Queensland, Australia, and half in Hossegor, France. He surfed for the U.K. in the 2002 World Surfing Games. Hargraves has appeared in about 10 surf videos, including *Oz on Fire* (1991), *Surfers of Fortune* (1994), and *Stash* (2002).

Harlow, Warren   Unheralded big-wave rider of the 1960s, originally from Manhattan Beach, California. Harlow began surfing waves in 1947 as a junior high school student on a 60-pound hollow board. He moved to Oahu in the late '50s to work in the navy shipyards, and rode big waves on the North Shore because "it was the only way to escape the crowded conditions." Harlow rented an oceanfront house at Waimea Bay in the early '60s in order to be as close as possible to the world's most famous heavy-water surf break, and by 1965, according to *Surfing* magazine, he was "one of the best" big-wave surfers in the world. "The kind of guy," Waimea pioneer Greg Noll said in 1997, "who's never had a minute in the spotlight and could care less."

Harris, Peter   Postal worker from Queensland, Australia, who at age 22 steamrolled the world's best pro surfers to win the 1980 Stubbies Pro contest, held in beautiful six-foot surf at Harris's home break of Burleigh Heads. Harris was born (1958) in Brisbane, and began surfing at age seven. The Stubbies was his first pro contest, and he gained entry at the last minute when one of the seeded surfers went missing. The easygoing local was defeated in his first match and had to fight his way up through the losers' rounds, defeating Cheyne Horan and Buzzy Kerbox, among others, on his way to a final heat against Hawaiian Dane Kealoha; the win paid $10,000 in cash and prizes. Harris, a rangy regularfooter, never won another international pro contest, but on the strength of his Stubbies victory finished the 1980 season ranked 15th in the world.

Harrison, Dru   Terrier-built regularfoot surfer from Hermosa Beach, California; winner of the 1966 Swami's Pro-Am, and runner-up in the 1969 United States Surfing Championships. Harrison began surfing at age 10 in Hermosa; as a young teenager he had the quickest feet on the coast, and often embellished his noserides by kicking his right foot into the air ahead of his board or turning around and hanging heels. His $500 win in the 1966 Swami's Pro-Am came in the predawn of surfing's professional era; later that year Rick Surfboards introduced the Dru Harrison Improviser signature model board. He also placed eighth in the 1966 World Surfing Championships, won the juniors division of the 1967 United States Surfing Championships, and was runner-up in the men's division of the 1969 U.S. Championships. After the late-'60s introduction of the shortboard, Harrison reinvented his surfing and rode in a curious feet-together "speed surfing" stance. He appeared in a small number of surf movies, including *Cosmic Children* (1970) and *Going Surfin'* (1973), and wrote a half-dozen articles for *Surfer* and *Surfing* magazines. Harrison died from alcohol-related causes in 2003; he was 52.

Harrison, Lorrin "Whitey"   Hot-rodding California surfer in the 1930s and '40s, and pioneering

Lorrin Harrison

geriatric surfer in the '80s and '90s. Harrison was born (1913) in Garden Grove, south of Los Angeles, and as a child traveled to and from the family summer house in Laguna Beach by horse and wagon. He began surfing in 1925 at age 12, and eight years later was among the first to ride San Onofre; in 1933 he won the Pacific Coast Surf Riding Championships. Harrison labored as a surfboard builder, lifeguard, dry cleaner, and night watchman, but the majority of his work life—for roughly 30 years, beginning in 1946—was spent as a lobster and abalone diver. In 1932, he stowed away on a cruise ship bound for Waikiki, but was caught and sent back to the mainland without having set foot on Hawaiian soil. Less than 24 hours after his return to California he again stowed away, and was again caught, but this time allowed to remain in Hawaii; during a return visit in the late '30s, he was among the first to surf the North Shore of Oahu. Harrison steeped himself in Waikiki beach culture, and decades later, when presented to a nationwide TV audience in 1990 as a lively senior citizen surfer—in a Nike ad campaign, a *Life* magazine feature, and as a guest on *Late Night with David Letterman*—he was usually outfitted with a brightly colored aloha shirt, a coconut palm-frond hat, and a ukulele.

In 1946, Harrison met and married Cecelia Yorba, a descendant from an old California Spanish land grant family, and they lived in her 18th-century adobe house in San Juan Capistrano, one mile inland from Dana Point in south Orange County. They had four children together; Harrison had two children from a previous marriage. He died from a heart attack in 1993 while driving home with his wife after a morning swim.

Harvey, Richard   Australian surfer and surfboard shaper from Queensland's Gold Coast; winner of the 1973 Australian National Titles. That same year, the 24-year-old Harvey visited Bali, where he likely became the first to ride the explosive but perfect left-breaking tubes of Padang Padang. (Australian Tony Eltherington has also been cited as the original Padang surfer.) "A barrel came into view that was so insane I staggered," Harvey wrote in *Australia's Surfing Life* magazine, recalling his first view of the dangerously shallow Padang. He rode three waves, made them all, and was relieved to call it quits. "I was scared. I didn't know where the take-off area was, didn't know if the reed would suck dry, didn't know if it was even makable..." Harvey Surfboards later became one of the most popular Gold Coast labels. Harvey appeared in a small number of surf movies, including *Splashdown* (1969) and *Freeform* (1972). *See also* Padang Padang.

Hasley, Chuck   Club organizer and surf society raconteur from La Jolla, California; founder of the Windansea Surf Club in 1963. Hasley was born (1934) in Oklahoma, moved with his family in 1941 to Seal Beach, California, and began surfing at age 10. He moved to La Jolla in 1958, one year after receiving a master's in education from Long Beach State College. In 1963 he picked up the long-moribund name of Windansea Surf and Ski Club in order to enter a team in the Malibu Invitational; Hasley then put together an all-star surf squad—including Joey Cabell, LJ Richards, Skip Frye, Mike Hynson, Rusty Miller, and Butch Van Artsdalen—rented a bus, and hired a band to play while they drove up the coast. The Windansea Surf Club's debut turned into a raucous beer- and prank-filled weekend odyssey. They also won the contest, placing five surfers in the six-man final. Under Hasley's direction, Windansea Surf Club was a force in California surfing for the next five years. In 1964, Hasley and Hynson opened Windansea Sport, a La Jolla surf shop. Hasley was convicted of wholesale marijuana drug dealing in 1970 and served four years on a 15-year sentence. In 1981 he opened Windansea

Silkscreen, a T-shirt business, which he still owns and operates. *See also* Windansea Surf Club.

Hawaii   Hawaii, located 2,090 miles southwest of the U.S. mainland, is commonly recognized as surfing's birthplace, as well as its spiritual home. "If there's a church of surfing like there's a church of baseball," novelist Kem Nunn wrote in 1993, "certainly Hawaii is its Mecca." Hawaii's four major islands (Kauai, Oahu, Maui, and Hawaii) have a combined 820 miles of coastline; air and water temperatures on each island average between 70 and 80 degrees from season to season; and with a few exceptions waves here break over shallow lava-lined reefs. Summer surf is generally between two and four feet; winter surf is often six to 10 feet, and can get up to 30 feet or bigger. Oahu is by far the most populated Hawaiian island, and also has the most surf breaks, including the gentle rollers of Waikiki, the variegated waves of Makaha, and the thundering arrangement of spots along the North Shore, including Pipeline, Sunset Beach, and Waimea Bay. Maui's best-known breaks are Honolua Bay, Jaws, and Maalaea; Kauai is home to Hanalei Bay. (The Hawaiian chain is actually composed of more than 130 islands and extends for 1,500 miles, ending to the northwest near the Midway Islands; the major islands are clustered together in the southeast.)

While it's likely that the Hawaiian surf was being ridden on bellyboards as early as A.D. 400, shortly after seafaring Polynesians first settled the islands, historians have suggested that stand-up surfing began around 1000. Lieutenant James King, an officer under British explorer Captain James Cook, was the first person to write about surfing, in 1778, after seeing a group of Hawaiian wave-riders at the Big Island's Kealakekua Bay, noting that "they seem to feel a great pleasure in the motion which this exercise gives." Reports from subsequent explorers and missionaries described surfing as an integral part of daily life for all islanders, male and female, old and young, royalty and commoners. Premodern Hawaiians are thought to have ridden at least 100 different surf breaks throughout the island chain, with the Kona coast of the Big Island being the most popular surfing region, followed by the Waikiki area of Oahu. Villages would empty during a good swell, with everyone picking up their wooden boards made of koa or wiliwili and heading for the surf. Most adults used the shorter *alaia* boards, measuring between seven and 12 feet; royalty sometimes used massive *olo* boards that measured up to 17 feet. Surfing was also a method of courtship (a man and woman might ride a wave together prior to lovemaking), a spectator sport (pigs, canoes, and textiles were often wagered; servitude, even life itself, was occasionally put on the line), and a source of myth and legend. Prayers were offered to bring the surf up, and to consecrate the trees from which surfboards were made.

The introduction of western culture was disastrous for the Hawaiians and for their favorite sport. By the mid-19th century, crippled by newly introduced diseases and humbled by the arrival of Calvinist missionaries who disapproved of surfing as licentious (the fact that it was practiced in the nude was particularly galling to the newcomers) and running "against the laws of God," Hawaiians for the most part gave up the sport. By 1892, as physician and missionary's son Nathaniel Emerson wrote, it was "hard to find a surfboard outside our museums and private collections."

Hawaii's surfing renaissance began in Waikiki in the early 20th century and was soon being led by future Olympic gold medal swimmer Duke Kahanamoku, along with Irish-Hawaiian surfer George Freeth and writer/organizer Alexander Hume Ford. Waikiki remained the center of the surf world until just after World War II. Much of America was introduced to the sport through Hawaii-based travel essays written by Mark Twain (published in 1866) and Jack London (1907). The sport was filmed for the first time in 1906 in Waikiki, two years before Ford chartered the Outrigger Canoe Club, the sport's first organized group (and by some reckoning the sport's first surf shop, as boards could be purchased at the Outrigger's palm-frond-covered Waikiki clubhouse). Waikiki was also the base from which surfing was exported to the rest of the world: Freeth introduced surfing to Southern California in 1907, and a few years later, Kahanamoku gave wave-riding demonstrations in California, New Jersey, New York, Australia, and New Zealand.

By the late '30s, Waikiki surfers John Kelly and Wally Froiseth were riding the bigger and faster waves at Makaha on the west side of Oahu; by the early '50s, a small number of surfers were regularly taking on the raw and powerful waves of the North Shore. The Makaha International Surfing Championships, the islands' first major surf contest, debuted in 1954, and was soon drawing entrants from California, Australia, and Peru. (Oahu would later become the crucible for professional surfing, as the home of International

Professional Surfers—founders of the world pro circuit in 1976—and as host island to dozens of events, including the Duke Kahanamoku Classic, the Pipeline Masters, the World Cup, the Smirnoff Pro, the Billabong Pro, the Gotcha Pro, and the Quiksilver in Memory of Eddie Aikau.) By the late '50s, the first generation of California transplant big-wave riders (most notably Buzzy Trent, Peter Cole, Ricky Grigg, and Fred Van Dyke) had moved to Hawaii, while dozens of other mainlanders were visiting for weeks or months at a time, a seasonal influx that would soon rise to hundreds, then thousands. Surf movies of the '50s and early '60s showed not only the more familiar Oahu spots like Makaha and Sunset, but ventured out to highlight more exotic breaks such as Honolua Bay on Maui or Kauai's Hanalei Bay. Hawaii continued to be viewed as the ultimate surf destination in the 1970s, where big-wave surfing and tuberiding were practiced at their highest levels and where cash prizes, reputations, and world championships could be won. By the early '80s, however, Indonesia was beginning to overtake Hawaii as the ultimate tropical surf destination, as perfect waves were discovered by the score up and down the gigantic Indian Ocean archipelago.

Hawaii continues to be a vital surf center today: thousands of tourists get their first and perhaps only taste of wave-riding while visiting resort-packed Waikiki; local surfers, like their island forebears, have made wave-riding an integral part of their everyday lives; the pro circuit ends each year with a series of events on the North Shore. Big-wave riding was reinvented in Hawaii in the early '90s as surfers began using personal watercraft to tow each other in to giant waves inaccessible by the standard paddle-in method, and the limits of big-wave surfing are tested nearly every winter in the giant Hawaiian surf. Maui has long been the creative wellspring for surf-associated sports like windsurfing, kiteboarding, and foilboarding.

Hawaii has regularly produced world champions (including Fred Hemmings, Margo Oberg, Lynne Boyer, Derek Ho, Rusty Keaulana, Sunny Garcia, Bonga Perkins), pro tour standouts (Michael Ho, Dane Kealoha, Shane Dorian, Kalani Robb, Rochelle Ballard, Keala Kennelly), big-wave riders (Peter Cole, Ricky Grigg, Eddie Aikau, James Jones, Darrick Doerner, Mark Foo, Ken Bradshaw, Laird Hamilton, Brock Little), first-rate surfboard shapers (Dick Brewer, Ben Aipa, Glenn Minami, Pat Rawson, John Carper), photographer/filmmakers (Warren Bolster, Steve Wilkings, Don King, Bill Ballard), and industry-leading surf companies (Lightning Bolt, Town and Country, Hawaiian Island Creations, Local Motion). Other Hawaiian surfers who've made indelible imprints on the sport include Rabbit Kekai, Joey Cabell, Gerry Lopez, Larry Bertlemann, Jeff Hakman, Barry Kanaiaupuni, Reno Abellira, Jock Sutherland, Paul Strauch, Rell Sunn, and Johnny-Boy Gomes.

As of 2003, Hawaii was home to about 110,000 surfers, 85 surf shops, two surfing magazines (*High Surf Advisory,* and *Tiaregirl*), and a small number of local surfing TV shows (including *Board Stories*). The Hawaii Amateur Surfing Association runs dozens of events annually. The Bishop Museum in Honolulu is home to the world's most extensive collection of pre-20th-century surfboards. Hawaii's surfers, surf history, and surf breaks have been detailed in dozens of books, including *Hawaiian Surfriders* (1935), *Surfing Hawaii* (1972), *Surfing: The Ultimate Pleasure* (1984), *Surfer's Guide to Hawaii* (1991), and *Surfing: A History of the Ancient Hawaiian Sport* (1996). *See also* Hawaii (the Big Island), Kauai, Maui, North Shore, Oahu, Waikiki.

Hawaii Five-O   Weekly one-hour CBS-TV police drama series, filmed on location in Hawaii, starring Jack Lord as the steely-eyed and taciturn detective Steve McGarrett. *Hawaii Five-O* ran from 1968 to 1980, making it television's longest-running police show. Surfing rarely figured into *Hawaii Five-O*, but surfers often tuned in to catch the title shot of a huge, empty, churning wave, famously set to a brass-heavy theme song recorded by the Ventures. The location of this wave has long been a surf world mystery. Its length suggests Ala Moana, in Honolulu, and that was the presumptive choice for years. Not so, said *Surfer* magazine in 1980. "The monster wave in the *Hawaii Five-O* tag is Sunset Beach, reversed." *Surfmovies,* an exhaustive book on surfing in movies, television, and video published in 2000, said it was Pipeline. California surf moviemaker Dale Davis was said to be the photographer, as was Don Brown, also from California. In 1990, the *San Diego Reader* newspaper reported that CBS cameraman Reza Badiyi filmed the wave on the North Shore, just off "a rocky peninsula"—Badiyi didn't know the break's name—which would almost certainly put the location at Rockpile, a reef just west of Pipeline. *See also* television and surfing.

Hawaii, the Big Island   Hawaii's Big Island is 93 miles long, 76 miles wide, and covers nearly 4,050 square miles—about twice the combined size of the remaining Hawaiian islands. Relative to the rest of the island chain, Hawaii is a quiet and out-of-the-way place to surf, with far fewer breaks per square mile than Oahu, Maui, or Kauai, and lacking even a single high-profile spot to compare with Pipeline (Oahu), Honolua Bay (Maui), or Hanalei Bay (Kauai); non-Hawaiian surfers would be hard-pressed to name even one Big Island break. But for hundreds of years prior to the 20th century, Hawaii's lava-fringed Kona coast was the island chain's surfing capital as well as its population center. About 50 different breaks are thought to have been ridden by ancient Big Island surfers, compared to fewer than 10 breaks in Oahu, and Kamehameha I, the unifying high chief and founder of the Kingdom of Hawaii at the turn of the 18th century, learned to surf on the southwest-facing Kona coast. Captain James Cook, the 18th-century English navigator/explorer and the person who introduced surfing to the English-speaking world, was clubbed to death by Kona coast natives in 1779.

Because Hawaii is positioned at the southeast tip of the island chain, its summer surf—produced by storms in the South Pacific or Central America—is bigger than that found on the other islands. But North Pacific winter swells, particularly from the northwest, are often much reduced in size once they thread past the other islands and hit Hawaii. Hilo and the mall-studded Kona coast are the Big Island's two most populated wave-riding areas. Surf breaks in Hawaii are for the most part widely dispersed, access to some areas is difficult, and local surfers spend much of their time driving in search of waves. Hawaii has by far the most diverse landscape in the Islands, with small plantation towns, enormous cattle ranches on low plains, wet and densely forested valleys, jagged-rock coastlines, black-sand beaches, and the 13,800-foot snowcapped Mauna Kea. Two of the island's five volcanoes are active; Mauna Loa and Kilauea on occasion will send long, slow-rolling rivulets of lava into the ocean. The Big Island has just over 150,000 residents; about half live in and around Hilo, the island's largest city.

"Why is it that the Big Island hasn't been written about?" *Petersen's Surfing* magazine asked in a 1968 feature article that introduced the island to the surf world at large. "And is there any surf there?" The magazine reported that, yes, there was surf on Hawaii, and that it hadn't been written about in part because local surfers preferred anonymity. Surf magazine writer/editor Steve Pezman in 1996 described the Big Island as "a last resort for those seeking the old Hawaii." While the Big Island produced talented surfers throughout the decades, virtually none came to the attention of the larger surfing world until Kona coast teenager Shane Dorian joined up with the New School surfers of the early '90s. Other Big Island standouts include Conan Hayes, Noah Johnson, and nine-time bodyboarding world champion Mike Stewart.

As of 2003, the Big Island was home to 13 surf shops and about 7,000 surfers. The Hawaiian Amateur Surfing Association each year holds seven contests on the Big Island; the Shane Dorian/Conan Hayes Keiki Classic and the Tiger Espere Longboard Classic are both popular local events. The Big Island is featured in a small number of surf movies and videos, including *Shock Waves* (1987), *The 5th Symphony Document* (2001), and *The Blueprint* (2002). Big Island surf is detailed in *Surfing Hawaii* (1973) and *Surfer's Guide to Hawaii* (1991).

Hawaiian Amateur Surfing Association (HASA)

Oahu-based amateur competitive surfing organization, a sanctioning body for a set of discrete island-contained circuits, and the managing group for the statewide amateur championships. The Hawaiian Surfing Association (HSA), forebear to the Hawaiian Amateur Surfing Association (HASA), was created in 1964 as a way to facilitate and promote organized competition among the dozen or so statewide surfing clubs. The HSA was reformatted and expanded in 1968, after the United States Surfing Association folded. The Hawaiians, however, seemed to be less interested than mainland surfers in clubs, associations, and contests. As HSA secretary Jan Husic wrote to *Surfing* magazine in 1968, sport often "loses its appeal, its excitement, when it becomes regulated. In Hawaii, complexity must always give way to simplicity." But the HSA carried on, running an annual slate of regional events leading to a state championship, held each June at Ala Moana in Honolulu. Top finishers in the state event were invited to the United States Surfing Championships. HSA champions of the '60s and '70s include two-time world champion Sharron Weber, 1966 world contest runner-up Jock Sutherland, 1974 Smirnoff winner Reno Abellira, 1973 U.S. champion Larry Bertlemann, and 1982 Pipeline Masters champion Michael Ho.

The organizationally adrift HSA was turned over in 1989 to Oahu businessman and surf contest director Reid Inouye, who changed the group's name to the Hawaiian Surfing Federation (HSF), and made clear his intention to operate the association as a for-profit business. While this was against the strictures of the governing United States Surfing Federation (USSF), Hawaii's presence was important to the American amateur surfing family, there was no alternative group, and Inouye was running a well-structured operation; the USSF put the HSF "under review" and left it at that.

In 1996, Wendell Aoki, contest judge for the Association of Surfing Professionals (ASP), took over as HSF executive director, renamed the association the Hawaiian Amateur Surfing Association, and returned it to nonprofit status. HASA had just over 400 members by 2001. The group sanctions a circuit of contests on four of the Hawaiian islands (Oahu, for example, has a nine-event series), all using the same rules as the ASP and all using ASP Hawaii judges, so as to help prepare top Hawaiian amateurs for a career in the pro ranks. Profits from membership and contest fees go into an account to help send the Hawaii state team to the biannual amateur World Surfing Games. *See also* competitive surfing.

Hawaiian shirt   *See* aloha shirt.

Hawaiian Surfing Association   *See* Hawaiian Amateur Surfing Association.

Hawaiian Surfing Federation   *See* Hawaiian Amateur Surfing Association.

Hawaiian Surfriders   Ninety-five-page book written by Tom Blake, part surf history and part instruction manual, originally published in 1935 as *Hawaiian Surfboard*; described by the *Surfer's Journal* as a "seminal volume of surf literature, [and] the sport's single most important document." Articles, essays, and journal entries were published before Blake's book, and in 1931 California's Ron Drummond wrote *The Art of Wave Riding*, a 26-page pamphlet on bodysurfing. But *Hawaiian Surfboard* was the sport's first book, and was written by surfing's most knowledgeable figure. The Wisconsin-born Blake was the winner of the 1928 Pacific Coast Surf Riding Championship, the first to surf Malibu, and the originator of the hollow surfboard, the sailboard, the surfboard fin, the waterproof surf-use camera, and the commercially made surfboard. *Hawaiian Surfboard* is illustrated with nearly 50 black-and-white photos, most taken by Blake (eight were published in a 1935 issue of *National Geographic*); Olympic swimming

champion and surf icon Duke Kahanamoku wrote the book's introduction. Chapter titles include "Ancient Hawaiian Legends of Surfriding," "Modern Surfriding," and "How to Use the New Hollow Surfboard." Blake's prose is dry, often clumsy, and occasionally pedantic, but he does convey the power and beauty of surfing in Hawaii.

> *The water is so warm one is not conscious of it. The view of the palm trees on shore, the [Waikiki] hotels, the mountains and clouds is marvelous and to me it is part of the pleasure of surfing. The hour before sunset is best of all, for then the mountains take on all the shades of green imaginable, while the clouds near them assume all shades of white and gray. Rainbows are often seen in the far off valleys.*

The blue-cloth-covered *Hawaiian Surfboard* was published by Honolulu-based Paradise of the Pacific, and the original press run was about 500. As a postpublication marketing tactic, Blake, at his own expense, added a tapa cloth dust jacket. In 1983, Bank Wright, a surf book publisher from Redondo Beach, California, reissued Blake's book as *Hawaiian Surfriders 1935*. By 2000, pristine first editions of *Hawaiian Surfboard* were priced around $4,000. *See also* Tom Blake, books and surfing.

Hawk, Sam   Rugged regularfoot surfer originally from Orange County, California; a standout power surfer of the early and mid-1970s. Hawk was born (1950) in South Gate, and began surfing at age 14 in Huntington Beach; along with brothers Tom and Chris, he was soon regarded as one of the area's top riders. Hawk moved to the North Shore of Oahu in 1967, and soon found that the big Hawaiian waves perfectly matched his aggressive but fluid approach. By 1971 he was among the pacesetters at Sunset Beach and Rocky Point, while at Pipeline he was regarded as by far the most advanced regularfooter. Photographs and film clips of the blond-haired Hawk squaring off against Pipeline's cavernous tubes on January 17, 1972—soon dubbed Huge Monday—sent shock waves throughout the surf world. "Sammy surfs with complete and total abandon," *Surfer* magazine reported in its Huge Monday article. "He gets into spots that no one else will go for. It's a miracle that he's lived as long as he has." Hawk's performances at Pipeline stood as a benchmark until the "backside attack" movement of 1975–76.

Sam Hawk

Never a keen competition surfer, Hawk nonetheless posted a few good results in the North Shore pro events, including a fourth in the 1972 Pipeline Masters and a third in the 1974 Duke Kahanamoku Classic. He was also invited to the 1971 Expression Session. Hawk appeared in a small number of surf movies, including *Oceans* (1972), *Five Summer Stories* (1972), *Going Surfin'* (1973), and *Super Session* (1975). A protégé of master surfboard shaper Dick Brewer in the early '70s, Hawk himself quickly became a highly regarded board-maker, first for the Brewer label, then with his own small business. He continued to surf through the decades, and was Australian Cheyne Horan's tow-in partner during the enormous Biggest Wednesday swell that hit the North Shore in January 1998. *See also* Huge Monday.

Hawk, Steve Raw-boned surf journalist from San Diego, California; *Surfer* magazine editor from 1990 to 1999. Hawk was born (1955) in Pensacola, Florida, raised in San Diego, and began surfing at age 14. Not long after earning a B.A. in English from U.C. Santa Barbara, Hawk took the first of a series of newspaper reporter jobs in north San Diego County, leading to full-time work with the *Orange County Register* from 1984 to 1990. He had also been submitting freelance articles to both *Surfer* and *Surfing* magazines, and in 1990 was hired as *Surfer*'s editor. Hawk was perhaps best known for his warm and often self-effacing monthly "Intro" column, where he used personal experience as a gateway into a more general surf world topic. A description in 1997 of how he scraped his forehead on a rock at his local surf break—"It didn't hurt too much, but for once in my life I looked kind of gnarly"—became an essay on how surfers generally

injure themselves in small waves, not big ones. Not convinced by his own logic, Hawk finishes by saying that before his next venture out into big surf, he intends to "find a piece of driftwood and knock on it till my knuckles bleed." Hawk was the executive director of Swell.com, a surfing Web site, from 1999 to 2001; he's freelanced surf-related articles to the *New York Times*, the *Los Angeles Times*, *Outside*, and *Harper's*. Hawk is married with two children; his younger brother is skateboard icon Tony Hawk.

Hawkins, Joey Flashy white-blond regularfoot longboarder from Huntington Beach, California; winner of the 1992 world longboard championships. Hawkins was a shortboarder on the Huntington Beach High School surf team when he herniated a disk and was out of the water for six months. He began riding a longboard to work his way back into surfing shape, but found he enjoyed applying his shortboard skills onto a longer medium. Hawkins became a rip-and-tear "progressive" longboarder, as differentiated from the smooth-riding "classic" school. His win in the 1992 world contest, held in Biarritz, France, was a first for an American longboarder in the pro era, as the first six championships had gone to Australian surfers. Hawkins was 22 when he won the championship, which paid $6,000. He's appeared in a number of surf videos, including *Longboards: The Rebirth of Cool* (1993) and *Full Cycle* (1994).

Hawkins, Mary Ann Eye-catching surfer from Costa Mesa, California; winner of the Pacific Coast Women's Surfboard Championships in 1938, 1939, and 1940. Hawkins had "the figure and looks of a movie star," surf journalist Jeff Duclos wrote in 1999, and was "grace personified in the water." Hawkins was born (1919) and raised in Pasadena, began swimming at age nine, and at 17 was the Amateur Athletic Union 500-meter freestyle champion. The Hawkins family moved to Costa Mesa in 1934, primarily so that Mary Ann could train in the ocean. But the plan "kind of backfired," as Hawkins recalled in 1991, "because I fell so in love with surfing and bodysurfing I never really did my best in swimming from that time on." Hawkins was taught to surf by pioneering Orange County wave-riders Gene "Tarzan" Smith and Lorrin "Whitey" Harrison. Between 1935 and 1941 she was the darling of the California surf scene, winning nearly every women's surfing and paddleboarding event she entered. She also served as a model for

Mary Ann Hawkins

the next generation of California female surfers, including Robin Grigg, Vicki Williams, and Aggie Bane. Hawkins was invited to compete in the 1939 Duke Kahanamoku Swim Meet in Honolulu, where she broke the Hawaiian record for the 220 meter freestyle and spent her days surfing at Waikiki with Olympic gold medal winner and surfing icon Duke Kahanamoku.

Hawkins was featured surfing in a 1938 issue of *Life* magazine, and not long afterward began getting work in Hollywood as a stunt double, standing in for Dorothy Lamour, Shirley Jones, and Lana Turner, among others. On ABC-TV's *You Asked For It,* Hawkins held her breath underwater for two minutes and 15 seconds, setting a world record. Hawkins moved to Hawaii in 1956 to work on a movie, and was hired to do a water show at the Hilton Hawaiian Village swimming pool, with special appearances by longtime friend Esther Williams. The show was popular, and helped publicize Hawkins's newly opened swim school. In 1973, Hawkins estimated that she had taught more than 10,000 people to swim.

Hawkins was married three times, and had two children. She quit surfing in 1983, not long after her son, Rusty, drowned while working in Alaska. "I felt that if I got out in the water again maybe I would be closer to him and closer to God," she recalled. "But it was so lonely because quite often Rusty and I surfed together. I haven't been surfing since." Hawkins died in 1993 at age 73. Several pictures of Hawkins surfing appear in John "Doc" Ball's 1946 book, *California Surfriders.*

Hayes, Conan   Introspective and heavily tattooed goofyfoot pro surfer from Kona, Hawaii; world-

ranked #12 in 1996. Hayes was born (1975) in Seattle, Washington, moved to Hawaii at age eight, began surfing the following year, and won three state amateur titles between 1986 and 1990. He turned pro at 15, and four years later qualified for the world tour. A first-rate tuberider, especially in bigger surf, Hayes was also known for his hooking backside off-the-lip maneuver. No longer a full-time competitor by 2000, he nonetheless scored his first pro tour victory that year with a win in the G-Shock Hawaiian Pro at Haleiwa, Oahu. Hayes had by that time proven himself to be a very different kind of pro surfer: he wrote poetry, spent six months of the year in New York, and told a surf magazine interviewer that he wanted to learn French and Japanese. He was regularly featured in surf videos, including *Momentum 2* (1993), *The Show* (1996), and *Thicker Than Water* (1999). On New Year's Eve, 1999, Hayes married surfer/model Malia Jones.

head dip   A small-wave maneuver, usually more theatrical than useful, where the surfer holds a tight angle near the crest and inserts himself partially or wholly into the whitewater as it crumbles down. As performed in the original longboarding hotdog era— from the mid-'50s to the mid-'60s—the head was tilted horizontally or completely inverted, then "dipped" into the breaking wave. Today's head dip often looks like a tuberide without the tube.

health and surfing   *See* fitness and surfing, injuries and surfing.

Hedemann, Hans   Dependable pro surfer from Kailua, Hawaii; world-ranked #4 in 1983. Surf journalist Derek Hynd described Hedemann in 1987 as a "tenacious, [and] physical customer," and also noted the Hawaiian's nonflashy "stoic approach." Hedemann was born (1959) in Honolulu, raised in Kailua, and began surfing at Waikiki in 1966. He started competing at age 17 with little success, turned pro at 18, and the following season, 1978, was named the world tour's rookie of the year after finishing #14 in the ratings. Hedemann opened the 1983 season with back-to-back victories in South Africa—the first two wins of his career—and led the ratings for the first third of the season. He won his last world tour event in 1989, and retired at the end of 1990. Friendly, reliable, and hardworking, Hedemann was sponsored at a higher level than many of the era's better-known surfers; in 1986 he listed Beach Towne, Hawaiian Island Creations, Victory Wetsuits, Primo Beer, Ray-Ban, Astrodeck, Freestyle Watches, and a local Honda dealership as his backers. Hedemann appeared in more than 20 surf films and videos, including *We Got Surf* (1981), *Follow the Sun* (1983), *Wave Warriors* (1985), and *Shock Waves* (1987); he also appeared in Universal's *North Shore* (1987) and Paramount's Frankie Avalon/Annette Funicello reunion movie *Back to the Beach* (1987). He founded the Hans Hedemann Surf School Hawaii at Diamond Head in 1992.

heels over   A hotdogging longboard-only variation on the noseride, usually performed after hanging ten, where the surfer does a quick half-turn and drapes both heels off the tip of the board. Extremely difficult and sometimes dismissed as showy by longboard purists. First performed in the mid-'60s. Also called "hanging heels." *See also* hang ten, noseriding.

Hemmings, Fred   Straight-talking square-jawed surfer/organizer/politician from Honolulu, Hawaii; winner of the 1968 World Surfing Championships; founder of the Pipeline Masters, as well as the International Professional Surfers world tour; Republican minority whip in Hawaii's House of Representatives in 1990. Hemmings was born (1946) and raised in Honolulu, one of six children delivered to a New York–born civil servant father and a Portuguese-American mother. The family was poor, and Hemmings, along with three of his siblings, contracted polio, though none suffered permanent debilitation. Hemmings began surfing in Waikiki at age eight; in 1961 and 1963 he won the juniors division of the Makaha International contest; in 1964 he took the Makaha men's title (while earning all-league honors as a center on the Punahoe High School football team), then finished runner-up in 1965, and won again in 1966.

Hemmings's strengths as a surfer were power and consistency; he rode in a fairly narrow regularfoot stance, drew elegant if somewhat predictable lines across the wave, and kept his maneuvers under control at all times, even while charging through the most critical sections. He appeared in *The Endless Summer* (1966), *Golden Breed* (1968), and other period surf movies. Because Hemmings had nothing but disdain for anything associated with the late-'60s counterculture movement, it wasn't surprising that he had little enthusiasm for the concurrent shortboard revolution. The short surfboards, he said in a 1968 interview, "are absurd for Hawaiian surf. They

don't work here." (Later in the same interview Hemmings railed against "pot and hippieism.")

In a result that surprised nearly everybody in the sport except for Hemmings himself, he then went on to win the 1968 World Championships, held in Puerto Rico. He used a longer and thicker board than the other competitors, but during the finals, held in beautiful six-foot surf, he rode without error to defeat 1964 world champion Midget Farrelly and 1966 world champion Nat Young, among others. "They were rock and rollers," Hemmings said of Farrelly and Young, in a remark that illustrated the distance between himself and surfing's psychedelic orthodoxy, "while I tried to waltz with the waves." Hemmings arrived at the world championships awards ceremony dressed in a blue blazer, tie, and leather loafers, looking, he recalls, "like an IBM salesman at a Cheech and Chong convention."

Hemmings retired from competition in 1969, and turned his attention to creating, promoting, and marketing professional surf contests. From 1970 to 1978 he did color commentary for ABC-TV's *Wide World of Sports* and CBS-TV's *Sports Spectacular* during their annual surf contest coverage in Hawaii. In 1971 he developed the Pipeline Masters, which was soon regarded as the sport's premier competition; in 1976 he was the driving force behind the formation of International Professional Surfers (IPS), the first worldwide surfing circuit and predecessor to the Association of Surfing Professionals (ASP) tour; in 1983 he founded Hawaii's Triple Crown of Surfing, a three-event minitour

Fred Hemmings

within the world tour. "Professionalism," as Hemmings called it, was a tough sell, particularly in the early years, and the iron-willed determination that earned Hemmings the nickname Dead-Ahead Fred, while indispensable to bringing his vision to life, often put him at odds with surf society at large. He returned to the subject of drugs in 1969, for example, saying, "there will be no room for dope" in the ranks of professional or amateur surfing. A majority of surfers at the time were drug users to one degree or another, and even non–drug users had doubts about lumping surfing in with baseball, basketball, and football as a competitive sport. Professional surfing would nonetheless be created more or less to Hemmings's specifications, and find a niche in the sports world, even if rank-and-file surfers continued to show at best a passing interest in competition.

Hemmings was ousted as the head of the pro tour in 1982, following a coup of sorts led by Australian surfer/organizer Ian Cairns, as the financially struggling IPS was replaced by Cairns's newly created ASP. Hemmings retained ownership of Hawaii's world tour contests, but devoted himself mostly to business and politics. In 1984 he accepted a seat on the Denver Broncos' NFL Board of Directors, and was elected to Hawaii's House of Representatives. He was a fiscal and moral conservative, and in 1988, returning to a favorite issue, wrote a letter to ASP Executive Director Graham Cassidy asking that the world tour "consider mandatory drug testing for competing surfers." The ASP declined. In 1990, one year after becoming minority floor leader, Hemmings won the Republican candidacy for the governor's race, then lost the general election. He hosted a conservative drive-time radio talk show in 1991 and 1992; in 2000 he was elected to the state senate.

Hemmings was Hawaii's top vote-getter in the 1967 *International Surfing* Magazine Hall of Fame Awards. He was inducted into the International Surfing Hall of Fame in 1991 and to the Hawaii Sports Hall of Fame in 1999; in 2002 he won the Surf Industry Manufacturers Association Waterman Achievement Award. He self-published a memoir titled *The Soul of Surfing is Hawaiian* in 1997. But Hemmings for the most part has kept his distance from—or been kept out of—the surfing mainstream. His relationship to the sport has in many ways been ambivalent. He hasn't surfed regularly since the mid-'70s, and has little interest in most forms of post-1968 surf culture. But at some level Hemmings remains a dedicated

surfer. In 1994, during his second run for governor, a campaign poster showed Hemmings leaning into a back-arch bottom turn, circa 1967, with the accompanying slogan: "Hemmings: He Doesn't Golf."

Hemmings has been married three times, and has three children. *See also* International Professional Surfers, Pipeline Masters, politics and surfing, professional surfing, Triple Crown of Surfing, World Cup, World Surfing Championships 1968.

Hening, Glenn   Surf activist and environmentalist from Santa Monica, California; cofounder of the Surfrider Foundation, and founder of the Groundswell Society. Hening was born (1950) in San Antonio, Texas, and began surfing Malibu in the mid-'60s. From 1975 to 1980 he worked as a schoolteacher in El Salvador, and in the early to mid-'80s worked on NASA's Space Shuttle program at Jet Propulsion Laboratories in Pasadena, California. He founded Surfrider in 1984 with Tom Pratte and Lance Carson, remained an integral part of the organization over the years, but eventually became ambivalent about the group and about surfing's media/industrial structure in general. The once-informative surf magazines, he said in 1997, had become "transient entertainment," and editors were afraid to do anything that might "step on the toes of advertisers." Surfrider had helped instill some degree of environmental consciousness among surfers, Hening continued, "but I'm disillusioned with teenagers in the surf industry who don't understand what their responsibilities are as corporate citizens. And some of those teenagers are millionaires in their 40s." In 1995, Hening founded the Groundswell Society, a surfing group dedicated to "critical thinking, ecology, fine art, history, equipment and leadership"; the group has self-published four books and hosted seminars; the Society's first surf education field trip, to Brazil, took place in 2002. *See also* environmentalism and surfing, Surfrider Foundation.

Heritage, Dan   New Jersey surfboard manufacturer whose career got started after he read a *Popular Mechanics* do-it-yourself article on surfboards in 1962, mail-ordered the materials, and built himself a board. Two years later, the 20-year-old Heritage opened Little Wave Surf Shop, his first retail outlet, in Sea Isle City, New Jersey; the company name was changed in 1971 to Heritage Surfboards. A second outlet opened in 1978 in Ocean City, at which time the Heritage board-making factory—with Dan overseeing the entire operation and shaping many of the boards him-self—was producing 500 boards a year. A third and final store was added in 1983, with Brian Heritage, Dan's son, taking over most of the shaping duties. Heritage was in the first group of surf world luminaries to be inducted into the East Coast Surfing Hall of Fame in 1996. "He legitimized surfing in New Jersey," *Surfer* magazine wrote in its Hall of Fame report. Heritage died of pancreatic cancer in 1997 at age 53.

Herring, Shane   Meteoric Australian pro surfer from Sydney's Dee Why Beach; world-ranked #4 in 1992. Herring was born (1971) in Manly, New South Wales, and began surfing as a toddler. As a teenager he developed a low, streamlined crouch, and cornered through turns with the precision of a Formula One driver; when he turned pro in 1991 he was described by *Waves* magazine as having "the purest style" of his generation. Herring's high point as a competitive surfer came in April 1992, when he defeated Kelly Slater in the finals of the Coke contest in Sydney: "The first strike of a new age," surf journalist Derek Hynd said of the Slater/Herring duel, which left the freckle-faced Australian regularfooter, then still living with his mother, on top of the world circuit rankings. "These two will battle for future championships," Hynd promised. Eight months later Slater won the 1992 world title, and went on to win another five before the decade was over. Herring never again won a world tour event, in part because he was unable to cope with the attention of surf stardom. Herring was described as a "lost surfer" in a short *Australia's Surfing Life* article in 1998. "I just chose me own path and nobody was going to stop me," he told the magazine. "Everyone tells me what to do. I hardly listen." Herring appeared in a small number of surf videos, including *Oz on Fire* (1991), *Madmen, Saints and Sinners* (1992), and *Rad Movez* (1993).

high-pressure system   A sunny, dry, storm-free weather system that, when located over the coast or just inland, greatly improves the quality of the surf. Air sinks in and around a high-pressure system, which inhibits cloud formation. A high-pressure system itself has nothing to do with wave creation; when located over the ocean, high pressure will in fact prevent swell-producing storms from forming nearby, and can also, if positioned near the coast, create a steady onshore wind. A land-hovering high

pressure system, on the other hand, will often create a glassy ocean surface—sometimes across hundreds of miles of coastline—or produce a light, wave-improving offshore wind. While land-based high pressure in summer or fall can send temperatures soaring, winter high pressure can push temperatures to far below normal. Meteorologically attuned surfers in California, along with checking data for swell height and period, often look just as carefully at a developing high-pressure system—which ideally will anchor itself somewhere along the eastern state line. A strong inland high pressure will sometimes remain almost stationary for five days or more; in spring, northeast Pacific Ocean high-pressure systems can last for weeks. The more-descriptive "anticyclone" is sometimes used in place of "high pressure." *See also* low-pressure system, surf forecasting.

hips   The lower portion of a surfboard, as viewed deck-on. Not so much a quantified specification, as with nose or tail measurements, "hips" is an informal term used to describe the amount of below-center curve. Hips become more pronounced as the board's wide point drops. *See also* outline.

Ho, Derek   Stylish Hawaiian goofyfoot pro surfer from the North Shore of Oahu; 1993 world champion; two-time winner of the Pipeline Masters, and four-time winner of the Triple Crown. Ho was born (1964) in Kailua, the son of a onetime beachboy and army enlisted man, and was second cousin to popular Honolulu nightclub entertainer Don Ho. He began riding waves at age three, following in the footsteps of his surf-obsessed older brother Michael, who went on to become one of the Hawaii's best-known and most durable pros. Derek was a talented but somewhat indifferent young surfer, became a small-time criminal during his teenage years, and was arrested several times. At age 18 he spent 10 days in prison, after which he dedicated himself to a career in surfing. The following year he placed third in the 1983 Pipeline Masters, and finished the pro tour season ranked 30th. For the next six years he climbed steadily up the ratings, all the way to runner-up in 1989; in 1990 he fell to sixth, however, and by 1992 he'd dropped all the way to 30th. His career at that point was already remarkable: he'd won the 1984 Duke Kahanamoku Classic (with brother Michael finishing second); won the Pipeline Masters in 1986 and finished second in 1991; and won the Triple Crown in 1984, 1986, and

Derek Ho

1988. In 1985, Derek and Michael Ho became the first siblings to both place in the prestigious year-end pro tour top 16. But following the 1992 season, it seemed obvious that Ho's career had peaked. "He's an artist who appears loath to butcher his style for a few decimal points more on the judges' cards," surf journalist Derek Hynd once said of Ho, finishing off by predicting the handsome 28-year-old Hawaiian had "no chance" at a world title. Kelly Slater of Florida had just won the first of what everyone assumed would be a long string of championships.

Ho was ranked fifth after nine events in 1993, with just the Pipeline Masters remaining. The final day of the event was held in excellent six to eight-foot surf, and as the four contenders ahead of him were all eliminated after the quarterfinals, Ho smoothly won the contest and the championship, along with a fourth Triple Crown title. He was the first male Hawaiian to win the pro tour, and at 29 he was the oldest men's pro tour winner up to that point. The 1993 Masters was his only win of the season, and the last pro tour win of his career. He dropped to 24th in the ratings the following year, and in early 1997 his world circuit career was ended by a knee injury.

The smallest male world champion at 5′4″, 125 pounds, Ho was quick-footed, with a sharp, angular, slightly formulated attack. Tuberiding was his strength, and in hollow waves, especially at Pipeline, he rode with sublime precision and elegance. Two-

time world champion Tom Carroll was Ho's equal at Pipeline, but the Australian's approach was rougher and more power-driven, whereas Ho time and again drew perfect lines through the deepest part of the wave—updating the approach invented by '70s Pipeline ace Gerry Lopez. Ho was an intense, withdrawn, sometimes prickly surf world figure. He was quietly and justifiably critical of the surf press in 1994, as magazine reporters all but ignored the defending world champion and focused instead on Kelly Slater. "Put it this way," Ho dryly told *Australia's Surfing Life* magazine, "I haven't been subjected to the overexposure a world champ normally gets."

Ho appeared in more than 50 surf movies and videos, including *Wave Warriors* (1985), *Shock Waves* (1987), *Surfers: The Movie* (1990), *Aloha Bowls* (1994), *TV Dinners* (1995), and *Side B* (1997). He is married and has two children.

Ho, Michael   Indestructible Hawaiian pro surfer from Sunset Beach, Oahu; world-ranked #3 in 1978, and the Triple Crown winner in 1983 and 1985; described by fellow Hawaiian Dane Kealoha as "the godfather of the North Shore." Ho was born (1957) in San Mateo, California, the son of a former Waikiki beachboy, raised in Waimanalo, Oahu, and first surfed at age three. He won the boys' division of the 1970 United States Surfing Championships, and the following year placed third in the juniors division. As a pigeon-chested 15-year-old, he took fifth in 1972 World Surfing Championships, and was praised as the event's most exciting and progressive surfer. He soon became one of Hawaii's first full-time professional surfers, and in 1975 finished runner-up in the Duke Kahanamoku Classic and the Pro Class Trials. Ho was already being called the world's finest "position" surfer, meaning he invariably placed himself in the most critical section of the wave using the simplest and cleanest line. He often rode with a ramrod straight back, knees apart, his right arm distinctively held out from his body, hand dangling at the wrist. (Younger brother Derek Ho, the 1993 world champion, surfed in much the same way.) At 5′5″, 135 pounds, Ho was never able to explode through a turn the way his heavier peers could, but nobody was quicker on his feet, and few were as innately stylish. He was one of the world's best tuberiders in the mid- and late '70s (he helped invent the "pigdog" tuberiding technique), and his skills only improved throughout the '80s. Gregarious around friends and

Michael Ho (left) with younger brother Derek

family, the mustachioed Ho kept a wary distance from the rest of the surf world, and was a shadowy figure during his 13 years (1976–88) on the pro tour.

Ho performed well at world tour venues around the world, but never won a pro circuit event outside of Hawaii. On the North Shore, however, he was a competitive force for more than 25 years: a five-time Pipeline Masters finalist (winning in 1982, even though hobbled by a cast on his right wrist); an eight-time Duke finalist (winning in 1978 and 1981); a four-time winner of the Xcel Pro (in 1988, 1990, 1991, and 1996); a two-time Triple Crown winner (1983 and 1985); and a four-time competitor in the Quiksilver in Memory of Eddie Aikau big-wave event at Waimea (finishing fourth in 1990). In one of pro surfing's most remarkable competitive achievements, the 40-year-old Ho finished runner-up in the 1997 Pipeline Masters.

Ho appeared in more than 35 surf movies and videos, including *A Sea for Yourself* (1973), *Super Session* (1975), *Free Ride* (1977), *Tales of the Seven Seas* (1981), *Follow the Sun* (1983), *Shock Waves* (1987), and *Aloha Bowls* (1994). A mainstay in the World Masters Championships, an annual event for ex-pros over the age of 36, Ho placed second overall in 1997, second in the over-40 division in 1999, first in 2000 and third in 2001. Ho is married and has a son and daughter, both of whom were among the country's top young amateur surfers in 2003.

Hobgood, Clifton "CJ" Tenacious goofyfoot pro surfer from Satellite Beach, Florida; winner of the 2001 world championship. Hobgood was born (1972) in Melbourne Beach, Florida, the son of a dental technician father and nurse mother, and began rid-

ing waves in 1984 with his identical twin brother Damien. Five years later he won the menehune division of the 1991 Eastern Surfing Association Championships (Damien placed second), setting up a long run at the top of the national amateur ranks: he was the National Scholastic Surfing Association (NSSA) East Coast boys' division champion in 1994, the NSSA national juniors' champion in 1995, and in 1997 he became the NSSA East Coast men's champion, and finished third in the prestigious Pro Junior contest in Sydney, Australia. Hobgood turned pro in 1998, and the following year qualified for the world championship tour. A middleweight surfer (5′8″, 150 pounds), Hobgood used a wide, stable, functional stance, his arms spread, head and chin lifted. He quickly earned a reputation as an all-conditions pro: a creative aerial technician in smaller waves and a fearless tuberider at places like Pipeline and Teahupoo. Hobgood finished the 1999 season ranked 18th in the world, and was named the pro tour's rookie of the year; the following year he rose to #7 in the rankings, earned his first big-league pro win (at the Hossegor Rip Curl Pro), and was named as "Breakthrough Surfer of the Year" at the *Surfer* Magazine Readers Poll Awards.

Hobgood's championship season in 2001 was diminished slightly by the cancellation of three of the tour's eight scheduled events after the 9/11 attacks, and because Hobgood was winless in the remaining five contests. His best result for the year was a second place in the Billabong Pro at Teahupoo. (A few months later, in a demonstration of grit on the opening day of the Op Pro/Mentawai Islands specialty event, held in cylindrical 8-foot tropical tubes, Hobgood bloodied his face on the reef after a wipeout, was patched up by an attending physician, then returned to the water where he quickly scored the day's longest tuberide and won the heat.) Hobgood was 22 when he became world champion. "I'm not super talented," the drawling-voiced surfer humbly told *Eastern Surf Magazine*. "I just work hard." In 2002, Hobgood dropped to #15 on the year-end ratings. The unmarried Hobgood has appeared in nearly 20 surf videos, including *Triple C* (1996), *Sacred Water* (1999), *The Bomb 2000* (1999), and *Momentum: Under the Influence* (2001). CJ and Damien Hobgood own a house together in Satellite Beach.

Hobgood, Damien Dynamic goofyfoot pro surfer from Satellite Beach, Florida; world-ranked #10 in

2001; identical twin brother to 2001 world champion CJ Hobgood. Damien was born (1979) in Melbourne Beach, Florida, raised in Satellite Beach, began body-boarding at age five and stand-up surfing at six. The Hobgoods both came to the attention of the surf world in 1991 by taking the top two slots in the menehune division of the Eastern Surfing Association Championships (CJ beating Damien). Both were top-rated amateurs over the next several years, with Damien placing second in the boys' division of the 1994 U.S. Championships, winning the 1995 East Coast National Scholastic Surfing Association juniors division ratings, and placing third in the juniors of the 1996 World Surfing Games. Not surprisingly, the Hobgoods developed similar wave-riding styles, each utilizing a low, spread-out stance, while making a study of all facets of the sport, with an emphasis on aerials, as well as tuberiding in thick, high-risk surf. Both were gently mocked by the surf press for being fans of country-western music. Damien Hobgood placed fifth in the 1999 World Qualifying Series of the pro tour; the following year he was world-ranked 25th, was named rookie of the year, and was de-scribed by surf journalist Jason Borte as one of five "replacement killers" who might fill in for then-retired six-time world champion Kelly Slater, also of Florida. In 2000, the Hobgoods became the first brothers to place simultaneously in the world tour top 10. Damien Hobgood has appeared in more than a dozen surf videos, including *Under the Same Sun* (1994), *Triple C* (1996), and *Momentum: Under the Influence* (2001).

Hobie Surfboards Dominating surfboard manufac-turer from the late 1950s to the early '70s, founded by surfer and ocean sports industrialist Hobart "Hobie" Alter, and headquartered in Dana Point, California. Alter started building and selling balsa boards out of his parents' Laguna Beach garage in 1950. Three years later, his father bought him a small plot of land on Pacific Coast Highway in nearby Dana Point, a town with only two other businesses at the time. Alter de-signed and built a small factory/retail building, and Hobie Surfboards opened in 1954—the first commer-cial surfboard outlet in Orange County and the first shop of its kind built from the ground up. Stock boards originally retailed for $65. Looking for an in-expensive and readily available replacement for balsa, Alter and surfboard laminator Gordon "Grubby" Clark spent several years experimenting with

polyurethane foam, leading to Hobie Surfboards going to an all-foam policy in 1958. (Clark left the company in 1961 to found Clark Foam.)

In 1962, firmly established as the industry leader in a small but booming market, with newly licensed Hobie Surfboard dealerships in San Diego, Honolulu, and Peru, Alter tore down his original Dana Point building and rebuilt with larger shaping facilities and a 1,200-square-foot, 150-surfboard display area. He began to heavily promote an all-star team of surfers that included Phil Edwards, Joey Cabell, Joyce Hoff-man, Gary Propper, and Corky Carroll (all of whom had signature model boards, another Hobie innova-tion), and expanded rapidly on the East Coast, licens-ing the Hobie name to nearly 20 dealers. Bruce Brown's original live-narration *Endless Summer* tour was brought into the Hobie marketing process, as a van full of Hobie-sponsored surf stars drove the perimeter of the country, giving demonstrations during the day, with Brown screening his movie in the evenings. The company also moved quickly on the mid-'60s skateboard craze, with the redwood laminate Hobie Skateboard and the juice-company-cosponsored Hobie/Vita-Pakt Skateboard Demonstra-tion Team. Surfboard sales continued to rise, peaking in the mid-'60s at about 6,500 boards per year. The Hobie surfboard, *Sports Illustrated* said in 1966, was "the Cadillac of the surfing world." Top surfboard craftsmen who worked for the Hobie label over the years included Edwards, Renny Yater, Mickey Muñoz, Joe Quigg, Terry Martin, Don Hansen, and the Patter-son brothers, Robert, Raymond, and Ronald.

The late-'60s shortboard revolution was a disaster for all the major board-makers of the period, Hobie included, as they were first stuck with an inventory of obsolete longboards, then unable to keep up with ca-reening shortboard design changes. Hobie Surfboards was still a force into the next decade, but nothing like it had been in the '60s. Alter himself meanwhile had all but left the surf industry after the 1967 introduc-tion of his Hobie Cat catamaran, which exploded in popularity after being featured in a *Life* magazine ar-ticle. By the mid-'70s, Hobie Surfboards—still with more than a dozen retailers—had switched its focus from surfboards to beachwear and skateboards, later adding a Hobie-brand line of sunglasses, bodyboards, snowboards, kayaks, sailboats, and wakeboards. Hobie was the second-largest producer of beachwear in America in 1987, behind Ocean Pacific, but ahead of Quiksilver and Gotcha. The Hobie stores were bought and sold several times, with Alter retaining ownership of just the original Dana Point site. By 2002, only two Hobie shops remained, in Dana Point and Laguna Beach. Hobie Industries, run by Alter's two sons, licenses the Hobie name and sells beachwear, sunglasses, skateboards, and novelty items. Collectors have paid up to $7,500 for an original Hobie balsa board. *See also* Hobie Alter, surfboard shop.

hodad   Bygone derogatory phrase for an unwelcome surfer of any kind, usually either a beginner, poser, or hot-rodder; sometimes used in reference to nonsurfers in general. The word's origins are unknown. Although the expression went out of use in the mid-'60s, "hodad" is one of very few words identified in the *Oxford English Dictionary* as "surfing slang." The *OED*'s definition: "An ill-mannered or boastful surfer." Spelling variations include "hodaddy," "hoedad," and "ho-dad." "Help Stamp Out Hodads" and "Wipe Out Ho-Dads" were two of the antihodad stickers printed in the mid-'60s. *See also* gremmie, kook.

Hodge, Harry   Hardworking, fast-talking surfwear executive and surf moviemaker, originally from Victoria, Australia. Hodge was born (1950) in Healesville, Victoria, outside of Melbourne, raised in nearby St. Kilda and Mornington Peninsula, and began surfing at age 14. From 1967 to 1973 he worked as a journalist and photographer for the Australian Associated Press, then began making surf movies; his first effort, *Liquid Gold,* a small but relatively successful first effort, was released in 1976. Hodge then overreached in spectacular fashion with his second effort, *Band on the Run,* a 35-millimeter travelogue funded in part by the Australian Film Commission and Coca-Cola. Filming began in 1977, but problems with funding and music rights pushed the film's release date back to 1981, when it met with tepid reviews and small audiences. "What was intended to be Australia's biggest surf movie ever," Albie Thoms wrote in his book *Surfmovies,* "ended up being just another surfing flick."

Hodge was hired as marketing director for Quiksilver Australia in 1982; two years later he became cofounder and president of newly licensed Quiksilver Europe, and by 2000 he'd guided the company into $150 million in annual sales. Hodge's marketing instincts have been sound throughout his Quiksilver career: *The Performers,* a 1983 film he produced for Quiksilver, is often mentioned as the original surf

video; in 1997 he hired Australian surf-journalist Phil Jarratt to produce the well-reviewed *Mr. Sunset,* a biography on '70s surf champion Jeff Hakman. Hodge has lived in Biarritz, France, since 1984. *See also* Quiksilver.

Hoffman, Philip "Flippy"   Gravel-voiced surfer and textile executive from Capistrano Beach, California; a pioneering big-wave rider on the North Shore of Oahu in the early 1950s, and one of the first surfers, in 1975, to ride Kaena Point. Hoffman was born (1930) in Glendale, California, raised in Hollywood and Laguna Beach, and began surfing at age 13 at San Onofre. In late 1952, after viewing an 8-millimeter reel of the big waves at Makaha filmed by his younger brother Walter—a surfer and navy enlistee stationed at Pearl Harbor—Hoffman made his first trip to Hawaii; he and surfboard designer Bob Simmons became the first surfers to rent a house at Sunset Point on Oahu's North Shore in early 1953. "There were just a few people out there; pig ranchers and shit," Hoffman recalled in 1992, in the blunt cadence that helped set the tone for nearly all hardcore big-wave riders. "We surfed and we'd sit and we'd argue. Then some guys would come over from Makaha or Honolulu and they'd surf and then leave and we'd stay and sit and argue. Pretty much the same shit as the surfers are doing today."

On January 19, 1975, with a 15-foot swell running, Hoffman and three others became the first to ride Kaena Point, a break regarded at the time as the final big-wave frontier. Four years later, Hoffman and surfer/board-maker Mickey Muñoz built themselves 16-foot boards and became the first surfers to ride the North Shore's outer reefs, taking off on relatively benign 18-foot waves about three-quarters of a mile from the beach.

Since the late '50s, Flippy and Walter Hoffman have owned and managed Hoffman California Fabrics, the 1924-founded family business that has for decades been a primary textile supplier to the surfwear industry. Hoffman has been married once; Marty Hoffman, his son, won the boys' division of the 1977 United States Surfing Championships, placed fourth in the juniors division of the 1980 World Amateur Championships, and was a competitor in the 1990 Quiksilver in Memory of Eddie Aikau big-wave contest at Waimea Bay.

Hoffman, Joyce   Dynamic regularfoot surfer from Capistrano Beach, California; world champion in

Joyce Hoffman

1965 and 1966, and arguably the world's best-known and most successful surfer of the mid- and late '60s. Hoffman was born (1947) in Los Angeles, California, raised in Newport Beach, and began surfing at age 13, not long after her mother married big-wave pioneer and surf textile magnate Walter Hoffman, and the family moved to Orange County's Capistrano Beach. A sparkly, attractive, easy-smiling blond fixated on competition, Joyce Hoffman often surfed for six hours a day in what amounted to a kind of free-form training routine. She later acknowledged that "soul-fulness" wasn't part of her surfing experience, and that her satisfaction came from being "the best pre-pared," which led to winning contests. "My daugh-ter's real weird," Walter Hoffman once said. "She wants to win. The other girls couldn't care less." By 1963 she was among the best women surfers in the state; from 1964 to 1967 she was all but invincible in competition, placing first in the United States Surfing Association's year-end ratings four years in a row, and posting multiple victories in the United States Surf-ing Championships (1965, 1966, and 1967), the Makaha International (1964, 1966), and the Laguna Masters (1965, 1967). Hoffman's 1965 World Champi-onships win in Lima, Peru, went virtually unnoticed by the surf press (*Surfer* magazine dispatched with the women's portion of the event in a single sentence), but earned her the first of dozens of general-interest magazine feature articles, including a *Sports Illustrated*

profile titled "An Odd Sport, and an Unusual Cham-pion," in which Hoffman is quoted as saying, "If I didn't think I was considered the best I'd quit." Fol-lowing her victory in the 1966 World Championships held in San Diego, the 19-year-old Hoffman made the cover of *Life* magazine, and was featured in *Seventeen, Look, Teen* (who described her as a "blonde surf god-dess"), and *Vogue,* and was named the sporting world's "Woman of the Year" by the *Los Angeles Times.* Hobie Surfboards introduced the Joyce Hoff-man signature model surfboard in 1967, while Tri-umph gave her a Spitfire coupe. With the exception of Florida's Lisa Andersen, four-time world champion in the mid- and late-'90s, no woman surfer has come close to matching Hoffman's popularity.

Hoffman was an athletic and kinetic hotdogger (5'7", 125 pounds), with lightning-quick feet, given at times to striking theatrical poses while riding. She also performed well in medium-large surf, and was the only woman in the '60s to ride Sunset Beach in Hawaii with any regularity. In 1968 she became the first women to ride Pipeline, the fearsome left-breaking wave located just to the west of Sunset. That was the year the short surfboard permanently changed the sport; it was also the beginning of the end of Hoffman's competitive reign, as she was up-staged by Margo Godfrey, a braces-wearing 15-year-old from La Jolla, California, who won the 1968 World Championships in Puerto Rico. Hoffman stayed active in surfing for another three years (plac-ing fourth in the 1970 World Championships and winning the 1971 United States Championships), then dropped off the surf scene entirely. She became a competitive motocross racer, then switched to auto racing, giving up in 1983 after spinning into a wall at 150 miles per hour. (More than a decade later, Hoff-man told *Longboard* magazine that her drive to com-pete was "horrible . . . the bane of my life.") She returned to surfing in 1987.

Hoffman appeared briefly in a few surf movies, including *Free and Easy* (1967) and *Five Summer Stories* (1972), and was featured in *Surfer Girl: A Century of Women in Surfing,* published in 2000. She was a four-time *Surfer* Magazine Readers Poll Award winner (1964–67), and was twice the top female vote-getter in the *International Surfing* Magazine Hall of Fame Awards (1966, 1967). She was inducted into the Hunt-ington Beach Walk of Fame in 1994. Hoffman is niece to gruff big-wave trailblazer Philip "Flippy" Hoffman, sister-in-law to longboard master Herbie Fletcher, and aunt to aerialists Christian and Nathan Fletcher. She's been married once, has one child, and lives in Laguna Beach, California. *See also* World Surfing Championships 1965, World Surfing Championships 1966.

Hoffman, Walter   Burly big-wave pioneer and beachwear industrialist from Laguna Beach, California; longtime president of Hoffman California Fabrics, surf fashion's biggest textile supplier; younger brother to surf world rapscallion Philip "Flippy" Hoffman, stepfather to two-time world champion Joyce Hoffman, and grandfather to aerial specialists Christian and Nathan Fletcher. Hoffman was born (1931) in Glendale, California, raised in Hollywood and Laguna Beach, and began surfing at age 14. He surfed Malibu starting in 1946, and was soon keeping company with Matt Kivlin, Joe Quigg, Bob Simmons, Buzzy Trent, and a number of other Malibu surfers who collectively helped shape the sport in the years following World War II. On the first day of his first visit to Hawaii in 1948, Hoffman and Hawaiian surfer George Downing rode beautiful 10-foot waves off Diamond Head, igniting in Hoffman a lifelong interest in big, powerful tropical surf. In 1951, after he enlisted in the navy and was stationed at the Pearl Harbor, Hoffman began surfing regularly at Makaha, the versatile break on the west side of Oahu, where the waves sometimes hit 20 feet or bigger. Hoffman soon mailed rolls of 8-millimeter film back to California, causing a stir among his surf mates back home, including his brother Flippy and Buzzy Trent. "The lights went out," Trent later said, recalling the first time he saw Makaha on film, "and here came the immortal Walter Hoffman driving through a gigantic 15-foot wave." Trent and Flippy joined Walter in Hawaii, and they were soon camping on the beach at Makaha, before moving into nearby wooden shacks and army-built Quonset huts. By 1953, Hoffman, Trent, Downing, along with Wally Froiseth, Woody Brown, and a few others, were riding their newly streamlined big-wave boards in waves up to 18 foot—half again the size of the biggest waves ridden just five years earlier. Explorations were also made along the North Shore of Oahu, where Hoffman often led the charge at Sunset Beach; by mid-decade the North Shore had replaced Makaha as the new big-wave epicenter.

In 1959, Hoffman took over Hoffman California Fabrics, the wholesale textile business his father had started in 1924. The surfwear industry was in large part built out of Hoffman fabrics; under Walter's stewardship the company would be the primary textile provider to Quiksilver, Billabong, and Gotcha, among other popular surfwear brands.

While Hoffman had only a passing interest in surfing competition, he and partner Joanie Jones won the tandem division of the 1954 Makaha International, and he judged the 1967 Duke Kahanamoku Invitational. Hoffman's stepdaughter, Joyce, was the women's world surfing champion in 1965 and 1966. His second daughter, Dibi, married longboard ace Herbie Fletcher, and is the mother of Christian and Nathan Fletcher. Walter Hoffman was given the Surf Industry Manufacturers Association Waterman Achievement Award in 1995. He's married and has four children. *See also* big-wave surfing.

Holland   *See* Netherlands.

Holland, Bob   Enduring goofyfooter from Virginia Beach, Virginia; cofounder of Smith and Holland Surf Shop in 1962, the first store of its kind in Virginia; winner of hundreds of state, regional, and nationwide amateur surfing contests, including seven United States Surfing Championship titles and 12 East Coast titles. Holland was born (1928) in Norfolk, Virginia, raised in both Norfolk and Virginia Beach, and began surfing at age nine on a paddleboard. His father, Captain Robert Holland, was a first-generation Virginia Beach lifeguard/surfer in the '30s. By 1959, Holland was importing California-made Jacobs Surfboards and selling them out of his garage; Holland Surf Shop opened for business in 1960; Smith and Holland Surf Shop, cofounded with Pete Smith, opened in 1962. When the Eastern Surfing Association was formed in 1967, Holland was one of the organization's first judges, and served as ESA head judge in the late '60s and early '70s. In 1972 he judged the World Championships, held in San Diego, California. Holland was among the first group of surfers to be inducted into the East Coast Surf Legends Hall of Fame, in 1996 and the following year he was elected to the Virginia Sports Hall of Fame.

Holland, Todd   Baby-faced pro surfer from Cocoa Beach, Florida; world-ranked #8 in 1991; "a scrappy pug," surf journalist Steve Barilotti said, "with a 'don't-cross-that-line' attitude." Holland was born (1968) in Winston-Salem, North Carolina, the son of an electrical contractor, and spent the first four years of his life traveling up and down the eastern seaboard and living for the most part in an Airstream trailer. In 1972, the Hollands built a log cabin in Emerald Isle, North Carolina, and settled down; Holland began surfing five years later at age nine. The garrulous Carol Holland, later described in the surf press as "the ultimate Surf Mom," took such an interest in Todd's surfing progress that she became a surf contest judge, and later opened a surfing travel agency. The family moved to Cocoa Beach in 1981. Holland had a good run as an amateur, particularly in the annual United States Surfing Championships, where he made the finals of the boys' division in 1982 and 1983, placed second in the juniors division in 1984, and won the juniors in 1986. He also placed third in the juniors division of the 1984 World Championships. Holland turned pro in 1987, three days after high school graduation, and made a slow but determined climb up the world tour ratings, finishing 27th in 1987 (earning rookie-of-the-year honors), 17th in 1988, 11th in 1990, and eighth in 1991. From there he dropped out of the top 10, and retired after finishing 39th in 1998. Not a supernaturally gifted surfer, the 5′8″, 165-pound Holland lifted himself into the first rank by force of will, and at his peak was able to shine in waves ranging from gentle two-foot Floridian beachbreak to raging 12-foot grinders at Pipeline in Hawaii. From 1989 to 1991 he was the only East Coast surfer in the world tour top 16. A career low point came during a 1994 competition in Brazil, when he used legal but heavy-handed tactics to defeat a popular local surfer, and was subsequently pelted with

Todd Holland

sand by an angry mob of spectators as he left the water; a police escort took him to the airport for a hastily arranged flight back to America.

Holland went without a surfwear sponsor for five years during his professional career, he said, because he didn't "kiss butt" and because he didn't fit the surfer image. A more prevalent notion was that Holland was sponsorless—and to some degree friendless—because he brooded regularly and often lost his temper. He distinguished himself from his peers with a jutting blond Sons of the Confederacy beard and an extensive country-western CD collection. He also loved muscle cars, and for a 1990 surf magazine portrait he stood proudly cross-armed in front of his supercharged cherry-red 1969 Mustang GT. Holland appeared in more than two dozen surf movies and videos, including *Gripping Stuff* (1987), *Atlantic Crossing* (1989), and *Mental Surfing* (1993). He's been married twice, and has two children. After leaving the pro tour, he was hired by Surf Express, his mother's travel agency.

Hollinger, Henry "Kimo"   Contemplative big-wave rider from Honolulu, Hawaii; a finalist in the 1965 Duke Kahanamoku Invitational who 10 years later became an eloquent anticontest crusader. Hollinger was born (1939) and raised in Honolulu, the son of a fireman, began surfing at age 16, and by the end of the decade was one of the best native-born riders in the heavy surf at Sunset Beach and Waimea Bay. Helped in part by his appearances in surf movies like *Barefoot Adventure* (1960) and *Surfing Hollow Days* (1962), Hollinger was invited to the 1965 Duke contest and placed eighth; for the next three years he served as a Duke judge, while working as a Honolulu city and county fireman. Two events changed Hollinger's life in the mid-'70s. On Thanksgiving Day, 1975, just prior to the final heats of the Smirnoff Pro, with the Waimea surf booming in at gorgeous 25 to 30 feet, Hollinger and a handful of other noncontestants were asked by Smirnoff officials to leave the water. Hollinger complied, but resentfully—in part because Waimea breaks just a few times each season, and rarely with the kind of form seen on this particular day, and in part because of the commercial intrusion on what Hollinger regarded as a sacred surfing area. "Powerboats and helicopters appeared," he wrote in *Surfer* magazine a few weeks later, "and [contest officials] started warming up on the loudspeaker. I couldn't believe it. Telling us who could ride and who couldn't. A surfer has trained himself to ride these waves. It is all he asks of life. Who the hell is Smirnoff to tell him he can't? God created those waves." Thirteen months later Hollinger was rescued from certain death at Waimea after a group of surfers formed a human chain and pulled him to shore; he never again rode big waves. Hollinger was married once, has two children, and lives on the North Shore of Oahu. *Kimo: A Collection of Short Stories,* his nonfiction surfing book, was published in 2002.

hollow A wave or section of wave whose crest loops out and down into the trough to form a tube. Hollow sections are usually created as the wave moves over a raised section of underwater topography—a high spot on the reef or sandbar, for instance—and almost always break with more power than nonhollow waves. Hollow waves are a prerequisite for tuberiding. *See also* tube, tuberiding.

hollow surfboard Type of wooden surfboard/paddleboard popular in the 1930s and '40s; invented and almost single-handedly developed by Wisconsin-born surfer and board designer Tom Blake. Judged on its wave-handing characteristics, the hollow board was at best a lateral step in the surfboard's design evolution. But because it was lighter than the solid-body plank redwood boards used in the early decades of the 20th century—the average plank weighed about 70 pounds, while a 12-foot hollow weighed about 45 pounds—surfing became accessible to those who otherwise might not have had the muscle to get a board from the parking lot to the water.

Blake made a hollow board of sorts in 1926 by drilling hundreds of holes through the deck of a plank, then sealing the board with a thin wood veneer. Three years later, in an effort to built a faster paddleboard, Blake designed the "chambered" hollow, bisecting a finished board, carving out the interior, and gluing the two pieces back together. In 1932 he introduced the transversely braced hollow, with wooden ribs in a design similar to that used in airplane wings. Blake added a last refinement to the hollow board in the early '40s, replacing the squared-off edges with a rounded-rail design.

Hollow surfboards and paddleboards (which doubled as lifeguard rescue boards) were manufactured commercially from 1932 to the early '50s; thousands of additional hollows were made in garages and backyards, and as school projects. As listed in a 1939 *Popular Science* magazine do-it-yourself article, a 13'9" by 21¾" combination paddleboard/surfboard could be made from either cedar, mahogany, spruce, redwood, or pine, along with 18 flathead brass screws, four gross of three-quarter-inch screws, a pint of marine glue, a brass yacht deck plug, and a quart of spar varnish. Nearly all hollow boards featured a streamlined silhouette, a pointed tail, and a rounded nose; boards 12 feet and under were thought of as surfboards; those over 12 feet were used primarily as paddleboards.

Beginning and intermediate surfers in the '30s and early '40s for the most part preferred the hollow board; advanced surfers were split between the hollow and the plank, but favored the latter. The plank was slower to paddle, but smoother riding and easier to control once on the wave. The lighter hollow caught waves with ease, but was tippy and skittish. Hollows, furthermore, were more fragile. A photo from a 1942 *Popular Mechanics* article, "Hitch-Hiking on the Big Waves," shows a dejected California surfer standing next to his splintered and peeled hollow board that had just received a "going over" from a big wave. An undetected crack or small hole in a hollow, moreover, meant the board would slowly fill up with water, and have to be drained regularly. By the mid-'30s, planks were being made of balsa, and were nearly as light as the hollows, and in 1937 the narrow-tailed hot curl solid board was developed, offering greatly improved handling over the plank. Board design after World War II was almost exclusively in the hands of Malibu-based surfers, who rejected outright the hollow board, and soon developed the finned balsa/fiberglass chip, which in turn led to a prototype of today's longboard. Hollow boards continued to be used by lifeguards and paddlers into the late '50s.

The hollow was known almost immediately as a "cigar board" or "cigar box," as it resembled a cigar in outline. By the late '40s, as the hollow was being phased out, it was often dismissed as a "kook box." In Australia, surfers forswore planks and used hollows (known there as "toothpicks" or "pencils") almost exclusively from the late '30s until 1956. By the early 1990s, hollow boards had become highly prized by surfboard collectors; in *Surf's Up: Collecting the Longboard Era,* a coffee-table book published in 2002, Blake hollows from the '30s are estimated to be worth between $6,000 and $12,000. *See also* Tom Blake, lifeguarding and surfing, paddleboarding, plank surfboard.

Hollywood and surfing   Although surfing was shown briefly in several movies of the 1930s and '40s, including *Bird of Paradise* (1932) with Dolores Del Rio and *Waikiki Wedding* (1937) with Bing Crosby, Hollywood didn't take a close look at the sport until *Gidget,* a frothy 1959 hit for Columbia Pictures. Hollywood's take on surfing in the decades since has been uneven at best (usually fun and bubbleheaded or heavy-handed and melodramatic), frequently unprofitable, and almost always unpopular with surfers as well as movie critics. "Make no mistake," the *Surfer's Journal* wrote in 1998, "the union between Hollywood and surfing has for the most part been a failure." *Gidget* spawned the beach movie phenomenon of the early and mid-'60s; *Beach Party, Beach Blanket Bingo,* and *How to Stuff a Wild Bikini* were among the roughly two dozen low-budget genre movies released between 1960 and 1967 (many produced by American International Pictures, and starring teen idols Frankie Avalon and Annette Funicello). Surfing was little more than a background activity to beachside twist parties, but popular '60s surfers like Mickey Dora, Johnny Fain, and Mickey Muñoz were employed as beach movie extras and stuntdoubles, and musical guest stars like Jan and Dean, the Righteous Brothers, the Animals, Stevie Wonder, and Dick Dale kept the soundtracks hopping. Some of the beach movies performed well at the box office; *Muscle Beach Party* cost $300,000 and grossed $12 million. The cartoonish beach movies were reviled by surfers in the '60s, embraced in the '80s as ironic camp, then—for some—cherished in the '90s and '00s as silly but likable tokens of a more innocent past. (*Ride the Wild Surf,* released in 1964 and starring Fabian, Tab Hunter, and Barbara Eden, was an exception to the beach movie formula, veering close to straightforward drama, and featuring some beautifully photographed Hawaiian surf sequences, including a climatic big-wave showdown at Waimea Bay.)

Hollywood stayed away from surfing in the 1970s, with one notable exception: 1978's *Big Wednesday.* Warner Brothers' $11 million coming-of-age California surf drama, starring Gary Busey, Jan-Michael Vincent, and William Katt, was a critical and box-office bomb ("melodramatic ... self-indulgent ... embarrassing," *Surfer* magazine wrote), then slowly found new life and stature in video release, with 1998 bringing a mini-blitz of *Big Wednesday* 20th-anniversary events and marketing. *Apocalypse Now,* the Vietnam War epic released the following year, wasn't a surf movie, but featured what many regard as

John Wayne and Hawaiian surfer Duke Kahanamoku, in 1948's *Wake of the Red Witch*

Hollywood's finest surfing character, the strutting Colonel Kilgore, played by Academy Award winner Robert Duvall. When questioned by an underling as to the necessity of taking out an entire "Victor Charles" (Vietcong) village so that a few of his men can ride a nearby pointbreak, Kilgore stares at the inquisitor and famously bellows, "Charlie don't surf!" (Hollywood produced its second and final well-done surf character in 1982, with Sean Penn playing the eternally stoned surf dude Jeff Spicoli in *Fast Times at Ridgemont High.*)

The year 1987 brought Annette Funicello's *Back to the Beach,* a flaccid beach movie encore, and the trifling *North Shore,* a drama in which a wavepool champion from Arizona flies out to Hawaii to compete against the world's best in the big annual contest at Pipeline. Supporting actor John Philbin provides comic relief as Turtle, but the *North Shore* characters are otherwise uniformly flat, including those played by pro surfers Gerry Lopez, Laird Hamilton, Robby Page, and Mark Occhilupo.

Point Break, 20th Century Fox's 1991 cops-and-robbers surf movie starring Patrick Swayze and Keanu Reeves, was a misfire, as was New Line's *Endless Summer II,* a fusion between Hollywood and the old school hardcore surf movies of the '60s, and the long-awaited follow-up to the 1966 crossover hit *The Endless Summer.* Far more ambitious was TriStar's $10 million big-wave saga *In God's Hands,* released in 1998, and starring top pro Shane Dorian, along with surfer/actors Matty Liu and Matt George (who also wrote the script). Much of the *In God's Hands* surf footage was breathtaking, but the plot dribbled and the characters' persistent brooding quickly and unintentionally became the movie's sole comic outlet. *Blue Juice* (1995), a bland romantic drama set in coastal England, is noteworthy only in that it stars precelebrity Catherine Zeta-Jones and Ewan McGregor. As with virtually every mainstream surfing drama, *Blue Juice* ends with a life-or-death surfing showdown. Hollywood has occasionally shown surfing to be meditative and calming (usually in the film's early acts), but far more often the sport is presented only in terms of thrills, challenge, and conflict, and almost never is it viewed as simply integrated into a person's life. This lack of balance is perhaps the main reason why Hollywood has yet to produce a first-rate surfing movie. *Blue Crush,* released in 2002, was the most expensive surf movie ever made, at $35 million, and put a slight twist on things by using young women in the starring roles.

Surfing has on rare occasion been well served by off-Hollywood movies, including the poignant *Ocean Tribe* (1997) and the wildly satirical *Psycho Beach Party* (2000). Surfing has also been presented to spectacular effect in the giant-screen IMAX format, in *Adventures in Wild California* and *IMAX Extreme,* both released in 1999. A short list of Hollywood actor/ surfers past and present includes Jackie Coogan, Cliff Robertson, Peter Lawford, Tom Hanks, Woody Harrelson, and Sean Penn. *See also* Apocalypse Now, Big Wednesday, Blue Crush, Fantastic Plastic Machine, Fast Times at Ridgemont High, In God's Hands, John Milius, North Shore, Point Break, Ride the Wild Surf.

Holmes, Paul   Cultured and erudite surf journalist from Laguna Beach, California, by way of Australia and Great Britain. Holmes was born (1949) in Bradford, England, grew up in Newquay, and began surfing at age 13, wearing a rugby shirt against the winter chill. In 1971, he was the founder, publisher, and principal writer of *Surf Insight,* England's second surf magazine, as well as a shaper for Bilbo Surfboards in Newquay. In 1972 he moved to Sydney, Australia, and shaped for Keyo Surfboards, and for the next four years he shaped for various Sydney-based boardmakers. *Tracks* hired Holmes in 1976 as a writer and ad salesman, and from 1977 to 1981 he served as the magazine's editor. For four years beginning in 1978, Holmes also worked as contest director for the Coca-Cola Surfabout contest, the world's richest surf contest, held in Sydney; in the 1979 event, Holmes airlifted the entire contest—hiring six small planes to do so, at Coke's expense—from Sydney to Bells

Beach, Victoria, prompting 1976 world champion Peter Townend to write that the Coke contest had become "worlds ahead of every other professional surfing event." Mobile surf contests would later become a pro tour standard. (In 1980, Holmes published *Surfabout: The Complete Story of Professional Surfing and the World's Richest Contest.*)

Holmes moved to Laguna Beach, California, in 1981, to work as the editor of *Surfer* magazine, a post he held until the end of 1989. He was also coproducer of *Surfer*'s ESPN television series, which debuted in 1985. From 1990 to 1995 Holmes worked a succession of marketing jobs for Gotcha surfwear, Action Sports Retailer, and Hang Ten surfwear; since 1995 he's been a freelance writer, working primarily for *Longboard* magazine. *See also* Coke classic.

Hong Kong   *See* China.

Honk   Six-piece country rock band from Laguna Beach, California, formed in 1971 and best known for their Granite Records soundtrack album for MacGillivray-Freeman's 1972 surf film *Five Summer Stories.* Honk toured with major acts such as Linda Ronstadt, the Beach Boys, Loggins and Messina, and Chicago, and released two more albums, but never again returned to their early level of popularity; the group broke up in 1975. "Pipeline Sequence," "Blue of Your Backdrop," "Made My Statement," and "Lopez"—the latter an instrumental named for Hawaiian Pipeline guru Gerry Lopez—were some of the most popular Honk songs from the *Five Summer Stories* album, which hit #1 on the charts in Hawaii. *See also* Five Summer Stories.

Honolua Bay   Dreamy right-breaking point surf located on the northwest corner of Maui, Hawaii; described by four-time world champion Mark Richards as "the ultimate wave; the best wave in the world." Beginning at an outermost section called Coconut Grove, the wave at Honolua bends into the cliff- and boulder-lined bay, passes through the Cove takeoff area, and arranges itself into a long, fast, perfectly foiled wall that spins through two or three bowl sections. The northeasterly tradewinds blow offshore at Honolua. Small surf is fairly common here from October to April (the summer months are waveless), and on sub-six-foot swells the area divides into three separate breaks. Incoming North Pacific swells have to thread the narrow Kalohi Channel between the

Honolua Bay

islands of Molokai and Lanai before moving into Honolua Bay, which means that only a few times a year does the break come into full form, linking all the waves from Coconuts to the final Cave section. When conditions do come together, the lineup is invariably choked with surfers, who often ride three or more to a wave.

Oahu surfers George Downing, Wally Froiseth, and Russ Takaki are credited as the first to ride Honolua Bay in 1947, but the break was rarely surfed until the early '60s. *The Performers,* a 1965 surf movie, featured a Honolua sequence filled with glorious six-foot waves, which helped put the break on the map, and Oahu-based surfers were soon beginning to fly over by the dozens when the swell got big enough. Still, a full day of waves might find the lineup nearly empty by late afternoon. "The place just ate surfboards," Hawaiian surfer Barry Kanaiaupuni recalled describing Honolua's cliff-lined shore, which is notorious for destroying lost surfboards. "Fifteen, 20 boards a day sometimes." Maui resident Joseph "Buddy Boy" Kaohi was regarded as the mid-'60s master surfer of Honolua; Oahu surfers Jeff Hakman and Jock Sutherland, who both briefly attended college in Maui in 1967–68, were also standout Honolua riders, as were Les Potts and Gary Birch.

Honolua is sometimes thought of as the coming-out location for the short surfboard, as Australians Bob McTavish and Nat Young rode the break in late 1967 on their new vee-bottom boards; footage of the two Aussies climbing and dropping across the transparent Honolua walls was used for the climactic sequence to *The Hot Generation* (1968), which introduced the shortboard to much of the surf world.

Honolua then became a favorite testing ground for the ongoing shortboard revolution. It also became an icon for surf mysticism (waves here were described by one surf magazine as "the road to Nirvana"), in part for its unspoiled beauty, but also for its connection to the LSD-based Maui drug culture. The development of the surf leash in the early '70s brought an end to the Honolua idyll, as the intermediate-level surfer could ride without ruining his board. *Surfer* magazine described Honolua as "paradise lost" by 1975; five years later, *Surf* magazine alerted its East Coast readership to steer clear of the break altogether, warning of crowds, fights, and car rip-offs.

Honolua was cited by *Surfing* magazine in 1981 as one of "The 10 Best Waves in the World." The break was featured in *Great Waves* (1998), an Outdoor Life Network documentary series, and has appeared in dozens of surf movies and videos, including *Angry Sea* (1963), *Cosmic Children* (1970), *Free Ride* (1977), *Follow the Sun* (1983), *Surfers: The Movie* (1990), and *Triple C* (1996). Second-tier men's division pro surfing contests have been held at Honolua since the late '80s; its also been the site of the Billabong Girls world pro tour event since 1999. *See also* Maui.

hook   *See* curl.

Horan, Cheyne   Creative and eccentric Australian pro surfer from Sydney's Bondi Beach; runner-up to the world championship in 1978, 1979, 1981, and 1982. Horan was born (1960) in Sydney, the son of a former national speed-skating champion, and grew up in the beachside suburb of Bronte. He began surfing at 11, and three years later was the juniors division state champion and one of the country's top skateboarders. In 1977, one year after finishing fourth in the juniors division of the National Titles, the 16-year-old Horan turned pro, placed seventh in his first world tour event, and finished the year ranked 29th. The following season Horan won the Waimea 5000 in Brazil, and astounded the surf world by finishing runner-up in the final standings to fellow Australian Wayne Bartholomew.

Horan was by then a full-blown teenage surfing sensation. He rode in a low, open-kneed squat, weight distributed evenly over a pair of enormous thighs (his surf trunks had to be custom-tailored to fit his legs) in what was sometimes called the "horse stance." Instantly recognizable by his white-blond hair and flamboyantly colored surfboards, Horan maneuvered almost exclusively in and around the wave pocket, turning constantly and often folding himself into a muscle-flexed tube stance. He's often credited as the inventor of the floater maneuver, in which the surfer rides laterally across the curl or the whitewater crown, and was an early proponent of the aerial. Photogenic and quotable—"I'm not into doing the same thing that's always been done," he told *Tracks* magazine, "I'm into evolution"—the young Horan was a surf media darling, turning up often on magazine covers and in surf movies. (His world tour peers were less enamored, often referring to him as the Bondi Brat or Cheyne the Pain.) He became a member of the high-profile Bronzed Aussies surf team in 1977, then quit acrimoniously the following year, saying he "wanted to make it as an individual." Horan again finished runner-up to the world title in 1979, this time to eventual four-time world champion and avowed Horan nemesis Mark Richards. In 1980 he dropped to fifth, then returned to finish second to Richards in 1981. Surf pundits had long been saying it was simply a matter of time before Horan won the championship, and in 1982 he shot to an early ratings lead by winning the first two events of the season. But Richards fought back and once again beat Horan for the title.

By that time Horan was being both celebrated and dismissed as a surf world crank. He rode experimental and frequently bizarre surfboards, including the wide-backed Lazer Zap (outfitted with a split-tipped "winged keel" fin) and a cigar-shaped double-ender. He rode 18-foot waves at Waimea Bay on a 5'8" single-fin. Horan also became a macrobiotic vegetar-

Cheyne Horan

ian, and a devotee of yoga, astrology, and the I-Ching; he lived in an all-male commune; he advocated for solar energy and for the release of jailed South African leader Nelson Mandela. Most conspicuously, he became a habitual user of marijuana and nonsynthetic psychedelics (or "mind food" as he called them), and went on record as supporting drug legalization.

Horan's world tour ranking slipped over the next five years, from third in 1983 to 24th in 1987. The 29-year-old then came back to win the season-ending 1987 Billabong Pro in Hawaii, earning $50,000—the sport's richest cash prize up to that point. His year-end rating went back to 14th, and he remained on the world tour for another four largely undistinguished seasons. He retired at the end of 1993 with 12 world tour career victories, including a popular win in the 1982 Op Pro in Huntington Beach. In the mid-'90s Horan reinvented himself as a big-wave surfer. He was a regular invitee to the Quiksilver in Memory of Eddie Aikau contest at Waimea Bay, and finished fifth in the 2002 Tow-In World Cup, held in 35-foot-plus surf at Jaws in Maui.

Horan won the 1983 *Surfer* Magazine Readers Poll Award. He's appeared in more than 50 surf movies and videos, including *Free Ride: Take 2* (1978), *We Got Surf* (1981), *Follow the Sun* (1983), *Waterborn* (1987), *Surfers: The Movie* (1990), and *Biggest Wednesday* (1998). *Scream in Blue,* a compelling and unvarnished documentary on Horan's 1985 world tour campaign, was released in 1986; in 2001 he was featured on *Biographies,* an Outdoor Life Network TV series. In the finals of the 1999 Quiksilver Masters World Championships, a pro event held for surfers 36 and older, Horan defeated Wayne Bartholomew—the surfer he'd finished second to in the world title race nearly 20 years earlier. Horan is married and has one child; in 2003 he was living on Queensland's Gold Coast. *See also* drugs and surfing, no-nose.

Horn, Christopher "Kit"   Unobtrusive big-wave surfer from Santa Monica, California. Horn was born (1929) in Los Angeles, raised in Santa Monica, and began surfing in 1941. He made the first of many visits to Hawaii in 1959, five years after receiving a B.S. in business from the University of Southern California, but most of his big-wave riding was done in northern California during the '60s and '70s, where he surfed 15-foot waves alone in 50-degree water. Horn had a good run in the United States Surfing

Championships: in 1965 and 1966 he finished runner-up in the seniors division; in 1969 at age 40, he won the kamaaina division (over 35), just before winning a paddle race in which he beat a field of surf-world headliners including Corky Carroll, Mike Purpus, and Gerry Lopez, all younger than Horn by at least 15 years.

Hornbaker, Jeff   Quiet, adaptable, peripatetic surf photographer from Los Angeles, California; among the best in his field throughout the 1980s and '90s. Hornbaker was born (1955) in Pomona, California, began surfing at age 13, and in 1975 published his first surf photos in *Surfer* magazine. He became a *Surfer* masthead photographer in 1979, then jumped to *Surfing* in 1987, where he remained until 1998. The gaunt and always watchful Hornbaker was perhaps the most versatile photographer of the period, equally skilled at action shots (water or land), portraiture, or sundry surf lifestyle images, with an artist's feel for color, light, and texture and a graphic designer's understanding of composition and framing. In the early '80s, Hornbaker and fellow California photographer Aaron Chang brought a quirky, sharp-edged New Wave sensibility to their peripheral surf-related photography, often using stark lighting, props (dead fish, spike-heel shoes, rusted NO SURFING beach signs), and industrial metallic or concrete backdrops. Hornbaker meanwhile became a favorite among top surfers, often traveling as the photographer of choice on long exploratory trips through Indonesia with world champion riders like Tom Carroll, Martin Potter, Tom Curren, Kelly Slater, and Sunny Garcia. *Australia's Surfing Life* magazine in 1990 named Hornbaker the world's best surf photographer. By then he was shooting film as well, producing or contributing to a number of surf videos, including *Strange Desires* (1990) and *The Hole* (1997); *No Destination* earned Hornbaker and film partner Don King a Best Cinematography Award in the 1998 *Surfer* Magazine Video Awards. His photography has been published in *Outside* and *GQ* magazines, and he has also contributed to a small number of illustrated surfing books, including *The History of Surfing* (1983) and *The Next Wave* (1991). The unmarried Hornbaker travels 10 months out of each year, and keeps houses in Hawaii, Sydney, and Los Angeles.

Hossegor   Holiday town on the southwest coast of France, 60 miles north of the Spanish border; world-

Hossegor, France

renowned for its tubing beachbreak surf, and the epicenter, along with neighboring Biarritz, of French surfing. Hossegor breaks from late summer to spring, but is best from September to December, as North Atlantic storms regularly send powerful three to eight-foot surf into the Bay of Biscay. Because the wave-forming sandbars along Hossegor's two-mile beachfront (connected to a near-endless stretch of beach to the north) change and shift frequently, and because wave quality is greatly affected by the area's extreme tidal changes, surfing here is a catch-as-catch-can experience, with flawless tubes often disintegrating within an hour into a churned-up riptide. Pro tour surfers nonetheless voted Hossegor the "Best Beachbreak in the World" in 1993, and *Australia's Surfing Life* magazine in 1997 listed it as one of the "Ten Waves Every Surfer Should Ride."

The Fosse de Capbreton—a narrow offshore canyon created by the river Adour—points directly at Hossegor and magnifies incoming swells, so that the waves here are dependably bigger than at beaches to the north and south. Hossegor gets 10 foot or bigger in fall and winter, but most of the sandbars overload when the waves get above eight feet. Popular surfing beaches in Hossegor include La Graviere, a right-breaking tube located at the south end of town that can hold bigger waves than anywhere in the area; Les Estagnots, home base for an annual world pro tour competition; and La Piste, a shallow, nearshore right tube just south in Capbreton.

Alain Weber was among the first of a small group of local and visiting surfers who began riding Hossegor in 1960, but the break remained something of a secret until 1969–70, when it was featured in two popular surf movies, *Evolution* and *Waves of Change*.

The latter film, made by California's Greg MacGillivray and Jim Freeman, featured Billy Hamilton, Keith Paull, and Mark Martinson riding dreamlike six-foot Hossegor tubes. The European Surfing Championships were held at Hossegor in 1973. In years to come, a surfing community—largely transient throughout the '70s, followed by the first all-year pioneers in the early '80s—began to take shape among Hossegor's beachfront pine trees and sand dunes; three-time world champion Tom Curren often surfed there while living in France from the mid-'80s to the early '90s. By 2002 there were more than a dozen surf shops in Hossegor, as well as three summer-season learn-to-surf camps. Surf industry giants Rip Curl and Billabong built their European headquarters in Hossegor; *Surf Europe* magazine, founded in 1999, is also headquartered there, along with the French Surf Federation and the Hossegor Surf Club. In early 2003, the Hossegor beaches, along with the rest of the south and southwest Bay of Biscay beaches, were closed due to an oil spill following the sinking of the tanker *Prestige* off the Spanish coast. About 1,500 full-time surfers live here (including touring pro Micy Picon), and thousands more visit during late summer and fall, often joining the masses of European tourists in nighttime revels. Hossegor has been featured in dozens of surf movies and videos over the decades, including *A Sea for Yourself* (1973), *Atlantic Crossing* (1989), *Beyond the Boundaries* (1994), and *E2K* (2001).

Hossegor Rip Curl Pro   World pro tour summer contest held in the mercurial beachbreak waves of Hossegor, France, a resort village just north of Biarritz; sponsored by wetsuit manufacturer Rip Curl. Australian Dave MacAulay won the first Hossegor Rip Curl Pro in 1987. A women's division was added in 1992. Tuberides are often a regular feature of the Hossegor Rip Curl Pro, as were the sweaty *après*-surf booze-ups at the local nightclubs. The 2000 Rip Curl Pro hit a high mark with $153,000 in prize money, but the following year the contest was reduced to a pro tour qualifying event. Winners of the Hossegor Rip Curl Pro:

1987:	Dave MacAulay
1988:	Tom Carroll
1989:	Tom Curren
1990:	Martin Potter
1991:	Tom Carroll
1992:	Kelly Slater, Wendy Botha
1993:	Damien Hardman, Kylie Webb
1994:	Flavio Padaratz, Lynette MacKenzie
1995:	Rob Machado, Layne Beachley
1996:	Kelly Slater, Serena Brooke
1997:	Rob Machado, Neridah Falconer
1998:	Damien Hardman, Layne Beachley
1999:	Michael Lowe, Rochelle Ballard
2000:	CJ Hobgood, Layne Beachley
2001:	Joel Parkinson, Melanie Redman
2002:	Richie Lovett, Pauline Menczer

hot coat   Second coat of resin applied to a surfboard, brushed on following the laminating coat (which saturates the board-covering layer of fiberglass) but before the finishing coat (or gloss coat). Hot coat resin, also known as sanding resin, contains styrene monomer, a wax-based sanding agent, which floats to the surface as the resin dries, resulting in an easy-to-sand surface. The hot coat puts a smooth, thin, hard layer over the fiberglass-dimpled laminating coat. By comparison, wax-free laminating resin is slightly gummy, even when dry. After the board is hot coated, the fin system is added: "glass-on" fins are attached to the board with resin and short lengths of fiberglass rope; boxes or plugs for removable fins are sunk into the bottom surface and set in place with fiberglass cloth and resin. The board is then machine and hand sanded. *See also* resin, surfboard construction.

hot curl board   Finless surfboard popular from the late 1930s to the late '40s, although used almost exclusively in Hawaii; invented in 1937 by Honolulu surfer John Kelly; often described as the first specialized big-wave board. Two types of stand-up surfboards were in use during the mid-'30s: the narrow-tailed block-edge hollow "cigar box" and the heavier (around 70 pounds) solid-wood square-tail plank. While the hollows paddled faster and were easier to carry, the solids allowed a slightly higher degree of control while riding, and as a rule most of the progressive Hawaiian surfers rode planks. In the summer of 1937, Kelly, Wally Froiseth, and Fran Heath were riding their redwood planks in six-foot surf at a break named Browns, near Diamond Head, when Kelly left the water, frustrated that he couldn't hold a tighter angle to the wave face. In the yard of his beachfront house, Kelly used an ax and a drawknife to reshape the back two-fifths of his board, narrowing the tail by about eight inches (as measured one foot up from the back), and carving a longitudinal rounded "boat-bottom" area down the real hull. That afternoon Kelly returned to Browns. The board floated lower in the water and was more difficult to paddle, but it did indeed grip better to the wave while on an angle. A few weeks later, Froiseth was so happy with his new board—which measured 10′11″ by 20″ and weighed 65 pounds—he shouted, "Hey, these things really get you in the hot curl!" The name stuck.

The surfboard fin, popularized in the late '40s, would allow surfers to ride at a far tighter angle. But the hot curl was nonetheless a huge improvement over the planks and hollows, and was at least partially responsible for the discovery in the fall of 1937 of Makaha, a versatile surf break located on the west side of Oahu. The new board seemed to demand a more challenging wave, and Makaha served beautifully. Kelly, Froiseth, Heath, and later Woody Brown and George Downing, were among a small group who all but invented big-wave surfing at Makaha in the '40s and early '50s while riding hot curls. In waves of all sizes, the hot curl tended to bring out a spare, often elegant posture from the rider, and encouraged a quiet, fast, "trim" style across the wave face. Waikiki's Albert "Rabbit" Kekai is often mentioned as the top hot curl performer. The limitations of the hot curl were made apparent when Downing, Froiseth, and Russ Takaki toured Southern California beaches in 1948. Surfers at Malibu, they discovered, were riding wide-tailed balsa chip boards, wrapped in a protective layer of fiberglass. The outline on the chip boards was wrong for bigger surf, but the fin allowed riders to climb and drop across the waves, while the redwood hot curl riders could do little more than hold an angle. The chip's balsa/fiberglass construction, furthermore, made the boards lighter. Back in Hawaii, Downing built what was in effect a balsa/fiberglass hot curl with a fin—a design that would shortly be known as a big-wave gun—and the original hot curl was obsolete. *See also* big-wave surfboard, Wally Froiseth, John Kelly.

hotdogging   Quick and flashy style of surfing, generally limited to small waves. The phrase "hotdogging" was popular in the 1950s and '60s, then all but dropped from the surfer's lexicon with the introduction of the short surfboard in the late '60s. While surfing has always had its share of animated performers (Waikiki surfer John "Hawkshaw" Paia performed headstands, spinners, and somersaults in the '30s),

hotdogging is often said to have originated with California's Dewey Weber in the mid-'50s. Riding a new wide-backed "pig" board, which made turning easier than it had been with the bulkier Malibu chip, the quick-footed Weber—known as "the little man on wheels"—was able to whip through as many as six or eight 90-degree turns per wave. By bleaching his hair white and using matching bright-red surfboards and trunks, Weber also gave hotdogging a distinctive look.

Hotdogging, or trick surfing, was practiced almost exclusively by small, light surfers (Weber was 5′3″), often at beaches full of onlookers. Masters of the genre included Californians Johnny Fain and Corky Carroll. Popular hotdog maneuvers of the '60s included the head dip (in which the surfer bends over and dips his head into the curl), the spinner (a pirouette, sometimes performed two or three at a time), the fin-first takeoff (starting the ride with the surfboard tail first, then quickly sliding it 180 degrees), as well as a series of flamboyant hunched-over positions including the butterfly and the quasimoto. The '60s-era hotdogger was compared, often disparagingly, to the "classic" or "functional" surfer. "A mature man," traditionalist Sam Reid famously wrote in 1966, "will never remain a hot-dogger." Dewey Weber didn't agree, describing the hotdogger as "the master surfer [and] a top waterman," and further arguing that "hot-dogging is the only style of surfing that allows the surfer to express himself as an individual." Hotdoggers, furthermore, inevitably become classicists. Hawaii's Gerry Lopez, long regarded as the surfing embodiment of less-is-more precision and smoothness, first came to the attention of the surf world in 1969 as the master of the "sideslip"—a hotdog move during which the rider bends over, jams a hand in the water, and drops sideways down the wave face. Although the language changes, the classic/hotdog argument is revisited by each generation of surfers, most recently in the early '90s, with deep-turning power surfers set against the aerial-launching, tail-sliding New School surfers. *See also* Dewey Weber.

Houston, James   Writer from Santa Cruz, California, best known to surfers as coauthor of *Surfing: A History of the Ancient Hawaiian Sport* (1966, revised in 1996) and *A Native Son of the Golden West* (1971). Houston was born (1933) in Fresno, and began surfing in the early '50s while working on a B.A. in drama from San Jose State. He met U.C. Berkeley student

Ben Finney at this time, and the two worked together in the mid-'60s to produce the scholarly *Surfing: A History of the Ancient Hawaiian Sport. A Native Son of the Golden West,* Houston's first novel—set mainly on Oahu, Hawaii, in the mid-'50s—is the alternately funny and disturbing coming-of-age story of Hooper Dunlap, a Southern California surfer and college dropout who travels to Honolulu to visit his maniac big-wave-riding friend, Jonas Vandermeer. The book's format is often unconventional, jumping back and forth in time, with long passages set in italics or in play format. But Houston also produces a number of lovingly rendered passages on surfing's wooden-board era, including the following on surf vehicles:

> *Cars lashed with balsa boards, stuffed with bedrolls and diving gear—rusty station wagons, rickety Model A's, abandoned laundry trucks, and taxicabs and hearses. They had to be old and battered and barely running. The closer to dead the better. The most trea-sured was the car that could travel the farthest on five cylinders, or four; three tires; or no lights. And the same measure applied to houses. And to clothing. And to food. Everything had to be old, or discarded, or cheap, or free.*

Houston is also the author of several novels, includ-ing *Gig* (1969), *Continental Drift* (1978), and *Snow Mountain Passage* (2001), and his essays have been published in the *New Yorker,* the *New York Times,* and the *Los Angeles Times.*

Hoy, Matt Beer-loving metal-head pro surfer from Merewether, New South Wales, Australia; winner of the Pro Junior in 1991, and world-ranked #5 in 1997. Hoy was born (1971) and raised in Newcastle, and said he decided to become a full-time touring surfer in 1989, even though he had no competitive record to speak of, when fellow Australian pro Luke Egan grabbed him by the shirt collar and told him, "C'mon, Hoyo, you're going out there with me." The regular-footed Hoy cast his lot with the tour's hard drinkers and hard rockers, and in 1991 said he was most in-spired by boxer Mike Tyson, Guns n' Roses, and the Al Pacino drugs-and-Mafia movie *Scarface.* He won three world circuit events over the course of his pro career, and was three times ranked in the top 10. The surf press meanwhile fed on Hoy's bad-boy image. In 1992, when a *Surfing* magazine subscriber wrote in to protest Hoy's use of the Hitler-associated Iron Cross

as a surfboard graphic, the magazine noted that Hoy was "neither a member of nor believer in the Nazi party." Two years later, *Australia's Surfing Life* offered Hoy $100 if he could "contain his satanic ways long enough to sit through a church service." He cheer-fully declined. Hoy appeared in more than a dozen surf videos, including *Surfers of Fortune* (1994) and *Performers III* (1999).

huaraches *See* slaps.

Huber, Rudy Cofounder in 1967, along with New Jersey surfer Cecil Lear, of the Eastern Surfing Associ-ation (ESA), America's biggest and best-run amateur competition organization. Huber was a 32-year-old Connecticut-based general manager of Party-Tyme Cocktail Mix in 1966 when he traveled to Lima, Peru, to talk with International Surfing Federation presi-dent Eduardo Arena about pulling together the un-manageable factions of East Coast competitive surfing. Huber's new organization was introduced in late 1967 as the East Coast Surfing Association, but the following year was renamed and aligned with the newly formed Hawaiian Surfing Association, Western Surfing Association, and the Gulf Coast Surfing Asso-ciation; in aggregate, the three groups took the place of the United States Surfing Association. Huber, a northeast surfer since 1958, served as the ESA's first executive director. In 1996, Huber was among the first group of inductees into the East Coast Surfing Hall of Fame. *See also* Eastern Surfing Association.

Huey Australia's god of the sea and surfing; similar to Hawaii's "Kahuna." The word's origins are un-known, although "Huey" was used by residents of the outback to describe the god of rain long before surfing was introduced to Australia. Old surfboards are sometimes burned as a sacrifice to Huey.

Huge Monday A spectacular day at Pipeline, on Oahu's North Shore, on January 17, 1972; still re-membered for producing some of Pipeline's biggest, smoothest, best-formed surf. Daybreak revealed a building eight-foot west swell; by late morning, 12 foot waves were fringing over Second Reef and streaming into First Reef, where they stood up and formed enormous tropical-blue tubes; by midafter-noon all surfers were beginning their rides on Second Reef waves measuring 20 feet from trough to crest. Hawaii's Gerry Lopez set the day's standard until he was hit in the face by his board during a wipeout and had to leave the water. Other Huge Monday standouts included Craig "Owl" Chapman, Sam Hawk, James Jones, Rory Russell, and Jock Sutherland. *Surfer* magazine editors dubbed the event "Huge Monday" for a subsequent feature article, and surfers around the world were awestruck by images of the Pipeline session. "Huge Monday," said 1978 world champion Wayne Bartholomew, who only experienced the event through magazine photographs and in surf films like *Five Summer Stories* and *A Winter's Tale,* "is still engraved on my mind as the single greatest day in surfing history." *See also* Pipeline.

Hughes, Russell   Handsome blond Australian regularfooter; winner of the 1967 Queensland state titles at age 20, and third-place finisher in the 1968 World Surfing Championships. The fluid-surfing Hughes was virtually the only top Australian to disavow the newly introduced short surfboards in 1967. "I don't like small boards," he told *Petersen's Surfing* magazine. "They're ridiculous, I think; even nine-footers. The

Russell Hughes

shortboard restricts you." The 1968 world titles were held in Puerto Rico, and Hughes, having by then made the switch to the shortboard, was a second-string member of the Australian team. But as teammate and 1966 world champion Nat Young later recalled, Hughes probably deserved higher than his third-place finish. "His smooth, flowing style suited the crumbling [Puerto Rican] walls so well," Young said. "I thought he had won." Hughes was featured in a small number of surf movies, including *The Hot Generation* (1967), *Evolution* (1969), and *The Innermost Limits of Pure Fun* (1970).

Hui Nalu Club   Beachfront surfing, canoeing, and watersports club in Waikiki, Hawaii; informally started in 1905 but not chartered until 1911; composed primarily of surfers of full or partial Hawaiian blood. Hui Nalu ("Club of the Waves") was a longtime rival to the 1908-formed Outrigger Canoe Club, the world's oldest surfing organization. The Outrigger was a social club as well as an athletic club; membership was almost entirely foreign-born *haole,* or white, and the ranks contained an ever-growing number of nonathletic Honolulu businessmen. Membership to Hui Nalu, in contrast, was by election, and the club, while social in its own way, was for athletes only. Olympic gold medal swimmer and surfing progenitor Duke Kahanamoku was a Hui Nalu cofounder, along with his five brothers and a number of other Waikiki regulars; John D. Kaupiko and Edward "Dude" Miller joined shortly; California surfing pioneer Tom Blake later became a member. In the early years, annual Hui Nalu membership dues were $1.

While members of the Outrigger Canoe Club gathered 100 yards up the beach in their comfortable clubhouse, Hui Nalu convened beneath a hau tree on Waikiki beach in front of the Moana Hotel, and used the hotel's basement bathroom for a changing room. Many early Hui Nalu members were among the first Waikiki beachboys, making a career as lifeguards, surf instructors, and surfboard builders, and also building a collective reputation as the unhurried masters of surf and seduction. Aside from providing competition against the Outrigger, mainly in well-attended paddling and canoe races, Hui Nalu invented surfboard water polo and free-boarding (riding a surfboard with a towrope from behind a boat), while club member Sam Kahanamoku was the first person to use swim trunks—made of East Indian batik cloth—rather than the one-piece torso-covering woolen bathing suit.

Duke Kahanamoku became an honorary lifetime member of the Outrigger Canoe Club in 1917, as the wealthier organization was able to sponsor his swimming trips to the mainland. In years to come, more Hui Nalu members followed Kahanamoku and joined the ranks of the Outrigger; many held membership in both clubs. Loyalty to Hui Nalu ran deep, and beachboys who were buried at sea were often serenaded with the Hui Nalu song:

> Where the wild ocean waves are foaming
> Our fellows are sure to be
> Where big rollers burst
> And the surf is the worst
> We'll be there and yell with glee
>
> With our surfboards we always are ready
> To leap in the deep blue sea
> Our royal black and gold
> In victory will unfold
> Always on the top
> Hui Nalu!

The Hui Nalu's hau tree and the Moana Hotel bathhouse were both gone by 1947, and the club's activities were limited to outrigger-canoe racing. "What happened to the Hui Nalu?" former member Sam Reid asked Duke Kahanamoku shortly before the latter's death in 1968. "They just drifted away, one by one," Duke answered. "After they cut down the hau tree we didn't even have a club house. This is what happened to the Hawaiians...." Hui Nalu did in fact survive, primarily as a small canoeing and paddling club, and in 2002 was based out of Maunalua Bay Beach Park in southeast Oahu. *See also* Duke Kahanamoku, Edward "Dude" Miller, Outrigger Canoe Club, surf clubs, Waikiki.

Hui, The Loosely organized club located on the North Shore of Oahu, Hawaii, put together in 1975, according to cofounder Eddie Rothman, because there were "too many people from too many places" visiting and not showing enough respect for local wave-riders. The club's full name is Hui O He'i Nalu (Club of Wave Sliders; no relation to Hui Nalu, the club Duke Kahanamoku cofounded in Waikiki in 1911). From the beginning, the Hui had a reputation for heavy-handedness, even thuggery. When 1978 world champion Wayne Bartholomew of Australia was publicly beaten at Sunset Beach by a group of resident surfers in 1976, after bragging to the surf press about his country's prowess in the big Hawaiian surf, it was understood to be the work of the Hui—also known as the Black Shorts, for the black surf trunks that served as the club's uniform. Whether or not the group deserved its underworld reputation is another matter. "Some of the members have been in trouble here and there," Rothman acknowledged to *Australia's Surfing Life* magazine in 1997. "But the club has never been any extortion ring, or into drug dealing or anything like that." Beginning in the late '70s, the Hui was hired as the "water patrol" for the North Shore pro contests (a service not required anywhere else on tour), and in 1995, a spinoff surfwear company called Da Hui was formed. Da Hui sponsored a series of professional surf contests in Hawaii, the best known being the Backdoor Shootout, held at Backdoor Pipeline in 1996, 1997, and 1999. The original club, according to the Da Hui Web site, is now "more family and community oriented." But visiting surfers, as they have for decades, still give black-short-wearing locals a wide berth. "When I go out and surf," Rothman said in 1997, "don't bother me, don't bother my kids, don't bother the other kids around here. Just stay out of the way." Asked about the Hui membership process, Rothman added, "I think membership is closed right now." *See also* Da Hui's Backdoor Shootout, violence and surfing.

Hunt, Al Fleshy, surf-erudite competition administrator from Narrabeen, Australia. Hunt was born (1950) in Sydney, grew up in the central New South Wales town of Epping, and began surfing at age 14. The following year he moved with his family to the Sydney beachfront suburb of Narrabeen. Hunt was a reserve for the New South Wales surf team in the 1974 Australian National Titles; when he didn't get a start in the competition, he was asked to judge. Two years later, during the inaugural year for the International Professional Surfers (IPS) world circuit, Hunt judged contests in Australia, Hawaii, and California; in 1982, when the IPS became the Association of Surfing Professionals (ASP), he was elevated to world tour head judge. From 1984 to 2002, the hardworking Hunt—known to pro surfers worldwide as Fatty Al—served as the ASP tour representative, acting primarily as a rating-points tabulator, media liaison, and general competition-site troubleshooter. Hunt meanwhile began collecting surf magazines, and as of mid-2002 owned roughly 7,300 issues of magazines from every known surfing nation, including Switzerland, Greece, and Nova Scotia. His collection is the largest in the world; about 70 new issues arrive at his Sydney post office box each month. Hunt is married and has three children. He was named as an honor roll member of the Australian Surfing Hall of Fame in 1991. *See also* Association of Surfing Professionals.

Huntington Beach Suburban Southern California beach town located 35 miles southeast of Los Angeles; longtime home to the United States Surfing Championships, as well as America's densest cluster of surf shops; often referred to as "Surf City USA." Although ridable two-way beachbreak peaks are found along the entire length of Huntington's nine-mile coastline, Huntington Pier—California's longest municipal pier at nearly 1,900 feet—has always been the area's surfing focal point. Huntington is arguably mainland America's most consistent break, receiving long-distance swells all year, from every available direction (northwest to southeast, with southern-based swells having poorer form), and even turning local wind swells into reasonably organized surf. Wave shape is better during west or northwest swells. The densely-packed Huntington Pier crowds are notoriously aggressive; moving away from the pier, the number of surfers drops steadily. Huntington Cliffs, to the north, is a popular beginner break. Average wave height in Huntington is two to four foot; six-foot or bigger surf is not uncommon, but paddling out becomes a problem, and wave shape tends to deteriorate with size. On higher tides, the surf will often break over "outside" sandbars, reform into a swell, then break again just off the beach. Average daytime air temperatures range from the low 70s in summer to the upper 50s in winter; water temperatures range from the upper 60s to the mid 50s. The Huntington beachfront environment has long been derided by visitors and even some residents. Oil derricks by the hundreds, built adjacent to a large tidal marsh, lined the shore in the early decades of the 20th century; decrepit brick buildings near the pier in the '60s helped give Huntington the nickname "Surf Ghetto"; remodeling in the '80s and '90s turned much of the town into a series of strip malls and condominiums. "Huntington," surf journalist Ben Marcus wrote in 2002, "is a gray, sprawling wasteland, built on an oil field built on a swamp."

Huntington Beach was likely first surfed by Hawaiian George Freeth, California's original beach lifeguard, who arrived in Los Angeles in 1907; Freeth

gave a surfing demonstration during the opening ceremonies for the just-built Huntington Pier in 1914, and eight years later the pier waves were ridden by visiting Hawaiian surfer Duke Kahanamoku. Delbert Higgins and Gene Belshe, the first Huntington lifeguards, had by that time built their own surfboards and were teaching others how to ride, and by the late '30s it was common to see as many as 15 surfers out at the pier. But the Huntington surf scene didn't begin booming until the mid-'50s: local surfer Gordon Duane opened Gordie Surfboards in 1956, the first shop of its kind in the area, and the debut West Coast Surfing Championships were held three years later. Six hundred surfers were counted in the water on a sunny weekend day in 1962, and it was understood that "Surf City," Jan and Dean's bouncy #1 hit from 1963—with the lyric, "They're either out surfing, or they got a party going"—was about Huntington. (City legislators tried in 1992 to have Huntington Beach recognized by the state of California as the official "Surf City," but were thwarted by their Santa Cruz counterparts who argued—not convincingly—that *their* town was the real Surf City.) The West Coast Surfing Championships were renamed the United States Surfing Championships in 1964, and the contest was held annually at Huntington Pier through 1972. The debut Katin Pro-Am Team Challenge in 1977 was Huntington's first international surfing event (with the exception of a four-year break in the early '90s, the Katin ran continuously through 1998), and helped set the stage for the inaugural Op Pro in 1982. The gaudiest and best-attended pro tour event throughout the '80s and most of the '90s, the Op over the years was won by a number of world champions, including Tom Curren, Mark Occhilupo, Kim Mearig, Frieda Zamba, Sunny Garcia, and Barton Lynch. Surfing associations founded in Huntington Beach include the American Surfing Association (1976), National Scholastic Surfing Association (1978), the Association of Surfing Professionals (1982), and Surfing America (1998); on any given weekend, areas on either side of the pier will be cordoned off for a surfing competition. Top Huntington Beach surfers over the decades include, in roughly chronological order, Rocky Freeman, Jack and Mike Haley, Jackie Baxter, Corky Carroll, Herbie Fletcher, David Nuuhiwa, Bud Llamas, Kim Hamrock, Jeff Deffenbaugh, and Joey Hawkins.

As of 2003, Huntington was home to 12 surf shops, more than a half-dozen surf-themed restaurants, the popular Surfline wave forecasting service, and a number of surf murals and surf statues. An estimated 11 million beachgoers visit Huntington each year; five Web cams are trained on the Huntington surf—more than at any other beach in the world. The Huntington Beach Surfing Walk of Fame is located near the foot of the pier, adjacent to the Huntington Beach Surfing Hall of Fame and the 2,000-square-foot Huntington Beach International Surfing Museum. The pier was condemned in 1988, and rebuilt in 1993.

The Huntington surf has been featured in dozens of surf movies over the decades, including *Barefoot Adventure* (1960), *Cosmic Children* (1970), *Five Summer Stories* (1972), *Ocean Fever* (1983), and *Bliss* (1996). Huntington was also included in *Great Waves,* a 1998 Outdoor Life Network documentary series, and is the setting for two surf novels: *Tapping the Source* (1984) and *Reef Dance* (2002). *See also* Katin Pro-Am Team Challenge, Op Pro Huntington Beach, Orange County, United States Surfing Championships.

Huntington Beach International Surfing Museum   Two-thousand-square-foot museum located in Huntington Beach, California, two blocks east of the municipal pier. The volunteer-operated Huntington Beach International Surfing Museum was founded in 1988 by local Realtor Natalie Kotsch, and moved to its present city-donated site in 1990. The museum features a primary exhibit, changed annually (past displays have honored surf filmmakers, surf music, women surfers, and pre-20th-century surfing), and dozens of smaller exhibits. A life-size bust of surfing pioneer Duke Kahanamoku is on permanent display, as is a 1935-built paddleboard from surfing innovator Tom Blake. Museum fund-raisers have included a "surf stomp" concert featuring Dick Dale and the Chantays and an *Endless Summer* reunion concert with the Sandals. Museum admission as of 2003 is $2 for adults and $1 for students. *See also* Bishop Museum, California Surf Museum, Santa Cruz Surfing Museum, Surfworld Museum.

Huntington Beach Surfing Walk of Fame   Surf-themed sidewalk memorial in Huntington Beach located at the intersection of Main Street and Pacific Coast Highway, near the base of the municipal pier, patterned after the Hollywood Walk of Fame; founded in 1994 by Mike Abdelmuti, owner of nearby Jack's Surfboards. The annual Huntington Beach

Surfing Walk of Fame induction ceremony takes place in August, in conjunction with the U.S. Open of Surfing, a world pro tour competition. The induction committee is made up of about 80 international surf industry notables who send in their choices for each of six categories: Surf Culture, Local Hero, Surf Pioneer, Surf Champion, Woman of the Year, and Honor Roll. Occasionally, more than one surfer will be picked for a given category. Hawaiian surfer Duke Kahanamoku was elected in 1994 as the Father of Modern Surfing. While inductees are generally thought of as worthy of tribute, and the induction ceremony itself is loose and easygoing, the Walk of Fame has at times been criticized, most notably by *Surfer's Journal* publisher Steve Pezman, who in 1999 described the nominee list as "incredibly random," and said the entire concept and its execution made him "cringe." (Pezman nonetheless accepted his 2002 induction.) Walk of Fame members have their names inscribed into a one-foot by one-foot piece of granite, along with their category, the year of induction, and the Walk of Fame logo. Honor Roll members are listed together on a single tile. (The Surfer's Hall of Fame, founded in 1996 and located in the nearby Huntington Surf and Sport shop, has a similar list of inductees.) *See also* Australian Surfing Hall of Fame, East Coast Surf Legends Hall of Fame, International Surfing Hall of Fame.

Huntington Beach Walk of Fame inductees are as follows:

1994:   Duke Kahanamoku (Father of Modern Surfing)
Bruce Brown (Surf Culture)
Robert August (Local Hero)
Tom Blake (Surf Pioneer)
Mark Richards (Surf Champion)
Joyce Hoffman (Woman of the Year)

1995:   John Severson (Surf Culture)
Herbie Fletcher (Local Hero)
Phil Edwards (Surf Pioneer)
Tom Curren (Surf Champion)
Margo Oberg (Woman of the Year)
Jack W. Hockanson (Honor Roll)

1996:   Bud Browne (Surf Culture)
Corky Carroll (Local Hero)
Greg Noll (Surf Pioneer)
Nat Young (Surf Champion)
Rell Sunn (Woman of the Year)
Tom Pratte (Honor Roll)
John Rothrock (Honor Roll)

1997: Rick Griffin (Surf Culture)
       Hobie Alter (Surf Culture)
       Gordon Duane (Local Hero)
       Dale Velzy (Surf Pioneer)
       Shaun Tomson (Surf Champion)
       Linda Benson (Woman of the Year)
       Bud and Gordie Higgins (Honor Roll)
1998: Jack O'Neill (Surf Culture)
       Chuck Dent (Local Hero)
       John "Doc" Ball (Surfing Pioneer)
       Peter Townend (Surf Champion)
       Frieda Zamba (Woman of the Year)
       Ann Beasley (Honor Roll)
       Natalie Kotsch (Honor Roll)
1999: Leroy Grannis (Surf Culture)
       Jack Haley (Local Hero)
       George Downing (Surf Pioneer)
       Tom Carroll (Surf Champion)
       Jericho Poppler (Woman of the Year)
       Chuck Allen (Honor Roll)
2000: Greg MacGillivray/Jim Freeman (Surf
       Culture)
       Bud Llamas (Local Hero)
       Eddie Aikau (Surf Pioneer)
       Gerry Lopez (Surf Pioneer)
       Mark Occhilupo (Surf Champion)
       Nancy Katin (Woman of the Year)
       Mike Abdelmuti (Honor Roll)
       George Fahquhar (Honor Roll)
2001: Simon Anderson (Surf Culture)
       David Nuuhiwa (Local Hero)
       Albert "Rabbit" Kekai (Surf Pioneer)
       Wayne "Rabbit" Bartholomew (Surf
       Champion)
       Janice Aragon (Woman of the Year)
       Max Bowman (Honor Roll)
2002: Steve Pezman (Surf Culture)
       Brad Gerlach (Local Hero)
       Mickey Dora (Surf Pioneer)
       Kelly Slater (Surf Champion)
       Kim Mearig (Woman of the Year)
       Andy Verdone (Honor Roll)

Hurley, Bob Cheerful but razor-sharp surfwear magnate from Huntington Beach, California; Billabong USA president from 1983 to 1998; founder and CEO of Hurley International. Hurley was born (1955) in St. John's, Newfoundland, Canada, the son of an air force staff sergeant father, and spent his early years growing up on or near military bases in Rhode Island, Texas, and Japan. He moved with his family in 1963 to Orange County, and began surfing at age 13. At 21 he learned how to shape surfboards, and in 1978—after shaping boards for Infinity, Wave Tools, Lightning Bolt, and other labels—he opened Hurley Surfboards, a small factory/retail outlet in Huntington Beach. He was still making boards when Australian-based Billabong surfwear, unheard of in America, awarded him the Billabong USA license in 1983. Hurley proved to have a first-rate business mind, with a particular talent for marketing, as he assembled a crackerjack surf team (including world tour pros Sunny Garcia and Richie Collins), sponsored a number of high-profile professional surf contests (including the Billabong Pro in Hawaii, one of the premier world tour events of the '80s), and produced or coproduced a series of popular surf videos, including *Surf into Summer* (1987), *Pump* (1990), and *Sik Joy* (1995). In mid-1998, when Hurley announced he was leaving Billabong, *Surfing* magazine called it "the biggest surf industry news in two decades," while the *Los Angeles Times* business section, in a two-column article, noted that Hurley was largely responsible for Billabong being carried in Nordstrom and other mainstream stores. Hurley took many of Billabong USA's best designers, marketers, and team riders with him when he formed Hurley International, as well as some of the Billabong USA patents. The aggressively marketed Hurley International, like Billabong, produced surfwear and wetsuits, and immediately became one of the sport's hottest lines. Footwear giant Nike bought the company in early 2002 for an estimated $120 million.

Hurley was named by *Surfer* magazine in 2002 as one of the "25 Most Powerful People in Surfing." Jeff Hurley, the oldest of Bob Hurley's three children, was the national collegiate surfing champion in 1997 and 1999, as well as the 1999 Pacific Surfing Tour of America champion. *See also* Billabong.

Hurricane Gloria, 1985 Robust and long-lasting 1985 North Atlantic storm; fearsome enough in its north-tracking approach that the New York Stock Exchange was shut down for a day, along with all eastern seaboard schools and three Connecticut nuclear power plants. Gloria was the first hurricane to come ashore in New England since 1960, and the source of powerful triple-overhead waves in New Jersey, as well as a seven-day run of prime early autumn surf in the southern states. Gloria began as a tropical disturbance just south of the Cape Verde Islands on September 16. Five days later it reached hurricane strength (defined as having sustained wind speed of at least 74 miles per hour), and on the 25th it peaked as a Class 4 hurricane (with sustained winds of 143 miles per hour), putting the entire East Coast on hurricane alert for the first time in history. Gloria headed directly for the Carolinas, turned north and tracked closely along the coast, hit Long Island midafternoon on the 27th, then fell back to tropical storm status on the 28th as it passed over southeast Canada—one of the longest tracks ever plotted by the National Hurricane Center. While high winds left 250,000 New Englanders without power, and $1 billion in damages were reported between North Carolina and Maine, Gloria caused few injuries and no deaths. Excellent four to eight foot surf rolled into Florida, Georgia, and parts of South Carolina during almost the entirety of Gloria's life span. In the northern states, the winds switched to offshore after Gloria moved inland, and for a few hours the surf at places like Manasquan Inlet, New Jersey, was big—up to 12 foot—powerful, and well-shaped.

Hurricane Iwa, 1982   Hurricane Iwa, amplified by strong El Niño conditions, with winds gusting up to 120 miles per hour, swept into Hawaii on the afternoon of November 23, 1982—the first hurricane to hit the islands in 23 years. Only one hurricane-related fatality was recorded, but the storm did more than $200 million in damage, mostly on the island of Kauai. The world pro tour had just arrived on Oahu's North Shore, and the contests were suspended for a week until the power grid was back up. Surf journalist Allston James was vacating his rented condo at Makaha on Oahu's west side, when the first big waves hit. "Then came the sound of exploding glass doors and television sets," James later wrote, "and the deep groan of dozens of couches, beds and bookcases being moved across rooms simultaneously."

hybrid   Any one of a number of medium-sized, full-figured surfboard designs, all located somewhere on the board design spectrum between high-performance shortboards (usually about six or six and a half feet long) and full-length longboards (usually between nine and 10 feet). A typical hybrid might be eight feet long and 22 inches wide. The "egg" and "mini-log" are two hybrid variations. Hybrids are also known as "midlengths" or "funboards." The hybrid is faster paddling and more stable than a shortboard, and less cumbersome than a longboard. Surfers of all levels and abilities ride hybrids, but they're favored by beginners, intermediates, and older surfers. *See also* egg.

Hyman, Nev   Cheerful redheaded surfboard shaper from the Gold Coast, Queensland, Australia. Hyman was born (1958) in Johannesburg, South Africa, grew up in the Western Australia city of Perth, began surfing at age 11 and shaping three years later. In 1973, one week after graduating high school, Hyman founded the Odyssey Surfboards factory showroom in Perth; five years later he moved to Burleigh Heads, Queensland, and in 1980 he began shaping under his own Nev Surfboards label. He opened a Gold Coast factory showroom in 1994, and as a promo stunt built the world's biggest surfboard: a 25-foot tri-fin, ridden simultaneously by 10 surfers in its one and only seagoing excursion. Hyman has over the years made boards for dozens of the world's best surfers, including world champions Kelly Slater, Wendy Botha, Mark Occhilupo, Sunny Garcia, and Wayne Bartholomew. In 2001, Hyman was featured in an *Australia's Surfing Life* magazine article called "Loaded: 10 Surfing Millionaires." Hyman's fortune, the magazine said, came largely from exporting boards to Japan.

Hynd, Derek   Bright, quirky Australian pro surfer and journalist from Newport, New South Wales; world-ranked #7 in 1981; author of hundreds of surf press articles and columns between the early '80s and the early '00s. Hynd was born (1957) and raised in the Sydney suburbs, moved with his family to Newport in 1966, began surfing in 1968, and earned a B.A. in economics from Sydney University in 1978. Joining the world pro tour the following year, he finished the season ranked #32, then jumped to #12 in 1980. Small and wiry (5'9", 145 pounds), with double-jointed elbows, Hynd liked to punctuate his laterally drawn lines with flashy 360-degree spins. Blinded in his right eye after being struck by his board during a competition in 1980, Hynd surprised everyone by finishing the 1981 season ranked #7. The following season he dropped to #20, and at age 25 retired from competition.

Hynd began writing for *Australia's Surfing World* in 1978; in 1983 he started writing for *Tracks,* and the following year began contributing to *Surfer.* His prose was by turns insightful, witty, obscure, raunchy, and

Derek Hynd

morbid. He wrote profiles and travel pieces, but is best remembered for his coverage of the world pro tour, particularly his annual *Surfer* analysis of the top-ranked surfers. Debuting in 1987 as "The New ASP Top 30" (changed to the "Top 44" in 1992), Hynd's article included each surfer's ratings from the previous three years, and a short, often critical paragraph on their performance from the previous season. For 15th-ranked Charlie Kuhn of Florida, Hynd wrote, in part: "He has lost the bastard desire to win, and there's not much purpose evident right now. A mellow, super-nice guy, obviously lacking in the necessary forward-advancing emotions: spite, jealous and ego." Hynd also gave a one- or two-word prediction for each surfer's future world title chances: usually "no chance," but occasionally "faint possibility," "possibility," or, rarer still, "definite." Hynd's predictions were usually accurate, but he was fallible at times; at the end of the 1988 season he gave South African–raised surfer Martin Potter "no chance" for the 1989 championship, then watched as Potter ran away with the title.

Hynd also worked as a pro surfing coach from 1984 to 1988, most notably with Australian power surfer and future world champion Mark Occhilupo. In 1992 he developed "The Search," a long-running marketing campaign for Rip Curl wetsuits that focused on exotic surf locations and kept retired world champion surfer Tom Curren in the media spotlight; in 1999 he made *Proland,* a surf video; in 2001 he organized the Hebridean Surf Festival in Scotland, on the Isle of Lewis, with attending surfers including Curren and Skip Frye. Hynd himself was featured in a small number of surf videos, including *Sultans of Speed* (1987) and *Litmus* (1997). He's been married once and has one child.

Hynson, Mike   Swaggering American surfer and surfboard shaper/designer from San Diego, California; costar of the 1966 crossover hit *The Endless Summer,* and creator of the popular Gordon & Smith–produced "red fin" signature model. Hynson was born (1942) in Crescent City, California, the son of a career navy man, and spent his early years moving back and forth between Hawaii and the mainland, before settling down with his family in the mid-'50s in San Diego's Pacific Beach, where he began surfing. Nimble and athletic, Hynson quickly became one of the area's best riders; visiting Hawaii for the first time in late 1961, he was one of the first to ride Pipeline on Oahu's North Shore. Two years later Hynson was looking for a reason to leave the country and avoid being drafted into the army; when filmmaker Bruce Brown asked if he wanted to go around the world to shoot *The Endless Summer,* he jumped at the chance. The blond-haired Hynson, a regularfoot, was paired with dark-haired goofyfooter Robert August; along with Brown, the two surfers visited Africa, Australia, New Zealand, Tahiti, and Hawaii. Hynson's sublime first ride at Cape St. Francis—the right-breaking point surf the group discovered in South Africa, memorably presented as the answer to "the search for the perfect wave"—was the movie's high point.

Hynson was a surfer of great composure, never straining, and subtly arranging his arms, legs, head, and torso into positions that would come to define proper surfing style. He was one of the sport's great masters of trim, often letting his board run on a straight, elegant line. Handsome and cocky, Hynson was also a trendsetter on the beach, with surf racks on his Jaguar sports car, a wardrobe full of stylish clothes, and his hair always combed neatly back from his forehead, even while in the water. "He was the golden boy," his former wife said in 2001, "and everyone wanted to be like him." (Never particularly interested in surfing competition, Hynson nonetheless had some good results throughout the decade, placing fourth in the 1963 Malibu Invitational, second in the 1965 Tom Morey Invitational, and second in the 1969 Santa Cruz Big-Wave Contest. He was also selected for the Duke Kahanamoku Invitational in 1965, 1966, and 1967, and was a founding member of the rowdy but highly competitive Windansea Surf Club in 1963.)

A commercial surfboard shaper since 1959, and a star on the Hobie Surfboards shaping roster in 1963, Hynson returned from his *Endless Summer* travels, jumped over to Gordon & Smith Surfboards, and soon released the tri-stringer Hynson Model, a signature board later known as the "red fin" for its distinctive bloodred skeg. Many of the era's best surfers rode Hynson's boards, including Billy Hamilton, Barry Kanaiaupuni, Butch Van Artsdalen, and Herbie Fletcher. Hynson also designed and built the HY-1 and HY-2 models for Gordon & Smith, helped develop the control-enhancing "tucked-under edge"

surfboard rail in the late '60s, and created the Dol-Fin in 1973, a popular fin design patterned after a dolphin's dorsal fin. In 1970, he opened the short-lived Rainbow Surfboards in La Jolla, a combination surf shop and juice bar.

Plagued by drug and alcohol problems since the late '60s, Hynson later spent time in jail and lived on the streets. A long-simmering feud with Bruce Brown led Hynson to sue the filmmaker in 1995 for a share of the *Endless Summer* profits (the lawsuit was dismissed in 2000); at an *Endless Summer* reunion in 2001, however, Hynson somewhat amicably joined Brown and August to meet fans and sign autographs. Aside from *Endless Summer*, Hynson appeared in more than a dozen other surf films, including *Surfing Hollow Days* (1962), *Angry Sea* (1963), *Inside Out* (1965), and *Cosmic Children* (1970). He's also featured in a surfing sequence for *Rainbow Bridge*, the 1972 documentary featuring Jimi Hendrix in concert on Maui. Hynson was cited by *Surfer* magazine in 1985 as one of "25 Surfers Whose Surfing Changed the Sport." He's been married once, and has one child. *See also The Endless Summer,* tucked-under rail.

ice cream headache Brief but intense headache caused by immersion in cold water, usually occurring when a surfer first begins paddling through broken waves; similar to the pain felt when eating cold food—like ice cream—too fast. Ice cream headaches usually begin when the ocean water drops below 60 degrees, although the threshold changes from person to person, and is affected by air temperature and wind. The pain goes away a few seconds after resurfacing, then comes back on the next submersion. The headaches begin to lessen after a few minutes, and will often disappear completely after 10 or 15 minutes. Painful but harmless, ice cream headaches are caused by the arteries in the brain constricting and relaxing, and are thought to be more common among surfers who suffer from migraines. A well-fitted neoprene hood will not only prevent ice cream headaches, but reduce a surfer's chances of developing a more serious condition known as surfer's ear.

Iceland Cold and rugged island country, slightly bigger than Ireland, located just below the Arctic Circle, 200 miles east of Greenland; known as the "Land of Fire and Ice" for its joining of glaciers and volcanoes. In 1970, *Surfer* magazine published a letter from a U.S. serviceman stationed in Iceland that read,

Iceland; California's Robert "Wingnut" Weaver

"The waves here are generally very good, and eight foot surf is common." Twenty-seven years later, a group of California surfers, including Robert Weaver, Donovan Frankenreiter, and Mark Renneker, discovered excellent waves at several breaks around the island. "A place with Hawaii's jagged volcanic skylines, Alaska's rivers of ice and the isolated powerful surf of northern California," accompanying surf writer Dan Duane noted. While Iceland is open to swells from any direction, predicting and catching waves here can be difficult. During the peak winter surf season, when south swells are powerful and consistent, the daylight hours are very short—on the north Icelandic coast, during the winter solstice, the sun doesn't rise at all—and water temperatures are just above freezing. Swells from the north are mostly blocked or heavily filtered by ice floes. In the summer, when water temperatures rise as high as 55 and daylight lasts for 20 hours or more, surfing is all but impossible due to heavy winds and lack of swell. Most Icelandic people live in coastal towns and have a respectful, even fearful, relationship with the ocean—not surprising, given the drowning deaths over the years of hundreds of local sailors and fishermen. When the California surfers asked about nearby wave conditions, they were always told to stay ashore, and often given the same simple warning; enter the water, and "you will die." As of 2003, there were no native Icelandic surfers.

Ige, Harold "Iggy" Stylish, meticulous, affable surfer and surfboard shaper from Hawaii; a top member of the Dewey Weber Surfboards design and production team from '64 to '71. Ige was born (1941) in Lahaina, Maui, moved with his family at age four to Oahu, started surfing at age nine in Waikiki, and began shaping surfboards two years later. In the early '60s, not long after graduating from high school, Ige moved to Southern California and worked for Greg Noll Surfboards and Velzy Surfboards; he began working for Weber in '63. Ige had meanwhile developed into a graceful and athletic surfer and was a finalist in the '65 Laguna Swimwear Masters, one of the sport's first professional contests. Weber introduced the Harold Iggy signature model in '66 and in December of that year, Ige was featured in a group portrait in *Surfing* magazine—alongside Weber, Mike Doyle, Phil Edwards, Hobie Alter, and others—for an article titled "The Signature Model Era." Ige returned to Hawaii in '69 and since the early '80s has worked primarily in sailboard manufacturing.

impact zone   Churning area just shoreward of where the wave folds and breaks; almost always the most dangerous place at any surf spot, and the site where virtually all surf-related injuries and deaths occur. The phrase "impact zone" generally isn't used until the surf is at least medium sized. The impact zone at any given spot can change in size and intensity from day to day or even wave to wave. It can be measured in acres (Hawaii's Sunset Beach) or yards (First Peak Sebastian Inlet, Florida). *The Impact Zone,* a young adult surfing novel by Ray Maloney, was published in 1986; *Journey to the Impact Zone,* a surf video by Jeff Neu, was released in 1989. A *Surfer* magazine man-on-the-street column in 1999 posed the question: "Is there such a thing as an atheist in the impact zone?" *See also* boneyard.

In God's Hands   Beautifully photographed but critically flayed 1998 TriStar big-wave movie, directed by Zalman King (*9½ Weeks*), starring California surf journalist Matt George (who also cowrote the script), top-rated pro Shane Dorian, and surfer/actor Matty Liu. Shaun Tomson, 1977 world champion, costars; big-wave surfers Brian Keaulana, Darrick Doerner, and Brock Little have small parts. The *In God's Hands* travelogue plot, such as it is, takes the three friends on a color-saturated surf quest to Madagascar, Bali, Hawaii, and Mexico. The thundering big-wave climax was filmed at Jaws on Maui, where Liu cheers on his friends, George commits underwater suicide, and Dorian stylishly conquers the heavies. A favorable notice in the *Los Angeles Times* called the PG-13-rated *In God's Hands* "compelling," but most reviews were harsh. "As pretty as a scenic calendar and about as exciting" (*New York Times*), "[An] abysmally turgid and pretentious mess of tepid adventure, ponderous philosophizing, unromantic romance, bogus mysticism and vapid travelogue" (*Box Office Movie Magazine*). *In God's Hands* cost $10 million, went into limited release, mainly in California, and was pulled from most theaters after one week. *See also* Shane Dorian, Matt George, Hollywood and surfing.

India   Predominantly Hindu country, with a 3,400-mile coastline, facing into the Bay of Bengal to the east, and the Arabian Sea to the west. Swells generated in the Indian Ocean arrive on both coasts during the March-to-June hot season; local monsoons produce wind swells during the rainy season, from June to September; the winter months generally have little or no surf. Sea temperatures in India range from the mid-70s to the low 80s, and local sea life includes crocodiles and poisonous sea snakes. The Andaman Islands, a chain of about 200 islands located 800 miles northeast of India's southern tip, were long off-limits to visitors, but a 1998 *Surfer* magazine article included photos of perfectly shaped overhead Andaman reef surf, similar to that found in nearby Indonesia. Further south, the nine islands of the Nicobar group offer similar waves and settings, but are still mostly unexplored. India has virtually no surf industry, and just a handful of native surfers.

It's not clear exactly when surfing was introduced to India. Regularfooter Jerry Bujakowski represented India in the 1966 and 1968 World Surfing Championships, but he was likely an Indian citizen living overseas. In mid-1968, reigning East Coast champion Claude Codgen, along with Marylou McGinnis and Bob Purvey of California, rode some gentle beach-break waves at a place they called Seventh Pagoda, near the city of Madras; they're generally credited as the first to surf India. The country's enormous coastline remains largely unexplored for surf spots, but an excellent pointbreak has been ridden near Bombay, and a 1986 *Surfer* magazine article noted that India was full of "smallish, fun waves mostly breaking over shallow reefs." *See also* Andaman Islands.

Indian Ocean   World's third-largest ocean, covering 42 million square miles, located between Africa, southwest Asia, and Australia; includes the Andaman Sea, the Arabian Sea, the Bay of Bengal, the Persian Gulf, the Red Sea, and many other tributaries. Along the Indian Ocean's 41,000 miles of coastline are some of the world's best surf breaks, including South Africa's Jeffreys Bay, Grajagan and the Mentawai Islands in Indonesia, and Gnaraloo in Western Australia.

Surface currents in the Indian Ocean are directed for the most part by a counterclockwise gyre in the south, along with a unique figure-eight current in the north. Wave-generating storms in the Indian Ocean often form along the notorious "Roaring 40s"—on or near the 40-degree latitude, between the tip of South

Africa and the southwest tip of Australia. From June to October, low atmospheric pressure over southwest Asia results in southwest-to-northeast winds and currents in the Indian Ocean; these conditions produce excellent surf in Indonesia and Western Australia. Between December and April, high-pressure systems over northern Asia result in northeast-to-southwest winds and currents, often creating excellent waves in South Africa, Madagascar, and the Seychelles. Tropical cyclones can meanwhile form in the northern Indian Ocean in May to June and October to November, and in the southern Indian Ocean during January and February. The Indian Ocean is home to a complete spectrum of coastal environments, from lushly tropical to barren desert. Some Indian Ocean islands, like Madagascar, are geologically ancient. Others, like Mauritius, are relatively new. The Indian Ocean holds an estimated 40 percent of the world's offshore oil.

The Indian Ocean was the last of the three major surfing oceans to be introduced to surfing. Surfers have mapped most of the Indian Ocean's coastline over the past 40 years, but hundreds of first-rate breaks remain secret, underutilized, or undiscovered.

Indonesia   Tropical archipelago, home to the world's largest Muslim population; regarded since the late 1970s as the world's most wave-enriched nation, filled with a seemingly endless array of perfectly foiled reefbreaks. While cities like Jakarta are crowded, and in some cases blighted, vast portions of Indonesia are lightly populated (less than half of its 13,000 islands are inhabited) and sublimely beautiful. Excellent waves are found along Indonesia's entire south- and southwest-facing coastline, with major surfing areas identified by islands, from west to east, as follows: 1) Sumatra and offshore islands, including the sloping tubes of Nias and the wave-fringed Mentawai Islands. 2) Java, including the long, racing, dangerous tubes of Panaitan Island in the far west, and the expansive left walls of Grajagan on the island's southeast corner. 3) Bali, home to the fabled left tubes of Uluwatu and Padang Padang, the sand-bottomed peaks of Kuta Beach, and the open-ocean right-breaking waves of Nusa Dua. 4) Lombok, including the temperamental but exquisite waves of Desert Point. 5) Sumbawa, including the blazing lefts of Scar Reef, the thin-lipped cylinders at Periscopes, and the consistent two-direction waves of Lakey Peak. Many other islands—including Sumba, Timor, Roti, and Su-

Indonesia; reef surf in the Mentawai Islands

lawesi—have first-rate surf as well, but as of 2002 lacked any kind of visitor infrastructure.

Indonesia receives surf all year, but the most consistent period is the June-to-September dry season, as Southern Hemisphere storms originating in the Roaring 40s regularly produce four to eight foot ground swells, which pour into the islands and are lightly burnished by southeast (offshore) tradewinds. Ten-foot or bigger surf hits a few times each year. The December-to-February wet season brings inconsistent swells, southwest winds, and rainstorms. Spring and fall can take on the characteristics of either the wet or dry season. Indonesia straddles the equator, and average daytime temperatures range from the high 70s to mid-90s, with water temperatures ranging from the mid-70s to the mid-80s. Sharks and sea snakes patrol the Indonesian reefs, but the great surfing hazards here are overcrowding at the more popular breaks (Uluwatu and Grajagan, for example), shallow reefs, and in some cases extreme isolation. Indonesia's unstable sociopolitical climate has also been cited as a danger for traveling surfers, and the Bali nightclub terrorist attacks in 2002 caused thousands of cancelled surf trips.

Indonesian children have long ridden waves on small wooden bellyboards, and America-born hotelier Robert Koke introduced stand-up surfing to the country in the 1930s at Bali's Kuta Beach. But surfing didn't really take root here until the late '60s, when visiting Australian and American flight attendants began testing the breaks around Kuta. Sydney surf moviemaker Bob Evans filmed Nat Young, Mark Warren, and Col

Smith riding the Kuta surf in 1971; a few weeks later, Australian Alby Falzon filmed Stephen Cooney and Rusty Miller riding the long lefts at Uluwatu, and the results showed up to reverberating effect in Falzon's 1972 surf movie *Morning of the Earth.* Within three years, Bali had become the hottest new spot for the global surf traveler; local surfers, including Ketut Menda and Made Kasim were meanwhile beginning to pick up the sport as well, and were soon traveling to Australia and Japan to represent their country in international pro contests. Joe's Surf Shop, the first of its kind in Indonesia, opened in 1974 in Kuta by local surfer Made "Joe" Darsana; the first Balinese Surfing Championships were held later that year at Legian Beach, near Kuta, and won by Wayan Sudirka. The Bali Surfing Club was formed four years later, and organized the first Indonesian Championships, won by Wayan Suwenda. The OM Bali Pro, staged at Uluwatu, was Indonesia's first pro contest, and was part of the world pro circuit in 1981 and 1982.

Surf travelers began to shift their attention from Bali to the outer Indonesian islands beginning in the late '70s, a few years after waves were first ridden at Java's Grajagan and Lagundri Bay on Nias, near Sumatra. New perfect-wave discoveries were a regular occurrence in the '80s and '90s; surf resorts opened by the dozens (following the lead of the hugely successful camp at Grajagan), and chartered surf tours allowed thousands of surfers to fan out across the island chain, changing local economies as well as the surf world's perception of high-quality surf. The big powerful Hawaiian waves had been the surf world ideal since the late 19th century. Indonesia's thinner, longer waves, it turned out, were more dependable, better groomed, and better suited for high-performance riding.

As of 2003, Indonesia was home to about 50 surf shops (mainly in Kuta), one domestically published surf magazine (*Surf Time,* founded in 1999), and 15,000 native surfers. The Bali Surfing Association hosts about 20 amateur contests each year. The Indonesian Surfing Association was formed in 1990, primarily to help organize international events such as the world pro circuit's Quiksilver Grajagan Pro (held from 1995 to 1997), the Nias Indonesian Open (1994–96), the Dompu Pro at Lakey Peak (1997), the Op Boat Challenge (2000–01), and the Bic One Design Challenge (2002). Balinese goofyfooter Rizal Tanjung, winner of the 1997 Dompu Pro, has become Indonesia's first internationally known surfer. The In-

donesian surf has been featured in hundreds of surf movies, videos, and documentaries, and is detailed in a number of guidebooks, including *Indo Surf and Lingo* (1992), *Surfing Indonesia* (1999), and the *World Stormrider Guide* (2001). *See also* Bali, Grajagan, Mentawai Islands, Padang Padang, Uluwatu.

injuries and surfing   Although surfing has been presented at times as a sport with a danger level comparable to mountain climbing or bullfighting, its injury rate is in fact statistically similar to that of fishing and well below that of cheerleading. A 1999 study conducted by the Surfer's Medical Association (SMA) put the frequency of surfing injuries at one per every 250 surfing days—an injury being defined as anything serious enough to cause the surfer to miss at least one day of surfing. Lacerations, the SMA report continued, are the most common surfing injury, accounting for 40 percent of the total, followed by contusions (12 percent), sprains (11 percent), and fractures (6 percent). Other SMA findings:

- About three in 10 injuries affect the lower extremities, with an equal number of head and neck injuries.
- Wipeouts account for just over 60 percent of injuries, followed by postwipeout (or postbailout) surfboard recovery (9 percent), paddling out (7 percent), entering or exiting the water (6 percent), and duck diving (6 percent).
- Sixty-six percent of injuries result from contact with a surfboard, with 55 percent of those caused by the rider's own board. Contact with fins is the leading cause of injury from a surfer's own board, while being struck by the surfboard nose is the most prevalent cause when it comes to another surfer's board. Surfboard leash recoil is involved in 13 percent of injuries.
- Poisonous marine life, such as sea urchins, stingrays, jellyfish, sea snakes, and stonefish—all found in shallow tropical or temperate waters—account for less than 3 percent of all surfing injuries. Shark attacks, often considered by nonsurfers to be surfing's greatest danger, are in fact rare. There were 441 reported attacks on surfers worldwide during the entire 20th century, including about two dozen fatalities.

Another study, from 2002, showed that 70 percent of all surf injuries occur in waves head-high or smaller.

Crowded surfing areas, inexperienced surfers, and a failure to obey the sport's unwritten rules—particularly against dropping in on another surfer's wave—are all primary causes of surfing injuries. Safety devices, such as rubber noseguards and rubber-edged fins, have been available for years, but are for the most part unused, either out of laziness or because such accouterment are regarded as uncool. Surfing helmets are even less popular.

Surf breaks are described in part by their capacity to injure; shallow, hard-breaking, coral- or rock-bottomed breaks are the most dangerous. Pipeline in Hawaii has without question injured more surfers than any break in the world. In a record-breaking day for surfing injuries, 30 people were hurt at Pipeline on December 22, 1998, during a six-to-10-foot swell. Two of surfing's most famous injuries took place in back-to-back heats of the 1983 Pipeline Masters contest: Floridian surfer Steve Massfeller fractured his skull after hitting the bottom, permanently impairing his sight and memory; California's Chris Lundy then had his left leg wedged into the reef, wrenching the knee so badly that his foot was pointing behind him. Virtually every collision with the bottom in tropical locations results in scrapes, cuts, or abrasions ("reef rash") to one degree or another. Sand-bottom breaks can be dangerous as well. Pioneering Delaware surfer Bill Wise wiped out headfirst in the shallow waters at Bethany Beach, in 1965, broke his spine, and became a quadriplegic. The explosive Newport Beach Wedge, in California's Orange County, popular with bodysurfers, bodyboarders, and kneeboarders, has likely produced more spinal injuries than any other surf break.

Chronic injuries such as shoulder and back pain, usually the result of too much paddling, are generally visited upon older surfers. But Chris Prosser, traveling chiropractor with the world pro tour, says that more and more younger surfers, including world champions Kelly Slater and Sunny Garcia, are experiencing chronic knee and ankle problems as a result of high-impact maneuvers like floaters and aerials. Injury rates are also going up for tow-in big-wave riders, not so much because of the giant surf they are launching into, but because they use footstraps, which create a wrenching effect on knees and ankles and also greatly increase the likelihood of being struck by the board during a wipeout. *See also* death and surfing, fitness and surfing.

inside   1) Shoreward of the wave zone, between the beach and the breaking surf, as opposed to the "lineup," located just beyond—or outside—the wave zone. After finishing a wave, the surfer is inside. Beginners learn to surf by riding already-broken waves on the inside. 2) Abbreviated form of "inside the tube." 3) A wave-catching designation. If more than one surfer is paddling for a wave, the surfer closest to the curl has the inside position, and holds right-of-way. Similarly, among a group of surfers sitting and waiting for waves at a reef, pointbreak, or sandbar—where incoming waves break in more or less the same place and in the same direction—the surfer sitting "deepest," or closest to where the wave will begin to break, is holding the inside position, and generally has first claim on the next wave. *See also* caught inside.

International Professional Surfers (IPS)   The original governing body of the world professional surfing tour, created in 1976 by former world champion Fred Hemmings and Randy Rarick, both of Hawaii. An informal circuit of pro contests in Hawaii, Australia, and South Africa—sometimes called the "gypsy tour"—had taken shape by 1975. Because the events weren't linked together, however, there was no year-end champion and little uniformity from contest to contest. Big-wave pioneer Fred Van Dyke in 1968 had tried to organize surfers into what he called the International Professional Surfers Association, but no progress was made and the effort died the following year. Hemmings then tried to launch the Professional Surfing Association, but again the idea went nowhere. Hemmings, world champion in 1968, turned instead to organizing individual competitions on Oahu's North Shore (founding the Pipeline Masters event in 1971, and taking control of the annual Duke Kahanamoku Classic and Smirnoff Pro contests), then returned in 1976 to the idea of a world tour and an integrated yearly ratings system. His first idea was to simply rate surfers by their aggregate prize-money totals for the season, and at the end of 1975 he went as far as to produce a top 15 list of surfers. (South Africa's Shaun Tomson came out on top, with $10,875; Hawaii's Eddie Aikau, in 15th, earned $25.) But 25-year-old journeyman pro surfer Randy Rarick, along with Australian pros Peter Townend and Ian Cairns, convinced Hemmings to switch to a points-per-placing system. International Professional Surfers (IPS) was signed into existence on Rarick's kitchen counter in October 1976, with Hemmings named as executive director. Nine previously unrelated contests from earlier in the year were retroactively tabulated into a midseason IPS ratings sheet, with five events still to come; in January of the following year, Peter Townend was announced as the 1976 IPS world champion. A women's division was added for the second season, and Hawaii's Margo Oberg—amateur world champion in 1968—won the first title.

While the IPS produced a number of popular world champions over the next five years, including Shaun Tomson, Wayne Bartholomew, Lynne Boyer, and Mark Richards, the organization evolved in fits and starts. The two most important developments were the introduction of the spectator-friendly man-on-man format in 1977 (as a replacement for heats consisting of anywhere from four to eight competitors), and the long-anticipated inclusion of California in the world tour schedule in 1981. The number of IPS men's division world tour events ranged from 10 to 13, and total yearly prize money went from $77,650 in 1976 to $338,100 in 1982. The women surfed in just four or five contests each season, and total prize money went from $19,500 to $42,000. By 1982, pro surfers and much of the surf media felt that the IPS wasn't growing fast enough—"terminal stagnation" was the expression used by *Surfer* magazine—and at the end of the year Ian Cairns led a revolt in which the IPS was replaced by the Association of Surfing Professionals (ASP), with Cairns named as executive director. The deposed Hemmings was left to operate his Hawaiian pro events, which, after some rugged political grappling, were integrated into the ASP schedule. Hemmings later reflected on the IPS's early years. "We didn't have a payroll, we worked out of our homes, Rarick and I covered expenses ourselves; I never made any money on the IPS—I *lost* money. But I've always thought surfers could be pro athletes like any other pro athletes, plus I wanted to sell surfing to the general public. With the IPS we got things started in that direction." *See also* Association of Surfing Professionals, competitive surfing, Fred Hemmings, professional surfing, Randy Rarick.

International Surfing Association (ISA)   Amateur surfing umbrella organization, formed in 1976 primarily to oversee the biannual amateur World Surfing Championships; currently headquartered in La Jolla, California. The International Surfing Association (ISA) was a near replica of the 1964-founded International Surfing Federation (ISF), which oversaw the World Championships in 1965, 1966, 1968, 1970, and 1972. The ISF folded in 1972, and the Championships were suspended for six years. Basil Lomberg, president of the South African Surfing Association, traveled to Hawaii in late 1976 with the idea of resurrecting both the ISF and the World Championships. When gaining title to the ISF proved difficult, Lomberg, along with amateur surfing representatives from England, California, Hawaii, and the American East Coast, instead created the ISA, with Lomberg elected president. It was further determined that the organization's home office would be located in the country of the reigning ISA president. In 1978, six countries competed in a small, one-day amateur World Surfing Championships in South Africa's East London; larger Championship events were held in years to come; in 1996 the World Surfing Games (still administered by the ISA) replaced the World Championships. The ISA became a member of the General Assembly of International Sports Federations in 1987, bringing the group a small step closer toward Olympic Games approval by the International Olympic Committee. ISA presidents have included Basil Lomberg (1976–80), Reginald Prytherch (England, 1980–88), Pepe Alvarez (Puerto Rico, 1988–94), Fernando Aguerre (Argentina/America, 1994–present). *See also* Fernando Aguerre, competitive surfing, International Surfing Federation, Olympics and surfing World Surfing Championships, World Surfing Games.

International Surfing Federation (ISF)   The first international surfing organization, based in Lima, Peru, founded in 1964 by former Peruvian national champion Eduardo Arena; created primarily to serve as the overseeing administrative body for the biannual World Surfing Championships. While visiting Australia in mid-1964 for the inaugural World Championships, Arena called together representatives from the United States Surfing Association and the Australian Surfriders Association and presented his idea for an international sanctioning body. The International Surfing Federation (ISF) was formed on May 17, 1964, the final day of the world contest, with Arena elected chairman. The ISF oversaw the next five world contests, in 1965 (Lima), 1966 (San Diego, California), 1968 (Rincon, Puerto Rico), 1970 (Torquay, Australia), and 1972 (San Diego). While Arena served as meet director in all but the 1972 event, the Championship contests were administered primarily by the host country's national organization. The ISF's job was to synchronize various national championships prior to each World Championship; to determine the size of each country's world contest team; to select a judging panel; and to help with international logistics. About 20 countries were affiliated with the ISF by the early '70s.

As the ISF's fate was tied to that of competitive surfing in general, the 1965 and 1966 Championship events—run during an era when surfing contests were nearly always met with approval—are rightfully thought of as the organization's best efforts. By 1970, the very concept of surfing competition was being questioned and even disparaged, and the ISF suffered accordingly. The rise of professional contests in the early '70s further reduced the importance of the prize money-free World Championships. As the poorly run 1972 Championships staggered to a close, with the title decided in two-foot windblown surf, the ISF itself expired. The next amateur World Championships, in 1978, were held under the auspices of the newly formed International Surfing Association. *See also* Eduardo Arena, competitive surfing, International Surfing Association, World Surfing Championships.

International Surfing Hall of Fame   Honors and formal-dress awards ceremony sponsored by *International Surfing* magazine—precursor to today's *Surfing*—held in 1966 and 1967. The Hall of Fame Awards were *Surfing*'s answer to the 1963-founded *Surfer* Magazine Poll Awards; while *Surfer* asked readers to cast votes for their favorite surfers, *Surfing* polled an international panel of 150 surfing experts. Also, whereas the *Surfer* Poll had just two categories, men's and women's, Hall of Fame Awards laurels were distributed to Hall of Fame inductees, as well as specialties and regional division categories, plus an Outstanding International Surfer division—more than 40 divisions in all, from New Zealand Women to Tandem to Motion Picture Photography. There was never an actual "hall" for the International Surfing Hall of Fame.

The first Hall of Fame ceremony took place on June 7, 1966, at the Santa Monica Civic Auditorium (home to the Academy Awards presentation from 1961 to 1968), and was one of the year's surf society highlights, attended by more than 2,000 people. Adam West, star of ABC-TV's *Batman,* was a presenter. Virtually all honored surfers were there in formal dress, including original inductee Duke Kahanamoku, who died 18 months later. Sponsors were relieved that the crowd behaved itself. Journalist Ron

Haworth's Hall of Fame report for the *Honolulu Star-Bulletin* made it plain that the awards presentation was in part a public relations move. "Surely," Haworth wrote, "the formal affair did much to alleviate the long-hair, juvenile delinquent image surfing has borne wrongly in the past." The 1967 presentation was held at the Hollywood Palladium. In 1991, the Balboa Park Hall of Champions in San Diego hosted a third *International Surfing* Hall of Fame awards banquet, with 26 surfers inducted. Major category winners for the *International Surfing* Hall of Fame:

1966
Hall of Fame: Duke Kahanamoku, Dewey Weber, Mickey Dora, George Downing, Greg Noll, Phil Edwards, Mike Doyle, Buzzy Trent, Bob Simmons, Hoppy Swarts, Pete Peterson
Women's International: Joyce Hoffman
Men's International: Mike Doyle
Junior's (under 18) International: David Nuuhiwa
World's Best Surfer: David Nuuhiwa
Small Waves: David Nuuhiwa
Big Waves: Jeff Hakman
Motion Picture: Bruce Brown
Still Picture: Leroy Grannis

1967
Hall of Fame: Dale Velzy, Tom Blake
Women's International: Joyce Hoffman
Men's International: Nat Young
Junior's (under 18) International: David Nuuhiwa
World's Best Surfer: David Nuuhiwa
Small Waves: David Nuuhiwa
Big Waves: Ricky Grigg
Motion Picture: Greg MacGillivray
Still Picture: Don James

1991
Hall of Fame: Kemp Aaberg, Ben Aipa, John "Doc" Ball, Duke Boyd, Bud Browne, Lance Carson, Colin Couture, Dick Dale, Mike Diffenderfer, George Freeth, Harry "Skip" Frye, Leroy Grannis, Fred Hemmings, Albert "Rabbit" Kekai, Charles "Snow" McAllister, Brennan "Hevs" McClelland, Margo Oberg, Rell Sunn, David Nuuhiwa, Jack O'Neill, Dorian Paskowitz, Joe Quigg, John "LJ" Richards, John Severson, Donald Takayama, Nat Young

See also Australian Surfing Hall of Fame, East Coast Surf Legends Hall of Fame, Huntington Beach Surfing Walk of Fame.

International Women Surfers (IWS)   Small California-based organization formed in 1999 by top female pro surfers Rochelle Ballard, Kate Skarratt, Layne Beachley, Megan Abubo, and Prue Jeffries, as a public relations tool for competitive women's surfing and a lobbying group for women members of the Association of Surfing Professionals (ASP) world tour. Precursors to International Women Surfers (IWS) include the 1975-formed Women's International Surfing Association (WISA) and the 1977-founded Golden Girls promotional group. In 2000, executive director and sole IWS staff member Christine Bent announced that the organization would first aim to establish a series of independent women's events on the ASP world tour, and to raise the women's pro tour prize money. Because the ASP was in a general state of flux at the turn of the decade, the impact of the IWS on the world tour has been hard to measure. The number of scheduled ASP women's events dropped from 14 in 1999 to five in 2001. With an effort backed by IWS members, however, the minimum women's prize purse was raised from $30,000 per event to $60,000.

Internet and surfing   The Internet—a noncentralized computer network invented by the U.S. Defense Department in the 1960s, and available to anyone with a modem-appended home computer by the early 90s—became part of the surfing world in the mid-'90s, when wired American surfers began accessing meteorological Web sites like the National Oceanic and Atmospheric Administration as an aid to wave forecasting. Carlsbad bodysurfer and computer programmer Ron Brivitch set up a video camera in a friend's beachfront home in 1994 to relay 10-second clips of surf conditions to his Surf Windows Web site, making the images, as well as direct links to other popular weather information sites, available to any Internet user. The following year, California-based surf forecasting services such as Surfline and Surfcheck—which had previously operated as phone and fax services—also went online, using live Web cameras or posting daily pictures to report conditions at dozens of American beaches. By the late '90s, surf break Web cams were so common that Internet users could within three or four minutes check the waves in Hawaii, Texas, California, Florida, Sydney, Queensland, Costa Rica, and Bali.

Surfer became the first publication of its type to launch an online surf magazine, in 1996, with a site featuring late-breaking news, contest results and photographs, video clips, Web links, bulletin boards, and e-mail contact to staff; virtually every other surfing periodical had followed by decade's end. All of the larger surf shops, along with surfboard- and wetsuit-makers, as well as surfwear companies, also developed Web sites—as marketing tools and to help customers contact, locate, and buy products. Sites also went up for surfing associations, competition leagues and clubs, and surf-related newsgroups (alt.surfing.com, surfinfo.com.au), along with sites for surf history (legendarysurfers.com, surfresearch.com.au) and surf travel (wavehunters.com, surftrip.net). Several pro surfers, beginning with six-time world champion Kelly Slater in 2000, developed their own official, commercial-driven Web sites.

Contributing to the Internet boom, meanwhile, tens of millions of dollars in venture capital were poured into three America-based mega-surfing sites—Swell.com, Hardcloud.com, and Bluetorch.com—beginning in 1999. Unable to match the salary and stock-option offers made by the digital newcomers, surf magazines stood by helplessly as their top employees abandoned ship. Swell, for example, hired *Surfer* publisher Doug Palladini, *Surfer* editor Evan Slater, former editors Steve Hawk and Matt Warshaw, *Surfer* writers Dave Parmenter, Ben Marcus, and Jason Borte, former *Surfing* editors Nick Carroll and Dave Gilovitch, *Surfing* photo editor Larry "Flame" Moore, and *Eastern Surf Magazine* editor Matt Walker. Swell also bought the popular Surfline forecasting service. All three of the new sites offered a mix of daily news, Web cam and forecasting services, live contest coverage, surf history, discussion groups, and online shopping; all three were unable to generate revenue. Hardcloud and Bluetorch both folded before the end of 2000; Swell, after burning through $24 million, broke away from Surfline in early 2001 and became an online surf store. By the end of the year, surfing's strongest presence on the Internet was through Surfline (one million unique viewers per month), as well as the online versions of *Surfer* and *Surfing* magazines. Smaller surfing sites of every description were also constantly being added to the Web.

Despite the vast sums of money, time, and energy poured into the surfing sector of the Internet over the years, wave- and weather-related sites were the most popular in 2003—just as they were in 1994. Not all surfers were happy with the Internet revolution. In California, locals at surf breaks from Trestles to Pacifica, believing that the Web cams trained on their breaks led to bigger crowds in the water, have vandalized cameras and sent angry messages to the surf-forecasting services who operate them, as well as the surf media. On a lighter note, some wave-riders resent the fact that "surfing" has become a much-overused Internet catchword. "Surfing the fucking web indeed," indignant Australian surf journalist D.C. Green wrote in 1999. "Give us back our verb!" *See also* swell.com.

interval   *See* swell period.

Ireland   Ireland's 1,700-mile coast is filled with long, deep bays and mountainous peninsulas covered in grass, moss, and rock. The weather is often blustery and damp, rarely below freezing or above 70; water temperatures range from the high 30s in winter to low 60s in summer. Ireland has surf on the north, west, and south coasts, most of it generated from North Atlantic storms. From August to May, the country's best surf is found on the north shore, particularly along the 26-mile "Causeway Coast," between Ballycastle and Magilligan Point, as waves pile onto a series of beachbreaks and the occasional rock reef. The west coast is best during spring and autumn, and can be divided into three regions: Donegal Bay, County Clare, and Dingle Peninsula. Donegal, to the north, has some of the country's best reefbreaks and a prevailing offshore wind; it is described in the *Stormrider Guide Europe* as nothing less than "a surfer's paradise." Donegal also has a well-established local surf club and a surf museum/bar. County Clare, south of Donegal, has a variety of surf spots, from easy-to-ride beachbreaks to powerful, board-snapping reefs. The beautiful but inconstant Dingle Peninsula, in the southwest, can provide excellent waves for those who know the complexities of local wave and weather patterns. The southern coast of Ireland usually gets waves only during winter. Most of the surf here is small- to medium-sized, breaking on long sandy beaches or rocky reefs. The Irish surf can get up to 15 foot or bigger, but generally shows best form between four to eight feet. For surfers accustomed to crowded suburban beaches, a visit to Ireland can be an adventure. "Overlooking Bomb Bay," surf journalist Ben Marcus wrote in 1995, "was a very cool, fully-functioning castle, with turrets and spires and flags waving. We were tempted to go up to the gate, ask to see the lord and hopefully get invited inside for a joint of mutton and a pint."

Surfing was introduced to Ireland in 1963, when Ian Hill, an English customs officer who'd been watching the sport in Devon, rode his British-made board alone for a summer near a jetty in the Northern Ireland town of Castlerock. At about the same time, Kevin Cavey, who often bellyboarded near the Republic of Ireland town of Bray, read a *Reader's Digest* story on surfing, built himself a plywood and plastic kneeboard, then sent away for a do-it-yourself balsa surfboard kit from England. Cavey also traveled to Hawaii to surf, and represented Ireland in the 1966 World Surfing Championships in San Diego, California. The Surf Club of Ireland was formed in 1966 in Bray; Cavey won the first Irish National Championships in 1967; and in the summer of 1969 an Irish team attended the first European Surfing Championships, held on the English Channel island of Jersey. By 1970 Ireland had five surf clubs, which combined to form the Irish Surfing Association (ISA), the current governing body of Irish competitive surfing. Ireland hosted the European Championships in 1972, 1985, and 1997, and the 2001 Masters World Championships. Surfing in Northern Ireland organized more slowly, as there were never more than 50 surfers in the area prior to the mid-'80s. Today, however, the wave-rich north coast is Ireland's most-surfed area.

By 2003, Ireland was home to about 4,000 surfers, 15 surf shops, and a dozen surf clubs. Ireland is featured in a small number of surfing videos, including *Litmus* (1997) and *Thicker Than Water* (1999), and the country's surf breaks are detailed in *The Stormrider Guide Europe* (1998) and *Surf U.K.* (2000). Ireland is scheduled to host the World Surfing Games in 2004.

Irons, Andy   Showstopping regularfoot pro from Hanalei, Kauai; winner of the 2002 world championship and the 2002 Triple Crown. "He has the miraculous combination of big-wave craziness and small wave ripping down better than any surfer in the world right now," *Surfing* magazine noted in 2003. "It's a horrifying skill range." Andy Irons was born (1978) in Lihue, Kauai, the son of California-raised surfer/carpenter Phil Irons, who moved to Kauai in 1970 and spent two years living out of a beachside tent on a diet of rice, bananas, and avocados. Andy began surfing at age eight, along with his younger brother Bruce, and went on to become a top amateur, placing third in the boys' division of the 1992 and 1993 U.S. Championships, winning the juniors division of the 1996 U.S. Championships, and

Andy Irons

taking both the juniors and men's divisions of the 1996 National Scholastic Surfing Association championships. Later that year, while still a high school senior, Irons launched his pro career with an astonishing win in the HIC Pipeline Pro, held in huge barreling waves. A few months later he won the 1997 Tahiti Pro at Teahupoo.

Irons became the most visible and versatile surfer in the world over the next three years. Well-proportioned at 6'0", 170 pounds, with superhuman reflexes, he was able to blast skyward into any one of a number of spiraling aerial maneuvers in smaller waves, as well as set well-defined turns and cutbacks in larger surf, and position himself like a standing Buddha deep within the tube. "You can't take your eyes off him," surf journalist Chris Mauro wrote, noting that the new arcs and lines Irons had developed represented nothing less than "a break from the dominant formula." Younger brother Bruce had progressed just as quickly, and their fractious, sometimes violent sibling rivalry became a regular source of amusement to the greater surf world. Bruce once tried to blow up Andy with fireworks; Andy once knocked Bruce unconscious with a karate kick to the head. "We try not to talk to each other too much," Andy said in 2000. "That way things don't get too irritating." (Volatility has been a problem for Irons throughout his pro career, and world tour officials fined him $1,500 in 2000 for his part in a beach brawl with Australia's Mick Campbell following a man-on-man heat in France.)

Irons qualified for the championship tour in 1998, won the World Juniors Championship, and halfway through the season posted back-to-back wins at Huntington Beach, California, in the U.S. Open and the Op Pro. He finished the year at #21, then dropped to #34 in 1999, at which point it was thought that he'd drank and partied himself into an early career flameout. But Irons reined in, finished the 2000 season at #16, and went to #10 the following year. In 2002, he won two of the first three events (the Rip Curl Pro and the Billabong Tahiti Pro), took the ratings lead, and sailed on to the title, closing the season with a victory in the Pipeline Masters. He also won the 2002 Triple Crown.

Irons has appeared in more than 30 surf videos, including *Voluptuous* (1996), *Rise and Shine* (1999), *Momentum: Under the Influence* (2001), and *Flight Academy* (2002); he also starred in *Raw Irons* (1998). Irons made news in 2001 when he signed a six-year contract with Billabong thought to be worth $650,000 a year, helping to make him one of the wealthiest surfers in the world. The unmarried Irons was voted the year's best surfer in the 2002 *Australia's Surfing Life* Peer Poll, and won the 2002 *Surfer* Magazine Readers Poll Award.

Irons, Bruce   Prodigiously talented regularfooter from Hanalei, Kauai, Hawaii; winner of the 2001 Pipeline Masters; the proudly dissolute younger brother of 2002 world champion Andy Irons. Bruce Irons was born (1979) in Lihue, Kauai, a three-and-a-half-pound preemie, the son of a California-raised surfer/carpenter and nephew to 1964 United States Invitational winner Rick Irons. Raised primarily in Hanalei, Irons began surfing at age seven, and went on to become one of the state's best amateur competitors: in the Unites States Surfing Championships, he won the menehune division in 1992, placed third in the boys' division in 1994, and finished runner-up to Andy in the juniors division in 1996. Irons turned pro just after high school graduation, and the following year, as surf journalist Chris Mauro wrote, he had "the entire surf industry eating out of his palm." Then and now, Irons seemed loath to attach much ambition to his extraordinary talent. "I don't think I have to prove anything to anyone," the mumbling 5'10", 165-pound surfer told Mauro, and added that he hoped to just "keep everything the same as before, keep hanging with the same people and keep the same routines."

While big brother Andy earned a spot on the world pro circuit in 1998, Bruce continued to be hit or miss as a competitor, often losing in the early rounds, but sometimes rocketing to a top finish: in the Pipeline Masters he placed second in 1998 and third in 2000; he beat six-time world champion Kelly Slater to take the 2001 Masters, then a few weeks later won the 2002 Gotcha Pro, also held at Pipeline. But contest results had little to do with Irons's rock-star reputation in the surf world. In the water he was fluid and limber—smoother than Andy, if not quite as powerful through his turns—deploying one spring-loaded aerial move after another in small-to-medium-sized waves, and riding the tube with insolent calm at places like Pipeline and Teahupoo. He was often described as having the best pure surfing style since Californian Tom Curren. On land, meanwhile, Irons was a devoted libertine. Exiting the water after winning the 2001 Masters, he hoisted a beer as he was lifted onto the shoulders of friends, and led to a beachfront house to help engineer, as *Surfing* magazine put it, "the biggest throwdown of the season."

Maybe the most photogenic surfer of his generation, Irons has appeared in more than three dozen surf videos, including *Voluptuous* (1996), *Side B* (1997), *Magnaplasm* (1998), *Loose Change* (1999), and *Changing Faces* (2001). The unmarried Irons was named Breakthrough Surfer of the Year in the 1999 *Surfer* Magazine Readers Poll Awards.

Isaka, Hiromi "Doji"   Enduring surf impresario from Chigasaki, Japan. Isaka was born (1948) and raised in Chigasaki, just south of Tokyo, began surfing in 1963, and became the Japanese national champion in 1969. He came to the attention of the California surf media later that year when he turned up in the offices of *Surfer* magazine, wondering where to check in for the World Championships, originally scheduled to be held in Baja California. The bewildered surfer was told the event had months earlier been postponed until 1970, and moved to Australia. Isaka became the All-Japan professional champion in 1976. From 1971 to 1981 he owned and operated the Cosmic Surf surfboard factory; from 1980 to 1982 he worked as the editor of Japan's *Surfin' Life* magazine; from 1981 to 1986 he ran the Marui Pro, a world pro tour competition; from 1982 to 1986 he served on the Association of Surfing Professionals board of directors. Isaka wrote *Try It: Surfing,* an instructional book, in 1978.

island pullout   A longboard-only variation on the pullout, in which the rider, crouched on the front third of the board, pushes the nose section under-water, swings the tail around toward shore, stalls, and lets the wave pass by. The island pullout is almost always performed in small surf. Probably developed in Waikiki in the 1920s or '30s—"island" refers to the Hawaiian Islands; California's Tommy Zahn is remembered as the first surfer to have mastered the island pullout, sometime in the late '40s. A more difficult variation is the standing island pullout, where the rider stays upright throughout.

Israel   Surfing arrived in Israel in 1957, when American surfer/physician Dorian Paskowitz, serving as a volunteer in the Israeli army, brought his 9′6″ Hobie balsa from Hawaii to Tel Aviv. Paskowitz invited local lifeguard captain Shamai "Topsi" Kancepolsky to help recruit surfers; the two men began giving surf lessons at Hilton Beach in Tel Aviv, and soon had to import more boards from California. By 1975, Hilton Beach had become the Malibu of Israel, and Kancepolsky was making surfboards with locally produced materials. "Polyester resin was something new to us," recalls Kancepolsky's son, Nir Almog, who later went to America to learn how to shape surfboards. "I remember doing the first ding repair. We used old cigarette filters instead of foam. Who had heard about foam?" In 1977 Nir Almog founded Almog Surfboards, Israel's first surfboard company. The sport continued to grow, and an international pro contest was held in Tel Aviv in 1984, with Derek Ho of Hawaii beating Australia's Wayne Bartholomew in the finals. The Israel Surfing Association was founded in 1986, and was soon running surf clinics and hosting contests.

Israel's temperate 170-mile beachbreak-lined coast is interrupted with a few rocky points and jetties, and faces out to the greatest fetch of any Mediterranean country. The surf rarely gets over four foot, and swells are generally short-lived and weak; winter usually brings the best and most consistent waves. Surfing enthusiasm runs high in Israel, and many surfers carry cell phones specifically to inform each other of swell conditions. The best breaks near Tel Aviv remained crowded with wave-riders even as the country's long-standing Palestinian conflict exploded in 2002. Israel is home to about 15 surf shops and 10,000 surfers.

Italy   Italy's rocky southwest-facing coastline, including the islands of Sardinia and Sicily, receive consistent small to medium-sized waves throughout the year, with the best surf arriving between September

Italy; an unidentified surfer at Varazze rights, Liguria

and June, as Atlantic Ocean storms cross western Europe and enter the Mediterranean. Capu Manu and Mino Capo, a pair of reefbreaks located on Sardinia's west coast, are among Italy's best surf spots, and both can produce tubing waves up to eight feet; beaches around Livorno, Viareggio, and Genoa to the north also have well-shaped surf. The east coast, facing the Adriatic Sea, receives sporadic short-lived wind swells, mainly during the winter. (The French-governed island of Corsica, located just north of Sardinia, is lined with a series of rarely surfed reefbreaks.) Italy is one of the few places in the surfing world where there is no tidal change. As of 2003, major portions of coastline in Sicily and the rest of southern Italy were still devoid of surfers and largely unmapped for surf. Average coastal air temperatures in Italy range from the upper 80s in summer to the low 50s in winter, with water temperatures ranging from the low 80s to the mid-50s.

Wave surfing in Italy (as distinct from the far more popular sport of windsurfing) began independently and halfheartedly in several places during the late 1960s on boards left behind by visiting surfers. The sport shot up in popularity after the 1978 release of Universal's *Big Wednesday,* which bombed in America but was a minor hit in Italy as a subtitled import. "We all made our own boards, as it was impossible to find a real board in Italy," recalls Alessandro Dini, who began surfing in 1978, just before the release of *Big Wednesday,* and shortly afterward opened Italy's first surf shop, Natural Surf, in Viareggio. Other pioneering Italian surfers include Rome-based Carlo Piccini and Fabio Gini, along with Maurizio Spinas and Giuseppe Meleddu from Sardinia. "We all

surfed in diving wetsuits and wool socks," Dini later recalled, "and used leashes made of rope." Dini also went on to found the Italia Wave Surf Team, which had 70 members by 1983.

By 2003 there were nearly 50 surf shops in Italy and about 20,000 surfers, half of them longboarders, with the highest concentration of shops and riders located in and around Rome. Five Italian-published surf magazines were founded in the '90s: *Surf Latino, Surf News, King Surfer, Surf,* and *Revolt.* The Italian Surfing Federation, chartered in 1994, has 30 affiliated clubs and organizes three or four contests annually, leading up to an Italian national championship. The Italian surf is detailed in *The Stormrider Guide Europe* (1998).

Ivory Coast   Relentlessly humid African country located about 400 miles north of the equator, in the south-facing Gulf of Guinea; Ivory Coast's 320-mile coastline is for the most part made up of palm-fringed lagoons and broad sandy beaches. Californian wave-hunters Kevin Naughton and Craig Peterson explored Ivory Coast in 1973, but chose not to give locations to any of the breaks they discovered in their subsequent article for *Surfer* magazine. Today, Ivory Coast's most popular surfing area is located at the eastern village of Assinie, near the Ghanian border, where a French-run surf camp overlooks a few nicely shaped and easy-riding sandbar breaks, most of which begin to overload when the waves hit five feet. November to April is the best season for waves in Assinie. Bigger swells provide overhead waves in late spring and summer at a half-dozen reef- and pointbreaks to the west, but none of them are first quality. The Ivory Coast water temperature remains near 80 degrees all year; in late spring and early summer the damp air often boils up to the high 90s; August, September, and January are the only months that provide relief from the heat. As of 2003, there were a pair of surf shops in the capital town of Abidjan, two hours west of Assinie. West Africans are generally nonswimmers, and just a handful of Ivory Coast natives have taken up surfing; most of the country's roughly 200 surfers are French, as Ivory Coast was a French colony from 1893 to 1960. Except for stingrays, which thrive in the sand-bottom shallows, and the roasting equatorial sun, there are few native surfing hazards. But malaria and yellow fever, along with a recent history of civil unrest and lack of prime breaks, contribute to Ivory Coast being a low-priority surfing destination.

J

Jackman, Dave Bluff and matey 1960s big-wave surfer from Sydney, Australia. Jackman was born (1940) and raised in the beachfront Sydney suburb of Manly Beach, and began surfing at age 12. He was a 21-year-old surfboard factory worker when he took on the Queenscliff Bombora, a much-feared reefbreak on Sydney's northside, on June 6, 1961. As the slender, blond-haired Jackman knee-paddled alone into the 15-foot surf, word spread quickly. "It was common knowledge in the local surfing fraternity that Jacko was going to ride the Bombie," 1964 world champion Midget Farrelly recalled 30 years later, "but that day people from everywhere came to watch. I rate it still as the greatest Australian surfing feat." Jackman rode two waves successfully, was pummeled on his third, swam in to recover his board, paddled back out, and rode a final wave to the beach. Local papers published photos of Jackman under headlines such as THE CONQUEROR and HE RODE WITH DEATH. After the news crossed the Pacific, Jackman became the first Australian surfer featured in *Surfer* magazine. He and fellow Sydney surfer Bob Pike were the first two Australians to ride the huge waves on the North Shore of Oahu.

Jackman appeared in a small number of surf movies, including *Angry Sea* (1963), *Cavalcade of Surf* (1963), and *Surfing the Southern Cross* (1963); *Australia's Surfing Life* magazine listed him in 1992 as one of Australia's "50 Most Influential Surfers." Jackman moved to Auckland, New Zealand, in 1963, and later opened Jackman-Way surfboards with burly big-wave Kiwi surfer Peter Way.

Jackson, Bruce South African surfer from Durban, described by neighbor and 1977 world champion Shaun Tomson as "one of the finest power surfers of the 70s." Jackson was born (1956) in Zimbabwe, spent his early years in England, and was seven when he moved with his family to a beachfront house in Durban, where he began surfing. He was a quarterfinalist in the 1973 Gunston 500, South Africa's premier professional event, and finished runner-up in the 1978 World Amateur Surfing Championships, held in East London, South Africa. At age 38, Jackson placed fourth in the 1994 World Longboard Championships. He appeared in the 1975 surf movie *Playgrounds in Paradise*.

Jacobs, Dudley "Hap" Gentlemanly surfboard manufacturer from Hermosa Beach, California; founder of Jacobs Surfboards. Jacobs was born (1930) in Los Angeles, the son of a plumber, moved with his family to Hermosa in 1938, and began surfing at age 16. He started shaping boards in 1953, after spending two years stationed in Hawaii with the Coast Guard; the following year he became partners with master board-maker Dale Velzy, and together they opened Velzy-Jacobs Surfboards in Venice Beach, California; four years later they split and Jacobs founded his own label, opening a factory-retail store in Hermosa Beach. The lean (6'2", 180 pounds), soft-spoken Jacobs was by then regarded as one of surfing's finest craftsmen, and his new company did well from the beginning; by the middle of the decade Jacobs Surfboards was making up to 125 boards a week, testing the stamina of the owner and six other full-time shapers—only Hobie Surfboards, Weber Surfboards, and Greg Noll Surfboards were producing more boards. The impeccably kept high-ceilinged Jacobs showroom was later described by surf publisher Steve Pezman as the "Notre Dame Cathedral" of surf shops. Jacobs had by that time assembled the period's most talented surf team, including Hawaii-born shaper Donald Takayama, noseriding ace Lance Carson, tandem champion Linda Merrill, *Endless Summer* star Robert August, Malibu icon Mickey Dora, 1964 world title runner-up Mike Doyle, and two-time U.S. champion David Nuuhiwa.

Jacobs left the business in 1971 and worked for 15 years as a commercial fisherman (the retail shop closed in 1981); in the early '90s he once again began shaping boards under the Jacobs label. He's married with two children, and has lived in Palos Verdes, California, since the 1970s.

Jamaica Small subtropical West Indies island nation, located 90 miles south of Cuba and 100 miles west of Haiti; the marijuana-infused spiritual center for Rastafarian religion and reggae music, and home to a budding surf culture. Jamaica's reef-lined eastern shore produces the best surf, with the biggest and most consistent waves—usually three to five feet, but occasionally bigger—arriving between November and April. Offshore winds are common in the mornings. The most popular surfing area in Jamaica is Boston Beach, a sublime horseshoe-shaped bay located on the island's eastern tip, featuring gentle right- and left-breaking waves. The Zoo, sometimes referred to as the Jamaican Pipeline, located near the capital city of Kingston, is generally regarded as the island's best break. Daytime air temperatures are consistently warm and pleasant, averaging between 85 and 90 degrees throughout the year, with water temperatures ranging from 75 to 80. Sea urchins and sharp reefs are the major Jamaican surf hazards, along with the occasional saltwater crocodile.

Surfing was introduced to Jamaica at Boston Beach in the early 1960s by traveling surfers from California and Florida, some of whom left their boards behind. First-generation Jamaican surfers included Cecil Ward, Robby Epstein, and Gordon Cooper. Terry Muschett began shaping boards locally during the late '70s, and was Jamaica's only board-maker until the early '90s. Local surfer/musician Billy Wilmot founded the Jamaican Surfing Association in 1998, and three years later started a small Jamaican surf camp near Kingston. Wilmot's children, Inilek, Icah, and Ishack, are some of Jamaica's top surfers; the former two—along with Jamaican national champion Drum Drummond—represented Jamaica at the 2002 World Surfing Games in South Africa. Jamaica first appeared in the American surf press in 2001, with *Surfer* magazine writer Chris Dixon describing the island as "manic-depressive . . . beautiful, beguiling and friendly, but also seething with discontent borne of generations of grinding poverty and politically inspired thuggery." There were roughly 100 native Jamaican surfers in 2003.

James, Dr. Don Laconic and durable surf photographer from Los Angeles, California; the sport's most widely published photographer during the 1960s. James was born (1921) and raised in Santa Monica, California, and began surfing in 1935. Influenced by the pioneering surf-photographers John "Doc" Ball and Tom Blake, James started taking surf photographs the following year, mainly in the Santa Monica Bay and at San Onofre in north San Diego County. James built himself a waterproof mahogany housing for his camera in 1938, and began shooting from the surf zone; he'd remove the camera from the box while he sat on his board, hit the shutter, then replaced the camera when a wave threatened to wash over him. Photography would always be a moonlight job for James; he worked as a lifeguard while attending dental school at the University of Southern California in the mid-'40s, then set up a practice in Beverly Hills where his patient list included Hollywood stars like Clark Gable and Cary Grant. Nevertheless, James took his camera to Hawaii each winter, and contributed to virtually all California surf publications in the early and mid-'60s. He photographed both Waimea Bay and Pipeline when the two famous Hawaiian breaks were ridden for the first time in 1957 and 1961, respectively, and in the early '60s he became the first to shoot Waimea from the water. James had a natural eye for composition and framing, and his later work was richly colorful; his photos were published in *Life, Time,* the *Saturday Evening Post,* and *Sports Illustrated,* and his 1963 shot of California surfer Rusty Miller racing down a huge wave at Sunset was reproduced on billboards across the country as part of a Hamm's Beer campaign. James won the Still Photography category of the 1967 *International Surfing* Magazine Hall of Fame Awards. He reduced his surfing output in the late '60s, but published on occasion, and in 1984 he turned in his final *Surfing* magazine cover shot.

James's photography was given new life in the '90s, beginning with a 10-page *Surfing* magazine retrospective in 1990, followed in 1994 by the release of *Surfing in the 1930s,* a video made up of James's 55-year-old movie footage of San Onofre, Malibu, and Palos Verdes. An elegant book of prewar Southern California surfing and beach images, *1936–1942: San Onofre to Point Dume, Photographs by Don James,* was published in 1996; the following year James's work was featured in the *New Yorker.* A 1962 James portrait of the preadolescent Jeff Hakman was used on the cover of *Mr. Sunset: The Jeff Hakman Story,* published in 1997; New York's Danziger Gallery presented an exhibition of James's work in 1998. His photos have also been featured in more than a half-dozen illustrated surfing books, including *Where the Surfers Are* (1968), *A Pictorial History of Surfing* (1970), *The History of Surfing* (1983), and *SurfRiders* (1997).

James was going blind from glaucoma in 1996 when he took his own life on Christmas Eve. He was 75. He'd been married twice and had three children.

jams *See* baggies, surf trunks.

Jan and Dean Clean-cut vocal duo from Los Angeles, California, best known for their 1963 #1 single "Surf City." By definition, Jan and Dean, like their friends and chart rivals the Beach Boys, don't belong to the reverb-soaked instrumental surf music genre. They instead recorded catchy, sing-along records about the teenage life in coastal Southern California that revolved around surfing, the beach, cars, and girls. Jan Berry and Dean Torrence, both born in Los Angeles in 1941, were football teammates in junior high school, and originally recorded in the late '50s as a moderately successful doo-wop group. After the Beach Boys hit the charts in 1961, Jan and Dean quickly began writing surf and car songs. Beach Boy Brian Wilson cowrote and sang backup on Jan and Dean's "Surf City," famous for its gremmie-fantasy opening line, "Two girls for every boy!" (Torrence returned the favor with the uncredited lead vocal on the Beach Boys' 1965 hit "Barbara Ann.") "Surf City" was the first surf song to hit #1 nationally. Jan and Dean in fact sold more records than the Beach Boys in 1963 and 1964, with hits like "Honolulu Lulu" (#11), "The Little Old Lady (From Pasadena)" (#3), "Ride the Wild Surf" (#16; the theme song from Columbia Pictures' like-titled movie), "Sidewalk Surfin'" (#25), and "Dead Man's Curve" (#8). Jan and Dean didn't have an artistic second act, the way the Beach Boys did, but their falsetto-loaded hits were as fun as anything produced at the time.

Berry did most of the duo's songwriting, and both somehow managed to remain full-time students during the height of their pop celebrity, Torrence as an architecture student at UCLA, Berry a graphic design student at USC. Berry crashed his Corvette into a parked truck in the spring of 1966, killing his three passengers, and leaving him brain damaged and partially paralyzed. For years afterward, he was taken to a nearby studio where he recorded demo tapes as therapy. Torrence's graphic design firm meanwhile went on to create album covers for the Beach Boys, the Nitty Gritty Dirt Band, and Linda Ronstadt, among others. Berry was able to perform again by 1973, and in 1982 Jan and Dean released *One Summer Night,* a live album. *See also* Ride the Wild Surf, surf music.

Japan Composed of four large islands and thousands of smaller islands, bordered to the west by the Sea of Japan and to the east by the Pacific Ocean, the Japanese chain extends for about 1,200 miles and features a tremendously diverse coastline. The northernmost island of Hokkaido has the smallest number of surfers, the coldest water (ranging from the high 40s to the high 50s), and is ridden primarily during summer, along the beaches and pointbreaks of the south and east coasts. Honshu is the largest and most-surfed island, with beachbreaks, rivermouths, and pointbreaks lining both the Pacific and Sea of Japan coasts. The domestic surf industry is also based on Honshu, along with the vast majority of Japanese surfers; Shonan (often called Japan's "surf city") and Chiba are the two most popular surfing areas in Japan; Malibu and Matsube, two of Japan's best reef breaks, are located directly in front of the coast highway at Katsuura Bay. The southwest coast of Shikoku, the smallest of Japan's main islands, has some of the country's finest breaks, including Niyodo Rivermouth, near Kaifu, a right-breaking sand-bottom tube that has been compared to Hawaii's Backdoor. Kaifu Rivermouth and Monobe Rivermouth can also produce strong, beautifully shaped tubes. Kyushu, Japan's subtropical southernmost island, has the warmest water (from 62 to 72 degrees) and powerful, if inconsistent, surf along the west- and east-facing coasts. As of 2003, roughly 20 percent of the Japanese coastline remains more or less uncharted for surfing potential. Climate varies dramatically from island to island, with subfreezing winters in the north and long, hot, sultry summers in the south. Seasonal monsoons blow cold from the northwest in winter and warm from the southeast in summer. Japan's best surf usually hits during the August-to-October typhoon season, as an average of 10 to 20 storms track north over or around Japan, each creating a short-lived swell in either the Pacific Ocean, the East China Sea, or the Sea of Japan. Two to four-foot surf is fairly common; 15-foot waves have been ridden. For the rest of the year, Japan receives small and irregular ground swells along east-facing coasts from storms in the North and South Pacific, and short-period windswells along the west-facing coast. Long waveless periods are common. Traveling surfers have traditionally steered clear of Japan, as it's expensive and culturally challenging, with some areas insufferably crowded and others nearly impossible to access.

Evidence suggests that Japanese fishermen were riding waves on small wooden bellyboards as early as the 12th century, but it's generally accepted that surfing was imported not long after World War II by Tokyo-stationed American servicemen. California surf filmmaker Bruce Brown visited Japan in 1963 while scouting locations for *The Endless Summer*; he found excellent waves, and a handful of native surfers. A few months later, California-born surfboard shaper Tak Kawahara, while traveling through Honshu, made further wave discoveries; on subsequent visits, Kawahara—sometimes called the Father of Japanese Surfing—organized surf lessons, taught several locals the fundamentals of surfboard shaping, and set up contacts to import surf equipment. The Nippon Surfing Association was founded in 1965, and that year brought the first All-Japan Surfing Championships. By the end of the '60s, a small but viable network of surf shops and clubs had been established in Shonan, an affluent (if surf-poor) beach town near Tokyo, as well as Chiba, a rural area located about 25 miles southeast of Tokyo. Five Japanese surfers entered Hawaii's prestigious Makaha International surf contest in 1969, and natives Hiromi "Doji" Isaka, Mikio Kawai, and Michio Degawa soon became big names on beaches in and around Tokyo.

A Japanese surf boom in the late '70s and early '80s brought an export windfall to dozens of American and Australian surf companies, and created a startling version of surf consumerism, with huge fluorescent-lit Japanese surf shops carrying items such as surf cologne, presurf high-protein drinks, and pro-surfer-endorsed stationery. Japan became part of the world pro tour in 1979, hosting four of the season's 13 events (Australia staged three contests, Hawaii and South Africa had two each); through the '80s and '90s, there were one or two circuit events per season in Japan, usually in the Chiba area, most of them sponsored by the Marui department store chain. Winners of the Marui Pro over the years included world champions Wayne Bartholomew, Pam Burridge, Frieda Zamba, Tom Curren, Kim Mearig, Kelly Slater, Derek Ho, Damien Hardman, and Lisa Andersen. The 1990 World Amateur Surfing Championships were held at Niijima, a wave-attracting island located a few hours off the central Honshu mainland.

In 2003, Japan was home to about 750,000 surfers, seven surfing magazines (including *Surfing Life, Nalu,* and *Surfing World Japan*), a number of smooth-running competitive surfing organizations (including the 1978-founded Japanese Professional Surfing Association), and roughly 900 surf shops (most of them surf-flavored boutiques). While the domestic surf scene has never lacked for enthusiasm, just a small number of Japanese surfers over the years—including Hiromishi Soeda, Shuji Kasuya, Satoshi Sekino, and Takoa Kuga—have drawn notice, and none has performed well at the international level. *Asian Paradise* (1984) was the first Japanese-produced surf movie; the Japanese surf is featured in *The World Stormrider Guide* (2001), as well as in more than 25 surf movies and videos, including *The Wet Set* (1990), *Rad Movez* (1992), *Surf Food* (1995), and *Smooth'n Casual* (2000).

Jaquias, Kaipo Compact regularfoot pro from Hanamaulu, Kauai, Hawaii; world-ranked #5 in 1996; described by 1990 world champion Pam Burridge as "a perfect little surfer." Jaquias was born (1971) and raised in a rough section of Lihue, on the east side of Kauai, and began surfing at age four. Jaquias later claimed that he trained to become a professional mainly to outsurf his father (just 16 when Kaipo was born) who "forced me into surfing, and forced me into big waves when I didn't want to go out." He joined the world tour in 1990 and retired at the end of 1999, having won two events (the Gold Coast Billabong Pro and the Lacanau Pro, both in 1996), as well as the 1996 Triple Crown, surfing throughout in a fast, stable, low-slung stance. Jaquias kept a lower profile than any of his professional contemporaries, but did appear in a few surf videos, including *Madmen '93: Changing of the Guard* (1993) and *Modern Legends in Hawaiian Surf* (1994).

Jarratt, Phil Smart, funny, mildly profane Australian writer, originally from Wollongong, New South Wales; editor of *Tracks* magazine from 1975 to 1978, and a regular contributor to *Surfer* from the late '70s to the late '80s. Jarratt was born (1951) and raised in Wollongong, began surfing in 1960, and published his first article in a 1968 issue of *Surf International,* a short-lived Australian magazine. From 1970 to 1973 he contributed articles to *Tracks,* a monthly surf tabloid published out of Sydney; in 1974 he became *Tracks'* assistant editor, and the following year began a three-year stint as editor. While Jarratt wrote eloquently on virtually all surfing-related subjects, he was at his best doing profiles, and his features on

Wayne Bartholomew, Gerry Lopez, Reno Abellira, Simon Anderson, Shaun Tomson, and other surf notables from the '70s and '80s are among the genre's best. "His self-assurance is almost frightening," Jarratt wrote of Tomson in 1978, one year after the South African had won the world title, "but there are times when you sense his vulnerability; times when you catch glimpses of the spoiled rich kid or the Jewish family boy who would rather not go home than go home a failure."

Jarratt later worked for the Australian editions of *Playboy* and *Penthouse,* and contributed articles to the *London Times, Vanity Fair,* and *Esquire.* He has written or cowritten more than 15 books, including surfing titles such as *The Wave Game* (1977), *The Surfing Dictionary* (1990), and *Mr. Sunset: The Jeff Hakman Story* (1997). From 1997 to 2000 he published and edited the Australian edition of the *Surfer's Journal* magazine. Shore Thing, Jarratt's at-home publishing house, produced *Surfmovies: The History of the Surf Film in Australia* (2000), with Jarratt serving as the book's editor. In 1992, *Australia's Surfing Life* magazine named Jarratt as one the country's 50 most influential surfers; two years later he was given a special media award by the Australian Surfing Hall of Fame. Jarratt created the popular Noosa Festival of Surfing in 1998. Since 1999, he's worked as the head of marketing for Quiksilver Europe. Jarratt is married and has three children; he has homes in Guethary, France, and Noosa, Australia. *See also* Tracks magazine.

Jaws Big-wave colossus located on the north coast of Maui in Hawaii; proving ground for the motorized tow-in form of big-wave riding, and site of the first successfully ridden 35-foot wave. "Before it was 'Jaws,'" Hawaiian surfer Gerry Lopez recalled, "we called it 'Atom Blaster' because it broke like an atomic bomb." Local surfers also know the break as *Peahi,* Hawaiian for "beckon." Jaws responds only to the biggest North Pacific storms and is best from late fall to early spring. It begins to break at 12 foot, but doesn't assume full form until 20 foot—an event that occurs about a half-dozen times a season—and will occasionally hit 40 foot or bigger. The leading edge of Jaws's spur-shaped lava reef is a half mile from shore, and the reef topography bends incoming waves into a classic "bowl" shape, which in turn produces a cyclonic tube that can spit and grind for up to 200 yards. The break is fronted by steep cliffs, adjacent to a grid of sugarcane fields.

Jaws, with Hawaii's Laird Hamilton

The sheer size of the waves, along with prohibitively strong tradewinds, kept Jaws from becoming a paddle-in surfing spot. It was first taken on in the late '80s and early '90s by a group of wave-riding sailboarders, including Mike Waltz, Rush Randle, Mark and Josh Angulo, and Dave Kalama. Meanwhile, on the North Shore of Oahu in 1992, Hawaiian surfers Laird Hamilton, Buzzy Kerbox, and Darrick Doerner invented tow-in surfing. Hamilton and Kerbox moved to Maui the following year, converted some of the local wave-sailors into tow-in surfers, and dedicated themselves to riding giant waves at Jaws. It was here that tow-in surfing took its present-day form, with the use of personal watercraft (outboard inflatables had been used up to that point), along with the development of short, narrow, heavy surfboards equipped with footstraps.

The surf world at large got its first look at Jaws in the September 1994 issue of *Surfer* magazine (although the break was identified only as a "heaving, deep-water outer reef in Maui"); a few weeks later, an extraordinary Jaws sequence was praised as the highlight of *Endless Summer II,* Bruce Brown's new surf film. Muscle-bound Hamilton was by far the best surfer at Jaws, and while he rode the break with amazing strength and flair, he also respected its power. "It vaporized me," he said after one of his first wipeouts there. "I felt like my body went into little particles." In late 1994, Dave Kalama rode a Jaws wave measuring 30 or 35 feet—the biggest wave surfed up to that point.

Jaws is featured in dozens of surf videos, including *Wake-up Call* (1995), *Liquid Thunder* (1999), *Biggest Wednesday* (1998), and *Swell XXL* (2001); Hamilton,

Doerner, and Kalama stunt-surfed at Jaws in the 2002 James Bond movie *Die Another Day. Jaws Maui,* a coffee-table photo book, was published in 1997. Hamilton was featured at the base of an enormous wave on the cover of the November 1998 issue of *National Geographic* for a story titled "Maui's Monster Waves: Jaws." The debut Tow-In World Cup, the first contest of its kind, was held in 25 to 35-foot surf at Jaws in early 2002, with the $70,000 first-place prize going to the team of Garrett McNamara (Hawaii) and Rodrigo Resende (Brazil); Hamilton, still regarded as Jaws's dominant surfer, didn't enter the event. A haven for a select few tow-in surfers in 1993, the Jaws lineup by the turn of the century was sometimes filled with as many as 20 personal watercraft, used by photographers as well as surfers. *See also* big-wave surfing.

Jeffreys Bay   Long, fast, exquisitely tapered right-breaking point surf, regarded for decades as one of the world's premier waves; located at the base of Cape St. Francis, South Africa, 45 miles west of Port Elizabeth. "It's an almost indescribable sight," South African pro surfer Marc Price said of Jeffreys in 1982. "Watching from the beach, you start off looking up to your right and end up facing left as the wave travels down the point. This 180-degree perspective is something no photograph can capture." Waves along the enormous point at Jeffreys Bay are broken into five connected but distinct surfing areas: the Point and Tubes are the two innermost breaks (the former shapely and long, the latter short and intense); Boneyards and Magnatubes are the outermost breaks, both shifty, hollow, and hard-breaking; Supertubes, the

Jeffreys Bay

magnificent centerpiece, located between Tubes and Boneyards, is the main draw and has become all but synonymous with Jeffreys Bay. A good Supertubes wave will last for about 250 yards. On the rarest of days a surfer can take off at Boneyards and carry on through Supertubes into an express section known as Impossibles, which shoots the rider into Tubes and through to the Point—a high-speed, 1,200-yard-long ride lasting nearly two minutes.

Waves occasionally roll into Jeffreys during summer, but it breaks primarily from May to September. Winter swells generated in the fabled Roaring 40s will often march toward shore in hypnotic procession, and 10-foot waves will spiral down the point at Jeffreys with a uniformity and precision that looks nearly machine-crafted. Winter air temperatures at Jeffreys range from the upper 40s to the low 70s, while ocean temperatures remain near 60. The wind here can be fickle, but often blows offshore or side-offshore for days at a time (usually as a result of the same storms that produce waves at Jeffreys); most surfers wear a full wetsuit against the wind-amplified cold and booties to protect their feet from the mussel-covered rocks that line the shore. Sharks are a constant source of worry at Jeffreys. As of 2001, there had been two nonfatal white shark attacks on surfers and dozens of sightings. Attacks, even fatalities, have been recorded at nearby St. Francis Bay surf breaks. At daybreak, dolphins are regularly seen leaping from wave faces at Jeffreys as they race down the point, often in groups of 100 or more.

Pioneering South African surfer John Whitmore spotted waves at Jeffreys Bay (named after local 19th-century hotel owner J.A. Jeffrey) in 1959, but the break wasn't ridden until Easter week 1964, when Gus Gobel, Brian McLarty, and four other Cape Town surfers tried their luck at what would later be called Supertubes. The waves proved too fast for their 9'6" longboards. Repositioning to the north, they had a better time at the Point, which soon became the featured surf break at Jeffreys. Supertubes wasn't regularly surfed until the late '60s. Meanwhile, California's Bruce Brown filmed Mike Hynson and Robert August in 1963 discovering and riding "the perfect wave" at Cape St. Francis, 18 miles by road south of Jeffreys, in what would be the highlight sequence to Brown's movie *The Endless Summer.* Three years later, as *Endless Summer* was being shown in theaters across America, a *Surfer* magazine article titled "Quest for the Perfect Wave" denounced Cape St. Francis as fluky and unreliable, and introduced the surf world at large to the far more dependable and consistent waves at Jeffreys Bay. Visiting surfers began to camp out along the undeveloped sand- and aloe-covered beachfront, and dine in the nearby Afrikaner fishing township, also called Jeffreys Bay.

Jeffreys was a showcase wave from the beginning. Gavin Rudolph, Jonathan Paarman, Peers Pittard, and Anthony "Bunker" Spreckels were among the early standouts. Terry Fitzgerald, the 1971 Australian champion and aptly nicknamed "Sultan of Speed," was magnificent at Jeffreys throughout the '70s, linking one blistering turn to the next. Shaun Tomson, 1977 world champion, was for years the most advanced Jeffreys rider, placing himself deep inside the tube almost at will and driving his board into a wide range of turns. Mark Occhilupo of Australia, during his world tour debut in 1984, was one of the first goofy-foot surfers to match the regularfooters at Jeffreys. Beginning in the early '90s, when high-performance shortboards became thinner and narrower, the performance level at Jeffreys among visiting pro surfers actually declined as their boards wouldn't hold the kind of sustained turns that Jeffreys demands. Tom Curren and Kelly Slater were able to find the right lines, however, and set a new Jeffreys standard before the end of the decade. The world pro tour included a stop at Jeffreys Bay in 1984 and 1996, and from 1998 to present day. The 2001 Oxbow World Longboard Championships were also held at Jeffreys, with the win going to California surfer Colin McPhillips.

Jeffreys has over the years been home to a small but richly talented number of expatriate surf world eccentrics, including Malibu legend Mickey Dora, Florida ace Mike Tabeling, and Australian surf journalist Derek Hynd. Once a remote but overwhelmingly beautiful break, Jeffreys, since the mid-'80s, has been crowded with South African vacationers and wave-seekers from around the world, and the rolling beachfront hills are now lined with houses, condos, and parking lots. Jeffreys has been featured in dozens of surf movies, videos, and documentaries, including *Freeform* (1970), *Fantasea* (1978), *Storm Riders* (1982), *The Search* (1992), *Endless Summer II* (1994), *Litmus* (1997), and *Great Waves* (1998). *See also* Billabong Pro (Jeffreys Bay).

Jenkins, Bruce   Straight-talking sportswriter for the *San Francisco Chronicle,* and contributor to *Surfer, Longboard,* and *Surfer's Journal* magazines; author of

1990's *North Shore Chronicles: Big-Wave Surfing in Hawaii.* Jenkins was born in Los Angeles (1948), raised in Malibu, and began writing sports columns for the *Chronicle* in 1973. While vacationing on the North Shore of Oahu in 1986, Jenkins, a lifelong bodysurfer, was flushed through his rented house in the dead of night by an enormous wave; shortly thereafter he began work on *North Shore Chronicles,* a series of profiles on big-wave surfers. Jenkins's "Buffalo's Soldiers" article for *Surfer,* about ageless Makaha surfer Buffalo Keaulana and his entourage, was published in the *Best American Sports Writing 1999* anthology, which includes essays by Richard Ford, David Mamet, and David Halberstam. Jenkins was also selected in 1999 as one of the top 10 sports columnists in the country by the Associated Press sports editors, and his coverage of the inaugural Quicksilver Men Who Ride Mountains competition at Maverick's that year was published as the *Chronicle*'s front page lead story. Jenkins is the author of two mainstream sports books; his surfing articles have been republished in *The Big Drop: Classic Big-Wave Surfing Stories* (1999) and *The Perfect Day* (2001). He also wrote the narration for the documentary *Maverick's* (1998).

Jennings, James "Chappy"   Australian goofyfooter from Queensland's Gold Coast; often remembered as the gnomish sidekick to world tour stars Wayne Bartholomew and Gary Elkerton, but a hard-charging surfer in his own right. Jennings was born (1965) in New Guinea, grew up in Victoria and South Australia, and began surfing at age 10. Three years later he ran away from home to live in the warm, wave-rich Gold Coast, where he was mentored by 1978 world champion Wayne Bartholomew; in 1980 he finished fourth in the juniors division of the Australian National Titles. Along with Bartholomew and fellow Queenslander Gary Elkerton, the spindly Jennings (5'5", 115 pounds) starred in *Kong's Island,* a popular 1983 Jack McCoy–made short film. Jennings finished runner-up in the Pro Junior in 1980 and 1981, and placed fourth on the 1985 Australian Professional Surfing Association tour, but had little success on the world tour. He was better known as a first-rate tuberider, utilizing a wide, low, crablike stance, and a photo of him racing through an enormous tube at Pipeline was used as a two-page spread in *A Day in the Life of Hawaii,* a 1984 coffee-table photo book. Jennings appeared in a small number of surf movies and videos, including *Wizards of the Water* (1982) and *The Performers* (1984).

Jepsen, Hal   Plucky surf moviemaker from Topanga, California; best known for *Cosmic Children,* his raw but energetic 1970 debut. Jepsen was born (1940) and raised in Los Angeles, and began surfing at age 17. He received a B.S. in business administration from UCLA in 1968, and was an unemployed real estate agent before he started filming *Cosmic Children,* which cost $18,000, was shot almost entirely in California, Hawaii, and Mexico, and showcased Hawaiian surfers Jeff Hakman and Barry Kanaiaupuni. Jepsen used his personal album collection to create all-bootlegged soundtracks for his movies, and *Cosmic Children* featured the Rolling Stones, B. B. King, Jimi Hendrix, Cream, and Dave Brubeck. "Jepsen's film is occasionally dark and fuzzy," *Surfer* magazine wrote in its *Cosmic* review, "but the 'full-juice' surfing is powerful." Jepsen followed with three more full-length surf movies: *A Sea for Yourself* (1973), *Super Session* (1975), and *We Got Surf* (1981), and three short-subject films, along with *Spinning Wheels* (1978), a feature-length skateboarding movie. Jepsen was the first surf moviemaker to give appearance fees to surfers. In 1997, he was profiled in *50 Years of Surfing on Film,* an Outdoor Life Network TV series.

Jet Ski   *See* personal watercraft.

jetty   Well-shaped waves often form on sandbars in front of or adjacent to jetties. Generally constructed out of boulders or preformed jack-shaped concrete "dolos," a jetty ("groyne" in Australia) is usually built either to interrupt lateral sand-flow and stabilize the nearby beach (as in Newport Beach, California) or serve as part of a harbor design (as with Santa Cruz Harbor). The line between jetties and breakwaters is often blurred. The surf spot known as Princeton Jetty in Half Moon Bay, for example, is in fact part of a breakwater. Wave form and quality at most jetty breaks is erratic. Storm surf will often create a wave-forming sandbar deposit near a jetty; the next storm might rearrange the sandbar or erase it altogether. Jetty breaks are common along much of the American eastern seaboard. *See also* breakwater.

Johnson, Jack   Easygoing surfer/filmmaker/musician from the North Shore of Oahu, Hawaii. Johnson was born (1975) and raised on the North Shore, began surfing at age five, was a finalist in the menehune division of the 1988 U.S. Championships, and as a high school senior made the finals of the 1992 Pipeline Masters Trials. After earning a B.A. in film studies from University of California at Santa Barbara in 1997, Johnson along with California surfer Chris Malloy made *Thicker Than Water,* a lush 45-minute travelogue surf video, originally shot with 16-millimeter film and sold with a 160-page companion book. *Thicker Than Water* won the *Surfer* Magazine Video of the Year Award in 2000. *September Sessions,* Johnson's follow-up, was described by *Surfer* as "a tribute to the glory days of surf films where images were savored like wine, not edited into tiny shots of adrenaline." Johnson's singing and songwriting talents had meanwhile gained him a contract with Virgin-owned Enjoy Records. *Brushfire Fairytales,* his soulful 2001-released debut CD, was a surprise hit, rising up to #34 on the Billboard charts in 2002, and earning Johnson profile articles in *Rolling Stone* and *Time* magazine; the latter described him as a "surf-folkie," and said he'd "perfected the art of contemporary beach music." *See also* surf music.

Johnson, Noah   Bantamweight big-wave rider from the North Shore of Oahu; winner of the 1999 Quiksilver in Memory of Eddie Aikau contest at Waimea Bay. Johnson was born (1973) in Hilo, the son of a University of Hawaii psychology professor, and began surfing at age 11. He moved to the North Shore after graduating high school in 1991, spent a fruitless two years on the world pro tour, then began to focus on big waves. Johnson competed in the 1995 Quiksilver/Aikau contest, which was cancelled at the halfway mark after the surf dropped below 20 feet. He started tow-in surfing two years later, and in early 1998 the slender regularfooter (5′6″, 140 pounds) rode 30-foot-plus waves during the magnificent Biggest Wednesday swell. The following year he won the Quiksilver/Aikau, and his $55,000 paycheck was at the time the biggest prize ever awarded in a surfing contest—but because Johnson had financed his big-wave career by going into debt to the IRS and MasterCard, virtually all the prize money was turned over to creditors. Johnson finished poorly in the 2001 Quiksilver/Aikau, but placed fourth in the 2002 contest. He also placed third in the 2001 Swell XXL competition, after towing in to a late-December 35-footer at Maverick's. Johnson has been featured in a small number of surf videos, including *Players* (1995), *The Moment* (1998), and *Speechless* (1998). He stunt-surfed in a blond wig and bikini for Universal's 2002 surf movie *Blue Crush.*

Jones, James Aloof big-wave rider from Honolulu, Hawaii; winner of the Duke Kahanamoku Classic in 1972 and 1976, and a key figure in the '80s-launched big-wave surfing renaissance. Jones was born (1952) and raised in Honolulu, the son of a construction equipment operator and bar owner, and began surfing in Waikiki at age nine. He first came to the attention of the surf world as an 18-year-old semifinalist in the 1970 World Surfing Championships, held in Australia; in 1970 and 1971 he was an invitee to the surfing showcase Expression Session events, held in Hawaii. Jones's winning performance in the 1972 Duke, as described by surf journalist Drew Kampion, was the result of his "clean, flowing, functional style," and for the next four years Jones was a consistent performer in the North Shore pro events. He was also the era's premier switchfoot surfer, able to lead with either his left or right foot.

Jones had meanwhile developed into one of the world's best big-wave riders, spreading his wiry 5'6", 140-pound frame out across his board in a low crouch while spearing across giant waves at Waimea Bay on the North Shore of Oahu. On February 4, 1977, Jones became the first surfer to ride inside the tube at Waimea; he later described the experience—in a grandiose style that many of his big-wave contemporaries found offputting—as one in which the "full potential for ultimate surfing was realized." Since 1970, big-wave riding had in fact been pushed to the background, as surfers and the surf media focused on professional contests (rarely held in giant surf), tuberiding (mainly at Pipeline, located just to the east of Waimea), and high-performance small-wave surfing. But in the winter of 1982–83, as North Pacific storms were pumped up by a strong El Niño condition and the Hawaiian surf became consistently huge and spectacular, big-wave surfing returned to prominence, with Jones appropriately viewed with new respect as a Waimea sage. Jones was himself impressed. "Let me say this," the handsome dark-haired Hawaiian told *Surfing* magazine in 1987, "I think I'm the best big-wave rider in the world. I feel like the fastest gun in the west, and every kid with a gun of his own is trying to shoot me down."

Jones wrote nearly a dozen surf magazine articles, mainly on big surf, between 1977 and 1987, and appeared in about 15 surf films and videos, including *Tracks* (1970), *Five Summer Stories* (1972), *Playground in Paradise* (1976), and *Atlantic Crossing* (1989). He finished 11th in the 1990 Quiksilver in Memory of Eddie Aikau big-wave contest at Waimea, and competed in the 1995 Quiksilver event, which was canceled due to failing surf at the halfway mark. Jones has worked as a stockbroker, commercial property manager, and a real estate agent; in '84 he made an unsuccessful bid for a seat in the Hawaii State House of Representatives.

Jones, Malia Lithesome surfer/model from Haleiwa, Hawaii; girls' division winner in the 1992 United States Surfing Championships; named by *People* magazine in 1998 as one of the world's "50 Most Beautiful People." Jones was born (1977) in Loma Linda, California, moved with her family to Hawaii at age one, and began surfing as a toddler. She competed briefly on the 1993 world pro tour. In 1996 she surfed in a $500 Chanel swimsuit for her first mainstream modeling assignment with *Elle* magazine, and since then she's appeared in *Glamour, Shape, Maxim, Fit, Women's Sports and Fitness, People,* and dozens of other magazines. Jones's cover story in the October 2000 issue of *Gear* magazine was titled "The Perfect Form." In 2001, she was featured surfing in a nationally aired commercial for VO5 shampoo. Jones's younger brother Daniel won the boys' division of the 1998 United States Surfing Championships, and in 2001 took the juniors division; older brother Mikala was described by *Surfing* magazine in 1999 as one of the "young bucks of the next millennium." Malia Jones married Big Island pro surfer Conan Hayes on New Year's Eve, 1999.

K

K2 Big-Wave Challenge A winner-take-all $50,000 photo-based competition for big-wave surfers, the first of its kind, developed in 1997 by former *Surfing* magazine editor Bill Sharp, and sponsored by equipment and clothing manufacturer K2. Guidelines for the K2 Big-Wave Challenge were simple: the surfer had to paddle into the wave (no personal watercraft–assisted tow-in takeoffs), the ride had to be documented on film, and the surfer had to get to the trough of the wave without falling. The contest was open to anybody. K2 entries could be submitted from November 1, 1997, to March 15, 1998, at which time an eight-man panel of judges—two editors each from *Surfer* and *Surfing* magazines plus four big-wave experts—would gather to view the photographic evidence and select a winner. Entries were posted as they were received on a special K2 Big-Wave Challenge Web site. For most of the winter Santa Cruz surfer Peter Mel was a consensus pick as front-

runner for an oversize wave he'd ridden at Maverick's. Then on February 17, 1998, at Todos Santos, Baja California, Mexico, during the semifinals of the Reef Brazil Big-Wave World Championships, San Diego surfer Taylor Knox dropped into an enormous near-vertical wall and completed a ride that would be featured simultaneously on the covers of *Surfer, Surfing,* and *Australia's Surfing Life* magazines. On March 31, at the Hard Rock Café in Newport Beach, judges voted seven to one to give the prize to Knox, with *San Francisco Chronicle* sportswriter Bruce Jenkins casting the lone vote for Mel (who at the last minute was awarded a $5,000 consolation prize). Knox's wave was estimated to be 52 feet high from trough to crest; Mel's was labeled 48 feet. Les Walker was awarded $5,000 as winning photographer. Results for the K2 Big-Wave Challenge were announced in the *Los Angeles Times, Time, Sports Illustrated,* and on CNN, as well as in the surf press.

Not everyone was excited about the K2 event. Some dissenters, including big-wave veteran Ken Bradshaw, thought the money would lure inexperienced riders into situations they couldn't handle. Others thought the K2 concept was simply crass and lurid, and counter to the traditionally noncommercial spirit of big-wave surfing. The like-formatted Swell XXL event was held in 2000–01, and won by California's Mike Parsons; it was followed by the Nissan Xterra XXL Big Surf Awards in 2001–02, won by Brazil's Carlos Burle. *See also* big-wave surfing, Taylor Knox, Bill Sharp, Todos Santos.

Kaena Point Narrow west-pointing finger of land located on the northwest tip of Oahu in Hawaii, fringed with black lava rocks and cliffs. On the biggest winter swells, Kaena will produce what appears to be ridable right-breaking 40-foot-plus waves on the southwest side of the point, and equally large but less organized left-breaking waves on the northwest side. From the late 1950s to the 1980s, Keana Point was thought of as big-wave surfing's final frontier. *Surf*

K2 Big Wave Challenge winner Taylor Knox

Guide magazine described it in 1963 as "near-mythical"; 10 years later *Surfer* said it was "surfing's ultimate challenge"; and another 10 years after that *Surfing* identified it as the focal point "for perhaps the greatest ocean energy on earth." In the early 1960s, George Downing, Buzzy Trent, and Greg Noll were among the first surfers to contemplate a run on Kaena. Downing said he'd try it for $2,500, but found no takers. Anticipating the tow-in method of big-wave surfing by more than 30 years, Trent said he'd have to be pulled into the wave from behind a boat. Jim Neece reportedly signed a $12,000 contract with a Los Angeles film company in 1973 to ride a 40-footer at Kaena; he said he would wear a small back-mounted canister of oxygen in case of a wipeout, and, like Trent, intended to be towed in to a wave. But Neece, like the rest before him, backed down.

On January 19, 1976, Flippy Hoffman, Roger Erickson, David Kahanamoku, and Jeff Johnson rode 15- to 20-footers at Kaena, using Johnson's boat to motor out to the break—but not to tow in to waves. Hoffman described it as "just a lot of fun," but noted that the heaviest section of the wave, located farther out from where they'd been riding, was still unmet. Mercenary big-wave rider Alec Cooke from Hawaii rode a half-dozen 18-foot waves at Kaena in 1984, with photographer Warren Bolster there to document each ride. A year later, Cooke recognized that the outer reefs on Oahu's North Shore offered more fertile big-wave possibilities. As breaks like Maverick's (California), Jaws (Maui), and Dungeons (South Africa) came to the fore, the impressive but erratic Keana Point was all but forgotten as a big-wave break. "Kaena" in Hawaiian means "the heat." *See also* North Shore.

Kahanamoku, Duke   The long-celebrated father of modern surfing, from Honolulu, Hawaii; an Olympic gold medal swimmer and Hawaii's beloved ambassador to the world through much of the first half of the 20th century. Kahanamoku was a skilled wave-rider, but his real gift to surfing was the way he presented the sport as something that could be practiced with grace, humor, and generosity. "You know," he said in 1965, "there are so many waves coming in all the time, you don't have to worry about that. Take your time—wave come. Let the other guys go; catch another one." The sport's greatest shortcoming may be that surfers have for the most part failed to live up to the Kahanamoku ideal.

Duke Kahanamoku

Kahanamoku was born (1890) and raised in Honolulu, a full-blooded Hawaiian, and the first-born son of a delivery clerk. Five male siblings followed; all were first-rate surfers, swimmers, and paddlers. Surfing, along with other native Hawaiian forms of recreation, had all but vanished at the time of Kahanamoku's birth, partly because the indigenous population had been decimated by a century's worth of Western-borne disease, and partly due to the work-not-play influence of homesteading Calvinist missionaries. By the time Kahanamoku was in school, however, agricultural and tourist interests had replaced the missionaries in setting the political and cultural tone in Hawaii, and surfing began to flourish in Waikiki. It soon became the romantic symbol of America's newest vacation destination. Kahanamoku was a natural at virtually all water-related activities—bodysurfing, board-surfing, diving, sailing, and outrigger canoe paddling—but he first came to national prominence as a short-distance swimmer. In the summer of 1911, at age 20, he broke the American 50-yard record by more than a second, and beat the 100-yard world record by more than four seconds. (Kahanamoku had earlier that year cofounded the Hui Nalu Club, the world's second surfing organization following the 1908-formed Outrigger Canoe Club.) In the 1912 Olympics, held in Stockholm, Sweden, the 6'1" 190-pound Duke used the already-famous "Kahanamoku Kick" to set another world record on his way to a gold medal in the 100-meter freestyle; he also won a silver medal in the 200-meter freestyle relay. In the 1920 Olympics in Antwerp, Belgium (World War I forced the cancellation of the 1916 Games), Kahanamoku won gold medals in both the 100-meter freestyle and the 400-meter freestyle relay; in the 1924 Olympics in Paris, the 34-year-old won a silver medal in the 100-meter freestyle. He was called the "human fish" and the "Bronzed Duke," and at age 42 Kahanamoku swam sprints as fast as when he was 21. In 1925, he made what the *Honolulu Star-Bulletin* described as a "superhuman rescue act," pulling eight fishermen out of heavy seas at Newport Beach, California.

Kahanamoku was by then the world's best-known surfer. In 1910, when virtually all Waikiki surfers were riding near the beach on six- or seven-foot boards, he'd made himself a smooth-riding 10-footer that he could take further offshore to pick up bigger, longer waves. He rode for the most part in an elegant, straight-backed stance, but played to onlookers at times by standing on his head as he approached the beach. In 1912, while returning from the Olympics, he brought surfing to the American East Coast, with exhibitions in New Jersey's Atlantic City; in late 1914 and early 1915, Kahanamoku introduced the Hawaiian form of surfing to Australia and New Zealand with demonstrations that attracted thousands; from 1915 to the early '30s, he helped popularize surfing in Southern California. It was Kahanamoku who inspired Wisconsin-born swimmer Tom Blake to move to California and learn how to surf; Blake later had a profound effect on the sport, inventing the surfboard fin, the hollow board, and surf photography.

Kahanamoku was celebrated for decades as a swimming and surfing hero (one female admirer described him as "the most magnificent human male God ever put on the earth"), and socialized with Charlie Chaplin, John Wayne, Babe Ruth, and other sports and entertainment giants. But he also knew financial and emotional hardship. He was a quiet, guileless ninth-grade dropout who at various times in his life worked as a stevedore, surveyor, gas-station owner, and City Hall janitor. While traveling across America in 1912, the dark-skinned Kahanamoku was regularly denied service at restaurants and hotels. He was given small roles in Hollywood films from the '20s through the '50s, but always as an impassive foreigner—a Sioux chief or Turkish sultan or Hindu servant. Kahanamoku served as the largely ceremonial "Sheriff of Honolulu" from 1934 to 1960. Throughout this period, Kahanamoku found solace in the ocean; Tom Blake later noted that "Duke attained his greatest surfing satisfactions and some of his greatest achievements as a rider after his 40th year." Surfing almost exclusively at Waikiki, he continued to ride into his late 60s, then sailed and swam into his mid-70s. Although he never made a job of it, as did dozens of renowned Waikiki surfers in the first half of the 20th century, Kahanamoku has nonetheless been called the ultimate beachboy. When disc jockey Kimo Wilder McVay became Kahanamoku's manager in 1961, the aging and dignified Hawaiian was suddenly the frontman for a small commercial empire that included Duke Kahanamoku's Restaurant, the Duke Kahanamoku Invitational Surfing Championships, and an array of Duke Kahanamoku signature merchandise, including floral-print tennis shoes, aloha shirts, surfboards, bellyboards, skateboards, ukuleles, and table glasses.

Kahanamoku died of a heart attack in 1968 at age 77. He was married, but had no children. Kahanamoku was the first inductee into the *International Surfing* Magazine Hall of Fame (in 1966), as well as the Huntington Beach Surfing Walk of Fame (1994). From 1964 to 1972, the Duke Kahanamoku Award was given to the best all-around surfer at the annual United States Surfing Championships. He was inducted into the International Swimming Hall of Fame in 1965 and the United States Olympic Hall of Fame in 1984. He's the only surfer to appear in portraiture on the covers of both *Surfer* and *Surfing* magazines; *Surfer* named him the "Surfer of the Century" in 1999. At Kuhio Beach in Waikiki, a 17-and-a-half-foot bronze statue of Kahanamoku standing in front of a surfboard was dedicated in 1990; a bronze statue of him surfing was unveiled at Sydney's Freshwater Beach in 1994 as the centerpiece of the Duke Kahanamoku Commemorative Park. The U.S. Postal Service issued a stamp honoring Kahanamoku in 2002. Biographies include *Duke of Hawaii* (1968), *Duke Kahanamoku: Hawaii's Golden Man* (1974), *Duke: The Life*

Story of Duke Kahanamoku (1994), and *Memories of Duke: The Legend Comes to Life* (1995). A small chain of Duke-themed restaurant/bars opened in Hawaii and California in the 1990s. *See also* beachboys, Duke Kahanamoku Invitational, Hawaii, Hui Nalu Club, Kimo Wilder McVay, Waikiki.

Kahuna Strictly defined as a Hawaiian word for priest, wise man, witch doctor, or sorcerer. Surfers in the mid-20th century playfully adopted Kahuna as their own pagan god of waves, and over the decades have ritually sacrificed thousands of surfboards—usually by immolation—to honor Kahuna and bring up the big surf. Kahuna was also the name of the sage older surfer in Frederick Kohner's 1957 novel *Gidget*. Two years later, when Kohner's book was turned into a movie, Kahuna was played with predatory cool by Cliff Robertson. Big Kahuna, a surf-themed bar/nightclub, opened in 1985 in midtown Manhattan, New York. Kahuna is similar to Australia's "Huey."

Kaio, Kealoha Quiet Hawaiian big-wave surfer rider from Laie, Oahu; third-place finisher in the 1963 Makaha International contest. Kaio didn't begin surfing until 1958 at age 23. Two years later he was riding Sunset Beach, the big-wave capital of Oahu's North Shore, and by 1963, with just five years of experience in the water, he'd almost magically become a refined and elegant big-wave rider. By keeping his arms and hands low through turns, Kaio invented "one of the keys to modern big-wave ripping," *Surfing* magazine noted in 1992, and the trait was passed to Hawaiian surfers like Eddie Aikau and Jeff Hakman, who in turn influenced virtually every big-wave rider that followed. In 1963, the same year he made the Makaha International finals, Kaio helped train Fabian, Tab Hunter, and the rest of the stars of Columbia Pictures' *Ride the Wild Surf*. Kaio competed in the inaugural Duke Kahanamoku contest in 1965, but by the end of the decade he'd left the surf scene and become a commercial fisherman.

Kalama, Dave Muscular waterman from Maui, Hawaii; "a polydimensional surfer," as described by *Longboard* magazine, expert in tow-in surfing, sailboarding, and longboarding. Kalama was born (1964) in Newport Beach, California, the son of West Coast Surfing Championships winner Ilima Kalama. He began surfing at age seven, moved to Maui at 21, and

soon became a top competitive wave-sailor, winning virtually every contest in Hawaii, including the 1991 Hard Rock Café World Cup. Kalama began experimenting with footstraps on his surfboard in the early '90s, and was soon able to perform a dazzling variety of small-wave aerials and flips. Meanwhile, surfers Laird Hamilton, Buzzy Kerbox, and Darrick Doerner were pioneering the tow-in method of big-wave riding on the North Shore of Oahu, getting a personal watercraft–assisted start on giant waves from behind Kerbox's inflatable Zodiac boat. When Hamilton and his group moved to Maui in 1992, they joined up with Kalama and his strapped-in surfing/sailboarding friends and were soon riding enormous waves at a break called Jaws. Tow-in leader Hamilton became partners with Kalama, and on December 20, 1994, Hamilton towed Kalama in to a 35-foot-plus Jaws wave, described by *Surfer* magazine as possibly "the biggest wave ever ridden." While Kalama rode bigger waves in the years to come, as did a growing number of tow-in surfers, he also became a top paddleboarder, surf canoeist, tandem surfer, kite surfer, and hydrofoil rider. "Dave is a *bad* man," Hamilton said in 2001. "Anything he tries he's proficient at in no time, and then before you know it he's pro." Kalama is featured in *Jaws Maui*, a 1997 coffee-table book. He appeared in the Hollywood-produced *Endless Summer II* (1994) and *In God's Hands* (1998), as well as a number of surf videos.

Kalama, Ilima Unheralded pure-blooded Hawaiian surfer from Oahu; men's division winner in the 1962 West Coast Surfing Championships. Kalama was born (1943) in Honolulu to one of the state's largest families—he was youngest of nine siblings, and his grandmother is said to have given birth to 21 children. Kalama began surfing at age six in Waikiki, and in 1959 he moved with part of his immediate family to Newport Beach, California, where his bodysurfing father helped form the California branch of the Outrigger Canoe Club. Kalama's functional upright wave-riding style helped earn him the 1962 West Coast title, as he defeated better-known American surfers like Mickey Muñoz, Rusty Miller, and Mike Haley; he also placed runner-up in the 1963 Pacific Coast Tandem Championships. Kalama appeared in a small number of surf films, including *Gun Ho!* (1963) and *A Cool Wave of Color* (1964). He's the father of champion sailboarder and tow-in surfing ironman David Kalama.

Kaluhiokalani, Montgomery "Buttons"   Loose and jiving regularfoot surfer from Waikiki, Hawaii; winner of the 1979 Sunkist Pro at Malibu, and generally regarded as one of the sport's most naturally gifted riders. He was born Montgomery Ernest Thomas Kaluhiokalani (1958) in Honolulu, the son of an army serviceman, and raised on Oahu's North Shore. At age five he moved with his two brothers and bartender mother to Waikiki; his grandmother said his black curly hair looked like buttons sewn to his head, and gave Montgomery his nickname. Kaluhiokalani began surfing at age nine; at 15 he placed second to future world tour powerhouse Dane Kealoha in the boys' division of the state titles, and also finished second in the United States Surfing Championships. Kaluhiokalani came to the attention of the surf world at large in 1975, when he and surfing partner Mark Liddell, riding their new split-rail stinger boards, set a new high-performance standard in small waves. Like Larry Bertlemann before him, Kaluhiokalani seemed to have spring-loaded legs and a riding style that was at once flamboyant and smooth. More so than Bertlemann—or virtually any surfer aside from six-time world champion Kelly Slater—Kaluhiokalani was spontaneous and innovative, stringing together turns, cutbacks, tuberides, tailslides, and 360s with offhanded genius.

Buttons Kaluhiokalani

Apart from his surfing, Kaluhiokalani was known for his enormous afro hairstyle (he once described himself as "half-Hawaiian, half black, a little bit Chinese"), and his chattering, laughing, often manic personality. He wore a curly blond wig for a surf magazine portrait shot, and ate sand in a brief but memorable surf movie clip. Along with his win in the 1979 Sunkist, Kaluhiokalani placed third in the 1975 Pro Class Trials, third in the 1981 Pro Class Trials, third in the 1981 Pipeline Masters, and first in the 1981 Peru International. For the most part, however, he was unable to focus on competition or any other facet of professional surfing. "He approached his career," surf journalist Phil Jarratt wrote, "with all the steadiness and good timing of a chicken with its head cut off."

Kaluhiokalani was featured on NBC's *Real People* in 1983, and the following year he appeared on the cover of *Surfing* magazine's "20 Who Rip" issue. Heavy cocaine use all but removed Kaluhiokalani from the surf scene, beginning in 1985. He reappeared suddenly in 1996, surfing better than ever, and announcing that "drugs are not where it's at for nobody." Nevertheless, Kaluhiokalani was arrested in early 1998 when Oahu police raided a North Shore crystal methamphetamine drug lab; charges were later dropped. One of the sport's most photogenic riders, Kaluhiokalani was featured in 1996, somewhat incongruously, as a surfer/model in the J. Crew summer catalog, and has appeared in dozens of surf movies, including *Playgrounds in Paradise* (1976), *Free Ride* (1977), *Fantasea* (1976), and *Ocean Fever* (1983). Kaluhiokalani has been married once, and has six children.

Kampion, Drew   Imperishable American surf writer and editor, best known for his work with *Surfer* magazine in the late 1960s and early '70s. Kampion was born (1944) and raised in Buffalo, New York, and began surfing in 1962, two years after moving with his family to Sunnyvale, California. He received a B.A. in English from California State University at Northridge in 1966, worked briefly for the *Wall Street Journal,* and was first published by *Surfer* in early 1968. By year's end, the 24-year-old Kampion had been hired as *Surfer*'s editor, and led the effort to transform the industry-leading magazine from a handsome but fairly straightforward sports publication into an innovative, mischievous, drug-influenced counterculture journal. He was the most protean of surf writers, shifting gears from contest reportage to editorials, equipment articles, environmental pieces, profiles, interviews, poetry, plays, reviews, and fiction. He could be murky and ponderous, but had a playful side as well, writing a coverline that read "First Annual End of the World Issue!" and an article titled "Picking a World Contest Team (It's Harder Than Picking Your Nose)." At his best, Kampion honored the sport by elevating it to a level above that of simple recreation. "It seems to me that surfing by itself is clean and basic and real enough to transcend this era of anarchy and unrest," he wrote in 1970.

> [And] when wars and flags and religions and nations and cities and rockets and taxicabs and monosodium glutamate and television are gone, there will still be an order to things far beyond the order of power-crazed men. It will be the order of a universe at equilibrium with all natural forces in balance. And that's what riding a wave is.

Kampion jumped from *Surfer* to *Surfing* magazine in late 1972. The bulk of his surf-related work over the next 15 years consisted of interviewing and profiling the world's top surfers, but he continued to make regular forays into fiction, essays, and comedy; he sometimes shot photographs to go with his article. Kampion later worked as advertising director for O'Neill Wetsuits (1978–81), editorial director of *Wind Surf* magazine (1982–89), associate editor of *New Age Journal* (1992), owner/publisher/editor of the Washington state–based *Island Independent* (1993–96), and contributing writer for Swell.com (2000–01).

Kampion has written articles for the *Surfer's Journal, Tracks, Surfing World, Surf Session, Longboard,* and other surf magazines around the world. He authored *The Book of Waves* (1989) and *Stoked: A History of Surf Culture* (1997), wrote voice-over script for the 1972 surf movie classic *Five Summer Stories* and for *20th Century Surfers,* a 2000 Outdoor Life Network cable television series, and also served as the editor for the *Stormrider Guide North America* (2002). Kampion lives on Whidbey Island, Washington. He's been married twice and has two children. *See also* Surfer magazine, Surfing magazine.

Kanaiaupuni, Barry   Revered power surfer from Haleiwa, Hawaii; world-ranked #9 in 1976, but best known for his innovative and never-duplicated approach at Oahu's Sunset Beach. Kanaiaupuni was

Barry Kanaiaupuni

born (1945) and raised in Honolulu, the son of a supervisor for the Honolulu Rapid Transit bus system, and began surfing at age eight in Waikiki. As a teenager he was briefly featured in Bud Browne's 1963 surf movie *Gun Ho!*; three years later Rick Surfboards introduced the Barry Kanaiaupuni Model, and in the 1967 Malibu Invitational, according to *Surfing* magazine, the handsome dark-haired Hawaiian "brought a quiet crowd to cheers with his power surfing unlimited." But Kanaiaupuni didn't come into full bloom as a surfer until the shortboard revolution of the late '60s, when boards went from unwieldy 10-footers to spearlike seven-footers. Sunset Beach had long been a North Shore favorite, but while longboard-riding surfers were for the most part forced to simply maintain speed and take an unbroken line from takeoff to pullout, Kanaiaupuni, atop a slivery "pocket rocket" of his own design, was able to swing up and down the big foaming Sunset walls. "He never had to look for a place to turn like the rest of us," California surfer Mike Armstrong recalled in 1992. "He turned anywhere he wanted to—and he really hit it hard." Kanaiaupuni constantly rode on the edge, and wiped out often; his style was a perfect contrast to that of Jeff Hakman, another power-turning Sunset master from Hawaii, whose specialty was precision and exactitude.

Kanaiaupuni was a hit-or-miss competitor. Virtually all of his best results came at Sunset, including a second in the 1973 Hang Ten Pro, wins in the 1975 and 1976 Pro Class Trials, and a fourth in the 1976 Duke Kahanamoku Classic. He competed in every Duke contest from 1968 to 1979, and was invited to the 1970 and 1971 Expression Session events. "But I was never really much of a contest surfer," he admitted in 1995. "I never had the mentality for it." While Kanaiaupuni also had little or no interest in the surf media spotlight, he was featured nonetheless in virtually every surf movie of the early and mid-'70s, including *Cosmic Children* (1970), *Morning of the Earth* (1972), *Five Summer Stories* (1972), *Going Surfin'* (1973), and *Tales from the Tube* (1975). A sequence of Kanaiaupuni riding Sunset to Jimi Hendrix's "Voodoo Chile" in 1973's *Fluid Drive* has been called the ultimate fusion of surfer and soundtrack. Kanaiaupuni was also featured on *Biographies,* a cable TV documentary series produced in 2001 by Outdoor Life Network.

Kanaiaupuni began shaping surfboards in 1967 and, in chronological order, he worked for Rick Surfboards, Country Surfboards, Surf Line Hawaii, and Lightning Bolt, before opening BK Ocean Sports in Haleiwa in 1979. Ten years later he opened a second BK retail outlet, in nearby Waianae, and in 1996 he opened Quiksilver Boardrider's Club, also in Haleiwa. He shaped boards for many of the best surfers in the '70s, including Ian Cairns and Shaun Tomson; he later made boards for Rusty Keaulana, his son-in-law and three-time longboard world champion. Kanaiaupuni is married and has four children. *See also* power surfing, Sunset Beach.

Kasuya, Shuji   Regularfoot pro surfer from Chiba, Japan; winner of the Japan Professional Surfing Association tour in 1989 and 1990. Kasuya was born (1961) and raised in Chiba, and began surfing at age 15, after becoming one of the country's top skateboarders. In 1980 he was Japan's second-ranked men's division amateur surfer; the following year he moved to Huntington Beach, California, and turned pro, returning to Chiba every three months because he didn't have a work visa. A fast, lithe, athletic surfer, Kasuya competed sporadically and with no great success on the world pro tour in the mid- and late '80s; on the domestic Japanese pro tour, however, he was in the top five from 1982 to 1987, champion in 1989 and 1990, and remained in the top 10 until late 1997. A near-fluent English speaker, Kasuya has worked since 1989 for Dropout Surfboards—one of Japan's biggest board-makers—as an interpreter/broker/scout to the American and Australian surf world. He's also worked for *Surfing Life,* a Japanese magazine, since 1999. Kasuya appeared in a small number of surfing movies and videos, including *Blazing Boards* (1983), *Asian Paradise* (1984), and *Freeze Frame* (1989). He's lived in Honolulu, Hawaii, since 1986.

Katin, Nancy   Owner and founder of Kanvas by Katin surf trunks, one of the original surfwear lines; known from the 1960s to the '80s as the "First Lady of Surfing"; Nancy Alexander was born (1900) and raised in Long Beach, California, and worked as a vaudeville dancer in the '20s and '30s. She married Sears & Roebuck salesman Walter Katin in 1951, and six years later they opened a small boat-cover business called Kanvas by Katin in Surfside, California, just north of Huntington Beach. The company began making a thick, rugged line of surf trunks in 1959, which were an instant hit with surfers up and down the coast. Katin sponsored a series of California "Underdog" amateur contests in the mid-'60s, open only to surfers who had never before won an event. The Katin Pro-Am Team Challenge debuted in 1977. Nancy ran Kanvas by Katin by herself after Walter died in 1967; the couple had no children.

Katin was regarded as a cheerful mother figure by three generations of surfers, and many Kanvas by Katin magazine ads in the '70s showed the diminutive Katin surrounded by a phalanx of stripped-to-the-waist surfers wearing their drawstring-fly Kapers, Kontenders, and Eyekatchers. She reminded people, as one surf journalist noted, "of the little old lady who ran the corner store down by the beach and let you slide when you didn't have quite enough change for milk and donuts." But the chain-smoking senior

Shuji Kasuya

also had a temper, and now and then let go with a slightly off-color remark. She once asked a surfer if he'd put sunscreen on his face; he said no, and asked if she had anything he could use to cover his nose. "Yeah, my fist," Katin replied. She died in 1986 at age 85; her service was attended by dozens of well-known surfers, including Peter Townend, Shaun Tomson, Jack Haley, Ian Cairns, and Dru Harrison. Katin won *Surfer* magazine's 1982 Surfer Cup Award for lifetime contribution to the sport; in 2000 she was inducted into the Huntington Beach Surfing Walk of Fame. *See also* Katin Pro-Am Team Challenge, surf trunks.

Katin Pro-Am Team Challenge   Pro-am surfing competition held in Huntington Beach, California, from 1977 to 1998, founded and sponsored by Kanvas by Katin surf trunks; California's premier international surfing event during its early years. Company owners Nancy and Walter Katin, parental figures to hundreds of Southern California surfers, organized a semiregular series of "Katin Underdog" contests in the mid- and late '60s, open only to surfers who hadn't yet won a competition. The Katin Pro-Am Team Challenge, conceived by Katin general manager Rus Calisch, was different from other surf events— and a throwback as well to the club contests of the '60s—in that teams were scored along with individuals. The inaugural Katin Pro-Am featured 38 four-man teams and a $10,000 purse, and was California's first big international pro contest. The six-day event was held in mid-February at the Huntington Cliffs, with the finals taking place in nearby San Pedro—the only time in the contest's history the site was moved from Huntington. The field included California favorites Mike Purpus and David Nuuhiwa and top Hawaiians Reno Abellira and Larry Bertlemann, but Shaun Tomson of South Africa went virtually unchallenged in winning the $4,250 first-place check. As the world pro tour didn't schedule an event in California until 1981, the first four versions of the Katin Pro-Am were the state's biggest and best-attended contests. With the founding of the richer and gaudier world tour–rated Op Pro in 1982, the nonrated Katin suffered a loss in prestige. But international surfers continued to enter, and winners included pro tour world champions Martin Potter, Tom Curren, and Kelly Slater.

When Katin went out of business in 1990, the Katin Pro-Am was suspended. In 1994, after the label was revived, the contest returned for another five years. With the exception of the 1977 event, the Katin

Pro-Am was always held at the Huntington Pier. In 1987, for one year only, a women's division was added (won by future world champion Lisa Andersen); other division and contest formats were picked up and discarded over the years. In 1997 and 1998, the Katin Pro-Am was a pro tour World Qualifying Series event. Individual and team winners of the Katin Pro-Am Team Challenge:

1977:	Shaun Tomson,	Kanoa Surfboards
1978:	Larry Bertlemann,	Bronzed Aussies
1979:	Greg Mungall,	Bronzed Aussies
1980:	Michael Ho,	Victory
1981:	Shaun Tomson,	Calvary Chapel
1982:	Tom Curren,	Body Glove
1983:	Martin Potter,	O'Neill
1984:	Joey Buran,	O'Neill
1985:	Willy Morris,	Body Glove
1986:	Martin Potter,	O'Neill
1987:	Tom Curren,	Gotcha
1988:	Dave Parmenter,	Body Glove
1989:	Richie Collins,	Quiksilver
1994:	Kelly Slater,	Focus
1995:	Pat O'Connell,	Quiksilver
1996:	Chris Brown,	Quiksilver
1997:	Sunny Garcia,	Doctor G
1998:	Jeff Deffenbaugh,	Body Glove

See also Nancy Katin.

Kauai   Rain-saturated Kauai is Hawaii's oldest and northernmost island. Long regarded as one of surfing's most localized areas, with some breaks virtually off-limits to visitors, Kauai has since the early '90s also become known as home to some of the world's most progressive and exciting surfers. Isolated somewhat from the rest of the Hawaiian island chain, Kauai's roughly circular shoreline is open to swells from nearly any direction. There are more than 50 charted breaks on Kauai, but many are temperamental or frequently windblown, leaving the island with far fewer dependable breaks than Oahu—the island against which all others in Hawaii are measured. Kauai's two primary surfing areas are the north shore, home to the sand-bottomed peaks of Pine Trees, the thumping right tubes of Tunnels, and the slingshot lefts of Cannons; and the southwest coast, which includes the long lefts of Infinities and the churning rights of Acid Drops. Magnificent Hanalei Bay, the broad and multifaceted right-breaking wave on Kauai's north shore—made famous as home to Puff the Magic Dragon, in the folk song of the same name—is the island's best-known surf spot, but is also mercurial and crowded. Average daytime temperatures on Kauai range from 70 to 80 degrees, with water temperatures in the mid- to upper 70s. (Mount Waialeale, the rainiest place on earth, located in the center of the island, receives more than 450 inches of rain annually.) Shallow reefs and foreboding local surfers are Kauai's biggest surfing hazards. Tourism here continues to grow, but much of Kauai remains rural or undeveloped, and the island is home to fewer than 40,000 residents.

Premodern Hawaiians rode at least five surf breaks on Kauai, including the gentle waves of Makaiwa, inside Wailua Bay on the east coast. Ancient legend holds that after a long sojourn from Tahiti, a chief named Mo'ikeha found the waves at Makaiwa so much to his liking that he never left the island and eventually became Kauai's chief. Captain James Cook landed here in 1778, and over the course of the following century, under missionary influence, surfing all but disappeared from the island. Visitors from Honolulu reintroduced the sport to Kauai in the 1930s. Hanalei was featured in the 1958 movie *Search for Surf,* but Kauai nonetheless remained a beautiful wave-riding backwater until the late '60s and early '70s, when it became the adopted home to a number of key surf world figures from the period—including Dick Brewer, Bill Hamilton, and world champion Margo Godfrey—all looking to escape the growing crowds on Oahu. In a largely successful effort to prevent Kauai from being overrun by surf tourism, locals enforced a ban on commercial surfing photography, keeping the island out of the surf press almost entirely, and made it clear that visitors were unwelcome. Kauai served as a launching pad for a set of electrifying high-performance riders during the '90s, beginning with Kaipo Jaquias, followed by Rochelle Ballard, Keala Kennelly, and brothers Bruce and Andy Irons. Kauai surfing godfather Titus Kinimaka had meanwhile long since established himself as the island's premier big-wave rider.

As of 2003, Kauai was home to 10 surf shops and roughly 3,000 surfers; the Hawaiian Amateur Surfing Association stages about a dozen events on the island each year. The Kauai surf has appeared in just a few surf movies and videos, including *Barefoot Adventure* (1960), *Free and Easy* (1967), *A Sea for Yourself* (1973), *Follow the Sun* (1983), *Filthy Habits* (1987), *Kauai Boys* (1996), and *On the Edge* (1997). The Kauai surf is detailed in *Surfing Hawaii* (1973) and *Surfer's Guide to Hawaii* (1991).

Kawahara, Tak   Entrepreneur from Santa Monica, California; surfing's original liaison to Japan, and often described as the "father of Japanese surfing." Kawahara was born (1940) in Los Angeles, raised in Santa Monica, and began surfing at age 17. He began shaping boards at Con Surfboards in Santa Monica; in 1961 he went on to work for Weber, Jacobs, Greg Noll, and Morey-Pope. Kawahara made the first of several biannual trips to Japan in 1964 to help organize the local surfing industry, and to scout for waves along the Shonan and Chiba coasts, near Tokyo; in 1968 he established the Japanese chapter of the Malibu Surfing Association. Kawahara founded California Hawaii Promotions (CHP) in 1976 in Los Angeles, and became the international wholesaler for the popular Town and Country line of surfboards and surfwear.

kayak   *See* wave ski.

Kealoha, Dane   Glowering power surfer from Honolulu, Hawaii; world-ranked #2 in 1980, remembered as the best tuberider of his generation, and often credited as inventor of the "pigdog" tuberiding stance. Kealoha was born (1958) and raised in Honolulu, the son of a pure-blooded Hawaiian carpenter father. He tried surfing for the first time at age ten at Waikiki, accompanied by his father; after wiping out on his opening wave, Kealoha swam for shore crying, ran across the street, and threw his arms around a tree. He didn't surf again until age 14. Francis Kealoha, Dane's older brother, had meanwhile become one of Hawaii's top amateur competitors; Dane himself proved to be a natural, winning the boys' division of the 1973 Hawaii state titles less than two years after he started surfing, and winning the juniors division of the 1976 United States Surfing Championships. Kealoha, Montgomery "Buttons" Kaluhiokalani, and Mark Liddell were the oft-photographed teenage protégés of high-performance surfing wizard Larry Bertlemann of Waikiki; all four were proponents in the mid-'70s of the split-railed stinger design surfboard. Nonetheless, it was a shock to the first-generation world tour pros in 1977 when Kealoha, a stone-faced 19-year-old rookie, placed third in the prestigious Duke Kahanamoku Classic at Sunset Beach, beating Reno Abellira, Mark Richards, Wayne Bartholomew, and Peter Townend in the final.

Dane Kealoha

At 5′9″, 185 pounds, with thighs like a fullback, Kealoha was a born power surfer. He rode in a wide stance, slightly hunkered over, pressing his board into a series of deeply chiseled turns and cutbacks. Kealoha also had an infallible sense of where to find speed on any given wave and Zen-like composure while inside the tube. South African surfer Shaun Tomson had in the mid-'70s invented a weaving method for tuberiding, allowing him to ride deeper and more creatively than any surfer before him; Kealoha improved on Tomson's technique and by the late '70s had taken over as the world's best tuberider, able to find his way out of the deepest caverns, especially at Backdoor Pipeline in Hawaii. In the early '80s, Kealoha developed a compact drop-knee method of riding the tube—originally called the "lay-forward," later known as the "tripod" or "pigdog"—that eventually allowed backsiders to ride nearly as deep inside the wave as frontsiders. Meanwhile, the dark Kealoha scowl frightened most surf journalists off, and convinced virtually all other surfers, even his world tour peers, to give him a wide berth. Australian surf journalist Tim Baker described Kealoha as "solitary and strangely quiet" while waiting for a wave. "He seems almost anchored, not bobbing around like the rest of us at the mercy of the temperamental Hawaiian waters, but somehow rooted to the spot."

Kealoha was a world pro tour mainstay from 1978 to 1982, finishing (in order) ninth, fourth, second (behind four-time world champion Mark Richards), third, and sixth. He made the finals of the Pipeline Masters contest four times, winning in 1983; he was in the finals of the Duke six times, winning in 1983. In what should have been his best season as a professional, 1983 instead brought a career crisis, as Kealoha was trapped in a political dogfight when the pro tour administration removed their sanction from the three Hawaiian events and banned the top-rated competitors from entering them; Kealoha defied the ban and won two of the three events, refused to pay the $1,000 reinstatement fine, and was stripped of his pro tour rating. Bitter and angry, he retired at age 25 from full-time competition. He continued to ride with consummate power and precision for the next few years, and his style was picked up on by a number of next-generation surfers, including Hawaiian strongman Johnny-Boy Gomes and 1990 world champion Martin Potter of South Africa. Kealoha was featured in more than 40 surf movies and videos in the '70s, '80s, and '90s, including *Fantasea* (1978), *Wave Warriors* (1985), *Gone Surfin'* (1987), and *Rolling Thunder* (1991). He finished runner-up to Mark Richards in the 1980 *Surfer* Magazine Readers Poll Awards; in 1990 and 1995 he competed in the Quiksilver in Memory of Eddie Aikau big-wave contest at Waimea Bay. Kealoha has been married twice (the first time to Carol Ching, a former Miss Hawaii), and has six children. *See also* power surfing.

Keating, Dick   Lithe regularfooter from Pacifica, California; the first homegrown San Francisco Bay Area rider to make an impression on the international surf scene as an invitee to the prestigious Duke Kahanamoku Invitational in 1967. Keating was born (1942) in San Francisco, and moved with his family to Pacifica's Pedro Point at age seven. He rode his first wave at age two, when his uncle, also named Dick, took him into the surf at Pedro Point. "Uncle Dick," as he was known to area surfers, had learned to surf while visiting Hawaii in 1936 for an Olympic swim team tryout; upon his return to San Francisco he became the Bay Area's first surfer, and in 1944 founded the Pedro Mountain Surf Club, housed in a ramshackle beachfront surfing clubhouse at the base of Pedro Point: "The only place we know," photographer John "Doc" Ball wrote in his 1946 *California Surfriders* book, "where you can practically step from your surfboard right smack into big patches of wild strawberries." The younger Dick Keating was featured in *The Natural Art,* a 1969 surf film, and briefly appeared in *Duke Kahanamoku's World of Surfing,* a 1968 CBS sports special.

Keaulana, Brian   Stone-faced Hawaiian big-wave surfer from Makaha, Oahu, described by surf journalist Dave Parmenter in 2000 as "the greatest all-around waterman alive." Keaulana was born (1961) and raised in Makaha, the son of Hawaiian surf icon Richard "Buffalo" Keaulana, and began riding waves with his father before he could walk. In keeping with long-standing Makaha tradition, Keaulana immersed himself in virtually all things ocean-related, becoming an expert bodysurfer, longboarder, kneeboarder, kitesurfer, canoeist, paddle- and tow-in big-wave rider, as well as a diver, sailboarder, fisherman, and Jet Skier. A lifeguard since 1976, he was awarded the United States Lifesaving Association medal of honor in 1993 for rescuing a drowning tourist trapped in an underwater cave. Keaulana trained for big-wave wipeouts by doing underwater sprints while carrying an 80-pound boulder. He's appeared in a half-dozen surf videos, including *Liquid Thunder* (1990) and *Full Cycle* (1994), and played himself in TriStar's 1998 big-wave movie *In God's Hands.* Keaulana competed in the Quiksilver in Memory of Eddie Aikau contest at Waimea Bay in 1990, 1999, 2001, and 2002, and was included in the 2001-launched Billabong Odyssey big-wave exploration project. *See also* waterman.

Keaulana, Richard "Buffalo"   Commanding Hawaiian surfer from Makaha, Oahu; winner of the 1960 Makaha International, and often referred to as the "Mayor of Makaha." Keaulana was born (1935) in Honolulu, and moved with his family to Makaha, on Oahu's west side, at age five. He learned to surf as a child at Waikiki, and made his first board by taking a machete to a blank assembled from glued-together railroad ties. Keaulana worked as a Waikiki beachboy in the '50s and earned the nickname "Buffalo" for his generously proportioned head and shaggy reddish-brown hair. A perennial favorite in the Makaha International contest, Keaulana placed third in 1957, second in 1958, and first in 1960. He was one of the most naturally gifted surfers of the period, ambidextrous in stance, smooth and fluid from one maneuver to the next, and unfailingly in the right place

Buffalo Keaulana

on the wave. He was also regarded as the world's best bodysurfer. (California big-wave pioneer Greg Noll once watched Keaulana bodysurf six-foot waves at Yokohama, near Makaha. "He looked so natural," Noll later recalled, "streaking across the waves like a seal. I actually expected him to turn and swim out to sea when he was done.") The barrel-chested Keaulana continued to place highly at the Makaha event, finishing third in 1961 and 1964 and fourth in 1965. He was also a semifinalist in the 1965 World Surfing Championships, held in Peru.

Keaulana was appointed head lifeguard at Makaha in 1969, a post he held until 1995. A statue of Keaulana was erected in 1972 in front of the Waianae Public Library, not far from Makaha. The Buffalo Big Board Classic debuted in 1977, a surf contest/beach party that immediately became a local institution. Keaulana—married with six children, including big-wave expert Brian and three-time longboard world champion Rusty—appeared in nearly a dozen surf movies between the mid-'50s and the mid-'70s, including *Trek to Makaha* (1956), *Cat on a Hot Foam Board* (1959), *Angry Sea* (1963), and *A Winter's Tale* (1974).

Keaulana, Rusty   Versatile Hawaiian surfer from Makaha, Oahu; three-time winner of the World Longboard Championships (1993, 1994, and 1995); middle son of Makaha surfing demigod Richard "Buffalo" Keaulana and younger brother to big-wave ace Brian Keaulana. Rusty was born (1966) and raised in Makaha, began riding waves as a toddler, and by his early teens was recognized as one of the island's best switchfooters, able to ride with either foot forward. He claimed his first longboard world title at age 27, in churning double-overhead surf at Haleiwa on Oahu's North Shore. His second title, won at Malibu, was controversial, as Keaulana and two Hawaiian teammates, while surfing in the four-man final, worked together to prevent the lone California competitor and odds-on favorite, Joel Tudor, from catching waves. Keaulana won his third and final title at St. Leu, on Réunion Island. Keaulana was both celebrated and criticized as a "progressive school" longboarder, filling his repertoire with dynamic shortboard-style turns, spins, and cutbacks. He had also developed into a first-rate big-wave rider, and placed fifth in the 1999 Quiksilver in Memory of Eddie Aikau big-wave contest at Waimea Bay. Keaulana has appeared in about 20 surf movies and videos, including *Blazing Longboards* (1994), *Adrift* (1996), and *Decade* (2002). *Rusty's World: Trip You Out,* a surf video travelogue, was released in 1999. Keaulana is married to Sunny Kanaiaupuni, daughter of venerated '70s Hawaiian power surfer Barry Kanaiaupuni. *See also* World Longboard Tour.

Kechele, Matt   Drawling but dynamic goofyfoot surfer and surfboard manufacturer from Cocoa Beach, Florida; aerial pioneer in the late '70s and early '80s, and winner of the 1992 ASP East circuit. Kechele was born (1962) and raised in Cocoa Beach, began surfing at age eight, and soon earned a spot near the top of the pecking order at Sebastian Inlet, Florida's best and most crowded break. He won the 1981 Stubbies Trials at the Inlet, at which point *Surfing* magazine noted that the curly-haired Kechele was a master at "flipping and hopping his board all over the waves"; one of his hopping moves was known as "Kech Air." He continued to develop aerial moves, but also said he hoped to "beat that trickster image," and by the late '80s, after more than a half-dozen extended visits to Hawaii, he'd become a first-rate Pipeline tube rider. Kechele began shaping surfboards at age 18, and founded Matt Kechele Surfboards at 23; one of his first team riders was the preadolescent Kelly Slater. Kechele appeared in about 15 dozen surf movies and videos, including *Amazing Surf Stories* (1986), *Gen X* (1990), and *Three Fins Firing* (1995). *See also* aerial.

Kekai, Albert "Rabbit"   Perennial regularfooter from Waikiki, Hawaii; often recalled as the best high-performance surfer of the 1930s and '40s; winner of the Makaha International in 1955; a senior surfing icon in the '90s and '00s. "Rabbit is the living link," as *Longboard* magazine put it in 1998, "to surfing's entire modern history." Kekai was born (1920) and raised in Waikiki, began surfing at age five, and was later given informal instruction by pioneering surfer and gold medal swimmer Duke Kahanamoku. Kekai earned the nickname "Rabbit" as one the island's fastest runners, and he's said to have run a 10-second 100 yard dash in high school. According to Kekai, the invention of high-performance surfing—turning up and down the wave face instead of just holding an angle—came about in the mid-'30s, as he and his friends began dodging the rocks at a Waikiki surf break called Publics. Kekai was one of Waikiki's best canoe steersmen as a teenager, and sometimes competed in canoe races against the aging but still formidable Kahanamoku. Kekai was also a Waikiki beachboy—a beachfront concession-stand worker who gave surf and canoe lessons to tourists, lounged on the sand, played the ukulele, traded stories, romanced the endless stream of vacationing women, and frequently engaged in small-time hustles and scams. Kekai has a black-and-white photograph of himself taken in the late '40s riding a small wave alongside actor David Niven, his student for the day. He also gave surf lessons or canoe rides to Red Skelton, Dorothy Lamour, Kirk Douglas, Gregory Peck, Sandy Koufax, and Gary Cooper. Meanwhile, the up-and-down lines Kekai drew on the waves had a big influence on the coming generation of surfers, including Californians Matt Kivlin, Joe Quigg, and Phil Edwards and Hawaii's Conrad Canha and Donald Takayama. "He was light-years ahead of anybody," Kivlin once said, recalling the first time he saw Kekai surf in 1947, further noting that the forthcoming "Malibu" style of riding was based on Kekai's high-performance technique. Kekai is sometimes also credited as the surfer who invented noseriding.

As a navy-trained underwater demolitions man, Kekai spent more than three years during World War

Rabbit Kekai

II planting explosives on island-based enemy defenses in Micronesia. Back in Waikiki after the war, his surfing continued to improve, first on the newly streamlined hot curl boards, which had become popular in the late '30s, and then on the California-designed Malibu boards of the early '50s. Kekai won the 1956 Makaha International contest (Jamma Kekai, his brother, won the following year), and was runner-up in 1961. He also won the tandem division with Heidi Stevens in 1958.

Kekai carried on as a beachboy, but also worked in construction and as a longshoreman. From the early '70s onward, he was hired each winter as a beachside official for the annual pro surfing contests held on the North Shore of Oahu. Meanwhile, year after year, he was the most active surfer of his age, winning his division in the United States Surfing Championships in 1973, 1980, 1984, and 1988. In the legends division of the 2000 U.S. Championships, surfing against men nearly 15 years his junior, the 79-year-old Hawaiian placed fourth.

Kekai was featured in two PBS-aired surfing documentaries, *Liquid Stage: The Lure of Surfing* (1995) and *Surfing for Life* (1999), both of which show him in his

70s riding waves with vigor and style. Kekai's endurance and enthusiasm, along with handsome lion-in-winter bearing, also attracted the attention of the nonsurfing world. He was profiled at length in the *Los Angeles Times* in 1999, and in a full-page ad for Springmaid Bed and Bath that appeared in the *New York Times Sunday* magazine in 2000, Kekai is posed at the edge of the water, wrapped in a sea-green sheet, next to a tag line reading, "I dream of the next wave." Kekai was inducted into the International Surfing Hall of Fame in 1991 and the Huntington Beach Surfing Hall of Fame in 2001. He was featured on *Biographies,* a 2001 cable TV documentary series produced by Outdoor Life Network. Kekai has been married twice and has four children. *See also* beachboys.

Keller, Charlie   Pioneering New Jersey surfer whose 1964-founded Keller Surf Shop, according to *Eastern Surf Magazine,* was "the prototype for all East Coast surf shops to follow." Keller was born (1934) and raised in Lavallette, New Jersey, and began surfing at age 23. He began making surfboards in 1958, and opened Keller's Surf Shop in Lavallette with a small stock of molded "popout" boards and, as store worker Bill Yerkes later recalled, virtually nothing else: "No trunks, no bikinis, and if you wanted a T-shirt you had to bring in your own and we'd be glad to spray-paint the shop logo on it—no charge." Keller's expanded the following year and began importing surfboards and surfwear from California. Around the same time, Keller also became one of the first surfers to visit and ride in Puerto Rico. He sold his shop in 1972, and it closed in 1973. Keller died of a heart attack in 1996 at age 61; an original 10-foot Keller surfboard was used as a bar during his wake. Keller was elected to the East Coast Surfing Hall of Fame in 1998.

Kelly, John   Lively and resourceful surfer/activist from Hawaii; inventor of the hot curl surfboard in 1937. Kelly was born (1919) in San Francisco, the son of artists, moved with his family to Honolulu at age four, and began surfing at six on his mother's discarded ironing board. Kelly got his first real surfboard at nine, a seven-foot redwood plank shaped by David Kahanamoku, Duke's brother. It was Kelly's idea in the summer of 1937 to streamline the tail section of the planks he and his friends were riding in order to lend more traction and control in bigger surf. Using a small ax and a drawknife, he reshaped a friend's board by narrowing the tail section and carving the rear planing surface into a rounded hull; the new design was named the "hot curl," and it was the foundation upon which modern big-wave surfing was built. Later in 1937, Kelly was among the first to travel to the west side of the island and ride Makaha. More than 25 years later, Kelly designed and marketed a split-bottom board he called the Hydroplane. *Surf and Sea,* Kelly's 304-page book covering virtually every aspect of the sport, was published by New York's Barns and Company in 1965; it was later described by the *Surfer's Journal* as "the most intelligent, well-crafted book ever written on surfing." Kelly also did color commentary for ABC-TV's *Wide World of Sports'* coverage of the Makaha International contest in the early '60s.

Kelly's nonsurfing life was just as rich and full, if more complicated and difficult. He received the Navy and Marine Corps Medal during World War II after diving 60 feet to recover an unexploded submarine torpedo; joined the Communist Party during the early years of the Cold War; graduated in 1950 with a B.A. in music from the Julliard School; formed Save Our Surf, one of the first ocean-based environmental groups, in 1961; was a guest lecturer in economic history at the University of Hawaii from 1974 to 1977; and became a tireless advocate for the Hawaiian sovereignty movement of the late '80s. The 81-year-old Kelly was featured in *Surfing for Life,* a 2000 PBS-aired documentary about geriatric surfers. The following year Kelly received the first annual Environmental Award from the Surf Industry Manufacturers Association. He lives with his wife of 57 years in the same house where he'd invented the hot curl in 1937. *See also* hot curl board.

kelp   Kelp grows from the ocean floor in both cold and temperate coastal waters around the world, and is distinguished by long vines, ridged and slippery leaves, and air-filled bulbs. Surfers like kelp because it helps keep the waves smooth; kelp canopies just outside the surf line will filter out small wind-chops, and the plant itself releases a mildly viscous oil that floats on the surface and further reduces any small wind ruffles. Kelp in the surf zone itself, however, can be a problem, as a ride can be checked or stopped altogether when the board's fins run across floating kelp vines. Beds of giant kelp (*Macrocysitis pyrifera*), and their self-contained kingdoms of algae, fish, and shellfish, are found across the American West Coast

from Washington to mid-Baja, but grows thickest and fastest—up to a foot a day—in the water just south of San Francisco. Kelp does best in depths between 10 and 60 feet; it won't grow in water above 75 degrees. Kelp harvesting in Southern California (algin, a kelp by-product, is used in beer, ice cream, salad dressing, and cosmetics) has long been a back-burner environmental issue. Storms will periodically decimate kelp beds. An El Niño storm in early 1983 reduced the Palos Verdes kelp canopy from 709 acres to 35, and a single day of heavy surf in 1988 wiped out an estimated 50 percent of the kelp plants off San Diego, leaving the beaches and beachfront sidewalks covered in drifts of slippery, decaying, fly-covered organic matter.

Kennelly, Keala   Rugged blond goofyfooter from Hanalei, Kauai; world-ranked #4 in 2002, with an untouchable reputation as the sport's most fearless female tuberider; described by *Rolling Stone* magazine as "Hawaii's big-wave amazon." Kennelly was born (1978) in Hanalei, raised in a geodesic dome handmade by her two surfing parents, and got her first surfboard at age five. She was a force as an amateur competitor; in the girls' division of the United States Surfing Championships she finished third in 1992, second in 1993, and fourth in 1994, and also placed third in the 1994 World Championships. Kennelly's blunt, hard-charging style wasn't a natural fit within the somewhat regulated confines of the world pro tour, but she nonetheless became one of the circuit's most compelling figures, launching aerials from which other women kicked out, and riding deep

Keala Kennelly

inside the tube at places like Pipeline and Teahupoo. She won her first major world tour event in 2000 at Teahupoo; the following year she won the Op Pro/ Mentawais specialty event, and in 2002 she again won at Teahupoo. Breaking rank from the girlish "surfette" look that all but defined women's surfing in the '90s and early '00s, Kennelly was a leather-clad and tongue-studded nightclubber who often looked, as surf journalist Alison Berkley put it, like "a sinister Disney cartoon character." Kennelly has appeared in more than a dozen surf videos, including *Empress* (1999), *Peaches* (1999), and *Tropical Madness* (2001). The unmarried Kennelly has lived in Honolulu, Oahu, since 1999.

Keogh, Denny   Australian surfboard manufacturer from Sydney's Manly Beach; founder of Keyo Surfboards, and an unheralded leader of the late-'60s shortboard revolution. Keogh was born (1937) in Dulwich Hill, Sydney, raised in Manly, began surfing at age eight, and in 1957 started making balsa boards out of his garage. Three years later he opened the Keyo Surfboards factory and retail shop in the north Sydney suburb of Brookvale, a neighborhood that quickly became the country's board-manufacturing hub. Midget Farrelly, winner of the 1962 Makaha International, was the first surfboard shaper Keogh brought in to help with the workload; in 1964, Keogh shaped the board that Farrelly rode to victory in the first World Surfing Championships, held at Manly.

Keogh hired Queensland-born surfer/shaper Bob McTavish in February 1967, and the following month McTavish shaped the first vee-bottom—a wide-backed nine-footer that kicked off the shortboard revolution. McTavish-designed Keyo Plastic Machine vee-bottom models were soon selling at the astonishing rate of 70 a week. Keyo followed up in 1968 with the Nat Young Tracker model; later in the year, however, the Keyo factory burned to the ground. Keogh became the Australian and New Zealand licensee builder for Hobie Cat catamarans in 1972, and Keyo Surfboards folded four years later.

Kerbox, Burton "Buzzy"   Famously handsome pro surfer from Hawaii; world-ranked #6 in 1978, and one of the original tow-in surfers of the early '90s. Kerbox was born (1956) in Indianapolis, Indiana, and was nine years old when he moved with his family to Kailua, on the east side of Oahu; he began surfing the following year. Kerbox won two major pro contests,

the 1978 World Cup at Sunset Beach and the 1980 Surfabout in Sydney; the latter earned him $12,000 and a new van—pro surfing's richest prize up to that point. Kerbox was ranked in the year-end top 10 in 1977, 1978, and 1980. Celebrated fashion photographer Bruce Weber, after seeing a small photo of Kerbox in a 1977 issue of *Surfing* magazine, arranged for the Hawaiian regularfooter to fly to New York, where he posed for *Vogue Men* and began a modeling career that would place him in nationwide campaigns for Levi's, Ralph Lauren, and United Airlines.

Kerbox and Maui-based power surfer Laird Hamilton invented tow-in surfing in 1991, using Kerbox's 15-foot Zodiac motorboat to pull each other into medium-sized waves on the North Shore of Oahu. Hamilton was intent on breaking all big-wave height and performance barriers; Kerbox was looking mainly to escape the growing crowds that had swarmed over Pipeline, Sunset, Waimea, and the rest of the famous North Shore surf breaks. "To ride waves without anyone else around," Kerbox later said, "that was what got the whole thing started for me." Oahu lifeguard Darrick Doerner soon joined Kerbox and Hamilton, they replaced Kerbox's Zodiac with personal watercraft, and by early 1994 the three surfers had completely reinvented big-wave surfing. Kerbox was featured in more than a dozen surf movies and videos, including *Fantasea* (1978) and *Radical Attitude* (1993). Kerbox is married and has three children. *See also* tow-in surfing.

kick   *See* rocker.

kick-stall   Braking maneuver in which the surfer shifts his weight to the rear foot and momentarily lifts the nose of the board. Shortboarders will occasionally use the kick-stall to slow down for a tube section, but in general it's a longboard maneuver, performed in small- to medium-size waves, often as a way to set up a noseride. Surfers in Waikiki may have been doing an early version of the kick-stall as far back as the 1930s, but it's generally thought to have developed in Southern California sometime in the '40s, not long after the introduction of the ride-stabilizing surfboard fin.

kickout   *See* pullout.

Kimoto, Naoya "Kin"   Soulful and well-traveled photographer from Osaka, Japan; described by the

Surfer's Journal in 1997 as "the dean of Japanese surf photography." Kimoto was born (1959) and raised in Osaka, began surfing in 1976, and shooting photographs not long thereafter. He studied photography and film at Kogei College in Tokyo, but abandoned the program at 21, moved to Hawaii, and began a career as a staff photographer for Japan's *Surfing World* magazine. His work has also been published in *Surfer* and the *Surfer's Journal, The Wonder Wave Land,* a book of Kimoto's photography, was published in 1991. Accomplished in all facets of surf photography, Kimoto has an affinity for long-angle shots, as well as moody, atmospheric, back-lit settings.

King, Don   Aquatic Hawaii-born cameraman from Kailua, Oahu; *Surfing* magazine staff photographer through the 1980s and early '90s; best known for his tight-angle action water photography. King was born (1960) in Honolulu, raised in Kailua, and began surfing in 1969 in Waikiki. He took his first water shots at age 14, swimming into the lineup at Pipeline on the North Shore of Oahu with a waterproof Kodak Instamatic—the equivalent, as *Surfing* magazine later phrased it, "to learning how to drive at the Indy 500." Two years later King got his first real camera, and within months was publishing in both *Surfer* and *Surfing* magazines; in 1980 he was put on the *Surfing* masthead, and in 1984 he became one of the magazine's elite senior staff photographers. The 6'2", 165-pound King meanwhile played water polo for Stanford University's national championship teams in 1980 and 1981—in high school he'd broken the state speed swimming record—and in 1983 graduated with a B.A. in psychology. While photographers throughout the '70s had moved steadily closer to both the surfer and the falling curl, King redefined the art in the early '80s, using a wide-angle lens and frequently shooting from inside the tube looking out, just inches from the passing rider.

King was hired by NBC Sports to shoot the 1982 World Cup of Surfing; he later contributed to Hollywood-made surf movies, including *North Shore* (1987), *Endless Summer II* (1994), and *In God's Hands* (1998). King also worked on surf movies and videos, including *Shock Waves* (1987) and *The Hole* (1997). His camera work on *Surfer Girl,* a documentary, won him a Best Cinematography Award in the 1995 Chicago Film Festival; *No Destination* earned King and fellow cameraman Jeff Hornbaker Best Cinematography honors in the 1998 *Surfer* Magazine Video Awards. King's work was featured in a 36-page *Surfer's Journal*

portfolio in 1992; he's also contributed to *Sports Illustrated* and *National Geographic,* as well as a number of illustrated surfing books, including *The Next Wave* (1991), *Aloha Blue* (1997), and *The Perfect Day* (2001). King won the 1992 Pipeline Bodysurfing Classic, the world's most competitive bodysurfing competition. He has been married twice and has three children.

King, Paul   Husky blond surf travel entrepreneur from Sydney, Australia; founder in 1987 of the Surf Travel Company, a boat charter service best known for its routes up and down the wave-rich Indonesian island chain. King was born (1958) and raised near the beachside Sydney suburb of Cronulla, and began surfing in 1970. He made his first visit to Java's soon-to-be-famous Grajagan surf camp in the early '80s, during a vacation from his entry-level job as a computer engineer in Sydney. In 1985 he began working full-time on surf travel, running his own boat out of Bali and making fantastic surf discoveries (including the King-christened Supersuck and Periscopes) on the coasts of nearby Lombok and Sumbawa. By the mid-'90s, the Cronulla-based Surf Travel Company was running boat tours through the Mentawai island chain off the coast of Sumatra; at the peak of the surf season, King would have as many as 11 charters running at once, using both company-owned boats as well as hired boats, with the average trip lasting 12 days and carrying 10 surfers. (The Surf Travel Company also had boats operating in Samoa, the Maldives, Tonga, New Caladonia, and other locations.) King has been damned as exploitative by surf adventure purists, but made wealthy by thousands of appreciative surfers who might otherwise have never seen or ridden Indonesia's remote but dependably perfect waves.

As the Mentawais began to attract other tour operators, most notably Australians Rick Cameron and Martin Daly, the political and marketing clashes between charter companies grew vicious, if not quite dangerous. By the early '00s, however, King seemed to emerge on top, and was saluted in "Loaded: Ten Surfing Millionaires," a 2001 *Australia's Surfing Life* magazine feature article. But King seemed ambivalent about his success. "Now here I am," he wrote at the time, "back in the office behind a desk, arranging for surfers to live the dream I once envisioned for myself."

Kinimaka, Titus   Imposing Hawaiian big-wave rider from Kalapaki, Kauai; a Quiksilver in Memory of

Titus Kinimaka

Eddie Aikau competitor in 1986, 1990, 1999, and 2001; regarded since the mid-'70s as the guardsman and figurehead of Kauai surfing. "People might think that I'm some kind of heavy," Kinimaka told *Surfer* magazine in 1986, "but I'm just holding heritage, holding roots." Kinimaka was born (1955) and raised on Kauai, began surfing at age three, and was invited to the last two Duke Kahanamoku Invitational contests in 1983 and 1984. On Christmas morning, 1989, Kinimaka broke his femur while surfing Waimea, and had to be airlifted from the lineup to a Honolulu emergency room for surgery. In 1995 he and Terry Chung became the first to tow-surf in Kauai, riding 35-foot-plus waves at King's Reef. Kinimaka has appeared in a small number of surf movies and videos, including *Bali High* (1981), *The Mondo X-treme X-periment* (1992), and *Wordz* (2002). He competed in the 2002 Tow-In World Cup, held at Jaws, Maui.

Kiriaty, Avi   Israeli-born artist who moved to Hawaii in his early 20s and began to produce oil paintings and knife-carved linoleum-block prints. Some of Kiriaty's pieces are surf-specific, but most are earthy, warm-toned depictions of traditional Polynesian life, in a style reminiscent of Paul Gauguin, filled with brown flesh, azure skies, and rich flora and fauna. Dale Hope, design coordinator for aloha shirt manufacturer Kahala, began using Kiriaty's work in fabric

patterns in 1991, and within five years Kahala had sold more than a quarter million shirts featuring Kiriaty's designs. In 1996, when Kiriaty was 39, his work was featured in an eight-page *Surfer's Journal* portfolio.

Kirra   Long, hollow, bullet-fast point surf located in southern Queensland, Australia, near the New South Wales border; one of the world's premier right-breaking waves. "Kirra is a barrel, a keg, a spitting pit," longtime Kirra local and former world champion Wayne Bartholomew explains. "That's all it is." The word "Kirra," which refers to the surf break and the surrounding neighborhood, is an aboriginal term for "gathering place." The Coral Sea cyclone season (December through March) generally brings the most consistent surf, but the winter months (May through August) can produce bigger waves along with steady offshore winds. Four to six feet is the ideal size. The wave at Kirra is divided into three sections of diminishing intensity—Big Groyne, the Point, and Little Groyne, as set from the top of the point to the bottom—and on bigger swells it's possible to link all three into a 300-yard-long ride; top surfers can easily ride inside a funneling sand-bottom Kirra tube for 10, 15, even 20 seconds at a time. Kirra demands intense concentration and frequent line adjustments, as the wave bends and scallops while passing different sections of the sandbar. While Queensland's balmy subtropical weather is an added bonus, enormous crowds—up to 200 surfers at a time—more often than not make Kirra one of the most frenzied and frustrating surf breaks in the world, and a dangerously shallow impact zone regularly sends riders to the beach (or the hospital) with sprained limbs and wrenched backs.

Members of the 1917-founded Kirra Surf Lifesaving Club began riding waves at the base of Kirra Point in the '20s, and the break remained the focal point of Queensland surfing in the decades ahead. The Kirra Surfriders Club was founded in 1962; the first surf contest held at Kirra was the inaugural Queensland state titles in 1964. Famous among Australian surfers for years, Kirra was relatively unheard of internationally until it was featured in Alby Falzon's popular 1972 surf movie *Morning of the Earth,* which showed local ace Michael Peterson—still regarded by most as the greatest Kirra surfer of all time—dashing across a series of aquamarine Kirra walls.

While Kirra hits peak form a few times each season, occasionally a cyclone—or cluster of cyclones—will produce a memorable long run of perfect surf.

Kirra

In April and May of 1972, Kirra turned on for nearly six consecutive weeks; the 1975 Queensland titles were held in flawless eight-foot Kirra tubes during the middle of a two-week swell; 1982's Cyclone Abigail produced 10 consecutive days of excellent surf. Top local riders at Kirra over the years include Graeme Black, national champions Keith Paull and Peter Drouyn, Wayne Deane, three-time national champion Michael Peterson, world champions Peter Townend and Wayne Bartholomew, and pro tour standouts Joe Engel, Michael Barry, Joel Parkinson, Dean Morrison, and Mick Fanning. Since the mid-'90s, Kirra has often been the site of an annual Queensland-based world pro tour contest; winners of the event include world champions Kelly Slater and Sunny Garcia.

Kirra was featured in *Great Waves* (1998), an Outdoor Life Network TV series, and has appeared in more than 50 surf films and videos over the years, including *Tubular Swells* (1977), *Surf Into Summer* (1987), *Cyclone Fever* (1994), *Snuff* (1999), and *Montaj* (2002). Kirra was listed by *Surfing* magazine in 1981 as one of the "Ten Best Waves in the World"; a 1997 issue of *Australia's Surfing Life* listed it as one of "Ten Waves Every Surfer Should Ride." *See also* Billabong Pro (Queensland), Gold Coast, Queensland.

kiteboarding   Watersport that combines elements of surfing, sailboarding, and paragliding. Using a platterlike board with footstraps or bindings, and harnessed to a large hand-controlled kite, kiteboarders use the power of the wind to ride, sail, and fly across the water. Kiteboarding began in the mid-1980s, when brothers Bruno and Dominique Legaignoux of Southern France and Oregon's Cory Roeseler simultaneously began experimenting with a kite-propelled

sailboard. Both inventions debuted in Maui, Hawaii, in the early '90s, creating a small sensation among local sailboarders, and inspiring others—including Hawaiian big-wave rider Laird Hamilton and French kiteboard pioneer Emmanuel Bertin—to create their own versions of the kiteboard. By the late '90s, kiteboarding was being labeled as an "extreme sport," and 2001 saw the debut of the Kiteboarding World Championship Tour, with stops in the Dominican Republic, Germany, Spain, Switzerland, and the United Arab Emirates. Competition is divided into three categories: freestyle, hang-time, and best trick. While the range of kiteboarding equipment is broad, the essentials are simple: a kite measuring roughly 10 to 30 feet wide and three to five feet across; a board, similar in shape and construction to a wakeboard; and a kite-control device consisting of a handheld bar with either two or four lines running to the kite. Kiteboards utilize wind in a similar fashion to sailboards, but with increased power and vertical lift; an expert kiteboarder can launch 60-foot-high aerials (sometimes performing complex flips and spins), re-

Kiteboarding

main airborne for as much as seven seconds, and sail laterally for up to 150 feet. *See also* sailboarding.

Kivlin, Matt   Elegant regularfoot surfer and surfboard-maker from Santa Monica, California; often cited as California's best wave-rider in the late 1940s and early '50s; creator of the slouched, knees-together, neatly synchronized "Malibu" surfing style. "He invented what I call performance cruising," next-generation Malibu ace Kemp Aaberg said. "He was gentlemanly, and rode that way, without a lot of yahoo around it." Kivlin was born (1929) in San Antonio, Texas, and raised in Santa Monica. He began surfing in 1943, when lifeguard and four-time Pacific Coast Surf Riding Championships winner Pete Peterson took the 14-year-old with him on a day trip to Palos Verdes Cove. Two years later, Kivlin and future big-wave rider Buzzy Trent began hitching rides to Malibu; they would sometimes get a lift with the Kohner family, whose diminutive youngest daughter Kathy would later show up at Malibu, where she was nicknamed "Gidget." Kivlin visited Hawaii for the first time in 1947, and was impressed by the agile close-to-the-curl riding style of Waikiki surfer Albert "Rabbit" Kekai. Back at Malibu, Kivlin, along with surfer/board-builder Joe Quigg, started designing and riding modified versions of Kekai's board—narrower, thinner, and lighter than what the Malibu surfers had been riding—and began to emulate Kekai's pronounced turns and active footwork. By the end of the decade, the 6'3" Kivlin had developed his own method, active but smooth, which would be directly copied by the next generation of Malibu surfers, including surf style icon Mickey Dora. In 1947, Kivlin made a pared-down 26-pound balsa board for his girlfriend that was lighter than any of the boards in use at the time. The "girl boards"—Quigg had also made one for his girlfriend—were soon in hot rotation among the Malibu men, who found them far easier to turn than their own boards; the upshot was the popular "Malibu chip" design. Kivlin and Quigg also developed the first narrow-based raked-back surfboard fin, a design idea that inexplicably went ignored until the mid-'60s.

Kivlin briefly went into a board-building partnership with eccentric California surfer/designer Bob Simmons in the late '40s, and just as briefly had a board-laminating shop with Quigg. While Simmons and Quigg have received most of the credit for design breakthroughs in the late '40s and early '50s, Kivlin

had the highest production rate. "When you're talking about Malibu boards of that time," Dave Rochlen, a Kivlin contemporary, said in 1998, "you're probably talking about Matt's boards." The handsome dark-haired Kivlin was also Malibu's social leader, driving carloads of people to beachfront luaus at which he cooked, poured drinks, and acted as informal host.

Kivlin quit surfing in 1962, and in 1971 opened Matt Kivlin AIA, a successful Santa Monica–based architecture firm. He never entered a surfing contest, went virtually unnoticed by the early surf media, and remains a largely forgotten name in surfing. "But if you had to name the most important people of [mid-20th-century surfing] on five fingers," Joe Quigg said in 1998, "Kivlin would be in there." Kivlin has been married twice and has four children. *See also* chip board, Malibu.

Klopf, Chris   Semi-reclusive American surf photographer and videographer from northern California. Klopf was born (1950) and raised in Mill Valley, just north of San Francisco, started surfing in 1965 at age 10, and began shooting photographs in 1967. Surf magazines began publishing Klopf's work in 1970, and he's since been featured in virtually every American and Australian surf magazine. With his still photography, Klopf often pulls back for a wider angle. "The wave comes first," surf journalist Steve Barilotti noted in a 1999 *Surfer's Journal* portfolio of Klopf's work. "The surfer is often seen merely as a player, reacting to the brief nexus of swell, rock and wind." The taciturn and mustachioed Klopf spent most of his 20s and 30s living and working in Santa Cruz, California, often photographing obscure surf breaks. (The Klopf-written "Ten Spots You'll Probably Never Surf" was published by *Surfer* in 1974.) He also made two 16-millimeter surf films, *Cycles of the Northern Sun* (1975) and *Time Tunnels* (1978). Since 1989, Klopf has produced roughly one surf video each year, including *Raw Power* (1991), *Wet Cement* (1997), and *Nomads* (2000).

Klyn, Vince   Muscle-pumped surfer/actor from Honolulu, Hawaii. Klyn was born (1964) in New Zealand, raised in Honolulu, began surfing at age 10 after finding an old Dewey Weber longboard lying by the side of the highway, and was among eight riders in *Surfer* magazine's "Pick of the Hot Young Crop" for Hawaii in 1981. Unsuccessful as a pro competitor, Klyn began working as a model in the late '80s, and was cast as the fearsome Fender Tremolo, leader of the Flesh Pirates cannibal gang, in the 1989 sci-fi cult hit movie *Cyborg*. Klyn made a career over the next 10 years as a television and B-movie heavy, appearing in *Bloodmatch* (1991), *Point Break* (1991), *Conflict of Interest* (1993), and *Urban Menace* (1999), as well as episodes of *Baywatch* and *Nash Bridges*. He also appeared in about a half-dozen surf movies and videos in the '80s and early '90s, including *Wave Warriors* (1985), *Ticket to Ride* (1986), and *Raw Power* (1991).

knee-paddle   Paddling a surfboard from a kneeling position, with both arms working in simultaneous motion; used by longboard surfers only; a slightly slower and more labor-intensive way of paddling, compared to the more commonly used prone position, but welcome as a change of pace and as a way to bring different muscles into play. Knee-paddling also affords a raised view, which helps the surfer to pick out incoming swells. Because knee-paddling is more effective on a long, stable, buoyant surfboard, it was virtually forgotten after the late-'60s shortboard revolution, when the average board length dropped from 10 feet to less than seven feet. The '80s-launched longboard resurgence brought a return to knee-paddling. Frequent knee-paddlers can develop half-dome calcium deposits on their knees and the tops of their feet—egg-size, in more severe cases—known as "surfer's knots." *See also* paddling.

kneeboarding   Form of surfing performed from a kneeling position, usually on a small, wide, blunt-nosed board; a popular and progressive alternative to stand-up surfing in the 1960s and '70s, but a fading practice by the turn of the century. Kneeboarders often say they chose their version of the sport over stand-up surfing because of the increased sensation of speed that comes from operating closer to the water surface. In decades past, kneeboards were more maneuverable by far than stand-up boards, were easier to fit into tight sections on the wave, and were thus the vehicle of choice at some of the world's most dangerous breaks, including the Wedge and Big Rock in California, and Shark Island in Australia.

Kneeriding likely originated in Polynesia in roughly 2000 B.C., along with bellyboarding and stand-up riding. The nonstanding versions of surfing were more popular during the sport's dark decades in the 19th century, when Western-borne disease and missionary influence vastly cut down the number of

Kneeboarding; California's Rex Huffman at Big Rock

surfers in Hawaii and other Pacific island groups. (All three surfers in "Sandwich Islanders Playing in the Surf," a 1841 drawing are riding on their knees.) But stand-up riding quickly became synonymous with surfing during the sport's early 20th-century renaissance; while kneeboarding was undoubtedly a part of the surf scene, it was all but unmentioned as a surfing subcategory until the late '50s, and didn't gain any kind of popularity until the mid-'60s.

Dominant kneeboarders over the decades included Rex Huffman of California and Australians Peter Crawford, Michael Novakov, and Simon Farrer. But kneeboarding was virtually defined by two people: George Greenough and Steve Lis. Greenough, a surfer/filmmaker/board-designer from Santa Barbara, California, became famous in the surf world in 1966, when surf magazines began publishing photos of him riding his newly designed "spoon"—a thin, semiflexible, five-foot kneeboard that allowed him to do advanced hairpin turns and cutbacks. Greenough's performances led directly to the shortboard revolution of the late '60s and early '70s, which can be seen as nothing more than a five-year effort by stand-up surfers to match Greenough's kneeboard-initiated standard. Steve Lis of San Diego, California, is best remembered for developing the wide, split-tailed, two-finned "fish" board in the late '60s and early '70s—a design that produced the stand-up twin-fin boards used in the late '70s, which in turn led to the wildly popular tri-fin.

Amateur kneeboarding contests were introduced in the late '60s, and the first professional kneeboarding event took place in Sydney, Australia, in 1976, with Sydney rider Steve Artis winning $1,000 for first place. Professional kneeboard events—including a small pro circuit founded in 1988—have since been held in Australia, New Zealand, and South Africa. Australians have always been the top force in competitive kneeboarding.

Performance and design contributions aside, kneeboarders have long been easy prey for offhand scorn and derision by conventional surfers. Kneeboarding sequences from '70s surf movies were often interrupted by shouts of "stand up!" from the audience, and the kneeboarder has been referred to as "halfman"; Australian surf journalist Phil Jarratt, while working as editor of *Tracks* magazine in the early '70s, authored a kneeboarding column titled "Cripple's Corner." But it wasn't the taunts and gibes that caused kneeboarding to drop in popularity; it was the mid-'70s introduction of the bodyboard, along with improved stand-up boards, that mitigated, then erased altogether, the performance advantage of the kneeboard. "Endangered Species," a lengthy 1998 *Surfer's Journal* article, noted that kneeriders in America were "caught in a black hole of diminishing numbers, diminishing talent and diminishing recognition." Kneeboarding dropped in popularity as well in Australia, but to a lesser degree. Kneeboard Surf Australia, a competitive organization, as well as the Australian Professional Kneeboard Circuit (consisting of four events in 2002), attest to the sport's relative health Down Under.

Average measurements for a kneeboard are about 5'6" by 23", roughly a foot shorter and five inches narrower than a small-wave shortboard. Kneeboards have between two and five fins, while virtually all shortboards are tri-fins. With few exceptions, kneeboarders use swim fins to propel themselves into waves. Australian kneeboarder Simon Farrer coproduced *The Sparrow Has Landed and Friends* (1998), the first full-length kneeboarding video; kneeriding has also been featured briefly in more than 50 surf movies and videos over the years. *See also* bodyboarding, bodysurfing, George Greenough, Steve Lis.

Knox, Taylor   Agreeable regularfooter from Carlsbad, California; world-ranked #4 in 2001, winner of the 1998 K2 Big-Wave Challenge, and the most accomplished power surfer of his generation. Knox was born (1971) in Thousand Oaks, California, grew up in Oxnard, and began surfing at age eight. He moved with his family to Carlsbad at 13; at 15, he had emergency spinal surgery to repair a lumbar vertebra damaged years earlier in a skateboard accident, and spent six months in a chest-to-thigh plastic wraparound body brace. Knox made a full recovery the following year, and finished fourth in the men's division of the 1990 World Amateur Surfing Championships. Over the next few years, the thick-chested Knox (5'10", 170 pounds) set himself apart from the Kelly Slater–led New School surfers by focusing on deeply set turns and cutbacks rather than aerials and tailslides. Knox could perform all the tricks, too, but at times he seemed to be a throwback to '80s power surfers like Richard Cram and Gary Elkerton. "It's a hard, efficient, uncompromising style," two-time world champion Tom Carroll said of Knox, "and I sometimes find myself wondering, How many G's is Taylor pulling out there?"

Knox has occasionally been spoken of as a world title contender, but he's been inconsistent on the pro circuit, going from 24th as a rookie in 1993 to fifth in 1995, then dropping to 35th in 1998 and failing to make the cut for 1999. Requalifying in 2000, Knox finished 28th, shot up to fourth in 2001, then dropped to 25th in 2002. Knox meanwhile won the 1995 Professional Surfing Association of America tour, and led the American team to a win in the 1996 World Surfing Games, finishing first in the men's division. He also won the winner-take-all $50,000 K2 Big-Wave Challenge in 1998, awarded to the paddle-in surfer photographed on the largest wave of the year. Knox's wave, caught at Todos Santos, in Baja California, Mexico, was estimated to be 52 feet. One of the most photographed and filmed surfers of his generation, Knox starred in *Arc* (2002), a surf video biography, and has appeared in more than 40 other surf videos, including *Momentum II* (1993), *What's Really Goin' Wrong* (1995), *The Show* (1996), *No Destination* (1998), and *Shelter* (2001). Knox finished runner-up to six-time world champion Kelly Slater in the 1998 *Surfer* Magazine Readers Poll Awards. In April 2001, the blond-haired, square-jawed Knox was featured on the cover of *Men's Journal* magazine. Knox is married and has two children. *See also* K2 Big-Wave Challenge.

Kohner, Frederick   *See* Gidget.

Kohner, Kathy   *See* Gidget.

kook   Timeless derogatory surfing term, generally applied to rank beginners, but also used for any surfer thought to be in violation of surfing's complex unwritten code of conduct; a world champion paddling out to a surf break for the first time and dropping in on a local, for example, would be shouted down as a "kook." Originally a Hawaiian slang expression, the surf-variant of "kook" was probably first used by mainland surfers not long after World War II. The surf leash is sometimes referred to as "kook cord"; in 1987, a California surfing novelty company developed Kook Repellent, an aerosol "silly string" knockoff. "Kook" is one of a select few genre words—"stoked" is another—to remain in usage through the decades. Occasionally spelled "kuk." *See also* hodad.

kook box   *See* hollow surfboard.

Kookmeyer, Wilbur   Dim-witted but perpetually optimistic cartoon character invented by Bob Penuelas, and presented in a self-titled *Surfer* magazine cartoon strip from 1985 to 2000. Penuelas, from Southern California's Pacific Beach, was cocreator of Maynard and the Rat, a cartoon strip published in *Surfer* from 1980 to 1987; in 1985, Penuelas began to work exclusively on Wilbur Kookmeyer, a gangly jug-eared character he'd introduced in a Maynard strip. Kookmeyer, outfitted in all the trendiest surf gear, including his high-top beach sneakers and "Kook Kind" tri-fin, spends most of his time in the water tangled in his surf leash and wiping out. But on land the droopy-eyed adolescent often falls into a happy and

Wilbur Kookmeyer

richly detailed surf-fantasy reverie. In a strip titled "Wilbur World," Kookmeyer imagines a "totally killer theme park" filled with perfect artificially made waves, a topless beach, "Mickey Dora Theater," live dolphin rides, and a nightclub "featuring all those insane Aussie bands that you see on MTV." Kookmeyer became the most popular American surf cartoon personality since Murphy, the mop-topped gremmie created by artist Rick Griffin in the early '60s. A line of Wilbur Kookmeyer calendars, posters, and greeting cards, and a Gumby-like Wilbur Kookmeyer bendable doll—all produced by the Penuelas-founded Yikes! company—were available by 1989; in 1995, *Surfer* magazine announced high school sophomore Jeremy Miller of Grass Valley, California, as the winner of its "Wilbur Kookmeyer Kookalike Contest." *Surfer* published 66 Wilbur Kookmeyer episodes altogether. Penuelas later described Kookmeyer as "the ultimate surfing pretender," and said his appeal came from the fact that "we're all kooks—or at least we've all been kooks at some time in our lives." *The Best of Wilbur Kookmeyer,* a softcover book, was published in 1999. *See also* Bob Penuelas, surf cartoons and comics.

Kuga, Takao   Hard-charging Japanese regularfoot surfer from Taito, on the island of Chiba; five-time Japanese Professional Surfing Association champion (1982, 1984–87), and Japan's first international big-wave rider. Kuga was born (1964) in Taito, began surfing in 1974, was the national boys' division champion in 1978 and juniors division winner in 1979. He was one of the first from his country to ride the big surf at Hawaii's Waimea Bay, and in 1990 finished 15th in the Quiksilver in Memory of Eddie Aikau contest at Waimea; he remains the only Japanese surfer to be invited to the prestigious Quiksilver/Aikau event. Kuga was also a semifinalist in the 1998 Reef Brazil Big-Wave Team Championships, held at Todos Santos, Mexico, and placed ninth in the Madeira Big Wave Challenge. Kuga has owned and operated Faith Surfboards in Chiba since 1994. He's appeared in a small number of surf movies and videos, including *Asian Paradise* (1984) and *Raw Power* (1991).

Kuhn, Charlie   Unassuming regularfoot pro surfer from Cocoa Beach, Florida; world-ranked #15 in 1986. Kuhn was born (1962) and raised in Cocoa Beach, and began surfing at age 11. In 1982, one year before turning pro, he won the men's division of both the Eastern Surfing Association Championships and the

United States Surfing Championships. On the world tour he won the 1985 Lacanau Pro in France, riding out of a driving, low-slung utilitarian stance, and connecting his turns smoothly. Kuhn retired from international competition in 1988, but continued to compete domestically. In 1990 he was the Association of Surfing Professionals' East Coast tour champion, and finished runner-up in the Professional Surfing Association of America tour. The low-profile Kuhn appeared in a small number of surf movies and videos, including *Wave Warriors IV* (1989), *Session Impossible* (1991), and *Panama Red* (1994).

Kukea, Ethel   Graceful regularfoot surfer from Honolulu, Hawaii; winner of the Makaha International contest in 1955 and 1956. Ethel Harrison was born (1914) in Garden Grove, California, raised in Santa Ana Canyon, and began surfing in the 1930s at Corona del Mar with her older brother and California surfing pioneer Lorrin "Whitey" Harrison. "Daddy was the rebellious one, and always running off to go surfing," Rosie Harrison, Lorrin's daughter, wrote in 1997, "and he usually conned Ethel into going with him. He and Ethel were so close in age they were almost like twins." Harrison married Joe Kukea, Honolulu fireman and full-blooded Hawaiian, in 1935, and settled in Hawaii. Kukea was a 41-year-old YWCA fitness instructor and mother of three in 1955 when she won Makaha for the first time.

Kwock, Danny   Enterprising surfer/executive from Newport Beach, California; leader of the brightly colored California New Wave surfers in the late 1970s and early '80s; marketing ace for surfwear giant Quiksilver since the mid-'80s. Kwock was born (1961) in Honolulu, began surfing in Waikiki at age eight, and moved with his family to Newport at 12. He became interested in fashion in 1978 after paging through some issues of *Vogue* magazine, and in 1980 he made the cover of *Surfer* riding a polka-dot surfboard and wearing a full-length red, white, and powder-blue wetsuit. Kwock's association with Quiksilver began in 1977 as a team rider, and by 1986 he was the company's marketing director. He helped develop the Quiksilver in Memory of Eddie Aikau contest at Waimea Bay, Hawaii (first held in 1986), as well as the Men Who Ride Mountains contest at Maverick's in California (first held in 1999). Kwock also helped sign Floridian Kelly Slater to the Quiksilver team in 1990; Slater went on to win six world titles before the decade was out. *See also* Quiksilver.

L

Lacanau Pro Midsummer world pro tour surfing contest held in the French resort town of Lacanau, located 120 miles north of the French/Spanish border; the original and longest-lasting European world tour event. Lacanau's beachbreak surf is generally unremarkable, but the Lacanau Pro has nonetheless produced exciting and hard-fought small-wave clashes, and pro surfers have traditionally looked upon the event—along with the rest of the French portion of the world tour—as an extended sun- and wine-soaked working vacation. The Lacanau Pro debuted in 1979 as a men's-only competition, and was won by Florida's Greg Loehr; in 1983 it was included on the men's world tour schedule, and a women's division was added in 1987. Quiksilver, Gotcha, Ocean Pacific, Oxbow, and Kana Beach, among others, have sponsored the Lacanau Pro over the years. Men's and women's combined prize money for the event peaked in 1999 at $150,600. The Lacanau Pro women's division became a second-tier pro event in 2000; the men's division followed in 2001. Winners of the Lacanau Pro:

1979:	Greg Loehr
1980:	Wayne Bartholomew
1981:	Thierry Fernandez
1982:	(cancelled)
1983:	Barton Lynch
1984:	Mark Occhilupo
1985:	Charlie Kuhn
1986:	Tom Curren
1987:	Barton Lynch, Wendy Botha
1988:	Tom Carroll, Wendy Botha
1989:	Martin Potter, Kim Mearig
1990:	Tom Curren, Wendy Botha
1991:	Damien Hardman, Pauline Menczer
1992:	Tony Ray, Lisa Andersen
1993:	Martin Potter, Pauline Menczer
1994:	Kelly Slater, Pauline Menczer
1995:	Victor Ribas, Lisa Andersen
1996:	Kaipo Jaquias, Lisa Andersen
1997:	Shane Powell, Rochelle Ballard
1998:	(cancelled)
1999:	Tim Curran, Megan Abubo
2000:	Rob Machado, Lynette MacKenzie
2001:	Joel Parkinson, Maria Tita Tavares
2002:	Flavio Padaratz, Julia Christian

Lagardere, Josette Nimble blond regularfoot surfer originally from Redondo Beach, California; winner of the 1966 Laguna Swimwear Masters contest and finalist in the 1966 World Surfing Championships. Lagardere was born (1947) in DeLand, Florida, raised in Redondo, and began surfing at age 13. Three years later she won the Santa Monica Mid-Winter Championships; not long after, she was given a slot on the prestigious Dewey Weber Surfboards surf team. Lagardere was 19 when she beat two-time world champion Joyce Hoffman in the Laguna Masters contest, which was televised on ABC's *Wide World of Sports*. At year's end, she was runner-up to Hoffman in the United States Surfing Association's final ratings. Lagardere moved to Queensland, Australia, in 1968; the following year she won both the Queensland state titles and the Australian National Titles. Lagardere maintains duel U.S./Australian citizenship, but lives in Queensland.

Lagundri Bay *See* Nias.

Laine, Wes Well-scrubbed regularfoot pro surfer from Virginia Beach, Virginia; world-ranked #9 in 1983 and 1985. Laine was born (1960) in Fort Belvoir, Virginia, the son of a U.S. Marine colonel. He first surfed at age five, then spent nearly 10 years living with his family on military bases in Italy, Rhode Island, and North Carolina, before settling in Virginia Beach. One of the East Coast's strongest amateur competitors in the mid- and late '70s—winning the boys' division of the 1974 East Coast Surfing Championships, the juniors kneeboard division of the 1976 U.S. Championships, and the juniors division of the 1978 East Coast Surfing Championships—Laine

Wes Laine

turned pro in 1979, and joined the world tour in 1982, finishing the year ranked #22. Laine was the top-rated East Coast surfer for the next three years, finishing ninth in 1983, 11th in 1984, and ninth in 1985. He left the world tour after the 1989 season to concentrate on the East Coast pro circuit, and finished the 1993 tour rated fourth.

Laine had functional and polished wave-riding style, connecting his turns smoothly and always keeping his long, thin limbs in balance. He was particularly skilled at frontside tuberiding, slotting his 6′4″, 170-pound frame into the wide-open cylinders at Off the Wall and Backdoor in Hawaii, and neatly folding himself into three-footers at preferred East Coast breaks such as North Carolina's Cape Hatteras. Laine was one of the most brightly accoutered surfers of the period, with hallmark orange-decked boards and wetsuits in preschool color combinations, including a fullsuit in canary yellow and hot pink with black accents. In his one and only brush with surfing politics, Laine said in a 1990 *Surfing* magazine interview that he didn't agree with a recently organized pro surfer boycott against South African surf contests to protest apartheid. "I'm not going to jeopardize my livelihood or miss out on a good surf trip for anything." Three months later, contest officials in the antiapartheid Caribbean country of Barbados prevented Laine from entering a pro event there. Laine responded by saying that he would organize a boycott against future contests in Barbados.

Laine appeared in about 20 surf movies and videos, including *The Performers* (1984), *Atlantic Cross-*

ing (1989), and *No Exit* (1992). Older brother Randy Laine competed briefly on the world pro circuit in the mid-'70s; in the early '80s he was celebrated and reviled as one of the first surfers to ride waves on a personal watercraft. Wes Laine, is married and has one child, and has been a surfwear salesman since 1990.

Lambresi, Mike Hardworking regularfoot pro surfer from Oceanside, California; Professional Surfing Association of America (PSAA) tour champion in 1987, 1988, and 1989. Lambresi was born (1964) in Loma Linda, California, grew up in Oceanside, and was a successful pro bodyboarder in the late '70s and early '80s. He began stand-up surfing in 1982, skipped amateur competition altogether, and won in 1983 the California Stubbies Trials, a pro event. Lambresi used a wide, stable, functional stance, and connected his moves beautifully. He competed on the Association of Surfing Professionals' (ASP) world tour in 1983, finished the 1984 season world-ranked #18 (named that year as the ASP's most improved surfer), then unexpectedly retired from international competition to stay home with his wife and newborn daughter. He dominated the PSAA circuit from 1987 to 1989. Lambresi later worked in the *Surfer* magazine ad department, then as publisher for *Action Sports Retailer* magazine. He appeared in a small number of surf movies and videos, including *Freeze Frame* (1989).

laminate The process of covering a shaped polyurethane foam blank with a resin-saturated layer of fiberglass; the first step in transforming a shaped blank into a finished surfboard. Virtually all major surfboard manufacturers from the 1950s to the '70s laminated their own boards, and some of today's shops still do the work in-house. Most contract out to a regional "glass shop" or "glass factory." ("Glassing"—short for fiberglassing—is often used synonymously with "laminating.") A top glass factory can laminate up to 20 boards a day. The process begins with the laminator, usually working in a large, well-ventilated room, distributing a set of shaped blanks bottom up and horizontal onto a row (or double row) of individual waist-high glassing racks. A length of fiberglass cloth is measured out and laid flat down the length of the board, then trimmed with a pair of garden shears so that it hangs down about two inches below the board's rail line. The cloth is then rolled back and the board-maker's label is affixed to the surface with a small amount of resin. For a short-board (about 6′6″), one quart of laminating resin is mixed in a bucket with approximately a half ounce of catalyst, which gives the laminator about 30 minutes to work before the resin begins to gel, or gum up. The respirator-wearing laminator "wets out" the cloth by making three or four walking passes up and down the board, pouring the resin from the bucket with one hand and using a squeegee with the other to distribute the resin and evenly saturate the cloth. The hanging cloth is then pressed around the curve of the rail with a smaller squeegee. While the resin is gelling, the laminator flips the board over and uses a razor blade to trim a clean line around the edge of the cloth. The entire process is then repeated on the deck, usually with two layers of cloth instead of one, to guard against the dents and troughs caused by a surfer's knees and heels.

Production-scale laminating is dirty, repetitive, decent-paying work, performed by a small clique, with a fairly low turnover rate. Glass factory conditions have improved over the decades, but there are nonetheless health risks associated with fiberglass, resin, and acetone solvent. Long-term exposure to the chemical styrene (resin's main ingredient) has been linked to liver damage, lymphoma, and leukemia, and fiberglass is also carcinogenic. Unlike surfboard shapers, who are often celebrated as craftsmen and gurus, glass factory workers are all but anonymous. Laminator Jack Reeves of Hawaii would likely be the only glass factory worker whose reputation extends—just barely—into the general surf world. *See also* fiberglass, surfboard construction.

Larkin, Joe   Pioneering Australian surfboard manufacturer and archetypal hard-drinking "surfie" of the 1950s and '60s. Larkin began surfing in 1943 at age nine at Sydney's Freshwater Beach. By the late '50s, Larkin, Barry Bennett, Bill Wallace, and Gordon Woods had each founded their own surfboard label, and collectively established the Australian board-making industry. In 1960, Larkin moved to Kirra Point in Queensland, where he opened a new shop. Some of Queensland's best surfers worked for Larkin over the next 12 years, including Keith Paull, Terry Fitzgerald, Michael Peterson, and Peter Townend; as 1978 world champion Wayne Bartholomew recalls in his autobiography, "It seemed like design breakthroughs were being made every week at Joe Larkin's factory during this time." Larkin had long since earned a reputation as a great man for the pub. "He

was the wildest guy in surfing," 1964 world champion Midget Farrelly once said. "Too drunk and too funny." In 1992, *Australia's Surfing Life* magazine named Larkin as one of the country's "50 Most Influential Surfers."

Larmont, Mike   Surfboard shaper and board manufacturer from Durban, South Africa; the country's dominant board-maker in the late '70s and early '80s. Larmont was born (1951) and raised in Durban, began surfing at age 12, and in 1972 was selected as a member of South Africa's team to the World Surfing Championships. His shaping career began in 1968, as the Australian-inspired shortboard revolution took hold in Durban, and Larmont found himself in possession of a brand-new but suddenly obsolete 9′4″ longboard. He sold the 9′4″, bought a polyurethane surfboard blank and a hand plane, borrowed a bread knife from his mother, and spent eight hours crafting himself a vee-bottom shortboard. The first Larmont Surfboards retail shop opened in 1973 in Durban, and was eventually joined by branches in Margate, East London, Port Elizabeth, and Cape Town. Larmont made boards for 1977 world champion Shaun Tomson, as well as Michael Tomson, Mike Esposito, Jonathan Paarman, Bruce Jackson, Peers Pittard, and Paul Naude—the cream of South Africa's surfers in the '70s and early '80s.

Larson, George "Peanuts"   Quirky pre–World War II surfer and board-builder from Laguna Beach, California; a model for the irrepressible and irresponsible Southern California surfer. Larson was born (1916) and raised in Laguna, and began surfing in the late '20s. During the depression he made surfboards, usually out of redwood and balsa, using a drawknife, for most of the two or three dozen Laguna surfers. In 1939, Larson rode a 12-foot wave at a break called Church, just south of San Clemente, that became legendary among Southern California surfers of the period. "The whole thing walled up and crashed on him," eyewitness Brennan "Hevs" McClelland recalled in 1953. "Nobody'd ever seen anybody ride a wave that big." Larson, a first-rate raconteur, later told a female friend, "My god, honey baby, that thing was 40-feet high! I was smokin' through the tunnel with my candle lit!" A photo of Larson on a smaller but still impressive wave at Dana Strand, taken around the same time by John "Doc" Ball, became an iconic image of early California surfing. Larson sometimes worked as a Laguna Beach lifeguard, but was essentially unemployed throughout his life. He died in 1986 at age 70, still living at his mother's trailer house in Laguna Beach. Larson is featured in two surfing photo books: Ball's seminal *California Surfriders* (1946) and Don James's *1936–1942: San Onofre to Point Dume, Photographs by Don James* (1996).

Larson, Merv Futuristic wave-ski surfer from Ventura, California; winner of the 1969 Rincon Surf-Ski and Kayak Championships. Larson was born (1940) in the city of Orange, California, raised in Huntington Beach, and began bodysurfing at age seven. In 1959 he saw kayaker Don Golden riding at Doheny Beach in Orange County, and was intrigued; in 1965 he installed footstraps, a small seat, and a seat belt to an old paddleboard, building his first wave-ski. The board originally had a fin, but when it broke off Larson found he preferred the wider range of motion allowed by a finless craft, and discovered that he could get more than enough forward thrust by using a paddle blade as a fin. Larson also wired a small waterproof transistor radio to his white plastic crash helmet, and was able to ride to music. By 1968, Larson and fellow Southern California experimental surfer George Greenough, a kneerider, were the two most advanced surfers in the world; from atop his buoyant nine-foot ski, Larson was able to mix long-arc carves, hairpin turns, spins, slides, reverses, and barrel rolls in a way that stand-up surfers wouldn't begin to match for 20 years. In *Surfer* magazine's 1970 spoof "End of the World" issue, Larson was chosen to be the only surfer allowed into the apocalypse-surviving time capsule. "Who," the magazine asked, saluting Larson as the New Adam, "is better equipped to carry the banner of surfing into time immemorial?"

Larson won the 1968 American Olympic trials for the one-kilometer kayak flat-water paddle sprint, and traveled that summer to Mexico City to compete in the Olympics, where he was eliminated in the early rounds. During the '70s, he won the wave-ski division of the Santa Cruz Surf Fest five times. From 1972 to 1996 he owned Merv Larson Aquatic Designs, a small wave-ski-building company in the Santa Barbara/Ventura area. Larson appeared in two surf movies, *Waves of Change* and *Pacific Vibrations,* both from 1970. *See also* wave-ski.

Lassen, Chris Hawaiian surfer/artist best known for his swirling, vividly colored oil or acrylic seascapes, many of them dense with animals, stars, planets, coral fans, and breaking waves. Lassen was 11 in 1967

when his family moved to Maui from Mendocino, California. He began surfing (and later took up sailboarding), taught himself how to paint and sketch, and sold his first hand-painted T-shirt design to a local gift shop while in the eighth grade. He was soon recognized as both an athlete and artist. Lassen appeared sailboarding in commercials for Swatch and Quasar in 1985, and three years later was featured on the cover of *Surfer* magazine. In 1991, he and agent/partner Jona-Marie Price opened the multimillion-dollar Gallerie Lassen in Lahaina, Maui's tourist capital. Additional Lassen galleries soon opened in Waikiki, Key West, Laguna Beach, San Francisco, Las Vegas, La Jolla, and Seattle. The blond-haired Lassen, who often dressed in skintight pants, unbuttoned shirt, and black leather jacket, was the subject of dozens of magazine features; he also appeared on *Baywatch* and *Lifestyles of the Rich and Famous.* In Japan—where he was treated as art royalty in the '80s and '90s and where his paintings sold for $100,000 each—he was the subject of a weekly television show. Lassen viewed himself as an environmental artist (he created a United Nations commemorative stamp in 1992 honoring the world's oceans), and once said that his work "expresses the interconnectedness between Earth's life forms and the creative forces of the universe." Not everyone agreed. *Surfer* called Lassen's work "narcoleptically banal," and said that his environmentalism "has the depth and power of Spice Girls feminism." *See also* surf art.

late takeoff Beginning the takeoff at the last possible moment. The late takeoff is often preceded by a rushed paddle up the wave face and a quick frog-kicking spin toward shore as the crest begins to fold over. The later the takeoff, the greater the chances of wiping out. *See also,* air-drop, no-paddle takeoff.

lay forward *See* pigdog, rail grab.

layback Spine-twisting maneuver in which the surfer, during a frontside cutback or backside tube-ride, bends the upper back and shoulders onto the wave face. The layback cutback was popularized in the mid-1970s by 1976 world champion Peter Townend of Australia. At the beginning of the cutback, the surfer would drop the rear arm, raise the front arm for balance, fall back onto the wave face, and direct the board in an arcing turn so that it ended up beneath his center of gravity, at which point the rider used leg strength to push back to a standing position. *Surfing*

Layback

magazine called it "surfing's newest, most radical maneuver" in 1979; two years later, *Surfer* declared it "a silly trick" and "a real dead dog." Surfers had meanwhile developed the backside layback tube stance ("backside" means the rider's back is facing the wave), using more or less the same body arrangement, but while trimming instead of turning to fit more snugly inside the tube. Australia's Simon Anderson memorably used the layback tuberide to win both the Surfabout and Pipeline Masters contests in 1981. The layback tuberide soon developed into the more functional lay-forward tuberide, with the surfer's weight shifted to the front leg. The New School surfers of the early '90s updated the layback cutback as part of their acrobatic, board-sliding repertoire.

Lazer Zap   *See* no-nose.

Lear, Cecil   Diligent surf contest organizer from Belmar, New Jersey; cofounder of the Eastern Surfing Association. Lear was born (1930) in Irvington, New Jersey, raised in nearby Caldwell, received a B.A. in economics from Drew University in 1952, and began surfing 10 years later at age 32. In 1963, Lear formed the Jersey Surfing Association. In late 1967, Lear and Rudy Huber of New York created the Eastern Surfing Association (ESA), and managed a six-event circuit the following year. Lear has served on the ESA board of directors throughout the association's history. In 1968 he was an official at the World Surfing Championships, held in Puerto Rico; from 1969 to 1971 he wrote articles and sold advertising space for *Petersen's*

Surfing magazine. Lear won the 1968 Surfer Cup Award and the 1974 Nancy Katin Outstanding Surfer Award, both for his contribution to organized surfing. In 1996 he was inducted into the East Coast Surf Legends Hall of Fame. Lear is married and has three children. *See also* Eastern Surfing Association.

leash   *See* surf leash.

leash plug   Circular plastic device set flush to the deck of a surfboard near the tail as a fastening point for a surf leash. The leash plug was invented by California surfboard manufacturer Con Colburn in 1971, and today's plug is much the same as Colburn's prototype: about one-and-a-quarter inches in diameter and three-quarter-inch deep, with a plastic cross-pin around which the nylon leash-end is tied. Before the plug was developed, leashes were usually threaded through a hole drilled into the fin or an eyelet screw behind a removable fin, or attached to a small fiberglass rope bridge (a "leash loop") laminated onto the deck of the board near the tail. The leash plug is also known as a "leash cup." *See also* surf leash.

left   A wave that breaks to the left, from the surfer's shoreward-facing perspective. As viewed from the beach, a surfer on a left will move from left to right. Pipeline, Grajagan, and Cloudbreak are famous left-breaking waves.

left-go-right   Ride-opening maneuver in which a surfer paddles into the wave while angling left, stands, and turns to the right. The expression "left-go-right" was popular in the '50s, '60s, and early '70s, and is today used primarily by longboarders. Similar to "fade" and "whipturn."

legrope   *See* surf leash.

Lennox Head   Rock-lined point located on the North Coast of New South Wales, about 70 miles from the Queensland border, featuring long, fast, hollow, right-breaking surf. Lennox Head was first ridden in early 1962 by two vacationing New Zealanders who came upon the break by chance, then spread the word that night at a pub in nearby Byron Bay. Five Byron surfers rode it the following morning. From the mid-'60s to the early '70s, Lennox was arguably the best-surfed wave in the world, as it became a favorite of shortboard revolution leaders Nat

Young, George Greenough, and Bob McTavish, as well as 1968 Australian national champion Keith Paull and 1968 World Championships finalist Russell Hughes. Lennox was at the time located at the end of a dirt track, in the heart of Australian dairy country, about seven miles from the highway. Because it was depicted as New South Wales's own version of Shangri-la in *The Innermost Limits of Pure Fun* (1970) and other period surf movies, Lennox became the first break in rural Australia to become insufferably crowded, and by the early '90s, it was common to find 100 surfers in the water, even on average days. Lennox breaks often, but is best during autumn and winter, with a powerful east-southeast swell running. The surf here doesn't often get over eight foot, but rides will occasionally last for more than 300 yards. Lennox has been featured in a number of surf movies and videos, including *The Young Wave Hunters* (1964), *Sultans of Speed* (1987), *Oz on Fire* (1991), and *Stash* (2002). A 1990 issue of *Australia's Surfing Life* magazine listed Lennox as one of the country's 10 best waves. *See also* North Coast, New South Wales.

Letham, Isabel   Lively and adventurous surfer from Sydney's Freshwater Beach; sometimes referred to as "the mother of Australian surfing." On December 23, 1914, the 15-year-old Letham rode tandem with surfer and Olympic gold medal swimmer Duke Kahanamoku during the Hawaiian's famous wave-riding demonstration at Freshwater. It was later revealed that the sport had been introduced to Sydney at least four years earlier, but for decades Letham was celebrated as the first native Australian surfer. Nearly amphibious as a child, Letham was nonetheless frightened when she paddled out with Kahanamoku at Freshwater. On the first of their four rides together, she later recalled, "He got me by the scruff of the neck and pulled up on the board." Two weeks later they again rode tandem at nearby Dee Why Beach, in front of several thousand spectators. Letham continued to surf after Kahanamoku returned to Hawaii, as did an ever-growing number of surfing newcomers, and the sport quickly became an established part of Australian beach life.

Letham later traveled to America (surfing in Waikiki on her way to the mainland) and lived in New York, Los Angeles, and San Francisco; she worked most of her life as a swimming instructor. A 1961 Manly Beach newspaper article noted that the 62-year-old Letham "still gets a thrill from riding a

Isabel Letham

breaker," and in 1978 the never-married Letham was named as "grand patron" of the newly formed Australian Women Surfriders Association. She was inducted into the Australian Hall of Fame in 1993; the following year she attended the unveiling of a Duke Kahanamoku statue at the north Freshwater headland, and gave a short but spirited interview to *Australia's Surfing Life* magazine. Refusing to give her age, Letham feigned shock when told she was 95. "Ah, no! I'm only about 65, surely!" Letham died in 1995, and her ashes were scattered just past the surf line at Freshwater.

Liberia   Tropical western African country founded in 1822 by freed American slaves, located about four degrees north of the equator and featuring 300 miles of rugged southwest-facing coastline. In 1975, California surf pilgrims Craig Peterson and Kevin Naughton, having already traveled much of the West African coast, discovered a perfectly shaped left pointbreak tube at Robert's Port, near the Liberian/Sierra Leone border. Braziers, a point located near the town of Marshal, is also first-rate—if somewhat inconsistent—as

Liberia; Kevin Naughton at Robert's Port

are another three or four Liberian points. Most of the coast, however, is filled with sandy jungle-lined beachbreaks. Liberia is open to Atlantic swells from the west, southwest, and south, and picks up small waves all year. The biggest surf, usually between four and eight feet, generally arrives from April to July. The Liberian coastal weather is often stifling, averaging 80 degrees for most of the year, then jumping to the mid- and high 90s, with 100 percent humidity, from March to June. Ocean temperatures remain near 80 all year. As of 2003, Liberia was home to fewer than a dozen native surfers.

Liddell, Mark   Fast-talking Hawaiian regularfooter from Honolulu who, along with best friend Montgomery "Buttons" Kaluhiokalani, all but defined Hawaiian hotdog surfing in the mid-1970s. Liddell was born (1960) in Hollywood, California, raised in Honolulu, and began surfing at Waikiki in 1968. His nimble, spidery style of riding was a perfect match for the fast-cornering stinger surfboard, introduced by Honolulu surfer/shaper Ben Aipa in 1974. Liddell and Honolulu neighbor Kaluhiokalani began surfing together in 1975, and were featured on the cover of *Surfer* magazine the following year, casually posed on the harbor rocks near Kaisers, a favorite Waikiki haunt. Neither Liddell nor Kaluhiokalani had much luck on the world pro tour, but they dominated the popular Waikiki breaks for more than five years, set a new small-wave performance standard—both mastered a looping 360-degree turn 15 years before Kelly Slater and his New School peers made the move famous—and in general seemed to be having a better time than anybody in the sport. Liddell began shaping surfboards in 1984, was soon hired by Wave Rid-

ing Vehicles and Blue Hawaii, and in 1990 opened his own shop, Island Energy Surfboards. He appeared in more than a half-dozen surf movies and videos, including *Playgrounds in Paradise* (1976) and *Many Classic Moments* (1978).

lifeguarding and surfing   Lifeguarding and surfing are now only casually linked, but in the first half of the 20th century the two grew and developed almost as one. As beachside recreation soared in popularity in America during the first two decades of the 1900s, aquatic lifesaving techniques and methods were developed by the Red Cross, the YMCA, and the Boy Scouts, then adopted by beachfront municipalities and beach-based entrepreneurs. Hawaiian surfer George Freeth, billed as "the man who walks on water," after he was hired by California railroad executive and land developer Harry Huntington in 1907, introduced the sport to Southern California by giving surfing demonstrations for tourists in front of Huntington's hotel in Redondo Beach. He also worked as a swimming instructor and lifeguard at Huntington's saltwater plunge, and was frequently called upon to make surf rescues; Freeth was hailed in late 1908 by the *Los Angeles Times* and other local papers after he helped save 11 Japanese fishermen during heavy surf at Venice Beach. Others had lifeguarded along the American coast in one form or another before, but Freeth is generally credited as the country's first full-time ocean lifeguard.

Primitive lifeguarding methods were being used on beaches in Sydney, Australia, in the late 19th century, and by 1910 ocean-rescue "surf clubs," with subsidized waterfront clubhouses, had been established on popular Sydney beaches. When Hawaii's Duke Kahanamoku gave the first in a series of Australian surfing demonstrations in 1914, he was escorted into the waves by the Manly Beach Surf Club; for decades following, the sport was practiced almost exclusively by Australian Surf Life Saving Association "clubbies."

Friction between lifeguards and surfers in Southern California began in 1959, when a newly commissioned lifeguard ordered Malibu surfer and beach kahuna Terry "Tubesteak" Tracy to extinguish his small beach fire. Depressed by the fact that law had moved onto his favorite beach, Tracy soon quit surfing. Other Malibu surfers also resented the new lifeguard presence, and through the years the wooden lifeguard tower standing near the top of the point was periodically set on fire. (Hollywood created its own Malibu surfer/lifeguard flashpoint in 1978's *Big Wednesday,* when guard Jack Barlow, speaking through a bullhorn, tells drunken friend Matt Johnson there's a "county ordinance" against sleeping in the sand. Johnson responds with "Stuff it, *lifeguard,*" gets decked, and is ordered off the beach.) Enmity between Southern California surfers and lifeguards grew in the '60s with the introduction of the surfing-prohibited "blackball" flag, flown from lifeguard towers during summer months.

A Los Angeles County lifeguard team led by Malibu surfer Tommy Zahn and big-wave rider Greg Noll visited Sydney, Australia, in 1956 to compete in an international lifeguard event. The Californians had brought their new Malibu chip surfboards—smaller, lighter, and far more maneuverable than the Australian-made hollow "toothpicks"—and during their free time they hit the surf and showed the Aussies how to do turns while angling across the wave face. Local surfers immediately picked up on what the Americans were doing; shortly thereafter, Australian surfing began to take on its own identity, separate from that of the surf lifesaving clubs.

Some of the world's best surfers have worked as lifeguards—particularly in California during the '40s and '50s and in Hawaii from the '70s to present day—including Tom Blake, Pete Peterson, Eddie Aikau, Butch Van Artsdalen, and Mike Cunningham. *See also* surf boat.

Lightning Bolt Surfboards   Surfboard and surf accessories company founded in Honolulu, Hawaii, in 1970, by Gerry Lopez and Jack Shipley, and turned into an industry powerhouse with the help of California surfwear executive Duke Boyd. Lopez and Shipley were both working at a Honolulu surf shop called Surf Line Hawaii in early 1970; the 21-year-old Lopez was on the cusp of becoming the universally acknowledged master surfer at Pipeline, the world's best-known surf break, and had been shaping surfboards since 1968; Shipley was an ace Surf Line Hawaii salesman and a surf competition judge. They bought the old Hobie Surfboards outlet on nearby Kapiolani Boulevard in the summer of 1970. Lopez had been using a colored lightning bolt emblem on his boards since 1969, and since the dark-haired goofyfooter was going to be the new company's one and only marketing tool, they named the new shop Lightning Bolt Surfboards. (Hansen Surfboards in

California had introduced a short-lived Lopez-designed Lightning Bolt model in early 1970.)

Bolt quickly became a kind of showroom/co-op for many of the best Hawaiian board shapers, including Bill Barnfield, Tom Parrish, Reno Abellira, Barry Kanaiaupuni, Tom Nellis, and Tom Eberly, all of whom worked out of their own houses (Bolt had no factory of its own) and brought their finished boards to the Bolt retail store, each one trimmed with the distinctive lightning bolt logo on the deck. Shipley opened a second Bolt outlet on Maui in 1972. He also began distributing free Bolt surfboards to nearly all the top surfers who visited the North Shore of Oahu each winter to compete in the pro contests, which meant the Bolt logo was endlessly featured on magazine covers, and in surf movies. The overwhelming majority of the world's best surfers rode Bolt surfboards from 1973 to 1978 while in Hawaii, including world champions Mark Richards, Wayne Bartholomew, Shaun Tomson, and Margo Oberg, and ace North Shore riders like Jeff Hakman and Rory Russell. Board sales never went above 2,500 units a year (mainly in Hawaii), but no board-making label before or since has dominated the surf media the way Bolt did in the mid-'70s. By 1975, the Bolt logo had been copied by so many board-makers around the world that the company placed a full-page ad in *Surfer* magazine asking that manufacturers "create their own symbols, and not use ours." (Bolt boards were even used to political ends during the tension-filled North Shore winter of 1976–77, when Hawaiian surfers, upset at the way visiting Australians had crowed after winning the big competitions the previous year,

Lightning Bolt surfboards; Australian Mark Richards with his 1975 Bolt quiver

demanded that Bolt no longer distribute free boards to visiting pros.)

Former Hang Ten surfwear magnate Duke Boyd had by that time come in as the controlling partner of what was now called the Lightning Bolt Corporation, and the company branched out into surfwear, surf wax, leashes, backpacks, wallets, skateboards, bodyboards, towels, even jewelry. ("We came out with some really shitty stuff," Lopez later acknowledged.) Friction between company heads caused Lopez to sell his share of Bolt in 1980; Shipley stayed on longer, but Bolt was soon viewed by most surfers as bloated and out-of-touch. Bolt products continued to sell well overseas, particularly in Japan, before sales tapered off mid-decade. As of 2003, Lightning Bolt was headquartered in Maui. *See also* Bill Barnfield, Duke Boyd, Gerry Lopez, Tom Parrish, Jack Shipley.

Linden, Gary   Good-natured American surfboard shaper and competition judge from Oceanside, California; founder and owner of Linden Surfboards. Linden was born (1949) in El Centro, California, in the Imperial Valley, raised in the San Diego suburb of Clairemont, and began surfing at age 13. Four years later he started shaping boards in the family garage, and soon founded his own label. Linden spent much of his time in the early and mid-'70s making boards in Brazil. In 1978 he opened Linden Surfboards, a factory/retail outlet in Oceanside, and over the years he made boards for dozens of world tour pros, including Todd Holland, Brad Gerlach, Margo Oberg, Taylor Knox, and Cheyne Horan. Throughout the '80s, Linden, Al Merrick, and Rusty Preisendorfer were regarded as the Holy Trinity of mainland American surfboard shapers.

From 1981 to 1991, while still running his surfboard business, Linden also worked as a judge on the world pro tour, and was meet director for the California-based Stubbies Pro contests. From 1996 to 1998 he served as president of the Association of Surfing Professionals, the world tour organizing group. A dedicated big-wave rider himself, Linden eventually organized big-wave competitions in South Africa, Madeira, and Brazil. His greatest success as a competition director came in 1998, as he supervised the Reef Big-Wave Team World Championships at Killers, on Mexico's Todos Santos Island.

Linden was hired in 2001 as logistics director for the Billabong Odyssey, a three-year search for a ridable 100-foot wave. He also served as the event direc-

tor for the 2002 Margaritaville Longboard Trophy Series. On January 9, 2002, the curly-haired 52-year-old was towed in to a 30-footer at Todos Santos. Linden is married and has two children.

lined up   A wave with a long, evenly tapered wall; the lined-up wave is in contrast to the triangular-shaped "peak" wave. The pointbreak surf found at Kirra, Rincon, and Jeffreys Bay is often beautifully lined up.

lineup   Area just beyond the surf zone where surfers wait for waves. A "tight" lineup is compressed and small; the lineup at Florida's Sebastian Inlet is smaller than a tennis court. In contrast, the lineup at Hawaii's Sunset Beach can stretch out for a hundred yards or more.

lining up   A fixed place in the takeoff area, usually maintained by visual cues on the shore. A good lineup means the surfer can return to a near-exact spot where the best waves are breaking, and allows him to hold position against currents or drift. A lineup can be determined by paddling to the desired spot, turning toward shore, and picking out two aligned landmarks—a beachfront house, for example, set in front of a notch on a distant hillside. By checking and rechecking his position, the surfer with a reliable set of lineup markers will be in the right spot for the next set of approaching waves, while other surfers may drift off unaware on the littoral current. At some breaks, lineup markers might change from day to day, or even hour to hour, depending on the tide, the size of the swell, or (particularly at beachbreaks) alterations in the sandbar. At other breaks, particularly reef- and pointbreaks, the lineup will remain fairly constant.

lip   The upper edge of a wave where it steepens, fringes, and begins to spill over. Although surfers regularly do off-the-lip maneuvers on soft, crumbling, easy-breaking waves, the expression "lip," used alone, generally refers to the cresting portion of a tubing wave. Two surf movies, *Hot Lips and Inner Tubes* (1975) and *Wet Lips* (1983), turned the word into an all-too-easy sexual double entendre. Similar to "curl."

Lis, Steve   Shadowy and undercredited kneeboarder and surfboard designer from San Diego, California; kneeboard division winner in the 1970 United States

Championships, and creator of the wide-backed, split-tailed "fish" design. Lis was born (1951) and raised in San Diego, and began surfing at age 10 at Ocean Beach. He made the original fish in 1967, working out of his family's garage. "I liked to ride pintails," he explained to surf journalist Gary Taylor in 2000, "but my swim-fins"—used by kneeriders to kick into waves—"hung over the side and created drag. So I designed a split-tailed board with the width to support my fins, but at the same time preserve the characteristics of the pintail." Riding almost exclusively at San Diego's highly territorial reefbreaks—Lis became an underground hero for his tuberiding, vertical off-the-lips, and arcing cutbacks. *Surfing* magazine called him one of "the world's best and faster wave-riders" in 1973. By that time a slightly longer version of the fish was being used by stand-up surfers, including Florida's Mike Tabeling, 1971 U.S. champion David Nuuhiwa, and 1972 world champion Jim Blears. Hawaiian pro surfer Reno Abellira brought a fish to Australia in 1976, showed it to young Australian pro Mark Richards, who in turn made some adjustments and developed the twin-fin design, which he used to win four world titles. Knee-joint damage forced Lis to quit kneeriding in 1991; he continues to stand-up surf. *See also* fish, kneeboarding.

Little, Brock   Unflinching big-wave surfer and world traveler from Haleiwa, Hawaii; runner-up in the 1990 Quiksilver in Memory of Eddie Aikau contest at Waimea Bay. Little was born (1967) in Napa, California, moved with his family to Hawaii at age three, and began surfing at age seven. He was a finalist in the menehune division of the 1980 United States Surfing Championships; just over six years later the 145-pound pencil-legged rookie pro placed fourth in the 1986 Quiksilver/Aikau event, held in ragged 20-foot surf at Waimea. Little was 19; Clyde Aikau, Mark Foo, and Ken Bradshaw, the three surfers who placed ahead of him, were 37, 28, and 34, respectively.

Although Little was runner-up to Hawaiian surfer Keone Downing in the 1990 Quiksilver/Aikau, held in spectacular 25 to 30-foot Waimea surf, he stole the show with a gladiatorial wipeout on the biggest wave of the day, and followed up by pulling into the tube on a 20-footer—a rarity in big-wave surfing at the time—and nearly making it out. Little's relaxed, loose-armed style made his big-wave bravado seem all the cooler; he and fellow Hawaiian Darrick Doerner were named as the best Waimea riders in peer polls

Brock Little

conducted in 1990 and 1993. Little went on to place highly in most of the big-wave events over the next few years.

Meanwhile, the sociable Little moonlighted as a photo trip pro, jetting off on dozens of sponsor-funded journeys to Tahiti, Fiji, South Africa, South Australia, France, Spain, Brazil, and Morocco, and to more exotic places like Alaska, Ireland, Nicaragua, Namibia, and Easter Island. Little's job was simply to get his photo in the magazines and to turn up in surf movies and videos. "People ask me what I do for a living, and I do *nothing*," the staccato-voiced surfer candidly told *Interview* magazine in 1991. "I pick up a check in the mail and go surfing. And when the waves aren't good in Hawaii, somebody pays me to surf somewhere else." Little authored nearly 30 articles for *Surfer* and *Surfing* magazines between 1989 to 1997, mainly travel stories and big-wave features. He was the informal mentor to a slightly younger generation of Hawaiian big-wave surfers, including Todd Chesser and Shane Dorian, and was the most vocal proponent of the idea that big-wave riding, rather than being a spiritual exercise or a test of character, was just hugely fun.

Little and fellow Hawaiian big-wave rider Mark Foo both rode Maverick's for the first time on December 23, 1994. Around noon, Foo wiped out on a 15-foot wave while dropping in; Little wiped out on the wave following, bumped into Foo underwater, and was washed into a nearshore rock outcropping, where he struggled mightily to get free and make it ashore. Foo had meanwhile been pushed to the bottom and drowned.

Little has been featured in more than 50 surf movies, videos, and documentaries, including *Amazing Surf Stories* (1986), *Surfers: The Movie* (1990), *The Search II* (1993), *Endless Summer II* (1994), and *In God's Hands* (1998). Working regularly as a Hollywood stuntman since 1999, the never-married Little appeared in *Pearl Harbor* (2001), *Orange County* (2002), and *Windtalkers* (2002). *See also* big-wave surfing.

Llamas, Bud   Barrel-chested goofyfooter from Huntington Beach, California; one of America's top domestic pro competitors in the early and mid-'80s. Llamas was born (1963) in Anaheim, California, and raised in Huntington Beach, where he began surfing at age eight. He won the inaugural National Scholastic Surfing Association (NSSA) championship in 1978, and the following year he won eight of 10 NSSA contests to retain his title. He turned pro in 1980 and won the California Stubbies Trials, and two years later became the Body Glove Grand Prix tour champion. Although he finished runner-up in the 1983 Op Atlantic City Pro, a world tour contest, for the most part Llamas's international career never got off the ground. His reputation had less to do with contest results and more with his gouging turns and first-generation aerials, and throughout the '80s he was Huntington Beach's most exciting surfer. Llamas was featured in the surf movies *Ocean Fever* (1983) and *Shock Waves* (1987); in 2000 he was nominated to the Huntington Beach Surfing Walk of Fame.

localism   Territorial practice whereby resident surfers in a given area try to exclude nonresident surfers through threat, intimidation, and occasionally violence; a predictable, if rarely defensible, surf world response to overcrowding. Localism wasn't named until the late 1960s, but the practice itself predates World War II. Visiting California surfers Gene "Tarzan" Smith and Tom Zahn were both harassed,

Localism; graffiti at Windansea, La Jolla, California

even beaten up, by Hawaiian surfers in the '40s during their visits to Oahu, and a *Surfer* magazine letter writer in 1963 noted that Honolulu surfers were "always fighting" with nonnatives. Two developments set the stage for localism's wider disbursement. First, post–World War II changes in board design encouraged the surfer to perform turns while riding at a tight angle across the wave, and to do so he needed to ride alone. Whereas surfers in previous decades often rode in congenial groups of five or 10 or more, "one surfer/one wave" became the new performance requirement, and put a higher demand on wave resources. Second, and more important, by the late '50s the sport began attracting hundreds, then thousands, of newcomers, which marked the beginning of an exclusionary "we were here first" attitude at some of California's better breaks.

As noted in a 1969 issue of *Sports Illustrated,* a professional surfing competition at Steamer Lane was sabotaged by a group of Santa Cruz locals—reasoning that the contest and the ensuing media coverage would bring new surfers to the lineup—who shoved an unmanned judges' stand over the beachside cliff onto the rocks below. Localism hit an apogee of sorts in Southern California during the 1970s: fights were relatively uncommon, but verbal harassment was rampant, and theft and vandalism were widespread, as nonlocal surfers had their car tires slashed, their windshields broken, or their wallets, boards, or wetsuits stolen. "If you don't live here, don't surf here," "locals only," and "go home" became popular graffiti slogans. Australian surfers meanwhile began writing letters to American surf magazines telling the "yanks" to "stay home or go to Mexico," while a thuggish gang of Hawaiian surfers known as the

Black Shorts began a long, low-grade terror campaign against surfers visiting the North Shore of Oahu.

Localism has since taken root to one degree or another in virtually all populated surfing areas, from Vancouver Island to the Basque country to Western Australia to Mauritius. In *The World Stormrider Guide,* a region-by-region guidebook to surfing breaks, the volatility of local surfers is noted under a "Hazards" section, along with notes on more customary perils such as rip currents, shallow reefs, and dangerous sea life. While California and Hawaii are both less localized than they were in the '70s (in part because the fight against crowds is now seen as hopeless), territorial pockets remain. Lunada Bay in southern Los Angeles County is generally recognized as the surfing world's most localized break, and in some instances—in Oxnard, California, as well as Lunada—law-breaking local surfers have been convicted of assault charges. Localism has been condemned for the most part by the surf press, who often refer to it as a "plague" or "cancer," but at a basic level it's proven to be an effective practice: fervently localized surf breaks such as Lunada are in fact less crowded while nonlocalized spots (Malibu, for one) are overrun with visitors.

A limited form of localism has meanwhile gained support among a small number of surf writers, most notably Australians Nick Carroll and Tim Baker. It's hard to argue against the idea that all waves belong equally to all wave-riders, but the local surfer, having spent years or decades learning and decoding a particular break, might justifiably expect a greater share of waves than a visiting surfer. (Particularly a visiting surfer who arrives in a large group, or one who changes the ambient mood in the water by aggressively taking waves, or one who "shadows" local surfers in the lineup—to name a few of the unwritten nonlocal violations.) Throwing punches and slashing tires to keep the lineup less congested, Carroll and Baker have written, is insupportable. "Dropping in" on nonlocals, or paddling around them to secure a better takeoff position—essentially going out of turn—may be acceptable.

Localism, particularly when accompanied by violence, has frequently attracted the attention of the mainstream news media; articles on localism have appeared in *Newsweek, Esquire, USA Today,* and the *Los Angeles Times.* The California state legislature, however, defeated the antilocalism California Open Waves Act in 1999, as it seemed redundant to laws already on

the books. *Locals Only* was the title of the second album by the California novelty rock band Surf Punks. *See also* Palos Verdes, surf rage, violence and surfing.

Lochtefeld, Tom   Inventive and entrepreneurial surfer/designer from La Jolla, California; architect of the FlowRider standing-wave machine, patented in 1990. Lochtefeld was born (1952) in San Diego, California, raised in Pacific Beach, and began surfing at 10. He graduated in 1974 from the University of San Diego law school, worked as a real estate developer, and cofounded in 1983 the Raging Waters theme park in San Dimas, California. Five years later, along with fellow La Jolla surfer/designer Carl Ekstrom and builder Jeff Clark, he began working on what would become the FlowRider. The wave is created by a thin layer of water shot over a hard-rubber hump, which throws the water up and over into a swirling, stationary wave. The first FlowRider opened in New Braunfels, Texas, in 1991; by 2000, Lochtefeld had designed and installed FlowRiders in Norway, Germany, Japan, Mexico, South Korea, the United Arab Emirates, and dozens of other locations worldwide. The more powerful machines are capable of producing a 12-foot-high wave. *See also* FlowRider.

locked in   *See* tuberiding.

Loehr, Greg   Hardworking surfer and surfboard designer from Brevard County, Florida; winner of the 1974 Eastern Surfing Association (ESA) Championships, and an early advocate of epoxy-made surfboards. Loehr was born (1952) in Brooklyn, New York, and began surfing at age 11 after moving with his family to central Florida. He was runner-up in the 1973 ESA Championships, then won the following year, just before taking fourth in the 1974 United States Surfing Championships. He also won the 1979 Lacanau Pro in France. Loehr's preference for longer, narrower boards served him well when he visited Hawaii in the early and mid-'70s, and the lanky goofy-footer quickly became a standout in the throttling tubes at Pipeline on Oahu's North Shore. Loehr appeared in a small number of surf movies, including *Directions* (1972) and *Fluid Drive* (1974). A surfboard shaper since 1967, Loehr started making boards out of styrofoam blanks and epoxy resin in 1981, and helped create a stronger, lighter, and slightly more expensive alternative to the standard polyurethane foam/polyester resin board. He was inducted into the East Coast

log Synonym for "longboard"; more specifically, a particularly heavy and cumbersome longboard. In 1987, *Surfer* magazine ran a short-lived cartoon strip called "Log," by Tom Finley, about an amiable, beer-bellied, middle-aged longboarder. A longboard surfer is sometimes called a "logger." *See also* longboard.

logjam Pre-1950s expression describing a multi-surfer wipeout that results in a tangle of heavy wooden surfboards. "I remember coming up from a logjam," California board-builder Dale Velzy recalled in 1996, "and my redwood would be halfway through a balsa board. And we'd have to go up on the beach, sit there and pull and tug to get the things loose." The phrase had already fallen out of use by the late '50s, when the newer and lighter polyurethane foam-core surfboards became popular. *See also* plank surfboard.

London, Jack Wildly popular American novelist (1876–1916) from the San Francisco Bay Area, best known as the author of adventure books such as *Call of the Wild* (1903) and *White Fang* (1907); also an early troubadour of surfing—or as London called it, the "royal sport for the natural kings of earth." As a teenager, London worked as a seal hunter in Siberia and as a gold miner in the Klondike; by the time he sold his first story, in 1899, he was an enthusiastic boxer, swimmer, fencer, high jumper, and cyclist. London was a national literary hero in 1907 when he arrived in Honolulu, Hawaii, where he met surfing promoter Alexander Hume Ford on the beach at Waikiki; Ford quickly convinced the famous writer to give the sport a try. On his second day in the water, the 30-year-old London, managed to ride prone for some distance; he remained in the surf for four hours, but wasn't able to stand, and was bedridden the following day with a terrible sunburn. London's 4,000-word account of his surfing experience was published in the *Woman's Home Companion* (then reprinted in London's 1911 *Cruise of the Snark* travelogue); it reads as a how-to guide, a primer on wave formation, and an ode to the surfer mystique. Waves are described as "bull-mouthed monsters," and Irish-Hawaiian surfing master George Freeth is a "sea-god, calm and superb . . . a brown Mercury." American writer Mark Twain, 40 years earlier, had also visited Hawaii, tried surfing,

and written about the experience. But where Twain's account is short, humorous, and offhanded, London's is long, reverent, and awestruck.

Soon we were out in deep water where the big smokers came roaring in. [Just] facing them and paddling seaward over them and through them, was sport enough in itself. One had to have his wits about him, for it was a battle in which mighty blows were struck, on one side, and in which cunning was used on the other side—a struggle between insensate force and intelligence. I soon learned a bit. When a breaker curled over my head, for a swift instant I could see the light of day through its emerald body; then down would go my head, and I would clutch the board with all my strength. Then would come the blow, and to the on-looker on shore I would be blotted out. In reality the board and I have passed through the crest and emerged in the respite of the other side. I should not recommend those smashing blows to an invalid or delicate person. There is weight behind them, and the impact of the driven water is like a sand-blast.

London's account of surfing was widely read, and contributed to the sport's early growth. "Arguably," a biographer later wrote, "Jack London's most enduring memorial was his successful transplanting of the sport of surfing form Waikiki to the West Coast of America." *See also* books and surfing.

long john Armless wetsuit design covering a surfer's chest, trunk, and legs, originally made for skin and scuba diving. The long john, along with the no-legs short john and the front-zip jacket, was one of the first wetsuits used by surfers. It was often worn by itself, but surfers looking for maximum insulation in the '50s, '60s, and early '70s would layer a wetsuit jacket over a long john. The long john's popularity began to wane in the early '70s, with the introduction of the one-piece fullsuit, and by the early '80s the surfing-designed long john was all but obsolete. *See also* short john, wetsuit.

longboard, longboarding Type of surfing performed on a blunt-nosed surfboard, generally over nine feet long, and often patterned on the smooth, style-conscious form of wave-riding popular in the early and mid-1960s. The terms "longboard" and "longboarding" were coined in the late '60s in response to the shortboard revolution, which put an end to what is sometimes referred to as the original longboard era. The return of longboarding—a slow-building trend in the mid- and late '70s that exploded in the '80s and '90s—is one of the most significant developments in surfing history, detested by some and celebrated by others. "There are only two authentically American artforms," California-born surfer and board-maker Dave Parmenter noted in 1998, "jazz and longboarding." By 2002, longboarders made up an estimated 40 percent of all surfers worldwide.

As the short surfboard went international in 1968, the previous year's models—generally measuring 9'6" by 23" and weighing about 25 pounds—were quickly rendered obsolete. A tiny percentage of surfers (including Malibu legend Lance Carson and *Endless Summer* star Robert August) continued to use longboards, but over the next 10 years the vast majority of surf breaks around the world were ridden exclusively by shortboarders. But during this period, as shortboards continued to get smaller, thinner, and lighter—putting greater demands on the surfer's timing and fitness, and dictating an active, nearly aerobic style of riding—some began to reconsider the easy-to-paddle, smooth-running longboard. In 1973, *Surfer* magazine published "Thinking Longer," a pro-longboard editorial; the following year brought the first ads for "modern longboards," as well as a few small but well-organized longboarding contests. A longboard division was added to the United States Surfing Championships in 1975.

The longboarding ranks swelled in the 1980s, fueled by an American nostalgia trend, by lapsed '60s-era surfers returning to the sport, by surfers looking to increase their wave count (longboards have a huge wave-catching advantage over shortboards), and by the fact that longboards worked beautifully in the kind of small, powerless waves—18-inchers at First Point Malibu, for example—that were all but useless for shortboarding. "There's just something about longboarding that makes you want to grin from ear to ear," California surf journalist Kevin Kinnear wrote in 1986. "The glide is effortless . . . it's like driving a Rolls instead of a Porsche." A men's-only longboard division was added to the Association of Surfing Professionals (ASP) world pro tour in 1986; ASP longboard champions include Nat Young, Stuart Entwistle, Martin McMillan, Rusty Keaulana, Bonga Perkins, Dino Miranda, Joel Tudor, Colin McPhillips, and Beau Young. Winners of the 1999-founded

Women's World Longboard Championships include Californians Cori Shumacher and Kim Hamrock and Daize Shayne of Hawaii.

Animosity between shortboarders and longboarders has been present to one degree or another since the 1970s. San Francisco surfer Mark Renneker wrote in 1997 that surfing is intended to be an adventure, while longboarding is generally "an act of acquiescence, a giving up, a process of resignation." Dave Parmenter responded by noting that most shortboarders were "Children of a Lesser Board who miss waves, flounder behind the curl line, and fling weak, fin-skidding twitch-turns." (A slow-growing percentage of surfers, meanwhile, ride both long- and shortboards.) A second ongoing schism, originating in the early '80s, pits the style-conscious "traditional" longboarders who mostly adhere to the form as it was practiced in the '60s (Joel Tudor is thought to be the group's exemplar) against the "modern" or "progressive" longboarders who borrow heavily from the shortboarder's repertoire, even mixing aerials into their performance. Noseriding is the ultimate maneuver for both groups. Finally, the definition of the longboard itself has been a source of debate, with "egg" and "funboard" hybrids straddling the line between short- and longboards. The narrow-nosed big-wave gun, while roughly the same length, is not a longboard, which is defined primarily by its wide, rounded nose. Sixties-era longboards were all single-fins; today's longboards are equally divided between single- and tri-fins. Today's average 9'6" longboard weighs about 14 pounds.

More than 100 longboard surf videos have been made since the early '90s, including *Longboarding: The Rebirth of Cool* (1993), *Powerglide* (1995), *Adrift* (1996), *Siestas and Olas* (1997), and *Cool and Stylish* (2001). A number of longboard-related books have been published as well, including *Longboarder's Start-Up: A Guide to Longboard Surfing* (1996) and *The Glide: Longboarding and the Renaissance of Modern Surfing* (1998). Longboard-only surf shops began opening in the early '90s. *Longboard,* founded in 1993, the first niche magazine of its kind, was followed by more than a half-dozen similar publications worldwide, including *Pacific Longboarder* in Australia and *Nalu* in Japan. More than 100 longboard clubs and organizations have been formed worldwide; longboard legends events, honoring longboard stars from the '60s, were frequently held in the '90s, and are still occasionally scheduled. Because of their inherent stability, longboards are the near-mandatory board for beginning surfers. *See also* Coalition of Surfing Clubs, *Longboard* magazine, shortboard revolution, Women's World Longboard Championships, World Longboard Tour.

Longboard Collectors Club   *See* surf collectors.

Longboard magazine   Well-crafted glossy surf magazine published out of San Clemente, California, focusing on longboard surfing past and present. *Longboard* was founded by photographer and surf press veteran Guy Motil, and debuted in the summer of 1993 as a quarterly. Former or current *Surfer* magazine editors John Severson, Drew Kampion, Paul Holmes, Jim Kempton, and Sam George have all contributed articles to *Longboard,* as have *San Francisco Chronicle* staff writer Bruce Jenkins and *Honolulu Star-Bulletin* writer Greg Ambrose. *Longboard*'s graphic design is conventional (or "classic," to use a favorite word of *Longboard* editors, writers, and advertisers), and the editorial mix also works within the established form, with an emphasis on travel, competition, and surfer profiles, along with plenty of photo essays. Articles on surfboard and surf memorabilia collections are a regular *Longboard* feature. Motil has served as *Longboard*'s publisher and editor in chief since the magazine's inception; Scott Hulet was editor from 1994 to 1999; Devon Howard has been managing editor since 2000. *Longboard*'s growth has been slow and steady, both in pages per issue (68 for the debut issue; up to 178 in 1999) and issues per year (five in 1994, eight in 2002). *Longboard*'s circulation in 2002 was 40,000. In 2002, the magazine began sponsoring the Longboard Trophy Series, a domestic professional longboarding circuit. *See also* Guy Motil.

Lopes, Pedro "Pepe"   Brazil's first internationally ranked surfer; a finalist in the 1976 Pipeline Masters, and winner of the 1976 Waimea 5000, held in Rio de Janeiro. The vigorous, risk-loving Lopes was born (1957) and raised in Rio, began surfing at age eight, and quickly developed into an accomplished rider in nearly all types of waves. He was 18 when he became the first Brazilian to be invited to the Masters, the world's most prestigious surfing contest; two months earlier, with his Waimea 5000 victory, he became the first from his country to win a world tour event—it was 16 years before Fabio Gouveia earned

Brazil a second world tour victory. From 1988 to 1990, Lopes produced and directed the Alternativa International, a world tour event. Lopes became the world hang-gliding champion 1980, and in 1991, he died in Japan while trying to win a second hang-gliding title.

Lopez, Cory   Nervy goofyfoot pro surfer from Indian Rocks, Florida; world-ranked #3 in '01; younger brother to easygoing Shea Lopez, also a top world tour pro. Lopez was born (1977) and raised on Florida's Gulf Coast, and began surfing as a preschooler. He placed third in the menehune division of the 1989 United States Surfing Championships, and won the boys' division of the 1991 Championships. Lopez qualified for the world pro tour in 1997; two years later during the Gotcha Tahiti Pro, the handsome dark-haired surfer rode deep inside the tube on a pair of big, thick, deadly lefts at Teahupoo, getting annihilated both times and failing to advance to the next round, but setting a world tour standard for reckless cool. Earlier that year, Lopez was part of a first-of-its kind surfing expedition to Cuba, which included his father (who is three-quarters Cuban) and brother. Asked by the surf press afterward if he'd gained a "new perspective on Communism," Lopez answered, "Well, we went to all the museums and stuff, which was cool. I understand it a lot more, but it still seems like a pretty bogus deal." Lopez was by that time known throughout the surf world not only as a fearless tuberider, but as a quick and flexible performance surfer, with gyroscopic balance that often guided him through the most ambitious tailslide and aerial maneuvers. Lopez's rating breakthrough came in 2001, when he returned to Tahiti to win at Teahupoo, and finished the year ranked third. Extremely photogenic, Lopez has been featured in more than 30 surf videos, including *What's Really Goin' Wrong* (1996), *Lost at Sea* (2000), *Iratika* (2001), and *Flight Academy* (2002).

Lopez, Gerry   Hawaiian tuberiding specialist, lauded for his cool-under-fire style at Pipeline in Hawaii, and still regarded as the model of wave-riding elegance and refinement. "What he does is poetry," fellow Pipeline ace Rory Russell once said. "For sheer beauty, no one else even comes close." Lopez was born (1948) and raised in Honolulu, the son of a newspaperman father and a high school teacher mother; he began surfing in Waikiki at age nine, but didn't take the sport up in earnest until high school, when he was greatly influenced by silky-smooth Hawaiian regularfooter Paul Strauch. He won the Hawaiian Junior Championships in 1966, was a three-time finalist in the state titles (1968, 1969, and 1972), and was a finalist in the U.S. Championships in 1969 and 1970. The shortboard revolution had meanwhile enshrined the tuberide as the ultimate surfing maneuver, and while Lopez was in the high-performance vanguard, ricocheting off the curl and doing hairpin cutbacks, he began to focus on riding as far back inside the wave as possible. Taking cues from Pipeline ace Jock Sutherland, Lopez taught himself how to take the simplest but deepest line through the tube, first making the near-vertical drop down the wave face, then turning and positioning himself beneath the curl with an absolute minimum of adjustments, and finally assuming a tranquil posture within the tube itself, knees slightly bent, arms and hands lowered, gaze steady. "One movement, one breath . . . very Zen," three-time world champion surfer Tom Curren said of Lopez's tuberiding at Pipeline. "Like an archer pulling back and letting the arrow fly."

By 1972, progressive surfing was all but defined by images of the sinewy (5'8", 135 pounds) and dark-haired Lopez atop a sleek pintail surfboard decorated with a narrow lightning bolt logo, racing deep inside the Pipeline. Asked a few years later by *Sports Illustrated* magazine how he was able to keep his cool while enclosed in a exploding funnel of water, Lopez said it was partly from choosing the right waves, but also a matter of focus and concentration. "The faster I go out there," the soft-voiced goofyfooter told the magazine, "the slower things seem to happen." He was easily the most-filmed surfer of his generation, and a protracted Lopez-at-Pipeline sequence was built into nearly every surf movie made between 1971 and 1978, including *Morning of the Earth* (1972), *Five Summer Stories* (1972), *Going Surfin'* (1974), *Super Session* (1975), *Tales from the Tube* (1975), and *In Search of Tubular Swells* (1977). While the yoga-practicing Lopez had doubts about the validity of surf competition—"Surfing's like a dance," he said, "and when you're trying to squash your opponents it kind of takes away from that whole experience"—he nonetheless entered most of the pro events in Hawaii, winning the Pipeline Masters in 1972 and 1973, and making the finals in a handful of the meets held at Sunset Beach. He also traveled to Australia to compete during the nascent years of the world pro circuit.

Gerry Lopez

Along with surf contest judge and board salesman Jack Shipley, Lopez opened the first Lightning Bolt Surfboards outlet in the summer of 1970. Mentored by board-making guru Dick Brewer, Lopez had been shaping for three years, and his boards were in demand. Bolt went on to become the decades' biggest and best-known surf company. Lopez sold his interest in Bolt in 1980, and for three years worked as the vice president of marketing for Pipeline surfwear. By that time he was spending at least a few weeks each year surfing in Indonesia, and was one of the first to stay in the tree-house camp at Grajagan in Java; he later said that he actually preferred the long tubes of Grajagan to the shorter, thicker, more intense waves at Pipeline. Lopez had meanwhile moved to Maui, where he continued to shape surfboards under his own Gerry Lopez label; in the mid-'90s, during the developmental years of tow-in surfing, he made boards for tow-in innovators Laird Hamilton and Darrick Doerner; *Surfing* magazine named him as Shaper of the Year for 2002.

In addition to the previously named films, Lopez has appeared in more then 30 other surf movies, videos, and documentaries over the decades, including *Surfers: The Movie* (1990) and *Endless Summer II* (1994). In 2001, he was featured on *Biographies,* an Outdoor Life Network TV series. Lopez also had costarring or cameo roles in nearly a dozen Hollywood films and TV shows, including *Big Wednesday*

(1978), *Conan the Barbarian* (1982), *North Shore* (1987), *Farewell to the King* (1989), and *Baywatch* (1989). *Lopez: The Classic Hawaiian Surfer,* a short illustrated biography, was published in 1982. Between 1969 and 2000, Lopez wrote about 20 surf magazine articles and columns on topics ranging from travel to yoga to tow-in surfing. The Surf Industry Manufacturers Association gave Lopez the Waterman Achievement Award in 1999, and the following year he was inducted into the Huntington Beach Surfing Walk of Fame. He was cited in 1999 as the ninth most influential surfer of the 20th century in a special issue of *Surfer* magazine. Lopez is married and has one child. In 1992 he moved with his family to Bend, Oregon, where he opened a small snowboard manufacturing company. *See also* Lightning Bolt Surfboards, Pipeline, soul surfing, tuberiding.

Lopez, Shea   Smooth and powerful pro surfer from Indian Rocks, Florida; world-ranked #11 in 2000 and 2002. Lopez was born (1974) and raised on the Gulf Coast of Florida, and began surfing as a toddler, along with younger brother Cory. Lopez was a versatile high school athlete, and received college baseball scholarship offers. He meanwhile performed well as a juniors division amateur surfer, winning the 1990 National Scholastic Surfing Association Nationals and placing third in the juniors division of the 1992 World Championships. Lopez had no trouble making it to the lower echelon of the Association of Surfing Professionals world pro tour ratings in the mid-'90s, but most observers thought he lacked the killer instinct to move up: "Pretty, nice hair, nice white teeth," as described by an anonymous competitor in 1996, after Lopez placed 34th for the season. "Surfs good but he's going to be eaten alive on next year's tour." Lopez instead jumped ahead 20 slots, finishing 14th in 1997 and three years later he hit #11 for the first time. A well-built goofyfooter (6'0", 170 pounds), Lopez is respected both for his muscular turns in bigger surf, as well as his flashy small-wave acrobatics. He's appeared in more than two dozen surf videos, including *Progression Sessions* (1994), *Voluptuous* (1996), and *Newborn* (1999).

Los Angeles, Los Angeles County   Sunny, crowded, history-rich surfing area located in central Southern California; the birthplace of modern surf culture; current or former home to surf world icons such as George Freeth, Pete Peterson, Mickey Dora, Dale Velzy, Gidget, Malibu, John "Doc" Ball, Bud Browne, Greg Noll, and the Beach Boys. The 76-mile Los Angeles County coastline can be divided into three general surfing areas: 1) The Palos Verdes Peninsula, a hilly 27-square-mile promontory located in southwest Los Angeles County, is home to the wealthy communities of Rancho Palos Verdes and Palos Verdes Estates, as well as a small number of reef- and pointbreaks, including Indicator, Haggerty's, and the highly localized Lunada Bay. 2) The sandy and densely suburban beach cities of Santa Monica Bay, including Redondo, Hermosa, and Manhattan (collectively known as South Bay), as well as Venice and Santa Monica, all of which can produce snappy beachbreak waves. 3) The Malibu area, home to a series of rock-lined pointbreaks, including Sunset, Topanga, and Surfrider Beach. The rarely surfed Catalina and San Clemente Islands are also part of Los Angeles County. Los Angeles receives surf all year: Malibu and a small number of other area breaks require swells from the south or southwest, which generally arrive in late summer and early fall; most L.A. breaks are best on north or west swells, which commonly hit between late fall and early spring. Summer surf in Los Angeles is generally between two and four foot, but can drop off to nothing; winter surf is dependably three to five foot, but gets up to eight foot a few times each year, and can go as big as 12 or 15 foot—most notably at Lunada Bay. Average midday coastal air temperatures range from the mid-70s in summer to the low 60s in winter; water temperatures range from the low 70s to the mid-50s. Crowds are the primary Los Angeles County surfing hazard.

Hawaii's George Freeth introduced surfing to Los Angeles in 1907 at Venice Beach. (Freeth was long believed to be mainland America's first surfer, but it was later discovered that three Hawaiian brothers had ridden in Santa Cruz in the mid-1880s.) Surfing patriarch Duke Kahanamoku visited the Los Angeles area in the 1910s and '20s and helped popularize the sport; by the early '30s, Santa Monica surfer and lifeguard Pete Peterson was regarded as the best surfer on the coast, while Hollywood's Gard Chapin soon earned a reputation as the sport's most progressive rider. Palos Verdes Cove and Long Beach Flood Control were two of the most popular breaks on the coast; Malibu, first ridden by surf innovator Tom Blake in 1927, was beginning to earn a reputation as well. The Palos Verdes Surf Club, founded in 1935 by pioneering surf photographer John "Doc" Ball (whose work was published in *Life,* the *Los Angeles Times, Popular*

Mechanics, and National Geographic), wasn't the first club of its kind in mainland America, but was the model for the era. The Art of Wave Riding, written by Hollywood bodysurfer Ron Drummond and sometimes referred to as the first book on surfing, was published in 1931; Ball's California Surfriders—filled primarily with photographs of Los Angeles–area waves and surfers—was published in 1946. Pacific Systems Homes in south Los Angeles had meanwhile become the first company to mass-produce surfboards.

The peak years for the Los Angeles County surf scene were just after World War II. Malibu, with its long and perfectly tapered waves, was by this time generally regarded as the world's best surf break; a group of Malibu-based board designers—including Bob Simmons, Joe Quigg, Matt Kivlin, and Dale Velzy—transformed the surfboard in just a few years from cumbersome 50-pound planks to foiled and tapered 25-pound "chips" that could be controlled and maneuvered. Los Angeles surfers like Kivlin, Dewey Weber, Mickey Muñoz, and Les Williams set and reset the performance standards in the mid-'50s; Mickey Dora, Mike Doyle, Kemp Aaberg, and Lance Carson came to the fore by the end of the decade, with the charismatic Dora also setting the parameters for the surfer/outlaw. Velzy had meanwhile opened what has been called the first surf shop (in Manhattan Beach in 1949), while Santa Monica school teacher Bud Browne debuted the first surf movie (Hawaiian Surfing Movies, in 1953). Dive N' Surf, founded in 1952 in Redondo Beach, is credited, along with Jack O'Neill's San Francisco Surf Shop, as the first company to manufacture and sell surfing wetsuits. The Los Angeles Surf Fair, held from 1962 to 1964 in Santa Monica, was the surf industry's original trade show; the 1965 KHJ Hermosa competition is sometimes cited as the first professional surf contest. South Bay's Hermosa Beach had by then become a surfboard manufacturing powerhouse, second only to Huntington Beach in neighboring Orange County, with companies owned by Hap Jacobs, Greg Noll, Dewey Weber, and Rick Stoner all producing thousands of boards per season.

Los Angeles writers, movie producers, and musicians began making regular contributions to surf culture, beginning in 1957 with the publication of Gidget by Brentwood novelist Frederick Kohner. Columbia Pictures' version of Gidget was released in 1959; the Hawthorne-raised Beach Boys hit the national charts in 1962 with "Surfin' Safari," and West L.A.'s Jan and

Dean followed the next year with "Surf City." (Surf music soon died out, but Hollywood would intermittently continue to produce surf movies, including Big Wednesday, North Shore, In God's Hands, and Blue Crush.)

Pacific Palisades surfer Rolf Aurness won the 1970 World Surfing Championships, but Los Angeles County had by that time lost its surf world preeminence. Overcrowding was partly to blame, along with a hard-to-define lack of drive—it's been said that the area is weighed down by its own history. Neighboring Orange County had by 1970 taken over as surfings industrial hub (Body Glove Wetsuits remained a big industry player; Syderboards would later become one of the country's biggest boardmakers; both are located in Hermosa Beach), while top riders in Orange County, San Diego County, and later Santa Cruz County soon eclipsed their Los Angeles contemporaries.

Los Angeles was home to both the United States Surfing Association (in the mid-'60s) and the Western Surfing Association (from 1968 to 1993). The Malibu Invitational was one of the biggest events of the early and mid-'60s; Malibu also hosted the 1981 Instinct U.S. Pro, the first world tour event held in California and the 1994 World Longboard Championships. Los Angeles has over the decades been home to dozens of surf world notables, including top surfers (Tommy Zahn, Vicki Flaxman, Johnny Fain, J Riddle, Mike Purpus, Allen Sarlo, Willy Morris, Jimmy Gamboa), writers (Bill Cleary, Peter Dixon, Craig Stecyk, Jamie Brisick), and photographer/filmmakers (Don James, Leroy Grannis, Hal Jepsen, Scott Dittrich, Mike Balzer, Jim Russi). Surf magazines published out of Los Angeles include the Surfer's Annual (1960), Surfing Illustrated (1962–67), So-Cal Surfing News (1963), Petersen's Surfing (1963–64, 1968–70), Surf Guide (1963–65), H2O (1979–2001), and Wahine (1995–2002). As of 2002, Los Angeles County was home to roughly 250,000 surfers and 90 surf shops. Los Angeles County surf breaks are detailed in Surfing Guide to Southern California (1963), Surfing California (1973), and The Stormrider Guide North America (2002). See also Hollywood and surfing, Malibu, Palos Verdes.

Los Angeles Surf Fair   The original surfing industry trade show, sponsored by Surf Guide magazine and radio station KRLA, held in 1962, 1963, and 1964 at the Santa Monica Civic Auditorium. The Los Angeles Surf Fair, precursor to today's Action Sports Retailer

(ASR) and Surf Expo trade shows, was designed to showcase the latest in surfing equipment, media, and paraphernalia. Because it was also meant to boost the sport's image (a 1962 issue of the *Saturday Evening Post* reported that many surfers were "roughnecks who ruin the ocean for swimming, drink and go on rampages . . ."), Surf Fair exhibitors for the most part looked the very soul of propriety, in ties, slacks, and blazers, and neatly combed hair. While a small number of Surf Fair booths were taken up by wetsuit companies, surfwear producers, surfing clubs, surf publications, or surf filmmakers, the majority of floor space in the exhibitors' hall was claimed by surfboard manufacturers, with well-known brands like Hobie, Con, Weber, and Jacobs vying for attention with start-ups like Diwain, Pacific Coast, and Skag. The event was open to the public, as well as retailers and manufacturers.

For the 1963 Surf Fair, attractions in the 3,000-seat main auditorium included surf movies by Bud Browne and Bob Evans; surf band performances by the Beach Boys, the Surfaris, and the Surf-Tones; a beauty contest; surf art; and exhibitions for woodies and vintage surfboards. A skateboard competition was held outside, while a skimboard contest was staged at the foot of nearby Pico Avenue, along with the Santa Monica Mid-Winter Surfing Championships. The Los Angeles Surf Fair was also known as the Surf-O-Rama. The third and final edition, in 1964, was presented by surf filmmaker Don Brown. *See also* Action Sports Retailer Trade Expo, Surf Expo.

Louisiana   *See* Gulf of Mexico.

low-pressure system   Storm-producing convergence of warm and cold air, circular or oblong in shape, filled with wet, windy, unstable weather; ocean-centered low-pressure systems create ground swell and are the world's primary source of high-quality waves. Low-pressure areas are formed as separate bands of cold and warm air meet and begin spiraling around each other, counterclockwise in the Northern Hemisphere and clockwise in the Southern Hemisphere. As the wind spiral rises it forms an atmospheric dome, which in turn lowers the barometric pressure. The rising air cools, condenses, and forms storm clouds. Swell generation, meanwhile, is the result of winds circulating along the perimeter of the storm. Generally speaking, swell size is determined by the duration and mobility of the low-pressure system (long-lasting, slow-moving storms produce bigger waves), how "deep" the low is (a lower millibar reading translates into higher winds), and the distance along the storm-front. As a rule, cold air will be found to the immediate north and west of a low-pressure system, while warm air will likely be found to the south and east. *See also* high-pressure system, surf forecasting.

Lowe, Michael   Husky pro surfer from Wollongong, New South Wales, Australia; world-ranked #6 in 2002, and a natural in large, hard-breaking tubes. Lowe was born (1977) and raised in Wollongong, began surfing at age eight, and won virtually every under-18 title available in Australia, including the juniors division of the 1995 National Titles. He was accepted to the Wollongong University law school, but turned it down to become a full-time pro surfer in 1996. A heavyset goofyfoot (5′9″, 180 pounds), Lowe rode best at powerful breaks like Teahupoo and Pipeline, and proved to be an inspirational tuberider. He meanwhile earned a reputation as the brightest and best-educated surfer of his peer group (he offhandedly quoted the Duke of Gloucester from Shakespeare's *Henry VI* in a 1995 *Australia's Surfing Life* interview), and as one of the most stubborn: after losing a man-on-man heat in the 1997 Pipeline Masters, Lowe walked up the beach, punched a tree, broke his hand, and spent Christmas in a cast. Lowe had his best pro season in 2002, winning the Quik-

Michael Lowe

silver Pro in Fiji, and runner-up in the Billabong Pro at Jeffreys Bay, to finish the year at #6. Lowe has appeared in a small number of surf videos, including *Thunder* (1997) and *E2K* (2000).

Lucas, Jimmy   Regularfoot surfer from Honolulu, Hawaii; a standout among the first wave of shortboarders in the late 1960s, known as the "Hawaiian Impala" for his graceful style. Lucas was born (1949) and raised in Honolulu, and began surfing as a schoolboy on a homemade board built by his mother. He was 17 when he competed in the 1966 World Surfing Championships, held in San Diego, California; by the turn of the decade he was described by some as the most naturally talented surfer in the world. Lucas used the open-knee stance popular with Hawaiian surfers of the period, linked his turns together beautifully, and was fearless at places like Haleiwa and Sunset Beach on the North Shore of Oahu. He continued to enter surf contests in his late teens and early 20s—finishing runner-up to Jeff Hakman in the 1973 Hang Ten American Pro—but otherwise was almost completely removed from the commercial surf scene. "You never hear of Jimmy Lucas," East Coast surfer Bruce Valluzzi said in 1971, "because he's not where they're taking pictures, and he's not endorsing anybody's surfboard." Lucas appeared in a small number of surf movies, including *The Natural Art* (1969) and *Super Session* (1975).

Lueras, Leonard   Writer, publisher, and photographer from Honolulu, Hawaii; best known as the author of the handsome and authoritative *Surfing: The Ultimate Pleasure,* a large-format illustrated history of the sport published in 1984. Lueras was born (1945) in Albuquerque, New Mexico, raised in Southern California, and began surfing in 1959. He received a B.A. in communications from California Western University in San Diego in 1967, then began a 15-year stint as a reporter for the *Honolulu Advertiser. Surfing,* Lueras's first surfing book, earned rave reviews from the surf press and was a steady seller for more than 10 years. The prose in *Surfing* is both thorough and heartfelt; in the book's introduction, Lueras recalls paddling out at Doheny, a popular Southern California surf break, and picking up his first wave. "I didn't fall; the board didn't 'pearl'; and together we didn't—as they say in Hawaii—make ass. Instead, we slid forward and maintained an improbable kinetic energy all our own, and, for the first time, I stood up and moved

into a new and exhilarating world that has held me transfixed ever since." One year after *Surfing* was published, Lueras moved to Bali, where he wrote, designed, and did photographic work for a series of large-format books on Indonesia and other southeast Asian countries. He later returned to his favorite sport with a pair of guidebooks—*Surfing Indonesia* (1999) and *Surfing Hawaii* (2001)—both cowritten with his son, Lorca. Lueras's work has also been published in *Time, Rolling Stone,* and *Vogue. See also* Surfing: The Ultimate Pleasure.

lull   Calm period between waves, or between sets of waves. Lulls tend to be longer the farther a wave-producing storm is from the break itself. In big beachbreak and pointbreak surf, lulls are often necessary to allow a surfer entry to the lineup. If succeeding lulls become longer in duration, it generally means the surf is fading.

Lunada Bay   See Palos Verdes.

Lynch, Barton   Bright, expansive, rubber-faced Australian pro surfer from Sydney's Whale Beach, 1988 world pro tour champion. Lynch was born (1963) in Sydney's Manly Beach, the son of a policeman, and raised in Whale Beach. He began surfing at age eight; in 1981 he finished runner-up in the juniors division of the Australian National Titles; two years later, just after turning professional, he won the highly competitive Pro Junior event. On the world pro tour, his year-end ranking shot up from 13th in 1983 to eighth in 1984 to runner-up in 1985; the following year he dropped to 12th, then charged back in 1987 to finish third. The slightly built Lynch (5'9", 147 pounds) wasn't possessed of natural talent on the order of fellow world champions Tom Curren or Kelly Slater, but he rode with great polish, flow, and intelligence, and had a wickedly effective set of backside turns in and around the curl.

Lynch's last-minute dash to the 1988 world title came on the final day of the final event of the season—the Billabong Pro, held in perfect eight to 12-foot tubes at Pipeline in Hawaii—and is counted as one of the pro tour's most thrilling episodes. Lynch was third in the ratings as the day began, behind fellow Australians Damien Hardman and Tom Carroll, both of whom were eliminated in dramatic fashion before midday. Lynch then defeated three-time world champion Tom Curren in the quarterfinals to earn a semifinal match against Glen Winton; a win would give him the championship, a loss meant Hardman would win. Winton built a solid lead through the first half of the match, but Lynch came back with a brilliant series of tuberides for the victory. He then won the final against Aussie teenager Luke Egan for good measure. Over the course of a 15-year pro career, Lynch placed in the top four eight times, a world tour record. He won 17 world tour events, including the Op Pro in 1987 and 1991, and the 1991 Rip Curl Pro. He competed in the 1990 Quiksilver in Memory of Eddie Aikau big-wave contest at Waimea Bay; in 1993 he won the World Qualifying Series tour. Lynch meanwhile earned a reputation as one of the sport's wittiest and most articulate figures, and for his willingness to express views outside what he correctly viewed as a narrow surf world orthodoxy. Surfing, he said in a 1989 interview, was nothing more than "another outlet for making yourself feel good," and shouldn't serve as "the be-all and end-all of your life." Surfers, he continued, were on the whole the most "self-righteous, cocky and judgmental group of people you'll find anywhere in the world."

Lynch appeared in more than three dozen surf movies, videos, and documentaries, including *Amazing Surf Stories* (1984), *Gripping Stuff* (1987), *Surfers: The Movie* (1990), and *Legends: An Australian Surfing Perspective* (1994). In 1989 and 1990 he wrote a monthly "Learn to Surf" column for *Surfing* magazine. In 1997, Lynch and fellow Sydney-born world champion Damien Hardman formed a management and consulting firm called the Surfers Group Limited. Since 2000, Lynch has produced *RA: The Boardriders Show,* a weekly half-hour program for the Foxtel network. He's also appeared on the Australian version of *Wide World of Sports, The Today Show, Sportsworld,* and *Good Morning Australia.* Lynch was inducted into the Australian Surfing Hall of Fame in 1998. He is unmarried and has one child.

Lynch, Wayne   Dynamic Australian goofyfoot surfer from Lorne, Victoria; teenage messiah of the shortboard revolution in the late 1960s and early '70s, and generally regarded as the inventor of "vertical" surfing. "He was the Future of Surfing incarnate," Hawaiian pro surfer Reno Abellira said of Lynch. "A boy wonder with searing eyes, a disarming choirboy smile, and an attacking style that often left him upside-down in the curl, only to recover in midair and land back on his wax." Lynch was born

Wayne Lynch

(1952) in the southwest Victoria town of Colac, the son of a fisherman/carpenter, and raised in the nearby town of Lorne, 25 miles west of Bells Beach, one of Australia's best-known surf breaks. He began surfing at age 10; the following year he entered and won a statewide open-age contest, but event organizers, flustered by the smooth-cheeked phenomenon, hastily gave him the "Best Wave of the Day" award rather than the first-place trophy, and banned him from competing the following year, saying he was too young. In 1965 he won the first of six consecutive juniors division Victoria state titles.

While surf magazines published some impressive black-and-white photographs of Lynch in 1968, his star-making moment came in 1969 with the release of *Evolution,* Paul Witzig's rough-hewn cult classic surf movie. Two years earlier, surfers on 10-foot-long boards were focused mainly on walking the board and hanging ten. Lynch, the 16-year-old master of the just-introduced short surfboard, featured in the opening sequence of *Evolution* riding a stubby 7'1" board, seemed to change the direction of the sport single-handedly, riding out of a low crouch, his thin legs collapsing and extending almost pneumatically from one tightly arced turn to the next. Although 1966 world champion Nat Young and 1968 Bells winner Ted Spencer costarred in *Evolution,* the film is remembered almost exclusively as a Lynch showcase.

Lynch won the juniors division of the Australian National Titles four straight times (1967 to 1970), appeared in a small number of surf films (most notably 1971's *Sea of Joy*), then suddenly dropped from public view, saying he "wasn't interested in fame or money," and that he wanted to be "just a surfer, not a star." Only later did he admit that he spent nearly three years avoiding Australia's then-mandatory military service. A motorcycle accident in Bali in 1972 put Lynch in an Indonesian hospital with a broken collarbone and sprained back; while there he caught malaria, was virtually bedridden for six months, and was unable to surf for all of 1973. He returned to the water in 1974, and the following year reentered the competition scene, placing sixth at Bells, then earning $3,500 for winning the Surfabout event in Sydney, the second-richest pro event of the year. Lynch competed part-time for the next three years (finishing 11th on the debut International Professional Surfers circuit in 1976, second at the 1978 Katin Pro-Am, and second in the 1978 Surfabout), then once again retired. In the 1978 short film *A Day in the Life of Wayne Lynch,* surf filmmaker Jack McCoy shows the one-time child star dividing his time between his quiet, woodsy house in Victoria and surfing alone—

and brilliantly—in the deepwater reefs nearby. Lynch was regarded by many as the ultimate "soul surfer." In talent and temperament he would in years to come be likened to three-time world champion Tom Curren of California.

Lynch continued to have a curious back-and-forth relationship with the surf industry and media. While he's been an eloquent spokesman against surfing's commercialization, he's also benifited from surf company sponsorship throughout his career, most notably by Rip Curl wetsuits and Quiksilver beachwear. His disinterest in the surf media seems genuine enough, but he's nonetheless turned up regularly in surf videos and documentaries, including *Legends: An Australian Surfing Perspective* (1994), *Litmus* (1997), *Great Waves* (1998), and *Biographies* (2001). Lynch continues to live a quiet life in coastal Victoria, designing and shaping surfboards for a living, as he has since the early '70s. In 2000 he became the long-distance president and the head designer of Evolution Surfboards, based in Del Mar, California.

Lynch was inducted into the Australian Surfing Hall of Fame in 1988, and was cited by *Surfer* magazine in 1999 as the 13th most influential surfer of all time. Making another return to competition, Lynch placed ninth in the 1997 Masters (for surfers 36 and over) and fifth in the 1999 Masters. He is married and has two children. *See also* Evolution, shortboard revolution.

M

Maalaea Temperamental right-breaking reef wave located on the south shore of Maui, Hawaii, renowned as the world's fastest ridable surf break. Although Maalaea breaks with machinelike perfect form, fewer than one in four rides here are completed; for most surfers, the object at Maalaea is to simply take a trim position inside the tube and try to keep pace with the falling curl for as long as possible. "It's just pure, unadulterated speed," Maui photographer Kirk Aeder noted, "that never, ever lets up." Maalaea usually comes into top form just once or twice a year, when a distant wave-producing storm lines up perfectly with an eight-mile-wide gap between the island of Kahoolawe and the southwest tip of Maui. Prevailing winds at Maalaea are straight offshore and usually blow at 20 to 30 knots; the bottom is coral-lined and fairly shallow. Maalaea rarely gets over six feet, and is best on an incoming tide. The wave itself is divided into five sections, beginning with Off the Wall (separate from the other four), then moving through Impossibles, Freight Trains, Down the Line, and Inside Section; a single ride from Impossibles to Inside Section—one of surfing's rarest feats—lasts for more than 300 yards.

Maalaea was first ridden in the early '60s, but the unwieldy longboards of the time weren't suited to the wave. Not until the shortboard revolution of the late '60s did surfers begin to cover any real distance at Maalaea. Local surfer Joseph "Buddy Boy" Kaohi was so highly regarded at Maalaea in the late '60s and early '70s that the break was sometimes referred to as "Buddy's Bay." Top Maalaea riders over the decades include Maui residents Brad Lewis, Lloyd Ishmine, and Chris Lassen. *Surfing* magazine in 1989 listed Maalaea as one of the "25 Best Waves in the World." No surf contests have been held here.

Maalaea has been featured in several surf movies, including *Angry Sea* (1963), *Adventures in Paradise* (1982), *Amazing Surf Stories* (1986), and Maui '99 (2000). Developers have periodically introduced plans to expand the 1952-built Maalaea Harbor, and it's generally assumed that any such expansion would either compromise or ruin the surf. *Maalaea: A Cry for Help,* a documentary on the break's ongoing problems with developers, was released in 2002. *See also* Maui.

MacAulay, Dave Even-tempered Australian pro surfer from Cowaramup Bay, Western Australia; world-ranked #3 in 1989 and 1993; best remembered as an evangelical Christian, and a deadly efficient small-wave rider. MacAulay was born (1963) and raised in Perth, began surfing at age nine, and was one of the country's best amateur performers in the early and mid-'80s, winning the state championships in 1982 and 1983, and finishing runner-up in the National Titles in 1983 and 1985. His rise up the pro ranks was steady as his year-end rating, between 1986 and 1989, went from 23rd to eighth (for two years), then to third. Few in the surf world were paying attention, however, as the slender goofyfooter went about his business quietly, almost anonymously. His wave-riding technique was fast, precise, and mistake-free, but predictable; he also shied away from Hawaii's reputation-making big surf. What little interest the surf press took in MacAulay generally stemmed from his devout born-again Christianity. *Surfer* reported in 1986 that just a few hours after his first world tour win, in Brazil, he went on a door-to-door proselytizing "crusade" through the streets of Rio; cheeky *Australia's Surfing Life* magazine offered MacAulay $100 in 1994 to walk into a Honolulu strip bar while visiting Hawaii that winter; he refused.

MacAulay dropped to 12th in the ratings in 1991, then came back to finish seventh in 1992 and third in 1993. He retired the following year at age 31, with seven total world tour victories, including an extraordinary three-in-a-row streak in 1986 that saw him win events in Brazil, Japan, and Australia. A surfboard shaper since high school, MacAulay returned to the craft full-time in 1995, making boards under his own label in the Margaret River area, near his home. He appeared in a small number of surf movies and videos during his pro career, including *All Down the Line* (1989) and *Raw Power* (1991). MacAulay is married and has three daughters. *See also* religion and surfing.

MacGillivray, Greg Fastidious and highly successful filmmaker from Laguna Beach, California, a two-time Academy Award nominee, best known to surfers as the cocreator of 1972's *Five Summer Stories*. MacGillivray was born (1945) in San Diego, California, the son of a navy officer and former lifeguard, and raised in Orange County's Corona del Mar. He began surfing at 13, and started making short surf films in high school, which he screened in his garage, charging 25 cents for admission. MacGillivray's first full-length film, the sparkly and well-photographed *A Cool Wave of Color,* came out in 1964 and featured California surf breaks exclusively. *The Performers,* MacGillivray's second film, followed in 1965, not long after he met Jim Freeman, another Orange County college-age surf filmmaker. MacGillivray-Freeman Films was formed in 1966, and *Free and Easy,* the pair's debut effort, came out the following year. *Waves of Change*—immodestly referred to as "Super Film" during its long three-year production—came out in 1970; surfboard design and surfing techniques were changing so fast at that time the film was dated upon arrival.

Technically and artistically, the MacGillivray-Freeman team had no rival. They invested in the best equipment, worked harder and longer than anyone, and were both fervent students of the craft; their movies were better framed, better edited, and more color-saturated than anything produced at the time. (*Waves of Change* was reissued as *Sunshine Sea* for a brief mainstream theatrical run in 1971.) *Five Summer Stories,* MacGillivray-Freeman's last surf film, originally released in 1972 and updated regularly until 1979, further advanced the duo's reputation and became a surf movie classic.

MacGillivray-Freeman was hired by Hollywood producers to do second-unit work on *Jonathan Livingston Seagull* (1973) and *The Towering Inferno* (1974). They made their first IMAX film, *To Fly!,* in 1976; just before the movie debuted in Washington, D.C., at the Smithsonian, Freeman was killed in a helicopter accident. MacGillivray went on to become the world's best-known IMAX film producer, creating 25 of the 70-millimeter movies between 1976 and 2002.

Two of his films—*The Living Sea* (1995) and *Dolphins* (2000)—received Oscar nominations for Best Documentary Short Subject. *Adventures in Wild California,* another MacGillivray IMAX film released in 2000, featured a big-wave surfing sequence filmed at Maverick's.

MacGillivray was a cameraman on *Big Wednesday* (1978) and *The Shining* (1980). Alone or with Freeman, he also made five surfing shorts: *The Day War Came to Malibu* (1965), *Moods of Surfing* (1967), *The Loser* (1968), *Who's Best* (1969), and *Expression Session* (1971). MacGillivray was the top vote-getter in the motion picture category of the 1967 *International Surfing* Magazine Hall of Fame Awards; at the 1996 *Surfer* Magazine Video Awards he received a Lifetime Achievement honor; in 1997 he was profiled in *50 Years of Surfing on Film,* an Outdoor Life Network documentary series; in 2000 he was inducted into the Huntington Beach Surfing Walk of Fame. *See also* Five Summer Stories.

Machado, Rob Laconic goofyfooter from Cardiff, California; world-ranked #2 in 1995, and generally regarded as the smoothest-riding surfer of his generation. Machado was born (1973) in Sydney, Australia, the son of an American general contractor/real estate agent father and a British school teacher mother, and began surfing at age nine, five years after his family moved to Cardiff. Machado compiled a string of good results in the U.S. Surfing Championships, placing first in the menehune division in 1986 and third in the juniors division in 1989 and 1990. In 1992, one year after placing first in the Op Pro Junior and turning professional, Machado began winning events on the Professional Surfing Association of America (PSAA) tour, and was also featured in *Momentum,* the debut video by San Diego filmmaker Taylor Steele. In 1993, Machado became PSAA champion, finished eighth on the world pro tour—the highest finish ever by a tour freshman—and was named rookie of the year.

As one of the founding New School surfers, the 5'10", 140-pound Machado was almost by definition aggressive and acrobatic in the water. But more so than any of his peers—and perhaps more so than any surfer of the shortboard era except Tom Curren and Gerry Lopez—Machado's riding was based on flow, form, subtlety, and composure. He often arranged his arms and legs into near-balletic positions, and occasionally slouched into a Zen-like motionless stance

Rob Machado

while racing across the wave face. Machado was tentative and ineffective in bigger, harder-breaking surf early in his career, but he eventually was able to draw his elegant lines in waves up to 12 or 15 feet. Meanwhile, his cool demeanor and angular features—"Catch his face at a bad angle," surf journalist Ben Marcus wrote in 1994, "and he looks like a Cubist portrait of himself"—helped make him a surf-chic trendsetter, featured in more beachwear ads than virtually anyone of the period.

Machado was world-ranked #5 in 1994. The following year, he and defending world champion Kelly Slater met in a championship-deciding semifinal heat at the Pipeline Masters, the last event of the season, traded tuberide after tuberide, and staged what was universally agreed to be the most exciting match in pro surfing history. Slater won the heat, the contest, and the world title; Machado finished the year ranked second. He placed 11th in 1996, fourth in 1997, 13th in 1998, 14th in 1999, and third in 2000. The following year he dropped to 46th, after missing part of the season due to a broken wrist, and failed to qualify for the 2002 world tour. By that time he'd won eight world tour events, including the 1994 Marui Pro in Japan, the 1995 U.S. Open, and the 2000 Pipeline Masters; he also won the 1995 Billabong Challenge in Western Australia. Machado placed runner-up to Slater in the *Surfer* Magazine Readers Poll Awards in 1994, 1996, 1997, 1999, and 2001.

Supremely photogenic, Machado has appeared in more than 50 surf videos, including *Momentum* (1992), *What's Next?* (1996), *Thicker Than Water* (1999), and *Shelter* (2001). *Drifting: The Rob Machado Chronicles,* a sponsor-funded video documentary, was produced in 1996. The Rob Machado Surf Classic, a contest and beach fair, was founded in 1997. In 1998, Machado, Slater, and La Jolla surfer Peter King, recording as The Surfers, released *Songs From the Pipe,* an Epic CD with Machado on guitar; that same year he performed onstage with Pearl Jam in Queensland, Australia. Machado is married and has one child.

Machuca, Jorge   Good-natured Machuca of Puerto Rico first came to the attention of the surfing world in 1967 at the age of 14 when he finished runner-up in the Puerto Rico International, behind reigning U.S. champion Corky Carroll, but ahead of American surf heroes like Rusty Miller, Claude Codgen, Gary Propper, and Dewey Weber. Flexible and creative in the water, Machuca was touted as a real threat to win the 1968 world contest, but lost early. "I get the coolies in a contest," he admitted a few months later. "I react too fast and tend to over-surf." In 1968 he became the only non-American on the prestigious Hobie Surfboards team. His competitive career stalled in the early '70s, but Machuca remains a surfing icon in his home country.

MacKenzie, Lynette   Fiery Australian pro surfer from Maroubra, Sydney, world-ranked #3 in 1994, and noted as the only pro circuit surfer ever suspended for fighting. MacKenzie was born (1974) and raised in the beachfront suburb of Maroubra, began surfing at age 10, and quickly developed a low, driving, athletic wave-riding style. In 1992 she won both the Australian National Titles and the World Amateur Championships, and was named Junior Female Athlete of the Year by the Confederation of Australian Sport. The following year she again won the Nationals, placed third in the final standings of the Australian Championship Circuit, and finished eighth on the world pro circuit; in 1994 she won two of 11 pro tour events to finish #3 in the world. Over the next few years her rating dipped as low as #15, but in 2002 the 28-year-old shot back up to #5. MacKenzie's competitive performances, however, have to a large degree been overshadowed by her violent temper. After a postmatch beach fight in 1999, she was fined $1,000, suspended for two months, and ordered to take anger management classes; two years later the redheaded goofyfoot was again fined for brawling during a competition. "What gets your blood boiling?" an interviewer asked MacKenzie in 2000. "Just about anything," she replied.

MacKenzie has appeared in a small number of surf videos, including 2001's *Tropical Madness*. Steve "Bullet" MacKenzie, Lynette's older brother, won the Australian pro bodyboarding tour in 1996 and 1997.

Madagascar   Tropical to subtropical African island nation, roughly two and a half times the size of Great Britain, located about 240 miles southeast of Mozambique in the Indian Ocean. Surfing's origins in Madagascar are unknown. An economically disastrous Marxist revolution in 1975 all but sealed off the country from visitors, and if any surfers explored Madagascar before that point their visits have gone undocumented. The government began to quietly encourage tourism beginning in 1987, with the hope that foreign currency would aid the economy, but Madagascar remains one of the world's poorest nations. Still, more than a dozen surf spots were mapped out across the country's 2,000-mile-long coastline by 1991, including a variety of reefs and white-sand beachbreaks, all of which have consistent medium-sized waves from April to June. Most of the reefs are located well offshore on the east coast of the island, and are reached by boat. Water temperatures are generally in the 70s. Sharks are a constant worry, as Madagascar averages 12 attacks annually.

Surf charter travel companies have begun offering boat excursions to Madagascar in 2001, and Madagascar waves have turned up in at least two surf videos—*Chocolate Barrels and Liquid Trips* (1999) and *Zagland 2* (2001)—and the opening scenes of TriStar's melodramatic 1998 big-wave surf film *In God's Hands* were set here as well. But Madagascar remains a strange and remote surfing frontier. "For every good wave you ride here," *Australia's Surfing Life* magazine reported in 1997, "you go through a lot of work. The country is poorer than poor and in the most unbelievable state of decay." As of 2003, it was thought that fewer than a dozen natives had taken up surfing.

Madeira   Rugged, subtropical, Portuguese-governed archipelago, known as "the Garden of the Atlantic," composed of two main islands and seven uninhabited islets, located 600 miles west of Lisbon. With its 6,000-foot peaks and near-vertical oceanfront cliffs, Madeira seems to fairly burst out of the ocean. North Atlantic winter swells regularly push thick, powerful, well-shaped waves onto Madeira's points and reefs. "What the place lacks," a 1994 *Surf Report* newsletter noted, "is relaxing small-wave breaks. Virtually every

spot is rocky and powerful, and none seem to break under six-feet." Madeira has no sand beaches, and negotiating the wave-battered rocks while entering and exiting the surf is one of the island's greatest surf hazards. On the plus side, Madeira has no sharks, mosquitoes, disease, or theft. The weather is warm and mild, with daytime air temperatures ranging from the mid-60s to the mid-70s and water temperatures from the low 60s to low 70s.

Surfers have been visiting here since the 1970s, but Madeira didn't come to the attention of the surfing world at large until 1994, when it was featured in a *Surfer* magazine travel article. A handful of locals have since picked up the sport, gamely learning how to ride waves in conditions that surfers elsewhere wouldn't try until they had a few years of water experience. Since 1996, top Portuguese surfers have flown here annually to compete in a regional edition of the Billabong Challenge; in 2001, the Madeira World Team Big Wave Championships were held at Ponto Jardim, the islands' premier surfing location—a long, winding, right-breaking wave. Madeira's surf is detailed in *The Stormrider Guide Europe* (1998). As of 2003, there were no surf shops in Madeira.

Maine   The rockbound coast of Maine, America's northeasternmost state—famous for its lobster, lighthouses, and tiny fishing villages—is home to dozens of temperamental surf breaks and a small but dedicated community of surfers. Maine's jagged 228-mile shoreline is filled with peninsulas, points, coves, and rivermouths, many of which contain surf spots that remain either uncharted or unexposed—especially in the rural area north of Portland, as well as hundreds of offshore islands. Established mainland breaks include Higgins Beach and Fortunes Rock in Biddeford and Gooch's Beach near Kennebunkport. Ogunquit Rivermouth, a sand-bottom wave featuring a long right and a shorter, faster left, is the state's best-known break, and the only spot that regularly draws a crowd. Maine's primary surf season is from August to early December, before the winter weather settles in. Winter surf can be excellent, but is more often stormy and always shockingly cold. Air temperatures range from 65 (summer) to 15 (winter); water temperatures range from the mid-60s to the low 30s. Winter surfers in Maine at times gain access to the water only after plowing through deep beachfront snowdrifts; many local surfers simply pack it in for the season or travel to warmer climes. Spring and summer are often waveless for weeks at a time. Tides in Maine can be extreme, particularly in the north, where water levels can change up to 30 feet in six hours. (The Bay of Fundy, just north of Maine, has the world's biggest tidal ranges; up to 52 feet.)

Ogunquit lifeguard Steve Watson introduced surfing to Maine in the summer of 1960, riding without a wetsuit on a 15-foot plywood paddleboard. Surfer Crow surf shop, owned by Watson, opened in 1966—the first shop of its kind in the state—and two years later Watson became the regional director for the just-chartered Eastern Surfing Association. The sport grew slowly in southern Maine during the '60s (the north remained virtually unsurfed), with small but loyal membership in groups like the Ogunquit Beach Surf Club and Drake's Island Surf Club, both established by 1967. The debut Maine Open Surf Contest was held in 1968. Maine surfing remained an outlier to East Coast surfing in general through the '70s and '80s; native Mike Morin formed Syco Surfboards, the state's first board factory, in 1984. Bill Woodward was the first Maine surfer to place in the finals of an Eastern Surfing Championship, taking third in the masters division (ages 25–34) in 1995. Only since the late '90s have adventurous surfers begun to systematically explore Maine's remote northern coast and outer islands. As of 2003, Maine was home to four surf shops and roughly 100 full-time surfers, most of whom are proud of their no-etiquette approach to the sport. "It's Neanderthal surfing around here," still-active surfer Steve Watson said in 2000. "Myself included."

Makaha   Historic surf break located on the arid west side of Oahu, 30 miles northwest of Honolulu; often described as the birthplace of big-wave surfing; home to the 1954-founded Makaha International Surfing Championships, the world's first international surf competition. Bordered by steep lava-ridged valleys and mountains to the east, Makaha (Hawaiian for "fierce") is one of the state's most consistent and variegated breaks; summer waves are generally below four feet, winter waves are frequently six feet, and can get up to 25. The predominant northeast tradewinds blow offshore, improving wave quality. The broad Makaha reef encompasses a group of interconnected breaks. During a medium-sized swell, the most popular takeoff zone is located at the Bowl, which produces a steep drop that quickly backs off into the Blowhole section, which in turn leads to the

Inside Reef—a zippy tube that funnels into a notorious backwash-amplified shorebreak just a few yards off the beach. When the surf is below eight foot, the Makaha lineup is filled with all manner of surf craft, from tandem boards to outrigger canoes, bodyboards, longboards, and shortboards. When the swell rises to 15 foot or bigger—which usually happens less than a half-dozen times each season—the crowd thins out considerably as the wave takes shape over a section of reef known as Point Surf. Makaha gets bigger than 20 feet perhaps once or twice a decade, but when it does it often shapes up as a thundering 200-yard-long wall that terminates at the looming and frequently nonnegotiable Bowl section, the "royal flaw," as described by *Surfer* magazine. (Big-wave surfer Fred Van Dyke had such a hatred of the Bowl section that in 1958 he planned to level the responsible area of reef with dynamite. The plan failed, and the Bowl remains the great challenge for Point Surf riders.) Makaha's large and close-knit surf community is often praised for upholding Hawaiian traditions and mores. The economically depressed area is also noted for its violence and crime, and outsiders are generally made to feel unwelcome. "You want to come to Makaha?" local surfer Melvin Puu told *Surfing* in 1991, addressing the magazine's readership. "Don't."

While Makaha was likely first ridden by premodern Hawaiians, 19th-century Makaha Valley landowner Kuho'oheihei "Abner" Paki is generally cited as the break's first surfer; after 1860, however, Makaha remained unsurfed for more than 75 years. In late 1937, just a few months after the development of the racy hot curl surfboard—sometimes called the original big-wave board—John Kelly and Wally Froiseth of Honolulu, along with a few others, rediscovered the Makaha surf. This new break was the perfect seasonal counterpart to Waikiki, where the surf is biggest in the summer and early fall. Teenager George Downing joined the original group of Makaha surfers in the mid-'40s, and soon gained a reputation as the island's finest big-wave surfer. Venturesome Californians like Buzzy Trent, Bob Simmons, and Walter Hoffman soon joined the Hawaiians, and by the early '50s the mainlanders were spending their winters living in a small row of army-built Quonset huts at the mouth of Makaha Valley, eating rice and peanut butter, and lying in wait for big Point Surf. America at large got its first look at Makaha in 1953, when newspapers across the country published an Associated Press photo of Trent, Downing, and Woody Brown shooting across the face of a sparkling 15-footer; inspired, dozens more mainland surfers packed their boards and headed for Oahu. The first annual Makaha International Surfing Championships were held the following year, and before decade's end the contest was known as the unofficial world championships. (It was also the world's first televised surfing event, running from 1962 to 1965 on ABC's *Wide World of Sports*.) By the late '50s, Oahu's North Shore had replaced Makaha as the capital of big-wave surfing. But the west side break still had its moments: Downing and Trent rode immaculate 25-footers there in early 1958, and in late 1969 California roughneck Greg Noll paddled out at Point Surf and caught the biggest wave ever ridden up that time, a 35-foot closeout that he was lucky to survive.

As Makaha faded somewhat from public view in the '70s, a colorful local surf culture continued to flourish, in large part thanks to longtime Makaha patriarch Richard "Buffalo" Keaulana, along with the "Queen of Makaha," Rell Sunn, who organized events like the Buffalo Big Board Classic meet and the Rell Sunn Menehune Contest. (Makaha also hosted the 1984 United States Surfing Championships, the 1997 World Longboard Championships, and the 2003 Masters World Championships.) When Sunn died in 1998 after a long fight with cancer, her ashes were scattered at Makaha.

Makaha has been home base for a number of world-class surfers since the late '70s, including three-time longboard world champion Rusty Keaulana, big-wave riders Brian Keaulana and Keone Downing, 1999 world tour champion Sunny Garcia, and power surfer Johnny-Boy Gomes. Makaha has been featured in more than 50 surf movies and videos, including *Trek to Makaha* (1956), *Slippery When Wet* (1958), *Cavalcade of Surf* (1962), *The Endless Summer* (1966), *The Golden Breed* (1968), *Five Summer Stories* (1972), *Ocean Fever* (1983), *Surfers: The Movie* (1990), and *Blue Shock* (1998). *Surfing* magazine named Makaha one of the "25 Best Waves in the World" in 1989. The break is detailed in *The Surfers Guide to Hawaii,* published in 1991. *See also* Richard "Buffalo" Keaulana, Rell Sunn, Swell of 1969.

Makaha International Surfing Championships

Annual surfing competition held at Makaha on the west side of Oahu, Hawaii, from 1954 to 1971, usually in November or December; regarded in the late '50s and early '60s as the unofficial world championships.

Makaha International; 1965 semifinalists

Created by Honolulu surfer and restaurant supplier John Lind, and sponsored by the Waianae Lions Club as well as the Lind-founded Waikiki Surf Club, the inaugural Makaha event in 1953 was a bust: the wave-riding events were cancelled due to lack of surf, leaving just the paddling races. Attendees were all from Hawaii or Southern California. California surfer Flippy Hoffman later recalled that the opening Makaha event was not without drama, as tensions flared between the Makaha surfers and the Waikiki surfers, then between the Hawaiians and the visiting Californians. "They had this big luau," Hoffman said, "and a big hassle developed over how to cook the pig. Things got pretty hot. That first contest had a lot of fist-fights and hassles."

The Makaha event steadied itself the following year, surfers from Australia and Peru joined in, and by the end of the decade it was the closest thing the sport had to a venerable competitive tradition. From 1962 to 1965, the contest was shown on ABC's *Wide World of Sports*. The Makaha competition structure was different from contests held on the mainland. In California and the East Coast, surfers usually were sent into the water in heats of six; Makaha heats contained as many as 24 surfers, each wearing an identifying number-stenciled T-shirt. There was no interference penalty for riding in front of another surfer, and a photo taken during the 1964 Makaha contest shows five riders clustered tightly together on the same wave. The Makaha scoring system was also unique, as each ridden wave was scored on a points system from one to 30, with an emphasis on ride length and wave height equal to that given to performance (turns, cutbacks, etc.). Finally, because the

Makaha event was open to all surfers, the number of contestants was enormous—more than 500 by 1965. Big-wave pioneer Wally Froiseth ran the event from 1960 to its demise in 1971.

The surf at Makaha International over the years ranged from two foot to 20 foot. The event peaked in 1963, as huge waves swept into the bay during the men's division final, won by Hawaii's Joey Cabell; *Time* magazine covered the event, calling it surfing's "supreme test." By the mid-'60s, however, the contest's reputation was nosediving. The first World Surfing Championships were held in 1964 in Australia, and 1965 brought the first Duke Kahanamoku Invitational at Sunset Beach—both events cut deeply into Makaha's prestige. The surf media meanwhile criticized Makaha for its crowded heats and judging favoritism (no California surfer even won the men's division), as well as its archaic scoring system. "Makaha is the Worst" was the title of a 1966 *Surfer* magazine article, while a *Surfing* editorial urged California surfers to boycott the event completely. In the late '60s and early '70s, the Makaha contest went all but unnoticed by the surf press.

Makaha International footage from the mid-'50s to the early '60s was often used in surf filmmaker Bud Browne's movies; later events are seen in *Golden Breed* (1968), *Tracks* (1970), and *Five Summer Stories* (1972).

Winners for the men's, women's, junior's and tandem divisions of the Makaha International Surfing Championships are as follows:

1954: George Downing, (no women's), Alan Gomes, Walter Hoffman/Joanie Jones
1955: Rabbit Kekai, Ethel Kukea, Alan Gomes, Ed Whaley/Nancy Boyd
1956: Conrad Cahna, Ethel Kukea, J. Raydon, Robert Krewson/Kahua Kea
1957: Jamma Kekai, Vicky Heldrich, Timmy Guard, (no tandem event)
1958: Peter Cole, Marge Calhoun, Joseph Napoleon, Rabbit Kekai/Heide Stevens
1959: Wally Froiseth, Linda Benson, Paul Strauch, Ed Whaley/Diana Moore
1960: Buffalo Keaulana, Wendy Cameron, Erick Romanchek, Mud Werner/Robin Grigg
1961: George Downing, Anona Napoleon, Fred Hemmings, Rabbit Kekai/Lucinda Smith
1962: Midget Farrelly, Nancy Nelson, Peter Kahapea, Joseph Napoleon/Sue Ellen Ketner
1963: Joey Cabell, Nancy Nelson, Fred Hemmings, Mike Doyle/Linda Merrill
1964: Fred Hemmings, Joyce Hoffman, Joey Gerard, Mike Doyle/Margie Stevens
1965: George Downing, Nancy Nelson, David Nuuhiwa, Mike Doyle/Danielle Corn
1966: Fred Hemmings, Joyce Hoffman, Reno Abellira, Pete Peterson/Barrie Algaw
1967: Joey Cabell, Martha Sunn, Reno Abellira, Bob Moore/Patti Young
1968: Joey Cabell, Margo Godfrey, Keone Downing, Leroy Achoy/Blance Benson
1969: Paul Strauch, Martha Sunn, Keone Downing, Bob Moore/Blanche Benson
1970: Peter Drouyn, Martha Sunn, Craig Wilson, Steve Boehne/Barrie Algaw
1971: Mark Sedlack, Bency Benson, Larry Bertlemann, (no tandem event)

Maki, Clarence Easygoing photographer from Honolulu, Hawaii, who shot many of the best-known surfing images of Waikiki and Makaha in the 1950s and early '60s. Maki was born (1924) in Kilauea, Kauai, raised in Honolulu, began surfing in 1944, and taught himself how to use a camera. His photos were first published in 1953 in the *Honolulu Star-Bulletin* and the *Honolulu Advertiser* newspapers; nearly all of Maki's work is in black and white. Some of his best images were candid or quickly posed beach shots, but he's perhaps best known for the water shots he took of the last great Waikiki beachboy surfers, including "Blue" Makua and "Scooter-Boy" Kaopuiki. In 1954, gray-haired surf pioneer Duke Kahanamoku, carrying a surfboard, approached Maki on the beach and told the photographer it was his 64th birthday. A few minutes later, Maki took a shot of Kahanamoku that was published the next day on the front page of the *Star-Bulletin*; it was the last photograph of Kahanamoku surfing. A Maki surf photo won $1,000 in a national photo contest sponsored by Kodak in 1957; another surf shot of his won the Kodak International Newspaper Snapshot Grand Prize in 1971. Maki's work has been used to illustrate more than a half-dozen surfing books, including *Surf Riding: Its Thrills and Techniques* (1960), *Surf and Sea* (1965), and *Waikiki Beach Boy* (1989).

Maldives The Republic of Maldives is made up of nearly 1,200 tiny low-lying coral islands (200 inhabited) strung along a 475-mile-long band in the Indian Ocean, just north of the equator and about 350 miles southwest of Sri Lanka; dozens of first-rate surf breaks are found among the Maldivian reef passes. The glimmering turquoise-colored waves here rarely get over 10 feet and lack the power found in Indonesia or Tahiti, but are shapely, perfectly groomed, and often hollow. Among the Maldives' best-known breaks are Pasta Point, a multifaceted left-breaking wave; Honky's, a speeding left that grows in size as it tracks across the reef; and Sultans, a right with three distinct tube sections. The Maldives has two monsoon seasons: the November-to-April northeast monsoon brings the best weather, as well as hundreds of tropics-loving tourists from around the world; the May-to-October southwest monsoon produces the best surf. Squalls are common in June and July; December and January often bring small waves and unfavorable winds for surfing. Average daytime high temperatures hold steady at 90 degrees; the water temperature remains near 80. The palm- and bamboo-covered Maldives are the world's flattest island group, and nowhere in the country is higher than 10 feet above sea level. The Maldivian government has a limited and carefully managed policy for visitors, with all resorts located in the North and South Male Atolls' "tourist zone." Surf breaks on the Outer Atolls can be reached only through government-approved charter tours.

Australian surfers Tony Hinde and Mark Scanlon were shipwrecked in 1973 near the capital city of Male—no injuries, surfboards and luggage unharmed—and soon became the first to ride the Maldivian surf. Hinde returned to stay the following year, and began searching out the best breaks in and around Male. He eventually married a local woman, converted to Islam, and became a naturalized Maldivian citizen, and for more than 15 years rode waves more or less by himself. "I ended up having to teach the locals how to surf," he later said, "so I'd have someone to join me in the water." In 1990, Hussein-Hinde (his Muslim name) founded the Atoll Adventures surfing resort in Tari Village.

Photographs of the Maldives were published in surf magazines as early as 1993; by 1997 most of the accessible breaks were mapped out in detail in an issue of the California-based *Surf Report* newsletter. The Maldivian Surfing Championships debuted in 1996, and four years later Hussein-Hinde opened the area's first surf shop. By 2002, there were a half-dozen Maldivian resorts that offered regular daily boat service to and from nearby surf breaks and a similar number of surf tour boat charters. Breaks near the re-

sorts can get crowded; those accessed by boat are less so. The Maldives are featured in a small but growing number of surf videos, including *Triple C* (1996), *Hit and Run* (2000), and *Surf Adventure* (2000). Santa Cruz big-wave surfer Jay Moriarity died while freediving off Lohifushi Island, north of Male, on June 15, 2001.

Malibu   Definitive California pointbreak, often described as the "original perfect wave," located on the northern arm of Santa Monica Bay in Los Angeles County; a surf-culture hothouse, and the center for much of the advancement in surfing performance and board design from the mid-40s to the mid-60s. "Malibu," surf journalist Paul Gross wrote, "is the exact spot on earth where ancient surfing became modern surfing." Malibu's south-facing cobblestone point is roughly 400 yards long from the famous wooden pier to Malibu Lagoon, and is divided into three connected surf breaks. First Point is the long, evenly breaking wave that made Malibu famous; Second Point produces bigger, faster, less predictable surf; waves at Third Point, farthest out, are bigger yet. First Point has since the mid-'80s been ridden almost exclusively by longboarders, while shortboarders dominate Second and Third Point. Malibu generally breaks best from late summer to early fall, in response to swells generated from Pacific Ocean storms located anywhere from Baja Mexico to New Zealand. The surf here is generally between two and four foot; on the rare days when it hits eight foot or bigger, waves can sometimes be ridden from Third Point to the pier. Warm, dry weather prevails throughout the surf season, with water temperatures usually in the mid- to upper 60s; afternoon westerly winds bring only a slight reduction in surf quality. Malibu is also an incorporated city, and a number of other surf breaks are located along its 21-mile coastline, including Topanga Beach, Big Dume and Little Dume, and Zuma Beach.

Chumash Indians lived in the area for 4,000 years and called it "Hamaliwu" ("the surf sounds loudly"); Malibu is the English version of the word. Surfing innovator Tom Blake, along with friend Sam Reid, was the first to ride Malibu in 1927, two years before this section of coast was open to the public; top California surfers like Pete Peterson and Gard Chapin rode Malibu in the '30s, and by the time America entered World War II, Malibu had earned a reputation among America's 200 or 300 surfers as the best wave on the coast. Newly-developed construction materials were available after the war,

Malibu

which encouraged new thinking in board design. Malibu-area board-makers—particularly Bob Simmons, Dale Velzy, Joe Quigg, Matt Kivlin, and Dave Sweet—quickly did away with the heavy, finless, redwood-lined plank, and developed the Malibu chip, an all-balsa board covered in fiberglass, thinner and lighter than the plank, with a stabilizing fin that allowed riders to maneuver, instead of just cutting a fixed angle across the wave. (Australian surfers still refer to all longboards as "mals"—short for Malibu board.) While Hawaii remained the last word for big, challenging surf, Malibu was viewed as the ultimate high-performance wave. Malibu surfers gave the sport a cultural makeover as well, with the regal archetype set by Hawaiian surfer Duke Kahanamoku replaced by the kind of bleach-blond, wise-cracking suburban California teenager who began piling into Malibu by the hundreds in the late '50s. The Malibu Colony, a private beachfront community located just past Third Point, gave the break a touch of glamour, and a few Colony movie stars—Peter Lawford and Cliff Robertson among them—were Malibu regulars. Columbia Studios producers soon recognized the sport's commercial appeal, and bought the rights to *Gidget,* Frederick Kohner's best-selling 1957 novel based on the experiences of Kathy "Gidget" Kohner, the author's plucky teenage daughter, who learned to surf at Malibu. *Life* magazine ran a photo feature on Kathy Kohner and Malibu in 1957, and two years later the movie version of *Gidget* debuted, kicking off an American surf craze fueled by beach movies and surf music, with Malibu holding position as Surfing

Mecca. Another precedent was set as Malibu became the first break to be spoiled by crowds, with up to 150 surfers in the lineup at the same time by the summer of 1961.

Hotdog innovator and surfboard magnate Dewey Weber was a Malibu regular in the '50s and '60s, as was noseriding king Lance Carson, and beachside master of ceremonies Terry "Tubesteak" Tracy. The Malibu Surfing Association, formed in 1962, counted among its members some of the best surfers in the state, including Butch Linden, Johnny Fain, J Riddle, and Jackie Baxter. But it was Mickey Dora—the dark-haired and cynical "Black Knight of Malibu"—who was and remains most closely associated with the break. Dora's jittery but elegant riding style is still being copied by longboard surfers, and his hustling antiestablishment disposition helped shape the basic surfer character. Since the early '60s, DORA (or DORA IS KING, or DORA RULES) has been graffitied again and again in huge letters on the beachfront wall at Malibu.

The Chevy Malibu, introduced in 1964, broadened the marketing possibilities for the world's most famous surf break, and Malibu Barbie, Malibu Gum, and Sizzler's Malibu Chicken Sandwich were among the dozens of like-named products that followed in the decades to come. Malibu meanwhile lost its position as a cutting-edge surf break in the late '60s, after the newly introduced shortboards encouraged surfers to ride more challenging breaks. The Malibu surf remained just as crowded (and locals like Allen Sarlo continued to ride impressively), but tuberiding had become the ultimate surfing maneuver, and the focus changed to hollow-breaking waves like Pipeline in Hawaii. The Malibu experience was further diminished when it was learned in 1969 that up-canyon runoff had fouled Malibu Lagoon with sewage and waste. The Surfrider Foundation environmental group was formed in 1984 as a response to Malibu's ongoing environmental problems.

The Malibu Invitational, held from 1962 to 1967, was the first major surfing tournament staged at Malibu; subsequent events included the 1973 United States Surfing Championships, the 1975 Hang Ten Women's Championships (mainland America's first women's pro surfing event), the 1979 Sunkist Pro, and the 1981 U.S. Pro (the first men's division world circuit event in California). As the longboarding renaissance began to pick up steam in the early '80s, the lineup at First Point Malibu, a shortboard break for nearly 15 years, was quickly filled with surfers on 10-foot noseriders. The 1986 Summer Reunion Longboard Classic honored Malibu longboard surfers of the '50s and '60s; the World Longboard Championships were held at First Point in 1994. Top longboarders at Malibu in 2003 include Jimmy Gamboa and Kassia Meador.

Malibu has been featured in more than 75 surf movies, videos, and documentaries over the years, including *Search for Surf* (1958), *Cavalcade of Surf* (1962), *Strictly Hot* (1964), *The Endless Summer* (1966), *Cosmic Children* (1970), *Going Surfin'* (1973), *Follow the Sun* (1983), *Legends of Malibu* (1987), *Great Waves* (1998), and *Super Slide* (1999). *Big Wednesday,* the Warner Brothers' box-office bomb in 1978 that later became a video cult favorite, was cowritten by Malibu surfer Denny Aaberg, and is a lightly fictionalized account of Malibu in the '60s. An exhibit on the history of Malibu surfing, including 40 vintage surfboards used at the famous break, was presented by the Santa Monica Heritage Museum in 1993. *See also* Lance Carson, Mickey Dora, Gidget, Matt Kivlin, Los Angeles, Malibu Invitational, Bob Simmons, Terry "Tubesteak" Tracy, Dale Velzy.

Malibu board   In America, a Malibu board is short for "Malibu chip," meaning virtually any of the balsa-core boards built between the late '40s and the mid-'50s by Bob Simmons, Matt Kivlin, Joe Quigg, and a small number of other Southern California surfer/board-makers who often rode at Malibu. A Malibu chip was usually about 10 feet long and 22 inches wide, with a blocky squared-off tail, and weighed between 25 and 30 pounds. In Australia and New Zealand, a Malibu, or "mal," is synonymous with "longboard." *See also* chip board.

Malibu Invitational   Annual surfing contest from 1962 to 1968, held in early fall; regarded as the second-biggest event on the West Coast competition calendar following the United States Surfing Championships. The Malibu Invitational was conceived and developed by the Malibu Surfing Association, a local club, and cosponsored by the Malibu Chamber of Commerce. Scores were kept for both team and individual entrants. Four five-man clubs competed on October 20, 1962, in small but smooth-faced waves, with local rider Dave Rochlen winning individual honors and the Malibu Surfing Association taking the team award. Over the next five years, waves for the Malibu Invitational ranged from two to five feet. The 1966 event drew more than 1,000 spectators, a medium-large turnout for a '60s-era surf contest. In 1964 and 1967, the contest was broadcast by Los Angeles–based TV station KHJ.

At least three episodes from the Malibu Invitational contests became small but cherished surf history footnotes. In 1963, the newly formed Windansea Surf Club rattled up on the morning of the event in a rented bus containing groupies and hangers-on, a generator-powered rock trio, a Dumpster's worth of empty beer cans, and a stumbling drunk all-star lineup of surfers including Butch Van Artsdalen, Joey Cabell, L. J. Richards, and Mike Hynson—who found their legs as the day went on and ended up placing five men in the six-man final for an easy, boozy Windansea victory. The 1965 contest was "The Day War Came to Malibu," as *Surfer* magazine described it, with longtime rivals Mickey Dora and Johnny Fain hustling, shouting, and shoving their way through the finals; Dora at one point whipped his board into a kickout that missed Fain's head by inches. In the semifinals of the 1967 event, Dora dropped his trunks and mooned the assembled judges and spectators. The surf magazines, having spent the previous seven years trying to convince the nonsurfing world that the sport had cleaned out the rowdies and hodads, couldn't bring themselves to describe Dora's ride ("he took the lotus position" was the best *Surfing* magazine could do); the Malibu Invitational was cancelled after the following year's event. A women's division was added in 1965 and 1966. Malibu Invitational winners are as follows:

1962:   Dave Rochlen, Malibu Surfing Association

1963:   Joey Cabell, Windansea Surf Club

1964:   Bobby Patterson, Windansea Surf Club

1965:   Buzz Sutphin, Charline Tarusa, Malibu Surfing Association

1966:   Steve Bigler, Joey Hamasaki, Windansea Surf Club

1967:   George Szegetti, Malibu Surfing Association

1968:   Angie Reno, Malibu Surfing Association

Malibu U   Short-lived 1967 ABC-TV prime-time music show, hosted by former teen idol and *Ozzie and Harriet* star Ricky Nelson. *Malibu U* was shot on a private beach north of the Malibu Pier. Nelson, introduced as the program's "Dean of the Drop-Ins"—a lame play on words; a "drop-in" surfer is a wave-stealer—would invite guest "professors" (pop singers) to "lecture" (sing their latest hit) to the "student body" (suntanned suburban high schoolers in trunks and bikinis, the latter known as "Malibeauties"). Surfing clips were occasionally used between songs. *Malibu U* debuted in late July and was canceled after five weeks. *See also* surfing and television.

Malloy brothers, Chris, Keith, and Dan   Photogenic surfing siblings from Ventura County, California. Chris (born in 1971), Keith (1974), and Dan (1977) grew up on a ranch in Ojai, 15 miles from the beach, and all began surfing before the age of six. Broad-shouldered Chris moved to the North Shore of Oahu at age 18, and within a few years had become one of the island's best all-around surfers, performing well in waves from two to 25 feet. He was featured in *Momentum* (1992), and more than a dozen other surf videos, then went behind the camera to coproduce *Thicker Than Water, Surfer* magazine's Video of the Year in 2000. He also worked on *The September Sessions* (2000), and coproduced *Shelter* (2002). Keith, smaller and quicker than his older brother, was one of the most photographed surfers of the '90s, turning up regularly in surf videos and surf magazine covers; he qualified for the world pro championship tour in 2000. Dan had the best competition results of the brothers, winning the Op Pro Junior in 1996 and placing second in the 2000 U.S. Open. He made surf world headlines in early 2002 by announcing that he was giving up his pursuit of a slot on the championship tour, because competition itself was causing him to "lose my love for surfing."

The Malloys were cofounders in 1996 (along with Taylor Steele, Taylor Knox, Ross Williams, and Shane Dorian) of the California-based surf accessories company On a Mission. The following year they were featured in *All for One,* a surf video documentary. The Malloys also appeared in a lengthy beach fashion shoot for a 2001 issue of *Vogue* magazine.

Malpartida, Oscar "Chino"   Thrill-seeking goofy-foot surfer from Lima, Peru; national champion in 1972, 1980, and 1981. Malpartida was born (1951) and raised in Lima, and began surfing in front of Club Waikiki at Miraflores in 1960 at age nine. Continuing a tradition started by fellow Peruvian surfer and 1965 world champion Felipe Pomar, Malpartida charged the big surf, first at Lima's Pico Alto, then on the North Shore of Oahu. He finished third in the 1972 Duke Kahanamoku Classic, beating international surf world notables such as Peter Townend, Gavin Rudolph, and Jeff Crawford in the finals. "Malpartida of Peru put on a marvelous show," surf journalist Roy Crump wrote in *Surfer* magazine. "His takeoffs were critical and usually followed by an explosive backside turn." The handsome Latino was a finalist in the big-wave division of the Peru International from 1967–70 and 1974. Malpartida earned a B.S. in business from the University of Lima, but continued his pursuit of dangerous sport, and died while skydiving in 1994, at age 43, after his parachute failed to open.

Mansted, Peter   Hot-tempered manager from Sydney, Australia; the first such full-time representative in the sport, employed by more than a dozen top pros in the 1980s and early '90s, including world champions Tom Carroll and Martin Potter. Mansted was 25 in 1982, and the sole employee of the ambitiously named Mansted Management Company, when he signed young Australian pro Tom Carroll as his first client. For 10 percent of Carroll's earnings (from sponsorships as well as contest prize money), Mansted negotiated contracts, made travel arrangements, and served as media manager, as well as informal coach. Mansted's bellowing confidence seemed to have a positive effect on Carroll, who won back-to-back world titles in 1983 and 1984. Mansted also signed a number of other pros, including Kim Mearig, Barton Lynch, Glen Winton, Simon Anderson, Gary Elkerton, and Richard Cram, but none of the relationships lasted more than a few months. Mansted negotiated a contract between Carroll and Australian airline giant Qantas in 1985; three years later he pushed through a groundbreaking five-year, $1 million deal for Carroll with Quiksilver surfwear, and in doing so invented the concept of "100 percent sponsorship"—meaning that Quiksilver became Carroll's sole sponsor. Meanwhile, as the redheaded Mansted himself acknowledged, he became "the most hated man in pro surfing." Surf magazines were cut off from his clients if they wrote anything other than fawning articles; surf company CEOs frequently received hysterical letters and faxes regarding contractual irregularities—both real and perceived. "I interviewed him once," Australian surf journalist Tim Baker later wrote, "and sat stunned as he screamed into the tape recorder, red-faced and banging the coffee table with both hands." Carroll left Mansted in early 1989, not long after the manager began feeding unauthorized stories about Carroll to the Sydney tabloids. Mansted (who had changed his last name to Colbert), then shifted his attention to Martin Potter, his one remaining client, who went on to win the 1989 world title. Less than a year later, Potter and Mansted split acrimoniously. Mansted then left pro surfing to manage Sydney-area rock bands.

Surfing magazine named Mansted as one of 50 "Surfing Leaders Who Are Changing Our Sport" in 1987. Five years later, *Australia's Surfing Life* magazine cited him as one of Australia's "50 Most Influential Surfers."

Margaret River   Thirty-mile stretch of coastal area on the southwest corner of Western Australia, 145 miles south of Perth, renowned for its powerful reef waves, translucent Indian Ocean water, and bucolic beachfront settings. Dozens of good to world-class waves are located in the area, including Margaret River (often called "the Point"), a left-breaking reef located just west of the small town that gives the area its name; the Box, a mauling right-breaking tube; and North Point, a temperamental but occasionally flawless right-breaking point in Cowaramup Bay. The picturesque Margaret area coastline is dotted with wide, sandy bays flanked by limestone cliffs, eucalyptus forests, rolling bushland hills, and small farms and wineries. February through June is the best time for surf here, as the weather is generally stable, while ocean storms in the Roaring 40s region frequently produce four to 10-foot waves. Dramatic weather changes are common to this part of the coast, particularly in winter. Average daytime air temperatures in Margaret River range from the low 70s in summer to the low 60s in winter; water temperatures remain in the 60s all year. Surfing hazards include shallow reefs, powerful waves, and sharks.

Perth surfers Cliff Hills and Rob Birch were the first to explore the Margaret River area for waves in 1961, riding just north in nearby Yallingup. Despite the area's excellent waves and proximity to Perth, Margaret River surf breaks remained uncrowded— in part due to inhospitable local wave-riders—until the real estate and winery boom of the mid-'90s. By 2002, Margaret River (population 10,000) was home to more than 300 full-time local surfers, a half-dozen surf shops, and the Margaret River Boardriders Club. It is also a popular weekend destination for Perth surfers. Internationally known surfers from the Mar-

garet River area include Mitch Thorson, Paul and Jake Paterson, Melanie Redman, and current world title contender Taj Burrow. Pro surfing pioneer Ian Cairns of Perth grew up surfing Margaret River.

The Australian National Titles were held at Margaret River in 1969, 1973, 1978, 1988, and 1994; world tour pro events were held there in 1985–90. The Margaret River surf has been featured in more than two dozen surf movies and videos, including *Evolution* (1969), *Gripping Stuff II* (1991), and *Sabotaj* (1999). The area's waves are described in *The Surfing and Sailboard Guide to Australia* (1986), Mark Warren's *Atlas of Australian Surfing* (1998), and *The World Stormrider Guide* (2001). *See also* Western Australia.

Margieson, Brenden   Rubber-limbed surfer from northern New South Wales, cited by *Australia's Surfing Life* magazine in 1998 as "the best free-surfer in the world." Margieson was born (1972) in Sydney, but raised in the bucolic wave-rich environs of Byron Bay, 60 miles south of the Queensland/New South Wales border. He had a spectacular win in the 1996 Nias Indonesian Pro, but his career was built almost exclusively on sponsor-paid promo visits to exotic surfing ports of call around the world. Professional "photo-trip" surfers have been a part of the sport since the mid-1980s, but Margieson, a bird-watcher and home gardener during his nonsurfing hours, has all but defined the role: superhuman in the water, always grateful for the job, and an easygoing travel companion. Margieson has appeared in more than a dozen surf videos, including *The Green Iguana* (1992), *The Sons of Fun* (1993), and *The Billabong Challenge* (1995).

Brenden Margieson

marine layer   A dense, low-lying stratum of clouds, often accompanied by fog; a regular occurrence on the American West Coast during late spring and early summer. A marine layer occurs when cold upwelling ocean water comes into contact with warmer air, forming condensation; it's often accompanied by a light to moderate onshore wind. Along certain areas of the coast, particular to the north, a marine layer can last for days or even weeks at a time. It's a particularly irritating condition to beachgoers, as the sun-blocking marine layer often dissipates less than a mile inland.

Marsh, Bette   Tireless surf contest official from Atlantic Beach, North Carolina; a mainstay of the Eastern Surfing Association (ESA) from its 1967 inception until 1992. Born Bette MacLachlan in Wisconsin in 1924, she married Jim Marsh at age 24, raised three boys (all surfers), and opened Marsh's Surf Shop in Atlantic Beach in 1972, by which time she was already being called the "Matriarch of East Coast Surfing." One of the original five ESA trustees, Marsh served as district director for the Carolinas from 1968 to 1979, and later coached the ESA team to the U.S. Championships. She also lobbied city councils on beach access issues, and in 1975 wrote "Who Controls the Beaches?" a *Surfing* magazine article on wave-riding restrictions in North Carolina. Marsh died in early 1992 of complications following a car accident. In 1998, Marsh was elected to the East Coast Surf Legends Hall of Fame. *See also* Eastern Surfing Association.

Marsh, Richard   Good-natured pro surfer from Cronulla, New South Wales, Australia; world-ranked #8 in 1992; known as "Dog" for his street-scruffy appearance. Marsh was born (1967) and raised in Cronulla, and began surfing at age nine. In 1986 he won the Australian National Titles and was runner-up to fellow Cronulla goofyfoot Mark Occhilupo in the prestigious Pro Junior; in 1987 he won the Pro Junior. Marsh broke the top 10 just once in his eight-year pro tour career, finishing eighth in 1992, the same year he won his only world circuit event, the Yoplait Pro on Réunion Island. He was also a finalist in the 1990 Pipeline Masters. The diminutive (5'7", 140 pounds) bleach-blond Marsh rode in a wide, low-slung stance; "not exactly a style-master," surf journalist Derek Hynd wrote, "but compensates with tenacity." Marsh appeared in a few surf movies and videos, including *Sultans II* (1989), *Rad Movez* (1992), and *Pure Filth* (1993). He opened Triple Bull Surf Shop in Cronulla in 1997.

Martin, Terry   Quiet and persevering Southern California surfboard shaper, credited with making 1,200 boards every year since 1963, totaling more than 45,000 boards to date. Martin was born (1937) and raised in San Diego County, California, began surfing at age 12, and shaped his first board—a balsa/redwood laminate—that same year. He spent the bulk of his long career working for Hobie Surfboards and Stewart Surfboards, and has made boards for David Nuuhiwa, Bill Hamilton, Gerry Lopez, Wayne Bartholomew, Shaun Tomson, and Mark Foo, among others. In 1965, on a lark, Martin shaped a 16-foot by 31-inch board—at that point the largest board ever made. Nine surfers were able to ride it at the same time.

Martinson, Mark   Barrel-chested regularfoot surfer from Long Beach, California; winner of the 1965 United States Surfing Championships, and globe-trotting lead in a series of surf movies made by Greg MacGillivray and Jim Freeman in the mid- and late '60s. Martinson was born (1947) and raised in Long Beach, the son of a mechanic and stock-car racer father, and began surfing at age 10. Six years later he placed runner-up in the 1962 West Coast Championships; in 1964 he won the United States Invitational, and in 1965 he won the men's division of the United States Surfing Championships. Martinson returned from a poor showing in the 1965 World Championships in Peru to find his U.S. Army induction notice. He deferred entry for as long as possible, then spent nearly seven years hiding from Selective Service agents. Martinson didn't quite go underground, as he continued to have a presence in the surf media, but had no phone number or mailing address and was virtually incommunicado. Much of his time from 1965 to 1969 was spent traveling with the MacGillivray/Freeman team—to Peru, Brazil, Argentina, France, Spain, Portugal, and Hawaii—while filming *Free and Easy* (1967) and *Waves of Change* (1970). Federal agents finally caught up with Martinson in 1971; an asthmatic, he washed out of basic training after three weeks.

Although Martinson never had a major contest result after 1965, he hit his peak as a surfer in the late '60s as one of the first California riders to fully adapt to the new short surfboards. Stocky and short (5′6″, 160 pounds), Martinson rode out of a low crouch, and occasionally pushed his turns past the breaking point at places like Sunset Beach in Hawaii. The amiable Martinson worked as a commercial fisherman from 1973 to 1992; since then he's shaped a line of longboards for Robert August Surfboards in Huntington Beach.

Marui Pro, Marui Japan Open   Professional World pro tour event held from 1981 to 1998, sponsored by the Tokyo-based Marui Department Stores, held at Chiba Beach or Hebara Beach, near Tokyo. From 1981 to 1990, and again from 1994 to 1998, the Marui was the only Japanese event on the world tour schedule; the 1991 Marui Pro, worth $195,000, was the richest event of the season. From 1984 to 1988 Marui sponsored a second men's-division-only season-opening event, the Marui Japan Open, held on semitropical Niijima Island, located about 100 miles south of Tokyo. (From 1986 to 1992 Marui also sponsored the Pipeline Masters contest in Hawaii; in 1988 it sponsored a one-off wavepool event in the Sports World complex in the city of Nagaoka.) Wave conditions for the Marui Pro were spotty; occasionally the surf was head-high or bigger and well-shaped, but about three-quarters of the Marui events were held in small, gutless waves. Three-time world champion Tom Curren earned his first world tour win at the Marui in 1982, and went on to dominate the contest over the next eight years, winning seven times altogether. The event was canceled in 1999. Marui Pro results:

1981:	Wayne Bartholomew (no women's event)
1982:	Tom Curren, Debbie Bowers
1983:	Tom Curren, Kim Mearig
1984:	Tom Carroll, Kim Mearig; (Niijima) Martin Potter
1985:	Tom Curren, Jolene Smith; (Niijima) Tom Carroll
1986:	Gary Elkerton, Pam Burridge; (Niijima) Tom Curren
1987:	Damien Hardman, Frieda Zamba; (Niijima) Tom Curren
1988:	Derek Ho, Jodie Cooper; (Niijima) Tom Curren
1989:	Dave MacAulay, Wendy Botha; (Niijima) Martin Potter
1990:	Tom Curren, Jodie Cooper
1991:	Derek Ho (no women's event)
1992:	Fabio Gouveia, Wendy Botha
1993:	Kelly Slater, Pauline Menczer
1994:	Rob Machado, Lynette MacKenzie
1995:	Rob Machado, Lynette MacKenzie
1996:	Shane Beschen, Pam Burridge
1997:	Kelly Slater, Lisa Andersen
1998:	Danny Wills, Serena Brooke

Maryland   Maryland surfing is generally friendly, safe, and uncomplicated. The state's 31-mile coastline is lined with a series of long, narrow, sand barrier islands; eastern Maryland is part of the Delmarva Peninsula, bordered by the Atlantic Ocean and Chesapeake Bay. The Maryland beachfront is divided into two main areas: the 10-mile strip in and around Ocean City, a famously manic summertime resort destination; and, in poetic counterbalance, the clean, empty, sand-and-shrub-filled Assateague Island National Seashore, located just south of the Ocean City Inlet. Ocean City has more than a dozen jetties that help create sandbars, and popular surfing areas here include 8th Street, 47th Street, and 80th Street. The surf along Assateague Island, which curves gently south for 20 miles into northern Virginia, is far less crowded than Ocean City, and will sometimes hold shape during larger swells, when Ocean City waves lose form. Winter air temperatures often drop below freezing, and the water dips into the mid-30s; air and water temperatures in summer both average about 75, but the relentless humidity makes it feel much hotter. Surfing is an all-year sport in Maryland, but best in fall and early winter, as the humidity falls, the Ocean City population drops almost 90 percent from its summertime high, and North Atlantic storms and hurricanes can produce clean surf with offshore winds.

Maryland lifeguard George Feehley occasionally surfed in front of his Ocean City post in the late 1950s, but surfing didn't really take hold here until 1962, when Delaware residents Bill Wise and George Pittman began riding Ocean City's North Beach, and were soon joined by Dan Herlihy, Bryant Hungerford, Jim Phillips, and the Johnson brothers, Richard and Al. The Eastern Surfer, Maryland's first surf shop, owned by Wise and Pittman and located in an Ocean City hotel basement, opened in 1964. On July 4th of that year, Bruce Brown did a live-narration screening at a local high school of his just-finished movie *The Endless Summer*; the morning before the show, *Endless*

Summer stars Mike Hynson and Robert August, along with top California surfer Corky Carroll, gave a surfing demonstration at 17th Street that drew nearly 5,000 spectators.

By 2003, Maryland had eight surf shops, all located in Ocean City, and about 1,500 resident surfers. The Eastern Surfing Association runs about a half-dozen surf contests here annually. Richard "Skill" Johnson, a first-generation Maryland surfer and finalist in the masters division of the 1980 United States Surfing Championships, is Maryland's best-known surfer, along with 1986 national champion bodyboarder Jay Reale. Jack Shipley, world pro tour judge and cofounder of Lightning Bolt Surfboards in Hawaii, was born and raised in Maryland.

Massachusetts   History-rich Massachusetts has by far the largest population of any New England state, and a fair number of worthwhile breaks along its crooked-finger mainland and offshore islands, but the surf scene here is nonetheless small and insular. Massachusetts can be broken into four surfing regions: 1) North of Boston, primarily around Cape Ann and Gloucester, offers a series of beachbreaks and cobblestone pointbreaks, most of which produce cold and mediocre surf, with the best waves usually arriving in winter and early spring. The area in and around the peninsula town of Nahant, on the north side of Boston Bay, is the area's best-known surf zone. 2) South of Boston is home to the state's most popular surfing areas, around the towns of Hull and Scituate, with a small number of surf shops and several Web cams focused on nearby breaks. As Cape Cod blocks incoming south and southeast swells, the area only receives waves generated by local winds or winter nor'easters. 3) The 65-mile east-facing arm of Cape Cod, positioned well into the Atlantic, contains dozens of beachbreaks, is best in fall and winter, but receives surf throughout the year. Beach crowds can be a problem in the summertime. 4) The offshore islands, primarily Martha's Vineyard and Nantucket Island, have a small number of breaks, with the best surf arriving during the fall. Famously exclusive and restricted, Massachusetts island surfing is generally practiced by wealthy visitors. Average coastal daytime air temperatures in Massachusetts range from the low 70s in summer to the mid-30s in winter; water temperatures range from the low 30s to the low 70s, although Cape Cod rarely gets above 62.

Bodysurfing and bellyboarding were popular on Cape Cod and the north coast of Massachusetts as far back as the early 1930s, but stand-up surfing wasn't introduced to the state until 1963, when native Bob Stevens began riding the beaches near his Nahant home. Nahant Beach Surf Shop, the first retail outlet of its kind in Massachusetts, opened the following year, and not long after the Short Beach Competition Team sponsored the state's first surfing contest in Nahant. Dave Williams of Nantucket Beach is believed to be the first person to ride the area south of Boston in 1963; surfers from Springfield helped introduce the sport to Cape Cod around the same time. "It's a little cool maybe in the spring," a founding Cape Cod wave-rider told *Surfing* magazine at the time, "but some of the boys wear rubber jackets [wetsuits], and others wear sweatshirts and baggies and we enjoy it to the fullest."

Massachusetts later became a novelty destination for a small number of East Coast surfers ("the place is so historic," surf journalist Any Vansant wrote in 1995, "even the squirrels live in ivy-covered brick houses"), but was for the most part left alone. By 2003, Massachusetts was home to seven surf shops and an estimated 1,000 surfers, most of them seasonal. Massachusetts is included in the New England district of the Eastern Surfing Association. The Massachusetts surf is detailed in *The Stormrider Guide North America* (2002).

Massara, Mark   San Francisco–based surfer/lawyer/environmentalist. Massara was born (1961) in Santa Barbara, California, began surfing at age 10, and graduated in 1987 from the University of San Francisco Law School. He began his most famous crusade in 1988, when he drove to northern California's Humboldt Bay to ride some waves and sniff out—literally—an ongoing toxic runoff problem with two local lumber-pulp mills, Simpson Paper and Louisiana-Pacific. "You could taste the pollution," Massara later told *People* magazine. In September 1991, Massara, on behalf of the Surfrider Foundation, won an out-of-court settlement from the two pulp mills to pay Clean Water Act government fines of more than $5.8 million, to redesign their outflow machinery, and to pay Surfrider $500,000. Massara was nicknamed "Messiah" and became a national media figure as the "surfing lawyer." The Humboldt case remains the second largest ever collected for Clean Water Act violations. Immediately after the victory, however, Massara and Surfrider began fighting over the group's $500,000 windfall, and in 1993 Massara and a handful of northern California Surfrider members broke away to form Surfer's Environmental Alliance (SEA). Massara also became director of the Sierra Club's California Coastal Program, and later founded the Surfing Attorneys' Association. "Surfers are environmentalists whether they want to be or not," Massara said in 2000. "People think we can be dismissed as surfers fighting for our right to surf, but we're fighting for clean water for everyone." Two years earlier, however, Massara admitted that organizing surfers "is like herding cats." *See also* environmentalism and surfing, politics and surfing.

Massfeller, Steve   Regularfoot surfer from Daytona Beach, Florida; a big-wave revivalist in the early 1980s, and very nearly the first world pro tour fatality, after a head injury in the 1983 Pipeline Masters. Massfeller was born (1955) and raised in Daytona Beach, began surfing at age nine, and moved to the North Shore of Oahu not long after graduating from high school. In 1978, he and fellow Floridian Pat Mulhern were the surprise winners in the World Team Challenge competition at Sunset Beach, beating Australians Peter Townend and Cheyne Horan in the finals. Massfeller was a finalist in the 1980 and 1983 Pro Class Trials, but was better known as one of a small group of surfers—and the only East Coaster—still interested in riding 20-foot-plus surf at a time when such outer-limit surfing had fallen out of fashion. "A big-wave rider," he said in early 1983, "can only take so many wipeouts until his number's up." Ten months later, after what appeared be a routine wipeout during the Pipeline Masters, Massfeller went headfirst into the reef, lost consciousness, was pulled to the surface some minutes later, and airlifted off the beach with a massive skull fracture over his right eye. Massfeller would have problems with his sight, memory, and speech, but after the damaged portion of his skull was reinforced with a steel plate he was able to surf again, and in 1987 he returned to the North Shore for the winter surf season. *See also* injuries and surfing.

Masters World Championships   Annual men's-only surfing competition for former world tour pros age 36 and over; founded in 1997 as the Oxbow Masters. Similar events had been staged as far back as 1982, when Peter Drouyn won the legends event of the Rip Curl Pro at Bells Beach, Australia, beating Nat Young, Midget Farrelly, and Wayne Lynch. In 1987, Hawaiian surfer Hans Hedemann won the $40,000 Stubbies Masters, for surfers 27 and over. The Masters World Championships, sanctioned by the Association of Surfing Professionals, is the first ongoing event of its kind. Twenty-four surfers attended the debut 1997 Masters, including former world champions Peter Townend, Shaun Tomson, and Wayne Bartholomew, and pro tour standouts Ian Cairns, Cheyne Horan, Dane Kealoha, Simon Anderson, and Wayne Lynch. The weeklong $50,000 event was held in churning six to eight-foot surf at Fiji's Cloudbreak, and Australian Terry Richardson defeated Michael Ho of Hawaii to win the $7,000 first-place check.

In 1998 the contest was moved to Puerto Escondido, Mexico, where the veterans (including Nat Young and Reno Abellira) again faced the somewhat daunting task of riding hollow eight-footers. While all ages had competed in a single division in 1997, this time the competitors were divided into two groups: Masters (36–40) and Grandmasters (over 40). Quiksilver Europe took over as event sponsor in 1999, inflated the name of the event to the Quiksilver Silver Edition Masters World Championships, lowered the age limit to 35, and moved the contest to the French Basque coast. Rob Buchanan, covering the event for *Outside* magazine, noted a division of sorts among the Masters contestants, between the "guys with the mortgages and haircuts and good jobs" and the "seekers, slackers and free spirits." The Masters division was changed to include surfers from 35 to 43, while Grandmasters was raised to age 44 and over.

Masters winners, Grandmasters winners, and event locations for the World Masters Championships are as follows:

1997: Terry Richardson (Cloudbreak, Tavarua)
1998: Joey Buran, Buzzy Kerbox (Puerto Escondido, Mexico)
1999: Cheyne Horan, Wayne Bartholomew (Lafetania and Anglet, France),
2000: Gary Elkerton, Michael Ho (Lafetania and Anglet, France)
2001: Gary Elkerton, Mark Richards (Bundoran, Ireland)
2002: Gary Elkerton, Wayne Bartholomew (Makaha, Hawaii)

mat-surfing   Type of surfing performed on a soft, inflatable, rectangular surf mat; wildly popular in the 1960s and early '70s with weekend beachgoers as well as preteen surfers-in-training. The all-rubber "surf-o-plane" was invented by a Sydney physician in 1934, and American-made surf mats—also called "surf rafts" or "floats"—were being used in Virginia Beach,

Mat surfing; California's George Greenough

Virginia, in the early '40s and in Southern California by the late '40s. Mat rental stands were a common sight at popular beaches on both American coasts by the early '60s, each stand featuring a small fleet of matching, numbered rafts, usually made by tennis shoe giant Converse. Each mat was four and a half feet long, with a laminated rubber/canvas body segmented into five longitudinal pontoons, hard rubber "bumpers" on either end, and a nylon rope threaded loosely around the perimeter as a handle. Mats were safe and easy to ride, approved for use in areas where board-surfing was not allowed, and a big hit with beach tourists of all ages, who generally rode straight to beach in a prone position. Meanwhile, as *Surfer* magazine noted in 1964, legions of school-age kids were "doing their surfing apprenticeship on the mats" by crouching on the raft deck and even angling across the wave face. Australian surfers were doing the same on their surf-o-planes. Most would graduate to surfboards by age 11 or 12, but a few continued to mat-ride, and discovered that the four-pontoon, red-white-and-blue Converse Hodgeman model outperformed the more expensive blue-yellow rental rafts. (California surf photographer Woody Woodworth, who bought his first Hodgeman for $14 in 1966, later noted that the price could in fact add up. When the surf was up at Corona del Mar jetty, Woodworth said, "it wasn't unusual to see the remains of several rafts strewn along the seawall and beach [after being] popped on the barnacle-encrusted jetty.")

Mat-riding's greatest supporter was California-born surfer and board designer George Greenough, best known as the creative force behind the late-'60s shortboard revolution. While Greenough was often

filmed and photographed riding his foam-and-fiberglass "spoon" kneeboard, he preferred riding prone on a surf mat—partly because of the heightened sensation of speed that comes from riding so close to the water surface, and partly because mats, unlike surfboards, can be ridden in windy, choppy, ugly surf. "The funny thing about mats," Greenough said in 2000, "is that they're the easiest thing to ride on a beginner level, but the hardest thing to ride on an advanced level. I've been riding mats for over 40 years, and I'm still learning things." *Rubber Duck Riders,* Greenough's short film on mat-riding, was produced in 1971; Greenough and surf journalist Paul Gross were featured riding their mats in the 1978 surf film *Fantasea.*

The surf mat disappeared from most beaches not long after the introduction of the Morey Boogie bodyboard in 1973, which was not only soft, safe, and easy to ride, but didn't pop and deflate. Paul Gross, however, citing the development of a high-performance three-pontoon raft, describes the mid-'80s as the "golden age of mat riding." By 2000, Greenough estimated that there were fewer than a dozen dedicated mat-riders in California, and just a few more in Australia—although the surf mat was reintroduced in Australia the following year. *See also* bodyboarding, George Greenough.

Matson line   San Francisco–based shipping service used by America's Hawaii-bound surfers from the 1930s through the 1950s. The Matson Steamship and Navigation Company introduced its first passenger ship, the steamer *Lurline,* in 1908. California surfing pioneer Tom Blake was almost certainly the first surfer to use the Matson line (whose boats were easily recognized by their red-brown hulls), making the six-day journey to Hawaii in 1924. "The ocean air was clean," Blake later recalled, "and the journey quite enjoyable." Sam Reid followed in 1925; Pete Peterson, Lorrin Harrison, and a small number of other surfers did so in the late '20s and '30s, as did virtually all Hawaii-bound American surfers until after World War II, when DC-6 planes cut the travel time to 12 hours. Even with air travel available, surfers in the late '40s and '50s often chose to sail. Matson-traveling surfers generally booked into the budget-priced below-deck steerage class (about $100 round-trip), then trespassed freely onto the upper levels. Meals, included with the ticket price, were a highlight of trip, and in one of Greg Noll's late-'50s

Search for Surf movies, a group of surfers are seen doing on-deck calisthenics in order to build an appetite for dinner. "The goal," Noll later recalled, "was to have the waiter hand you a menu and you'd look the whole thing up and down, hand it back and say, 'Yes, that will do.'"

Maui The second-largest Hawaiian island, Maui is 48 miles long, 26 miles wide, covers over 720 square miles, and is called the Valley Isle for its beautiful volcanic basins and cliff-lined canyons. Maui is fringed by about 70 surf breaks of varying quality and consistency. Because the island is flanked to the southwest by the Big Island and to the northwest by Molokai and Oahu, incoming swells are often blocked or reduced; winter surf on Maui is generally about half the size of that found on Oahu's North Shore, and most of its south shore waves demand a rare southeast swell. Maui's main surfing areas include the north shore town of Kahului (near the consistent waves of Ho'okipa), the west coast resort towns of Lahaina and Kaanapali, and the burgeoning south coast town of Kihei. Maui is home to three of the world's best surf spots: the hypnotically perfect right-breaking winter waves at Honolua Bay; the bullet-fast rights of Maalaea on the south shore; and the horrific right-breaking tubes at Jaws, a tow-in-only big-wave break located on the north coast. Steady northwest tradewinds bring moisture in from the northeast. The east, north, and upper northwest corners of the island are lushly vegetated and often windy and cloudy; the other side of the island is fairly dry and arid. Haleakala, the world's largest dormant volcano, 10,000 feet high, dominates Maui's eastern half. Temperatures on Maui range from 70 to 80 degrees (except for the upper slopes of Haleakala Crater, which can drop to 40), and water temperatures are in the mid- to upper 70s. About 120,000 people live on Maui, making it Hawaii's second-most populated island, following Oahu.

Premodern Hawaiian surfers frequented at least six breaks on Maui, with hundreds riding at a time in the gentle waves off Lahaina as late as 1823. Thirty years later surfing continued to be an enthusiastically practiced sport on Maui even though it had been all but eradicated on the other Hawaiian islands by visiting missionaries. By the end of the century, however, the sport had faded here as well, and it didn't return until the early 1930s. Maui remained a virtually unheard of surfing destination until the early and mid-'60s, when Honolua Bay was presented in surf movies and magazines as the unspoiled tropical version of Malibu. A mini-surf boom followed, as a small number of famous surfers—including *Surfer* magazine founder John Severson and ace tuberider Gerry Lopez—took up residence on Maui, while thousands of others flooded in looking for a quick hit of paradise; HERE TODAY, GONE TO MAUI, as the tourist-hawked T-shirts would later proclaim. Honolua was one of the great testing grounds of the late-'60s shortboard revolution, and longtime Maui resident Joseph "Buddy Boy" Kaohi held his own as the best surfers in the world, riding their new "pocket rockets" and vee-bottoms, began carving radical new lines across the wave face. (Maui also became known around this time as the LSD-infused psychedelic Babylon, a part of the island's culture best documented in the Jimi Hendrix concert movie *Rainbow Bridge,* filmed largely in Haleakala Crater—with added Maalaea surfing clips—three months before Hendrix's death.) Maui's strong and predictable tradewinds had by the late '70s turned the island into the sailboarding capital of the world, which in turn led to the late-'90s development of kiteboarding. Sailboarders were the first to ride at Jaws in the late 1980s, and were an important part of the Jaws tow-in push in the mid-'90s. Foilboarding was also invented on Maui.

As of 2003, Maui was home to 15 surf shops and about 5,000 resident surfers. The Hawaiian Amateur Surfing Association sponsors five contests here yearly. Maui has also hosted a number of pro events, including the 1999-founded Billabong Girls Pro and the 2002 Tow-In World Cup. Maui is home to a number of surf world notables, including artist Chris Lassen, photographer Erik Aeder, big-wave masters Laird Hamilton and Dave Kalama, and aerial surfer Randy "Goose" Welch. The Maui surf is detailed in the *Surfing Hawaii* (1973), *Surfer's Guide to Hawaii* (1991), and *The World Stormrider Guide* (2001). *See also* Honolua Bay, Jaws, Maalaea.

Mauritius Small subtropical Indian Ocean island nation located 330 miles east of Madagascar; best known to surfers as home to Tamarin Bay, the fickle but magnificent left-breaking reef wave featured in the 1974 surf travel film *The Forgotten Island of Santosha.* Mauritius gets its best surf between May and September, from swells originating in the Indian Ocean's Roaring 40s. Most of the two dozen surf breaks located along the island's 110-mile coastline are reef-pass waves that are often compromised or made unridable by the prevailing southeast tradewinds. While Tamarin Bay, located on the southwest coast, is angled so that the winds blow offshore, incoming swells have to bend sharply around the coast before hitting the reef, and the waves are thus much smaller here than almost anywhere else in the area: Tamarin only hits peak form about 20 days on an average season, and rarely gets above eight foot. But when conditions are right, the wave at Tamarin peels dreamlike across the reef for nearly 300 yards, in a series of exquisite tube sections. A 1989 issue of *Surfing* magazine named Tamarin Bay as one of the "25 Best Waves in the World." Average midday temperatures in Mauritius range from the low 70s to the mid-80s; water temperatures range from 70 to 80. Sharp reefs are the island's primary surfing hazard, and many of the breaks are too shallow to ride at low tide.

Pioneering French surfer Joel de Rosnay was the first to ride Tamarin Bay in 1958, using an old Australian-made plywood surfboard. De Rosnay wrote about Mauritius in a 1963 *Surfer* magazine article, and the unnamed Tamarin lefts were featured in *Sea of Joy,* a 1971 surf film. Three years later California surfer/filmmaker Larry Yates wrote "The Forgotten Island of Santosha," a *Surfer* cover story featuring Hawaiian champion Joey Cabell. "Santosha," a Hindustani world for "peace," was Yates's pseudonym for Tamarin Bay, and both the article and the like-titled film presented the island as the ultimate exotic surf destination. Yates noted that "Santosha is not a place, but a state of mind," striking a phrase that would become a mantra for the hundreds of Santosha-inspired surfers who set out to find their own perfect wave. The Yates/Cabell excursion itself was listed by *Surfer* in 1995 as one of the top 10 surf trips of all time.

Mauritius had two surf shops and more than 100 native surfers by 2003, most of them French Mauritian and local Creole. Resident surfers have earned a reputation as being among the most territorial in the world, particularly a loosely formed group known as the "White Shorts," and visiting surfers can expect to be ignored, harangued, or worse.

Maverick's   Fearsome big-wave surf break located just west of the Pillar Point headland in Half Moon Bay, California, 25 miles south of San Francisco; the heavily publicized focal point for West Coast big-

Maverick's; Peter Mel of California

wave riding since the early '90s. Daytime winter air temperatures in Half Moon Bay range from the low 40s to the mid-60s; the water temperature remains at or near 50. The Maverick's wave season usually begins in October and lasts through March; it begins to break at 10 feet, but doesn't really hit form until 15 feet. When the surf hits 35 or 40 feet—which happens roughly every other year—the wave begins to break over a different and far less predictable set of reefs located further offshore. Maverick's is a right-breaking wave for the most part, although lefts are ridden when the surf is below 20 foot. The terraced reef at Maverick's produces a two-speed wave: a fast, hollow, tremendously explosive opening section— the heart of the Maverick's ride—spills into a yielding "shoulder" area, which often leads to another near-vertical section known as Second Bowl, then another flat spot, and occasionally a third steep section. Most rides at Maverick's last less than 15 seconds. A ride connecting all sections might last up to 50 seconds and run for 400 yards. The shoreward edge of the Maverick's surf zone is marked by a jagged stand of rocks, and surfers occasionally get filtered through the rocks into the nearshore lagoon. Maverick's waves are greatly affected by tide (lower tides generally make the waves steeper and more dangerous) and the direction of the swell (northwest swells produce longer, easier waves; west swells produce shorter, steeper waves).

Three Half Moon Bay surfers rode the inside waves at Pillar Point in the winter of 1961, and the break was named after Maverick, a white-haired German shepherd who followed the group into the water. But it was 18-year-old goofyfoot surfer and local carpenter Jeff Clark, beginning in 1975, who did the real pioneering work at Maverick's. Remarkably, Clark rode the break alone for 15 years, teaching himself how to ride as a regularfooter, so as to give him a front-on view while riding the rights. Clark introduced Maverick's to surfers from Santa Cruz and San Francisco in the early '90s; the break made its surf world debut in "Cold Sweat," a 1992 *Surfer* magazine cover story. When reknowned Hawaiian big-wave rider Mark Foo drowned at Maverick's on December 23, 1994, after wiping out on a 15-footer, the break became a mainstream media sensation, with coverage in the *New York Times, Rolling Stone, Outside, Spin,* Dateline, and MTV Sports. Jeff Clark, in his late 30s, was still Maverick's central figure and spokesman, even if younger riders like Peter Mel and Darryl "Flea" Virostko of Santa Cruz had become the break's premier surfers. "It just goes to show," Clark told the *Times,* in one of his many gruffly theatrical quotes, "that no matter how prepared you are, [at Maverick's] you're in Neptune's playground."

In tow-in surfing, a rope-holding rider gets a running start at the wave from behind a personal watercraft, was introduced at Maverick's in 1994, but didn't really catch on here until 1999. Tow-in allowed surfers to ride much bigger waves than ever before, and by 2000 Maverick's tow-in riders, led by Mel, Clark, Virostko, and Ken Collins, were riding waves 40 feet and bigger. (The legality of tow-in surfing in the Monterey Bay Marine Sanctuary, which includes Maverick's, was in question as of early 2003.) The $55,000 Quiksilver Maverick's Men Who Ride Mountains contest had meanwhile debuted in 1999, and was won by Virostko, who defended the title in 2000.

Maverick's has been the subject of more than a dozen surf videos and documentaries since the mid-'90s, including *Heavy Water* (1995), *Twenty Feet Under* (1998), *Maverick's* (1998), and *Whipped!* (2001). Maverick's was also featured in *Great Waves* (1998), an Outdoor Life Network television series. Chronicle Books published *Maverick's: The Story of Big-Wave Surfing* in 2000. With the launch of Mavsurfer.com in 1995, Maverick's became the first break to have a dedicated Web site. "Mavericks," a modern dance interpretation of big-wave surfing, performed by the Keith Glassman Company, toured through California in 2001. A photograph of Brazilian surfer Carlos Burle riding an enormous Maverick's wave was picked in 2002 as the winner of the Nissan Xterra XXL Big Surf

Awards. *See also* big-wave surfing, Jeff Clark, Mark Foo, Peter Mel, Darryl "Flea" Virtostko.

Mayes, Jack "Bluey" Loud, strutting Australian surfer from Sydney's Bondi Beach; generally regarded as the country's best wave-rider from the early 1940s to the mid-'50s. Mayes was born (1922) in Sydney, raised in Bondi, and began surfing at age six, after stripping the cloth from his mother's ironing board. He earned notice in his early 20s, riding a 15′ hollow board he nicknamed the "Golden Hawk." A turning point in Mayes's surfing life came in '56, when a group of Southern California surfers-lifeguards visited Australia and brought along their balsa-core "Malibu" boards, which were infinitely more maneuverable than the hollow plywood boards used by the locals. The red-headed, barrel-chested Mayes adapted faster than anyone to the new Malibu-design boards and developed a flamboyant style that included deep-knee bends and scything arm movements, as well as a stance that switched frequently from regularfoot to goofyfoot. On land, Mayes was by turns belligerent and affable. "He knew everyone on the coast," friend and surf-travel partner Peter Bowes told *Tracks* surfing magazine in '97. "We would stop in some little town, everything would be closed, and Jack would go into the pub and in a couple hours come out half-drunk with the keys to the local surf club."

Mayes wrote a semi-regular surfing column for the weekly *Sunday Telegraph* in the early- and mid-'60s, and placed runner-up in the senior men's division of the '68 Australian Titles. He was featured briefly in *Surf Down Under,* a 1958 surf movie, and in a 1985 TV documentary titled the *History of Australian Surfing.* Brad Mayes, Jack Mayes's son, was one of Sydney's best surfers in the early- and mid-'70s and a semifinalist in both the '74 and '75 Coca-Cola Surfabout contests. Brad Mayes died of a heart attack at age 37. Jack Mayes died in 1997, at age 75.

McAlister, Charles "Snow" Robust and sociable Australian surfing pioneer from Manly Beach, New South Wales; a three-time Australian surfing champion in the 1920s; often referred to as the "father of Australian surfing." McAlister was born (1904) and raised in Sydney's Broken Hill, the son of a mailman, and took to the surf immediately when his family moved to Manly Beach in 1914—just in time to see Hawaiian swimmer and surfer Duke Kahanamoku give his famous wave-riding demonstration at nearby

Snow McAlister

Freshwater Beach. "I was staggered," McAlister later said of Kahanamoku's performance. "Everyone just clapped and clapped." McAlister, then 11, had been using his mother's castoff ironing board to ride nearshore waves, but after seeing Kahanamoku at Freshwater he made himself a wooden board similar to the one the Hawaiian used.

Fellow Manly surfer Claude West became the country's first dominant surfer, winning the first of six national surfing championships beginning in 1919, before losing to McAlister in 1926, who then repeated in 1927. The following year's championships were held in Newcastle, and in the final round McAlister did a headstand while riding a small wave all the way to shore, maintained his position as the wave receded and left him docked on beach, and didn't kick down until a contest official tapped him on the calf and said he'd won.

A small, stocky, cheerful man, McAlister continued to be active on the Australian surf scene throughout his life, but was particularly busy in the early and mid-'60s, writing the "Surfing with Snow" column for *Surfing World* magazine, barnstorming from surf club to surf club with filmmaker Bob Evans to do live-narration surf movie screenings, and cofounding the Australia Surfrider's Association.

McAlister traded in his stand-up board for a surf ski in the mid-'50s, which he operated from a sitting position, using a double-bladed paddle. He continued to ride waves into his early 80s. McAlister and four-time world champion Mark Richards were the first two inductees into the Australian Surfing Hall of Fame in 1985. The never-married McAlister died three years later at age 84, and the following year a plaque in his honor was placed into the Manly beachfront promenade.

McCabe, Peter   Ace tuberider from Newcastle, New South Wales, Australia; best known as one of the first surfers to make extended visits to Indonesia, living half of each year in Bali between 1974 and 1984. McCabe was born (1955) in the south coast New South Wales town of Narooma, moved with his family to Newcastle at age eight, and began surfing shortly thereafter. He finished runner-up in the juniors division of the 1974 Australian National Titles (losing to Newcastle neighbor and future four-time world champion Mark Richards), and placed fifth in the men's division the following year. McCabe founded Tradewinds Surfboards in Newcastle in 1976, doing all the board-shaping himself, and working just enough to finance his trips to Bali, where he quickly earned an international reputation for his well-groomed tuberiding at Uluwatu and Padang Padang. McCabe was also one of the first surfers to ride Grajagan in Java, where he and Hawaiian surfer Gerry Lopez would occasionally perform high-speed crisscross "go-behinds." McCabe was arrested in New Caledonia in 1984 for smuggling cocaine, and spent 20 months in a French prison. He still lives in Newcastle and shapes surfboards, and continues to visit Indonesia for a few weeks each year. McCabe appeared in nearly a dozen surf movies, including *Tubular Swells* (1977), *Bali High* (1981), and *Storm Riders* (1982).

McCaul, Brad   Clean-cut goofyfooter from Newport Beach, California; men's division winner in the 1970 United States Surfing Championships. McCaul was born (1952) in Alameda, California, raised in Newport Beach and Capistrano Beach, and began surfing at Huntington Beach at age 13. By 1968, when he was the juniors division national champion, McCaul was grouped with fellow Californian Rolf Aurness and Wayne Lynch of Australia as the best of the new-generation goofyfooters. In 1970, McCaul competed in the World Surfing Championships and the Duke Kahanamoku Classic. While visiting South Africa to compete in the 1971 Gunston 500, which he won, McCaul became one of the first Americans to ride long, spinning right-breaking waves at Jeffreys Bay. A small, quick, agile surfer, McCaul appeared in *Pacific Vibrations* (1970), *Five Summer Stories* (1972), and *Tales from the Tube* (1975). He received a B.A. in psychology from Southern California College in 1976 and a Ph.D. in clinical psychology from the California School of Professional Psychology in 1988.

McClelland, Brennan "Hevs"   Big, loud, jovial surf world toastmaster and organizer from Laguna Beach, California; founder of the United States Surfing Association in 1961, and host of the *Surfer* Magazine Readers Poll Awards ceremony from 1964 to 1968. McClelland, born (1920) and raised in Livingston, Montana, began bodysurfing not long after moving to Laguna with his family at age 11. After serving in the navy during World War II, the 230-pound McClelland received a football scholarship to the University of Southern California, where he befriended young big-wave surfer and football teammate Buzzy Trent. It was Trent who pushed McClelland into board-riding, and later introduced him to surf filmmaker Bud Browne, who, in the early and mid-'60s, frequently cast McClelland in the short comedy skits used to break up the action in his movies. In a star turn from 1962's *Cavalcade of Surf,* a demure McClelland, dressed in a wig and formfitting white one-piece woman's bathing suit, prances into the shorebreak with Hawaii's James "Chubby" Mitchell, and the two oversize men ride tandem.

McClelland founded the United States Surfing Association in large part as an advocacy group to try to prevent or repeal board-riding restrictions enacted by city councils throughout Southern California. But crusading was always second to entertaining; McClelland once performed an impromptu strip tease while announcing a surf contest, and dressed up for a *Surfer* Poll banquet as "the famous Maharishi Laguna." But by the end of the '60s, surfing had draped itself in high counterculture seriousness, and McClelland, who made a living as a liquor store owner, was all but forgotten. He died from diabetes-related problems in 1992 at age 72. McClelland married twice—the first time to 1958 Makaha International women's division

champion Marge Calhoun—and had one child. He was inducted into the International Surfing Hall of Fame in 1991. The *Surfer's Journal,* reporting on his death, reprinted a bit of doggerel McClelland had read at an early '60s surf function:

> *High in the crook of a hot little hook*
> *Salt spray singeing my toes*
> *I ought to be home with my nose to the stone*
> *Instead of here where the tradewind blows.*
> *For how can a man*
> *Amount to a damn*
> *Playing with these kids in the sea?*
> *Where would it end?*
> *I'll tell you my friend:*
> *When the last line is writ*
> *Who gives a shit?*
> *Except when will the next wave be*

See also United States Surfing Association.

McCoy, Geoff   Creative and cocksure Australian surfboard designer/shaper from the North Coast of New South Wales; best known for his 1980 reverse-teardrop Lazer Zap design and for his professional association with top Aussie pro Cheyne Horan. McCoy was born (1948) in Gosford, New South Wales, the son of a farmer, began surfing at age 14 and shaping at 17. He made boards for Sydney mainstays Bennett Surfboards and Keyo Surfboards in the late '60s, and was cofounder of the short-lived M&M Surfboards. In 1970, the blond-haired shaping prodigy founded McCoy Surfboards in the Sydney suburb of Brookvale, and shortly thereafter became the first Australian to make twin-fin boards. McCoy team riders over the years included world tour standouts Mark Warren, Larry Blair, Pam Burridge, and Damien Hardman, but his partnership with Horan—initiated in 1976, three years after McCoy moved his company to Avoca Beach, just north of Sydney—brought both to their career peaks. The Lazer Zap (generically known as the "needle-nose" or "no-nose") was developed in part because McCoy, as he later said, "always had this vision of surfboards looking like triangles." The strange wide-backed craft, with its drastically reduced nose area, dropped the board's wide point well below center, creating a small-wave board that pivoted effortlessly but was incapable of holding a sustained turn. The prodigiously talented Horan nonetheless rode the Lazer Zap to a second-place finish on the world tour in 1981 and again in 1982. The pure no-nose design itself was nearly obsolete by 1982, but the tri-fin board—introduced in 1981 by fellow Australian shaper Simon Anderson—incorporated a narrow McCoy-style nose. McCoy Surfboards meanwhile became one of the surf-world's hottest labels, with outlets in California, Hawaii, and Japan, but in 1984 the company went bankrupt after a business associate vanished and left McCoy with debts totaling nearly $400,000. McCoy continued to shape, but never regained his place in the surfboard manufacturing hierarchy. His self-esteem, however, did not flag. "McCoy-Horan was the most dominant force in surfing around the world," he stated in 1992. "We were doing all this new, exciting stuff, [and] the opposition were just cringing." Later that year McCoy was named as one his country's 50 most influential surfers by *Australia's Surfing Life* magazine; he was also listed in a poll by his fellow shapers as surf history's fourth most significant board-maker. In 2003, McCoy was living in Byron Bay, New South Wales. He's been married once and has two children. *See also* no-nose.

McCoy, Jack   Masterful surf film and video-maker from Australia; winner of the *Surfer* Magazine Video of the Year Award in 1996 and 1999, and widely regarded as the sport's premier cinematographer. McCoy was born (1948) in Los Angeles, the son of a radio and TV show host, spent his early childhood in Hollywood, and moved with his family in 1954 to Hawaii, where he soon began surfing. The preteen McCoy worked in the early '60s hanging movie handbills on telephone poles for touring surf filmmakers. He moved to Australia in 1970, and with encouragement from surf filmmaker Alby Falzon began shooting still photographs; McCoy's work was soon featured regularly in *Tracks* magazine. After McCoy teamed up with Australian photographer Dick Hoole in 1975, both began shooting 16-millimeter film, and *Tubular Swells,* their well-reviewed first surf movie, was released the following year. *Storm Riders* (1982), their follow-up, premiered at the Sydney Opera House. After splitting with Hoole, McCoy went on to make *Kong's Island* (1983), a short film featuring Australian powerhouse surfer Gary Elkerton; *The Performers* (1984), one of the first surf videos; a documentary on the 1986 Quiksilver in Memory of Eddie Aikau big-wave contest at Waimea; and *Surf Hits,* vol. 1 (1988), an "album" of video shorts released on video. McCoy continued to shoot still photographs as

well, and from 1977 to 1995 was listed on the *Surfer* magazine masthead.

McCoy—at 6′3″, lanky smooth, well-spoken, and sometimes imperious—was hired in 1990 by Australian-based surfwear company Billabong to produce the first in a series of marketing videos that would define his career. Traveling often to exotic locations with Billabong team riders (including Mark Occhilupo, Shane Dorian, Ross Williams, Luke Egan, and Michael Barry), doing much of his best filming from the water, and working closely with art director Graham Davey and film editor Calli Cerami, McCoy turned in one beautifully crafted video after another, including *Bunyip Dreaming* (1990), *The Green Iguana* (1992), and *Sik Joy* (1994). Released into the '90s flood of surf video titles, the huge majority of which were raw, loud, and abrasive, McCoy's work existed on a different artistic plane altogether; he shot in 16-millimeter film, rather than video, and used world music on the soundtrack, rather than neopunk. He also had a feel for pacing, color-matching, visual humor, and peripheral shots.

McCoy developed and directed the 1995 Billabong Challenge surf contest, held in remote Western Australia and featuring an elite group of seven surfers, including Kelly Slater, Rob Machado, and Sunny Garcia. McCoy's *Billabong Challenge* documentary brought him a *Surfer* Magazine Video of the Year Award in 1996; he earned another award three years later for *Occy: The Occumentary,* about 2000 world champion Mark Occhilupo.

McCoy has lived in New South Wales, Victoria, Queensland, and Western Australia. He's married and has two children. He was featured in *50 Years of Surfing on Film,* an Outdoor Life Network documentary TV series. As of 2003, McCoy had made 21 full-length or short-subject surf movies and videos, including *A Day in the Life of Wayne Lynch* (1978), *The Sons of Fun* (1993), *Psychedelic Desert Groove* (1997), *Sabotaj* (1999), and *To': Day of Days* (2001). *See also* surf movies.

McKnight, Bob   Shrewd and occasionally excitable surfwear industrialist from Laguna Beach, California; cofounder and CEO of Quiksilver USA; named by *Surfer* magazine in 2002 as the sport's single most powerful figure. McKnight was born (1953) in Pasadena, California, began surfing at age 12, and received a B.S. in business administration from the University of Southern California in 1976; later that year he and Hawaiian pro surfer Jeff Hakman became the first foreign licensees for the Australian-founded Quiksilver company, and began an instantly successful business importing the company's surfing trunks—or "boardshorts," in Aussie surfspeak. By the early '80s, Quiksilver had become one of the surf industry's leading manufacturers, and in 1986 Quiksilver USA, under McKnight's guidance, became the first surfing company to be listed on the New York Stock Exchange. McKnight also helped develop most of the Quiksilver's best-known marketing ideas, including the Quiksilver in Memory of Eddie Aikau big-wave contest at Waimea Bay; the Quiksilver Maverick's Men Who Ride Mountains big-wave contest; the early '90s push into female surf apparel with Roxy, a Quiksilver offshoot; and the Crossing, a 1999-launched surf-exploration boat journey.

McKnight became the president of the Surf Industry Manufacturers Association (SIMA) in 1989. Eleven years later, he gave the keynote address at the 2000 SIMA Summit in Cabo San Lucas, Mexico, introducing himself as a "non–garmento, non–Wall Street type" who was "scared shitless to get a real job," before going on to warn against "the enemy . . . Tommy Hilfiger, Nike, Guess, Old Navy and Gap," who were "sucking off us [surfers], trying to take away our customers, creeping in and copying our vibe with checkbook marketing." The following year, Quiksilver retail sales rose above $600 million. McKnight is married and has three children. *See also* fashion and surfing, Quiksilver.

McLaughlin, Isabel   Light-footed American surfer from New Smyrna Beach, Florida; winner of the 1974 United States Surfing Championships, and the only woman to compete regularly against men on the East Coast pro tour. McLaughlin was born (1957) in Daytona Beach, raised in New Smyrna, and began surfing at age 14. In 1974 she won the Florida State Championships, the East Coast Championships, and the United States Championships, then all but vanished from the surf scene while earning a B.A. in biology from the University of Central Florida and a master's in education from Nova University. McLaughlin returned to competition in 1981, testing her speedy, low-crouch style on the all-male East Coast pro tour, and finished the 1982 season ranked 22nd. The following year, while working full-time as a teacher at New Smyrna High School, she placed ninth in the hotly contested Sundek Classic, held at Florida's Melbourne Beach. Interviewed by *Eastern Surf Magazine*

in 1994, McLaughlin said she didn't mind hustling waves in the overcrowded New Smyrna lineup, but admitted that her comfort level was aided by a second-degree black belt in tae kwon do.

McLeod, Hugh   Inventive surf photographer and graphic designer from Sydney, Australia; co-owner of the luxuriant *Australian Surfing World* magazine from 1979 to 1998. McLeod was born (1951) and raised in Melbourne, Victoria, moved with his family to Sydney in 1960, and began surfing four years later. He worked as an advertising designer for three years before he started taking photographs professionally in 1970; three years later he was hired as a designer/photographer for *Surfing World,* the country's best-known surf magazine. Fellow photographer Bruce Channon became *Surfing World*'s editor the following year; the two bought the magazine in 1979, changed the title to *Australian Surfing World,* and produced each issue virtually unassisted. McLeod often used gold- or silver-foil embossing on the cover, scattered thumbnail-size photographs across a page, and had paint splatters dripping across the margins of photographs. But he just as often ran photos completely unadorned, and made beautiful use of portraiture and landscapes. The Channon/McLeod team also published two coffee-table books, *Surfing Wild Australia* (1984) and *Surfing the Chain of Fire* (1986). McLeod's photography has been featured in *Surfer, Surfing, Longboard,* the *Surfer's Journal,* and other surf magazines internationally. McLeod won a silver medal in the Nikon International Photography Awards in 1976; he also won a bronze medal in 1982. *See also* Australian Surfing World magazine.

McMillan, Martin   Australian longboarder from Newcastle, New South Wales; winner of the 1991 Longboard World Championships. McMillan was born (1961) and raised in Newcastle, hometown of four-time world pro tour champion Mark Richards, and began surfing at age eight. In the '80s he rode both shortboards and longboards; in 1990, as a longboard tour rookie, he finished second in the final ratings behind Nat Young by riding boards shaped by hometown hero Richards and using an attacking style with exaggerated body language. McMillan, a career sewing machinist, didn't win any of the four longboard tour events in 1991, but consistently placed high to win the championship. He's featured in *Full Cycle,* a 1994 surf video.

McNamara brothers, Liam and Garrett   Hard-charging brother duo from the North Shore of Oahu, Hawaii. Younger brother Liam was born (1969) in Berkeley, California, and began surfing at age nine after moving with his family to Hawaii. By 1991 he was gaining notice for his deep, fearless, if ungainly, attack at Pipeline. He also took more than his share of waves, was a brutal tactician during surf contests, complained often that world tour contest officials were conspiring to keep him from the top ranks, and was often mentioned as the sport's most disliked figure. "He's a good person inside," fellow Hawaiian pro Sunny Garcia once said. "He's just too much of a loudmouth." California surfer Jeff Booth got fed up with McNamara's hassling tactics during the preliminaries of the 1992 Pipeline Masters and, in front of a beach full of spectators, punched the Hawaiian in the face. McNamara, a goofyfooter, won the 1996 Tavarua Island Tuberiding Classic, held in Fiji.

Older brother Garrett (born 1967) began surfing at age 13. He was a respected North Shore semi-pro in the 1990s, but went about his business quietly. By 2000, however, he'd developed into one of the world's best tow-in surfers, and the following year he and Brazilian teammate Rodrigo Resende won the debut Tow-In World Cup, held in 35-foot-plus surf at Jaws in Maui. Garrett continued his big-wave push in 2002, towing into a mauling left at Teahupoo (Tahiti) and getting the season's biggest and longest tube at Jaws. He also found his voice, which, not surprisingly, turned out to be a few levels short of humble; in early 2003 he founded GarrettMcNamara.com, which sells autographed T-shirts for $25.

Liam has appeared in more than two dozen movies including *Session Impossible* (1991) and *Madmen, Saints and Sinners* (1992); and he filmed and produced *The Bomb 2000* (2000). Garrett has appeared in a similar number of videos, including *Gripping Stuff* (1987) and *Voluptuous* (1996).

McPhillips, Colin   Kinetic longboard surfer from San Clemente, California; three-time winner of the World Longboard Championships (1999, 2001, and 2002), described by *Longboard* magazine as "one of the hardest-working, smartest competitors around." McPhillips was born (1975) in Santa Monica, California, moved with his family to San Clemente at age one, and began surfing at five. He placed fourth in the shortboard juniors division of the 1992 United States Surfing Championships, and was selected for the National Scholastic Surfing Association's 1993 national team. As a longboarder, he finished fourth in the 1991 U.S. Championships and runner-up in the 1993 Championships. A hard-turning "progressive" longboarder (as opposed to the smooth-riding "traditional" school), McPhillips has competed in every longboard world title event since 1993; in 1999 he was also the Professional Surfing Tour of America champion; in 2002, along with his third world title, he edged out California rival Joel Tudor to win the debut Margaritaville Longboard Trophy Series. McPhillips has appeared in more than two dozen surf videos, including *Nomads* (2000), *From This Day Forward* (2001), and *Wordz* (2002). He's married and has one child.

McTavish, Bob   Cheerful Australian surfer and surfboard designer; inventor of the vee-bottom surfboard, and a key figure in the 1967-launched shortboard revolution. McTavish was born (1944) in Mackay, Queensland, the son of an accountant, and began surfing on a 16-foot plywood paddleboard at age 12, not long after moving with his family to the south Queensland city of Brisbane. At 15 he dropped out of high school, and two years later he moved to Sydney and began shaping surfboards; he eventually worked for most of the major Sydney-based board manufacturers of the period, including Larkin Surfboards, Dillon Surfboards, and Keyo Surfboards.

Although McTavish later became one of the first surfers to renounce competition, he was Queensland state champion in 1964, 1965, and 1966; finished third in the Australian National Titles in 1965 (behind national surf heroes Bernard "Midget" Farrelly and Nat Young); and was runner-up to Young in the 1966 Nationals. Small and barrel-chested (5'5", 140 pounds), McTavish was a fast, dynamic, arrhythmic surfer, keeping board and body in motion at all times. "Because there's so much going through his mind," former Queensland champion Russell Hughes said, "the guy is never still on his board." McTavish and Young, along with California-born kneeboarder/designer George Greenough, had formed the core of the "involvement" school of surfing by mid-1966, and were all looking to ride more actively in and around the curl. As the garrulous McTavish explained, the idea was to "use the power part of the wave, [and] to maneuver really fast without any loss of speed." The average 9'6", 25-pound board, McTavish knew, was far too bulky to allow this kind of riding. In the fall of

Bob McTavish

1966 he helped Young design Magic Sam, the thinner, lighter longboard Young used to win that year's World Championships; in early 1967 McTavish began working on an entirely new bottom design, and in March he produced the first vee-bottom—a wide-tailed nine-footer with a deep vee-shaped keel through the back third of the board—that he nicknamed the Plastic Machine. He then built a series of vee-bottoms over the next seven months, each getting progressively smaller and lighter, dropping all the way down to 7′6″ and 14 pounds.

McTavish flew to Hawaii in December to compete in the Duke Kahanamoku Invitational, held at Sunset Beach. For the bigger Hawaiian surf, he'd made himself a nine-foot vee-bottom; riding it for the first time during his opening Duke match in 12-foot surf, McTavish showed flashes of brilliance, but also wiped out often, didn't advance, and was laughed at by old guard longboarders. McTavish and Young then rode their vee-bottoms to great effect a few days later in eight-foot surf at Maui's Honolulu Bay, and footage of their rides was used in the final sequence of *The Hot Generation,* an Australian-made surf movie that helped introduce the surfing world to the high-performance possibilities of the shortboard. McTavish did some more design work the following year (much of it for California's Morey-Pope Surfboards), but short surfboard development over the next few years was for the most part done by Americans, particularly Dick Brewer of Hawaii.

In the early '70s, McTavish got married for a second time, became a Jehovah's Witness, moved with his new family to the north coast of New South Wales (he eventually had five children), and had little to do with the surf industry. In 1977, once again

ahead of his time, he began writing articles for surf magazines extolling the virtues of both the long-board and the midrange board. McTavish returned to the surf design vanguard in 1989 by introducing Pro Circuit Boards—machine-molded replicas of the boards used to top pro surfers. The business failed, but molded boards would catch on toward the end of the following decade, by which time McTavish had created a line of best-selling longboards.

McTavish appeared in about 10 surf movies in the '60s and early '70s, including *The Young Wave Hunters* (1964), *The Hot Generation* (1968), *Fantastic Plastic Machine* (1969), and *The Innermost Limits of Pure Fun* (1970). *Australia's Surfing Life* magazine selected him as the "Most Influential Shaper of All Time" in 1992; four years later he was inducted into the Australian Surfing Hall of Fame, where the still-nimble 51-year-old disarmingly spoke of himself during the awards ceremony as "just an old toymaker." *See also* molded surfboard, shortboard revolution, vee.

McVay, Kimo Wilder   Surfing promoter from Honolulu, Hawaii; manager of Olympic swim champion and surfing legend Duke Kahanamoku from 1961 until Kahanamoku's death in 1968; founder of the Duke Kahanamoku Invitational Surfing Championships. Australian surf journalist Phil Jarratt wrote that McVay, a disc jockey in the late '50s, was, "in the nicest possible way, a hustler." McVay's great-great-grandfather was a missionary to Hawaii and an official in King Kamehameha III's court. McVay himself was born in Washington, D.C., but raised in Honolulu. As president of the 1961-formed Duke Kahanamoku Corporation—a for-profit enterprise, but also an altruistic project to help the nearly impoverished Kahanamoku—McVay opened Duke Kahanamoku's Restaurant in Waikiki's International Market Place, and formed the Duke Kahanamoku Surf Club, with team members including top surfers Paul Strauch, Joey Cabell, Fred Hemmings, Jeff Hakman, and Butch Van Artsdalen. After attending the 1962 West Coast Championships in Huntington Beach with Kahanamoku, McVay had the idea for an elite made-for-TV surf contest at Sunset Beach; the resulting Duke Kahanamoku Invitational was the first major competition on Oahu's North Shore. *See also* Duke Kahanamoku, Duke Kahanamoku Invitational.

Mearig, Kim   Even-tempered regularfoot surfer from Santa Barbara, California; world champion in

1983, and described by surf journalist Bob Yehling as "Pretty, serene, stylish and athletic—the California beach girl about which dreams and movies are made." Mearig was born (1963) in Apple Valley, California, moved with her family to Santa Barbara when she was six months old, and began surfing at age 12. She at first had no interest in competition, but was talked into it by her parents, and encouraged by local surfboard shaper Al Merrick, and surfer Tom Curren—Mearig's junior high school classmate and future three-time world champion. Curren and Mearig each had a complete repertoire of flashy, high-performance surfing maneuvers, but sacrificed none of the polish or composure that had long been hallmarks of the Santa Barbara surfer. Mearig won the 1981 United States Surfing Championships, turned pro the following year, and finished a disappointing 18th in the final ratings. She went on a tear in the middle of the 1983 season, at one point winning three of four events, and later the championship when the 10th and final event of the season was canceled at the last minute, with Mearig holding a lead over Frieda Zamba of Florida.

Mearig was a pleasant, cooperative, utterly noncontroversial world champion, with surfboards and wetsuits rendered in matching yellow, pink, and light-blue pastels. But she had a harder side. She once listed *The Killing Fields* and *Platoon* as her two favorite movies, and when asked if she had any regrets, she noted that she'd been a fairly regular drop-in (a surfer who drops in front of an already-riding surfer and steals the wave), and apologized "to all the people in the lineup who I've yelled at." Mearig's fluid wave-riding technique was often noted and praised. "She uses her legs and hands to create the closest thing to a wave-dance a surf contest will ever see," *Surfer* magazine wrote. But aggressive "ride-like-a-man" surfing was the next trend for the women pros, and in 1984 Mearig finished second to the harder-turning Zamba. She finished sixth in 1985 and 1986, bounced back for a runner-up finish in 1987 (to South African Wendy Botha), then placed fifth in 1989 and 1990. She retired from competition in 1991. Altogether, Mearig won six career world tour events; she also won the *Surfer* Magazine Readers Poll Award in 1984. Mearig appeared in a small number of surf movies, including *Off the Wall II* (1982) and *Shock Waves* (1987). She was inducted into the Huntington Beach Walk of Fame in 2002. Mearig is married and has two children.

Mediterranean Sea   The Mediterranean Sea measures 2,200 miles east to west and 1,000 miles north to south; its western tip is connected to the Atlantic by the Strait of Gibraltar. A vast majority of the sublimely beautiful Mediterranean coastline is rocky and notched, creating excellent setups for surf breaks. Because of the sea's limited area, however, waves throughout the region are usually small and soft. Most Mediterranean surf is the result of locally generated wind, which regularly produces short-lived, one- to three-foot waves. North Atlantic winter storms, however, will occasionally track east across western Europe and enter the Mediterranean, broadcasting swells of up to 10 foot. Northerly sirocco and southerly mistral winds provide more reliable sources of midsized Mediterranean surf, particularly in the west. Waveless conditions are the rule here throughout summer. Water temperatures range from the high 50s in winter to the high 70s in summer; the Mediterranean has virtually no tide change, and a high evaporation rate caused by the warm and dry climate means the water has a greater salinity than that found in the oceans.

California surfer/physician Dorian Paskowitz introduced surfing to the Mediterranean in 1956 while visiting Israel. Little is known about surfing conditions in Mediterranean countries such as Turkey, Syria, Algeria, Egypt, and Tunisia; early surf reconnaissance reports from Greece suggest that the islands of Mani and Páros have small but ridable waves, with crystal-clear water. The Mediterranean's best surf is found on the southwest coast of Italy, as well as on the islands of Sardinia and Corsica. *See also* France, Israel, Italy, Morocco, and Spain.

Meistrell brothers, Bob and Bill   Unassuming identical twin-brother surf industrialists from Manhattan Beach, California; cofounders of Body Glove wetsuits. The Meistrells were born (1928) and raised in Boonville, Missouri, where at age 14 they crafted a dive helmet from a five-gallon vegetable can, a pane of glass, and tar. The Meistrell family moved to Manhattan Beach when the twins were 16; two years later they began surfing, not long after buying for $25 a genuine dive helmet—the original owner drowned while using it—which they used for underwater explorations around the Redondo Beach breakwater. In 1951, the Meistrells were both given prototype diving wetsuits from Bill's friend Bev Morgan, who produced the first commercial wetsuits that year and not long afterward opened a shop called Dive N' Surf in Redondo Beach. The brothers became partners in Dive N' Surf in 1953, and began selling the occasional diving wetsuit to local surfers—although '50s surfers in general rejected the rubber suits as both uncomfortable and unmanly. The Meistrells founded Body Glove in 1965 (the line was initially called Thermocline), just a few years after the general surfing population at last did an about-face on wetsuit use. Body Glove, located in Redondo Beach, went on to become an industry leader, second only to O'Neill Wetsuits. From 1986 to 1993 Body Glove underwrote the Professional Surfing Association of America tour; the $1,000 Body Glove Surf Bout II, held at Trestles in 1989, offered what was then the richest first-place prize in surfing history—$31,725. The Meistrells were both inducted into the Diving Hall of Fame in 1990. Bob has been married once and has three children; Bill has been married twice and has two children. *See also* wetsuit.

Mel, Peter Lucid and likable regularfoot big-wave rider from Santa Cruz, California; masterful at both the paddle-in and tow-in methods; a finalist in the Quiksilver Maverick's Men Who Ride Mountains contests in 1999 and 2000, and generally regarded as the best mainland American big-wave surfer of his generation. Mel was born (1969) and raised in Santa Cruz, the son of board shaper and manufacturer John Mel, and began surfing at age six. At 15, he placed third in the juniors division of the 1984 United States Surfing Championships, and by the end of the decade he was recognized as one of the state's best all-around surfers: an aerialist in small waves and a steady hand in 10-foot-plus surf at local reefbreaks like Steamer Lane and Mitchell's Cove. Mel was influenced by Richard Schmidt, the blond-haired Santa Cruz native who had been since the mid-'80s California's undisputed top big-wave surfer. Mel, like Schmidt, seemed to have an inborn composure in heavy surf, but his style was more fluid and expressive. Well-proportioned at 6′2″, 200 pounds, Mel drew polished and powerful lines on the wave, and rode with his long arms extended and often swept back; he was known as "The Condor" years before coming into big-wave fame.

Mel first rode Maverick's, the soon-to-be famous big-wave break located between Santa Cruz and San Francisco, in 1990. Within four years the 25-year-old Mel had quietly become the break's most accomplished rider. (Smiling and easygoing, Mel kept himself at a friendly remove from abrasive Santa Cruz "West Side" big-wave faction led by Vince Collier and two-time Men Who Ride Mountains winner Darryl "Flea" Virostko.) Mel finished runner-up in the K2 Big-Wave Challenge in 1998; the following year he placed fourth in both the Quiksilver in Memory of Eddie Aikau big-wave event at Waimea Bay and the Men Who Ride Mountains contest. He also finished fourth in the 2000 Men Who Ride Mountains.

A turning point in Mel's surfing life came in late 1999, when he began tow-in surfing waves at Maverick's. Using a 7′4″ board (three feet smaller than his paddle-in big-wave board), Mel was able to carve long, elegant high-speed turns, the likes of which had been performed in big waves only by Hawaii's Laird Hamilton. On October 28, 1999, he caught what was up to that point the biggest wave ever ridden outside of Hawaii—a 40-footer, by some estimations. Mel has appeared in more than three dozen surf videos, including *Gravity Sucks* (1994), *Voluptuous* (1996), *Monstrosity* (1999), and *Whipped* (2001). Mel is married and has two children.

Melanesia Variegated region of tropical islands in the South Pacific Ocean, located for the most part between the equator and the Tropic of Capricorn, and between Australia and Hawaii; includes New Guinea, the Admiralty Islands, the Solomon Islands, the Santa Cruz Islands, New Caledonia, Vanuatu, Fiji, and hundreds of smaller islands. Air and water temperatures in Melanesia are dependably warm, and the surf is often fast, well-shaped, powerful, and hollow, usually breaking over island-fringing coral reefs. Melanesia is open to a wide variety of swell directions; May through September generally produces clean, long-lasting surf from the south and east, while November to April brings less-reliable surf from the North Pacific.

Melville, Debbie *See* Debbie Beacham.

Menczer, Pauline Feisty Australian pro surfer from Bondi Beach, Sydney; 1993 world champion, and described by surf journalist Jodie Young as "the epitome of the Aussie battler." Menczer was born (1970) in Sydney, and came into hardship at age five when her

Pauline Menczer

taxi driver father and milkman grandfather were killed in separate car accidents, leaving her mother to take care of four children and a parent on a monthly welfare check. She began surfing at age 14, after she was given one-half of her brother's recently broken surfboard; four years later she won the 1988 World Amateur Surfing Championships, quickly joined up with the pro tour, and finished the year ranked #5. The diminutive Menczer (5′2″, 105 pounds) was an attacking surfer, with only a passing interest in flow and finesse, but ready at all times to place herself into critical positions on a wave—bigger waves included. She was a regular world tour event winner (finishing third overall in 1989, sixth in 1990, second in 1991, and sixth in 1992), while fending off recurring bouts of rheumatoid arthritis, a chronic and painful joint-inflammation.

Menczer's 1993 championship remains one of the sport's great achievements. Sponsorless and forced to spend $25,000 of the $30,000 she earned that year in prize money just to get from contest to contest, Menczer won three of the first 11 events, and had a slender ratings lead going into the 12th and final contest in Hawaii. Two weeks before the deciding event, the 23-year-old Menczer had an arthritis attack that put her temporarily in a wheelchair; seven days later she began paddling her surfboard in a pool as a warm-up; on the day of the contest—held in windblown eight-foot surf at Sunset Beach—she scraped into the finals, and won the title. "I couldn't even brush my own hair," she said of her pretitle attack. "My body had just shut down."

The following year brought the first of Florida-raised Lisa Andersen's four world championships,

and runner-up Menczer was all but ignored, despite the fact that she won five of the tour's 11 events, including the final three. As the freckled and tomboyish Menczer put it, "I don't have sponsors, because I don't have big boobs, blonde hair and blue eyes." At the end of 1995, with the popularity of women's surfing shooting up in large part due to a massive pretty-surfer-girl marketing campaign, Menczer decorated one of her surfboards with a hand-drawn surfing "bushpig" (Australian slang for an unattractive woman), in mordant celebration of her own nonglamorous looks. Menczer continued to be a top-ranked world tour performer for another four years, finishing fifth in 1995, second in 1996, sixth in 1997, and seventh in 1998, before slipping out of the top eight, having won a total of 20 world tour events, with one added in 2001 for good measure. "I think I deserve a lot more than I got," she said with a philosophical shrug. "But I've still got a lot more than I ever thought I'd have." In 2002, the 32-year-old focused on second-tier pro events, and won both the World Qualifying Series tour, and the Foster's Pro Surfing Tour.

Menczer was the top vote-getter in *Australia's Surfing Life* Magazine's 1993 Peer Poll. She's appeared in about 15 surf movies and videos, including *Surfers: The Movie* (1990) and *Tropical Madness* (2002), and is featured in *Girl in the Curl* (2000), an illustrated history of women's surfing. Menczer is unmarried; in 2003 she was living in Ocean Shores, New South Wales.

Menda, Ketut   Loose-limbed Balinese regularfooter from Kuta Beach; the first Indonesian surfer to compete on the world pro tour. Menda was born (1964) in Cannanguu, near Kuta, and began riding waves at age 10, while working as a board-carrier for visiting surf world dignitaries like Gerry Lopez and Peter McCabe. No more than a dozen Balinese had picked up the sport by that time. In 1981, Menda became the first surfer from Bali to compete on the world tour. He didn't place high in the standings, but learned about the surf retail business, and upon his return to Bali opened his first surfboard shop in Kuta. By 2000, Menda owned three shops in and around Kuta.

Mentawai Islands   Small, low-lying chain of islands located 75 miles off the west coast of the Indonesian island of Sumatra, just below the equator; generally considered to be the world's richest wave zone. The 200-mile-long Mentawais consist of four main islands—Siberut (a national preserve), Sipura, North Pagai, and South Pagai—and dozens of smaller islets, some of which are populated by animistic tribesmen. The May-to-September dry season is the best time for surf on the Mentawais, as the islands receive frequent four to six-foot waves generated from storms tracking across the Indian Ocean's Roaring 40s (bigger storms can produce surf up to 12 feet), and inexhaustible two to four-foot waves from smaller, closer storms. The October-to-April wet season brings smaller waves and intermittent stormy weather. Average daytime air and water temperatures remain in the low '80s all year. The Mentawaian surf takes shape along the dozens of perfectly tapered coral-lined lava reefs around the islands. Two of the area's best-known breaks are Lance's Rights (or Hollow Trees), a shifting, tubing, and sometimes dangerously shallow wave located at the south end of Sipura; and Macaroni's, a near-mechanical left tube that has been described as the world's best high-performance wave. Reef cuts and scrapes are the most common Mentawaian surf hazard; malaria is a risk for anyone on land from dusk to dawn.

Australian teenage surfers Scott Wakefield, Chris Goodnow, and Tony Fitzpatrick, all from Sydney, boated out to the Mentawais in 1980, camped for five weeks, surfed more than a half-dozen breaks, including Macaroni's, and didn't tell anybody about their discovery for years. Australian salvage diver and boat captain Martin Daly, working out of Jakarta, began trolling through the Mentawais in 1989 and 1990, and over the next year rode a handful of world-class surf spots, including what would later be called Lance's Rights (named after New South Wales surf traveler Lance Knight, who was dropped off on Sipura one month prior to Daly's arrival in 1990). The following year, after Daly began telling others about the newly discovered surfing paradise, a group of famous surfers—including former world champions Tom Carroll and Martin Potter—visited the Mentawais. The Carroll/Potter visit went all but unreported in the surf press, but word was spreading nonetheless, and by 1994 the first surf charter tour boats were taking groups of surfers out to the Mentawais on 12-day excursions. More breaks were discovered, and photographers and videographers began feeding a stream of ravishing Mentawaian images to the surf media. The surf charter tour outfits, primarily Great Breaks International and the Surf Travel Company, began looping

constantly from Sumatra to the Mentawais during the dry season, while sparring among themselves for exclusive reef-use rights, and engaging in endless political dealings with Indonesian officials and politicians. By 2002, as many as 30 surf charter boats were circulating through the Mentawais, carrying an aggregate total of 300 surfers at any given time. A berth on a 12-day budget charter boat (airfare to Sumatra not included) can cost about $1,500; slots on a plush air-conditioned cruiser cost as much as $4,000. A number of land-based surf camps were in the works as of mid-2002, but none had yet opened. The Bali nightclub terrorist attacks in 2002 brought a steep reduction in the number of surfers travelling to Indonesia, and it was reported that up to a third of Mentawai charter boats have been taken out of service.

Ocean Pacific surfwear and *Surfer* magazine sponsored a $102,000 "floating" pro surf contest in the Mentawais in 2000, won by Mark Occhilupo of Australia and Rochelle Ballard of Hawaii. Sports journalist Rob Story, covering the Op/*Surfer* event for *Outside* magazine, was impressed by the perfect surf and the magnificent performances by the pros, but described the general push into the Mentawais as "good old surf imperialism." (Occhilupo won the Op/*Surfer* event again in 2001, along with Hawaiian Keala Kennelly.) The Mentawaian surf has been featured in dozens of videos, including *The Search II* (1993), *Feral Kingdom* (1995), and *September Sessions* (2000). Books featuring the Mentawais include *Surfing Indonesia* (1999) and *The World Stormrider Guide* (2001). *See also* Indonesia, Op Pro Mentawai Islands.

Merchant, Gordon Australian surf-world executive; founder of Billabong, the Queensland-based beachwear and wetsuit giant. Merchant was born (1943) in Sydney, grew up in the beachfront suburb of Maroubra, began surfing as a teenager in the late '50s, and was a well-traveled surfboard shaper by the late '60s. While living in Queensland in 1970, he made a new board for himself and fine-tuned the rails into what would later be called the "tucked-under edge"—a significant design improvement (independently developed by Hawaii's Dick Brewer and California's Mike Hynson) that blended the fast downrail and the easy-turning 50-50 rail. The 29-year-old Merchant and his wife began making surf trunks in 1973, which he sold from the back of his station wagon. ("Billabong," as the fledgling company was called, is an Aboriginal word for dry or dead river). His first-generation trunks, Merchant told *Deep* magazine in 1996, "were bloody horrible. The only people who bought them were really only feeling sorry for us." The design and craftsmanship improved, as did Merchant's business skills, and by the mid-'80s he'd turned the company into Australia's hippest challenger to Quiksilver. While Merchant is quiet to the point of reclusiveness, he's also proven to be a marketing and PR whiz, and has built up the Billabong name in large part by underwriting dozens of big-money, high-profile surf contests, sponsoring some of the world's best surfers—including Wayne Bartholomew, Mark Occhilupo, Sunny Garcia, Taj Burrow, and Layne Beachley—and by producing a popular series of surf videos. When Billabong opened on the Australian Stock Exchange in 2000, *Australia's Surfing Life* magazine reported that Merchant's net worth was $98 million. *See also* Billabong.

Merkel, Dan   Gruff and disciplined surfing cameraman from Southern California, best known for the high-impact still photography he shot for *Surfing* magazine in the '70s, and as the primary water photographer for 1977's era-defining surf film *Free Ride.* Merkel was born in Belgium (1948), the son of an army serviceman. He grew up in North Dakota and the San Francisco Bay Area, began surfing in 1963, moved to Southern California the following year, bought his first professional-quality camera in 1968, and had his first surf photos published in 1969. He was, as a *Surfing* editor noted, "untrained and uneducated in the art of photography." He was also determined, hardworking, and single-minded, and by 1974 his water shots—taken primarily on the North Shore of Oahu, the sport's main arena—were setting the industry standard. (He meanwhile continued to surf regularly, and in 1972 finished fourth in the masters division of the United States Surfing Championships.) Merkel was one of surfing's first exercise fanatics, and spent his nonshooting days swimming, pumping iron, and jogging with weights taped to his arms and legs; he was sometimes referred to as "Man-Mountain Merkel." In the winter of 1975–76, with virtually no film experience, he shot the mesmerizing and technically perfect slow-motion North Shore water sequences for *Free Ride* using a 20-pound camera and housing. Two years later he did much of the water photography for the 1978 Warner Brothers' surf film *Big Wednesday.* Merkel's still photography was featured in a small number of illustrated surfing

books, including *Pure Stoke* (1982) and *The History of Surfing* (1983). A 21-page retrospective of his work was published in a 2002 issue of *The Surfer's Journal.*

Merrick, Al   Low-key surfboard shaper from Santa Barbara, California; founder and owner of Channel Islands Surfboards, and the board-making industry's dominant figure since the 1980's. Merrick was born (1944) in New Jersey, moved with his family to north San Diego County at age seven, and began surfing at 14. He moved to Santa Barbara in 1965, and was in the water at Rincon in late 1967 when Australian Bob McTavish introduced his newly designed short surfboard to California. The performance possibilities offered by the smaller boards—average length dropped from just under 10 feet to eight feet, and continued to fall steadily over the next two years—inspired Merrick to begin shaping; by 1969 he was making boards

Al Merrick

under the Channel Islands label, and selling them through local surf-retail outlets. Merrick came to the attention of the surf world at large in the late '70s, when he made boards for 1977 world champion Shaun Tomson; at that time he also began working with junior-high-school surfer Tom Curren, also of Santa Barbara. As Curren's reputation grew—at 15 he was winning pro-am contests and being hailed as the savior of California surfing—so, too, did the fortunes of Merrick and Channel Islands.

Merrick pushed his advanced water-channeling double-concave tri-plane hull design in the late '70s and early '80s, but his boards generally haven't been innovative so much as models of synthesis and refinement. It was Australian Simon Anderson who introduced the tri-fin board in 1981, for example, but it was the soft-voiced Merrick who did much of the subsequent fine-tuning that saw the design become the near-universal board choice by mid-decade. "I'm a designer but I haven't discovered anything," Merrick admitted in 1987. "I'm just using what's been around before . . . and I'm sure I'll take more ideas from somebody in the future." Curren won three world titles using Merrick's boards, with the shaper also acting as Curren's father figure and part-time agent. Just after Curren left the pro tour in 1991, Floridian marvel Kelly Slater rode Merrick's boards to the first of six world titles. Four-time world champion Lisa Andersen (1994–97) also used Merrick's boards, as did world champion Kim Mearig (1983), and dozens of topflight riders including Rob Machado, Taylor Knox, and Shane Beschen.

Merrick, a devout born-again Christian, opened his first retail shop in 1978, and in the early '90s he became one of the first shapers to switch over to computer-programmed machine shaping, although each board was hand-finished. By 2003, Merrick and his small cadre of machine-assisted Channel Islands shapers (including son Britt Merrick) were producing roughly 12,000 boards annually, and distributing them to retail outlets around the world. Merrick has been married twice, and has two children. He was named the top shaper in the world by *Australia's Surfing Life* magazine in 1992, 1993, and 1994. *See also* tri-plane hull.

Merrill, Linda   Stylish goofyfoot surfer from Oceanside, California. Merrill was born (1945) and raised in Oceanside, daughter of longtime California surfer Benny Merrill, and began surfing at age 12. She finished runner-up in the 1961 West Coast Championships, and two years later, at 18, she teamed up with California surfing ironman Mike Doyle to win the tandem division of both the West Coast Championships and the Makaha International. In 1964, Merrill became the first woman featured on the cover of *Surfer* magazine.

Meseroll, Dick   Wisecracking surf photographer and magazine publisher, originally from New Jersey; cofounder in 1991 of the impudent *Eastern Surf Magazine*. Meseroll was born (1952) and raised in Point Pleasant, New Jersey, began surfing in 1963, and started taking surf photos in 1971 with an inexpensive department store camera. He became a masthead photographer at *Surfing* magazine in 1976, and in 1987—after earning a reputation as the first top-quality surf lensman from the East Coast—he switched to *Surfer* magazine. Some of Meseroll's best work was done in the late '80s and early '90s; his action shots were tight and razor-sharp, while his wide-angle lineup shots presented East Coast surf spots, for the first time, in full panorama—not just waves and surfers, but sand dunes, jetties, buildings, piers, and parking lots. The never-married Meseroll cofounded the rambunctious and instantly popular newsprint giveaway *Eastern Surf Magazine* with fellow photographer Tom Dugan and Lally Collins. *See also* Eastern Surf Magazine.

Mexico   Mexico can be divided into three main surfing areas: 1) Baja California, the arid, scrub-covered finger of land extending 750 miles south from the U.S. border, is lined with coves, points, rivermouths, and beaches. Baja has for decades been a favorite destination for traveling Southern California surfers; some of the peninsula's best-known breaks include the point surf at San Miguel and Scorpion Bay, and the entire Cabo San Lucas area; the oversize reef waves on Todos Santos Island; and the wind-blasted beachbreak tubes on Isla Natividad. 2) Mainland Mexico's 2,500-mile coast, including harsh desert beaches in the north and jungle-lined coves to the south, encompasses vast tracts of unpopulated beachfront and several well-developed tourist areas, as well as several dozen popular surf breaks, including the thundering beachbreak tubes of Puerto Escondido. 3) Mexico's Gulf Coast is rimmed in marshlands and tropical rainforest, has fair surf during the winter months and late summer hurricane

Mexico; Salsipuedes, Baja California

season, but little in the way of an established surf scene. Most surfing here takes place around popular resort areas like Cancún and Cozumel.

Mexico's Pacific coastline is open throughout the year to swells from both the North and South Pacific. There are exceptions, but summer is generally better in the southern areas, while winter is better for the northern breaks. Wave height in mainland Mexico from June to October is consistently three to six foot, with swells occasionally hitting 10 to 12 feet or bigger. With the exception of Todos Santos, a wave magnet that produces some of the world's biggest waves—up to 35 feet—the Baja surf doesn't often get over eight or 10 feet. Sharks are a concern along the mainland, especially around rivermouths and fisheries; other Mexican surfing hazards include urchins, stingrays, and jellyfish, shallow reefs at some breaks, and isolation.

Surfing was introduced to Mexico in the late '40s by San Diego surfers making day- or weekend-long forays into northern Baja. Mainland Mexico came to the attention of the surf world in the late '50s via California surf filmmakers Bud Browne and Greg Noll, who drove together to Mazatlán and Acapulco and presented their finds in *Surf Crazy* (Browne) and *Search for Surf* (Noll). Virtually everything about Mexico—its language and laws, its poverty and sanitation levels, its barely tracked upon remoteness—was a challenge to the well-ordered suburban lives led by most American surfers. Still, many thrived under these conditions, and Mexican surf exploration over the years continued apace. Mexican locals began to surf as well. Baja surfers Carlos Hernandez and Ignacio Felix Cota competed in the 1966 World Champi-

onships in San Diego; the Baja Surf Club hosted a well-attended surf contest at San Miguel from 1966 to 1969; and the debut Mexican National Surfing Championship, also hosted by the Baja Surf Club, was held in 1967. The first Mexican surf shops opened in the mid-'70s. By the late '70s, Puerto Escondido, the "Mexican Pipeline," located in the state of Oaxaca, had become a top draw for thrill-seeking surfers from around the world. A small surf industry was built in Puerto Escondido over the next 20 years, complete with retail shops, surf contests, surf resorts, even a locally made line of surfwear. Big-wave riders meanwhile discovered the huge winter waves on the northwest corner of Todos Santos Island. Cabo San Lucas has since the early '80s been home to a colony of semiretired Southern California surfers, including big-wave pioneers Pat Curren and 1968 Duke Kahanamoku Classic winner Mike Doyle.

In 2003, there were roughly 30 surf shops and 30,000 native surfers in Mexico, and nearly a dozen surf camp or tour outfits; regional and national surfing contests are organized under the auspices of the 1987-founded Mexican Surfing Association. Raul Noyola of Puerto Escondido is often cited as the country's top rider, and in 2001 he became the first Mexican surfer to win a World Qualifying Series pro tour event. The Mexican surf has been detailed in a number of books including *The Surfer's Travel Guide* (1995), *The Stormrider Guide* (2001), *The Stormrider Guide North America* (2002) and *A Surfer's Guide to Baja* (2001). *See also* Baja California, Cabo San Lucas, Puerto Escondido, Todos Santos.

Micronesia   Region in the Pacific Ocean, north of Melanesia and mostly north of the equator, encompassing about 2,000 tropical islands and island groups, including the Caroline Islands, Guam, the Mariana Islands, Nauru, the Marshall Islands, and the Gilbert Islands. Micronesia means "tiny islands," and a majority of the region's landforms are indeed nothing more than low-lying coral atolls. Waves move across Micronesia from almost every direction, but the best seasons for surf are December to April (featuring north and northwest swells) and May to September (south and southeast swells). Waves in Micronesia are often fast, hollow, and powerful, breaking over sharp coral reefs. The surf here is smaller and less consistent than that found in better-known surf destinations in the tropical Pacific—Hawaii and Tahiti, for example—but excellent nonetheless when conditions come together. Air and water temperatures in Micronesia are warm all year. Except for Guam, there is virtually no surf industry throughout the region, and Micronesians have so far shown little interest in surfing.

midlength *See* egg, hybrid.

Mignogna, Bob New York–born surf media magnate; publisher of *Surfing* magazine since the mid-1980s. Mignogna was born (1949) in New York, New York, grew up in Long Island, and began surfing at age 17. He moved to Hawaii in 1973, and soon began contributing photographs to *Surfing*. The following year he moved to Laguna Beach, California, and started working in the magazine's advertising department; in 1975 he became advertising manager, and from there he advanced to business director, associate publisher, and, in 1985, publisher. Under Mignogna's direction, *Surfing* targeted a younger audience than archrival *Surfer* magazine. *Surfing* took on a hard-edged, brightly colored graphic look, created by top designer Michael Salisbury; published articles by surf world favorites Nick Carroll, Dave Parmenter, and Sam George; and consistently featured the best surf photography, by staff members like Aaron Chang, Jeff Hornbaker, Don King, Larry Moore, Bob Barbour, and Chris Van Lennep. Mignogna served as a founding adviser to the National Scholastic Surfing Association, as well as the Surf Industry Manufacturers Association. In 2001, four years after *Surfing* was bought by New York media conglomerate Primedia, Mignogna became Primedia's outdoor group publisher, overseeing *Surfing, Surfing Girl, Bodyboarding, Climbing,* and *Volleyball* magazines; that year, Primedia bought *Surfer*'s parent company, Emap, further consolidating Mignogna's surf world power base. Mignogna was married once and has three children. *See also* surf magazines, Surfing magazine.

Milius, John Battle-obsessed Hollywood writer/director/producer, best known to surfers as the creative force behind 1978's *Big Wednesday*, a Warner Brothers' film that drew on Milius's experiences at Malibu in the late '50s and early '60s. Milius was born (1944) in St. Louis, Missouri. He enlisted in the army, but was released due to his asthma; he then enrolled in the University of Southern California School of Cinema, along with George Lucas (Steven Spielberg and Francis Ford Coppola were also apprentice filmmakers in

John Milius with Gerry Lopez (left) and Jan-Michael Vincent, during *Big Wednesday* shoot

Los Angeles at the same time), and graduated in 1967. *Big Wednesday* did poorly at the box office, but eventually became a popular video rental. Milius, a self-described "Zen-fascist," had greater success as the screenwriter for *Magnum Force* (1973), *Conan the Barbarian* (1982), and *Clear and Present Danger* (1994). "Go ahead, make my day," the Clint Eastwood/Dirty Harry challenge, was a Milius-written line. In his Vietnam War screenplay for *Apocalypse Now* (1979), Milius created Hollywood's best and most believable surfing character, Colonel Bill Kilgore. Played to perfection by Robert Duvall, Kilgore orders a massive napalm drop on a seaside Vietcong village, so that a handful of surfer/infantrymen can safely ride waves at a nearby pointbreak. Warned beforehand that the point belongs to "Charlie"—short for Victor-Charles, code name for Vietcong—Kilgore angrily responds: "Charlie don't surf!" Another Milius line. *See also* Apocalypse Now, Big Wednesday.

Miller, Edward "Dude" An original Waikiki beachboy, the first captain of the 1911-formed Hui Nalu Club; owner of the concession stand at the Moana Hotel, Waikiki's first major resort. Aside from being a top surfer, fisherman, and canoeist (it was his idea to take tourists into the surf on outrigger canoes), the part-Hawaiian Miller was one of the Islands' best musicians; he played piano, wrote a popular booklet on ukulele, led the Dude Miller Band at the Moana, and was invited in 1929 to perform in New York. The beachboy system in Waikiki, which gave tourists a safe but exciting taste of the ocean, kept the beaches clean, and allowed the beachboys to act as casual oceanfront ambassadors—was in large part invented by the Miller-led Moana Bathhouse Gang. Miller died in 1935 at age 49. *See also* Hui Nalu Club, Waikiki.

Miller, Rusty   Loquacious, regularfoot surfer originally from Encinitas, California; the top-ranked surfer in America in 1965. Miller was born (1943) in La Jolla, California, the son of an aeronautical engineer, moved with his family at age five to the north San Diego County beach town of Encinitas, and began surfing at age 10. In the early and mid-'60s, Miller put together a sturdy competition record: in the West Coast Championships he finished runner-up in 1961 and fourth in 1962; in 1965 he was awarded a color TV set for winning the KHJ Hermosa event, was invited to the inaugural Duke Kahanamoku Invitational, and at the end of the season was the United States Surfing Association points leader. He competed in the 1966 World Championships, and was a Duke finalist in 1967 and 1968. Miller furthermore became one of the country's best big-wave riders; a dynamic 1962 photograph of the well-muscled Miller (5'11", 165 pounds) bombing down the face of a giant wave at Sunset Beach was bought by Hamm's Beer and used on billboards across the country.

The freckle-faced Miller received a B.A. in history from San Diego State College in 1964; while in school he occasionally attended surfer parties dressed in a tweed jacket and loafers, took to smoking a pipe, and tried with little success to engage other surfers in conversations about art, politics, and world affairs. He then spent two semesters with the University of the Seven Seas, boating with 350 other students to Tahiti, New Zealand, Japan, Australia, the Middle East, and the Mediterranean. Back in Encinitas in 1968, Miller and top California surfer Doyle cofounded the Surf Research accessory company and introduced Wax-mate, the first commercially successful surf wax. Miller sold his interest in the business in 1969, spent two years living the counterculture life on the Hawaiian island of Kauai, then moved to Sydney, Australia. In 1971 he was among the first to ride the beautiful and soon-to-be world-famous waves of Uluwatu.

Miller was featured in several surf movies in the '60s, including *Gun Ho!* (1963), *Angry Sea* (1963), and *Golden Breed* (1968); as a superbly fit man in his 50s, he also appeared in two longboard surf videos, *Full Cycle* (1994) and *Powerglide* (1995). Miller has worked as a surf instructor near his home at Byron Bay,

northern New South Wales, since the early '70s. He's married and has two children.

Miller, Sonny   Gravel-voiced surf filmmaker from north San Diego County, California, best known for directing the Search video series in the 1990s. Miller was born (1960) in San Jose, California, and learned to surf at age 11 after moving with his family to north San Diego County. He began his career as a still photographer for *Surfer* and *Breakout* magazines in the mid-'80s. During the surf video explosion of the early and mid-'90s, Miller and a few other quality-minded holdouts shot on 16-millimeter film rather than videotape; the resolution and contrast were better, the colors more realistic, and film, unlike videotape, could be shot in slow motion. Edited versions of Miller's movies were then transferred to video, resulting in a far higher quality product than the programs originally shot on videotape. In 1992, Miller began working on a series of promotional videos for Rip Curl wetsuits, as part of the company's long-running "The Search" marketing campaign, in which Rip Curl team members rode perfect waves in exotic locations around the world. Miller's *Searching for Tom Curren* won the *Surfer* Magazine Video of the Year Award in 1997. Miller's other videos include *Breakin' on Thru* (1992), *The Search* (1992), *The Search II* (1993), *For the Sea* (1994), *Beyond the Boundaries* (1994), *Feral Kingdom* (1995), *Aloha Bowls* (1996), and *Tripping the Planet* (1996). Miller also did water photography for *In God's Hands* (1998), and appeared onscreen as a surf contest announcer in *Blue Crush* (2002).

Minami, Glenn   Precise, dependable Hawaiian surfboard shaper from Honolulu; founder of Blue Hawaii Surfboards in 1984. Minami was born (1950) in Honolulu, raised in central Oahu, and began surfing at age 14. He started shaping boards at 18, during the beginning of the shortboard revolution in the late '60s. After earning earned a B.A. in accounting from the University of Hawaii in 1973, he went to work full-time as a shaper, spending 10 years with manufacturing powerhouse Town and Country, then founding his own Blue Hawaii Surfboards label in 1984. Minami was by that time known as "Xerox" for his board-to-board consistency; his semi-guns—boards used for medium to medium-big waves—were especially valued. A peak in Minami's career came in 1989, when Martin Potter won the world title using a quiver of Minami boards, and Cheyne Horan, after a near-five-year absence from the winner's circle, won the season-ending Billabong Pro just after picking up his first Minami-made Blue Hawaii. "A lot of shapers share my dream of being able to surf as well as the top guys," Minami said at the time. "I can't win the world championship myself, but it's satisfying to know I can shape the boards that can do it." Minami has made boards for Shaun Tomson, Johnny-Boy Gomes, Sunny Garcia, and Mark Foo, among others.

mini-board   *See* shortboard revolution, shortboard.

mini-tank, mini-log   *See* hybrid.

Miranda, Dino   Longboard surfer from Makaha, Oahu; winner of the 1997 World Longboard Championships. Miranda was born (1964) and raised in Makaha, and began surfing in the early 1970s in Waikiki, with informal instruction from ageless senior surfer Rabbit Kekai. At 26, Miranda switched from shortboards to longboards. The finals of the 1997 longboard titles, held in punishing 12-foot surf at Makaha, saw Miranda matched against Bonga Perkins—his first cousin and 1996 longboard world champion. Miranda's tuberiding gave him an early lead, and he simply outlasted his relative as they were both washed, rinsed, and spun in the big Makaha surf. "The only reason I won was because Bonga cracked right before I did," the hard-charging regular-footer told *Longboard* magazine. "We were both dead tired." Miranda has appeared in a number of surf videos, including *From Full Cycle* (1994), *Adrift* (1996), and *From This Day Forward* (2001).

missionaries   Christian-based religious proselytizers who travel to foreign lands to set up semipermanent installations—missions—for the purpose of converting natives to their faith. As known to the surf world, missionaries were a group of primarily American-born Calvinists who for most of the 19th century presided over a catastrophic decline in the health and well-being of native Hawaiians, and brought about the near termination of surfing.

In 1779, British explorer Captain James Cook became the first westerner to land in Hawaii. Indigenous Polynesians were then living by the *kapu* system, which regulated everything from agriculture to weather forecasting to surfboard and canoe-building. The *kapu* system was shaken during 40 years of post-Cook contact with western explorers, whalers, and traders, and the entire system broke down in 1819. The first boat of American missionaries sailed into

Honolulu the following year, with group leader Hiram Bingham, in a journal entry filled with pious shock and disgust, describing the Hawaiians as "chattering and almost naked savages," who had the effrontery to meet the incoming brig with bare feet and uncovered heads. Bingham's group, and several who landed in Hawaii the next few decades, built churches, gave sermons, translated the Bible into Hawaiian, and in general set about remaking the natives into industrious suit- and dress-wearing Calvinists. Surfing, along with most other traditional pastimes, amusements, and recreations, wasn't prohibited per se, but frowned upon as dangerous, time-consuming, and licentious (gambling and sexual maneuvering were both by-products of the sport), and thus against the will of God. Hawaiians died by the thousands of Western-borne diseases like measles and smallpox, and may have been too sick or depressed to think about surfing or any other form of recreation. Missionary leader Bingham nonetheless wrote that "the decline and discontinuance of the use of the surfboard, as civilization advances, may be accounted for by the increase in modesty, industry and religion. . . ." Nineteenth-century missionaries stationed in New Zealand, Tonga, and elsewhere in the Pacific had much the same effect on local natives. But small numbers of Hawaiians continued to surf, and by the late 19th century missionary influence was fast waning. American-led agriculture and tourism would soon replace religion as the driving forces of Hawaiian politics and culture, and when the first generation of Waikiki hoteliers recognized that surfing could be used as a marketing tool for vacationing mainlanders, the sport was quickly turned into a symbol of Hawaiian beauty, romance, and pride.

Surprisingly, only about 100 missionaries total were dispatched to Hawaii in the 19th century, mainly to Honolulu, Lanai, and Hilo. Most brought their families or began families in Hawaii. Much of James Michener's best-selling 1959 book *Hawaii* takes place during the missionary period. *See also* Hawaii, religion and surfing.

Mississippi   *See* Gulf of Mexico.

Mitchell, James "Chubby"   Big, nimble, easygoing regularfooter from Honolulu, Hawaii; surfing's double-extra-large embodiment of aloha spirit in the 1950s and early '60s. Mitchell was born (1933) and raised in Honolulu, the son of a fireman, and began

Chubby Mitchell

surfing at age 12. He moved to California in the early '50s, where he played football for San Jose State College; in the late '50s and early '60s he lived in the southwest Los Angeles County town of Manhattan Beach. Slow moving on land, with near-narcoleptic sleep patterns (he once fell asleep leaning against a Waikiki surfboard locker while checking the waves), the 5′9″, 300-pound Mitchell was a dynamo in the water, whip-turning his 11-foot Jacobs surfboard, deftly walking the nose, and dropping into an elegant and rock-solid crouch while shooting through whitewater sections. The jazz-loving Mitchell was noted for his enormous appetite, his light-fingered ukulele playing, and his sharp wit. Asked how much he weighed by an airline hostess, Mitchell gently smiled, motioned for her to come closer, then shouted the answer into her ear: "282!" The never-married Mitchell appeared in a half-dozen surf movies of the late '50s and early '60s, including *Spinning Boards* (1961), *Cavalcade of Surf* (1962), and *Angry Sea* (1963). He died of heart failure in 1972 at age 40.

Moir, Mike   Barrel-chested surf photographer from Newport Beach, California; a *Surfer* staffer from 1977 to present day, best known for crystalline close-up action shots, often taken in Orange County. Moir was born (1946) in British Columbia, Canada, moved with his family to Orange County in the mid-'50s, and by 1964 was an avid surfer and a hobbyist photographer. He had his first photo published in *Surfer* in 1967, but in the late '60s and early '70s he was all but completely off the surf beat, first doing service with the National Guard, then becoming a testifying Jehovah's Witness. Moir returned to surf photogra-

phy in 1972, this time as a career. Unlike virtually all his peers, the quiet and genial Moir avoids the annual winter surf scrimmage on the North Shore in Oahu, Hawaii. In 1999, he photographed the first surf trip to Russia; the results were published the following year in *Surfer* and the *Surfer's Journal*. Moir has also contributed to a number of illustrated surfing books, including *Surfing: The Ultimate Pleasure* (1984), *Stoked: A History of Surf Culture* (1997), and *The Perfect Day* (2001).

molded surfboard   General description used for a surfboard produced by any one of a number of machine-molding methods, as opposed to conventional polyurethane-core custom boards. Diwain Surfboards, located in a converted gas station in Huntington Beach, California, produced a two-piece molded plastic surfboard in the early 1960s that sold for $86 (customs sold for about $125), and was advertised as "ding proof." The 1963-founded Dextra also produced a line of molded plastic boards, as did a half-dozen other companies in the '60s. Molded boards were disparaged in the surf press as shoddily built (true in some cases) and poor performing (true when used by advanced surfers, not true for beginners and most intermediates). Early molded boards were commonly known as "popouts."

Molded board manufacturers in the 1970s—including Hansen Surfboards, W.A.V.E., Aqua Jet Honeycomb Surfboards, and Powerboards—did their best to remove the molded board stigma by hiring top surfers and board designers, and by utilizing complex aerospace construction methods. (W.A.V.E. boards were made from a heat- and pressure-bonded honeycombed composite of epoxy resin, fiberglass, urethane, and nylon.) Nonetheless, the new molded boards often leaked or delaminated, and were generally denounced as a soulless industrial intrusion on what was often depicted as a near-sacred relationship between surfer and shaper. Again, they didn't catch on. A third generation of molded boards, also doomed to failure, came in 1988, when renowned Australian surfboard shaper Bob McTavish introduced his Pro Circuit Boards, which were molded replicas of famous surfers' "magic" boards. Sailboard manufacturers had meanwhile taken to the molding process enthusiastically.

The idea of a durable and replicable surfboard remained intriguing, and as machines were more often used to create "hand-shaped" foam boards, the molded model was further pursued. Surftech, founded in 1997 in Santa Cruz, California, became the first viable producer of molded surfboards. The Surftech manufacturing process is a more intricate version of the '70s molding method: a foam core is wrapped in a layer of high-density sheet foam, along with multiple layers of epoxy resin and fiberglass, then topped with a coat of polyurethane paint. The resulting board is more expensive than a conventional board, but is marginally lighter and five times stronger; by 2003, Surftech's $12 million facility had a 75-model line of shortboards, longboards, and big-wave guns, designed by such notable surfers and shapers as Glenn Minami, Bob McTavish, Dale Velzy, and Reynolds Yater. BiC and Soloman, both European-based companies, have meanwhile produced alternative versions of molded boards, as has California-based Acme Boardworks. Experimental and custom boards remain the sole province of traditional foam-and-fiberglass manufacturers. But the molded board has at last found a permanent place in the surf market; what remains to be seen is just how quickly its market share will expand in the years ahead. *See also* popout board, surfboard construction.

Momentum   Low-tech, high-energy 1992 surf video filmed, edited, and produced by 20-year-old San Diego filmmaker Taylor Steele. The 40-minute *Momentum* was a punk-rock-scored calling card for a group of rising teenager pros, including Shane Dorian, Ross Williams, Rob Machado, and Kelly Slater. The footage was shot exclusively in Hawaii, California, and Mexico, and was edited into a series of minifeatures: one- or two-minute segments on a particular surfer, or a slightly longer feature on a surf break. *Momentum* cost about $5,000 to produce, and doesn't have any narration, surfer interviews, ambient beach or ocean noises, slow motion, or water photography; the soundtrack is filled with loud, fast, jackhammering songs by Southern California neo-punk bands like Offspring, Pennywise, Bad Religion, and Sprung Monkey. Steele's debut effort was a hit, described in a *Surfing* magazine review as "a vital document of contemporary surfing," and sold more than 15,000 copies at a time when few videos hit the 5,000 mark. *Momentum*'s energy was undeniable. So was the fact that it had no interest in the sport's grace, texture, versatility, and sensuality, and was all but humorless in the bargain. Age, more than anything, seemed to determine how a surfer felt about

Momentum. "Most surfers over 25 found it to be crude and exhausting," the *Surfer's Journal* noted. "Most surfers under 20 took to it like a new religion." Dozens of young aspiring filmmakers, recognizing that they, too, could make a movie more or less as good as *Momentum,* flooded the market with *Momentum*-style copycat videos throughout the '90s. *Momentum II,* Steele's follow-up, was released in 1993. Steele and *Momentum* were featured in *50 Years of Surfing on Film* (1997), an Outdoor Life Network cable TV special.

Slater, Machado, and the rest of the *Momentum* stars, while most often referred to collectively as the "New School," are sometimes called the *Momentum* crew, just as Shaun Tomson, Wayne Bartholomew, and Mark Richards were known as the *Free Ride* generation, after the 1977 movie that helped make them famous. *See also* Taylor Steele, surf video.

Moniz, Tony   Powerful but easygoing regularfoot surfer from Honolulu, Hawaii; an invitee to each of the five Quiksilver in Memory of Eddie Aikau big-wave competitions from 1985 to 2002. Moniz was born (1959) and raised in Honolulu, and began surfing at age five. At 14, one year after winning a boys' division state title, he all but quit surfing and took up motocross, becoming a two-time state champion in the 125cc expert division. At 18 he left motocross and became a Golden Gloves boxer; the following year he returned to full-time surfing, and two years later was competing professionally on the world pro tour. In the early '80s, Moniz was one of the first to master the lay-forward stance, which allowed the backside-riding surfer to get nearly as deep inside the tube as a frontsider. In 1982, 1983, and 1984 he was a finalist in the Duke Kahanamoku Classic, held at Sunset Beach, Hawaii; by the mid-'80s, Moniz was concentrating on big surf, and he placed sixth in both the 1999 and 2001 Quiksilver/Aikau events at Waimea Bay. The gentle but fierce-looking Moniz appeared in more than a dozen surf movies and videos, including *Wave Warriors* (1985), *Ticket to Ride* (1986), and *Liquid Thunder* (1990). He founded the Faith Riding Company clothing brand in 1996.

Monster from New Zealand Swell, 1975   Memorable 1975 south swell lasting from September 20 to 29, hitting beaches primarily in Southern California and Baja California, Mexico; the result of a nearshore Baja hurricane swell combining with a cyclone swell originating a few hundred miles northeast of New Zealand. The 1975 West Coast summer surf season had been dreary, and after a weekend of moderate three to four-foot waves—bigger than nearly anything seen in the previous eight weeks—most surfers expected the swell to once again taper off. But on Tuesday, September 23, the surf unexpectedly bumped up to four to six feet; on Wednesday it increased to eight to 10 feet; and on Thursday the swell peaked at 12 foot at a few prime south-facing beaches. Offshore winds and 90-degree weather prevailed throughout. Wave-starved surfers made the most of it, and Southern California's premier summer breaks were all jammed; Malibu had as many as 300 riders circulating through the lineup at once, with spectators bunched together on the sand, as surf journalist Richard Safady reported, "like the Sgt. Peppers album cover." The biggest surf was found at the Newport Wedge, a vicious bodysurfing/kneeboarding break located at the south end of Newport Beach, where waves hit 18 feet. Lower Trestles, a pointbreak near the Orange County/San Diego County border, didn't get over 10 feet but was "as good as it gets," according to longtime California surfer Mickey Muñoz. At a beach in Sonoma County, just north of San Francisco, an unknown surfer named Dale Webster rode the swell for seven days in a row and decided afterward to see how long he could keep his streak going. In 2003, 28 years later, Webster had marked off more than 10,000 consecutive days.

Southern California lifeguards prevented most swimmers and some surfers from entering the water during the biggest two days, but more than 400 rescues were nonetheless made between Venice Beach and Will Rogers State Beach in Los Angeles County. In large part because the annual summer sand buildup acted as a buffer, there was virtually no property damage. *Surfer* magazine covered the swell in its December 1975 issue, calling it "the Monster from New Zealand." The big California surf was featured in two surf movies: *A Matter of Style* (1975) and *We Got Surf* (1981).

Moon, JJ   *See* Ned Eckert.

Moondoggie   Fictitious character in Frederick Kohner's 1957 teen novel *Gidget;* played by teen idol James Darren in Columbia's 1959 like-titled movie. In Kohner's book, "Moondoggie" is the nickname for Jeff Griffin, a college-age Malibu surfer from a wealthy oil family. As described by Gidget, the lively 15-year-old narrator, Griffin drives a Corvette with red leather upholstery, and thinks of himself as "the sharpest-looking guy this side of Baja California." Moondoggie introduces Gidget to surfing, she falls in love with both the sport and her instructor, and the story climaxes as Moondoggie and surf sage Kahuna brawl over Gidget's honor. The Moondoggie character was loosely based on Kansas-born Malibu surfer Billy Al Bengston, who later became an internationally recognized pop artist. Bengston is said to have taken his nickname from blind American avant-garde composer Louis "Moondog" Hardin.

In the book, Moondoggie invents the name "Gidget" (a fusion of "girl midget"), and eventually gives the chirpy teenager his class pin. Asked by *Longboard* magazine in 1997 if there was in fact any romantic relationship between himself and Kathy Kohner—the real-life Gidget and daughter of author Kohner—Bengston dismissed the thought. "She brought sandwiches to the beach. We ate them." *See also* Gidget, Malibu.

Moore, Larry "Flame"   Industrious California-based surf photographer, and longtime *Surfing* magazine photo editor. Moore began shooting surf photos in 1970 at age 22 while living in a trailer near Orange County's Santa Ana River Jetties, and had his work published for the first time the following year. In 1973 he was hired as *Surfing*'s darkroom technician, and in 1976 he became photo editor. Moore's specialty is crisp, front-lit, tight-action water photography, shot for the most part in Southern California and Mexico. For years, the redheaded Moore, aware of potential charges of opportunism arising from his duel roles as *Surfing* photo editor and photographer, published his work under the alias "Flame." Not until "Larry's Army," a 1997 *Surfing* photo feature, was it made clear that Moore and Flame were the same person.

In February 1990, Moore and small-plane pilot Mike Castillo flew 100 miles out from San Diego, California, to the Cortes Bank, an open-ocean reef, where Moore photographed empty waves that appeared to be at least 30 foot. Cortes Bank was revisited in January 2001, by the Moore-led "Project Neptune," a complex one-day surf adventure involving two boats, a plane, three Jet Skis, six cameramen, and six surfers, which resulted in the year's most spectacular big-wave surf session.

More than any other surf photographer, Moore has let discipline and order guide his career. "He's the Oxford English Dictionary of surf imagery," surf journalist Evan Slater once said of the lean and highly emotional lensman, "peerless in his technical knowledge of surf photos." Moore moonlighted briefly in 2000 as photo editor for Swell.com, an Internet surf site. In 2002, *Surfing* magazine introduced the Golden Flame Awards, with Moore selecting winners in 14 separate photographic categories. Moore has also contributed to a number of illustrated surfing books, including *Pure Stoke* (1982), *The History of Surfing* (1983), and *The Next Wave* (1991). Moore is married and has one child. *See also* Surfing magazine.

Morey Boogie   Short, soft, flexible wave-riding craft introduced in 1973, touching off a wildly popular surfing subspecialty known as bodyboarding. "The Morey Boogie," *Surfer* magazine wrote in 1999, "is the most popular wave-riding vehicle of the century." Southern California surfer and board designer Tom Morey, working out of a friend's garage on the Big Island of Hawaii, made the prototype bodyboard in 1971, using an electric carving knife to shape a 4'6" by 23" beveled-rail board from a slab of Dow Chemical polyethylene packing foam. He called his new invention the SNAKE Machine—a cryptic acronym for "Side, Navel, Arm, Knee and Elbow." Two years later, Morey was in Carlsbad, California, creating a business around his newly renamed Morey Boogie. Early advertisements for the Boogie noted that the board was designed to ride where surfboards couldn't—over shallow reefs, in board-prohibited zones, and in closeout shorebreak surf. The safety advantages of the Boogie were obvious, as the unbreakable three-pound board was no more dangerous than a big, wet sponge ("sponge" would in fact become a derisive nickname for the bodyboard). Morey would later take a far more expansive view of his product, comparing the Boogie to the spoon and the Gutenberg printing press as one of mankind's greatest inventions.

The original Morey Boogie cost $45 assembled or $25 for a do-it-yourself mail-order kit that arrived with Morey's own hand-lettered assembly instructions. It was a commercial success, and something of a democratic one as well, introducing wave-riding to hundreds of thousands of people who otherwise would have likely remained on the beach. "The Boogie was a great equalizer," the *Surfer's Journal* said in 1999. "If you could ride one at all, you were riding it correctly."

Morey sold the Boogie to toymaker Kransco in 1977; Kransco was bought by Mattel in 1994; Mattel was purchased by Wham-O in 1998—with Morey brought along the whole time as a consultant. Dozens of other bodyboard companies have meanwhile come and gone since the mid-'70s. It was estimated that as of 2003 more than 20 million bodyboards had been sold worldwide. *See also* bodyboarding, Tom Morey.

Morey, Tom   Creative and eccentric surf designer/inventor/theorist from Southern California; organizer of the first professional surfing contest, and creator of the Morey Boogie bodyboard. Morey was born (1935) in Detroit, Michigan, and moved with his family at age nine to Laguna Beach, California. He started riding a surf mat at 12, and five years later, after moving to Santa Monica, began stand-up surfing. Morey became a Douglas Aircraft engineer in 1958, one year after getting a B.A. in mathematics from the University of Southern California; in 1964 he quit Douglas to open Tom Morey Surfboards, and the following year he formed Morey-Pope Surfboards with San Diego surfer/designer Karl Pope. Over the next four years, Morey-Pope introduced a small number of popular board models, including the Snub, the Peck Penetrator, the Blue Machine, and the Camel. (The Trisect, an early Morey-Pope creation—a travel-ready three-piece board that came with its own suitcase—was a brilliant idea that sank without a trace when introduced in the mid-'60s, then was resurrected 30 years later.) Morey helped develop Slipcheck in 1965, a surfboard traction aerosol spray-on used as an alternative to surfboard wax. Two years later he introduced W.A.V.E. Set, the first commercially successful removable fin system. The year 1965 also brought the $1,500 Tom Morey Invitational, surfing's first prize-money contest. Morey again put a new twist on things: the Invitational was a noseriding-only contest, and instead of receiving a subjective score between one and 10 for each ride, each surfer was timed while riding the nose of the board and ranked according to highest time totals. Mickey Muñoz beat Mike Hynson for first place by seven-tenths of a second, although Morey admitted years later that a timer's error had in fact robbed Hynson of the win.

Morey published articles for surf magazines on a wide range of topics, including surf contests, wave formation, riding technique, health, and artificial surf. His most interesting and quirky pieces were

Tom Morey

about surfboards and board design. "Hello, I'm a spaceman," Morey wrote in the first paragraph for "Spaceboards," his 1971 *Surfer* article. "I am the spirit of Albert Einstein, Thomas Edison, Alexander Graham Bell and [board designer] Bob Simmons, taking possession, temporarily, of the innocent body known here on earth as Tom Morey." Surfboards, he goes on to say, "are junk." Morey's suggestions for improvement included rubbing a coat of liquid detergent on the bottom surface of the board, air-intake vents, and a small rubber-band-powered engine lodged inside the board's core.

Morey introduced the bendable soft-skinned Morey Boogie in 1973, selling units in mail-order do-it-yourself kits for $25. The bodyboard, as all Boogie-type craft would soon be called, was more than just a fun and easy-to-use wave-riding device, according to its inventor. "For anybody to become a graduate of this planet," he once said, "it is essential that they learn to enjoy this activity." Millions of Boogies and Boogie knockoffs were in the water by the mid-'80s.

Morey had meanwhile sold his interest in Boogie in 1977, just before the bodyboard became hugely popular; one year earlier he and California surfer Mike Doyle had codeveloped the Morey-Doyle soft surfboard, the offspring of which became the standard for beginning surfers. Morey again went to work as an engineer, this time with Boeing, then returned to surf manufacture and retail in 2000 with a nine-foot soft-tipped longboard called the Swizzle.

Morey has appeared in a small number of surf movies and documentaries, including *Golden Breed* (1968), *Blazing Longboards* (1994), and *Liquid Stage: The Lure of Surfing* (1995); in 1966 he served as president of the United States Surfing Association. Morey was listed by *Surfer* in 1999 as one of the "25 Most Influential Surfers of the Century." That same year, he sent out a press release announcing that he'd changed his name to "Y," in part because "it's easy to say and hear" and because he found "the symmetric look of 'Y' quite pleasing." Morey has been married twice and has six children. *See also* bodyboarding, fin box, Morey Boogie, Tom Morey Invitational.

Morgan, Bev   Resourceful and overlooked surf world figure from Santa Barbara, California, regarded by some as the inventor of the commercially made surfing wetsuit; also a mid-1960s *Surfer* magazine photographer, writer, and editor. Morgan was born (1933) in Los Angeles, raised in Southern California and Kentucky, began riding waves in 1946, and soon became close friends with future big-wave icon Greg Noll and future surfboard manufacturing giant Bing Copeland. In 1951, Morgan got a copy of a just-completed U.C. Berkeley study on wetsuit design and construction, and the following year began making full-length neoprene wetsuits for his scuba-diving friends at the beachfront Scripps Institution of Oceanography in La Jolla. Morgan soon opened Dive N' Surf in Redondo Beach, out of which Body Glove Wetsuits was later formed. In 1959, when the general consensus among surfers was that wetsuits were for sissies, Morgan helped organize a one-day gathering of the top Southern California surf teams, who then received free wetsuits, and the entire group was ordered into the water. Two weeks later, Morgan later recalled, Dive N' Surf had 2,500 wetsuit orders.

Morgan, a weekend writer and enthusiastic self-taught photographer, worked as associate editor at *Surfer* magazine in 1963 and 1964, producing six feature articles and three cover photographs; his shot of

Oceanside surfer Linda Merrill was the first photo of a woman to be used on a *Surfer* cover. Morgan has lived in Santa Barbara since 1964, where he builds molded fiberglass helmets for commercial diving. He has been married three times and has two children. *See also* wetsuit.

Moriarity, Jay   Cheerful longboarder and big-wave rider from Santa Cruz, California; introduced to the surf world in 1994 as the 16-year-old innocent who endured the most spectacular wipeout of the year; widely mourned following his untimely drowning in 2001, the day before his 23rd birthday. Moriarity was born (1978) in Augusta, Georgia, and began surfing at age nine one year after moving with his family to Santa Cruz. Six years later, on a late December morning in 1994, Moriarity found himself airborne just after standing up on a windy 20-footer at Maverick's, the newly famous big-wave break, located between Santa Cruz and San Francisco. Moriarity floated for a moment, then was pulled over the falls into a cataclysmic explosion of whitewater. Dazed for a few moments, he regrouped, paddled back out, and rode eight consecutive waves without falling. But it was the wipeout that caught everyone's attention, as it made the cover of *Surfer* magazine, and was featured in the *New York Times,* as well as on NBC's *Nightly News.*

Moriarity generally used a longboard when he wasn't riding Maverick's, and earned a reputation as one of the sport's most friendly and least affected pros. He competed in the Quiksilver Men Who Ride Mountains contests at Maverick's in 1999 and 2000. He also appeared in more than a dozen surf videos, including *Mental Surfing* (1993), *Gravity Sucks* (1994), *Super Slide* (1999), and *Whipped!* (2002). He coauthored *The Ultimate Guide to Surfing* in 2001.

Moriarity lost consciousness and died while doing underwater breath-holding exercises in the Maldive Islands. His ashes were scattered at Pleasure Point, his home break in Santa Cruz, and at Maverick's.

Morning of the Earth   Lustrous and mildly psychedelic 1972 Australian surf film made by Sydney photographer Alby Falzon. Along with coproducer David Elfick, Falzon secured a $20,000 grant from the Australian Film Development Corporation—an unheard-of bonanza for surf moviemakers. *Morning of the Earth* had no narration, subtitles, or plot, but was earthy and well-crafted nonetheless, with an excellent soundtrack. *Surfer* magazine described it as being "about the Garden of Eden, plus waves, minus serpent." The featured surfers were mostly Australian, and memorable sequences included Queenslander Michael Peterson at his home break of Kirra; Terry Fitzgerald at Hawaii's Rocky Point; and former world champion Nat Young at Byron Bay, New South Wales. Young and a number of other Sydney-area surfers had at that time left the city for their short-lived but romantic back-to-nature "country soul" period, and Falzon framed the experience lovingly. He also brought the long, perfect surf of Bali's Uluwatu to the screen for the first time, setting off a period of Indonesian surf discovery that is ongoing. The Warner Brothers soundtrack album sold well in Australia, with G. Wayne Thomas's "Open Up Your Heart" single hitting #1 on the charts. *Morning of the Earth* was the most successful Australian-made surf movie up to that time, grossing more than $200,000 during its first domestic run. *See also* Alby Falzon, surf movies.

Morocco   Muslim country in northwestern Africa, bordered by the Atlantic and the Mediterranean, and separated from Spain by the eight-mile-wide Strait of Gibraltar. The Moroccan coastline is similar to that of Baja California, Mexico—rugged, dry, and desolate. The main surfing area extends south from Casablanca to Agadir, and is filled with high-quality reefs and points; the area around Taghazoute is particularly rich in surf. Roughly 20 good to excellent breaks are located along the 600-mile stretch of coast between Casablanca to Tangiers. The Moroccan south offers vast tracts of surf-filled coastline, but is largely unexplored as it crosses into the Sahara. Winter is the best time to surf in Morocco, as North Atlantic storms produce consistent four- to six-foot surf along the entire west-facing coast, along with the occasional 10-foot-plus swell. Winter air and water temperatures average about 70 and 60 degrees, respectively. Anchor Point, Morocco's most popular break, located just northwest of Taghazoute, offers a long and somewhat irregular right-breaking wave. Boats Point, 50 miles south of Agadir, produces hollow rights within a beautiful cliff-lined cove. Spring and fall waves are just as well-shaped, but generally smaller. Summer air and water temperatures are 10 degrees warmer on average than in winter, but the surf often goes flat for days or even weeks at a time. The Moroccan surf in general is powerful, and often breaks over barnacle-covered reefs, but the biggest dangers to surfers exist on land: local surf lore is filled with tales of snakes and giant black scorpions, as well as scams, hustles, and thievery. Weak, short-lasting waves can also be found on Morocco's 400-mile Mediterranean coast.

Surfing was introduced to Morocco in the late 1950s by U.S. soldiers stationed at Mehdia Plage, about 75 miles northeast of Casablanca. In the late '60s and early '70s, visiting surfers passed through regularly while on the Euro-African "hippie trail" that more or less had its southern terminus at Agadir. "We lived for a time in the hut of an Arab named Baraque," a 1968 visitor wrote, "drinking mint tea, surfing, talking, and listening to Baraque play his three-string Moroccan guitar." Australian surfers Nat Young, Wayne Lynch, and Ted Spencer were filmed riding empty waves in Morocco for the 1969 surf movie *Evolution*. The first Moroccan national surfing championships were held in 1992 at a left-breaking point in Dar Bouazza, 15 miles south of Casablanca. Two years later, at the same beach, the European Professional Surfing Association staged the first pro contest in Morocco, with native surfers Hamza Benaidi and Christophe Delval both making the quarterfinals. In 1994, King Mohammed VI helped found the Rabat Surf Club and sponsored a Moroccan team to the World Amateur Championship in Rio, Brazil. By 2003, there were two surf shops and about 2,000 surfers in the country, with surf clubs established in most of the bigger coastal cities. The Moroccan surf is detailed in *The Stormrider Guide Europe* (1998), and *The Wold Stormrider Guide* (2001).

Morris, Willy   Media-friendly surfer from Woodland Hills, California; winner of the 1985 Katin Team Challenge. Morris was born (1962) and raised in the San Fernando Valley, and began surfing at age eight. He was a force in the United States Surfing Championships, finishing second in the boys' division in 1977, second in juniors in 1980, and winning the men's division in 1981. Morris launched onto the world pro circuit with great fanfare—*Surfing* magazine ran a four-part series, "I'm Getting My Act Together and Taking it on the Road," about Morris's rookie season—then retired at the end of 1986 without ever having cracked the year-end top 25. He was nonetheless one of the most visible surfers of the era (few surfers turned as forcefully; none accoutered themselves in brighter colors), featured on magazine covers, in surf product advertisements, as well as in surf movies and videos, including *Totally Committed* (1984) and *Ticket to Ride* (1986). Morris earned $6,000 for his 1985 Katin win, after defeating world tour stars Tom Curren, Mark Richards, and Michael Ho, among others.

Morrison, Dean   Smooth but explosive Australia regularfooter from Coolangatta, on Queensland's Gold Coast; winner of the 2003 season-opening Quiksilver Pro, at which point he became a darkhorse world title contender. Morrison was born (1980) to a low-income family in Tweed Head, a small New South Wales town located next to the Queensland border, and began surfing at age eight. At 15, when his parents divorced, Morrison moved into a Gold Coast beachfront apartment with 1978 world champion Wayne "Rabbit" Bartholomew, his mentor, coach, and surrogate father; Morrison's refined tuberiding style is a direct reflection of his time spent with Bartholomew. In 1998, Morrison won the Queensland state championship, the Australian National Titles, and the World Surfing Games; he turned pro the following year and in 2000 won the Pro Junior, in Sydney. By that time he was known throughout the Australian surfing world as one of the Coolangatta Kids, along with fellow teenage sensations Mick Fanning and Joel Parkinson. The other two earned more attention in the early years of the new decade, in part because Morrison is small (5'6", 142 pounds), quiet and unobtrusive: when standing around with his world tour peers, as Australian surf journalist Tim Baker put it, "you could easily mistake him for just another grom chasing autographs." In the water, Morrison is full of speed, energy, grace, and flair, with body language resembling that of six-time world champion Kelly Slater. Morrison qualified for the world tour in 2002 and finished the year ranked #29; the following season, in front of a wildly cheering hometown crowd at a Gold Coast point-break named Snapper Rocks, he defeated former world champions Slater and Mark Occhilupo, among others, to win the Quiksilver Pro. Morrison has appeared in more than a dozen surf videos, including *Momentum: Under the Influence* (2001), *Shelter* (2002), and *Amplified* (2002).

Morrison, Peter   No-nonsense outdoor sports magazine publisher from the Gold Coast, Queensland, Australia, founder in 1985 of *Australia's Surfing*

Life (ASL), a colorful and lightly ribald monthly magazine regarded by many since the early '90s as the country's premier surf journal. Morrison was born (1955) and raised in Westport, New Zealand, began surfing in 1967, and moved to Australia in 1973. He formed Morrison Media just prior to launching *ASL,* and soon became known for running a tight business operation, while keeping a trusting distance from the magazine's day-to-day editorial management and direction. By 2003, Morrison Media titles included *Australian Snowboarder, Powerhound, Kiwi Surf,* and *Freerider MX.* Morrison also serves as *ASL*'s publisher. *See also* Australia's Surfing Life magazine.

Motil, Guy   Earnest and reserved surf publisher and photographer from San Clemente, California; founder of *Longboard* magazine in 1993. Motil was born (1950) in Enid, Oklahoma, began surfing in Daytona Beach, Florida, in 1963, and moved to Southern California in 1969. Surfboard-maker Dewey Weber bought Motil his first camera in 1970, when Motil was a Weber Surfboards team rider. Two years later he published his first surf photos in *Surfer* and *Surfing* magazines. Motil had no formal training, but nonetheless became a superb photographic technician, with an eye for richly colored beach life details: seagulls, glistening kelp bulbs, empty waves, shells, windswept beaches, and dusky back-lit lineups. In 1976 he was hired to work in the *Surfer* darkroom; for a six-month period in 1978 he worked as *Surfer*'s photo editor, while also listed as a masthead photographer for *Powder* and *Skateboarder* magazines. From 1980 to 1985, and again from 1987 to 1989, Motil was the editorial director for *Breakout,* a magazine designed for California surfers. In 1985 and 1986 he was the production manager for *Surfing* magazine. While in his second phase at *Breakout,* Motil also worked as the founding photo editor for *Transworld Snowboarding. Longboard* magazine, founded in 1993 as a handsome nostalgia-tinged quarterly, brought Motil's career itinerancy to an end; he serves as the magazine's president, publisher, and editor in chief. Motil's photographs have appeared in surf magazines around the world, as well as in *Time, Newsweek, Playboy,* and *GQ. See also* Longboard magazine.

Mozambique   Battle-scared subtropical country in southeast Africa, often described as the "world's poorest nation"; home to at least six top-quality point- and reefbreaks. After decades of civil or cross-border warfare, Mozambique became relatively safe for travel in 1992, and surfers for the first time began exploring the country's long (1,500-mile), sandy, swampy, wave-rich coastline. American pros Tom Curren and Shane Beschen, along with photographers Ted Grambeau and Sonny Miller, made a two-week boat journey up the southern end of Mozambique in 1993, and discovered a handful of perfectly shaped right-breaking points. They also found the remnant chaos of a nation still recovering from war: orphans, amputees, corrupt officials, ruined towns, millions of unexploded land mines, and a national flag emblazoned with an AK-47 rifle. The Mozambique weather is dependably mild, with air and water temperatures both ranging in the 70s; May through September is the best season for surf, as Indian Ocean swells often produce six to 10-foot surf. As of 2003, the northern half of the country remained almost entirely uncharted for surf, and just a handful of natives have picked up the sport. Mozambique is featured in a small number of surf videos, including *The Search II* (1993). The Gotcha Experienca, a World Qualifying Series pro tour contest, was held at Ponta do Ouro in 1998.

Mullis, Kary   Quirky, freethinking scientist and surfer from La Jolla, California; winner of a 1993 Nobel Prize in chemistry. Mullis was born (1944) and raised in South Carolina, and received a Ph.D. in biochemistry from U.C. Berkeley in 1972. He began surfing in 1990; three years later, after taking a six A.M. phone call from the Royal Swedish Academy of Sciences announcing that he'd won a Nobel for his work in gene replication, Mullis left his La Jolla apartment and went straight to nearby Tourmaline Beach to ride a few. "I'm a pretty fast learner, and I've got good balance," he told a surf magazine interviewer in 1994. "I'd probably say I'm one of the best surfers in the world, maybe in the top four." He also said he hoped to market a series of trading cards embedded with bits of celebrity DNA, including some from Michael Jackson and Albert Einstein. Mullis went from colorful to controversial in the mid-'90s, as a potential friendly witness for the defense in the O. J. Simpson murder trial (he wasn't called to the witness stand), and by stating that HIV wasn't the sole cause of AIDS. *Time* magazine, in a snide 2000 article titled "The Worst and the Brightest," took Mullis to task for his choice of recreation as well as his ideas. After winning the Nobel Prize, *Time* wrote, "Mullis became a beach bum, a surfer, [and] also took a lot of LSD."

Mundaka   Spectacularly fast and hollow left-breaking rivermouth wave located near the fishing village of Mundaka in Spanish Basque Country; long regarded as Europe's best surf spot. The exquisitely foiled sandbar that forms the wave at Mundaka is created by sediment washed down the Guernica River. September through December is the best time for surf here, as the sandbar is completely filled in, air and water temperatures are still relatively mild, the winds are frequently offshore, and the North Atlantic produces with some regularity storms of required size and duration to push waves into this corner of the coast. Six to 10-foot surf is optimal; smaller waves are shorter and less hollow, while bigger surf will crumble and break before hitting the sandbar. Weeks can pass during the surf season where the waves don't get over four feet; when the surf is up, high tide will almost always erase the waves for four or five hours. When Mundaka is at its magical best—just a dozen times per year—surfers can fit as many as four separate tuberides into the same 300-yard-long wave. Later in the season, the air and water temperatures can be uncomfortably cold (into the mid-40s and mid-50s, respectively), and the sandbar is often thrown out of alignment, creating a less predictable wave. Wetsuits are almost always required at Mundaka; a full wetsuit and booties are often used later in the season.

Exactly when Mundaka was first ridden, and by whom, is unknown, but it was a favorite among a small network of travelling surfers by the late '60s. *Surfer* magazine published a two-page overview photograph of Mundaka in 1973, showing ruler-edged waves peeling across the rivermouth, with a charm-ing Old World hillside village in the background. Mundaka quickly became a must-ride break for any surfer traveling through Europe. "You can't really see the break until you're almost on top of it," California surf journalist Kevin Naughton wrote in 1993, describing the approaching drive. "But when you round the final bend, it's one of the greatest sights in a surfer's life." Not surprisingly, the lineup at Mundaka has been crowded—often insufferably so—since the early '80s. A small number of regional, national, even international, surf contests were held at Mundaka in the 1980s; the 1999 Billabong Pro, won by Australian Mark Occhilupo, put Mundaka on the world pro circuit for the first time. Mundaka Surf Shop was opened in 1984 by expatriate Australian Craig Sage, and has long been the focus of the local surf community; the 1988-founded Mundaka Surf Club, with nearly 50 members as of 2003, has an office in city hall, overlooking the break.

Mundaka has appeared in a dozen surf movies and videos, including *Atlantic Crossing* (1989), *Lost . . . On the Road with Spike* (1995), and *Surf 365* (1999). *Surfing* magazine picked Mundaka as one of the "25 Best Waves in the World" in 1989, and *Australia's Surfing Life* magazine in 1997 cited it as one of "Ten Waves Every Surer Should Ride." British-published *Surfer's Path* magazine devoted its entire December 2000 issue to Mundaka. *See also* Spain.

Mungall, Greg   Big-voiced, barrel-chested regular-foot surfer from Cocoa Beach, Florida; winner of the 1976 Waverider Florida Pro and the 1979 Katin Team Challenge in Huntington Beach. Mungall was born (1955) in Newport News, Virginia, moved with his family to Cocoa Beach at age five, and began surfing at age nine. The 1976 Florida Pro was Mungall's first professional event, and was held in the debut year of the world circuit. In the 1979 Katin final, Mungall defeated world champions Peter Townend and Wayne Bartholomew; in a bit of psychological gamesmanship, he surfed through the frigid midwinter event without a wetsuit. Mungall remained in California after his Katin win and became a loud, laughing, sometimes obnoxious presence on the statewide surf scene. "I scream and yell and get people hyped up," he told surf journalist and future *X-Files* creator Chris Carter in 1981. "Everybody's so dead sitting out there . . . I set the pace." Mungall freely admitted that he had a limited range. "I don't ride big waves, and I'm not afraid to say it. Four-foot and under, espe-

Mundaka

cially around three foot, that's where I'm deadly."
Mungall founded Altra Surfboards in 1985, specializing in Styrofoam/epoxy resin boards. He appeared in a small number of surf movies, including *We Got Surf* (1981) and *Wizards of the Water* (1982).

Muñoz, Mickey   Quick-footed regularfoot surfer from Capistrano Beach, California; among the first group of surfers to ride Hawaii's Waimea Bay in 1957; runner-up in the 1965 United States Surfing Championships. Muñoz was born (1937) and raised in New York City, the son of an opera singer father, moved at age six with his family to Santa Monica, California, began surfing at 10, and soon developed into one of the hottest young riders at Malibu. In 1956 he dated a neophyte teenage surfer named Kathy Kohner, better known to the Malibu surf set, and soon to America at large, as "Gidget." (The 5′4″, 130-pound Muñoz wore a bikini and blond wig as the surfing stunt double for Sandra Dee in the 1959 movie version of *Gidget*.)

While Muñoz earned a reputation in the late '50s as an enthusiastic big-wave rider, he was also highly regarded as a snappy and playful small-wave expert: the 1960 debut issue of *Surfer* magazine features him riding three-to-a-board at Malibu, and spontaneously inventing moves like the "mysteriouso," "el telephono," and, most famously, the "quasimoto." In the early and mid-'60s, Muñoz developed into one of California's best competitors, finishing runner-up in the 1962 and 1963 West Coast Championships and third in the 1964 United States Championships. In 1965 he was invited to the inaugural Duke Kahanamoku Invitational, won the Tom Morey Invitational noseriding contest, placed second in the U.S. Championships, and fourth in the World Championships.

In the summer of 1963, when 10-foot boards were the rule, Muñoz often used a 6′8″ board he made for his four-year-old son. Muñoz went on to design and shape for Hobie Surfboards. Unlike many surfers of his generation, Muñoz continued to surf regularly if anonymously through the '70s and '80s. He returned to the public eye in the '90s as a sage, cheerful, and at times poetic elder statesman. "It's the process of surfing that's important," he told *Longboard* magazine in 1997. "It's sitting in the water, looking into the depths, watching the colors change, sensing the rhythm of the ocean and knowing you're not tied to your wristwatch." Muñoz was featured in more than a dozen surf movies, including *Search for Surf* (1958),

Angry Sea (1963), *Stop the Wave, I Want to Get Off* (1965), and *Fantastic Plastic Machine* (1968). He was also featured in *Liquid Stage: The Lure of Surfing,* a 1995 PBS-aired documentary. Muñoz has been married twice and has two children.

Munro, Mimi   Diminutive blond child-star surfer from Ormond Beach, Florida; third-place finisher in the 1966 World Surfing Championships at age 14. Munro was born (1952) in Daytona Beach, Florida, raised in Ormond, and began surfing at age 10. Two years later she became Florida's state champion, and in 1965 and 1966 she won the East Coast Surfing Championships. Munro never got over a childhood fear of big surf, but had near-perfect balance and exceptionally quick feet, and by 1965 she was the best female noserider in the world. She quit surfing in 1968 at 16, in part because she'd been teased in school for being a tomboy. At 18 she joined a commune, at 20 she was married, at 33 she had four children, and at 40 she "began to dream about surfing" and started riding a longboard. In 2001, at age 49, she won the women's pro division of the Cocoa Beach Easter Surfing Festival. Munro was inducted into the East Coast Surfing Hall of Fame in 1996.

Murph the Surf   *See* Jack Murphy.

Murphy   Short, blond, perpetually stoked cartoon surfer created in 1961 by 17-year-old California artist Rick Griffin. Murphy made his debut in the third issue of *Surfer* magazine. He was "the archetypal Everysurfer," as surf journalist Steve Barilotti wrote in 1988. "A potbellied little grem, and an instant surf world hit." *Surfer* published 28 Murphy strips between 1961 to 1987, with 22 strips running in near-consecutive issues up until mid-1965. For Griffin and Murphy both, the early '60s consisted mainly of a long series of surf adventures ("Murphy and the Caveman," "Murphy and the Surf Spy," "Murphy and the Lost Continent of Atlantis"), with Murphy often shouting out "Cowabunga!" and "Yes, I'm stoked!" As *Surfer* founder John Severson later recalled, "It was hard to tell where Griffin ended and Murphy started." Murphy made the *Surfer* cover in 1962; Murphy stickers, T-shirts, and coffee cups were soon available; and Murphy was used on handbills for Southern California surf bands like the Challengers and the Belairs. Murphy went on hiatus in 1965, just before Griffin moved to San Francisco where he helped

Murphy

create the psychedelic rock-art poster genre. Murphy
returned in 1969, still upbeat, but reconfigured, as
Griffin had been, by drugs and born-again Christianity. In a 1969 strip, Murphy rips into an overhead
wave while wearing a stylized Hopi Indian mask, is
visited by human-size rats, and briefly turns into a
flaming eyeball. For his final appearance in 1987,
Murphy was sadly pushed to the background of his
own strip as Griffin's pen-and-ink panels wandered
from astrology to mermaids to Easter Island tiki
heads, vortex theory, Alfred Tennyson, Merlin the
Magician, and other "geographistoric enigmas." In
the final panel, Murphy walks into a new morning,
surfboard under arm. "But enough for now!" he ex-
claims. "It's dawn . . . I'm goin' surfin'!" Griffin died in
a 1991 motorcycle accident. *See also* Rick Griffin, surf
cartoons and comics, Surfer magazine.

Murphy, Jack   Florida surfing champion and convicted jewel thief/murderer. Los Angeles–born Jack
Murphy arrived in Miami Beach in 1955 at age 18,
where local lifeguards, impressed by his wave-riding
skills, nicknamed him "Murph the Surf." Murphy
won the 1962 Daytona Beach Surfing Championships, one year after making a short appearance
in Bruce Brown's film, *Surfing Hollow Days.* Murphy
owned a south Florida surf shop and also promoted
surf movies at local halls and auditoriums. When his
shop failed he turned to crime, and on a rainy October night in 1964 he and a partner broke into New
York City's Museum of Natural History and stole the
563-carat Star of India sapphire; "a chapter in crimi-

nal history," the *New York Daily News* reported the
following day, "that rivals anything in fiction." Murphy was caught and convicted, and served two years
at Rikers Island penitentiary. He was later arrested for
a double murder in Florida, again convicted, and returned to prison for 16 years. A born-again Christian
when he was released in 1986, Murphy began a mobile prison ministry, and also made his return to surfing. "It's always good to go someplace where we can
both evangelize and surf," one of Murphy's ministry
associates said in 2000. "It's sort of a double bless-
ing." Murphy was featured in *Gangs and Gangsters:
The Illustrated History of Gangs from Jesse James to
Murph the Surf,* published in 1974. *Murph the Surf,* a
low-budget Hollywood thriller starring Don Stroud,
was released the following year. Murphy was inducted into the East Coast Surf Legends Hall of Fame
in 1996, where it was noted that he was "a much better surfer than he was a jewel thief."

Murphy, Matthew "Spider"   Quiet and diligent
surfboard shaper from Durban, South Africa; best
remembered for providing the boards upon which
fellow Durbanite Shaun Tomson in the mid-1970s
reinvented both the frontside and backside forms of
tuberiding. Murphy was born (1947) and raised in Durban, began surfing at age 12, and started shaping at 16.
He cofounded War Surfboards in 1970, and in 1972
began shaping for Safari Surfboards. A Safari board
that Murphy shaped for Tomson in late 1974—measuring 7′10″ by 18″ by 3¼″, with a coral-colored swirl design on the deck—was initially written off as a mistake
for having too much rocker (lift in the nose and tail).
"I took it out for the first time at [Hawaii's] Sunset
Beach," Tomson later recalled, "and it was a dog. No
speed—just a dreadful board." Unable to get another
board on short notice, Tomson tried the pink board at
Pipeline, and it was magic. The added rocker not only
allowed Tomson to drop cleanly down the steep-faced
Pipeline waves, but encouraged him to maneuver
while inside the tube, something that had never been
done. A blue-bottom, seven-foot Murphy-made board
worked just as well for Tomson at Backdoor Pipeline
and nearby Off the Wall. Murphy later shaped boards
for world champions Martin Potter, Mark Richards,
Tom Carroll, Peter Townend, and Wendy Botha, as
well as dozens of other first-rate surfers.

mushy   Surf that crumbles along the crest, then
rolls down the wave face. Mushy waves are contrasted

with hollow waves, whose crests launch out from the wave face and pour down to form a tube. While generally soft-breaking, and best suited for beginning surfers, mushy surf can also invite big, innovative performance maneuvers: the annual world pro tour contest held in the dependably mushy waves of Bells Beach, Australia, for example, can produce some of the year's hottest surfing. Old Man's reef at San Onofre, in north San Diego County, is a famously mushy break; a soft-rolling wave on the North Shore of Oahu, about a half-mile west of Sunset Beach, is called Monster Mush. Waves are often made mushy by an onshore wind. Mushy waves are sometimes called "mushburgers" or just "burgers."

Myanmar   Military-ruled country in tropical Southeast Asia, located in the Bay of Bengal, surrounded by Thailand, Laos, China, India, and Bangladesh. Myanmar, formerly called Burma, came to the surf world's attention in 2001, when the *Surfer's Journal* published "On the Edge of Burma," documenting a short visit made by American surfers Randy Rarick and Tor Johnson, who endured 16 separate tear-apart luggage searches but also found some small but well-shaped waves peeling off the nearshore islands adjacent to Gwa, about 150 miles north of Pagada Point. Myanmar has three distinct seasons: the May-to-October wet season, which produces nearly 200 inches of rainfall; the cool months from October to February, when temperatures drop to the high 60s; and the hot season, February to May, when temperatures often hit 100. Sea temperatures range from the mid-70s to the low 80s. Indian Ocean storms push small- to medium-sized surf into the Bay of Bengal throughout the year, with the biggest and best waves usually arriving between March and June. Myanmar's exotic 1,650-mile coastline, decorated with hundreds of gilded pagodas, remains almost entirely uncharted for surf breaks. "We only saw a tiny portion of Burma, mystical and backward, full of gracious people and despotism," Johnson wrote in his *Surfer's Journal* article. "It's also got some good surf. I'll go back, if they'll give me a visa."

mysto break   A surf spot that rarely breaks, and is even less-frequently surfed; often a deep-water, big-wave-only offshore reef, but the term can also be applied to any spot that requires a highly unusual set of conditions—a minus tide, a huge swell, and a rare wind direction, for example. "Mysto" is short for mysterious. *See also* bombora, cloudbreak.

N

Namibia Sandy and vaguely sinister diamond-rich country in southwestern Africa, bordered by Angola to the north, Botswana to the east, and South Africa to the southeast, with a 950-mile Atlantic-facing coast. French journalist and surf photographer Arnaud de Rosnay, while working on a diamond mining story for *Paris Match* magazine in 1968, reported seeing a "surfer's paradise" of empty waves in southern Namibia. He discovered that a few of the miners were also surfers, but weren't allowed in the water because it was assumed they would hide gems in their surfboards. To guard against diamond theft, much of Namibia's coast, particularly in the south, is still patrolled by dogs, boats, and planes, and lined with electric fences.

"Namibia" means "land of no people," a fair description for a gray and desolate coastline, dotted with shipwrecks, that averages 340 days of fog per year. Air temperatures range from freezing to 95; ocean temperatures, lowered by the chilly Benguela Current, drop to the mid-50s in winter, and rarely get higher than 68 in summer. White sharks feed on the coast's enormous seal population. Most of the accessible surf breaks are located around the resort town of Swakopmund, near the center of Namibia's coastline, and six to 10-foot waves are common here from May to September. The surf drops off during the rest of the year, and is often windblown. The most popular spot, located 12 miles south of Swakopmund, is a pointbreak called Guns, a long, steep, perfectly shaped left. More high-quality pointbreaks are found 80 miles north on the Fur Seal Reserve at Cape Cross, and dozens of other spots up and down the coast are either undiscovered or kept secret. "If you don't mind surfing alone in the kind of chilly waters that scream WHITE SHARK," California surfer/shaper/writer Dave Parmenter wrote of Namibia in 1994, "and if you don't object to the odd X-ray and personal body search, this place is for you."

The Namibia Surfing Association was formed in 1996, and later that year staged the first Namibia National Surfing Championships. Two years later the country sent a team of surfers to the biannual World Surfing Games. As of 2003, Namibia was home to about 200 resident surfers and one surf shop.

Narrabeen Dynamic beachbreak located in the northeast suburbs of Sydney, New South Wales, Australia; home to the area's most consistent waves and a hotbed for talented, creative, highly competitive surfers. The Narrabeen sandbars are in a constant state of flux, but there are three semipermanent breaks, from north to south: 1) The Alley, a wedging right that breaks into a channel and connects through to nearby Narrabeen Lake. 2) North Narrabeen, the premier break, a high-performance left with a tubing end section; if conditions are right, the wave can run for up to 100 yards. 3) Carpark Rights, just south of North Narrabeen, occasionally creates a thick tubing wave during south swells. Narrabeen (an Aboriginal word meaning "place of eels") has ridable surf all year, as the area is open to a wider range of swells than anywhere in Sydney, but generally sees its best waves from April to October during the South Pacific storm season. Nearshore cyclones can also produce good surf during February and March. Wave height is consistently between two and four foot; a few times a year the surf gets six or eight foot. Average daytime air temperatures range from the high 70s in summer to the low 60s in winter. Average water temperatures range from the low 70s to the low 60s. Snarling, tightly packed crowds are the only real Narrabeen surfing hazard.

The Narrabeen waves were being put to use by resident Surf Lifesaving Club members as far back as the 1920s; Bob Pike and other top Sydney surfers from the beaches to the south began riding there often during the '50s and early '60s. In April 1963, Narrabeen was visited by a flawless eight-foot swell, and photographs of the day—with the hollow lefts looking very much like Hawaii's Pipeline—created a small sensation when published in the American surf press. ("Australia's Narrabeen" was the only non-American break cited in the Beach Boys' 1963 hit "Surfin' U.S.A.") Local surfers Owen Pilon and Bob "Doc" Spence formed the Narrabeen Boardriders Club in 1964, and by the end of the decade the "Narra boys" had a reputation as loud, rowdy, and hostile to outside surfers. (A commemorative 30th-anniversary Narrabeen Boardriders Club album proudly states that the group "invented localism.") Hazing of grommets (younger surfers) was also a Narrabeen specialty, with cheeky pubescents often stripped naked and lashed to the beachfront "grommet pole" for public viewing. But the competitive nature of Narrabeen's surfers meant that they welcomed the arrival in 1974 of the debut 2SM/Coca-Cola Surfabout pro contest; the event ran continuously until 1999, almost always at Narrabeen, and from 1975 to 1982 it was the world's richest surf contest. Surfabout winners include world champions Mark Richards, Margo Oberg, Wayne Bartholomew, Tom Carroll, Kelly Slater, and Layne Beachley. Narrabeen is also home to the 1977-founded Pro Junior event.

Narrabeen-area surfboard shaper/designers Terry Fitzgerald and Geoff McCoy both left a mark on board design in the '70s. Simon Anderson—later named "the best surfer ever at Narrabeen" by *Australia's Surfing Life* magazine—initiated a sea change in board design history in 1981 by riding his newly developed tri-fin Thruster surfboard to consecutive wins at the Bells Beach Rip Curl Pro and the Surfabout. A short list of other Narrabeen notables includes Australian champion Col Smith, world pro champion Damien Hardman, surf industrialist Bruce Raymond, pro surfers Mark Warren, Greg Anderson, Mark and Brett Bannister, Nathan Hedge, and Nathan Webster, aerialist Ozzie Wright, and world kneeboarding champions Mike Novakov and Simon Farrer. Narrabeen has been featured in about 20 surf movies and videos, including *The Young Wave Hunters* (1964), *Tracks* (1970), *A Winter's Tale* (1974), *The Swell* (1983), and *Madmen '93* (1994). Narrabeen was featured in *Great Waves* (1998), an Outdoor Life Network documentary series. *See also* Sydney.

National Scholastic Surfing Association (NSSA)

Domestic amateur competitive surfing association formed in 1978 in Huntington Beach, California, focusing primarily on student surfers; regarded as the gold standard for American amateur surfing, particularly during its '80s heyday. National Scholastic Surfing Association (NSSA) alumni include world pro tour champions Tom Curren and Kim Mearig, big-wave rider Mike Parsons, and pro tour standouts Rob Machado and Andy Irons. Founded by Huntington Beach bank executive and high school surf coach Chuck Allen, along with teacher/coaches John Rothrock and Tom Gibbons, the NSSA lifted most of its rules and bylaws from the American Surfing Association, a short-lived organization formed in 1976, when amateur surfing in American lay virtually fallow. The new organization was different from previous groups in that it was linked to the classroom. "The NSSA was created," Allen later said, "for the sole purpose of keeping surfers in school." To compete in the NSSA, the surfer/student had to maintain a not-very-demanding 2.0 grade point average. While the NSSA was popular from the beginning, it took a jump in prestige in 1980 when Allen hired Australians Peter Townend and Ian Cairns (first and second, respectively, on the 1976 world pro tour) as executive directors, and for the next few years a slot on the NSSA's elite National Team, coached by Townend and Cairns, was the Holy Grail for America's young amateur competitors.

The NSSA has been defined by its relationship to the United States Surfing Federation (USSF), founded in 1979 in an attempt to oversee, organize, and unify six separate U.S. amateur surfing organizations. Leaders of the one-year-old NSSA, already thinking of their group as a cut above the rest, signed on as a USSF member with reluctance. Problems arose after NSSA surfers captured nine of the 10 slots on America's 1980 World Amateur Surfing Championships team; the USSF maintained—and won the point—that all six American amateur groups should contribute equally or commensurably to future U.S. world teams. In 1993, NSSA executive director Janice Aragon pulled her organization out of the USSF, forcing amateurs to choose between competing in the better-organized and talent-superior NSSA or working toward a coveted U.S. world team slot through a USSF affiliate. (The NSSA Nationals event was already more prestigious than the USSF-run U.S. Championships.) The NSSA grew and prospered under Aragon's leadership in the mid- and late '90s. USSF teams, meanwhile, won the renamed World Surfing Games in 1996, then finished sixth in 1998 and an embarrassing 10th in 2000. Efforts by the USSF to bring the NSSA back into the fold have so far been rejected.

The NSSA is divided into seven regional conferences (six on the mainland and one in Hawaii), and funds itself through membership and contest fees and corporate sponsorship. Each conference holds its own championship event, with the cumbersome Nationals—the event features 32 separate divisions—held each summer at California's Lower Trestles. The NSSA had roughly 2,000 members in 2003.

The National Scholastic Surfing Association Nationals were held twice a year from 1978 to 1980; a juniors division was added in 1981. Nationals winners for the men's, women's, and juniors divisions are as follows:

1978:	(summer): Bud Llamas, Francine Hill
1978:	(winter): Mark McDandel, Alisa Schwarzstein
1979:	(summer): Jeff Johnson, Kathy Wilson
1979:	(winter): Bud Llamas, Alisa Schwarzstein
1980:	(summer): Todd Martin, Debbie Rooney
1980:	(winter): Doug McKenzie, Kim Mearig
1981:	Chris Frohoff, Debbie Rooney, Chris Frohoff
1982:	Kelly Gibson, Crystal Roever, Brad Gerlach
1983:	Chris Frohoff, Jolene Smith, Noah Budroe
1984:	Scott Farnsworth, Jolene Smith, Jeff Booth
1985:	Dino Andino, Christine Gillard, Jeff Booth
1986:	Jim Pinkerton, Christine Gillard, Kirk Tice
1987:	Todd Miller, Janel Anello, Kaipo Jaquias
1988:	Taylor Knox, Rochelle Gordines, Donavan Frankenreiter
1989:	Joey Zintell, Nea Post, Rob Machado
1990:	Mark Austin, Nea Post, Shea Lopez
1991:	Barry Deffenbaugh, Hoey Capps, Jeremy Sommerville
1992:	Bryan Doonan, Falina Spires, Kalani Robb
1993:	Kalani Robb, Jayme Lee, Kalani Robb
1994:	Kalani Robb, Megan Abubo, Chris Ward
1995:	Eric McHenry, Megan Abubo, CJ Hobgood
1996:	Andy Irons, Melanie Bartels, Shaun Burrell
1997:	Bruce Irons, Jessica Earl, Michael Losness
1998:	Michael Losness, Sena Seramur, Bobby Martinez
1999:	Fred Pattachia, Sena Seramur, Dustin Cuizon
2000:	Anthony Petruso, Kristen Quizon, Travis Mellem
2001:	Greg Long, Holly Beck, Patrick Gudauskas
2002:	Dustin Cuizon, Karina Petroni, Jeremy Johnston

See also Chuck Allen, Janice Aragon, Ian Cairns, competitive surfing, Peter Townend.

Native Son of the Golden West, A   *See* James Houston.

naturalfoot   *See* regularfoot.

Naude, Paul   Multifaceted surfer and surf entrepreneur from Durban, South Africa; third-place finisher in the 1976 Pipeline Masters, the same year he cofounded *Zigzag* surf magazine; CEO of Billabong USA since 1998. Naude was born (1955) and raised in Durban, and began surfing at age 10. He won the 1975 Smirnoff Amateur at Sunset Beach, Hawaii, became the South African national champion the following year, then spent three relatively unsuccessful years on the world pro tour. From 1974 to 1981 Naude was partners with Mike Larmont in Larmont Surfboards; in 1976, Naude, Larmont, and editor Doug McDonald founded *Zigzag,* with Naude serving as publisher. He worked briefly as a freelance photographer in 1981, contributing to both *Surfer* and *Surfing* magazines, then became co-owner of Gotcha South Africa, an outgrowth of the Gotcha USA beachwear company. Naude moved to Laguna Beach, California, in 1992, and spent five years as executive vice president with Gotcha USA, before taking over in 1998 as CEO and president of Billabong USA.

Naughton, Kevin   Easygoing surfer and surf journalist from Laguna Beach, California; coauthor, along with Craig Peterson, of a series of popular *Surfer* magazine travel articles in the 1970s and '80s. Naughton was born (1953) in Philadelphia, Pennsylvania, the son of a psychiatrist, moved with his family in 1959 to Long Beach, California, and began surfing at age 11. After high school, Naughton traveled north to Oregon and Washington, then flew to Hawaii for the winter; the following year he visited France and Central America. He returned to Central America in 1973, this time with 17-year-old surf photographer/writer Craig Peterson of Huntington Beach, and over the next 11 years the peripatetic duo regularly mailed off packages of handwritten text and color slides to *Surfer,* documenting their adventures in places like Senegal, Ghana, Liberia, Morocco, France, Spain, Ireland, Mexico, Barbados, and Fiji. Traveling for weeks or months at a stretch, sometimes with just the vaguest itinerary, Naughton and Peterson pioneered dozens of breaks worldwide, and their articles captured the boredom, strangeness, joy, misadventures, and comedy of the dedicated surf traveler. Peterson took the photos, mostly of the husky (6′, 200-pound) but smooth-surfing Naughton. They took turns writing, always referring to themselves in the third person. "We entered the bar and situated ourselves at a table in the corner," Naughton wrote in 1975, describing their arrival in the El Salvadorian beach town of La Libertad, after a harrowing eight-hour bus ride.

> *The place reeked of stale booze and soaked armpits. Our talk revolved around finding a place to stay, how to get ahold of more money, where the waves were, and could we stomach another drink. Within a couple of hours, both our tongues felt numbed from the local tonic. Kevin scanned the bar. It was certainly no place for two scholars to talk serious business. Five mean-looking studs hung around a torn, faded, green-lit pool table. People in the back room were engaged in some sort of game that involved money. Right next to us a woman in a blonde wig was hustling a young drunk. Kevin did a double-take on Craig, who was slumped in his chair and swiping fingerfuls of a chocolate bar that had melted in his shirt pocket. Places like this attract a very special breed, and Craig was clearly one of them. Flies buzzed, chairs creaked, bottles clinked, talk clocked away the time: the harmony of a Latin cantina.*

Naughton received a B.A. in English literature from UCLA in 1975; two years later he took a graduate degree in Anglo-Irish literature from Trinity College in Dublin; in 1983 he opened a nursery and gardening supply store in Laguna Beach. Naughton and Peterson wrote 13 travel articles for *Surfer* from 1973 to 1989; an 18-page retrospective of their articles was published in a 1993 issue of the *Surfer's Journal* magazine, and two of their journeys were listed in *Surfer's* 1995 article "The 10 Greatest Surf Trips of All Time." *The Far Shore,* a documentary on the Naughton/Peterson travels, came out in 2002. Naughton is married

and has two children. *See also* Craig Peterson, surf travel.

Neece, Jim   Flash-in-the-pan regularfooter from Hawaii, nicknamed "Wildman," who made news in 1973 when he announced his intention to ride a 40-foot wave at Keana Point, the unconquered big-wave break on the western tip of Oahu. Neece, then 21, reportedly signed a $12,000 contract with a Los Angeles film company to make good on his Keana claim, money due only if he rode a 40-footer successfully. He planned on wearing a five-minute "mini-lung" supply of oxygen strapped to his waist, and had a pair of special yellow-and-red 12-foot boards built, one of which he broke at Waimea Bay in late 1973 during a practice session. To make the Keana takeoff easier, Neece hoped to be pulled into his giant wave from behind a speed boat; he tested what he called the "water-ski takeoff" in the fall of 1974, predating the tow-in movement by more than 15 years. In December of that year, however, Neece abandoned the project, overwhelmed, according to *Surfer* magazine, by "constant pressure and anxiety." In a brief "whatever happened to" follow-up notice three years later, *Surfer* reported that Neece was working as a ski instructor in the Italian Alps. Neece appeared in a small number of surf movies, including *Fluid Drive* (1974) and *A Winter's Tale* (1974).

needle nose   *See* no-nose.

Neilsen, Paul   Sociable first-generation pro surfer and tuberiding virtuoso from Queensland, Australia; winner of the event in 1971, as well as that year's Australian National Titles; present-day surf retail magnate. Neilsen was born (1951) and raised on Queensland's Gold Coast, the son of the first fulltime lifeguard in the resort area of Surfer's Paradise. Neilsen's first surfing experience went badly, as the 10-year-old, along with older brother Rick and a friend, team-paddled a 19-foot hollow wooden surf-ski into a shorebreak wave, pearled, and broke the board in two. An aggressive regularfooter, Neilsen peaked as a competitor surfer in 1972 when he won the $5,000 first-place prize in the Smirnoff Pro in Hawaii, by far the richest purse in surfing history up to that point. "What's your goal in the sport?" Neilsen was asked by *Surfing* magazine a few weeks later. "Dollar signs on a wave," he replied. Neilsen was also a finalist in the 1972 Hang Ten Pro and the

Paul Neilsen

1976 Bells. He appeared in a small number of surf movies, including *Oceans* (1972) and *Fluid Drive* (1974). Brothers Neilsen Surfboards, founded by Paul and Rick, opened in Surfer's Paradise in 1971, and was an instant success; by 2001 there were 27 Brothers Neilsen outlets in Australia, making it the country's largest surf shop retailer.

Nelson, Nancy   Baby-faced goofyfoot surfer from San Clemente, California; winner of the Makaha International in 1962, 1963, and 1965, and runner-up in the 1965 World Surfing Championships. Nelson was born (1946) and raised in San Clemente, and got her first surfboard at age 12. Four years later, while living in Honolulu for eight months with her family, she placed third in the Makaha contest; the following year she won at Makaha and placed second in the West Coast Championships; in 1963 she again won Makaha and finished third in the West Coast Championships. Small, compact, and quick-footed, with excellent wave sense, Nelson was nonetheless overshadowed throughout the mid-'60s by two-time world champion and media darling Joyce Hoffman, who lived just a few miles to the north. After a slow year in 1964, Nelson returned the next year for a final victory at Makaha, then finished runner-up to Hoffman in both the United States Surfing Championships and the World Championships.

Netherlands   The Netherlands' 230-mile coastline faces the North Sea; summer waves are small or non-existent, but fall and winter swells produce chilly midsize surf at more than two dozen breaks up and down the coast. Average midday temperatures along Dutch beaches range from the low 40s in winter to the upper 60s in summer; water temperatures range from the upper 30s to the low 60s. Scheveningen, a soft-breaking but dependable beachbreak not far from Rotterdam, has been referred to as the country's own Surf City. "But try to stay away from Scheveningen," advised local surfer Macario Gomes in a 1998 issue of *Surfing.* "It's too crowded; up to 60 people on any day." The surf in the Wadden Islands to the north meanwhile remains largely untapped, although it is believed that some of the country's best waves are located here.

Native beachgoer Jan Nederveen began riding a homemade wooden board in the Netherlands in the late 1930s, but Dutch surfing didn't really catch on until the mid-'60s. "The sport is new in the Netherlands," *Surfer* magazine wrote in early 1968, next to a tiny black-and-white photograph of a surfer riding a minuscule wave, "but growing." Go Klap, one of the first local surfers to own a foam board, opened the Netherlands' first surf shop in 1973; the Holland Surfing Association was formed later that year. As of 2003, there were about 4,000 surfers and 10 surf shops in the Netherlands, with the Holland Surfing Association counting nearly 500 members. The Netherlands are informally known as Holland.

New Guinea   Large, remote, exotic tropical island in the Pacific Ocean, located about 100 miles north of the northeastern tip of Australia. The western half of New Guinea is called Irian Jaya, and is a province of Indonesia; the independent nation of Papua New Guinea takes up the eastern half. As a surfing area, New Guinea was described in a 1994 issue of the *Surf Report* newsletter as "practically a virgin land," and just enough discoveries have been made in the years since to identify the island as a repository for good, consistent, easy-to-ride reef waves. Portions of mainland Papua New Guinea's south coast pick up vestiges of the cyclone swells that hit Australia and New Zealand. New Guinea's north coast, however, has more consistent surf—at least from November to April, as monsoon storms to the northwest produce swells—especially around the towns of Wewak, Aitape, and Vanimo. New Guinea's best surf is found on the offshore islands to the northeast. Kavieng, on New Ireland Island, is New Guinea's most popular surfing area, and includes a reefbreak named Piccin-niny that can produce a hollow 200-yard-long right. Dozens of breaks scattered among New Guinea's is-lands remain either undiscovered or secret; access, in nearly all cases, is by boat only. Two small foreign-run surf camps were in operation in New Guinea by 1998, one at Vanimo and the other on New Ireland Island; enough natives had taken up the sport by 2003 that a small number of breaks were beginning to get crowded.

New Guinea is a kaleidoscope of mostly premod-ern cultures, and home to more than 700 native lan-guages. The weather is hot and humid all year, with an annual rainfall of 200 inches. Air temperatures range from 75 to 85; water temperatures are usually in the low 80s. Sharks, stonefish, sea snakes, and croco-diles are common in New Guinea waters, but the biggest concerns for visiting surfers are malaria and staph infection from reef cuts.

New Hampshire   This rustic New England state funnels down to a mere 13 miles of coast, but is nonetheless home to more than two dozen surf breaks, some of them first quality. New Hampshire's beachbreaks often get crowded during the summer season, when the surf is generally small and crumbly but ridable. The point- and reefbreaks—as well as the beachbreaks—are best in fall and winter; six to eight-foot surf is fairly common during the coldest months, and 12-foot waves are not unheard of. Aver-age daytime air temperatures in New Hampshire range from the upper 60s in summer to the low 30s in winter; water temperatures range from the low 70s to the low 30s. Rye on the Rocks, the state's best-known break, is a fast, powerful, predominantly left-breaking reef that handles nearly any size wave. Other favorite New Hampshire breaks include the point surf at Fox Hill, the consistent beachbreak waves at Wall, and a foreboding deep-water reef called Boar's Head. Tidal changes of up to 13 feet have a dramatic effect on all New Hampshire breaks. Surfers in Maine, New Hampshire, and Massachusetts regularly drive from state to state in search of waves.

University of New Hampshire professor Pete Laslow and Maine schoolteacher Steve Watson were the first to surf in New Hampshire in the early 1960s. Brother's Surf Shop opened in Rye in 1963, and three more shops opened shortly thereafter in Seabrook, Rye, and Hampton. Each put together a small compe-tition squad, and team events were common. By the

late '60s, surfing was restricted at several popular New Hampshire beaches, if not banished outright; just 25 surfers at a time were allowed in a 300-foot-long stretch of water at Rye Beach, and everyone had to wear a brightly colored lifeguard-issued belt to in-dicate they were registered to surf. A 1969 *Sports Illus-trated* article meanwhile noted that the winter surfers of New Hampshire had to deal with "sub-zero tem-peratures, blizzards, small-craft warnings and insinu-ations of dementia."

By 2003, New Hampshire was home to two surf shops and an estimated 500 surfers. The state is part of the New England District of the Eastern Surfing As-sociation, which includes Maine and Massachusetts; the district hosts about seven contests annually. Six-time national amateur surfing champion Kevin Grondin is the state's best-known surfer; in 2000 Grondin was listed in *Sports Illustrated* as one of New Hampshire's "50 Greatest Sports Figures of the Cen-tury." The New Hampshire surf has been featured in a small number of surf videos, including *Granite State of Mind* (1996), *Fade* (1998), and *Surfing the Soul* (2002), and is detailed in *The Stormrider Guide North America* (2002).

New Jersey   The jetty-studded beaches of New Jer-sey produce some of the East Coast's finest waves, but surfing difficulties here are manifest, with long flat spells, brutally cold winter temperatures, highly reg-ulated beaches, and teeming summertime crowds. New Jersey's 130 miles of east/southeast-facing coast-line is made up almost entirely of beachbreaks, with the most reliable waves forming next to jetties, piers, and inlets. Popular breaks include Manasquan Inlet to the north, States Avenue in Atlantic City, and Broadway Beach in Cape May. New Jersey's southern beaches are better known and more crowded than the northern beaches; Sandy Hook, a long right-breaking wave in the extreme north of Jersey—with a direct view across Lower New York Bay to the Man-hattan skyline—is one of the state's only pointbreaks. Waves arrive throughout the year from a variety of Atlantic Ocean sources, including tropical hurricanes (usually forming in late fall) and powerful nor'easter storms (fall through spring), either of which can pro-duce waves from three to eight feet and sometimes bigger. Fall is generally the best surf season; winter brings bone-chilling temperatures and erratic surf; spring is also hit or miss; summer waves are often small, weak, and in many places cordoned off for

New Jersey; Manasquan Inlet

hundreds of thousands of visiting beachgoers. Average daytime air temperatures along the New Jersey coast range from the mid-70s in summer to the upper 30s in winter; water temperatures range from the mid-70s to the low 30s.

Hawaiian surfer/swimmer Duke Kahanamoku introduced surfing to New Jersey with a well-attended demonstration at Atlantic City in 1912, but the sport didn't really take root here until the mid-'30s, when surfing pioneer Tom Blake visited Ocean City and taught local lifeguard captain John "Bull" Carey how to ride his 13-foot paddleboard. Before and after World War II, Carey built a small number of surfboards and gave informal surf lessons along the Jersey Shore. Still, just a few dozen hardy surfers were counted in Jersey by the late '50s, and not until the lighter foam-core boards were imported from California in the early '60s did surfing take off. Cecil Lear formed the Jersey Surfing Association in 1963, and soon began holding local and statewide surfing contests; the Ocean City Surfing Association was founded in 1964, and was soon running contests featuring more than 100 surfers and up to 3,000 spectators. Keller Surf Shop, owned by pioneering New Jersey surfer Charlie Keller, also opened in 1964; *Surfing East* magazine was founded in 1965, in Ridgewood, New Jersey, and was published for nearly three years. Cecil Lear cofounded the Eastern Surfing Association in 1967, and over the next three decades organized hundreds of surf contests up and down the East Coast. The Grog's Seaside Pro event, held in Seaside Heights, debuted in 1973, and was included on the world pro tour schedule in 1978 and 1979. Surfboard

shaper Dan Heritage meanwhile opened Little Wave Surf Shop in 1964 in Sea Isle; the name was later changed to Heritage Surfboards, and by the end of the '70s the company was producing 500 boards a year. Beach communities across the state had by that time enacted the strictest surfing codes in America, with surfers having to pass a swimming test in order to gain a wave-access registration number. New Jersey's reputation took another hit in the mid- and late '80s, as toxic runoff forced a number of well-publicized beach closures.

Notable New Jersey surfers include pro surfer Dean Randazzo, indomitable amateur competitor George Gerlach (winner of the grandmasters division of the United States Surfing Championships in 1982, 1987, and 1995), Ron Jon Surfboards founder Ron Di-Menna, surf moviemaker and Sundek founder Bill Yerkes, and photographer/publisher Dick Meseroll. By 2003, New Jersey was home to 25 surf shops and roughly 10,000 surfers. The Eastern Surfing Association holds about 12 contests in New Jersey each year. New Jersey has appeared in several surf movies and videos, including *Atlantic Crossing* (1989), *Flail* (1996), and *What Exit?* (2001). The New Jersey surf is detailed in *The Stormrider Guide North America* (2002).

New School A loosely affiliated group of surfers led by Florida's Kelly Slater, who began asserting themselves, while still teenagers, in the early 1990s. The New School surfers rode thin, narrow surfboards. They concentrated on aerial and tail-slide maneuvers, preferred short, hollow, quick waves (making Pipeline/Backdoor, rather than Sunset Beach, the hot spot on the North Shore of Oahu), and were featured in rough-edged, punk-scored videos like Taylor Steele's *Momentum* and *Focus*. New Schoolers were seen as both rivals and heirs to an older group of surfers—including Tom Curren, Tom Carroll, Martin Potter, and Gary Elkerton—who had long dominated the surf media and the world tour ratings. Aside from Slater, New School surfers included Shane Beschen and Rob Machado from California, Shane Dorian and Ross Williams from Hawaii, and Shane Herring and Shane Powell from Australia. A slightly younger group of up-and-comers, including Hawaii's Kalani Robb, were sometimes called Pre-Schoolers.

New South Wales This Australian state's intricate 750-mile beachfront contains hundreds of surf breaks of all description, and can be divided into four general surfing areas: 1) The less-developed South Coast, from the Victorian border to just south of Sydney, has a generous number of shallow rock-lined reef-breaks, including the spitting left tubes of Black Rock. 2) The headland-studded coast of the Sydney area, stretching from working-class Cronulla to the affluent Northern Beaches, is home to a few walloping reefbreaks such as Shark Island and Little Avalon, and dozens of temperamental sand-bottom breaks like Narrabeen, Manly, and Bondi. 3) The central coast, which includes the crowded beachbreaks of Newcastle and the more isolated beaches and bays north to Coffs Harbour. 4) The pastoral North Coast, from Yamba to the Queensland border, is dotted with a series of outstanding right-breaking point waves, including Angourie, Lennox Head, and Byron Bay. New South Wales (NSW) has reasonably consistent surf all year, but generally gets its biggest and best waves from April through October, during the South Pacific storm season; nearshore cyclones in February and March can also produce excellent surf. Wave height throughout the state is regularly between two and four foot; a few times a year powerful swells will push the surf up to eight to 10 foot, or bigger. Temperate air and water conditions prevail from season to season.

New South Wales was bodysurfed as far back as the early 1900s and board-surfed as early as 1910, but the sport didn't catch on here until surfer and Olympic gold medal swimmer Duke Kahanamoku of Hawaii gave a small number of well-attended surfing demonstrations in late 1914 and early 1915—most notably with a debut performance at Sydney's Freshwater Beach. Frank Adler of Maroubra introduced the Tom Blake–style hollow surfboard to Australia in 1934, which greatly helped to popularize the sport. Surfing was for the most part regarded as an offshoot of lifeguarding, but after World War II, a rift developed between the "surfies" and the Surf Life Saving Association "clubbies."

New South Wales surfers were the first in their country to see the hot new American style of wave-riding in 1956, when a group of California surfer/lifeguards—visiting the country for a lifeguarding festival associated with the Melbourne Olympics—gave a series of impromptu demonstrations on their all-balsa "Malibu" boards. Local surfers quickly exchanged their Blake-style hollows for Malibu-style balsas. (Sydney board-maker Gordon Woods opened Australia's first surf shop a few weeks later in Bondi

Beach; a board originally belonging to one of the Americans was passed on to Sydney surfer Bob Evans, who went on to become the country's first surf film-maker, as well as the founder in 1962 of *Surfing World* magazine.) Americans meanwhile got their first look at the waves in New South Wales in 1958, with the release of Bud Browne's *Surf Down Under.*

Sydney was and remains both the state and national surf capital. By the mid-'60s, Sydney had produced world champions (Midget Farrelly and Phyllis O'Donell won the 1964 championships, held at Manly Beach) and top big-wave riders (Dave Jackman and Bob Pike), while Sydney board-builders like Gordon Woods, Scott Dillon, and Barry Bennett had a near monopoly on domestic surfboard manufacturing. Surf clubs across the country banded together in 1963 to form the Sydney-headquartered Australian Surfriders Association (now Surfing Australia); the inaugural New South Wales Surfing Championships were held that year in Manly, just before the first Australian National Titles at Bondi. New South Wales's bucolic North Coast became the world's hot spot for progressive surfing and surfboard design in the mid- and late-'60s, as Queensland-born shaper Bob McTavish, along with Sydney's Nat Young and George Greenough of California, launched a movement that would first see Young crowned as world champion in 1966, then create the prototype boards for the short-board revolution. Greenough's 1970 film *The Innermost Limits of Pure Fun,* shot largely in the North Coast, documented the new aggressive style of surfing that was already the trademark Australian style. The North Coast was also featured in Alby Falzon's 1972 movie *Morning of the Earth,* which focused on Australian surfing's back-to-nature "country soul" period. Attention shifted back to Sydney in the mid-'70s with the advent of professional surfing; the 1974-founded 2SM/Coca-Cola Surfabout, which found a semipermanent home at Narrabeen, soon became the sport's biggest and richest contest. Surfers from other areas of the state also made their presence felt. Mark Richards of Newcastle won the 1978 Surfabout riding a twin-fin surfboard of his own making—a design that soon became the world's most popular small-wave board—and went on the following year to win the first of four consecutive world titles.

New South Wales has by far produced more first-rate surfers than any state in the world, including world champions Midget Farrelly, Phyllis O'Donell, Nat Young, Mark Richards, Tom Carroll, Damien

Hardman, Barton Lynch, Pam Burridge, Pauline Menczer, Mark Occhilupo, and Layne Beachley; longboard world champions Stuart Entwistle, Marty McMillan, and Beau Young; and kneeboard world champions Simon Farrer and Mike Novakov. As of 2003 New South Wales was home to about 250 surf shops, 50 surf clubs, and roughly 350,000 surfers. Dozens of amateur and professional contests are held in the state yearly. The New South Wales surf is detailed in a number of books, including *The Surfing and Sailboarding Guide to Australia* (1993), *Atlas of Australian Surfing* (1998), *Surfing Australia* (1998), and *The World Stormrider Guide* (2001). *See also* Narrabeen, North Coast.

New York   The diverse New York surf scene ranges from the hustling concrete-lined boardwalk setting at Long Beach to the affluent sea-grass-covered dunes of the Hamptons. Temperamental southwest-facing beach breaks make up the vast majority of surf spots along New York's 127-mile-long Long Island coast, with the most reliable waves found adjacent to jetties, piers, and inlets. (Surfing is also practiced along the New York shorelines of Lake Ontario and Lake Erie; *see* Great Lakes.) The state's largest and most consistent surf usually breaks along Long Island's northeast shore in the Hamptons or the rugged Montauk region, where the state's only pointbreaks are found; the easy-breaking waves of Montauk's Ditch Plains have been called the "Mecca of New York surfing." The sheltered southwestern beaches offer better waves when huge swells have rendered the northern breaks unridable. Rockaway Beach, immortalized in a like-titled song by New York punk band the Ramones, is the only New York surfing beach accessible by subway, and offers a particularly urban surfscape. "One Brooklyn surfer was famous for surfing with a knife taped under his board," the *New York Times* magazine reported in 1997, before commenting on tensions between local Irish, Haitian, Italian, Hispanic, and Jewish surfers.

New York generally gets its best surf in fall and spring, as Atlantic storms and hurricanes produce fairly steady two to four-foot waves, broken up by an occasional six-foot-plus swell. Summer can bring waveless conditions for weeks at a time; the winter surf gets excellent, but is cold and often prohibitively stormy. Average daytime air temperatures in coastal Long Island range from the low 80s in summer to the upper 30s in winter; water temperatures range from the low 70s to the low 30s.

Surfing was introduced to New York in 1912 by reknowned surfer/swimmer Duke Kahanamoku of Hawaii, who gave a wave-riding demonstration at Rockaway while traveling from Honolulu to compete in the Stockholm Olympics. Wisconsin-born surfer Tom Blake visited Jones Beach in the summer of 1934, rode with local lifeguards, and shared with them his latest hollow surfboard designs. A few more locals picked up the sport, but it developed slowly over the decades, practiced mainly by lifeguards at Babylon, Jones Beach, and Gilgo Beach. In 1959, Long Island surfer John Hannon began selling surfboards out of his garage, and the following year Hannon opened a surf shop near Gilgo, with protégé Charlie Bunger soon to follow. Lido Beach was the site of New York's first surf contest, held in the summer of 1960; the *New York Times* covered the event, which was attended by more than 10,000 people. The first East Coast Surfing Championships were held at Gilgo the following year. (Since 1965, the Championships have been held in Virginia Beach.) Westhampton surfer Rick Rasmussen won the 1974 United States Surfing Championships, and was still regarded as New York's hottest surfer eight years later when he was shot and killed during a Harlem drug deal. Other notable New York surfers include surfing novelist Allen Weisbecker and Eastern Surfing Association founder Rudy Huber. *Atlantic Surfing* magazine was published in Brooklyn from 1965 to 1968, and *Competition Surf* was published in Long Island in 1966 and 1967. *Surfing* was published in Manhattan from 1969 to 1971.

The waves were up during the terrorist attacks on September 11, 2001, and a half-dozen surfers who worked for businesses housed in the World Trade Center had skipped work that morning and gone to the beach; at least one New York surfer/fireman, however, died when the buildings collapsed.

As of 2003, New York was home to roughly 25 surf shops and 5,000 surfers. The Unsound Pro, New York's only pro tour surf contest, was held annually from 1999 to 2002; the Eastern Surfing Association runs about 10 amateur contests in New York each year. The New York surf has been featured in a small number of surf movies and videos, including *Flowing Free* (1980), *Sun Waves* (1982), *Surfing NY* (2002), and *Couch Tour* (2002).

New Zealand   New Zealand is located 1,000 miles southeast of Australia, and is composed of two large islands (North Island and South Island), each trimmed with hundreds of surfing spots, including several world-class point- and beachbreaks.

The lush variegated New Zealand coastline runs for more than 3,200 miles. Weather conditions throughout the country are mild and moist, with air temperatures ranging from 65 to 85 degrees in summer and 35 to 55 in winter, and water temperatures ranging from 50 to 70. Beachbreaks make up the majority of surf spots. Shapely 10-foot or bigger surf is rare in New Zealand, but three to six-foot waves are common, and the sunny afternoons produce waves with a glistening transparent green finish. South Island surf is consistent, with waves produced by Antarctic Circle storms, as well as local wind swells. Mangamaunu, a long, tapering right point located 10 miles north of Kaikoura on the northwest coast, is South Island's best-known wave. The majority of surf spots here are found on the east coast, but the remote northeast, west, and far south coasts contain some beautiful breaks as well, many of them rarely surfed. North Island is home to 75 percent of New Zealand's population, and also has waves throughout the year. The west coast is best in the winter months (June to September), as Tasman Sea storms generate south and southwest swells, while the east coast is best in summer (January to March), when tropical storms push swells in from the northeast. Westerly winds are common to both islands. Raglan, a majestic point located near Auckland, is New Zealand's best known surf spot: a long, walling, left-breaking wave with three distinct sections that can link together on a big southwest swell. Rocks and unfiltered sunlight—New Zealand is home to the world's highest rate of skin cancer—are the main surfing hazards. Aside from the breaks in and around Auckland, this remains a relatively uncrowded surfing nation.

Dutch explorers landed in New Zealand in the mid-17th century and noted that the indigenous Maori were riding waves using canoes and unrefined surfboards; in the late 1800s, Calvinist missionaries arrived from England and, as part of their proselytizing efforts, effectively brought an end to Maori surfing, just as Hawaii-posted missionaries had done a few decades earlier. Hawaiian surfer and Olympic gold medal swimmer Duke Kahanamoku reintroduced the sport to New Zealand in 1915 by putting

New Zealand; South Island's Merken Point

on a surfing demonstration at Lyall Bay in the North Island city of Wellington. Over the next several decades, members of New Zealand "surf clubs"—lifeguard organizations—rode with limited success on surf-skis and weighty hollow surfboards.

New Zealand surfing changed quickly following a 1958 visit from Southern California lifeguard/surfers Bing Copeland and Rick Stoner, who arrived with the latest Malibu-style balsa-and-fiberglass boards. "Upon returning to the beach," Copeland said later, recalling the first time he and Stoner rode at Piha, a beachbreak near Auckland, "we were surrounded by guys wanting to give our boards a go. I believe our boards never left the water during the daylight hours for the next few weeks." Piha tomato farmer Pete Byers helped Stoner and Copeland build several boards during their visit; Byers then went on to become New Zealand's first commercial surfboard manufacturer. A small number of local surfers had meanwhile visited Australia and returned with Australian-made boards. In 1960 New Zealand was home to about six board-makers and 75 surfers; by 1967, there were a dozen board-makers and about 15,000 surfers. The first New Zealand National Surfing Championships were held in 1963, with Peter Way winning the men's title and Wayne Butt taking the juniors (there was no women's division); the New Zealand Surf Riders Association formed shortly afterward. Australian-born John McDermott competed for New Zealand in the 1964 World Surfing Championships, held in Sydney, Australia. The bimonthly *New Zealand Surfer* magazine debuted in 1965 (lasting for six issues), just before the publication of Wayne Warwick's *A Guide to Surfing in New Zealand*; North Island surf filmmaker Tim Murdoch soon began producing New Zealand's first homegrown surf films, beginning with *Out of the Blue* in 1968. Top riders of the decade included Peter Way, Wayne Parks, and Cindy Webb. Regional surf clubs had meanwhile sprung up by the dozen, and New Zealand surfers in general had embraced whole-heartedly the California- and Australian-style surf culture—its music, language, fashion, and habitually wild behavior—and were raising eyebrows among staid natives. Over time, however, the New Zealand surfing identity became reserved, even inconspicuous. A small number of New Zealanders have developed international surf/world reputations (most notably board-maker Allan Byrne), but for the most part native surfers have been content to ride their beautiful and relatively isolated waves without drawing undue attention to themselves or their nation. "We don't have to worry anymore about projecting a bad image to the wider public," local surf journalist/photographer Logan Murray wrote in 1995. "Surfing in New Zealand simply does not have an image."

As of 2003, New Zealand was home to about 150 surf shops, 100,000 surfers, and two glossy monthly surfing magazines, *New Zealand Surfing* and *Kiwi Surf*. Surfing New Zealand, the country's governing body for competitive surfing and heir to the New Zealand Surfriders Association, oversees 64 affiliated surf clubs and produces a national pro-am contest circuit, along with separate longboarding and body-boarding events and an annual big-wave contest. In 2002, New Zealand won the World Surfing Games, while Maz Quinn, a smooth-riding regularfooter from Gisborne, became the first Kiwi to qualify for the world pro championship circuit. *New Zealand Surfers* and *Gone Surfing: The Golden Years of Surfing in New Zealand* were both published in 2002 by Penguin Books. New Zealand has been featured in dozens of surf movies and videos, including *The Endless Summer* (1966), *Coastal Disturbance* (1994), and *Static* (2001). *See also* Raglan.

Newport Beach   Wealthy and crowded Southern California beach city, featuring six miles of west-southwest-facing coastline, located in Orange County, just south of Huntington Beach. From north to south, Newport's main surfing areas are: Santa Ana River Jetties, 56th Street, 36th Street, Blackies, the Point, the Wedge, and Corona del Mar. With the exception of the Wedge—the towering shorebreak wave adjacent to Newport Harbor—the surf here is made up of semipowerful two-way beachbreak peaks. River Jetties, 56th Street, and 36th Street are ridable all year; Blackies is best in winter; the Point and the Wedge require an oversize south swell.

The long, easy-breaking waves at Corona del Mar, located between the original Newport Harbor jetties, were regarded in the 1920s and 30s as among the best in California, ridden by pioneering surfers like Duke Kahanamoku and Tom Blake. The Corona del Mar Surfboard Club, formed in the late '20s, was the mainland's first surf organization and early editions of the 1928-founded Pacific Coast Surf Riding Championships were held at Corona del Mar. A jetty extension in 1938 rendered the surf unridable for the type of boards used at the time.

Newport's high surf-world profile is largely due to the fact that it's located in the backyard of the California surf industry, with magazines to the south (*Surfer, Surfing,* the *Surfer's Journal,* and *Longboard* are all based in nearby San Clemente) and surfwear company headquarters to the east (Quiksilver, Gotcha, Hurley, and Billabong are based in nearby Costa Mesa). Huntington Beach has meanwhile been American surfing's competition hub since the late '50s. While Lenny Foster, Ed Farwell, John Van Ornum, and the rest of Newport's original early and mid-'70s standout surfers were relatively unaffected by surfing's commercial forces, the next generation, led by Danny Kwock, Preston Murray, and Jeff Parker, at times seemed to be holographic creations of marketing and media. "Newport Beach: The Hottest 100 Yards" was the title of a 1980 *Surfer* magazine article describing the insular, hyperactive New Wave surf scene at 56th Street, led by Kwock in his fluorescent-colored wetsuit and polka-dot surfboard. Richie Collins later became Newport's most successful competitive surfer, finishing #8 in the world ratings in 1989 and 1990.

Newport has some of the country's most restrictive surfing laws, with board surfing prohibited city-wide between noon and 4 P.M., from mid-June to mid-September. *See also* Huntington Beach, Orange County, Pacific Coast Surf Riding Championships, the Wedge.

Nias   Palau Nias Island is located 80 miles off the west coast of Sumatra, and is home to Lagundri Bay, a silky right-breaking tube located on the island's south end. Lagundri—the first world-class right discovered in Indonesia—is commonly and mistakenly referred to as Nias. The May-to-October dry season is the best time for surf at Lagundri; because the break is tucked nearly a half-mile inside a bay, waves here lose size on the approach and are one-third to one-half smaller than those found at Grajagan (Java) or Uluwatu (Bali). But when swells do finally bend in and reach the flat seaweed-covered Lagundri reef, the resulting wave is a smooth, perfectly tapered wall that dependably spills over into an almond-shaped tube. Other surf breaks in the area include Indicators, a stronger and more erratic wave just outside Lagundri's main break; the Machine, a speeding left further inside the bay; and the consistent Hinako Islands, just northwest of Nias, which include the steam-rolling left tubes of Asu and the deep-water right walls of Bawa. Tropical air and water temperatures across the island are generally in the '70s and '80s. Although getting to Nias still requires a great deal of time and effort, and malaria remains a threat throughout the area, Lagundri's many "homestay" lodgings are often full during the dry season, and crowds of 100-plus surfers are common.

Lagundri was first ridden in 1975 by intrepid Australian surf travelers Kevin Lovett, Peter Troy, and John Geisel. "The search was over, the dream was for real," Lovett later wrote, before describing Geisel's death from malaria nine months after the Lagundri discovery. Nias became an international surf world sensation after it was showcased in a 1979 issue of *Surfer* magazine; Lagundri natives took to the waves in earnest in the mid-'80s, when Australian Mark Flint became making boards locally, and the Nias Surf Club was founded soon after. Nias farmer and landowner Ana Dalin began to develop Lagundri Bay for surf tourism in the early '80s, and helped organize a series of international contests in the mid to late '90s, including the Nias Indonesian Open (which ran from 1994 to 1997) and the O'Neill Deep Jungle Open (2000). But as longtime visitor Peter Reeves later noted, "by the late '80s, the magic was gone. Lagundri had turned into an eroded, polluted, hygienic nightmare." The break nonetheless remained popular with international surf travelers, and much of the local economy was built on surf trade.

Asian Paradise (1981) and *Stormriders* (1982) were the first two surf movies to feature Lagundri Bay; it's since been seen in dozens of movies and videos, including *The Golden Pig* (1996), a documentary chronicling the discovery of the break and surf-related development in Lagundri. It was overcrowding at Lagundri that prompted '90s-era surf travelers to look for surf in the wave-rich Mentawai Islands, about 300 miles south. The Lagundri surf is detailed in a small number of guidebooks, including *Indo Surf and Lingo* (1992), *Surfing Indonesia* (1999), and *The World Stormrider Guide* (2001). In 1989, *Surfing* magazine listed Nias as one of the 25 best waves in the world.

Nicaragua   Central America's largest country, bordered by Honduras to the north and Costa Rica to the south, with 215 miles of west-facing Pacific Ocean coastline and nearly 300 miles of coastline along the Caribbean Sea. While a small number of surf explorers passed through coastal Nicaragua in the '70s and early '80s, including California kneerider George Greenough and fabled *Surfer* magazine travel correspondents Kevin Naughton and Craig Peterson, the country's civil war encouraged most wave-hunters to keep their visits short. When Brazilian surfer Adrian Kojin rode a motorcycle from California to deep South America in 1987, virtually nothing was known about the Nicaraguan surf. Kojin discovered beautifully groomed five-foot beach- and pointbreak surf, and said he'd been "made to feel welcome every place I went." Democratic elections were held in Nicaragua in early 1990, bringing an end to the civil war, and Southern California–launched surf expeditions soon followed, including a well-publicized one-week visit in 1992 by pro surfers Matt Archbold and Brock Little.

Surfing in Nicaragua is practiced for the most part in the country's dry and dusty southwestern corner, near the town of San Juan del Sur. Altogether, more than 50 surf spots have been mapped out along the mountainous and largely inaccessible southwest-facing Pacific coast—including a number of high-quality point- and reefbreaks—with dozens more either undiscovered or being kept secret. Four to six-foot surf regularly hits the Nicaraguan Pacific coast from February to October; air and water temperatures are both around 80 all year, and the prevailing wind is offshore. Much of Nicaragua's wet, low-lying, rainforested Caribbean shore is inaccessible by land, the prevailing wind is onshore, and portions of the coast are all but waveless due to barrier reefs or extended shoaling. But late summer/early fall Caribbean hurricanes can send waves toward Nicaragua, and it's likely that good surf will be discovered in the near future, perhaps near the Honduran or Costa Rican border areas, or among the country's scattered off-shore islands.

By 2003, Nicaragua was home to roughly 150 native surfers and three lightly stocked surf shops (one each in Managua, León, and San Juan del Sur). Surf charter boat trips along the Nicaraguan Pacific coast began in 1997, and in 2001 a small surf resort opened in Las Salinas, just north of San Juan del Sur. Poverty and crime remain a problem, however—Nicaragua is the second poorest country in the Western Hemisphere after Haiti—and surfers exploring on their own are advised to do so with a hired guard. The Nicaraguan surf has been featured in a small number of surf videos, including *Panama Red* (1994) and *Killing the Pier* (2000).

night surfing   Night surfing goes back nearly as far as modern surfing itself. Honolulu surf booster Alexander Hume Ford, in his 1909 *Collier's* magazine article "Riding the Surf in Hawaii," describes a feature of the annual Waikiki beachside carnival, in which surfers fasten acetylene lamps to their boards and then go in the late evening "to ride the breakers in a circle of light." Night surfing is usually done under the light of a full moon, at easy-to-read breaks that are prohibitively crowded during the day. Malibu, Rincon, and Trestles, all California pointbreaks, are thought to be the three most popular night surfing locations. Young surfers around the world will sometimes peel away from a beach party, especially in warmer weather, for a drunken round of night surfing. (Hawaii's Jock Sutherland became a night surfing legend by riding 20-footers at Waimea Bay long past sundown while high on an extra-large dose of Orange Sunshine LSD.) Reduced visibility makes judging incoming waves difficult, and the night surfer depends as much on "feel" as on the usual sight cues—turns and cutbacks will generally be toned down. The sense of speed, meanwhile, is greatly amplified compared to daytime surfing. Apart from the satisfaction of riding without a crowd, night surfing has its own moody if slightly ominous charm, particularly when the red tide outlines each breaking wave with a blue-green phosphorescence. Collisions between riding and paddling surfers are night surfing's biggest hazard; night surfers should regularly make their position known with shouts, whistles, or yells.

Efforts are sometimes made to use artificial lights for night surfing. Riders in Huntington Beach, California, have for decades been surfing by the lamppost

light of the municipal pier, and in 1967 the city adjusted the wattage and light angle for improved visibility in the water. In 1972, a California company introduced Nite-Lites, a nylon belt with two hip-mounted waterproof battery-powered lights. Portions of the 1984 Beaurepaire's Open, a world pro tour event held in Sydney, Australia, were run under huge crane-raised floodlights, in front of more than 30,000 spectators. The waves at Arpoador beach in Rio de Janeiro, Brazil, are currently lit by stadium-style floodlights.

Ninth Wave, The   Eugene Burdick's gloomy 1956 novel follows the young adult years of Mike Freesmith, a teenage surfer from Southern California who turns into a venal and murderous political power broker. In the book's first chapter, high school senior Freesmith is dropped off at the local surf break by Miss Bell, his English teacher and lover. Hank Moore, Freesmith's devoted friend, is already in the water, patiently waiting for "the ninth ninth wave," based on the surfing superstition that eight waves will build up to a bigger ninth wave, and that the ninth wave in the ninth set of waves will be even bigger still. Years pass as Freesmith ruthlessly accumulates power and rises to the top of state politics. In the book's penultimate chapter, "The Last Green Hump," Freesmith and Moore, now enemies, return to the surf during a huge winter swell, and duel to the death.

> They started to paddle. Hank looked over at Mike.
> "Don't take it, Mike," Hank called. "Let it go. It's too big for you. You can't ride it."
> And Mike grinned. His arms kept pumping. They felt the sea rise beneath them, push against the boards, lift them high. Then, just at the tip of the wave, the mass of water gripped them and they started to shoot forward. The roar, the grinding, tearing, rumbling, fundamental sound, grew louder. Mike was getting to his feet. He grinned over at Hank. He was going to ride down the crash.

Moore lives; Freesmith drowns. Eugene Burdick (1918–65) was a Rhodes scholar at Oxford and taught political science at U.C. Berkeley. *The Ninth Wave*, his first book, published by Houghton Mifflin, was a Book-of-the-Month Club selection; he later became famous for a pair of novels, *The Ugly American* (1958) and *Fail-Safe* (1962). Burdick also wrote short stories for the *New Yorker, Harper's,* and *Collier's.* In 1963, he wrote "They Ride the Big Surf" for *Reader's Digest,* who described the author as "an ardent surf-rider." *See also* books and surfing.

no-nose Single-fin surfboard design introduced in 1980 by Australian shaper Geoff McCoy and championed by four-time world title runner-up Cheyne Horan; the no-nose dropped the board's wide point below center, increasing the tail area while decreasing the nose area. "Visually," *Surfing* magazine wrote, "it is almost triangular." The no-nose—sometimes called a needle-nose while the McCoy model was known as the Lazer Zap—allowed for lightning-quick turns in small waves, but there were problems. "[The boards] lack projection; they don't seem to reach far enough out of a turn," *Surfing* noted. "This could probably be solved with minor modifications." But the problems weren't solved, and while Horan continued to ride no-nose boards for the next few years, the design was passé by early 1982, after the three-fin board was introduced—although the tri-fin did incorporate a modified version of the no-nose.

no-paddle takeoff Wing-and-a-prayer method of entering a wave, generally performed at the last possible second, as the surfer, while paddling up the face of an approaching wave, stops and spins around, then gives a single frog-kick down the wave face before standing up. Audacious, and often disastrous, when attempted in big surf.

Noll, Greg Boorish but charismatic big-wave rider originally from Manhattan Beach, California; generally regarded as the first person to ride Hawaii's Waimea Bay, in 1957; founder of Greg Noll Surfboards. Noll was born Greg Lawhead (1937) in San Diego, California, moved to Manhattan Beach at age six with his just-divorced mother, and changed his name when she married chemical engineer Ash Noll. He began surfing at age 10, and by the early '50s was one of the Los Angeles area's best hotdoggers. He visited Hawaii for the first time in 1954 at age 17, stayed for seven months in a Quonset hut at Makaha on Oahu's west side, and finished his senior year at nearby Waipahu High School. Noll generally rode Makaha, but also made his initial foray to the wave-lashed North Shore, a seven-mile rural strip of coastline already known for its dangerous and potentially deadly big surf. It was during his first trip to Hawaii that Noll developed a taste for bigger waves; on sub-

Greg Noll

sequent visits he began spending more time on the North Shore, riding ever-bigger waves at breaks like Sunset Beach and Laniakea. By late 1957 he was ready to try Waimea Bay, the deep-water wave where Honolulu surfer Dickie Cross had died in 1943 after paddling down the coast from Sunset during a fast-building swell. Cross had sprinted for shore at twilight, but was caught by a set of waves and drowned. Surfers in years following had seen beautiful big waves at Waimea, but were too scared to ride them.

Noll convinced his friend Mike Stange to paddle out with him at Waimea on November 7, 1957, when the surf was about 15 foot. Another six surfers followed. It's never been clear exactly who rode the first wave, but all agree that Noll led the charge, and thus he gets the credit for opening Waimea Bay—the break that would all but define big-wave riding for the next 35 years. (Noll had made a pioneering effort of a different sort one year earlier, as a member of the American lifeguard team that visited Australia during the 1956 Melbourne-held Olympic Games. Noll and his surfing teammates arrived with their Malibu chip boards, and their impromptu wave-riding demonstrations yanked Australia into the modern surfing age. "We hit 'em like a comet," Noll later recalled. "Took 'em from the horse and buggy straight to the Porsche.")

Noll had meanwhile decided to make a career in surfing any way he could. He published the *Surfer's Annual* magazine in 1960, followed by the *Surfing Funnies* (1961) and the *Cartoon History of Surfing* (1962). He made five surf movies, from 1957 to 1961, each titled *Search for Surf*. But his main business was Greg Noll Surfboards, founded in the early '50s as Noll began shaping boards out of his family garage. In late 1965, Noll opened in Hermosa a brand-new, custom-built, 20,000 square-foot factory—the biggest board-building operation in the world at the time—which included a separate room for making polyurethane foam blanks, eight shaping stalls, and a 40-board-capacity laminating room. Noll Surfboards produced more than 200 boards weekly in 1966, about half of which were shipped across the country to dealers on the eastern seaboard. Noll also produced Da Cat, Mickey Dora's signature model surfboard; an instantly notorious print ad featured Dora hanging Christ-like from a cross made of two Da Cat surfboards.

Noll had by that time become almost synonymous with big-wave surfing. He was nicknamed "The Bull" for his size (6'2", 230 pounds), as well as his implacable head-down charging style in heavy surf. He was seen riding Waimea in virtually every surf movie of the late '50s and '60s, including *Surf Crazy* (1959), *Gun Ho!* (1963), *Strictly Hot* (1964), and *Golden Breed* (1968), and was instantly recognizable in his trademark black-and-white-stripe jailhouse surf trunks. He also stunt-doubled for James Mitchum in Columbia Pictures' big-wave movie *Ride the Wild Surf* (1964), and was featured in Bruce Brown's crossover hit *The Endless Summer* (1966). Never particularly interested in competition, Noll nonetheless entered in the Duke Kahanamoku Invitational from 1965 to 1969, and was a finalist in 1966. The big-voiced Noll had also earned a reputation as a drinker and a brawler, with a sometimes-macabre sense of humor. A Greg Noll Surfboards employee once cut off his thumb while on the job; after Noll took the man to the hospital and found out the thumb couldn't be reattached, he returned to the factory and placed the severed digit in a cup full of resin to make a paperweight.

Noll was 32 when he dropped into a churning 35-footer at Makaha on December 4, 1969, jumping off the back of his board just as the giant wall exploded around him. It was the largest wave ever ridden and remained so for more than 20 years. It was also Noll's last big-wave hurrah. "That day at big Makaha," he wrote in *Da Bull: Life Over the Edge,* his 1989 autobiography, "was like looking over the goddamn edge at the big, black pit. Some of my best friends have said it was a death-wish wave. I didn't think so at the time, but in retrospect I realize it was probably bordering on the edge."

In short order, Noll quit riding big waves, liquefied Greg Noll Surfboards, and moved to Alaska, where he lived in a motor home. He then spent 20 years working as a commercial fisherman in Crescent City, California. Beginning in the late '80s, as interest in surfing's history began to grow, Noll again became a popular surf media figure, appearing in *Surfers: The Movie* (1990), the PBS-aired *Liquid Stage: The Lure of Surfing* (1995), and *50 Years of Surfing on Film* (a 1997 Outdoor Life Network documentary series). Noll's commercial sense remained keen: he founded Da Bull clothing company, then Greg Noll Oceanwear, and in 1992 released *Search for Surf,* a video compilation of his old surfing movies. He began making wooden surfboards similar to those he'd shaped in the '50s, selling them to collectors for up to $10,000 apiece, and also produced a limited edition of signed and numbered Da Cat models. In 1991, in Costa Rica, he sponsored the first of five annual Da Bull Surf Legends Classic, a seven-day surf contest and social gathering for older surfers. In 1996 he founded the East Coast Surfing Legends Hall of Fame.

Noll was voted the top big-wave rider in a 1965 *Surfing Illustrated Readers Poll,* was inducted into the Huntington Beach Surfing Walk of Fame in 1996, and was given the Waterman Achievement Award by the Surf Industry Manufacturers Association in 1998. At the 1999 *Surfer* Magazine Video Award banquet, he was presented with a Lifetime Achievement Award for his work in surf films. Noll has been married twice and has three children. *See also* big-wave surfing, Swell of 1969.

Noosa Enchanting set of tropical right-breaking Australian point waves located inside Noosa Heads National Park, 150 miles north of Brisbane, on Queensland's Sunshine Coast. "Noosa" is a local Aboriginal word meaning "a place of shade." The coast here faces almost due north; from west to east, Noosa's five separate breaks are as follows: Main Beach (or First Point) and Johnson's, a pair of sheltered small-wave spots; National Park, Noosa's premier surfing break, with a dramatic takeoff at a section called Boiling Pot, funneling into a long sand-bottom performance wave; the boulder-lined Ti Tree Bay, a more consistent break than National Park; and Granite Bay, the most exposed, least-groomed, and least-crowded of Noosa's waves. Occasionally rides can be connected from National Park all the way through to Main Beach—a distance of more than 500 yards.

Noosa is maddeningly inconsistent, as it faces away from the South Pacific storms that generate waves for Australia's southeast coast. The best surf generally hits Noosa during the December-to-May Coral Sea cyclone season, but waves here generally reach the six-foot mark no more than a dozen times per season. But between swells the points are often filled with beautifully formed small waves, perfect for longboarding. Average midday air temperatures at Noosa range from the low 80s (summer) to the low 60s (winter); water temperatures range from the low 80s to the high 60s. The leafy and tranquil Noosa setting has long been cherished as among the finest in the world. "Surfing at Ti Tree Bay," Australian surfboard shaper Bob McTavish said, "is like having a cup of tea with God."

Board-maker Hayden Kenny of the nearby town of Maroochydore was the first to surf Noosa in the late 1940s, and he later introduced the break to visiting surf world luminaries such as McTavish, Bob Evans, Bob Cooper, and George Greenough. Noosa was one of the country's best-known and –loved breaks by the late 60s, and a primary testing grounds for the new short surfboards. In 1989, *Surfing* magazine named Noosa as one of the "25 Best Waves in the World." Noosa also earned a reputation for crowds, with good days featuring hundreds of surfers spread across the points at the same time, on all manner of surf craft. The annual Noosa Festival of Surfing, a rollicking seven-day longboarding event, debuted in 1993; virtually no other contests have been held here. Despite Noosa's popularity, it's waves have been featured in just a handful of surf films and videos, including *The Young Wave Hunters* (1964), *Hot Generation* (1967), and *Super Slide* (1999).

North Carolina   North Carolina's 300-mile coastline is fronted almost entirely by a chain of sandy islands, or "banks." The state's best surf—and arguably the best surf on the entire East Coast—is located along the Outer Banks, long, narrow, lightly devel-oped islands known as the "Graveyard of the Atlantic" for the hundreds of ships that have run aground and sunk on its offshore sandbars. Jutting into the Atlantic Ocean, surf along the Outer Banks is often bigger than anywhere else on the eastern seaboard; 12-foot-plus waves have been ridden here, but the ideal size generally ranges from three to six feet. Sandbars adjacent to piers and jetties invariably create the most consistent and best-shaped waves. Cape Hatteras is the most popular Outer Banks area, and the jetties near the Cape Hatteras Lighthouse in Buxton produce shifty, hollow, hard-breaking waves. The relaxed setting, composed almost entirely of water, sky, sea grass, and rolling dunes, greatly adds to the Outer Banks experience. "I defy any surfer to walk out to the tip of sand that is the Cape," Australian surf journalist Nick Carroll wrote in 1997, "and not leave aware that the Banks is one of the world's greatest surfing areas; as unique as the North Shore of Oahu, or the Gold Coast of Queensland."

The fall hurricane season is generally the best time to catch waves in North Carolina, seconded by powerful but erratic nor'easter winter swells. Spring surf is inconsistent, and summer brings long periods of small, gutless waves. The southern half of the North Carolina coast bends to face the southeast and is fronted by a broad continental shelf, and thus often receives a much-dissipated version of the swells that move head-on into the Outer Banks. High-quality waves can nonetheless be found at fairly regular intervals in the south at places like Wrightsville Beach, Masonboro Island, and Bogue Banks. Average daytime air temperatures in North Carolina range from the mid 80s in summer to the mid-40s in winter; water temperatures range from the high 70s to the high 40s; temperatures in the north are generally a few degrees cooler. Jellyfish, stingrays, and sharks are North Carolina's main surfing hazards.

Lifeguards at Carolina Beach and Wrightsville Beach introduced surfing to southern North Carolina in the late '40s and early '50s. Carolina Beach lifeguard/surfer Lank Lancaster cofounded East Coast Surfboards, the state's first surf shop, in 1964, making boards on the side porch of a converted meat market, and selling trunks and T-shirts in the front. The state's first two surf contests were held in 1966, one at Carolina and the other at Wrightsville. Restrictions on surfing imposed in the mid- and late '60s (the sport was outlawed altogether in tiny Surf City) soon had wave-riders searching for breaks in outlying areas. Meanwhile, North Carolina native Tom Fearing began riding waves along the Outer Banks in the early '30s, but surfing didn't catch on there until the early '60s (just a few years after Cape Hatteras became the first protected National Seashore Park), when teenagers Buddy Hooper and John Ochs of Buxton took up the sport. After the Oregon Inlet Bridge was completed in 1962, the Buxton/Hatteras area grew in popularity as a summertime vacation spot, and Hatteras local John Conner was soon renting boards to visitors; in 1968, Conner converted a mobile home into the region's first surf shop. Before the decade was out, top East Coast surfers like Gary Propper, Claude Codgen, and Mike Tabeling had all named the Outer Banks as the eastern seaboard's hottest wave. Cape Hatteras, easily identified by its 19th-century black-and-white barber-pole lighthouse, hosted the annual Eastern Surfing Association (ESA) Championships for the first time in 1971, and the event has returned to Hatteras (or nearby) each year. The $3,000 1972 ESA Pro at North Carolina's Atlantic Beach was the East Coast's first professional surf contest. The United States Surfing Championships were held at Cape Hatteras in 1974, 1978, and 1982.

By 2003, the once-sleepy Outer Banks had become a seasonal surfing boomtown, with 25 surf shops catering to tens of thousands of surfers visiting from up and down the East Coast. North Carolina's resident surfing population is thought to be around 10,000. North Carolina's top surfers include Ben Bourgeois, Noah Snyder, and Jesse Hines. The North Carolina surf has been featured in more than a dozen surf movies and videos, including *Atlantic Crossing* (1989), *Surf NRG,* Vol. II (1991), *Hatteras Surf-Fest* (1991), *The Foundation Project* (2001), and *The Wrong Side* (2002). The Eastern Surfing Association holds about 15 contests each year in North Carolina.

North Coast, New South Wales, Australia

Wave-rich subtropical coastal zone in New South Wales, Australia, running approximately 350 headland-studded miles from Newcastle up to the Queensland border. Reefs, rivermouths, beachbreaks, and jetty breaks are included among roughly 200 North Coast surf spots, but the area is best known for its right-breaking point surf, including Lennox Head, Byron Bay, Crescent, and Angourie—all of which produce long and frequently hollow high-performance waves. March through October is the best time for surf on the North Coast, but waves of one type or an-

other can be found throughout the rest of the year. Midday air temperatures average from the low 60s in winter to the upper 70s in summer. Ocean temperatures range from the low 60s to the low 70s. The North Coast's dependably pleasant weather is counterbalanced somewhat by the threat of shark attack. Local surfer Marty Ford died in 1982 after a white shark attacked him at Byron Bay's Tallows Beach.

The rural North Coast was a shortboard revolution staging area in the late '60s and early '70s, as Nat Young, Bob McTavish, George Greenough, Chris Brock, Russell Hughes, and David Treloar were among a small but progressive group of surfers either living here or visiting regularly, always riding new and sometimes experimental boards. The surfing counterculture they formed, often identified as Australia's "country soul" period, was perfectly captured in Alby Falzon's 1972 surf film *Morning of the Earth.* The North Coast still has nothing resembling an urban center. But virtually every North Coast town, including Mullumbimby, Yamba, Ballina, Coffs Harbour, and Port Macquarie, now has at least one surf shop, and once-sleepy Byron Bay—Australia's easternmost point—has become a small but vigorous Australian surf industry outpost, with board manufacturers, surfwear companies, and surf schools. The North Coast surf has been featured in dozens of surf movies and videos, including *The Innermost Limits of Pure Fun* (1970), *Sea of Joy* (1971), *Sultans of Speed* (1987), *Oz on Fire* (1991), and *Stash* (2002). North Coast surf breaks are detailed in *The Surfing and Sailboarding Guide to Australia* (1993), *Surfing Australia* (1998), and *Atlas of Australian Surfing* by Mark Warren (1998). Pro surfers Danny Wills, Trent Munro, Jock Barnes, and Brenden Margieson are among today's top North Coast–based surfers. *See also* Angourie, Byron Bay, Lennox Head.

North Sea Wide and relatively shallow branch of the North Atlantic Ocean, between Great Britain and mainland Europe, bordering the shores of Norway, Sweden, Denmark, Germany, Belgium, the Netherlands, England, and Scotland. The North Sea is about 600 miles north to south and 350 miles west to east. Surfing is practiced throughout the year in every North Sea–facing nation. Small to medium-sized waves funnel into the North Sea as Atlantic storm fronts travel north or northeast past Scotland toward Scandinavia, with the best surf usually occurring from September to April. Summers are mild, as air and water temperatures climb to the low 70s and the low 60s, respectively, while winter conditions are brutally cold, with a few hardy rubber-encased surfers trudging through beachfront snowdrifts into 38-degree water. *See also* Belgium, Denmark, Germany, the Netherlands, Norway, Sweden, and United Kingdom.

North Shore   Good-natured but far-fetched 1987 Universal Studios coming-of-age movie about Rick Kane (played by Matt Adler), an 18-year-old Arizona surfer who wins a local wavepool contest and flies west to test his skills on the North Shore of Oahu. Kane falls in love, gets beat up by local heavies, acquires a wise and predictably full-bearded surfing guru, and makes the finals of the big contest at Pipeline. The surfing sequences were beautifully photographed by Dan Merkel and Don King, while pro surfers Gerry Lopez, Mark Occhilupo, Laird Hamilton, and Robbie Page all have speaking roles. Some comic relief is provided by John Philbin as Turtle, Kane's sidekick. The PG-rated *North Shore* did poorly at the box office and was pilloried by film critics. "Waves get shredded," as a *Washington Post* reviewer notes, but "they probably should have shredded the script as well." *See also* Hollywood and surfing.

North Shore   World-renowned stretch of Hawaiian coastline located on the north side of Oahu; the undisputed capital of big-wave surfing from the 1950s to the early '90s; home to about 40 surf breaks, many of them hallowed. "If the surfing world has a shared mythology," American essayist William Finnegan wrote in 1997, "then the North Shore of Oahu is its Olympus." The North Shore's thin coastal plain is backed by steep lava-ribbed hills and fronted by a dazzling system of nearshore reefs. Because the coast faces northwest, the reefs are open to virtually all North Pacific storm-generated swells from September to May (the biggest usually arriving between November and February), and breaking waves are groomed by side-offshore northeast tradewinds. Air and water temperatures are pleasant and balmy all year. While the north side of Oahu technically extends about 20 miles from Kahuku Point to Kaena Point, what surfers know as the North Shore begins at the town of Haleiwa and runs east for seven miles to Sunset Beach. North Shore breaks include Haleiwa, Laniakea, Off the Wall, Rocky Point, and Velzyland; Pipeline, Waimea Bay, and Sunset are among the world's best-known surf spots—Pipeline for its ex-

North Shore, Oahu; reef surf at Off the Wall

ploding tubes, Waimea for its fearsome size, Sunset for its consistency and complexity. Winter surf on the North Shore averages between four and eight foot; 10- to 15-foot surf might hit two or three times a month; three or four times a season the waves will get 20 foot or bigger. About twice a decade, the North Shore's outer reefs will produce ridable 40- or 50-foot waves. (Surfers have long used their own peculiar measuring system scale, so that a wave with an actual trough-to-crest height of 20 feet, for example, will be described as 10 or 12 feet. When the surf exceeds 30 foot, measurement sometimes reverts to the actual trough-to-crest height.) The power of the North Shore surf, combined with shallow reefs, crowded lineups (pressuring surfers to try marginal waves), and near-constant surf media presence (encouraging them to take star-making risks), made this the most dangerous surf area in the world. About 30 surfers have died on the North Shore since the early 1960s, and hundreds more have been severely injured.

Although Sunset Beach was surfed in ancient times, and the nearshore waves at Haleiwa were surfed as far back as the 1920s, it is generally accepted that the modern era of North Shore surfing began in 1938, when Wally Froiseth and John Kelly of Hawaii, along with California-born Gene Smith and Lorrin Harrison, began driving out from Honolulu to ride Sunset Beach. In the mid- and late '40s, teenager George Downing of Hawaii began pioneering western sections of the North Shore, including Laniakea; Walter Hoffman, Henry Preece, Buzzy Trent, and others joined in during the early '50s. (Many surfers avoided the North Shore completely in the '40s and '50s, remembering that 17-year-old Dickie Cross of Honolulu had paddled out at Sunset one afternoon in 1943, got caught outside during a fast-rising swell, and drowned while trying to get ashore through 35-foot surf at Waimea Bay.) By the mid-'50s, the North Shore was still lightly populated, mostly by field workers and small-acreage farmers; some of the beachfront houses were vacation homes belonging to the Honolulu elite.

Waimea was ridden for the first time in 1957 by a group of California surfers including Greg Noll, Mickey Muñoz, and Pat Curren. California's Phil Edwards is credited as the first to ride Pipeline, in 1961. Surf movies and surf magazines were by that time filled with images shot on the North Shore; the cover of the first issue of *Surfer,* published in 1960, showed Jose Angel of Hawaii dropping into a huge Sunset Beach peak. The annual winter surfer migration to the North Shore began in earnest in the late '50s, with dozens of mainland surfers renting houses and staying for weeks, or even months, at a time, and the number of visitors increased steadily over the years. Crowded lineups have been a problem on the North Shore since the early '60s, and by the early '70s local surfers were using scare tactics—and the occasional punch-out—to secure waves for themselves.

Surfboard-maker Dick Brewer opened Surfboards Hawaii, the North Shore's first surf shop, in 1961; the Dick Brewer Surfing Championship, held two years later, was the area's first surf contest. The Duke Kahanamoku Invitational debuted in 1965, and was the first in a long line of prestigious international surfing contests held on the North Shore, including the Pipeline Masters (which debuted in 1971) and the World Cup (1975). The North Shore's influence on the surfing world at large was perhaps strongest from the late '60s through the late '70s, as resident surfers like Jock Sutherland, Gerry Lopez, Barry Kanaiaupuni, Lynne Boyer, Reno Abellira, and Jeff Hakman set the standard for high-performance riding. Pipeline meanwhile became the world's most-photographed and –filmed surf break. The International Professional Surfers organization, creator of the world pro tour, was founded on the North Shore in 1976.

Big-wave surfing, pushed to the background in the '70s and early '80s, roared back in 1983, and the North Shore's Waimea Bay once again found itself in the spotlight. The Quiksilver in Memory of Eddie Aikau big-wave contest was first held at Waimea in 1986; subsequent versions were held in 1990, 1999,

2001, and 2002. North Shore big-wave riders like Mark Foo, Ken Bradshaw, Darrick Doerner, and Brock Little became surf world icons; Laird Hamilton and Buzzy Kerbox, along with Doerner, invented tow-in surfing on the North Shore in 1992; Bradshaw in 1998 was towed in to a wave at Outside Log Cabins, located just east of Waimea, that was estimated to be 60 feet from trough to crest—the biggest wave ever ridden up to that point. Dungeons in South Africa, along with Maverick's and Todos Santos on the North American west coast, have broken up the North Shore's big-wave monopoly, while Indonesia with its perfect waves has to a large degree replaced the North Shore as the ultimate surf destination. But this relatively short piece of coastline remains in many respects the center of the surf world. World champions are crowned here in December; giant waves are ridden throughout the winter; hundreds of high-performance boards are produced by North Shore shapers each month—no other surf zone in the world can match the North Shore for intensity.

Although visited by thousands of surfers annually, the North Shore is home to fewer than 1,000 resident surfers, including world tour standouts Kalani Robb and Megan Abubo, surfer/musician Jack Johnson, surf photographers Don King and Bernie Baker, videographer Larry Haynes, shapers John Caper and Pat Rawson, and contest organizer Randy Rarick. Nineteen surf shops are located on the North Shore; more than two dozen surf contests, amateur and professional, are held here annually. The 1997-launched TV show *Board Stories* is produced near Sunset Beach. The North Shore surf has been featured in hundreds of surf movies, videos, and documentaries. *North Shore,* Universal Studios' coming-of-age surf drama, was released in 1987; sportswriter Bruce Jenkins's *North Shore Chronicles: Big-Wave Surfing in Hawaii* was published in 1991. North Shore surf breaks are detailed in *Surfing Hawaii* (1985), *Surfer's Guide to Hawaii* (1991), and *The World Stormrider Guide* (2001). *See also* big-wave surfing, Haleiwa, Outside Log Cabins, Pipeline, Rocky Point, Sunset Beach, Triple Crown of Surfing, Velzyland, Waimea Bay.

Norway Long, narrow, oil-rich Scandinavian country on the northwestern edge of the European continent. Norway's weather-battered coastline is a breathtaking assemblage of mountains, cliffs, and fjords, difficult to traverse, but wide open to surf generated from storms near the Arctic Circle and Greenland. The Jæren region, a stretch of coast near the southern tip of Norway between Stavanger and Eigersund, has nearly 30 charted surf spots—mostly rocky pointbreaks or broad sandy beachbreaks, many of which produce first-rate waves from two to 12 foot—and is the center of the Norway surf scene. Waves hit the area regularly from midfall to early spring; the best surf usually arrives in December and January, but limited daylight makes deep-winter surfing a hit-and-run operation. Heavy winds are often a problem. Average winter air and water temperatures are 45 and 35 degrees, respectively. During the summer months, when temperatures are mild and daylight is plentiful—Norway is known as the "land of the midnight sun"—the surf is generally small and unpredictable. Novelty-seeking surfers can detour to the Sommerland waterpark in Bo, 30 miles from the coast, home to the world's most powerful FlowRider machine, which produces a chlorinated standing wave up to 12 foot high. The FlowRider, however, is for bodyboarding only, and each 30-second ride is more often than not preceded by a 15-minute wait in line.

Roar Berge, a fireman from Skeie, along with several visiting American oil workers, were Norway's first surfers, testing the chilly waves in the southern part of the country in 1982. A handful of natives took up the sport in the late '80s—while Berge became his country's sole representative in the 1988 World Amateur Surfing Championships in Puerto Rico—but surfboards weren't retailed in Norway until 1993. Norway came to the attention of the surf world at large in 2000, as a group of surfers from Santa Cruz, California, rode some small but well-shaped waves for a *Surfer* magazine travel article. In 2001, British pros Spencer Hargraves and Sam Lamiroy, toured above the Arctic Circle and discovered "perfect waves and world-class barrels" beneath the Northern Lights. As of 2003, Norway was home to just one surf shop and about 250 surfers. The Norweigan surf is detailed in *The Stormrider Guide Europe* (1998).

nose The front end of a surfboard. As a board design specification, nose width is measured at right angles to the board's longitudinal "stringer," one foot down from the tip. In general terms, however, nose is used to describe roughly the front third of the board. While surfboard noses have changed and evolved through the years—variations include the concave nose, the spoon nose, the hyper-kick nose, and the no-nose—this area has traditionally held less

interest for designers than the board's bottom contour, tail section, and fin configuration. *See also* the surfboard.

nose drip An abrupt release of water from the paranasal sinuses, the bone-encased hollows located behind the forehead ridge and above the eyes. Nose drip often occurs just after leaving the surf, particularly if induced by inverting then slowly raising the head. It can also happen hours later, and most surfers have experienced the terrible thrill of a poorly timed spontaneous nose drip—onto the table linen at a dressy dinner party, for example, or while leaning over to kiss an aged relative. The amount of expelled water generally ranges from a few drops to a quarter ounce. Trapped water in the sinuses, along with barotrauma (injury due to sudden underwater pressure changes, a danger in big surf) can lead to a painful bacterial infection known as sinusitis, which is treated, according to severity, with externally applied heat (from a washcloth or shower nozzle), decongestants (nasal sprays and tablets), or antibiotics. Nose drip is also called postsession nasal drip, faucet nose, saltwater drip, or nasodrain.

noseguard Soft silicone-rubber bumper affixed to the tip of a finished surfboard with quick-dry adhesive. The Nose Guard was developed by Hawaiian surfboard shaper Eric Arakawa and insurance salesman David Skedeleski in 1986, and first marketed by SurfCo products. Noseguard soon became a generic description. While the noseguard helps protect the surfboard, its main purpose is to prevent or reduce puncture-wound injuries. The original nose guard was V-shaped and about two inches long. Today's shortboard noseguard is diamond-shaped, while the longboard noseguard—developed in 1990—is elliptical. *See also* injuries and surfing.

noseriding Surfing maneuver in which the rider, moves to the front of the board while angling across the wave face, and assumes one of a half-dozen or so positions. Noseriding, described by California surf journalist Bill Cleary in 1965 as "a sport within a sport," can be an act of transcendent elegance and subtlety, and is most often performed in small waves while riding a longboard. The exact origins of noseriding are unknown. Hawaii's Albert "Rabbit" Kekai is sometimes identified as the first surfer to consistently ride the nose, doing so in the 1940s at

Queens Beach in Waikiki, while on a finless hot curl surfboard. California surfer and pioneering wetsuit manufacturer Bev Morgan, however, claims that surfboard-maker Dale Velzy not only invented noseriding in 1951 at Manhattan Beach, but that he was also the first to hang five (placing the toes of the lead foot over the tip of the board) and hang ten (placing all the toes over the tip). By the late 1950s, noseriding had become the ultimate small-wave maneuver, and "hang ten" was about to become the first surfing phrase recognized by nonsurfers.

The science of noseriding—the hydrodynamics that allow the board's nose to glide along the wave rather than sink beneath the rider's weight—has baffled surfers for decades. A U.C. Irvine physics professor explained in 1991 that noseriding is possible in part because the tail of the board is pressed down by the falling curl and acts as a counterweight. Expert noseriders, however, can move to the front of the board even on an unbroken wave. An alternative explanation is that the upflowing water on the wave face gathers against the bottom surface of the nose and forms a kind of supporting cushion.

Because the surfboard is best controlled from the rear, the basic surfing stance is assumed over the back third of the board. Beginning and intermediate surfers move to and from the nose using a shuffle step; advanced surfers use the more difficult cross-step. Hanging five and hanging ten are the two most common noseriding positions; experts will occasionally levitate one foot out ahead of the board, or turn and "hang heels" off the tip. The peak of what is sometimes referred to as the golden age of noseriding came in the mid-'60s. David Nuuhiwa, Lance Carson, Joey Cabell, and Mickey Dora were among those celebrated for their smooth noseriding skills. The 1965 Tom Morey Invitational, held in Ventura, California, was the first contest in which each surfer was judged solely on the amount of time spent on the front one-quarter of the board; later that year, in 10-foot surf at Sunset Beach, 17-year-old Jeff Hakman of Hawaii astounded the surf world by executing a flawless "cheater five"—squatting on his rear haunch while extending his front foot to the tip—to win the inaugural Duke Kahanamoku Invitational. Surfboard manufacturers soon began to make specialized noseriding models, including the Wing Nose, the Ego Builder, the Nose Specializer, the Cheater, and the Ugly.

Noseriding hit its apex during the first round of the 1966 World Surfing Championships, when fa-vorite David Nuuhiwa of California spent 10 graceful back-arching seconds perched at the tip of his board. Power-turning Nat Young of Australia, however, came back and won the contest, then declared the noseriding era to be over. "If you just stand on the nose from start to finish," Young noted, "you've defeated creativity and individualism—the very essence of surfing!" Noseriding all but vanished in the 10 years following the shortboard revolution of the late '60s; as the longboard began its slow but steady return through the '80s and '90s, noseriding was again recognized as a sublime surfing manouver. By the mid-'90s, pencil-thin teenage goofyfooter Joel Tudor of San Diego, California, was being described as the finest noserider in the history of the sport. *See also* cheater five, hang five, hang ten, heels over, Tom Morey Invitational.

Nova Scotia   *See* Canada.

Novakov, Mike   Invincible kneeboarder during the early and mid-'80s from Narrabeen, Australia; winner of the World Amateur Surfing Championships in 1982, 1984, and 1986. Novakov was born (1961) in Manly Beach, raised in Sydney, and began surfing in 1975. He became the New South Wales kneeboard champion in 1981—and was the first kneerider to use a tri-fin board—then went on to win dozens of regional, state, and national titles over the next eight years. "Smart money was on Mike Novakov," *Surfing* magazine wrote in its coverage of the 1986 World Championships, "who slammed and carved his way to victory in a style every bit as exciting as stand-up surfing." Novakov was featured in *The Swell*, a 1983 surf movie. *See also* kneeboarding.

nudity and surfing   Surfing developed across Polynesia as a nude activity, and remained so until top-coated 19th-century missionaries shamed the natives into covering themselves, even while at play in the ocean. (The dress code was often ignored; a British engraving from 1874 shows a set of waves being ridden by nearly a dozen Hawaiian surfers, male and female, all of them naked.) No other sport lends itself to nudity as easily as surfing; clothes shedding is required, and the act itself, a product of the tropics, is often described as sensual. Pre–World War II photos of early American surfers like Tom Blake and George "Peanuts" Larson lounging nude on the beach, published for the first time in the late '90s, didn't raise an eyebrow among contemporary surfers.

Nudity and surfing; a visiting European's sketch of native Hawaiians, 1819

A more aggressive style of nudity was often cited as part of the "surfer problem" in the late '50s and early '60s, when rock-and-roll-fueled baby-boom teenagers began strafing the beachfronts of Southern California and Sydney with bent-over "BAs," often shot from car windows. "Undressing in public," California surfer John Severson wrote in his 1964 book *Modern Surfing Around the World,* was a hallmark of the gremmie or hodad surfers who were "giving the sport a bad name." (The forces of decency and nudity would occasionally clash in the years and decades to follow. After receiving complaints about surfers not covering themselves while changing in and out of their wetsuits, city lawmakers in Pacifica, located just south of San Francisco, passed an ordinance in 1997 under which naked surfers could be fined up to $500.)

The mid-'70s were a golden era for surfing nudity. Top California surfers Mike Purpus and Angie Reno both posed and surfed naked for *Playgirl* magazine in 1974; the following year pro surfer Wayne Bartholomew of Australia shed his boardshorts for an in-the-buff *Tracks* surf magazine cover shot, while reigning Smirnoff Pro women's division winner Laura Blears of Hawaii was featured in a *Playboy* spread and posed topless for a best-selling surfing poster. (Precedent set, four-time world pro tour champion Wendy Botha did an Australian *Playboy* layout in 1992, while Hawaiian pro Megan Abubo posed for a relatively demure nude shot in a 2001 issue of *Rolling Stone.*)

Male Australians have far and away proven to be the most fervent surfing nudists. A group of Sydney surfers formed Club INT—In the Nude—in 1984 (later changing their name to Even Nuder); 28 surfers entered the inaugural Ungawa Nude Classic, held at Southside Beach in Victoria in 1994 (with first place going to a Torquay local dressed in suspenders and stockings who surfed atop a wooden door); while the Bondi Nude Night Surfing Expression Session drew more than 2,000 spectators in 1996. "Why are we obsessed with public nudity and silly games involving our genitals?" *Australia's Surfing Life* magazine asked in 1993, putting the question to a Sydney psychologist. She replied that surfers seemed to have taken normal "sexually flavored" early-adolescent bonding games and continued them "well beyond the usual age range," probably as a form of "narcissism and ego-investment."

Nunn, Kem   Soft-spoken California noir novelist; author of *Tapping the Source* (1984) and *The Dogs of Winter* (1997), both gloomy but well-crafted books set in the surfing world, each with a memorable cast of gangsters, hustlers, rogues, and murderers carefully lifted, as the *Los Angeles Times* put it, "from the Boschian hothouse of Nunn's imagination." Nunn was born (1948) and raised in Pomona, and began surfing at 15. "I discovered Jack Kerouac not long after discovering Mickey Dora," he later said, "and the two interests, surfing and writing, have competed for the honor of my ruins ever since."

Tapping the Source protagonist Ike Turner, an 18-year-old Central California innocent looking for his long-missing older sister, arrives in Huntington Beach and takes up residence among the local surfers and biker thugs. In the market for a first board, he nervously enters a local surf shop and finds a young sun-blond salesman and a pair of surf groupies.

> *Ike knelt beside the board and tried to pretend he knew what he was looking for. The board looked like it had once been white, but was now a kind of yellow. It was long and thin, pointed at both ends. Around him the frantic beat of the music filled the shop. He was aware of one of the girls dancing near the counter, her small tight ass wiggling beneath a bikini bottom. He turned to the salesman. "This would be good to learn on?"*
>
> *"Sure, man. This is a hot stick. And I can make you a good deal on it. You got cash?"*

Ike nodded.

"Fifty bucks," the kid said. "It's yours.". . . Ike stood by the cash register as the kid rang up the sale. He picked up the board. "Rip 'em up," he heard one of the girls say as he went back outside, into the brilliant light. He heard one of the girls laugh, and he had not guessed that buying a board could turn out to be such a humiliating experience.

Tapping the Source sold fewer than 10,000 copies, but earned Nunn high critical praise, along with an American Book Award nomination. *In The Dogs of Winter,* Nunn's fourth novel, an aging surf photographer travels north at the behest of a retired messianic surfer to capture the first-ever images of Heart Attacks, a deadly big-wave break on a menacing, undeveloped area of coast near the Oregon border. "Too much space is devoted to epic slogging along deserted beaches," a *New York Times* reviewer noted, although Nunn had also produced "many stretches of confident and lyrical writing."

Nunn wrote a profile on three-time world champion Tom Curren for *Rolling Stone* in 1987, and contributed an article to *Surfer* in 1993. He lives in Laguna Beach, California. *See also* books and surfing.

Nuuhiwa, David Quintessentially smooth goofyfoot surfer from Southern California; best known as a noserider, but regarded by many as the finest surfer of the 1960s; winner of the United States Surfing Championships in 1968 and 1971, and runner-up in the 1972 World Surfing Championships. Nuuhiwa was born (1948) in Honolulu, Hawaii, the son of a Waikiki beachboy and martial arts instructor, and began surfing at age five, one year after his mother died. In 1961, after living with various relatives, the 13-year-old Nuuhiwa moved to San Francisco to live with an uncle, then two months later left for Southern California to look for his remarried father in Anaheim. He moved to Hermosa Beach in 1962 and lived with surfboard-makers Donald Takayama and Harold Iggy, and soon after began to compete in the juniors division of the United States Surfing Association, where he was nearly unbeatable, topping the year-end standings in 1964, 1965, and 1966. He won the juniors division of the 1965 United States Surfing Championships, then flew to Hawaii and took the juniors division of the Makaha International.

By that time, the 17-year-old Nuuhiwa was universally regarded as one of the world's best surfers, he

David Nuuhiwa

rode in a pliable open-knee stance, deftly blended one turn to the next, and cross-stepped with cool self-possession across the deck of his board. Expert in all facets of the sport—save big-wave riding—Nuuhiwa was a preternaturally gifted noserider, able to suspend himself on the tip for seconds at time. When *Surfer* magazine asked Phil Edwards to pick the world's 10 best noseriders in 1965, he placed Nuuhiwa on top. "He was a pharaoh," fellow Hawaiian-born surfer Reno Abellira later said. "David was surfing itself, noseriding to the adoring masses." A first-generation surfing professional, Nuuhiwa signed endorsement deals in 1967 that were said to be worth $25,000.

American surfers expected the slender goofyfoot to cruise to a world title in 1966—he won the *Surfer Magazine* Readers Poll Award that year, and the David Nuuhiwa Noserider signature model by Bing Surfboards was the season's hottest-selling board—but Australian regularfooter Nat Young, turning his board forcefully up and down the wave instead of riding the nose, won the championships easily (Nuuhiwa finished 12th), setting the stage for the late-'60s shortboard revolution. Nuuhiwa receded into the background somewhat in 1967 and early 1968, then returned as a psychedelic glam-surfer with a quiver full of ornately airbrushed boards. He began to compete again, arriving at events behind the wheel of a paisley-covered Porsche 911, wearing aviator shades and a mink-trimmed coat, with one or two board-carrying lackeys in tow. Nuuhiwa's presence, as *Sports Illustrated* noted in 1969, was in part because the darkly handsome 6′1″ surfer was "one of the most unusual-looking young men in sport, [with] the imperious look of an Aztec king." He won the U.S. Championships in 1968 and 1971, and was invited to the 1970 and 1971 Expression Session events. He was the consensus favorite going into the 1972 World Championships, where he appeared to edge out Hawaiian surfer Jimmy Blears in the finals, but was instead given second place. Nuuhiwa more or less dropped off the scene for 10 years (making a brief public appearance in 1977 to win the Grog's Seaside Pro contest in New Jersey), developed a drug habit and quit surfing, then returned in the early '80s as a part-time patriarch for the longboard renaissance.

Nuuhiwa appeared in more than a dozen surf movies of the '60s and early '70s, including *The Performers* (1965), *Golden Breed* (1968), *Wave of Change* (1970), and *Five Summer Stories* (1972). He was also featured in *Rainbow Bridge* (1971), a documentary on rock guitarist Jimi Hendrix. David Nuuhiwa Surfboards opened in Huntington Beach in 1968 and folded before the year was out; Nuuhiwa later worked as a surf shop manager, then as a union laborer for trade shows and expositions. He was named World's Best Surfer in *International Surfing* Magazine's Hall of Fame Awards in 1966 and 1967. In 1991 he was inducted into the International Surfing Hall of Fame in San Diego; 10 years later he was inducted to the Huntington Beach Surfing Walk of Fame. Nuuhiwa is married, has a son, and lives in Sunset Beach, Orange County, California. *See also* noseriding, World Surfing Championships 1966, World Surfing Championships 1972.

O

O'Connell, Pat Pro surfer from Laguna Niguel, California, best known as the skipping, giggling, permanently cheerful shortboarder from Bruce Brown's 1994 surf movie *Endless Summer II*. O'Connell was born (1971) and raised just outside of Chicago, Illinois, and began surfing at age 12, just after moving with his family to Southern California. Eight years later he was getting good results in the local pro contests, and in 1992 and 1993 he and Santa Cruz longboarder Robert Weaver spent 18 months shooting on location at surf breaks around the world for *Endless Summer II*. When O'Connell qualified for the world championship pro tour in 1995 (he also won that year's Katin Team Challenge), the blond-haired regularfoot was thought of as too nice to ever be a contender. "I want to be everybody's friend," he told *Surfer* magazine in 1998. "I suppose that's a character flaw in pro surfing." He also said that he'd recently gotten in touch with "my inner asshole"—and his 11th-place finish that year was indeed a career best. O'Connell is featured in most of Taylor Steele's surf videos, including *Momentum* (1992), *Focus* (1994), and *The Show* (1997). *See also Endless Summer II.*

O'Donell, Phyllis Wispy regularfooter from Sydney, Australia; winner of the 1964 World Surfing Championships. O'Donell was born (1937) and raised in Sydney, the daughter of an auto mechanic father and stenographer mother, and began surfing at age 23. Four years later she was the surprise winner of the Australian National Titles, and just a few weeks after that, at Sydney's Manly Beach, she defeated American national champion Linda Benson of California to win the sport's first-ever World Championships. "Phyllis was completely at ease on the swell," the Australian-published *Surfing World* magazine wrote at the time. "Her placement in the wave was ideal and her trimming and arching through the hollow sections pretty to watch. O'Donell was a decisive winner." The diminutive O'Donell (5′2″) was a steady presence on the surf scene over the next few years: in

1965 she repeated as national champion; in 1966 she placed third in the Makaha International and in the National Titles; in 1968 she was third in the World Championships; in 1970 she was third in the Nationals Titles; and in 1971 she placed fourth. "I was horribly, horribly aggressive," the bob-haired O'Donell recalled in 2001, "and I swore like a trooper." She lived for a few months in Redondo Beach, California, in 1968, and worked in the showroom at Dewey Weber Surfboards in nearby Hermosa Beach. She was a judge at the Australian Women's Surfing Association's 1980 National Championships.

O'Donell appeared in a small number of surf movies, including *Surfing the Southern Cross* (1963) and *The Young Wave Hunters* (1964). In 1996 she became the second woman to be inducted into the Australian Surfing Hall of Fame. O'Donell never married. *See also* World Surfing Championships 1964.

O'Neill, Jack Low-key and savvy surf industrialist from Santa Cruz, California; founder of O'Neill Wetsuits, the world's leading manufacturer of surfing wetsuits. O'Neill was born (1923) in Denver, Colorado, and raised in Southern California and Oregon. He started bodysurfing in the late 1930s, and continued to do so after moving to San Francisco in 1949, where he got his B.A. in liberal arts from San Francisco State. O'Neill opened the prosaically titled Surf Shop out of a beachfront garage in San Francisco in 1952, and a few months later—inspired, he later said, by the neoprene foam flooring of a DC-3 passenger plane—he made his first neoprene wetsuit vest. (The original wetsuit prototypes were made in 1951 by a U.C. Berkeley physicist; Southern California's Dive N' Surf company, like O'Neill, began making wetsuits in 1952.) O'Neill opened a second Surf Shop in Santa Cruz in 1959, just prior to the first American surf boom. Surfboards were the primary sale item at first, but wetsuits became the shop's defining product in the early '60s, and by the end of the decade O'Neill was the industry leader.

Jack O'Neill

O'Neill lost sight in his left eye in 1971 after his leash-tethered surfboard snapped back and hit his face; the surf leash, ironically, had been invented the year before by Pat O'Neill, Jack's son. (A stylized piratelike image of O'Neill with a full beard and eye patch would later be used as the company logo.) O'Neill was by that time the consummate behind-the-scenes operator of what was turning into a small international empire, hiring talented managers so that he could continue to surf and sail around Santa Cruz. He never brought attention to himself, and on the rare event when he spoke to the surf press he modestly attributed his success to little more than good timing. Industry insiders, however, regards O'Neill as perhaps the coolest and shrewdest surf businessman alive—the "rubber baron," as surf journalist Ben Marcus later called him.

O'Neill was inducted into the International Surfing Hall of Fame in 1991 and the Huntington Beach Surfing Walk of Fame in 1998. *Surfer* magazine in 1999 named him as one of the "25 Most Influential Surfers of the Century," and in 2000 he was given the Water-

man Achievement Award from the Surf Industry Manufacturers Association. O'Neill is married and has six children. *See also* O'Neill Wetsuits, Santa Cruz, wetsuit.

O'Neill Wetsuits   Industry-leading wetsuit company founded by Jack O'Neill, based in Santa Cruz, California. O'Neill opened the Surf Shop in Santa Cruz in 1959, seven years after he began making wetsuit vests. The shop focused on surfboards, but O'Neill was already shifting attention to the development and marketing of his wetsuits; by the late '50s he was visiting boat trade shows, at which he would launch his three young neoprene rubber-clad children into a tank of ice water to demonstrate the wetsuit's effectiveness. A breakthrough came in the early '60s, when O'Neill introduced wetsuits featuring a thin layer of elastic nylon jersey laminated to the neoprene, facing the user's skin, which made the suit more durable and easier to wear; many '50s-era surfers had rejected the front-zip long sleeve "rubber jacket" (the most common type of surfing wetsuit) as being nearly impossible to put on and take off.

Other surf-directed wetsuit companies were up and running in the '60s (most notably Dive N' Surf in southwest Los Angeles County), but O'Neill was established as the industry leader by decade's end. The company continued to innovate, producing the first single-piece fullsuit in 1970. It also continued to lead the field in marketing, with the industry's best slogan, "It's Always Summer on the Inside"; a talented roster of team riders (Shaun Tomson, Dane Kealoha, Martin Potter, Brad Gerlach, Shane Beschen, Rochelle Ballard, and Cory Lopez); and dependably eye-catching ad campaigns, including a sexy but tasteful 1970 print ad featuring a bare-breasted female surfer putting on a short john wetsuit.

O'Neill Incorporated celebrated its 50th anniversary in 2002, the first major surf-related business to reach the half-century mark. The business by then had 28 foreign distributorships. Surfing wetsuits remained the company lifeblood, but O'Neill had long since branched into diving, sailing, skiing, snowboarding, wakeboarding, and waterskiing, as well as sportswear of every description. Custom-made O'Neill wetsuits were used by a group of surfers who traveled to the Antarctic in early 2000, where they rode waves in sub-30-degree water near ice floes. *See also* booties, fullsuit, long john, Jack O'Neill, short john, spring suit, wetsuit.

O'Rourke, Chris   Smooth-riding but combative regularfooter from La Jolla, California; lauded in 1976 as California's best surfer by Pipeline ace Gerry Lopez. O'Rourke was born (1959) in New Jersey, began surfing at age 10 after his family moved to California, but didn't really take to the sport until he began riding Windansea, La Jolla's best-known break, at age 12. His talent was instantly recognizable—as were the shrill, obscenity-laced rants he directed to nonlocal surfers at Windansea—and in 1975, at age 16, he was the top-rated surfer in the Western Surfing Association's elite AAAA division. California surfing was then in the middle of a decade-long, territorial, anticontest, antimedia period, and O'Rourke's gift was under-appreciated, if not quite entirely unseen. He had brief appearances in two surf movies, *A Matter of Style* (1975) and *Playground in Paradise* (1976).

O'Rourke was diagnosed with Hodgkin's disease in 1977, and over the next four years he made at least three unexpected recoveries—in between surgeries, radiation treatments, and chemotherapy—during which he regained his dazzling form in the water. He placed third in the 1979 California Pro at Oceanside, the state's biggest surf event of the year, missing chemo treatments to compete. O'Rourke announced in 1980 that he was cancer-free, but in the spring of 1981 he relapsed and died, at age 22, leaving behind a wife and infant son. *See also* Windansea.

Oahu   Hawaii's best-known island measures roughly 30 by 40 miles, is home to state capital Honolulu as well as 80 percent of the state's population, and is ringed with excellent waves, including more than a half-dozen of surfing's most historic breaks. Oahu can be divided into four main surfing areas: 1) The rural North Shore, surfing's most storied coastline, sometimes referred to as "the seven-mile miracle," is home to Sunset Beach, Pipeline, Waimea Bay, and Haleiwa. The North Shore breaks best from October to March in response to cold-season North Pacific storms, and produces the world's most consistent and ridable big waves; six to eight-foot surf is common, and most seasons bring at least three 20- to 30-foot swells. 2) The highly developed South Shore (often called "Town," as distinguished from the North Shore "Country") includes Waikiki's easygoing reefbreaks and the dependably hollow waves at Ala Moana and Kaisers. Waikiki was the center of the surf world in the early decades of the 20th century, and was home to surfing pioneer Duke Kahanamoku. The waves

here are best from May to September, and don't often get over six feet. 3) The arid Leeward coast, generally known as the West Side, covers a lesser number of dependable and weather-sheltered breaks, including the famed Makaha. The West Side is Oahu's most consistent surf area, as it draws in swells from both North and South Pacific storms. 4) The Windward coast is often battered by the northeast tradewinds, but is home to a number of high-quality breaks when the wind switches direction or drops off. Average daytime temperatures on Oahu range from 70 to 80 degrees all year, with water temperatures in the '70s. Intensely crowded lineups and jagged reefs are the island's biggest surfing hazards.

Premodern Hawaiians are thought to have ridden at least 18 breaks on Oahu, with Kalehuawehe (now called Outside Castles) on the South Shore one of the most popular breaks, along with Paumalu (Sunset Beach). In the early 20th century, as surfing rebounded after a missionary-imposed fallow period, Waikiki became the sport's epicenter, and remained so for more than four decades. Waikiki was home to the 1908-formed Outrigger Canoe Club, surfing's first organization, and the sport originally came to the world's attention through photographs and newsreels of wave-riders steaming for shore with Diamond Head in the background. Oahu's other coasts weren't regularly surfed until the '40s and '50s. By the time Makaha International Surfing Championships made its debut in 1954 as the sport's first major competition, Oahu's surfing focal point had shifted from the South Shore to Makaha; the second change, from Makaha to the North Shore, took place in the late '50s. The inaugural Duke Kahanamoku Surfing Championships, held at Sunset Beach in 1965, replaced the Makaha event as Hawaii's most prestigious contest. Oahu went on to become the sport's most-booked site for professional surf contests, hosting the Pipeline Masters, the World Cup, the Smirnoff Pro, and the Quiksilver in Memory of Eddie Aikau, among other events; the United States Surfing Championships, an amateur event, were held on Oahu seven times between 1976 and 2000.

Over the decades, Oahu has been home to many of the sport's greatest big-wave riders (George Downing, Buzzy Trent, Peter Cole, Joey Cabell, Ricky Grigg, Eddie Aikau, Reno Abellira, Darrick Doerner, Brock Little, Shane Dorian), high-performance pioneers (Albert "Rabbit" Kekai, Conrad Canha, Paul Strauch, Barry Kanaiaupuni, Jock Sutherland, Montgomery

"Buttons" Kaluhiokalani, Johnny-Boy Gomes, Rusty Keaulana), and competition surfers (Joey Cabell, Jeff Hakman, world champions Fred Hemmings, Sharron Weber, Lynne Boyer, Derek Ho, and Sunny Garcia), as well as a number of influential surfboard designers, surf photographers, and surf filmmakers.

In 2003, Oahu was home to more than three dozen surf shops and approximately 45,000 surfers, as well as the Bishop Museum, the first museum to recognize surfing. The Oahu-based *H₃O TV,* Hawaii's first television show dedicated solely to surfing, began in 1989, and was followed by three other locally aired programs including Board Stories. Oahu-based surf magazines include *H₃O, High Surf Advisory,* and *Tiare Girl.* Guidebooks to Oahu surf breaks include *Surfing Hawaii* (1972), *Surfer's Guide to Hawaii* (1991), and *The Surfer's Travel Guide* (1995). *See also* Ala Moana, Haleiwa, Kaena Point, Makaha, North Shore, Outside Log Cabins, Pipeline, Rocky Point, Sandy Beach, Sunset Beach, Triple Crown of Surfing, Velzyland, Waikiki, Waimea Bay.

Oberg, Margo   Gifted and resilient pro surfer from the Hawaiian island of Kauai; world champion in 1968, 1977, 1980, and 1981, and often cited as the original female big-wave rider. Born Margo Godfrey in Pennsylvania in 1953, the daughter of an aerospace engineer, she moved with her family at age five to the wealthy San Diego beachfront community of La Jolla, and began surfing at age 10. Two years later the reed-thin regularfoot beat an all-boy field to win the 12-year-old division of the Windansea Surf Club menehune contest; at 13, mentored by power surfer Mike Doyle, she was a finalist in the Makaha International and runner-up in the United States Surfing Championships. Fellow Californian Joyce Hoffman was then the reigning queen of women's surfing, but in 1968 Godfrey repeatedly finished ahead of Hoffman, placing first in three of seven events on that year's elite AAAA-rated California circuit, and winning both Makaha and the East Coast Surfing Championships. Near the end of the year, the birdlike but intensely competitive ninth grader was an easy winner in the World Surfing Championships, held in Puerto Rico. The following year she swept all four AAAA-rated events, and became the first women surfer to earn a prize-money check, taking $150 for her win in the Santa Cruz Pro-Am. Godfrey then placed second in the 1970 World Championships, which led to a breakdown of sorts. "I had to go back

Margo Oberg

to high school and live through the 11th and 12th grades not being world champion," she later recalled. "People kept asking, 'What happened, why didn't you win?' It was all so devastating that I retired."

Godfrey dropped off the surf scene entirely. She married San Diego accountant and church pastor Steve Oberg in 1972 and became a fervent born-again Christian, and the couple soon moved to Kauai. Oberg made a seemingly effortless competitive comeback in the summer of 1975, winning the Women's International Professional Surfing Championships at Malibu. Her surfing had improved during her five-year seclusion. She rode in a function-first style, crouched and ready, arms spread evenly; she was aggressive in her choice of maneuvers, but stayed within herself and rarely fell. Oberg had meanwhile discovered a talent for riding larger surf, and by mid-decade was a winter season fixture at Sunset Beach on the North Shore of Oahu, where she excelled in waves up to 15 feet. She also reclaimed a self-confidence that at times veered into arrogance: she described herself as "the women's Gerry Lopez," and said she was her own favorite surfer.

A women's division was added to the world pro tour in 1977, and Oberg set the competitive standard, winning the title that year and finishing runner-up to fellow Hawaiian Lynne Boyer in 1978. She took 1979 off, returned to take a third world title by winning both events on the abbreviated 1980 world tour, then won three of four events in 1981 to earn her fourth and final championship. She then retired permanently from full-time competition at age 29. Oberg continued to enter events in Hawaii, and placed second in the 1982 World Cup just three months after giving birth to her first child. In 1983 she earned her final pro tour victory, at the World Cup, held at Sunset.

In the late '70s, Oberg wrote a weekly surfing column for the *Honolulu Advertiser,* as well as a semi-regular column on the women's pro tour for *Surfing* magazine, and also did surfing event color commentary for ABC's *Wide World of Sports.* She won the *Surfer* Magazine Readers Poll Award in 1968, 1969, 1978, 1980, and 1981, and was the only woman included in a 1985 *Surfer* article titled "25 Surfers Whose Surfing Changed the Sport." She was inducted into the International Surfing Hall of Fame in 1991, the Huntington Beach Surfing Walk of Fame in 1995, and the Hawaii Sports Hall of Fame in 2001. She was profiled in *20th Century Surfers,* a 2001 Outdoor Life Network documentary series; she was also featured in *Girl in the Curl: A Century of Women's Surfing,* published in 2001. Oberg appeared in about a dozen surf movies and videos, including *Waves of Change* (1970), *Five Summer Stories* (1972), *Adventures in Paradise* (1982), *Shock Waves* (1987), and *Surfers: The Movie* (1990). A 2000 issue of *Sports Illustrated for Women* included Oberg among the "Top 100 Women Sports Figures of the Century." She's owned and operated the Margo Oberg Surfing School since 1977. She's been married once and has two children. *See also* religion and surfing, women and surfing, World Surfing Championships 1968.

Oberholzer, Frankie   Camera-friendly pro surfer from Warner Beach, South Africa. Oberholzer was born (1972) in Port Elizabeth, raised in Warner Beach, south of Durban, and began surfing at age nine on a discarded ironing board. He proved to be a surfer of rare talent, with only a passing interest—and virtually no skill—in organized competition. In 1991 the amiable and somewhat aimless regularfooter signed a four-year contract with Rip Curl International (later extending for another six years) to be photographed and filmed at exotic surfing locations around the world; through the early and mid-'90s he was protégé to three-time world champion Tom Curren of California. As a condition of his Rip Curl agreement, Oberholzer was not permitted to enter surf contests. The handsome longhaired surfer traveled often with Curren, further developed a technique based on equal parts grace, power, and flash, and was featured in more than a dozen surf videos throughout the '90s,

including *The Search* (1992), *Beyond the Boundaries* (1994), and *Tripping the Planet* (1996).

Occhilupo, Mark   Revered Australian power surfer from Sydney, Australia; a teenage phenomenon in the mid-1980s who suffered a physical and mental breakdown in the early '90s, then rebounded in spectacular fashion to win the 1999 world championship. Occhilupo was born (1966) and raised in the Sydney suburb of Kurnell, the son of an Italian-born civil engineer who'd emigrated to Australia as a young adult. He began surfing in 1974 at age nine, and through his early teenage years was greatly influenced by Tom Carroll—another stocky goofyfoot from Sydney. When Carroll won the first of his two world titles in 1983, it obscured the fact that 17-year-old Occhilupo, having dropped out of the 10th grade to surf full-time on the world tour, finished his rookie season ranked #16. The high-voiced, lantern-jawed goofyfooter with the hard-to-pronounce name soon proved himself to be one of the world's most exciting surfers, as well as a shrewd competitor, and in 1984 his rating jumped up to #3. In 1985 he finished fourth, then went back up to third. He won the 1985 Pipeline Masters, and was a two-time winner in the Op Pro (1985, 1986) and the Pro Junior (1984, 1986). While Carroll was still the more complete surfer, and American Tom Curren (world champion in 1985 and 1986) was the sport's ultimate stylist, Occhilupo rode with unmatched vigor and passion, planting his stumpy legs in a wide utility stance and directing his board through deeply chiseled turns, hands and open fingers extending out from his body like balance sensors. Occhilupo was celebrated for his tremendous raw strength—at 5′9″, 175 pounds, he was nicknamed "Raging Bull"—but finesse was in fact his greatest asset, and no surfer has ever had a more natural feel for the vectors and planes of a breaking wave. (As of 2003, in his 30th year as a surfer, he's never once been seriously hurt while in the water.) Less effective in tiny surf, and not particularly interested in waves over 15 feet, Occhilupo rides best in long, fast, broad-based four to eight-foot waves, and has turned in some of his best performances while riding backside at Bells Beach in Australia and South Africa's Jeffreys Bay.

Occhilupo had become one of the sport's most beloved and unique figures: warm, childlike, giggly, easily upset by violent movies, and a routine mangler of words and phrases ("I really wanted to win a contest last year," he once noted, "but it deluded

Mark Occhilupo

me...”). In 1987 however, he began showing signs of instability: he bought a penthouse in Cronulla and sold it a few months later, moved temporarily to the North Shore of Oahu, announced his retirement, made a comeback, then quit again. He was drinking and regularly using cocaine. In 1990 he moved into his parents' house and gained 50 pounds; in 1992 he trimmed down and rejoined the world tour, but suffered an insomnia-related breakdown while in France, and again retreated to Australia, this time taking an apartment in Queensland's Gold Coast, where he quit surfing and put on 80 pounds (topping out at 245), before spending a year in therapy being treated for bipolar disorder. In 1993 he married Beatrice Ballardie, a single mother, and the following year, under her care—along with that of his therapist, as well as surf moviemaker Jack McCoy—he began to lose weight and regain his surfing form. In 1997 he completed his first full year on the world tour since 1987, and finished runner-up to Kelly Slater for the championship. The following year he dropped to seventh, then in 1999 he won three of 13 events (in Tahiti, Fiji, and Spain) and at age 33 won the world title with hundreds of ratings points to spare, culminating what former world champion Wayne Bartholomew justly called "one of the greatest comebacks in the history of sport." Occhilupo was and remains pro surfing's oldest world title holder.

Occhilupo slipped to 20th in 2000, then bounced back the following year to finish runner-up behind world champion CJ Hobgood; in 2002, he finished 10th. By that time he'd won 12 world tour contests and dozens more nonrated events, including back-to-back victories in the 2000 and 2001 Op Pro, both held in Indonesia's Mentawai Islands. One of surfing's most photogenic figures, Occhilupo has appeared in nearly 75 surf movies and videos, including *Amazing Surf Stories* (1986), *Filthy Habits* (1987), *Pump!* (1990), *The Green Iguana* (1992), *The Billabong Challenge* (1995), *Psychedelic Desert Groove* (1997), *Nine Lives* (1999), and *Inspired* (2000). Occhilupo played himself in Universal's 1987 surf movie *North Shore*; in 1998 he was featured in the Australian version of *60 Minutes*; in 1999, a Jack McCoy feature titled *Occy: The Occumentary* won Video of the Year in the *Surfer* Magazine Video Awards. Occhilupo was inducted into the Huntington Beach Surfing Walk of Fame in 2000. *Occy: A Surfer's Year* was published by HarperSports at the end of the 2000 season. *See also* Op Pro Huntington Beach, Op Pro Mentawai Islands, power surfing.

Ocean Pacific   Southern California–based surfwear company founded in 1972 by San Diego surfboard shaper Jim Jenks. Ocean Pacific was originally the name of Jenks's surfboard line, established in 1969 while he was moonlighting as a sportswear rep to surf shops up and down both American coastlines. Launching his own surfwear three years later, Jenks continued to use his "Op" surfboard logo. Op was an instant success, with the company's high-cut corduroy "walkshorts" becoming a ubiquitous American surfing fashion item by 1974. Five years later, however, newer surfwear lines—particularly Australian-based Quiksilver—had made Op obsolete among trendsetting surfers; Jenks had by then placed Op into department stores and was licensing the name out for other products and other active-wear sectors. Op sales in 1979 were $40 million, bigger by far than any other surfwear manufacturer. Looking to keep its connection to surfing, Op became the primary financial backer of the world pro tour in late 1982, the same year it first sponsored the Op Pro surf contest in Huntington Beach. Op sales continued to build through the '80s, peaking at $370 million in 1987. By 2000, Op was owned by the Doyle and Boissiere investment firm, and sales that year were reported to be $175 million, with licensees in 83 countries making a range of Op-labeled items, including sunglasses, watches, hats, footwear, wetsuits, body lotions, and fragrances. Op has sponsored a number of high-profile surfers over the years, including Larry Bertlemann and Tim Curran. *See also* fashion and surfing, Op Pro Huntington Beach, Op Pro Mentawai Islands.

ocean temperature   Ocean temperature, as it relates to surfing, is no longer the all-determining factor it was prior to the development of the wetsuit, but it still has a profound effect on the sport. Surfing developed in Polynesia probably in part due to the warm and inviting mid–Pacific Ocean water temperature. By the same token, the sport failed to catch on when it was first introduced to mainland America in the 1880s in Santa Cruz, a beach city located about 75 miles south of San Francisco, almost certainly because the water temperature was prohibitively cold. When surfing was reintroduced to the mainland in 1907, this time in warmer south Los Angeles County, it caught on immediately. Wetsuits have mitigated the problem of cold-water surfing to the point that Santa Cruz surfers now spend as much time in the water as their counterparts in Los Angeles—or Hawaii, for that matter. Surf travel is nonetheless greatly skewed toward warm-water destinations, and surfing styles in general tend to be more relaxed as the water heats up. A successful O'Neill wetsuit ad campaign from the 1970s played on this idea of the subliminally warm environment, rather than cold-water protection, with the slogan, "It's Always Summer on the Inside."

Because water transmits heat (body heat included) at a much greater rate than air, the two elements, even while giving the same temperature reading, can feel entirely different. An air temperature of 66 degrees, for example, is warm enough to wear shorts and a T-shirt, while 66-degree water will quickly bring goose bumps to a trunks-wearing surfer. While ocean water temperatures are coldest at the poles and warmest along the equator, the gradient isn't uniform. This is due in part because of wind and upwelling, both of which allow colder subsurface water to rise to the surface, but mostly because of transoceanic currents. The warm North Pacific Current, for example, keeps water temperatures along Southern California higher than those found in much of Baja Mexico, which is closer to the equator. The crisp Humboldt Current, meanwhile, can bring water temperatures in the equator-straddling Galápagos Islands down to the mid-60s. Currents also explain how beaches on the same latitude can have wildly disparate water temperature ranges. San Fran-

cisco water temperatures, for example, stabilized by the North Pacific Current, range from the upper 40s to the low 60s, while temperatures in Ocean City, Maryland, located on roughly the same parallel, drop to the mid-30s and peak in the mid-70s.

The surf-affecting El Niño condition raises water temperatures across most of the Pacific and slightly reduces temperatures in the Atlantic. The coldest regularly surfed breaks in the world are found in Maine, New Hampshire, and Massachusetts, where the water can drop into the upper 20s in late winter. (Salinity lowers the freezing point in ocean water to about 28 degrees; nonsaline water freezes at 32.) The warmest regularly surfed breaks are found in Sumatra and northern Brazil, where the water often rises into the mid-80s.

Oceanside   Beachbreak in north San Diego County, located on the edge of the city of Oceanside; one of Southern California's most consistent surf spots, ridable on all swells and tides, but best on a peaky four- to six-foot west swell with a medium-low tide and strong offshore wind. Oceanside Pier and South Jetty, the two most popular surf areas, are separated by about a half-mile.

Because of its dependable waves, its location near the heart of Southern California's surf industry, and its infrastructure (beachside parking lots and bathrooms; nearby hotels, markets, and restaurants), Oceanside has long been one of America's most popular contest venues. The United States Surfing Championships were held in Oceanside in 1981, 1989, 1993, and 1997, and annually from 1998–2002; Oceanside also hosted the early rounds of the 1972 World Championships and a portion of the 1984 World Championships. Professional contests held in Oceanside include the 1979 California Pro (one of the state's first pro contests), the California Stubbies Pro (held from 1984 to 1988), and the 1990 Life's a Beach Surf Klassic. The Professional Surfing Association of America, the Professional Surfing Tour of America, and the Foster's Pro Surfing Tour have all used Oceanside as a contest venue.

Located in the flatlands between Carlsbad and Camp Pendleton Marine Corps Base, Oceanside is one of Southern California's least-glamorous beach cities; a favorite hell-raising haunt for Pendleton's enlisted men, and fertile ground for car vandals. Well-known surfers from Oceanside include 1963 *Surfer* Poll winner Phil Edwards, 1964 world contest finalist

LJ Richards, and three-time Professional Surfing Association of America champion Mike Lambresi. The California Surf Museum has been located just east of the Oceanside Pier since 1997. *See also* San Diego, United States Surfing Championships.

off the top Catchall phrase for virtually any kind of nonaerial cornering maneuver performed on or near the wave crest. "Off the top" can be used instead of "off the lip," "roller coaster," "re-entry," "snap," "snap-back," or "rebound." The first deliberate off-the-top moves were probably done in the mid- or late-1940s at Malibu, California, as the heavy plank boards, along with the skittery "cigar-box" hollow boards, were replaced by the lighter and more maneuverable all-balsa chip.

offshore wind Land-to-sea wind, treasured by surfers. Unless it's overpowering (about 25 miles per hour or stronger), an offshore will groom and clean the surf, hold the curl up so that it's more likely to pitch over into a tube, and lends a dreamy quality to the wave zone. Offshore winds are common during the early morning hours in California and Australia; in Indonesia and other tropical surf zones, offshores will often pick up in the late morning and hold through the afternoon. Santa Anas (or Santanas) are the hot, gusting, days-long offshore winds that often hit Southern California in fall and early winter, and sometimes contribute to hugely destructive brushfires. Offshore was also the name of a popular surfwear company of the '70s and '80s. *See also* onshore wind, sideshore wind.

Ogden, Bill California artist from Laguna Beach; best known to surfers for his splashy and mildly psychedelic pen-and-ink work in American surf magazines in the late '60s and early '70s. Ogden was born (1943) in Los Angeles, the son of Oklahoma sharecroppers, and began surfing at age 18. A self-taught artist, his cartoon work was first published in *Surf Guide* magazine in 1963. In the late '60s he did T-shirt and decal designs for Hobie Surfboards and other surf companies; from 1971 to 1975 he did a series of Jantzen swimwear ads that appeared on the back cover of *Surfer.* He also created the poster art for *Forgotten Island of Santosha,* a popular 1974 surf travel movie, and contributed to the 1972 surf comic book *Tales from the Tube.* Ogden is a definitive underground artist whose work has been featured in just

a handful of art shows and exhibitions. For better or worse, his style would inspire the phantasmagoric surfscapes of Chris Lassen and Robert Wyland. *See also* surf art.

Olivenca, Jojo Gracious Brazilian regularfoot pro surfer from São Paulo, Brazil; world-ranked #11 in 1994. Olivenca was born (1968) and raised in São Paulo, began riding waves at age 11, and developed into a rangy, limber, unpolished, but explosive surfer. Brazilian national pro champion in 1991 and 1993, Olivenca was a 10-year minor league pro veteran in 1994 when he finally earned a slot on the world tour, during which the 27-year-old lifted his performance to finish the season rated 11th and earn rookie-of-the-year honors. He didn't finish higher than 16th over the next three seasons, and retired at the end of the 1997 tour. The smiling and devoutly Catholic Olivenca was never interviewed by either the American or Australian surf media, and with the exception of a few short appearances in Brazilian-made videos, was all but ignored by '90s surf moviemakers and videographers. "If quietly spreading goodwill was rewarded on tour," the usually acerbic surf journalist Derek Hynd wrote in 1997, "he would be world champ."

olo board A long, thick, narrow surfboard, usually built from *wiliwili* wood, thought to have been used exclusively by pre-20th-century Hawaiian royalty. The largest of the three *olo* boards in Honolulu's Bishop Museum is 17 feet long, 16½ inches wide, nearly six inches thick, and weighs 150 pounds. (*Alaia* boards, used by royalty and commoners alike, were between seven and 12 feet long, slightly wider than the *olo,* and much thinner.) The fast-paddling *olo* allowed royals to pick up unbroken waves well beyond the normal takeoff area; the boards cut through the water with luxuriant smoothness, but were nearly impossible to turn, and required a cautious deep-water approach to the lineup, as they couldn't be pushed through broken waves. *See also alaia* board.

Olympics and surfing As of 2003, surfing remains firmly excluded from the Olympic Games. This fact torments contest organizers and industry boosters who have been trying since the mid-1960s to convince the International Olympic Committee (IOC) to accept surfing, but pleases many others who cherish the idea of wave-riding being independent from the larger world of sport. The history of surfing's courtship of the IOC is one of cyclical hope and disappointment. "It shouldn't be long before surfing is entered on the Olympic calendar," *Surfer* magazine wrote in 1964, in the first of dozens of optimistic surf press articles to appear over the decades, with headlines including "The Olympics at Last" (*Surf* magazine, 1977), "Surfing's 1984 Olympic Bid" (*Surfing,* 1984), and "Surfing Takes Its First Big Step Toward the Olympics" (*Surfer,* 1995).

Sports looking for Olympic acceptance have to meet national and international IOC guidelines, then work through a series of IOC approvals. Early efforts, including the establishment of the United States Surfing Federation and the International Surfing Association (in 1979 and 1976, respectively), were preludes to a vigorous and well-organized mid-1990s effort—led by ISA chairman Fernando Aguerre of Argentina—to gain IOC sanction in time for the 2000 Olympic Games in Sydney, Australia. The IOC granted provisional recognition to the ISA in 1995; in June 1996, Aguerre met with IOC president Juan Antonio Samaranch in Lausanne, Switzerland, and was told by Samaranch that "the door is not closed" for surfing's chances in 2000. In October of 1996 the ISA staged the World Surfing Games (replacing the World Surfing Championships), complete with Olympic-style flag-waving march-and-review opening ceremonies, hoping to impress visiting IOC and U.S. Olympic Committee members. But when the IOC released its official 2000 Games program in November, surfing didn't make the cut, though beach volleyball was approved.

Olympic naysayers had by that time found a voice in the surf press. *Surfer's Journal* publisher Steve Pezman described the Olympics as "a harsh and politically corrupt area, rife with crap," and further noted that "surfing can't be shrink-wrapped and taken to market without losing its character, spontaneity and appeal." Wondering how surfing might fit into the Olympic format, *Surfer* editor Steve Hawk commented that, "There's a good chance it would be an embarrassment." But Aguerre remained undaunted, saying in 1999 that surfing's acceptance into the Olympics was "only a matter of time," and that he was on a committee looking into building a wavepool to allow surfing's inclusion in the 2004 Olympic Games in Athens, Greece. *See also* Fernando Aguerre, competitive surfing, International Surfing Association, World Surfing Games.

Oman

Oman   Small, dry, rocky desert country on the eastern corner of the Arabian Peninsula, bordered by Saudi Arabia to the west, the Gulf of Oman to the north, and the Arabian Sea to the southeast. Oman was introduced to the surfing world in a 2001 *Surfer* magazine travel feature. Five California surfers, including former *Surfer* photo editor Jeff Divine, rode tiny but perfectly shaped right-breaking point waves just outside the town of Salalah, home to the tomb of Job. They also found tubing head-high beachbreak peaks near the Yemeni border, and drove across an empty stretch of coast that featured more than a half-dozen likely pointbreak setups. The June-to-September monsoon season is rumored to produce waves up to 12 feet, but the Omani surf is small to nonexistent for the rest of the year, and the beaches are impossibly hot. A late–'80s *Surf Report* dispatch for the United Arab Emirates, Oman's neighbor in the Gulf of Oman, begins: "Mean wave height: flat. Air: 120 degrees: Water: 90 degrees."

onshore wind   Sea-to-land wind, detrimental to wave quality. A light to moderate onshore puts a ruffle on the water surface, makes the wave crest break unevenly, and in general takes the sparkle out of things, though the surf usually remains ridable. A strong onshore, however, will ruin the surf outright. In popular surfing coastlines around the world—including Australia and mainland America—the wind is often still or offshore (a desirable land-to-sea breeze) at daybreak, before turning onshore mid- or late morning. The one advantage of an onshore wind is that it reduces the number of surfers in the lineup, no mean feat at some of the more crowded breaks. *See also* offshore wind, sideshore wind.

Op Pro Huntington Beach   Clamorous midsummer professional surfing contest held between 1982 and 1998 at California's Huntington Beach Pier. California had previously hosted international pro events (the Katin Team Challenge, the Sutherland Pro, and the U.S. Pro, among others), but this was the first time the sport was tied into high-end West Coast marketing and promotions. For its first 10 years, the Op Pro was the world's biggest and best-publicized surfing contest, covered by local and network news, reported in newspaper sports pages, and analyzed to extravagant detail by the surf press. It was often referred to as the "Super Bowl of Surfing." The Op Pro generally ran for five days, and by the weekend finale nearly 50,000 spectators would fill up bleachers on the south side of the pier and along the beachfront. "The Op," as California surfboard manufacturer

Op Pro; California's Tom Curren, 1986

Rusty Preisendorfer put it, "sticks the pros right in the face of the consumer."

Combined prize money for the men's and women's divisions of the 1982 Op Pro was $35,000. The men's event featured 120 nonseeded surfers, two wild cards, and 16 world tour pros; one of the wild cards was 18-year-old Tom Curren, who had turned professional just 10 days earlier. Australia's Cheyne Horan completed a backside 360 to beat South African Shaun Tomson in the final; Curren placed 5th. Becky Benson of Hawaii took the women's division. Over the next few years, it was nearly automatic that Curren and Australian Mark Occhilupo would turn in the best performances of the meet; Curren won in 1983, 1984, and 1988, Occhilupo in 1985 and 1986. Four-time women's world champion Frieda Zamba of Florida was by far the most dominant Op Pro contestant, winning six times between 1984 and 1994.

The summertime surf was generally poor for the Op Pro, and the event's nonstop marketing Sturm und Drang helped make the event unpopular with competitors. There were two options at the Op Pro, as surf journalist Nick Carroll put it: "suffer horribly, or win." The Op Pro made national headlines in 1986 when hundreds of spectators rioted during the finals, setting three police cars and a lifeguard Jeep on fire.

The Op Pro was a world championship tour event from 1982 to 1991, and again in 1998; from 1992 to 1995 it was a second-tier pro event. The Op Junior debuted in 1989, and was won by future six-time world champion Kelly Slater. Other Op Junior winners included Rob Machado (1991), Kalani Robb (1994), and Tim Curran (1995). A longboard division was added in 1993, 1994, and 1995, with Joel Tudor winning all three years. A team format was used for the 1992 Op Pro. The 1995 Op Pro was the largest in the series, with just over 400 entrants; the 1998 Op was the richest, at $120,000. Op Pro winners:

1982:	Cheyne Horan, Becky Benson
1983:	Tom Curren, Kim Mearig
1984:	Tom Curren, Frieda Zamba
1985:	Mark Occhilupo, Jodie Cooper
1986:	Mark Occhilupo, Frieda Zamba
1987:	Barton Lynch, Wendy Botha
1988:	Tom Curren, Jorja Smith
1989:	Richie Collins, Frieda Zamba
1990:	Todd Holland, Frieda Zamba
1991:	Barton Lynch, Frieda Zamba

1992: Team USA: Kelly Slater, Richie Collins, Todd Holland, Mike Parsons, Alisa Schwarzstein
1993: Sunny Garcia, Kim Mearig
1994: Rob Machado, Frieda Zamba
1995: Sunny Garcia, Lisa Andersen
1996: (not held)
1997: (not held)
1998: Andy Irons, Layne Beachley

See also Ocean Pacific, Op Pro Mentawai Islands.

Op Pro Mentawai Islands   Elite, oceangoing professional surfing competition held in Indonesia's Mentawai Islands in 2000 and 2001; sponsored primarily by Ocean Pacific beachwear, with support from *Surfer* magazine. The Op Pro Mentawai Islands, also known as the Op Boat Trip Challenge, debuted in 2000 as a nonworld tour event, meaning it offered no points toward the world championship. Four surf charter boats were hired for the event, and the total prize purse was $102,500. The concept was to put the world's best surfers in the world's best surf, and present the results to the surfing public through magazines, cable TV, the Internet, and video. (Surfwear giant Billabong had done much the same thing with a series of contests in the mid- and late '90s called the Billabong Challenge.) Six men—Andy Irons, Bruce Irons, and Sunny Garcia from Hawaii; Mark Occhilupo from Australia; Tim Curran and Shane Beschen from California—competed for a winner-take-all $65,000, the biggest cash prize in surfing history. Four women—Layne Beachley and Serena Brooke from Australia; Rochelle Ballard and Megan Abubo from Hawaii—competed for a winner-take-all $37,000. The format was different from the standard pro contest: in the men's division, four two-hour heats were held at various breaks across the 200-mile-long Mentawai island chain, with all six competitors surfing at once. The winner of each round received 10 points, second-place earned 9 points, third received 8 points, and so on. The surf was flawless throughout the event, and 34-year-old Occhilupo, who just months earlier had been declared the 1999 world champion, took first. The women surfed in three two-hour rounds, with 29-year-old Ballard coming out on top. Inspired by the friendly vibe among the competitors, Occhilupo and Ballard surprised everyone by pooling their winnings and distributing the money evenly among the 10 en-

trants. Occhilupo later said the 2000 Op Pro was "the best contest I've ever been involved with."

Occhilupo, Bruce and Andy Irons, Curran, CJ Hobgood of Florida, and Hawaii's Shane Dorian made up the men's field for the 2001 Op Boat Trip event; the women's division consisted of Beachley, Brooke, Ballard, and Hawaii's Keala Kennelly. The purse was raised to $127,500, with $30,000 going to repeat-winner Occhilupo, $22,500 going to women's division winner Kennelly, and the remainder distributed among the rest of the competitors. Once again, the surf was first-rate.

Outside magazine covered the 2000 Op Pro; *Sports Illustrated*, *GQ*, and the *Men's Journal* covered the 2001 Op Pro. The event was also covered online, on cable television, and in video specials. *See also* Ocean Pacific, Op Pro Huntington Beach.

Opper, Ira   Tireless producer of surf videos, documentaries, and television shows from Solana Beach, California; best known as producer/director for the acclaimed *Surfer's Journal* cable TV series, which aired on the Outdoor Life Network from 1997 to 2001. Opper was born (1949) in Hollywood, California, and began surfing at age 15. He received a B.S. in television from Arizona State University in 1971, and five years later produced Solo Sports, cable television's first surfing series. Opper formed Frontline Video and Film in 1982, and from 1987 to 1991 he produced a weekly prime time *Surfer* magazine TV series for ESPN, America's first national weekly prime time surfing show. His shows for the *Surfer's Journal* were broken into four documentary series: *50 Years of Surfing on Film* (1997) spotlighted surf movie- and video-makers, *Great Waves* (1998) focused on the world's most popular surf breaks, and *20th Century Surfers* (2000) and *Biographies* (2001) both looked at famous surfers, past and present. Opper has received four Emmy Awards—two for his surfing programs—between 1982 and 1991. He has also made about two dozen feature-length surf videos, including *Vaporware* (1994), *Powerglide* (1995), *Super Slide* (1999), and *Wordz* (2002). *See also* television and surfing.

Orange County   Sprawling suburban county in Southern California, located between Los Angeles County and San Diego County; the surf world's industrial and media hub since the 1950s. Orange County has 42 miles of shoreline, and includes the coastal towns of Seal Beach, Huntington Beach, Newport

Beach, Laguna Beach, Dana Point, and San Clemente. Surfing was likely introduced to Orange County in 1908 by Hawaiian-born George Freeth, not long after he first rode Los Angeles's Venice Beach. By the mid-'20s, Corona del Mar, on the south end of Newport, had become one of the state's most popular surf breaks and in 1928 it was the site for the inaugural Pacific Coast Surf Riding Championships. (The Corona del Mar Surfboard Club, host group for the event, was the mainland's first surfing club.) Trestles, the Wedge, and Huntington Pier eventually became the area's three best-known surf breaks.

Orange County surf industry got under way in earnest when Hobie Surfboards, the first all-service surf shop, opened in Dana Point in 1953. More than a half-dozen shops would open in Huntington Beach alone before the end of the decade. In 1959, Kanvas by Katin in Seal Beach began making surf trunks, surf guitarist Dick Dale began playing at Newport's Rendezvous Ballroom, and the West Coast Surfing Championships debuted at Huntington Pier; one year later *Surfer* magazine began publishing in Dana Point. Surf moviemaker Bruce Brown was also living and working in Orange County by that time, as was polyurethane foam innovator Gordon "Grubby" Clark. The United States Surfing Association, America's first national surfing group, was formed in Laguna Beach in 1961.

Orange County consolidated its industrial-commercial position in the surf world over the decades, as home to beachwear giants (Ocean Pacific, Quiksilver, Gotcha, Hurley), surf magazines (*Surfing,* the *Surfer's Journal, Longboard*), surf organizations (the National Scholastic Surfing Association, the Association of Professional Surfers, the Surf Industry Manufacturers Association, the Surfrider Foundation), and major surf contests (the Op Pro, the NSSA Nationals, the Stubbies US Pro). Commercial surf forecasting was born in Orange County in the mid-'80s, with Huntington Beach–based companies such as Surfline and Wavetrak. Orange County has also produced dozens of world-class surfers (including Phil Edwards, Corky Carroll, Joyce Hoffman, Mike Parsons, Matt Archbold, Christian Fletcher, Shane Beschen, Pat O'Connell, and Colin McPhillips), as well as a commensurate number of surf filmmakers and photographers (Bud Browne, Greg MacGillivray, Jim Freeman, Ron Stoner, Art Brewer, Larry Moore, and Jeff Divine), and top surfboard shapers (Robert August, Rich Harbour, Bill Stewart, Jeff "Doc" Lausch, Timmy Patterson, Matt Biolos).

By 2003, Orange County was home to an estimated 200,000 surfers and 80 surf shops. The Orange County surf is detailed in *Surf Guide to Southern California* (1963), *Surfing California* (1973), and *The Stormrider Guide North America* (2001). *See also* Huntington Beach, Newport Beach, Op Pro Huntington Beach, Trestles the Wedge.

Oregon   Oregon's ruggedly beautiful 300-mile redwood-lined coast contains a small number of first-rate surf spots and dozens of other serviceable breaks, all frequently made unridable by high winds, gigantic waves, and land-bound North Pacific storms. Fall is the best season for surfing in Oregon, as the skies are often clear and wind-free, while early season storms in the Gulf of Alaska regularly produce three to six-foot surf, with stronger swells hitting 10 feet or bigger. Winter conditions are often prohibitively stormy; spring brings ocean-shredding northwest winds; summer is less windy, but often lacking for waves. The average daytime air temperatures along the Oregon coast range from the low 60s in summer to 50 in winter; ocean temperatures range from the mid-50s to the mid-40s. Most surf breaks in central and northern Oregon are accessible by car; breaks in the south are all but unreachable as the area is part of the Siskiyou National Forest. The most popular breaks in Oregon are those in the wind-protected lee of a headland or promontory. Seaside Point, a long, fast, spinning left tube located on the north coast, is Oregon's best and best-known surf spot. Rare but perfect sand-bottom tubes form on the south side of Cape Lookout on the north-central coast; Otter Rock and Agate Beach, just north of Newport, are both popular and generally easy-to-ride beachbreaks. Sharks and rocks are Oregon's two primary natural surfing hazards; local surfers have also earned a reputation—justified in some areas (particularly Seaside), unjustified in others—for being territorial, even macabre. In 2001, a group of visiting pro surfers woke up to find a severed deer's head next to their car, along with an order to leave the state.

Determined Agate Beach ocean divers, protecting themselves against the cold by wearing a full set of woolen underclothes, began riding waves on small wooden bellyboards in the late 1930s. Stand-up surfing came to Oregon in the early '60s at Agate, Coos Bay, and Seaside, with much of the pioneering work done by Southern California transplants Chris Brodeson, Chuck Garland, and Dana Williams. The Surf

Shack in Portland and Serb's Surf Center in Coos Bay were Oregon's first surf shops; both opened in 1964. A number of local surfing groups were also founded that year, including the Seaside Surfing Association, the Agate Beach Surf Club, and the North Shore Surf Club of Portland—all were defunct by the end of the decade. Wetsuits were popular at the time, but not universally used, as some early Oregon surfers rode in Levi's, sweaters, and tennis shoes. The Agate Beach Surf Capades, Oregon's first statewide surfing competition, was held in 1964, with Agate Beach local Marty Scriver coming out ahead of California surf hero Corky Carroll to win the final. California surf moviemaker Bruce Brown helped judge the event, and also screened his just-completed new movie, *The Endless Summer.* The 1979-founded Oregon Surf Shop was the beginning of a second small wave of Oregon-based surf retail outlets.

By 2003, Oregon was home to about 20 surf shops and 2,500 surfers, with both numbers rising steadily. There are no shortboard surfing contests in the state and fewer than a half-dozen longboard events. Local surfers have for the most part kept the surf media at bay, but the Oregon surf has nonetheless been featured in a small number of surf movies and videos over the years, including *Out of Control* (1961), *Going Surfin'* (1973), *Tales of the Seven Seas* (1981), and *Oregon Green* (1998). The Pacific Northwest Surfing Museum, located inside the Lincoln City Surf Shop, opened in 1992.

Outer Banks   *See* North Carolina.

outline   The perimeter of a surfboard as viewed from the deck or bottom. When making a board, the first task is to either draw an outline directly onto the polyurethane foam blank or key the outline into a software program that drives a board-shaping machine. A board's outline has four primary measurements: the widest point; placement of the wide point relative to the board's center point; nose width, as measured one foot from the tip; and tail width, as measured one foot from the back end. "Template" and "planshape" are often used interchangeably with "outline." *See also* the surfboard.

Outrigger Canoe Club, The   Beachfront club in Waikiki, Hawaii; the world's oldest surfing organization, founded in 1908 by eccentric Hawaii booster and former New York newspaperman Alexander Hume Ford. The Outrigger Canoe Club was chartered on one

and a half acres of land between the Seaside and Moana hotels, and the original clubhouse consisted of two grass shacks purchased from a nearby zoo. Surfing had become almost moribund in the late 19th century, and Ford, since his arrival in Hawaii in 1907, had become the sport's top patron; thousands of Americans first learned about surfing by reading Ford's 1909 *Collier's* magazine article "Riding the Surf in Hawaii." The Outrigger Canoe Club, Ford's biographer later wrote, was conceived and developed "for the purpose of reviving and preserving the ancient Hawaiian sport of surfing on boards and in outrigger canoes."

By 1910, construction had begun on a new Outrigger clubhouse with a dance pavilion and added storage space for surfboards. The all-male club had been instantly popular; it was, however, almost exclusively *haole,* or Caucasian. Hui Nalu ("Club of the Waves"), open to native-born Hawaiians, was formed in response and lodged in the Moana Hotel bathhouse next door. Hawaiian surfer and gold medal swimmer Duke Kahanamoku was a Hui Nalu cofounder, although in 1917, while retaining his membership in Hui Nalu, he became an honorary lifetime member of the Outrigger; dozens of people would hold duel memberships over the years. The Outrigger's first captain, George "Dad" Center (later an Olympic swim coach), and Hui Nalu's John D. Kaupiko were early sources for new and secondhand surfboards. "The Outrigger's grass shack on the beach," the *Surfer's Journal* wrote in 1996, "was one of the first places where surfboards were built in the modern era, and probably the very first place where a *haole* tourist, attracted to the sport of kings by Ford's promotional blitz, could obtain a surfboard."

The Outrigger Canoe Club had 1,200 members by 1915, with hundreds of people on a waiting list; in 1926 the club opened its membership to women; in 1941 it built another new clubhouse, with a dining room and cocktail lounge; and in 1964 it moved again, to a lavish new $1.25 million clubhouse at Diamond Head Beach, about a mile to the east. By 2003 the Outrigger Canoe Club had 4,500 members, each paying between $11 to $100 in monthly dues, according to a 12-tiered membership structure. Canoe racing, more so than surfing, has long been the club's main athletic focus. *The Outrigger: A History of the Outrigger Canoe Club* was published in 1971. *See also* Alexander Hume Ford, Hui Nalu Club, surf clubs, Waikiki.

outside   The region just beyond the breaking surf; a staging area where surfers wait for incoming waves, as differentiated from the "inside"—the broken-wave area leading to the shore. "Outside," in this usage, is synonymous with "lineup," or the Australian-derived "out the back." "Outside" is also used to signal an approaching bigger-than-average set of waves, and is sometimes spoken or shouted as a warning to unaware surfers. To get "caught outside" on a big day of surf is to be trapped beyond the surf zone, with no easy route to the beach. *See also* lineup, set.

Outside Log Cabins   Majestic but inconsistent big-wave surf spot located on the North Shore of Oahu, Hawaii, between Waimea Bay and Pipeline. Outside Log Cabins is the site of one of the biggest waves ever surfed, a 40- or 45-footer (about 60 or 70 feet from trough to crest) ridden by Hawaiian big-wave veteran Ken Bradshaw in 1998. A right-breaking wave, Outside Log Cabins—also known as Outer Logs—forms over a reef located about three-quarters of a mile offshore. It requires a huge North Pacific winter swell, doesn't begin to take shape until the waves are nearly 20 feet, and might come into full-blown form just two or three times a decade. Shiftier and more lined up than the waves found at Jaws on Maui, Log Cabins can produce rides of more than 400 yards, with the curl often pitching out to form monolithic tube sections.

Big-wave zealot Jose Angel built a house in front of Log Cabins in the early '70s, choosing the location in part so that he could study the break and see if it could be ridden. He never tried. In early December 1986, with a 25-foot swell running, Bradshaw and local surfer Trevor Sifon became the first to surf Outer Logs, each paddling into a 20-foot wave before getting caught inside and washed ashore by a 30-foot set. "It's probably the ultimate big wave," surf journalist Leonard Brady wrote of Log Cabins two years later, insightfully adding that the break probably wasn't ridable "using standard paddling take-offs." Fewer than a half-dozen attempts were made on Outer Logs over the next nine years. In the early '90s, a small group of big-wave surfers did in fact discard the paddling take-off and towed each other in to huge waves from behind personal watercraft; on January 28, 1998, with Outer Logs producing crystalline 35-footers, it was ridden by tow-in surfers only. Bradshaw caught his enormous wave at about 10:00 A.M.; six other tow-in teams rode throughout the day. Video footage from January 28 was used in *The Moment* (1998), *Biggest Wednesday* (1998), and other surf videos; 70-millimeter film shot from a helicopter was used to create a breathtaking 10-minute sequence for *Extreme,* a 1999 IMAX movie.

Over the falls

over the falls   A type of wipeout, or stage in a wipeout, in which the surfer is embedded in the crest as it hooks over and drops into the trough. Regarded as the sport's most dangerous type of wipeout for a number of reasons: the surfer has little or no control of his body position or where he'll land; he's generally delivered into the wave's exploding core; and momentum gained in descent will often drive him to the bottom. A surfer can also go over the falls after paddling up the wave face and trying unsuccessfully to punch through the curl. Hawaiian big-wave rider Mark Foo died at Maverick's in 1994 after going over the falls on a 15-foot wave. "Sucked over" is a variation on "over the falls." *See also* wipeout.

overgunned   Riding a surfboard that is too big for prevailing wave conditions. "Gun" is shorthand for "big-wave gun" or "elephant gun." Being overgunned is often the result of misreading the surf: a surfer may take out his 7'6" board, thinking the waves are eight feet; when the surf turns out to be six feet, the rider will feel overgunned, wishing he brought a faster-turning 6'10". At particularly crowded breaks—Rincon in California, for example, or Hawaii's Sunset Beach—surfers will sometimes overgun as a tactical ploy, using the longer board's paddling advantage to outmaneuver other surfers in the lineup and catch more waves.

overhead   A wave that is slightly bigger than the height of a surfer, or roughly six to 10 feet from trough to crest. Double-overhead is twice the surfer's size, and so forth. This method of assessing wave height, while imprecise—overhead to tiny Australian pro Pauline Menczer might not be overhead to Maverick's surfer and one-time Trinity College power forward Grant Washburn—was developed to lend some measure of consistency to an area of the sport where numbers have become almost meaningless. A 10-foot wave in California, for example, might be called six-foot in Hawaii and 15-foot in Florida. "Overhead," or "double-overhead" by comparison, provides something close to a standard surf world measurement. *See also* wave height and measurement.

Owens, Bobby Congenial freckle-faced Hawaiian pro surfer from the North Shore of Oahu; world-ranked #10 in 1982, but best known for his fast and fluid riding on the North Shore of Oahu. Owens was born in Italy (1957), the son of a lieutenant colonel in the U.S. Army, and moved with his family to Oahu in 1966, where he began surfing. Ten years later he turned professional. Owens placed second in the 1977 Duke Kahanamoku Classic at Sunset Beach; in 1980 he won the Pro Class Trials also at Sunset, and the Quiksilver/Bells Beach Trials in Australia. He made the prestigious year-end top 16 four times, placing 12th in 1977, seventh in 1978, 12th in 1981, and 10th in 1982. An unlikely looking surf hero, at 5'8", 140 pounds, with incandescent red hair, Owens was nonetheless the most respected surfer at Sunset Beach in the late '70s and the '80s. He was featured in more than a dozen surf movies, including *Fantasea* (1978) and the original *Wave Warriors* (1985).

Oxbow World Longboard Championship
See World Longboard Tour.

P

Paarman, Jonathan   Fearless regularfooter from Cape Town, South Africa; world-ranked #15 in 1976. "An awesome surfer," journalist Derek Hynd said of Paarman in 1989. "He is to the beastly waves of Cape Town what [Hawaii's] Barry Kanaiaupuni is to Sunset Beach." Paarman was born (1954) and raised in Cape Town, and began surfing at age 10. Donald Paarman, his older brother, was one of the country's original high-performance surfers and was elected to the *Surfing* Magazine International Hall of Fame in 1966; John Whitmore, his uncle, often described as the "father of South African surfing," was Cape Town's first surfboard builder. Jonathan Paarman won the boys' division of the national surfing championships in 1967 and 1968; competed in the 1970 World Surfing Championships; and was runner-up to former world champion Midget Farrelly in the 1970 Gunston 500, held in Durban. Paarman served his two-year mandatory military service in 1974–75, then returned to competition; in 1976 he placed second in the Gunston, and made the finals of the Duke Kahanamoku Invitational and the Smirnoff Pro, both at Sunset Beach. Paarman's reputation, however, is based less on competition results and more on his forceful big-wave performances, often alone, at a number of frightening reefbreaks near his Cape Town home. In the mid-'90s, he became one of the first to regularly surf the massive deep-water waves at Dungeons. Paarman appeared in a small number of surf movies, including *Going Surfin'* (1973) and *Playgrounds in Paradise* (1976).

Pacific Coast Surf Riding Championships   Mainland America's first major surfing competition, held sporadically in Southern California between 1928 and 1941. The first Pacific Coast Surf Riding Championships (PCSRC) took place at Corona del Mar in Newport Beach, and were organized in part by pioneering California surfer Tom Blake, under the auspices of the Corona del Mar Surfboard Club. It was a one-day contest, held in mid-summer. "Fifteen surfboard artists have signed up," the *Long Beach Press-Telegram* reported in its preevent coverage, "some from as far away as San Francisco." (Top-billed entrant Duke Kahanamoku of Hawaii was a no-show.) The contest involved both paddling and wave-riding. Entrants lined up with their boards on the beach, and at the sound of a firing pistol ran into the water, paddled 500 yards out to a buoy, turned for shore, and rode a wave to a finish marker on the beach. Surfers were eliminated over the course of a few rounds. The contest had been well-promoted, and the sand was crowded with several hundred spectators, along with the local press corps, including a newsreel team. Blake later recalled that the surf was about head-high. Along with Kahanamoku, Blake had been touted as the man to watch, and at the start of the race he ran to the water's edge with a 15-foot, 120-pound semihollow paddleboard, then surprised everyone by turning back to get his 9'6" wave-riding board. He then placed the smaller board atop the deck of his paddleboard and set out after the other contestants, already 50 yards distant. Paddling his sandwiched boards past the entire field, Blake discarded the paddleboard after rounding the buoy, and moved into the surf zone on his 9'6" to wait for a wave. Some of the other surfers caught up—Gerald Vultee, soon to become one of the nation's top aircraft designers, in fact rode a wave before Blake, but angled to the left and lost momentum—but Blake was first to the beach. Later that day he also won the 440-yard paddleboard race. Other attractions in the 1928 event included canoe tilting and an ocean lifesaving demonstration.

In years to come, the PCSRC were sometimes referred to as the Southern California Surfing Championships. The event was moved to San Onofre in 1938, at which point the number of contestants had risen to almost 50 (all from California), and the rules and scoring system were overhauled. Two buoys were set up, one outside the surf line and another near the beach and about 50 yards to the north of the first buoy. At a signal, everyone began to surf; contestants received a point every time they were able to complete a ride from south of the outside buoy to north of the inner buoy. The event lasted for about two hours. A photograph in John "Doc" Ball's seminal *California Surfriders* shows a phalanx of surfers riding the same wave during the 1940 PCSRC, all angling for the finish buoy. "Here are 17 men hell-bent for a trophy," Ball wrote in a caption. "The boards fly and they pile up in droves, but somehow out of the mess comes the new champ." The PCSRC was held nine times between 1928 and 1941, when it was canceled after America's entry into World War II; four-time winner Pete Peterson was the event's dominant surfer. Winners of the Pacific Coast Surf Riding Championships:

1928:	Tom Blake
1929:	Keller Watson
1932:	Pete Peterson
1934:	Gardner Lippincott
1936:	Pete Peterson
1938:	Pete Peterson
1939:	Lorrin Harrison
1940:	Cliff Tucker
1941:	Pete Peterson

See also Tom Blake, competitive surfing, Lorrin Harrison, Newport Beach, Pete Peterson, San Onofre, Cliff Tucker.

Pacific Ocean   The world's largest ocean, covering 103 million square miles, or nearly half of the earth's ocean surface. The Pacific runs along 83,000 miles of coastline, and is bordered by Asia, Australia, Russia, North and South America; tributary bodies of water include the Bering Sea, the Coral Sea, the East China Sea, the South China Sea, the Gulf of Alaska, the Gulf of Tonkin, the Yellow Sea, the Philippine Sea, the Sea of Japan, the Sea of Okhotsk, and the Tasman Sea. Geographers disagree as to whether the Pacific extends to Antarctica or stops at the Antarctic Ocean. The equator divides the North Pacific from the South Pacific; surface currents in the North Pacific are dominated by a clockwise warm-water gyre and in the South Pacific by a counterclockwise cold-water gyre. The westerlies and the tradewinds are the Pacific's two primary wind belts; the westerlies form between 30 and 60 degrees latitude in both the North and South Pacific; the tradewinds also form on both sides, blowing in toward the equator from about 30 degrees latitude.

Thousands of islands are spread across the Pacific Ocean. "Continental" islands, like Taiwan, New Guinea, and Australia—the largest islands in the world—are located primarily in the east. The volcanic and coral islands of Micronesia, Melanesia, and Polynesia are scattered primarily between the Tropic of Cancer and the Tropic of Capricorn. The Challenger Deep, the lowest point on earth at almost 36,000 feet below sea level, is located in the North Pacific, near Guam, in the Mariana Trench. Water temperatures in the Pacific range from 84 degrees near the equator to 28 degrees near the Antarctic Circle.

The Pacific is the birthplace of surfing and home to many of the world's best-known surf destinations, including Hawaii, California, Fiji, Tahiti, and the east coast of Australia. It is believed that Polynesians have been riding waves since 2,000 B.C.; fishermen in northern Peru may have practiced a form of surfing as far back as 3,000 B.C. North Pacific winter storms broadcast a regular supply of waves to the shores of the North America and many of the Pacific islands; breaks such as Maverick's in California and Jaws on the Hawaiian island of Maui produce the world's largest ridable waves. From September to February, cyclones and typhoons along the western band of the North Pacific often send high-quality surf to Asia's east-facing shores; from June to October, hurricanes forming south of Mexico bring waves to Central America, Mexico, and California. The biggest and most durable South Pacific storms are formed between June and September, sending waves into the central and eastern Pacific, as well as the west-facing coastline of South America.

Pacific System Homes surfboards   Home construction company located in south Los Angeles; producer of the Swastika model surfboard in the 1930s, the sport's first commercially made board. Pacific System Ready-Cut Homes (as it was originally known), founded in 1908, made a line of prefabricated houses that were delivered and assembled on-site by company workers. In 1929, Meyers Butte, the college-age son of one of the Pacific System Homes cofounders, persuaded the company to build and market a line of surfboards. Surfing had been introduced to Southern California 22 years earlier, but not until the late '20s was board demand high enough to encourage production-line assembly. Little is known about the first Pacific System Homes boards, produced either in late 1929 or early 1930, except that they were made from redwood strips held together with lag bolts, and were probably 10 feet long and weighed about 70 pounds. Pine/redwood boards replaced the all-redwood boards by 1932; full-length redwood-edged balsa boards, weighing as little as 45 pounds and costing less than $40, were introduced in the mid-'30s. The swastika symbol—used by American Indians, Vikings, and Greeks as a sign of good luck and harmony—was wood-burned or print-marked onto the back of all Pacific System Homes's Swastika model boards up until 1937. The following year, after the swastika-decorated German military invaded Austria, Pacific System changed the line name to "Waikiki Surf-Boards."

The 1939 Waikiki board came in 10-, 11-, and 12-foot models, as well as a 14-foot paddleboard model, and five- or six-foot "kiddie boards." All were typical of the plank period: blunt-nosed, squared off at the tail, with near-parallel sides. Pacific System Homes boards were made in production runs of 15 on sawhorses in a designated dust-free area of the company's 25-acre site, and were sold in beach clubs, sporting good stores, and high-end department stores like Robinson's and the Broadway. Custom-made Pacific System Homes boards were also available, built by top California surfer/board-makers such as Pete Peterson and Lorrin "Whitey" Harrison. California board-maker Dale Velzy, who introduced the popular "pig" design in 1955, remembers that the Pacific System boards were among the finest on the coast. "Most of us had homemade jobs or hand-me-downs, while the rich guys down there at the Bel Air Bay Club, or the Balboa Bay Club, had the Waikiki models. So we'd sneak down to Balboa and steal 'em."

Pacific System Homes surfboards were promoted with illustrated brochures and magazine advertisements. The boards had a one-year guarantee on workmanship and materials. In 1938, the Waikiki model became the official board of Honolulu's renowned Outrigger Canoe Club. Pacific System Homes stopped producing surfboards not long after America's entry into World War II. *See also* plank surfboard.

Padaca, Myles   Soft-spoken Hawaiian regularfooter from Kona, on the Big Island of Hawaii; winner of the 2001 Triple Crown of Surfing. Padaca was born (1971) in Kona, the son of Tom Padaca, a highly respected surfer of the late '60s and early '70s, and began riding waves at age 11. By the time he'd moved to the North Shore at age 20, Padaca had developed into a smooth, rangy, powerful surfer. Although Padaca had some good results in minor pro contests (first in the Asahi Pro at Sunset Beach in 2000, runner-up in the HIC Pipeline Pro in 1997), his 2001 Triple Crown win—which included a victory in the Rip Curl Cup—was a minor upset, as he finished ahead of perennial favorites including Sunny Garcia, Kelly Slater, and Johnny-Boy Gomes. Padaca has appeared in a small number of surf videos, including *Fluid Combustion* (1995) and *Sudden Rush* (1996).

Padang Padang   Exquisite left-breaking reef wave located in Bali, Indonesia; an emerald-green tropical tube described by photographer Aaron Chang as a "rare, treasured and magical spot." Richard Harvey, 1973 Australian national champion, is credited as the first person to ride Padang in August 1973. Harvey picked his way down the rocky coast by himself one morning from nearby Uluwatu, the break that just two years earlier had introduced the surfing world to the miraculous Indonesian coastline. "The wave that came into view," He later said, recalling his first look at Padang, "was so insanely hollow I staggered." He successfully rode three waves and retreated, happy to have steered clear of the reef. American surf movie audiences got their first look at Padang in the 1977 film *Free Ride,* although it was unidentified and vaguely located on the "island of a thousand temples." Padang wasn't named in the surf press until 1980; just one year later it was cited in a *Surfing* cover story as one of the "Ten Best Waves in the World."

Padang is located about one mile northeast of Uluwatu. In contrast to Uluwatu—one of the world's most dependable surf spots, breaking from two to 12 foot over a broad field on virtually any tide—Padang requires a huge Indian Ocean–born swell (most likely to occur from May to September) and a medium-low tide. The ride at Padang is short, the takeoff zone is cramped, and the crowd can get surly. Padang is best at six foot; smaller waves break too close to the reef—which remains a constant hazard, even under ideal conditions—while bigger waves break too far outside. "Padang" means "grass" or "grasses." Padang has been featured in more than two dozen surf movies and videos, including *Bali High* (1981), *Raw Power* (1991), and *Year of the Tiger* (1999).

Padaratz, Flavio   Cheerful, fitness-minded goofy-footer from Florianópolis, Brazil; world-ranked #8 in 1994, and one of his country's first internationally

Flavio Padaratz

recognized surfers. Padaratz was born (1971) in the landlocked town of Blumenau, near Florianópolis, began surfing at age 12, was a semifinalist in the juniors division of both the 1986 and 1988 World Amateur Surfing Championships, and turned pro in 1988, along with just-crowned men's world amateur champion and fellow Brazilian Fabio Gouveia. Despite the fact that the two were, as surf journalist Ben Marcus wrote, "the oddest of odd couples," Padaratz and Gouveia were presented as a package deal to the rest of the surf world. The shy, swarthy Gouveia, a regular-footer from a poor family, initially had more success on the pro tour, and was world-ranked #5 in 1992. The garrulous blond-haired Padaratz, raised in an upper-middle-class family, lived in Huntington Beach in 1987, where he learned English and groomed himself for a career in surfing. When he won the 1991 Alternativa International event in Rio, beating future world champion Sunny Garcia in the finals, he became a national celebrity. "There is President Fernando Collor De Mello," Australian surf journalist Derek Hynd wrote the following year, without a trace

of irony. "There is Formula One world champion Ayrton Senna. There is Flavio Padaratz." He further bolstered his reputation by winning the World Qualifying Series tour the following year.

Padaratz rode with equal parts flash and power, rounding off each turn and smoothly connecting one move to the next. In 1994 he beat Kelly Slater in the finals of the Rip Curl Hossegor Pro in France, and finished the year rated #8. He slipped to 36th in 1996, then dropped off the world tour for three years—breaking his arm in 1997 after falling down in a drunken pile while dancing, and breaking it again the following year playing soccer—then came back in 2000 at age 29, after winning the 1999 World Qualifying Series. He finished the 2000 season world-ranked #10. Padaratz had remade himself into one of the sport's most disciplined athletes, combining daily swimming, cycling, surfing, yoga, and meditation into what he called "the Process." Padaratz has appeared in more than 20 surf videos, including *La Scene* (1994), *Beyond the Boundaries* (1994), and *Metaphysical* (1997). Neco Padaratz, his tongue-studded younger brother, also became a world tour pro. Flavio Padaratz is married and has two children.

Padaratz, Percy "Neco"   Volatile pro surfer from Florianópolis, Brazil; world-ranked #13 in 1997, and described by *Surfer* magazine in 2000 as "the first legitimate world-title contender from Brazil." Percy "Neco" Padaratz, younger and wilder brother of world tour pro stalwart Flavio Padaratz, was born (1976) in Blumenau, Brazil, began surfing at age nine, and turned pro in 1995 at 18. A broken ankle kept him out of the water for three months in 1996, but he qualified nonetheless for the world tour, and the following year finished at #13. Halfway through the 1998 season he suddenly quit the circuit and returned to Brazil, due either to a stomach ailment or—as reported in the surf magazines—because his wife, upset at the amount of time Padaratz was spending on the road, had put a voodoo curse on him. He returned to the tour in 1999, with close-cropped bleached-white hair, new tattoos, and an oblong lime-green stud piercing his lower lip. His stomach was healthy (or the curse had been lifted), and he won the Gotcha Pro, America's richest contest, in Huntington Beach. Australian surf journalist Tim Baker described Padaratz, a regularfoot, as "vague, laidback and confused on land . . . puffing and snorting with a terrifying will in the water." Padaratz has appeared in a number of surf videos, including *Sarge's Scrapbook, Take 7* (1995), and *Feral Kingdom* (1995).

Paddleboard Cove   *See* Palos Verdes.

paddleboarding   Seagoing activity invented by surfers but performed almost exclusively beyond the surf zone, using a long, narrow, streamlined craft similar to a surfboard, which is paddled for exercise or in competition. A paddleboard is usually between 12 and 20 feet long, about 20 inches wide, and weighs between 25 and 35 pounds; paddleboarders switch between the prone and kneeling positions; paddleboard races usually range from two to 32 miles. Wisconsin-born surf innovator Tom Blake used a board templated from an ancient Hawaiian *olo* surfboard in the paddling portion of the 1928 Pacific Coast Surf Riding Championships; Blake's 110-pound semihollow board has been cited as the first paddleboard. Blake's boards got lighter and faster over the next few years, and he won virtually every paddle race he entered, with half-mile and 100-yard sprint times that stood as world records until the mid-'50s. Presaging what would later become the sport's most popular race, Blake paddled 26 miles from Palos Verdes Peninsula to Catalina Island in 1932; he was accompanied by Santa Monica lifeguard/surfers Pete Peterson (California's best paddler and maker of exquisite paddleboards) and Wally Burton. Blake finished in five hours and 23 minutes. Meanwhile, scaled-down versions of his hollow "cigar-box" paddleboard—or "toothpick"—were being adopted for wave-riding, and put to use by lifeguards; Blake-style surf- and paddleboards were mass-produced and marketed beginning in the early '30s. The *Los Angeles Times* described a Peterson-built chambered mahogany paddleboard in 1939, noting that it had 15 coats of varnish and was held together with more than 1,500 screws. "All in all," the *Times* surmised, "it's a pretty delicate creature. If you rode one through waves it would bust up quicker than a house of cards."

Balsa/fiberglass paddleboards were introduced in the '40s; in 1955, California-born surfer Ricky Grigg beat 12 other paddlers to win the inaugural 32-mile International Paddleboard Race from Catalina to Manhattan Beach Pier. While no longer an intrinsic part of wave-riding competitions, paddleboarding races were instead held on their own, or as an adjunct to surfing contests, and renowned California surf-

board shapers like Greg Noll, Hobie Alter, and especially Dale Velzy—mentored by Blake—made constant design improvements to their paddleboards. Paddleboard races were divided into two board-size classes, which ran simultaneously: stock (for boards under 14 feet; later changed to 12 feet) and open (or "unlimited," with most boards checking in between 16 and 18 feet). The Catalina-to–Manhattan Beach race continued to be the sport's premier event, but in 1961 it was canceled halfway through due to high winds, and remained dormant until returning in 1982 as the Catalina Classic. Now separated almost completely from surfing and surfing competition, paddleboarding became its own internationally practiced sport, and by the early '90s there were several events in Hawaii (most notably the Molokai Channel race), an all-year circuit in California, and spectator-friendly two-mile races in Australia. Escort boats are required of each competitor for long-distance races. Equipment innovations continue apace, with designers always balancing the same performance characteristics: longer boards are faster but unwieldy; narrower is faster but less stable; round bottoms are faster but difficult to balance.

Paddleboarding remains a fairly obscure sport, practiced seriously by just a few dozen men and women. Long-distance paddling has virtually no spectator appeal, and thus little appeal to potential sponsors; professional paddleboard racing made a quiet debut at the 1999 Molokai Channel race (32 miles from Molokai to Oahu), with surfwear giant Quiksilver putting up a $2,000 purse. As of 2002, the unlimited division record for the Catalina–Manhattan Beach race was 5:02.12, set by Tim Gear. Unlimited

Paddleboarding; a competitor in the 1998 Catalina Classic

boards are now made with styrofoam, carbon fiber, and epoxy resin, and weigh as little as 15 pounds. *See also* Tom Blake, Pete Peterson, Gene "Tarzan" Smith.

paddling   Tow-in surfing excepted, any given hour of a surfer's water time is more or less divided equally between paddling and sitting in the lineup, with just a few seconds spent riding waves. The surf world paid a lot of attention to paddling in the early and middle decades of the 20th century: paddleboarding was a featured event at all the big surfing competitions, and some of the world's best surfers, including Tom Blake and Pete Peterson, were as renowned for their paddling as their wave-riding skills. Since the late-1960s shortboard revolution, however, paddling has been viewed as little more than a dull necessity to wave-riding. While efficient paddling—including all the different methods, routs, and techniques used in getting through the surf zone—continues to signify expertise in the waves as surely as a beautiful cutback or a long tuberide, modern surfers, as editor and journalist Steve Hawk wrote in 1998, "look forward to paddling out about as much as they look forward to waiting in line at the DMV."

Shortboard surfers paddle exclusively from a prone position. Longboarders, with their stable high-floating equipment, occasionally use a kneeling position while maneuvering into and around the lineup, but almost always go prone while catching waves. Shortboarders use an alternating arm stroke; longboarders often use a two-arm simultaneous stroke. The most common physical feature among dedicated surfers is a set of overdeveloped broad-back *latissimus* muscles, often pumped to flaring bat-wing proportions by tens of thousands of paddling strokes. Most surfers utilize at least three different paddling techniques: a charging head-lowered sprint stroke usually is required while launching into a bigger wave, or when driving into a hard-to-catch smaller wave; a slow and relaxed stroke is used to conserve energy while paddling over smooth water out beyond the surf zone; an arrhythmic stop-and-go stroke is needed when heading out through sandbar-formed beachbreak waves. By the late '90s, as a result of the thin, narrow, low-flotation boards used by high-performance shortboarders, some surfers—particularly the pros—began augmenting their sprint paddle by kicking their feet. In a 1999 *Surfer* magazine how-to column, surfers were advised to squeeze the butt and thighs and to draw in the belly button while sprint paddling to support the spine and prevent lower-back overuse injury.

Paddling's biggest shortcoming was revealed in the late 1950s, as big-wave surfers found they were unable to generate enough takeoff speed to make the drop on waves over 30 feet. The problem was solved in the early '90s with the advent of tow-in surfing, which eliminated paddling altogether, as the rider got a running start at the wave from behind a personal watercraft.

Page, Robbie   Entertaining gravel-voiced pro surfer from Wollongong, New South Wales, Australia; winner of the 1988 Pipeline Masters. Page was born (1967) and raised in Sydney, began surfing at age nine, and at 13 moved with his mother into a rough Wollongong public housing development; he later cheerfully described his family as "the trash of the trash." The rapid-fire banter that earned Page a reputation as the funniest man in pro surfing was a survival mechanism, he said, to keep from getting pummeled by the big kids in the neighborhood. At 17, Page won the juniors division in the New South Wales state titles, then turned pro; in 1987 the blond-haired goofy-footer earned his highest year-end finish of his decade-long pro career, at #23. Page won one world circuit event, the 1988 Masters, defeating world champions Tom Curren and Damien Hardman in the finals. In 1992, he spent 66 days in a Japanese prison (including four weeks in solitary confinement) after being arrested for LSD possession.

Page rode in a wide stance, arms frequently akimbo, and was an excellent tuberider. He played himself in Universal's 1987 surf movie *North Shore*; he was also the featured surfer in 1991's *Rolling Thunder,* one of the last barnstormed surf movies.

paipo board   *See* bellyboarding.

Pakistan   Dry and rocky Muslim country in South Asia, bordered by Iran, Afghanistan, China, and India, and featuring more than 600 miles of desolate south- and southwest-facing Arabian Sea coastline. "The Pakistani embassy near enough laughed in our faces when we said we wanted to go surfing in the Makran desert," English surfer Stuart Butler reported to surfing Web site Swell.com in 2001, just after he and fellow Brits Dan Haylock and Ben Clift, along with French surf photographer Antony Colas, became the first wave-riders in Pakistan. (Sailboarding had come to Pakistan years earlier, and in 1998 the Windsurfing Association of Pakistan was formed in the eastern port city of Karachi.) It was hoped that the Pakistani surf during the June–August monsoon season might be good enough to outweigh the hassles and dangers of exploring a roadless, lawless, sandstorm- and bandit-filled coastline. The surfers crossed 150 miles of shoreline in three weeks, traveling by Jeep, boat, and camel; midday temperatures regularly hit 100, and the ocean was 80 degrees and dirt brown. The group nonetheless surfed nearly every day, mainly in windblown six-foot beachbreak waves or refined but minuscule pointbreak rights. The Pakistani government insisted that the visitors employ armed guards, and at one point the group came across a heavily armed convoy waiting to transfer hashish, heroin, and firearms to ships waiting offshore. The surfers also encountered a 17-year-old fisherman living in a tiny coastal village near Karachi who was using a wooden plank to ride the nearby shorebreak waves.

Palos Verdes   Affluent hill-covered peninsula located in southwest Los Angeles County; home to more than a dozen surf breaks, including Palos Verdes Cove and Lunada Bay. The cliff-lined Cove, with its four distinct reefbreaks, was first ridden in 1929, and quickly became a favorite among prewar American surfers like Hoppy Swarts, John "Doc" Ball, Bud Morrissey, and Tulie Clark. The Cove was sometimes called "California's Little Waikiki" for its easy-rolling waves and dramatic cliffs that faintly resembled Diamond Head in Hawaii. Surfers of all abilities rode the Channel, an easy-breaking wave in the middle of the Cove; during bigger swells, top riders moved either to Ski Jump, a right-breaking wave to the north, or Indicator, a left-breaking wave to the south. A visit to the Cove (also known as Paddleboard Cove) was often an all-day affair, as the surfer had to shoulder his 60-pound wooden plank board down a half-mile dirt trail from the road to the beach. The carefree California surfing idyll was in part created on the beach at the Cove, as surfers caught abalone and lobster in the nearshore waters, and cooked over open fires on the beach, while drinking jug wine and playing ukuleles. The Palos Verdes Surfing Club, the second club of its kind in California, was formed in 1935 by Cove riders Doc Ball and Adolph Bayer. Nearly a quarter of Ball's *California Surfriders* photo book, published in 1946, is dedicated to the Cove.

Palos Verdes; Tom Blake (left) and Gard Chapin at Palos Verdes Cove

Lunada Bay, located on the northwest tip of the Palos Verdes Peninsula, less than two miles south of the Cove, gained notoriety in late 1962 after California-born big-wave rider Greg Noll tackled some 18-footers there that he later compared to Hawaii's Waimea Bay. Lunada remains Southern California's premier big-wave break. It is also the state's best-known area for localism. Visiting surfers since the early 1970s have had rocks thrown at them while walking down the cliff-side Lunada trail, and returned from the water to find their car windows broken and their tires slashed—the work of local surfers, the sons of millionaires, determined to keep their break free of outsiders. Palos Verdes surfer Peter McCollum was arrested in 1996 on misdemeanor assault charges after threatening and pushing a nonlocal surfer who'd arrived at Lunada with a camera crew from a local TV station. The 34-year-old McCollum was convicted, fined $15,000, and given two years' probation. Another Palos Verdes localism-related assault case was pending as of early 2003.

In *The Tribes of Palos Verdes,* Joy Nicholson's 1997 novel about the corruption of wealth and privilege and the redemptive power of surfing, the 14-year-old narrator describes a conversation at the local tennis club between her mother, a newcomer, and a group of longtime club members. " 'The surfers. They destroy the ice plant. They drag their boards across the ice plant and ruin everything. What's wrong with this place? How come the children roam around in packs?' This is my mother's first faux pas. The ladies of PV don't want to hear complaints about their children. The drinking, the smoking, the violence. No one wants to think about *that*." *See also* localism, Palos Verdes Surf Club.

Palos Verdes Surfing Club   California surfing club formed in 1935 by John "Doc" Ball, dentist and surf photographer, and Adolph Bayer; the second such club in mainland America, following the short-lived Corona del Mar Surfboard Club, formed in the late '20s. Bayer wanted to name the group the Cove Paddleboard Riders Fraternity, but Ball demurred—as a USC student he'd had his fill of fraternities—and countered with Palos Verdes Surfing Club (PVSC), which was unanimously chosen by the club's seven original members. Twenty-one additional surfers were admitted to the PVSC over the next six years, including Leroy Grannis, Cliff Tucker, E.J. Oshier, and Tulie Clark; all were issued a matching letterman-style jacket with a circular PVSC patch stitched to the left breast. Weekly club meetings were held in south Los Angeles at Ball's five-room apartment/dental office, which was decorated with trophies, surf paintings, and dozens of black-and-white photos of club members on the beach or riding waves. The hand-lettered club credo, suspended within a yellowing set of shark jaws tacked to the wall, read in part: "I, as a member of the Palos Verdes Surf Club, do solemnly swear to be steadfast in my allegiance to the club . . . and at all times to strive to conduct myself as a club member and a gentleman. So help me God." Smoking was not permitted in the clubhouse. Members usually adjourned from their weekly meetings to the nearby Zamboanga Club (where a four-feet by five-foot Ball surfing photograph hung on the wall) for beer and pretzels; weekend trips were made up and down the coast to compete and socialize with California's other newly formed surf clubs. *Ye Weekly Super Illustrated Spintail* was the title of the club newsletter, published from 1936 to 1940. The PVSC was unofficially disbanded with America's entry into World War II, as virtually all members went off to military duty. In September 1988, 24 PVSC members gathered at the Camp Pendleton Marine Base, near San Onofre, for a weekend reunion. *See also* John "Doc" Ball, surf clubs.

Pan, Peter   Energetic surfer/retailer/contest director from Narragansett, Rhode Island. Born Peter Panagiotis (1950) in New York, New York, Pan moved with his family to Narragansett as a child and began surfing at age 13. He started competing in 1967 and has over the decades amassed hundreds of regional titles, while entering every possible division, including longboard, bodyboard, shortboard, and kneeboard. Pan has directed contests in New England for the Eastern Surfing Association from 1972 to present; since 1976, he's owned and operated the Watershed Surf Shop in Wakefield, Rhode Island. Hobie Surfboards introduced in 1980 the Peter Pan Slug signature model—a wide, thick, blunt-nosed, easy-to-ride hybrid—and an estimated 8,000 Slugs sold over the next 20 years, mostly in New England and Florida. The small and wiry Pan holds a B.A. in fine arts from the University of Rhode Island, and has long styled himself a surf world gadfly. "My favorite time to surf," he told *Eastern Surf Magazine* in 2000, "is when it's small, windy and there's a blizzard. When it's like that there's no kooks out and no attitudes. The only things that ruins waves are humans."

Pan American Surfing Association (PASA)   Competition group for amateur surfers from North, South, and Central America, and the Caribbean; founded by Argentinean-born Reef sandal owner Fernando Aguerre in 1992. Aguerre said the Pan American Surfing Association (PASA) was formed in part because the International Surfing Association paid so little attention to South and Central American nations. The first Pan American Surf Championships were held on Isla Margarita in Venezuela in 1993, and featured more than 200 surfers from the United States, Brazil, Puerto Rico, Chile, the Dominican Republic, Ecuador, Trinidad and Tobago, and Uruguay. Brazil won, followed by Venezuela and the United States. Competing surfers included future world tour stars Maria Tavares and Shea Lopez. Subsequent Pan-American Surf Championships were held in Guadeloupe (1995), Brazil (1997), Argentina (1999), and again in Venezuela (2001). The PASA is based in San Diego, California; as of 2003, Aguerre was still the organization's president. *See also* Fernando Aguerre.

Panama   Small and narrow Central American country located between Costa Rica and Colombia, with tropical coastlines facing the Pacific Ocean and the Caribbean Sea. Panama is sometimes called the "Crossroads of the World," as it connects North America and South America, as well as the Atlantic and Pacific oceans via the Panama Canal. Panama's

750-mile Pacific coastline features a variety of point-, reef-, and beachbreak surf, and regularly produces three to six-foot waves between June and November, with prevailing offshore winds blowing from December to April. Larger surf hits the nearshore islands. Five popular breaks are located in Panama City, and high-quality waves of almost every description are distributed evenly from border to border; Playa Santa Catalina, a right-breaking point located 175 miles southwest of Panama City, is one of Central America's most popular surf spots. Waves along the 400-mile north-facing Caribbean coast are best from December to April, with several first-rate coral reefbreaks found near the mouth of the Panama Canal and dozens more rarely surfed spots located to the east and west, particularly among the nearshore islands. As Panama forms a rough S shape, the Pacific side picks up swells from the south and west, while the Caribbean coast is open to swells from the north and east. Traveling from coast to coast generally takes only two hours, but beach access along both coasts is often a problem. Daytime air temperatures in Panama City average about 80 degrees throughout the year, as do water temperatures on both coasts. Some breaks are shallow, but for the most part surfing in Panama is relatively hazard-free.

Americans living in the U.S.-governed Panama Canal Zone were the first to surf in Panama in the early '60s. Rio Mar, a resort beach located 60 miles west of Panama City, was the first regularly surfed area; a beautifully shaped rivermouth break called Tits, located at the end of Rio Teta, just east of Rio Mar, soon became known as the country's finest wave, and was featured in a 1971 *Surfing* magazine travel article. A small team of native Panamanians, meanwhile, competed in the 1968 world contest, held in Puerto Rico. As the country labored under sometimes-volatile military rule in the '70s, the surfing population remained tiny, and America's involvement in Panamanian affairs—even after the United States agreed in 1977 to cede control of the Canal—bred resentment toward visiting U.S. surfers. President George Bush's 1989 decision to invade Panama and extract dictator General Manuel Noriega was regarded by many natives as further violation. "But," as Australian surf photographer Ted Grambeau pointed out in 1992, "it helped keep the crowds down." Four years later the Panamanian tourist board invited a delegation of American longboarders to visit a newly built surf camp on the Pacific coast of north Panama, and American surfers have since been made to feel more welcome.

As of 2003, Panama was home to about 700 resident surfers, four surf shops, and 10 surf camps. An early version of the Panama Surfing Association was formed in 1987; amateur surfing contests are now held regularly in Panama, and a Billabong-sponsored pro contest has been held at Playa Venada, on the Pacific coast, since 1998. Panama has been featured in a small number of surf videos, including *Session Impossible* (1991), *Panama Red* (1994), and *NRG 2000* (2000).

Pang, Dennis   Quiet Hawaiian surfer and surfboard shaper from the North Shore of Oahu. Pang was born (1953) and raised in Honolulu, began surfing at age nine, and competed in the 1970 World Surfing Championships. He started making boards in 1969 at age 16, in much the same way many apprentice shapers did during the shortboard revolution—by stripping the fiberglass off his outmoded 9′6″ longboard and reshaping the foam core into a streamlined "pocket rocket." Pang got his first steady shaping job in 1976 with Surf Line Hawaii, just after receiving a B.S. in psychology from the University of Hawaii. He shaped briefly for Lightning Bolt Surfboards, then in 1979 switched to Town and Country Surfboards, where he still works. Over the years Pang has shaped boards for world champions Martin Potter, Sunny Garcia, and Wayne Bartholomew, as well as Dane Kealoha, Larry Bertlemann, Michael Ho, Christian Fletcher, and dozens of other first-rate surfers. Pang himself was invited to the Quiksilver in Memory of Eddie Aikau big-wave events in 1985, 1986, and 1990.

Papua New Guinea   *See* New Guinea.

Parkes, Wayne   Domineering New Zealand surfer and surfboard shaper from Takapuna Beach, New Zealand; national men's division champion from 1966 to 1970. Parkes was born (1950) in Whangarei, raised in Takapuna, and began surfing at age 12. He won the juniors division of the 1965 New Zealand national titles, and went on to compete in the World Surfing Championships in 1966, 1968, and 1970. The sure-footed, smooth-turning regularfooter quit competition in late 1970, not long after winning his fifth consecutive New Zealand men's division title. Parkes had meanwhile apprenticed under Australian board shaper/designer guru Bob McTavish in 1966 and 1967; he's since had a long and successful board-making career, based out of Takapuna, and opened Wayne Parkes Surfboards in 1980. Parkes was featured in a small number of surf movies in the late '60s and early '70s, including *Out of the Blue* (1967) and *Seven Sundays* (1970). He was New Zealand's top vote-getter in *International Surfing* Magazine's 1967 Hall of Fame Awards.

Parkinson, Joel   Self-assured Australian regular-footer from Queensland's Gold Coast; World Junior Championship winner in 1999 and 2001, and world-ranked #2 in 2002. Parkinson was born (1981) and raised in Nambour, Queensland, and began surfing at age three during weekend family visits to the beach. At 13 he moved with his family to the Gold Coast, and by the late '90s, Parkinson, Mick Fanning, and Dean Morrison were being touted as the supernaturally talented "Coolangatta Kids," as all three teenagers lived in or near the small Gold Coast town of Coolangatta. The beaky, dark-haired Parkinson had by then developed into an aggressive and innovative surfer, loose-armed but never flailing, and always riding with what surf journalist Nick Carroll called an "oddly hypnotic grace." In small waves Parkinson is

Joel Parkinson

fast and acrobatic; in larger surf he's cool-handed and faster yet. His grinning and offhanded demeanor was occasionally taken by many as a sign of arrogance; his goal in 2000, he told *TransWorld* magazine, was to "win everything." One year earlier, at age 18, he'd taken the World Junior Championships and become the youngest nonseeded surfer to ever win a world tour contest, winning the prestigious Billabong Pro at Jeffreys Bay and commenting afterward that "it's not as hard as it seems." Parkinson had his first full year on the world tour in 2001, finished the season ranked #21, and also won another World Junior title. He opened the 2002 season with a win in front of a Gold Coast home crowd at the Quiksilver Pro, and won the year's final event, the Rip Curl Cup in Hawaii. He was runner-up to Andy Irons for the world title. Parkinson has appeared in more than two dozen surf videos, including *Feeding Frenzy* (2000), *Momentum: Under the Influence* (2001), and *The Rising* (2002).

Parmenter, Dave   Dissident American surfer/writer/surfboard shaper; world pro tour competitor in the mid- and late 1980s; once described by *Surfing* magazine as "the most interesting surfer in the world." Born in Southern California in 1961, the son of an X-ray technician single mother, Parmenter began surfing at age 13 after moving with his mother and younger brother to Newport Beach. Three years later the family moved again, to the central California town of Cayucos, where the already-caustic Parmenter nearly failed to graduate from high school after refusing to participate in gym class on "religious grounds." In 1982, the square-jawed 21-year-old established himself as one of California's best pro surfers, winning or placing highly in a string of statewide events. He also gained a reputation as a trenchant surf world observer with his *Surfer*-published article titled "Raiders of the Lost Coast," in which he dismissed the tribal surfers of his home region who rejected anything—surf-related or otherwise—that was "newer, lighter [or] shinier." Parmenter himself used brightly colored boards and wetsuits, planted his feet in a wide stance across his board, generated as much lateral velocity as any surfer of the period, and often reversed direction with a scything roundhouse cutback. He joined the world tour in 1983, finished the 1985 season ranked #14—his highest rating—then quit the circuit three years later. In a 1988 *Surfer* interview titled "Iconoclast Now," published just before he left the tour, Parmenter railed against commercialization and the loss of surfing purity. Young surfers, he said, were concerned only with "stickers and freebies, [and] their first sponsorship deal is put right up there with losing their virginity. In the meantime, they're missing out on surfing. Competing is just a tiny sliver of what the sport has to offer...." Parmenter voiced similar opinions in the nearly 50 articles he wrote for the American surf press between 1989 and 2001.

Parmenter shaped his first surfboard in 1977, took up the craft in earnest in late 1988, and was soon making and selling boards under his Aleutian Juice label. Bucking a general trend toward narrower and thinner boards, Parmenter developed a spacious blunt-nosed board he called the Stub Vector; by the mid-'90s, virtually every shaper was offering a Stub-influenced model. While on a surf trip to Christmas Island in 1994, Parmenter met graceful Hawaiian surfer Rell Sunn; they were married the following year, and Parmenter moved into Sunn's home in Makaha, on the west side of Oahu. Sunn had been diagnosed with metastasized breast cancer in 1983; when she died in 1998 at age 47, Parmenter scattered her ashes into the ocean at Makaha. He remained in Hawaii, shaping surfboards for a living, and remarried in 1999.

Parmenter appeared in a small number of surf movies and videos, including *Shock Waves* (1987) and *Just Surfing* (1989). "The Land That Duke Forgot," Parmenter's *Surfer*-published article on wave-riding in Alaska, was included in 1993's *Best American Sports Writing* collection, published by Houghton Mifflin. John Parmenter, Dave's younger brother, a stocky blond regularfoot, was the 1985 Professional Surfing Association of America tour champion.

Parrish, Tom   The world's most popular surfboard shaper of the mid-1970s, and a virtual one-man equipment source for the era's top pros; described by *Surfing* magazine as the "Man With the Red-Hot Planer." Parrish was born (1951) and raised in Southern California, began surfing at age 12 while on vacation in Waikiki, and started making boards at 17. He moved to Hawaii in 1969 and over the next three years worked for Surf Line Hawaii and Country Surfboards, before moving to Lightning Bolt. In 1975, Parrish made full quivers for Jeff Hakman, Mark Richards, Ian Cairns, Shaun Tomson, Peter Townend, Wayne Bartholomew, and Margo Oberg, among others. Parrish was best known for his elegant rounded-pintail big-wave guns and semi-guns; he also devel-

oped into an excellent surfer, and often shared the lineup with his patrons at breaks like Sunset Beach and Honolua Bay. Parrish mentored or influenced dozens of shapers, including Phil Byrne, Bill Barnfield, and Jim Banks. He later moved to Maui, earned a law degree, and became a lawyer. *See also* Lightning Bolt Surfboards.

Parsons, Mike   Freckle-faced pro surfer from Laguna Beach; winner of the 1991 Professional Surfing Association of America tour, as well as the 2001 Swell XXL Big Wave Awards. Parsons was born (1965) and raised in Laguna, began surfing at age six, and was runner-up in the juniors division of the 1983 United States Surfing Championships. He had few spectacular moments during his 12-year Association of Surfing Professionals career (1984 to 1996), but he was smooth, consistent, and tactically sound, and finished the 1987 season ranked 15th. He also won the 1991 Professional Surfing Association of America tour, coming out ahead of future world tour stars like Shane Beschen, Taylor Knox, and Rob Machado. But Parsons attracted more attention for his clean-cut looks and relentlessly agreeable disposition. "Needs more spontaneity," surf journalist Derek Hynd once wrote of Parsons. "Needs a punk haircut. Needs to shock someone. Anyone." Parsons did in fact shock people by regularly manhandling 25-foot surf at Baja's Todos Santos in the late '80s and '90s, and after retiring from the competition circuit he began to devote even more time to big-wave riding, eventually becoming tow-in partners with former nemesis and top-ranked pro Brad Gerlach. In January 2001, Parsons rode a 60-foot-plus wave at Cortes Bank, an open-ocean reef located 100 miles west of San Diego. Two months later, a photograph of Parsons's giant wave earned him the $60,000 first-place check in the Swell XXL Big Wave Awards—the biggest cash prize in surfing history. The following year, Parsons and Gerlach placed second in the first Tow-In World Cup, held at Jaws, Maui.

Parsons appeared in more than two dozen surf movies and videos, including *Shock Waves* (1987), *Overdrive* (1993), and *The Reef at Todos* (1998). He was cofounder of Realm clothing in 1998 and Von Zipper sunglasses in 1999. *See also* big-wave surfing, Cortes Banks, tow-in surfing.

Paskowitz, Dorian   Beatific and enduring Southern California surfing patriarch; runner-up in the

1941 Pacific Coast Surf Riding Championships; founder of the Paskowitz Surf Camp; lifelong advocate for improved health and diet among surfers, and a staunch believer in the health benefits of surfing itself. "When he's away from the ocean he's an old man," Paskowitz's wife said in 1990, looking at her then–68-year-old husband. "He's a boy when he surfs." Paskowitz was born (1921) and raised in Galveston, Texas, and began surfing at age 12. He moved with his family to San Diego in 1934, where he worked as a lifeguard at Mission Beach, helped revive the area's flagging surf scene, and became one of the first regulars at San Onofre; in the 1941 Pacific Coast Surf Riding Championships he finished second to surfing ironman Pete Peterson.

Paskowitz divided his time throughout the '40s between surfing (in Hawaii and California), school (earning a B.A. in biology from Stanford University in 1942, and an M.D., also from Stanford, in 1946), and military service (stationed aboard the USS *Ajax* in 1946–47). When he moved to Israel in 1956, Paskowitz took his Hobie Surfboards pintail, hoping, he later said, "to get Arabs and Jews surfing together." After founding a small surfing colony in Tel Aviv, he paddled out to a likely-looking break near the Gaza Strip just as the Suez Canal crisis brought live fire to the area; an Israeli solider ordered him out of the water and confiscated his board, thinking it was a cleverly disguised missile. Paskowitz was at that time married to his second wife, and had already fathered three children.

In the '60s and '70s, Paskowitz and his ever-growing family (a third marriage produced nine children) lived in a mobile home and traveled often from one side of America to the other, with family practitioner Paskowitz working ad hoc at various medical clinics, and wife Juliette home-schooling the kids. The Paskowitzes spent much of the year living in the beachfront parking lot at San Onofre. In 1975 Paskowitz wrote the first of nearly 30 columns for *Surfer* magazine, in which he skillfully mixed surf history with health, diet, and fitness advice. Also in 1975, the three-year-old Paskowitz International Surf School, founded in Tel Aviv, was relocated to San Onofre, with weekend learn-to-surf camps offered from June to February. In the early '80s, the camp was renamed the Paskowitz Surfing Psychiatric Clinic, specializing in kids with drug problems and/or personality disorders; in 1985 it made a final change to the Paskowitz Surfing Camp, offering

weeklong surfing seminars administered by the Paskowitz family, with guest appearances by pro surfers. The Paskowitz Surf Camp wasn't the first of its kind, but it was by far the most popular and durable. Clothes designer Tommy Hilfiger signed on as a Paskowitz Surf Camp corporate sponsor in 1997; the following year the camp was featured in a lengthy *New York Times* article, with Paskowitz described as "the 78-year-old camp founder whose body looks like that of a man 40 years younger." Paskowitz had indeed kept himself in marvelous shape, and, along with Hawaiian surfer Rabbit Kekai, was at that point the world's best septuagenarian wave-rider. Both were still surfing in 2003. Paskowitz and his surf camp have been featured in articles by *People, GQ,* and *Sports Illustrated.*

Israel and Jonathan Paskowitz, two of Dorian Paskowitz's sons, became nationally known longboarders in the late '80s; by the mid-'90s Israel had taken over the Paskowitz Surf Camp's day-to-day operations. Dorian Paskowitz was inducted into the International Surfing Hall of Fame in 1991; *Surfing and Health,* his memoir/medical advice book, was published in 1998. *See also* surf schools.

Paterson brothers, Jake and Paul   Rough-and-tumble regularfoot brothers from Yallingup, Western Australia, whose surfing seems to improve in direct proportion to the size and danger of the waves. "The sort of blokes," Steve Smith, Jake's trainer, said in 2000, "you'd want in your bunker during wartime." In 1996, 23-year-old Jake won the Association of Surfing Professionals World Qualifying Series tour; in 1998 he won the Pipeline Masters and ended the season world-ranked #9; in 2000 he won the Billabong Pro at Jeffreys Bay, South Africa, and finished the year at #5. Although relatively small (5'9", 155 pounds), Jake was described by *Surfer* magazine as having a "quietly menacing presence," nurtured in part by years of riding the board-snapping reefbreaks in and around his hometown. Jake returned to Jeffreys and successfully defended his Billabong crown in 2001, and again finished the season at #5.

Paul Paterson, older than Jake by just over a year, won the 1996 World Cup held at Sunset Beach and the 1999 Reef Big-Wave World Championship. He also finished third in both the 2001 and 2002 editions of the Quiksilver in Memory of Eddie Aikau big-wave events at Waimea Bay, Hawaii. Presumably to illustrate the Paterson brothers' earthiness, they were photographed covered head to toe in mud for their 2000 *Surfer* magazine profile, "Snake and the Antman." Paul Paterson is featured in *Psychedelic Desert Groove* (1997), *The Moment* (1998), and a small number of other surf videos; Jake is featured in *Outside In* (1999) and *Farsiders* (2000).

Patterson brothers, Robert, Raymond, and Ronald   Good-humored brother trio originally from Honolulu, Hawaii; the Pattersons moved to Southern California as teenagers in the 1950s and served for decades as live-in ambassadors of the casual, beachboy-influenced surfing lifestyle. All three spent much of their adult lives in the Dana Point/ Laguna Beach area, working at the Hobie Surfboards factory.

Oldest brother Robert "Flea" Patterson was born in 1934, and moved in 1952 to Santa Monica, California, where he lived with hotdogging ace Mickey Muñoz and his family. The quick-footed 130-pound Patterson was then regarded by many as the best small-wave surfer in the world; he and Muñoz would be lifelong friends. Patterson finished third in the 1963 West Coast Surfing Championships, and won the 1964 Malibu Invitational. From 1962 to 1971 he lived in Dana Point and worked as a glosser for Hobie; in the early '70s, wanted by the FBI, he fled the country for Thailand, and spent the rest of his life as a fugitive. He died in Bangkok in 1994 at age 60.

Middle brother Ronald, born in 1936, was one of the original members of the Windansea Surf Club. He moved to Dana Point in the early '60s, worked as a sander at Hobie, earning distinction of a sort by chain-smoking up to five packs of Marlboros a day and working without a dust-filter mask. Not surprisingly Ronald died of cancer in 1996 at age 60.

Younger brother Raymond was born in 1938, and was regarded as one of Hawaii's premier ukulele players when he moved to Laguna Beach in 1956. He also began working for Hobie in the early '60s, as a laminator, and was a member of the San Onofre Surfing Club. Raymond died of heart failure in 1989 at age 51.

The Patterson brothers together wrote the pidgin English "Da Kine Chreesmess Fairystory" for *Surfer* magazine in 1965. The story ends with the surfing "Sandy Claws" making a Christmas Eve toy stop in Waikiki. "He went cut bak and ride da curl, an no queeka den you can say 'Duke Kahanamoku' he went put all da toy stuffs in front da Royal Hawaiian Hotel. Queek like one jax rabbits, he jump on hes bawd, and even wen he was far away we went hear him excreem, 'Merry Chreesmess to all you guys, an Alohaaa!' "

Paull, Keith   Square-jawed regularfoot surfer from Queensland, Australia; winner of the 1968 Australian National Titles, and described by 1978 world champion Wayne Bartholomew as having "the most beautiful style in surfing." Paull was born (1946) and raised on Queensland's Gold Coast, and began surfing at age 14. The master of what was called the "power-crouch" style, Paull defeated world champions Midget Farrelly and Nat Young to win the 1968 Australian National Titles, prompting *Surfing* magazine to introduce the well-built vegetarian as "the most powerful all-around performer in Australian waters today." He also finished runner-up in the 1968 Bells Beach event, won the small-wave portion of the 1969 Peru International, and finished third in the 1970 Australian National Titles.

Paull's paranoid-schizophrenic mental breakdown in the early and mid-'70s was unexpected, and at times perversely funny. At a preevent gathering for a 1974 surf contest, he drove his panel van up the stairs and halfway through the front door of a hotel pub in Queensland, then stepped out of the car wearing silver knee-high boots and blue Superman briefs, with concentric blue circles painted on his shaved head. A respected surfboard shaper, Paull opened Keith Paull Surfboards and Harmony Surfboards in the Gold Coast during the early '70s. He then quit surfing and shaping altogether in 1976, as his mental problems grew worse. Paul appeared in a

Keith Paull

small number of surf movies, including *A Life in the Sun* (1966), *The Way We Like It* (1968), *Evolution* (1969), and *Waves of Change* (1970). Paull still lives in Queensland.

Peahi   *See* Jaws.

peak   A triangle-shaped wave, shouldering in both directions, offering both a right and left slide. "Peak" surf is at the opposite end of the wave spectrum from "wall" or "lined-up" surf, in which the crest of the wave runs virtually parallel to the trough. Peak waves are much shorter than lined-up waves, but under the right conditions can produce excellent tubes. Duranbah in Australia and Mexico's Puerto Escondido are often described as peaky. Local winds often create peaky waves, especially at beachbreaks. "Peak" also describes the highest point on any given wave.

pearl, pearling   When the nose of the surfboard dips underwater, checking or completely stopping the board's forward motion; usually the result of the rider putting too much weight on the front of the board, or from hitting a ridge of water known as a "chop." Pearling is short for "pearl diving," meaning the surfer is about to find himself down among the pearl beds. Pearling is a sudden and sometimes dangerous way to fall, almost always resulting in a wipeout, and is common to beginning surfers.

Peck, John   Brightly burning surfer from Costa Mesa, California; the first regularfooter to ride inside the tube at Pipeline in Hawaii. Peck was born (1944) in Los Angeles, the son of a navy pilot, and was raised on or near military bases in Virginia, Texas, California, and Hawaii. He began surfing at Coronado, California, at age 15; later that same year his family moved back to Waikiki, Hawaii. Peck placed fourth in the juniors division of the 1960 Makaha International, and returned the following year to finish third, but was virtually unknown in the surf world until New Year's Day, 1963, when he and California switchfooter Butch Van Artsdalen put on a fantastic display at Pipeline, with Peck spontaneously inventing a low-crouch stance, his right hand grabbing the rail of his board, that allowed him to ride high and tight to the curl. That summer, Peck's thrilling Pipeline rides were the highlight of three surf movies, *Angry Sea, Gun Ho!,* and *Walk on the Wet Side.*

Peck developed into one of surfing's most unusual characters. He was arrogant enough to wear a

T-shirt with YES, I'M JOHN PECK stenciled across the back, and honest enough to admit to a surf journalist that he'd become "schizoid; I'm completely repulsed by the whole fame situation, yet I still seek it and I don't understand why." Peck finished fifth in the 1963 West Coast Championships, second in the 1963 Malibu, and third in the 1966 United States Championships. A victory in the 1966 Laguna Masters earned him a new Honda motorcycle. The Peck Penetrator, a noseriding model made by Morey-Pope Surfboards in Ventura, debuted in late 1965 with ads and brochures featuring Peck dressed as a well-groomed British mod. (Extant Penetrators would become high-priced collectors' items in the late '90s.) Peck had meanwhile set out on a lengthy course of alcohol and drug abuse, including a seven-year LSD phase beginning in 1965. He was involved in the Brotherhood of Eternal Love, a Laguna Beach consciousness-raising group that quickly evolved into a drug ring; he also lived in a tree in front of Sunset Beach on the North Shore of Oahu, served six months in solitary confinement on Maui on drug convictions, and was institutionalized. He gave up drugs and drinking in 1984, four years later began surfing again, and in the mid-'90s was reintroduced to the nostalgia-hungry surfing world as a thin, weathered, flexible yoga master who claimed he could levitate. Peck surfed constantly, and traveled often to Baja California, Mexico, paying for his trips by building neoclassic Penetrator models and selling them for $1,200 each. Peck was married once, and has no children.

peel, peeling, peel off   A fast, clean, evenly falling curl line, perfect for surfing, and usually found at pointbreaks. A peeling wave has no sections or flat spots. Not all great waves peel off: Hawaii's Sunset Beach is thought of as one of surfing's most challenging breaks in part because it changes shape and speed as it goes. But as a rule, the best waves in the world—including Rincon, Kirra, Grajagan, and Jeffreys Bay—are long-peeling waves.

Penuelas, Bob   Surf cartoonist from San Diego, California; creator of the vapid but optimistic Wilbur Kookmeyer cartoon character. Penuelas was born (1957) and raised in San Diego, the son of a technical illustrator, and began surfing in 1970. He took junior college commercial art classes and worked briefly as a technical illustrator, but is for the most part a self-taught artist and cartoonist. In 1980 he teamed up with fellow San Diego surfers Rich Bundschuh (his brother-in-law) and Tom Finley to produce Maynard and the Rat, a comic strip about a middle-aged mustachioed soul-surfer and his young rip-and-tear sidekick. *Surfer* magazine published 29 Maynard and the Rat episodes from 1980 to 1987 (the last four produced without Penuelas); in 1985, the strip introduced Wilbur Kookmeyer, a jug-eared, spike-haired, wipeout-prone adolescent who often slips into a fantasy world of surf magazine covers and world title victories. Penuelas wrote and drew the Kookmeyer strip unassisted—his work is filled with neatly crafted and often satirical jabs at surf culture, particularly surf consumerism—and it quickly became a hit; *Surfer* published it until 2000. Penuelas has also been a surfboard airbrusher since the late '70s, working for more than a dozen San Diego–based surfboard companies, including Rusty and Gordon & Smith. *See also* Wilbur Kookmeyer, surf cartoons and comics.

perfect wave, the The "perfect wave" is subjective, changing from person to person, but it nonetheless takes on a collective shape and form defined by each new generation of surfers. As surfing was exported from country to country in the first few decades of the 20th century, Waikiki, the sport's homeland, was unanimously regarded as having the world's best surf. After World War II, with the new easier-handling boards encouraging surfers to ride faster and more sharply angled waves, Southern California's Malibu became the ultimate break. While the best waves at Waikiki and Malibu were no doubt referred to as "perfect," it was California filmmaker Bruce Brown who brought "the perfect wave" into the lexicon with his wildly popular 1966 surf movie travelogue, *The Endless Summer*. Three years earlier, Brown had set out with surfers Mike Hynson and Robert August in search of a Malibu-like wave with no crowds. In South Africa, at a boulder-lined point located on Cape St. Francis, the group discovered a beautifully tapered chest-high wave, and an ecstatic Brown filmed what would become the high point for his upcoming film. "On Mike's first ride, the first five seconds," Brown said in his *Endless Summer* narration, with Hynson trimming across a long Cape St. Francis wall, "he knew he'd finally found that perfect wave." Brown also shot photographs of Cape St. Francis for a 1964 *Surfer* magazine article titled, "Africa: The Perfect Wave." The quest for the perfect wave has since become a permanent surf world trope. After the introduction of short surfboards in the late '60s, riding inside the tube became the ultimate in high-performance surfing, and the cylindrical waves at Hawaii's Pipeline became the "new" perfect wave. Almost by definition, the perfect wave had to have an element of difficulty. Just as the geographic distance between South Africa and the rest of the surfing world made Cape St. Francis all but unreachable, the dangerous sheer-faced tubes at Pipeline were off limits except to the most skilled. The perfect wave was diffused somewhat beginning in the mid-'70s, although breaks like Jeffreys Bay (South Africa), Grajagan (Indonesia), and Kirra (Australia), each of them long and hollow, might be viewed as Malibu/Pipeline hybrids. *See also* Cape St. Francis, The Endless Summer.

period *See* swell period.

Perkins, Gregory "Bonga" Strong and agile longboarder from Honolulu, Hawaii; winner of the 1996 World Longboard Championships. Perkins was born (1972) and raised in Honolulu, began surfing at age five, and developed into an all-around talent, equally skilled on a bodyboard, shortboard, and longboard. By his late teens, Perkins was spending most of his water time on a longboard, and he placed runner-up in the longboard division of the 1989 United States Surfing Championships. Perkins lived in Japan for two years during the early '90s, where he was an English language tutor and did publicity work for a Tokyo-area surfboard shop. He returned to Hawaii in 1993 as a virtually unknown surfer, but nonetheless finished fifth in that year's World Longboarding

Bonga Perkins

Championships, held in brutal conditions at Haleiwa on the North Shore of Oahu. The well-muscled Perkins (6′1″, 185 pounds) was an excellent noserider, but for the most part used a modified shortboard style. He had a remarkable run in the World Longboard Championships through the mid- and late '90s, finishing second in 1994, third in 1995, first in 1996, second in 1997, fifth in 1998, and third in 1999; in the 2002 Championships he placed runner-up to California's Colin McPhillips. Perkins also became the dominant longboard surfer in the hollow and powerful waves at Pipeline/Backdoor on the North Shore of Oahu. Perkins has appeared in more than a dozen surf videos, including *Blazing Longboards* (1994), *Adrift* (1996), and *From This Day Forward* (2001). *See also* World Longboard Tour.

Perrow, Kieren   Articulate regularfooter from Byron Bay, New South Wales, Australia; world ranked #7 in 2002 and regarded as one of the sport's most fearless riders. Perrow was born (1977) and raised in Byron Bay, started surfing at age seven, was a high school honor student, and in 1997 was runner-up in the Pro Junior. He began his pro career in earnest in 1999, by which time he'd earned a reputation for his fast, balanced approach in point surf and for an almost unnatural calm when the waves became dangerous. In 2001, the slender blond-haired Perrow paddled into what many consider to be the gnarliest right-breaking wave ever ridden, a double-up 12-footer at Shipstern Bluff in Tasmania; Perrow went airborne on the drop, reconnected, turned just beneath a horrific tube section and set a line inside, but was unable to make it out. He surfaced without injury. Perrow qualified for the world tour in 2002 and surprised pundits by charging directly to the #7 position. He has appeared in a small number of surf videos, including *Holy Water* (1999), *Evolve* (2002), and *Speed* (2002).

Perry, Mike   Sharp-witted surfboard shaper/journalist/forecaster from Queensland, Australia, by way of Southern California; board-maker for dozens of manufacturers from 1964 to 1997, and editor of *Australia's Surfing Life* magazine from 1985 to 1991. Perry was born (1946) and raised in Culver City, Los Angeles, began surfing at 13, and was taught the basics of surfboard shaping in 1964 by Hawaiian big-wave surfing pioneer George Downing. Perry started working for Roberts Surfboards in 1964, and went on to make boards for Hobie, Blue Cheer, Con, and Natural Progression; the Mike Perry Surfboards label was founded in 1970. Two years later, just eight weeks after publishing his debut surf article, Perry began a two-year associate editor term at *Surfer* magazine; in 1974 he made the first of several long visits to Queensland, and moved there permanently in 1989. Perry was the first editor of *Australia's Surfing Life*; he has also freelanced articles to the *Surfer's Journal, Surfing,* and *Deep*. He continued to shape surfboards for a number of different companies, while moonlighting as a radio and TV surf forecaster.

Persian Gulf   Warm, shallow, kidney-shaped body of water, about 500 miles long and 125 miles wide, bordered by Iran, Iraq, Kuwait, Saudi Arabia, Qatar, and the United Arab Emirates. No chartered surf tours will be offered to the Persian Gulf anytime soon, but a small underground surf culture has taken root, with perhaps a dozen or so American and Australian expatriates foraging for waves along the Gulf's sandy beaches and rocky inlets. Winter is the only time to surf here, as northwest *Shamal* winds can push head-high waves with some regularity into the Gulf's southeast coast. "Good month for the Gulf," American surfer Ian Roberts said in a 1991 *Surf Report* newsletter, noting that there had been 12 days of ridable waves in January. "Discovered a new break halfway between Dubai and the Straits of Hormuz at Umm Al Quawain; a left pointbreak with good, hollow waves breaking on a sandstone bottom." Gulf summers are waveless, with air temperatures reaching 120, and water temperatures in the low 80s.

personal watercraft   Inboard water-jet-powered craft often referred to as a Jet Ski, and generally thought of as the motorcycle of the boating world; used for recreation and lifeguarding; celebrated and reviled among surfers as the motorized component of big-wave tow-in riding. In 2003, the average tow-in surfing personal watercraft (PWC) was eight feet long and weighed 600 pounds, with a two-stroke 155-horsepower motor. PWCs are usually ridden by one person, but larger models can seat three; they go as fast as 65 miles per hour on flat water. PWC drivers don't need to be licensed, but must be 16 or older in most American states.

Motocross rider Clayton Jacobsen of Arizona developed the one-man Sea-Doo PWC prototype in 1968, but it was motorcycle manufacturer Kawasaki who popularized the new machine in 1973, introducing the Jet Ski, a gas-powered 34-horsepower stand-up model with handlebar steering. The sit-down, multi-passenger PWC was introduced in the late '80s. California longboarder Herbie Fletcher had by then used a PWC to ride places like Pipeline and Waimea Bay in Hawaii. PWC usage in the United States increased 400 percent between 1990 and 1996.

As of 2003, a PWC cost between $5,000 and $9,000. The vast majority of PWC users are weekend and vacation riders on lakes and rivers; some compete in regional, national, or international races. Ocean lifeguard agencies adopted PWCs in the early '90s for rescue and patrol use. Shortly afterward, a handful of surfers in Hawaii reinvented big-wave riding by attaching a 30-foot towline to the rear of the craft to give a rope-holding surfer a whip-start into gigantic waves. Whereas paddle-in surfers were unable to catch waves bigger than 30 feet, tow-in surfers—riding the Yamaha WaveRunner GP1200R model almost exclusively—would soon be riding 50-footers. PWCs have also been used during world pro tour events to quickly shuttle contestants back to the take-off area after riding a wave.

PWCs had meanwhile become hugely unpopular among some groups. U.S. Coast Guard statistics show that while PWCs represent less than 10 percent of total boats, they consistently account for more than 25 percent of annual boating accidents; the two-stroke engine used on virtually all PWCs dumps as much as one-third of its fuel load unburned into the water; a 1999 issue of *Time* magazine listed the PWC as one of "The 100 Worst Ideas of the Century." San Francisco big-wave rider Mark Renneker spoke for all surfers who value a quiet, smoke-free surfing environment when he described the PWC as "sickening" and "rapacious." PWCs in America are subject to a series of ever-changing state and local regulations (rarely enforced during heavy surf), and have been banned outright in some areas, including Marin County in California, San Juan County in Washington, and the Cape Cod National Seashore. *See also* big-wave surfing, tow-in surfing.

Peru South America's third-largest country has a rich surfing history to go with its 1,500 miles of mostly dry and rugged Pacific-facing coastline. The surf in Peru is remarkably consistent, with wave height averaging between three to six foot throughout the year, thanks to long-distance north swells during the summer, a steady feed of powerful south swells in winter, and a balance of the two during spring and fall. About 80 percent of Peru's surf spots are lefts, most of them breaking along rocky points spilling onto sandy beaches. Daytime coastal air temperatures generally range between the low 70s in summer and the low 60s in winter; water temperatures around the capital city of Lima, chilled by the Humboldt current, range from the upper 60s to the mid-50s. While surfing in Peru is centered in Lima—home to one-fifth of the country's total population—crowded lineups and dirty water at popular spots like Punta Rocas and Miraflores have long encouraged native wave-riders to search for breaks beyond the city limits. Peru's wave-rich northern tip faces northwest (the rest of the coast faces southwest), warmed by the Panama Current, is home to an assortment of points and reefs, including the high-acceleration tubes at Cabo Blanco. Chicama—the arid left-breaking point known as the longest ocean wave in the world, with rides sometimes lasting more than a mile—is located about 200 miles south of Punta Negra, and is flanked by at least four other high-quality breaks. Lima's Pico Alto is the country's premier big-wave spot, with well-shaped rights and lefts (rights preferred) breaking up to 25 feet. The country's southern coast is lightly populated, hard to access, and rarely surfed. The number and quality of surf breaks, however, is thought to be nearly equal to that found in the north.

A few surfing historians argue that the sport originated in what is now called Peru, with pre-Inca fishermen as far back as 3000 B.C. riding waves on their recreation-designed *caballitos* ("little horses") made of bundled reeds. Modern surfing in Peru was practiced briefly in the early 1920s at Barranco, north of Lima, and natives riding homemade boards were featured in a 1924 issue of *Aire Libre,* a Peruvian sports magazine. But surfing didn't catch on here until 1939, when wealthy sugarcane heir Carlos Dogny, after learning to surf in Waikiki, returned to Lima with a board given to him by Hawaiian surfing legend Duke Kahanamoku. Dogny founded Club Waikiki at Lima's Miraflores in 1942, just after a local furniture company began producing a small number of hollow paddleboard/surfboards. (No other country had such a higher concentration of rich surfers, and the Peruvians generally shunned the locally made boards, preferring to ride imports from California or Hawaii; the country's first surf shop didn't open until 1975.)

Peru's first National Surfing Championships were held in 1955 and won by Alfredo Granda; other top Peruvian surfers of the '50s included Piti Block and Eduardo Arena. Club Waikiki hosted the first annual International Peruvian Surfing Contest in 1956, and by the end of the decade the renamed Peru International was second in surf world prestige only to the Makaha International. The contest ran continuously until 1974.

The Peruvian Surfing Federation (PSF) was formed in 1962, two years before Arena created the Lima-headquartered International Surfing Federation. As chairman of the organization, Arena brought the 1965 World Surfing Championships to Punta Rocas, Lima, with local big-wave specialist Felipe Pomar winning the event. Pomar, Hector Velarde, Sergio "Gordo" Barreda, and Oscar "Chino" Malpartida were the country's top performers in the '60s and early '70s. The PSF launched *Tabla Hawaiiana,* Peru's first surfing magazine, in 1970, and also hosted a number of surfing events, including the international Carlos Dogny Pro Surfing Classic in the early '80s, a series of second-tier pro tour events in the '90s, and the annual National Championships. (Lima surfer Magoo de la Rosa won the Nationals seven times between 1983 and 2001.) A small number of big-wave contests have been held at Pico Alto since 1993.

By 2003, Peru was home to 10 surf shops and about 10,000 surfers, with the 1985-founded *Tablista* serving as the country's only surfing publication. Surfing here remains a sport for the wealthy, and while poor surfers aren't discouraged from riding, expensive equipment keeps most out of the water. *Kon-Tiki: Surfboard Museum,* a history of Peruvian surfing by native surf historian Jose Schaffino, was published in 2001; the Peruvian surf is detailed in *The World Stormrider Guide* (2001). Peru has been featured in more than two dozen surf movies and videos over the decades, including *The Young Wave Hunters* (1964), *A Sea For Yourself* (1973), *We Got Surf* (1981), *Atlantic Crossing* (1989), *Jacked* (1995), and *Lunar Road* (2002). *See also* Chicama, Pico Alto, Waikiki Surf Club.

Peru International Surfing Championships
Annual surfing competition held in Lima, Peru, from 1956 to 1974, usually in February or March; the first international contest outside of America, and for many years one of the sport's biggest and most prestigious events. The Peru International Surfing Championships were conceived, developed, and underwritten by Club Waikiki, the upscale Lima beachfront surfing association, and directed by club member Carlos Rey y Lama. The 1956 debut event was little more than a friendly scrimmage between Club Waikiki and the San Onofre Surfing Club of California; it was held at Kon Tiki, and won by future International Surfing Federation president Eduardo Arena. For the 1957 event, the Peruvians competed against a team of Hawaiian surfers. A small group of Californians attended the third edition of the contest in 1961, won by *Surfer* magazine founder John Severson. The Makaha International had been running for several years by that time, but the 1962 Peru International—attended by teams from California, Hawaii, Australia, France, and Peru—represented, as Severson later wrote, "the first successful event where teams from most of the leading surfing areas of the world were represented." The contest also pointed out the need for an international set of surfing competition rules, as the Peruvians judged solely on speed and length of ride instead of maneuvers and form; changes were made in 1964. Two milestone Peru International events took place before decade's end: the 1965 contest doubled as the World Surfing Championships (won by Lima surfer Felipe Pomar and Joyce Hoffman of California), while the 1969 contest was the first professional surfing event outside of America (winner Mike Doyle of California earned $1,000). The site of the big-wave portion of the Peru International was changed to nearby Punta Rocas in 1965.

Divisions and events multiplied quickly in the Peru International, and by 1964 the weeklong event produced winners in Kon-Tiki (big surf), Waikiki Shorebreak (hotdogging), Waikiki First Break (midsize), Women's Hotdogging, Tandem Surfing, and nine different paddling races. (An overall champion was declared in the early versions of the contest, but the Kon Tiki winner has over the years come to be synonymous with the Peru International winner.) The Peruvians meanwhile became famous throughout surfdom for throwing the best surf parties, with local surfers—"bored rich kids, outrageous partiers," as Doyle later described them—insisting that their visitors fight bulls, race cars, drink endless rounds of *pisco* sours, and visit high-end brothels.

The Peruvian Surfing Federation replaced Club Waikiki as the overseer for the Peru International in 1973, the contest suffered an immediate drop in both prestige and attendance, and in 1975 the event was canceled. A series of international surfing contests held in Lima from 1979 to 2000, under different titles, are sometimes grouped together with the Peru International. Kon-Tiki winners of the Peru International are as follows:

1956:	Eduardo Arena
1957:	Conrad Canha
1961:	John Severson
1962:	Felipe Pomar
1963:	Paul Strauch
1964:	Fred Hemmings
1965:	Felipe Pomar
1966:	Felipe Pomar
1967:	Corky Carroll
1968:	Joey Cabell
1969:	Mike Doyle
1970:	Joey Cabell
1971:	Sergio Barreda
1972:	(unknown)
1973:	Sergio Barreda
1974:	Jeff Hakman

Peterson, Craig   Affable surf photographer and writer, best known for a popular series of *Surfer* magazine travel articles written with surf partner Kevin Naughton in the 1970s and '80s. Peterson was born (1955) in Washington, D.C., the son of an air force officer and artist mother, grew up in Maryland and Puerto Rico, moved with his family in 1962 to Huntington Beach, and began surfing at 10. At 16 he met Naughton, a slightly older Laguna Beach surfer, and a few months later the two were traveling through Central America in Peterson's 10-year-old VW Bug. *Surfer* magazine published the first installment of what would soon be called the "Naughton/Peterson adventures" in 1973. Both surfers wrote the text while Peterson—who'd had his first photo published in a 1970 issue of *Surfing* magazine—took pictures. *Surfer* ran 13 Naughton/Peterson stories between 1973 to 1989 (nine of them prior to 1979), each one a light, funny, good-natured account from an exotic or semi-exotic port of call, including Senegal, Ghana, Liberia, Morocco, France, Spain, Ireland, Mexico, and Barbados. Peterson became a staff photographer at *Surfer* in 1973, remained on the masthead until 1984, and produced six cover shots, three of them from his travels with Naughton. "Fiji: A South Pacific Wave Garden," Naughton and Peterson's 1984 *Surfer* feature, introduced the surf world at large to the perfect surf at Tavarua, Fiji. During his travels, Peterson worked as a gemologist in Sydney, a ski lift operator in Switzerland, and a boat captain in western Africa. He later worked as the photo editor for *Windsurf* magazine and for *Action Sports Retailer* magazine; in 2001 he founded the Cyberian Group, an online insurance company.

An 18-page retrospective of the Naughton/Peterson trips was published in a 1993 issue of the *Surfer's Journal* magazine, and two of their journeys were listed in *Surfer* magazine's 1995 article "The 10 Greatest Surf Trips of All Time." Peterson's photography has appeared in a number of illustrated surfing books, including *Stoked: A History of Surf Culture* (1997), *SurfRiders* (1997), and *The Perfect Day* (2001). *The Far Shore,* a documentary on the Naughton/Peterson travels, was produced in 2002. *See also* Kevin Naughton, surf travel.

Peterson, Michael   Pyrotechnic Australian regular-footer from Queensland's Gold Coast; winner of the Australian National Titles in 1972 and 1974; regarded by many as the world's most advanced high-performance surfer during the mid-'70s. Peterson was born (1953) and raised in the Gold Coast town of Kirra, and brought up by a single mother who ran a local pool hall. He began surfing at age 11, dropped out of school at 16, and the following year, competing in the juniors division, won the 1970 Bells Beach event and placed third in the 1970 Australian National Titles. Peterson was by then regularly surfing the bullet-fast point waves of Kirra and Burleigh Heads with local teenagers Wayne Bartholomew and Peter Townend, both of whom would win world pro titles before the end of the decade. Peterson won the

Michael Peterson

first of three Queensland state titles in 1971; in 1972 he won the first of two national titles; in 1973 he won the first of three consecutive Bells Beach men's division titles; in 1974 he won the debut Coca-Cola Surfabout, the richest pro contest ever held up to that point, earning $3,000 for the victory.

By that time, according to friend and rival Bartholomew, the darkly charismatic Peterson, "was flat-out the best surfer in the world." His surfing style was patterned directly on that of former world champion Nat Young—both surfers were tall, rangy, and powerful—but by 1974 he'd evolved into a completely unique performer. Energy seemed to radiate from Peterson's body while he surfed; his legs folded and straightened almost pneumatically, while his hands twitched and shook in response to an inner rhythm that put him onto fresh new angles, routes, and trajectories on the wave face. The effect was sometimes choppy, even frantic, but always thrilling; others rode with equal abandon and spontaneity, but none had Peterson's measure of raw talent. He could also channel his energy into the long, fast, subtle lines necessary to ride deep inside the tube at places like Kirra and Burleigh, and it's likely that he was the first surfer in the world to travel inside the barrel for more than 10 seconds at a stretch. Peterson visited Hawaii just three times, and proved to be just as electrifying in 15-footers as he was in small surf. His form was in many respects too eclectic to become mainstream, but a number of next-generation Australian surfers—most notably three-time world champion runner-up Gary Elkerton—adopted the Peterson style.

Tense and introverted, Peterson usually arrived on the beach just seconds before a match was due to start; he gave mumbled, head-down acceptance speeches at contest awards presentations, or didn't bother showing up at all. (He also had an explosive temper, and the public brawls he had with younger brother Tom—who later became one of Queensland's best surfboard shapers—were the stuff of local legend. Fighting in the water once as teenagers, Michael ripped Tom's board away from him and paddled it out past the shark nets; Tom then swam to shore, opened the hood of Michael's car, and hurled his brother's distributor and battery into the surf.) "I don't know why I have a lot of these problems," Peterson once told an Australian surf magazine. "I try to be like everybody else, but it's hard." By 1975, his paranoia was such that he hid in the parking lot after winning his third consecutive Bells Beach title, con-

vinced that if he walked up to accept his prize check, spectators "were going to start throwing things at me." Peterson—who earned a living by shaping surfboards—meanwhile wanted nothing to do with the sanitizing that went with professional surfing; he kept his hair long, hid behind mirrored aviator sunglasses, and wore dark and frequently grungy clothes.

Peterson won the first contest of the debut world pro tour in 1976, finishing the season world-ranked #7, but by the end of the year he'd become a near recluse. Twice in early 1977 he surfed through the prelims at local pro events, then vanished without competing in the finals. The 1977 Stubbies Pro at Burleigh would be Peterson's last hurrah. The surf was five foot and perfect, and while Peterson went through the event, as contest organizer Peter Drouyn later recalled, looking "shell-shocked, nervy and twitchy," he surfed brilliantly to take first place. Peterson rarely entered the water after that, turning up only when conditions at Kirra or Burleigh were at their best, and he quit surfing altogether in 1982. The following year he was arrested after a high-speed car chase from Kirra to Brisbane; he told police he was a CIA agent and was being followed by Russian spies. Diagnosed as paranoid schizophrenic, Peterson was institutionalized, then released to the care of his mother, with whom he still lives. He never married.

Peterson appeared in more than a dozen 1970s-era surf movies, including *Tracks* (1970), *A Sea for Yourself* (1973), *A Winter's Tale* (1974), *Playgrounds in Paradise* (1976), and *Tubular Swells* (1977). He was also briefly interviewed for the documentary *Legends: An Australian Surfing Perspective* (1994). Peterson was inducted into the Australian Surfing Hall of Fame in 1992; *Surfer* magazine named him in 1985 as one of "25 Surfers Whose Surfing Changed the Sport"; in 1999 the magazine cited him as one of the "25 Most Influential Surfers of the Century." *See also* Gold Coast, Kirra, Stubbies Classic.

Peterson, Pete   Gruff and durable surfer/paddler/lifeguard from Santa Monica, California; four-time winner of the Pacific Coast Surf Riding Championships (1932, 1936, 1938, and 1941), and tandem division winner in the 1966 World Surfing Championships. "He was muscular and lean, but didn't look like anything special," one of Peterson's contemporaries said. "But when he got in the water he was the best." Peterson was born (1913) in Rockport, Texas, and moved with his family to Santa Monica in the early '20s, where his parents built and ran the Crystal Beach Bathhouse. He began surfing at age eight, and started lifeguarding at the bathhouse pool three years later. In 1932 he was included among the first group of Santa Monica lifeguards, and his reputation over the next 15 years was built on his rescue work as much as his surfing and paddleboard accomplishments. Peterson invented a galvanized rescue flotation device, resembling a small buoy, which evolved into the modern rubber rescue tube, and he was twice the winner of the Pacific Coast Lifeguard Championships.

Paddleboard racing was then closely allied to both lifeguarding and surfing—the waterman ethic was, and largely remains, a combination of the three—and Peterson was a masterful paddler. He was described in Los Angeles–area newspaper articles as a "paddleboard and aquatic star," and "the bronzed paddle star of Santa Monica," and from the early '30s until the late '40s he consistently set and reset paddling marks in all categories, from 100-yard sprints to 26-mile open-ocean marathons. In a 1939 meet he was victorious in the 100 (his 30.7-second time beat a nine-year mark set by Sam Kahanamoku, Duke's brother), the 880, the one-mile, and the relay. Arlene, his wife, won the women's 100- and 440-yard sprints.

The quiet and reserved Peterson was also a first-rate craftsman. He designed and built a popular line of surfboards and paddleboards for Pacific System Homes in the late '30s, working mainly with balsa and redwood, and also made and sold boards out of his own house for $35 (or $45 with a five-coat spar varnish finish). As surf photographer Don James later noted, Peterson was particular, almost neurotic, about the condition of his own boards. "He was a neat freak," James remembered, "who never used any wax on the surface of his board for traction because he felt it violated the pristine look he so admired." Peterson dominated the Pacific Coast Surf Riding Championships, early modern surfing's biggest event, winning four times between 1928 and 1941—nobody else won more than once.

Peterson didn't surf competitively in '50s, then returned with spectacular results in the early and mid-'60s as a tandem rider. With various partners (including Patti Carey, Sharon Barker, and Barrie Algaw), he won the 1960 and 1962 West Coast Championships, the 1964 and 1966 United States Surfing Championships, the 1966 Makaha International, and the 1966 World Championships. *Life* magazine ran two photos of Peterson and Algaw winning the Worlds. "Every gremmie on the beach knows that surfing is a sport mainly for teenagers," the *Life* caption read. "But this in no way inhibited [Pete] Peterson, the nearly bald 53-year-old businessman from Santa Monica who specialized in tandem surfing." *Life* went on to note that the 6'2", 200-pound Peterson was "bigger than most competitors," and that over the past few years he'd outlasted "more partners than Fred Astaire."

Peterson occasionally worked as a Hollywood stuntman, but for 25 years, beginning in 1958, his primary occupation was the marine salvage business he owned and operated from the Santa Monica Pier. Much of Peterson's shop, along with many of his personal effects, were lost as the end of the pier collapsed during the El Niño storms of 1982 and 1983; on May 10, 1983, the 70-year-old Peterson died of a heart attack on his boat in nearby Marina del Rey. Peterson was inducted into the *International Surfing* Magazine Hall of Fame in 1966. He was married three times, and had two children. *See also* lifeguarding and surfing, Pacific Coast Surf Riding Championships, paddleboarding, tandem surfing.

Pezman, Steve Beatific surf magazine publisher from San Clemente, California; publisher of *Surfer* from 1971 to 1991, and cofounder of the *Surfer's Journal* in 1992. Pezman was born (1941) in Los Angeles, California, the son of a juvenile probation officer father and an actress mother, and raised in Hollywood and Brentwood. He took up surfing in 1958 at age 16, not long after his family moved to Long Beach; in 1966 he began shaping surfboards, and was soon doing freelance work for Hobie Surfboards and Weber Surfboards; in 1967 he cofounded Creative Design Surfboards in Newport Beach. Pezman's first surf articles were published by *Petersen's Surfing* in 1968; the following year he was hired by the magazine as an associate editor, and in mid-1970 he took the same title at *Surfer*. With a grand total of 11 months in the magazine field, Pezman was offered the publisher's job at *Surfer* after founder John Severson sold the magazine. Pezman helped *Surfer* maintain a gently counterculture editorial slant as the sport was "professionalized" in the '70s, then oversaw a period of enormous ad revenue growth in the late '80s, when issues for the first time topped 200 pages. He also served briefly as publisher for *Powder* and *Skateboarder* magazines, both issued by Surfer Publications; in 1980 he launched the *Surf Report,* a popular newsletter—and another *Surfer* title—that mapped out surf breaks around the world.

Pezman was 50 when he left *Surfer* in 1991; the following year he and his wife, Debbee, produced the first issue of the *Surfer's Journal,* a glossy quarterly targeted for older surfers. In 1997, Pezman and videographer Ira Opper produced *The Surfer's Journal: 50 Years of Surfing on Film,* a 12-part Outdoor Life Network cable TV series; *Great Waves,* the follow-up series, was produced in 1998, then *20th Century Surfers* (2000) and *Biographies* (2001). Pezman himself was featured in a 1995-aired PBS documentary *Liquid Stage: The Lure of Surfing.* Regarded as one of the last purists in surf publishing, Pezman has editorialized against surfing becoming an Olympic event, and was the lone voice of nonchalance after the American team finished a lowly 10th in the 2000 World Surfing Games. "Who cares?" Pezman wrote in a letter to *Surf News* magazine. "Why is it so important for the States to field the world's dominant surf team? What does it prove except to further turn wave riding into pro football? Let's just pick up our trash and go surfing." Pezman was inducted into the Huntington Beach Surfing Walk of Fame in 2002. He has been married twice, and has three children. *See also* surf magazines, Surfer magazine, Surfer's Journal magazine.

Philippines   The tropical and mountainous Philippines consists of more than 7,000 islands (900 inhabited) and is home to dozens of first-rate but fickle reefbreaks. The Philippine surf is generated by strong but sporadic typhoons, which in turn are influenced by the tropical monsoon season: the November-to-April northeast monsoon sends waves to the west side of the islands in the South China Sea, while the May-to-October southwest monsoon provides waves to the east side in the Pacific Ocean. The Philippines are divided into three main surfing areas: 1) Luzon, the large northernmost island, has the greatest number of surfers and surf breaks, including Charlie's Point, a reef wave made famous in the 1978 film *Apocalypse Now.* 2) Catanduanes, a small island just south of Luzon, features the speedy right-breaking wave called Majestics—the Philippines' first internationally known break. 3) Siargao, a small wave-filled island in the southeastern part of the archipelago, is home to Cloud Nine, often described as the country's best wave. There are hundreds of other breaks scat-

tered across the Philippine island chain, but difficult access and lack of consistent swells—a typical season produces 15 to 20 typhoons, each bringing between two to 10 days of head-high or larger surf—have kept many spots undiscovered. Water and air temperatures both range between the high 70s and low 80s. Sharp, shallow reefs are the primary surfing hazard, and many of the breaks are well removed from any kind of medical facility. The Philippines are also struck by an average of five typhoons per year, more than any other country.

The Philippines were first surfed by American servicemen stationed in Subic Bay on the island of Luzon in the early '60s. Photographs of the Philippine waves began turning up in surf magazines as early as 1980, but the country wasn't really noticed until a 1993 *Surfer* story featured California pros Evan Slater and Taylor Knox pulling into the flawless right-breaking tubes at Cloud Nine. (American-born surf explorer and convicted drug smuggler Mike Boyum had discovered the break four years earlier, and died on a nearby beach after a 45-day fast.)

Four surf camps opened in the Philippines in the mid-'80s. By 2003, the country was home to roughly 15 surf camps and five makeshift surf shops, as well as a native-born surfing population of about 1,200. The annual Siargao International Cup, an Australian-administered pro surf contest ran in 1996 and 1997. The Philippine waves are featured in a small number of surf videos, including *Overdrive* (1993) and *Surf Adventures* (1990); Catandvanes area surf breaks are detailed in *The World Stormrider Guide* (2001). *See also* Cloud Nine.

Phillips, Walt   Baby-faced surf media impresario from Los Angeles, California. Phillips spent two years in the marines just after high school, then quickly made his first surf movie, *Sunset Surf Craze,* in 1959. He went on to produce another half-dozen films, including *Surf Mania* (1960), *Once Upon a Wave* (1963), and *Dr. Strangesurf* (1965). He founded *Surfing Illustrated* magazine in 1962, serving as publisher, editor, photo editor, art director, and distributor; Phillips himself was the subject of two *Surfing Illustrated* features, including "The Four Faces of Walt Phillips," in which he's immodestly nicknamed "Mr. Surfer." Just over a dozen episodes of his *Surf's Up* television show were aired in the Los Angeles area in 1964, and another short-lived nationally syndicated show, *Walt Phillips' Surfing World,* debuted the following year.

Surfing Illustrated folded in 1967. Phillips wrote articles for *Surfing* in 1970, and in 1978 worked briefly for *Surf,* a Florida-based magazine.

Pico Alto   Peru's top big-wave reefbreak, located about 27 miles south of Lima; often compared to Sunset Beach in Hawaii. Pico Alto begins to take shape at about eight to 10 foot, can hold virtually any size, and has been seen maintaining form at 35 foot, with waves cresting nearly one mile from the rock- and cliff-lined shore. It breaks both left and right, but rights are preferred; rides can last for up to three hundred yards. Pico Alto is generally biggest from March to August, and an average year will produce at least 10 days of 15-foot or larger surf. Although Pico Alto has tube sections, the wave is broad-based and sloped, unlike the vertical walls of Hawaii's Waimea Bay or Maverick's in California. Surfers aren't pushed down to the reef after a wipeout at Pico Alto, but are often held underwater for a lung-testing period of time, up to 20 seconds or more, and rolled violently shoreward. The midwinter water temperature in the Lima area is about 60, while the average daytime air temperature is 65. Gray skies and a light haze can partially obscure the view of Pico Alto from the beach.

Peruvian big-wave goofyfooter Joaquin Miro Quesada named the break "Pico Alto" (High Peak) minutes after he became the first to ride it on June 29, 1965. (Quesada was killed two years later while surfing at Pipeline in Hawaii.) Reigning world champion Felipe Pomar of Lima rode some 15-footers at Pico Alto in 1966, and wrote "Pico Alto is Better Than Sunset," a short *Surfer* magazine feature that introduced the

Pico Alto

break to the surf world at large. Pomar, along with big-wave specialist Ivo Hunza and a few other Peruvians, occasionally surfed here over the next 12 years; from 1979 to 1986, as big-wave surfing fell out of fashion, the churning Pico Alto peaks went unridden. In 1987, Lima surfers Titi de Cole, Max de la Rosa, Magoo de la Rosa, Tony Maldi, and veteran Felipe Pomar—all with big-wave experience from Hawaii—"rediscovered" Pico Alto when a 15-foot swell moved in during Easter week. A few days later, as the surf hit 20 foot, the Peruvians were joined by American big-wave riders Mark Foo, James Jones, and Richard Schmidt, along with photographer Robert Beck, who became the first to shoot Pico Alto from the water. The break has since been surfed regularly. The 1993 Jose Rizo Patron Invitational, named after the contest organizer and won by local surfer Fernando Paraud, was the first surf contest held at Pico Alto. Pico Alto is featured in *Atlantic Crossing,* a 1989 surf movie.

pier   Piers were originally built as cargo transfer points, long before they were used for strolling and recreational fishing. They've also been a part of the surfing environment for more than a century; in a Waikiki photograph taken in the late 1890s, a small pier juts into the water between a solitary loincloth-wearing surfer and Diamond Head. First-generation Southern California surfers in the 1920s rode waves adjacent to piers in Hermosa, Venice, and Santa Monica; surfing patron Duke Kahanamoku rode on the west side of the Huntington Beach Pier in 1924, and two years later surfboard designer Tom Blake and friend Sam Reid became the first to surf Malibu, ending their rides about 50 yards from the Malibu Pier. All piers were then made of wood, and might be broken like so much kindling if met by a full-strength winter storm. Beginning in the 1940s, piers were more often made from steel and concrete.

Piers can have a direct effect on the surf, as littoral currents react to pilings and form nearby channels and sandbars. During a heavy swell, surfers will sometimes avoid the paddle-out by making a quick and illegal jump from the pier into deeper water beyond the surf line. Piers have also long served as a gathering place for surfers. "We didn't ride at State Park to the north and we didn't surf at Golden West Street to the south," Huntington Beach regular and 1959 West Coast Surfing Championship winner Jack Haley once said. "We surfed the pier. It was an honor; you had people standing up there, looking down, applauding and yelling." Haley also recalled the pre-wetsuit era of the '50s when he and his friends, during winter months, would tie a gallon of red wine to a rope and lower it off the pier railing; the surfers drank wine between rides to keep warm. Huntington Pier was the site of the West Coast Surfing Championships from 1959 to 1963 and the United States Surfing Championships from 1964 to 1972, with contestants in the latter having to wear plastic crash helmets to guard against possible injuries from "shooting" the pier (threading the pilings). San Diego's Ocean Beach Pier was the site of the 1966 and 1972 World Surfing Championships. Surf photographers often used piers as a framing device or backdrop, or as an elevated vantage point from which to shoot. Piers have also been rendered in all manner of surf art, and used in dozens of surf world stickers, decals, and logotypes. Piers have contributed to thousands of surfer injuries, and a small number of surfer deaths. Twenty-year-old Nick Gabaldon, America's first black surfer, was killed when he ran into Malibu Pier following a long ride from the top of the point in 1951; 16-year-old Huntington Beach High School student Joshua Hall died after trying to shoot the Huntington Pier in 1997.

pig board   Wide-hipped, blunt-tailed surfboard, generally about 10 feet long and weighing 25 to 30 pounds, invented and popularized in the mid-1950s by California board-maker Dale Velzy. The pig design is often cited as the modern longboard prototype. By putting more area in the tail and less in the nose, the pig, compared to the more parallel-railed boards of the time, turned faster and fit into more critical sections on the wave. Hotdog surfing was more or less invented on the pig by riders like Dewey Weber. "Those boards changed everything," Velzy later recalled. "We just went nuts from then on." The Weber Pig, made by Weber Surfboards in 1970–71, was essentially a smaller, lighter version of the Velzy pig. Weber's version didn't catch on, but wide-backed boards would periodically return to fashion over the years. *See also* chip board, Malibu board.

pigdog   A backside tuberiding stance in which the rider crouches, drops the rear knee, brings the trailing arm forward, and grabs onto the board's shoreward-facing rail, adjacent to the front foot. The pigdog is an updated variation on the rail-grab stance made popular by California surfer John Peck in the

early '60s. Hawaiian surfer Dane Kealoha is often given credit for inventing the pigdog technique, if not the name, in the early '80s. "Pigdog" is Australian slang for pitbull or bull terrier; the connection between the animal and the surfing maneuver is unclear, except perhaps for the fact that the crouching rail-grab tuberide requires a kind of dogged determination. While the pigdog is both functional and popular, the upright, no-rail-grab stance is considered the ultimate form of backside tuberiding. *See also* rail grab.

pigment   Highly concentrated coloring agent added to resin, usually during the fiberglass lamination process. Pigments are either translucent (tints) or opaque, and are generally used to color broad areas of the surfboard—often the entire board. Pigmented boards were popular in the '50s, '60s, and '70s; airbrushing has since become the board-coloring standard.

Pike, Bob   Intrepid and somewhat reclusive regular-footer from Manly Beach, Sydney; often described as the original Australian big-wave surfer. Pike was born (1940) and raised in Sydney, began surfing at age 14, and in 1961 made his first visit to the North Shore of Oahu—the big-wave Mecca, then and now. "I felt like I'd discovered where my umbilical cord was connected to," Pike later said of his introduction to the tropics. American surfers got a look at Pike's driving

Bob Pike

big-wave style in *Surfing Hollow Days* (1962), *Angry Sea* (1963), and other early '60s surf movies. Pike won the small-wave portion of the 1962 Peru International, the first overseas win by an Australian surfer. As the Australian surf industry blossomed in the mid-'60s, Pike removed himself almost entirely from the commercial surf scene and became a fireman. "If nobody had ever heard of me," Pike said in a 1998 interview with *Australian Longboarding* magazine, "if no one had ever known if I'd surfed or not, it wouldn't have mattered one iota. I did it because I loved doing it." The following year, the 59-year-old Pike killed himself by asphyxiation.

pinstripe, pinline   Thin, decorative stripe on the deck of a surfboard, typically running one or two inches inside the board's perimeter. Pinstriping (or pinlining) was introduced to board-making in the early '50s; by the early '60s it had become an art form of sorts. Originally pinstriping was done after the sanding coat and before the gloss coat, and consisted of pigmented resin brushed between carefully laid strips of masking tape. Resin-based pinstriping all but disappeared in the late '70s, when airbrushing was introduced as a faster and lighter board-coloring alternative. Pinstripes on today's boards are nearly all done by airbrush. *See also* gloss coat, resin.

pintail   Narrow, streamlined, pointed tail design, used almost exclusively on paddle-in (as distinct from tow-in) big-wave surfboards. Average tail width for a 10-foot pintail surfboard, measured one foot from the rear tip, is nine or 10 inches—about four inches narrower than the tail width of a small-wave board—and this reduced area is in large part what allows the board to adhere to the face of a giant wave. Hawaiian surfer George Downing made one of the first pintail boards in 1951. The Mike Hynson Gun model, made by Gordon & Smith Surfboards in the mid-'60s, was one of the only stock-made pintails. The rounded-pintail (or round pin), a blunter version of the pintail, has long been the most popular tail design for boards used in medium-sized waves, and is often used for small-wave boards as well. *See also* roundtail, squaretail, squashtail, swallowtail.

Pipeline   Beautiful but ferocious Hawaiian surf break located on the North Shore of Oahu, regarded since the early 1960s as the sport's premier tube; site of the venerable Pipeline Masters competition.

Pipeline, with Australian Tom Carroll

Pipeline is best on a westerly swell, and along with the rest of the North Shore, breaks most often from October to March. While "Pipeline" specifically refers to the left-breaking wave, it can also be used to include Backdoor, the right-breaking wave attached to the Pipeline peak that opens up when the swell angles in from the north or northwest; surfers will often take off side by side, one riding Pipeline, the other riding the Backdoor right. Off-the-Wall, a break similar to Backdoor, is located a short distance to the west. Pipeline itself is made up of a series of reefs. First Reef, a flat lava plateau broken up by a few narrow crevasses and located less than 75 yards offshore, is the premier break; an incoming wave, shaped into a peak by outside reefs, will abruptly strike First Reef and pitch out into the hallmark Pipeline tube, which usually spins and grinds for about seven seconds, tapering down the whole time, before expiring over a sandy area to the east. Most Pipeline waves will "spit"—eject a misty horizontal blast of water from the mouth of the tube—at least once. Sand deposits sometimes affect the shape of the wave at First Reef; the break is temperamental as a rule, and might come into top form just a half-dozen days a season. Second Reef Pipeline is located about 75 yards out from the regular Pipeline lineup, and comes into play when the surf hits 10 or 12 foot. Waves here often do little more than fringe along the crest, which allows the rider to make an early entry and set the ride up as the swell moves toward First Reef. Third Reef Pipeline, a shifty and foaming big-wave break located another 300 yards offshore, is rarely surfed. Pipeline has justly earned a reputation as the world's most dangerous surf spot; waves here break with tremendous force over a shallow reef (usually between six and 10 feet deep), and can be difficult to read; the omnipresent photo gallery attracts surfers, and helps create an aggressive mood in the lineup, which in turn leads to bad wave selection, insane risk taking, injuries, and even death. It is estimated that a surfer dies at Pipeline every other year. On a single day in December 1998, there were 30 injuries at Pipeline, including a near fatality.

There are competing claims as to who was the first surfer to ride Pipeline, but the honor is generally given to Phil Edwards of California, who paddled out on a four-foot day at what was then called Banzai Beach in mid-December 1961, then returned the following morning with filmmaker Bruce Brown, when the waves were six to eight foot. Edwards rode a beautiful eight-footer that showed up on Brown's 1962 surf film *Surfing Hollow Days*. It was board-maker Mike Diffenderfer, also of California, who suggested to Brown that he call the break Pipeline, after noticing that the waves looked like the giant concrete pipes being used in a nearby construction project. By the end of the following year, California surfers Butch Van Artsdalen and John Peck had set the early standard for Pipeline surfing; Van Artsdalen's tuberiding earned him the title of "Mr. Pipeline." In 1963 the break gained recognition even among nonsurfers, as the Chantays' "Pipeline" instrumental went to #4 on the national charts; the following year Pipeline was featured in Columbia Pictures' *Ride the Wild Surf*. As tuberiding became the focus of high-performance surfing in the late '60s during the shortboard revolution, Pipeline became the sport's ultimate break. Tom Stone and Jock Sutherland of Hawaii were riding completely behind the curl by 1969; Gerry Lopez, another Hawaiian, not only went deeper the following year, but did so with a pared-down style that became a benchmark for surfing grace and elegance. "You're always right on the edge at Pipeline," Lopez later remarked, admitting that he was never quite as serene as he appeared. "You're always hanging by your fingertips; you never really have it under control. But I guess that's the appeal of the place." (Rory Russell, second-in-command to Lopez at Pipeline in the early and mid-'70s, and given to earthier phrasing, once described the takeoff at Pipeline as "a goddamn heart-stopper.") Regularfoot surfers, long at a disadvantage to goofyfooters at Pipeline as they ride with

their backs to the wave, made a strong bid for parity during the Shaun Tomson–led "backside attack" season of 1975–76. The Pipeline Masters was by then in its fifth year, and well on its way to becoming the sport's premier surf contest. Pipeline continued the crossover into the mainstream: *Sports Illustrated* published a 1982 cover story on the break, "Thunder from the Sea," while the Masters was featured each year on ABC's *Wide World of Sports*. Surfers continued to ride deeper and longer in the tube at Pipeline. Regularfooters, led by six-time world champion and five-time Masters champion Kelly Slater of Florida, had by the mid-'90s all but equaled the goofyfooters' performances.

Aside from those already mentioned, a short list of top Pipeline surfers over the decades, in roughly chronological order, would include Jackie Eberly, Rory Russell, Sam Hawk, Jeff Crawford, Jackie Dunn, Michael Ho, Larry Blair, Dane Kealoha, Tom Carroll, Ronnie Burns, Mike Cunningham, Tom Curren, Mike Stewart, Derek Ho, Johnny-Boy Gomes, Sunny Garcia, Liam McNamara, Rob Machado, Andy Irons, Bruce Irons, and Tamayo Perry.

The surf world's most photographed and filmed wave by far, Pipeline has been featured in roughly three-quarters of all surf movies and videos ever made, and been listed on every surf magazine's best waves list. Pipeline was also featured in *Great Waves*, a 1998 Outdoor Life Network documentary series. Aside from the Masters, Pipeline-held competitions include the HIC Pipeline Pro, the Pipeline Bodysurfing Classic, and the Mike Stewart International Pipeline Pro. *See also* Gerry Lopez, Pipeline Masters, tuberiding.

Pipeline Masters   Annual men's-only professional surfing competition held in December at Pipeline on the North Shore of Oahu; founded in 1971 by former world surfing champion Fred Hemmings of Hawaii. Because the explosive tubes at Pipeline are regarded as one of the great wonders of the surfing world, and because the waves here break just 75 yards off the beach, the Pipeline Masers has long been regarded as the sport's top surfing contest. Different from every other surfing contest in the world—with the exception of the Tahiti Pro, held in Pipeline-like barrels at Teahupoo—the Masters is designed primarily as a tuberiding event. Turns and cutbacks are scored, but if the surf is cooperating (about one in seven Masters is plagued by nonhollow waves), the win goes to the surfer who can ride deepest in the tube for the longest period of time in match after match. Virtually every edition of the Masters has produced at least a few moments of high drama, and more often than not it proves to be the best event of the pro tour.

The Hawaiian Masters, as it was originally known, was conceived and developed by Fred Hemmings three years after he won the 1968 World Surfing Championships. Continental Airlines contributed the $1,000 prize purse to the inaugural Masters. Just six surfers were invited to the single-heat event, held December 16 in "a rather docile six-foot-plus swell," as Hemmings later recalled. The Masters officials area consisted of some plastic bunting, 10 metal folding chairs, and a card table; fewer than 50 spectators were scattered across the beach. Hawaiian pro surfer Jeff Hakman took the $500 first-place check in an event that went completely unreported in the surf press. The most intriguing aspect to the debut Masters is that Pipeline prodigy Gerry Lopez of Hawaii was a no-show—allegedly because third-place finisher Corky Carroll of California told Lopez the event had been postponed. The Masters evolved slowly; it was a single-heat event until 1975, and the prize purse didn't exceed $10,000 until 1980. The Masters was included in the world pro tour's debut season in 1976, and has been part of the tour every year except 1983, 1984, 1985, and 2001. It was the world tour's season finale in 1992 and 1993, from 1995 to 2000, and in 2002.

Surf history has often been made at the Masters. Australian Simon Anderson won in 1981 and showed that his new tri-fin surfboard, already proven in smaller surf, worked just as well in the big, powerful Hawaiian waves. Hawaiian surfer Michael Ho won the following year with his right wrist in a cast. In 1983, competitor Steve Massefeller was nearly killed after suffering a massive head injury during a heat. World champions Derek Ho and Tom Carroll both won multiple Masters titles, but it was six-time world champion Kelly Slater of Florida who became the dominant Masters surfer, winning the event five times during the '90s, including a victory in 1995 that is still regarded as the most thrilling afternoon in pro surfing history.

The surf video, *25 Years of Pipeline,* was released in 1995 to commemorate the Masters 25th anniversary; *The Pipeline Masters,* a one-hour documentary in honor of the event's 30th anniversary, came out in 2001. ABC-TV's *Wide World of Sports* covered the Masters from 1972 to 1982; NBC aired the 2001 event.

Pipeline Masters

Pipeline Masters sponsors over the years have included Primo, O'Neill, Offshore, Marui, Chiemsee, Mountain Dew, and X-Box; the event is part of the Triple Crown of Surfing, a three-contest series held on the North Shore. Prize money for the Masters topped $100,000 in 1991; the 2002 event was worth $250,000. Pipeline Masters winners:

1971:	Jeff Hakman
1972:	Gerry Lopez
1973:	Gerry Lopez
1974:	Jeff Crawford
1975:	Shaun Tomson
1976:	Rory Russell
1977:	Rory Russell
1978:	Larry Blair
1979:	Larry Blair
1980:	Mark Richards
1981:	Simon Anderson
1982:	Michael Ho
1983:	Dane Kealoha
1984:	Joey Buran
1985:	Mark Occhilupo
1986:	Derek Ho
1987:	Tom Carroll
1988:	Robbie Page
1989:	Gary Elkerton
1990:	Tom Carroll
1991:	Tom Carroll
1992:	Kelly Slater
1993:	Derek Ho
1994:	Kelly Slater
1995:	Kelly Slater
1996:	Kelly Slater

1997:   Johnny-Boy Gomes
1998:   Jake Paterson
1999:   Kelly Slater
2000:   Rob Machado
2001:   Bruce Irons
2002:   Andy Irons

Piter, Didier   Cosmopolitan pro surfer from Hossegor, France; three-time European champion (1992, 1994, and 2000), and winner of the 1996 European Professional Surfing Association tour. Piter was born (1971) and raised in Dakar, Senegal, and began surfing at age 12. He moved to Paris in 1989 to attend Lincoln International Business School, and won the first of four French National Championships the next year (winning again in 1993, 1994, and 2000). The dark-haired goofyfooter also won the California National Scholastic Surfing Association college title in 1993 while completing his master's degree in international business and marketing at San Diego State University. He meanwhile discovered an affinity for big, powerful surf, and put in world-class performances at breaks like Pipeline and Teahupoo. He appeared in nearly a dozen surf videos, including *On the Road with Spike* (1996), *The Moment* (1999), and *Better Days* (2000). Since 2000, Piter has worked in marketing for Gotcha Europe.

planer   Handheld, rotary-blade, chain- or belt-driven power tool used by surfboard shapers to sculpt a board from a polyurethane foam blank. Planers, originally used by carpenters for tasks like trimming doors to fit into doorjambs, were first used on surfboards in 1951 by Southern California board-building pioneer Dale Velzy. Previously, boards were shaped with axes, knives, hand planers, Surforms, and sandpaper. The shoe-box-sized power planer is held in both hands and run along the length of the surfboard blank, removing layers of foam in a series of "cuts" with the depth of each cut determined by adjusting the planer's blade setting. Sandpaper is then used to smooth out the flats and angles left by the planer. While Velzy maintains his original chain-driven, dual-blade Mall planer was both "the first and the best," virtually all contemporary shapers agree that the belt-driven Skill 100 is tops—despite the fact that it was discontinued in the mid-'80s. *See also* surfboard construction, surfboard shaping.

planing surface   A surfboard's bottom surface; more specifically, the area of the board that planes across the water—a definition that may exclude the last foot or so of the nose section. A board's planing surface is usually made up of some combination of flat area, concavity (single concave or side-by-side double concave), convexity, or vee panels. While post–World War II California board-maker Bob Simmons paid attention to the surfboard's bottom configuration, the planing surface was for the most part an ignored aspect of board design until the late-'60s shortboard revolution, when all design elements were rethought and reconfigured. It was quickly discovered that a board's planing surface was as important to its performance as outline, foil, rocker, and fin setup. *See also* belly, bonzer, bottom, channel bottom, concave, reverse vee, vee.

plank surfboard   Type of finless solid-wood surfboard used from antiquity until the 1940s. While it's been argued that the ancient Peruvian reed-bundled *caballito* ("little horse") is the original surf craft, the surfboard as it exists today traces its roots back to the ancient Hawaiian *olo* or *alaia*—plank-style boards made of wiliwili, koa, or breadfruit wood. (The word "plank" didn't come into use until the early 1930s, with the popularization of the hollow "cigar-box" board.) As surfing was exported from Hawaii to mainland America, Australia, New Zealand, and South Africa during the first few decades of the 20th century, few changes were made to the basic plank board, except for weight. Surfing patriarch Duke Kahanamoku of Hawaii crafted a blunt-nosed, square-tailed redwood board for himself in 1910 that was 10 feet long, 23 inches wide, 3 inches thick, and weighed

Plank surfboard

70 pounds. Three decades later, the commercially made Pacific System Homes "Waikiki" model, with roughly the same measurements as Kahanamoku's board, but made primarily out of pine, weighed just over 43 pounds.

Post–19th-century planks were made from either a single piece of wood (usually redwood) or a glued-together wood composite (often pine or balsa, edged in redwood). Boards were shaped by saw, drawknife, hand planer, and sandpaper, sometimes stained, then finished with multiple coats of varnish. A design of some sort—the board-owner's name, or the name and logo of his club—was often painted, inlaid, or burned into the board's deck, near the nose. Angling across the wave face (as opposed to riding straight for shore) came into vogue around 1910, but that was more or less the plank's performance limit. Surfing maneuvers, such as they were, more often included bicep-flexing poses, backward riding, headstands, and other tricks.

Wisconsin-born surfer/board-maker Tom Blake introduced the lighter and buoyant hollow board in 1929, and it quickly became a popular alternative to the plank. A group of teenage Hawaiian surfers led by John Kelly and Wally Froiseth invented the hot curl in 1937, a narrow-tailed version of the plank that al-lowed a tighter angle on the wave face. The hot curl is the prototype big-wave board. After World War II, a group of Malibu-based surfer/shapers including Bob Simmons, Joe Quigg, and Matt Kivlin, began working on a series of finned balsa boards that rendered the plank obsolete.

Plank-board riding is featured in *Surfing in the 1930s,* a video documentary released in 1994, and can be glimpsed in more than a half-dozen pre–World War II Hollywood movies, including *Waikiki Wedding* (1937) and *Honolulu* (1939). Plank boards had become collectible by the early 1990s, and by the turn of the century were selling at auction for up to $10,000. The plank board is occasionally referred to as a "slab." *See also* hollow board, hot curl board.

planshape   *See* outline.

pocket   Steep section of the wave face just ahead of the whitewater; more closely defined as the area within the shadow of the falling curl. "All pockets are not the same," Hawaiian big-wave surfer Mark Foo wrote in 1979. "At Burleigh Heads [Australia] the pocket is low on the wave face, at Uluwatu [Indone-sia] it's high, and at Backdoor [Hawaii] the entire

wave face is a pocket." The surfer riding "in the pocket" is almost but not quite in the tube. Skilled surfers will perform hairpin turns in the pocket or begin midair maneuvers by launching up and out of the pocket. Narrow, streamlined surfboards in the late '60s and early '70s were often called "pocket rockets." *See also* tube.

Point Break   Melodramatic 1991 R-rated thriller from 20th Century Fox starring bleach-blond Patrick Swayze as Bodhi, a surfer/philosopher/bank robber, with Keanu Reeves as FBI agent and surf acolyte Johnny Utah. James Cameron (*Titanic*) was *Point Break*'s executive producer and an uncredited writer. Gary Busey, familiar to surfers as Leroy in 1978's *Big Wednesday,* costars as Reeves's partner. Utah becomes a surfer after going undercover to infiltrate Bodhi's gang of wave-riding criminals, and his learning process leads to *Point Break*'s one good line: When an angry FBI superior demands to know if Utah has "anything even *remotely* interesting" to report after spending days with Bodhi on the beach and in the surf, Utah solemnly answers, "I caught my first tube today." The *Washington Post* called *Point Break* "gor-geous but dumb," and noted that Reeves "seems per-petually on the verge of a thought that can't quite work its way to the surface." Utah chases Bodhi to Bells Beach, Australia, where the bad guy paddles out to meet a watery death in huge surf. The "Bells" surfing footage was in fact shot at Waimea Bay, with Hawaiian surfer Darrick Doerner earning $10,000 for the stunt wipeout. *See also* Hollywood and surfing.

pointbreak   Type of wave that breaks around a point of land. Pointbreak surf is generally long, evenly tapered, and predictable, and surfers who ride pointbreaks often develop a smooth and elegant style. It's often noted that three-time world cham-pion Tom Curren developed his fluid technique in the point surf near his home in Santa Barbara, Cali-fornia. Pointbreaks are often lined with rocks and boulders and are located almost exclusively on coasts bordered by hills or mountains. Low-lying sandy coastlines, as found in the southern half of the east-ern seaboard, are virtually pointbreak-free, as are the reef-fringed islands in the tropics. Pointbreaks on a given stretch of coastline, all formed under the influ-ence of the same dominant nearshore current, tend to produce waves that break in the same direction. Nearly all pointbreaks in California and on the east coast of Australia, for example, break to the right.

A majority of pointbreaks, including Malibu and Rincon in California, are formed by rivermouth alluvial fans; unlike most reef breaks, which tend to break further off shore, pointbreaks are often affected by sand deposits. Kirra Point, in Queensland, Australia, while justly regarded as one of the world's best pointbreaks, is in fact a combination point-jetty break, and is greatly affected by sand flow.

Pointbreaks as a rule aren't big-wave spots. Because pointbreak waves are generally longer and easier to read than beachbreak waves, and less hazardous than reefbreaks—the other two primary categories of surf breaks—they tend to be the most crowded type of surf spot. Jeffreys Bay in South Africa is regarded by many as the world's premier pointbreak. *See also* beachbreak, reefbreak.

politics and surfing   Surfing and politics intersected for the first time in the early 1960s, as Southern California beach communities—responding to the injury risk posed by mixing board-riders and swimmers, and to counter a perceived threat from "surf hooliganism"—began passing legislation to ban or restrict surfing along popular beaches. The United States Surfing Association (USSA) was founded in 1961 as an advocacy group for the sport, and representatives from the USSA's Committee for Legal Action on Surfing Legislation spoke at city council meetings at which surfing-related issues were debated. Draconian antisurfing measures (outright bans, for example) were repealed, but surfing restrictions were for the most part left in place. Politics had meanwhile proven to be a tough sell on surfers, and by mid-decade the USSA reinvented itself as an administrative group for surfing competition. Similar mid-'60s legislative fights, with similar results, were also waged in Australia, New Zealand, and the American eastern seaboard.

Beach access issues were the main concern of surfing activists in the '70s, with issues laid out region by region in "Who Controls the Beaches?," a mid-decade series published by *Surfing* magazine. The 1967-founded Eastern Surfing Association (ESA) had become the sport's most politicized group, speaking out at hearings against developers, commercial fishermen, municipalities, oil companies, and anyone else who might keep East Coast surfers out of the water. The ESA produced the Beach Access and Preservation survey in 1974, which sought to "identify areas where surfing is being treated unfairly and to develop methods of correcting inequities," often

by lobbying regional, state, and national politicians. Another front was opened in 1984 with the formation of the Surfrider Foundation environmental group, and clean-water politics—demonstrating, lobbying, and campaigning—have been a part of the sport ever since.

South Africa's race-segregating apartheid policies produced a low point in surfing's political history. When dark-skinned surfers, including Hawaiian big-wave master Eddie Aikau, were prevented from riding South Africa's whites-only beaches in the '60s and '70s, it was of little concern to the surf world at large. "I read the article and noticed the bit in there about the Negro on the segregated beach," a Floridian wrote in response to a *Surfer* magazine article on South Africa. "It bothered me some, but I figured I'd let it slide." World pro circuit contests were held in South Africa long after other sports groups began boycotting the country to protest apartheid. When top pro surfers Tom Curren, Martin Potter, and Tom Carroll all boycotted the 1985 world circuit events in South Africa, the tour's executive director responded by saying, "We don't have a political position," and that the events would continue. Surfing and politics met again in the '90s as Fijian surf resort owners clashed with government officials over exclusive reef-use rights—an issue that to this day remains unresolved.

A small number of surfers have become politicians, the best known being 1968 world champion Fred Hemmings from Hawaii, a Republican who served in the state House of Representatives from 1984 to 1990, and was elected to the state senate in 2000. Other surfers have mounted political campaigns of one kind or another over the years: former world champion Nat Young of Australia ran as a state parliament Labor Party candidate in 1986; boardmaker Maurice Cole, also of Australia, rallied surfers to help vote race-baiting conservative legislator Pauline Hanson out of office in 1998. But the sport's rank and file have remained politically static—an "immovable do-nothing majority," as described by *Surfer* magazine in 2000. It's thought that while surfers are nearly all left-leaning on environmental issues, they nonetheless split their vote—in America—between the Democrat and Republican parties. *See also* environmentalism and surfing, Fred Hemmings, Surfrider Foundation.

Polynesia   Vast island group in the Pacific Ocean, encompassing about 300 islands and extending roughly 5,000 miles from the Midway Islands in the north to New Zealand; includes the Hawaiian Islands, the Cook Islands, Christmas Island, Tonga, and Easter Island. While land and climate differ greatly throughout the region, Polynesia ("many islands") is justly famous for its white-sand beaches, gentle ocean breezes, swaying palm trees, and wave-fringed reefs. Polynesia is also generally regarded as the birthplace of surfing.

polyurethane foam Light, rigid, gritty, chemical-based material molded into ready-to-shape surfboard shaped blanks; the core element for the vast majority of surfboards produced since the late 1950s as a replacement for balsa wood—a changeover often described as the single most important technological breakthrough in surfboard construction. Multipurpose polyurethane was invented by American chemists during World War II, and would later be used as upholstery material, heat insulation, carpeting, and safety padding. Other types of foam were invented around the same time. Los Angeles surfboard design innovator Bob Simmons was the first to use foam for surfboard construction, making a "sandwich" board in 1947 by layering plywood over a core of polystyrene foam—better known as Styrofoam. Working with fellow board-makers Matt Kivlin and Joe Quigg, Simmons sold more than 100 sandwich boards before decade's end, then gave up on the process as too labor-intensive. South African surf pioneer John Whitmore made a few similar boards in 1954. Styrofoam, as all interested board-makers of the period quickly learned, dissolves beneath the polyester resins used in the fiberglassing process. Balsa had meanwhile proven hard to find at times, as well as inconsistent in density. Surfboard manufacturers needed a core material that was cheap, consistent, and plentiful.

Experimentation with polyurethane foam—which unlike Styrofoam does bond with polyester resins—began in the mid-'50s, primarily by Santa Monica surfer Dave Sweet, who designed and built a wood-clamped concrete mold in his rented apartment. Sweet figured out through trial and error the precise chemical mixture (foam components come in a liquid state), as well as the amount of liquid required to make a blank (the combined and poured solution expands to about 20 times its original volume). Air pockets in blanks were a problem; fiberglass laminators in the early years of foam regularly covered air-pocket blemishes by mixing a light

opaque color into the resin during the laminating process; the resulting light blue, violet, and yellow surfboards of the late '50s were referred to as "Easter boards." For added strength, blanks were soon bisected lengthwise and glued back together with a thin strip of wood known as a "stringer." Sweet introduced the first commercially made polyurethane foam boards in 1956. Two years later, leading board manufacturer Hobie Alter—partners with laminator Gordon "Grubby" Clark in a secret foam-making plant in Laguna Canyon—abruptly changed the core material used in all Hobie Surfboards from balsa to foam, and by the end of the decade balsa boards had been phased out almost entirely. (Clark broke away from Hobie in 1961 to form Clark Foam, and eventually all but cornered the market on blanks.) Some surfboard shapers resisted the new synthetic material; most embraced it. "After balsa," Alter later said of the wood-to-foam switch, "it was like shaping a stick of butter."

While today's blanks are far lighter and less dense than those produced in decades past, the basic chemical recipe and molding process for polyurethane foam is virtually unchanged. As the outer layer is generally the strongest part of the blank, molds now produce blanks that closely resemble a finished shape. Foam blanks are sold wholesale for about $40 to $80 per unit. As of 2003, about 90 percent of all boards were made with polyurethane foam. Alternative core materials include wood (usually balsa), polystyrene (used with epoxy resin), polyethylene, and EVA foam. It's estimated that about 350,000 blanks worldwide are produced annually. *See also* Hobie Alter, balsa, Gordon Clark, Clark Foam, epoxy surfboard, molded surfboard, surfboard construction, Dave Sweet.

Pomar, Felipe Debonair regularfoot surfer from Lima, Peru; winner of the 1965 World Surfing Championships, and one of the 1960's most dependable big-wave performers. Pomar was born (1943) to a wealthy Lima family, and began surfing at age 14. He won the Peru International in 1962, 1965, and 1966 (placing second in 1963 and 1967), was a four-time finalist in the Duke Kahanamoku Invitational between 1965 and 1969, and finished second in the 1970 Smirnoff Pro. All of these events were held in oversize surf.

The 1965 World Championships were held at Punta Rocas, just outside of Lima, in thick, gray, shifty waves. Pomar rode in his usual fashion—squat,

Felipe Pomar

utilitarian, and nearly mistake-free—and defeated a strong finals field that included Midget Farrelly, Nat Young, and Fred Hemmings, all of whom earned world titles in the '60s. Pomar was the first Latin American surfing champion. His win at Punta Rocas, while not undeserved, was a surprise, and down-played somewhat by the surfing elite. "Felipe did a better job at riding the wave the way the judges wanted," Farrelly said, in a plainly backhanded com-pliment. The surf press meanwhile described Pomar's riding as "unstylish," but liked the Latin angle. "On the beach," *Surfer* magazine wrote, "Pomar is a quiet and soft-mannered Peruvian aristocrat. But in the water, he's a fierce go-for-broke competitor who faces the big surf like a matador working a giant bull."

The strangest moment in Pomar's surfing life took place on October 3, 1974, when he and fellow big-wave rider Pitti Block rode a tsunami. The two had been getting ready to surf some three-foot waves off a small island near Lima, when the area was hit by a violent earthquake. An hour later, after deciding against an immediate return to Lima, the two men paddled into the surf; 15 minutes later they were sud-denly transported more than a mile out to sea amid giant whorls and boils; perhaps a half-hour later, Pomar was able to catch and ride a 10-foot wave. A quarter mile from shore, Pomar lost the wave as it again backed down into an unbroken swell. "As I paddled to the beach," he later said, "the wave I'd been riding kept going, then jacked up a fishing boat and threw it above a retaining wall into a building." Pomar made land a few minutes later, with Block,

having ridden a subsequent wave, joining him shortly thereafter.

In 1987, Pomar began a one-man crusade to have the fishermen of ancient Chan Chan, a pre-Inca em-pire located in what is now Peru's northern territory, recognized as the original surfers. Chan Chan fisher-men from as far back as 3,000 B.C., Pomar said, used reed-built *caballitos* ("little horses") to ride waves; a 15th-century warrior, furthermore, on a seagoing mission to expand Inca territory, may have intro-duced the *caballito*—and surfing—to Polynesia. "While there is much room for speculation," Pomar said in a surf magazine article, "there seems to be a distinct possibility that the embryonic form of modern-day surfing was born off the coast of north-ern Peru."

Pomar appeared in a small number of surf movies, including *Golden Breed* (1968), and was featured in *Duke Kahanamoku's World of Surfing,* a 1968 CBS sports special. He was Peru's top vote-getter in the 1966 and 1967 *International Surfing* Magazine Hall of Fame Awards. The never-married Pomar has lived in Hawaii since 1963, and has worked in real estate since 1971. *See also* tsunami, World Surfing Championships 1965.

Pope, Karl   Southern California surfboard acces-sory designer and manufacturer. Pope met surfer/ designer Tom Morey at the University of Southern California in the mid-'50s, and in 1965 they formed the Morey-Pope company in Ventura. One of their first products was the Trisect, a travel-ready three-piece surfboard that Pope designed and engineered. More board models followed, including the Snub, the Peck Penetrator, the Blue Machine, and the Camel surfboards. Other Morey-Pope products included Slipcheck, an aerosol traction spray; Lock Set, an anti-theft device for surfboards; and, the W.A.V.E. Set in-terchangeable fin system. Morey-Pope earned more than $1 million in gross revenue in 1968, but the part-nership fell apart in 1970. Two years later, Pope de-signed and marketed a molded epoxy-finished line of boards called Hollow W.A.V.E.—a noble failure that more or less drove him from the surfing business in 1974. Just over 20 years later, after Pope had founded, developed, and sold a Ventura tennis club, he came back to the idea of a multipiece surfboard, and in 1996 introduced the Pope Bisect Travelboard, a re-worked version of the Trisect (which itself had been a noble failure, having sold less than 50 units in the mid-'60s). The new Bisect cost about $1,200, and found a niche with older, wealthier, convenience-minded longboarders. *See also* molded surfboard, Tom Morey.

popout board   General term used to describe a range of quickly made, mass-produced inexpensive surfboards. "Popout" was coined in the early '60s as a dismissive name for bargain foam-core boards, and was sometimes applied as well to injection-molded plastic boards introduced later in the decade. The popout was invented in 1959 by the short-lived Robertson/Sweet Surfboards company (a partnership between Hollywood actor Cliff Robertson and Roger Sweet, brother of pioneering surfboard manufacturer Dave Sweet); the typical Robertson/Sweet was built with a single layer of 20-ounce fiberglass laid over a virtually unshaped polyurethane foam core, and finished with a layered-fiberglass fin; it cost $99.50—about $30 less than a custom board. Another early popout manufacturer, Diwain Surfboards in Huntington Beach, built its surfboards from two molded "ding-proof" plastic halves that were fused together with a foam core. Ventura International Plastics launched more than a half-dozen popout brands in the '60s, including Duke Kahanamoku, Sting Ray, Ten Toes, and Inland Surfer. Other early and mid-'60s popout brands included the Malibu Competition (sold at Shell gas stations throughout Southern California) and Dextra. Some popouts were shoddily made; others were perfectly serviceable as low-priced beginner boards. Popout boards were also available in do-it-yourself kits. Nonpopout surfboard manufacturer and retailers viewed popouts as a threat to business and, with editorial support from the surf press, kept the boards from gaining any kind of serious market share, even for entry-level surfers. A 1965 *Surfer* magazine editorial called popouts a "disease" visited upon surfing by "get-rich-quick manufacturers." *See also* molded surfboard.

Poppler, Jericho   Lively regularfoot surfer from Long Beach, California; world-ranked #2 in 1979. Poppler was born (1951) and raised in Long Beach, and began surfing at age nine. She was a women's division fixture in the United States Surfing Championships from the mid-'60s to the early '70s, finishing fifth in 1966, sixth in 1967, fifth in 1969, first in 1970, third in 1972, and fourth in 1973. She also placed sixth in the 1970 World Championships, won the Western Surfing Association's elite AAAA division in

1971, and placed third, with partner Hal Sachs, in the tandem division of the 1971 U.S. Championships. Poppler then became one of the original full-time female pros, winning the 1976 Gunston 500 and the 1977 Smirnoff Pro, among other events. She was second to Hawaii's Lynne Boyer in the 1979 title race, and retired after the 1981 season.

Poppler was the original media-savvy female surfer, presenting herself as a confident and well-muscled athlete ("I'm dynamic," she in a 1980 *Surfer* profile, "I mean, look at me, I look great!"); as a sexy ingenue (lounging in a bubble bath with a bottle of champagne for her *Surfer* portrait); and as a part-time feminist who said that men look to "conquer" waves while woman prefer to "dance, and just be part of this kingdom." Along with top surfers of the '60s and '70s, Poppler said she was influenced by Marc Chagall, Rudolf Nureyev, Clara Bow, and Cyd Charisse. In 1975, Poppler cofounded the Women's International Surfing Association, the first all-women's competition organization, and in 1978 she cofounded the Golden Girls promotional group. She turned her attention to environmental causes in the mid-'80s as a founding member of the Surfrider Foundation (later serving on its board of directors), and by working with Surfers Environmental Alliance, the Algalita Marine Research Foundation, and Kids for Clean Waves.

Poppler is featured in a small number of surf movies, including *Waves of Change* (1970) and *Five Summer Stories* (1972). In 1999, she was inducted into the Huntington Beach Surfing Walk of Fame. Poppler is married and has five children. *See also* Golden Girls, Women's International Surfing Association.

Pororoca   Series of quirky inland surfing breaks in northern Brazil created as an incoming tidal surge runs up the various tributaries of the Amazon River, forming waves over shallow sandbanks. The name "Pororoca" comes from the native Tupi Indian dialect and means "great noise." The mud-colored river surf is in fact dangerous; a ship belonging to French oceanographer Jacques Cousteau was sunk by a wave during a Pororoca field expedition in 1984. Other dangers include uprooted trees swirling in the wave zone and wildlife that includes alligators, anacondas, piranhas, and the dreaded candiru, a tiny fish that can swim up the human penis and lodge its spiny fins so firmly in the walls of the urethra that removal usually requires amputation. The Pororoca wave comes into full form just a few times each season, during the February and March full moon low tides, and is ridable in numerous spots, up to 120 miles from the ocean. The two most frequently ridden Pororoca breaks are Rio Araguari, first surfed in 1997 by Brazilians Noelio Sobrinho and Gilvandro Junior, which can get up to six foot and is the most dangerous wave in the region, and Rio Guama, a more accessible wave and the site of the 1999-founded Pororoca Surf Championships. Brazilian surfer Eraldo Gueiros rode a Pororoca wave in 2000 for a leg-numbing 17 minutes—a record for this particular tidal bore. The Pororoca has been featured in *Surfer* and *Surfer's Journal* magazine articles, and in 2002 was the subject of a National Public Radio report. *See also* Severn Bore, tidal bore waves.

Portugal   Along with having one of Europe's best surfing coastlines, Portugal is also home to one of the world's fastest-growing surf cultures. Portugal has ridable surf all year, but the biggest and most consistent waves arrive from October to March, in response to the North Atlantic storm season. The country's 530-mile coast can be divided into two surfing areas: the mountainous and craggy region north of Lisbon is rich in surf—including a handful of world-class breaks—and can be rainy and cool; the rolling bay-lined coast south of Lisbon has a Mediterranean climate and fewer surf spots, many of which break only in winter. Coxos, a fast and hollow right-breaking reef/point, located 30 miles northwest of Lisbon, is Portugal's best and best-known surf spot. Other spots include Cabedelo, a wedging jetty break in Figueira da Foz; the sand-bottom tubes at Lisbon's Carcavelos; and the rock-lined point surf at Arrifana in the south. Portugal also governs two sets of Atlantic islands, Madeira and the Azores, both more than 500 miles off the coast, volcanic in origin, and containing a small number of first-rate surf breaks. The air temperature in Portugal ranges from the low 50s in winter to the high 70s in summer, while the water stays cool all year—between 52 in winter and 67 in summer—due to upwelling and chilly north-to-south Atlantic currents. Hazards include urchins and sharp volcanic rock reefs.

The Portuguese surf was first ridden by native-born sailor Pedro Martins de Lima and Olympic pentathlete Antonio Jonet, who brought a wooden surfboard back from a visit to Hawaii in 1958 and began surfing at Costa de Caprica, just south of Lisbon. (Martins was still surfing as of 2002.) Portugal came to the attention of the surf media in the late '60s and early '70s, first in a small number of magazine articles, then in two of the era's most popular surf films, *Evolution* (1969) and *Waves of Change* (1970). The first Portuguese surf contest was held in 1977, at Ribeira D'ilhas in Ericeira; the Portuguese Surfing Federation was founded in 1988; the first surf shops opened in the early 1980s. The Buondi Pro, held in 1989 and 1990 in the Portuguese surf capital of Ericeira, near Lisbon, brought world tour competition to Portugal; the Figueira Pro, held in Figueira da Foz, has been part of the pro tour since 1996. Portugal hosted the 1998 World Surfing Games.

As of 2003, Portugal was home to about two dozen surf shops, six surf camps, and 20,000 resident surfers and bodyboarders. "Surfers here don't travel much," according to João Valente, editor of the 1987-founded *Surf Portugal* magazine. "They know how good they have it in their backyard." Tiago Pires, the country's top surfer, won rookie-of-the-year honors in the 2000 Triple Crown series in Hawaii. The Portuguese Surfing Federation runs about 40 regional and national contests annually, with no distinction made between professionals and amateurs. American-born Nick Uricchio of Semente Surfboards, in Ericeira, has meanwhile become one of Europe's best-known surfboard shapers. Portugal has been featured in over a dozen films and videos, including *Lost . . . on the Road with Spike* (1995), *Bliss* (1996), and *E2K* (2000). The Portuguese surf is detailed in *The Stormrider Guide Europe* (1998). *See also* the Azores, Madeira.

Potter, Martin   Volatile regularfoot surfer from Durban, South Africa; world pro tour champion in 1989, and an early proponent of aerial surfing. "Many young surfers today are still slightly scared of Potter," *Surfing* magazine noted in "Pottz: Last of the Wildmen," an article published in 1995, one year after Potter retired from the pro tour. "He's a big, hulking, hairy beast with a tough-guy snarl and the ineffable air of cool." Potter was born (1965) in Blyth, England, the son of an engineer father and barmaid mother; the family moved to Durban when Potter was two, and he began surfing at age 10. He won the 1981 National Scholastic Surfing Association International Team Challenge, beating future three-time world champion Tom Curren in the final. Ten weeks later, the 15-year-old Potter entered and won his first pro contest, a local event in Durban, beating former

perbolic aerial move. He favored brightly colored surfboards; a 1984 *Surfing* magazine cover shot showed him airborne four feet above the crest on his trademark green-and-yellow board, wearing a magenta wetsuit. He was a mercurial presence on the world-tour—brooding and angry at times, acting like a spoiled child, then festive, loud, and matey, drinking until the bars closed and later carrying the party into the streets and hotel rooms. "The scary thing for me," Potter said later, "was that I could go out and have a big night, drink heaps of beer, and wake up the next morning without a hangover. My body dealt with everything. There were contests I won after staying up all night." Potter moved to Sydney, Australia, in 1985. In what would be the only political gesture of his career, he later that year refused to compete in South Africa because of apartheid. World champions Tom Carroll and Tom Curren also boycotted the South African contests.

Potter began non-surfing fitness training for the first time in 1989, and charged into the season by winning an unprecedented four out of five contests, and picked up two more victories on his way to the championship. With contest prize money added to his sponsor salaries and bonuses, the 24-year-old Potter earned nearly $300,000 in 1989—a record at the time.

The following year was a minor disaster. Potter started a surfwear company that immediately lost money, while the Australian government presented him with a notice for $300,000 due in unpaid taxes. He also had an acrimonious split with his long-time manager, the effective but fiery-tempered Peter Mansted. The stress was reflected in Potter's surfing, and he finished the year ranked a disappointing 15th. He later said the world title year itself had drained him. "I was the fittest I'd ever been, but it took so much out of me, and after I won I just couldn't get myself back to the same level." Potter came back and finished fifth in 1993, then retired after 1994, skills intact, rated 10th. He'd spent a record 14 years in the world tour Top 16. His unfettered approach to aerial surfing had meanwhile long since been adopted and amplified by younger riders like Matt Archbold, Christian Fletcher, and six-time world champion Kelly Slater.

Potter was featured in more than 40 surf movies and videos, including *Follow the Sun* (1983), *Shock Waves* (1987), *Surfers: The Movie* (1990), and *The Hole* (1997). *Strange Desires,* a 25-minute video documentary on Potter, was released in 1990; in 1999, he was

Martin Potter

world champion Shaun Tomson in the final. The following week, riding a 5'6" twin-fin, he placed second in the Gunston 500, his first world tour event, and a week later he placed second in the Mainstay Magnum, another world tour contest. It was a world tour debut the likes of which has never been equaled. Potter—"Superkid," as named by the Durban press—finished eighth on the year-end rankings.

Potter was a hit-or-miss competitor over the next seven years, winning a half-dozen events (including the 1983 Stubbies Pro, the 1984 Marui Pro, and the 1987 U.K. Surfmasters), and usually finishing the year rating in the middle of the top 10. But his position in the surf world was in fact much higher—particularly among young surfers—as he constantly and flamboyantly pushed the limits of high-performance surfing. Not a stylist like world tour peers Tom Curren and Tom Carroll, Potter was a model of kinetic energy, his short legs pumping constantly, arms extended winglike from his torso as he ripped into a series of big, fast, gouging turns, or launched off the curl into a hy-

featured in *The Theory,* a surfing training and fitness video. From 1994 to 1996, he hosted *NRG,* a weekly half-hour surfing variety show produced in Sydney. Potter has been married twice, and has one child. In 2000, he moved to Biarritz, France. *See also* aerial.

Powell, Shane   Inconspicuous Australian pro surfer from Avoca, New South Wales; world-ranked #2 in 1994. Powell was born (1972) in Sydney, and raised in the north Sydney beachfront suburb of Avoca, where he began surfing at age eight. He turned pro in 1990, after an undistinguished run as an amateur, and made a steady rise up the world tour ratings, going from 49th in his rookie season to ninth in 1993. Powell was a slender, rubber-limbed, splay-fingered surfer, quick and precise, and occasionally criticized for lacking power. Raising his level again in 1994, the dark-haired regularfooter finished runner-up to Florida's Kelly Slater for the world title, only to be dropped by his primary sponsor, Rip Curl, 18 months later as he headed for a 15th-place finish in the 1996 ratings. Powell battled his way back to third in 1997, then over the next four years again dropped out of the top 10. Powell won five world tour events during his career, including the 1993 Quiksilver Surfmasters in France and the 1994 Coke Classic in Australia; he also won the 1995 World Qualifying Series tour. Powell appeared in more than three dozen surf videos, including *Overdrive* (1993), *Panama Red* (1994), *Beyond the Boundaries* (1994), and *The Billabong Challenge* (1995).

power surfing   Type of surfing characterized by strong, deeply set turns. "Good surfing," Australian Gary Elkerton, three-time runner-up to the world title and power surfing virtuoso, said in 1992, "is power, speed and flow. The rest of it doesn't attract me at all." The expressions "power surfing" and "power surfer" have been used since the early '60s; Phil Edwards of California and Australian Nat Young are often cited as the original power surfers. In the late 60s, Hawaiians Barry Kanaiaupuni and Jeff Hakman took their newly streamlined surfboards and reconfigured the lines that could be drawn at places like Oahu's Sunset Beach, setting a new power surfing standard in the process. Power surfers aren't necessarily huge, but tend to be stocky and strong; Hakman, just 5'7" and 140 pounds, was nicknamed "Surf Muscle." Master power surfers over the years include Ian Cairns, Tom Carroll, Simon Anderson and Mark Occhilupo of Australia; Dane Kealoha, Johnny-Boy Gomes, Laird Hamilton, Sunny

Garcia, and Pancho Sullivan of Hawaii; and Taylor Knox of California. In the early '90s, power surfing was positioned as the older—and, some felt, more respectable—method of wave-riding, as compared to the quick, light tailslide/aerial approach used by the teenage New School surfers led by Kelly Slater. Tom Carroll in 1993 said he appreciated the New School method, but that power surfing hadn't yet run its course. "Power is about burying the rail, holding it—fins in the water—and driving the turn as far as possible. And I don't think we've gone as far in the direction as we can go." The younger surfers agreed. "We all want to surf with power," California new schooler Shane Beschen said. "But that comes with age. You fill out. You're older. You're more of a man."

Pratte, Tom   Soft-spoken but emotional environmentalist from Huntington Beach, California; co-founder of the Surfrider Foundation, and the group's executive director from 1986 to 1990; often described as the "father of surf environmentalism." Pratte was born in 1948, began surfing in the early '60s, and graduated from Humboldt State University with a B.S. in a self-designed program called coastal studies. In the early '70s he took a nonpaying job as the environmental director of the Western Surfing Association, a competition group. In 1984, along with surfer/engineer Glenn Hening and Malibu surfing legend Lance Carson, he helped organized the Surfrider Foundation, surfing's first major environmental organization. As Surfrider's first paid employee, Pratte was instrumental in halting a mile-long breakwater project at San Diego's Imperial Beach, which would have ruined the nearby waves; he also worked on public right-of-way beach access. In 1987, Pratte received the Ocean and Coastal Management Award from the Coastal Zone conference, and was named by *Surfing* magazine as one of 50 "surfing leaders who are changing our sport." An activist rather than an administrator, Pratte found himself at odds with his growing managerial duties at Surfrider, and the board voted him out as executive director in early 1990; he responded by throwing his vintage 9'8" Yater longboard out of the second-story window of the Surfrider offices, and resigned from the group completely. Pratte did consulting work for a variety of environmental groups over the next three years. He died of cancer in 1994 at age 45; he never married.

Pratte had battled Chevron Oil for years over a wave-compromising jetty the company had built at

El Segundo, a southwest Los Angeles County surf break. Just before Pratte died, Chevron agreed to fund the construction of what was later nicknamed "Pratte's Reef," an artificial reef about one mile north of the jetty. In 1996, Pratte was inducted into the Huntington Beach Surfing Walk of Fame. *See also* artificial reefs, environmentalism and surfing, Surfrider Foundation.

Preisendorfer, Rusty   Full-sized, even-tempered surfboard shaper and surfwear CEO from La Jolla, California; founder and owner of Rusty, one of the sport's largest surfboard and surfwear labels. Preisendorfer was born (1953) in Los Angeles and raised in La Jolla, the son of a Scripps Institute research mathematician father and occupational therapist mother. He began surfing at 13 and shaping boards three years later, setting up a "factory" in a neighbor's backyard chicken coop. He continued to shape while going to college at U.C. San Diego (where he took a B.A. in visual arts), freelancing for San Diego mainstay Gordon & Smith Surfboards, then for Canyon Surfboards, and

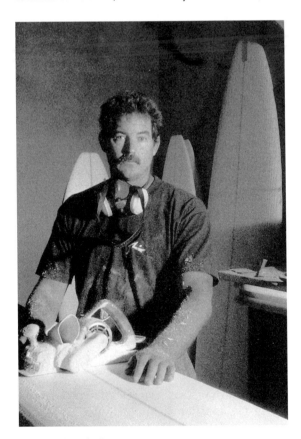

Rusty Preisendorfer

earning a reputation among the sport's elite by making boards for 1976 world champion Peter Townend and 1978 world champion Shaun Tomson. But Preisendorfer's real breakthrough came in 1983 when he shaped a plain-looking tri-fin for 16-year-old Mark Occhilupo of Australia, who rode it to electrifying effect as a world pro tour rookie. Preisendorfer founded Rusty Surfboards two years later, and in 1988 he moved into clothing. The company's simple "R." script logo (designed by Preisendorfer) soon became a national, then international, beachwear icon.

Preisendorfer built his shaping reputation by making basic, slightly full-templated tri-fin boards, favored by power surfers such as Occhilupo. "I'm not interested in coming up with the next major breakthrough in surfboard design," he once said. "Trying to be consistent is what's most important." But Preisendorfer had a creative streak as well, best exemplified by his five-finned C-5 model, introduced in the late '90s; Preisendorfer shrewdly promoted the board by staging the 1999 Rusty C-5 Challenge competition at Lower Trestles, in which all entrants had to ride a five-fin design. Wes Laine, Kalani Robb, Taylor Knox, Serena Brooke, and Shane Powell are among the dozens of top world tour pros who have used Preisendorfer boards over the years, along with big-wave riders Mike Parsons and Darryl "Flea" Virostko; Florida surfer CJ Hobgood rode Preisendorfer's boards to a world pro tour championship in 2001. Preisendorfer has informally mentored a number of popular shapers, including John Carper and Dave Parmenter.

In a 1993 *Australia's Surfing Life* magazine poll, the burly but genial Preisendorfer (6′ 4″ 240 pounds) was named the second-best shaper in the world, behind fellow Californian Al Merrick. The Rusty company sold more than 14,000 boards worldwide in 2001, more than any other manufacturer; combined sales of Rusty boards and surfwear in 2001 was just over $40 million. A *Forbes* magazine feature on Preisendorfer, "Beach Bum Makes Good," was published in 1995. Preisendorfer is married and has two children.

Prestage, Todd   Thin, loose-limbed Australian pro surfer from Gerringong, New South Wales; world-ranked #12 in 1996. Prestage began surfing in 1980 at age eight; 10 years later he moved to Oceanside, California, to take advantage of America's superior minor-league pro circuit, and was regarded as a turncoat by most of Australia's often-nationalistic surfing population. Prestage first defended himself as a "true-blue Aussie," and later, in a more belligerent mood, said that he'd "stick the finger up to anyone" who questioned his Australian authenticity. In 1996, Prestage finished third in the World Surfing Games, was runner-up in the World Qualifying Series tour, and took second in the Bells Beach Rip Curl Pro. He appeared in more than a dozen surf videos, including *Momentum II* (1993), *Bliss* (1996), and *The Ritual* (2000).

Price, Mark Debonair surfer and surfwear entrepreneur, originally from Durban, South Africa; world-ranked #17 in 1981; founder of Tavarua beachwear in 1994. Price was born (1961) and raised in Durban, began surfing at age 13, and was the second-ranked surfer on the South African domestic pro tour in 1979. He appeared in a small number of early '80s surf movies, including *Wizards of the Water* (1982), and from 1982 to 1984 he wrote more than a dozen features and columns for the American surf press. In 1983 he moved to Laguna Beach, California, and began working for surfwear giant Gotcha; by 1987, with Gotcha annual sales at $100 million, Price was promoted to the vice president of marketing, and had become, as later described by *Beach Culture* magazine, the "consummate surf executive." Price's Tavarua company, taking its name from the famous wave-fringed Fijian island, performed well in the late '90s, but folded in 2001. Price finished second in the 36-to-40 division of the 1998 Oxbow Masters World Championships.

Pro Class Trials Professional surfing contest held at Sunset Beach, Hawaii, from 1975 to 1983, usually in early November. Although the 1976 Pro Class Trials were part of the pro tour schedule, and counted toward the world championship, the contest was designed as a feeder event to place a small number of top-finishing surfers (between six and 12) into the elite North Shore pro events, including the World Cup, the Smirnoff, and the Duke Kahanamoku Invitational. Surfers already seeded into the big-ticket events were not allowed in the Trials. Bernie Baker of Hawaii produced and directed all of the Pro Class Trials contests. Forty-five surfers competed in the first Trials in 1975; the 1982 event had 142 entrants. Winners of the Pro Class Trials:

1975:	Barry Kanaiaupuni
1976:	Barry Kanaiaupuni
1977:	Col Smith
1978:	Ian Cairns
1979:	Jim Banks
1980:	Bobby Owens
1981:	Richard Cram
1982:	James Mahelona
1983:	Fielding Benson

Pro Junior Hotly contested Australian professional competition for young male surfers, held each January since 1977, almost always at Narrabeen in Sydney; long regarded as a bellwether event for up-and-coming pros. The Pro Junior was sponsored originally by Pepsi, then by domestic surf industry mainstays Ocean and Earth, and Hot Buttered. The Pro Junior is distinguished in part by its low-key presentation. The first edition was a single-division event for surfers 18 and under, with future two-time world champion Tom Carroll winning the $500 first-place check. More age categories were later added to the contest, and the open division age limit was raised to 19 and under. As the line between amateur and professional surfers was hazy in the late '70s, Pro Junior winners received prize money but were still able to compete in amateur events. Pro Junior winners have included pro tour stars-in-the-making like Mark Occhilupo, Barton Lynch, Gary Elkerton, Luke Egan, and Mick Fanning. While overseas surfers weren't prohibited from entering the Pro Junior (American surfer Joey Buran competed in 1979), foreign pros paid little attention until the 1987 event, which was attended by Americans Sunny Garcia, Jeff Booth, and John Shimooka, along with Vetea David of Tahiti. Kelly Slater became the first non-Australian Pro Junior winner, in 1992.

The starting field for the Pro Junior is made up of roughly 100 prequalified surfers. While challenge and prestige have always been the event's main attractions, Pro Junior prize money has risen steadily through the decades, and Adrian Buchan earned $3,000 for his 2001 Pro Junior win. The contest is run by Sydney surf collector and event organizer Michael Mock. As the Pro Junior formula proved successful, similar events were developed throughout the surfing world in the '90s, leading to the inauguration in 1998 of an Association of Surfing Professionals juniors world tour.

Open division Pro Junior winners are as follows:

1977:	Tom Carroll
1978:	Joe Engel
1979:	Joe Engel
1980:	Tom Carroll

1981: Stuart Cadden
1982: Gary Elkerton
1983: Barton Lynch
1984: Mark Occhilupo
1985: Mark Sainsbury
1986: Mark Occhilupo
1987: Richard Marsh
1988: Luke Egan
1989: Michael Barry
1990: Marcus Brabant
1991: Matt Hoy
1992: Kelly Slater
1993: Jake Spooner
1994: Nathan Webster
1995: Beau Emerton
1996: Taj Burrow
1997: Drew Courtney
1998: Phil MacDonald
1999: Mick Fanning
2000: Dean Morrison
2001: Adrian Buchan
2002: Bede Durbridge

Proctor, Edward "Pop" Southern California's original geriatric surfer, Proctor didn't start riding waves until the late 1940s, after retiring at age 56 from his job as an oil field engineer. His life to that point hadn't lacked for excitement or flair, as he had at various times worked as a gold prospector, steamboat engineer, merchant marine, and Prohibition rumrunner. Surfing, however, was at the center of Proctor's life for most of the next five decades. He was a self-described hobo and vegetarian, and became a fixture at Orange County's Doheny State Park, living out of a 1950 Dodge camper. Proctor vowed that he'd still be riding waves at 100, but at 97 his driver's license was revoked due to failing eyesight. "After that," *Life* magazine later wrote in a feature on senior surfers, "he spent most of his time in the bathtub." Proctor died in 1981 at age 99.

professional surfing Professional surfing, originally defined almost exclusively in terms of prize-money surf contests, is often said to have two starting points: 1965 and 1976. The 1965 Tom Morey Invitational, held in Ventura, featured a $1,500 purse—gathered largely from the $50 per surfer entry fee—and was the first in a small, unconnected series of prize-money events held in California, Hawaii, Peru, and South Africa. (Other contests included the 1966 Swami's Pro-Am, worth $500; the 1966 U.S. Profes-

Professional surfing; California's Richie Collins wins the 1988 O'Neill Coldwater Classic

sional Surfing Championships, worth $5,000; the 1968 Duke Kahanamoku Classic, worth $1,000; the 1969 Peru International, worth $1000; the 1969 Smirnoff Pro, worth $4,350; and the 1970 Gunston 500, worth $720). Pro contests disappeared from California in 1970, but continued in Hawaii and South Africa. Australia's first significant pro event was the 1973 Rip Curl Pro, held at Bells Beach, Victoria. The first pro women's contest was held in Hawaii in 1974.

Although sales from signature model surfboards technically created a low-paying professional class of surfer in 1966, 1967, and 1968, such profits generally weren't at the time included in discussions on pro surfing.

"Professionalism" was the sport's most contentious topic from the late '60s to the mid-'70s. Supporters claimed that money events would "legitimize" the sport, while purists argued that cash prizes debased an activity that was uniquely free and natural. Fred Hemmings of Hawaii, the 1968 world champion, was the most active supporter of pro surfing, envisioning a time when money contests would be "seen by millions on television," help "project a clean, healthy image for the sport," and "vastly increase the advancement of surfing techniques." Naysayers included Santa Cruz surfer John Scott, who wrote that pro surfers "exchange their wild freedom for wave limits, time limits, area, age and sex limits . . . all for a token benefit." Top surfers themselves had mixed feelings about pro contests. Hawaii's Bill Hamilton cashed checks worth a combined $1,500 for his runner-up finishes in the 1971 Duke and Smirnoff events, just a few months after telling *Surfer* magazine that "surfing should not fit into contests, and contests should not fit into surfing." There was no such thing as a fully professional surfer in the early and mid-'70s; most earned a living by working in the surfboard industry.

Professional surfing is often said to have originated in 1976, when Hemmings and fellow Hawaiian Randy Rarick spearheaded the formation of the International Professional Surfers (IPS) world tour, bringing together 14 previously unassociated men's-only pro contests into what was sometimes referred to as a "grand prix" circuit. (The Australian Professional Surfing Association, created one year earlier, ran a similarly formatted domestic tour in 1975; an IPS women's division was added in 1977. The short-lived Beachcomber Bill's Grand Prix tour, which virtually mirrored the IPS tour, was founded in late 1976.) Australia's Peter Townend became the 1976 IPS world champion; adding his prize money to his sponsorship income, he earned just over $25,000 for the year—barely enough to cover travel costs. Aggregate prize money for the 1976 IPS circuit was $77,650.

The Association of Surfing Professionals (ASP) took over from the IPS in 1982, the circuit grew in fits and starts over the years, and professionalism became an accepted fact of surfing, with an ever-larger number of surfers earning a living solely through prize-money winnings and sponsorship deals. The combined worth of the men's and women's world pro circuits in 1980 was $218,400; in 1990 it was $2,145,000; in 2000 it was $3,967,300. Nearly a dozen domestic pro tours were operating around the world by 2000; pro events were regularly held for longboarders and bodyboarders, and occasionally kneeboarders, bodysurfers, and skimboarders. Surf contest promoters began creating specialty pro events for big-wave surfing (the Quiksilver in Memory of Eddie Aikau, the Tow-In World Cup), tuberiding (the Tavarua Tuberiding Classic), and for the biggest photographed wave of the season (the K2 Big-Wave Challenge). Some pro contests were held in exotic locations, such as the Mentawai Islands in Indonesia or the Western Australian desert, without spectators, and presented to the surf world via surf magazines, TV shows, and videotaped specials. Others were held in front of tens of thousands of beachside onlookers at places like Huntington Beach and Rio de Janeiro. The Swell XXL Big Wave Awards offered the richest first-place prize in the sport's history at $60,000.

Meanwhile, the surf industry—particularly beachwear manufacturers—had long since replaced the contest circuit as the pro surfer's primary source of income. Australian goofyfooter and two-time world champion Tom Carroll became the first million-dollar surfer in 1988 after signing a five-year deal with surfwear giant Quiksilver; six-time world champion Kelly Slater of Florida was thought to be earning a million dollars a year from Quiksilver by 1995. By the late '80s there were also small but growing cadres of surf-media-directed "big-wave pros" and "travel pros," paid by their sponsors not to compete, but to ride giant waves, or to travel in search of exotic breaks. Beginning in the '90s, the top-ranked amateur surfers were in fact pros, as they received money from contests and sponsors, usually in the form of contributions to the surfer's "travel fund."

But the number of professional surfers overall remained small. It was estimated that about 2,500 people worldwide were paid a monthly retainer of some kind to ride waves in 2002, with fewer than 200 of those earning more than $25,000 a year, and about 20 making over $100,000. Professional surfing's impact on the sport, meanwhile, has been difficult to measure. Advances in equipment and wave-riding technique have no doubt been accelerated by having a paid class of surfers, although commensurate advances were made in the decades before pro surfing. Indifference seems to be today's main response to professionalism. "The thing to remember about Kelly Slater's million bucks a year," former world champion Nat Young said in 1996, "is that the vast majority of people who surf don't give a shit if he gets it or not." *See also* Association of Surfing Professionals, Australian Professional Surfing Association, competitive surfing, International Professional Surfers, Professional Surfing Association of America, Professional Surfing Tour of America.

Professional Surfing Association of America (PSAA)

America's first domestic professional surfing tour, formed in late 1984 by San Diego County surfer Joey Buran to serve as an intermediary step between amateur competition and the pro world circuit. While the 23-year-old Buran—a top-rated world tour pro and winner of the 1984 Pipeline Masters—drew up an ambitious schedule for the opening Professional Surfing Association of America (PSAA) season, with stops on the East Coast, the Gulf Coast, and Hawaii, it turned out that all 19 events took place in California. Prize money for the entire season was just under $50,000; central California surfer John Parmenter and Jorja Smith were the year-end champions. In 1986, Buran sold the PSAA to Dive N' Surf, owners of Body Glove wetsuits, the tour was pared down to six events, and the women's division was canceled. Buran stayed on as executive director, but resigned in midsummer after being hospitalized following a tour-related emotional breakdown.

At the end of the 1986 season, Dive N' Surf brought Budweiser on as the PSAA umbrella sponsor ($370,000 for three years, tripling the prize money); while the tour was now officially known as the Budweiser United States Professional Surfing Tour, it was still administered by the PSAA. The 1987 tour featured contests in Hawaii and the East Coast, and bigger prize purses attracted some of the world's top pros. In 1988, cable sports network Prime Ticket signed a five-year, 50-event deal with Meistrell Sports Productions (a division of Dive N' Surf) to cover the PSAA/Bud Tour contests, and by 1990, with a $500,000 annual prize purse, regular nationwide television event coverage, and a group of young pros that included future world-beaters Kelly Slater, Shane Beschen, Taylor Knox, and Rob Machado, the PSAA/Bud Tour set a domestic pro circuit standard that hasn't yet been matched.

In 1993, Meistrell Sports Productions sold the PSAA/Bud Tour to Prime Ticket, who then hired Association of Surfing Professionals (ASP) founder Ian Cairns to direct the contests. The next five years brought a succession of primary sponsors, and each name change (Bud Tour to the Clarion Surf Tour to the Panasonic Shockwave Tour) was accompanied by a decreasing number of events and competitor interest. (The women's division, however, returned in 1995.) By the end of 1998, all remnants of the PSAA tour were extinguished. The Professional Surfing Tour of America, and the Foster's Pro Surfing Tour, launched in 1999 and 2002, respectively, have both tried to restore the American competitive vigor once found in the PSAA.

Winners of the PSAA/Budweiser Pro Tour:

1985:	John Parmenter, Jorja Smith
1986:	Mike Cruikshank
1987:	Mike Lambresi
1988:	Mike Lambresi
1989:	Mike Lambresi
1990:	Dino Andino
1991:	Mike Parsons
1992:	Shane Beschen
1993:	Rob Machado
1994:	Chris Brown
1995:	Taylor Knox, Alisa Schwarzstein
1996:	Shaun Sutton, Alisa Schwarzstein

See also Joey Buran, Foster's Pro Surfing Tour, Professional Surfing Tour of America.

Professional Surfing Tour of America (PSTA)

California-based pro-am competition tour launched in 1999 by sports event manager Jeff Grell. The Professional Surfing Tour of America (PSTA) was created more or less in the image of the 1984 Professional Surfing Association of America, and is designed to serve as a minor league to the Association of Surfing Professionals (ASP) World Championship Tour. The inaugural PSTA tour was made up of five contests, each worth about $10,000 in prize money; each event was composed of three divisions: men's, women's, and longboard. Grell also contracted with Outdoor Life Network to broadcast PSTA contests on cable TV. Prize money went up as the surf industry began sponsoring events: the Rip Curl Pro, event #4 on the 2001 schedule, was worth $60,000. All six PSTA events in 2001 were sanctioned as ASP World Qualifying Series contests. In 2002, the Foster's Pro Surfing Tour, also based in California, was founded as an alternative to the PSTA. Men's, women's, and longboard PSTA tour champions are as follows:

1999:   Jeff Hurley, Holly Beck, Colin McPhillips
2000:   Jeremy Sommerville, Mindy de Armond, Brendan White
2001:   Ryan Simmons, Julia Christian, Josh Mohr
2002:   Ryan Simmons, Jodie Nelson, Josh Mohr

prone-out   Escape maneuver generally performed on a medium-size or larger closeout wave, in which the surfer aims for shore, drops to his stomach, grips the board's rails, and tries to ride out the whitewater explosion. Prone-outs were common before the introduction of the surf leash in the early 1970s, as it gave the surfer a chance to avoid a board-retrieving swim. The prone-out is still used as an alternative to ejecting off the board's tail section; a badly executed prone-out, however, can turn what might otherwise have been a routine wipeout into something more dangerous, as the rider is far more likely to strike his board.

Propper, Gary   Baby-faced surfer from Cocoa Beach, Florida; winner of the 1966 East Coast Surfing Championships; the first international-caliber surfer from the eastern seaboard, and the top-paid surfer of his generation. Propper was born (1946) in the Bronx, a borough of New York City, raised in Miami Beach, and began surfing at age 13 after moving with his family to Cocoa Beach; five years later the fast-talking regularfooter won the juniors division of the 1964 East Coast Surfing Championships. Propper rarely left the East Coast, and was frightened of waves over eight feet, but from the mid-'60s to the early '70s he was omnipresent on the surf scene, partly as a successful contest surfer—in the finals of the 1966 East Coast Championships he beat West Coast stars Dewey Weber and Tom Leonardo; he also competed in World Championships in 1966, 1968, and 1970—but also as a surf products promoter. The Gary Propper signature model surfboard, made by Hobie Surfboards and introduced in 1966, went on to become one of the world's best-selling model, with virtually all sales made between Florida and Maine. It was estimated that of the 6,000 surfboards Hobie made in 1967, nearly half were Propper models. He later claimed that his 1967 board royalties, added to the money he earned as a salesman for Katin surf trunks and O'Neill wetsuits, amounted to almost $100,000 for the year. "I put down 'Professional Surfer/Athlete'

Gary Propper (right) with Hawaiian surfer Ben Aipa

on my '64 tax returns," Propper said in 1996. "It was the coolest." The reason he almost never turned up in '60s-era surf movies, Propper also said, is that he demanded appearance fees from filmmakers, most of whom refused. Propper meanwhile earned a reputation as one of the sport's most volatile figures. "You never knew what he was going to do next, in or out of the water," longtime Florida surfboard builder Dick Catri later recalled. "I saw him throw away a trophy because it was only for second place, or turn around right there at the presentation ceremony and give it to some girl he'd never met."

Propper became an entertainment promoter in the early '70s, mentored by legendary San Francisco rock impresario Bill Graham, and was soon booking little-known bands like Devo, Blondie, and The Police into Florida clubs and halls. Later, as a manager, he represented comedians Gallagher and Carrot Top. Propper made a small fortune in the early '90s after securing the film rights to the Teenage Mutant Ninja Turtles comic book characters.

Propper was the top East Coast vote-getter in *International Surfing* magazine's 1967 Hall of Fame Awards, and was inducted into the East Coast Hall of Fame in 1996. He's been married twice and has three children.

pterygium   A flat yellow-white fibrous growth originating on the sclera (white) section of the eye, caused by UV sun rays, and exacerbated by wind, sea-spray, and glare. Virtually all longtime surfers have pinguecula (where the growth is contained within the sclera) or pterygium (where the growth has crossed over onto the cornea) to one degree or another, as do most longtime sailors and beach volleyball players. Pterygium, if left unchecked, can interfere with vision. Pterygium growth can be checked by using UV-blocking sunglasses, by applying eyedrops after surfing, and by reducing sun exposure in general. The outpatient eye surgery required to remove an advanced pterygium is relatively easy, and virtually risk-free, but the condition can return.

Puerto Escondido Savage two-way Mexican beachbreak tube located on the northern tip of the Gulf of Tehuantepec, in the state of Oaxaca; often called the "Mexican Pipeline." The broad, sandy beach at Puerto Escondido ("Hidden Port") is fronted by an underwater canyon that amplifies incoming swells from the south and southwest so that the waves here are bigger than those found virtually anywhere else on the Mexican mainland. From May to October, the surf at Puerto Escondido rarely drops below four foot, is often six to eight, and occasionally 15 foot or bigger. Waves here break close to shore, over a sandy bottom, but hazards are nevertheless plentiful, including swift riptides and currents, exploding tubes, and aggressive crowds. Heat and humidity can also be a problem: midday air temperatures in the summer are usually in the upper 80s, with the water temperature in the low 80s. Because wave shape is dependent on mutable sandbars, days and weeks can pass where the majority of waves are closeouts. Puerto Escondido has two main breaks: a wedging right, sometimes called Carmelita's or Wheelchair Bar, and a looping left about 200 yards to the south known as Far Bar. A softer-breaking point wave along the rock-lined southern headland is also surfed. The wind at Puerto Escondido blows offshore dependably from dawn until mid- or late morning, then turns onshore for the afternoon, and occasionally switches back to offshore just before sunset. High-performance surfing of every description is done on smaller days, but surfers come to Puerto Escondido—sometimes loaded with as many as six boards, with the knowledge that the entire set might be broken over the course of a weeklong visit—to ride inside the tube.

Traveling surfers rode Puerto Escondido as far back as 1959, but it remained a virtually unknown break until the early '70. The surf press began running photos of spherical Puerto Escondido tubes in 1974, by which time increasing numbers of surfers from California, Texas, and the eastern seaboard were beginning to file into the small hotels in the fishing/resort town to the immediate north. The number of visitors shot up with the opening of the Puerto Escondido International Airport in 1986. By the early '90s, Puerto Escondido's local economy had been so pumped up by incoming surf tourism dollars that the city council erected a statue of a surfer embedded into a looping concrete tube. Native surfers meanwhile took to the water in earnest in the early '80s, held the first Puerto Escondido National Surf Contest in 1981, and opened the first local surf shop in 1988. Top local surfers in 2003 included Raul Noyala, Celistino Diaz, Omar Diaz, Carlos Nogales Escalante, Rogelio Ramirez, and Kalle Carranza.

The Oxbow Masters surf contest took place here in 1998 in grinding six to eight-foot tubes, with a field that included surf icons like Reno Abellira, Michael Ho, Ian Cairns, Cheyne Horan, and Nat Young. A small number of international pro longboard events have been held here as well. Puerto Escondido has been featured in dozens of surf movies and videos, including *Ticket to Ride* (1986), *Momentum* (1992), *Siestas and Olas* (1997), and *Reflection* (2002), as well as the *Puerto Underground* video series (1995, 1996, and 1998). *Australia's Surfing Life* magazine named Puerto Escondido in 1997 as one of "Ten Waves Every Surfer Should Ride." *Surfer* magazine in 2002 cited it as one of the "World's Most Dangerous Waves." *See also* Mexico.

Puerto Rico Tropical Spanish-speaking American commonwealth island located 1,000 miles southeast of Miami, Florida, measuring about 100 miles by 35 miles; often referred to by surfers as the "Hawaii of the Atlantic." Puerto Rico produces the biggest and most consistent surf in the Caribbean; its north coast is open to all manner of storm-generated waves in the Atlantic (particularly from November to April), while its south coast receives infrequent but often-powerful surf from Caribbean Sea hurricanes (typically between August and October). An average winter season brings between 20 and 30 swells, with wave size ranging from four to 20 feet. Puerto Rico's 310-mile coastline is lined with dozens of coral and rock reefs that produce a wide variety of waves, many of them fast, hollow, and hard-breaking. Although the north coast sees the most swell activity, northeast tradewinds often render the area all but unsurfable. Breaks in and around the beachfront towns of Aguadilla and Rincón in the northwest are regarded as the best on the island in large part because they're positioned so that the tradewinds blow offshore. Puerto Rico's eastern shore is fringed with small wave-blocking islands.

Gas Chambers, a temperamental right-breaking tube located just outside Aguadilla, is Puerto Rico's most famous wave. Other popular breaks include Domes, a high-performance right, and Tres Palmas, a deep-water reef generally thought of as the west Atlantic's premier big wave, holding form up to 20 feet. "If Puerto Ricans consider Gas Chambers to be their version of Pipeline," surf journalist Mitch Varnes wrote in 1993, further drawing comparisons to Hawaii, "Tres Palmas is surely their Sunset Beach." More than 100 Puerto Rican surf breaks are located within a three-hour drive. Ocean temperatures here range from the high 70s to the low 80s; average mid-day air temperatures range from 70 to 85. The island's primary surfing hazards are shallow reefs, urchins, and sewage near the capital city of San Juan. Local surfers can be aggressive, even hostile, toward visitors.

Surfing in Puerto Rico began in the late '50s, with natives Jose Rodriguez, Guille Bermuda, and Rafy Viella all taking to the waves of the north and northwest coasts around the same time. American surfer Gary Hoyt opened the island's first surf shop in the capital city of San Juan in 1960. Malibu surfers Johnny Fain and Butch Linden visited Puerto Rico in 1965 and were warmly received by the 50-or-so resident surfers, but the sport didn't really take off here until after the 1968 World Surfing Championships (held mostly at Domes, and won by Fred Hemmings and Margo Godfrey). Fourteen-year-old Puerto Rico surfing savant Jorge Machuca also emerged in 1968 as the island's first great wave-riding talent. By 1969, American surfers from across the eastern seaboard were flying into balmy Puerto Rico by the hundreds during the winter months—not always to the island's benefit. "The trickle of visiting sportsmen in search of the perfect ride," *Surfing* magazine wrote in 1970, "has turned into a veritable tidal wave of escaping hippies, runaways and dopers." (Puerto Rico's drive for national independence over the decades has further complicated the relationship between locals and tourists, surfers included.)

Puerto Rico continued to produce talented surfers in the '70s and '80s, including Edwin Santos and Juan Ashton. San Juan's Jose "Pepe" Alvarez was the president of the International Surfing Association from 1988 to 1990; he was responsible for bringing the World Amateur Surfing Championships to Puerto Rico in 1988. By 2002, there were nearly a dozen internationally recognized Puerto Rican surfers, including big-wave riders Alberto Licha and Waldo Oliver, 2000 HIC Pipeline Pro winner Carlos Cabrero, 1996 Haleiwa International winner William "Chino" Sue-A-Quan, Pipeline charger Otto Flores, and teenage pros Dylan Graves and Brian Toth. Puerto Rico is home to about 25,000 surfers and bodyboarders and more than 20 surf shops. The 1984-founded Puerto Rico Surfing Federation hosts over a dozen surfing contests annually, both professional and amateur. *Low Pressure,* founded in 2000, is the country's only surf magazine. Puerto Rican waves and surfers have often been featured in surf movies and videos, including *Evolution* (1969), *Gone Surfin'* (1987), *La Bruja* (1996), and *Epiphany* (2000). The Puerto Rican surf is detailed in *The World Stormrider Guide* (2001). *See also* World Surfing Championships 1968.

pullout   Exit maneuver used at wave's end, or as a way to escape a closed-out or otherwise badly shaped wave. Surfers didn't often pull out of waves prior to the 1940s, as it was nearly impossible to break a long, heavy, finless board out of its shoreward track. (Riders would sometimes shuffle to the rear of the board, sit, straddle the tail section, and use their legs as brakes.) Boards designed after World War II were lighter and had a stabilizing fin, and the pullout was developed along with other basic surfing maneuvers, like the bottom turn and cutback. Most pullouts, then and today, are done by simply angling or pivoting the board up and over the wave crest. In the stalling pullout, common for beginners, riders shift their weight rearward, lift the nose of their boards, and stall as the wave passes. More attention was given to the pullout before the development of the surf leash in the early '70s, as a badly executed pullout meant surfer and surfboard would likely be separated. "Nowadays," as California surf journalist Devon Howard scornfully noted in 2000, "a lot of surfers dive off or fling the board out from underneath them to avoid the extra effort needed to complete the wave." Also known as a "kickout," "cut out," "flick off," or "flick out." *See also* flying pullout, island pullout, reverse pullout.

Pump House Gang, The   Clever, cutting essay by American novelist and pop culture critic Tom Wolfe, describing the mid-1960s surf scene at Windansea, a popular California surf break located in north San Diego. A dandified Virginia-born Yale graduate, Wolfe became a national literary figure after the 1965 publication of *The Kandy-Kolored Tangerine-Flake Streamline Baby,* a collection of essays that helped define the often snide and showy new journalism. His 7,000-word "The Pump House Gang" was originally published in a 1966 issue of the *New York World Journal Tribune* Sunday magazine; in 1968 it was the lead piece in *The Pump House Gang,* a collection of Wolfe's essays published by Farrar, Straus and Giroux. Midway through the piece Wolfe describes a "surfing life [that] floats over the 'real' world, or the square world, or whatever one wants to call it." Wolfe elaborates as a few members of the Pump House Gang head off to a *"very Dionysian"* party.

> The [surfers] are not exactly off in a world of their own, they are and they aren't. What it is, they float right through the real world, but it can't touch them. They do these things, like the time they went to Malibu, and there was this party in some guy's apartment, and there wasn't enough legal parking space for everybody, and so somebody went out and painted the red curbs white and everybody parked. Then the cops came. Everybody ran out. At [a party] in Manhattan Beach . . . somebody decided to put a hole through one wall, and everybody else decided to see if they could make it bigger. Everybody was stoned out of their hulking gourds, and it got to be about 3:30 a.m. and everybody decided to go see the riots. These were the riots in Watts. The Los Angeles Times and the San Diego Union were all saying, WATTS NO-MAN'S LAND, but naturally nobody believed that. Watts was a blast, and the Pump House gang was immune to the trembling gourd panic rattles of the LA Times.

Surfers were generally dismissive of Wolfe and his essay, in part because he mangled a few surf expressions (describing a "reverse kick-up," for example, instead of "reverse kickout"), but mostly because the Pump House Gang surfers are unflatteringly—and honestly—portrayed as arrogant, indulgent, and mildly criminal. After the essay was published, La Jolla surfers spray-painted TOM WOLFE IS A DORK across the cement beachfront pump house structure that gives the story its title. *Surfer* magazine later called "The Pump House Gang" a "bit of low-rent pop soci-

ology," but acknowledged that the Windansea surfers, who once dressed up as Nazi storm troopers and goose-stepped down to the beach for a laugh, were in fact viewed as "savages" by the rest of California surf society. Wolfe went on to write a number of best-sellers, including *The Right Stuff* (1979), *Bonfire of the Vanities* (1988), and *A Man in Full* (1998). *See also* books and surfing, Windansea, Windansea Surf Club.

Purpus, Mike Flamboyant regularfoot surfer from Hermosa Beach, California; a seven-time finalist in the United States Surfing Championships, and the West Coast's most progressive and entertaining surfer of the 1970s. Purpus was born (1948) in Santa Monica, California, raised in Hermosa Beach, and began surfing at age 10. He placed fourth in the juniors division of the 1965 U.S. Championships; moving up to the men's division, he finished sixth in 1967, fifth in 1968, third in 1969 and 1970, and sixth in 1972 and 1975. (In the 1975 event he won both the kneeboarding and longboarding divisions.) Purpus also won the small-wave event in the 1970 Peru International, placed second in the 1971 Makaha International, and competed in World Surfing Championships in 1968, 1970, and 1972.

The short surfboard, introduced in the late '60s, was a good match for Purpus's kinetic riding style. Not overly concerned with finesse or nuance, he rode in a squat, with a ramrod-straight back. A hotdogger in the best sense of the word, he taught himself how to switch stance, developed a tremendous 270-degree cutback in the early 1970s that was far and away the best of its kind in the sport, and mastered a series of frontside and backside side-slips and 360s.

The blond-haired and mustachioed Purpus meanwhile established himself as one of the sport's most colorful characters, accoutered in a puka-shell necklace and floppy-brimmed leather hat, wearing brightly colored surf trunks over his full wetsuit, and putting a life-size airbrush of Raquel Welch on the bottom of his favorite board. In 1968 he made the first of three appearances on ABC's *The Dating Game* (winning a chaperoned trip to Scotland in his debut outing), and in 1974 he posed nude for *Playgirl.* Purpus had the misfortune of being a surfing harlequin at a time when the sport had become oppressively earnest and solemn. Almost alone among his contemporaries, he kept his sense of humor. In a 1970 magazine poll in which top surfers were asked "What other experiences parallel surfing?," his answers ranged from "ballet dancing" to "love" to "being filled with the Holy Spirit." Purpus said, "Riding my Makaha skateboard after getting sauced on a gallon of Red Mountain."

The only California surfer to compete regularly as a professional in the early and mid-'70s, Purpus was a five-time invitee to the Duke Kahanamoku Classic and a finalist in the 1972 Hang Ten American Pro. He appeared in nearly all of the American-made surf movies of the late '60s and '70s, including *Fantastic Plastic Machine* (1969), *Pacific Vibrations* (1970), *Five Summer Stories* (1972), and *Super Session* (1975). From 1974 to present day, he's written a surf column for the *Easy Reader,* a weekly regional newspaper. In 1979 and 1980 he lent his name to the ill-fated Mike Purpus Hot Lips Surfboards; since 1978 he's worked as a bartender. Purpus is unmarried. *See also* nudity and surfing.

Q

quad *See* four-fin.

quasimoto Goof-around hotdog maneuver invented by California surfer Mickey Muñoz in 1959, in which the rider hunkers over while angling across a small wave, head just above the knees, and stretches both arms out horizontally in line with the surfboard. Named after the lead character in Victor Hugo's *Hunchback of Notre Dame.* A black-and-white photo of Muñoz doing a quasimoto was used on the Packards' 1980 album *Pray for Surf.* Also spelled "quasimodo." *See also* hotdogging.

Queensland Warm and sprawling Australian state located in the continent's northeast corner, facing the Pacific Ocean to the south and the Coral Sea to the north; home to nearly a dozen exceptional right-breaking point waves and thousands of prodigiously talented surfers past and present. Only the southernmost 200 miles of Queensland's 1,500-mile Pacific-facing mainland coastline receives surf, as the Great Barrier Reef filters out virtually all incoming swell along the northern beaches. Queensland can be divided into three main surfing areas: 1) The remote

Quasimoto by Mickey Muñoz of California

Great Barrier Reef—the world's largest coral reef; long known as one of the Seven Natural Wonders of the World—contains several dozen temperamental and hard-to-access surf breaks. 2) The relaxed Sunshine Coast is home to a collection of tropical beachbreaks, the stunning right-breaking point surf of Noosa Heads, and the isolated sand-bottomed pointbreaks on Fraser Island. 3) The frenetic Gold Coast has five excellent sand-bottomed right-breaking points, including the Kirra and Burleigh Heads, as well as a handful of beachbreaks, the best known of which is Duranbah. The Gold Coast is also the industry and media center for the state's surf industry. Queensland has reasonable surf all year, but breaks best during the December-to-March cyclone season, as nearshore storms produce an average of two to three northeast swells per month. Some south-exposure Gold Coast breaks—most notably Burleigh Heads and Duranbah—can also show excellent form between March and July. The Queensland surf hits six foot a few times a year, and can get up to 10 foot. Average daytime air temperatures range from 90 (summer) to 65 (winter); water temperatures range from the low 80s to the mid-60s. Hazards include sharks, bluebottle jellyfish, aggressive crowds, and shallow sandbars.

Surfing was introduced to Queensland in the early '20s by a group of Kirra Lifesaving Club members, including Sid Chapman, Bill Davies, Eric Lane, Lance Powell, and Laurie Powell, and a small number of surfers continued to ride here over the next four decades. Adler's Surfboards, opened in Brisbane in 1959 by Frank Adler, was the state's first surf shop. But not until the early '60s did Queensland surfing really take off; 1963 saw the formation of the Australian Surfriders Association/Queensland Branch (now Surfing Queensland), as well as the Kirra Surfriders Club; 1964 brought the first Queensland state titles (won by Ken Adler, Billy Stafford, and Phyllis O'Donell); and in 1966 the Australian National Titles were held in Queensland for the first time. Sunshine Coast board-maker Bob McTavish meanwhile spent a good part of the mid-'60s in Noosa, along with California kneeboarder George Greenough and 1966 world champion Nat Young of Sydney, developing ideas that would in 1967 produce the groundbreaking vee-bottom surfboard—the prototype for the late-'60s shortboard revolution. Other top Queensland riders of the '60s and early '70s included Keith Paull, Peter Drouyn, Paul Neilsen, and Josette Lagardere.

Queenslanders were a domineering force in professional surfing throughout the '70s: Peter Townend placed third in the 1972 World Championships and won the 1976 world pro tour; Michael Peterson won the Rip Curl Pro three times from 1973 to 1975, as well as the 1977 Stubbies Pro; and Wayne Bartholomew took the 1978 world pro tour. (Joe Engel, Peter Harris, Gary Elkerton, Michael "Munga" Barry, Mick Fanning, Joel Parkinson, Trudy Todd, Serena Brooke, and Dean Morrison are among the dozens of post-'70s world-caliber Queensland surfers.) The long, hypnotic tubes at Burleigh and Kirra meanwhile became a shared fantasy for the rest of the surf world, in much the same way Waikiki had been for surfers in the '30s and '40s. Queensland was host to the 1982 World Amateur Surfing Championships.

As of 2003, Queensland was home to about 150 surf shops (mainly on the Gold Coast and the capital city of Brisbane), 33 surf clubs, and more than 100,000 surfers. Over 50 amateur and professional contests are held in the state yearly, including professional world tour events. *Australia's Surfing Life* magazine, Queensland's first nationally distributed surf publication, started at Burleigh Heads in 1985; the Association of Surfing Professionals moved its offices to the Gold Coast in 1999. The Queensland surf is detailed in a number of books, including *The Surfing and Sailboarding Guide to Australia* (1993), *Surfing Australia* (1998), Mark Warren's *Atlas of Australian Surfing* (1998), and *The World Stormrider Guide* (2001). *See also* Burleigh Heads, Great Barrier Reef, Gold Coast.

Quigg, Joe Virtuoso surfboard designer and craftsman, originally from Santa Monica, California; cofounder of both the modern longboard and the specialized big-wave board, and credited by many as the most influential midcentury board-maker. Quigg was born (1925) in Los Angeles, raised in Santa Monica, and began surfing at age four, after building himself a small wooden bellyboard. At 13 he made a redwood board that had slightly upturned nose and tail sections (later called "rocker"), which allowed

greater maneuverability and made the board more forgiving in tight places; the solid-wood plank boards in use at the time, as well as the hollow paddleboard/surfboards, were flat from bow to stern. Quigg would later say that the rocker was his greatest contribution to surfboard design.

After four years in the navy, Quigg returned to Santa Monica in 1947, bought a surfboard that didn't perform well, and vowed to make his own boards from that point forward. He became part of a small group of surfer/designers, including Bob Simmons and Matt Kivlin, who used Malibu as a test track. Quigg's boards immediately earned a reputation as sleek, fast, and well-made; in keeping with the times, however, his shapes were wide, heavy, blunt, and buoyant. In 1947, Quigg built a balsa/redwood board for Darrylin Zanuck, a beginning teenage surfer and the daughter of Hollywood mogul Darryl Zanuck, that was thinner and lighter than anything yet seen; the 25-pound "Darrylin board," as it was soon called, was then passed from one Malibu surfer to the next as the hottest-turning board on the beach, and thus became a prototype for the popular Malibu chip board. That same year, Quigg built in succession the first polyurethane foam-core board, an all-fiberglass fin, and a narrow-base raked-back fin; each idea would become standard in years to come.

In 1948, after dreaming about a board fast enough to make a wave from the top of the point at Rincon—a Malibu-like wave near Santa Barbara—Quigg cut his board in half longitudinally, removed two inches (reducing the board's width from 23 to 21 inches), glued it back together, and created the first pintail board, designed to hold traction at higher speeds; Quigg's pintail was a forerunner of the big-wave board. He made boards for Tom Zahn in the late '40s and early '50s—Zahn being one of the best riders at Malibu, along with Kivlin and Les Williams—and for pioneering big-wave surfer Buzzy Trent in the mid-'50s. When Trent ordered a 12-foot big-wave board from Quigg, he memorably asked the shaper to build him an "elephant gun," to be used for hunting down giant waves. Big-wave boards have since been known as guns.

Quigg founded a production-retail surfboard shop in Santa Monica in 1950, then opened a similar shop in Honolulu in 1953, after moving to Oahu. Years earlier, Quigg had taken photography classes at the Art Center College of Design in Los Angeles; he quit one semester before graduating, but went on to shoot some of the best surf photos of the late '40s and '50s. Quigg lived in Newport Beach, California, from 1959 to 1969, then moved back to Hawaii, where he built boats, canoes, and paddleboards until retiring in 1987. He was known as one of surfing's slowest and most meticulous workers, and made just 4,000 boards in his career—tens of thousands fewer than some other long-term shapers. Quigg married Aggie Bane, one of the first and best female surfers at Malibu, in 1950; they have two children. He was inducted into the International Surfing Hall of Fame in 1991. *See also* big-wave surfboard, chip, Malibu board.

Quiksilver Surfing's biggest, richest, and most successful company; maker of surfwear, wetsuits, and all manner of surfing accessories; founded in 1973 in Victoria, Australia, by Torquay surfers Alan Green and John Law. After a brief run manufacturing sheepskin ugg boots, Green and Law came out with their instantly popular surfing trunks (or "boardshorts"), featuring a unique scalloped-leg cut and color contrasting waistband. The Quiksilver name was lifted from acid-rock band Quicksilver Messenger Service. Green and Law licensed the brand in 1976 to Hawaiian pro surfer Jeff Hakman and University of Southern California business school graduate Bob McKnight, who began producing Quiksilver trunks in Southern California; five years later, Quiksilver USA's annual sales were approaching $5 million. Quiksilver Europe was established in 1984; licensees were soon set up in Brazil, Japan, and South Africa, among other nations, and by the end of the decade, new lines were developed for skiing, snowboarding, windsurfing, and skateboarding. With some notable exceptions (including the color-burst Echo Beach line in the early '80s), Quiksilver has produced a refined, handsome, easy-to-wear line of clothes. Quiksilver Wetsuits were introduced in 1990.

The company's marketing department has for more than two decades been without equal in the surf world. Teamriders over the years include world champions Wayne Bartholomew, Tom Carroll, Lisa Andersen, Kelly Slater, and Layne Beachley. (Carroll's five-year contract with Quiksilver, signed in 1986, made him the first million-dollar surfer; Quiksilver began paying Slater something close to $1 million a year—another first—in the mid-'90s.) In 1994, Quiksilver team riders won the men's and women's pro surfing world tours (Slater and Andersen), the pro longboard tour (Rusty Keaulana), the men's world

amateur title (Sasha Stocker), as well as snowboarding and sailboarding world titles (Bertrand Denervaud and Robbie Naish, respectively). Quiksilver has also developed and produced some of the sport's most memorable surfing contests, including the Quiksilver in Memory of Eddie Aikau big-wave event at Waimea Bay; the Men Who Ride Mountains big-wave contest at Maverick's; the Quiksilver Pro, held at Grajagan, Java; and the Quiksilver Airshow World Championships in Sydney, Australia. The year 1999 brought the launching of the Quiksilver Crossing, a seagoing effort designed primarily to discover, surf, and photograph uncharted waves 21 degrees north and south of the equator. In 2000, Quiksilver sponsored skateboarding hero Tony Hawk and bought his company, Hawk Clothing Inc. Union* the Boardriding Channel, a Quiksilver-backed VOD (video-on-demand) program, was launched in 2002.

Quiksilver subsidiary brands have performed well over the years, especially Roxy, the company's 1991-founded entry into the women's surfwear market. By 2002, the Roxy line—originally T-shirts and female-cut boardshorts—had expanded to include shoes, sheets, lamps, luggage, and beauty products, and its annual sales had topped $150 million. Other Quiksilver-owned companies or spin-offs include Mervin, Raisins, Radio Fiji, Leilani, and Teenie Wahine. Quiksilver is sold in retail surf shops, major department stores, company-owned retail stores (Quiksilver Boardriders Club, Quiksvilles, and Roxyvilles), and flagship stores in Paris, London, and New York. The Quiksilver line has expanded to backpacks, boardbags, watches, sandals, and sunglasses. In 1986, Quiksilver USA became the first publicly traded surfing company. Quiksilver's international sales in 2001 totaled more than $1 billion—a surfworld first. *See also* fashion and surfing, Alan Green, Jeff Hakman, Danny Kwock, Bob McKnight, Quiksilver in Memory of Eddie Aikau, Quiksilver Maverick's Men Who Ride Mountains, Quiksilver Pro, Roxy.

Quiksilver in Memory of Eddie Aikau, The
Professional big-wave surf contest held at Waimea Bay, Hawaii, in honor of Eddie Aikau, the revered pure-blooded Hawaiian big-wave rider who died in a 1978 boating accident; conceived and developed by company marketing chiefs Danny Kwock and Jeff Hakman, along with Quiksilver USA CEO Bob McKnight and Aikau family friend Eddie Rothman. The Quiksilver in Memory of Eddie Aikau (or "The Eddie"

as it's frequently called), wasn't initially planned as a big-wave contest, and the all-but-forgotten inaugural was held in 1984 in six to eight-foot surf at Sunset Beach, with Hawaiian surfer Denton Miyamura winning the $5,000 first-place check. The contest was refashioned the following year into a Waimea-targeted event, with 30 surfers invited, and a minimum wave-height requirement of 20 foot, as determined by newly hired event director and Hawaiian big-wave pioneer George Downing. Waimea, at that point the world's most famous big-wave break, had been Eddie Aikau's favorite spot, and he was considered to be the best rider there from the mid-'60s until his death. Surf contests had previously been held at Waimea—including the 1974 Smirnoff, the 1980 Duke Classic, and the 1985 Billabong Pro—but in each case the decision to run at Waimea had been made spontaneously.

Big-wave riding was coming back into vogue in the mid-'80s after a 15-year low period, and the 1986 Quiksilver encouraged the trend. The Waimea surf was rough and windblown, and just barely 20 foot. Surfers were divided into three groups, and each 10-man heat rode for an hour; the process was repeated, but with 45-minute heats, and each contestant's first- and second-round scores were combined for a final tally. The contest ended in a draw between Mark Foo and 36-year-old Clyde Aikau, Eddie's younger brother, with Aikau winning on a tiebreaker. Ken Bradshaw finished third. Clyde rode a 10-year-old board that had belonged to Eddie.

For three years, the surf at Waimea didn't meet the minimum Quiksilver/Aikau requirements. The 1990 version of the event, however, was magnificent—"A monumental day in surfing history," as described by *Australia's Surfing Life* magazine—with smooth-faced waves up to 30 feet. Hawaiian surfer Brock Little rode inside the tube on one wave, not long after taking a spectacular wipeout on the day's biggest wave, but Keone Downing—George Downing's son—was the most consistent performer and took the $55,000 winner's check, the richest prize in surfing history up to that point. Little was second; Richard Schmidt of Santa Cruz finished third.

The first round of competition was finished in 1995, with Brock Little leading, before the contest was called off for lack of surf. Diminutive Hawaiian surfer Noah Johnson won the 1999 Quiksilver/Aikau, held on New Year's Day, earning $55,000. Second place went to Tony Ray, third to Johnny-Boy Gomes.

New developments in big-wave surfing—the introduction of Maverick's, a break near San Francisco that killed Mark Foo in 1994, the advent of tow-in surfing, and the introduction of other big-wave contests, like the 1998 Reef Brazil Big-Wave World Championships—had meanwhile reduced the impact of the Quiksilver/Aikau. It would continue as one of the sport's most venerated contests, but never again would it have the honor of being the world's only big-wave surfing event.

In 2001, Ross Clarke-Jones of Australia became the first non-Hawaiian to win the Quiksilver/Aikau, held this time in smooth 20-foot surf. Shane Dorian was runner-up; Paul Paterson finished third. Indicative of the state of big-wave surfing, however, *Surfer* magazine's coverage of the event ran in the back of the magazine, while a tow-in shot of Noah Johnson on a 30-foot-plus wave at Maverick's was used on the cover. First-place Quiksilver prize money, moreover, was reduced for the first time to $50,000. The starting field for the 2002 Quiksilver was suddenly narrowed down when it was announced the day before the contest that the inaugural World Tow-In Cup would be held the same day in Maui; six-time world pro tour champion Kelly Slater stayed at Waimea and won the Quiksilver, just ahead of Aussie Tony Ray.

Quiksilver in Memory of Eddie Aikau results:

1984:	Denton Miyamura
1986:	Clyde Aikau
1990:	Keone Downing
1999:	Noah Johnson
2001:	Ross Clarke-Jones
2002:	Kelly Slater

See also big-wave surfing, Waimea Bay.

Quiksilver Masters World Championships
See Masters World Championships.

Quiksilver Maverick's Men Who Ride Mountains
Single-day professional big-wave surfing competition held at Maverick's, in Half Moon Bay, California; inaugurated in 1999, and sponsored by beachwear giant Quiksilver. The Men Who Ride Mountains event was conceived and produced by Quiksilver executives Bob McKnight and Danny Kwock, along with pioneering big-wave surfer George Downing and original Maverick's rider Jeff Clark; it was the second event designed specifically for big waves, following the Quiksilver in Memory of Eddie Aikau contest, held at Hawaii's Waimea Bay. Like the Aikau contest, the Maverick's

event has a months-long waiting period, with invited surfers standing by to appear on a 24-hour notice. Both contests are paddle-in only.

The debut Men Who Ride Mountains event was held on February 18, 1999, in wind-ruffled 15- to 20-foot surf. Rambunctious Santa Cruz surfer Darryl "Flea" Virostko, surfing with a close-cropped bleached-polka-dot hairstyle, was an easy and popular winner, and earned $15,000 of the $55,000 prize purse. In the finals, Virostko successfully launched an air-drop on one of the biggest waves of the day, earning a 98 out of a possible 100 from the judging panel—the highest score for the event. Thirty-eight-year-old big-wave veteran Richard Schmidt, also from Santa Cruz and thought to be past his prime, finished runner-up. Twenty surfers competed altogether; five of the top six were from Santa Cruz. The contest was the front-page lead story in both the *San Francisco Chronicle* and the *San Francisco Examiner,* was covered in the *New York Times, Sports Illustrated,* and the *Los Angeles Times,* and was featured on ESPN and San Francisco Bay Area news stations. On-site spectators numbered fewer than 500, as local police, for safety reasons, kept people off the flat bluff above the beach.

The second Men Who Ride Mountains event was held on March 3, 2000, in well-groomed 20-foot-plus surf, and Virostko again won convincingly, this time taking $30,000 of a $75,000 purse. In a mildly controversial placing, six-time world champion Kelly Slater from Florida, riding Maverick's for the first time, finished second. Jeff Clark served as contest director, as he had in 1999. For the next three years, wave conditions didn't meet Quiksilver standards, and the event was postponed. Meanwhile, not everyone in the surf world was glad to see competition and commercialization imported to Maverick's, a harshly beautiful break that had remained a surf world secret until 1992. "A few years ago Maverick's was surfed by the right people for the right reasons," a *Surfer* magazine reader said in a letter to the editor. "Now they want to bottle it, can it, and sell it on the shelf at Safeway. They just can't let the beast be." *See also* big-wave surfing, Darryl "Flea" Virostko.

Quiksilver Pro (Grajagan)   Men's-only world pro tour surfing contest held from 1995 to 1997 in the long, thrilling, left-breaking waves at Grajagan on the Indonesian island of Java; described by *Surfing* magazine as "the ultimate event," and by *Surfer* as "the greatest contest ever." The inaugural Quiksilver

Pro was worth $105,000, and featured a nearly surreal week-long run of perfect four- to eight-foot waves. Reigning world champion Kelly Slater of Florida won, getting a perfect 10 score after pulling into five distinct tubes on a single wave in his final heat against Californian Jeff Booth.

The vast majority of world tour surf contests prior to the Quiksilver Pro were designed mainly to attract a big on-site audience, with wave quality usually given no more than a passing thought. The surf, as a result, was often dreadful. The Quiksilver Pro, held on the edge of a Javanese jungle preserve, was the first contest to do away with on-site spectators entirely (attendance was limited to competitors, photographers, journalists, and contest staff) in exchange for high-quality surf and a media-only public presentation. The plan worked. The Quiksilver Pro was lavishly covered by the surf media, and was shown on cable TV, while nearly every pro nominated the event as their favorite.

The 1996 and 1997 versions of the Quiksilver Pro (won by Shane Beschen and Luke Egan, respectively) also met with excellent surf; a women's demonstration heat, featuring reigning world champion Lisa Andersen and champion-to-be Layne Beachley, was added to the 1996 event. Civic unrest in Indonesia forced the cancellation of the 1998 Quiksilver Pro, and as of 2003 the event had yet to return to the tour schedule. *See also* Grajagan.

Quinn, Maz   Smooth-riding regularfoot pro from Gisborne, New Zealand; the first surfer from his country to qualify for the World Championship Tour (WCT). Quinn was born (1976) in Hamilton, New Zealand, raised in Gisborne, and began surfing at age 11. Five years later he became the national juniors division champion; in 1996 and 2000 he won national titles in the men's division; in 2001 he finished third on the World Qualifying Series tour and made the big jump to the WCT. Quinn's siblings also performed well in 2001: younger brother Jay became the first New Zealand surfer to win a world championship by taking the Quiksilver World Grommet Titles; younger sister Holly was national women's champion. Maz Quinn appears in *Fifth Symphony Document* (2001) and a small number of other surf videos.

quiver   A surfer's personal collection of surfboards, usually numbering from three to six, but occasionally going up to 20 or more, with each board designed for a specific kind of wave. A "quiver" of boards is the surfing equivalent to the archer's quiver of arrows. Prior to 1968, surfers generally rode all-purpose boards, about 10 feet long, and rarely kept more than two boards at a time. After the late '60s shortboard revolution, as designs became increasingly specialized, avid surfers began assembling a graduated set of boards—often from the same shaper—so as to be ready for any type of surf. Generally speaking, the bigger the wave, the bigger the board. Mark Richards, for example, used a six-board quiver in Hawaii in 1975, with boards ranging from a 6'9" stinger for small waves up to an 8'6" pintail for 25-footers at Waimea Bay.

R

racism and surfing   While sexism has long been a surf culture hallmark, the sport for the most part has been free of racism. San Diego–raised surf photographer Aaron Chang, for example, remembered being treated "viciously" in the schoolyard during the early 1970s for being Asian, and said that surfing became the most important thing in his life in large part because "there was no racism in the water, just ability." This is likely due to the fact that the sport was conceived and to a great degree developed in Hawaii, among a racially mixed population. Many of modern surfing's best-known figures are dark-skinned pure-blooded Hawaiians (Eddie Aikau, Dane Kealoha), Asian (Mark Foo), or a polyglot mix (Sunny Garcia, Gerry Lopez, Rell Sunn). With Duke Kahanamoku as the sport's grand patriarch, it was all but guaranteed that racism wouldn't be a defining characteristic.

Surfing and race issues have nonetheless intersected at times. It can be argued that imperialist-based racism was the root cause of surfing's collapse in the 19th century, as English-speaking missionaries in Hawaii, in an effort to "civilize," as Calvinist Hiram Bingham put it, the islands' "chattering, almost naked savages," did everything they could short of legislation to discourage the sport. When Hawaii's civic leaders began to promote surfing in the early 20th century as a tourist-enticing symbol of romance and excitement, skin-color distinctions were sharply drawn. "The white man and boy are doing much in Hawaii to develop the art of surf-riding," Hawaii booster Alexander Hume Ford wrote in 1909. "[Surfing] games and feats never dreamed of by the native are being tried." Racial dissonance between mainstream and surf cultures echoed now and then in the years ahead: Kahanamoku was often treated poorly by white-owned hotels and restaurants while traveling through America on his way to the 1912 Olympics in Sweden; Eddie Aikau, after flying to South Africa to compete in the 1972 Gunston 500 event, was turned away from the whites-only Malibu Hotel in Durban.

Racism within the sport, while rare, is not unheard of. Wayne Bartholomew of Australia, the 1978 world champion, describing a hot and crowded summer day at Burleigh Heads, Queensland, in 1983, said that the beach was "crawling with ethnics," and complained that he was able to "walk from one end of the [Burleigh] park to the other without hearing a word of English." In a 1984 *Surfer* magazine portrait, half-black surfer Montgomery "Buttons" Kaluhiokalani is shown sitting in a beach chair wearing a comic frown while an unidentified person holds a photograph of a gorilla next to Kaluhiokalani's face. There can be no denying, furthermore, that surfing has in fact long been a white-dominated sport. Since the founding of the world pro circuit in 1976, all 10 women's champions have been white, as have 11 of the 13 men's champions (the exceptions being Derek Ho and Sunny Garcia, both from Hawaii); and as of 2003, virtually all owners and executives of major surfing-related companies were white. Japan and South America alone have produced hundreds of thousands of surfers, but the sport overwhelmingly reflects not just the blond-haired/blue-eyed physiology of Southern California and the Australian east coast, but the culture and aesthetic that goes with it. (The number of black surfers worldwide was microscopic in 1979 when *H2O* magazine published "Why Blacks Don't Surf"—primarily due to lack of surfing tradition, access, and role models, the article concludes—and just slightly less so in 1998, when San Diego County black surfer Sal Masekela, son of jazz trumpeter Hugh Masekela, was stopped while leaving the water by a family of tourists who asked him to pose for a photograph. When Masekela asked why, the father said, "We just want to show the folks back home that there's Negroes who surf.")

But a racially unbalanced sport is a long way removed from a racist sport. Surfers have dependably set themselves against racism. Eddie Aikau, after being turned away from the hotel in Durban, was taken in by Ernie Tomson, respected Durban businessman and father of 1978 world champion Shaun Tomson. World champions Tom Carroll, Martin Potter, and Tom Curren boycotted the pro circuit events in South Africa in 1985 as a protest against apartheid. In 1998, Australian surfer/board designer Maurice Cole led a spirited surf world campaign to help unseat right-wing politician Pauline Hanson, leader of the anti-immigrant One Nation party. If surfing isn't quite poised to become a multiracial promised land, it's nonetheless well ahead of the general sociological curve. "In its essence," Sal Masekela noted, "surfing blends cultures as well as music or art or anything like that." *See also* politics and surfing.

radio and surfing   Beach city radio stations were broadcasting short regularly scheduled reports on wave and beach conditions as far back as the mid-1960s, with the information usually phoned in by a well-known surfing personality. Radio surf reporters from the '60s and '70s include South Africa's John Whitmore, Australians Shane Stedman and Mark Warren, Hawaii's Lord Blears and Joe Teipel, and California's Mike Purpus. Radio surf reports continued to be popular even after the mid-'80s introduction of telephone pay-per-call reports, which were far more detailed. In 1990, *Surfing* magazine published a list of 17 American radio-broadcast surf reports, ranging from Waikiki to San Diego, Houston, Long Island, and Lake Michigan.

Surf radio shows, as distinct from surf reports, have been few and far between. Four-time South African champion George Thomopolous hosted a 15-minute surfing variety show called *High Wave* from 1971 to 1973. In late 1981, Hawaiian surfer Mark Foo launched a one-hour Sunday evening program on Honolulu's 98 Rock called *Surf Scene,* featuring surf contest updates, interviews with local and visiting surfers—Dane Kealoha, Shaun Tomson, Simon Anderson, and Dick Brewer all made appearances—and a call-in segment.

Radio stations have occasionally sponsored surf contests, including the 1965 KHJ Hermosa Beach event, one of the sport's first professional contests, and the Coca-Cola/2SM event in Sydney, the world's richest surf contest from 1977 to 1982.

America's only surfing radio show as of 2003 was *Let's Talk Surfing,* hosted by Marc Kent, from his home in Shell Beach, and broadcast through most of central California and parts of Hawaii. The one-hour weekly show, started in 1997, features interviews with famous surfers (guests have included Gerry Lopez, Sunny Garcia, and Joel Tudor), board-builders, surf magazine editors, and even anonymous world-traveling surf gypsies. Radio Fluminense in Brazil also

has a weekly surfing program. *See also* television and surfing.

raft surfing   *See* mat surfing.

Raglan   Left-breaking point wave located on the west coast of New Zealand's North Island, near Auckland; the country's most famous break, capable of producing rides of nearly surreal length; named in a 1989 *Surfing* magazine article as one of the "25 Best Waves in the World." Raglan is made up of five separate surf spots—a beachbreak, a reefbreak, and three points—along the perimeter of a huge rock- and shrub-lined bay. Raglan Point, the innermost left-breaking wave, was the first area to be ridden, in 1959 by local surfer Peter Miller, who three years later opened the region's first surf shop. Raglan's remaining breaks came into play as the crowds grew. On the biggest and best-shaped days, the three point waves will occasionally link together to form a continuous wave in excess of two miles. On such occasions, local surfers take turns waiting at the base of the point to drive groups of their friends back to the starting area. Raglan is generally best during summer and fall, when four- to six-foot surf is fairly common and the water temperature is in the mid-60s.

Raglan, named after a nearby town, first came to the attention of the surfing world in 1964 when it was featured in an early version of Bruce Brown's hit film *The Endless Summer.* "The rides are so long it's ridiculous," Brown narrates as the camera follows California surfer Robert August. "This is the middle part of the ride," he continues, before cutting to a second shot of August. "Later in the day, here's some more of the middle part of the ride." *The Endless Summer* crew surfed Raglan alone on Christmas Day, 1963, but crowds were moving in by the end of the decade. Within a few years, as a New Zealand surf journalist/photographer later wrote, a good day of surf would be met by surfers "scrambling down the hill like termites exiting a smoking tree."

Raglan is host site to an annual event on the New Zealand Championship Circuit. The Raglan surf has been featured in a number of surf movies, including *Coastal Disturbance* (1994) and *Static* (2001). Local standouts as of 2003 include Luke Cederman and Sam Wills.

rail   The surfboard's rounded perimeter; elliptical on both axes, from nose to tail and from deck to bottom surface. Rails are a fundamental element in surfboard design, along with outline, thickness, bottom contour, and volume distribution. In general, a soft and rounded rail makes the board slower but easier to handle; a dropped-profile rail with an edge along the bottom increases board speed but makes it more difficult to turn; a full rail lends stability at the expense of maneuverability; a thin and tapered rail promotes quick turns but doesn't carry momentum, and can make the board feel jittery. For high-performance shortboards, rails tend to be thin, boxy, and hard-edged along the rear of the board, full and soft-edged in the middle, thin and rounded in the nose. Longboard rails are often soft and medium thin from nose to tail.

Little attention was given to rails until the late '60s; nearly all boards up to that point had some variation of a soft, egg-shaped rail, in which the deck-to-perimeter curve more or less matched the curve coming up from the bottom. The 1967-launched shortboard revolution, which in two years saw boards redesigned from lumbering 10-footers to streamlined sub-seven-footers, brought attention to rail design. The "down rail," which dropped the rail's apex toward the board's bottom surface, was an early and improved result, giving surfers greater traction and control, and allowing them to ride deeper inside the tube. (American board-builder Dave Parmenter went so far as to say that the down rail "represents the continental divide in surfboard development.") The "tucked-under edge," a modification of the down rail, with the rail curve bending around the perimeter and brought to a wide-angle edge by the board's bottom surface, became the rail of choice in the late '70s.

"Rail" is used in a number of surfing-related phrases. To "bury a rail" is to set a deep, powerful turn. To "dig a rail" is to have an edge sink into the water unexpectedly, often resulting in a wipeout. A "rail grab" is when the surfer grips the rail for added stability. *See also* chine rail, egg rail, 50/50 rail, outline, the surfboard, tucked-under rail.

rail grab   Holding the rail of the surfboard as a stabilizing technique, often with the trailing hand on the board's shoreward-facing outside edge; usually performed in tight situations while riding backside (back to the wave). California surfer John Peck made the rail grab famous in the winter of 1962–63, as he blasted through the hollow sections at Hawaii's Pipeline in a low, three-point stance, right hand locked on the edge of his board for balance. Aerial surfers often use one of nearly a dozen rail grab varia-

Rail grab by Hawaii's Bruce Irons

tions—single- or double-handed—while in flight; gouging midface turns can also be guided by a one-handed rail grab. *See also* pigdog.

rail line   *See* outline.

rail sandwich   Dreaded variation of wipeout in which a rider's board tilts sideways and flies up between the legs toward the genitals.

rail saver   Thin, rectangular piece of high-strength nylon, more or less the shape and size of a watchband, looped at each side, designed to prevent a surf leash from gouging into the surfboard's tail section. Invented in the mid-'70s, the rail saver was originally sold as a separate unit. One end was attached to the nylon cord found at the end of the leash, the other end was attached to a nylon cord loop anchored to the board, usually by means of a deck plug. Today's leash comes equipped with a rail saver. *See also* surf leash.

rail turn   A deep, sustained, water-displacing turn, generally performed at high speed, during which the engaged rail of the surfboard is said to be "buried" in the wave face. The rail turn is the mark of the power surfer; since the early 1990s it has been the surfing traditionalists' most popular example of "real" surfing, as compared to the New School–developed array of tailslides, aerials, and other "neutral rail" maneuvers. Australians Tom Carroll, Gary Elkerton, and Mark Occhilupo, pro surfers who all came of age in the '80s, are celebrated for their rail turns. *See also* power surfing.

Ranch, The   Fourteen-thousand acres of privately owned and virtually undeveloped land, located just north of Santa Barbara, California, featuring almost nine miles of pastoral wave-filled coastline. Adjacent to the surf world's most densely populated surf zone—the Southern California coast from San Diego to Santa Barbara—the fiercely protected Hollister Ranch has for decades been viewed by most American surfers as a kind of inaccessible earthly paradise. About 100 surfers own property on the Ranch, and another few hundred sometimes boat in from the south when the surf is up. Tens of thousands, meanwhile, stand by and hope the state will eventually open the Ranch up to public access.

About a dozen high-quality reef- and point-breaks are located on the Ranch between Gaviota to the south and the tip of Point Conception (part of the adjacent Bixby Ranch) to the north. Among the best breaks are the long and beautifully paced rights of Cojo Point, the short, pinwheeling tubes at Rights and Lefts, and Little Drakes. Cojo is one of the few Ranch spots that break best during the southwest swells of late summer and early fall; most of the spots require cold season swells from the west and northwest. The Channel Islands effectively block incoming swells from the south, and Ranch waves in general are smaller than those found to the north and south, rarely getting above eight feet. The prevailing westerly wind blows up to 30 miles per hour, but strikes side-offshore at some Ranch breaks.

Named after the Hollister family, who owned and farmed the Ranch for four generations dating back to the mid-19th century, the Ranch has never been part of surfing's public domain. In 1959, a group of 20 Santa Barbara surfers, including surfboard manufacturer Renny Yater, formed the Santa Barbara County Surf Club for the express purpose of gaining access to the Ranch; part of the club's deal with the Hollister family was to post a guard at the south entrance to keep other surfers from gaining access. The Hollisters sold the 14,000-acre "home" portion of their land in the late '60s to a developer, who in turn divided the land into 140 100-acre parcels. (A beachfront parcel went on the market in 2001 for $7.9 million.) A 1976 California state law ordered public access to the Ranch, but wealthy and well-connected Ranch owners have so far not only managed to keep the law

from being acted upon, they have made their corner of the world almost disappear. "Hollister Ranch" doesn't appear on most California road maps, and there are no Hollister off-ramp signs along Highway 101. Surfers can legally boat into the channels near the breaks, or walk in along the beach from below the high-tide line. Once in the surf, however, they are generally given a cold reception by property-owning surfers.

The Ranch first came to the surf world's attention in John Severson's 1961 surf film *Big Wednesday; Surfer* magazine first wrote about the Ranch in 1968, describing the oak- and canyon-lined coast as "clean and raw and silent, with the best waves to be found anywhere in America proper." *Surfer* also warned that trespassers would be prosecuted "to the limit of the law" by a local parcel-owning judge. In a 1998 issue of the *New York Times Sunday Magazine* devoted to status items among various groups, access to the Ranch was cited as the ultimate surf status token.

The Ranch has occasionally been featured in surf movies and videos, including *The Natural Art* (1969), *Cosmic Children* (1970), *Pacific Vibrations* (1970), and *Rolling Thunder* (1991). The "Malibu" scenes from Warner Brothers' 1978 surf movie *Big Wednesday* were filmed at Cojo Point.

Randazzo, Dean   High-energy regularfooter from Atlantic City, New Jersey; a world tour surfer in 1996, and described by Swell.com as "one of the fastest and most entertaining surfers in the world." Randazzo was born (1969) and raised in Atlantic City, began surfing at age 10, and by 17 had developed a low, racy, eye-pleasing style. He became a member of the prestigious National Scholastic Surfing Association's National Team in 1985, but in general he surfed below form during competition. In 1991, he moved to Oceanside, California; four years later, after serving what amounted to the sport's longest professional apprenticeship, the dark-haired 27-year-old at last qualified for the world pro circuit—then failed to make the cut the following year. Randazzo was treated with chemotherapy after being diagnosed with Hodgkin's disease in 2001; fully recovered in 2002, he finished #4 in the year-end standings for the Foster's Pro Surfing Tour. Randazzo has appeared in a handful of surf videos, including *110/240* (1992), *Players* (1995), and *Lost Across America* (1999).

Rapa Nui   *See* Easter Island.

Rarick, Randy   Authoritative surf traveler/organizer/board-maker from Sunset Beach, Hawaii; semifinalist in the 1970 World Surfing Championships; executive director of the Triple Crown of Surfing since its 1983 inception. Rarick was born (1949) in Seattle, Washington, moved with his family to Honolulu at age five, and began surfing at 10, under the tutelage of fabled beachboy Rabbit Kekai. He won the juniors division of the 1967 state surfing championships; three years later he nearly made the finals of the 1970 World Championships, held in Victoria, Australia, and was invited to the Duke Kahanamoku Classic and Smirnoff Pro-Am.

Rarick's first overseas surf trip was in 1968, just after high school, when he flew to Australia and stayed for nearly a year, in part to avoid the draft. He began making annual visits to South Africa in 1971, and in the decades to come the ruddy-faced regular-footer traveled to coastlines near and far, eventually surfing in more 60 countries, including Angola, Greece, Namibia, Albania, Colombia, Sri Lanka, Ghana, India, and Lebanon. Rarick was the only candidate when Bruce Brown hired a location scout in 1992 for his new movie *Endless Summer II*.

Rarick always returned from his travels to be on the North Shore of Oahu for the winter surf season, and in 1976, at age 26, he and 1968 world champion Fred Hemmings were the two principal organizers of the International Professional Surfers (IPS) world circuit, precursor to today's Association of Surfing Professionals (ASP) tour. Hemmings for the most part dealt with contest sponsors and the media; Rarick was liaison to the pro surfers and general troubleshooter. Both lost money on the IPS; both had to retrench following the 1982 ASP takeover, with Rarick going on to become an ASP board member and head of the Triple Crown, the circuit-within-a-circuit made up of three North Shore contests, and long regarded as surfing's second-most coveted title, after the world championship. Rarick was by then known as one of the sport's more reliable figures. "Of all the surfers who made a difference over the past 30 years," sports writer Bruce Jenkins wrote of Rarick in "Mr. Clean," a 1998 *Surfer's Journal* profile, "he's among the handful who never changed. Never took drugs, never bailed out, never lost his stoke, never stopped ripping." Rarick's income has meanwhile been drawn almost exclusively from surfboard shaping, a craft he learned as a teenager from master Hawaiian shapers George Downing and Dick Brewer. In the late '60s and '70s,

he worked for Surf Line Hawaii, Dewey Weber Surfboards, and Lightning Bolt, and made boards for big-wave rider Buzzy Trent, 1972 world champion Jimmy Blears, and Hawaiian surf icon Rell Sunn, among others.

Rarick appeared in a small number of early- and mid-'70s surf movies, including *Tracks* (1970), *Oceans* (1972), and *A Winter's Tale* (1974); since 1970 he's written more than three dozen surf articles and columns, mainly for *Surfer* and *Surfing* magazines. Rarick has been married twice. *See also* International Professional Surfers, professional surfing, Triple Crown of Surfing.

rash guard   Snug, flexible, long- or short-sleeve Lycra shirt worn by surfers for protection against sunburn or cold, and to prevent chafing caused by an ill-fitting wetsuit or gritty surfboard deck. Prior to the mid-1980s, a T-shirt was often used for the same purpose. Professional surfers began using brightly colored Lycra tank tops during competition in early 1985, and by the end of the year a short-sleeve version was being sold as an antirash garment. By the early '90s, lightweight Lycra (five or six ounces per yard) was being used for sun protection rash guards, while heavier material (seven or eight ounce, often laminated with heat-retaining polypropylene) was used for under-wetsuit rash guards. *See also* wax rash, wetsuit rash.

Rasmussen, Rick   Hard-charging, fast-talking goofyfoot surfer from Westhampton, New York; winner of the 1974 United States Surfing Championships. Rasmussen was born in 1955, the son of an aerospace test pilot and former pro basketball player, raised in Maine, and began surfing at age 10, not long after his family moved to an affluent Westhampton neighborhood. As a juniors division surfer he placed fourth in the 1972 U.S. Championships, first in the 1973 East Coast Championships, and third in the 1973 U.S. Championships; moving up to the men's division in 1974, the blond-haired 18-year-old finished fifth in the East Coast Championships, then became the first East Coast male to win a U.S. surfing title—taking the kneeboard division for good measure. Rasmussen was known by that time not only for his aggressive small-wave style, but as a hellfire tuberider, gaining praise from surfers like Gerry Lopez after threading his way through some enormous barrels at Pipeline in Hawaii. He was also one of the first East Coast surfers to travel Indonesia, riding Uluwatu in Bali in early 1976, then visiting Java's Grajagan the following year. Along with New Jersey pro surfer Linda Davoli and TV actor Gregory Harrison, Rasmussen was filmed at Grajagan in 1980 for an episode of ABC-TV's *American Sportsman*. He also appeared in six surf movies, including *Fantasea* (1978) and *Bali High* (1981). Throughout the '70s, Rasmussen shaped surfboards for Clean and Natural (his own label) and Rick Rasmussen Surfboards.

In 1979, after being charged with possession of a kilo of cocaine while in Bali, Rasmussen spent three months in prison awaiting trial, then won an acquittal. Two years later he was arrested after selling $500,000 worth of heroin to a New York undercover agent. Less than 10 months later, and one week before he was to be sentenced on trafficking charges, Rasmussen was shot and killed in Harlem, following a Times Square–initiated drug deal. He was 27. Rasmussen was inducted into the East Coast Surf Legends Hall of Fame in 2000. *See also* drugs and surfing.

Rawson, Pat   Good-natured surfboard shaper from Sunset Beach, Hawaii; regarded by many, since the mid-1980s, as the maker of the world's finest big-wave boards. Rawson was born (1954) and raised in Santa Monica, California, began surfing at age nine and shaping at age 12. In the early '70s he started working for Southern California surfboard companies, including Rick, Blue Cheer, and Wilken; he moved to Oahu in 1974, and soon found work with Downing and Local Motion. Rawson meanwhile made boards under his own label, and eventually began distributing them to retail outlets worldwide. Rawson himself has never owned a surfboard shop. While he makes first-quality boards of all sizes and shapes, he's best known for midlength guns (big-wave boards) ranging in size from seven to 10 feet; his boards can look almost rudimentary, but are in fact masterworks of blended rocker, outline, bottom curves, and volume distribution. Nearly every world champion surfer since 1976 at one time or another has ridden Rawson's boards, usually while in Hawaii; longtime Rawson devotees include Mark Richards, Tom Carroll, and Kalani Robb. Rawson was named the world's best shaper in a 1991 peer poll taken by *Australia's Surfing Life* magazine; *Surfer* magazine cited him in 1994 as "the man who makes the best 7'6" in the world." Rawson is married and has three children; Ryan Rawson, his only son, earned a reputation

in the early '00s as one of Hawaii's best up-and-coming big-wave riders. *See also* big-wave surfboard.

Ray, Tony   Unassuming big-wave rider from Torquay, Victoria, Australia, described by surf journalist Steve Hawk as the "Forrest Gump of giant waves"; world-ranked #11 in 1992, and runner-up in the 1999 and 2002 editions of the Quiksilver in Memory of Eddie Aikau contest at Waimea Bay in Hawaii. Ray was born (1965) in Torquay, moved with his family to Coolangatta, Queensland, in 1970, and began surfing at age seven. In 1983—five years after moving back to Torquay—Ray placed third in the juniors division of the Australian National Titles; the following year he was runner-up in the men's division to future world tour powerhouse Gary Elkerton. The slender-framed Ray was a precision surfer, and had a beautiful line through the tube. He won his only world tour event in 1992, beating future six-time world champion Kelly Slater in the Lacanau Pro in France.

After retiring from the tour after the 1995 season, Ray began to concentrate on big-wave surfing, and quickly developed a smooth, almost laconic approach to both paddle-in and tow-in riding. He placed second in the 1998 Reef Big-Wave World Championships at Todos Santos, Mexico; the following year he finished ninth in the Quiksilver Men Who Ride Mountains contest at Maverick's and second in the Quiksilver/Aikau event; in 2000 he placed third in the Quiksilver/Maverick's contest. On January 28, 1998, Ray and tow-in surfing partner Ross Clarke-Jones rode a series of 30-foot-plus waves at Outside Log Cabins, on the North Shore of Oahu, during what soon came to be known as the "Biggest Wednesday" swell. Ray was announced as the winner of the 2002 Quiksilver/Aikau event just after the contest finished, but a tabulating error was discovered a few hours later, and he ended up finishing second to six-time world champion Kelly Slater.

The soft-spoken Ray has kept a friendly distance from the surf media, and appears in just a few surf videos, including *Mental Surfing* (1993), *Players* (1995), *Twenty Feet Under* (1998), and *Biggest Wednesday* (1998). He's been married once and has one child.

Raymond, Bruce   Australian pro surfer and surf businessman from Sydney's Bondi Beach; world-ranked #16 in 1977, and the managing director for Quiksilver International surfwear from 1979 to present day. "He has that dark-eyed sinister air about him

Bruce Raymond

that appeals to women and makes men wonder," surf journalist Phil Jarratt said of Raymond in 1977. "He would have made a good con man, hustler or gigolo." Raymond was born (1954) in Wauchope, New South Wales, moved with his family to Sydney at age four, and began surfing at 10. He lied about his age and became a fireman at 17, then resigned three years later to join the fledgling pro surfing tour. Raymond wasn't an especially good competitor, but put in first-class performances each winter on the North Shore of Oahu, where he earned a reputation as a brave and sometimes reckless big-wave rider. "I didn't think I had a death wish," Raymond later said, "but everyone around me thought I did." For Warner Brothers' 1978 surf movie *Big Wednesday,* Raymond was hired as the stunt surfer for the climactic wipeout sequence. He also starred in *Band on the Run* (1981), *Adventures in Paradise* (1982), and a few other period surf movies.

Raymond quit the tour at 25 to work with Quiksilver, but continued pushing the limits. In one of the company's early full-page color ads, he is slouched bare-chested against the hood of a car, with the tag line reading, "If You Can't Rock and Roll, Don't Fuckin' Come." He helped Quiksilver with licensing agreements around the world, launched the Quiksilver Pro at Grajagan in 1995, conegotiated Quiksilver's contracts with world champions Kelly Slater and Lisa Andersen, and was identified in a 1997 *Deep* magazine article as "one of the most powerful figures in the multi-billion-dollar global surfing industry." *See also* Quiksilver.

Red Sea Long, narrow arm of the Arabian Sea, slightly larger than the state of California, separat-

ing the Arabian Peninsula from northeastern Africa. Although windsurfing is popular in the warm waters of the Red Sea, little is known about its surf. The sea's average width is about 200 miles, however, providing more than enough fetch for waves to take shape; monsoons cross the area from both northeast and southwest, and both the east and west shores of the Red Sea are lined with vibrant coral reef—a combination that virtually guarantees surfable waves.

red tide Nearshore bloom of single-cell algae called dinoflagellates; sometimes miles long, usually occurring during summer months. Red tide has nothing to do with tides, and the color it gives off isn't so much red as an unattractive brown-rust. But at night, the microorganisms, when tossed around in the foaming part of a breaking wave, produce a mesmerizing blue-green phosphorescent glow; night surfing during a red tide is a mildly psychedelic experience. Scientists have suggested a number of explanations for red tide—that it's caused by upwelling of cold water mixing with warmer surface water, from a sudden increase in nutrients from land-based runoff, or from a sedimentary disturbance of some kind on the ocean floor—but the exact causes remain a mystery. While health experts say red tide is harmless, many surfers and swimmers say it causes sore throats, earaches, and other infections. Red tides are more common in nontropical areas, generally last a few days, and are dispersed either by wind, heavy seas, or from being eaten by other plankton.

Red Triangle Roughly triangular region of ocean along the central California coast, known to have the world's highest concentration of white sharks; bordered by Tomales Bay to the north, Monterey Bay to the south, and the Farallon Islands (28 miles off San Francisco) to the west. The 150-mile stretch of coastline between Monterey and Tomales includes some of mainland America's best surfing areas, including Maverick's and all of Santa Cruz. It is also home to thousands of full-time surfers, all of whom worry to one degree or another about shark attacks, even though just a microscopic percentage have in fact been hit. Two of the Red Triangle's best-known incidents took place almost 20 years apart. On December 19, 1981, 25-year-old Pacific Grove kneeboarder Lew Boren, while surfing alone at Asilomar Beach in Monterey, was killed by a white shark estimated to be 21 feet long. On September 29, 2000, Santa Barbara surfer Peck Euwer, while sitting on his board in the channel at Maverick's, was bucked into the air—but left unharmed—by a 13-foot white shark. There were 51 documented shark attacks in the Red Triangle between 1926 and 2000, five of them fatal. A surf video titled *Waves of Adventure in the Red Triangle* was released in 1993; *Sharks of the Red Triangle,* a nonsurfing Discovery Channel documentary, aired in 1996. *See also* sharks and surfing.

Redman-Carr, Melanie   Plain-spoken regularfoot pro surfer from Busselton, Western Australia; world-ranked #2 in 2001. Redman-Carr was born (1975) and raised in Busselton, and began surfing at age 10. Raised on the punishing reef surf of the Margaret River area, Redman-Carr performs best when conditions get extreme; she's the only woman to regularly surf the notoriously shallow waves at the Box, not far from her home. She became a full-time pro in 1993, and won her first world tour pro event—the Billabong Pro at Jeffreys Bay—in 1999. She's been critical of the world tour, and seems genuinely unimpressed with her own achievements. "Sometimes I think I used to surf better when I was 17," she told *Surfing* in 1999. "You've got more confidence when you first start out. You haven't been beaten and put down so much." Redman-Carr continued to place well on the world tour, finishing fourth in 1999, sixth in 2000, second in 2001, and third in 2002. She's appeared in a small number of surf videos, including *Our Turn* (2000) and *Tropical Madness* (2001).

Melanie Redman-Carr

reef rash   Scrapes, cuts, and abrasions resulting from contact with a reef; especially common at shallow-water breaks in the tropics, where surfers ride with little or no wetsuit protection. Even mild cases of reef rash can be worrisome, as any break in the skin while in the tropics can lead to a staph infection. *See also* injuries and surfing.

reef walkers   Low-cut rubber booties with hard rubber soles and thin, sometimes-ventilated uppers; designed for walking over shallow inshore coral- or urchin-covered reefs, and to protect the surfer's feet during a wipeout. Reef walkers—a generic name—were introduced in the mid-1980s, as the sharp-bottom breaks in Indonesia, Tahiti, and Fiji became popular. *See also* booties.

reefbreak   Type of surf break centered around a permanent high spot in the underwater topography—a reef—almost always formed by either rock or coral. Although reefbreaks are found worldwide, their dispersion varies greatly from coastline to coastline. Sandy nontropical or subtropical areas such as the southern half of the American East Coast have few reefbreaks; tropical islands—Fiji and Hawaii, for example—feature reefbreaks almost to the exclusion of all other breaks. Reefbreaks have a wider range of characteristics than either point- or beachbreaks (the other two primary types of surf spot), creating virtually every kind of wave from the long, slow, gentle rollers of California's San Onofre to the abruptly explosive tubes of Teahupoo, Tahiti. Other well-known reefbreaks include Sunset Beach, Pipeline, and Maverick's. Virtually all big-wave locations are reefbreaks. In the early decades of 20th century, the world's premier surfing area was a set of reefbreaks in Waikiki; in the early decades of California surfing, the reefs of Palos Verdes's Paddleboard Cove—sometimes referred to by locals as "little Waikiki"—were thought of as the state's most elegant surf. Because many of the world's most beautiful and challenging waves break over shallow reefs lined with coral heads or sharp-edged rock, reefbreaks are to blame for a good portion of the surf world's collective scrapes, cuts, and scars. *See also* beachbreak, pointbreak.

reentry   Maneuver in which the surfer ricochets off the curl, just as it starts to break; a harder and more powerful version of the "roller coaster" and synonymous with "off the lip." While surfers began using the word "reentry" in the mid-1960s, it was and remains a misnomer, as rider and board stay in contact with the wave—aerials didn't come into play until the early '80s—and don't really "reenter" at all. A "vertical reentry" occurs when the rider rides straight up the wave face before cornering back down.

reform   A foaming whitewater wave that first moves into deep water, so that it reverts back to an unbroken swell—or the whitewater is reduced to a fringe along the crest—then onto a shallow area where the wave once again steepens and breaks. Reforms come in all sizes and shapes. Waves at Second Reef Pipeline in Hawaii almost always reform into a gaping tube on the nearshore reef; waves at Huntington Beach in California often reform into an undistinguished shore-break closeout.

regularfoot   A left-foot-forward stance on a surf-board. Regularfooters make up about 65 percent of the surfing population, as compared to right-foot-forward goofyfooters. A tiny percentage of surfers are switchfoots, and ride either regularfoot or goofy-foot. Famous regularfoot surfers include Phil Edwards, Shaun Tomson, Tom Curren, Lisa Andersen, Kelly Slater, and Andy Irons. Called "naturalfoot" in Australia and New Zealand. *See also* goofyfoot, switchfoot.

Reid, Sam   American surfing pioneer from New Jersey; the first person, along with Tom Blake, to ride Malibu. Reid was seven years old in 1912 when Hawaiian surfer/swimmer Duke Kahanamoku gave a surfing demonstration in Atlantic City, near Reid's home; the following day Reid began riding waves on his mother's ironing board. He traveled to California at 19 and became a lifeguard at the Santa Monica Swimming Club. In 1925, he made the first of many visits to Hawaii. In the early fall of 1926, Reid and Tom Blake drove up Pacific Coast Highway in Blake's Essex, stopped at a private-property gate at the mouth of Los Flores Canyon, pulled their redwood boards from the rumble seat, and paddled one mile north to a never-before-surfed break at what was then known as Malibu Ranch. They rode their first Malibu wave together, and Reid later said that the experience "made you feel like a king!" Writing for *Surfer* maga-

zine in 1966, Reid, a surfing traditionalist who preferred an understated style of wave-riding, noted that "a mature man will never remain a hot-dogger." He died in 1978 at age 73.

religion and surfing   Religion played a significant role in the surfing lives of ancient Hawaiians: tree trunks were prayed over before they were shaped into surfboards, surf-dedicated temples were built (suggesting that there was a god unique to surfing, although the deity's name remains unknown), waves were called forth with chants and prayers, and competing surfers always made offerings prior to entering the water. Calvinist Christianity trumped native religion in Hawaii in the 19th century as the islands came under the influences of American and British missionaries, and surfing was discouraged (although not banned outright) as an act that encouraged sloth, gambling, and sex.

Religion played little or no role in the early decades of modern surfing, but returned in the 1970s as surfers by the thousands converted to born-again Christianity. Surf magazines featured advertisements with Jesus "fish" symbols and psalm quotes (a San Fernando Valley surf shop offered free bibles to new customers), and published articles like "Surfing as Prayer"; the Jesus Classic surf contest was inaugurated in Australia, and the Christian Surfing Association was formed in Southern California. *Tales from the Tube,* a 1975 surfing movie, ended with a group of top surfers discussing the apocalypse, the Second Coming, and salvation. "Surfing," four-time world champion Margo Oberg of Hawaii told a surf journalist, "is a way of humbling ourselves before God and praising Him for such an abundant life." (*Surfing* magazine satirized the surfing born-again movement in its 1974 Comedy Annual, offering the *Guide to Sacred Surf Spots* book, which guaranteed to show each buyer the "silver stairway to heaven-sent tubes.") Born-agains continued to make up a small but active percentage of surfers, quietly led by three-time world champion Tom Curren of California, who guided the Calvery Chapel surf team to an upset victory in the 1981 Katin Pro-Am. Curren spoke before 40,000 born-agains at the Harvest Crusade at Anaheim Stadium in 1997, and signed bibles afterward. Other well-known born-again surfers include Brad McCaul, Yancy Spencer, Joey Buran, Chris Brown, Tony

Moniz, Dave MacAulay, Mike Lambresi, Tim Curran, and CJ Hobgood.

While nonevangelical religions and sects count surfers among their members, few have tried to establish any kind of beachhead within the sport. "Why Don't Jews Surf?," a 1980 *H2O* magazine article, noted that surfing was the preserve of "the young, blonde, tanned, be-muscled Gentile. No others need apply; few do." (Jewish surfers are in fact not uncommon; South Africa's Shaun Tomson flew to Hawaii in 1969 as a bar mitzvah present, and eight years later won the world title; Nachum Shifren, the "surfing rabbi," was profiled in *People* magazine and the *L.A. Times* in the '90s.) Australian surfer Ted Spencer, two-time winner of the Bells Beach contest in the late '60s, became a follower of Swami Bhaktivedanta in 1970 and later said, "When I surf, I dance for Krishna." Sixties pointbreak stylist Bob Cooper, a lifelong Mormon originally from California, said in 1999 that he still "got a buzz" from surfing, but that he was more interested in "things that sustain the spirit." Pioneering big-wave surfer George Downing of Hawaii meanwhile saw no reason why surfing and spirituality couldn't be more closely fused, and suggested in the early '90s, only half-jokingly, that wave-riding itself could serve as the basis of a religion.

Religious-based surfing groups in 2003 included Christian Surfers USA, Christian Surfers Australia, Christian Surfers U.K., and Surf and Soul (for Jewish surfers). Religious-themed surf videos include *Son Riders* (1988), *Changes* (1999), and *The Outsiders* (2002).

Rendezvous Ballroom   Concert venue and dance hall in Newport Beach, California; launching pad for surf music innovator Dick Dale, and point of origin for the no-finesse-required "surfer stomp" dance step. The block-long two-story beachfront Rendezvous Ballroom, located just west of Balboa Pier, opened in 1928, and quickly became known as the "West Coast Home of the Big Band Sound," featuring acts like Guy Lombardo and Benny Goodman. It had a 12,000-square-foot wooden dance floor, and could accommodate 4,000 people. The Rendezvous faded along with the big band era, and was all but shuttered in 1959 when guitarist Dick Dale, one year after recording his debut single, played his first show there—to an audience of 17. Dale persisted, and the following year word spread among local high school students that his Rendezvous shows were hot. "It was a place you could go to be a surfer," said Righteous Brothers

drummer Tracy Longstreth, who played the Rendezvous in the early 1960s and remembered it as being loud, sweaty, and rowdy. Other surf bands took up the slack after 1961, when Dale left his semiregular Rendezvous gig to tour the country, but by 1965 the ballroom, along with surf music in general, was fading fast. The Rendezvous burned down in 1966, and never reopened. Condominiums now fill the lot, although a bronze plaque, unveiled in 1986 at what was once the Rendezvous's southeast corner, notes the location as Orange County Historical site #34. "The music and dancing have ended," the plaque's inscription reads, "but the memories linger on." *See also* Dick Dale, surf music, Surfer Stomp.

Renneker, Mark   Loquacious big-wave rider/explorer/health advocate from San Francisco, California; founder of the Surfer's Medical Association. Renneker was born (1952) in Chicago, Illinois, the son of a psychiatrist, moved with his family to West Los Angeles at age four, and began surfing at 10. He received a B.S. in biology and epistemics from U.C. Santa Cruz in 1975; four years later he took his M.D. from U.C. San Francisco; in 1990 he began a private practice specializing in research and advocacy for patients with life-threatening illness. Renneker founded the Surfer's Medical Association (SMA) in 1987 during the First International Medical Conference on the Sport of Surfing, held on Fiji's Tavarua Island; from 1988 to 1995 he was the principal contributor to the SMA's "Surf Docs" question-and-answer health column in *Surfer* magazine.

Renneker began riding Maverick's, the big-wave break located between San Francisco and Santa Cruz, in 1990; over the next 12 years, he surfed there more than anyone else. He also began looking for breaks along the world's coldest and most remote coastlines, and by 2001 the tall, bearded, hawk-nosed regular-footer had ridden waves off the Aleutian Islands, mainland Alaska, Iceland, and Tierra del Fuego. He's the only person to have surfed both Spitsbergen (800 miles from the North Pole), as well as Antarctica.

Renneker had neither the interest or the skills to be a competition surfer, but he nonetheless accepted an invitation to the debut Quiksilver Men Who Ride Mountains contest at Maverick's in 1999. The oldest entrant at 47, he finished 12th in a field of 20; in 2000 he chose not to accept his Quiksilver invite. After tow-in surfing became popular at Maverick's in the late '90s, Renneker became the voice of opposition. "The noise and the stink," he said in 2001, beginning a list of the reasons he felt personal watercraft should be banned from local waters. "They're tearing up kelp; they scare the crap out of the birds, seals, sea lions and sea otters; they leave the water coated with that horrible oil."

Renneker was the title subject in 1992's "Playing Doc's Games," a two-part *New Yorker* article, and the following year he was featured in an episode of the Ed Bradley–hosted *Street Stories* newsmagazine show on CBS-TV. In 1998 he appeared in the documentary film *Maverick's,* as well as the Maverick's episode of *Great Waves,* a Outdoor Life Network documentary series; in 2000 he was featured in *Maverick's: The Story of Big-Wave Surfing,* published by Chronicle Books. He coauthored the medical advice book *Sick Surfers: Ask the Surf Docs* (1993), and wrote the foreword to Peter Dixon's *The Complete Guide to Surfing* (2001). Renneker lives with Jessica Dunne, an artist whose surf-themed work was featured in a 1995 issue of the *Surfer's Journal. See also* Antarctica, personal watercraft, Surfer's Medical Association.

Reno, Angie   Hyperkinetic switchfooter from southwest Los Angeles County. A 1968 issue of *Surfing* magazine noted that the 15-year-old Reno "surfs like a young Dewey Weber, always on the go, climbing and dropping, and driving hard on every move." Reno was the surprise winner of the Malibu Club Invitational competition that year, and was featured in three of the most popular surf films of the early '70s:

Angie Reno

Pacific Vibrations (1970), *Five Summer Stories* (1972), and *Going Surfin'* (1973). He stunt-surfed in Warner Brothers' 1978 movie *Big Wednesday,* and was buffed yet coy for his photo spread in the June 1973 issue of *Playgirl,* which included a shot of him surfing nude at Hawaii's Velzyland. *See also* nudity and surfing.

resin   Syrupy polyester chemical compound, which is mixed with catalyst, a hardening agent, and spread across the surface of a fiberglass-covered surfboard to form a light, brittle, protective shell. Three types of polyester-based resins are commonly used, one after the other, in surfboard construction. Laminating resin is used to saturate the fiberglass; it contains no wax, and therefore can't be sanded. The paraffin wax added to sanding (or "hot-coating") resin, the second coat, rises to the surface, resulting in a "soft" and easy-sanding layer. Finishing (or glossing) resin also contains wax, but is harder, so it can be polished to a high shine, and thinner, to keep weight down. Most shortboards are made without a gloss coat. Surfboards can also be made with epoxy resin (over a styrofoam core rather than polyurethane foam), which is stronger than polyester resin, and somewhat more environmentally friendly, but harder to work with and more expensive. A versatile urethane-based resin came into play in 2001, developed by a college-age Texas surfer named Mark Tolan.

Resin-making is a complex, industrial process. Coal, natural gas, petroleum, wood, salt, water, and other organic materials are processed into alcohol, formaldehyde, glycerol, ammonia, and other chemicals, which in turn are combined, cooked, and strained in different ways to form the hundreds of polymer compounds known as synthetic resin—as opposed to the organic resins secreted by trees and plants—including most plastics. Bakelite, the first synthetic resin, was patented in 1909. *See also* epoxy, fiberglass, gloss coast, hot coat, laminate, surfboard construction.

Restaurants   *See* Tavarua.

Réunion Island   Mountainous French-governed subtropical island located about 400 miles east of Madagascar; home to the long and magnificent left-breaking waves of St. Leu. Réunion was first surfed by two visiting Australians in 1967, and while photos of the waves appeared in the surf press as far back as 1980, it didn't really come to the attention of the surf

Réunion Island; reef waves at St. Leu

world at large until 1988, when it was featured as a cover story in the *Surf Report* newsletter. Réunion is roughly circular, and measures 30 miles across at its widest point. Peak daytime air temperatures range from the high 60s to the mid-70s; water temperatures range from the low to mid-70s. The volcanic island's western side is dry, rocky, and cactus-filled, while the eastern side and central mountains are subject to heavy rainfall. (The Réunion mountain village of Cilaos recorded the most rainfall ever in a 24-hour period—74 inches—in March 1952.) About 650,000 people live on Réunion, and the island is for the most part friendly, clean, cultured, and expensive.

Réunion generally gets its best surf between June and August, as Indian Ocean storms southeast of South Africa often send powerful six-foot and bigger waves to Réunion's west coast, where most of the island's roughly 30 surf breaks are located. Shallow reefs, sharks, and urchins are the primary surfing hazards. St. Leu is the island's best and most famous break, a hollow wave that actually grows in size as it winds down the reef. "An easy wave to ride," *Surfing* magazine said in 1992, in an article naming Réunion as one of the 20 best surf trips in the world, "so long as you're comfortable tucking into tubes over razor sharp coral." From 1992 to 1996 (with the exception of 1993), St. Leu was the site of one of the world pro tour's best surfing events; winners included world champions Kelly Slater, Sunny Garcia, and Lisa Andersen. St. Leu was also the site of the 1995 Longboard World Championships, won by Hawaii's Rusty Keaulana.

In 2003 there were an estimated 2,000 surfers on the island and about 12 small surf shops. Amateur Réunion Island surfers compete internationally as part of the French B Team (which also includes surfers from Tahiti and Guadeloupe). Réunion waves have been featured in several surf videos, including *Overdrive* (1993), *Factory Seconds* (1995), and *Where's Wardo?* (2001). The west Réunion breaks are detailed in *The World Stormrider Guide* (2001).

reverse   A skateboard-influenced move popularized in the early 1990s by the Kelly Slater–led New School group, in which the surfer briefly disengages the board's stabilizing fins and rides backward. Not so much a maneuver in itself, the reverse is the final phase to a variety of off-the-top, cutback, or aerial maneuvers; variants include the roundhouse reverse, the backside 360 reverse air, and the floater-to-reverse. While the reverse had a precedent of sorts in the mid-'60s, when California longboard surfers David Nuuhiwa and Mike Purpus began doing fin-first take-offs—paddling into the wave tail first, standing, then turning the board 180 degrees to a regular position—the reverse, in name and practice, was copied from pool- and half-pipe-riding skateboarders. *See also* tailslide.

reverse pullout   A longboard-only variation on the kickout, almost always performed while riding backside (back to the wave); the rider turns his board over the crest, simultaneously twirls his body into an opposite-direction 180-degree half-spinner, and finishes in a paddling position. A classic hotdog maneuver. Mislabeled in Tom Wolfe's 1966 surfing essay, "The Pump House Gang," as a "reverse kick-up."

reverse takeoff   *See* fin-first takeoff.

reverse vee   A type of surfboard bottom contour. With standard vee, a low-profile V-shaped convexity is located in the tail section, beneath the surfer's back foot, while the middle of the board is generally flat or slightly rounded. The reverse vee design puts a slight inversion in the middle of the board, and usually feeds into two subtle parallel concaves through the board's back end. Developed by Australian surfboard shaper Maurice Cole primarily as a way to increase board speed, reverse vee was a new and much-talked-about design concept in the early 1990s. *See also* concave, vee.

rhino chaser   *See* gun.

Rhode Island   Rhode Island's rugged 40-mile coast-line is trimmed with a disproportionately high number of good surf breaks, along with yachts, polo fields, lobster traps, 50-room summer "cottages," and free-range old-money aristocrats. Weather extremes are a hallmark of the all-year Rhode Island surfing experience, with average air and water temperatures hitting 70 degrees in summer, then plummeting to the low 30s in winter, at which time determined local surfers in head-to-toe wetsuits will sometimes pick their way across snow-covered rocks and beaches to get to the waves. "You don't get any better in winter," a Rhode Island surfer told *Sports Illustrated* magazine in 1969, "because if you try anything new you might fall off."

Fall is usually the best time to surf in Rhode Island, as the state's south-southeast-facing coast is particularly receptive to seasonal hurricane swells. Autumn surf will sometimes hit six foot for days in a row, and can occasionally pump up to 12 foot or bigger. Rhode Island's famously notched and jagged shoreline meanwhile not only houses a full range of beach-, reef-, and pointbreaks, but ensures that the wind will always be blowing offshore or sideshore at one break or another. Top Rhode Island surf breaks include the variegated peaks and walls in Matunuck, the sand-bottom tubes of Narragansett Town Beach, and the inconsistent but soul-stirring Ruggles Avenue, a right-breaking reef in the heart of blue-blood Newport generally regarded as the East Coast's premier big-wave break.

Although Hawaiian surfer and gold medal swimmer Duke Kahanamoku gave a surfing demonstration in Rhode Island in 1924, the sport didn't take hold here until 1960, when natives Chuck Fogerty and Matt Chrostowski returned from a visit to Southern California with a pair of new surfboards and began driving the harbor- and inlet-filled coast in search of breaks. A Hobie Surfboards outlet opened in Narragansett in 1963; two years later the inaugural New England Mid-Winter Surfing Championships were staged at Narragansett Town Beach. Rhode Island beach communities had meanwhile issued some of the toughest surfing laws in America, demanding that all surfers have a swimming certificate and a full wetsuit (in winter only), and ride with a partner at all times. Rhode Island was in the grips of a mini-surf boom by 1967, with five surf shops in Cranston, six in

Rhode Island surfer Peter Pan

Narragansett, and two in Newport; four years later there were no surf shops open anywhere in the state. Sid Abruzzi opened the Surf Store in Newport in 1973; Peter Pan followed two years later with the Watershed in Narragansett; both shops are still open.

As of 2003, Rhode Island was home to 10 surf shops and about 500 resident surfers; hundreds of out-of-state surfers, mainly from Connecticut and Massachusetts, drive in regularly. Pan, the garrulous regional longboard champion from the mid-'70s to the early '00s, is Rhode Island's best-known surfer, along with the late Colin Couture, president of the Eastern Surfing Association (ESA) in the '70s and '80s. The ESA holds about seven contests in Rhode Island each year. The state is featured in *Couch Tour,* a 2002 surf video; *The Stormrider Guide North America* (2002) details the Rhode Island surf.

Ribas, Victor   Flyweight Brazilian goofyfooter from Rio de Janeiro, world-ranked #3 in 1999, making him the highest-placed Brazilian in the history of pro surfing. Ribas was born (1971) and raised in Cabofria, Brazil, and began surfing at age 10. At 5′4″, 125 pounds, he was a small-wave dynamo, fast and flashy, gliding and pivoting when his peers seemed to be riding through mud; "he surfs like a scalpel," Florida pro Shea Lopez said. Ribas turned pro in 1990, moved steadily up the ratings to finish sixth in 1995, dropped all the way to 37th by 1998, then rocketed up to his #3 finish in 1999. More fluctuations followed, as over the next three years he placed 32nd, 12th, and 45th. Ribas's career was unusual in other ways. He became the first and only male surfer in world tour history to turn in a zero-points performance after failing to catch a wave during an early heat of the 1998 Pipeline Masters. After losing a close match in a 2001 contest, Ribas left the water and began throwing fist-sized rocks at the tournament's head judge; he was later fined $2,000. Ribas has appeared in more than a dozen surf videos, including *Surf Espetacular* (1992) and *Euro Trash* (1995).

Richards, John "LJ"   Regularfoot surfer from Oceanside, California; fourth-place finisher in the 1964 World Surfing Championships. LJ (Little John) Richards was born (1939) and raised in Oceanside and began surfing at age 13, often riding with schoolmate and mentor Phil Edwards. In 1963 he won the West Coast Surfing Championships and the following year placed runner-up in the United States Invitational. Richards was invited to Sydney, Australia, for the first World Championships; in the semifinals he fell on his board and opened a cut on his lip that was stitched closed just minutes before the finals. "His concentration seemed to suffer," Australia's *Surfing World* magazine reported, describing Richards's fourth-place performance, "and it was only toward the end that his best form returned." Richards was an original member of La Jolla's 1962-founded Windansea Surf Club. He later worked as a lifeguard and a fireman. Richards appeared in a small number of surf movies, including *Surf Crazy* (1959), *Cavalcade of Surf* (1962), and *Angry Sea* (1963). Richards was nominated to the International Surfing Hall of Fame in 1991.

Richards, Mark   Pro surfer from Newcastle, New South Wales, Australia; electrifying in the water, mannerly and easygoing on land; the first person to win four consecutive world championships (1979–82); described by *Australia's Surfing Life* magazine as the country's "surfing saint." Richards was born (1957) and raised in Newcastle, an industrial city located 100 miles north of Sydney. Ray Richards, Mark's father, was a surfer and used car salesman who, in 1961, opened Newcastle's first surfboard shop. The younger Richards was in the surf as a toddler, soon graduated to a surf mat, and began riding a surfboard at age six. He placed second in the juniors division of the 1972 Australian National Titles (losing to future tri-fin innovator Simon Anderson), and made the national team for that year's World Surfing Championships in California. The following year he won the national juniors title, and in 1974 he placed fourth. A nonaffiliated set of professional contests were in

Mark Richards

place by 1975, and the 18-year-old Richards made a splashy international debut by traveling to Hawaii to win both the Smirnoff Pro-Am at Waimea Bay and the World Cup at Sunset Beach, earning a total of $9,000—a nearly unimaginable sum for a pro surfer at the time.

Surf filmmaker Bill Delaney was in Hawaii at the time shooting his debut movie, *Free Ride*. The film had been conceived mainly as a showcase for Australian Wayne Bartholomew and Shaun Tomson of South Africa, both future world champions, but Richards—riding a flashy yellow-and-red surfboard and wearing brightly colored surf trunks—was too good to leave out. *Free Ride* showed a generational change in the sport, as the established Hawaiians (Jeff Hakman, Gerry Lopez, Barry Kanaiaupuni, and Reno Abellira) were overshadowed by the newcomers from Australia and South Africa; Richards, Bartholomew, and Tomson and a number of their peers have long been collectively known as the "Free Ride generation."

Richards had a peculiar surfing style: knees often braced together, even through sharp turns, hunched shoulders, long arms fully extended, with both hands frequently bent up at the wrist. He was nicknamed the "Wounded Gull," and his unorthodox body mechanics were all but ignored by the next generation of surfers. But the lines he drew across the wave face were fast, balanced, smooth, and flexible, and punctuated often with spectacular, deep-set turns. He meanwhile came to be loved in the surfing world for being confident (wearing a silver wetsuit and decorating his boards with a giant Superman logo), but also humble and self-effacing. He also looked different from other pro surfers: large (6′1″, 175 pounds) but unimposing, with a baby face, thin shoulders, and an extra-long torso. When *Surfer* magazine asked, "What's makes you happy?" Richards endeared himself to thousands of young wave-riders with his sensible reply: "Sex and tuberides."

Richards was thought of as unstoppable during his world title years. In 1979 he skipped four of the scheduled 13 events (two in South Africa, two in Florida), and was ranked fourth going into the World Cup in Hawaii, the final event of the year. In what would turn out to be the decade's most thrilling title finish, the three front-runners faltered one after the other, and the 22-year-old Richards won both the World Cup and the championship. He won four of 10 events in 1980 to easily defend the title. The 1981 and 1982 seasons were closer, but without the drama of 1979. Australian Cheyne Horan was Richards's main rival, finishing runner-up to the championship in 1979, 1981, and 1982.

A key to Richards's world tour success was his refashioning of the twin-fin surfboard. He'd been shaping his own boards since age 15 (in early 1977 he had a two-month-long shaping seminar with Hawaiian board-making guru Dick Brewer), but was struggling to keep up with smaller, lighter pros when the waves dropped below three feet—which happened often on the world tour. Richards took notes in 1976 when Hawaiian surfer Reno Abellira came to Australia with a wide, blunt-nosed 5′3″ board with two fins; the following year Richards produced a longer and more streamlined version of the twin-fin, saying later that the boards were "fast and maneuverable," and that he "felt like he could do anything on them." Twin-fin fever swept through the surf world in the late '70s and early '80s, then was stopped cold by the 1981 introduction of the tri-fin surfboard.

Richards retired from full-time competition surfing at the end of the 1982 season. He'd won Rip Curl Pro at Bells Beach four times (1978–80, 1982), twice won the Stubbies Pro (1979 and 1981), twice won the Gunston 500 (1980 and 1982), been a four-time Duke Kahanamoku finalist (winning in 1979), and a four-time Pipeline Masters finalist (winning in 1980). In 1985 he entered and won the Billabong Pro, held at Waimea Bay and Sunset Beach, and in 1986 he defended his Billabong title—a competitive surfing career epilogue that has no equal.

Richards won the *Surfer* Magazine Readers Poll Award in 1979, 1980, and 1981, and was selected as *Surfing* magazine's Surfer of the Year in 1979, 1980, and 1982. In 1985 Richards and pioneering surfer Charles "Snow" McAlister were the first two inductees into the Australian Surfing Hall of Fame; in 1994 he received the Order of Australia medal (similar to a British knighthood), and was elected to the Huntington Beach Surfing Walk of Fame. Richards finished runner-up in the grandmasters (42-and-over) division of the 2000 Quiksilver Masters Surfing Championships; the following year he placed first; in 2002 he was runner-up.

Richards appeared in dozens of surf films and videos during the '70s and '80s, including *A Matter of Style* (1975), *Playgrounds in Paradise* (1976), *In Search of Tubular Swells* (1977), *Fantasea* (1978), *Wizards of the Water* (1982), and *Ocean Fever* (1983). He was also featured in the American-made cable TV series *20th Century Surfers* (2000) and the Australian-aired documentary *Legends: An Australian Surfing Perspective* (1994). *The Mark Richards Tapes,* a video biography, was released in 1987. *Mark Richards: A Surfing Legend,* written by *Sydney Sunday Telegraph* journalist David Knox, was published in 1992. The Mark Richards Newcastle City Pro, a World Qualifying Series pro tour event, has been held annually since 1995. As of 2002, Richards was running the Newcastle surf shop his father opened 40 years earlier. He's married and has three children. *See also* twin-fin.

Richardson, Terry Easygoing vegetarian goofyfoot pro surfer from Wollongong, New South Wales, Australia; winner of the 1980 Australian National Titles, and world-ranked #7 in 1982. Richardson was born (1956) and raised in Wollongong. A chronic late bloomer, he didn't begin surfing until age 15, didn't turn pro until 25, and posted his biggest win—at the 1997 Oxbow Masters, a contest for retired world tour pros—at 40. He later attributed his success in part to a wife-and-children-centered home life that placed him in what amounted to an alternative universe compared to the typical '80s pro surfer/satyr. "All I ever really wanted to do was be married and have children," he told *Surfing* magazine in 1987. "And I couldn't have married a better woman or have better-looking kids. Because of that, it's a lot easier to be content with my surfing." Richardson built his own surfboards, and is remembered as one of the era's great tuberiders. He appeared in a small number of surf movies and videos, including *Free Ride* (1977), *We Got Surf* (1981), and *Wizards of the Water* (1982).

Riddle, J   Good-looking, media-savvy regularfoot surfer from Santa Monica, California; a dominating presence at Malibu from the late '60s to the late '80s; cofounder in 1967 of Natural Progression Surfboards. The summer of 1970 was a high point in J Riddle's surfing life, as the 20-year-old was simultaneously on the covers of *Surfer* and *Surfing* magazines, and starred in *Cosmic Children*, Hal Jepsen's first and most popular surf film. In 1972, Riddle invented a cutaway template design called the "fangtail"—a forerunner to the winger or "bump" tail design used on virtually all shortboards made in the '80s. He was the surfing stunt double for Jan-Michael Vincent in Warner Brothers' 1978 film *Big Wednesday,* which Riddle later dismissed as "a pie in the face of surfing." Riddle appeared in a small number of other surf movies, including *A Sea for Yourself* (1973), *Fluid Drive* (1974), and *Tales of the Seven Seas* (1981). *See also* wings.

Ride the Wild Surf   Frothy and lightly sermonizing 1964 Columbia Pictures movie about three California surfers visiting Oahu's North Shore in search of big-wave thrills and tropical romance. Jody Wallis, Steamer Lane, and Chase Colton (Fabian, Tab Hunter, and Peter Brown, respectively) find plenty of surf, and Jody wins the climactic big-wave showdown at Waimea Bay, but each comes to realize that full-time surfing just isn't compatible with responsible adult living. Shelley Fabares (*Coach*) and Barbara Eden (*I Dream of Jeannie*) play the two female leads. *Ride the Wild Surf* was a big step removed from Hollywood's beach movie franchise (*Beach Blanket Bingo, Muscle Beach Party*), but the filmmakers nonetheless strayed often from surf world realities. "For instance," *Surfing* magazine asked in its 1964 review, "how is it that whenever the stars are wiped out and come to the surface the board is always there?" But *Surfer* also noted both agreed that the action sequences—shot with expensive 35-millimeter cameras at places like Sunset Beach, Pipeline, and Haleiwa, and spread generously throughout the movie—were first-rate. The stunt-surfing was performed by many of the day's top riders, including Greg Noll, Mickey Dora, Mike Hynson, Butch Van Artsdalen, Rusty Miller, and Phil Edwards. Jan and Dean's "Ride the Wild Surf" theme song was a Top 20 hit on the Billboard charts. *See also* Hollywood and surfing.

Rielly, Derek   Mischievous surf journalist originally from Perth, Western Australia; editor of *Australia's Surfing Life* (*ASL*) magazine from 1995 to 1999. Rielly was born (1967) in Perth and raised in the nearby suburb of Willetton, the son of a pro wrestler father and a diplomat mother, and began surfing at age 12. After working as a blackjack dealer and a barman, Rielly moved in 1989 to Burleigh Heads, Queensland; two years later he published his first article in *ASL*; later that year he was hired as the magazine's associate editor. Rielly soon became the *ASL*'s leading voice, and helped turn what had been a glossy but fairly staid monthly into surfing's funniest and naughtiest publication. Later acknowledging that his two greatest literary influences were *Mad* magazine and *National Lampoon,* Rielly often put his cheerful and profanity-laced writing style to use in short bursts of schoolboy comedy. In "The 48-Hour Surf Movie Marathon," he subjected himself to two sleepless days of nonstop video viewing: "6:17 A.M. Band on the Run finished. Think I might take a dump and watch the '89 Billabong Pro . . . might even risk a wank once my flatmate leaves for the beach." But Rielly also wrote longer well-crafted articles on subjects like the elitism of surf resorts and how surf competitions force local wave-riders out of the water.

Rielly moved in 1999 to Hossegor, France, and worked for two years as the editor for a start-up magazine called *Surf Europe.* In 2001 he moved to the Sydney beachside suburb of Bondi, and became a staff writer for *Waves* magazine. Rielly has published articles in *Surfer, Tracks,* and *Penthouse* magazines; he also contributed an essay to *Surf Rage* (2000), a book on surf-related violence. Rielly is married and has one child. *See also* Australia's Surfing Life magazine.

Rietveld, Rick   Southern California artist, best known in the surf world for his brightly colored and mildly surreal ads for Maui and Sons surfwear in the mid- and late '80s. Rietveld was raised in Los Angeles, and graduated from Pasadena Art Center in 1977. He was a cofounder in 1980 of Maui and Sons, and the company was all but built on Rietveld's ads, including his airbrush interpretation of the famous photo of Muhammad Ali gloating over a fallen Sonny Liston, with both fighters wearing radiant surf print trunks instead of boxing shorts. A billboard campaign in 1988 earned Rietveld an Outdoor Advertising Association of America OBIE Award. He founded his own surfwear company, Rietveld USA, in 1995. "I like to think I have a loose imagination," he told *Beach Culture* magazine in 1990. "And I do dream in Technicolor." *See also* surf art.

right   A wave that breaks to the right, from the surfer's shoreward-facing vantage point. As viewed from the beach, a surfer on a right moves from right to left. Malibu, Kirra, Jeffreys Bay, and Waimea Bay are famous right-breaking waves.

right-go-left   Ride-opening maneuver in which the surfer paddles into the wave angling to the right, stands, and turns to the left. The expression "right-go-left" was popular in the '50s, '60s, and early '70s, and is today used primarily by longboarders. Similar to "fade" and "whipturn."

Rincon   Long, elegant right-breaking point wave located on the border between Ventura and Santa Barbara counties; nicknamed "Queen of the Coast," and regarded as America's gold-standard pointbreak. "At times the wave is so close to perfection," surf journalist Bill Cleary wrote of Rincon del Mar (Little Corner of the Sea) in 1966, "that maneuvering—nose rides, turning and cutbacks—seems inappropriate, an insult to the dignity of the wave."

Rincon breaks best from late fall to early spring, during the west and northwest swell season, and is composed of three overlapping sections. 1) The Indicator, located at the top of the point, produces a bigger and slightly thicker wave that often runs for 75 yards before hitting a section in front of the Rincon Creek rivermouth. 2) The Rivermouth, or Second Point, marginally smaller than Indicator, breaks for about 50 yards. 3) The Cove, in the lee of the point, is the premier Rincon break; smaller, thinner, and less powerful than the Indicator or the Rivermouth, but far longer—up to 300 yards—and so perfectly tapered as to be nearly hypnotic. All three breaks at Rincon improve as the tide drops; tube sections often appear at low tide. (Backside Rincon, a modest left-breaking spot located just north of the Indicator, is a summer wave.) Rincon is best from four to eight foot; it can get up to 12 foot, but waves of that size are often stormy or weather-beaten. Five-hundred-yard-long, 90-second rides from the Indicator through to the Cove are rare but possible on bigger swells. Rincon has been viewed since the early '50s as the winter counterpart to Malibu, the famous Los Angeles County pointbreak located 75 miles to the south,

Rincon

but while the Malibu surfing experience is warm and sun-washed, Rincon is usually chilly, with air temperatures in the 50s or low 60s and water temperatures in the low to upper 50s. Crowded since the early 1960s, Rincon on a good day will see as many as 200 surfers out at once. Sewage runoff has also been a problem: the Rincon surf was declared off-limits 84 times by county officials between 1996 and 1998 due to high fecal bacteria counts.

Santa Barbara County lifeguard Gates Foss is credited as the first to surf Rincon, in either 1938 or 1939; he called the break "Three Mile," as it was located three miles below the town of Carpinteria. After World War II, Rincon became popular with virtually all of the top Malibu surfers, including Bob Simmons, Joe Quigg, and Matt Kivlin, then later Mickey Dora, Lance Carson, and Kemp Aaberg. (Quigg designed what many people regard as the first specialized big-wave surfboard in 1948, after waking from a dream in which he had connected a wave from the Rivermouth into the Cove.) By the early '60s, local surfer Renolds Yater had developed what would later be identified as the Santa Barbara point-surf style, riding with a cool minimalism. Protohippie Bob Cooper, another influential Rincon surfer of the period, was more flamboyant.

Kneerider and surfboard builder George Greenough, from the wealthy Santa Barbara enclave of Montecito, used Rincon as a test track for board designs and surfing maneuvers that would lead directly to the late-'60s shortboard revolution. In December 1967, Australian surfer/designer Bob McTavish made the first California-built shortboard while visiting

Greenough, and rode it at Rincon during a monumental six-week run of surf. Future world champion Tom Curren began surfing Rincon in the mid-1970s, riding boards made by Santa Barbara surf shop owner and design-guru-in-the-making Al Merrick.

With the exception of a few local events, including the 1997-founded Clean Water Classic fund-raiser, Rincon residents have kept the point off-limits to surfing competitions. Rincon has appeared in more than 40 surf movies and videos over the decades, including *Surf Crazy* (1959), *Inside Out* (1965), *Pacific Vibrations* (1970), *Fluid Drive* (1974), *Amazing Surf Stories* (1986), *Powerglide* (1995), and *Super Slide* (1999).

Rio de Janeiro   Sprawling Brazilian metropolis and resort city; the beachbreak-lined birthplace of surfing in this country, and home to a dense, competitive, highly charged surf scene. The Rio surf is best from April to October, as South Atlantic storms generate fairly consistent three- to six-foot waves. From east to west, the city's best-known breaks include the left-breaking rock-studded peaks of Arpoador (lit by stadium-style floodlights for night surfing); the close-to-shore closeout tubes of Ipanema; the rare right-breaking big waves of Canto do Leblon; the shallow left tubes of Pepino; the breakwater-formed sandbar peaks of Quebra Mar; the longboard-friendly rollers of Macumba Beach; and the high-performance peaks inside the cove at Prainha. Rio's average daytime air temperatures range from the upper 80s (summer) to 70 (winter); water temperatures range from the mid-70s to the low 60s. Crowded lineups are by far the city's greatest surf hazard.

Surfing was introduced to Rio (and Brazil) in 1928 by an unknown American riding a redwood board, and virtually all early development in Brazilian surfing, including the establishment of a domestic surf industry, came about here. (*See* Brazil.) The mix of wealth and poverty within Rio's 30-mile coastline has meanwhile allowed for genuine class diversity in the water. "Who are you and where do you live?" Brazilian surf journalist Carlos Lorch asked rhetorically in 1984. "Doesn't matter. Do you rip? That matters." Beginning in the late '80s, the southern city of Florianópolis overtook Rio as the country's top producer of pro-grade surfers, although Rio, as of 2003, was home to world tour competitors Renan Rocha and Victor Ribas. Rio contains about 50 surf shops and 40,000 surfers; *Realce,* a popular nationally broadcast Rio-based surfing television show, was launched in 1982.

Rip Curl   Australian-based wetsuit/surfwear/surfboard company, headquarted in Torquay, Victoria, founded by Doug Warbrick and Brian Singer. Rip Curl Surfboards began as a backyard board-making operation in 1968; wetsuits were introduced the following year. The company was a half step behind Torquay neighbor Quiksilver in the great Australia-to-America surf culture export of the late '70s and early '80s, when the understated and laid-back California/Hawaii ethos was for the most part dropped—especially by younger surfers—for the loud, colorful, hyperenergetic Aussie style. While California's O'Neill wetsuits had the Sunline model in 1979, available primarily in black and dark blue, Rip Curl offered the Aggrolite in hot pink with canary-yellow accents. In 1977, after the company had added lines for sailing, sailboarding, and waterskiing, it was given statewide and national government export awards.

Rip Curl's promo department has in many ways been the company's greatest strength. Over the years, its surf team roster has included Wayne Lynch, Michael Peterson, Terry Fitzgerald, Larry Bertlemann, Wayne Bartholomew, Mark Richards, Tom Carroll, Tom Curren, Cheyne Horan, Damien Hardman, Pam Burridge, and Mick Fanning. Rip Curl began sponsoring the annual Easter surf contest at Bells Beach in 1973; in 1987 it founded the Rip Curl Pro at Hossegor, France, and in 1997 began sponsoring the World Cup in Hawaii. Marketing just as diligently to the sport's noncompetitors, the company in 1992 launched a long-running print and video campaign called "The Search," focusing on empty, exotic, perfect surf. Rip Curl first licensed its name to America and France in 1981 and 1985, respectively, and by 1995 it had 10 licensees around the world. The name "Rip Curl" was taken from a vee-bottom surfboard that cofounder Warbrick bought in 1968, upon which he'd written "Rip Curl Hot Dog." The words didn't mean anything, he later admitted. "Except ripping was groovy; surfing the curl was groovy; we wanted to be groovy—so that was it." As of 2002, Warbrick and Singer retained a 50 percent interest in Rip Curl; international sales in 2001 were estimated to be $163 million. The Rip Curl line has expanded to include watches, mountain gear, backpacks, and travel bags. *See also* Rip Curl Pro, Doug Warbrick, wetsuits.

Rip Curl Cup   *See* World Cup.

Rip Curl Pro, Bells Beach   Venerable surfing competition held at Bells Beach, Victoria, Australia, during Easter Week; inaugurated in 1962, it became Australia's first significant professional surf contest in 1973, and remains the sport's longest-running pro contest. The Rip Curl Pro is also the only event to appear on every world pro tour season schedule since the circuit's 1976 founding. Closely linked to the nearby surf industry city of Torquay, set amid the cold, wet, dramatic Victorian coastline, "Easter at Bells" has for decades been one of the great surfing/ social experiences. Local surfers Peter Troy and Vic Tantau, cofounders of the Bells Beach Boardriders Club, staged the inaugural Bells contest in January 1962, armed with two folding bridge tables and a small box full of inexpensive trophies. It was a single-division, men's-only contest, won by Sydney surfer Glen Richie, with local George Smith awarded a special cash prize of one Australian pound for riding the day's biggest wave. The Bells contest soon earned a reputation for providing bigger-than-average surf, with six to eight-foot waves common; the 1965 event was met with steel-blue 18-footers. Torquay-based Rip Curl Wetsuits signed on as the primary Bells sponsor in 1973 and put up $2,500 in prize money, with Queensland surfer Michael Peterson winning the $1,000 first-place check; the women's division went pro two years later, with winner Gail Couper awarded a brazenly inequitable $200. (By far the event's dominant surfer, Couper won Bells ten times between 1966 and 1976.)

Bells was part of the debut world tour pro circuit in 1976, with Hawaii's Jeff Hakman becoming the event's first foreign-born winner. Hundreds of dramatic world tour matches have since taken place at Bells, in front of tens of thousands of bundled-up spectators; a 1986 semifinal duel between Tom Curren and Mark Occhilupo is often cited as one of pro surfing's greatest bouts. The 1981 Bells contest, however, is rightfully thought of as the event's high-water mark, as the second-to-last day of competition was met with perfectly groomed 12- to 18-foot surf, and Sydney regularfooter Simon Anderson changed the course of surfboard design history by riding his just-invented tri-fin Thruster surfboard to victory. *Bells '81*, a short documentary surf movie, was released a few weeks later.

Bells was the opening event on the men's world tour schedule from 1992 to 1995, (in 1994 it was the opening event for the women's), and by 2001 the men's winner earned $30,000 of a combined men's–women's prize purse of $275,000. Poor surf at Bells forced a last-day relocation in 1993, 1995, 1996, and

2000, usually to Johanna, a sand-bottom break 95 miles to the southwest. The annual induction ceremony for the Australian Hall of Fame is held in conjunction with the Bells contest. A Bells juniors division (17 and under) was held from 1963 to 1972, with the 1965 event canceled due to heavy surf; the women's division was added in 1966 and dropped after 2001. The 1967 and 1971 Bells events counted as the Australian National Titles. Bells winners:

1962:	Glen Ritchie
1963:	Doug Andrews, Glen Ritchie
1964:	Mick Dooley, Nat Young
1965:	Robert Conneeley
1966:	Nat Young, Gail Couper, Wayne Lynch
1967:	Nat Young, Gail Couper, Wayne Lynch (Australian Titles)
1968:	Ted Spencer, Gail Couper, Wayne Lynch
1969:	Ted Spencer, Vivian Campbell, Wayne Lynch
1970:	Nat Young, Gail Couper, Michael Peterson
1971:	Paul Neilsen, Gail Couper, Simon Anderson (Australian Titles)
1972:	Terry Fitzgerald, Gail Couper, Simon Anderson
1973:	Michael Peterson, Gail Couper
1974:	Michael Peterson, Gail Couper
1975:	Michael Peterson, Gail Couper
1976:	Jeff Hakman, Gail Couper
1977:	Simon Anderson, Margo Oberg
1978:	Mark Richards, Margo Oberg
1979:	Mark Richards, Lynne Boyer
1980:	Mark Richards, Margo Oberg
1981:	Simon Anderson, Linda Davoli
1982:	Mark Richards, Debbie Beacham
1983:	Joe Engel, Helen Lambert
1984:	Cheyne Horan, Frieda Zamba
1985:	Tom Curren, Frieda Zamba
1986:	Tom Carroll, Frieda Zamba
1987:	Nick Wood, Jodie Cooper
1988:	Damien Hardman, Kim Mearig
1989:	Martin Potter, Wendy Botha
1990:	Tom Curren, Lisa Andersen
1991:	Barton Lynch, Pauline Menczer
1992:	Richie Collins, Lisa Andersen
1993:	Damien Hardman, Pauline Menczer
1994:	Kelly Slater, Layne Beachley
1995:	Sunny Garcia, Lisa Andersen
1996:	Sunny Garcia, Pauline Menczer
1997:	Matt Hoy, Neridah Falconer
1998:	Mark Occhilupo, Layne Beachley

1999:   Shane Dorian, Layne Beachley
2000:   Sunny Garcia, Megan Abubo
2001:   Mick Fanning, Neridah Falconer
2002:   Andy Irons (no women's event)
See also Bells Beach, Rip Curl.

riptide   A current flowing from nearshore waters back toward the open sea, gentle in some cases, violent in others. While riptides can contribute directly to good waves, they are frequently dangerous to swimmers and novice surfers. Riptides are generally formed when waves break consistently over a shallow sandbar or reef, and the incoming lines of whitewater, unable to return seaward by the same route, instead briefly traverse the shore, then turn 90 degrees, often into a topographical low spot. Riptides adjacent to reefbreaks (like Hawaiis Sunset Beach) flow along permanent channels; riptides at beachbreaks often form temporary channels—which in turn can produce first-rate surf. Riptides are usually about 30 to 50 yards wide, are more common during lower tides, and tend to dissipate not far beyond the surf zone. Because they produce chops and eddies as they flow outward, riptides are fairly easy to spot. Nonetheless, a majority of beachside lifeguard rescues worldwide are made when swimmers, and sometimes beginning surfers, wander into a riptide and are pulled out to sea. Swimming or paddling directly against a riptide is often futile; the easiest and most direct way out is to angle laterally across the current, into the nearby breaking surf.

Surf band Jon and the Nightriders, recorded "Riptide" for *Surf Beat '80,* their debut album. A riptide is also known as rip current or run-out. "Riptide" is something of a misnomer, as it's influenced but not caused by tide. *See also* current.

rivermouth   Rivermouth-created surf break, with waves breaking along sandbars in front of or alongside a river-cut channel. Most pointbreaks are in a sense rivermouth breaks—Malibu and Rincon in California, for example—as the points were created by river-flow alluvial deposits. But surfers generally view a rivermouth break as having a more immediate connection between river and wave. Rivermouth waves come in nearly all shapes and sizes, and each break can vary greatly from season to season—or even week to week—depending on river volume and flow. The Santa Cruz rivermouth only produces a sandbar after heavy rains, and is completely inactive as a surf break during drought years. Mundaka, Spain, with its long, fast, left-breaking waves, is perhaps the world's best and best-known rivermouth break. Rivermouths are the most polluted category of surf break (as compared to point-, beach, or reefbreaks), with industrial or agricultural chemical and bacterial matter often flushed downriver and into the lineup. Furthermore, because rivermouths tend to be rich feeding grounds, they often attract sharks.

Roaring 40s   *See* Indian Ocean.

Robb, Kalani   Lightning-fast goofyfoot pro surfer from the North Shore of Oahu, Hawaii; world-ranked #6 in 2001. Robb was born (1977) in Kailua, Oahu, the adopted son of a landscaper/surfer father, began surfing in Waikiki at age seven, and moved with his family to the North Shore at 10. He had a remarkable career as an amateur competitor, winning the menehune division of the 1989 United States Surfing Championships, finishing second in the boys' division of the 1992 U.S. Championships, winning both the juniors and men's divisions of the 1993 National Scholastic Surfing Association Nationals, and taking the juniors division of the 1994 World Amateur Surfing Championship. Robb by that time had developed into one of the sport's quickest and flashiest small-wave riders, skimming effortlessly over flat spots, and able to launch a variety of high, spiraling aerial maneuvers. He later became an expert Pipeline rider, calmly placing himself deep inside the tube, then drawing a smooth, almost tranquil line to the

Kalani Robb

exit. The spidery Robb (5′8″, 140 pounds) wasn't able to put much power into his turns, but few surfers of any era had his measure in terms of balance and finesse.

Described—and perhaps burdened—in the mid-'90s as "the next Kelly Slater," Robb qualified for the world circuit in 1995 and finished the season ranked 20th, earning rookie-of-the-year honors. The following year he jumped up to #7, and indeed looked set to challenge Slater for the title. Robb then contracted malaria while surfing in Indonesia in 1997, spent a week in the hospital, and seemed to lose focus. He finished the year ranked 11th, then dropped to 26th in 1998. (A bright spot came as he earned $30,000 for winning the 1997 Da Hui Backdoor Shootout at Pipeline.) He returned to form over the next three years, going from 17th to ninth to sixth.

The dark-haired and boyishly handsome Robb has been featured in more than 50 surf videos, including *Good Times* (1995), *Triple C* (1996), *These Are Better Days* (1999), and *Revelation* (2000). Robb sounded wise beyond his 21 years in a 1999 interview with *TransWorld Surf* magazine; when asked about the next phase in high-performance surfing, he noted that "everyone forgets that it's more of a lifestyle and an expression—so it's not the moves, it's the people." Amending the thought a few moments later, he allowed that the future of surfing was in the hands of "the psycho kids out there who want to do some crazy shit." Surf gossips were titillated in 1999 when surfer/model Malia Jones, named by *People* magazine a few months earlier as one of the world's "50 Most Beautiful People," left Robb for fellow Hawaiian surfer Conan Hayes. Robb is unmarried.

Rochlen, Dave   Entrepreneurial surfer from Santa Monica, California; one of the original post–World War II Malibu regulars; cofounder in 1963 of Surf Line Hawaii, a surfboard retail outlet, and founder of Jams beachwear in 1964. Rochlen was born (1924) and raised in Santa Monica, and began surfing at age 15. After serving in the Marine Corps, he returned to Santa Monica in 1946 where he surfed, worked as a lifeguard, and began building a line of surfboards that soon became popular among Malibu Colony movie celebrities, including Gary Cooper and Peter Lawford. Along with fellow surfer/designers like Joe Quigg and Matt Kivlin, Rochlen helped develop the popular Malibu chip board in the late '40s and early '50s. Rochlen received a B.A. in psychology from

UCLA in 1954, worked as a systems analyst for the Santa Monica–based RAND Corporation think tank, then moved to Honolulu, Hawaii, in 1962, where he founded Surf Line Hawaii with California surfer Dick Metz. Rochlen and his Hawaiian-born wife created the Jams line the following year; the loose-fitting and brightly colored surf trunks were an instant success, and soon available in department stores across America. Rochlen was also known as one of surfing's most thoughtful and articulate voices. "It's simple," he said when asked by American surf writer Leonard Lueras in 1984 to explain the sport's attraction. "The ocean is the most wondrous thing on the planet, and a breaking wave is the single most exciting thing happening in the ocean." Riding a wave, Rochlen said, allowed you to "reach out and touch the face of God."

rock dance   Walking over an intertidal area of rocks while entering or exiting the surf. Some can make the rock dance look graceful and smooth, but for most surfers it's a tedious, wobbly, even painful process; moss, seaweed, urchins, and barnacles can slow progress to a virtual and sometimes literal crawl. Rock dancing was a regular part of the sport before the introduction of the surf leash in the early '70s, as surfers at many popular breaks—including Malibu, Burleigh Heads, Jeffreys Bay, and Rocky Point—had to clamber over rocks to pick up each and every lost surfboard.

rocker   The curve of a surfboard from nose to tail, as viewed side-on. Variables such as foil, rail design, and bottom configuration will influence the way rocker acts, but its hydrodynamic effect at a base level is easy to define: less rocker means greater speed and reduced maneuverability, more rocker means greater maneuverability and reduced speed. Board-makers for decades had only a passing interest in rocker. During the late-'60s shortboard revolution, however, when boards became lighter, quicker, and faster-turning, rocker was given its due as a key design element, and by the early '90s it was regarded by many as a board's single most important feature. Polyurethane foam blanks (the surfboard's core material) are molded with rocker already in place, and many shapers now use computer-programmed rocker templates to further ensure consistency from board to board. For shortboards, rocker is most pronounced in the front third and the rear sixth. *See also* foil, volume.

Rocky Point   Crowded, aggressively ridden, camera-friendly surf break on the North Shore of Oahu, between Sunset Beach and Pipeline. Rocky Point has been described as "the crossroads of the Pacific" and "Hawaii's most photographed wave." The surf here hits top form between October and March, when the swell is three- to six-foot. Left-breaking waves come off the east side of the point, and are best if the swell is from the west-northwest. Rights off the west side of the point require the swell to be from the north or northwest. Lefts and rights often break at the same time. A few times each year the surf at Rocky Point is perfect, but in general waves tend to shift and section off—particularly on the rights, as a well-shaped set of waves is often followed by a set of closeouts. The lava-rock reef is flat, with a few submerged rocks and boulders on the west side of the point. Barry Wilson, a 25-year-old pro surfer from Ventura, California, drowned at Rocky Point in 1990 when his surf leash got tangled on a rock and he was held underwater.

Because the waves break close to shore and the lighting is often flawless, Rocky Point has for decades been a favorite with surf photographers, who line up like fence posts on both sides of the point when conditions are right. The cameras in turn bring out an international throng of media-hungry surfers. Rocky Point begins to lose form at six or eight foot, at which point attention shifts to any one of two dozen other North Shore breaks, much to the relief of those pro surfers who view a session at Rocky Point as a necessary career evil. "I hate Rocky Point," Hawaiian surfer Todd Chesser said in 1994. "I'm going to fill it up with kerosene and light a match." *See also* North Shore.

rogue wave   Gigantic, unpredictable, nonsurfable midocean wave, usually solitary, thought to be the result of two or more waves meeting up from intersecting swells. A rogue wave is also known as a "nonnegotiable wave." Ships and ocean liners occasionally come across a rogue wave. Just after four A.M. on September 11, 1995, the *Queen Elizabeth II,* sailing from France to New York, ran into a wave whose crest was level with the bridge, 100 feet above the waterline. The ship pushed through with minor damage and no injuries to passengers or crew. Rogue waves, while huge, tend to dissipate quickly, and are unrelated to fast-moving, low-in-the-water tsunamis—also known as tidal waves—whose power is stored below the surface.

Roland, Joe   Frizzy-haired regularfooter from Jacksonville Beach, Florida; the 17-year-old winner of the hotly contested 1968 East Coast AAAA circuit. Roland began surfing in 1964 at age 13 in Jacksonville; four years later the Eastern Surfing Association debuted its elite AAAA division, and Roland's victory—over internationally known East Coasters like Mike Tabeling, Claude Codgen, and Bruce Valluzzi—was a surprise. The slender and easygoing Roland competed in the World Surfing Championships in 1968 and 1970; he also won the 1969 East Coast Surfing Championships. Roland was elected to the East Coast Surf Legends Hall of Fame in 1998. Vincent, Brad, and Paul Roland, Joe's younger brothers, were all highly regarded East Coast surfers.

roller coaster   Arcing maneuver during which the surfer rides at an angle up the wave face, banks off the crest, and drops back down to the trough; an up-and-down movement that resembles the path of a roller coaster. "Roller coaster" first came into use in the early 1960s, not long after polyurethane foam core surfboards replaced the heavier solid balsa-wood models; the phrase has to some degree been replaced by newer expressions, including "off the lip," "rebound," and "reentry."

Romanosky, Ron   Battered but durable kneeboarder/photographer from Newport Beach, California; a fixture since 1964 at the infamous Newport Wedge. Romanosky was born (1948) in the Dominican Republic, the son of a career U.S. Marine officer, and was raised on or near a series of American military bases. He first rode the throttling Wedge waves as a bodysurfer, graduated to a bellyboard, then a kneeboard. Few surfers in history have been so devoted to a single break. A big swell at the Wedge, Romanosky wrote in 1979, renders him "practically

Roller coaster by California's Dale Dobson

insane with longing, adrenaline and anticipation. I'm addicted to the place. I cannot foresee a time when I won't be this way." Romanosky made a side career from the Wedge as a photojournalist (*Surfer* published his first Wedge article in 1970; his latest ran in the 1999 issue of the *Surfer's Journal*), and by making Wedge-designed kneeboards. As of 2003, he was still riding the Wedge on big days, despite a long history of Wedge-inflicted injuries, including torn knee cartilage, broken teeth, a broken nose, and back sprains that have left him temporarily paralyzed. *See also* kneeboarding, the Wedge.

Rommelse, Michael   Quiet, curly-haired Australian goofyfoot surfer from the Sydney suburb of Avalon; world-ranked #10 in 1996, and Triple Crown winner in 1997. Rommelse was born (1967) in Sydney, began surfing at age eight, and was greatly influenced by two-time world champion Tom Carroll, also of Sydney. Rommelse, like Carroll, was a dedicated power surfer, and filled his repertoire with muscle-flexing turns and cutbacks. He placed fifth in the 1986 Pro Junior contest, and finished second in the 1988 Australian National Titles. After seven middling years as a world tour pro, the 29-year-old Rommelse unexpectedly burst forward in 1996 for a top 10 finish, then followed the next year with his Triple Crown win. He retired after the 1997 season. Flying beneath the media radar throughout his career, Rommelse made a few brief appearances in surf videos, including *All Down the Line* (1989), *Oz on Fire* (1991), and *Primal Urge* (1995).

Ron Jon Surf Shop   American retail chain founded in 1961 by New Jersey surfer Ron DiMenna; includes a Cocoa Beach, Florida, branch long recognized as the sport's largest and gaudiest retail outlet. DiMenna began surfing in 1959, and two years later, on the advice of his father, began paying for his own surf gear by ordering custom boards from California and reselling them out of his parents' attic. DiMenna opened his first shop in 1961 in a trailer parked near the shore in Long Beach Island; two years later he opened a second shop in Cocoa Beach. In the early '90s, the Cocoa Beach location—already 19,000 square feet and covering an entire block on the city's main street—was given a $2.2 million overhaul, raising the square footage to 52,000. The remodel included a floor-to-ceiling fish tank, an elevator, and hundreds of yards of neon tube–light ornamentation, and the store was now open 24 hours a day, 365

days a year. A $1.5 million outdoor sports park was added in 1996; it features 10 sand-and-resin statues, including a 21-foot replica of six-time world champion and Cocoa Beach resident Kelly Slater. The Florida Ron Jon complex, described by one surf magazine as a "frightening monument to consumerism," covers two acres, and sells Jet Skis, boats, dive equipment, wakeboards, snowboards, bicycles, and camping gear, as well as surfing equipment and beachwear. Additional 25,000-square-foot Ron Jon outlets are located in Orange, California, and Fort Lauderdale, Florida. Ron DiMenna was inducted into the East Coast Surf Legends Hall of Fame in 1998. *See also* surfboard shop.

Rosa, Peterson   Raw, relentless pro surfer from Matinhos, Brazil; world-ranked #7 in 2001. Rosa was born (1974) in Guaraja, Brazil, and began surfing at age nine. He turned pro in 1988 at 14, and by 1992 he'd earned a reputation as one of the most entertaining, go-for-broke members of the world tour, picking up nicknames such as "The Animal" and "Bronco." Surf journalist Derek Hynd once said that the tattooed and wild-haired Rosa "doesn't so much perform maneuvers as have collisions with the wave." Or as Florida pro Shea Lopez put it, "If the Cookie Monster could surf, he'd surf like Peterson Rosa." Rosa, a regularfooter, scored his one and only world tour win in Rio in 1998. He has appeared in more than a dozen surf videos, including *Surf Espetacular* (1992), *Beyond the Boundaries* (1994), and *Primal Urge* (1995). He was featured in *The Animal: Peterson Rosa* (2002), a Brazilian-made video. Rosa owns a surf shop in Florianópolis.

Roth, Ed "Big Daddy"   Southern California artist, cartoonist, and custom-car builder; best remembered by male baby boomers as the creator of Rat Fink, a bug-eyed, fly-covered, teeth-baring comic-monster rodent, sold in plastic model kits by Revell in the mid-'60s and printed on tens of thousands of T-shirts. Surf Fink, Surf Monster, Sidewalk Surfer, and a whole retinue of similar Roth-invented cartoon characters soon followed. In 1965, the 35-year-old Roth, a former barber with four years' service in the U.S. Air Force, began to mass-produce "The Surfer's Cross"—a replica of the German Iron Cross military award—on decals and pendants. *Surfer* magazine, worried that the new products were bad for the sport's image, quickly labeled Roth's wares as "The Sign of the Kook." Roth himself looked like an oversized cartoon

Ed "Big Daddy" Roth (lower left) on Revell model box cover

figure at 6'4", 275 pounds, with what *Surfer* described as "an unpruned goatee clinging desperately to a craggy chin." But teenagers and preteens alike loved his creations. "It really upsets your parents," a 15-year-old California surfer admitted to *Time* magazine in 1966, speaking about his new Surfer's Cross pendant. "That's why everyone buys them." Roth carried on for the next few years as a pop culture renegade; his follow-up to the Surfer's Cross was a plastic replica of the German Wehrmacht iron helmet. "You know," he told *Time,* "that Hitler really did a hellavua public relations job for me." Roth later became a Mormon, and worked as a graphic designer for Knott's Berry Farm amusement park in California. He died in 2001, age 69, of a heart attack.

roundhouse   *See* cutback.

roundtail, rounded-pintail   A blunt, elliptical tail-section outline, popularized during the short-board revolution of the late 1960s. The squaretail was used on virtually all boards for small- and medium-sized waves in the pre-1967 longboard era (the wide-backed pintail came into play in the mid-'60s), while big-wave guns featured either a squaretail or a pintail. The roundtail was presented as the easiest-turning tail design, and was more or less the second big step in the shortboard revolution, following the introduction of the vee-bottom; virtually every surfboard manufacturer in 1969 introduced a roundtail model. The twin-point swallowtail cut into the roundtail's popularity beginning in the early '70s, and 15 years later the rounded-square tail (or "squashtail") became the shortboard standard—just as the rounded-pintail, a narrower version of the roundtail, became

the standard on big-wave guns and semi-guns. *See also* pintail, squaretail, squashtail, swallowtail.

Rowland-Smith, Rob   Zealous surf fitness instructor from Sydney, Australia, known as the "Sand Hill Warrior"; trainer to dozens of top surfers in the 1990s and '00s. Rowland-Smith was born (1952) and raised in Sydney. He'd been working for more than 10 years as a gym teacher and rugby trainer when reigning world pro champion Wendy Botha came to him in 1988 to help her rehabilitate following a knee injury. After Botha went on to win two more championships—and to display her buffed Rowland-Smith–sculpted body in a nude Australian *Playboy* pictorial—other pro surfers began to hire the garrulous ruddy-faced trainer. Rowland-Smith clients include world champions Kelly Slater, Tom Carroll, Layne Beachley, Martin Potter, and Lisa Andersen, and pro tour standouts Mick Campbell, Danny Wills, Jeff Booth, and Gary Elkerton. Rowland-Smith's training rhetoric bounces back and forth between military dictums ("You've always got to be in the trenches with your troops," "Your muscles are your suit of armor") and self-help platitudes ("Be a giver, not a taker"), and he's renowned for directing beach exercise programs that leave unprepared surfers doubled up and vomiting in the sand. Rowland-Smith and Quiksilver executive Harry Hodge coauthored 1999's *Fit for Business. See also* fitness and surfing.

Roxy   Bright and casual young women's clothing line; an offshoot of surfwear giant Quiksilver, and the leading force behind women surfing's rapid commercial expansion in the 1990s and '00s. Roxy was quietly launched in 1991 with a limited line of bathing suits, with denim and snow-wear items soon to follow. The company assumed its present form in 1993, when marketer Randy Hild took over as Roxy head and helped develop the instantly-popular girls' "boardshort." Hild also repackaged the label, creating the Roxy Boardriders Team—with world champion Lisa Andersen leading a group of young, sexy, athletic female surfers including Megan Abubo, Daize Shayne, and Kate Skarratt—and by building the company image on laughing, sunny, good-time recreational surfing. Roxy sales doubled each year through 1999, when annual revenue from the brand surpassed $100 million.

Roxy has sponsored dozens of women's surf contests since 1992, including many world pro tour events; from 1996 to 2000 the Roxy Pro was the tour's season-ending event; since 2001 it's been the season-opener. The Roxy line has meanwhile expanded to include luggage, sheets, lamps, jewelry boxes, license plate holders, steering wheel covers, beauty products, and perfumed surf wax. The company has also produced a learn-to-surf video and sponsored Roxy Surf Camps. Hild was listed in 2002 by *Surfer* magazine as one of the "25 Most Powerful People in Surfing." Roxy sales in 2002 topped $150 million. *See also* fashion and surfing, Quiksilver, women and surfing.

Rudolph, Gavin   Regularfoot surfer from Port Elizabeth, South Africa; surprise winner of the 1971 Smirnoff Pro-Am at Sunset Beach, Hawaii, and one of the first to ride Supertubes at Jeffreys Bay. Rudolph began surfing in 1962 at age nine near his Port Elizabeth home; not long after his 15th birthday he flew to Puerto Rico to compete in the 1968 World Surfing Championships. Later that year, he and 1968 Australian champion Keith Paull became the first surfers to ride long, spiraling waves at Supertubes—located just a half-hour's drive from Rudolph's home—and in 1969 he won the Gunston 500 in Durban. The following year Rudolph competed in the 1970 World Surfing Championships. The 18-year-old was visiting Hawaii for the first time when he won the 1971 Smirnoff contest, held in challenging 12-foot Sunset Beach surf, in what was probably the greatest upset of the early pro era. In 1977, Rudolph entered about half of the scheduled world pro tour events and finished the season ranked #15. His surfing style was both efficient and flowing, and he rarely made mistakes; he appeared in just over a half-dozen surf films, including *Freeform* (1970), *Tracks* (1970), and *Oceans* (1972).

Russell, Rory   Happy, hedonistic tuberiding specialist from the North Shore of Oahu, Hawaii; Pipeline Masters winner in 1976 and 1977. Russell was born (1953) in Würzburg, West Germany, the son of an army attaché, and grew up in military bases in Kansas and Pennsylvania before moving to Oahu with his family at age 10. He began surfing the following year, and in 1968 at age 15, Russell and his family moved to the North Shore beachfront, next door to Jock Sutherland, the just-crowned winner of the Duke Kahanamoku Invitational. Sutherland, the era's best tuberider, became Russell's informal mentor. Russell had some decent competition results early

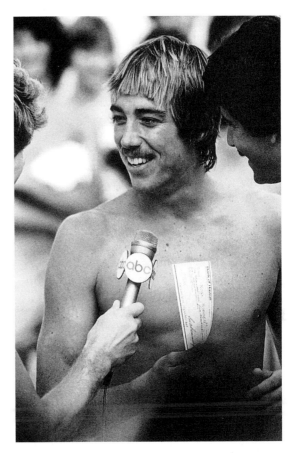

Rory Russell

in his career, including a finals berth in the juniors division of the 1970 Hawaii State Championships, but made his reputation with a series of surf movie appearances in the early '70s, riding deep inside the tube at Pipeline. The super-smooth Gerry Lopez, however, had established himself as the dominant Pipeline surfer, and Russell—who rode in spindly swayback stance, until lowering into a deadly efficient tube crouch—would never fully step out from Lopez's shadow.

Russell won two events on the inaugural world pro circuit in 1976 to finish the season ranked #8, the highest of the Hawaiian pros. He finished eighth the following year as well, in large part due to his second Masters win. (Russell's record in the Pipeline Masters from 1973 to 1978 was untouchable, as he finished third, second, second, first, first, second.) Known throughout his career as "The Dog," the smoky-voiced Russell had meanwhile earned a reputation as the ultimate surf world Bacchus. "No matter what time of day or night it is," surf journalist Phil Jarratt wrote in 1980, "chances are he'll be talking, surfing, or partying at full throttle." Russell never won a pro tour contest after 1977, and was off the tour by 1980. In the early and mid-'80s, he was paid to be the jet-setting bon vivant surfer/frontman for Lighting Bolt, the fading Hawaii-based surfboard and surfwear giant. He later earned a living by running North Shore fishing charters.

The never-married Russell appeared in more than two dozen surf movies, including *Cosmic Children* (1970), *Five Summer Stories* (1972), *Fluid Drive* (1974), *Super Session* (1975), and *Fantasea* (1978).

Russia   In the fall of 1999, Southern California surfers Shayne McIntyre and Jon McClure, along with Newport Beach photographer Mike Moir and Australian surfer Marc Lesoki, introduced surfing to Russia. The group visited the largely uninhabited Sakhalin Island at the bottom of the Russian-held Kuril Islands, between the Sea of Okhotsk and the North Pacific Ocean, not far from the northern tip of Japan. Most of the beaches were reachable only by logging roads; the surf breaks the group found were "often stark and desolate," as Moir reported, but also "pristine and utterly beautiful." Waves in the Sea of Okhotsk proved to be inconsistent (access to the Pacific was limited), but when typhoon-generated surf did arrive, getting as big as eight foot, a stunning variety of high-quality breaks were discovered; one reminded the surfers of Rincon in California, another broke like Australia's Lennox Head, while yet another resembled Bali's Uluwatu. "There were so many spots to choose from," Moir said, "it was confounding." While the air temperature often dipped into the 30s, the water temperature remained in the mid- and upper 50s. Accounts of the trip were published in *Surfer* and the *Surfer's Journal* magazines. Domestic surfing didn't exist in Russia as of 2003, although the word *daska,* for "surfboard," had some years before come into the lexicon.

S

S-turn Linked set of turns usually performed directly after takeoff on a medium-sized or bigger wave; consisting of an opening turn toward the wave's shoulder, a matching turn back into the steeper and more critical portion of the wave, then a bottom turn. A variation of the "fade" and an elegant way to set up a tuberide.

sailboarding Popular surfing/sailing hybrid sport using a surfboardlike hull and a universally mounted mast supporting a boom and sail. Early American surfer Tom Blake created a prone-position "sailing surfboard" in the 1930s, but the stand-up version of the sport was invented in 1965, when Southern California surfer/sailors Hoyle Schweitzer and Jim Drake developed a prototype for their 1970-patented Windsurfer. The new craft was an instant hit in Europe, and by the end of the decade had begun to catch on in America as well; it was estimated that 100,000 sailboards were sold worldwide prior to 1980. In Europe, the sport was practiced almost exclusively on lakes and rivers, while in America it was for the most part an ocean activity, with wave-riding and -jumping emerging as the main attraction. Sailboarders in Hawaii were soon angling across huge waves; when the surf was smaller, they used waves to launch into spinning midair loops, flips, and rolls. Sailboarding equipment evolved quickly over the years, becoming ever lighter and stronger. Today's high-performance boards (usually between seven to nine feet long, resembling a thick surfboard with footstraps) are generally made from Styrofoam blanks covered in fiberglass and epoxy resin, the mast from carbon-aluminum composites, and the sails (used in various sizes according to wind speed) from some combination of monofilm, Dacron, Mylar, and Kevlar.

The first Sailboarding World Championships were held in France in 1975, the sailboarding Pro World Tour was founded in 1983, and the sport became an Olympic event in 1984. Today's competition categories include slalom racing, distance racing, wave-riding, aerials, and free-riding. There are dozens of local, domestic, and international windsurfing leagues and circuits, topped by the Professional Windsurfing Association's (PWA) pro tour, which sanctions 14 to 18 annual international events a year; aggregate PWA prize money in 2001 was just over $500,000. Robbie Naish of Maui is almost universally acknowledged as sailboarding's all-time greatest rider, having won more than 20 overall and individual discipline world titles in the '70s, '80s, and '90s, including six PWA championships. Wind- and wave-filled Hookipa Beach on Maui has long been regarded as sailboarding's Mecca. By 2003, there were an estimated 10 million sailboarders worldwide, eight million in Europe alone.

Some of California and Hawaii's best-known surfers, including Gerry Lopez, Richard Schmidt, and Laird Hamilton, became avid sailboarders in the '80s and early '90s; virtually all of the best wave-riding sailboarders, meanwhile, are accomplished surfers. In the early '90s, sailboarders Mike Waltz, Dave Kalama,

S-turn

and Rush Randall were among the first group to ride a Maui big-wave surf break called Jaws; Hamilton, along with fellow Hawaiian surfer/sailboarders Buzzy Kerbox and Darrick Doerner, recognized the advantage of a wind-aided takeoff for big-wave riding, and in the early 1990s took the process a step further by developing motorized tow-in surfing, thereby revolutionizing big-wave riding completely.

Sailboarding is also known as windsurfing, boardsailing, and surf-sailing. *See also* kiteboarding.

Sainsbury, Mark   Spike-haired Australian regular-footer from Avoca, New South Wales; men's division winner in the 1986 World Amateur Champions, and an early master of the floater maneuver. Sainsbury was born (1966) and raised in Avoca, began surfing at age 11, and by 1985 was an unbeatable amateur competitor, winning the Australian Professional Surfing Association title, the Pro Junior contest, and the Australian national championship. He had less luck on the pro tour. He won a world circuit event (the 1989 4X International in Queensland), but otherwise his six years on the tour were unremarkable. On August 6, 1992 the 26-year-old Sainsbury died suddenly of a brain aneurysm while surfing Avoca. Bill Cilia, Sainsbury's surfboard shaper for 13 years, described him in a surf magazine obituary as "a dynamo; like a little atom in the water, he paddled so fast." Sainsbury was featured in a small number of surf movies and videos, including *Mad Wax* (1987), *Water Slaughter* (1988), and *Oz on Fire* (1991).

saltwater   Saltiness in the oceans and seas is caused by the introduction of dissolved chemicals eroded from the earth's crust. Scientists believe that hundreds of millions of years ago, before the onset of rainfall, the primeval seas were only slightly salty. Over millions of years, rains flushed salt-bearing minerals from the earth into the oceans. Today, rivers worldwide annually transport an estimated four billion tons of dissolved salt to the oceans, while an equal amount of salt is deposited on the ocean floor. A cubic foot of seawater will evaporate down to just over two pounds of salt. Salinity is the amount of salt found in water, and is generally measured in grams per kilogram; the average ocean salinity is 35 parts per thousand, or 3.5 percent, but the number varies from 32 to 37. Salinity increases where there is high evaporation (water evaporates, salt doesn't) and little rainfall, as is the case in the Red Sea and the Persian Gulf. Saltier water is both denser and heavier, and thus more buoyant; a surfboard will float higher in the water at Rye Beach, New Hampshire, than it will at Silver Beach at the south end of Lake Michigan. Water is less salty in areas where it is diluted with freshwater—near rivermouths, in areas of high rainfall, or around melting icebergs. Winds and ocean currents help keep the world's oceans and seas circulating, which in turn maintains a fairly consistent salinity rate from ocean to ocean. Salinity also causes ocean water to freeze at a lower temperature than fresh water—at about 28 degrees rather than 32. Saltwater is mildly corrosive, and is particularly hard on wetsuits, which should be washed in fresh water after each use.

saltwater drip   *See* nose drip.

Samoa Islands   Group of volcanic islands in the tropical South Pacific Ocean, located roughly halfway between New Zealand and Hawaii; American Samoa, made up of the eastern islands, is a United States territory; Western Samoa is an independent nation. The bountiful Samoan surf is powerful, well-shaped, and lined with sharp coral reefs. Many of the best reefs are set in near-complete isolation. The weather is tropically warm from season to season, with water temperatures averaging about 80 degrees; the Pago Pago harbor area, on American Samoa's main island of Tutuila, gets nearly 200 inches of rain a year. Swells arrive from the south and east between May and October and from the north and northwest from November to April. Samoa was one of the surf world's best-kept secrets in the '70s and '80s, and even today retains much of its quiet, even mysterious allure—and all its beauty. "The contrasts in color are amazing," Australian pro surfer Pru Jeffries said after visiting in 1998. "A black-lava-lined point is fringed with deep green vegetation, and cerulean blue lefts wall up and spin over a fan-coral bottom." Lauli'i Tuai is one of American Samoa's best waves, a fast, tubing, spitting left. Aufaga's long right-breaking waves are among the best in Western Samoa. Poisonous reef fish are a worry throughout the entire area, but nothing like the shallow coral-covered reefs, which are regarded as among the most dangerous in the surfing world.

Surfing was a part of ancient Samoan culture, but was quashed under the influence of visiting 19th-century missionaries. Unlike Hawaiians, the Samoans didn't pick the sport back up in the early decades of the following century. In the 1990s, however, a handful of young natives began surfing, and since 2000 American Samoa has fielded a small team in the Pacific Cup, the Oceania Cup, and other competitions. Two small Australian-owned surf resorts opened on the islands in the late '90s, while travel companies began offering oceangoing Samoa surf boat charters. Surfing is prohibited on Sundays in Western Samoa, along with nearly all other activities, except for church services and feasts. Samoa is featured in a small number of surf movies and videos, including *Ticket to Ride* (1986) and *Follow the Leader* (1998).

San Diego, San Diego County   Temperate and largely suburban area in California's southwest corner, including just over 75 miles of Pacific Ocean coastline; encompasses the coastal towns and communities of Oceanside, Carlsbad, Leucadia, Encinitas, Cardiff, Del Mar, La Jolla, Pacific Beach, Mission Beach, Ocean Beach, Coronado, and Imperial Beach. San Diego County offers a wide range of surf breaks, including the point-reef rights at Swami's, the two-way beachbreak waves at Oceanside, the quirky peaks of Windansea, and powerful sand-bottom tubes at Blacks Beach. (Trestles, one of the state's best-known breaks, straddles the border between San Diego and Orange counties, but is generally regarded as Orange County territory.) The two most popular surfing regions in San Diego proper are the reef-lined Sunset Cliffs, along Point Loma, and the wealthy La Jolla area. San Diego County receives waves all year, but the best and biggest surf generally arrives between late fall and early spring; four-foot surf is common during this period, and the biggest winter swells can produce waves up to 12 feet or bigger at places like Blacks, La Jolla Cove, and Tijuana Sloughs. Summer surf is generally small. San Diego has been described as having the world's best climate, with daytime air temperatures along the coast rarely dipping below 60 or above 90; water temperatures range from the mid-50s to the low 70s. San Diego surf lineups can be maddeningly crowded, and areas in La Jolla and Sunset Cliffs have earned a reputation for localism. Because most San Diego surf breaks are relatively soft and easy to ride, the entire area has for decades been popular with longboarders and beginning surfers.

Surfing was probably introduced to San Diego in 1916, when lifeguard Charlie Wright borrowed a redwood surfboard from visiting Hawaiian Duke Ka-

hanamoku and rode a few waves at Ocean Beach. (Hawaiian-born George Freeth, a Los Angeles County lifeguard, may have surfed in San Diego sometime between 1907 and 1909.) Wright began making surfboards and giving surf lessons, and wave-riding communities were founded up and down San Diego County in the '20s and '30s. The annual Pacific Coast Surf Riding Championships—the state's first all-regions surfing event—was held from 1936 to 1941 in the easy-breaking waves at San Onofre, near San Diego County's northern border. In 1959, San Diego surfers Larry Gordon and Floyd Smith opened Gordon & Smith Surfboards in Pacific Beach, the county's first full-service surf shop. (Hansen Surfboards, another first-generation shop, opened two years later.) Windansea by that time had earned a reputation for producing some of America's loudest, rowdiest, and most talented surfers. Looking to channel some of that energy, local surfer Chuck Hasley formed the Windansea Surf Club in 1963—with a roster that included Skip Frye, Mike Hynson, LJ Richards, Pat Curren, Butch Van Artsdalen, and Rusty Miller—and it soon became the best-known organization of its kind in America. Other top San Diego county riders of the era include power surfer Phil Edwards, 1964 World Championships runner-up Mike Doyle, 1968 World Champions hips winner Margo Godfrey, two-time U.S. Champion Linda Benson, and surfboard shaper Mike Diffenderfer. (Other influential San Diego designer/shapers include Steve Lis, Rusty Preisendorfer, and Gary Linden.)

San Diego County made up one of the original competition districts in the 1961-formed United States Surfing Association, and in 1966 the city hosted the wildly successful World Surfing Championships, won by Australian Nat Young and Joyce Hoffman of California. The Championships returned to San Diego in 1972, with titles going to Jimmy Blears and Sharron Weber of Hawaii, but the contest was an organizational disaster. Localism by that time had become the rule on many San Diego County beaches: David Nuuhiwa, top contender for the 1972 title, had his board stolen by Ocean Beach–area surfers during the early rounds of the contest, and on finals day it turned up mangled and spray-painted, hanging from a piece of rope off the Ocean Beach Pier. The California Pro, one of the state's first international pro contests, was held in Oceanside in 1977 (earning a special place in surf contest history when all the winners' checks bounced); the Stubbies Pro, also held in Oceanside (from 1984 to 1988), was the biggest world pro tour event held in San Diego County. The United States Surfing Championships were held in Oceanside in 1981, 1989, and 1993, and annually from 1997 to present day; Oceanside also hosted portions of the 1984 World Surfing Championships. Noteworthy San Diego–area surfers of the past 30 years include world tour pros Joey Buran, Debbie Beacham, Brad Gerlach, Rob Machado, and Taylor Knox; style exemplar Chris O'Rourke; and longboarders Dale Dobson and Joel Tudor. Tenured surf photographers Jeff Divine and Aaron Chang are also from San Diego.

By 2003, San Diego County (population 2.5 million) was home to about 60 surf shops and 200,000 surfers. Local surf companies include Gordon & Smith, Rusty, and TransWorld Surf. The San Diego surf is detailed in *Surf Guide to Southern California* (1963), *Surfing California* (1973), and *The Stormrider Guide North America* (2002). *See also* Oceanside, San Onofre, Windansea, the Windansea Surf Club.

San Onofre   Relaxed, tradition-rich Southern California surf break located at the north end of San Diego County, adjacent to San Clemente; home to the Pacific Coast Surf Riding Championships from 1938 to 1941; regarded since the end of World War II as a surfing sanctuary for families and old-timers. Origins for the name "San Onofre" are unclear, but it's been suggested that the area was named after the desert-dwelling hermit Saint Onuphrius. California goofyfooter Bob Sides, driving through what was then part of the Rancho Santa Margarita in 1933, noticed good waves across the tracks and down the dirt cliffs from the San Onofre train station; Sides quickly convinced Lorrin "Whitey" Harrison and a few others at Newport Beach's Corona del Mar jetty—a favorite break for early generation California surfers—to make a two-day San Onofre surf exploration. After a jetty extension shut down the waves at Corona del Mar in 1935, San Onofre became one of California's most popular surf breaks; "a meeting place," as longtime San Onofre regular Dorian Paskowitz later recalled, "for surfers from San Diego's Tijuana Sloughs to Steamer Lane in Santa Cruz." Weekend camp-outs, Paskowitz continued, were filled with "Hawaiian guitar, Tahitian dancing and no small amount of boozing." Virtually every notable surfer in California from the mid-'30s to the early '40s rode often at San Onofre, including Tom Blake, Cliff Tucker, Tulie

San Onofre Surfing Club decal

Clark, Gard Chapin, John "Doc" Ball, and L. E. "Hoppy" Swarts. Santa Monica's Pete Peterson, the era's best surfer, won two of his four Pacific Coast Surf Riding Championships at San Onofre in 1938 and 1941.

After World War II, with the development of shorter, lighter surfboards, performance-minded California riders began seeking more challenging waves at places like Malibu and Windansea. San Onofre, along with hundreds of square miles of inland property, had meanwhile been turned over to the U.S. Marines; when it looked as if the marines would shut San Onofre down to surfers, Orange County surfer/ dentist Barney Wilkes led the drive in 1952 to establish the San Onofre Surfing Club, whose members were allowed beach access. By the early '60s, San Onofre was all but enshrined as a warm, nostalgic, easygoing family-style surf break. Club members were singularly devoted to their beach. "This is our life," as one put it in 1961. "All the days in-between are bare existence." A palm-frond shack in front of the main surf break became a surf-world icon, as did the yearly San Onofre Surf Club car window sticker. By 1965 there were 800 club members, including *Los Angeles Times* publisher Otis Chandler and TV star James Arness. In 1973 San Onofre became part of the California State Parks system, and was opened to the public. Five years earlier the break lost a measure of its wilderness cachet with the opening of the looming San Onofre Nuclear Generating Station; otherwise the marine-operated area remained almost completely undeveloped.

While San Onofre State Park stretches along nearly two miles of wave-filled beachfront, there are two main breaks, both located in the northern half of the park: Old Man's (also called Outside), the traditional San Onofre break and onetime home to the Pacific Coast Surf Riding Championships, features a broad, generous, multitiered wave field, similar to that of Waikiki. Small rocks fill the shoreline, and the break is often crowded with longboard-riding novices, but the surf is otherwise easy-breaking and hazard-free. Waves at the Point, located a quarter mile north of Old Man's, break closer to the beach, and are steeper, smaller, and marginally harder-breaking. Old Man's and the Point are ridden almost exclusively by longboarders; shortboard surfers ride further to the north at Church, Trestles, and Cottons. The 1977 United States Surfing Championships were held at San Onofre; hundreds of regional, national, and international longboard contests have been held here since the mid-'80s, including the Hobie San Onofre Classic and the all-female Roxy Wahine Classic.

The prewar San Onofre surfing scene is featured in John "Doc" Ball's seminal 1946 photo book *California Surfriders*. Lorrin Harrison and Dorian Paskowitz were among the still-active senior San Onofre surfers featured in "Endless Summer," a 1990 *Life* magazine feature. "The cosmic forces of San Onofre made me," Paskowitz told *Life*. "In these waves I found a power that took a nice Jewish boy and made him a nobleman." *See also* Pacific Coast Surf Riding Championships.

sandbar   A raised area of underwater sand that sculpts and directs breaking waves; sandbars are usually dome- or plateau-shaped, and are often formed by littoral or outgoing currents. While some sandbars are more or less fixed—as with Mundaka, Spain, the world's premier rivermouth sandbar—mutability is the classic sandbar trait. Sandbars are often created during a big swell, and erased just as quickly by the next big swell; sandbars lasting for just one or two days are not unheard of. Australia's Narrabeen and Hossegor in France produce some of the world's best sandbar waves. Sandbars can also be a hindrance to good surf; at Pipeline in Hawaii, sand will occasionally fill in the channel adjacent to the reef so that the famed left-breaking waves funnel into a vicious close-out section. *See also* beachbreak.

sandboarding; sand surfing   Ancient Egyptians used planks made of pottery or wood to slide down sand dunes, and sandboarding photos date back to the 1940s, but this was a virtually unknown recreation until the mid-'60s, when it slipstreamed in behind the original surfing and skateboarding boom. A 1964 *Petersen's Surfing* magazine article described sand surfing as "four or five lads pouring down the side of what looks like a 150 foot wave, pulling off almost every surfing gimmick in the book." Sandboarding expanded in the '70s, largely due to the efforts of Colorado's Gary Fluitt and Jack Smith from California. Borrowing technology from snowboarding, the sandboard evolved from cardboard sheets, snow discs, and old surfboards to customized wooden boards (about four feet long and 10 inches wide) with footstraps and slick Formica bottoms. *Sandboard,* an online magazine, debuted in 1995. "We found that there were several thousand sandboarders out there," magazine founder Lon Beale said, "making boards and carving dunes completely unknown to each other, and thinking they were the only ones doing this crazy sandboarding thing." Sandboarding is practiced in Australia, New Zealand, Namibia, Egypt, Saudi Arabia, Argentina, Germany, Uruguay, Brazil, Canada, and nearly every state in America. In 2000, Dune Rider International, the sport's organizing body, hosted eight worldwide professional events, and the sixth World Sandboarding Championships— a five-day event held in Monte Kaolino, Germany— drew about 200 competitors and 20,000 spectators.

Sandy Beach   Arid sand-and-rock-lined surf break located on the east side of Oahu, Hawaii; known primarily as a bodysurfing and bodyboarding spot. The board-surfing area at Sandy Beach is divided into three humdrum breaks—Full Point, Half Point, and Generals—and from 1986 to 1989 the world pro tour Gotcha Pro event was held here, primarily because its beachfront parking lot is big enough to handle an influx of 5,000 spectators. The shorebreak located just west of Half Point has been one of the world's most popular bodysurfing areas since the 1950s, with bodyboarders joining in during the mid-'70s. While the entire gently curved stretch of beach is utilized, local bodysurfers and bodyboarders identify at least four different breaks: Cobbles, Middles, Gas Chambers, and Insanities. Waves here are usually shapeless and rarely over four feet, but massively thick and powerful, often exploding in just inches of water. Sandy Beach is reputed to have put more wave-riders in the hospital—with separated shoulders, strained backs, and occasionally paralyzing spinal injuries—than any other break in the world. Sandy Beach has surf of one kind or another all year, but is biggest and most consistent between May and September. Sandy Beach made headlines in 1985, when England's Prince Charles, visiting Hawaii with Lady Diana, snuck past dozens of reporters, donned a pair of borrowed surf trunks, and spent 20 minutes bodysurfing Middles. Sandy Beach has been featured in more than a dozen surf movies and videos, including *Slippery When Wet* (1958), *Shock Waves* (1987), *Surfers: The Movie* (1990), and *Pure Blue* (2001). *See also* bodysurfing.

Santa Cruz, Santa Cruz County   Cliff-lined surfing hub located in north central California, about 70 miles south of San Francisco; the 19th-century birthplace of surfing in mainland America; a magnificent wave haven now filled with dozens of partially overlapping groups of longboarders, aerialists, kayakers, big-wave riders, and rank beginners. "Nowhere else in the world," *Surfing* magazine noted, "will you find so many different types of waves packed into such a short coastline: big surf and small surf, long glassy walls, steep curling peaks, and fast-breaking shorebreak." More than 65 surf breaks are found along Santa Cruz County's 45-mile S-shaped coast, which can be divided into four main surfing areas: 1) The rugged and largely undeveloped North Coast, extending from the Santa Cruz city limit up to Año Nuevo. 2) The West Side, located along Santa Cruz's western border, home to Steamer Lane. 3) The East Side, centered around Pleasure Point. 4) The often-overlooked South Beaches. With the exception of Moss Landing, the area's southernmost break, the waves in Santa Cruz County generally get progressively smaller from north to south. The area receives surf all year, but is biggest and most consistent in late fall and winter. Summer surf is dependably small, often flat, and sometimes fogged in. The spring months are windy and cold, although nearly all "town" breaks—those located within Santa Cruz city limits—are protected from the prevailing northwesterlies. Winter air temperatures range from the mid-40s to the mid-60s, and the mid-50s to upper 70s in the summer. Water temperatures range from the high 40s to the mid-60s. The multifaceted Steamer Lane, at the near center of Santa Cruz County, has always been the area's best-known break. Pleasure Point,

Moss Landing, the Harbor, the Rivermouth, Stockton Avenue, Mitchell's Cove, Swift Street, Ledges, Año Nuevo, and a half-dozen other city and county breaks can produce world-class surf. Cowells, just east of Steamer Lane, is one of the state's best beginner areas. Breaks within Santa Cruz city limits have for decades been notoriously crowded.

American waves were surfed for the first time by Hawaii's Kawananakoa brothers, Jonah (heir to the royal throne), David, and Edward, who attended a San Mateo boarding school and in 1885 rode homemade redwood plank boards at the San Lorenzo Rivermouth in central Santa Cruz. A small group of locals continued to board-ride along the city's southern beaches as far back as the 1890s, but the sport really took root here in 1938, in part thanks to an inspiring visit by Hawaiian surfing patriarch Duke Kahanamoku. That same year, a group of Santa Cruz High School surfers, including Harry Mayo, Bill Grace, and Buster Stewart (who used sweaters layered over woolen bathing suits to guard against the cold), founded the Santa Cruz Surfing Club. Pleasure Point was first surfed in 1940. Peter Cole, Fred Van Dyke, and Rick Grigg, who would all go on to ride the huge Hawaiian surf, developed their taste for big waves at Steamer Lane in the early and mid-'50s.

Surfing in Santa Cruz became more comfortable in 1959, when budding wetsuit magnate Jack O'Neill relocated his business from San Francisco to Santa Cruz. Top surfers from the area in the early and mid-'60s included Danny Anderson, Doug Haut, Gene Hall, Gary Venturini, and Rod Lundquist. In the 1961 surf movie *Angry Sea,* Santa Cruz regularfooter Jim Foley is shown riding a 7'10" board—seven years before the shortboard revolution. Roger Adams, Mark Angell, Michael Junod, Joey Thomas, Pat O'Neill, and Robbie Waldamar were all part of the talented if somewhat provincial Santa Cruz front line in the late '60s and '70s. In 1970, Adams and Pat O'Neill (son of Jack O'Neill) invented the surf leash. "Localism," surfing's belligerent no-outsiders policy, meanwhile flourished in Santa Cruz during this period; just before the start of a big surfing competition in 1969, local surfers, under cover of night, pushed the judges' scaffolding off the cliff at Steamer Lane, and the following day they refused to give way to the competitors in the water, yelling to the visitors that they were "goose-stepping pigs." Nonetheless, hundreds of amateur surf contests have been held in Santa Cruz since the early '60s. Professional surfing was introduced here in 1967 when Corky Carroll won $300 in the Santa Cruz Pro-Am; of the dozens of succeeding pro contests—with nearly all shortboard events taking place at Steamer Lane and most longboard events staged at Pleasure Point—the biggest and richest was the world tour O'Neill Coldwater Classic, held from 1988 to 1990. Long-running local events include the 1980-founded Yeah Now No-Cord Classic, first held in 1980, and the Big Stick Surf-o-Rama, first held in 1989.

Aside from Chris Gallagher and Adam Replogle, who both briefly qualified for the world pro tour, Santa Cruz surfers, as compared to their Southern California peers, have been less interested and adept in competition. Shortboard surfers here have earned distinction as high-flying aerialists (starting with Kevin Reed in the late '70s) or as big-wave riders. Decades before the early '90s introduction of Maverick's, the big-wave break located in nearby Half Moon Bay, Santa Cruz had been known as California's premier big-wave training ground, and by the early '80s local surfers Richard Schmidt and Vince Collier together had set a Santa Cruz big-wave-riding standard: Schmidt for his cool-handed technique and Collier for his loud, crude, swashbuckling disposition. Peter Mel, Darryl "Flea" Virostko, Josh Loya, and Kenny "Skindog" Collins were among the city's best big-wave riders as of 2003.

About a dozen or so shark sightings are made each year in and around Santa Cruz County surf breaks. San Jose surfer Eric Larsen needed 400 stitches and 200 surgical staples after being hit by a 15-foot white shark while surfing Davenport in north Santa Cruz County in 1991; big-wave master Peter Mel, while waiting for a wave at a north county break in 1997, found himself hunching over his board beneath a jumping "flock of seals," who were being chased by a shark.

In the mid-'90s, city officials from both Santa Cruz and Southern California's Huntington Beach squabbled over the rights to the title of "Surf City," to no final result. As of 2003, the fast-growing city of Santa Cruz was home to an estimated 50 surf shops and 8,000 surfers. Roughly 15 to 20 percent of the local surf population are women, a higher figure than anywhere in the world. Santa Cruz surf world notables include longboarder and *Endless Summer II* star Robert "Wingnut" Weaver, videographer Tony Roberts, photographer Patrick Trefz, and big-wave rider/aerialist Shawn "Barney" Barron; the 1992-

founded Surftech board-making company is located in the town's industrial center. The Santa Cruz surf is detailed in *Surfing California* (1973) and *The Stormrider Guide North America* (2002). Daniel Duane's memoir *Caught Inside: A Surfer's Year on the California Coast* (1996) is set in Santa Cruz; Trefz's photo book *Santa Cruz: Visions of Surf City* was published in 2002. *See also* Jack O'Neill, O'Neill Wetsuits, Steamer Lane.

Santa Cruz Surfing Museum   Five-hundred-and-fifty-square-foot surfing museum inside the Mark Abbott Memorial Lighthouse, located in Santa Cruz, California, overlooking the surf break Steamer Lane. The Santa Cruz Surfing Museum, the first museum of its kind in America, opened in 1986 and was founded by the Santa Cruz Longboard Union surf club, along with the local chapter of the Surfrider Foundation environmental group. The museum is dedicated to Santa Cruz's own long and rich surfing history, and permanent displays include a pair of redwood plank surfboards used locally during the '30s and '40s, and the first wetsuit made by Santa Cruz–based wetsuit titan Jack O'Neill. The original Santa Cruz lighthouse was built in 1869 and torn down just before World War II; the current lighthouse was built in 1967 to honor local surfer Mark Abbott, who died at age 18 while surfing Steamer Lane. *See also* Bishop Museum, California Surf Museum, Huntington Beach International Surfing Museum, Surfworld Museum.

Santa Monica Civic Auditorium   Performing arts center located a few hundred yards off the beach in Santa Monica, California; America's premier surf movie venue in the 1960s and 1970s, and site of the 1966 *International Surfing* Magazine Hall of Fame Awards ceremony. The 3,000-seat white-on-white pop-futuristic Santa Monica Civic Auditorium was built in 1958, and is fronted by a row of distinctive Tomorrowland-style space needles. From 1961 to 1968 it was home to the Academy Awards ceremonies; in the late '60s and '70s it was a popular midsize venue for rock acts like Frank Zappa, David Bowie, the Eagles, Eric Clapton, and Tom Petty. John Severson's *Surf Safari* was the first surf movie to play the Civic, in 1960; a majority of California-made surf movies over the next 20 years also screened there, including *Going My Wave* (1962), *Free and Easy* (1967), *Cosmic Children* (1970), and *Free Ride* (1977). Surfing's biggest and most-anticipated surf movie premiere took place at the Civic March 24, 1972, with the showing of

Greg MacGillivray and Jim Freeman's long-awaited *Five Summer Stories.* Surfboard display booths were set up in the lobby, Laguna Beach country/surf band Honk played before the screening, and at least 500 counterfeit tickets were sold. "People were seated in the aisles, on the stairs, standing along the back," MacGillivray later recalled. "Every nook and cranny was filled—no one could move." Surf movie bookings at the Civic began tapering off in the late '70s and dried up altogether in the mid-'80s as the surf movie was replaced by surf video.

The Los Angeles Surf Fair, trade show precursor to the Action Surf Retailer and Surf Expo events, was held at the Civic from 1962 to 1964. Duke Kahanamoku, Pete Peterson, Greg Noll, Joyce Hoffman, Mickey Dora, Dewey Weber, Bruce Brown, and Phil Edwards were among the 2,000 attendees to the 1966 *International Surfing* Hall of Fame formal-dress invitation-only gala, also held at the Civic. *See also Five Summer Stories,* Los Angeles Surf Fair, Sydney Opera House.

Santos, Edwin   Top Puerto Rican surfer from the mid-'70s to the mid-'80s. Santos, the son of an engineer, began surfing in 1968 at age 12, after watching the World Surfing Championship, held that year on Puerto Rico's west shore. He never broke out of the middle of the pack during his years as a world tour pro, but did earn a footnote in tour history by beating Dane Kealoha in a preliminary heat of the final contest of the 1979 season, thus denying the heavily favored Hawaiian a world title. The victory was a huge upset, as 1978 world champion Wayne Bartholomew later remembered. "You would have got 100 to 1 on Edwin before the heat." *Surfer* took a kinder view, saying the win showed a "progressing ability to think out the right moves while under fire." Santos was featured on the cover of the August 1983 issue of *Surfing* magazine.

Santosha   *See* Mauritius.

Sargeant, Paul   Indefatigable surf photographer, videographer, and writer from Cronulla, New South Wales, Australia; a constant presence on the world pro tour since 1987. Sargeant was born (1955) in Sydney, raised in the nearby suburb of Cronulla, and began surfing in 1970. He was a *Sydney Daily Mirror* photographer from 1975 to 1982 (in 1979 he was named Australian Press Photographer of the Year), then went freelance. Sargeant began attending surf

contests regularly in 1984, and three years later he became a full-time surf photographer, submitting his work mainly to *Tracks* and *Surfer* magazines. His work has also appeared in *Reader's Digest* and *Newsweek.* The often cantankerous Sargeant has also written more than 200 surf press articles and columns, mainly contest coverage and surfer interviews. Nine editions of the Sargeant-made *Sarge's Scrapbook* video series came out between 1989 to 2001, each documenting a portion on the world pro tour; a majority of the footage is surfing action, but the videos are better known for their lightly ribald behind-the-scenes candids. "With a few obvious exceptions," surf journalist Derek Rielly noted in his review for *Sarge's Scrapbook: Take Five,* in a backhanded compliment to the filmmaker's intentionally crude cinematic style, "Sarge seems to have mastered the art of focusing a video camera." Sargeant moved to Queensland's Gold Coast in 1995.

Sato, Denjiro Hiroshi   Discerning and unassuming Japanese-born surf photographer. Sato was born (1952) in Niigata, on the island of Honshu, got his first camera in 1966 at age 14, and began surfing in 1970. Sato, a self-taught photographer (and former sushi chef), whose work was first published in 1978, became a *Surfer* masthead photographer in 1983, not long after the magazine used two of his pictures of Hawaiian big-wave surfer James Jones on the cover. "His water photos," *Surfer* later noted, "are quickly becoming the standard by which others are judged." Sato went on to concentrate more on ocean texture and patterns, rather than action shots, and was able to frame empty waves so that they appeared to be massive, intricately detailed sculptures. His work has appeared in *Surfing, Surfer's Journal, Longboard, Surfing World, Nalu,* and *Surf Trip.* He also contributed to a number of illustrated surfing books, including *The History of Surfing* (1983), and *Surfing: The Ultimate Pleasure* (1984), and worked as a cameraman for two Hollywood surf movies: *North Shore* (1987) and *In God's Hands* (1998). *Aloha Waves,* Sato's tranquil short film, produced in 1995, was an award winner in Japan.

Schmidt, Richard   Soft-spoken and methodical big-wave rider and surf instructor from Santa Cruz, California; runner-up in the 1999 Quiksilver Maverick's Men Who Ride Mountains contest, and founder of the Richard Schmidt Surf School. Schmidt was born (1960) in San Francisco, the son of a Lutheran minister, raised in Santa Cruz, and began surfing at

Richard Schmidt

age eight. He came to the attention of the surf world in 1980, after *Surfing* magazine published photos of him tuberiding the thick, explosive waves of Puerto Escondido, Mexico. Schmidt's friend and fellow Santa Cruz surfer Vince Collier also gained notice at this time, and the two were often spoken of as a unit. But whereas the barrel-chested Collier was loud and coarse, the slender, white-blond Schmidt (5′8″, 155 pounds) was quiet and focused. He rode in a narrow stance, with arms and hands extended somewhat rigidly out to the sides, rarely backed down from the waves he paddled for, and made few mistakes. Bottom turns were a specialty. "There are top pros," Australian surf journalist Nick Carroll later wrote, "earning six times his money with 20 times the ego, who curl up and die upon witnessing the Richard Schmidt big-wave bottom turn."

Schmidt visited the North Shore of Oahu for the first time in 1979, and steadily built a reputation as a cool hand in larger surf. In 1989 he won the XCEL Pro and placed third in the World Cup, both held at Sunset Beach; he placed third in the 1990 Quiksilver in Memory of Eddie Aikau contest at Waimea Bay, and a

photo of Schmidt racing down a 25-foot gray-blue Waimea wall during the Quiksilver finals was published on the cover of *Surfer* magazine. The following year, he was one of the first Santa Cruz surfers to ride Maverick's, the terrifying big-wave break located between Santa Cruz and San Francisco; Schmidt was 38 when he finished runner-up to Santa Cruz surfer Darryl "Flea" Virostko in the inaugural Quiksilver Maverick's Men Who Ride Mountains contest. Virostko and fellow Santa Cruz big-wave ace Peter Mel have both cited Schmidt as a primary influence.

While working as a Santa Cruz Parks and Recreation lifeguard In 1983, Schmidt began giving individual and group surfing lessons at Cowells Beach, near the Santa Cruz pier, and in 1990 he began running weeklong summer surf camps. In 1998, he incorporated as the Richard Schmidt Surf School. *Learn to Surf and Ocean Safety with Richard Schmidt,* a one-hour instructional video, was released in 1997, and updated in 2002. Schmidt himself has appeared in more than two dozen surf movies and videos, including *Amazing Surf Stories* (1986), *Gone Surfin'* (1987), *Mental Surfing* (1993), and *Twenty Feet Under* (1998). Schmidt is married and has two children. *See also* big-wave surfing, Santa Cruz, surf schools.

Schroff, Peter   Wry surf artist, board-builder, and surfwear manufacturer from Venice Beach, California. Schroff was born (1954) and raised in Newport Beach, began surfing at age 12, and shaping boards at 18. From 1981 to 1986 he made surfboards under the Peter Schroff Designs label; from 1983 to 1987 he produced the edgy and fleetingly popular Schroff Clothing, which he called an "anti-surf" line of surfwear, in sartorial opposition to what he called "the brown corduroy walk shorts/flowered print T-shirt syndrome." Schroff's best-known art pieces are highly stylized surfboards—some devious, others seductive, most of them humorous—including *Pink Whale* (1988), a lustrous, pastel-colored, 15-foot-long "artboard" that includes a '50s-era clock, radio, and television, a pair of lamps, a Schlitz beer tap, and chrome exhaust pipes. *Pink Whale* was shown at *Surf Trip,* a well-reviewed 2000 surf art exhibit at San Francisco's Yerba Buena Center for the Arts. *See also* surf art.

Schumacher, Cori   Bright-smiling regularfooter from San Diego, California; winner of the Women's Longboard World Championships in 2000 and 2001. Schumacher was born (1977) in Huntington Beach, learned to surf in San Diego, and was a top amateur shortboarder in the mid-'90s. She won her first world longboard title at age 23 (after finishing runner-up the year before) just one week after triple-rolling her car on the freeway near her home. She competed with a mild concussion and stitches in both legs. "I couldn't see straight," Schumacher later recalled, describing her first heat. "I was seeing stars and getting light-headed, and when I got to the shore I almost passed out." The following day she revived, and won the final going away. Two months earlier she'd been voted the most popular woman longboarder in *Longboard* magazine's first annual readers poll. Schumacher successfully defended her title in 2001. She has appeared in a small number of surf videos, including *Costa Rica: Land of Waves* (2001) and *The Road* (2001). *See also* Women's World Longboard Championships.

Schwarzstein, Alisa   Well-ordered surfer and surf contest organizer from Laguna Beach, California; women's division winner in the 1980 World Amateur Surfing Championships. Schwarzstein was born (1964) in Tarrytown, New York, moved with her family to Laguna at age nine, and began surfing two years later. At 15 she placed runner-up in the girls' division of the United States Surfing Championships, and a few weeks later, in Biarritz, France, she won the 1980 world amateur title. Schwarzstein also placed third in the 1982 world titles. Later that year she became a part-time competitor on the pro tour, while attending college at UCLA, where she would receive a B.A. in sociology. In 1984 Schwarzstein was named the world tour's rookie of the year, and in 1985 she was world-ranked #4. Schwarzstein began working as a Professional Surfing Association of America tour judge in 1991; she went on to judge events for the Association of Surfing Professionals tour and the Professional Surfing Tour of America, and also worked as an administrator and events manager for U.S. Surfing. In 1996, Schwarzstein married 1976 world tour runner-up Ian Cairns of Australia.

Scotland   Scotland's rugged and wind-lashed coastline can be divided into four surfing regions: 1) The western isles, primarily the Inner and Outer Hebrides, contain dozens of forlorn rocky points and untouched beaches, with chilly Atlantic waves rolling in from the north, west, or south. Many breaks here are not yet fully charted. 2) The mountainous north shore area features huge slabs of flat

Scotland; California's Joe Curren rides the Bowl, just west of Thurso

gray stone jutting into the ocean to form granite-bottom reefbreaks, some producing beautifully shaped waves. The inshore waters are criss crossed by huge seals and occasionally killer whales. Castle Reef, a hollow, right-breaking wave near the north shore town of Thurso, is Scotland's best-known wave. 3) The east coast, facing into the North Sea, is lined with a variety of beach-, reef-, and pointbreaks, all of which are best during winter. 4) The cliff-lined Orkney Islands, to the north, contain additional tracts of remote high-quality surf breaks, while the Shetlands—a cluster of about 100 mostly uninhabited islands located between Scotland and Norway—stand as one of Europe's final surfing frontiers. Water temperatures in Scotland range from the low 40s to the mid-50s; coastal air temperatures range from 10 to 80; wind, fog, rain, and drizzle are common. In spring, melting ice blocks will sometimes float downriver and drift into the surf zone. Summer surf is generally three foot or below; four- to six-foot waves are common from fall to spring, and winter can bring surf up to 12 foot or bigger. Around the summer solstice, north shore surfers can hit the water at twilight after the pubs close at 11 P.M.

Aberdeen teenager Andy Bennetts became Scotland's first surfer in 1968, after he returned from Newquay, England, with a surfboard, and began riding it with some friends on the beaches near his home. The Scottish Surfing Federation, located in Aberdeen, was formed in 1973; the 1988 British Surfing Championships were held in Thurso. By 2003, Scotland was home to about 900 surfers and nearly a dozen surf shops, most located on the east coast. The Scottish surf is detailed in *The Stormrider Guide Europe*

(1998) and *Surf UK* (2000), and is featured in the surf video *Made in Britain* (2001).

Scott-Rogers, Brenda   Rugged surfer and gender-breaking surf executive from Santa Cruz, California; winner of the 1978 Hang Ten World Cup, and co-founder of Hotline USA Wetsuits. Scott was born (1957) in Lausanne, Switzerland, raised in Gilroy, California, began surfing at age eight, and moved with her family to Santa Cruz at 12. An Amateur Athletic Union short-distance swimming champion from age eight to 14, Scott also swam in the 1972 Olympic Trials, and was an All-American backstroker in 1977. Her victory in the 1978 World Cup, held in testing conditions at Hawaii's Sunset Beach, was worth $3,000—a record for women's surfing at the time. Scott was ranked fifth in the 1978 pro standings, and was named the world tour's rookie of the year; in 1981, the year she married Santa Cruz surfer Craig Rogers, she finished the season ranked #3. From 1977 to 1985, she ran the Brenda Scott Surf School in Santa Cruz, and in 1979 she and Japanese exporter Hiro Iida formed the Santa Cruz–based Hotline wetsuit company; Scott-Rogers was for years the surf industry's only woman CEO.

Scott-Rogers's father is Dr. Robert Scott, president of the Western Surfing Association in the late '60s and early '70s, and inventor of Doc's Pro Plugs, used to prevent surfer's ear. Craig Rogers made news in 1987 after surviving a white shark attack while surfing just north of Santa Cruz.

screwfoot   *See* goofyfoot.

sea urchin   Spiny round-bodied marine animal, found on intertidal rocks and reefs worldwide; generally dark purple or black in color, but also brown, green, red, or white. Urchins are harmful to surfers, as the spines can break off and lodge into the skin. The common nonpoisonous purple urchins in California have small, blunt, solid spines. The spines on many tropical urchins, however, are longer—up to 12 inches—hollow, brittle, and filled with a venom that can produce swelling and severe pain, and sometimes temporary paralysis. The old salt's method for on-site urchin wound treatment is perverse but effective: remove the spines as best as possible and urinate on the affected area. Urchin punctures are most common on the feet and hands. *See also* injuries and surfing.

seaweed   *See* kelp.

Sebastian Inlet   Wedging sand-bottom jetty break adjacent to the north side of Sebastian Inlet State Park, 15 miles south of Melbourne Beach, Florida; one of the surf world's high-performance hot spots, and home to at least three generations of world-class surfers, including Mike Tabeling, Kelly Slater, and Lisa Andersen. "Part talent show," Swell.com said of the notoriously crowded Sebastian Inlet scene in 2000, "part photo studio, part boxing ring." Sebastian is a man-made wave, created in 1969 with the completion of a south-angling rubble jetty extension; the wave's wedging effect is the result of a rebound swell bouncing off the jetty and running across the following wave, which in turn creates a another rebound swell, and so on. First Peak, Sebastian's premier spot, is a frequently hollow right-breaking wave that forms just a few yards north of the jetty. Three more spots—Second Peak, Third Peak, and OK Signs—follow just to the north, and are usually less defined and shapely than First Peak, but also less crowded. Monster Hole, the outside break located beyond the south jetty, is occasionally ridden on bigger swells. The Sebastian surf is generally best in late summer and early fall; low tides are preferred, and west winds are straight offshore. Sebastian is one of the Florida coast's most consistent breaks, and can hold form even on the rare six- to eight-foot days. The flat-topped Sebastian jetty, usually lined with fishermen casting perilously close to the surfing lineup, makes an ideal vantage point for spectators and surf photographers, which in turn drives the surfers to fever pitch.

Sebastian Inlet; Florida's Lewis Graves at First Peak

Rides here are generally fast and short, with waves often spilling into an oncoming section; Sebastian has been called the birthplace of aerial surfing.

Sebastian Inlet came to the attention of the surfing world in 1969, when locals Mike Tabeling, Kiwi White, and Gary Hook were arrested and fined for illegally surfing within 200 feet of the jetty. Resident board-maker Dick Catri then led a successful crusade to have Sebastian opened to surfers. The first Eastern Surfing Association Championships were held at Sebastian Inlet in 1970 (although the contest was aborted at the halfway mark); Sebastian also hosted the Waverider Magazine Florida Pro, mainland America's only world pro tour event in 1976 and 1977; the 1981 Stubbies Pro East; the United States Surfing Championships (in 1986, 1990, and 1994); and the annual Quiksilver King of the Peak contest, founded in 1995. Florida's best surfers have always been drawn to Sebastian, beginning with Tabeling, Greg Loehr, and Jeff Crawford, moving on to Matt Kechele, Jeff Klugel, and Charlie Kuhn, followed in turn by Kelly Slater, Lisa Andersen, CJ and Damien Hobgood, Shea and Cory Lopez, David Speir, Bill Hartley, and Phillip Watters.

Surfing magazine named Sebastian in 2002 as one of "15 Waves that Fuel Surfing's Future." The break has been featured in more than a dozen surf movies and videos, including Wet Lips (1983), *Kelly Slater in Black and White* (1991), *Flail* (1996), and *The Times* (2002). A part-time treasure hunter, diving in eight feet of water about 100 yards out from First Peak in 1994, found $1 million worth of jewels and gold coins from a Spanish galleon that sank there more than 250 years earlier. *See also* Cocoa Beach.

secret spot   A surf break known by a few, but undiscovered by the surfing masses. Until the early 1960s, newfound breaks were regularly presented in the surf press, sometimes even with location maps. In a 1964 issue of *Surfing World,* however, editors reported that a New Zealand correspondent had just found a great new spot, but the discovery was "so secret that he didn't even tell us where it is." While hundreds of new breaks would be charted and revealed in the decades to come, a corresponding number—obviously an unknown quantity—were kept hidden. Secret spots have always had currency, as all surfers long not only for uncrowded waves, but for in-the-know cachet. *Surfer* magazine played on this idea in 1973 with a smugly titled article, "Ten Spots You'll Probably Never Surf." Secret spots can be ephemeral (a temporary sandbar), hidden in plain sight (Maverick's, the long-secret northern California big-wave break, is easily seen from the hilly roads above Half Moon Bay), or virtually unreachable (Parsons Point, on the southernmost tip of the Indian Ocean's Great Nicobar Island, is off-limits to visitors). Secret spots are often given aliases or protected by territorial locals. More often they're just quietly and deeply cherished. "To be completely honest," surf journalist Nick Carroll wrote in 1998, "I'd have to say that nothing, not my family, bank account, country, or even my species, brings out quite the same combination of feelings—a weird mix of selfishness, dedication and worship—as my secret spot."

section   A portion of a breaking wave that drops ahead of the primary curl line; common to all surf breaks, including the best-formed waves in the world. A section can produce a number of results, good and bad. If the section is hollow—forming a tube section—the surfer can angle through for a tuberide. If the section is crumbly, the surfer can rebound off the fringing crest, skim laterally across the top of the section in a floater, or launch off the section into an aerial. The surfer can also drop low on the wave and bottom turn around a section. Often a section is too long to be surfed around by any method, and the rider has to exit over the top of the wave, jump off his board, or angle toward shore. A wave that "sections off" is generally defined as being unmakable. "Sectiony" surf means the sections are plentiful, and almost all the rides will be short.

Sekino, Satoshi   Flashy small-wave specialist from Shonan, Japan; the 1991 Japan Professional Surfing Association ratings champion. Sekino was born (1964) in Yokohama, raised in Shonan, near Tokyo, and began surfing at 13. He won the 1981 All-Japan Junior Championships; two years later he moved to Australia for a year to train for a career on the world pro tour, and further develop his tight-cornering, low-to-the-water style. Sekino finished the 1985 world tour season ranked #45, his highest year-end finish; in 1991 he placed 13th in the Pipeline Masters event in Hawaii. Sekino appeared in a small number of surf movies and videos, including *Modern Legends in Hawaiian Surf* (1995).

semi-gun   *See* gun.

Semmens, Nigel   Lanky regularfoot surfer from Newquay, in Cornwall, England; Britain's dominant surfer in the early late '70s and early '80s. Semmens was born (1957) and raised in Newquay, the hub of English surfing, and began riding waves at age 12. He won four consecutive English national titles from 1977 to 1980, was the European amateur champion in 1981, and placed seventh in the 1980 World Surfing Championships. Semmens then became one of the first European pro surfers, competing briefly on the world tour in 1982 and 1983. He began shaping surfboards in 1975, and has been shaping for Ocean Magic Surfboards since 1977.

Senegal   Small and dry west African nation located just below the Sahara, facing the North Atlantic Ocean. Senegal was brought to the attention of the surf world in 1964, when California filmmaker Bruce Brown toured an early version of his soon-to-be-classic travelogue *The Endless Summer*; the first surf break encountered by Mike Hynson and Robert August, the film's two stars, was N'gor Rights, a reef near the end of the Almadies Peninsula, Africa's westernmost point and home to most of Senegal's best waves. At least five distinct reef- and beachbreaks are located on the Almadies's northwest side, with another six on the southwest; most are within walking distance of each other. Onshore winds on one side mean offshores on the other. North of the peninsula lies 100-

Senegal; reef waves at Oaukam, near Dakar

plus miles of mostly undistinguished beach break; the entire Senegalese coastline is just 310 miles long. A limited number of breaks, all requiring heavy swell, are found south of Almadies. The Senegal surf rarely gets over 10 foot, but the best breaks are fast, tubing, and powerful; Oaukam, not far from the capital city of Dakar, is a world-class peak, with long, tubing rights. November to May is the best time for waves in Senegal, as Atlantic storms generate swells from the north and northwest; August to October sees the arrival of south swells from hurricanes located off the African west coast. Average daytime air temperatures in coastal Senegal range from the low 70s in winter to the mid-80s in summer; water temperatures range from the low 60s to the low 80s; the cold and dry harmattan wind, blowing down from the northeast during winter, often deposits great dusty clouds onto Senegal's coastline. Dense fields of sea urchins are the only real surfing hazard, making booties or reefwalkers a necessity. In 2003, there were about 250 Senegalese wave-riders, mostly bodyboarders. Tribal Surf Shop, located just east of N'gor, is the country's only surf shop; a small surf camp opened at N'gor in 2002, and is used primarily by French surfers.

Servais, Tom   Finicky surf photographer from Dana Point, California; longtime senior staff photographer for *Surfer* magazine; best known for his work in the South Pacific, including five *Surfer* magazine cover shots from Fiji's Tavarua Island in the 1990s. Servais was born (1953) in Miami, Florida, began surfing at 13, and started taking surf photos in 1977, four years after moving to San Clemente, California. Aside from enrolling in junior college photography classes, Servais is primarily self-taught. In 1979, two years after being hired at *Surfer* as a darkroom assistant, he was given a masthead position, and while he didn't became a marquee name like Art Brewer, Jeff Divine, Aaron Chang, or Jeff Hornbaker, he steadily worked his way to the top rank, and by the mid-'90s was among the sport's busiest, best-traveled, and most-published photographers. Servais's versatile work has appeared in *Outside, Men's Journal*, and *Sports Illustrated*; his best-known shot, of Florida surfer Cory Lopez in the tube at Tahiti's Teahupoo, was used on the cover of *The Perfect Day: 40 Years of Surfer Magazine*, published in 2001. He has also contributed to a number of other illustrated surfing books, including *The History of Surfing* (1983), *Surfing: The Ultimate*

Pleasure (1984), *SurfRiders* (1997), *Girl in the Curl* (2000), and *The Perfect Day* (2001).

set   A group of larger-than-average waves, usually numbering between two to five, but sometimes up to 10 or 15. While set frequency from day to day varies—from one set every five minutes to one per hour—over a short period of time it is generally consistent. Surfers checking the waves on big days will often time the interval between sets, to get a rough idea of what to expect once they're in the water. Sets are formed as individual open-ocean waves cluster together and essentially take turns "drafting" off a lead wave to conserve energy; similar to a group of cyclists drafting off a lead rider. A "swing set" is a set of waves that breaks adjacent to the usual takeoff area. The disappointing "one-wave set" is self-explanatory. *See also* clean-up set.

Severn Bore   British surf created by an incoming tidal surge running up the lengthy (220 miles) and picturesque River Severn, about 100 miles west of London. The bore rolls upriver one hour before high tide, twice a day, approximately 130 days a year, with the biggest and best waves—usually waist-high, but sometimes up to six feet—arriving just after the full and new moons around the spring equinox. Wave height is determined primarily by the tide differential, which goes as high as 40 feet (the greater the differential, the bigger the wave), and to a much lesser degree by local winds and the level of freshwater runoff. The best part of the wave is along the river banks, as opposed to midstream. Switchbacks near Gloucester, particularly the bend at Stonebench, create the hottest Severn surfing waves. Two-mile rides are fairly common, and 40-minute rides have been recorded; on big bore days, hazards include uprooted trees and dead sheep. British surfer Rodney Sumpter described the experience of riding the Severn Bore in a 1968 *Surfer* magazine article, and in 1994 it was the cover story for the April issue of the *Surf Report* newsletter. "Bear in mind," the article noted, "that if you lose the wave you can always jump in your car and catch up to it." The Severn Bore has been featured in a small number of surf movies and videos, including *Playgrounds in Paradise* (1976). *See also* Pororoca, tidal bore waves.

Severson, John   Seminal surf world writer, editor, publisher, photographer, filmmaker, and artist from

John Severson

San Clemente, California; best known as the founder in 1960 of *Surfer* magazine. "Before John Severson," surf journalist Sam George wrote in 1999, "there was no 'surf media,' no 'surf industry' and no 'surf culture'—at least not in the way we understand it today." Severson was born (1933) in Los Angeles, raised in North Fair Oaks and Pasadena, and began surfing at age 13, after his family moved to the Orange County beach town of San Clemente. He received a B.A. in art education from Chico State College in 1955 and an M.A. in art education from Long Beach State College in 1956; Severson's paintings and sketches from this time have been called the original surf art. After being drafted by the army in 1956, he was stationed in Honolulu and assigned to the army surfing team. *Surf,* Severson's debut film, was released in 1958, while he was still in the military. *Surf Safari* followed in 1959, after he returned to California; *Surf Fever* came out in 1960. Severson was among the first group of surf moviemakers, along with Bruce Brown, Greg Noll, and genre originator Bud Browne; with the exception of *Surf,* Severson barnstormed his films up and down the coast from Santa Cruz to San Diego. His movies were similar to the others—plot-free, colorful, filled with lots of wave-riding action and a few short comedy routines—but his pen-and-ink handbills and posters were eye-catching and unique.

In the summer of 1960, as a promotional piece for *Surf Fever,* Severson put together a 36-page horizontally formatted magazine, consisting of black-and-white photographs, pen-and-ink sketches, a short fiction article, a map of Southern California surf breaks, and a how-to article for beginning surfers. He called it *The Surfer,* and the debut issue sold 5,000 copies. In 1961 he published four editions of what he now called the *Surfer Quarterly,* and the magazine grew steadily from issue to issue. It was at first a one-man production, with Severson doing all the editing and much of the writing, photography, and design work; he later hired a number of people who went on to become the surf media's icons, including cartoonist Rick Griffin; photographers Ron Stoner, Jeff Divine, and Art Brewer; writer/editors Drew Kampion and Steve Pezman; and graphic designers John Van Hamersveld and Mike Salisbury. Severson continued to produce surf movies, including *Big Wednesday* (1961), *Going My Wave* (1962), *Angry Sea* (1963), and *Surf Classics* (1964). He also competed in surf contests (in 1961 he placed fifth in the West Coast Surfing Championships and won the Peru International), and became a surfing spokesman to the general-interest media (as the subject or author of feature articles in the *Saturday Evening Post, Life, Sports Illustrated,* and *Paris Match*). Doubleday publishers in New York during this time produced two Severson books: *Modern Surfing Around the World* (1964) and *Great Surfing* (1967). Severson guided *Surfer* through the social and economic whirlpools of the late '60s, and produced one final surf movie, 1970's beautiful but overly serious *Pacific Vibrations.* He sold *Surfer* in 1971 and moved with his wife and two daughters to Maui, and for the most part returned to painting, sketching, and surfing.

Severson was inducted into the International Surfing Hall of Fame in 1991 and to the Huntington Beach Surfing Walk of Fame in 1995. In 1997 he was given the Waterman Achievement Award by the Surf Industry Manufacturers Association, and was profiled in *50 Years of Surfing on Film,* an Outdoor Life Network documentary series. He was ranked sixth in *Surfer* magazine's 1999 list of the "25 Most Influential Surfers of the Century"; the following year the *Surfer's Journal* published "John Severson Presents," an exhaustive profile; *Surf Fever,* a 240-page hardcover retrospective of Severson's early work, was published in 2003. Various Severson art pieces have been used on the cover of *Surfer* magazine (in 1963, 1969, and 1979), the *Surfer's Journal* (1993), and *Longboard* (2000 and 2001). *See also* surf art, surf magazines, surf movies, Surfer magazine.

sex and surfing The undercurrent of sex and sexuality that runs through surfing has at times overshadowed the act of wave-riding itself. Prior to the early

1800s, men and women surfers in Hawaii often used the wave zone as a venue for flirting and display, and a shared wave often amounted to a hands-off type of foreplay. Westerners got their first look at surfing through sketches of nude Polynesian women riding gracefully for shore; crusading American missionaries in the middle and late decades of the 19th century railed against the "evil pleasures" associated with surfing.

Surfing was only a few degrees less sexualized during its resurrection in the early 20th century. The Waikiki beachboys, a raffish, semiorganized band of surf instructors and entertainers (described by one writer as the "tumescent playboys of the Pacific"), were known to be great seducers of visiting mainland women, and "surf lessons" sometimes included a half-submerged coupling out past the lineup while using a surfboard as a flotation device. Meanwhile, Hawaiian gold medal swimmer and surfing proponent Duke Kahanamoku—broad-shouldered, perfectly muscled, often photographed stripped to the waist and gleaming wet—might be regarded as the first beefcake pinup: in an advertisement for the 1914 Mid-Pacific Carnival, a smiling Kahanamoku is shown riding for shore atop his redwood surfboard with hips tilted forward and arms, legs, and chest flexed. Sex has always been an integral part of surf-related marketing, from the surfboard-holding bathing beauty used on the sheet-music cover of "My Waikiki Mermaid" in 1903, to the poster for 1964's *Muscle Beach Party* ("When 10,000 biceps go around 5,000 bikinis, you *know* what's gonna happen!"), to the early '90s-launched Reef Brazil sandal ads featuring young thong-bottomed models.

Surfers in the '50s and early '60s, like rock and rollers or bikers, were often portrayed as sexual deviants; "peroxide boys and girls," as *Time* magazine wrote in 1963, with "outlandish hairdos; throbbing to guitars at midnight twist parties, [and] fond of nudity." The 15-year-old female narrator of *Gidget,* a 1957 best-seller, is surprised by the raunchy *après* surf conversation on the beach. "I pretended not to listen," Gidget confesses, "but lapped up every word of that sexy talk, every last single syllable of it." Mid- and late-'60s pulp books like *Surf Broad* (described as "A Searing Story of the Free Love, Free Sex, Surfing Generation!") further added to the surfer's reputation as a sexual provocateur, as did a mid-'70s mini-explosion of nude pictorials featuring well-known surfers, with California's Mike Purpus and Angie Reno posing in separate issues of *Playgirl* and Hawaii's Laura Blears appearing in *Playboy*. (Whether or not surfers were having more sex, or better sex, than nonsurfers is debatable, although Purpus later boasted that he "had to put a drive-through door in my bedroom" to handle the increased flow after his *Playgirl* spread.) The surfing/sex nexus reached a media peak of sorts in 1998—10 years after a *Wall Street Journal* article described surfing as "the sexiest sport in America"—when six-time world champion Kelly Slater and voluptuous girlfriend Pamela Anderson were featured in a mildly erotic *Interview* magazine photo spread.

While today's surfers continue to have a permissive and easygoing attitude toward sex, there are limitations; homosexuality, for example, is either ignored or vilified. A small number of lesbian surfers have come out (including former world champion Lynne Boyer), but the sport as a whole has stayed resolutely homophobic, and when a 1988 surf magazine article intimated that former world title contender Cheyne Horan was gay, he lost sponsors and friends. Filling out a *Surfer* magazine questionnaire in 1996, teenage surfer Shane Dorian of Hawaii listed "dykes and fags," along with "diseases, food poisoning, the Devil, and flat spells," as things he'd banish if possible. "The big question is," an anonymously written *Surf News* magazine article asked in 1999, "where are all the gay surfers? And the obvious answer: sitting right next to you in the lineup, hoping nobody will ask so they won't have to tell." *See also* nudity and surfing.

Sex Wax "Mr. Zog's Sex Wax" is the full name of Frederick Herzog's 1972-founded surfboard wax company, based in Carpinteria, near Santa Barbara. Herzog, better known as Zog, later said he chose the mildly racy company name because it both mocked and utilized the "sex sells" axiom. In a 1974 surf magazine ad, beneath the slogan "Expose Yourself to Sex Wax," a grinning Herzog looks over his shoulder while he opens his trenchcoat to a pair of wide-eyed preadolescent girls. For the early batches of sex wax, ingredients were heated in a 50-gallon drum, mixed with a boat propeller, then poured into empty tuna-fish and soup cans to cool. Aside from Sex Wax's name, its round container set it apart from its square-molded competitors. The product caught on immediately, as did the Sex Wax logo T-shirts, which sold by the tens of thousands in the '70s and early '80s, and were banned from some school districts. A related trend developed in the early '80s, as teens and pre-

teens began chewing Sex Wax—composed, like all surf wax, primarily of nontoxic food-grade paraffin wax, but also containing a host of chemical-additive scents and softeners—leading to a DO NOT EAT OR CHEW label disclaimer. Sex Wax today is sold worldwide and comes in four scents (strawberry, pineapple, grape, and coconut) and three basic formulas for surfboards (Original, Quick Humps, and Really Tacky), with four subformulas for different water temperatures. Just over two million bars of Sex Wax were produced in 2002. Other Sex Wax products include wax remover, wax containers, wax combs, logo towels, rash guards, hats, and the still-popular T-shirts. *See also* surf wax, traction pad.

sexism and surfing *See* women and surfing.

Seychelles Tiny, densely foliated African island nation, located 1,000 miles east of Tanzania, consisting of about 90 islands scattered across a 400,000-square-mile area of the Indian Ocean. Mahé, the Seychelles' main island, was revealed to the surfing public in a 1967 *Surfer* magazine article and described "as a goofyfooter's paradise." True, if the goofyfooter likes small, safe, easy-riding waves. The Seychelles Banks, a wide apron of reef extending out from Mahé, filters out much of the size and power from incoming swells, and generally keeps the surf below five foot. From late April through October, however, monsoon storms will push warm and well-groomed left-breaking waves into Mahé's exquisitely tropical bays. The outer Seychelles islands have larger surf, and are full of uncharted or unpublicized breaks. Crowds are never a problem. The Seychelles' tourist economy has flourished for years, but international traveling surfers for the most part have gone exploring elsewhere, and locals so far have shown little inclination to pick up the sport.

Seymour, Allan Avuncular surf historian and entrepreneur from Capistrano Beach, California; founder of the Pacific Coast Surf Auction for buyers and sellers of vintage surfboards and memorabilia. Seymour was born (1943) in Santa Monica, California, and began surfing at age 12. He was a lifeguard in Southern California beach cities from 1959 to 1969, then worked as a publicist, salesman, and cameraman. From 1978 to 1981, the witty and big-voiced Seymour was given the World's Worst Surfer Award at the annual *Surfer* Magazine Readers Poll Awards. In

December 1986, he organized the first one-day surfing swap meet, held in Costa Mesa, California. Allen Seymour Productions was formed in 1990 to produce special events for sports and recreation trade shows. In 1997, responding to the growing market for surf memorabilia, Seymour created the Pacific Coast Vintage Surf Auction, an annual event held at the Long Beach Convention Center, in conjunction with the Action Sports Retail trade show. Aside from surfboards, the Surf Auction also sells surf magazines, posters, books, aloha shirts, and other surfing collectibles. Seymour serves as host and auctioneer. *See also* surf auctions, surf collectors.

shaping machine   Expensive and at one point mildly controversial computer-programmed machines designed to shape a polyurethane foam blank into something very close to a ready-to-fiberglass surfboard. The shaping machine does in a few minutes what the planer-wielding shaper does in about an hour. The prototype noncomputerized shaping machine—an elliptical wooden jig used to guide an electric planer—was being used by a few Southern California board-makers as far back as the mid-1950s, but the device didn't come to the attention of the surf world at large until early 1968, when Dewey Weber Surfboards began advertising their "precision quality" machine that allowed them to "guarantee the dimensions on all of our shapes to $1/32$ of an inch." But shapers by that time were already giving up on the jigs, as the wild design fluctuations of the just-started shortboard revolution were better met by traditional hand-shaping.

French board-maker and engineer Michel Barland developed the first computerized shaping machine in 1979. Barland's fully mechanized invention allowed the shaper to preprogram virtually every board measurement, and could rough-shape a board in 15 minutes. By the mid-'90s, top surfboard-makers including Al Merrick and Donald Takayama, while still fine-shaping their boards, were using machines to increase their production rate. Fundamentalists argued that the new computer-shaped boards lacked "soul." But as Merrick told the *Los Angeles Times* in 1996, "There's no soul in foam. The soul of surfing is to get out into the waves and have a good time." Machine-aided, Merrick was able to produce 150 boards a week.

By the early '00s, there were two primary methods of computerized shaping: computer-aided manufacturing (CAM), which replicates existing boards, and computer-aided drafting (CAD), developed in large part by Brazilian shaper Luciano Leao, which allows the shaper to design a board from scratch entirely on a computer. Once a board is machine-shaped, with dimensions exact to $1/100$th of a millimeter, a small amount of fine-sanding by hand is still required before the board can be fiberglassed. By 2003, an estimated 85 percent of major board-makers (those producing more than 2,000 boards a year) were using computerized shaping machines. A top-of-the-line shaping machine costs roughly $500,000. *See also* Michel Barland, surfboard construction, surfboard shaping.

shaping, shaper   *See* surfboard shaping.

sharks and surfing   There were 441 recorded shark attacks on surfers between 1900 and 1999, about two dozen of which were fatal. Despite these relatively small numbers, sharks have always cruised freely and often luridly through the surfing world's collective imagination. "No matter how gruff and grim," San Francisco writer Daniel Duane noted in his 1996 surfing memoir *Caught Inside,* nearly every surfer "is scared witless at the thought of being torn apart while conscious, of watching a spreading slick of one's own blood." A holdover from the predinosaur Paleozoic era, sharks first appeared 400 million years ago (395 million years before man), and have evolved into roughly 370 species, ranging in size from six inches to 40 feet. Some eat plankton or other plant life, but most are predatory; all have cartilage-formed skeletal systems, with skin made up of a thin crosshatched layer of teethlike denticles. A nose-to-tail system of

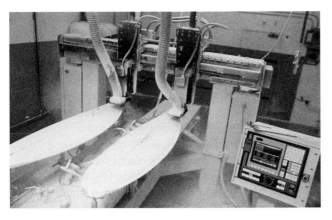

Shaping machine

electric-current-measuring sensors gives sharks what amounts to a panoramic view of their immediate surroundings, and allows them to navigate by the earth's magnetic fields. The shark's triangular teeth are serrated along the edges, and line both the upper and lower jaws in multiple rows; the jaws of a great white can exert up to 2,000 pounds of pressure per square inch. Sharks are thought to be the world's only pre-birth predators; shark eggs hatch in utero, with off-spring attacking and eating each other until just one is left. The average life span of a white shark remains a mystery; estimates range from 25 to 100 years.

A Surfrider Foundation report in 2000 stated that one shark attack can be expected for every one million individual surfing days. Attacks are rare enough that scientists believe they occur only when the shark mistakes a human for its normal prey (seals, sea lions, sea turtles, or fish) or when it feels territorially threatened. Nonetheless, attacks on humans are rising, from 180 worldwide in the '70s to 280 in the '80s to 520 in the '90s. The increase is generally attributed to a rise in the number of surfers, bodyboarders, divers, and ocean swimmers rather than an increase in the number of sharks; roughly 10 percent of attacks in the '90s were fatal. The surfer may be more vulnerable than anyone else in the water, as his below-surface silhouette, while sitting on his board, resembles that of an idling seal.

Glorified and demonized in the 1975 movie *Jaws,* the great white has since been regarded by surfers and nonsurfers alike as the overlord of the shark world. Great whites can exceed 20 feet in length and weigh more than 4,000 pounds. They prefer cooler water, account for more than half of all confirmed attacks on humans, and are the most lethal of the species. Great whites are concentrated in what is called the Red Triangle, a heavily surfed 150-mile-long region in central California that includes the beginning of Monterey Bay, Santa Cruz, and San Francisco. In 1981, Monterey kneeboarder Lew Boren was killed by a 20-foot great white; documentary filmmaker Peck Euwer in 2001 was thrown from his board by a 13-footer while sitting in the deep-water channel adjacent to Maverick's, the big-wave break in Half Moon Bay. (Boren remains the only surfer killed by a shark in California waters.) Nearly all great white attacks on humans follow the same pattern: an initial lunging strike from below, then a quick retreat as the shark realizes the targeted animal isn't in fact a blubber-rich sea mammal. The shark is particularly likely to vanish if it gets a taste of surfboard. In most great white–caused fatalities, the victim isn't devoured, but instead bleeds to death from the first hit.

Tiger sharks (usually 10 to 15 feet long) and bull sharks (around 10 feet) can also be deadly. Both prefer warm water. Tiger sharks generally hunt at night, live in tropical climates, and are responsible for virtually all attacks on surfers in Hawaii, including the 1992 death of a bodyboarder on the North Shore of Oahu. Unlike great whites, the tiger shark will bite and return, and is an indiscriminate eater; tiger shark stomach contents have included driftwood, coiled wire, coal, boat cushions, beer bottles, unopened cans, birds, dogs, smaller sharks, and dolphins. The bull shark has the highest testosterone of any animal, will attack prey as large as itself, and can live in salt- and freshwater. Bull sharks born in the Mississippi delta eventually migrate to the Gulf of Mexico, then the Florida Keys, and are responsible for many of the surfer-related attacks in Florida. An eight-foot bull is thought to have been responsible for killing a 10-year-old surfer at Virginia Beach, Virginia, in September 2001.

Surfers and nonsurfers have for decades tried to guard against shark attacks. Popular swimming and surfing beaches in Australia have been lined with mesh nets as a deterrent since the early '30s; in South Africa, researchers developed an electric barrier designed to keep sharks outside the surf zone without killing marine life the way nets do. The surf press suggested in 1982 that an antishark wetsuit made of Kevlar might be a possibility, but the idea was never pursued. In 1993, two South African scientists developed a one-pound electromagnetic pulsing device that, in tests, caused sharks to veer away; two years later the $300 plastic-encased, battery-powered POD (Protective Ocean Device) was marketed—but to divers, not surfers. (A two-pound, ankle-strapped, Australian-made electromagnetic Shark Shield was marketed to surfers in early 2002, but a diver was killed in South Australia a few months later while wearing a similar device.) Surfers were left with few options to reduce the chances of attack, beyond the normal set of recommendations: stay away from rivermouths and muddy water, don't surf at dawn or dusk, don't surf at breaks near seal colonies, don't surf alone. More than 100 million sharks are killed each year, primarily by fishing nets, and great whites have been protected by federal laws in America and Australia since 1997. A *Time* magazine article in 2002 noted that from 1986 to 2000 the white shark population may have been reduced by more than 75 percent.

The surf world has responded to sharks in almost every conceivable way, including brute conquest (a shark is speargunned in the head and left to flop to its death in the 1967 surf movie *The Hot Generation*), humor (the satirical 1982-released "Shark Attack" single by the Surf Punks), gore fetishism (surf magazines regularly publish photos of surfers' open or just-sutured shark wounds), and solid reportage (with "Sharks: Myth or Menace," "Sharks: Why Not to Worry," and other well-researched surf press articles). *Surfer* magazine published more than 75 features, columns and short items on sharks from 1960 to 2001, compared to just 27 pieces on wetsuits and fewer than 50 on Malibu. *See also* death and surfing, injuries and surfing, Red Triangle.

Sharp, Bill   Tireless bottle-blond writer/publisher/executive/promo man from Newport Beach, California; *Surfing* magazine editor in 1989 and 1990; co-owner of Kanvas by Katin beachwear from 1991 to 1997; founder of *Surf News* magazine, and creator of the K2 Big-Wave Challenge and the Billabong Odyssey. Sharp was born (1961) in Novato, California, the son of a fighter pilot, raised in Newport, and began surfing in 1974. As National Scholastic Surfing Association's top-rated kneeboarder in 1982, he was invited to that year's World Amateur Championships, where he placed fourth. He began an internship at *Surfing* magazine in 1983, just after earning a B.A. in business administration from San Diego State University; in 1987 he became managing editor, and two years later was promoted to editor. *Surfing* magazine, which grew to produce 200-plus-page issues during the late '80s, was animated and flashy under Sharp's watch, full of exclamation points, bikini-clad girls, and neon boldface cover blurbs. Sharp himself provided some of the magazine's most incisive and well-crafted articles.

After leaving *Surfing* in early 1991, Sharp became co-owner of Kanvas by Katin, a popular surf trunk line in the '60s that had lay moribund since the early '80s; in 1997 the company did $4 million in wholesale business. That same year, Sharp began working for ski equipment giant K2, for which he developed the K2 Big-Wave Challenge, a provocative first-of-its-kind competition offering $50,000 to the surfer photographed riding the largest wave of the winter sea-

son. Critics thought the much-hyped event was demeaning and potentially dangerous, saying the cash prize might cloud a rider's judgment. Sharp and K2 ignored such remarks, and hit the marketing jackpot, as the Big-Wave Challenge—won by San Diego surfer Taylor Knox, for a 50-footer he caught at Mexico's Todos Santos—was covered by the *Los Angeles Times,* CNN, *Time,* and *Sports Illustrated.* Sharp left K2 in 1998, and the following year launched *Surf News,* a cheeky monthly tabloid, with headlines reading "Red-Hot 3-Way All-Girl Interview," "Are Pro Surfers All Overpaid Kooks?," and "Chow Time! Shark Attack at Maverick's." *Surf News*'s coverage of the Southern California surf scene, particularly the surf industry, was always more timely and often more pointed than that produced by *Surfer* and *Surfing* magazines. In early 2001, Sharp helped photographer Larry Moore organize a group of tow-in surfers for a one-day visit to Cortes Bank, an eerie open-ocean reef located 100 miles west of San Diego, where Mike Parsons caught and rode a 50-foot-plus wave. Later that year Sharp developed the Odyssey, a three-year international hunt sponsored by surfwear giant Billabong in search of a ridable 100-foot wave.

Sharp is married and has two children. He's not related to William Sharp, the Oxnard-based surf photographer. *See also* Cortes Banks, K2 Big-Wave Challenge, Billabong Odyssey, Surfing magazine.

Shaw, Bill (Flea)   Freckle-faced goofyfooter from Florida who came to the attention of the surf world at age 10 with a cameo in Greg MacGillivray's 1965 movie *The Performers.* That same year Shaw won the boys' division of the Florida state championships, and was *Surfing* magazine's "Personality of the Month" for October. In 1987 he married four-time world professional champion Frieda Zamba, and in 1998 he was inducted into the East Coast Surf Legends Hall of Fame.

Shayne, Daize   Stunning-but-wholesome goofy-foot surfer from Hawaii; winner of the 1999 Women's World Longboard Championship, and runner-up in 2000. Daize (pronounced "Daisy") Shayne was born (1977) in Ukiah, California, moved with her family to Hawaii at age six months, and began surfing at 16. In 1996 she was hired by Roxy, the Quiksilver-launched women's beachwear line, and soon became the near-ubiquitous poster girl for the women's surfing explosion; a popular magazine ad featured Shayne cross-stepping on a small wave in Hawaii dressed in a bikini, hula skirt, and a palm-frond hat; a 1997 *Longboard* magazine article called her the "surfing supermodel." When Shayne won the inaugural women's longboard world title, she was dating 1998 men's longboard world champion Joel Tudor. She has appeared in a number of surf videos, including *Super Slide* (1999), *The Road* (2001), and *Contours* (2002). *See also* Women's World Longboard Championships.

Shepherd, Bob   Reticent, detail-oriented surfboard shaper of the late 1950s and '60s from Honolulu, Hawaii; best known for his sleek balsa-core big-wave guns. Shepherd was born (1934) in Upland, California, near Los Angeles, and began surfing in 1955, two years before moving to Hawaii. He started shaping in 1959, and almost immediately became the second-most popular big-wave gun maker, behind fellow Californian Pat Curren. Shepherd, who favored the concave-nose design, learned from master craftsman Joe Quigg, and went on to shape boards for Hawaiian stylist Paul Strauch and California-born big-wave charger Buzzy Trent. He was also the primary influence on shaping guru Dick Brewer. In the early '60s, Shepherd founded and briefly owned the oddly named Swim Boat Surfboards in Honolulu. A regular-foot surfer, he appeared in a small number of surf films, including *Surf Safari* (1959) and *Angry Sea* (1963). Shepherd worked as a fireman in Honolulu from 1961 to 1989.

Shifren, Nachum   Media-savvy, longboard-riding Hasidic Jew; author of 2001's *Surfing Rabbi: A Kabbalistic Quest for Soul.* Born Norman Shifren in Los Angeles in 1951, the lanky regularfooter began surfing at age 13, lived in Hawaii in the early '70s, and worked as a Los Angeles County lifeguard from 1973 to 1977. Shifren moved to Israel in 1977 and served in the Israeli Defense Forces; in 1990 he received his rabbinical ordination. While living in Israel, Shifren gave surf lessons and founded the *Surf and Soul* newsletter; he returned to Southern California in 1999. Shifren has been profiled in *Surfer* magazine, *Longboard,* and the *Surfer's Journal,* as well as in *GQ,* the *Los Angeles Times,* and *People,* and on CNN, NPR, *Good Morning America,* and the *Phil Donohue Show.* He founded Jewish Surfers International in 1995, and later set up Surfingrabbi.com. An elementary school teacher as well as a rabbi, Shifren is a regular at Malibu, leaving his yarmulke, Torah, and beach towel in a bag under the lifeguard station. The only conflict between surfing and Hasidism, Shifren noted, is that he often steps on his beard while jumping up on his surfboard. But the rewards, he says, are infinite. "You're going 50 miles an hour," he told the *Los Angeles Times,* describing a good ride at Malibu, "to a point where it's like rapture." *See also* religion and surfing.

Shipley, Jack   Phlegmatic surf competition judge from Hawaii, and cofounder of Lightning Bolt Surfboards. Shipley was nine in 1961 when he moved with his family from Baltimore, Maryland, to Oahu. He later worked for the Hobie Surfboards outlet in Honolulu, and in 1966 judged his first surf contest. Shipley and Pipeline master surfer Gerry Lopez opened the first Lighting Bolt Surfboards shop in Honolulu in 1970; Bolt would dominate the Hawaiian big-wave board market for the rest of the decade. Shipley continued to judge surf contests at every level—he's worked the Pipeline Masters event since its 1971 inaugural—and was soon regarded as one of the most knowledgeable and trenchant observers of the Hawaiian surf scene. Hired by the world pro tour, Shipley was director of judging from 1976 to 1982, and head judge for Hawaii from 1982 to present day. *See also* Lighting Bolt Surfboards.

shoot the pier   Riding a wave from one side of a pier to the other by threading the pilings. In their 1962 hit "Surfin' Safari," the Beach Boys sang "At Huntington and Malibu they're shooting the pier...," and in fact the pier shot is a regular part of surfing at dozens of breaks around the world. For the

Shooting the pier at Huntington Beach, California, during the 1965 US Championships

most part, riders who wipe out near the pilings surface unharmed, or come away with minor scratches, bumps, and bruises. But pier-related injuries and even deaths are not unheard of. Santa Monica City College student Nick Gabaldon died after hitting the Malibu Pier in 1951, and 16-year-old Joshua Hall died in a similar manner at Huntington in 1997.

shoot the tube   *See* tuberiding.

shorebreak   Technically speaking, "shorebreak" is defined as any wave that breaks close to shore, but surfers generally use the word to describe a particularly hollow, hard-breaking, usually closed-out wave just off a sandy beach. At places like Pipeline in Hawaii, the shorebreak can be an energy-draining (and sometimes board-breaking) impediment to better surf farther off the beach. While shorebreak surf for the most part is useless to board surfers—and often dangerous to unaware swimmers and waders—bodysurfers, bodyboarders, and skimboarders have long put these explosive waves to good use at places like Makapuu, Sandy Beach, and Waimea Bay in Hawaii, and Oak Street in Laguna Beach, California.

short john   Minimum-protection shoulder-strap wetsuit design, covering a surfer's trunk, chest, back, and thighs, usually constructed with two-millimeter neoprene and a small back zipper. The short john—or "shorty"—is one of the original surfing wetsuits, along with the legs-covered long john and the front-zip long- or short-sleeve jacket. From the mid-'50s until the mid-'60s, short johns were often used from fall through spring, as surfers more or less braved the cold as best they could. Today, with full-coverage wetsuits available for virtually every climate, temperate to arctic, the short john is most often used in tropical or subtropical areas. *See also* long john, wetsuit.

shortboard revolution   Surfboard design phase lasting from roughly 1967 to 1970, when average board specifications dropped from 9′6″ by 22″ and 26 pounds to 6′6″ by 20″ and 10 pounds; accompanied by an equally radical shift in wave-riding styles and techniques. Shortboard revolution details are complicated in places, with key figures still in disagreement as to who contributed what, but the accepted view is that the movement began with Australian Bob McTavish and Californian George Greenough, with Nat Young and Wayne Lynch of Australia as the main test

riders, and was then refined by Hawaii's Dick Brewer. There is no disagreement as to the profound change the shortboard revolution brought to the sport. Surf journalist Paul Gross called it "a mass desertion from everything that had gone before." *Surfer* magazine editor Drew Kampion described it as the "greatest conceptual shift in surfing history."

Experimental short surfboards had been used prior to 1967. Jim Foley of Santa Cruz rode a 7′10″ in the early '60s, Southern California surfer Mickey Muñoz used a 6′8″ board in 1964, and Hawaii's Wally Froiseth often stood up while riding a 4-foot bellyboard in the '40s and '50s. But the seeds of the shortboard revolution, along with the turn-activated shortboard style of wave-riding, were planted in 1965 just after Santa Barbara kneerider George Greenough arrived for a long stay with Queensland-born surfer/board-maker Bob McTavish in the North Coast of New South Wales. Riding a thin, flexible, dished-out 4′10″ "spoon" kneeboard with a narrow-based fin patterned from the tail of a bluefin tuna, Greenough was able to climb and drop across the wave face while remaining close to the curl. Stand-up surfers were turning also, but not with any proximity to the curl, and were more concerned with riding the nose—hanging ten was regarded then as the ultimate surfing maneuver. McTavish himself for the most part was content to ride in the traditional manner, but watched Greenough with great interest and wondered what kind of equipment a stand-up surfer would need to be able to draw up-and-down lines across the wave. In the fall of 1966, Australian surfer Nat Young, riding a thin 9′4″ board with a Greenough-made fin, won the World Surfing Championships in San Diego by turning harder and sharper than anybody else in the event. Noseriding, Young said afterward, had led the sport into a blind alley; "involvement" was the phrase he and close friend McTavish used to describe a more active style of riding that put the surfer closer to the curl, and it became a buzzword for the upcoming shortboard revolution.

McTavish later said that "three-quarters of the development of the shortboard" took place in 1967. In March, he built the first vee-bottom board, a 9′ by 23″ wide-backed squaretail he nicknamed the "Plastic Machine," featuring a two-panel V-shaped planing surface along the rear section that more or less forced the board to tip over into a turning position. Six months later a group of elite California surfers including Skip Frye and Mickey Muñoz, all riding boards 9′6″ or bigger, visited Sydney and were astounded to find local surfers on vee-bottom shortboards, some as short as 7′6″. McTavish and Young then flew to Hawaii in December for what amounted to the international debut of the vee-bottom design. Competing in 12-foot Sunset Beach surf during the Duke Kahanamoku Invitational, McTavish and his strange-looking board were a washout. But a few days later, in six- to eight-foot waves at Maui's Honolua Bay, the vee-bottoms worked beautifully for both McTavish and Young, and their best rides formed the ending sequence to *The Hot Generation,* a 1968 surf film that captured the transformation from longboard surfing to "involved" shortboarding. (John Witzig's follow-up movie, *Evolution,* released the following year, presented 17-year-old Wayne Lynch as the first true master of the shortboard.)

Board-maker Dick Brewer, generally regarded as the world's best longboard shaper, was living and working on Maui in 1967, and was at Honolua when McTavish and Young showed up with their vee-bottoms. Brewer was then developing what was called the "pocket rocket" or "mini-gun" design, essentially a light, narrow-backed pintail longboard that some (Brewer included) view as the genuine shortboard prototype, rather than the vee-bottom. It's probably closer to the truth to say that his contribution to the shortboard revolution came in 1968–70, following the movement's initial phase, as he figured out how to make the new boards work in Hawaii's big surf by streamlining the templates, making subtle but crucial changes in the board's nose-to-tail thickness, and helping reconfigure the rail profile.

The new push in surfboard design was first referred to as a "revolution" in the April 1968 issue of *Petersen's Surfing* magazine, just a few weeks after the vee-bottoms were introduced in California. By early 1969 the vee-bottoms were phased out as board manufacturers shot off in all directions looking for the next groundbreaking design, creating 5′8″ by 23″ double-ender blobs and 7′ by 16″ stilettos; using 12″ narrow-base fins and 3″ "finger" fins; and marketing their latest board ("stick," "tool," "surfing utensil," or "kinetic vehicle" in the going argot) with semitechnical ad copy referencing displacement hulls, rail camber, and S-rocker. The shortboard revolution was disastrous for the big-label surfboard companies, all of whom were caught with a huge inventory of obsolete longboards. It was the low-overhead boardmakers working out of backyards and garages who got the early jump on short surfboards, and industry titans of the mid-'60s either scaled back their operations or shut down altogether.

As quickly as surfboard design was changing, so, too, were surfing techniques, with riders angling up and down across the wave face, rebounding off the whitewater, and riding ever deeper inside the tube— an area of the wave that had been virtually inaccessible on longboards. The entire sport was also being reshaped by Woodstock-era drugs, music, language, graphics, fashion, and politics. *Surfer* magazine cover captions went from "Jock Sutherland charges down the face of a Pipeline giant (1966)" to "Tom Stone suspended in the Pipeline vector complex (1970)."

At the 1970 world championships, held in Victoria, Australia, the heavily favored Australians rode balky sub-six-foot "mind machines" and were beaten by Californian Rolf Aurness, who used a sensible-looking 6′10″ roundtail. Board experimentation would continue in the years and decades ahead, but Aurness's win in Victoria effectively brought the shortboard revolution to an end. By the mid-'70s, the revolution was in a sense coming undone. "Re-enter the longboard," Bob McTavish wrote in a 1977 *Surfer* magazine article, saying how he'd returned to a 9′ by 22″ board when the waves were small. "It's good to see them back." *See also* Dick Brewer, George Greenough, Bob McTavish, vee, Nat Young.

shortboard, shortboarding   Category of short, light, high-performance surfboard; shortboards are patterned for the most part on equipment used by professional surfers, and a small-wave shortboard used by a 150-pound rider would likely be about 6′3″ long, 18½″ wide, 2¼″ thick, and weigh just under seven pounds. Virtually all shortboards are tri-fins. The word "shortboard" came into use during the late-'60s shortboard revolution, when average board length dropped from roughly 10 feet to seven feet (early shortboards were often called "mini-boards"). "Shortboard" nearly disappeared from the lexicon in the '70s as virtually all boards were in fact short, then it reappeared late in the decade as longboards once again returned to fashion. Shortboards are also differentiated from hybrids, including funboards, minitankers, and eggs. Streamlined big-wave guns are generally categorized as shortboards, not because they're short—some guns are 10 feet or longer—but because they're not longboards (characterized by a round nose), and are generally ridden by shortboard surfers. In general, shortboarders tend to favor tight-radius turns and cutbacks, while the longboarder's method is straighter, smoother, and more flowing. Shortboarders tend to be younger than longboarders, although the distinction is less marked than it was in the '80s. Because the longboard's buoyancy allows users to paddle faster and catch waves earlier than surfers on shortboards, and because the easy-riding longboard brought more bodies into the water, the two groups have a long history of mild friction. Film-maker Bruce Brown turned the animosity into a run-ning gag in his 1994 travelogue *Endless Summer II* by pairing longboarder Robert Weaver with short-boarder Pat O'Connell. *Surfer* magazine addressed the issue with a 1997 cover story, headlined "Can't We All Just Get Along?" The answer seemed to be "no," as San Francisco shortboarder Mark Renneker described longboarding as "an act of acquiescence, a process of resignation" and longboarders as "glinty-eyed, barrel-shaped, middle-aged surfers wearing T-shirts bearing the names of their surf clubs." Longboards have a place in small, sloppy waves, Renneker concludes, but shortboarding is the only way to fully take advantage of what he describes as "the delirious pleasures of surfing." *See also* longboard, shortboard revolution.

shoulder   Downward-sloping area of the wave adja-cent to the crest and the whitewater. A shouldering wave is either temporarily slowing down or giving out altogether; waves often shoulder into a deep-water channel. In general, the shoulder is what al-lows a surfer to angle across the face. Surfers inside the tube aim for the shoulder, and surfers on the shoulder often perform a cutback to return to the more powerful area of the wave. "Sitting on the shoulder" means a surfer has taken a watching posi-tion off to the side of the wave zone, scared or other-wise not ready to move into the thick of things.

shoulder hopper   An inexperienced or overly ag-gressive surfer who takes off in front of an already rid-ing surfer, compromising or ruining the original surfer's ride. The expression "shoulder hopper" comes from the fact that the interfering surfer usually begins his ride not at the wave's peak, but somewhere on the easier-to-manage shoulder. Shoulder-hopping

Shoulder-hopper (right) at Blacks Beach, California

is a serious breach of etiquette, and can result in ten-sion, arguments, even fights. Southern California novelty band the Surf Punks wrote a song called "Shoulder Hopper" for their 1980 album *My Beach*.

shuffle   Method of advancing toward the front of the surfboard, generally used by beginning- and intermediate-level longboarders, in which the back foot always remains behind the front foot. The shuffle is set apart from the more elegant and diffi-cult cross-step, in which the feet and legs cross and uncross as the rider moves forward.

side-slip   Low-speed, forward-weighted maneuver generally performed in small surf, during which the surfboard fins are disengaged, allowing the board to drop sideways down the wave face. Hawaiian surfer Gerry Lopez side-slipped his way to a fifth-place fin-ish in the 1969 United States Championships, and de-scribed the maneuver as a "controlled fin drift." The uncontrolled fin drift is generally referred to as a "spin-out"—which nearly always results in a wipe-out. The spin-out (or "sliding ass") was especially common prior to the mid-1940s, when boards were finless. California surfer Mickey Dora is often cred-ited as the inventor of the side-slip in the mid-'50s, but the maneuver didn't really catch on until 1969, when Lopez, along with fellow Hawaiian goofyfooter Jock Sutherland and California favorite J Riddle, all added it to their repertoire and triggered a minor fad.

California surfer Mike Purpus took things further in the mid-'70s by often pushing his side-slip into a 360-degree spin, but the surfing world by that time had dismissed the move as trickery. The neutral-railed floater, popularized in the early '80s, borrowed from the side-slip, as did the entire collection of tail-slide maneuvers first practiced by the Kelly Slater–led New School teenagers in the early '90s. *See also* reverse, tailslide.

sideshore wind   Wind blowing parallel to the incoming waves; generally detrimental to wave quality. A slight shift in wind angle can produce either an improving side-offshore wind or a wave-crumbling side-onshore wind. The mid-Pacific tradewinds generally blow sideshore across the North Shore of Oahu in Hawaii. *See also* offshore wind, onshore wind.

Sierra Leone   Small country located on Africa's western bulge, north of the equator; diamond-rich but impoverished due in large part to a long and violent civil war. For safety reasons, Sierra Leone has been almost completely ignored as a surfing destination, and only portions of the country's 210-mile swamp-lined coastline have been mapped for waves. The biggest and best surf coincides with the April-to-November rainy season, with windless conditions prevailing in the morning, followed by an afternoon offshore breeze. Visiting American surfer John Ford, in a 1983 note to the *Surf Report* newsletter, wrote of "hundreds of pointbreaks, beachbreaks and river-mouths with potential" in Sierra Leone, and just one surfer—presumably himself—in the entire country. He added that the waves are generally under six feet; that the capital city of Freetown is lined with surf breaks; and that the rest of the Sierra Leone coastline is largely inaccessible by car.

Silva, Jacqueline   Freckle-faced regularfooter from Florianópolis, Brazil, world-ranked #2 in 2002, and winner of the 2001 World Qualifying Series (WQS) tour. Silva was born (1979) in Florianópolis, began surfing at age 10, and in 1996 she placed 3rd in the World Surfing Games. She turned pro the following year, qualified for the World Championship Tour in '99, failed to hold position in 200, requalified the following year and finished at #11, then jumped all the way to #2 in 2002, when she was also named as the world tour's Most Improved surfer. Dismissed in years past as a small-wave-only breachbreak specialist, Silva

showed beautiful form while engineering her debut world tour victory, in 2002, at the season-ending Billabong Pro Maui at Honolua Bay, held in tubing overhead point surf.

Silver Surfer   Gleaming, space-surfing Marvel Comics superhero, created by comic-book legend Stan Lee along with Jack Kirby in 1966, and later developed by John Buscema. Born on planet Zenn-La, Silver Surfer was initially sent to destroy earth as a retainer of the evil warlord Galactus. "I made him into a *receptacle* for the ambient energies of the universe," Galactus says by way of introducing Silver Surfer. "I created for him a *wondrous board* which obeys his *every thought*. My herald was one of the more *powerful* and *unique* beings in all creation." After rebelling against Galactus, Silver Surfer was for years exiled on earth, where he did battle against Mephisto, Doctor Doom, and Obliterator, among other villains, and fell in love with blind earthling Alicia Masters. Nearly 200 "main appearance" Silver Surfer comic books,

Silver Surfer

annuals, and graphic novels were published between 1968 and 1998; 13 half-hour animated *Silver Surfer* television episodes were made in 1998. *See also* surf cartoons and comics.

Simmons, Bob   Seminal post–World War II surfboard designer and shaper from Pasadena, California; a primary architect of the modern surfboard who almost single-handedly brought into play the now-fundamental principles of nose-lift, foil, and finely sculpted rails; often described as the sport's only true design genius. Simmons was born (1919) in Los Angeles, the son of a postman, and raised in the Los Angeles communities of Silverlake and Pasadena. He developed a cancerous tumor in his left ankle at age 16, and nearly had the limb amputated before the growth went into remission. Bicycling to rehabilitate his leg, Simmons was hit by a car and broke his left elbow, and the joint had to be fused at a 45-degree angle. While in the hospital recuperating, he was advised by another patient to take up surfing to help strengthen his arm. Simmons eventually became a skilled if ungainly surfer, limited somewhat by his bad arm, and riding in a straight-backed legs-together goofyfoot stance. Malibu was his favorite break, as it was with virtually all Southern California surfers in the '40s and '50s.

A high school dropout, Simmons nevertheless passed an admittance test to the California Institute of Technology, and became a part-time engineering student for nearly five years, earning straight As. When America entered the war in 1941, he quit his classes and became a machinist, and for two years after the war he worked on and off as a mathematician for Douglas Aircraft. (He later attended San Diego State College for one semester and earned a B.S. in mathematics.)

California surfers in the mid-'40s rode either long, flat, blunt-nosed plank boards, usually about 10 feet and weighing almost 60 pounds, or the longer, lighter, more streamlined "cigar-box" hollow boards. (Progressive Hawaiian surfers had meanwhile developed a modified plank design called the hot curl.) The planks were lumbering and unresponsive, the cigar-boxes were tippy, and the lanky 6′2″ Simmons was compelled, almost from the moment he began surfing, to create better equipment. He learned the basics of board-building in the mid-'40s from the talented but surly Gard Chapin (stepfather to surf icon Mickey Dora); in 1946 he acquired a copy of a lengthy MIT study on planing hulls, and began applying its complex equations and theories to surfboards. By 1949, the typical Simmons board was wide (up to 24 inches), with a thin, squared-off tail, finely turned and calibrated rails, and a broad spoonlike nose. Prewar boards for the most part had been redwood/balsa composites coated in varnish; Simmons, working out of his garage in Pasadena, used balsa only and was one of the first to cover his boards with a layer of resin-saturated fiberglass. He also produced a small number of Styrofoam/balsa "sandwich" boards, predating the commercial production of polyurethane foam surfboards by nearly 10 years. The "Simmons spoon" board weighed about 25 pounds; it wasn't particularly maneuverable, but was faster and more controllable by far than either the planks or the cigar-boxes, and could be put on a more acute angle across the wave face. Simmons also made the first double-finned boards, and experimented with bottom-surface concaves as well as a split-rail "slot" design.

Joe Quigg, Matt Kivlin, Dale Velzy, and other Malibu-based board-makers incorporated many of Simmons's design features into their own boards, and by 1950 were producing the easier-to-turn Malibu chip design, which in turn led to the development of the modern longboard. Simmons had meanwhile earned a reputation as loud, scruffy, opinionated, and frequently unpleasant. "He was dunked and beaten up at Malibu," San Diego surfer and Simmons test pilot John Elwell later recalled. "He was punched down at San Onofre, and stoned on the trail to Palos Verdes Cove." (An ax-wielding Simmons returned to the Cove under cover of night and retaliated by de-

Bob Simmons (left) and Matt Kivlin at Malibu

molishing a row of paddleboards left on the beach.) Simmons spent much of his time in the early '50s driving the coast alone in his rusted-out 1937 Ford Tudor sedan with black-painted side windows, in which he kept hydrographic charts and abstruse hand-drawn graphs and computations, along with cans of baked beans, a bag of oranges, weather maps, unpaid speeding tickets, a quiver of homemade boomerangs, and a sleeping bag. In October 1953, the never-married Simmons sailed to Hawaii, became the first visiting surfer to rent a house on the North Shore of Oahu, and discovered that his wide-tailed boards didn't work very well in larger surf.

On September 26, 1954, in eight-foot surf at San Diego's Windansea, Simmons was struck in the head by his own board and drowned. He was 35. Simmons was posthumously inducted into the *International Surfing* Magazine Hall of Fame in 1966. Almost 35 years later, a Simmons sandwich board sold at auction for $18,500—the highest amount ever paid for a surfboard. *See also* chip board, death and surfing, fiberglass, Malibu board, the surfboard, twin-fin.

Sims, Craig   Well-spoken surf journalist and editor from Durban, South Africa; owner and publisher, since 1988, of *Zigzag* surfing magazine. Sims was born (1964) in Durban, raised in the inland suburb of Westville, and began surfing in 1976. He finished runner-up in the South African Championships in 1982 and 1985, spent just over two years on the world pro tour, and was the Association of Professional Surfers Africa champion in 1989. Sims had no publishing experience whatsoever when he bought the 12-year-old bimonthly *Zigzag* in 1988—average issue size at the time was 48 pages; circulation was just over 4,500—and worked for the first few years as publisher, editor, layout artist, photo editor, and janitor before he could afford to hire a modest staff. By 1997, when *Zigzag* was given a "best consumer magazine" award by the Print Media Association of South Africa, average issue size was 110 pages, and circulation had grown to 14,000. Sims wrote a weekly surfing column for the *Natal Mercury* for 11 years, beginning in 1989; in 1999 he cofounded the Surfer's Environmental Association. He graduated from Natal University in 1985 with a B.A. in economics.

single-fin   A surfboard with one fin, as compared to boards with anywhere from two to five fins. Surfboards were finless until Wisconsin-born surfing

Single-fin surfboards

prodigy Tom Blake attached a low-profile metal boat keel to the back of one of his paddleboards in 1935. Blake's invention didn't catch on until after World War II; from the mid-'40s to the early '70s, with a few rare exceptions, all boards had one fin. The expression "single-fin," however, didn't become part of the surfing lexicon until the early '70s, with the introduction of the short-lived first-generation twin-fin board. When four-time world champion Mark Richards of Australia brought out his version of the twin-fin in 1977, there was a split between single-fin and twin-fin advocates as to which was the better small-wave performance board. The singles were more stable and predictable; the twin-fin allowed for a wider tail, which increased the planing area and made for a faster and more maneuverable board in small waves. When the surf hit about six foot, however, the addition planing surface began to work against the twin-fin, making the board skittish and difficult to control; single-fins were the rule in bigger surf.

The single-fin was all but phased out on high-performance shortboards, including big-wave guns, in the early '80s, after the new tri-fin design proved to be stable, fast, and maneuverable, trumping both the single and the twin. But the longboard renaissance, which began in the late 1970s and grew through the '80s and '90s, ensured that single-fin boards remained in production; longboards are more or less equally divided between single- and tri-fins. *See also* fin, four-fin, tri-fin, twin-fin.

Sizemore, Ron   Lanky blond hotdogger from Laguna Beach, California; surprise winner of the 1961

West Coast Surfing Championships. Sizemore was born (1944) in Long Beach, California, and began surfing at age 10. He jitterbugged his way through the 1961 West Coast titles, switching stance frequently, doing spinners, angling toward the pier and riding backward, and otherwise deploying a full bag of tricks. Other finalists included Rusty Miller, Mike Doyle, Ilima Kalama, and John Severson. It was Sizemore's only big win. He was featured in a small number of surf movies, including *Cavalcade of Surf* (1962) and *Gun Ho!* (1963).

skateboarding While forerunners to the skateboard date as far back as the early 1900s, when American preteens made scooters by attaching metal roller skate wheels to wooden planks and vegetable crates, skateboarding as it exists today was developed and popularized by surfers in the late '50s and early 1960s. Roller Derby introduced the first commercially made skateboard in 1959: it measured 24" by 4", had clay-composition wheels spinning on ball bearings, and sold for just under $10. As surfing's popularity grew in the early '60s, so, too, did "sidewalk surfing," with Makaha Skateboards and Hobie Skateboards emerging as industry leaders by 1964, and 50 million skateboards sold in America by mid-decade. Skaters often rode barefoot, and performed surfing-inspired tricks (back-arch turns, cross-stepping, noseriding, spinners, and coffins), along with pinwheeling 360-degree spin turns. The first organized skateboard contest was held in Hermosa Beach, California, in 1963, and attracted about 100 competitors; the 1965 International Skateboard Championships, held in Anaheim, were featured on ABC's *Wide World of Sports*. Meanwhile, Jan and Dean's bouncy single "Sidewalk Surfing" peaked at #25 on the Billboard charts, while the *Quarterly Skateboarder* magazine was founded in 1965, the same year *Skater Dater* received a best live action short Academy Award nomination. A 1965 *Life* magazine cover story called the skateboard "the most exhilarating and dangerous joy-ride device this side of the hot rod"; the American Medical Association that year called the sport "a new medical menace."

Skateboarding slumped in the late '60s and early '70s, then roared back following development of the smooth-riding urethane wheels and encased precision bearings. America's first skateboard park opened in 1976 in Florida; three years later there were an estimated 300 parks open across the country. Home-made plywood ramps were also popular, as were empty swimming pools and any other type of wave-like asphalt or concrete embankment; skateboarders were soon able to get vertical on the upper regions of ramps and pools, and by the late '70s were launching and completing aerial maneuvers. While a few years earlier skateboarders took style cues from top surfers, particularly Hawaiian ace Larry Bertlemann, surfers began to copy them in an effort to bring aerials to the water. Meanwhile, Jay Adams and Tony Alva, two working-class surfer/skateboarders from Santa Monica, California—an area better known to skate fans as "Dogtown"—helped give the sport a new rowdy outlaw image. (The documentary *Dogtown and Z-Boys*, narrated by actor Sean Penn, won the Audience Award and the Director's Award at the 2001 Sundance Film Festival.)

Skateboarding took to the streets in the early '80s, in part because skyrocketing insurance premiums had shut down the vast majority of skateparks. Pools and plywood "half-pipes" remained popular. Three skateboard manufacturers—Powell-Peralta, Vision/Sims, and Santa Cruz—dominated the industry, each promoting a team of high-profile riders, some of whom earned as much as $10,000 a month on royalties and contest winnings; the 1981-founded *Thrasher* magazine celebrated the sport's renegade image. Fourteen-year-old Tony Hawk of San Diego, California, won his first pro contest in 1982, and over the next 17 years won nearly 75 percent of the contests he entered. Following an early '90s economic downturn, skateboarding's popularity once again shot forward when the sport became a main attraction in the X-Games, ESPN's teen-marketed answer to the Olympics. Skate-style shoes were by that time accounting for an ever-growing portion of youth market footwear sales; more than 12 million copies of the 1999-launched Tony Hawk's Pro Skater video game series had sold by 2002.

Today's basic skateboard is symmetrical, about 30 inches long, eight inches wide, concave and up-turned at both ends, and made of seven-ply sugar maple topped with traction-providing grip tape. Adjustable metal trucks are located about five inches from either end; each urethane wheel has a pair of encased bearings. A ready-to-ride board costs about $100. Skateboarding is generally divided into street skating and vert skating; both incorporate a broad and constantly evolving array of tail-, nose-, and rail-slides, truck "grinds," and aerial maneuvers, executed on any variety of specially designed ramps (half-pipes, quarter-pipes, or launch ramps) or street obstacles (curbs, handrails, or benches). Specialized forms of skateboarding have also developed: downhill "street luge" skateboarders reach speeds up to 80 miles per hour; "dirt-boarders," using oversized rubber-wheeled boards, take the sport off-road; flexible longboards are used for a smooth, stately, old school street ride. By 2003, there were an estimated 11 million skateboarders in America and an enormous worldwide network of skateboarding organizations, industries, and media outlets. *See also* aerial.

skeg   *See* fin.

skimboarding   Riding a thin, flat board made of wood or foam over sand covered by a thin layer of water. The skimboarder begins his ride by running at an angle toward the surf, just behind an ebbing wave; at full sprint, he shoots the board onto the film of water just ahead of him, jumps on, and begins gliding. For intermediate and advanced riders, the sand-skimming portion of the ride is a prelude to a surfing-like maneuver—or short series of maneuvers—performed on an approaching shorebreak wave. It's likely that ancient Polynesians practiced some form of skimboarding, but Laguna Beach lifeguards are credited as inventing the sport, sometime in the late 1920s.

By the time *Peterson's Surfing* magazine published "How to Build a Skimboard" in 1964 (cut a 30-foot-

Skimboarding

diameter disk from a piece of plywood, sand the edges smooth, and water-seal the entire board), Laguna skimmers were already making elliptical-outlined plywood boards, roughly three feet long and 18 inches wide at the center, which were better suited than disks for making the transition from wet sand up and onto a wave. In 1975, Tex Haines and Peter Prietto, both skilled riders at Victoria Beach, Laguna's hottest skimboard spot, founded Victoria Skimboards. Five years later they began making boards from polyurethane foam covered in fiberglass and resin—the same materials used to make surfboards. The faster, lighter foam-based boards raised performance levels. Skimboarders had long been doing big, flashy turns against the wave face; tuberides were now part of the advanced skimmers' repertoire, and a 1987 *Sports Illustrated* cover featured a skimboarder doing an aerial. Laguna Beach remains the sport's hub, but top skimmers have for years been riding the sand-smashing waves at Hawaii's Waimea Bay and the Wedge in Newport Beach, California. The first annual World Skimboard Championships were held in 1976 at Aliso Beach in Laguna, with Haines directing; the 2002 championships had a $4,500 purse. Skimboarding is covered by Skim Online and *Skim* magazine, founded in 1995 and 1999, respectively. Skimboard videos include *The Bomb* (1995), *Sand Crabs* (1997), and *Vortex Children* (2001).

skin cancer   General name for different types of epidermal cancer, most often formed on the face, ears, back, chest, hands, and forearms. Skin cancer is caused or triggered by overexposure to the sun, or, more specifically, sun-produced ultraviolet (UV) rays. Skin cancer rates have been on the rise for decades, almost certainly because industrial emissions have depleted the earth's UV-screening ozone layer; as surfers spend so much time in the sun, they contract skin cancer at rates higher than that of the general population. "Unfortunately," writes Dr. Geoff Booth in *Sick Surfers: Ask the Surf Docs,* a health and medicine book for surfers, "we're in the box seat for cumulative skin damage." UV rays, Booth notes, are reflected off the sand, and unaffected by cold weather (although greatly affected by the angle of the sun), and will penetrate a light cloud cover at something close to full strength. Saltwater also washes away the skin's natural protection—urocanic acid—and a sea breeze will intensify the UV rays' burning effect. Skin cancer prevention is a matter of staying out of the sun as much as possible, and while in the sun, protecting the skin with clothes, wetsuits, and rash guards (as required), and a high SPF (sun protection factor) sunscreen.

There are three types of skin cancer: 1) Basal cell carcinoma, the most common and benign form, is nonmetastasizing, generally appears as a small raised, ulcerated, pimplelike bump, and is easily removed with a scalpel or frozen off with cryosurgery. 2) Squamous cell carcinoma takes shape as a firm, fleshy, hard-surfaced, lump, and is also slow growing and easily removed, but capable, if left too long, of metastasizing. 3) Malignant melanoma is much rarer than the other types, but quick to metastasize, and fatal if not caught early. The two primary factors determining a person's likelihood of contracting skin cancer are skin pigmentation (light-skinned people are more at risk than dark-skinned) and sun exposure at an early age (childhood sunburns are a predictor for adult-contracted skin cancer). Regular use of sunscreen from ages one to 18 is thought to reduce the lifetime incidence of skin cancer by as much as 80 percent.

Australia's Wayne Bartholomew, 1978 World surfing champion, had a malignant melanoma diagnosed in 1988. The cancer was removed before it spread, and Bartholomew became a part-time health crusader, setting up skin cancer testing sites at surfing competitions near his Queensland home, and speaking about prevention on Australia's *60 Minutes.* Stuart Entwistle, 1987 longboard world champion also from Australia, died of skin cancer in 2002. *See also* sunscreen, zinc oxide.

skysurfing   Free-falling extreme sport in which the skysurfer jumps from a plane with a surfboard-like device strapped to his feet, and rides the uprushing wind before releasing a parachute. Invented in 1987 by French skydiver Joel Cruciani, using a surfboard outfitted with snowboard bindings, skysurfing appeared in early '90s television commercials for Reebok and Coca-Cola. American skysurfer Jerry Loftis formed the first skysurfing company, Surflite, in 1992, making specialized parachutes and graphite/Kevlar composite skysurf boards; two years later the first Skysurfing World Championships were held in France. Skysurfing was also featured in the opening ceremonies for the 1994 Winter Olympics, and in 1995 it became part of the wildly popular X-Games. The Skysurfing Pro Tour was inaugurated in 1996,

with four events worth a total of $85,000. Competitive skysurfing is a two-man team effort, with a skysurfer and video cameraman working together; winners are picked from video footage of the skysurfer's loops, spins, and drawn-out surfing-style turns.

Slabbert, Lance   Dependable freelance photographer from Cape Town, South Africa; regarded, since the early '90s, as his country's premier all-around surfing lensman. Slabbert was born (1964) in Johannesburg, raised in Cape Town, started taking photographs in 1976, and began surfing in 1981. The South African surf magazine *Zigzag* began publishing his work in 1988; the American surf press soon followed. Slabbert is a multifaceted talent, adept at water- and land-based angles, action shots, and portraiture, but has a particularly keen eye for landscapes and local color. His photos have appeared in the *London Times,* Italy's *L'umo Vogue,* and the South African editions of *Cosmopolitan, Elle,* and *GQ,* as well as *Surfer, Surfing, Australia's Surfing Life, Tracks, Trip Surf,* and *Japan Surfing Life.* Slabbert graduated from the University of Stellenbosch in 1988 with a B.A. in commerce.

slaps   Comfortable and durable neoprene-soled sandals with a nylon flat-weave Y-shaped toe strap; called "slippers" in Hawaii. Slaps are a rugged version of the inexpensive all-rubber flip-flops, also known as "go-aheads," "thongs," or "zorries." Footwear—with an emphasis on minimal coverage and smooth slip-on/slip-off action—has always been high on the surfer's admittedly short list of fashion concerns. The California surfer of the 1950s and '60s often returned from visits to Baja Mexico wearing a new pair of heel- and toe-strap Mexican huaraches, featuring recycled tire-tread soles. The Japanese straw-thatched *tatami* thong, with its distinctive oval shape, was briefly popular in the early '70s. The slap sandal as it exists today was developed in 1974 in the central California beach town of Avila, and was an instant local hit. The following year, a new company called Beachcomber Bills, located a few miles north in San Luis Obispo, began mass-producing the new footwear, with brightly colored nylon straps and laminated neoprene soles featuring between one and three horizontal bands of color sandwiched between the top and bottom layers of black. Copycat slaps followed immediately, and the international surf world had a clothing item that would remain virtually unchanged through the decades. Beachcomber Bills folded in the late 1970s, but Rainbow Sandals (established in 1974) and Reef Brazil (1984) have each sold millions of pairs of Beachcomber-style slaps. Leather-topped slaps were introduced in early '80s, Teva-style straps were later added to surf market slap lines, and dozens of other design alternatives have been introduced and discarded—including a model with an Astro Turf insole—but the original rubber-sole/nylon-strap slap remains the popular choice. A high-quality pair of slaps can last eight years or more, even with heavy use. *See also* fashion and surfing.

Slater, Evan   Enterprising surfer/writer/editor from Ventura, California; the only person to hold the editor's post at both *Surfer* and *Surfing* magazines. Slater was born (1971) and raised in the San Francisco Bay Area, moved with his family to Ventura at age seven, and began surfing at nine. At 15 he was the Western Surfing Association boys' division champion; he later became a three-time member of the National Scholastic Surfing Association's National Team. After receiving a B.A. in sociology from U.C. San Diego in 1994, Slater moved to San Francisco, where he became a regular in the Maverick's lineup and earned a reputation as one of California's best big-wave riders.

Slater was hired as *Surfer*'s associate editor in 1997; the following year he became managing editor; in 1999 he was promoted to editor, a title he held for just six issues—the shortest editor's tenure in the magazine's history—before jumping over to start-up surfing Web site Swell.com to serve for 15 months as its managing editor. When the Internet bubble burst, Slater made a nimble return to paper-and-ink publishing in 2001 to become editor of *Surfing* magazine. As a surf journalist, Slater has focused on competition and big-wave riding; the two converged in 1998 when he covered the first Reef Brazil Big-Wave Team World Championships, held in 30-foot surf at Todos Santos Island, Baja California. Slater himself competed in the 1999 Quiksilver Men Who Ride Mountains contest at Maverick's. He has appeared in nearly a dozen surf videos, including *Overdrive* (1993), *Gravity Sucks* (1994), and *Puerto Underground* (1997). He's married and has two children. *See also Surfer* magazine, *Surfing* magazine, Swell.com.

Slater, Kelly   Supernaturally talented pro surfer from Cocoa Beach, Florida; a record-breaking six-time world champion (1992, 1994–98) who rein-

vented virtually every aspect of high-performance surfing. Slater was born (1972) and raised in Cocoa Beach, the son of a bait-and-tackle shop owner father, and began surfing at age five. By 11 he was an unstoppable amateur competitor, and in 1984 he won the first of four consecutive United States Surfing Championships titles, two in the menehune division and two in the boys' division. At 14, mentored by aerialist pioneer and surfboard manufacturer Matt Kechele, Slater won not only the boys' division of the Easter Surfing Festival at Florida's Canaveral Pier, but the pro division as well—turning down the money to keep his amateur status. (Meanwhile, he was never able to post a good result in the World Amateur Championships.) Slater beat California's Rob Machado in the 1989 Op Junior event held at Huntington Beach. Turning pro at 18, Slater won the $100,000 Body Glove Surf Bout contest at Trestles in 1990, and signed a six-figure contract with beachwear giant Quiksilver. "Believe the hype," surf journalist Ben Marcus wrote. "He is a certified phenomenon." Slatermania, as it was soon being called, was helped by the fact that the brown-haired, green-eyed Floridian was incredibly handsome. *Surfer* magazine compared him to a young Elvis Presley. Surf journalist Derek Rielly, playing on the newcomer's deification—but as astounded by his talent as anyone—wrote that seeing Slater surf for the first time was "like being led by the infant Jesus to the promised land." *People* magazine included Slater in its 1991 "50 Most Beautiful People" issue.

Slater's surfing range and repertoire would expand in the years ahead, but at age 18 the basics were already in place. His stance and balance were similar to those of three-time world champion Tom Curren of California. Slater would never match Curren for fluidity, but his legs had more spring, his body was more limber, his approach was more innovative, and he had matchless coordination and reflexes. Wiry but strong (5′9″, 160 pounds), Slater could adjust his line from virtually anywhere on the wave; he was faster than any of his peers going into maneuvers, and the angle of his turns was more acute. Frequently pushing his moves just past the edge of control—often in the form of a drifting tailslide—Slater trusted that he could find his way back to stability before falling off. He also brought aerial surfing in from the sport's fringes, not just because his success rate was higher than anybody else's, but because he smoothly mixed aerials into the ride along with deep-set turns and cutbacks.

Kelly Slater

Slater ran hot and cold during his rookie world tour year in 1991, finished the season ranked 43rd, and was regarded as a longshot contender for the 1992 championship. But he moved into the ratings lead halfway through the 1992 season, pulled away from his rivals, won the title with room to spare in the second-to-last event, then punctuated with the season-ending victory in the Pipeline Masters. At 20, he was pro surfing's youngest-ever world champion. Meanwhile, his moves were being studied and dissected by tens of thousands of young surfers around the world, as he starred in *Momentum* (1992), as well as *Kelly Slater in Black and White* (1992), the first sponsor-funded video biography. Just weeks after winning the championship, Slater announced that he had taken a supporting role on *Baywatch,* the banal but hugely successful lifeguard drama TV show starring the buxom Pamela Anderson. Slater left the show a little over a year later, having appeared in 10 episodes as Malibu High School surfer Jimmy Slade; he would be romantically linked to Anderson for the next seven years. After dropping to sixth in the year-end ratings for 1993, Slater came back the following year to win the first of five consecutive championships. In the mid-'90s, Slater's surfing was in part defined by his protean tuberiding skill; with aplomb that only occasionally shaded into arrogance, he tracked ever deeper and longer inside the barrel, perfecting the no-hands backside tube stance, and sometimes pivoting around to ride as a goofyfooter. It was sublime tuberiding that won him another four Pipeline Masters titles (in 1994, 1995, 1996, and 1999),

as well as the 1995 Quiksilver Pro at Grajagan and the 1995 Billabong Challenge at Jeffreys Bay. Quiksilver fittingly raised his annual salary to a rumored $1 million a year. The even-tempered and surprisingly unaffected Slater continued to have a strong presence in the nonsurfing world: he was profiled by the *Los Angeles Times Magazine* in 1995, and made the cover of *Interview* magazine in 1996; two years later he was again featured in *Interview,* in a provocative series of photos with Pamela Anderson.

Slater retired from full-time competition at the end of the 1998 season, having just won his sixth world championship, along with a total of 21 world tour events, and the 1995 and 1998 Triple Crown titles. He formed a musical group the Surfers with world tour friend Rob Machado and La Jolla surfer Peter King, with Slater playing guitar and singing lead. Their 1998 release *Songs from the Pipe,* produced by Grammy winner T Bone Burnett, was released to indifferent reviews and low sales. (Slater also revealed in 1998 that two years earlier he'd fathered a child out of wedlock.) He entered a few world tour contests over the next three years, winning the Masters in 1999 and the Gotcha Pro at Teahupoo in 2000. He also competed in big-wave contests, finishing runner-up in the 2000 Men Who Ride Mountains event at Maverick's and winning the Quiksilver in Memory of Eddie Aikau at Waimea Bay in early 2002. Slater's much-anticipated return to full-time world tour competition in 2002, however, was something of a disappointment, as he finished the year rated #9.

Slater won a record eight consecutive *Surfer* Magazine Readers Poll Awards from 1993 to 2001; he was profiled in *20th Century Surfers* (2000), an Outdoor Life Network documentary series, and additionally has been featured in more than 150 surf movies and videos, including *Atlantic Crossing* (1989), *Surfers: The Movie* (1990), *Endless Summer II* (1994), *Focus* (1994), *Voluptuous: The Big Movie* (1996), *Kelly Slater in Kolor* (1997), *No Destination* (1998), *Nine Lives* (1999), *September Sessions* (2000), and *Shelter* (2001). In 2000, Slater became the first pro surfer to have his own official Web site. The year 2002 brought his induction into the Huntington Beach Surfing Walk of Fame and the release of Kelly Slater's Pro Surfer video game, patterned on the best-selling Tony Hawk's Pro Skater; *Pipe Dreams,* Slater's autobiography, is due out in 2003. Slater is part owner of K-Grip, a surf accessories company.

Slater is unmarried, and lives in Cocoa Beach. Older brother Sean was a top East Coast amateur competitor in the mid- and late '80s; younger brother Stephen is regarded as one of America's best longboarders.

slide   1) The act of "sliding," or angling, across the wave face. While surfers at the turn of the 19th century rode straight to the shore, by 1910 they were beginning to trim their boards at an angle to wave. For almost 40 years, sliding was the measure of high-performance surfing; in a 1940 flyer for the Palos Verdes Surf Club Hula Luau get-together, surfers were exhorted to "get out of the soup [whitewater] and slide." A basic part of the surfer's lexicon until the mid-'60s, "slide"—as a synonym for "angle"—was phased out during the late-'60s shortboard revolution. 2) The direction the wave itself is breaking, either "left slide" or "right slide." 3) Loss of traction between surfboard and wave; shortened from "slide-out" or "slide-ass," and analogous to "spin-out." 4) Shorthand for "tailslide."

Slipcheck   *See* traction pad.

Smirnoff Pro-Am   Early professional surfing contest, held from 1969 to 1977, often at Sunset Beach on the North Shore of Oahu. As noted in a *Sports Illustrated* feature story, when the Smirnoff Pro-Am made its 1969 debut in Santa Cruz, its $4,350 prize purse was "an all-time high for a surfing contest." Men's division winner Corky Carroll earned $1,500; women's division winner Margo Godfrey had to settle for $150. The following year the Smirnoff contest went to an all-male format (women were reintroduced six years later), and was moved to the North Shore, where it remained until 1977. The Smirnoff was regarded throughout its nine-year history as one of the sport's most prestigious events, but its reputation was made on Thanksgiving Day, 1974, when the final four heats were held in gigantic 25-foot-plus surf at Waimea Bay, for what was later described by Australia's *Tracks* magazine as "the most spectacular day in surfing history." Five of the 18 Smirnoff competitors had never ridden Waimea before, and some made it clear they wanted nothing to do with the huge waves. Contest director and 1968 world champion Fred Hemmings finessed the situation by offering to paddle out and catch the first wave, to prove it could be done. Not wanting to be shown up in front of 5,000 spectators, the com-

petitors agreed to surf. Hawaii's Reno Abellira, described by surf journalist Drew Kampion as the event's "most graceful, composed and sophisticated surfer," beat Jeff Hakman in the finals by a half point to take the $5,100 first-place check. Smirnoff Pro winners and locations:

1969:	Corky Carroll, Margo Godfrey (Steamer Lane)
1970:	Nat Young (Makaha)
1971:	Gavin Rudolph (Sunset)
1972:	Paul Neilsen (Haleiwa)
1973:	Ian Cairns (Laniakea)
1974:	Reno Abellira (Waimea)
1975:	Mark Richards (Sunset)
1976:	Mark Warren, Jericho Poppler (Sunset)
1977:	Reno Abellira, Jericho Poppler (Sunset)

Smith, Col (Newcastle)   Hard-charging Australian goofyfooter from Newcastle, New South Wales, described by two-time Pipeline Masters winner Rory Russell in 1977 as the "most underrated surfer in the world." At the end of that year, Smith, a world tour rookie, won the Pro Class Trials held at Sunset Beach, then finished seventh in the Pipeline Masters. He was labeled the "new" Col Smith, to distinguish him from Sydney's Col Smith—another Australian goofyfoot and the winner of the 1977 Australian National Titles. Newcastle Col Smith finished second in the Nationals in 1977, then won in 1978. He also won the 1978 Quiksilver Trials at Bells Beach, Australia, then quickly faded from the pro scene. Smith died of stomach cancer in 1986 at age 31. He was featured in *Fantasea* (1978) and a small number of other surf movies.

Smith, Col (Sydney)   Tall, flexible, dynamic Australian goofyfoot surfer from Narrabeen, New South Wales; winner of the 1977 Australian National Titles, and progenitor in the late '60s and early '70s, along with fellow Australian Wayne Lynch, of high-performance backside surfing. "I just started going up and down the wave instead of along it," he later said with a shrug. Smith came on the scene like a Viking, with long, blond hair and a jutting goatee—*Surfing* magazine called him "a 1972 version of Errol Flynn"—and locally was nearly as famous for public nudity as for his exploding through-the-lip turns. *Australia's Surfing Life* magazine in 1992 named Smith as one of Australia's 50 most influential surfers. He was featured in several surf movies of the late '60s

Col Smith

and '70s, including *Splashdown* (1969), *Freeform* (1970), and *Over Under Sideways Down* (1970).

Smith, Davey   Fast, compact, innovative goofy-footer from Santa Barbara, California, best known as a pioneer of the floater maneuver in the late 1970s. Smith was born in Los Angeles (1958), moved with his family to Santa Barbara at age three, and began surfing at 10. His method of "whitewater ripping," as *Surfing* magazine described it, was in part a response to Santa Barbara's small, crumbly, almost shapeless summer waves; whereas other surfers had little use for the wave after it closed out, Smith began banking, or "floating," off the foam. (World pro tour surfer Cheyne Horan was doing the same thing at his home beach in Bondi, Australia.) Smith was a washout on the pro circuit, but was nonetheless regarded as one of California's best surfers in the early '80s. He was featured in a small number of surf movies, including *Off the Wall II* (1982) and *Follow the Sun* (1983), and was an early test pilot for guru-to-be board-maker Al Merrick. *See also* aerial, floater.

Smith, Gene "Tarzan"   Pugnacious California-born surfer, described by the *Surfer's Journal* as "the greatest ocean paddler of the 20th century." In 1938 at age 24, during one of his many visits to Hawaii, Smith and fellow Californian Lorrin Harrison were among the first modern surfers to ride waves on the North Shore of Oahu. Two years later, Smith paddled his 14-foot, 90-pound hollow board from Oahu to Kauai—a distance of almost 100 miles—hallucinating late in the 30-hour journey that he was floating down Hollywood Boulevard. Smith paddled, it was said, to work off aggression. Perhaps he didn't paddle enough, as Malibu surfing pioneer Tom Blake said he personally knew six people who had their jaws broken by the well-muscled, frequently drunk, 6'4" Smith. In the late '70s, Smith left the beach for the California desert and was never seen again. *See also* paddleboarding.

Smith, Jorja and Jolene   Blond-haired identical twin sisters from San Clemente, California, who dominated the women's division of the National Scholastic Surfing Association in 1983 and 1984. Jolene won a world tour event in 1985; Jorja, between 1985 and 1987, was world-ranked fifth, fourth, and fifth, respectively, and in 1988 won the circuit's opening two events. "There's actually a lot of difference in our personalities," Jorja told *Surfing* magazine in 1989. "But the best way to tell us apart is that Jolene is a goofyfoot and I'm a regularfoot."

snake   *See* drop-in.

Snake River   Lunch Counter is the name of the stationary wave located on the Snake River near Jackson Hole, Wyoming; the break is formed as water pushes into a group of submerged boulders, rises up, and folds over. A surfer performs a "takeoff" at Lunch Counter by hiking 100 yards upriver, jumping into the 48-degree salt-free water, drifting backward, then paddling furiously against the current as he's pulled into the breaking wave. When the CFPS (cubic foot per second) flow hits 10,000, the wave is about three foot high and 20 foot wide, with an oscillating right-breaking shoulder. Cutbacks, top turns, and other maneuvers can be strung together for as long as the surfer's legs and wind hold out—usually about four minutes. At less that 8,000 CFPS, the Lunch Counter wave is too small to ride; a second set of boulders, located about 30 feet behind Lunch Counter, then offers a larger, steeper, more difficult wave. At 12,000 CFPS, Lunch Counter turns mushy; at 15,000 it's unridable. Lunch Counter is usually in top form for just two to six weeks a year, from May to August. The Snake River was first surfed in the mid-'80s, and by the early '90s it had been all but commandeered by river kayakers. *See also* tidal bore waves.

Snapback by California's Taylor Knox

snap, snapback   Cornering maneuver performed on or just under the crest; after angling up the wave face, the surfer turns quick and sharply, then aims back down to the trough. "Snap" is often used synonymously with "off-the-top," "roller-coaster," or "reentry," although the snap can also describe a situation in which the rider doesn't actually ricochet off the crest. "Snap" is an abbreviation of "snapback," which first came into usage in the mid-'70s to describe the signature move of Australian power surfer Ian Cairns. In the mid-'80s, *Surfing* magazine published four separate snap-related Surf Clinic columns: "The Backside Snap," "The Frontside Snap," "The Under-the-Lip Snap," and "The Backside Under-the-Lip Snap." Other variations include the "layback snap" and the "tailslide snap."

sneaker set   *See* clean-up set.

snowboarding   Hybrid sport that combines surfing, skateboarding, and skiing; performed for the most part at mountain resorts on a double-ended board ridden in a surfing-like stance. In 1965, Michigan chemical engineer Sherman Poppin invented the "Snurfer," a narrow plywood stand-up board with footstraps and a rope handle tied to the nose, as a snow toy for his daughter. A half million Snurfers sold the following season, and the boards remained popular for years to come. Throughout the '70s, sev-

eral different innovators—including skier Jake Burton in Vermont, skateboard manufacturers Chuck Barfoot and Tom Sims in California, and former East Coast surfer Dimitrije Milovich in Utah—independently produced early versions of the snowboard. (California surfing champion Mike Doyle tried and failed in the early '70s to market the "single ski," or "mono-board," a wide-beamed ski with side-by-side boot bindings.) By 1980, commercial snowboards were being made from hard wood coated in polyurethane, and featured a sturdy boot-binding system; Burton and Sims, in that order, were the two largest snowboard companies. Attendant media soon followed, with *International Snowboard Magazine* launched in 1984, followed by *TransWorld Snowboarding* and *Snowboarder*. The sport by that time was borrowing liberally the moves and the rebel attitude of skateboarding, and its popularity exploded over the next decade, particularly in the early and mid-'90s: in 1985 snowboarding was permitted at less than 10 percent of American ski resorts. By 1995 it was allowed virtually everywhere, with a majority of resorts providing snowboard-only "half-pipes": long, U-shaped inclines that riders use to launch a variety of skateboard-inspired aerial maneuvers. Hundreds of companies—including many crossovers from the surfing, skateboarding, and skiing industries—began manufacturing snowboard equipment and clothing lines, sponsoring top riders and events, and producing videos. The International Snowboard Federation was formed in 1989 (the USA Snowboard Association was also formed that year), and held its first world championship event in 1993; two snowboarding events—half-pipe and parallel slalom—were included in the 1998 Winter Olympics. (Frustrated international surfing competition boosters, in contrast, have been trying for 40 years to get their sport Olympic-certified.) American snowboarders won the gold, silver, and bronze medals in the 2002 Olympics.

A small percentage of snowboards are designed for downhill/speed riding; the vast majority are for half-pipe/trick riding. The average snowboard is about 150 to 160 centimeters long, side-cut and cambered, rounded and upturned at both ends, and made from the same polyethylene-composite materials as snow skis. Snowboards, like surfboards, have a nose and tail; unlike surfboards, they're designed to be ridden in either direction; backward riding is called "fakie." Riders wear padded boots, which attach to the snowboard by one of a few different boot-specific binding systems. A high-end snowboard setup—board, bindings, and boots—costs about $1,000.

Snowboarding feels more like surfing than any other sport, and tens of thousands of surfers are also proficient snowboarders, including Pipeline icon Gerry Lopez, big-wave riders Laird Hamilton, Brock Little, Darrick Doerner, and Mike Parsons, and aerial wizards Nathan and Christian Fletcher. The early '90s saw the introduction of combined two-day surfing/snowboarding events, such as the Op Wintersurf Pro in California and the Quiksilver Boardriders Pro in France, which included professionals from both sports. But a majority of rank-and-file snowboarders, along with many top sponsored pros, have little interest in contests, viewing the sport instead as a free-form activity; snowboarding's inclusion in the Olympics in 1998 was met by indifference and even scorn in most quarters. Snowboarding has moved toward the mainstream over the past few years, but to a large degree it remains a scruffy and rebellious alternative to skiing.

Soeda, Hiromisha   Pioneering Japanese professional surfer; winner of the Japanese Professional Surfing Association circuit in 1978, and world-ranked #30 in 1979. Soeda was born (1956) and raised in Hiratsuka, a coastal town located just to the southwest of Tokyo. He began surfing at age 10, and in 1974 won the juniors division of the All-Japan Surfing Championships. Soeda rode aggressively, using a low-slung stance, and was comfortable in hollow, hard-breaking waves. He was Japan's best-traveled surfer in the '70s and early '80s, making annual trips to Hawaii, visiting Indonesia and mainland America; he starred in 1984's *Asian Paradise,* the first Japanese-made surf film. He founded Soeda Surfboards Japan in 1979, the year after he won the national pro title.

soft racks   *See* surfboard racks.

soft surfboard   Safe, spongy boards used almost exclusively by beginning surfers. The Morey-Doyle soft surfboard was invented in 1976 by California surfer/designers Tom Morey and Mike Doyle, inspired by the flexible soft-skinned Morey Boogie, the original and wildly popular bodyboard introduced three years earlier. Five Morey-Doyle models were offered, ranging from five to nine feet. Like the Boogie, the soft surfboard's core was made of polyethylene, a flexible packing foam, with a second thinner, denser layer of polyethylene heat-bonded to the core's surface. Unlike the Boogie, the Morey-Doyle had a fin, and the board was stiffened with a quarter-inch longitudinal fiberglass stringer. Morey-Doyle made some fairly outrageous claims as to the soft board's performance capabilities, trying mistakenly to sell it to intermediate and even advanced surfers, as well as beginners. By the end of the decade, the Morey-Doyle—along with knockoffs such as BZ, Mason-Smith, and Bronzed Aussies—were being used almost exclusively as start-up boards, and as surf schools began opening by the dozens in the late '80s, it was all but mandatory for each school to assemble a fleet of soft boards.

The hard-soft combination board was introduced in 1980, vanished immediately, then reappeared in modified form when epoxy board-maker Surftech introduced the Softops line in 1997; a Softop board has a hard-bottomed epoxy layer, with a soft EVA (ethylene vinyl acetate) foam rubber layer on the deck and rails.

Solomon Islands   Equatorial Pacific Ocean island nation located directly southeast of Papua New Guinea, composed of 922 islands—the largest are rugged, heavily wooded, and mountainous; the smallest are tiny low-lying coral atolls—spread over 230,000 square miles of ocean. Most of the known surf breaks in the Solomons are found among the coral reefs of the country's Western Province, and require boat access. Waves here break in some of the world's warmest, clearest water. The best surf generally arrives between December and April, in response to south-moving cyclones and low-pressure systems in the Tasman Sea and the Coral Sea; the surf is usually small- to medium-sized, and fairly powerful. Skull Island, located near the western tip of New Georgia Island, is one of the Solomons' best breaks: a long, hypnotic right wall that finishes up in a beautiful lagoon. Surfing hazards include sea urchins, stonefish, and stingrays; malaria is also common. There is virtually no surf industry in the Solomon Islands, and widespread lawlessness and civil strife have plagued the country's major cities—especially the capital of Honiara—following a coup in June 2000.

soul arch   Upright, chest-out, back-bending surf pose, meant to denote mastery in a way that can be either subtle or arrogant, depending on the rider. A soul arch is generally performed while in trim across

Soul arch by Australia's Peter Townend

the wave face or during a frontside bottom turn. The expression "soul arch" originated in the early 1970s, and the move was made famous by 1976 world champion Peter Townend, who later confessed that he stole it from an iconic 1961 black-and-white photograph of California surfer Kemp Aaberg back-arching at Rincon.

soul surfing   Durable if overused expression generally used to describe the type of riding practiced by noncommercial, noncompetitive surfers; the soul surfer is often thought of as the "pure" surfer. Although Southern California surf guitarist Johnny Fisher wrote and recorded the instrumental "Soul Surfer" in 1963 (perhaps with the intention of drafting off the growing popularity of soul music), the origins of soul surfing are rooted in the late '60s, as the sport aligned itself with the counterculture. In "Blue Barefoot Soul," a 1968 *Petersen's Surfing* magazine article, writer Duke Boyd praises "the man upon his board who shuts out the world and its clamor," then encourages the surfer to "trip through the sunshines of time and eternity with bare feet and blue soul." Never defined by tenets or principles, soul surfing nonetheless came into its own in the mid- and late-'70s as the catchall opposition philosophy to professional surfing, which encompassed not only

prize-money competition, but much of the surf industry and surf media. Some went much further with the soul surfing concept than others. In Australia's small but celebrated "country soul" movement, dozens of Sydney-based surfers, including 1966 world champion Nat Young, took up residence in abandoned country farmhouses in the northeast corner of New South Wales, grew their own vegetables, made their own surfboards, and for two or three seasons rode uncrowded point surf. In California, soul surfing was in many places crossbred with territorial localism; surfers in a particular area banded together to discourage nonlocal surfers from visiting, by means of intimidation or violence. Eventually there developed what might be called the pragmatic soul surfer, exemplified by Wayne Lynch of Australia, Gerry Lopez of Hawaii, and California's Tom Curren; each had soul credentials of the highest order, but nonetheless remained involved with the surf industry, the surf media, and surfing competition. A dedicated surfing life, it turned out, required compromise; Lynch, Lopez, and Curren, like nearly everyone else, had mortgages to pay and families to raise, and the unfiltered back-to-nature version of soul surfing didn't provide enough. The phrase "soul surfing" had in fact lost much of its currency by the time *Surfer* magazine published "Soul Search" in 2000, with author Sam George first noting that "the perimeters of 'soul' in surfing have, for the past two generations, been stretched and shrunk and tugged like the rubber of an ill-fitting wetsuit," then closing with the notion that "we're all soul surfers; and so there's no such thing as soul surfing."

Australia's country soul period is beautifully captured in Alby Falzon's surf movie classic *Morning of the Earth.* Hollywood-produced soul surfers include the Kahuna, played by the hut-dwelling Cliff Robertson in 1959's *Gidget,* and Chandler, the bearded surf sage played by Gregory Harrison in 1987's *North Shore.* Dark-side soul surfers are found in Kem Nunn's California noir novels *Tapping the Source* and *The Dogs of Winter.*

soup   *See* whitewater.

South Africa   South Africa's kaleidoscopic 1,800-mile coastline is bordered to the east by the Indian Ocean and to the west by the South Atlantic Ocean, and is trimmed with first-rate surf breaks of every description. South Africa is also home to the oldest and best-established surf culture outside of America and Australia. The country can be divided into four main surfing regions: 1) The warm KwaZulu-Natal Coast in the northeast, anchored by the resort town of Durban, is home to a series of right-breaking reefs and points as well as dozens of beachbreaks; Durban's three piers (Bay of Plenty, North Beach, and New Pier) have long been the hub of South African surfing. 2) The rocky shark-patrolled East London area includes powerful Nahoon Reef. 3) The Port Elizabeth area, filled with cooler point- and reefbreaks, includes world-renowned Jeffreys Bay and Cape St. Francis. 4) The Cape Town area includes Dungeons, a terrifying big-wave break often compared to Maverick's in California.

South Africa's best surf comes from Atlantic-born storms that move east along the Roaring 40s region into the Indian Ocean. While the central and west coasts generally produce the country's biggest surf, waves on the southeast coast are usually smoother and better formed. South Africa has ridable waves all year, but prime surf season is from March through September. Tropical cyclones can also bring snappy, short-lived swells to the Durban area between January and March. Shallow reefs are a surfing hazard throughout South Africa, but sharks are the biggest worry; 1998 brought a record-breaking 15 attacks (one fatal) on South African swimmers and surfers.

Durbanites began riding homemade wooden bellyboards in the early 1920s, and Australian surfing champion Charles "Snow" McAlister gave Durban beachgoers a surfing demonstration in 1928, just as local surfers began making redwood boards for stand-up riding. But surfing didn't really catch on here until the late '30s, when surf lifesaving clubs began making 18-foot hollow "cigar-box" boards; even so, there were fewer than 100 surfers in the country when the South Beach Surfboard Riders Club, the first of its kind in South Africa, was chartered in 1948. Six years later, Cape Town surfer and abalone diver John Whitmore—often called the father of South African surfing—began to build foam-core surfboards and deliver them to Durban. When California moviemaker Bruce Brown flew into South Africa in late 1963 to shoot a South African sequence for an upcoming surf travel film, it was Whitmore who told him to look for waves in the Cape St. Francis area. *The Endless Summer,* Brown's movie, became a huge crossover hit, and helped put South African surfing on the map—thanks to the small but immaculate point waves Brown discovered and filmed at Cape St. Francis (known to this day as Bruce's Beauties). Surfers found that Cape St. Francis rarely showed the kind of form seen in *Endless Summer,* but they soon discovered Jeffreys Bay, another pointbreak, located just a few miles to the north. Jeffreys quickly gained an international reputation as one of the world's longest, fastest, best-shaped waves.

Safari Surfboards, South Africa's first surf shop, opened in Durban in 1963; the following year, Safari cofounder Max Wetteland represented South Africa in the debut World Surfing Championships, held in Sydney, Australia. In 1965, George Thomopolous of Durban won the first competition held in South Africa, while fellow Durbanite Anthony van der Heuvel made the semifinals of the World Surfing Championships (held in Peru); the South Africa Surfriders Association was formed (with Whitmore as chairman); and Harry Bold of Durban launched *South African Surfer* magazine. Robert McWade won the first South African Championships, held in 1966. The Durban 500 international pro contest (later renamed the Gunston 500) debuted in 1969 at the Bay of Plenty, and became a mainstay of the world pro circuit. (International pro events have also been held at Nahoon Reef, Jeffreys Bay, and Dungeons, among other South Africa breaks; the 1978 World Amateur Surfing Championships were held in East London.)

Port Elizabeth surfer Gavin Rudolph was the first South African surfer to win an international event overseas, taking first place in the 1971 Smirnoff Pro-Am at Sunset Beach, Hawaii. Cape Town power surfers Jonathan Paarman and Peers Pittard, along with Durbanite Mike Esposito, also proved themselves as world-class talents in the early '70s. Shaun Tomson of Durban then set out on a wildly successful pro career, winning the 1977 world title, starring in the era-defining *Free Ride* surf movie, and single-handedly reinventing the way surfers ride inside the tube. Michael Tomson, Shaun's cousin, was also a top pro of the mid-'70s, then moved to California to found Gotcha surfwear. Other influential South African surfers include Durban-raised Martin Potter, winner of the 1989 world title; four-time world champion Wendy Botha; '80s pro tour standouts Marc Price and Mike Burness; photographic free-surfer Frankie Oberholzer; competition organizers Basil Lomberg, Peter Burness, and Graham Stapelberg; pro surfer-turned-photographer Pierre Tostee; ace water photographer

Chris Van Lennep; and surfwear executive Paul Naude. Greg Emslie, Paul Canning, and Heather Clarke represented South Africa on the 2002 world pro tour; other top pros included Travis Logie, David Weare, and Simon Nicholson.

Shaun Tomson went on record in 1988 to say that he was "totally opposed to any political interference in sport," but South Africa's race-segregating apartheid policy brought surfing and politics together like nothing before or since. Visiting Hawaiian pro surfer Eddie Aikau, after arriving to compete in the 1972 Gunston 500, was barred from Durban's whites-only hotels and turned away from a whites-only beach; world champion surfers Tom Curren, Tom Carroll, and Martin Potter (who emigrated to Australia in 1985) took an anti-apartheid stand by refusing to compete in South Africa beginning in 1985; South African surfers often had difficulty entering antiapartheid countries during the '70s, '80s, and early '90s. By the mid-'90s, with apartheid dismantled, South Africa again took its place in the league of surfing nations, but racial volatility remained, and a devaluation of the national currency made it difficult for South African surfers to travel abroad. In 1999, however, Cape Town Rastafarians Cass Collier and Ian Armstrong won the team event in the Reef Big-Wave World Championships, held in Todos Santos, Mexico. Collier, half East Indian, had once been forcibly removed from a whites-only Cape Town beach.

As of 2003, there were roughly 50,000 surfers in South Africa, serviced by about 120 surf shops. The 1976-founded *Zigzag* was the country's most popular surfing magazine. Cape Town contest organizer Paul Botha inaugurated in 1986 the South Africa Surfing Series, a domestic pro tour; the United Surfing Council of South Africa was chartered in 1992 (renamed Surfing South Africa in 2002) to unify the country's disparate amateur surfing associations. A small number of South African surfing guidebooks have been published, including *Hitting the Lip: Surfing in South Africa* (1974), *Surfing in Southern Africa* (1989), and *Surfing in South Africa* (2001). The Timewarp Surfing Museum, located in Durban's Dairy Beach and the first museum of its kind in South Africa, opened in 1993. *See also* Cape St. Francis, Dungeons, Durban, Jeffreys Bay.

South Australia This rugged and somewhat isolated Australian state faces the chilly Southern Ocean, and is best known among surfers for its shark-patrolled reefbreaks to the west. South Australia's 900-mile coastline can be divided into five main areas: 1) The southeast coast, characterized by dry salt plains, pine forests, and dozens of broad, empty beachbreaks. 2) The Fleurieu Peninsula, including the mediocre but well-used beachbreak waves near the capital city of Adelaide, as well as the more consistent beaches and reefs of the south-facing Victor Harbour area. 3) The desolate Yorke Peninsula, featuring a half-dozen excellent spots, including a powerful left-breaking reef wave called Chinaman's, located on the southwest tip of the peninsula. 4) The cliff-lined Kangaroo Island, home to a few temperamental reefbreaks. 5) The Eyre Peninsula, a series of parched sand-and-rock-filled bays stretching west into the Nullarbor Desert, including the world-class reefs of the Cactus/Point Sinclair area, near Streaky Bay. South Australia generally receives its best waves from March to June, as storms from the Roaring 40s region generate surf while the coastal weather remains pleasant. Average daytime air temperatures on the coast range from the high 70s (summer) to the mid-50s (winter); water temperatures range from the low 70s to the mid-50s. Sharks are an ever-present hazard in South Australia; Cactus has been called the most shark-infested break in the country, and as of 2002 there had been nearly 50 attacks statewide, including a 48-hour period in September 2000 that saw two surfer fatalities.

Adelaide natives began riding waves on paddleboards in the 1930s, but surfing in South Australia didn't catch on until the late '50s, after members from local lifeguarding clubs came together to form the South Coast Surf Chasers and began looking for waves near Victor Harbour. Jay Bee Surfboards, the first shop of its kind in the state, opened in 1960 in Adelaide; the first state titles were held three years later. The waves at Cactus were explored by Victoria teenage surfing phenomenon Wayne Lynch and filmmaker John Witzig in 1968, while shooting footage for Witzig's new movie *Evolution*. South Australia hosted the Australian National Titles for the first time in 1975; the event returned in 1980, 1985, and 1991.

By 2003, South Australia was home to nearly 20 surf shops, most located in Adelaide, and roughly 15,000 surfers. The 1962-founded Surfing South Australia oversees about a dozen amateur and professional surf contests a year across the state. While the area receives a steady flow of good waves, it has yet to produce an internationally known surfer. The South Australian surf—mainly the Cactus area—has been featured in more than a dozen surf films and videos, including *Evolution* (1969), *Rolling Home* (1974), and *Storm Riders* (1982). South Australian surf breaks are detailed in *The Surfing and Sailboarding Guide to Australia* (1993), Mark Warren's *Atlas of Australian Surfing* (1998), *Surfing Australia* (1998), and *The World Stormrider Guide* (2001).

South Bay   *See* Los Angeles.

South Carolina   Surfing off the gently shoaling South Carolina coast, in keeping with the state's natural disposition, is for the most part loose, friendly, and slow-rolling. South Carolina generally gets its best and most consistent waves during the North Atlantic hurricane season in late summer and fall; midwinter and midspring can also produce surf. South Carolina summers are hot, humid, and filled with afternoon thunderstorms, and for the most part waveless. Because the state is fronted by a particularly wide and shallow apron of continental shelf—extending out more than 60 miles from shore in some places—South Carolina waves rarely gets over six feet. Low tide can further drain off whatever surf is running, and swells rarely last for more than two days. Most South Carolina surfers are travelers by necessity, making regular visits into neighboring North Carolina. The water temperature in South Carolina usually rises to 70 in May, at which point surfers may ride wetsuit-free for the next six or even seven months. In midwinter, the water temperature can drop to the upper 40s. The Washout at Folly Beach, directly south of Charleston, is by far South Carolina's best and most popular surf break. Folly Beach itself is eight miles long and studded with sandbar-producing jetties; the Washout sandbars in part are formed by the remnants of houses lost to hurricanes in decades past. Pawleys Island, to the north, the oldest beachfront in the country with vacation houses built as far back as the early 19th century, is also a popular surfing area. (Land-strike hurricanes provide the infrequent but jolting exception to the relaxed South Carolinian coastal experience: on September 21, 1989, Hurricane Hugo blew into Charleston with wind speeds up to 140 miles per hour, and did more than $7 billion in statewide damage. Portions of the older and funkier South Carolina beach scene were erased permanently, and clusters of million-dollar beachfront homes filled the void.)

Wooden paddleboards could be rented at Folly Beach as far back as the late 1930s, but surfing didn't really get started in South Carolina until California-born surfer and U.S. Air Force serviceman Rick Ficthman, while stationed in Charleston in 1963, introduced the sport to local Folly Beach teenagers. Corky's Surf Shop opened the following year, also in Folly Beach, while Ficthman formed the West Coast East Surf Club. McKevlin's Surf Shop (originally called Folly Surf Shop) opened in 1965, and was still in business as of 2003. The state's first surf contest took place in 1966 at Folly Pier: a South Carolina versus Georgia team match, won by South Carolina.

By 2003, there were a dozen surf shops in South Carolina, servicing approximately 8,000 surfers statewide. A short segment on Folly Beach appeared in the video *Surf NRG 2000*; in 1998, South Carolina Educational TV produced and aired a 30-minute documentary called *Beach Break: A History of Surfing in South Carolina*. The Eastern Surfing Association each year runs about 10 events in South Carolina.

South Padre Island   Barrier island located on the southeast tip of Texas; home to the state's best waves. Although the island is more than 100 miles long, surfers referring to "South Padre" mean a relatively small region near the resort town of Port Isabel, about 15 miles north of the U.S./Mexico border. Autumn hurricanes in the Gulf of Mexico tend to produce the area's best surf, and the most popular breaks—the Jetty, the Cove, Steamers, and Boca Chica—are clustered around a pair of half-mile-long harbor jetties at the south end of Port Isabel. The United States Surfing Championships were held on South Padre in 1975, 1979, 1983, and 1995. The South Padre Island visitors bureau touts the area "the hottest place to be for Spring Break, with 125,000 bikini-clad coeds"; it's also home to 45,000-acre national wildlife refuge. *See also* Texas.

spaghetti arms   Postsurfing condition brought on by too much paddling, in which the overexerted muscles in the back, shoulders, and arms become leaden and unresponsive. Usually won't prevent a surfer, once back on the beach, from gesturing expansively to describe a particularly good ride. Synonymous with "rubber-arms" or "noodle-arms."

Spain   Small but ridable waves occasionally roll ashore along the Spanish Mediterranean, and the arid southwest coast around Cádiz can produce good surf on occasion, but the heart of surfing in Spain is found on the 350-mile north-facing coastline known as El

Cantabrico, in the Bay of Biscay. On this coast, the best-known area is the Pais Vasco, near France, home to more than a dozen premium surf spots, including the long and cylindrical left-breaking rivermouth waves at Mundaka. Waves in this area of Spain are bigger than nearly anywhere else in the Bay of Biscay, due to a deep offshore trench. While the north coast of Spain has waves all year, prime surfing season begins in September and ends in December, as North Atlantic storms regularly provide waves, while air and water temperatures are still temperate. Spanish winters are often cold and stormy; spring surfing is hit or miss, and the pleasantly warm summers are generally waveless. Average daytime air temperatures along the northern Spanish coast range from the high 60s in summer to the high 40s in winter; water temperatures range from the high 60s to the low 50s. Aside from Mundaka, other top breaks along the north-facing coast include the big-wave rights at Roca Puta, the Mundaka-like Rodiles, and the snappy beachbreak tubes at Pantin. El Palmar, a tubing beachbreak, is one of the best waves in the Cádiz area. Surf hazards in Spain are for the most part limited to a few shallow rock reefs and pollution near the cities.

Bellyboarding was practiced in the Spanish Basque country as far back as the 1940s, but stand-up surfing wasn't introduced here until the late '50s, when a small number of boards were imported from Biarritz, France; Cantabrian surfer Jesus Fiochi began exploring the waters of the Basque coast in earnest beginning in 1962. By the end of the decade, native surfer José Merodio began shaping the first surfboards in Spain, and by the mid-'70s there were several hundred Spanish surfers, mainly in the Basque country. Foreign surfers traveling through Europe generally steered clear of Spain until Fascist-supported dictator General Francisco Franco died in 1975. By that time, photos of the incredible Mundaka lineup had been published in both the American and Australian surf press, and the Spanish Basque country soon became a favorite stop for virtually all European surf tourists. The Spanish surf industry also got started in earnest, with the first Pukas Surfboards retail outlet opening in 1977 in Zarautz; Pukas remains the biggest outfit in the still-growing Spanish surf industry. The first Spanish National Surfing Championships were held in Zarautz in 1968. World pro tour events have been held in Spain since 1988, first at Zarautz and other area beachbreaks, then at Mundaka, beginning in 1999.

By 2003, there were roughly 50 Spanish surf shops and about 8,000 stand-up surfers, plus 7,000 bodyboarders. The 2002-founded Basque Country Surfing Federation has 1,300 members and stages over a dozen amateur events annually. There are surf schools in Zarautz and San Sebastián. *Tres 60,* Spain's best-known surf magazine, was founded in 1987. Other Spanish surf magazines include *Surf Time* and *Surfer Rule.* Young Spanish surfers ruled the 2002 Quiksilver World Grommet Titles, held in Sydney, Australia, with regularfooter Gony Zubizarreta of Zarautz placing first, while friend and neighbor Hodey Collazo finished runner-up. Environmental catastrophe was visited upon Spain's entire north- and west-facing coastlines in late 2002, as the tanker *Prestige* sank off Cabo de Fisterra, spilling more than 50,000 tons of heavy fuel oil. By early 2003, beaches from Portugal to southwest France were closed, as the oil slicked fanned out. The Spanish surf is detailed in *The Stormrider Guide Europe* (1998). *See also* Mundaka.

speed surfing   A wave-riding concept from the late 1960s, more talked about than practiced, in which the surfer crouched while keeping the legs nearly locked together, and essentially rode the wave as if it were a downhill ski run, with long, fast, gradual turns. Speed surfing was developed by three-time Makaha International winner Joey Cabell of Hawaii, a competitive downhill skier in the early and mid-'60s. During the first few months of the shortboard revolution, Cabell returned to the beach and applied his ski techniques to the newly streamlined "pocket rocket" surfboards. His rank as a surf world guru helped win converts. "Cabell showed me how to use the ski stance," California surfer Dru Harrison said in 1969, "and it put me onto the most righteous surf trip of my life." But waves aren't mountains, and most top surfers understandably couldn't resist doing the big, sharp, flashy turns that were anathema to the speed surfing method; Cabell's technique was passé by 1971.

Spencer, Ted   Dynamic bowlegged regularfooter from Sydney, Australia; New South Wales state champion in 1968 and 1969, when he also won back-to-back Bells Beach events. In the early phase of the shortboard revolution, Spencer and his stubby 5′6″ Shane Surfboards White Kite model—a top seller in Australia—pushed the limits of small-wave high-performance surfing with more vigor than anyone, save fellow Australian Wayne Lynch. The stocky, dark-haired Spencer was featured in nearly a half-dozen Australian-produced surf movies, including *Hot Generation* (1968), *Evolution* (1969), and *The Innermost Limits of Pure Fun* (1970). He became a dedicated follower of Swami Bhaktivedanta by 1970, and in a 1974 *Tracks* magazine interview he said, "When I surf, I dance for Krishna."

Spencer, Yancy Energetic regularfoot surfer and surf shop owner from Pensacola, Florida; winner of the East Coast Pro in 1972, and founder of Innerlight Surf Shop; sometimes referred to as the "godfather of Gulf Coast surfing." Spencer was born (1950) in Roanoke, Virginia, moved with his family at age two to Pensacola, and began surfing at 14. Two years later he won the juniors division of the Florida Gulf Coast Championships. Greg Noll Surfboards in California produced the Yancy Spencer signature model in 1970, making Spencer the first and only Gulf Coast surfer to have his own model; two years later the cherubic Floridian with the blond curls went undefeated on his way to a $1,000 first-place finish in the East Coast Pro, the first professional surf meet held in the Atlantic Ocean, besting a tough field of American heavyweights including David Nuuhiwa, Mike Tabeling, Dale Dobson, and Jeff Crawford. Spencer's wave-riding form, as reported by surf journalist David Sledge, was "cerebral, precise, delicate, [and] smooth." The line between professional and amateur was all but nonexistent at the time and Spencer finished runner-up in the 1975 United States Surfing Championships, an amateur event.

Spencer opened the first Innerlight Surf Shop in 1972, in the town of Gulf Breeze, near Pensacola; a second Innerlight outlet opened in Pensacola three years later; a third shop opened in Fort Walton Beach in 1981. More than a half-dozen Innerlight outlets have since opened and closed, but as of early 2003 just the original three remained, along with a fourth in Navarro, Florida. Spencer's born-again Christianity was a big part of Innerlight's marketing throughout the 1970s; one ad showed a portrait of him with a boldface tag line reading, "Whoever Imagined That I Would Be a Surfing Preacher!?!"

Spencer appeared in a small number of surf movies, including *The Natural Art* (1969); from 1972 to 1981 he authored a half-dozen articles for *Surfer* magazine, including a 1979 editorial on the importance of good style in surfing. "Doing a maneuver with style," he wrote, "is doing it the right way and

not the easy way, and is the difference between mediocrity and greatness." He continued to compete as an amateur: in 1986 he won the senior men's division of the United States Surfing Championships, and in 1987 he finished runner-up in both the senior men's and the longboard divisions. Spencer is married and has three children; his two sons, Yancy IV and Sterling, are both highly regarded East Coast surfers. Yancy Spencer was inducted in 1996 into the East Coast Surf Legends Hall of Fame. *See also* religion and surfing.

Spicoli, Jeff *See* Fast Times at Ridgemont High.

spinner Longboarding hotdog maneuver during which the surfer, without altering the course of his board, quickly pirouettes in a full circle; distinct from the 360, in which surfer and board both move in a circle. The spinner is probably one of the original trick moves, as it was easily performed on the long, blunt, heavy wooden boards used in the early 20th century. A 1914 photograph shows California surfing pioneer George Freeth riding backward at Redondo Beach, perhaps halfway through a spinner. *See also* hotdogging.

spinout Type of wipeout in which the tail section of the board loses traction with the wave face and quickly spin sideways. A spinout generally happens during a turn, but can also occur if a rider, while trimming, hits an abruptly steep section of wave. Spinouts are for the most part caused by riding a board too small for the conditions; by overpowering a turn or turning too quickly; or by turning through ocean-surface bump or "chop." The spinout can be dangerous, particularly in big waves, because it's almost always unexpected and therefore uncontrollable. *See also* wipeout.

spiral vee *See* vee.

spit, spitter Compressed and aerated water that blasts horizontally out from the mouth of a tubing wave. As the ceiling and walls of the wave's interior collapse, usually about 10 feet back from the curl line, a bellows effect is created and for two or three seconds air and water are funneled out of the tube opening. If a surf break features spitting waves with good form, it's generally open to deep tuberiding. Pipeline and Teahupoo, two of the world's best-known tuberiding

Spitter at Teahupoo, Tahiti

breaks, both notoriously powerful, spit regularly and prodigiously. The amount of spit isn't so much a function of the span and breadth of the tube, but rather a measure of a wave's thickness and power. A thin, circular tube may produce a gentle puff of spit, while the spit from a broad-based, solid-lipped tube can belch out with enough force to temporarily blind the tube-riding surfer, sting his back, neck, and legs, and perhaps even lift him off the surface of the wave. A wave can spit more than once, and a long, hollow point wave—like Kirra or Jeffreys Bay—might spit three or four times from start to finish. The phrase "spitting peak" is used to describe a near-symmetrical wave that tubes, tapers, and spits in both directions. *See also* tube.

sponge   Derogatory term for a bodyboard, lampooning the board's soft, safe, pliable form. Permutations include "sponger" and "spongehead" (bodyboarder) and "sponging" (bodyboarding). Board-using surfers worldwide traditionally have looked down on bodyboarding; surf magazines have reflected this attitude, usually with gentle humor—magazine-published expressions for the bodyboard include "lid" and "speed-bump"—but occasionally with real derision: "Fuckin' Spongers!" was the title of a 1998 *Eastern Surf Magazine* feature story. *See also* bodyboarding.

spoon kneeboard   Flexible, thin-hulled, single-fin kneeboard design invented in 1965 by George Greenough of Santa Barbara, California. Velo, Greenough's breakthrough spoon board, was 4′10″ long, just over 20 inches wide, and weighed six pounds; a

ridge of fiberglass-covered polyurethane foam was laid around the board's nose and rails, but the midsection and tail areas were built solely from layered fiberglass, and were semitransparent. A radical departure from the fairly sluggish 10-foot stand-up surfboards in use at the time, Velo was designed to carve up and down the wave face and fit inside the tube; Greenough's dynamic performances on Velo and subsequent spoon boards led directly to the 1967-launched shortboard revolution. By the early '70s, when stand-up surfers and kneeboarders alike were finally able to ride as Greenough had done 10 years earlier, the spoon kneeboard—nearly impossible to paddle due to its lack of buoyancy—had been replaced by wider, thicker, higher-floating, multifinned kneeboard designs. *See also* George Greenough, kneeboarding.

spoon nose   A wide, round, upturned longboard nose, designed primarily to keep the front of the board from pearling (digging into the water). California board designer Bob Simmons is often credited with inventing the spoon nose, not long after World War II. Surfboard-maker Renolds Yater of Santa Barbara introduced a popular spoon nose model in 1964; in the Vietnam War epic *Apocalypse Now,* Robert Duvall, playing the surf-mad Colonel Kilgore, instructs a soldier to "bring me my Yater Spoon! The 8′6″!", before incinerating a North Vietnamese coastal stronghold in order to score a few waves.

Spreckels, Anthony "Bunker"   High-born surfing hedonist of the late 1960s and early '70s; heir to the Spreckels Sugar fortune and stepson to Hollywood actor Clark Gable; contributor to the shortboard revolution. Spreckels was five when his mother married Gable in 1955; he learned to surf while spending time in Waikiki, not long after Gable's death in 1960. An uncontrollable teenager, Spreckels was temporarily cut off from the family money, but soon came into a multimillion-dollar inheritance, and in the early '70s was said to own more surfboards than anyone in the world. Spreckels is primarily remembered as mysterious, decadent, and sometimes violent; surf magazines published photos of him standing shirtless with a rifle over a just-killed antelope, being chauffeured while wearing a mink-lined overcoat, and inserting a hypodermic needle into his arm. He made an important surfboard design contribution in 1969 by helping invent the "down" rail, a feature that remains all but universal on short surfboards. Spreckels was also one of the first to ride the dangerous waves at Backdoor Pipeline in Hawaii. He died of a drug overdose in 1976, at age 27. A moody soft-lit portrait of Spreckels was used on the cover of *Masters of Surf Photography: Art Brewer,* a 2002-published photo book. *See also* tucked-under rail.

springsuit   A single-piece, medium-protection wetsuit design, covering the surfer's trunk, chest, and thighs, available in either a long- or short-sleeve cut; usually made from two-millimeter neoprene and featuring a back zipper. The springsuit was introduced in the early 1970s, and quickly replaced the "beavertail" wetsuit jacket as the top choice for cool-but-not-cold water conditions. *See also* wetsuit.

squaretail   Surfboard tail design in which the end of the board is squared off. Longboards often feature a squaretail. It was fairly common on shortboards in the late 1960s and early '70s, as it was believed to open up the board to quicker pivoting; the swallowtail and the roundtail or roundpin tail soon made the squaretail obsolete, although it made a return of sorts in 1981, with the introduction of the soft-cornered squashtail. *See also* pintail, roundtail, squashtail, swallowtail.

squashtail   Type of surfboard tail outline; essentially a squaretail with rounded corners. The squashtail became popular in the early '80s as the tail of choice for the newly introduced tri-fin surfboard, and remains a favorite tail design for high-performance shortboards. The expression "squashtail" is said to have originated after a just-shaped roundpin-tail surfboard blank was dropped tail first to the ground, squashed, then fiberglassed. *See also* pintail, roundtail, squaretail, swallowtail.

Sri Lanka   Tear-shaped tropical island nation in the Indian Ocean, about 270 miles long and 140 miles wide, located 20 miles off the southeast coast of India; formerly known as Ceylon. California's Rusty Miller, the 1965 United States Surfing Association champion, visited Sri Lanka in 1964, rode some "clear, glassy three-foot waves" near the southwest town of Kalutara, and described the setting as "a true Shangri-La for surfers." The American surf audience got its first look at Sri Lanka in a 1968 *Petersen's Surfing* magazine article titled "India and Ceylon's For-

bidden Waters." Although Sri Lanka has been riven by civil war since 1983, surfing has nonetheless become increasingly popular. A 1993 issue of the *Surf Report* charted 19 surf breaks in the southern part of the country (much of the rest of Sri Lanka's 1,000-mile coastline is unsuitable for surfing), and notes the "warm water, cheap accommodations, and a laid-back lifestyle." Arugam Bay and Hikkaduwa are Sri Lanka's two most popular surfing spots: Arugam, a beachbreak in the southeast, generally has the best surf during the May-to-October monsoon season; Hikkaduwa, a pointbreak in the southwest adjacent to a holiday town, is best from November to April. Hikkaduwa is also the center of Sri Lanka's budding surf industry, which includes a surf shop and surf tour company. In 2001, Hikkaduwa was the location for the first annual Sri Lanka Airlines Cup, an international pro contest—an Israeli won the event; the remaining finalists were from Japan, the Maldives, and Sri Lanka. As of 2003, there were two surf shops and about 150 native surfers in Sri Lanka.

St. Leu   *See* Réunion Island.

stall   Catchall term for any kind of board-slowing maneuver. The stall is generally used to keep the rider in the steep section of the wave, adjacent to the curl. Longboarders often use a kick-stall, a kind of surfing wheelie, just prior to a noseride; shortboarders often use an arm-stall (digging the rear arm into the wave face as a break), a delayed-turn stall (a slower, wide-arced bottom turn), or a butt-stall (dragging the

Tube stall by Australia's Terry Richardson

posterior in the wave face) as a way of setting up a tuberide; any of these moves can be described as a "tube stall." Early versions of the stall were performed in the late 1940s, after the development of the chip—the lighter, easier-turning board design that replaced the unwieldy prewar planks and "cigar-box" boards. To "stall out" means the surfer has slowed to the point that the wave passes him by altogether.

stance   Primarily refers to the basic position of a surfer's feet while riding: either a left-foot-forward regularfoot stance or right-foot-forward goofyfoot stance. Switchfoot means the surfer can ride either way. A more detailed stance reading takes into account the arrangement of feet and legs, and to a lesser degree the rest of the body; a rider's stance can be described as narrow, wide, knock-kneed, straight up, or stinkbug. *See also* goofyfoot, regularfoot, switchfoot.

stand-up tube   Advanced maneuver during which the surfer comes up from a crouch to stand at full height while inside the tube; the ultimate form of tuberiding. Hawaii's Gerry Lopez is often credited with inventing the stand-up tube at Pipeline in the early 1970s.

standing island pullout   *See* island pullout.

Stapelberg, Graham   Soft-spoken and reliable competition judge and world tour organizer from Durban, South Africa; Association of Surfing Professionals (ASP) executive director from 1995 to 1998. Stapelberg was born (1962) and raised in Durban, began surfing at age 13, received a bachelor of commerce degree from the University of Natal in 1983, and four years later became a CPA. He was hired as a full-time world pro tour judge in 1987 (later assuming as well the title of financial controller), and in 1995 was promoted to executive director. During his four years as ASP chief, Stapelberg helped bring world tour competition to American cable-sports giant ESPN and to other TV outlets around the world. He was also instrumental in signing watchmaker G-Shock as a world tour underwriter, and in founding popular new "prime wave" contests at Jeffreys Bay in South Africa and Grajagan in Indonesia. Stapelberg has lived in Orange County, California, since 1988; he's married and has two children, and as of 2003 was working as vice-president of marketing for surfwear giant Billabong USA. *See also* Association of Surfing Professionals.

Starr, Rusty   Regularfoot surfer from Hawaii; winner of the juniors division of the 1969 Hawaii State Championships. The 17-year-old was described in a *Surfing* magazine profile as "a Zorro and a flash, completely free-flowing, always radical." The article concluded by saying that "Rusty Starr is too dedicated to have any other future direction than up and ahead . . . and he has his whole life ahead of him." The following year Starr died of a drug overdose, and his passing—along with that of close friend Tommy Winkler, another teenage Hawaiian surfing ace—came to symbolize the small epidemic of drug-related casualties that thinned the surfing ranks in America and Australia from the late 1960s to the mid-'70s. *See also* drugs and surfing.

Steamer Lane   Multifaceted reefbreak located in Santa Cruz, California; the epicenter of Santa Cruz surfing since the 1940s. Steamer Lane, named for the steam-powered boats that motored past in the 1930s on their way to the nearby Santa Cruz wharf, is made up of four separate but overlapping breaks: 1) The Point, a shifty right-breaking wave located to the north, is best from four to six foot, favors a south or southwest swell, and often produces hair-raising take-offs as the wave explodes off a jutting rock point. 2) The Slot, another right, is located just a few dozen yards south of the Point, and breaks best on west or northwest swells. While the Point and the Slot sometimes offer tube sections, both are for the most part thick-based waves that invite high-performance maneuvers. 3) The eye-catching Middle Peak breaks left and right, with incoming waves humping up across a series of reefs projecting out more than a mile to sea. Middle Peak breaks dependably on north and northwest swells, but is best on a southwest. 4) Indicator, in the lee of Middle Peak, is best on a five- to eight-foot north or northwest swell, can produce 300-yard-long rides, and spills into an easy-breaking wave known as Cowells. The waterfront cliffs that make Steamer Lane perhaps the world's most spectator-friendly surf break would regularly, in the pre-surf-leash era, devour lost surfboards. The surf leash was in fact invented in 1970 by local surfers Roger Adams and Pat O'Neill—son of wetsuit magnate Jack O'Neill—more or less in direct response to the high material cost of riding Steamer Lane. All Steamer Lane breaks are protected from the brutal northwest winds that shut down virtually every surf break north of Santa Cruz in spring. Summer brings long periods of small to nonexistent surf; water temperature ranges from the upper 40s to the mid-60s.

While members of the 1938-formed Santa Cruz Surfing Club may have strayed up the point toward Steamer Lane on occasion (native Lloyd Ragon rode there as far back as 1937), they usually stayed at Cowells, and the Lane wasn't regularly surfed until after World War II. First-generation Middle Peak surfers included Peter Cole, Rod Lundquist, Fred Van Dyke, Bob Teitsworth, and Carl Vesper. In the '50s and '60s, Steamer Lane was presented in the surf media as one of California's gnarliest breaks, not only featuring big waves, as *Surfer* magazine wrote in 1961, but "the coldest water available, giant bull kelp to bring your ride to a screaming halt, an occasional killer whale, a few sharks, and several miscellaneous forms of sea life to scare the pants off you." Steamer Lane has been known for decades as one of the sport's most crowded breaks—particularly since the advent of the surf leash—and today up to 150 longboarders, shortboarders, bodyboarders, and kayakers will be out at the same time during a good swell.

While Steamer Lane produced dozens of talented surfers in the '60s and '70s, including Roger Adams, Joey Thomas, Robert Waldemar, Kevin Reed, and Vince Collier, none had any real impact on the national or international surf scene (aerial progenitor Reed excepted) until soft-spoken Richard Schmidt began a steady climb in the early '80s that would eventually land him in the elite rank of big-wave riders. By the end of the '90s, a group of punkish Lane regulars—including Darryl "Flea" Virostko, Shawn Barron, Jason Collins, and Ken Collins—were known to surfers worldwide as first-rate aerialists or big-wave riders, or both.

Steamer Lane was the site of the $700 Santa Cruz Pro-Am in 1967, the first shortboard-era pro contest; from 1988 to 1990 it hosted the world pro tour O'Neill Coldwater Classic. Hundreds of other amateur and pro events have been held at the Lane over the decades. In 1986, the Santa Cruz Surfing Museum opened in the Mark Abbott Memorial Lighthouse, located just to the east of the Point. Steamer Lane has been featured in more than 40 surf movies and videos, including *Barefoot Adventure* (1960), *The Endless Summer* (1966), *Totally Committed* (1984), *Players* (1995), and *The Kill 6* (2002). "Steamer Lane" was the name of Tab Hunter's character in Columbia Pictures' 1964 movie *Ride the Wild Surf. See also* Santa Cruz.

Stecyk, Craig   Habitually cryptic artist, photographer, and writer from Santa Monica, California; longtime contributor to *Surfer* and the *Surfer's Journal* magazines; architect of the punkish and still-echoing mid-1970s Dogtown skateboarding scene. Stecyk was born (1950) and raised in Santa Monica, and was 26 when *Surfer* published his 1976 article "The Curse of the Chumash," his best and best-known article, which described—in dated, separated, nonlinear paragraphs—the history of Malibu surfing and beach culture. Stecyk's deadpan prose was alternately lyrical and obfuscating. His art installations include 1983's *Road Rash,* for which Stecyk scraped dead animals from Pacific Coast Highway, had them bronzed, then returned and glued them back to their original positions on the asphalt; and *Papa Moana,* his 1989 walk-through exhibit at a Laguna Beach Museum of Art annex, featuring mostly Hawaiian objects and images, and described in a catty *Surfer* review as being "little more than window dressing . . . [and] about as significant as Banana Republic's African safari outfitting rooms." Stecyk wrote the foreword for *1936–1942: San Onofre to Point Dume,* a photo book featuring the work of Don James; he was also cowriter and production designer for *Dogtown and Z-Boys,* a skateboarding documentary narrated by Sean Penn that won the Audience and Best Director awards at the 2001 Sundance Film Festival. Stecyk helped curate *Surf Culture: The Art History of Surfing,* a 2002 exhibit at the Laguna Art Museum in Laguna Beach, California. He has published more than a dozen articles under the pseudonyms Carlos Izan and John Smythe.

Stedman, Shane   Extroverted and industrious Australian surfboard manufacturer; founder of Shane Surfboards, the nation's top-selling board-maker in the early '70s. Stedman grew up in rural Crescent Head, New South Wales, received an industrial engineering degree from the University of New South Wales, and began making surfboards commercially in 1965 at age 22. "But my first boards were so rough," he later recalled, "that I used to wax them straightaway and advertise them as second-hand." Just five years later, Stedman had four surfboard factories— three in New South Wales and one in Queensland— and was beginning to advertise his immensely talented pool of shapers and surfers as the Shane Gang. Ted Spencer, Russell Hughes, Michael Peterson, Terry Fitzgerald, Butch Cooney, Judy Trim, and dozens of other top '70s-era Australian surfers worked for, or were sponsored by, Shane Surfboards. Spencer's stubby White Kite signature board, introduced in 1969, remains the best-selling model ever produced in Australia. Tri-fin innovator Simon Anderson also began his shaping career with Stedman. A separate line of mass-produced Shane Surfboard "popouts," designed for beginners and offered at discount rates in sporting goods and department stores, caused Stedman to fall out of favor with Australia's surfing tastemakers in the early '70s. But he remained with the surfing public, doing radio surf reports in Sydney for nearly 20 years, beginning in 1975. Luke Stedman, Shane's son, was a minor-league Australian pro surfer in the late '90s. *See also* popout board.

Steele, Taylor   Reticent and industrious surf video producer/distributor from Solana Beach, California; creator of the genre-changing *Momentum* in 1992, and by far the best-selling surf video entrepreneur of the '90s and '00s. "Basically, we don't know what we like," young pro surfer Kalani Robb said in 1998, when asked to comment on the popularity of Steele's videos. "Taylor knows what we like, and puts it in the video, and goes, Hey, this is cool. He *makes* it cool." Steele was born (1972) and raised in north San Diego County, and began stand-up surfing at age 12, one year after his surfer parents bought him a video camera. He received a C in a video production class during his junior year of high school, but in a similar class the following year he made *Seaside and Beyond,* starring classmate and future world title contender Rob Machado, and got an A. In 1991, a few months after graduation, Machado introduced Steele to Kelly Slater, Shane Dorian, Ross Williams, and a number of other teenage surfers who would soon collectively be known as the New School. Steele filmed them in Hawaii, California, and Mexico, edited the footage into brief segments, and scored the footage with fast, raucous songs from his favorite neopunk bands, including Bad Religion, Pennywise, and Sprung Monkey. *Momentum* cost about $5,000, and had no plot, narration, slow-motion photography, or water photography. Australian surf journalist Tim Baker described it as a "loud, no-frills production," while the *Surfer's Journal* called it "a 40-minute shot of adrenaline," and *Momentum* did in fact make other releases from that year seem slow and stodgy. Steele sold about 15,000 copies of his movie; few video titles, up to that time, had sold more than 5,000 copies.

Steele produced a long string of successful if formulaic videos, including *Focus* (1994), *Good Times*

(1996), *Drifting* (1997), *All for One* (1997), *The Show* (1998; winner of *Surfer* magazine's Video of the Year), *Loose Change* (2000), *Hit and Run* (2000; the first independent surfing DVD), and *Momentum: Under the Influence* (2001). Steele's videos became a measuring stick for professional surfers. "If you don't rate a segment in a Taylor Steele flick," *Surfer* magazine noted, "there's not much to talk about." Video-makers throughout the '90s meanwhile copied his method, and flooded the market with similar rough, harddriving product. Steele also proved an adept businessman, setting up a production company (Poor Specimen) and a distribution company (Steelehouse), and overseeing more than two dozen other video projects, including *Factory Seconds* (1995), *Reef@Todos* (1998), and *Arc* (2002). He was also a cofounder in 1996 for On a Mission, a surf accessories line. In something of a stylistic departure, Steele worked with Chris Malloy and Jack Johnson to make the fluid and easygoing *Shelter* (2001).

Steele was profiled in *50 Years of Surfing on Film* (1997), an Outdoor Life Network cable TV series. His music video for Unwritten Law's "Teenage Suicide" was nominated for Billboard's Alternative Music Video of the Year in 1999. By 2001, Poor Specimen had seven full-time employees and a 20-title backlog, and Steele was cited in an issue of *Australia's Surfing Life* magazine as one of "Ten Surfing Millionaires"; the following year *Surfer* magazine named him as one of the "25 Most Powerful People in Surfing." *Hallowed Ground,* Steele's skateboard video, was named as the 2002 EXPN Sports Video of the Year. Steele is unmarried, and divides his time between Solana Beach, Los Angeles, and Byron Bay, Australia. *See also Momentum,* surf video.

stepdeck   Longboard design developed in the mid-1960s in which approximately 40 percent of the volume on the front third of the board is planed off during the shaping process, with the idea that the thinner forward section allows the board to ride "shorter" than its actual size. The step itself is cut in a V shape along the deck, rather than longitudinally, with the point aiming toward the nose to prevent the board from breaking in half on the demarcation line. Popular first-generation stepdeck boards included the David Nuuhiwa Lightweight by Bing Surfboards and Mickey Dora's Da Cat model by Greg Noll Surfboards.

Stewart, Bill   Mustachioed surfer/artist/boardmaker from San Clemente, California; an early backer of the longboard resurrection, and owner of Stewart Surfboards. Stewart was born (1951) in Bowling Green, Kentucky, grew up in Hollywood, Florida, began surfing in 1963 and shaping boards in 1967. He moved to Southern California in 1971, worked for Hobie, Rick James, and South Shore, and opened Stewart Surfboards in 1979 in Laguna Beach. When Stewart moved his business to San Clemente, his boards were best known for their extravagant Stewart-applied airbrush designs; in 1990 CNN commemorated the end of the Cold War by presenting Soviet leader Mikhail Gorbachev with a Stewart surfboard decorated with airbrushed Soviet and American flags. In 1984, Stewart developed the Hydro Hull, a double-concave bottom design he used on longboards and shortboards. An Office Depot television ad, with close-up water shots of Stewart riding at San Onofre, aired nationally during *60 Minutes* and the 1994 NFL playoffs.

Stewart, Mike   Friendly and utterly dominant bodyboarder and bodysurfer from Kailua-Kona, on the Big Island of Hawaii; nine-time bodyboarding world champion (1983, 1985, 1987–92, 1995). "Stewart has transcended the bodyboarding genre," sports journalist Bruce Jenkins wrote in 1991, after acknowledging that bodyboarding in general is often viewed as a lesser version of surfing. "His performances have established him as one of the best surfers in the world, period." Stewart was born (1963) in Honolulu, raised in nearby Nuuanu, started bodysurfing at age four and bodyboarding regularly at 13. He moved with mother to the Big Island in 1976, not far from the home of Morey Boogie inventor and expatriate California surfer Tom Morey, who became the wiry blond teenager's father figure and part-time employer. Often riding alone in the late '70s and early '80s, Stewart developed a progressive new set of maneuvers, including the aerial 360. Many of the top bodyboards at the time used a half-standing drop-knee stance; Stewart remained prone, continued to string together ever-more complex moves, and learned how to ride deeper inside the tube than anybody in the world.

Stewart attended the University of Southern California for two years in the early '80s, dropped out, became one of bodyboarding's original professionals, and by the early '90s was earning more than $100,000 a year in prize money and sponsorship retainers. Easygoing in most circumstances, Stewart nonetheless earned a reputation as a ruthless and cunning

competitor. In 1987, he became the first and only bodyboarder to receive a full-length *Surfer* magazine profile; the magazine followed up in 1991 with an article titled "Is Mike Stewart the Best Surfer in the World?" Most *Surfer* readers agreed that Stewart's performances were astounding. But some, speaking for the tens of thousands who regard the easy-to-learn sport of bodyboarding as a crowd-making pestilence on surfing, dismissed him as a "spongerider" or "speedbump." Meanwhile Stewart-invented maneuvers such as aerial flips and barrel rolls were inspirational to stand-up New School surfers like Kelly Slater, a six-time world champion in the '90s.

Stewart and fellow Hawaiian bodyboarder Ben Severson are credited as the first to ride bigger surf at Tahiti's Teahupoo in 1986; in the early '90s, Stewart was the first bodyboarder to ride the 20-foot-plus waves on the outer reefs of Oahu's North Shore; in 1993 he became the first bodyboarder to ride Jaws on Maui. Stewart spent seven days following a big summer swell in mid-1996 as it moved northward, riding first in Tahiti, then on to Hawaii, Southern California, and central California, finally ending up in Alaska. Stewart also took up competitive bodysurfing, and was just as dominant as he was in bodyboarding; he won the prestigious Bodysurfing Classic at Pipeline eight times between 1991 and 2002. Stewart has appeared in nearly two dozen surf movies and videos, including *Shock Waves* (1987), *No Exit* (1992), *Endless Summer II* (1994), and *Primal Surf* (2000). He's married and has one child. *See also* bodyboarding, bodysurfing.

stinger   Small-wave surfboard design, invented in 1974 by Hawaiian surfer Ben Aipa, whose main feature was a bifurcated outline: two-thirds of the way from the nose, the rails abruptly cut in about one inch toward the board's center strip, then continued down to the tail. The stinger was a hybrid, grafting the narrow tail section of a big-wave gun onto the wider hips and nose of a small-wave hotdog board. A narrow-base single fin, placed further up from the tail than conventional single-fin boards, was another stinger design component, as were the beveled (or "chine") rails along the front section. *Surfing* magazine claimed "the stinger's theory and basic template are patterned after the hydrofoil boat," but Aipa later admitted he invented it after accidentally dropping a Masonite template onto the rail of a just-shaped board, which he then salvaged by narrowing the tail outline. (California board designer Dale Velzy had twice before introduced the split-outline board, first with the "Bump" in 1956, then with the Jacobs Surfboards "422" model in 1965; neither caught on.) By luck or design, Aipa's new board was in fact quicker turning than conventional boards then on the market, and his amazing Hawaiian test pilots—Larry Bertlemann, Dane Kealoha, Mark Liddell, and Buttons Kaluhiokalani—helped fuel the stinger's burst of popularity in the mid-'70s. Its decline, however, was just as fast, as the twin-fin became the hot small-wave design in 1977. *See also* Ben Aipa.

stinkbug stance   Crouched and splay-limbed surfing posture, stable but ugly, often used by beginners. By strict definition, the stinkbug stance should also include a raised butt, in imitation of the eponymous cloud-spraying insect.

stoke   Enduring surf slang expression meaning excited, pleased, happy, thrilled. "Stoke" is an English adaptation of the 17th-century Dutch word *stok,* used to describe the rearrangement of logs in a fireplace in order to bring up the heat. California surfers began using the word in the early or mid-'50s, and it never went out of fashion. Variations include "stoker," "surf-stoked," "stoke-um," "stokaboka," and "stoke-arama." Surf magazines have run articles such as "Murphy Gets Stoked," "Low on Stoke," "Investing in Stoke," "The Five Laws of Eternal Stoke," and "Digital Stoke." *Pure Stoke,* a collection of surfing essays by journalist John Grissim, was published in 1982; Drew Kampion's *Stoked: A History of Surf Culture* came out in 1997.

Stone, Tom   Stylish Hawaiian goofyfooter surfer, best known for his clean, cool lines at Pipeline. Stone was born (1951) in Honolulu, and began surfing at age four in Waikiki. He twice made the cover of *Surfer* magazine in the early 1970s, was invited to the 1970 and 1971 Expression Session events, and was featured in period surf movies including *Pacific Vibrations* (1970), *Cosmic Children* (1970), and *Five Summer Stories* (1972). Stone was addicted to cocaine by 1973, and was sent to prison after a drug bust in which he held a half-dozen people at gunpoint, including two policemen. He enrolled in college after his release, and in 1998, at age 46, received a B.A. in Hawaiian studies from the University of Hawaii. In 2001 he earned an M.A., also from UH, after writing a thesis paper on the ancient Polynesian practice of riding *holua*

boards—streamlined 12-foot wooden sleds used to "surf" down grassy mountains.

Stoner, Ron   Gifted but troubled 1960s surf photographer from Dana Point, California; best known for his tranquil, well-composed, color-saturated images of Southern California, Mexico, and Hawaii. Stoner was born (1945) in Long Beach, California, raised in Pasadena, and began surfing at 14, just before he started taking photographs. He was a masthead photographer at *Surfing Illustrated* magazine in 1963 at age 17, jumped to *Surf Guide* magazine in mid-1964, then moved to *Surfer* a few months later. Over the next six years—all spent working for *Surfer*—Stoner's life dramatically peaked and crashed. In mid-1965 he was awarded the magazine's powerful and expensive Century 1000-millimeter lens, along with a gas card, food allowance, and a $500 monthly retainer, an unheard-of annuity at the time for a surf photographer. Stoner's formal training consisted of just a few city college photography classes, but he had an infallible eye for color and action, worked hard, and immediately justified *Surfer*'s investment. At one point in 1967–68, his photos were featured on six consecutive *Surfer* covers; many

Ron Stoner

Stoner images—particularly those from a series of trips he made to the Hollister Ranch, near Santa Barbara—remain surf world icons. "The best moments of a surfer's life," next-generation photographer Art Brewer later said, "Stoner caught 'em. His view of surfing was so generous." From early 1965 to mid-1967, Stoner worked with *Surfer* cartoonist Rick Griffin and editor Patrick McNulty to produce what came to be known as the "Griffin-Stoner adventures," a loopy fictitious series written by McNulty, with Stoner playing the wide-eyed innocent to Griffin's hustling surfer/beatnik.

Stoner did some of his best work in 1968, after he'd become a regular LSD user. By the end of year, however, drugs had amplified his congenital insecurity and anxiety, and he had a mental breakdown—at one point dressing up as Jesus and dragging an enormous wooden cross through the streets of his Dana Point neighborhood. Stoner was 23 when his family committed him to a mental hospital in Santa Ana, California, where electroshock therapy left him docile and nearly mute, but functional. He continued to work, returning to Hawaii in late 1968, and shooting in California the following summer. Beginning in 1969 he went into a kind of self-exile, first in Maui, then in his Dana Point apartment; by early 1971 he was off the *Surfer* masthead, in 1978 he was listed as a missing person, and in 1994 he was declared dead. Ellen Hawley, Stoner's younger sister, seemed to tacitly acknowledge that the never-married Stoner had lived most of his life in a kind of richly colored fantasy world. "He wanted to make people look beautiful," she told the *Surfer's Journal* magazine in 1997, "and he wanted to put them in beautiful places." Stoner's work has appeared in more than a dozen illustrated surfing books, including *Surfing: The Ultimate Pleasure* (1984), *Stoked: A History of Surf Culture* (1997), and *The Perfect Day* (2001). *See also* drugs and surfing, surf photography, Surfer magazine.

straighten out   A yielding maneuver in which the surfer, faced with a fast-breaking and unmakable section, veers off perpendicular to the wave—or "straightens out" the angle he'd been holding across the wave face—and rides toward shore just ahead of the whitewater. A surfer usually straightens out only when he can't exit the wave by kicking out over the crest. The maneuver can also be forced, when another surfer drops in ahead of the rider and breaks his line. In bigger surf, a rider straightening out will

sometimes drop to his stomach and ride prone ("prone-out") for added stability. The surf leash, popularized in the early '70s, made straightening out largely a matter of form, not function, as the leash-wearing surfer can simply eject into the water as the wave closes out, then reel in his board after the wave passes by. *See also* prone-out.

Strauch, Paul   Quiet and graceful regularfoot surfer from Honolulu, Hawaii; winner of the 1963 Peru International, and creator of the cheater five (or "Strauch crouch") noseride. "He was the best surfer in the world," Hawaiian power surfer Barry Kanaiaupuni later said of Strauch. "It was like Star Trek; like something out of the future." Strauch was born (1943) and raised in Honolulu, began surfing as a goofyfooter at age four, then switched to regularfoot at 12. While Strauch is best remembered as an effortless freestyle surfer, he competed often and well: he finished second in the juniors division of the 1958 Makaha International, then won in 1959; he won the

Paul Strauch

1963 Peru International, placed second in the 1965 Duke Kahanamoku Invitational and third in the 1965 World Surfing Championships; he also won the 1966 state titles and the 1969 Makaha, and competed in the 1966 and 1970 World Championships.

Strauch has been credited as the first surfer to do bottom turns in bigger waves, something he began working on in the late '50s. At about the same time he developed a noseriding stance in which the rider squats on the rear haunch and extends the front foot to the board's tip—mainly as a way to increase stability. It was called the "cheater five" or "stretch five" because, unlike a vertical-stance hang five noseride, the rider's weight is almost completely on the back foot, well away from the nose. The Strauch crouch is the only type of noseride used in large surf. Strauch finished third in the 1963 and 1965 *Surfer* Magazine Readers Poll Awards, and appeared in a small number of surf films, including *Barefoot Adventure* (1960), *Gun Ho!* (1963), and *The Endless Summer* (1966). For the most part, however, Strauch politely steered clear of the surf media spotlight.

Strauch was co-owner of Alii Surfboards in Honolulu from 1963 to 1965; he received a B.A. in business from the University of Hawaii in 1968, and made a career first in real estate, then marketing. He lived in New York from 1985 to 1991, then moved to Southern California. Strauch has been married once, and has two children. *See also* cheater five.

stretch five   *See* cheater five.

stringer   A thin strip of wood bisecting a polyurethane foam surfboard blank, running from nose to tail; added primarily for strength, but sometimes regarded as part of the board's aesthetic makeup. The stringer (also known as "stick") was invented in 1958 by California surfboard manufacturer Gordon Duane as a way to remove flex from the new polyurethane-core boards that were replacing balsa-core boards. The stringer-insertion process that soon developed remained virtually unchanged over the decades: after a just-molded (or "blown") blank is cut lengthwise, wood glue (sometimes colored, usually blue or black) is applied to the cut surfaces, the stringer is dropped in, and the blank is clamped back together. Basswood is the most common wood type for stringers, followed by cedar, redwood, and balsa. High-performance shortboards usually have a 3/16"-wide stringer; longboards and big-wave guns usually have

a 3/8" stringer; stringer widths rarely go over two inches. The "T-band" stringer is made up of three strips of wood laminated together, with the flanking strips of a different wood type than the center strip. With the triple-stringer design, used mostly on longboards, three parallel cuts are made into the blank, with the flanking cuts set about six inches from the center cut, and three stringers are added. With some triple-stringer boards the flanking cuts are made at an angle, so that the stringers are bunched together at the nose, and set wider apart at the tail. *See also* Gordon Duane, polyurethane foam.

Stubbies Surf Classic   Sun-baked world pro tour contest held from 1977 to 1986 at Burleigh Heads, Queensland, Australia, usually in March; created by former Australian national champion Peter Drouyn, who used the event to introduce the now-standard man-on-man competition format. The Brisbane-based Edward Fletcher clothing company, makers of a bargain-priced line of surf trunks called Stubbies, put up $14,400 to sponsor the inaugural Stubbies Surf Classic in 1977, making it the second-richest event on the tour schedule, behind the $16,000 Coca-Cola Surfabout in Sydney. Fletcher also hired the eccentric but charismatic Drouyn, winner of the 1970 Australian National Titles, as event producer/director. It was Drouyn's decision to stage the contest in the beautiful point surf at Burleigh; he also developed a tennis-tournament-style man-on-man format to replace the five- or six-man heats then favored by the world tour.

Because the tour had been somewhat hastily conceived just a few months earlier, resulting in a slapdash 1976 season, many of the 44 men-only invitees viewed the 1977 Stubbies as the world tour's official debut. Given the new competition format, the higher-than-average prize money, and Burleigh's reputation for good waves, the Stubbies was in fact one of the most anticipated surf events of the decade. None of the contest organizers or competitors, however, could have predicted the long run of clear skies, light offshore winds, and long, tubing six-foot surf that rolled in day after day during the weeklong event. "Drouyn obviously has a direct line to The Creator," Australian surf journalist Phil Jarratt wrote, reporting from the spectator-packed Burleigh beachfront. "There's an air of excitement building around this contest like no other." Virtually every match from the quarterfinals on was a high-performance

Stubbies Surf Classic; 1979 winner Mark Richards of Australia

cliff-hanger, filled with long tuberides and gouging turns, and in the end the $5,000 winner's check went to local surfer Michael Peterson, in what would turn out to be the last win of a storied career.

None of the Stubbies Classic events in years to come matched the 1977 contest, but it remained the season opener in 1978, 1979, and 1981, and as such carried a built-in excitement. One year after the final Stubbies Classic was held in 1986, a Stubbies Masters event was staged for pro surfers 27 and over, the first "old-timers" event of its kind. Stubbies also sponsored a series of regional trials events in California, Florida, and Hawaii in the early '80s, with the winners qualifying for the Stubbies Classic. Tom Curren's first win as a professional came in the 1982 California Stubbies Trials. From 1984 to 1988, the Stubbies Pro was held in Oceanside, California. A Stubbies Classic women's division was held in 1978, 1985, and 1986; due to a world tour scheduling change, two Stubbies Classic events were held in 1986. Combined men's and women's Stubbies prize money in the second 1986 event was $85,000. Stubbies Surf Classic results are as follows:

1977:	Michael Peterson
1978:	Wayne Bartholomew, Margo Oberg
1979:	Mark Richards
1980:	Peter Harris
1981:	Mark Richards
1982:	Cheyne Horan
1983:	Martin Potter
1984:	Tom Carroll
1985:	Tom Curren, Liz Benavidez
1986:	Tom Curren, Wendy Botha
1986:	Damien Hardman, Wendy Botha

See also Burleigh Heads, Peter Drouyn.

Stussy, Shawn   Southern California–based clothes designer; founder, in 1982, of Stussy Surfboards, which three years later evolved into Stussy surfwear, and then into what online encyclopedia Altculture.com described as "the most influential street-fashion label of the '90s." Stussy's original surf line—identified by the owner's attractive calligraphic signature—was elegant and understated, at a time when surfwear in general was at its loudest and gaudiest. Stussy surfwear did $5 million in sales in 1989, and Stussy, 35, by then was regarded by many as the world's hippest surfer/ entrepreneur. *See also* fashion and surfing.

suck-out   A wave, or section of wave, that suddenly becomes extremely steep, hollow, and hard-breaking. Suck-outs are almost always caused by the wave moving abruptly over a shallow area of sandbar or reef. Suck-out waves often "double up" or even "triple up," meaning a scalloped ridge appears on the wave face. A manageable suck-out can provide a great tuberide, while a difficult or unexpected suck-out can be dangerous—and the line between the two is often blurry. Maverick's in California and Teahupoo in Tahiti, two of the world's hairiest breaks, are both regarded as suck-outs.

sucked over   *See* over the falls.

Sugarman, Martin   *See* H2O magazine.

Sullivan, Pancho   Bespectacled Hawaiian power surfer, born (1973) in a bamboo treehouse located on a seven-acre commune on Kauai's dreamscape Napali Coast. Sullivan and his mother moved to Oahu in 1980, he got his first surfboard the following year, and by age 15 he was riding big waves at Sunset Beach on the North Shore. By the mid-'90s, Sullivan had packed 190 muscle-laden pounds onto his once-lanky six-foot frame, and was turning his board with as much force as anybody in the sport. He had no contest record to speak of, but didn't need one. "In waves that matter," *Surfing* magazine noted, "Pancho has become one of the best surfers in the world." Sullivan has appeared in nearly two dozen surf videos, including *Aloha Bowls* (1994), *Feral Kingdom* (1995), and *Tripping the Planet* (1996). *See also* power surfing.

Sumpter, Rodney   Nation-hopping surfer and surf entrepreneur from Cornwall, England; 1960s title-winner in Australia, America, Great Britain, and Ireland, and the sport's only quad-national champion. Sumpter was born (1947) in Watford, England, the son of an insurance salesman, moved with his family at age five to Sydney, Australia, and began surfing in 1961 at 14. Two years later the gangly regularfooter won the juniors division of the Australian Invitational Surfing Championships. Sumpter (long known as "Gopher" for his oversized front teeth) began dividing his time between Sydney and Southern California; in 1964 he won the juniors in the United States Surfing Championships, and in 1965 he competed with the American team at the World Surfing Championships in Peru. He also traveled to Jersey in the British Channel Islands, winning the inaugural Great Britain National Championships. Sumpter moved back to England in 1966, and with his aggressive Aussie-style turns and a gift for noseriding—complemented by a smooth-talking raconteur charm—he made a profound impression on the budding English surfing scene. Sumpter was hired by Bilbo Surfboards in Cornwall and began shaping his own Union Jack signature model, which became a huge success following his fifth-place finish (while representing Great Britain) in the 1966 World Championships in California. Two years later, in a complicated set of circumstances, Sumpter won the Irish National Championships and rode for Ireland in the 1968 World Championships in Puerto Rico. For the 1970 World Championships in Australia, he once again represented Great Britain. He dropped out of competitive surfing not long after finishing third in the 1971 Makaha International.

Sumpter also filmed and produced surf movies, releasing seven titles between 1967 and 1979, including *Come Surf With Me* (1967), *Freeform* (1970), and *Oceans* (1972). The critics weren't impressed. "Rodney Sumpter," one surf magazine reviewer noted in a review for *Freeform,* "proves he's more polished in the waves than behind the camera." (David Sumpter, his brother, fared much the same with his 1974 surf movie *On Any Morning.*) Sumpter also gained notice in 1967, when he rode a tidal bore wave up the Severn River, west of London, for more than two miles. Two years later Sumpter produced *British Surfer,* the first domestic surf magazine; it lasted just six issues. He made a brief return to competition with the British Amateur Team at the 1990 World Contest in Japan, but was eliminated in the early rounds.

Not counting his own films, Sumpter appeared in several surf movies, including *Surfing the Southern Cross* (1963), *The Endless Summer* (1966), and *The Hot Generation* (1968). *International Surfing* magazine named him as Britain's top surfer in its 1966 Hall of Fame Awards, and he's featured prominently in *You Should Have Been Here Yesterday: The Roots of British Surfing,* published in 1994. Sumpter is married, has one child, and lives in Cornwall. *See also* Severn Bore.

sunburn   *See* skin cancer.

Sunn, Martha   Lithe and graceful regularfoot surfer from Makaha, Hawaii; one of the best female competitors of the late 1960s and early '70s, and older sister of Hawaiian surf icon Rell Sunn. Sunn was born (1948) and raised in Makaha, and began surfing at age nine. She won the Makaha International in 1967, 1969, and 1970 (placing second in 1966 and 1968), finished fourth in the 1968 World Surfing Championships, and fifth in the 1970 Championships. A regularfooter, Sunn was noted for her refined and relaxed wave-riding style.

Sunn, Rell   Soulful regularfoot surfer from Makaha, Oahu; a top-ranked pro in the 1970s and '80s, but better remembered as the embodiment of Hawaiian grace and warmth, and for her defiant but ultimately futile struggle with breast cancer. Sunn was born (1950) in Makaha, the daughter of a beachboy, and

Rodney Sumpter

raised along with four siblings in a Quonset hut. She began surfing at age four; at 16 she won the Hawaiian Junior Championship and was invited to the 1966 World Championships, in San Diego. Two years later she moved to Oklahoma with her boyfriend, where she got married, had a child, and got divorced. When she returned to Makaha with her daughter in early 1972, she hadn't surfed for nearly five years. Surfboard designs had changed radically during that period, but Sunn regained her form within months, and was soon counted among the first group of professional women surfers: she placed third in the 1975 Lancers Cup, held at Sunset Beach, and in 1977—the first year of the women's pro tour—she finished the year ranked #6. For the next seven years, she was regularly in the top eight, and finished #3 in 1979 and 1982. The slender, dark-haired Sunn, by then known as the Queen of Makaha, wasn't an attacking surfer like her Hawaiian peers Margo Oberg or Lynne Boyer; she was smooth, cool, and composed, taking few risks, but often riding waves from beginning to end in a perfectly fluid motion. *Surfing* magazine called her "the sport's premier female stylist." Sunn developed in other areas as well: in 1975 she became Hawaii's first female lifeguard, in 1976 she got a B.A. in cultural anthropology from the University of Hawaii, and in 1977 she founded the annual Rell Sunn Menehune surf contest at Makaha. She also had a brief second marriage in the late '70s.

Sunn was diagnosed with breast cancer in 1983, and began a 15-year battle that would involve chemotherapy, radiation, bone-marrow transplants, and a mastectomy. She fell into a coma in 1988 and recovered; she was given six months to live in 1991. But months and sometimes even years passed by with Sunn in seemingly perfect health, as she surfed daily, rode her bike, and traveled (including a first-of-its-kind surfing expedition to China in 1986). She worked as a radio DJ, computer operator, and physical therapist. Sunn married for a third time in 1994, to Dave Parmenter, a former pro surfer from California, 10 years her junior. As Sunn continued her fight against cancer, she was often presented in the surf media as nothing less than a beatific wave-riding saint. But there were other sides to her: she had a black belt in judo, told filthy jokes, and occasionally displayed a fearsome temper. She could be sweet and carnal in the same breath. "Four- to five-foot surf at Makaha is such a nice sound," she told surf journalist Bruce Jenkins in 1994, "it's almost sexual." Sunn was 47 in

Rell Sunn

early 1998 when she died at her home in Makaha. Three thousand people gathered for her beachside memorial service during which her ashes were scattered into the Makaha surf, and her passing was noted in a three-column article in the *New York Times,* in which she was called "a state treasure."

Sunn appeared in about a dozen surf movies, videos, and documentaries, including *Super Session* (1975), *Liquid Stage: The Lure of Surfing* (1995), and *Modern Legends in Hawaiian Surf* (1995). *Heart of the Sea: Kapolioka'ehukai,* a documentary on Sunn, was released in 2002. She was inducted into the International Surfing Hall of Fame in 1991. In 1996 she was inducted into the Huntington Beach Surfing Walk of Fame, and given the Surf Industry Manufacturers Association's Waterman Achievement Award; the following year she was inducted into the Hawaii Sports Hall of Fame. Sunn coauthored *A Guide to Beach Survival* (1986) and two children's coloring books, *The Waves You Ride* and *Who is a Surfer,* both published in 1995. *See also* Makaha.

sunscreen   Topical-use product designed to protect the skin from damaging ultraviolet (UV) sun rays, which burn the skin, reduce its elasticity and moisture levels, and lead to a higher risk of skin cancer. Surfers—along with sailors, skiers, snowboarders, and beach volleyball players—are prone to sun damage, and sunscreen has for decades been a surf culture essential. Sunscreens function by either blocking UV light, as with zinc oxide cream, or by chemically absorbing and dispersing UV light. The first commercially available sunscreen was produced in 1936 (by French chemist and L'Oréal cosmetics founder Eugene Schueller), but in the decades that followed it was the tan-promoting products that earned millions for companies like Coppertone and Bain de Soleil. In the late '50s, surfers and lifeguards began using zinc oxide to help prevent sun-blistered lips, cheeks, and noses. As skin cancer became a worldwide health concern in the late '70s, other forms of sunscreens became popular. Coppertone developed the first UV-absorbing sunscreen in 1980; sweat- and waterproof versions soon followed. All sunscreens are labeled with an SPF (sun protection factor) number that indicates the strength of the product. A sunscreen with an SPF of 15, for example, properly applied, means the person who would normally begin to burn in 10 minutes would instead start to burn in 150 minutes. SPF 45 is generally the highest level of protection. Surfers almost exclusively use a cream or gel form of sunscreen; it also comes as a lotion, spray, lip balm, or makeup. Sunscreens marketed for surfers include Bullfrog, Aloe Gator, and Headhunter. *See also* skin cancer, zinc oxide.

Sunset Beach Famously complex Hawaiian surf break located on the North Shore of Oahu; regarded by many as the center of the surfing universe from the 1950s to the '80s. "Sunset Beach," California surf journalist Drew Kampion wrote in 1980, "is the standard by which other waves are measured, and the best surfers here are the best surfers, period." Sunset's enormous lava-rock reef faces to the northwest, and contains at least six named sections, roughly west to east as follows: 1) Val's Reef, named after local surfer Val Valentine, draws small northwest swells into a short right-breaking peak just a few yards off the beach. 2) The Bowl breaks over a shallow patch of reef along the edge of Sunset's deep-water channel; a slabbing, ferociously hollow tube section on a six- to 12-foot north swell, and all but nonexistent on a west swell. 3) West Peak, the classic Sunset Beach wave, takes shape over a double finger of reef that stretches

out to the northwest and draws approaching west and northwest swells into the distinctive Sunset peak; a shifting, fast-moving wave that breaks from six to 18 foot. 4) Sunset Point, located on the tip of the bay's eastern arm, only breaks up to five foot; well-shaped on occasion, but often broken up and lumpy. 5) The North Wall is a broad area of reef between West Peak and Backyards, where north swells bigger than eight feet steamroll for up to 300 yards; sometimes handles the overflow crowd. 6) Backyards is a series of tricky, shallow peaks, mainly right-breaking, along a 300-yard-long stretch north of Sunset Point.

The Sunset Beach surf is generally biggest and best from October to February, as the break acts as a funnel for virtually all North Pacific storm-generated swells. One of only a few spots in Hawaii that breaks on swells ranging from the west to the northeast, Sunset is probably the world's most consistent producer of good eight- to 12-foot surf. A vast wave field and endlessly shifting peaks mean that surfers have to paddle almost constantly to get into takeoff position, and often get caught inside; the tradewinds blow hard on this particular stretch of coast and hit Sunset side-offshore, which can make the take-off even more difficult. Crowds are also a problem. Few breaks in the world put a greater demand on a surfer's fitness, as well as his strategic and tactical know-how, and even the world's best often leave the water in boiling frustration. But the classic Sunset ride is long and exhilarating, as the wave whorls and explodes, then flattens and tilts back up, sometimes running through four or five distinct stages as it moves across the reef. "It's fabulously imperfect," San Francisco sportswriter Bruce Jenkins once noted. "It can give you the ride of your life, but you've got to earn it."

Premodern Hawaiians knew the break as Paumalu ("taken secretly"), and it was one of about 20 Oahu spots ridden prior to the 19th century, when visiting missionaries brought the sport to near extinction. (*Paumalu: A Story of Modern Hawaii,* a surf-themed novel by journalist Rus Calisch, was published in 1979.) "Sunset Beach" was the name given to the area in 1919 by a real estate developer hoping to sell weekend getaway homes to wealthy Honolulu residents. Sunset was rediscovered as a surfing break by California-born riders Lorrin "Whitey" Harrison, Gene "Tarzan" Smith, and John Kelly, who ventured north from Waikiki in 1939 and surfed six- to eight-foot Sunset waves on their finless hot curl boards; Honolulu surfers Wally Froiseth and George Downing began riding there in the '40s; Walter Hoffman, Buzzy Trent, and others joined in the early '50s. As the North Shore replaced Makaha (on the west side of Oahu) as the sport's big-wave capital, Sunset Beach remained the area's surfing centerpiece. The advent of surf media in the '50s and early '60s underscored the point; Sunset was prominently featured in nearly every surf film of the period, and a photograph of a thundering West Peak wave, with Jose Angel charging down the face, was used on the cover of the first *Surfer* magazine in 1960. Sunset became the primary North Shore competition break, beginning in 1965 when it hosted the debut Duke Kahanamoku Surfing Classic, an annual event for two decades. When the world pro circuit was formed in 1976, four of the 14 events for the season were held at Sunset. Pro contests held at Sunset over years include the Pro Class Trials, the XCEL Pro, the World Cup, the Billabong Pro, the Chiemsee Women's Masters, and the Rip Curl Cup.

A short list of top Sunset surfers, in roughly chronological order beginning in the late '50s, would include George Downing, Ricky Grigg, Peter Cole, Paul Gebauer, Paul Strauch, Jock Sutherland, Reno Abellira, Terry Fitzgerald, Ian Cairns, Simon Anderson, Mark Richards, Ken Bradshaw, Bobby Owens, Michael Ho (voted "Best Surfer at Sunset" by his peers in a 1992 *Surfer* poll), Tom Carroll, Gary Elkerton (voted "Best Surfer at Sunset" by his peers in a 1992 *Australia's Surfing Life* magazine poll), Johnny-Boy Gomes, Sunny Garcia, and Pancho Sullivan. The two surfers most closely identified with Sunset are both '70s-era Hawaiians: Barry Kanaiaupuni, the free-form master who all but defined power surfing, and three-time Duke winner Jeff Hakman, whose 1997 biography is justifiably titled *Mr. Sunset*.

Listed as one of the "Ten Best Waves in the World" by *Surfing* magazine in 1981, Sunset fell somewhat out of fashion beginning in the early '90s, as pro surfers on the North Shore began focusing more on the short, explosive tubes at nearby Pipeline, Backdoor, and Off-the-Wall. "Has anybody else ever noticed that Sunset is just not that good of a wave?" surf journalist and regular North Shore visitor Sam George wrote in 1990. Older surfers disagreed vehemently, but the surfing world at large seemed to agree. After hosting a total of 19 men's division world tour events from 1976 to 1991, Sunset didn't again figure in the men's world championship tour schedule until 2001. *See also* North Shore, World Cup.

Sunshine Coast   *See* Queensland.

surf   *See* waves and wave formation.

surf art   Modern surfing and art have always been connected to one degree or another. Lyrically rendered images of the sport were used in a small number of 19th-century travel or adventure books, including a line drawing of three nude Polynesian nymph surfers used on the cover of American writer Charles Warren Stoddard's 1874 travelogue *Summer Cruising in the South Seas*. In the early decades of the 20th century, surfers often decorated their wooden boards with illustrations, usually painted or inked, but sometimes wood-burned or inlaid.

Surfer magazine founder John Severson, however, is generally regarded as the modern-day inventor of "surf art." He began with surf-themed wood-block prints and cartooning as a high school student in the early '50s, then sharpened his skills by taking fine art courses in college (earning a master's in art education from Long Beach State), working in advertising design, and serving as a draftsman in the army. His surfing work was representational but highly stylized, with wavy-limbed surfers and needlelike surfboards set among color-washed skies and beaches. Severson was selling surf-themed watercolors and oils out of a Laguna Beach gallery by 1956, and four years later the debut issue of *Surfer* magazine was trimmed with more than a dozen of his ink drawings. While a small

Surf art; the Laguna Art Museum's 2002 show, Surf Culture: the Art History of Surfing

number of artists (including Bernhard Zalusky, Tom Yasuda, and Gene Studebaker) continued to produce mildly experimental surf-related art in the years to follow, surf art, then and now, has never defined a particular school or style; it's used instead as a catchall for any kind of art associated with surfing. Perhaps the type of work most connected with surf art is the airbrush fantasy landscape, popularized in the 1980s and '90s by Hawaiian artists Chris Lassen and Robert Wyland, often featuring planets, stars, galaxies, lava reefs, waterfalls, tropical fish, and perfectly formed empty waves. Individual Lassen canvases such as *Mystic Eternity* and *Crystal Waters of Maui* sold for up to $100,000. More subdued works of surf art were being produced by Ken Auster, Michael Cassidy, Avi Kiriaty, and others, much of it focusing on either the sport's preshortboard past or soothing images of the tropics.

More challenging surf art has meanwhile been gathered and put on public display with some regularity, beginning with California-born Mike Parker's *Surfrealism* show—featuring blond-haired hypermuscled surfers—at the Fun Gallery in New York in 1987. Three years later, at Corcoran Gallery in Santa Monica, California, more than 100 artists, musicians, and surfers (including pop art luminary and former Malibu regular Billy Al Bengston, architect Frank Gehry, and Peter Max) each displayed a surfboard of their own design and making. Two ambitious and successful surf-themed art exhibitions were staged in the early '00s. *Surf Trip,* at the Yerba Buena Center for the Arts in San Francisco in 2000, featured paintings, video, photographs, and surfboards, and included Jessica Dunne's *Taraval Rights,* an oversize oil showing the wintry urban surfscapes of San Francisco; Peter Schroff's *Pink Whale,* an all-in-one deluxe surfboard loaded with a Schlitz beer tap, TV, palm fronds, and chrome exhaust pipes; and Kevin Ancell's *Aloha 'Oe,* consisting of 25 life-size motorized polyurethane Hawaiian hula dancers outfitted with grass skirts, leis, and ukuleles, as well as machine guns, bloodied mouths, and hypodermic needles. *Surf Culture: The Art History of Surfing* opened at the Laguna Art Museum in the summer of 2002, and was even broader in scope, with artifacts dating back to the 18th century. A *New York Times* review of *Surf Culture* noted that the sport has become not just "a colorful part of American culture," but also "a symbol of cultural imperialism." The exhibition catalog suggested that surfing itself is nothing less than "painted arcs done without a brush on an ever-changing canvas." Celebrated New York artist Robert

Longo was by that time creating huge canvases (up to six foot by 10 foot) of breaking waves. Other surfers who have made noteworthy contributions to surf art, or the art world in general, include Los Angeles installation artist Craig Stecyk, Orange County curator Bolton Colburn, sketch master Russell Crotty, and neoclassicist Sandow Birk. The Surf Gallery, the first retail store dedicated to surf art and surf photography, opened in 2001 in Laguna Beach.

Surf art continued to have a participatory element: *Surfer* magazine sponsored a Surfer Art Contest in 1969 (and later held a number of reader collage contests), while six-time world champion Kelly Slater started a decorative trend in 1994 when he began using opaque paint pens to illustrate the decks of his boards. *See also* Kevin Ancell, Ken Auster, Sandow Birk, David Carson, Rick Griffin, Avi Kiriaty, Chris Lassen, Bill Ogden, Rick Rietveld, Peter Schroff, Craig Steyck, surf cartoons and comics.

surf auctions   In 1996, Southern California surfboard fiberglasser Danny Brawner auctioned off his personal collection of '50s- and '60s-era longboards—more than 100 boards total—and grossed $117,000. The auction idea caught on, and six months later jovial surf entrepreneur Allen Seymour staged the first Pacific Coast Vintage Surf Auction (PCVSA), held at the Countryside Inn in San Clemente, California. Items for sale included vintage surf magazines, books, prints, posters, and Hawaiian silk shirts; a Duke Kahanamoku Invitational trophy sold for $1,500, a first edition of Tom Blake's 1935 book *Hawaiian Surfriders* went for $950, and a Hawaiian redwood-pine laminate plank surfboard from the '20s brought $7,500. The PCVSA moved to a banquet room in the San Diego Marriott Hotel in 1998, then to the Long Beach Convention Center, where it has been held annually during the first week in February, as an adjunct to the Action Sports Retailer Trade Expo. The one-day event is divided into two parts: about 30 less-expensive items, or "lots," are put up for silent auction in the late afternoon, with all comers welcome to bid. In the evening, authorized bidders, after paying a $25 registration free, make offers on about 100 premium lots, with Seymour serving as host and auctioneer. As of 2002, the highest-priced item sold at a Pacific Coast Vintage Surf Auction was a Simmons "sandwich" balsa board, which went for $18,500 in 2000. Other surf world auctions include the Hawaii Islands Vintage Surf Auction, developed by world pro tour cofounder Randy Rarick, and the Sydney Surf Auction, run by Australian surf magazine and memorabilia collector Michael Mock. Both debuted in 2001. New Jersey surfer Mike "Miggs" Migliorisi hosted the debut Premier Auction in 1999, where a late-'50s Greg Noll Surfboards balsa sold for $13,000. A surfing auction Web site, www.surfnhula.com, went online in 2002.

Not everybody was happy with how the sport's history was being bought, sold, and collected. "Surfing's past is shacked up in a posh hotel in San Diego," surf journalist Paul Gross wrote after attending the 1998 PCVSA, "with a generation of aging enthusiasts who were willing to pay for it, and together they cultivated a subculture which was wholly unfamiliar to me. In this lineup, what mattered wasn't how deep in the pocket you surfed, but how deep your pockets were when you bid." *See also* surf collectors.

surf boat   Round-bottomed fiberglass-constructed rowboat, usually manned by four rear-facing rowers and an aft-positioned "sweep steer." The surf boat, descended from the rugged wooden dory boats long used by fishermen and whalers, was adapted for res-

surf boats

cue purposes by the Surf Life Saving Association of Australia (SLSA) in the late 1800s, and is now used only for lifeguard training and competitions. The average surf boat is 22 feet long, four to five feet wide, and V-shaped at both ends; buoyancy chambers in the front and back make the boats virtually unsinkable, even in heavy surf. Surf boat racing started among Sydney-area SLSA clubs during the early 1900s, and a century later the sport remains essentially unchanged. Teams launch their boats from the beach, paddle through the surf and around a buoy anchored about 300 yards past the surf line, and race back to shore, trying to pick up waves on the way. Pioneering surf moviemaker Bud Browne thrilled audiences in the 1950s with footage of wooden surf boats riding 10-foot waves and smashing into each other during a Sydney club meet. Surf boat races were also a crowd favorite during the United States Surfing Championships held in Huntington Beach from the mid-'60s to the early '70s, and continue to be a popular part of lifeguard competitions around the world. Surf boating is physically demanding and sometimes dangerous: Australians joke that the best way to pick a surf boat crew is to line prospects up in a row and throw bricks at them; the ones who don't duck are selected. *See also* canoe surfing, wave ski.

surf bum   Disdainful phrase when used by nonsurfers to describe surfers; generally humorous, affectionate, or ironic when used by surfers to describe themselves. "I'm a surf bum," Kahuna says in the 1959 movie *Gidget.* "You know, ride the waves, eat, sleep, not a care in the world." In "How to be a Surf Bum!," a one-page cartoon panel from a 1967 issue of *SurfToons,* hodads are advised to step into a pair of baggies, rub on some wood stain "for that fast-fast-fast supertan!," drive around in a woody, "and presto! You, too, will be a surf bum!" The surf bum image is based on lack of industry—real or perceived. "Surfing was missing a general acceptance, a business acceptance," Hawaiian big-wave surfer Mark Foo said in 1986. "I've had my own mother telling me, 'You're nothing but a surf bum.' I just never believed it."

surf bunny   Mildly derogatory phrase, popular in the 1960s, for a young and usually voluptuous bikini-clad beauty; sometimes defined as a surfer, but more often synonymous with the resolutely nonsurfing "beach bunny." *Beach Blanket Bingo, Beach Party,* and the rest of the Hollywood beach films of the '60s were loaded with surf bunnies, often dancing the Twist, the Watusi, and the Hitchhiker.

surf camp   *See* surf schools; surf resorts.

surf cartoons and comics   Surfing is a natural for cartoon and comic book treatment, given its popularity with teenagers and preteens. Published surf cartooning dates back to at least 1937, when New Adventures Comics put an anonymous redheaded surfer crouched atop a redwood board against a giant sun. Batman, Robin, and Superman ride side by side (with Robin doing a headstand) on the cover of a 1948 issue of *World's Finest Comics.* The American surf boom of the early and mid-'60s was reflected in the comics, as Peanuts creator Charles Schultz gave Snoopy a pair of jams in 1965 and launched him into a hot right slide along with a boldface COWABUNGA! thought bubble, while *Mad* magazine, that same year, lampooned the sport in a six-page Al Jaffe feature titled "Surfing." (Alfred E. Neuman himself is seen shooting the curl on the cover of the September 1983 issue of *Mad.*) Marvel Comics introduced the buffed and grimly heroic *Silver Surfer* in 1966.

Surfer magazine founder and surf-art innovator John Severson sprinkled more than a dozen of his

Surf cartoon; panel from Gonad Man strip by Australian Mark Sutherland

own cartoons in the magazine's 1960 debut issue; high school cartoonist Rick Griffin meanwhile did artwork for the *Surfer's Annual,* the *Surfing Funnies,* and the *Cartoon History of Surfing,* then in 1961 began publishing his Murphy strip in *Surfer.* Short, smiling, bushy-blond-haired, and endlessly stoked, Murphy was a huge hit, eventually appearing on the cover of *Surfer* magazine, as well as on T-shirts and coffee mugs. Griffin, a fine artist as well as a cartoonist, would later design album covers for the Grateful Dead and the Eagles, and create the first *Rolling Stone* magazine logotype; he also did playful illustration work for the *Surfer*-published "Griffin-Stoner" adventures in the mid-'60s. *Surfer* meanwhile ran a semi-regular feature in the '60s titled "Surftoons," with reader-drawn single-panel cartoons. Petersen's Publishing also produced 28 issues of *Surftoons* magazine—unrelated to *Surfer*'s column—between 1965 and 1969.

The emphasis in American surf cartooning switched in the '70s from humor to fantasy, as epitomized by Glen Chase's Hobbitesque *Surfer*-published "Quest for Infinite Truth" series in 1974, featuring Prince Aquadau doing battle against the Flying Demons of Morlok. Griffin and Close, along with San Francisco underground cartoon legends S. Clay Wilson and R. Crumb and others, contributed to *Tales from the Tube,* a popular surf cartoon comic book published as a *Surfer* insert in 1972. That same year saw the debut in Australia's *Tracks* magazine of Captain Goodvibes, the raunchy surfing pig created by Tony Edwards. Goodvibes was an instant hit, and was later featured on a radio show, in comic books, and on records; *Hot to Trot,* a short animated Goodvibes film, was produced in 1977.

Maynard and the Rat, a strip by Tom Finley, Bob Penuelas, and Rick Bundschuh, debuted in *Surfer* in 1980 and brought joke-driven cartooning back to the American surf press; Penuelas broke from his partners in 1986 to create the vastly more popular Wilbur Kookmeyer strip, about the misadventures of a dim-witted but likable teenage surfer. "Surf Crazed Comics," by Roy Gonzales and Salvador Paskowitz, borrowing shamelessly from the bug-eyed Surf Fink and Surf Monster characters invented in the '60s by Ed "Big Daddy" Roth, debuted as a strip in *Surfing* magazine in 1992, and was shortly followed by three comic books—including one in 3-D. Australia contributed two popular strips in the mid-'90s: Gonad Man, the darkly humorous antihero created by Mark

Sutherland, and the dashing ASL Man, outfitted in tights, mask, and cape, and rendered with a light dose of irony by Paul Collins for *Australia's Surfing Life* magazine. Steve Cakebread's gross-out Felch strip debuted in *ASL* in 1999. Rock guitarist and cartoonist Reg Mombassa began a series of eccentric, frequently scatological, and always compelling cartoon ads for the Australian-produced Mambo clothing line beginning in the late '80s; dozens of his best pieces were gathered in the 1998-published *Mambo: Still Life with Franchise* coffee-table book. Mombassa, Sutherland, and Cakebread all had their work shown in *Tubular Cels: A Wild and Wet Exhibition of Loons, Goons and Surfin Toons,* an Australian surfing cartoon retrospective that opened at Sydney's Silicon Pulp Animation Gallery in August 2001. Surf cartooning was also featured in the 2002 Laguna Art Museum show, *The Art History of Surfing. See also* Captain Goodvibes, Rick Griffin, Wilbur Kookmeyer, Murphy, Bob Penuelas, Silver Surfer, surf art, Mark Sutherland.

Surf City   Chart-topping 1963 single for Los Angeles–based singing duo Jan and Dean, cowritten and cosung by Brian Wilson of the Beach Boys; "Surf City" opens with the immortal Southern California male teen surfer fantasy line, "Two girls for every boy!" While Jan and Dean weren't in the same creative league as the Beach Boys, their best work was just as sunny and tuneful as the Beach Boys' early hits; aside from being the first surf song to reach #1 nationally, "Surf City" is the perfect Kennedy-era beach anthem. The opening verse describes the singer's board-carrying 1934 Ford woody, while the second verse gives a brief outline of the promised land. While the lyrics specify no exact location for Surf City, and the song is in fact an ode to Southern California beaches in general, it was nonetheless associated from the beginning with Orange County's Huntington Beach, home to the West Coast Surfing Championships and the United States Surfing Championships. California state assemblyman and former Huntington Beach mayor Tom Mays wrote a bill in 1992 that the state of California officially recognize Huntington as "Surf City." Santa Cruz assemblyman Sam Farr, in turn, pointed out that surfing was introduced to mainland America at the Santa Cruz rivermouth in 1885, and that Santa Cruz had also long thought of itself as Surf City. As the two men turned the issue into a half-joking political fight, it was covered by the syndicated tabloid news program *A Cur-*

rent Affair, and earned comment from Hillary Rodham Clinton, who noted, while campaigning in Santa Cruz on behalf of her president-to-be husband, that "This is the real Surf City where only real surfers surf." Huntington Beach congressman Dana Rohrabacher responded by saying "Surf City isn't supposed to be a laid-back place with laid-back people." But Farr had the last word, as he was able to exile the Huntington/Surf City bill in committee. "The reason I killed it," he later said, "is because we all know the surfers in Huntington Beach are barneys. And not even soul-barneys at that." The township of Surf City, New Jersey, home to some of the state's first surfers, remained above the fray. *See also* Huntington Beach, Jan and Dean, Santa Cruz, surf music.

surf clubs   While surfing is for the most part correctly regarded as a sport for individuals and nonjoiners, surf clubs have played a small but sometimes influential role throughout the sport's history. The Outrigger Canoe Club, founded in 1908 in Waikiki, was created by former New York newspaperman Alexander Hume Ford "for the purpose of reviving and preserving the ancient Hawaiian sport of surfing on boards. . . ." Outrigger was a social and athletic club, whose membership consisted almost entirely of mainland-born *haoles* (whites); the group had 1,200 members in 1915, with hundreds more on a waiting list. Hui Nalu ("Club of the Waves"), a rival group chartered in 1911, was composed mostly of native Hawaiians and competed regularly against Outrigger in organized paddling, surfing, and canoeing events.

The 1935-founded Palos Verdes Surf Club was the second organization of its kind in California (following the short-lived Corona del Mar Surfboard Club), and another half-dozen surf clubs formed between San Francisco and San Diego prior to World War II. Club members of the period often had matching letterman-style jackets, held regular meetings, and frequently traveled to compete and socialize with other surf clubs. Nearly all mainland American surf clubs disappeared in the early '40s, after America entered the war. Meanwhile, in Lima, Peru, surfer and polo player Carlos Dogny founded Club Waikiki in 1942 as a convivial beachside meeting place for Peruvian surfer/socialites.

The American surf club revived and flourished in the early and mid-'60s, fueled in part by the same domestic surf craze that produced Gidget and the Beach Boys. More than 200 clubs were founded during this period, about a third of them on the East Coast. Virtually all the organizations solemnly vowed to do their part to help rid the sport of hodads, hooligans, and surf bums. "I pledge to keep surfing a clean sport," the Peninsula Surf Club membership oath read, "by setting a good example of behavior on the beaches, in school and in my community." Clubs such as the Malibu Surfing Association, the Long Beach Surf Club, the Salt Creek Surfing Society, the Rincon Raiders, the West Valley Surfing Association, and the Ventura Paddlebugs often wore matching T-shirts and nylon jackets, threw keg parties—behavior oaths were generally dropped on weekends—and met for interclub competitions. An organization's status was based on both the surfing and social skills of its members. (The 1952-formed San Onofre Surf Club and the 1959-formed Santa Barbara County Surf Club both fell outside the traditional model in that they were created primarily to gain exclusive beach access rights to, respectively, San Onofre and the Hollister Ranch.) The Windansea Surf Club, based in La Jolla, San Diego, was the best-known and most notorious group of its kind in the '60s, often arriving at surf contests with a live band, a cheering section, stacked cases of beer, wine, and liquor, and an all-star team of surfers including Skip Frye, Mike Hynson, Mickey Muñoz, Donald Takayama, Butch Van Artsdalen, and Rusty Miller. In late 1967, as the shortboard revolution got under way and the sport fused with the drug-influenced counterculture, American surf clubs—with their bylaws, uniforms, and typed-up competition schedules—vanished almost overnight.

In Australia, "clubs" had for decades been shorthand for local cells of the 1906-founded Surf Life Saving Association of Australia (SLSA), and early generations of Australian surfers were nearly all counted among the ranks of "clubbies." The Australian Surf Board Association was formed in Sydney in 1945 as a way for surfers to differentiate themselves from the somewhat autocratic SLSA; friction between "surfies" and clubbies grew in the '50s and hit a peak in the early '60s with a series of beach-brawling "club wars." By that time, as veteran Sydney surfer James Twight later recalled, "You were either a boardrider or a clubbie, and there was very little crossover." The developing network of boardrider clubs led to the first Australian state- and nationwide surfing associations (formed in 1963 and 1964), and helped Australia develop into the surf world's most successful competitive nation; virtually every top Australian rider

learned contest skills through his local boardriders club. The '80s and early '90s represented a peak for Australian boardrider clubs, with events such as the Kirra Teams' Challenge and the Surf League Championships providing forums for club rivalries—some of them 30 years old—between groups like Newport Plus, Narrabeen Boardriders, Snapper Rocks, and Merewether. While the competitive pace began to slow in the mid-'90s, by 2003 there were still more than 100 boardrider clubs in Australia operating under the umbrella of Surfing Australia.

Back in America, the '80s-launched longboard revival brought a renewed interest in surf clubs. Six clubs united in 1987 to form the Coalition of Surfing Clubs; five years later the organization had grown to include 30 clubs. The Coalition hosts six competitions each year, separate from the dozens of local events, get-togethers, surf trips, community projects, and fund-raisers organized by individual clubs. Niche clubs have also formed in California for black surfers, women surfers, gay surfers, and born-again surfers, while general membership clubs have taken root in places like England (the London Surf Club), the West Indies island of Guadeloupe (the Arawak Surfing Club), and Silicon Valley (Silicon Valley Surf Club).

See also Coalition of Surfing Clubs, Hui Nalu Surf Club, Outrigger Canoe Club, Palos Verdes Surf Club, Windansea Surf Club.

surf collectors Collectors have wanted to own a part of surfing for decades. A short item in a 1974 issue of *Surfer* magazine noted that California surfer Nathan Parrish was selling a pristine 1966 World Surfing Championships event program to the highest bidder (no follow-up as to what the winning bid was), while *Surfing,* a few months later, named "paper" collectors Richard Safady and Mark Fragale as the top two finishers of the Magazine Freak Awards; Safady, a longshoreman from Hermosa Beach, California, had been collecting surf magazines and memorabilia since the late '50s. In the early '90s, however, surf collecting began to transform into a more serious, expensive, and regimented hobby, and by the end of the decade items were no longer culled from garage sales and flea markets, but from auctions, specialty stores, and online trading posts. Driven for the most part by nostalgia-affected baby boom surfers looking for a connection to the sport's oft-cited but vaguely described "golden age" (best described as anything prior to the late '60s shortboard revolution), the

Surfboard collector Danny Brawner of California

boom in surfing collectibles was loud enough that a 2000 issue of the *Financial Review* listed surf memorabilia as one of America's top five collectible investments. Wooden surfboards were thrown away by the thousands in the late '50s and '60s; those that survived to the end of the century could be sold for anywhere between $1,000 and $18,000.

Although not technically a surfing item, the loose-fitting aloha shirt (or Hawaiian shirt) set a precedent of sorts in the mid-'70s by gaining collectible currency in the fashion world. Surf music albums soon followed, with a 1981 *Surfer* article, "Turn Your Surf Music Into Gold!," notifying readers that mint condition Beach Boys albums were worth more than $200. Surfboard collectors began ratcheting up their prices a few years later, buying and selling Pipeliners, Trestles Specials, and other signal mid-'60s model surfboards for up to $600.

California surf entrepreneur Allen Seymour, who in the mid-'80s organized the first surfing swap meets, took surf collecting to the next logical level in 1997, by staging the first-of-its-kind Pacific Coast Vintage Surf Auction featuring surfboards, surf magazines, posters, books, and other surf-related collectibles. Most collectors became specialists. British surfer Nick Cox filed and cataloged nearly 500 surf wax labels; Santa Monica surfer Lee Nichol collected about 150 mid- and late '60s boards, each featuring a floral design. One of the most valuable surfboard collections in the world is owned by the Hoffman family, headed by California surfing patriarchs Walter and Flippy Hoffman, and is thought to be worth about $350,000. (Not everybody was impressed by the growth or tenor of professional surf collecting.

"Been a lot of talk about collector surfboards lately," Australian surf magazine editor Derek Rielly wrote in 1998. "So much so that I feel like grabbing an ax and driving its blade through their overpriced decks.")

The Longboard Collectors Club was founded in Southern California in 1992; by the end of the decade the club had 147 members, and held regular meetings/board shows up and down the West Coast. In 2001, surfer and collector owner Mark Blackburn wrote *Surf's Up: Collecting the Longboard Era,* a lush coffee-table book with photographs and estimated values for surfboards (a 1940 redwood hot curl is listed at $6,000 to $8,000), books and magazines ($1,200 to $1,800 for a first-edition copy of John "Doc" Ball's *California Surfriders*), decals and cloth patches ($60 to $90 for a green 1966 United States Surfing Association decal), and sundry surf-related effects and paraphernalia, including postcards, movie tickets, teacups, print ads, flyers, and booklets. Blackburn describes surfing in the book's introduction as one of life's "most pleasurable and spiritual experiences," and invites readers to pick up on the sport's "joy and Nirvana through the following pages" of his book. Translating Nirvana into equity, the *Surf's Up* fine-print reveals that hundreds of the displayed items are available at Blackburn's own Big Island art gallery. *See also* surf auctions.

Surf Expo Bustling and slightly debauched three-day surf industry trade show held twice yearly in Orlando, Florida; the largest regular gathering of the sprawling East Coast surf community, and the oldest event of its kind anywhere. "Surf Expo," as former *Eastern Surf Magazine* editor Matt Walker once noted, "is part trade show, part Grateful Dead show." Surf Expo offers the chance for companies to show off their newest products—surfboards, trunks, sunglasses, video games, traction pads, wall clocks, key chains—to retailers and the surf industry at large; the show has expanded to include all manner of board sports, including skateboarding, wakeboarding, windsurfing, and snowboarding. Enormous quantities of beer and liquor are consumed at Surf Expo's after-hours parties, and many exhibitors spend virtually the entire 72-hour period either drunk or hungover.

A precursor to Surf Expo took place at the 1975 Eastern Surfing Association (ESA) Board of Directors meeting in Virginia Beach, when a dozen or so industry representatives rented hotel rooms to show their newest wares. ESA representative Ross Houston organized the first official Surf Expo the following January, staging the event in a Cocoa Beach hotel banquet hall; 30 exhibitors set up booths to display surfboards, wetsuits, surfwear lines, and accessories. (Surfing Expo, a one-off trade show held in Southern California in 1977, was unrelated.) By 1981, the number of Surf Expo booths had grown to 150; four years later a second annual show was added. Surf Expo moved to its current host site at Orlando's Orange County Convention Center in 1988; *Preview,* the Surf Expo trade magazine, began publishing in 1994.

Surf Expo employed over a dozen full-time event organizers by 2002, and the shows themselves had grown to include more than 850 companies occupying 2,050 booths. Surf Expo is not open to the general public, but nonetheless draws more than 15,000 people per show. Since 1993, Surf Expo has also organized the Back to School: East trade show in Virginia Beach (formerly called the Radshow); Back to School: West, held in Anaheim, California, began in 2002. Induction ceremonies for the East Coast Surf Legends Hall of Fame have been held at Surf Expo since 1996. *See also* Action Sports Retailer Trade Expo, Los Angeles Surf Fair.

surf forecasting   Surf forecasting—being able to predict when the surf is coming, where it will hit best, its duration, as well as wave-affecting local weather conditions, all in the name of getting more quality time in the water—has long been a Holy Grail for most surfers. The basic elements of surf forecasting are fairly straightforward, involving a series of measurements that include the breadth and strength of an open-ocean storm, the distance and angle between the storm and shoreline under consideration, secondary (or "interfering") storms, and nearshore weather conditions. The range of outcomes within this wave-making formula, however, are enormous, and while surf forecasting accuracy continues to improve, actual conditions often stray, sometimes greatly, from forecasters' predictions.

Modern surf forecasting began in the early 1940s, when Allied forces in World War II enlisted oceanographers from the Scripps Institution in La Jolla, California, to predict wave conditions for amphibious assaults in France and North Africa—including the D-Day landing in Normandy. An early connection between weather science and wave-riding came in 1965, when *Surfer* magazine announced wave prediction with the aid of storm-recording weather satellites as "the latest wrinkle in the surfing world." Big-wave

rider Fred Van Dyke invented his own personal phone-service wave forecasting system in 1967 by calling the Honolulu Weather Bureau to find out if a North Pacific storm had peaked, and using the information—which the Bureau gathered from wireless-transmitted shipping reports—to determine when he should paddle out at Waimea Bay. A small number of people continued to work on wave forecasting for surfers, and by the mid-'70s reasonably accurate forecasts were being issued by Hawaiian meteorologist George Mason and Southern California meteorologist Roger Pappas. In 1977, California surfer/meteorologists Vic Morris and Joe Nelson published *The Weather Surfer,* the first book of its kind for wave-riders, and forecasting from that point on became a regular part of the experience for all dedicated surfers. (The downside of wave prognostication was also pointed out at this time, as complaints were made against the *Honolulu Advertiser*'s surf report for increasing the crowds at Waikiki surf breaks.)

By the early '80s, Seal Beach surfer and self-taught forecaster Sean Collins had begun working on a new and improved wave-predicting formula based in large part on information downloaded via fax machine from the National Oceanic and Atmospheric Administration (NOAA). Collins and other surf forecasters were also using wave height/period information available from a series of open-ocean weather buoys. By 1982, Collins was working with *Surfing* magazine photo editor Larry "Flame" Moore to plan "sure thing" photo assignment surf trips. Commercial surf forecasting was introduced three years later, as Collins cofounded the pay-per-call Surfline phone service for the Los Angeles County area, which offered a 72-hour forecast along with regularly updated surf reports. Surfline was an instant hit, and the next few years brought a number of competing services, as well as an ever-expanding area of coverage that soon included much of the California coast and portions of the eastern seaboard and the east coast of Australia. When Surfline merged with competitor Wavetrak in 1991, the new service received more than one million calls in its first year. But there were critics. California surf journalist Scooter Leonard in 1999 praised the "instant empowerment" of wave forecasting, but lamented that it had to a great degree brought on the "death of mystery" in surfing. Uncrowded days at popular surf breaks in Southern California, Sydney, and Hawaii were all but unheard of, as surfers all knew days ahead of time when the waves would arrive. As with weather forecasting in general, surf forecasting accuracy tapers off as the prediction date is pushed back. Three-day predictions are extremely accurate; seven-day predictions are less so; 20-day predictions are just about useless.

With the rise of the Internet in the late '90s—and, most specifically, with the introduction of NOAA's ultra-detailed Wavewatch III Model—amateur surf forecasters had access to much of the data Surfline was using, which prompted the formation of local Web sites, such as Stormsurf.com in northern California and Swell-Forecast.com in Europe. Many of the sites have animated color- and time-coded models to show predicted storm intensity and wave height. But Surfline remained the primary source for wave forecasting, and as of 2002 the company offered detailed forecasts for almost every coastline in the world. *See also* buoy reports, Sean Collins, Surfline, swell period, wave height and measurement.

Surf Guide magazine   Handsome and occasionally provocative monthly surf magazine published by R. L. Stevenson and Associates in Santa Monica, California, from 1963 to 1965. The debut issue of *Surf Guide,* in January 1963, was produced as a marketing device for the Huntington Beach Surf Fair; the first three issues were on newsprint. *Surf Guide* was in fact wholly unexceptional until October 1963, when associate editor and Topanga Beach surfer Bill Cleary was promoted to editor and ran a cover story on Mickey Dora titled "The Angry Young Man of Surfing," as well as "The Surf Fad," a caustic article on surfing's exploding commercialization. While other magazines tried to coax surfing into the sporting mainstream, Cleary preferred to see it as loose and freewheeling, and *Surf Guide* soon became the genre's smartest and at times most poetic voice. "Surfing is more than waves and water," Cleary wrote. "It has a depth, a personality and a meaning. This is the surfing tradition—unconscious, beautiful and unsure." In November 1963, *Surf Guide* became the first surf magazine to put a woman on the cover (two-time U.S. champion Linda Benson), and devoted more than half of the issue's editorial space to women-themed articles. Unlike *Surfer, Surfing Illustrated,* and *Petersen's Surfing, Surf Guide* for the most part played down the contest scene; its report from the 1964 United States Surfing Championships, moreover, was the first surfing article to offer real contest analysis and criticism. Whereas *Surfer* described the 1964 event as an "awesome spectacle, [with] spectators kept on the edge of their seats," *Surf Guide* led by saying the contest was "a miserable fiasco of disorganization," and went on to explain why.

Cleary and Malibu surfer Kemp Aaberg, along with Australian Peter Rae, did much of the *Surf Guide* writing. The magazine began using color in early 1964, and a few months later graphic designer John Van Hamersveld (creator of the iconic *Endless Summer* poster) left *Surfer* to became *Surf Guide*'s art director, and quickly made it the best-looking publication of its kind. Bud Browne, Don James, and Ron Church were *Surf Guide*'s main photographers.

In the December 1964 issue, in a satire column written as a children's fable, *Surf Guide* author Robert Feigel mocks "Prince John the Stingy" and "Foul John," in what were plainly references to *Surfer* publisher John Severson. Legal action was threatened, and *Surf Guide,* already on shaky ground financially, folded after producing two issues in 1965. Twenty-two issues of the magazine were produced altogether. Cleary went on to become an associate editor at *Surfer. See also* Bill Cleary.

surf guitar   *See* Dick Dale, surf music.

Surf Industry Manufacturers Association (SIMA)   Trade group made up of about 350 surf industry manufacturers and distributors; founded in 1989 and headquartered in Dana Point, California. Before the formation of the Surf Industry Manufacturers Association (SIMA), the collective voice of the American surf industry manifested itself primarily through the Action Sports Retailer trade show in California and the Surf Expo trade show in Florida. Because both shows are owned by corporations outside the surf industry, surf company executives were concerned that the events might someday move away from their beach origins; SIMA in large part was created to address these concerns. O'Neill Wetsuits marketing director Kelley Woolsey proposed the idea for a surf industry trade group in 1988, and one year later, for the inaugural SIMA meeting, more than 50 companies had signed up as members. (Failed pre-SIMA trade groups include the 1965-founded Association of Surfing Industries, the 1966-founded Surfboard Manufacturers Association, and the 1972-founded Surfing Industries of America.)

SIMA's 2001 advisory board included the publishers of *Surfer, Surfing, TransWorld Surf,* the *Surfer's Journal,* and *Surf News,* as well as the presidents of the Association of Surfing Professionals and International Surfing Association. The SIMA directors' board traditionally includes the biggest names in the American surf industry. SIMA has independently budgeted committees that address environmental issues, trade shows, membership, and the Waterman's Ball, an annual promotional event and fund-raiser. In 1997 SIMA held its first annual Surf Summit in Cabo San Lucas, Mexico, a three-day event bringing together industry leaders for a series of meetings and panels. SIMA also founded Surfing America in 1997 as an umbrella group for domestic competitive surfing organizations.

Bob McKnight was the first SIMA president, followed in order by Michael Tomson, Tom Knapp, Jimmy Lomes, Tom Holbrook, Bonnie Crail, Peter Townend, and Dick Baker. Total international surf industry sales for 2002, as estimated by SIMA, were $4.5 billion. *See also* Waterman's Ball.

surf leash   Tethering device used to keep a surfboard from being washed toward shore after rider and board are separated, usually after a wipeout. Today's surf leash is made from a length of pliant and mildly elastic urethane cord. One end is attached to a thin rectangular nylon rail saver (to keep the cord from gouging into the edges of the board), which in turn is connected by a looped and knotted piece of nylon rope to a leash plug sunk into the deck of the surfboard near the tail. The other end is attached to a Velcro strap that loops around the surfer's rear ankle. Small metal swivels are added to each end of the urethane cord to prevent it from twisting and kinking. Surf leashes come in about eight basic sizes and styles, from light, quarter-inch-thick, six-foot-long "string" leashes used on most high-performance shortboards to sturdy 10-foot cords used by longboards, as well as $1/3$-inch-thick, 18-foot "monster cords" used by paddle-in big-wave surfers. Because the leash trails in the water behind the board's wake and cause a small amount of drag, most surfers try to use the smallest and lightest leash possible. Bigger waves require a longer, thicker leash, because the surfer needs to put more distance between himself and the breaking wave while still strapped to what in effect is a flotation device. Added thickness increases the leash's strength.

An early version of the leash was invented in the mid-1930s when American surfboard designer Tom Blake attached a 10-foot length of cotton rope from a belt on his waist to the stern of his board; he gave the device up as too dangerous. Other homemade rope-

Surf leash

constructed surf leashes were occasionally produced in the '50s and '60s. But credit for the invention of the surf leash is rightfully given to Santa Cruz's Pat O'Neill, son of wetsuit kingpin Jack O'Neill, who in 1970 fastened a length of surgical tubing to the nose of his board with a suction cup, and looped the other end to his wrist. Aside from the leash keeping the board nearby after a wipeout, it was initially thought that the surfer could use the new handheld product to leverage turns and cutbacks; by late 1971, however, the leash was connected to the ankle and the board's tail section, and was being sold—first by Control Products and Block Enterprises, both from Southern California, then by dozens of companies worldwide—simply as a board saver. Advertised as safe, the prototype rubber versions were in fact dangerous: Jack O'Neill permanently lost the sight in his left eye in 1971, after his tethered board snapped back and hit his face. Surfers by the thousands were meanwhile crafting their own leashes from lengths of marine surplus bungee cord.

"To Leash or Not to Leash, That is the Question" was the title of a 1972 *Surfing* magazine article, and for two or three years the question divided the surf world. Purists correctly noted that leashes encouraged less-skilled riders to try spots they would have otherwise avoided (board-damaging rocky breaks in particular), and that by removing the swim time from the surfing experience, lineups were more crowded than ever. Also, by relying on their leashes, surfers in general were becoming less water-savvy.

"Leashes are for dogs" was the unofficial motto of the no-leash group. Leash advocates said it was more fun to surf than swim, and that leashes promoted a freer, more progressive brand of surfing. By 1975 the pro-leash group had carried the debate (although it was a few more years before leashes would be used in large waves), and by 1980 it was rare to find a surfer not using a leash.

Leash construction and reliability improved steadily through the years, most significantly in 1975 with the introduction of the Control Products Power Cord, which threaded eight feet of nylon cord inside six feet of rubber tubing and thus limited the amount of tensile stretch; and in 1978, when urethane became the primary material. A small number of surfers have drowned after their leashes became tangled on an underwater rock or reef, and leash-recoil is estimated to be the cause of over 10 percent of surf-related injuries. Untold thousands of injuries, however, have been avoided as boards no longer fly spearlike toward shore after each wipeout. Many big-wave riders, furthermore, claim to have saved their own lives after a long wipeout when they were able to use their leash to "climb" to the surface.

Australians call the surf leash a "legrope," or "leggie." Dozens of surf leash synonyms, many of them derogatory, have been used over the years, including "ding string," "surf strap," "shot cord," "shock cord," "power cord," "kook connector," "kook cord," "sissy string," "dope rope," and "goon strap." A six-foot leash costs between $15 and $25. Most full-time surfers break between two and 10 leashes a year. *See also* injuries and surfing, leash plug, rail saver.

surf magazines   It's difficult to overestimate the loyalty and passion surf magazines inspire among readers. California surf writer Sam George once compared surf magazines to the Koran, the Book of Tao, and the Bible as the printed means to "reaffirm faith in a philosophy, a way of life. The only difference is that surf mags come out monthly."

While a handful of Southern California–based publications debuted in 1960 (including *Reef,* the *Surfers' Annual,* and *Surfing: The Voice of the Surfing World*—all short-lived), *Surfer* is generally credited as the sport's first magazine. California surf filmmaker John Severson produced the first issue of *The Surfer* (its original title) as a 36-page promo piece for his new film, *Surf Fever;* 5,000 copies sold, enough for Severson to begin publishing a quarterly version of *The Surfer* in 1961; two years later the magazine went bimonthly, and in 1964—firmly established as the field leader—the name was shortened to *Surfer.* More than a half-dozen Southern California–based surf magazines came and went in the early and mid-'60s; *International Surfing* (later shortened to *Surfing*) was founded in late 1964, and survived to become *Surfer*'s main competitor. Surf publishing was meanwhile taking root elsewhere with titles including *Surfing Hawaii* (founded in 1964), *Atlantic Surfing* (1965), *Surfing World* (Australia, 1962), *New Zealand Surfer* (1965), *South African Surfer* (1965), *Surf Atlantique* (France, 1964), and *British Surfer* (1969).

While surfing itself was regarded as something new, different, and untamed, first-generation surf magazines were generally conventional, even staid. Feature articles rotated almost without deviation from competition reports to travel pieces and surfer profile/interviews; column space was filled with equipment reports, cartoons, how-to articles, and the occasional short fiction piece. Even surf photography—the most important and compelling element in surf publishing, then and now—was often predictable, featuring the same riders at the same surf breaks. (Photographers nonetheless quickly became the stars of surf publishing. Top surf journalists over the decades, including Drew Kampion, Nick Carroll, Phil Jarratt, and Sam George, are merely admired and respected, while photographers like Don James, Jeff Divine, Art Brewer, and Aaron Chang are celebrated and glorified.) Surf magazine publishers and editors, as well as advertisers, meanwhile pulled together as one in an effort to "clean up" the sport and save it from the "gremmies and ho-dads" (as one editorial phrased it), "with their oiled hairdos and general unkempt appearance." *Surf Guide,* published out of Santa Monica, California, was the only magazine at the time to present surfing as removed from the larger world of sport, with editor Bill Cleary publishing naysaying articles on surf contests as early as 1964, and describing "the surfing tradition" as "unconscious, beautiful, unsure and elusive."

Surf magazines were liberated in the late '60s by both the shortboard revolution as well as the broader counterculture movement. Surf photographers tried new angles, shutter speeds, and development processes; editors, publishers, and writers gave up trying to domesticate the sport, and opened up the editorial palette, producing issue articles on topics such as localism and professionalism, and moving further afield to touch on drug use, the Vietnam War, and environmentalism; art directors were given freer reign and more color-use pages. (David Carson, John Van Hamersveld, and Mike Salisbury are among the surf magazine art directors who went on to have successful careers in mainstream graphic design.) *Tracks,* the 1970-founded black-and-white Australian tabloid, was the most progressive surf magazine of the '70s. Industry leader *Surfer* changed from bimonthly to monthly in 1978, and *Surfing* followed in 1979; they continued as the field's two best-selling magazines.

As the beachwear-led surf industry rocketed toward billion-dollar annual sales in the mid- and late '80s, surf publishing grew as well, with brightly colored, ad-packed issues—sometimes with foldout covers and free posters—topping 200 pages. After a brief early '90s slump, the surf industry once again expanded, publishing included; by the middle of the decade, surf magazines were being produced in nearly two dozen countries worldwide, including France (*Surf Session*), Germany (*Surfers*), Brazil (*Fluir*), Japan (*Surfing World*), Italy (*Surfer News*), Venezuela (*Surf Caribe*), Spain (*Surfer Rule*), and Canada (*Northern Swell*). Surf publishing in America and Australia was largely defined by niche marketing, with new titles aimed at female surfers (*Wahine, Surfing Girl*), longboarders (*Longboarder, Pacific Longboarder*), middle-aged surfers (the *Surfer's Journal*), and surfers in their early teens (*TransWorld Surf*). *Surfer* and *Surfing* magazines remained on top, each distributing about 110,000 copies internationally per issue, and each launching a successful Web site by decade's end. The October 1999 issue of *Surfer,* at 340 pages, remains the largest surf magazine ever published. The 1992-founded *Surfer's Journal,* a plush quarterly, had meanwhile broken new ground by booking fewer than a half-dozen advertisements for each 130-page issue, earning revenue instead from the magazine's $12.95 cover price. At the other end of the spectrum, rough-and-ready tabloids like Florida-published *Eastern Surf Magazine* were given out free at surf shops. *Australia's Surfing Life,* the potty-mouthed monthly from Queensland's Gold Coast, was prized by English-speaking surfers worldwide as the funniest and sharpest surf periodical.

Surf magazines were affected by the merger trend of the '90s and '00s. New York–based publishing giant Primedia bought *Surfing* magazine in 1997, while *Surfer* was bought by Petersen Publishing in 1998, which in turn was bought by Emap Publishing

in 2000. When Primedia bought Emap in 2001, *Surfer* and *Surfing* were brought into the same publishing house. Early surf magazines had meanwhile become valuable as collector's items. The "Magazine and Poster" issue of the *Surfing Collectibles Guide,* published in 2000, listed mint-condition prices for magazines of the '60s, with the debut issue of *Reef* (1960) priced at $600 and the second issue of *Surfer* (1961) marked at $1,500. According to surf magazine collector Al Hunt of Australia, 422 separate surf magazine titles were founded between 1960 and 2002. *See also* Australia's Surfing Life, Australian Surfing World, Deep, Eastern Surf Magazine, H2O, Longboard, Surf Guide, Surfer, Surfer's Path, Surfing, the Surfer's Journal, Tracks, TransWorld Surf, Wahine, Waves.

surf mat   *See* mat-surfing.

surf memorabilia   *See* surf collectors.

surf movies   Feature-length movies made by and for surfers, generally shot on 16-millimeter film, and filled for the most part with a series of surf-action montages. More energetic than artful, surf movies from the late 1950s to the late '70s were nonetheless greeted with wild enthusiasm from beach city audiences. "The surf movie is a high-energy situation," surf journalist Jack Heart wrote in 1975. "Next to actually being in the water, it can provide the most intense moments of our surfing lives."

The surf movie got started in 1953, when 41-year-old schoolteacher and former lifeguard Bud Browne premiered *Hawaiian Surfing Movies* to a full house at John Adams Junior High School in Santa Monica, California. The response to Browne's 45-minute film was enough for him to quit his teaching job and make a career of sorts by producing one surf movie a year—in similar fashion to ski moviemaker Warren Miller. Three more filmmakers had joined in by 1957: John Severson (*Surfer* magazine founder in 1960), Bruce Brown (creator of the 1966 hit *The Endless Summer*), and Greg Noll (board manufacturer and big-wave rider). Together they invented a surf movie format that remained virtually unchanged through the decades, and transferred easily into the '80s-launched era of surf video. The surf movie design was simple: two or three dozen surf-action montages interrupted periodically by a comedy sketch or an on-the-road vignette; later movies often had brief surfer interviews, an animated short, an alternative sport

Surf movies; handbill for 1960 double feature

detour (skiing, hang gliding, skateboarding), or an environmental-message sequence. Early surf movies, almost without exception, were filmed exclusively in California, Australia, Mexico, and Hawaii; all of them finished with a big-wave sequence shot on the North Shore of Oahu—usually at Waimea Bay. Each filmmaker worked as a one-man production company, shooting, editing, and scoring, then barnstorming the movie from one beach city to the next, with one- or two-night live-narration screenings at local vet halls, high school auditoriums, and community centers. The work was sometimes fun, but just as often exhausting. "I can't think of a worse business," Noll later said, "then trying to rent auditoriums, hammer up posters and handbills, and go through all the bullshit of making surf movies, the way it was done in the old days." Early surf films cost about $5,000 to produce, and filmmakers generally met costs and living expenses, and had just enough left over to begin the next movie. Undeterred, the roster of surf moviemakers grew in the early and mid-'60s, with newcomers Walt Phillips, Bob Evans, Dale Davis, Grant Rohloff, Jim Freeman, Greg MacGillivray, Paul Witzig, and others all for the most part working on the same one-a-year schedule. As the surf industry was based in

Southern California, so, too, were most of the surf filmmakers. *Cat on a Hot Foam Board, Slippery When Wet, Cavalcade of Surf, Going My Wave, Surfing Hollow Days, Strictly Hot,* and *A Cool Wave of Color* were among the best of the early surf films. (Meanwhile in the wake of Columbia Studios' 1959 hit *Gidget,* Hollywood produced more than two dozen low-budget teen-romp beach films, including *Beach Blanket Bingo* and *Muscle Beach Party,* which always included a few brief surf shots.)

Surf movies as a rule were less interesting than the gatherings they attracted while on tour, as surfers—mainly beer-soaked suburban teenagers—filed into the theater to whistle, shout, cheer, boo, hiss, stomp their feet, roll beer bottles down the aisles, throw paper airplanes, and occasionally sprint onstage to moon the audience. "Mass assembly was the real attraction of surf movies," the *Surfer's Journal* said in 1998. "Here was a chance to define and validate yourself as a surfer, not just in a group of two, or five, or 20, down on the beach where you were supposed to be, but in a crowd of 200, or 1,000, or even 3,000."

The Endless Summer, after touring in the usual fashion in 1964 and 1965, was blown up to 35-millimeter in 1966 and put into general release, earning glowing reviews in *Time, Newsweek,* and the *New Yorker.* Brown had gone much further afield in his "search for the perfect wave" (memorably found at Cape St. Francis, South Africa), with sequences from Ghana, Senegal, Tahiti, and New Zealand, and his film had a travelogue plot of sorts. It featured less wave-riding than any other surf film up to that point, and Brown was obligated to explain most aspects of the sport to a nonsurfing audience. But dedicated surfers embraced *Endless Summer* just as readily as the landlocked surf dreamers in Des Moines and Minneapolis, and it remains the one and only surf movie masterpiece.

While surfing began taking itself more seriously in the '70s, and the number of filmmakers continued to grow—with Hal Jepsen, Scott Dittrich, Alby Falzon, Yuri Farrant, Chris Bystrom, Steve Soderberg, and Alan Rich among the contributors—surf movies didn't much stray from the tried-and-true format. *The Endless Summer* had turned the search for the perfect wave into the sport's Holy Grail; surfers fanned out by the thousands, looking for their own Cape St. Francis, and surf movies reflected the trend: France, Spain, Morocco, South Africa, and Indonesia had all been featured by the early '70s. Photography and editing were uneven through the decade, but Bill Delaney, Jack McCoy, and the MacGillivray-Freeman team set a high quality standard. Surf movie soundtracks, meanwhile, were often fantastic—and nearly always bootlegged. Bruce Brown used West Coast jazz master Bud Shank to score two of his early films, but nearly all surf movies from the '60s and '70s were backed with rock and roll lifted straight from the filmmaker's record collection. California's Scott Dittrich scored his 1974 film *Fluid Drive* with Led Zeppelin, Jimi Hendrix, the Rolling Stones, and Lou Reed; Hoole-McCoy's 1978 release *Tubular Swells* had Fleetwood Mac, the Allman Brothers, T. Rex, Steve Miller, Joni Mitchell, and the Temptations. Audio-synch sound, another popular '70s surf film feature, which allowed filmmakers to present surfers speaking onscreen, for the most part did nothing more than show surfers looking uncomfortable in front of the camera. *Five Summer Stories* (1972), *Morning of the Earth* (1972), *Going Surfin'* (1973), and *Free Ride* (1977) were the standout surf films of the period.

Audiences were nonetheless more rambunctious than ever. "An unhappy crowd," *Surfer* magazine said in a 1975 surf movie notice, "eager for the film to end, hurled the projector and the film reels from a balcony into some empty seats below. The reels rolled down the aisle, unraveling the film, and the audience cheered and left." Production costs, meanwhile, were going up. *Free Ride,* the last great surf movie, cost about $70,000; *Surfers: The Movie* cost about $400,000. With a few exceptions—including *Storm Riders* (1982) and *Surfers: The Movie* (1990)—surf movies went into a steady decline over the next few years. Threatened lawsuits from music companies forced moviemakers to abandon the bootleg soundtrack, and instead buy cheap original music, and the results were an audio disaster. The 1984 video release of *The Performers,* meanwhile, signaled the upcoming wholesale change in surf cinema from celluloid to videotape, theater to living room. A small number of surf movies have been released since the early '90s, but the surf movie era was more or less finished by the early '80s. About 275 surf movies were made altogether from 1953 to 1990, including 50 short-subject films.

A 12-part documentary series, *50 Years of Surfing of Film,* produced in 1997 by the *Surfer's Journal* and Outdoor Life Network and later released in a four-video set, provides a surf movie historical overview;

a more detailed survey is found in *Surfmovies: The History of the Surf Film in Australia,* a 192-page coffee-table book published in 2000 by Albie Thoms. A few dozen surf movies themselves, including *Endless Summer,* are available on video.

See also Bruce Brown, Bud Browne, Chris Bystrom, Dale Davis, Bill Delaney, Scott Dittrich, David Elfick, Bob Evans, Alby Falzon, The Endless Summer, Endless Summer II, Evolution, Free Ride, Jim Freeman, Five Summer Stories, Hal Jepsen, Hollywood and surfing, Morning of the Earth, Greg MacGillivray, Jack McCoy, Greg Noll, Walt Phillips, John Severson, Paul Witzig.

surf music   Influential rock music genre, developed and recorded almost entirely in California, second only to Motown as the country's most popular music during the pre-Beatles '60s. Surf music is divided into two categories: the pulsating, reverb-heavy, "wet"-sounding instrumental form exemplified by guitarist Dick Dale, and the smooth-voiced, multitracked harmonized vocal style invented by the Beach Boys. Purists argue that surf music is by definition instrumental. Both forms have echoed clearly through the decades in pop music. (In the early and mid-'60s, instrumental and vocal surf music were both closely associated with—in some cases nearly indistinguishable from—"hot rod music." Jan and Dean, for example, recorded "Surf City" and "Drag City.")

Dick Dale of Southern California and the Ventures, a four-piece band from Seattle, Washington, have both been credited as inventing instrumental surf music. The Ventures hit the charts first with "Walk Don't Run," which went to #2 in 1960, but the song didn't have an intrinsic "surf" feel—and four years later the Ventures in fact released a second, more surfed-up version titled "Walk Don't Run '64." Dale's bouncy "Let's Go Trippin'," a Southern California regional hit in 1961, is more often cited as the original surf song. Dale was influenced by the guitar-driven sound of Duane Eddy and Johnny and the Hurricanes, as well as the Middle Eastern folk music played by his Lebanese family. A surfer himself, Dale built a loyal local following among Southern California wave-riders in 1960 and 1961 for his raucous shows at the Rendezvous Ballroom in Newport Beach, where the foot-pounding Surfer's Stomp dance step was ritualistically practiced. With the success of "Let's Go Trippin'," Dale was immediately billed as the "King of the Surf Guitar," and a photo

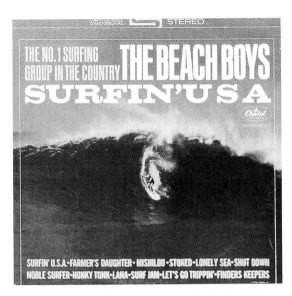

Surf music; the Beach Boys' 1963 album *Surfin' USA*

of him surfing was used on the cover of his 1962's *Surfer's Choice* album. With Dale's new single "Misirlou" (1962), his music became louder, faster, denser, and more intense—he was now running his Fender Stratocaster guitar through a Fender Duel Showman Amplifier and reverb unit—and the song become a surf music standard, along with the Surfaris' "Wipe Out" (1962) and the Chantays' "Pipeline" (1963). Dale later said the inspiration for his hurling guitar sound was "to match the feeling I had while surfing, a feeling of vibration and pulsification." Other popular instrumental surf bands of the period included the Bel-Airs, the Challengers, and the Astronauts.

The Los Angeles–based Beach Boys began recording what Dale and other surf musicians disdainfully called "surf songs" in the fall of 1961, but the group hedged its bet somewhat on their first single, which featured a vocal track on one side and an instrumental on the other ("Surfin'" and "Luau," respectively). By 1962, it was already obvious that while surfers liked the hard-charging instrumentals, teenagers nationwide preferred smoother, melodic, lyric-based pop tunes, and Beach Boy songwriting genius Brian Wilson, ambitious as he was creative, was soon turning out beautifully orchestrated records about the Southern California beach life, filled with sun, waves, fast cars, and bikini-wearing girls. "Surfin'" was a local hit in late 1961, but only went to #73 nationally, and the follow-up "Surfin' Safari" peaked at #14 in 1962. It was Jan and Dean, another Los Angeles vocal group, who took the surf song national, with a

Wilson-penned tune called "Surf City" that went to #1 for two weeks in July 1963. For the next 18 months, the Beach Boys and Jan and Dean almost single-handedly defined the surf song, with records like "Honolulu Lulu," "Ride the Wild Surf," "Sidewalk Surfin'" (Jan and Dean), "Surfin' U.S.A.," Surfer Girl," and "Catch a Wave" (Beach Boys). Meanwhile, a string of *Gidget*-inspired Hollywood beach movies did their part, along with instrumental and vocal surf bands, to export the warm, cheerful, mildly sexy vision of Southern California surfers and beaches. The surf sound was also popular in Australia, Great Britain, New Zealand, South Africa, and Japan. The Beatles-led British Invasion brought the American surf music era to a fast end, with the Beach Boys the only group to move on creatively in the years ahead, producing heaven-sent tracks like "God Only Knows," "Caroline, No," and "Good Vibrations."

A modest surf music revival took place in the late '70s and early '80s, led by neotraditionalists Jon and the Nightriders and the Surf Raiders, along with the Surf Punks, a novelty act whose song list included "Punchout at Malibu," "Can't Get a Tan," and "Somebody Ripped My Stick." Dick Dale returned in the early '90s to make two critically praised albums, and his original version of "Misirlou" was used as the opening song in the 1994 hit film *Pulp Fiction.* New surf bands like the Mermen, the Halibuts, the Phantom Surfers, and the Blue Hawaiians also made albums; none were best-sellers, but the genre was kept alive. In 1996, Rhino Records released *Cowabunga! The Surf Box,* a four CD compilation that included a detailed history of surf music.

Surfers and surfing, meanwhile, have always maintained a connection to music. Three-time U.S. surfing champion Corky Carroll recorded folk and novelty albums in the '70s, including *A Surfer for President* in 1979; six-time world champion Kelly Slater, along with pro surfers Rob Machado and Peter King, playing together as the Surfers, released their T Bone Burnett–produced *Songs From the Pipe* in 1998; Sunchild, featuring Orange County pro surfer and guitarist Donavan Frankenreiter, opened for aging rockers Peter Frampton and Ted Nugent in the mid- and late '90s; ace Hawaiian surfer Jack Johnson released *Brushfire Fairytales* in 2001 to critical and popular acclaim. The Surfrider Foundation environmental group, capitalizing on the small but influential number of famous rockers who also surf, released three *Music for Our Mother Ocean* compilation albums in the mid-'90s, featuring surfer/musicians such as Chris Isaak, Eddie Vedder of Pearl Jam, and Perry Farrell of Jane's Addiction, along with the Beach Boys' Brian Wilson and the eclectic but nonsurfing Butthole Surfers. A number of books on surf music have been published over the years, including *The Illustrated Discography of Surf Music* (1978), *Surfin' Guitars: Instrumental Surf Bands of the Sixties* (1988), and *Surf City: The California Sound* (1995). According to Web site Reverb Central, there were more than 500 instrumental surf bands playing and recording worldwide in 2002, in nations from Canada (the Treblemakers) to Finland (the Surfing Spacemen), Israel (the Astroglides), Japan (the Surf Coasters), Russia (the Spoilers), Sweden (the Seventh Wave), and Uruguay (Reverberockets). *See also* Beach Boys, the Chantays, Dick Dale, Honk, Jan and Dean, Jack Johnson, Rendezvous Ballroom, Surf Punks, the Surfaris, "Surfer Joe," Surfer Stomp, "Surfin' Bird," "Surfin' Safari," the Ventures, "Wipeout."

surf Nazi   Description for a hyperdedicated surfer, usually adolescent or preadolescent; sometimes derogatory, but just as often used as a backhanded expression of respect. American surfing has a long, intermittent, and for the most part innocuous association with wartime Nazi imagery. In the early 1930s, the Pacific System Homes company in Los Angeles introduced the "Swastika" model surfboard—the first commercially available board, featuring a small swastika emblem near the tail. The mark had been a symbol of good luck and harmony before being adapted by Hitler's Third Reich; in 1938, after Germany invaded Austria and pushed the world closer to war, Pacific System Homes changed the name of their line to "Waikiki Surf-Boards." Nearly 20 years later, a small group of surfers from La Jolla, California, dressed up in German military uniforms and marched along the beachfront holding Nazi flags. "We just did things like that to be outrageous," big-wave surfer Greg Noll recalled years later. "You paint a swastika on your car, and it would piss people off. So what do you do? You paint on two swastikas." Artist and custom car builder Ed "Big Daddy" Roth, creator of the popular Rat Fink character, marketed American teenage rebellion as well as anybody in the 1960s, and in 1965 he introduced a line of Surfer's Cross decals and pendants, each modeled after the German Iron Cross military award. The surf press railed against the new accouterment, but Roth was unrepentant. "That Hitler," he told *Time* magazine,

just before releasing a plastic copy of the German army iron helmet, "really did a hellava public relations job for me."

"Surf Nazi," however, didn't enter the surfing lexicon until the late '70s, as punk-inspired rebelliousness spread across the country on down to the beaches. "Wayne Lynch at 25: A Very Experienced Surf Nazi" was the perhaps badly chosen title of a 1978 *Surfer* magazine profile on one of the sport's more peaceable and noncompetitive figures, and it earned the magazine a number of angry reader's letters, including one from Stephen Bruce of Atlanta, Georgia: "Doesn't the term [surf Nazi] call forth images of cruelty, callousness and the worst kind of sadism?" *Surfer* disagreed, and followed up with a competition report titled "Storm Troopers Hit Surf City." "Surf Nazi" had for the most part fallen out of use among surfers by the late '80s, but the sport continued to make odd little connections with World War II Germanic symbols. In the early '90s, young Australian pro surfer Matt Hoy began airbrushing an enormous Iron Cross on the deck of his surfboards. *Surfing* magazine, clumsily moving to Hoy's defense, reported that while the Australian recognized the Iron Cross to be a "symbol of Nazi power," to him it represented only "strength and winning." *See also* Ed "Big Daddy" Roth.

surf photography   Photographs of surfers and surfing were taken in Waikiki as far back as the late 19th century, but surf photography as a genre was invented during the depression by Americans Tom Blake and John "Doc" Ball. Blake, the Wisconsin-born surfer/board designer who spent much of his young adult life in Hawaii, built a 10-pound wooden-box housing for his Graflex camera in 1929, rested the two-foot-high apparatus atop his board, and began to shoot surfing images from the water. The *Los Angeles Times* ran one of Blake's shots in 1931 as a full-page image, and in 1935 *National Geographic* published the duotone "Waves and Thrills at Waikiki," an eight-page Blake portfolio that included a shot of Amelia Earhart riding in an outrigger canoe with Diamond Head in the background. Southern California dentist and surfer John "Doc" Ball, inspired by Blake's work, took nearly 1,000 surf-related photographs between 1931 and 1941; *National Geographic* published Ball's eight-page black-and-white "Surf-Boarders Capture California" portfolio in 1944, two years before he self-published his 108-page *California Surfriders* photo

Surf photographers at Lower Trestles, California

book. Don James, another Southern California surfer/ dentist, began taking surf photos in 1936. While Blake, Ball, and James all worked hard at their craft, they were hobbyists, with careers outside of photography, and made little or no money from their camera work.

California surf filmmaker John Severson began publishing *Surfer* magazine in 1960, filling the pages almost exclusively with his own land-shot black-and-white photographs. (The second issue of *Surfer* offered $5 for each published reader-submitted photo.) More than a dozen surf magazine titles were founded worldwide in the early and mid-'60s, but most were shoestring operations, so that while the demand for surf photographs shot up, pay rates remained low. Southern California photographer Ron Stoner, hired by *Surfer* in 1964, became the first full-time professional surf photographer in mid-1965, earning $500 a month along with a gas and food allowance; he was also awarded the magazine's coveted Century 1,000-millimeter lens—far and away the best and most expensive piece of equipment used in surf photography at the time—and utilized it to beautiful effect, taking rich, well-composed, color-saturated images, primarily in Southern California and Hawaii.

Water shots have always been the genre's gold standard, and much of the development in surf photography over the years has involved getting closer to the rider and the breaking wave. In the early '70s, Steve Wilkings of Hawaii put viewers at the very perimeter of the tube at places like Pipeline; photographers Dan Merkel, Aaron Chang, and Don King, among others, went deeper still in the years to follow, and eventually began taking shots while completely inside the tube. Tight-angle water photography is by

far the genre's most demanding form, requiring great fitness, patience, timing, and surf sense. It can also be dangerous, as the photographer positions himself in the tiny margins between the curl, surfer, surfboard, and in many cases a shallow, coral-covered reef. Along with the water shot, other familiar surf photography standards include the telephoto land shot, the pulled-back surf break overview portraits, candids, and the rapid-fire motordrive sequence. Surf photos are sometimes taken from helicopters or from underwater, and from cameras mounted on raised poles or bolted to the deck of the surfboard itself. Surf photographers have experimented with shutter speeds, f-stops, and film stocks, and later with digital enhancement.

The surf photograph has since the mid-'60s been much more of a fantasy version of the sport rather than a documentary item. "They create desires," California surf journalist Steve Barilotti wrote in 1997, "fuel journeys, inspire, titillate, and transport us mentally and spiritually from our plodding and land-bound existence." The surf photographer's stock-in-trade image is of a perfectly front-lit wave, usually tropical, sometimes empty, but more often with one of the world's best surfers captured at the absolute peak of action—inside the tube, or carving a deep turn, or flying airborne above the crest. Photographers who can dependably produce such images have since the early '70s been awarded a surf world celebrity status just below that of their most famous subjects: Californians Art Brewer, Jeff Divine, and Leroy Grannis each have had their work gathered and published in lavish eponymously-titled photo books; Aaron Chang was profiled in an *American Photographer* cover story; surf magazines have featured lengthy portfolios from photographers like Warren Bolster and Don King (from Hawaii); Larry Moore, Jeff Hornbaker, Bob Barbour, and Tom Servais (California); Ted Grambeau, Peter Crawford, Bruce Channon, and Hugh McLeod (Australia); Dick Meseroll (America's East Coast); Denjiro Sato (Japan); Pierre Tostee (South Africa); and Sylvain Cazenave (France). "All-photo issue" surf magazines have been a mainstay since the early '70s. Surfing photo books have been published for decades, and include *California Surfriders* (1946), *A Pictorial History of Surfing* (1970), and *Aloha Blue* (1997).

Surf photography has always been a nearly exclusively male pursuit; Hawaii's Shirley Rogers, working for *Surfing* magazine in the early and mid-'80s, is one of a tiny number of women who have earned a surf magazine masthead credit. Surf photography wages, meanwhile, remain low in most cases. Of the roughly 80 full-time surf photographers worldwide in 2002, only about 25 were earning more than $25,000 annually. A starting investment in first-rate equipment—including a good auto-focus camera, 600-millimeter telephoto lens, 20-millimeter wide-angle fisheye lens, five-shots-per-second motordrive, waterhousing, tripod, carrying case, and accessories—costs about $20,000; film and processing run about $20 per roll.

See also Erik Aeder, Scott Aichner, Bernie Baker, John "Doc" Ball, Bob Barbour, Warren Bolster, Art Brewer, Sylvain Cazenave, Aaron Chang, Bruce Channon, Peter Crawford, Jeff Divine, Ted Grambeau, Leroy Grannis, Jeff Hornbaker, Don James, Kin Kimoto, Chris Klopf, Clarence Maki, Hugh McLeod, Dan Merkel, Mike Moir, Larry "Flame" Moore, Craig Peterson, Paul Sargeant, Denjiro Sato, Tom Servais, Lance Slabbert, Ron Stoner, Chris Van Lennep, Steve Wilkings, Woody Woodworth.

Surf Punks Loud, crude, satirizing Southern California rock band of the late 1970s and '80s. The Surf Punks added members as needed for live performances, but were essentially a two-man act consisting of drummer/producer Dennis Dragon (younger brother of Daryl Dragon, of Captain and Tennille fame) and guitarist Drew Steele. *My Beach,* the Punks' first album (1980), played off the increasingly aggressive vibe found on Southern California surf beaches. It sold more than 100,000 copies, and featured songs like "Shoulder Hopper," "Punchout at Malibu," "Can't Get a Tan," and "Somebody Ripped My Stick." Vocals for "My Beach," the album's two-chord opening track, were nasally and spare, and set a tone for the cuts that followed: "My beach / My wave / My chick / Go home!" Later Surf Punks albums included *Locals Only* (1982) and *Oh No! Not Them Again!* (1988). Younger surfers got a chuckle out of the Punks, as did a portion of the larger rock community, but the laughs turned to sighs of resignation as the band shouldered on. "What are you going to do?" *Surfer* magazine wrote of the Punks in 1982. "They're part of the family, good or bad, so tolerate them if you must and enjoy them if you can." *See also* surf music.

surf rage Mainstream media phrase coined in 2000 as a spin-off on "road rage," used to describe surfing-related hostility and violence. Fighting in the surf hadn't gone up proportionately since the '70s heyday of virulent turf-based localism. But when former world champion and international surfing icon Nat Young, 52, was beaten nearly unconscious in 2000 while riding in front of his house in northern New South Wales, Australia, news outlets—including the *Sydney Sun-Herald,* USA Today, the *New York Times,* CNN.com, and *A Current Affair*—produced a small flood of often-lurid "surf rage" stories. In America, *USA Today*'s Michael Hiestand reported, "Surf rage is now seen as a serious and growing national problem." Young himself, after recovering from two broken eye sockets, played up the idea of rampant beachside violence by writing a book of essays titled *Surf Rage* (2000), with an introduction describing surf rage as "burning like a brushfire everywhere in the world."

Surf journalist Sam George, meanwhile, wasn't convinced that disorder in the lineup was on the rise. "Is surfing really a violent sport?" he asked in 2000. "Recognize that in almost every situation, surfers are placed in direct competition with each other for a very limited resource [waves], all of them armed with a potentially dangerous weapon [surfboards], yet all cooperating to some degree. Harsh words occasionally, and plenty of tempers flaring, but over the years, only isolated instances of actual violence." *See also* localism, violence and surfing.

Surf Report, The Monthly surf-travel newsletter published from 1980 to 1998 by *Surfer* magazine in San Juan Capistrano, California; conceptualized by *Surfer* publisher Steve Pezman; developed and produced by founding editor Rus Calisch. Each issue of the *Surf Report* was nearly identical in format. A surfing area was featured on the cover (usually a country, state, island or island group, or region), with mapped and detailed spot-by-spot information on the next few pages, followed in turn by summaries of the area's culture and history, transportation and accommodations, as well as typical wave and weather conditions. The *Surf Report*'s text-heavy back pages contained short surf updates from around the world for the previous month, essays on wave formation and forecasting, classified ads, minifeatures on surfing areas, and condensed news items from the world of the traveling surfer. Each *Surf Report* was 10 or 12 pages long; black-and-white photographs were added to the design in 1997. The newsletters editorial voice was both knowledgeable and surfed out. "Slow, mellow righthander," a 1997 issue says of a break called

Piddlies in the Maldive Islands. "Any swell over four-foot tends to mush it out." The *Surf Report* was available by subscription, but most surfers sent away for back issues ($3.00 per issue in 1980, $6.00 per issue today) once they had a destination in mind. Assembled from a single office within the *Surfer* magazine publishing complex, the *Surf Report* was an instant low-overhead success, embraced by traveling surfers. Like Bank Wright's 1973-published guidebook *Surfing California*, the *Surf Report* was also regarded by many surfers as nothing less than heretical, as it revealed, in just a few short pages, information that had taken local surfers years to accumulate. Along with all the familiar wave-riding domains—Hawaii, Australia, Indonesia, and mainland America—*Surf Report* cover features over the years included El Salvador, Congo, Okinawa, Scotland, Papua New Guinea, Namibia, Madagascar, Sri Lanka, Hong Kong, and Senegal.

Calisch served as the *Surf Report* editor from 1980 to 1986, followed by Donna Oakley (1987 to 1996) and Chris Dixon (1996 to 1998). Four issues of the *Surfer Travel Report,* similar to the *Surf Report* and edited by Will Pennartz, were published in 1999, each focusing on a different region in California. *See also* Rus Calisch, surf travel.

surf sacrifice Beachfront pyrotechnic ritual performed in order to bring up the surf. The exact sequencing of events is often made up on the spot, but the final result is the nighttime immolation of an old, discarded surfboard or stack of surfboards. A surf sacrifice is often crowned with a beery salute to Kahuna, the Hawaiian god of waves and surf (or Huey, if the sacrificing party is Australian), but just as often the event goes off with no formal invocation. The number of surf sacrifices began to tail off in the late '80s, after it was pointed out that the column of black smoke rising off a burning pyre of fiberglass and polyester resin is in fact highly toxic.

surf schools Surfing has traditionally been a self-taught activity, partly because it's an individual rather than a team sport, and partly because the surf world's view of itself as rebellious and autonomous tends to squelch group activity—even at the introductory level. An overwhelming majority of surfers are introduced to the sport by a surfing friend or relative, given a few basic instructions, and are then left to learn at their own pace. Surf schools have

Surf schools; California instructor Richard Schmidt

nonetheless been part of the sport for decades, and since the early 1990s their popularity has been rising steadily.

The beachboys of Waikiki, Hawaii, working primarily for the expensive seafront hotels, put together impromptu surf schools for visiting mainland tourists as far back as the 1910s. But surf schools as they exist today came into being in the early '60s, with the founding of the San Diego Surf School and the West Coast Surf School in Dana Point. Dozens of surf schools came and went in California, Hawaii, and Australia over the next 25 years, while a small number became mainstays—including the Paskowitz Surf Camp in Southern California, the Nancy Emerson School of Surfing in Hawaii (both founded in the '70s), and the 1984-founded Manly Surf School in Sydney, Australia. Surfing began its second great boom in popularity during the early '90s, fueled in large part by baby boomers' preteen offspring, along with middle-aged first-timers and females of every age; all of these groups were less likely than previous generations of surfers to be concerned with the sport's go-it-alone ethos, and thus ideal candidates for the growing number of surf schools. By 2002, there were an estimated 100 surf schools in America and another 100 internationally.

Most surf schools use roughly the same pedagogical methods, especially for beginning classes. (Some schools offer intermediate and even expert classes, as well as multiday clinics or camps, but a vast majority of surf school classes are made up of first-timers.) Surf schools generally meet on a sandy beach with small, gentle waves. Class size typically ranges from six to 12; each student is provided with a soft-skinned longboard and, if necessary, a wetsuit. In a typical two-hour introductory session, half the time will be spent on shore, with the instructor covering basic rules of surf safety and etiquette (how to recognize and avoid a rip current; an explanation of the "drop-in" rule), and the students doing a paddle/stand-up "dry run" while lying atop their boards. During the second half of class, students are usually taken out one at a time and pushed into a series of waves. Many surf classes guarantee that the newcomer will ride a wave standing up during the first lesson. Surf schools charge about $30 to $70 per person for a two-hour introductory group lesson; longer and more expensive sessions might include yoga classes and massages, visits to a surf shop or surf museum, and videotape review of the day's lesson. Surf instructors in Australia can be certified by the Surfing Australia organization; the rest of the surf world, as of 2003, has no such certification process.

A prototype all-female surf school began in 1982, when world pro tour champion Debbie Beacham of California gave a series of free hour-long lessons to 150 women surf hopefuls at La Jolla Shores, San Diego. Surf Diva, a 1996-founded San Diego surf school, has since become the best-known all-female surf school. Niche surf schools have also targeted Christians, autistic children, business executives, and upscale vacationers. It's estimated that preteens make up about half of all surf school enrollees. Surf schools are occasionally sponsored by surf-related companies as a promotional device: in 1997 wetsuit manufacturer O'Neill Europe began holding four-day O'Neill Surf Academy sessions, free of charge, in England, The Netherlands, Belgium, Spain, Portugal, and Italy. In Sydney, Australia, the Manly Surf School gave lessons to an estimated 25,000 surfers in 2002. *See also* Dorian Paskowitz.

surf ski   *See* wave-ski.

surf slang   Invented or redefined words and phrases have been a part of the surf culture as far back as the 1920s, when surfers in Waikiki scanned the horizon for "bluebirds" (big waves), steered clear of the "soup" (whitewater), and did their best to keep their finless wooden boards from "sliding ass" (losing tail-end traction). As slang-happy American teenagers began surfing by the thousands in the 1950s, surf lingo output shot up as well; for nonsurfers, part of the humor and charm of Columbia Pictures' 1959 movie *Gidget*

was the casual saltwater-inflected patois used by characters with names like Moondoggie and Kahuna. A few years later, the Beach Boys' hit "Surfin' U.S.A." introduced pop music fans across the country to words like "baggies" and "surfari." General audience magazine articles on surfing over the decades have invariably made reference to surf slang (often using it to poke fun at surfing in general), and sometimes even included a short glossary, as was the case with *Look* magazine's 1964 feature "West Coast Surfers: The Look, the Living, the Lingo." The magazine either coyly or naively defined "brown-out"—surfspeak for a BA or "mooning"—as "riding backwards to shore; very difficult." Surf slang was also exported to the mainstream in Frank Zappa's 1982 hit song "Valley Girl" and in 1989's *Fast Times at Ridgemont High*.

Surf slang evolves constantly. Over the decades, the tuberiding surfer has been described as "locked-in" ('60s), "in the green room" ('70s), "barreled" ('80s), "shacked" ('90s), and "kegged" ('00s). Although English is the overwhelming language of choice for surf slang, with non-English speakers often using American- or Australian-coined phrases, specialized surf culture jargon is an international phenomenon. "Kook," the disparaging English word for a beginning surfer, is translated to Spanish *boludo* in Argentina, *doos* in Afrikaans, and *ao ni said* in Japanese. (Surf slang can also change, sometimes radically, from region to region: "kook" becomes "tranny" in Santa Cruz, "donkey" in Maui, "niner" in San Clemente, and "egg roll" in Sydney.)

A small number of expressions either created or reconfigured by surfers have found their way into general usage, including "wipeout," "stoke" (excited or thrilled), "gremmie" (young surfer), and "jams" (long, lose-fitting trunks), all of which are included, with surf culture attribution, in the fourth edition of the *Oxford English Dictionary*. Surf expressions that go mainstream often do so long after falling out of common use among surfers. "Cowabunga," an all-purpose expression of excitement used by surfers in the '50s and '60s, was recycled in the '80s by the animated cartoon heroes Teenage Mutant Ninja Turtles, and in the early '90s by Bart Simpson.

Surf slang is comprehensively gathered and ordered in *The Surfin'ary: A Dictionary of Surfing Terms and Surfspeak* by Trevor Cralle (revised edition, 2001). *Surfing: The Dictionary,* by Australian surf journalist Phil Jarratt, was published in 1985. *TransWorld Surf* magazine has published a regular "Surf Slang" column since 1999.

surf travel   There's no great mystery why surfing is enhanced, and to some degree defined, by travel, as both activities answer to the call of adventure, escape, even rebelliousness. "Surfers are the best-traveled sportsmen in the world," California-born wave-rider Dave Parmenter wrote in 1999, going on to note that "we've become the widest-flung tribe of fanatics since the Jesuits."

Surfing and travel have always been linked: Hawaiian royalty often brought surfboards with them during interisland visits; Hawaiian-born surfers Duke Kahanamoku and George Freeth both sailed out of Oahu in the early 20th century to bring surfing to the rest of the world, and California surfers began trickling over to Waikiki in the '20s. But surf travel as it exists today didn't really take form until after World War II, when surfboards became lighter and more transportable, and as crowded lineups began to push wave-riders to look for undiscovered breaks. "Traveling surfers," '70s surf nomad Kevin Naughton said, "picked up where the Beat Generation left off." Surfers launched weekend trips out of surf hub cities like Los Angeles, Sydney, and Durban, often sleeping in ramshackle panel vans or woody station wagons and eating beans cooked over a beach fire; all dreamed of one day making a pilgrimage to Hawaii. A few ambitious travelers set their sights even higher: Australian surfer Peter Troy began a four-year journey in 1963 that took him to coastlines in France, Spain, Morocco, the Canary Islands, the Virgin Islands, Peru, Argentina, Angola, and South Africa.

Travel has been a surf media cornerstone since the beginning: early surf movies included *Trek to Makaha* (1956) and *Surfing the Southern Cross* (1964), while the Beach Boys' 1962 hit "Surfin' Safari" was a bouncy ode to wave-hunting. "Around the World on a Surfboard," "Surfing 3,000 Miles from Anywhere," and "The Ecstasy of Travel!" are among the hundreds of travel-related articles published in the surf press over the years. (More than 10 percent of *Surfer* magazine's "Surfer Tips" advice columns have been about travel, and *Surfer* reader survey results unfailingly record travel stories as the favorite type of article, well ahead of contest reports, profiles/interviews, or board design features)

The surf travel ideal was distilled and presented unforgettably in Bruce Brown's 1966 surf movie *The*

Endless Summer, which followed two California surfers—Robert August and Mike Hynson—on their easygoing, sun-drenched "search for the perfect wave." Sickness, customs hassles, injuries, language problems, dislocation, and the rest of the usual travel hardships were almost completely filtered out of *Endless Summer,* but the spirit and magic of the quest were captured perfectly, with the highlight coming as the surfers discovered flawless pointbreak waves at remote Cape St. Francis in South Africa. Brown's film encouraged thousands of surfers to seek out other versions of the perfect wave, and in the years to come magnificent discoveries were made in Indonesia, the Philippines, Western Australia, and along tropical islands spread out across the Pacific Ocean. Immeasurable amounts of time, money, and energy meanwhile were spent on trips that were all but waveless.

The style and attitude of the traveling surfer were exemplified by Kevin Naughton and Craig Peterson, two empty-pocketed California teenagers who set out in 1972 on the first of a decade-long series of wave-hunting adventures, with *Surfer* publishing 13 of their cowritten articles. Naughton and Peterson occasionally found great waves, but the real pleasure in following their travels came as the two suburban-raised surfers cheerfully placed themselves into new and frequently exotic settings. In 1975's "Eleven Chapters of an African Surfari," they're arrested and jailed in Ghana for urinating in public, bribe their way out, and then are stuck in their beachfront camp next to a flat ocean trying to figure out how to distract themselves from the heat. "Count your malaria pills," Peterson suggests to himself, "read another book, write letters. Go for a swim in the 80-degree ocean, which is nice, but when you come out the sun dries you so fast you're caked with salt, and all the little kids run 'cause they think you have leprosy." By 2002, outer-limits surf explorers, professional and amateur, had ridden waves in Antarctica, Russia, Pakistan, and Iceland.

Commercial surf tourism was up and running by the early 1980s, as a small number of the surf-related camps, resorts, and tours opened for business. Today, the Grajagan surf camp in Java (a pay-to-surf prototype, opening in 1978) attracts an international clientele, as does the more upscale Tavarua Island Resort in Fiji. Twelve-day chartered boat trips through Indonesia's Mentawai Islands have been popular since the late '90s. More than 250 commercial surf travel businesses were in operation around the world by

2002, grossing an aggregate $120 million, and the camp/resort/tour is projected to be the fastest-growing sector of the surf economy over the next few years.

If prearranged surf travel has greatly increased the odds of hitting good waves, it has also insulated the surfer, sometimes almost entirely, from the kind of cultural adventures experienced by Troy, Brown, Naughton, and Peterson. The surf industry meanwhile supports a small professional class of surfers who are paid solely to travel the world with a hired retinue of photographers and videographers. (Surf journalist Dave Parmenter, righteously disgusted with both the theory and practice of for-hire surf travelers, called them "idiot savant surfwear mannequins, herded into surf camps by team managers, babysat by worldly photographers, and released like baby ducklings into perfect waves. . . .") The Rip Curl and Quiksilver companies both launched multiyear surf travel marketing campaigns in the 1990s.

The Surf Report, a monthly newsletter mapping out surf breaks across much of the known surfing world, was published between 1980 and 1998; more than two dozen guidebooks on surfing areas near and far have been published since the '60s, including California surf journalist Chris Ahrens's *The Surfer's Travel Guide: A Handbook to Surf Paradise* (1995). The all-travel *Surfer's Path* magazine, a bimonthly published out of England, was founded in 1997. *See also The Surf Report.*

surf trunks   Premodern Hawaiian surfers rode in the nude, and surfers in the early decades of the 20th century for the most part used the same type of bathing suits worn by nonsurfing beachgoers. Sometime in the late '20s or early '30s, Sam Kahanamoku, Outrigger Canoe Club member and brother of Hawaiian surfing pioneer Duke Kahanamoku, is said to have discarded the woolen two-piece tank top "swimming togs" in favor of the chest-baring swimsuit. The new Outrigger-style trunk was high-waisted, with a cinch belt to prevent it from slipping off while in the surf.

But as big-wave surfer Greg Noll later recalled, it was Southern California surfboard-maker Dale Velzy, along with his friends at the Manhattan Beach Surf Club, who in the late '40s invented the surf trunk as it exists today by cutting the legs off their white Salvation Army–bought sailor pants, just above the knees. As a practical matter, the extra-long cut prevented the surfers' thighs from rubbing and chafing

against the decks and rails of his board; as a slightly racy fashion statement, the trunks were worn low on the hips. Commercial surf trunks were introduced in the early 1950s by two small Hawaiian manufacturers: the H. Miura General Store and M. Nii's, both in Oahu. The Makaha Drowner trunk by M. Nii's is considered to be the first trunk marketed to surfers. In 1958, Noll ordered a pair of black-and-white–striped jailhouse trunks from M. Nii's. Noll used his new trunks that season while riding enormous surf at Waimea Bay, and soon adopted them as a kind of surfing uniform; they remain the sport's most famous trunk design. (Trunks have also been used as gang-style "colors," most notably by the infamous Black Shorts organization in Hawaii and the White Shorts in Mauritius.)

Southern California became the hub of trunk design and manufacturing beginning in the late '50s; by the early '60s, Kanvas by Katin, Birdwell Beach Britches, and Hang Ten were the sport's primary trunk-makers, with the brightly colored, balloon-legged Jams line added in 1964. Cotton and sailcloth were the original surf trunk materials, followed by nylon and then polyester. The surf trunk hemline has periodically dropped and risen over the decades, while the silhouette has expanded and contracted; snug, high-legged trunks were popular from the mid-'70s to the mid-'80s. Colors and prints have gone through similar fashion cycles. Fasteners have evolved from buttons and hooks to snaps, drawstrings, and Velcro. All surfing-designed trunks have a ventilated wax pocket, to hold a bar of surf wax; most are double-stitched for strength and designed to dry quickly; none makes use of the mesh-material "built-in underwear" feature or the elastic waistband. Female-cut trunks were introduced in the early '90s.

Australian-made Quiksilver "boardshorts" took the American surf market by storm in the late '70s, and remain the world's most popular surfing trunk; a new pair of Quiksilvers in 2003 cost between $40 and $50. Some observers meanwhile have imbued the surf trunk with cultural significance; surf journalist Sam George in 1993 labeled the item "as much a philosophy as a garment," and viewed trunk choice as "the ultimate statement on who's shooting the curl and who's shooting the shit." *See also* baggies, fashion and surfing, Hang Ten, Nancy Katin, Quiksilver.

surf video   General description for an assortment of commercially sold home-use surf features; the surf video became the sport's primary cinematic medium in the 1980s, replacing the once-popular theater-screened surf movie. Videotape was developed in the '50s as an instant-playback alternative to celluloid film. It was introduced to the surf world in the early '80s as an instructional aid for surfers, who could watch tapes of themselves and study their technique, and as a marketing tool for surfing trade shows. It was also used for cable TV coverage of professional surfing contests. As the mainstream video rental industry exploded, with Hollywood studios racing to convert films to videos for VCR home viewing, Bruce Brown's classic 1966 film *The Endless Summer* was released on video in 1984, along with California underground surf favorite *Off The Wall II*. More than a dozen converted surf movie titles were available by the end of the year, with an average unit cost of about $50.

The surf video was bad news for a surf movie industry that already had been brought to its knees by skyrocketing production costs. "It doesn't make any sense for a guy like me to spend $100,000 making a full-blown surf film," Santa Barbara surf filmmaker Greg Huglin said, "when kids now can just go to the local video store and rent a surf film they can watch over and over for a buck." Surf magazine articles in 1985 had titles like "Video Killed the Surf Movie," and announced that the heyday of raucous surf tribe gatherings for the latest theatrical surf film were over. *The Performers* (1984) and *Wave Warriors* (1985), surfing's first made-for-video efforts, meanwhile were released to good reviews and fairly wide distribution. Produced by Quiksilver surfwear and Astrodeck traction pads, respectively, *The Performers* and *Wave Warriors* also introduced the concept of the surf video as a corporate marketing device.

The surf video customized the viewing experience, as titles were collected, watched at leisure, paused, rewound, and studied. The moviemaking process was also democratized, as surf videographers—freed from the high cost of film and processing, as well as town-to-town barnstorming—could produce work at a fraction of the cost spent by their surf moviemaking predecessors. Video-makers generally stuck to cheaper, shorter versions of the format worked out decades earlier by surf filmmakers, often using an on-screen caption to announce a topic—usually a surfer, surf break, or surfing event—followed by a sub-three-minute fusillade of action. Short comedy sequences were sometimes used as filler. But if the surf video had great production-cost advantages over the surf

film, the quality almost always suffered by comparison, as video cameras in the '80s and most of the '90s generally produced a toneless "flat" image, were unable to shoot in slow motion, and were too large to fit into camera housings for water use. (A small number of quality-minded surf movie auteurs continued to shoot 16-millimeter film and had the footage transferred to video.)

Surf video took a big step toward its present-day form in the early 1990s. On the corporate side, Quiksilver in 1991 brought down the standard $40 unit price by releasing its *Kelly Slater in Black and White* promotional video for $9.95, and encouraging buyers to make bootleg copies for their friends. The Billabong company, meanwhile, hired ace surf filmmaker Jack McCoy to produce the first in a series of videos that would set a quality standard for the field, and Rip Curl soon followed by recruiting Sonny Miller to make a series of videos as part of a long-running marketing campaign known as "The Search." In the meantime, San Diego's Taylor Steele set the pace for independent surf video-makers with his raw 1992 release *Momentum*. Filmed on low-resolution tape, scored by Steele's favorite punk bands, and introducing New School surfers like Kelly Slater, Rob Machado, and Shane Dorian, *Momentum* sold 15,000 copies at a time when 5,000 in sales was thought of as being close to market saturation. By the time Steele released his follow-up *Momentum II* in 1993, the surf market was about to be flooded by loud, cheap, abrasive *Momentum*-style copycat videos. (Steele later said that he himself "rarely watched" surf videos, while six-time world champion Slater said he avoided them altogether, citing "bad editing and shitty music.") The video market began to subdivide by the middle of the decade, and titles were soon aimed at longboarders (*Super Slide, Soul Patrol*), women (*Peaches, Empress*), big-wave fans (*Biggest Wednesday, Year of the Drag-In*), and pro contest fans (*The Billabong Challenge, The Reef at Todos Santos*). Video biographies, the vast majority of which were produced by the featured surfer's main sponsor, included features on world champions Tom Curren, Margo Oberg, Mark Occhilupo, Andy Irons, and Sunny Garcia.

As many as 75 commercially sold surf videos are made worldwide each year, with production costs ranging from $250,000 to less than $500. Improved technology—including relatively inexpensive digital cameras, video camera water housings, and digital at-home computer editing—have in recent years helped to raise the general surf video standard. The *Surfer* Magazine Video Awards were founded in 1996 to honor the year's efforts in more than a dozen categories; Video of the Year winners have included Jack McCoy, Sonny Miller, Taylor Steele, Chris Malloy, and Jack Johnson. Surf videos generally run from 20 to 90 minutes and cost about $20. The first surfing DVDs were released in 2000; the DVD is expected to pass the videocassette as the most popular surf cinema format by 2005. *See also* Bill Ballard, Tim Bonython, Chris Bystrom, Jack McCoy, Sonny Miller, Momentum, Taylor Steele, surf movies.

surf wax Paraffin-based compound rubbed on the deck of a surfboard to provide foot traction, used by virtually all surfers worldwide since the 1940s. Surf wax is sold in three-ounce plastic-wrapped bars and is usually applied before each surf session. In the first few decades of the 20th century, surfers often coated their boards with a thin layer of sand-infused varnish, which increased traction, but also scraped their knees, chest, feet, and thighs—sometimes to the bleeding point. In 1935, teenager Alfred Gallant, from Palos Verdes, California, applied a small amount of liquid floor wax to his surfboard and liked the results. On the advice of his mother, he then tried paraffin wax (widely used at the time to seal jam jars for storage), and the traction was even better. Paraffin was used by surfers everywhere for more than 25 years. In 1965, Jack's Surfboards in Huntington Beach had an exclusive on a locally made product called Surf Wax, which was essentially repackaged paraffin. Three years later, top California surfers Mike Doyle and Rusty Miller introduced Waxmate, which consisted of paraffin softened by motor oil (making it easier to rub onto the board), bayberry scent, and purple dye. Reaction among surfers was at first tepid—a one-pound block of paraffin cost 30 cents, while Waxmate cost 25 cents a bar—but within two years the product was selling well.

In 1972, former Doyle/Miller associate John Dahl created the Wax Research company in Encinitas, California, and began producing an orange-tinged wax under the company name. In Carpinteria, meanwhile, U.C. Santa Barbara graduate Rick Herzog (also known as "Mr. Zog") founded the tiny but provocatively named Sex Wax company, pouring his heavily scented product into tuna cans to produce the first round bars of wax. By the early '80s, both Wax Research and Sex Wax—now competing with more than a dozen surf wax start-ups such as Southern Cal-

ifornia's Waxx On and Australia's hugely popular Mrs. Palmer's—were each producing more than a million bars of wax a year. The growing popularity of stick-on polyurethane traction pads had wax-makers scrambling in the late '80s and early '90s to improve and diversify their product, resulting in bars that were stickier, as well as specialized for different water temperatures. Wax formulas also became more complicated and were treated as highly confidential trade secrets. More than 10 million bars of surf wax were produced worldwide in 2002.

Paraffin is still the main surf wax ingredient, with small amounts of beeswax added for pliability, along with petroleum-derived products (such as Vaseline) for lubrication, synthetic rubber or petrochemical resin for added stickiness, plastics for temperature control, and chemical-based scenting. The ingredients are mixed and heated to 130 degrees, then poured into a metal mold; industrial molds can produce as many as 2,500 bars of wax at a time. A "hard" wax adheres best to the surfboard and is often used as a base coat upon which a softer coat of wax is applied. Hard wax is used in warmer water; softer waxes are designed for mild or cold water. Wax comes in a variety of shapes, colors, and scents (Sex Wax is available in strawberry, pineapple, grape, and coconut), and usually sells for a dollar per bar at surf shops as well as many coastal convenience stores. Surfers rub wax on their boards using a light, circular motion to build a small-beaded skein of wax bumps. Wax-makers advise surfers to strip the built-up wax from their boards every two weeks; most surfers strip their boards once or twice a year, if at all.

Despite the common malady of "wax rash" (skin abrasions caused by too much rubbing against a wax-covered board surface) and an uncountable number of wax-splotched clothes and car interiors, surf wax has over the years become a favorite surfing accouterment—far more so than the surf leash, for example, or the fin. "We like to have a little moment with our board before we go out," Sex Wax founder Herzog once said, "and waxing our boards gives it to us." Wax is referred to in songs by '60s acts like the Beach Boys and Jan and Dean, and postpunk band Weezer recorded a song in 1994 called "Surf Wax America." Surfers, while generally uncommunicative to surfers they don't know, will universally lend and borrow wax from each other. *See also* Sex Wax, traction pad.

surf's up Originally a straightforward declaration that the waves have suddenly gotten bigger; appropriated by the mainstream media in the early '60s as a headline prefix for virtually any surfing-related article or feature, including "Surf's Up: The Wet-Set Revolution" (*Newsweek,* 1967), "Surf's Up in a Pennsylvania Steel Town" (*People,* 1985), "Surf's Up at Center for the Arts" (*San Francisco Arts Monthly,* 2000). "Surf's Up" was also used by the Beach Boys in 1971, both as an album and song title.

Surf's Up   Half-hour weekly variety show produced by KHJ-TV Channel 9 in Los Angeles; broadcast locally in 1964 and 1965. *Surf's Up* was originally hosted by KHJ radio DJ and programmer Stan Richards, who also did a hot-rodding show called *Wheels.* The New Jersey–raised Richards was introduced to surfing at the 1964 Malibu Invitational, which he covered for a 90-minute KHJ-TV special. ("Now tell me, Bob," the uninformed Richards reportedly said on air to cohost and surf journalist Robert Feigel, "can a goofyfooter do the hotdog, and if so, what foot does he use?") Each episode of *Surf's Up* featured clips from the latest surf movies, an in-studio interview with a surfing celebrity, news on upcoming surf world events, and a Q&A session with studio and phone-in viewers. Surf moviemaker Jim Freeman was Richards's cohost on *Surf's Up*; the show was briefly hosted in 1964 by surf moviemaker/publisher Walt Phillips.

Surf-O-Rama   *See* Los Angeles Surf Fair.

surfari   A compound of "surfing" and "safari," used to describe a surf travel adventure, particularly to someplace remote. The opening lines to "Surfin' Safari," the Beach Boys' 1962 single, was a call to good-time surf travel: "Let's go surfing now, everybody's learning now / Come on a surfari with me." Surf magazine editors over the years have often used the word in article titles, from "Surfari to Baja" (*Petersen's Surfing,* 1964), "Eleven Chapters of an African Surfari" (*Surfer,* 1975), "Snake River Surfari" (*Surfing,* 1986), and "Glasnost: On Surfari Behind Russia's Rusty Iron Curtain" (*Surfer,* 2000). The Surfaris, a teenage surf band from Glendora, California, had a #2 hit with "Wipe Out" in 1963. *Surfari,* a Hollywood-made surf movie starring big-wave riders Rick Grigg and Greg Noll, had a brief theatrical release in 1967. *See also* surf travel.

Surfaris, The   Surf band from Glendora, California, best known for their drum-heavy 1963 single "Wipe Out." The original Surfaris, formed in mid-1962, consisted of three 15-year-old guitarists—bassist Pat Con-

nolly, rhythm guitarist Bob Berryhill, and lead guitarist Jim Fuller—and 17-year-old Ron Wilson on drums. They'd been together just four months when they recorded "Wipe Out," with its famous hard-driving drum solo, as the B side to "Surfer Joe," their first single. "Wipe Out" was composed in 15 minutes, recorded on the second take, and went to #2 on the national charts in June 1963. ("Surfer Joe" peaked a few weeks later at #62.) "Point Panic," the Surfaris' follow-up single, stalled at #49 in the fall of 1963, and was the band's last song to chart. The Surfaris unsuccessfully remade themselves as folk rockers in the mid-'60s, disbanded, then reunited periodically over the years, with several different lineups. "The Surfaris were not extraordinary," music critic Richie Unterberger wrote in 1997, "but they were more talented than the typical one-shot surf band, [and] drummer Ron Wilson's uninhibited splashing style sounds like a direct link to Keith Moon." *See also* surf music, "Wipe Out."

surfboard construction   The finless solid-wood boards used in the first half of the 20th century were all constructed in essentially the same way, by hand-shaping a slab of wood (usually redwood or a redwood/balsa laminate) with a saw, drawknife, hand planer, and sandpaper, then sealing the board with varnish. Hollow boards, popular in the '30s and '40s, were built from traverse-braced panels of cedar, mahogany, spruce, redwood, or pine, the pieces held together with glue and screws. Hollows were also finished with varnish. Both solid and hollow boards were commercially made in the '30s and '40s, but most were built in private garages and backyards; do-it-yourself surfboard articles were published in *Popular Mechanics* and *Popular Science* magazines. A strengthening resin-saturated fiberglass skin was added to the board-making process in the mid-'40s, along with a fiberglass-attached stabilizing fin; polyurethane foam blanks replaced balsa as the board's core material in the late '50s.

Machine-molded surfboards have made up a tiny fraction of all boards produced since the early '60s—newer versions of the molded board have steadily become more popular since the late '90s—but the vast majority of surfboards for more than 50 years have been constructed by the same basic five-step method, as follows:

1) Shaping. A precast foam blank is first roughed out by a shaper using a saw and an electric planer (or by a computer-programmed shaping

machine, in common use since the mid-'90s). The board is then fine-shaped with a sanding block and sanding screen. As shaping brings together the blend of curves, contours, and volume distribution, which determines how a board rides, this has traditionally been the only part of the board-making process to capture the surfing public's attention.

2) Airbrushing. An optional step; the airbrusher, spraying water-soluble acrylic paints onto the shaped foam blank, can render nearly any design, from a simple color accent along the board's rails to a full wraparound nose-to-tail panorama.

3) Laminating, or "glassing." The process of enveloping the foam blank in fiberglass. A sheet of fiberglass is pulled from a roll, laid flat on the bottom surface of a horizontally resting board, then trimmed so that it hangs about two inches below the rail line. A catalyst-infused coat of resin is then spread evenly into the fiberglass with a rubber squeegee, and the process is repeated on the board's deck, usually with a double layer of fiberglass. "Glassing" often refers to the entire postshaping construction process.

4) Hot coating, or sand coating. A second application of resin, brushed on, contains a wax-based sanding agent, which rises to the top as the resin dries, creating an easy-to-sand surface. Fins or fin boxes are added after the hot coat is dry; the board is then machine- and hand-sanded.

5) Gloss coating. A third and optional coat of resin is also brushed on. After the board has been hand-sanded and machine-polished, the gloss coat gives it a lustrous shine. Most longboards are glossed, while most short-boards are not because the extra few ounces of gloss coat weight can make a difference in performance.

As the sport itself has grown, the surfboard construction site has evolved from backyards, garages, workshops, and beachfronts to surfboard retailer back rooms and sprawling industrial factories that do manufacturing work for up to two dozen retailers. Boards are often shaped off-site, then shipped to a factory for glassing. There are health risks associated with surfboard construction, as virtually every board-building material is toxic to one degree or another.

Polyurethane foam dust can irritate the airways, which over a long period of time can result in chronic lung problems and perhaps cancer. Styrene, resin's main component, evaporates easily and quickly, and can irritate lungs, airways, and skin; long-term exposure has been linked to liver disease and cancer. Catalysts contain known carcinogens; fiberglass particles can irritate skin, and fiberglass dust (caused by sanding) may cause cancer. Surfboard factories have become much safer in recent years, equipped with high-tech ventilation systems. Board-makers themselves, once notoriously lax, have learned to consistently wear filtering masks and regulator masks.

Books on surfboard construction include 1994's *Surfboard: How to Build Surfboards and Related Watersport Equipment* (formerly titled *The Surfboard Builder's Manual*), *Surfboard Design and Construction* (1975), *Making a Surfboard: The Complete Manual* (1985), and *Essential Surfing* (1987); videos include *Carve It Up* (1996), *Shaping 101* (1997), and *Glassing 101* (1998). *See also* epoxy surfboard fiberglass, molded surfboard laminate, polyurethane foam, resin, shaping machine, surfboard shaping.

surfboard racks   Devices used to fasten one or more surfboards to a vehicle, usually a car or truck, for transportation. When Hawaiian surfer and gold medal swimmer Duke Kahanamoku visited Australia in 1914, he used rope to tie his wooden surfboard across the cab of a horse and buggy; the few dozen surfers in Hawaii and Southern California at that point were likely already using rope in similar fashion to lash boards to the roofs of their Model A Fords. (Although in the early decades of the 20th century, boards were often left at the beach, in a clubhouse, or storage area.) California surfers in the '30s sometimes towed boards in trailers behind their cars; they also began to bolt a pair of two-by-fours horizontally across their car roofs and secure the boards with old tire inner tubes. In the early '40s, the Los Angeles Ladder Company, makers of the Tom Blake signature model hollow surfboard, introduced the Octopus Luggage Carrier, an adjustable sledlike rooftop device advertised as "indispensable to fishermen, hunters, campers, skiers, vacationists and surf-board riders." The homemade "ladder rack" was introduced in the '50s: a long, wide, ladderlike device made of two-by-fours, which propped the trunk of the car open and provided horizontal shelves for the boards extending out of the trunk. The year 1961 saw the introduction of the Bertelen Surfboard Rack, which attached to the top of a car with four suction cups.

In 1963, California surfboard-manufacturing titan Hobie Alter convinced former Volkswagen designer Gerhard Landgraf to create a dependable, adjustable, easy-to-use roof rack for surfboards. Landgraf produced the Aloha rack, made by Bay Standard. Clamps on either end of two rubber-covered metal bars were fastened to the car's rain gutters, with the bars spaced about three feet apart. Surfboards were placed in two parallel rows, up to three boards per row, and fastened to each bar with a strap made of high-density rubber or containing a plastic-encased spring. Dozens of copycat racks were introduced over the decades, but the Aloha rack, which passed the million-sold mark in 1990, remains surfing's most popular "hard rack." Shortly after the introduction of the Aloha rack, similar commercially made devices were introduced for motorcycles and bicycles; the motorcycle racks placed the board off to one side or overhead; most bike racks lodged the board on a two-wheel rickshaw-style conveyance that trailed behind the rider.

"Soft racks" were introduced by the California-based Rax company in 1975. This new system was light and easily transportable (making it a boon to traveling surfers), but more difficult to use than the hard racks. Soft racks feature thin, flat, adjustable nylon straps, cylindrical foam cushions for the boards, and plastic-covered metal clips that fasten to door openings. Soft racks, easily removed and stowed in the trunk, were introduced partly in response to rack theft. (Hard rack thefts were so common in the '70s that *Surfing* magazine in 1979 published a three-page illustrated article, "How to Protect Your Racks".) As SUVs and minivans became popular with surfers in the '80s, boards were often simply loaded into the car, eliminating the need for surf racks.

surfboard shaping, shaper   The surfboard shaper uses an assortment of techniques and tools to craft a preformed blank—usually made of polyurethane foam—into a ready-to-laminate surfboard. The shaping process in premodern Hawaii also had a spiritual component. Boards were made of wood, and after a suitable wiliwili or koa tree was felled, the shaper would lay a recently caught fish inside the root cavity as an offering to the gods. The board was shaped with an ax and a chunk of handheld dried coral, then rubbed out and smoothed with stones. In the early

Surfboard shaping

decades of the 20th century, boards were made from blanks of redwood or redwood in combination with balsa or pine. Before the introduction in 1951 of the power planer, shapers worked with a saw, a hand planer, and a drawknife. As polyurethane foam blanks became the core material of choice in the late '50s, shapers inaugurated a basic six-part board-making process that remained unchanged until the early '90s, when computer-programmed shaping machines took over much of the work. Allowing for variation from shaper to shaper, the basic steps, in brief, are as follows:

1) "Skinning." The shaper uses a power planer to "skin" the blank and get its thickness to within 1/8″ of the desired finished shape. For the entire process, the board rests on a pair of support racks; professional shapers use sidelighting, which throws shadows across the board's surface to indicate high and low spots on the blank.

2) Creating a template. Using a tape measure for length and a T square for width, and working from a set of rigid parabolic template forms (usually made of plastic, fiberboard, or Masonite), the shaper pencils the board's outline on the blank.

3) Outline cut. The shaper uses a handsaw, jigsaw, or router to cut just outside of the pencil-marked outline, then squares off the rails (edges) using a rough-grit sanding block.

4) Planing. Using a power planer, with the board facing bottom up, the shaper uses the planer and the sanding block to set the "rocker" and "lift." He then flips the board over and takes

several dozen passes with the planer, first "turning" the rails, then working in toward the center.

5) Fine-tuning. More passes are made over the entire board, using a Surform or 40-grit sandpaper block.

6) Blending. Using progressively finer sandpaper, the shaper blends together the rocker, rails, and bottom to remove all bumps and ridges. A typical 6′6″ shortboard, prior to fiberglassing, weighs just under two pounds.

Thousands of hobbyist shapers, and an ever-smaller number of professionals, still follow the above procedure. By 2002, however, an estimated 85 percent of major shapers—those producing more than 2,000 boards a year—were using computerized shaping machines to take their board all the way to the fine-tuning stage. Given that a shaping machine costs between $100,000 and $500,000, many shapers contract with a machine-owning facility.

Because they understand all the complex board-design variables (rocker, foil, bottom curves, plan shape) and how to mix them—and are therefore responsible for producing the "magic" boards sought by all dedicated surfers—shapers have always occupied a vaunted place in the surfing hierarchy as artists, craftsmen, even gurus. A partial list of influential shapers through the decades, in roughly chronological order, would include Bob Simmons, Joe Quigg, Dale Velzy, Renolds Yater, Dick Brewer, Harold Ige, Mike Diffenderfer, Bob McTavish, Tom Parrish, Mike Eaton, Dick Van Straalen, Bill Barnfield, Matthew "Spider" Murphy, Geoff McCoy, Simon Anderson, Allan Byrne, Al Merrick, Pat Rawson, Glenn Minami, John Carper, Rusty Preisendorfer, Eric Arakawa, Nev Hyman, and Matt Biolos. As of 2002, there were roughly 2,000 full-time shapers worldwide, about half of them living in America. Only a few women have taken up shaping; none as yet has branched out beyond her local area. *Surfboard: How to Build Surfboards and Related Watersport Equipment* (revised in 1994; formerly titled *The Surfboard Builder's Manual*) has for decades been the standard handbook for the beginning shaper. Videos on the subject include *Carve It Up* (1996) *Shaping 101* (1997), and *The Masters Shaping Series* (2002). *See also* planer, polyurethane foam, surfboard construction.

surfboard shop   Retail outlet for surfing equipment and paraphernalia, as well as a time-tested cul-tural stronghold. "Surf shops," journalist Craig Stecyk wrote in 1996, "function as the sport's information centers, supply depots, halfway houses, classrooms, libraries, churches, banks and museums." California surfboard shaper Dale Velzy is sometimes credited as the inventor of the surf shop, opening his first Velzy Surfboards outlet in 1950 in Manhattan Beach, California, not long after the city closed the board-making operation he ran from beneath the municipal pier. Surfboards at the time were generally built in garages or backyards, and many of the sport's first shops—including those founded by Hobie Alter, Greg Noll, Ron DiMenna, and Bing Copeland—opened as a result of aggravated parents shutting down their children's smelly and messy in-house operations. Surf shops began as tiny single-item stores, where surfboards were shaped, fiberglassed, and sold in the same room. "There were saw horses," surf journalist Patrick McNulty recalled, "and bare electric light-bulbs hanging from the ceiling." As the sport grew, board manufacturing was separated from the retail showroom, first to an adjacent room, then off-premises altogether. Jack O'Neill, who would later make his name as a wetsuit magnate, opened what he called the Surf Shop in San Francisco in 1952; because O'Neill sold wetsuits as well as surfboards, it's been argued that this was the first true surf shop. The original Hobie Surfboards in Dana Point, a factory/retail store that opened in 1953, was the first custom-designed and -built surf shop—and was in fact so far advanced compared to Velzy's and O'Neill's rudimentary operations that it's also been called the original surf shop. As the surf industry expanded, so, too, did the shop's inventory list: by 1961, T-shirts, trunks, magazines, and wetsuits were sold alongside boards (new and used) and board-making supplies. The number of shops grew steadily as well; 41 outlets are listed in a directory of Southern California surf shops published in the 1963 *Petersen's Surfing Yearbook*; dozens more were open in northern California, the American eastern seaboard, Hawaii, Australia, and New Zealand. First-generation shops had also opened by that time in England and South Africa.

From the beginning, patrons have viewed the surf shop as something far grander than a specialty retail store. Young surfers in particular were awestruck by the new boards and the bawdy stories told by older customers; the shop clerk, furthermore, often had a local—or national or even international—reputation as a hot wave-rider. Surf posters and photos covered the shop walls; trophies lined the shelves; stickers were plastered on windows and countertops. By the early '90s, surf videos played constantly on a wall-mounted TV.

Until the late '70s, most surf shops carried only the house brand of surfboard. Today, shops usually carry at least three brands, and sometimes as many as a dozen, despite the fact that boards have long been the surf retailing industry's least-profitable item. Most shops additionally stock several brands of wetsuits and surfwear, surf leashes, wax, and an array of surf magazines and videos. Neatly kept surf shops began turning up in suburban malls and shopping centers in the mid-'80s, proportionally reducing the number of "core" (short for "hard-core") operations. The concept of the all-service surf shop was meanwhile greatly expanded. The 52,000-square-foot Ron Jon's Surf Shop in Cocoa Beach, Florida, is open 24 hours a day, and stocks equipment for snowboarding, skateboarding, windsurfing, Rollerblading, skimboarding, bodyboarding, wakeboarding, diving, Jet Skiing, waterskiing, bicycling, camping, and volleyball, in addition to its near endless racks of beachwear and wetsuits.

As of 2003, there were an estimated 2,000 surf shops worldwide, in places as diverse as the Great Lakes, Italy, Thailand, Nicaragua, Senegal, Israel, and Nova Scotia. America is believed to be home to about 700 shops selling 50 or more boards a year; half are located in California. The '90s and early '00s saw the development of specialty surf shops for women and longboarders, while online-only shops began competing for business with adjunct Web sites built by the larger brick-and-mortar shops. Some American shop owners were up in arms in mid-2002 as membership giant Costco began selling a mass-produced Taiwanese-made board called the Realm for $244.99—about $100 less than the average shop board.

Surf shops often sponsor top local riders and underwrite local surf competitions. Some offer board repair services and surf lessons. Surf shops have been featured in novels (Kem Nunn's 1984 book *Tapping the Source*), movies (1978's *Big Wednesday*), literary magazines (William Finnegan's 1992 *New Yorker* feature, "Playing Doc's Games"), and television (1993's short-lived sitcom *Big Wave Dave's*).

surfboard stacking   Diversion in which surfers lash down as many surfboards as possible to the roof of a car. As it originated in Southern California,

Surfboard stacking in the late 1970s

board-stacking involved bodies as well as boards. "Larry Stephens of Dana Point," as noted in a *Surfer* magazine caption next to a black-and-white photo of a parked wood-paneled Country Squire, "challenges anyone to produce a picture of a surf car with more boards than this. Total sticks on the roof: 9! Bodies in the car: 10!" There were challengers in early 1962, one from Malibu and another from Fullerton, each with 13 boards and 13 surfers. Australia checked in before the year was out, with a group from Southern Australia loading 14 boards and 15 surfers, and a Brisbane entry coming in at 22 and 22. The year ended with a group from San Diego, California, loading 32 boards, 35 surfers, and a dog.

Board-stacking disappeared for more than 15 years, then returned, with modifications, in 1978. The game now was boards only; onboard surfers (and pets) counted for nothing. Furthermore, the board-loaded car had to be driven a short distance under its own power. Former U.S. surfing champion Corky Carroll stacked 40 boards on a customized VW Bug in 1978 and did the requisite drive. Surfers from Byron Bay, Australia, the following year piled 60 boards atop a Morris Minor. In 1981, in the Malibu parking lot, 72 boards were loaded onto an American-made sedan (model unknown), but as *Surfing* magazine noted, the car "was sitting on its differential and oilpan." The entry was disqualified. Surf instructors at San Diego's Mission Bay Aquatic Center made a strong bid in 1988, with 115 boards loaded onto a Plymouth Galaxy 500. There was general agreement by this time that the board-stacked car had to be driven for 100 feet with no dropped boards, and that all structural support had to originate from the roof of the vehicle.

Close scrutiny of the Aquatic Center's entry showed that a board had been propped sideways on the Galaxy's trunk, providing a disqualifying support strut. Again, no record. Three months later the Aquatic Center was back with a perfectly executed 141-board effort. In 1998, a group from Santa Barbara, California, thatched together 282 boards on top of a Humvee—doubling the record—smoothly drove 100 feet across the Rincon parking lot, and apparently brought the game to an end. No attempts at the record have since been made.

surfboard, the   The definition of "surfboard" can be expanded to include nearly all types of wave-riding devices, including kneeboards, bellyboards, and bodyboards, but it most often describes only those boards meant for stand-up surfing. Machine assistance comes into play to one degree or another during the board-making process (*see* surfboard construction), but surfboards as of 2003 are still by and large hand-made. Looked upon as a sleek repository of function and design, built to exacting measurements taken from a set of hydrodynamic principles, the surfboard nonetheless continues to have an element of mystery or alchemy; longtime surfers will look back and often pick out just two or three nonreplicable "magic boards" owned over the course of their surfing lives. Molded surfboards, a once-disgraced idea, began gaining popularity in the early 2000s, and may eventually make boards as interchangeable as tennis rackets. But until that time, as California-born surfboard shaper Dave Parmenter once phrased it, "each board is mortal and completely original."

Peruvian fishermen as far back as 3,000 B.C. rode waves while straddling a high-prowed, bundled-reed craft called the *caballito* ("little horse"). Bellyboard riding, too, was almost certainly practiced on temperate coastlines around the world thousands of years ago. But boards for stand-up surfing are thought to have been invented around A.D. 1000 in Hawaii, although the date could be off by hundreds of years, as the first written description of stand-up surfing wasn't made until 1778, and the oldest extant surfboards date back only as far as the early 1800s. Hawaiian stand-up boards came in two basic designs: the popular *alaia,* ranging in size from seven to 12 feet, and the longer, heavier *olo.* Both were finless, had a blunt, rounded nose and a squared-off tail, with convex deck and bottom surfaces, and both were shaped from a single piece of koa or wiliwili

wood. Board-makers started and finished the construction process with rituals, rites, and prayers; a red fish, for example, as an offering to the gods, would be buried among the roots of the newly chopped-down tree used to make a surfboard.

Stand-up surfing all but vanished during the 19th century, as the Hawaiian race was brought down by western-borne disease, and the sport itself was discredited by visiting missionaries as licentious and dangerous. Boards produced during surfing's renaissance in the first years of the 20th century were almost exclusively made of varnished redwood; in 1910, surfing patriarch Duke Kahanamoku used a 70-pound flat-bottomed redwood board measuring 10' by 23" by 3"—a soon-to-be common design, wide in the tail, known as a "plank" or "slab." Heavier plank boards weighed up to 100 pounds or more. Board styles were virtually unchanged until 1929, when Wisconsin-born surfer Tom Blake developed the square-railed "cigar-box" hollow board, also flat-bottomed, but longer and more streamlined than the plank. The hollow board was light enough (as little as 40 pounds) to encourage hundreds of people to take up the sport in mainland America and Australia. Less popular than the cigar box, but more important from a design standpoint, was the hot curl board, invented in Hawaii in 1937. The hot curl, like the plank, was finless and made of solid wood—redwood or a balsa/redwood laminate—but had a narrower tail and a rounded yacht-style hull. It was designed to hold a tight angle across the wave face; planks and hollows both lost traction quickly when set on an angle. Because the hot curl was able to handle larger surf, it is regarded as the first big-wave surfboard design. In 1932, the Thomas Rodgers Company in Venice, California, bought Blake's hollow-board designs and produced the first commercially made line of surfboards. In the mid-'30s, the retail cost for a Pacific Homes Systems plank board, made in nearby Santa Monica, was just under $40. A 1935 *Popular Science* article offered blueprints and instructions for do-it-yourself board-builders, as did a Blake-written 1939 article in *Popular Mechanics.*

Malibu, California, was the primary surfboard design center and test track in the years immediately following World War II, as Bob Simmons, Joe Quigg, and Matt Kivlin collectively invented what was called the "Malibu chip," and Dale Velzy followed with the "pig" design—a prototype for the modern longboard. No other era brought such fundamental change in board design. Balsa was by this time the core material, and boards were wrapped in a hard, brittle, protective skin of resin-saturated fiberglass. Board weight was trimmed to 25 pounds. The biggest design change, however, was the addition of a stabilizing fin, which allowed riders to hold a higher, tighter angle across the wave, and to begin doing turns and cutbacks. In 1950, at Manhattan Beach Pier in southwest Los Angeles County, Velzy opened what many regard as the world's first surf shop; three years later, in Orange County's Dana Point, Hobie Alter opened Hobie Surfboards, the first custom-built surfboard factory/showroom; an off-the-rack Hobie cost about $65. Polyurethane foam began to replace balsa as the surfboard's core material in 1956, and by 1961 balsa boards were all but obsolete.

The American surf craze of the early and mid-'60s was a boom period for Southern California board manufacturers, led by Hobie, Bing, Jacobs, Weber, Greg Noll, and Con, and each produced about 3,000 boards a year during the mid-decade peak. Signature models became popular in 1965, with best-sellers over the next two years including the David Nuuhiwa Lightweight (made by Bing), Mickey Dora's Da Cat (Greg Noll), the Ugly (Con), the Lance Carson Model (Jacobs), and the Gary Propper East Coast Model (Hobie). Nearly all the boards were between 9′6″ and 10 feet long, 22 inches wide, and weighed about 27 pounds; average retail price was $150. The Australian board-making industry was doing nearly as well, led by manufacturers Gordon Woods, Barry Bennett, and Joe Larkin; smaller interests were up and running in South Africa, France, Japan, and other emerging surf nations worldwide.

Bob McTavish of Australia developed the vee-bottom surfboard in 1967, with assistance from California-born kneeboarder/designer George Greenough. The vee-bottom featured a wide tail above a distinct V-shaped double-panel planing surface, and launched what was soon known as the shortboard revolution. Constant design experimentation, some of it innovative, much of it absurd, marked the next three years, and while the field was still unsettled by the decade's end, the newly reduced small-wave surfboard was between six and seven feet long, 18 to 21 inches wide, and weighed between 10 and 15 pounds. The dropped-profile "down" rail, while less celebrated than many other new features, has since been called the most significant board design development of the late '60s, as it offered plenty of traction but also al-

lowed for sharp turns and cutbacks. Surfboard fins, blunt through most of the '60s, were now narrow based and swept back, like the tail fin on a bluefin tuna. Virtually all major board manufacturers were slow in responding to the shortboard revolution design free-for-all, and either went out of business or scaled back their operations. Small labels and backyard/garage outfits meanwhile offered the latest designs (sometimes crudely interpreted and produced) at below-retail prices. Specialized big-wave surfboards, less affected by fads and fashion, continued to develop at a slight remove from everyday board design, with Dick Brewer of Hawaii taking over from Pat Curren and Mike Diffenderfer as the genre leader.

New designs were introduced, modified, and/or discarded in the '70s, including the swallowtail, the split-rail winger (in the tail section) and stinger (just below midpoint), and the concave bottom (used years earlier in the nose section of longboards, now installed along the middle and tail section). The twin-fin appeared briefly in the early '50s and the early '70s, and early versions of the tri-fin were introduced in 1971 and 1974, but the multifinned board didn't really catch on until 1978, when Australian Mark Richards began tearing up the pro tour on a swallowtail twin-fin. For nearly four years, the fast but skittish twin-fins were popular in small waves. The workhorse board throughout the '70s and early '80s, however, was the unadorned roundpin-tail single-fin, usually measuring about 6′8″ and weighing about 10 pounds. Lightning Bolt was the marquee surfboard manufacturer through the '70s, particularly for boards used in Hawaii, with featured shapers like Bill Barnfield and Tom Parrish. American-made surfboards retailed for about $225.

In 1981, Australian pro surfer and board-builder Simon Anderson debuted the Thruster, a new tri-fin design, and within two years virtually every shortboard surfer in the world was on a three-finned board—and the same holds true today. Meanwhile, in the early '80s, California shaper and Channel Islands Surfboards owner Al Merrick, by providing equipment for soon-to-be world champion Tom Curren, established himself as the era's preeminent shaper/designer; Pat Rawson and Glenn Minami, both from Hawaii, were often cited as the best big-wave board-makers. Design changes in the '80s and '90s were largely a matter of shading and detail, with a trend to thinner, narrower, lighter boards. The board Kelly Slater used to win the 1995 Quiksilver

Pro in Grajagan, Java, measured 6′5″ by 17″ by 2 ¾″, and weighed just over six pounds. Retail prices went up to more than $400 for a shortboard and $500 for a longboard.

Having returned to the sport in the mid-'70s, longboards steadily gained in popularity through the '80s and '90s, and by the turn of the century accounted for half of all surfboard sales. A few longboards were near replicas of boards used in the mid-'60s; most were updated and modified—lighter than their predecessors, and often made as tri-fins. Hybrid boards, including the "egg" and "fun board," were also developed. It was estimated that just over 500,000 new surfboards were sold worldwide in 2002.

The 1992-invented tow-in method of big-wave surfing, with the rider getting pulled into huge waves from behind a personal watercraft, brought the single greatest break in surfboard design history. Every surfboard up to this point had in a sense been a paddleboard, as the wave, first and foremost, required a paddle-in entry. The tow-in board was the first to be built solely for wave-riding, not paddling, and is fashioned more after the water ski and snowboard; footstraps were added in 1993, and by the late '90s the average tow-in board measured about 7′6″ by 16″. To help stabilize the boards at high speed, extra layers of fiberglass were added, bringing the weight up to as much as 25 pounds.

The surfboard has long been recognized as having value beyond its intended recreational function. Peter Max and Billy Al Bengston were among the artists who contributed painted or sculpted boards to a 1990 gallery exhibition in Santa Monica. In *Icons: Magnets of Meaning,* a 1997 show at the San Francisco Museum of Modern Art, a surfboard was included along with an Armani suit, a Kitchenaid stainless-steel mixer, and a BMW, as an example of a mass-produced item that has become, as explained in a *New York Times* review, "a repository for our memories, inspirations and fears." *Surfer* magazine meanwhile described the surfboard as "our orthodox religion's primary fetish." Surfboards have also been given a Freudian reading, going back at least to the mid-'60s, with the introduction of the Penetrator model surfboard, and carrying on with Simon Anderson's tri-fin Thruster design. In "Playing Doc's Games," William Finnegan's 1992 *New Yorker* article, one surfer looks at another board-holding surfer and notes, "Obviously, it's erotic. That big board's his prick." Wealthy surfers in the mid-'90s began commissioning famous board-makers

to create "modern classics," or "wall-hangers"—beautifully detailed, fully functional boards, made solely for display and costing up to $7,500. Surfboard collecting and surfboard auctions grew in popularity through the '90s and early '00s, with vintage wooden boards selling for as much as $18,000. "Stick," "blade," "shooter," "cue," "ride," "vehicle," and "tool" are some of the euphemisms used over the decades for "surfboard." *See also* big-wave surfboards, surfboard construction.

"Surfer Joe" Absurd but mysteriously catchy 1962 song by the Surfaris, a teenage surf band from Glendora, California. "Surfer Joe" was a rock-and-roll novelty record in the style of 1960's #1 hit "Itsy-Bitsy Teeny-Weeny Yellow Polka-Dot Bikini," but generations of surfers either didn't understand or appreciate the joke, and *Surfer* magazine, in 1989, called "Surfer Joe" the "undisputed worst surf song ever to gain mass popularity." Laid over a basic mid-tempo 12-bar progression, the "Surfer Joe" lyrics are delivered in a fey male voice—which probably explains why surfers, a dependably homophobic group, kept their distance. The song originally had five verses, but only three were used for the song's national release.

"Surfer Joe" peaked at #62 on the national charts. ("Wipe Out," the Surfaris' spontaneously composed instrumental B side on the "Surfer Joe" single, went to #2.) But the phrase "Surfer Joe" nonetheless stayed in the mainstream lexicon, and turned up in at least two more pop songs. "Surfer Joe and Moe the Sleaze," on Neil Young's 1981 *Re-ac-tor* album, opens with "Here's a story about Surfer Joe / He caught the big one and let it go." The Replacements' 1989 single "I'll Be You," contains the lyric, "Well, I laughed half the way to Tokyo / I dreamt I was Surfer Joe / And what that means I don't know." *See also* surf music, the Surfaris.

Surfer magazine Authoritative monthly surf magazine published out of San Juan Capistrano, California, founded in 1960 by surfer/artist/filmmaker John Severson; the longest continuously published surf magazine, and sometimes referred to as the "Bible of the sport." Severson was a high school teacher with two surf films to his credit when he began to write and design *The Surfer,* a 36-page, black-and-white, horizontally formatted marketing piece for *Surf Fever,* his third movie. He sold 5,000 copies, enough to

Surfer magazine, 1965

convince him to produce *The Surfer Quarterly* in 1961. (Often labeled as the first publication of its kind, *Surfer* was in fact preceded by at least two other short-lived surf magazines.) Color pages were introduced in 1962, as Severson stepped up to a bimonthly publishing schedule (monthly issues were introduced in 1978), and the name was shortened to *Surfer* in 1964. *Surfer* was firmly established as the sport's leading voice by the mid-'60s, fending off challenges from a half-dozen other California-based surfing magazines, and serving as a template for a small but growing number of surf magazines around the world. For several years, the magazine's tone and layout were fairly conservative, with a features mix consisting almost entirely of travel articles, contest reporting, surf spot profiles, big-wave pictorials, and surfer interviews. Severson was pictured in a "meet the staff" page wearing a coat and tie, and the magazine often railed against gremmies and hodads and others who didn't adhere to the surf industry's rigid "clean-up-the-sport" dictums. Meanwhile, Severson hired knowledgeable surf writers (including Bill Cleary, Craig Lockwood, and Fred Van Dyke), top photographers (Leroy Grannis, Ron Stoner), and first-rate graphic designers (John Van Hamersveld, Mike Salisbury). *Surfer*

by far produced the best comedy of any '60s-era surf magazine, with Rick Griffin's Murphy cartoon series, and the fictitious rants of JJ Moon, self-appointed "number-one surfer in the world." John Witzig's 1967 essay, "We're Tops Now," proclaiming Australian surfing superiority over the Americans, went on to become the sport's single best-known article.

Surfer's biggest transformation came in 1968, after Severson hired Drew Kampion to not only edit the magazine but make it relevant to the times. Kampion, an outspoken 24-year-old Buffalo-born journalist, took *Surfer* deep into the counterculture for three years, with anticontest articles, drug references, environmental features, oblique fiction pieces, and free-verse poetry. Severson sold *Surfer* in 1972 to For Better Living Inc., and handed over publishing duties to editor/writer Steve Pezman, who remained with the magazine for two decades. (Pezman would later found the San Clemente–based *Surfer's Journal*.)

Surfing, published nearby, had by the mid-'70s emerged as *Surfer*'s main rival, in both sales and content. Both magazines took a fairly middle-of-the-road editorial position as the sport's popularity grew in the late '70s, then exploded in the mid- and late '80s; *Surfer* aimed at readers in their late teens and early 20s, while *Surfing* targeted a slightly younger audience. *Surfer* hired many of the best surf journalists, including Phil Jarratt, Kevin Naughton, Craig Peterson, Derek Hynd, Matt George, Matt Warshaw, Ben Marcus, and Steve Barilotti, along with celebrated surf photographers like Art Brewer, Steve Wilkings, Jeff Divine, Warren Bolster, Peter Crawford, Don King, Ted Grambeau, Jeff Hornbaker, and Tom Servais. Graphic designer David Carson was *Surfer*'s art director in 1991 and 1992, giving the magazine a contemporary makeover (criticized by many, including founder Severson, as dark and stifling) before going on to become one of the design world's best-known figures. Surfer had two major scoops in the early '90s, first with "Cold Sweat," the debut feature article on Maverick's, California's soon-to-be-famous big-wave break, followed shortly by "The Next Realm?," the first feature on tow-in surfing. "The New ASP Top 30," Derek Hynd's critical assessment of the world pro tour's ranking surfers, quickly became a popular annual feature (later renamed the "The New ASP Top 44"); from the mid-'90s to the early '00s, editors Steve Hawk and Sam George produced a series of lengthy and well-researched topical articles on subjects like localism, surf resorts, and drugs and surfing.

The October 1999 issue of *Surfer,* at 340 pages, remains the largest surf magazine ever published.

Surfer spin-off magazines over the years include *Skateboarder, Powder, Action Now, Snowboarder,* the *Surf Report,* and *Beach Culture.* Special issues include *Surfer Style,* the *Surfer Photo Annual,* and the *Whole Ocean Catalog.* The annual *Surfer* Magazine Readers Poll began in 1963, and the *Surfer* Magazine Video Awards were founded in 1996. *Surfer Magazine Video,* a half-hour cable TV show, premiered on ESPN in 1986; www.surfermag.com debuted in 1995. *The Perfect Day: 40 Years of Surfer Magazine* was published by Chronicle Books in 2001; *Surfer* also copublished 1989's *The Book of Waves.* For Better Living, longtime parent company of Surfer Publications, sold the magazine group to Petersen Publishing in 1998; Petersen in turn was bought by Emap Publishing. In 2001, Primedia, *Surfing* magazine's parent company, bought Emap, bringing the longtime rivals *Surfer* and *Surfing* into the same publishing house. *Surfer*'s 2002 monthly circulation was 118,500. *See also* Drew Kampion, Steve Pezman, John Severson, surf magazines.

Surfer Magazine Video Awards   *See* Surfer Poll Awards.

Surfer Poll Awards   Surf world popularity poll held annually since 1963, with winners selected by the readers of *Surfer* magazine; the awards are announced at a semiformal banquet ceremony. The *Surfer* Poll Awards were introduced by the magazine with a self-important flourish as "a historic first in the sport." First place in the all-male 1963 Poll debut went to power surfer Phil Edwards, 25, from Oceanside, California. A women's division was added the following year. The late-'60s shortboard revolution, combined with a general surf world drift into the counterculture, had the surf industry eager to do away with anything associated with the sport's longboarding past, and the *Surfer* Poll was suspended following the 1969 awards. It returned in 1978. From 1987 to 1995, Poll awards were announced, but there was no awards ceremony. The banquet returned in 1996, augmented by the *Surfer* Video Awards, with magazine staff members picking winning video clips in categories such as Best Tuberide, Humor, Worst Wipeout, Best Segment (Male), and Best Segment (Female). A Video of the Year is also selected. Since 1999, Surfer has also awarded a Breakthrough Surfer of the Year award: winners include Bruce Irons (1999), Laird Hamilton (2000), and Mick Fanning (2001).

Surf News magazine described the 2000 Poll banquet as "the best large-scale surf party in history," filled with 1,500 mostly young, drunk, dressed-up and sexed-up attendees. Women's third-place finisher Layne Beachley of Australia brought the house down when, extending her leg so that master of ceremonies Sam George could adjust one of her spike-heel shoes, lasciviously purred, "Sam, while you're down there . . ." Winners of the *Surfer* Poll receive trophies, and have their names added to the bronze and wood perpetual *Surfer* Poll trophy. California's Tom Curren won eight Polls in a row, from 1985 to 1992, while Florida's Kelly Slater won eight times from 1993 to 2001. Margo Oberg, Frieda Zamba, and Lisa Andersen all won five Polls apiece, while Joyce Hoffman won four.

Surf magazines worldwide have introduced similar reader-selected awards. The *ASL* Peer Poll, held by *Australia's Surfing Life* magazine and inaugurated in 1991, has the top surfers themselves pick winners rather than the magazine's readership.

Results of the *Surfer* Poll Awards:
- 1963:   Phil Edwards (no women's division)
- 1964:   Mike Doyle, Joyce Hoffman
- 1965:   Mike Doyle, Joyce Hoffman
- 1966:   David Nuuhiwa, Joyce Hoffman
- 1967:   Corky Carroll, Joyce Hoffman
- 1968:   Nat Young, Margo Godfrey
- 1969:   Jock Sutherland, Margo Godfrey
- 1970–77: (not held)
- 1978:   Shaun Tomson, Margo Oberg (née Godfrey)
- 1979:   Mark Richards, Lynne Boyer
- 1980:   Mark Richards, Margo Oberg
- 1981:   Mark Richards, Margo Oberg
- 1982:   (not held)
- 1983:   Cheyne Horan, Debbie Beacham
- 1984:   Tom Carroll, Kim Mearig
- 1985:   Tom Curren, Frieda Zamba
- 1986:   Tom Curren, Frieda Zamba
- 1987:   Tom Curren, Frieda Zamba
- 1988:   Tom Curren, Frieda Zamba
- 1989:   Tom Curren, Frieda Zamba
- 1990:   Tom Curren, Wendy Botha
- 1991:   Tom Curren, Wendy Botha
- 1992:   Tom Curren, Lisa Andersen
- 1993:   Kelly Slater, Wendy Botha
- 1994:   Kelly Slater, Lisa Andersen
- 1995:   (not held)
- 1996:   Kelly Slater, Lisa Andersen
- 1997:   Kelly Slater, Lisa Andersen

surfer population   Estimating the number of surfers in a given region, citywide to worldwide, has always been a difficult task, starting with the most basic defining terms. What constitutes a surfer? Do bodysurfers count? Bodyboarders? Wave skiers? Do people who rent surfing equipment count? What separates an active surfer from an inactive surfer? Or phrased another way, how many times a year does somebody have to surf to be a surfer? A 1965 *Sports Illustrated* article canvassed some of the top names in the surf industry to find out how many surfers there were in America; answers ranged from 200,000 to "several million." Thirty years later, little had changed. "Hell, we don't know the answer to these questions," *Surfer* magazine admitted in 1996, saying the only certain thing was the sport had been growing steadily throughout the 20th century. "And we don't know anyone else who knows."

Surfing population numbers continued to be elusive. The Superstudy of Sports Participation Survey, conducted by American Sports Data in early 2000, estimated the American surfing population (with a surfer defined as somebody who rode waves at least once in the previous year) to be 1,736,000. In a 2002 survey, Boardtrac, a surf industry group, estimated the American surf population to be 2.4 million. (The Australian Sports Commission in 2002 put the number of surfers nationwide at just under two million.) Estimates for worldwide surfing population in the early '00s differ greatly, from five million (Surf Industry Manufacturers Association) to 17 million (Surfing Australia) to 23 million (International Surfing Association). As of 2002, women were said to make up anywhere from 5 to 22 percent of the total American surf population.

Surfer Stomp   Artless but irresistible foot-stomping dance step created in 1960, almost certainly at Dick Dale's early "surf stomp" shows at the Rendezvous Ballroom in Newport Beach. The Surfer Stomp was a coast-to-coast hit in America in the early '60s, and later jumped to Australia and New Zealand. As described in a 1963 learn-at-home dance instruction guide, the intricacies of the Surfer Stomp are explained in six easy steps:

1) Feet slightly apart, straight ahead.
2) Partners stand about one and a half feet apart, facing each other; both partners at the same time:
3) Snap your fingers.
4) Slide your right foot back, then forward stomp, do it again.
5) Slide your left foot back, then forward stomp, do it again.
6) Repeat.

The Stomp was performed to up-tempo 2/4 rock-and-roll numbers, and was often used as a segue between the Watusi, the Twist, the Hitchhike, and other period dance steps. In Bud Browne's 1963 surf movie *Gun Ho!,* as a group of bathing-suit-wearing teenagers do a spirited Stomp on the beach at Huntington during the West Coast Championships, a mock-serious narrator describes the music as having "aroused primitive emotions in the natives as they move into weird ritualistic dances practiced by their ancestors hundreds of years in the past." The Surfer Stomp can be seen as a forerunner to the punk-era Pogo dance step.

"Surfer's Stomp," a sax-heavy instrumental track by the Mar-Kets, went to #40 on Billboard charts at the end of February 1962. One year earlier, the Beach Boys recorded "Surfin'," their first single, which included the lyric, "And when the surf is down, to take its place / We'll do the Surfer Stomp, it's the latest dance craze." The dance hit Australia hard in 1963–64, with more than 30 Stomp-titled singles released in 1963–64, including "Bondi Stomp" by the Dave Bridge Trio, "Everyone Let's Stomp" by Jay Justin, and Little Pattie's unforgettable "He's My Blond-Headed Stompy Wompy Real Gone Surfer Boy." *See also* Rendezvous Ballroom, surf music.

surfer's ear   Common medical condition for surfers worldwide, consisting of bone deposits formed under the skin of the ear canal, primarily from repeated exposure to wind and water; formally known as exostosis. While surfer's ear is painless in itself, the narrowed canal can trap water and wax in the inner ear, increasing the likelihood of infections and tinnitus (ringing in the ears); hearing loss may result if left untreated. The skin of the ear canal is the only place on the body where bone meets skin with no insulating layer of fat or muscle. When the ear is repeatedly exposed to cold, wet air and saltwater, it walls itself off from the elements with added bone growth in the ear canal. "It's a stupid affliction," surf journalist Steve Hawk wrote in 1995, noting that shrinking the ear canal "makes about as much biological sense as blocking a harbor entrance with rocks to keep the boats safe." As early as the 1940s, small numbers of exostosis-affected surfers, sailors, divers, and ocean swimmers were having their ears "drilled," a painful surgical procedure requiring general anesthesia, in which the ear is incised from behind and pulled forward, the ear canal skin cut and peeled back, and the exposed bone growths removed with a series of fine drills and burrs. In 1972, California surfer/physician Dr. Robert Scott, after having his own ears drilled, introduced Doc's Pro Plugs, a set of soft-plastic earplugs attached to a thin nylon tether looping over the surfer's neck to prevent the plugs from washing away. Earplugs were the first preventive measure against surfer's ear, and are still regarded as the best line of defense. Neoprene hoods also help in prevention, as does coating the inner ear with olive oil before surfing (a less-than-popular practice), and rinsing with rubbing alcohol afterward. *Surfer* magazine reported in 1978 that nearly half of all avid surfers had at least 30 percent obstruction of the ear canal due to surfer's ear. Virtually no ill effect is felt until the ears are at least 75 percent closed, however, and a huge majority of surfers get by for the remainder of their surfing days without medical treatment. Bone scraping and laser surgery are now used as alternatives to drilling; all procedures are expensive—between $3,000 and $5,000 per ear—and will keep a surfer out of the water for two to 12 weeks. Once treated, the condition is likely to return, and quickly, unless preventive measures are taken.

Surfer's Journal magazine, The   Elegant magazine geared toward adult surfers, published five times a year out of San Clemente, California; sometimes referred to as the "*National Geographic* of surfing." Founded and copublished by Steve and Debbee Pezman, the *Surfer's Journal* debuted in 1992. Steve Pezman had been the publisher of *Surfer* magazine from 1971 to 1991; his wife-to-be Debbee Bradley had been *Surfer*'s marketing director. The *Journal* was conceived

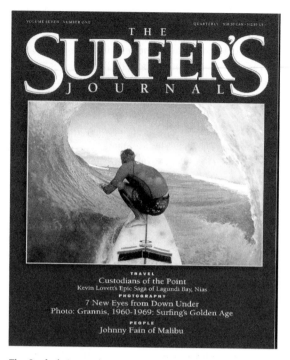

The Surfer's Journal, 1998

and developed as a glossy high-end quarterly with a strict limit on advertising (four advertisers in the early issues, six in later issues), with the idea that readers would pay a premium newsstand rate of $12.95 for a mature, low-hype periodical. Art director Jeff Girard, another *Surfer* alum, gave the journal a refined, squared-off, traditional look that instantly set the magazine apart from the clamorous design found in all other surf magazines of the period. Columns were kept to a minimum; surf contests were ignored entirely; the number of action photos were reduced to make room for a broader range of surf images. Feature articles, including profiles and interviews, travel stories, and photographer/surf artist portfolios, were often given exhaustive treatment—the 40,000-word "Animal Tracks" profile on 1966 world champion Nat Young consumed 45 pages in a 130-page issue—and the frequently solemn-voiced magazine switched back and forth from historical to contemporary pieces. The *Surfer's Journal* was also the first publication to divide its coverage more or less equally between longboarding and shortboarding. Durable surf writer Drew Kampion has been a frequent contributor to the *Journal*, as have Craig Stecyk, Paul Gross, Sam George, Ben Marcus, Matt Warshaw, Gerry Lopez, and Chris Ahrens.

Pezman has maintained a small staff and kept his overhead down, which has allowed the *Journal* to become a modest but steady commercial success, despite a circulation of just 15,000—about a 10th that of *Surfer* and *Surfing.* Longtime *Surfer* photo editor Jeff Divine was hired in 1998, and *Longboard* editor Scott Hulet was hired the following year. Continuity meanwhile has been a *Surfer's Journal* hallmark, and after 11 years the magazine has only slightly altered its look and voice. In 2000, the magazine began publishing five issues a year. The *Journal* remains one of the last independently owned surf glossies.

In 1997, the *Journal* and Opper Sports Productions produced *50 Years of Surfing of Film,* a 12-part documentary series that aired on Outdoor Life Network; *Great Waves, 20th Century Surfers,* and *Biographies* followed. The *Surfer's Journal* has also produced a series of lavishly illustrated coffee-table books, including *Photo: Grannis* (1998), *Masters of Surf Photography: Jeff Divine* (2000), and *Masters of Surf Photography: Art Brewer* (2001). Other magazines have followed the *Journal*'s high-price, low-ad-page model, including *Deep* and *Pacific Longboarder,* both from Australia. *Water* magazine, founded in 2002 and produced just a few miles from Pezman's offices, has been described as "a *Surfer's Journal* for groms." Circulation for the *Surfer's Journal* in 2003 was 30,000. *See also* Steve Pezman, surf magazines.

surfer's knobs   Fibrous half-domed lumps of thickened skin and overgrown connective tissue, located just below a surfer's kneecaps or on the bony ridge of the feet, and less often on the joints of the toes; caused by the friction and pressure of knee-paddling a surfboard. Surfer's knobs were a widely reported malady in the 1960s, during the later stages of the original longboard era. Essentially painless and rarely infected, surfer's knobs were in fact regarded as a status symbol, with a surfer's commitment and dedication to the sport measured in direct proportion to the height and circumference of his knobs. The American Medical Association did a study on surfer's knobs in 1965, while *Time* magazine reported on a San Diego doctor who cut into a golf-ball-size knob, discovered "cords of pearly white material," and was paying $15 per surgically removed specimen. *Time* also noted that the knobs were unrelated to "housemaid's knee," a form of bursitis, and that the growths would retract and disappear entirely within four to six months, once the surfer gave up knee-paddling. Surfers meanwhile discovered that foot knobs, if big enough, would prevent an army recruit from fitting into standard-issue GI boots, and thus could be used to prevent a tour of

duty in Vietnam. In the army induction scene from Warner Brothers' 1978 surf film *Big Wednesday,* a cane-wielding surfer takes a whack at his friend's knee-knob in order to bring it up to the appropriately disqualifying size.

Surfer's knobs vanished entirely in the late '60s with the introduction of the prone-paddle-only short surfboard, then reappeared about 15 years later—in far lesser numbers—as the longboard again became popular. Surfer's knobs are also known as surfer's knots and surf bumps. *See also* injuries and surfing.

Surfer's Medical Association   Organization of surfing doctors and fellow surf health travelers, founded in 1987 during the First International Medical Conference on the Sport of Surfing, held on Fiji's Tavarua Island, with Dr. Mark Renneker of San Francisco elected as president. For eight years, beginning in 1988, the Surfer's Medical Association's (SMA) "Surf Docs" advice column was a regular feature in *Surfer* magazine—with subjects ranging from wax rash to coral cuts, surfer's ear, and brain surgery—and in 1993 a collection of SMA columns written by Renneker, Dr. Kevin Starr, and Dr. Geoff Booth were gathered into a softcover book titled *Sick Surfers.* Twenty-one issues of *Surfing Medicine: Journal of the Surfer's Medical Association* were published between 1987 and 2002. SMA membership in 2002 was 600. *See also* fitness and surfing, injuries and surfing.

Surfer's Path magazine   Lucid, uncluttered bimonthly British surf magazine founded in 1997 by former Reuters reporter Alex Dick-Reed and published out of Cornwall, England. *Surfer's Path* focuses almost exclusively on the joys, trials, and tribulations of worldwide travel, and has little or no interest in surf magazine staple features, including competition reports and surf-star interviews. A 2002 issue was dedicated to Indonesia's Mentawai Islands; it looked at the history of the native people, described in detail how the islands came to the attention of the surf world, and told of a woman surfer working her way from one end of the island chain to the other. Environmental concerns also are featured prominently in *Surfer's Path.* The magazine's look and tone is vaguely New Age (a mandala is featured in the logo), but the writing is often sharp and witty. UK circulation for the glossy-paged *Surfer's Path* in 2003 was 28,000, with an additional 20,000 copies exported to America. Editor and publisher Dick-Reed also contributed to the 2001 *Stormrider Guide Europe.*

surfers rule   Cocksure phrase often shouted or spelled out by surfers and would-be surfers in the early and mid-'60s. "Surfers Rule" was graffitied onto walls, scrawled into drying squares of sidewalk concrete, and inked in block letters onto school folders and notebooks. "Surfers Rule" is also the title of a 1963 Beach Boys song, which begins: "It's a genuine fact that surfers rule / It's plastered on the walls all over school / Take it or leave it, but you'd better believe it / Surfers rule."

"Surfin' Bird"   Gibbering single by the Trashmen, a Minneapolis–St. Paul quartet; #4 on the American charts in February 1964. "Surfin' Bird" was a hybrid of two 1962 songs by Los Angeles R&B group the Rivingtons, "The Bird's the Word" and "Papa-Oom-Mow-Mow" (the Rivingtons rightfully sued the Trashmen for copyright infringement), and was covered by New York proto-punk band the Ramones in 1977. The chord progression is simple; the lyrics are essentially "The bird is the word" stuttered and repeated again and again in a kind of high-speed lunatic chant, and the song had little or no relation to the '60s surf scene. "Surfin' Bird" nonetheless remains one of rock's wildest rides. *See also* surf music.

"Surfin' Safari"   Simple but catchy 1962 song by the Beach Boys, containing a short checklist of popular early '60s surf breaks, maneuvers, and lingo. "Surfin' Safari" was the Beach Boys' first Top 20 hit, peaking at #14 on the Billboard charts. It was cowritten by Brian Wilson and Mike Love, with Love on lead vocal. The song's references were supplied to nonsurfers Wilson and Love by Jimmy Bowles, a surfer from Manhattan Beach and brother of Judy Bowles, Wilson's new girlfriend. "Surfin' Safari" appeared on the Beach Boys' debut album, also called *Surfin' Safari*. Hoping to cast as wide a net as possible across the youth culture, the "Surfin' Safari" single was backed with a hot rod song called "409." *See also* the Beach Boys, surf music.

Surfing America   Surfing organization based in Huntington Beach, California, formed in 1998 by the Surf Industry Manufacturers Association (SIMA) as an alternative to the fractious United States Surfing Federation (USSF), the group that has since 1979 acted as overseer for the disparate groups making up American amateur surfing. Modeled on the successful Surfing Australia program, and created primarily by

Surfing America logo, featuring three-time world champion Tom Curren

former SIMA president and 1976 world surfing champion Peter Townend, Surfing America was a paper organization until July 2000, when it was turned over to SIMA Surfing America committee chairman and Body Glove marketing director Scott Daley. Meg Bernardo, appointed as Surfing America's administrative director, said that the organization's main objective was to "provide a clear path from novice to professional competition." To do so, Surfing America supporters have said, requires all groups within the American competitive surfing structure, amateur and professional, to work together—in contrast to the backbiting and infighting that had for decades all but defined competitive surfing in the United States. While Surfing America has the support of the surfing industry and is linked to the Association of Surfing Professionals—the directors of the world pro tour—as of 2003 the USSF remained the national governing body for surfing in America. *See also* Surfing Australia, Peter Townend, United States Surfing Federation.

Surfing Australia   National governing body for amateur and professional surfing in Australia, formed in 1993 to replace the 1963-founded Australian Surfriders Association (ASA). While not an on-site manager, Surfing Australia sanctions, coordinates, and oversees dozens of domestic surfing associations, most of them competition-based, and through its Web site serves as a clearinghouse for national—and to a lesser degree international—surf-related information. From within the Surfing Australia network, an ambitious young competitive surfer can map a route from neighborhood competition to the world circuit.

In contrast, young American surfers have traditionally had to pick their way through a fractious amateur system, then graduate to an unrelated domestic pro system, which in turn isn't connected to the international pro system.

In 1993, ASA's board of directors, having just taken over operations of the Australasia branch of the Association of Surfing Professionals, as well as the newly founded Australian Championship Circuit domestic pro tour, elected to change its name to Surfing Australia. To extend the group's purview, new board member seats were created, including longboard director, kneeboard director, and bodyboard director. As of 2002, Surfing Australia represented 26,000 board-riding club members and 4,500 "elite" competitors. Its clinics coach an estimated 200,000 people annually in surf safety, surfing technique, and contest preparation. Surfing Australia is recognized by the Australian Government Sports Commission, the International Surfing Association, the Australian Olympic Committee, and the Association of Surfing Professionals. *See also* Australian Surfriders Association.

Surfing California   Popular 1973 guidebook to California surfing breaks; researched, written, and self-published by Bank Wright. *Surfing California* charts more than 400 spots, and is illustrated with hand-drawn maps and black-and-white photographs. Each entry is short and concise, and many are written in fairly heavy surfspeak. Little Drake's, a reef located in the Hollister Ranch, north of Santa Barbara, is described as "A hairball right. Peak sucks out across a shallow rock shelf and grinds either left or right. Works on any winter swell. Starts to smoke around 8 feet." Wright's book was released during the high epoch of California surfing territorialism—better known as localism—and surfers up and down the coast were outraged that their breaks had been named, described, and mapped. With this point of view in mind, *Surfing California,* as *Surfing* magazine half playfully described it in a review, "could very well be the Root of All Evil." A notice in a 2000 issue of *Surf News* magazine was kinder, saying that *Surfing California*—still in print, virtually unchanged from the first edition—is "the one book every California surfer should own." About 70,000 copies of the book have sold altogether. *Surfing Hawaii,* Wright's previous book, published in 1972, was an island-by-island guidebook to Hawaiian surf breaks. *See also* books and surfing, localism, Allan "Bank" Wright.

Surfing magazine   Active and colorful teen-oriented monthly surf magazine published in San Clemente, California; founded in 1964 by Hermosa Beach photographer Leroy Grannis and ex-marine Dick Graham. *International Surfing* (shortened to *Surfing* in 1974) emerged from a scrum of early and mid-'60s Southern California–based surf magazines—including *Surf Guide, Petersen's Surfing,* and *Surfing Illustrated*—as the sole challenger to American surf media dominator *Surfer. Surfing* began as a fairly conservative bimonthly, had a brief but innovative semi-psychedelic phase in 1967, then fell onto hard times, publishing just two issues in 1968. The magazine in its early years was carried in large part by the first-rate photography of Grannis and Don James; the load was admirably transferred in the early and mid-'70s to photographers Dan Merkel, Bob Barbour, and long-time photo editor Larry "Flame" Moore. Former *Surfer* editor Drew Kampion began writing for *Surfing* in 1973, and for a few years almost single-handedly kept the editorial tone in league with *Surfer*; erudite South African pro surfer Michael Tomson began regularly submitting features and columns in 1976; world champions Peter Townend and Wayne Bartholomew

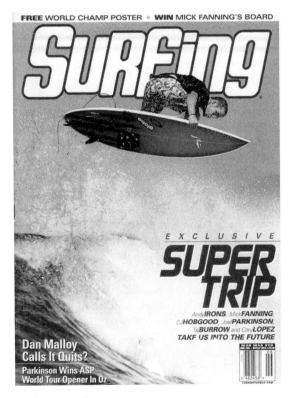

Surfing magazine, 2002

also contributed in the years to come. *Surfing,* more so than *Surfer,* focused on the competition scene—particularly the burgeoning world pro circuit. The magazine switched ownership five times from 1964 to 1979 (the year it went to a monthly publishing schedule), and was headquartered in Hermosa Beach, Panorama City, Laguna Niguel (all in Southern California), and New York City, before moving in 1976 to San Clemente.

Graphic designer Michael Salisbury gave *Surfing* a bright, active look in the early '80s, and the magazine, creatively and financially, pulled up almost neck and neck with archrival *Surfer. Surfing* staffers Aaron Chang and Jeff Hornbaker became something close to the Lennon and McCartney of surf photography (with Don King making valuable contributions as well), while the magazine's voice was strengthened with the addition of Dave Parmenter, Sam George, future *X-Files* creator Chris Carter, and editors-to-be Bill Sharp and Nick Carroll. Parmenter's 1987 article "Big Time," on Mexico's Todos Santos Island, was a coup for the magazine, as it showed that West Coast surf might in fact rival that found in Hawaii for size and power. *Surfing*'s rise during this period was in large part guided by the steady hand of Dave Gilovich, hired as associate editor in 1975, and later serving as editor or editorial director from 1979 to 1991. Publisher Bob Mignogna, also hired in 1975, meanwhile proved to have one of the sport's canniest business minds.

Surfing's target audience grew progressively younger through the '90s and early '00s, with grommet (young surfer) features published regularly, and a special late-2001 issue with cartoon figures on the cover, next to a blurb reading "KRAAK! 20 Surfing Superheroes Blast Into Battle." After the introduction in 1992 of the decorous and semiformal *Surfer's Journal, Surfer* had also lowered the age of its target audience—but not to the degree *Surfing* had. As *Surfing* advertising director-turned-publisher Peter Townend noted in 1996, "*Surfing* is *Teen Beat, Surfer* is *National Geographic.* And that's the way it should be." *Surfing* continued to find new material virtually in its own backyard, and on January 19, 2001, photo editor Moore led a one-day expedition to Cortes Banks, a reefbreak 100 miles off the coast of San Diego, and came back with the sport's biggest story of the year, as tow-in surfers rode 40-foot-plus waves.

Surfing's 2002 monthly circulation was 120,000. *Surfing* spin-off magazines over the years include *Surf*

Reflections (first published in 1971), *Bodyboarding* (1985), and *Surfing Girl* (1998). Special issues include the Surfing Comedy Annual (1974), the three-issue How to Surf series (1993), Surf Guide (1996), and an annual calendar. In 1996, *Surfing* introduced the Airshow, a popular series of pro surfing contests in which entrants are judged solely on aerial maneuvers; copycat Airshow events were soon being held around the world. Surfingthemag.com, *Surfing*'s Web site, was launched in 1999. In 1997, just a few months before *Surfer* was bought by Emap publishing, *Surfing* was bought by New York–based publishing giant Primedia. In a move that stunned surf magazine insiders, Primedia in 2001 bought Emap, bringing both titles into the same publishing house, and leading *Surf News* magazine to announce, just slightly tongue in cheek, that it was "the end of the world as we know it." *See also* Dave Gilovich, Dick Graham, Leroy Grannis, Bob Mignogna, Larry Moore, surf magazines.

surfing resorts   Surf resorts were the fastest-growing segment of the surf industry in the early 2000s, and remain so today, for understandable reasons: they provide escape from crowded lineups, supply the most waves per vacation dollar, and offer a reduced-risk exotic adventure. "The brute reality," celebrated American surf traveler Kevin Naughton said in 1999, discussing surf resorts, "is that the surf world is now one of increasing demand and diminishing resources. Surf resorts are the inevitable outcome." In 1978, California's Mike Boyum received permission from the Indonesian government to build a rustic surf camp near the jungle-rimmed village of Grajagan, in southeast Java. For $200 a day—with a one-week minimum stay, and a 10-surfer capacity—visitors to the Grajagan camp were able to ride long, hollow, perfectly shaped waves for as long as they could paddle. It wasn't illegal for others to ride there, but the break's remote location was a nearly insurmountable barrier for nonresort surfers. Camp amenities were basic: wooden huts, bedding, mosquito nets, food, bottled water, beer, hot showers, towels, and first aid. Transportation from Bali was included in the price. By the mid-'80s, the Grajagan resort was earning an estimated $250,000 in annual profit during its four-month season.

While a number of similar low-amenity resorts opened in the early '80s at places like Isla Natividad in Mexico and Tonga's Ha'atafu Beach, the next real development—arguably the first surf "resort," as compared to the surf "camp"—arrived in 1983 with the launch of Fiji's Tavarua Island Resort, built on a 30-acre site featuring three prime surf breaks. The American-operated Tavarua resort quickly established itself as the surf world's premier vacation spot. A $100 daily rate (transportation not included) included private cabin accommodations, first-rate food, a fan-cooled lounge/restaurant area, television, refrigeration, flush toilets, fishing and snorkeling gear, windsurfing equipment, and live entertainment.

Tavarua eventually found itself in the center of a legal and ethical controversy. In 1991, after reportedly muscling nonpaying surfers out of the lineup at Cloudbreak—Tavarua's primary surf spot—resort owners found themselves trying to defend how enforced exclusive rights to a particular break fit into a sport that has always cherished the idea of a playing field that is free, natural, and unregulated. "The notion that ownership rights can extend to reefs is foreign to surfers," journalist Steve Hawk said, "maybe even repulsive." In practice, however, most surfers seemed to approve of the idea of paying for a crowd-free surfing environment. Meanwhile, the issue of the Tavarua resort's exclusivity, pursued by local Fijian surfers and surf charter boat operators, was picked up by government officials and the national media. As of 2003, the legal status of Tavarua Island Resort's reef ownership remained uncertain. No nonresort surfers have been prosecuted yet for riding a resort-"owned" wave.

New surf resorts continued to open at a steady rate through the '90s and early '00s, some of them inexpensive low-amenity operations looking to attract the younger, more hard-core traveler, but most catering to the middle-aged surfer with a career and family looking to maximize his surf vacation time; baby-boom longboarders are a particularly sought-after demographic. (Resorts don't offer a guarantee of good surf, however, and some of the more popular destinations have become victims of their own success; the lineup at Grajagan, by the late '90s, was often filled with as many as 100 surfers staying in three separate resorts.) Niche resorts were developed by the early '00s, aiming for families, beginners, New Agers, born-again Christians, and other groups. The line between the surf resort and regular vacation resorts, meanwhile, became blurred, as the latter began to tap into a fast-growing market by offering surf packages. Chartered boat trips, furthermore, became popular in

the '90s as an alternative to surf resorts. As of 2003, there were roughly 100 surf resorts worldwide, located in Indonesia, all across the tropical Pacific Ocean islands, Costa Rica, the Maldive Islands, El Salvador, the Philippines, Australia, and elsewhere. Day rates for most surf resorts range from $50 to $200. *See also* Grajagan, Tavarua.

surfing T-shirt The surfing T-shirt is by far the sport's most enduring and popular fashion contribution. Surfboard manufacturer Floyd Smith of San Diego, California, is sometimes credited as the inventor of the surfing T-shirt. As a marketing ploy in 1961, Smith invited local surfers to bring their white T-shirts into the Gordon & Smith Surfboards shop, where he applied the company logo across the back using a newly evolved silk-screen process. By the end of the year, single-color Makaha International Surfing Championships T-shirts were also available, as were five-color O'Neill Surf Shop T-shirts; within three years, silk-screened surf company T-shirts were being made by the tens of thousands; as surf journalist Paul Holmes later wrote, the shirts were "symbols of the casual and free-spirited surfing lifestyle." The classic surfing T-shirt, then and now, features a large graphic on the back, usually a logo or illustration, and often has a smaller graphic over the left breast. Surf industry team T-shirts, signifying membership on a board manufacturer's competition team, were highly coveted throughout the '60s; top riders had their name screened above the pocket. Also prized were the competitor T-shirts given to entrants in high-profile meets like the Duke Kahanamoku Invitational or the World Surfing Championships. (T-shirts were also used as competition jerseys in the '50s and early '60s.) Hobie Surfboards and Weber Surfboards produced the best-selling surfer T-shirts of the period. By the mid-'70s, the California T-shirts company began selling their hugely popular semipsychedelic line of surfer shirts in department stores across America. By 2002, annual worldwide surfer T-shirt production was thought to be 300 million.

Surfer T-shirts have occasionally found their way into the entertainment world. Teenybopper Mackenzie Phillips wore an oversize Weber Surfboards T-shirt in 1973's *American Graffiti,* while Robert Duvall wore an army-green Yater Surfboards T-shirt for his Academy Award–nominated performance as Colonel Kilgore in 1979's *Apocalypse Now.* Rock and roller Eddie Vedder of Pearl Jam often performs in a surfer T-shirt, as do members of neopunk bands Blink-182 and Pennywise. *See also* fashion and surfing.

Surfing: The Ultimate Pleasure   Sumptuous large-format book on the sport's history and culture, written by former newspaperman Leonard Lueras of Honolulu and published in 1984 by New York's Workman Publishing. Lueras, a writer/editor who began surfing in California and moved to Hawaii in 1963, didn't break much new ground in *Surfing: The Ultimate Pleasure,* but his presentation was beautifully distilled and ordered, his analysis sharp, and his writing clear and often eloquent. The book's photographs and artwork range from 18th-century engravings to a depression-era *Vogue* cover shot of three surfers and one of world champion pro surfer Tom Carroll airborne in a spectacular wipeout. *Ultimate Pleasure* chapter titles include "Lyrical Polynesian Origins," "The Duke: Surfing's Father," "A Cult is Born," and "Waves from Abroad." A *Surfer* magazine review praised the book as "definitive . . . fascinating in content, lavish in production values, scholarly in approach and execution, and stoking in its sensitivity and perspective." A French edition, *Surf: Plaisir Des Dieux,* was published in 1986; more than 70,000 copies of the book, French and English editions combined, had sold by 1992. *See also* books and surfing, Leonard Lueras.

Surfing World   Weekly half-hour syndicated surfing variety show, produced by Los Angeles station KTLA Channel 5 and hosted by Southern California surf magazine publisher/moviemaker Walt Phillips. *Surfing World* aired in 1965, and was syndicated to coastal areas across the country. The *Surfing World* format was identical to the small number of other Los Angeles–area surfing shows of the mid-'60s: host Phillips greeted his TV audience, showed a few minutes worth of clips from the latest surf movie, interviewed a surf world "guest celebrity," and took questions from viewers. Surf music pioneers the Ventures were *Surfing World*'s in-house band. In 1964, Phillips hosted *Surf's Up,* a similar show, on rival station KHJ-TV Channel 9. *See also* Surf's Up, television and surfing.

Surfing World magazine   *See* Australian Surfing World magazine.

Surfline   Surf report and forecasting company launched in 1985 by Southern Californians Jerry Arnold, David Wilke, Craig Masuoka, and wave-prognosticating guru Sean Collins, based in Huntington Beach. Surfline began as a Los Angeles–area pay-per-call phone service (213-976-SURF; 55 cents per local call), utilizing California's newly approved 976 customer-toll numbers. Surfers looking for wave reports had previously either contacted a surf shop near the break they were interested in (hoping the shop clerks wouldn't lay bogus information on them) or called a recorded message—often outdated—at the local lifeguard headquarters.

Surfline employed a freelance network of on-the-beach surfers, trained by Collins, who relayed information on wave height, swell period and direction, weather conditions, and crowds. Surfline employees blended this eyewitness data with what they already knew about current swell direction, swell interval, water temperature, and tides, then digitally recorded a series of beach-by-beach messages that callers accessed by punching keys on their Touch-Tone phone. The morning report was posted 15 minutes after sunrise, the afternoon report at 2:15. Digital recording hardware allowed Surfline to field hundreds of calls at once. Surfline also offered a three-day forecast, as determined by Sean Collins, the self-taught surfing meteorologist who used satellite photos and National Oceanic and Atmospheric Administration (NOAA) millibar charts, among other sources, to make consistently accurate surf predictions. Surfline was an instant hit, and by 1987 it was covering all major surfing areas from the Mexican border to Santa Cruz. Collins left the company that year to form Wavetrak, his own pay-per-call service, but in 1991 the two businesses merged, and in 1998 he bought the combined operation. A *Los Angeles Times* article on Collins that year reported that Surfline was receiving one million calls annually. Similar report/forecasting companies, meanwhile, had come and gone, including 976-WAVE, 900-PRO-SURF, and 900-HOT-SURF. Surfax, one competitor that did survive, offered a twist on Surfline's service by faxing daily forecast information to subscribers. Surfline countered with Wavefax. In 1995, the company launched Surf Alert, a pay service that beeped pager-equipped surfers when the waves were about to turn on in a predesignated county.

In late 1997, two years after going online (www.surfline.com), Surfline began using stream live footage from strategically placed video cameras at Pipeline and Huntington Beach; the number of surf break Web cams quickly multiplied. Many surfers saw the cameras as an invasion of privacy, while a lesser number viewed professional surf reporting/forecasting in general as a crutch. "They really serve the rich and unimaginative," as San Francisco big-wave surfer Mark Renneker phrased it. But there was never any doubt that surf forecasting would only expand in the years to come. In 2000, when Swell.com bought Surfline (Collins stayed on as president and Chief Weather Officer, overseeing 10 full-time Surfline employees), the number of Surfline Web site users was doubling every nine months; by 2001 that meant about a half-million individual visits per week. Surfline broke away from Swell.com during the Internet bust of 2001, and Collins once again became part owner of the company. As of 2003, Surfline employed 15 people. *See also* Sean Collins, surf forecasting.

Surfrider Foundation   The world's first, largest, and most successful surfing-based environmental organization, headquartered in San Clemente, California, with chapters worldwide; founded in 1984 by spacecraft computer systems engineer Glenn Hening and activist Tom Pratte, along with Malibu surfing icon Lance Carson. Hening, who came up with the Surfrider name, later said he originally envisioned the group as "a sort of Cousteau Society for surfers," with surf schools and outreach programs, a surf movie production house, and a geologic design department to build artificial reefs. Budgetary realities and pressing surf-related environmental problems—beginning with river runoff contamination in Malibu lagoon—immediately turned Surfrider into a more narrowly defined educational/activist group. In addition to annual membership dues, Surfrider hoped to tap into corporate surfing's skyrocketing profits, but aside from a few medium-sized donations—Yvonne Chouinard of Patagonia and Gordon Clark of Clark Foam each gave $10,000—the surf industry was more interested in environmental sloganeering than financing. Surfrider scored an early victory in 1986 when it helped stop a mile-long breakwater project at San Diego's Imperial Beach. By 1990, however, despite a steady flow of surf media advertising and supportive editorial copy, the nonprofit Surfrider had fewer than 15,000 members, and was nearly bankrupt.

Surfrider made national headlines the following year as sole staff attorney Mark Massara, fighting a classic David-versus-Goliath case against two ocean-polluting pulp mills in Humboldt County, California, won the second-largest Clean Water Act suit in U.S. history. In addition to $5.8 million in government fines and a multimillion-dollar outflow renovation

tag, the pulp mills paid Surfrider $500,000 in legal fees. The sudden windfall threw the organization into turmoil, however, as Massara battled Surfrider over his fee. He eventually garnered $125,000, but left Surfrider—taking several board members with him—to form the Surfers' Environmental Alliance in 1993.

Surfrider soon developed two new and popular nationwide programs: Respect the Beach, an educational program for students, and the Blue Water Task Force, a volunteer ocean-water quality testing and monitoring program. Surfrider also changed from a central- to chapter-based organizational structure, essentially dividing itself into dozens of linked regional groups. A Surfrider chapter had already been formed in France; seven East Coast chapters opened in early 1992.

The group again made headlines in 2000, first by issuing its debut "State of the Beach" report, assessing the condition of America's beaches as measured by public access, water quality, shoreline structures, beach erosion, and recognition of surfing areas. Less successful was the long-delayed completion of a Surfrider-led artificial reef project in southwest Los Angeles County. Chevron Corporation years earlier had been ordered by the California Coastal Commission to "replace" the waves it had ruined in 1983 by building a jetty extension in front of its El Segundo beachfront refinery; Surfrider was eventually given $300,000 to build what it later called "Pratte's Reef"—named in honor of Surfrider cofounder Tom Pratte, who died of cancer in 1994. The 120-sandbag reef was installed just to the north of the Chevron refinery in September 2000; by midwinter it was embarrassingly obvious that the reef was having little or no effect on the surf. A $200,000 "phase two" sandbag extension was added in the spring of 2001, to no discernible change. Surfrider also helped with the passage in 2000 of the Beach Bill, mandating states to test and post water-quality results.

Surfrider marketers had meanwhile put together a set of three *Music for Our Mother Ocean* (MOM) benefit albums, with contributions by Pearl Jam, Jane's Addiction, Brian Wilson, Chris Isaak, and Beck, among others, collectively raising more than $300,000. (The MOM albums were preceded by *In a Blue Room,* a 1990 compilation featuring songs by top surfers including Tom Curren, Wayne Bartholomew, Frieda Zamba, Lance Carson, Pam Burridge, and Corky Carroll, with a percentage of profits donated to Surfrider.) By 2002, Surfrider had just over 35,000 U.S. members spread out over 60 chapters, with international affiliates in

France, Spain, Japan, Brazil, and Australia. The group has 18 full-time employees and brought in more than $6 million in 2002, almost exclusively from membership dues and small donations. Chris Evans, former assistant district attorney of Orange County, was named Surfrider's executive director in 1999; *Surfer* magazine in 2002 named him one of the "25 Most Powerful People in Surfing." *Making Waves,* Surfrider's newsletter, is published every other month. *See also* environmentalism and surfing, Glenn Hening, Mark Massara, politics and surfing, Tom Pratte.

Surfworld Museum   Well-appointed 4,500-square-foot surfing museum located in the Surf Coast Plaza shopping mall in Torquay, Victoria, Australia; home to Australian Surfing Hall of Fame. Surfworld, the world's largest surfing museum, opened in 1994, the result of a joint effort by the Surf Coast Shire (a local council), Surfing Victoria (state organizing body for surfing), and the Torquay-based surf industry, which includes Rip Curl, Quiksilver, and Oakley. Building costs were $1.3 million. Permanent Surfworld exhibits include a hall of historic surfboards, a scale-model glass-sided wave tank, and a functioning surfboard-shaping room. Each Australian Surfing Hall of Fame inductee is noted with a special board shaped in his or her honor. Surf art and surf photography are also featured in museum halls and galleries, and vintage surf movies show continuously in an 80-seat theater. Surfworld hosts surf-related book launches, movie screenings, and surf industry conferences. The museum is located five miles from Bells Beach, one of Australia's best-known surf breaks. About 20,000 people visit Surfworld each year; adult admission in 2002 was $6.50. *See also* Australian Surfing Hall of Fame, Bishop Museum, California Surf Museum, Huntington Beach International Surfing Museum, Santa Cruz Surfing Museum.

Sutherland, Jock   Quirky switchfoot surfer from Haleiwa, Hawaii; winner of the 1967 Duke Kahanamoku Invitational, and the first tuberiding virtuoso of the shortboard era. Sutherland was born (1948) in Long Beach, California, the son of a fisherman and World War II navy officer. The Sutherlands moved to the North Shore of Oahu in 1952, and Jock began surfing in 1956 at age eight; at 17 he was a finalist in the 1965 Duke event. Just days later, Sutherland was caught in traffic and missed the opening 40 minutes of the juniors division finals in the Makaha Interna-

Jock Sutherland

tional; paddling out with only 15 minutes left, he blitzed the lineup to gain his five-wave minimum, and finished runner-up to David Nuuhiwa by a single point. In the 1966 World Surfing Championships, held in San Diego, California, Sutherland finished second to Australian Nat Young. A few months later he won the small-wave division of the 1967 Peru International, and in December of that year won the Duke. (He was featured prominently in ABC's coverage of the 1968 Duke, and a violent Sutherland wipeout from that year's event was later used in the *Wide World of Sports*' opening credits to illustrate "the agony of defeat.") He also won the Hawaiian State Championships three times, from 1967 to 1969.

But it wasn't competition results that elevated Sutherland to the top spot on *Surfer* magazine's 1969 Readers Poll Awards; it was his newly honed skills as a tuberider, especially at Pipeline in Hawaii. The late-'60s shortboard revolution, with board sizes dropping quickly from 10 feet to seven feet, played to Sutherland's strengths. He'd long been the world's best switchfoot surfer, able to perform difficult maneuvers with either foot forward, but he'd never been particularly fluid, riding in a splay-legged stance with a rigid back, arms nearly locked in position. The short surfboards loosened up Sutherland's style, and he developed an efficient new way to get inside the tube, by stalling and angling his board just after takeoff instead of dropping to the bottom of the wave. He'd meanwhile become one of the sport's most interesting characters, with a love of phrasing and description; he memorably recalled the inside of a big Pipeline tube as looking "just like the Pope's living room." Sutherland's wave-riding creativity expanded further—possibly amplified by his regular intake of LSD—as he mixed conventional turns with side slips, noserides, and flying kickouts. He also became the first surfer, in late 1969, to ride the big surf at Waimea Bay at night. "We used to call him 'the Extraterrestrial,'" fellow Hawaiian surfer Jeff Hakman later said, "because he was so good at everything. He could beat anyone at chess or Scrabble; he could smoke more hash than anyone, take more acid, and still go out there and *surf* better than anyone." In early 1970, for reasons never made clear, Sutherland abruptly left the North Shore and joined the U.S. Army. He didn't see active duty, and returned to Hawaii in November 1971, but the surf world had passed him by. His tuberiding mantle had been picked up by Gerry Lopez, who improved upon Sutherland's methods and had become the new Pipeline master.

Sutherland appeared in nearly a dozen surf movies, including *Golden Breed* (1968) and *Pacific Vibrations* (1970); he was also featured in *Duke Kahanamoku's World of Surfing,* a 1968 one-hour CBS-TV sports special. Sutherland has been married once and has two sons; firstborn Gavin Sutherland won the men's division of the 1996 United States Surfing Championships and by the early '00s had become one of the world's top aerialists. *See also* drugs and surfing, switchfoot, tuberiding.

Sutherland, Mark Artist, animator, cartoonist, and writer from Sydney, Australia; best known as the creator of Gonad Man, a biting and intelligent surfing cartoon strip that made its *Waves* magazine debut in 1993. Sutherland was born (1961) in Canada, moved with his family at age two to Sydney, began surfing at seven, and started work as a professional animator at 21. His crudely drawn Gonad Man character was a scruffy, bandolier-wearing, hard-living, antisuperhero surfer with a prodigious set of testicles, and a tendency toward heavy drinking and philosophical musing. Gonad Man T-shirts and comic books soon appeared, and the cartoon had a short run in *Surfing* magazine beginning in 1998, after which the character was retired. Sutherland coproduced *Litmus,* a thoughtful, original, and occasionally pretentious 1997 surf video; a *Litmus* highlight is his six-minute short "Dream," a semiautobiographi-

cal slice of animated noir contrasting the life of a surfer with that of a junkie—Sutherland himself was a heroin user in the mid-'80s. "Dream" played at the 1993 Sydney Film Festival. Sutherland wrote regularly for the surf press throughout the '90s, with features and columns appearing in *Tracks, Waves, Surfer,* the *Surfer's Journal,* and *Australia's Surfing Life.* He wrote a column for the men's magazine *FHM* in 1998 and 1999. Sutherland's surfing cartoon work was featured in *Tubular Cels: Surf Cartoon and Comic Art,* a 2001 exhibition at the Silicon Pulp Animation Gallery in Sydney. *See* surf cartoons and comics.

swallowtail Split-tailed surfboard design, refined by Hawaiian surfer/board-maker Ben Aipa in 1972 as a way to add traction while loosening up a board's turning characteristics. Prototypes for the W-shaped swallowtail were developed in the early and mid-'50s by California board makers Tom Blake and Bob Simmons, and a twin-fin version was introduced in 1967 by La Jolla's Barry "Bear" Mirandon, but it was Aipa who reconfigured the design and made it popular. Most early swallowtails measured between four and six inches from tip to tip, with a wedge depth of one to five inches. (The fish design, introduced around the same time, had a wider tail, two fins, and was less popular—except among kneeboarders—than the swallowtail.) The swallowtail was one of three standard tail designs used through the mid- and late '70s, along with the roundpin and diamond-tail. The swallowtail was also incorporated into the bump-railed stinger, another Aipa design, introduced in 1974 and ridden by top high-performance Hawaiian surfers like Larry Bertlemann, Buttons Kaluhiokalani, and Mark Liddell. With the early '80s introduction of the trifin, which for the most part used a boxy squashtail, the popularity of the swallowtail began to fade. *See also* pintail, roundtail, squaretail, squashtail.

Swarts, Lewis "Hoppy" Fair-minded California surfer and surf contest judge/organizer from Hermosa Beach, California; the first president of the 1961-founded United States Surfing Association. Swarts was born (1916) in Tulsa, Oklahoma, the son of an oil businessman, moved with his family to Redondo Beach, California, and began surfing at age 14 in nearby Hermosa. He was known throughout his life as "Hoppy," the nickname given to him by his father, who was reading a Hopalong Cassidy book at the hospital on the day of Lewis's birth. Swarts became a

Hoppy Swarts

member of the Palos Verdes Surfing Club in 1934, along with lifelong friend and surf photographer Leroy Grannis. The smooth-riding Swarts, a regular-footer, placed seventh in the 1938 Pacific Coast Surf Riding Championships, took fifth in 1940, and was featured prominently in John "Doc" Ball's seminal 1946 photo book *California Surfriders*. Friends later said that Swarts's go-for-broke approach in the surf was in part because he was the most nearsighted surfer on the coast, and often didn't know what he was getting into. Photos of Swarts appeared in *National Geographic* and *Popular Mechanics*. He received a B.S. in math from Occidental College in 1941; in the mid-'40s he lived in Boston and attended MIT; he received an M.S. in engineering from U.C. Berkeley in 1949. Swarts worked for the navy, did spacecraft research for aerospace giant TRW, then became a high school math teacher.

In the post-*Gidget* surf boom years of the early '60s, American beach town city councils were passing antisurfing legislation in part due to the loud, crude, and sometimes-malicious behavior of teenage surfers. Swarts's interest in surfing competition, surf journalist Rus Calisch later noted, was more than anything

a public relations ploy. "Give society a winner, a champion, no matter what the sport," Calisch said, restating Swarts's original idea, "and it will become something they could not only understand, but cheer, and hopefully protect." To that end Swarts became the first president of the first public surfing organization, the United States Surfing Association (USSA), formed in 1961. For four years the USSA worked as a political action group, fighting surfing restrictions on both the East and West Coasts; the USSA changed course in 1965 and began to concern itself almost exclusively with surfing competition, using the format and judging system devised primarily by Swarts. The USSA split into regional groups at the end of 1967, with Swarts—an orderly, ethical, gentle-natured manager—serving as president of the Western Surfing Association (WSA); he remained active in WSA administration and judging for the rest of his life. In 1979 he drafted documents that became the framework for the United States Surfing Federation, an umbrella group for American amateur surfing.

On his way to a WSA contest in Santa Cruz in mid-1988, the 71-year-old Swarts had a stroke and died; he was then the executive director of the WSA. Swarts was inducted into the *International Surfing* Magazine Hall of Fame in 1966. He was married once and had three children. *See also* United States Surfing Association, Western Surfing Association.

Sweden   Sweden's two dozen mapped surf spots consist mainly of rocky pointbreaks and a few beach-breaks, all of them best in autumn and winter; most are located in the Baltic Sea, along the southern portion of the country's east coast and on the islands of Gotland and Öland. Ridable surf is also found on Sweden's west coast, facing the Kattegat Sea. Weak, blown-out, short-interval waves, produced by local winds, are the rule on both coasts. The beachbreak peaks at Torö Stenstrand, Sweden's most popular surf spot, are located 12 miles south of the capital city of Stockholm. The average winter air temperature in the south is 32 degrees, with the water temperature at near freezing; average air and water temperatures in summer are 63 and 45 degrees, respectively.

Stockholm's Jan Ekstedt was the first to surf Sweden, in 1982, and three years later he founded the Swedish Surfing Association. Surfers Paradise, a sailboard shop in Varberg, began retailing surfboards in 1989; the country's first surf contest was held in 1991 at Torö Stenstrand; the first annual Swedish Surfing

Championships were held in 1994. As of 2003, Sweden was home to six surf shops and about 3,000 surfers. The Swedish surf is detailed in *The Stormrider Guide Europe* (1998). *Edge,* a Swedish action sports magazine that features surfing, began publishing in 1995.

Sweet, Dave Innovative and irascible surfboard manufacturer from Santa Monica, California; an originator of the polyurethane foam surfboard blank and the first, in 1956, to bring a polyurethane board to market. Sweet was born (1928) in Seattle, Washington, moved with his family to Southern California at age 11, and began surfing at 16. Two years later he started building balsa surfboards on the beach at Malibu, and helped develop what was soon known as the Malibu chip—essentially the first board designed for turning and the progenitor to today's longboard. Sweet hit a turning point in 1953, just a few weeks after he received a B.S. from University of Southern California, when a friend handed him a block of just-developed Dow Chemical Styrofoam, and Sweet began wondering how to put the material to use in surfboard construction. For three years he poured nearly all his time, energy, and money into a research and development project that would eventually produce a board-shaped foam blank that was lighter and much less expensive than balsa. It was a long and difficult design process: Styrofoam was abandoned in favor of polyurethane foam; metal and fiberglass molds were built; hundreds of faulty blanks were produced. Sweet sold his car and went into debt to fund the project, and at one point was operating an 11-foot-long highly pressurized mold from his basement-level boardinghouse room in Hollywood. Meanwhile, 60 miles to the south, in Laguna Canyon, board-makers Hobie Alter and Gordon Clark were going through a similar trial-and-error foam-making process.

Finally able to mold blanks with some consistency, the Dave Sweet Surfboards retail store opened in Santa Monica in 1956 and began selling foam-core boards. (Months later, Roger Sweet, Dave's brother, formed Robertson/Sweet Surfboards along with actor Cliff Robertson—soon to play Kahuna in the 1959 film *Gidget.* Purveyors of inexpensive "popout" foam boards, Robertson/Sweet failed almost immediately.) Dave Sweet Surfboards became the hot label among Hollywood-connected surfers in the late '50s and '60s, and Sweet made boards for Clark Gable, Dick Van Dyke, Eddie Albert, Peter Lawford, and Jack Lem-

Dave Sweet

mon. In the late '60s, Sweet and the rest of the old guard manufacturers were weakened or toppled by the backyard board-makers during the shortboard revolution, and Dave Sweet Surfboards closed in 1974. Through it all, Sweet had a reputation as brilliant, fair-minded, and prickly. "He was highly protective of his foaming process," an employee recalled in 2000, going on to describe an incident from the late '50s when a customer wandered across the factory and reached out to open the door of Sweet's foaming room. "I heard a yell then saw a bucket of liquid foam hit and shoot out the door. Dave had thrown it to keep the guy out."

An early Dave Sweet Surfboards model, noted as the first board of its kind, was put on display by the Smithsonian Institution in Washington, D.C., in 1987. Sweet was married once and has one child. *See also* Clark Foam, Gordon Clark, polyurethane foam.

swell Generally refers to the entire output of waves generated by a storm, or combination of storms; also used to describe a single unbroken wave. Swells are identified primarily by their incoming direction (north swell, south swell, northwest swell, etc.) and by wave period (the amount of time it takes two successive waves to pass a stationary point). "Ground swell" refers to a swell generated from a distant storm; "wind swell" is created by local winds. Swells can last from a few hours to two weeks or longer, although multiday swells usually are generated as the result of two or more overlapping storms. Prior to the 1970s, swells arrived with little or no notice. Today, weather satellite photos and other methods of wave forecasting, combined with new information outlets—particularly the Internet—serve to announce swells days before their arrival. Memorable swells are used as surfing timeline markers, and are often recalled by their date (the Swell of 1953, the Swell of 1969), or some other identifying characteristic (the Halloween swell, generated by an enormous 1991 North Atlantic hurricane that later gained infamy as "the Perfect Storm"). *See also* ground swell, surf forecasting, waves and wave formation, and wind waves.

Swell.com   Surfing Web site based in San Juan Capistrano, California; founded in 2000 by East Coast surfers and financial analysts Jeff Berg and Nicholas Nathanson. Plugging into the late-'90s Internet boom, Berg and Nathanson were able to raise more than $20 million in venture capital to produce what they described as a "comprehensive surfing Web site." Swell.com quickly hired some of the biggest names in surf publishing, including writers Nick Carroll, Steve Hawk, Ben Marcus, Evan Slater, Dave Parmenter, and Matt Warshaw, and photo editor Larry Moore, in addition to a dozen or so top names in Web design, management, and marketing. Swell also purchased Surfline.com, the popular surf report and forecasting Web site, and created a skateboarding site (monsterskate.com) and a snowboarding site (crossrocket.com).

An expensive print ad campaign announced the Swell.com launch in October 2000. Web surfers on opening day were able to choose from an extensive content menu that included a 10,000-word feature on the history of tow-in surfing, a daily news feature, a contest report page, dozens of highly detailed surf break maps, an environmental section, surf product reviews, and an A-to-Z surfing almanac. Bluetorch.com and Hardcloud.com, Swell's primary rivals, had also spent millions putting together comparable all-purpose surf sites; all three expected to generate revenue through online surf shop sales. The Bluetorch and Hardcloud sites, however, were both gone by late 2000. Swell fared better, even during the beginning of the Internet bust, attracting more than one million unique monthly visitors by the summer of 2001 (a majority going directly to Surfline's popular onsite surf break Web cams), and winning a Webby Award for Best Sports Web site in July. The 2001 Swell XXL Big-Wave contest, with entrants judged on photographic evidence of their biggest wave from the previous winter, was won by California surfer Mike Parsons, and earned Swell a burst of mainstream press coverage. But deep editorial staff cuts had already been made and by the end of summer the company was divided into three somewhat-related sites: Surfingthemag.com (*Surfing* magazine's Web site) took much of Swell's editorial content, including daily features, reviews, and competition reports; Surfline.com retained the Web cams, surf spot maps, and almanac pages; and Swell.com became an online and mail-order surf shop. *See also* Internet and surfing.

Swell of 1939   Not so much an isolated swell as a long season of big waves; the sport's first year-identified big-surf milestone, beginning a chain that continues with the Swell of 1953 and the Swell of 1969. "On May 17th, 1939, the waves got large. I mean, *large*," surfing pioneer Wally Froiseth enthusiastically recalled in an interview decades later. "And then they got *big*, and then they got *huge*, and then they got *monstrous*. I haven't seen anything like that before or since." Weather records from the period are scarce, but scientists now believe that 1939–40 produced the third-strongest El Niño condition in the 20th century. The big surf started on the last weekend of September 1939, when 15-foot waves from a huge storm off Baja California moved into Southern California. The swell began on Saturday evening and by Sunday morning most Southern California beaches were washed out and unridable. At Corona del Mar in Orange County, surf photographer John "Doc" Ball filmed lifeguards making rescues while moored boats were swamped by giant waves. Perhaps fewer than two dozen surfers in the state tried their luck in the heavy surf. At Malibu that morning, Grannis and others rode 15-footers from the top of the point to near the end of the municipal pier; by early afternoon, strong winds and heavy rain chased everyone from the water, then washed out many of the coastal roads. Another giant swell hit California on Thanksgiving Day, this one from the west. "I counted 13 breaks [separate lines of broken-wave whitewater] from the shore all the way out to Carpinteria reef," Santa Barbara surfer Mike Sturmer later recalled. The surf was back up again on New Year's Eve, and Grannis remembers watching a school of dolphins riding 20-footers out past the end of Hermosa Beach Pier.

Swell of 1953   Magnificent long-lasting winter swell that buffeted the American West Coast for several days in 1953, peaking on Friday, January 10. "For a time Friday night," the *Los Angeles Times* reported, "the seas were so mountainous that they went over the roofs of houses." In south Los Angeles County's Redondo Beach, 30 families were evacuated from their beachfront homes and apartments, dozens of which were flooded. In nearby Hermosa Beach, the water rushed past Hermosa Avenue, more than 200 yards east of the beach, causing power outages across town. Several fishing boats in Santa Monica were swept ashore during the night. Lifeguards all across Southern California patrolled the beaches during the warm and balmy daylight hours to keep hundreds of spectators well away from the nearshore surge.

As the swell came directly from the west, virtually every surf break in the state was big, although the waves were too much for all but a dozen or so riders. "I was with some really good surfers," California's Mickey Muñoz recalled in 1998, "really experienced riders, and we drove to Sunset Point, just north of Santa Monica. The waves were so big and radical, and I can't remember if anybody got any great rides. It was like nothing else." Muñoz later went to Malibu and on three waves was able to ride past the end of the pier. In Santa Cruz, young big-wave surfer Peter Cole paddled out alone at Steamer Lane and got just one ride—a re-formed 15-footer that he took from Middle Peak, past Cowells, into the bay adjacent to the Santa Cruz pier. "My best and longest ride ever on the California coast," Cole later said. California surfer/board-builders Matt Kivlin and Joe Quigg, along with budding big-wave rider Rick Grigg, surfed at Rincon, just south of Santa Barbara. "That was the day I caught my first triple-overhead wave," Grigg later wrote in his autobiography. "I also got pounded, squashed, rolled underwater and terrified." *Surfer* magazine published three photos of the swell in "Old Timer's Album," a 1965 photo feature, and a photo of Kivlin riding Rincon appeared in 1963's *Surfing Guide to Southern California.*

Swell of 1969   Benchmark big-wave swell, sometimes referred to as the "swell of the century," producing waves up to 50 feet in Hawaii and 20 feet in Southern California during the first week of December 1969. Meteorologists later determined that the weather during the winter of 1969–70 was affected by a strong El Niño, the mid-Pacific ocean-warming phe-

Swell of 1969; La Jolla, California

nomenon that tends to produce bigger, stronger open-ocean storms. The Swell of 1969 was in fact the peak event in a wave season filled with a disproportionately high number of big-surf days. The famous swell itself was the result of three overlapping North Pacific storms; the first was identified on November 27, off the Kamchatka Peninsula. On the 28th, the fast-growing east-moving storm met with another low-pressure area and doubled in size, and by the following day 60 mile per hour winds were blowing across a front measuring about 2,000 miles, from just north of Hawaii to the Aleutian Islands. Furthermore, the storm remained nearly stationary for more than 24 hours, helping to generate even bigger swells. Meanwhile, a third storm, smaller but still powerful, began tracking along the initial storm's wake.

Thirty-foot surf hit the north shore of Kauai mid-afternoon on December 1; at midnight, hundreds of beachfront residents along Oahu's North Shore were ordered to evacuate. Sixty North Shore homes were destroyed or badly damaged over the next 72 hours, Kamehameha Highway was flooded, utility poles were flattened, and a small number of boats were flushed from their berths at Haleiwa Harbor and deposited more than 100 yards inland; debris-crusted high-water marks were later measured at 38 feet above sea level. Two people were washed from shore and drowned. The waves were unridable along the North Shore; top Hawaiian surfers Jeff Hakman, Jock Sutherland, and Bill Hamilton were among those who flew to Maui to ride 10- to 15-footers at Honolulu Bay. On the morning of December 4, a small group of surfers including Wally Froiseth, Fred Hemmings, Jim Blears, Randy Rarick, and Rolf Aurness all rode glassy 20-foot-plus waves at Makaha, on the west side of Oahu; later that day, as the largest waves from the second storm began piling ashore, big-wave leatherneck Greg Noll sat out at Makaha by himself and eventually bombed down the face of a 35-footer—the largest wave ever ridden up to that point.

The big surf first hit Southern California on December 4. Oceanographer and 1966 Duke Kahanamoku Invitational winner Ricky Grigg rode 18-foot waves at La Jolla Cove in San Diego County; at Rincon in Santa Barbara, board shaper Al Merrick, U.S. champion David Nuuhiwa, and world contest finalist Reno Abellira all rode oversize point surf. Conditions that day, Merrick later recalled, were almost supernaturally aligned: "Like perfect six-foot Rincon, except it was 20-foot." A mild Santa Ana condition was in place, pushing the temperatures into the mid-70s, and creating a light offshore breeze. As reported in the *Los Angeles Times,* the heavy surf, which lasted until December 8, was responsible for the drowning of two men near Santa Barbara. Piers and parking lots were damaged, and a number of beachfront homes in Ventura, Rincon Point, Oxnard, and Seal Beach were flooded, but not destroyed. To the north, a small group of Santa Cruz surfers worked their way around the biggest waves at Steamer Lane, and managed to ride some 15-footers.

Exceptionally large waves have at times rolled across the Pacific Ocean (most notably in 1953, 1983, and 1998), but 1969 stands as the milestone big-wave swell. While it's been said that surfers from the period remember the Swell of 1969 as bigger than it really was, satellite images of the great swell, along with atmosphere-gauging millibar charts and on-the-beach photographs, all prove that the swell was in fact the most powerful on record. Waves from the Swell of 1969 are featured in a small number of surf movies, including *Cosmic Children, Pacific Vibrations,* and *Tracks,* all released in 1970. *See also* big-wave surfing, Makaha, Greg Noll.

Swell of 1983 A period of moderate-to-huge winter surf along the American West Coast and Hawaii, lasting roughly from mid-January to mid-March, generated by a chain of El Niño–fortified storms in the North Pacific. Along with hundreds of millions of dollars in property damage, the Swell of 1983 marked the beginning of a new era in big-wave riding. In December 1982, the North Pacific jet stream—a west-to-east stratospheric current that moderates weather over much of the hemisphere—suddenly dropped 1,200 miles south, placing a series of low-pressure storm systems that much closer to mainland America and Hawaii. In early February, after five consecutive big-wave swells hit California, the *Los Angeles Times* reported that more than 1,200 structures along the Southern California coast had been damaged (including the end portion of the famed Santa Monica pier, which collapsed); it was later reported that a single wave had demolished 17 houses in Santa Cruz, and that the piers in Seal Beach, Oceanside, Pacific Beach, and Redondo were damaged or destroyed. President Ronald Reagan designated 17 California counties as federal disaster areas; public property damages along the coast were thought to be about $100 million; private property damages were thought to be in excess of a half billion. "While hundreds of surfers joined beachfront residents in sandbagging buildings," *Surfing* magazine added, "thousands more turned to the double and triple overhead surf. As this issue goes to press, there have been 25 consecutive days of overhead surf, and the weather maps show more to come." Many days were rainy, windy, and unridable, but an equal number were met with sunshine and light offshore winds. Some of the best waves were found at Swami's and Blacks Beach in San Diego County and Rincon in Santa Barbara County, but every winter break along the coast was in top form at one point or another during the wave-filled weeks. The El Niño condition in 1982–83 was later said to be the second strongest on record.

Hawaii also saw its biggest waves since the fabled winter of 1969. Roads were closed and beachfront houses were flooded, but the damage was mild compared to California. Waimea Bay, then the world's best-known big-wave break, located on the North Shore of Oahu, had what is still regarded as its best season. "It wasn't so much about sheer size as consistency," the *Surfer's Journal* wrote years later, marveling at how the surf had funneled into Waimea for up to three weeks at a time. "For the first time ever, big-wave riders actually got their fill." After years of concentrating on professional surf contests and zippy small-wave performance surfing, the surf media, for the first time since the late '60s, began to refocus on big-wave riding. *Surfer* ran a Waimea photograph on the cover of the July 1983 issue (the first Waimea shot so used since 1965), and published two articles, "Whatever Happened to Big-Wave Riding?" and "Dinner at Charlie's," both loaded with 1983 Waimea photos. Interest in big-wave surfing would continue to grow in the years ahead. *See also* big-wave surfing.

Swell of 2001 Large, orderly, sun-drenched winter weekend swell along the east coast of Australia, running from July 6 to 8, 2001, the result of a nearly undetected gale between New Zealand and New Caledonia. While the Australian Bureau of Meteorology had forecast modest three-foot waves for Friday, July 6, surfers from Queensland's Gold Coast to southern New South Wales woke up to find most spots breaking at a still-growing eight to 10 feet. "Easily the biggest waves I've seen ridden here," claimed David Treloar, a 35-year veteran at Angourie, one of north New South Wales' premier point breaks, after the waves peaked that afternoon at 12 to 15 feet. The big surf was complemented by sunny skies and a light offshore breeze, as the storm's perimeter was anchored 1,000 miles offshore, allowing waves to proceed, but holding back all storm-related wind, clouds, and surface chop. The relentless flow of surf, however, kept thousands of would-be challengers on the beach as they failed to break through the inshore waves. Many surfers who did gain position in the lineup still had a rough time. "Three hours, three rides, 15 hold-downs," was the summation of a frustrated Sydney local. Two or three dozen tow-in teams used personal watercraft to blast through the shorebreak and pull each other into some of the biggest waves ever ridden in Australia.

Over the weekend, two New South Wales fishermen were swept off the beach and drowned. A rumor quickly spread that former world tour pro surfer Cheyne Horan had been killed in a Queensland tow-in mishap; he was awakened from an afternoon nap by his best friend, who was weeping over the news. Property damage for the most part was limited to a half-dozen Queensland fishing boats, which were pulled from their moorings and rolled onto the beach. At a surf break in Newcastle, New South Wales, 27 boards were broken in half on Saturday alone. *Australia's Surfing Life* magazine devoted virtually its entire September issue to coverage of the "Three Days That Rocked Our World," and quoted four-time world champion Mark Richards as saying, "This could have been as good as it's ever going to get."

swell period In the simplest terms, "swell period" is the amount of time it takes for two consecutive wave crests to pass a stationary point. Period (also known as "interval") is one of two fundamental measurements, along with swell height, that surfers use to calculate the size and quality of incoming surf. Period and height data are measured by sophisticated transmitting sensors, offshore platforms, and high-tech buoys placed by the dozens in nearshore and offshore waters around the world. Surfers can access raw data on period and height or use surf-forecasting services that sort and interpret the data.

Swell period increases as open-ocean waves move farther from their storm-generated point of origin. Keeping in mind that local winds can make an enormous difference in wave quality for better or worse, it generally holds true that the surf improves with a longer swell period—particularly at big-wave breaks like Waimea Bay and Maverick's. An eight- or 10-second swell period means the surf is being generated from close range, or that two swells are overlapping. Either way, the resulting waves will likely be of low quality. A 20-second period generally translates into long, smooth, evenly spaced waves. Because wave energy is stored more effectively in long-period waves, swell period has as much to do with the size of the surf as swell height. If a swell is 10 foot with a 14-second period as it approaches the North Shore of Oahu, for example, the resulting average wave height might be 12 foot. If a swell is 10 foot with a 20-second period, average wave height could be 20 foot or bigger. Wave speed increases along with swell period, which means that in any given swell, the longer period waves arrive first. Although swell period has long been understood as intrinsic to wave formation and forecasting, surfers for the most part have been aware only of its importance since the mid-'80s. Swell period nonetheless remains one of the most complex and least-understood areas of wave formation. *See also* buoy reports, surf forecasting, wave height and measurement, waves and wave formation.

swell window A set of coordinates between a wave-producing storm and a surf break—the angle and distance between the two, as well as the storm's intensity—that when met will produce the best surf at that particular break. California's Huntington Beach has a near-panoramic Pacific Ocean swell window and breaks all year. Maalaea, in Hawaii, has a tiny swell window and might turn on for just two or three days in a season.

switchfoot, switch stance The vast majority of surfers ride in either a left-foot-forward regularfoot stance or a right-foot-forward goofyfoot stance; the switchfooter can ride comfortably in either position.

Shortboard switchfooters usually take a regularfoot or goofyfoot stance for the entire wave, while longboard switchfooters often swing back and forth from one to the other as they go. Switching stance is comparable to switch-hitting in baseball, only less common, as just a handful of surfers—including Butch Van Artsdalen, Jock Sutherland, James Jones, Jeff Clark, and Rusty Keaulana—learned to become truly ambidextrous. *Surfer* has often reminded its readers of the benefits of switchfoot surfing (primarily that a surfer can ride in a frontside position in either direction), and the magazine has published a number of how-to columns on the subject over the years, including a 1996 article titled, "Switching Stance: Are You Man Enough to Go Both Ways?"

Sydney   Sprawling Australian city located in central New South Wales, facing the Pacific Ocean's Tasman Sea; the birthplace of Australian surfing, and the country's reigning surf culture capital. Sydney's convoluted 36-mile coastline can be divided into two main surfing areas: 1) The headland-studded Northern Beaches, home to a diverse group of the sand-bottom waves like Narrabeen and Manly Beach, and a number of rock-lined reefs, including Dee Why Point. 2) The urbanized Southside, home to the famous and famously temperamental waves of Bondi Beach, as well as the powerful rock-lined reefbreaks in and around Cronulla. Sydney has fairly consistent surf all year, but generally gets its biggest and best waves from April through October, during the South Pacific storm season. Nearshore cyclones can also produce good surf during February and March. Wave height is often between two and four foot, but occasionally gets up to 10 foot or bigger. Average daytime air temperatures range from the high 70s in summer to the low 60s in winter. Average water temperatures range from the low 70s to the low 60s. The introduction of shark nets in 1936 made Sydney a safer place to ride, but the area is not without its hazards, including shallow rock reefs and stinging bluebottle jellyfish, as well as densely crowded lineups.

Sydney was bodysurfed as far back as the turn of the 20th century, and board-surfed as early as 1910 by a small group including Manly Beach resident Tommy Walker. But the sport didn't catch on here until 1914, after Hawaiian surfer and Olympic gold medal swimmer Duke Kahanamoku gave a surfing demonstration at Sydney's Freshwater Beach, capping his performance by riding tandem with 15-year-old local Isabel Letham, who has long been celebrated as Australia's first native surfer. A few days later, Kahanamoku gave his surfboard to 16-year-old Manly resident Claude West, who would later become Australia's first surfing champion, winning the title from 1919 to 1925. Charles "Snow" McAlister, another Manly rider, often called the father of Australian surfing, won the title from 1926 to 1928. Surfing's popularity in Australia shot up in the late '30s, after Southside surfer Frank Adler introduced the easier-to-ride Tom Blake–style hollow boards, then dropped off sharply during the later years of World War II, as many of Sydney's beaches were militarized against a feared Japanese invasion. Hollow boards were still being used exclusively in Australia in 1956, when a group of visiting American surfer/lifeguards (including Tom Zahn and Greg Noll) introduced Sydney to the lighter balsa-core Malibu boards, which quickly became standard throughout the country. Gordon Woods Surfboards, Australia's first surf shop, opened in Bondi Beach before the end of the year.

Americans got their first look at the Sydney surf in 1958, with the release of the Bud Browne film *Surf Down Under*. Four years later, Sydney's Midget Farrelly won the Makaha International, and became the first Australian surfer to earn international acclaim. Bob Pike and Dave Jackman, also of Sydney, were meanwhile tackling the heavies at Waimea Bay and Sunset Beach, on the North Shore of Oahu, giving the country a presence on the big-wave scene. That same year, 1962, brought the debut of *Surfing World* magazine, published by Sydney beachside impresario Bob Evans, who was also the country's first surf filmmaker, as well as the founder of the Australian Surfriders Association and the animating force behind Australia's staging of the first World Surfing Championships at Manly in 1964. (The first New South Wales titles, and the first Australian National Titles, were both held in Sydney in 1963.) Evans also helped ease the growing rift—in coastal communities around Australia, but particularly along Sydney beaches—between surfers and members of the Surf Life Saving Association, a popular and well-established beach lifeguarding group. Sydney was ground zero for the mid-'60s Australian surf scene explosion, marked by "surfie-rocker" brawls at Manly Beach, "surfer stomp" parties (often put together by Evans), and a flood of surf music singles, including Little Pattie's "He's My Blond-Headed Stompy Wompy Real Gone Surfer Boy."

Just a few months after Sydney surfer Nat Young won the 1966 World Championships, board-maker Bob McTavish of Queensland moved to the Northern Beaches and became the key figure in the shortboard revolution—the rich late-'60s design period that produced smaller, narrower, lighter, and infinitely more maneuverable surfboards. The landlocked Northside suburb of Brookvale by that time was known as the nation's board-building capital, housing companies like Bennett, Gordon Woods, Keyo, and Dillon. In the years ahead, surfboard design would be greatly advanced by Sydney-based surfer/board-makers like Geoff McCoy and Simon Anderson. Narrabeen's Terry Fitzgerald met with great business success after launching his Hot Buttered Surfboards business in 1971.

The Sydney competition scene kept pace with the surfboard industry. The 2SM/Coca-Cola Surfabout debuted in 1974, soon became the richest pro contest in the world, and ran continuously until 1999. Dozens of regional, statewide, and national amateur and pro contests are now held in Sydney annually. While surfers from Queensland and North Coast New South Wales had by the early '70s established themselves as equal—in some cases even superior—to the Sydney standard, riders from the "Big Smoke" more often than not continued to set the pace. Sydney has without question produced more first-rate surfers than any city in the world, including world champions Midget Farrelly, Phyllis O'Donell, Nat Young, Tom Carroll, Damien Hardman, Barton Lynch, Pam Burridge, Pauline Menczer, Mark Occhilupo, and Layne Beachley; longboard world champion Stuart Entwistle; and kneeboard world champions Simon Farrer and Mike Novakov. Sydney has also been home to a number of renowned surf journalists (John Witzig, Phil Jarratt, Nick Carroll, Derek Hynd), surf movie- and video-makers (Paul Witzig, Alby Falzon, Jack McCoy, Tim Bonython), photographers (Bruce Channon, Hugh McLeod, Peter Crawford, Paul Sargeant), and surf industrialists (Bruce Raymond).

As of 2002, Sydney was home to about 125 surf shops, over a dozen surf clubs, and roughly 150,000 surfers. *Tracks, Waves,* and *Surfing World* magazines are all published out of Sydney. The Sydney surf is detailed in *The Surfing and Sailboarding Guide to Australia* (1993), Mark Warren's *Atlas of Australian Surfing* (1998), *Surfing Australia* (1998), and *The World Stormrider Guide* (2001). *See also* Narrabeen.

Sydney Opera House   Famous scallop-roofed performing arts center, located on the south side of Sydney Harbor, Australia; site of more than 30 surf movie premieres between 1973 and 1991, including *Crystal Voyager, Rolling Home, Salt Water Wine, Hot Lips and Inner Tubes, Free Ride, Tubular Swells, Wizards on the Water, Storm Riders* (which played for seven weeks), and *Rolling Thunder*. The Sydney Opera House was designed by Danish architect Jorn Utzon, took 14 years to build, and opened in 1973. It has five main auditoriums, 60 dressing rooms, a reception hall, five rehearsal studios, four restaurants, and six bars, and has long been recognized as the busiest theater complex in world. Surf movies were screened in the Music Room, which seats 424 people. About 3,000 events are held at the Opera House each year (mainly theater, dance, and live performances from all genres of music), bringing in more than two million annual visitors. The Opera House is open 24 hours every day, except Christmas and Good Friday. *See also* Santa Monica Civic Auditorium.

T

T-band stringer   A stringer is the narrow strip of wood that laterally bisects a polyurethane foam surfboard blank. A T-band stringer consists of three strips of wood laminated together, with the flanking strips of a different wood type than the center strip; it strengthens the board slightly, but is valued more as a style accent. T-band stringers are most often found on longboards, and are usually about a half-inch wide. *See also* stringer.

Tabeling, Mike   Lanky regularfooter from Cocoa Beach, Florida; runner-up in the 1968 United States Surfing Championships, and often referred to as the

Mike Tabeling

East Coast's first international-caliber surfer. Tabeling was born (1949) in Memphis, Tennessee, the son of a navy pilot, and began surfing in Cocoa Beach in 1962, at age 12, not long after his family settled in the area. In the mid-'60s, Tabeling and Floridian surfer Bruce Valluzzi were among the first to ride Sebastian Inlet, which soon became the state's best-known break. Gary Propper, another Florida surfer, had by that time already made his mark on the national surf scene with lightning-quick small-wave performances and a best-selling signature model surfboard. Tabeling went further: as a contest surfer he won the juniors division of the East Coast Championships in 1966 and 1967, the juniors division of the 1967 Laguna Masters in Redondo Beach (becoming the first East Coaster to win an event on the West Coast), and placed second to David Nuuhiwa in the men's division of the 1968 U.S. Championships. He competed in the World Championships in 1966, 1968, and 1970, and was invited to the 1970 and 1971 Expression Session events. Tabeling was also the first East Coaster to make the cover of *Surfer* magazine (in 1971), and was featured in *Pacific Vibrations,* the definitive 1970 surf movie. With "I Love Cocoa Beach: An Erotic East Coast Confession," a *Surfer* article published in 1970, Tabeling also put the media spotlight for the first time on an area that would soon be famous for producing first-rate surfers, including six-time world champion Kelly Slater.

At 6′4″, 195 pounds, with a gaunt, hatchet-nosed face, Tabeling himself cut an impressive, even imposing figure. He rode for the most part in a straight-up style, folding up his body just prior to turning, then spreading his long arms out like wings during his trademark cutback. For a brief period in the early '70s, according to 1974 East Coast surfing champion Greg Loehr, "Mike was the best surfer in the world— and I saw them all." Tabeling traveled often in the '70s, surfing throughout Europe, Australia, and Africa. From 1978 to 1986 he owned the Creative Shaping surfboard-making factory in Merritt Island,

Florida; in 1989 he moved to Jeffreys Bay, South Africa, where he lived for 10 years, working as a salvage diver, real estate agent, and paragliding instructor. (Tabeling broke his leg, wrist, pelvis, and elbow in a 1994 paragliding accident.)

Tabeling appeared in a small number of surf films in the late '60s and early '70s, including *Oceans* (1972), *Pacific Vibrations* (1970), and *Directions* (1972). He was one of the original group of inductees into the East Coast Surf Legends Hall of Fame in 1996. In 1998, after living in South Africa for 10 years, he moved back to Cocoa Beach to work as an insurance salesman. Tabeling has been married once and has three children.

Tahiti   Tahiti is composed of two circular islands, Tahiti Nui and Tahiti Iti, joined by the narrow isthmus of Taravao; it's part of the Society Islands, and the largest body of land in volcano-formed French Polynesia. Tahiti is renowned in the surf world for the big, tubing, powerful waves that break over its distant coral-lined reef passes. On the north coast—which receives consistent three to five-foot swells primarily during the November-to-February rainy months—popular breaks include the hollow rights at Point Venus Reef and the left at Papeete Harbor, near the capital city of Papeete. Tahiti's biggest and best waves are found on the south and west coasts, where four to eight-foot surf hits regularly between March and October, with 10- to 15-foot swells moving through on occasion. World-class breaks here include Taapuna, Maraa, and Vairao: all are exploding, expert-level, left-breaking tubes. Teahupoo, another left, located just southeast of Vairao, has been regarded since the late 1990s as the world's most challenging and dangerous wave. (The small island of Moorea, located nine miles northwest of Tahiti, is home to nearly a half-dozen high-quality surf breaks.) Daytime air temperatures in Tahiti range from the mid-70s to the mid-80s throughout the year, and the water temperature remains at or near 80. Immensely powerful waves, along with jagged, shallow reefs, are the main surfing hazards in Tahiti; a local surfer was killed at Teahupoo in 2000 after being driven into the reef by a 10-foot wave.

Tahiti's surfing history, like that of Hawaii, stretches back hundreds of years. British explorer Captain James Cook was the first to write about Tahitian surfing, in 1777, noting that the sport was practiced on bellyboards and canoes, mostly by roy-alty. Stand-up riding, however, didn't develop in Tahiti as it did in Hawaii. English missionaries arrived in Tahiti in 1797 and surfing was soon discouraged as being anti-Christian; the sport didn't reemerge here until the 1950s. (Western-borne diseases meanwhile ravaged the island in the early decades of the 18th century, with the native population dropping from an estimated 20,000 to 6,000.) Tahitian waves were introduced to the surf world at large in 1964, when Bruce Brown toured American beach cities with an early edition of *The Endless Summer,* his new movie, which included a section filmed in Tahiti. But Brown and his surfers only rode the poorly shaped inshore waves, and didn't venture out to the reef passes. The Tahiti Surf Club was formed in 1969, and held the first Tahitian Championships that year at Papara, a beachbreak on the south coast. The Taapana Surf Club and Central Surf Club were formed in 1973 and soon combined with the Tahiti Surf Club to form the Polynesian Committee of Surfriding, headed by local surfer Edgar Galenon. Papeete local Arsene Harehoe won 15 Tahitian juniors and men's national titles between 1973 and 1989 (and opened the island's first surf shop in 1982). Harehoe also mentored his neighbor Vetea David, who won the juniors division of the 1986 World Amateur Surfing Championships, then went on to a long and successful professional career. Heifara Tahutini won the men's division of the 1990 World Amateur Championships. Current Tahitian standouts include Manoa Drollet, Hira Terinatoofa, Alain Riou, and Nicolas Leetham.

The Papeete-based Tahitian Surfing Federation was founded in 1989 by Papeete surfer Patrick Juventin, and since has overseen most local competitions, including the national titles. The Tahitian Pro, held at Teahupoo, debuted in 1997 as a second-tier world tour pro contest, and two years later became a championship tour event. By 2003, Tahiti was home to 12 surf shops and an estimated 3,000 surfers. *Tahiti Waves,* the country's first and only surf publication, was founded in 2001. The Tahitian surf is detailed in *The World Stormrider Guide* (2001), and has been featured in nearly two dozen surf movies and videos since the mid-'70s, including *The Forgotten Island of Santosha* (1974), *Amazing Surf Stories* (1986), *Tahitian Dreams* (1989), *Quiksilver Country* (1996), and *Holy Water* (2000). *See also* Tahiti Pro, Teahupoo.

Tahiti Pro   Annual Association of Surfing Professionals (ASP) world pro tour competition, founded in

1997; held in the beautiful but deadly left-breaking reef waves at Teahupoo, Tahiti; regarded as the world's most thrilling surf contest. Teahupoo was virtually unheard of when the Black Pearl Horue Pro, as the Tahiti Pro was first known, debuted as a World Qualifying Series event in 1997. (The WQS is the ASP's minor league tour, below the premier World Championship Tour.) Surf magazine coverage of the 1997 Black Pearl Pro, in fact, identified the break as Waterworld. Nearly 200 surfers competed in the $80,000 men's-only contest, including venerated pros Sunny Garcia, Gary Elkerton, and Vetea David. The surf was thrilling, the rides spectacular, and the biggest waves were enough to unman the entire field, and passed by untouched. A dramatic high point came on the third day of competition, when the *Aremiti,* a $1.5 million catamaran being used as a floating hospitality suite for competitors, judges, and VIP spectators, ran aground—"coral heads disemboweling her inch by screaming inch," as an Australian surf journalist reported. All 150 *Aremiti* passengers were ferried safely to shore. Teenager Andy Irons from Hawaii won the contest.

The contest returned the following year as the Gotcha Tahiti Pro; a women's division was added (won by Hawaii's Keala Kennelly); and the contest ended in chaos when Conan Hayes of Hawaii, the apparent winner after charging fearlessly through a series of Teahupoo barrels, was announced as runner-up to Australia's Koby Abberton. Hayes stormed off the presentation stage and later said he'd put his "life on the line, and got robbed." A contest judges' scaffolding, built on the reef adjacent to the break, collapsed halfway through the event.

The 1999 Gotcha Tahiti Pro was elevated to World Championship Tour status, and became the sensation of 13-event tour. The biggest waves for the most part continued to roar through with no takers, and *Surfer* magazine described Teahupoo as "a still-unconquered field of play." Australians Kate Skarratt and Mark Occhilupo won; Occhilupo was on his way to a world title. The judges' scaffolding once again collapsed. One week before the start of the 2000 Tahiti Pro, local surfer Briece Taerea broke his back in three places and died after getting caught inside by a 15-foot wave at Teahupoo. Six-time world champion Kelly Slater of Florida came out of semiretirement to win the men's division; Keala Kennelly took the women's. The contest was renamed the Billabong Pro Teahupoo

in 2001, and the prize purse was raised to $310,000, with Florida's Cory Lopez and Layne Beachley of Australia winning. Andy Irons and Keala Kennelly won in 2002.

Results of the Tahiti Pro:

1997: Andy Irons
1998: Koby Abberton, Keala Kennelly
1999: Mark Occhilupo, Kate Skarratt
2000: Kelly Slater, Keala Kennelly
2001: Cory Lopez, Layne Beachley
2002: Andy Irons, Keala Kennelly

See also Tahiti, Teahupoo.

tail   The back section of a surfboard, referring either to tail width or shape. Tail width is measured at right angles to the board's stringer, one foot up from the tip; average tail width for a 6′6″ shortboard is about 14 inches. Increased tail width means greater speed, particularly in smaller surf, but less control; wide-tailed boards tend to lose traction and spin out during a hard turn. Narrow tails don't maneuver as well, but adhere better to the wave face, and are standard on big-wave boards and those boards designed specifically for tuberiding.

Tail shape is the outline the board takes in the last few inches. The roundpin, squashtail, and swallowtail are common tail shapes. The "winger" ("bump" or "flyer" in Australia) is a symmetrical stepped-in break along the board's rails, usually about a foot from the rear tip, creating a narrower outline in the tail section. Tail designs are identified by both features: winger-squash, for example, or double-wing swallow. Tail shape was a hot design component in the 1970s; thickness, foil, and bottom contour have since overtaken tail design as the key elements to a board's performance. *See also* fish, roundtail, pintail, squaretail, squashtail, swallowtail.

tailblock   Generally defined as the back quarter of a surfboard. Also used to describe a strip of wood, laminated or a single piece, usually one or two inches wide, set perpendicular to the stringer at the tail end of a board, usually a longboard. The tailblock is cut and sanded to be of a piece with the shaped polyurethane blank, and is added partly for strength, partly as adornment.

tailslide   Type of cutback or top-turn maneuver during which the fins and tail section of the board

Tailslide by Florida's Cory Lopez

are disengaged and pushed into a sideways or backward drift. Finless wooden boards from the 1940s back to antiquity slid to one degree or another on virtually every wave, while controlled sideslip moves were popular with '60s-era longboarders and early '70s shortboarders. The modern tailslide, however, was developed and popularized in the early '90s by Kelly Slater, Ross Williams, Shane Beschen, and the other teenage New School surfers, who preferred the kind of thin, narrow, high-rocker boards that allowed the tail to come untracked with just the smallest change in foot-directed pressure. Tailslides are generally performed in waves under six feet, in dozens of variations, including the "reverse" and the full 360-degree slide. A tailslide move is often described as "throwing the tail." Tailslides have been lambasted by power surfers who believe that the gouging, deep-set, no-slide turns are the building blocks of good surfing. *See also* reverse, sideslip.

Taiwan   Subtropical island nation, about 350 miles long and 100 miles wide, located 90 miles off the Chinese coast; also known as Formosa, which means "beautiful island." Taiwan was first surfed in 1965 by native high school student Jeff Sun, who still rides today and is regarded as the island's top surf guru. Sun opened Jeff Surf Shop, the first in Taiwan, in 1979; the Chinese Surfing Association was founded in Taipei, Taiwan, in 1992, and the island's first surf contest was held that same year. Virtually all surfing is done on the island's Pacific-facing east coast, which consists for the most part of steep-faced headlands and forested bays, and a limited number of beaches.

Ridable waves break in Taiwan all year, but the best surf—up to 10 foot—arrives during the November-to-February winter monsoon season, and gets put to use by about 500 locals, plus a like number of visitors from Japan, Australia, Europe, mainland China, and America. The most popular surfing area in Taiwan is located at Tahsi, a small town near Honeymoon Bay, on the Northeast Coast National Scenic Area. Surf travel here for the most part is done by train. "Not in the major leagues of surfing," according to a 1994 *Surf Report* newsletter, which mapped out 12 Taiwanese surf breaks, "but the vibrancy and culture of the area makes for a truly rewarding experience." There were five surf shops in Taiwan as of 2003.

Takayama, Donald   Baby-faced surfer and surfboard shaper originally from Waikiki, Hawaii; runner-up in the 1966 and 1967 United States Surfboard Championships; founder of Hawaiian Pro Designs surfboards. Takayama was born (1944) and raised in Honolulu, began surfing at age seven and shaping surfboards shortly after. He's often been cited as the sport's original, and perhaps greatest, child phenomenon: in 1957, at age 12, he saved money from his paper route and bought a plane ticket to Los Angeles, where he got a job shaping for Velzy-Jacobs Surfboards in Venice Beach. The following year, when his employers split and formed their separate business, Takayama chose to work at Jacobs Surfboards in Hermosa Beach, and over the next few years he made boards for some of the state's hottest riders, including Lance Carson and Mickey Dora. Jacobs introduced the Donald Takayama Model in 1965 (later described by *Longboard* magazine as "one of the most functional and aesthetically appealing boards ever made"); Takayama then jumped to Bing Surfboards and designed the David Nuuhiwa Noserider in 1966; he moved on to Weber Surfboards a few months later, and helped shaper Harold Iggy design the wildly popular Weber Performer. The bantamweight Takayama (5'4", 130 pounds) worked hard and made enough money to indulge his passion for hot rods, keeping two fully tricked-out cars running at the same time. Meanwhile, he became one of the country's best competitive surfers; in the United States Surfing Associations' year-end ratings he placed fourth in 1964, third in 1965 and 1966, and fifth in 1967; he also finished runner-up to Corky Carroll in the U.S. Championships in 1966 and 1967. A bowlegged goofyfoot with lightning-fast reflexes, Takayama matched speed and flash with classic Hawaiian poise, often striking a back-arch pose while holding trim through a steep section of the wave. He was among a tiny number of top surfers from the 1950s who made a successful transition to short surfboards in the late '60s. Takayama continued to compete, and won the masters division of the U.S. Championships for three years running in 1971, 1972, and 1973. Near the end of the decade, he founded Hawaiian Pro Designs, and was making boards for world pro tour surfer Joey Buran; by the mid-'80s, in response to the growing longboard revival, he produced longboards almost exclusively, and made signature models for '60s-era longboard stars David Nuuhiwa and Dale Dobson.

In 1985 Takayama was arrested, along with 65 other people, in connection with a massive cocaine smuggling operation, and later served 13 months in federal prison. Upon release, he made a quick return to surfboard-manufacturing prominence, and in the early '90s began a celebrated association with California longboard whiz kid Joel Tudor.

Takayama appeared in nearly a dozen surf movies, including *Surf Crazy* (1959), *Barefoot Adventure* (1960), and *Cavalcade of Surf* (1962). As a sage surfer/shaper of the new longboard era, he was also featured in surf videos, including *On Surfari to Stay* (1992), *Powerglide* (1995), *Adrift* (1996), and *The Seedling* (1999). *Surfer* magazine in 1985 named Takayama as one of "25 Surfers Who Changed the Sport"; in 1991 he was inducted into the International Surfing Hall of Fame; in 2000 he was the second-place vote-getter in the legends division of the *Longboard* Magazine Readers Poll. Takayama has been married twice and has one child.

takeoff   Ride-opening maneuver in which the surfer quits paddling, pushes up into a standing position, and begins to drop down the wave face. Timing a takeoff correctly is one of the most difficult aspects of the sport. A misjudged or overly ambitious takeoff, furthermore, can result in a spectacular and potentially dangerous wipeout; a 1982 *Surfer* magazine article introduced the expression TOADS (Take Off And Die Syndrome) with a 10-page pictorial of surfers getting tumbled and thrashed. Tips for a successful takeoff include keeping an eye on the wave during the early stages of paddling; keeping the head close to the board while paddling, just prior to standing up; and in larger surf, taking an extra stroke or two beyond

the point at which the wave seems to be caught. Takeoff variations include the late takeoff and the no-paddle takeoff. The tow-in method of big-wave riding whips surfers into enormous waves from behind a personal watercraft, essentially doing away with the takeoff altogether.

Tales from the Tube   Twenty-page comic book insert, bound into the February 1972 issue of *Surfer* magazine, featuring the work of well-known San Francisco underground cartoonists (and *Zap* contributors) R. Crumb and S. Clay Wilson. *Tales from the Tube* was conceived and developed by Rick Griffin, creator of *Surfer*'s popular Murphy cartoon strip; surf world artist/cartoonists Bill Ogden, Jim Evans, and Glenn Chase also contributed strips, which ranged from whimsical fantasy (Chase's "Cosmic Shangri-La") to gritty and borderline offensive (Crumb's "Salty Dog Sam Goes Surfin'!"). In Griffin's untitled strip, a Murphy-like surfer gets swallowed whole by the fearsome Tube Monster, only to be regurgitated onto the beach just in time for the next showing of the Jumbo Stoke-a-Rama surf flick. *Tales from the Tube* has long been a collector's item. *See also* Rick Griffin, Bill Ogden, surf cartoons and comics.

Tamarin Bay   *See* Mauritius.

tandem surfing   Although tandem surfing is technically defined as any two people riding the same board at once, it's generally recognized as a particular surfing subgenre involving opposite-sex partners, with the man hoisting the woman into a series of lifts and poses. Pre-20th-century Hawaiians almost certainly practiced some form of two-to-a-board surfing, but tandem riding was more or less created in the 1920s by the tourist-serving Waikiki beachboys, who paddled visiting women into the gentle nearshore surf, then rode toward shore with the passenger either propped up in front, nestled in their arms, or sitting atop their shoulders. California surfers Lorrin Harrison and Pete Peterson introduced tandem riding to the mainland after visiting Waikiki in the '30s, and it was soon practiced by small numbers of devotees at places like San Onofre, Doheny, and Malibu. A tandem division was included in the 1954 Makaha International Surfing Championships, the era's most prestigious surf event; it was also part of the inaugural West Coast Surfing Championships in 1959, as

Tandem surfing; Pete Peterson and Barrie Algaw, 1966 Makaha International

and the Makaha Invitational. A *Life* magazine feature in 1964 described tandem surfing as a "sea-going version of an adagio dance."

Tandem surfing all but disappeared during and after the late-'60s shortboard revolution: *Surfer* magazine described it as "a dying sport" in 1969, and filmed tandem flubs were gathered for comedy sequences in surf movies like *Evolution* (1968) and *Waves of Change* (1970). "By 1970," recalled Southern California tandem surfer Steve Boehne, "you couldn't walk across Huntington Beach with a longboard without dying of sheer embarrassment." Boehne and his wife, Barrie Algaw, stuck with tandem, winning the 1970 Makaha, the 1971 U.S. Championships, and the 1972 World Championships, and helped keep the form alive through the '70s and early '80s, when there were fewer than a half-dozen tandem teams worldwide and virtually no tandem contests. The '80s-launched longboard revival eventually brought a mild renewed interest in tandem surfing, with much of the attention going to flamboyant tandem daredevils Bobby Friedman and Ana Schisler, California surfers who took on high-risk breaks like Pipeline and Waimea Bay in the '90s, assuming a four-footed spoon-stance on their 13-foot flame-airbrushed tri-fin. Meanwhile, trying to sort out point valuations between acrobatic lifts and board-turning maneuvers has become the pressing issue in the limited world of competitive tandem surfing. *The Art of Tandem Surfing,* an instructional video featuring Steve and Barrie Boehne, was released in 1997. *See also* Mike Doyle, Pete Peterson.

Tanjung, Rizal   Tall, thin, rubber-limbed goofy-footer from Bali, Indonesia, who gracefully captured the public eye in 1995 by slotting himself deep inside an enormous silver-blue tube at Pipeline in Hawaii— a sublime moment that ended up on the cover of *Surfing* magazine. Tanjung was born (1975) in a small town on Bali's Bukit Peninsula, and soon moved with his family to Kuta Beach, where he began surfing at age eight. At 13 he started riding Uluwatu, Bali's famous left-breaking reef; two years later he won an international 16-and-under grommet contest at Kuta—beating young surfers from America, Australia, and New Zealand—and at 18 he was invited by Pipeline deity Gerry Lopez to spend the winter season at his Pipeline beachfront house. Later that year Tanjung went face-first into the reef and lost two front teeth, but for the most part he maneuvered his lanky body through

well as the 1964-founded United States Surfing Championships. A tandem demonstration was included in the 1964 World Championships, and a tandem division was added to the Worlds in 1965.

Custom-made high-buoyancy tandem boards were first produced in the early '50s, and by the end of the decade the average two-person board was 11 feet long, 25 inches wide, and five inches thick. Tandem surfing was generally practiced by older, huskier men, who used a series of young, light, limber partners. First-generation tandem champions included Pete Peterson (West Coast Championships winner in 1960 and 1962 with Patti Carey; U.S. Championships winner in 1964 with Sharon Barker; U.S., Makaha, and World Championships winner in 1966 with Barrie Algaw) and Mike Doyle (winner, with Linda Merrill, of the Makaha and West Coast Championships in 1963, and the U.S. Championships and World Championships in 1965). Tandem surfers of the period mixed and matched about eight standard lifts, including the knee mount, the swan, and the shoulder stand, which were usually performed one or two per ride.

While virtually all surfers at one time or another try riding two to a board, only a tiny fraction have made a practice of formal tandem surfing; the surfing mainstream has in fact regarded tandem with a combination of amusement and disdain. But tandem was popular in the '60s with nonsurfers, who watched it during network coverage of the U.S. Championships

Rizal Tanjung

the hollows with total aplomb. The easygoing Tanjung has appeared in a small number of surf videos, including *The Loose Change* (1999), *Hit and Run* (2000), and *The Ombak* (2002).

tank   *See* longboard.

tanker surfing   Novelty form of the sport utilizing tanker ship–generated waves, which fan out from the bow and break over sandbars near the edges of a shipping channel. Tanker surfing began in the mid-1960s, when Michigan's Tobe Couture and friends rode freighter-generated waves in Lake St. Clair, near Detroit; dozens of local surfers followed Couture before the sandbars washed away in the early '70s. A small number of surfers in Galveston, Texas, had by that time picked up on the sport.

Tanker surfing wave quality is determined by the water depth along a given channel shoreline (low tide is optimal); the size, weight, speed, and direction of the ship (bigger, heavier, faster, incoming are best); and the width and shape of the channel (narrower is better). As of 2003, Galveston is thought to be the only place where tanker surfing is regularly practiced. Local surfers usually ride in the shipping channel about three times a month; the average tanker-generated wave is only about two foot once it breaks, but rides of up to a half mile have been recorded. Tanker surfing is featured in the surf video *Step Into Liquid* (2003). *See also* Texas.

Tasmania   Australia's storm-lashed and well-forested island state, located 170 miles below the southeast corner of the continent, is flanked by the Bass Strait, the Tasman Sea, and the Southern Ocean, and is home to a wide variety of cold water surf breaks. Tasmania's 2,000-mile coastline can be divided into three main regions: 1) The crowded beach- and pointbreaks of the Hobart area on the temperate south coast, including the reliable sand-bottomed peaks of Clifton Beach and the long right-breaking point waves at Seven-Mile Beach. 2) The pastoral east coast, which includes a number of high-quality but temperamental beachbreaks. 3) The weather-battered west coast, home to Shipstern Bluff, the horrific right-breaking reef widely publicized by the surf media in the early '00s as one of world's most dangerous waves. Tasmania receives its best surf from November through April, as the weather is relatively mild and Roaring 40s storms send out regular pulses of three- to six-foot waves, with 10-to-15-footers possible in March and April. Average daytime temperatures range from 70 in summer to 50 in winter; water temperatures range from the low 60s to the high 40s. Tasmanian surfing hazards include sharks, dangerously shallow reefs, powerful waves, and lack of emergency services along much of the coast.

While it's believed that the Swansea area of Tasmania was surfed as far back as the early 1900s, the sport was not practiced regularly on the "Apple Isle" until visiting Sydney surfer Cedric Cane began riding Clifton Beach in 1926. (Boardless at the time, Cane allegedly took to the surf on a fence post he wrestled out of the ground.) Local auto salesman Ken von Bibra began selling surfboards out of his car in the late '50s; Sea World, Tasmania's first surf shop, didn't open until 1971. The Tasmanian Surfriders' Association (later renamed Surfing Tasmania) was formed in 1963. The first state championships contest was held at Clifton in 1964; Tasmania hosted the Australian National Titles in 1989 and 2000.

As of 2003, Tasmania was home to 12 surf shops, a dozen surfboard shapers, and about 3,000 surfers, most of whom live in or near the state capital of Hobart. Despite an abundance of surf, Tasmania surfers for the most part have remained anonymous; top riders in 2002 included big-wave ace Andrew Campbell, along with minor league pros Dara Penfold and Simon McShane. Tasmanian Surfing Adventures, a surf tour operation focused mainly on the difficult-to-access west coast, including Shipstern Bluff, was opened in 2000. The Tasmanian surf has been featured in a handful of surf movies and videos, including *Under Down Under* (1998) and *Taz Zero One* (2002). Tasmanian surf breaks are detailed in *The Surfing and Sailboarding Guide to Australia* (1993) and Mark Warren's *Atlas of Australian Surfing* (1998).

Tavares, Maria Flashy regularfooter from Titanzinho, Brazil; world-ranked #4 in 2000. Tavares was born (1975) and raised in Titanzinho, an equatorial fishing village near Fortaleza, atop Brazil's eastern horn. She began surfing at age five on a finless surfboard carved from a discarded wooden door, and was riding the same board three years later when she entered her first competition. At 19 she was the Pan American amateur champion; at 21 she became a full-time pro, and in 1999, her first full year on the world circuit, the slender 4′11″ Tavares finished the season ranked #6, and was named rookie of the year. A great natural talent and a whiz in tiny surf, she was one of the first females to regularly complete aerial maneuvers. Tavares has been featured in a small number of surf videos, including *Tropical Madness* (2001).

Maria Tavares

Tavarua Tiny heart-shaped Fijian island located just off the western shore of Viti Levu; home to Cloudbreak and Restaurants, two of the world's best left-breaking reef waves; site of the Tavarua Island Resort, often called "the Club Med of surfing." Tavarua breaks best from May to October, as Southern Hemisphere storms generate consistent surf, which is often met by side-offshore winds. Coral Sea cyclones from February to March can also produce excellent surf, but much less frequently. Cloudbreak (a shortening of "Thunder Cloud Reef," which is translated from "Nakuru Kuru Malagi") is a powerful open-ocean reef located nearly a mile south of Tavarua; waves here often subdivide into three main sections—the Point, the Middle, and Shish Kebabs—which occasionally link up to offer a screaming 200-yard-long ride, with a number of tube sections. Like many tropical reef-pass breaks, Cloudbreak tends to get faster, shallower, and more critical as it goes. Waves here are regularly four to six feet, and it's been ridden up to 18 feet. Restaurants, the nearshore spot named after its proximity to the resort's kitchen and dining area, funnels around the western edge of the island; it breaks in extremely shallow water over sharp-edged coral heads, with waves usually half the size of those found at Cloudbreak. But the shape is perfect, and skilled riders are able to ride inside the tube at Restaurants for 10 or even 15 seconds at a time. Cloudbreak Rights, a temperamental right-breaking tube on the southeast side of the island, is best from November through March. Tavarua is tropical and humid, with water temperatures in the high 70s or low 80s.

American yachtsman John Ritter noted the likely-looking waves at Tavarua in 1982, and passed the information on to friend and surf traveler Dave Clark, who was teaching on nearby American Samoa. Later that year, Clark and his cousin camped and surfed on Tavarua for two months. They also met with three local Fijian tribes, and secured what they hoped would be exclusive surfing rights to the area's surf breaks. Clark and California surfer Scott Funk quickly built an early version of Tavarua Island Resort, which offered limited occupancy (24 surfers maximum), private cabin accommodations, and a number of amenities for $100 a day. The Tavarua surf and the Tavarua Surf Resort both came to the attention of the surfing world in a 1984 *Surfer* magazine cover story featuring legendary California wave-hunters Kevin Naughton and Craig Peterson. The island immediately became a favorite destination for high-end surf vacationers, and was soon booked solid months in advance. The resort's exclusive rights to Cloudbreak were tested through the '90s, however, as surfers staying on nearby islands sometimes boated over to ride the perfect surf. Clark had procured fishing rights to Cloudbreak's reef, but the legal and ethical grounds of Tavarua Resort's exclusivity was challenged by some Fijian officials as well as surfers. The issue remained unresolved as of 2003.

Tavarua has hosted more than a dozen pro surfing contests since the late '80s, including the 1995 Tavarua Tuberiding Classic (won by Shawn Briley), the 1997 Oxbow Masters (Terry Richardson), and the 2002 Roxy Pro Fiji (Melanie Redman). The Quiksilver Pro Fiji, a world tour event, has been held at Cloudbreak since 1999, and winners include Mark Occhilupo and Luke Egan. Tavarua also hosted the inaugural meeting of the Surfer's Medical Association in 1987. The island's stunning blue tubes have been featured in dozens of surf movies, videos, and documentaries, including *Gone Surfin'* (1987), *Endless Summer II* (1994), *Surfer Girl* (1994), *Great Waves* (1998) and *Tavarua: Pressure Drop* (2002). Cloudbreak was also used as the raft-smashing stunt site for the Tom Hanks movie *Cast Away* (2000). *Surfing* magazine named Cloudbreak one of the 25 best waves in the world in 1989, and an *Australia's Surfing Life* magazine poll of the world's top pros in 1991 found Cloudbreak tied with Hawaii's Pipeline as the world's best surf break. In 2003 a week on Tavarua Island Resort cost roughly $2,500 per person not counting transportation. *See also* Fiji, surfing resorts.

Teahupoo   Cyclonic left-breaking reef wave located near the southwest tip of Tahiti Iti; regarded since the late '90s as the world's most challenging and dangerous surf break. "Teahupoo isn't a wave, it's a war zone," surf journalist Gary Taylor wrote in 2000. "A freak of nature that some bastard decided to call a surf spot."

Waves at Teahupoo (pronounced *"cho-pu"*) break about one-third of a mile offshore, and are biggest and best between May and September. Riders usually arrive by boat; paddling from the beach takes about 15 minutes. About 50 yards beyond the Teahupoo reef, the water depth abruptly drops to more than 300 feet. The crescent-shaped perimeter of the Teahupoo reef gives the wave its basic form, with each swell bending in on itself as it refracts around the reef. But it's the sudden deep-to-shallow change in water

Teahupoo, with Florida's Cory Lopez

depth that creates the roaring, water-smashing tubes. Waves as small as three feet can be ridden at Teahupoo, and at six feet it still has a reasonable shape and demeanor. Above eight feet, however, Teahupoo gets exponentially stronger, thicker, rounder, and more malevolent: each ride begins with a vertical entry; each wave transforms into a thick-walled cavern, which in turn collapses with enough force to send shock waves running through the still water of the nearby channel. The ride on a 10-foot Teahupoo wave isn't particularly long, usually about 75 yards, but is relentless from start to finish, with the only objective being to get inside the tube early, hold a line toward the channel, and exit as the waves momentarily slow before shutting down across the reef.

Tahitian surfers rode small waves at Teahupoo in 1985, but Hawaiian bodyboarders Mike Stewart and Ben Severson are credited as the first to ride the break at full strength in 1986. By the early '90s, visiting pros began making semiregular forays out to what was then known only as the break at "the end of the road." (Teahupoo is located directly offshore from the end of a paved road.) As seen in the imperiously titled *Quiksilver Country* video from 1996, world champions Kelly Slater and Tom Carroll rode bravely and stylishly in eight-foot Teahupoo surf, although the break again went unidentified. The Tahiti Pro debuted at Teahupoo as a second-tier pro event in 1997, and became a men's and women's world tour contest in 1999. Winners of the contest over the years include Slater, Andy Irons, Mark Occhilupo, and Keala Kennelly. Tahitian surfers Manoa Drolliet, Vetea David, and Manoa David meanwhile have ridden Teahupoo with verve and style equal to or greater than most of the world tour pros.

One week prior to the opening of the 2000 Tahitian Pro, local pro Briece Taerea was caught inside by a 15-foot set wave and driven into the reef, breaking his neck and back in three places. He went into a coma and died two days later. Four months later Hawaiian big-wave surfer and tow-in ace Laird Hamilton launched into a 18-foot Teahupoo wave that nearly beggared description; photographer Jack McCoy saw the 6'3", 220-pound Hamilton as "a little speck of human, charging for his life, doing what none of us ever imagined possible" as the wave poured over him "like liquid napalm." Hamilton made the wave, then sat and wept in the channel.

"The Horror: Deconstructing Teahupoo," an 18-page article, ran in the *Surfer's Journal* in 2000, and a Teahupoo photo was used for the cover of the 2001-published *The Perfect Day: 40 Years of Surfer Magazine.* Teahupoo can be seen in an ever-growing number of surf videos, including *Sacred Water* (1999), *Trinity* (2000), and *Laird* (2001). *See also* Tahiti, Tahiti Pro.

television and surfing   Surfing began turning up with some regularity on both network and locally aired American television in the early and mid-1960s. The Makaha International surfing contest was televised on ABC's *Wide World of Sports* from 1962 to 1965, and the 1964 Malibu Invitational was shown on Los Angeles–area KHJ-TV. Surfing characters—usually jargon-talking hooligans or outright criminals—were written into top-rated network dramas, including episodes of *Dr. Kildare* and *Burke's Law* in 1964. *Surf's Up,* a weekly half-hour variety show hosted by radio DJ Stan Richards, debuted on KHJ-TV that year as well (just before the Bill Burrud–hosted *Let's Go Surfing* on KTTV), and was the first show dedicated to the sport. *Surf's Up* featured clips from the latest surf movies, an interview with a surfing celebrity, and questions from a small studio audience or from call-in viewers. *Surfing World,* a like-formatted show produced by KTLA Channel 5 and hosted by surf moviemaker/publisher Walt Phillips, premiered in 1965. All three shows were off the air by 1967. ABC's short-lived surf-themed musical variety show *Malibu U,* hosted by singer Ricky Nelson, came and went in mid-1967. Meanwhile, Australian television began to focus on surfing in 1962, and the Sydney-held 1964 World Surfing Championships were broadcast

nationwide. *The Midget Farrelly Surf Show* and the Nat Young–hosted *Let's Go Surfing*—an instructional series—both aired on Australia's ABC-TV in 1967.

Wide World of Sports and CBS Sports continued to produce surf contest coverage in the '60s and '70s, most notably with the Duke Kahanamoku Invitational and the Pipeline Masters events. Surfing also continued to make an occasional appearance on network shows, both drama and comedy: in a 1967 episode of *Batman,* the Caped Crusader dueled with the Joker in a Gotham Point surf-off; in a 1972 episode of the *Brady Bunch,* eldest son Greg nearly drowned after entering a Waikiki surf contest wearing a cursed tiki-head necklace. Perhaps the most telegenic surfing moment during this period was the opening shot for the CBS police drama *Hawaii Five-O,* which showed a big, empty, hypnotic tube, backed by trumpeting theme song written and recorded by the Ventures. (Surfing was seen on a number of other popular shows over the years, including *The Flintstones, Gilligan's Island, The Simpsons, Lou Grant, Scooby-Doo* and *Magnum PI.*)

Surfing's TV presence expanded in America and around the world during the '80s and '90s, along with the medium itself. Cable TV in particular helped bring more surfing to a larger audience. *Surfer* magazine made the jump to television in 1986 with its *Surfer* Magazine on Video series on ESPN—the first "magazine"–style surfing TV show. *H3O,* produced in Honolulu and hosted by pro surfers Mike Latronic and Mark Foo, debuted in 1990. TV-aired surf travelogues were occasionally produced, including a 1980 episode of ABC's *American Sportsman,* with former U.S. champion Rick Rasmussen riding the long lefts of Grajagan, Java, and a 1993 ESPN-aired show featuring big-wave riders Laird Hamilton and Brock Little charging into rock-fringed 15-footers on Easter Island. A number of first-rate surfing documentaries found their way onto Public Broadcasting System and cable, including *Liquid Stage: The Lure of Surfing* (PBS, 1995), *50 Years of Surfing on Film* (Outdoor Life Network, 1997), *Great Waves* (Outdoor Life Network, 1998), and *Surfing for Life* (PBS, 2000). Surf contest programming also increased, with domestic and international events covered in depth on ESPN and Prime Ticket. MTV meanwhile occasionally featured surfing in its original programming. Surfing characters appeared on *Beverly Hills 90210* (with Luke Perry as a brooding "soul surfer") and the short-lived *Top of the Hill* (William Katt as a boyish surfer-turned-U.S. congressman); *Big Wave Dave's,* a CBS sitcom about three friends from the Midwest opening a surf shop on the North Shore of Oahu, lasted just over a month in 1993 before it was canceled. NBC's *Wind on Water,* about a family of Big Island rancher/surfers, starring Bo Derek, only lasted two episodes in 1998. Far more engaging was Nickelodeon's surf-heavy cartoon series *Rocket Power,* a Rugrats takeoff premiering in 1999. The most talked-about surf-related TV event of the '90s was world champion Kelly Slater's decision in 1992 to take on the role of Jimmy Slade, Malibu High's top surfer, on the wildly popular lifeguard drama *Baywatch.* Slater appeared in 10 episodes, was for the most part panned by critics and surfers alike, and quit in 1993. The following year, TV news programs across the nation and around the world covered Mark Foo's drowning at Maverick's in California. Brazil's Globo TV coverage of the 1994 World Surfing Championships in Rio, meanwhile, reached six million viewers nationwide. Surfers in general proved to be ambivalent about the sport's TV presence. "The realness of surfing doesn't survive the television corporate process," John Berliner of San Francisco wrote in a 1992 letter to *Surfer* magazine. "A little of the essence rubs off every time a memo gets circulated, a board meeting convenes, a draft gets proofed."

Surfing had also become a regular part of Australian TV, with high-quality domestic contest coverage (for the Surfabout in Sydney, the Stubbies Pro in Queensland, and the Rip Curl Pro in Victoria) complemented by documentaries like *A Surfing Odyssey* (1972) and *Legends: An Australian Surfing Perspective* (1994). Former world champion Martin Potter hosted *NRG,* a weekly surfing variety show produced in Sydney from 1994 to 1998; former world champion Barton Lynch has produced and hosted *Ra! The Boardriders Show* since 1999.

As of 2003, surfing TV shows were being produced in a small number of countries around the world, including Brazil (*Surf TV* and *Surf Adventures*) and Japan. Popular American surfing shows included *Board Stories* and *Bluetorch TV,* as well as Union* the Boardriding Channel, a video-on-demand program backed by surfwear giant Quiksilver. (*Boarding House: North Shore,* a WB network reality show, similar to MTV's *The Real World* and starring pro surfers Sunny Garcia, Damien Hobgood, Veronica Kay, Holly Beck, Myles Padara, Danny Fuller, and Chelsea Gorgeson, was scheduled to air in the summer of 2003.) *See also* Baywatch, Big Wave Dave's, Hawaii Five-0, Malibu U, radio and surfing, Surfing World, Surf's Up.

template   Tracing guide, usually made of thin plastic, fiberboard, cardboard, Masonite, or plywood, used by surfboard shapers to draw a board's outline on an polyurethane foam blank. Templates can be one-piece, full-length, nose-to-tail outlines, but more often come in the form of an asymmetric, half-length "spin template," something like a French curve, which can be used to create new outlines, depending on how it's positioned. The template is placed alongside the board's stringer (the narrow wood strip that runs longitudinally down the center), traced in soft lead pencil, then flipped over and traced in mirror image on the opposite side. Templates were set aside—although never discarded outright—by high-volume board manufacturers in the '90s with the advent of computer-programmed shaping machines. "Template" is also used synonymously with "outline" and "planshape."

Texas   Texas surfing culture runs deeper than expected, despite the fact that wave quality suffers greatly from the broad continental shelf tracing the state's entire 365-mile-long coastline, and by the Gulf of Mexico's limited fetch. Fall is high season for Texas surfing, as hurricanes and passing cold fronts semi-regularly generate three- to five-foot waves. Winter surf is less consistent, but often bigger; summer is all but waveless. Average midday coastal air temperatures in Texas range from the mid-80s in summer to the high 50s in winter; water temperatures range from the low 80s to the low 60s. Surfing in Texas takes places almost entirely on the string of narrow, sandy barrier islands that trace the mainland; the southern tip of South Padre Island, near the Mexican border, generally produces the state's best surf. Top breaks on South Padre include the Jetty, the Cove, Steamers, and Boca Chica—all located within and around a pair of half-mile-long harbor jetties at the south end of Port Isabel. Other popular Texas surf spots include Bob Hall Pier in Corpus Christi, the beachbreaks at Port Aransas, and Surfside Jetty near Freeport. There are no reef- or pointbreaks in Texas. Outflow from dozens of rivers often turns the Texas surf a muddy brown color.

Italian-born deaf-mute lifeguard Leroy Columbo is credited with introducing surfing to Texas in 1930, in Galveston, and he was soon renting a pair of flexible Firestone-made surfboards constructed from inflated inner tubes wrapped in canvas. Other '30s-era Texas wave-riders included Dorian Paskowitz and Babe Schwartz, both of Galveston. But surfing remained a cult activity along this stretch of coast until the early '60s, when the sport had a miniboom, with dozens of surf shops and surf clubs established in coastal towns like Galveston, Corpus Christi, and Port Aransas, as well as Houston. *Surfing* magazine reported in 1964 that it was not uncommon to see more than 200 surfers out at Galveston Beach. Two years later there were two separate state championship events in Corpus Christi and Galveston, both attracting hundreds of competitors and thousands of spectators. By 1970, Galveston locals had discovered "tanker surfing," as they rode waves produced by tanker ships passing through the 25-mile channel at Galveston Bay. The Gulf Coast Surfing Association, the state's first competitive association, was formed in 1968; a number of other regional competition groups followed. The United States Surfing Championships were held on South Padre Island in 1975, 1979, 1983, 1991, and 1995.

In 2003, Texas was home to an estimated 20,000 surfers and 25 surf shops. The 1988-founded Texas Gulf Surfing Association has nearly 300 members and holds nine events annually, as well as the Texas State Championships. The state has been featured in a small number of locally produced surf videos, including *Primo Days* (1995) and *Isla Blanca* (1998); *Surfing the Texas Gulf Coast,* a guidebook, was published in 2000. Pioneering surfers Pete Peterson, Dorian Paskowitz, and Matt Kivlin, along with big-wave rider Ken Bradshaw and world champion Debbie Beacham, were all born in Texas. The first FlowRider wave machine was installed at the Shilitterbahn Water Park in New Braunfels, Texas, in 1991, and two more FlowRiders have since opened in the state. *See also* South Padre Island.

Texas Gulf Surfing Association   Small American amateur competitive surfing association, formed in 1988, and covering much of the Gulf of Mexico coastline. The history of the Texas Gulf Surfing Association is tangled and chaotic, in keeping with the general theme of American amateur surfing. The area's first competitive organization, the Gulf Coast Surfing Association (GCSA), was formed in 1968, after the United States Surfing Association split into four regional groups. Rival associations followed, and in 1975, after the overseeing United States Surfing Federation, for the first time, named Texas as host state for the U.S. Championships, infighting broke out between the GCSA, the Florida-based Southern Surfing

Association (SSA), and the just-formed Gulf Surfing Association (GSA) as to who would host the contest. The USSF stepped in and dissolved the GCSA entirely, then split the SSA in two, giving half to the Eastern Surfing Association (covering the eastern seaboard) and half to the newly dominant GSA. The GSA again hosted the U.S. Championships in 1979, but in 1983 the Championships were awarded to the Texas Surfing Association (TSA), a new group created by former GSA members. Four years later, as tension mounted between the TSA and the GSA over which group would host the 1988 U.S. Championships, the USSF again intervened and ordered the two organizations to merge, and June 1988 brought the formation of the Texas Gulf Surfing Association (TGSA), run primarily by members of the GSA, with five-time Texas State Surfing Champion Cliff Schlabach as president.

The Corpus Christi–based TGSA covers the Texas/Louisiana coastline from the Mexican border to the Mississippi, and is divided into north and south districts. Nine regular-season surf contests are held between September and April, prior to the Texas State Championships. The TGSA hosted the 1991 and 1995 U.S. Championships. It had roughly 300 members in 2003.

Thailand   Thailand, formerly called Siam, covers nearly 200,000 square miles, including a long southern peninsula—bordered by the Andaman Sea to the west and the Gulf of Thailand to the east—extending to Malaysia. Surfing in Thailand began in the early '80s when Australian and American expatriates discovered ridable waves on the vacation island of Phuket in the southwest. Two reefs and nearly 20 beachbreaks have been charted so far on Phuket, and the tropical west coast of the mainland, north of Phuket, contains roughly 60 miles of mostly unexplored warm-water beachbreaks. The surf in Thailand, while generally small and weak, is best during the April-to-September monsoon months. In September 2000, the inaugural Phuket/Quiksilver Surfing Contest at Kata Yai Beach featured 48 local and international surfers, and was won by Thai surfer Chalong Tanus. In 2003 there were an estimated 300 native surfers in Thailand, as well as a surfing school and surfboard-rental business.

Thomas, Marty   Polished, methodical regularfoot surfer from Haleiwa, Hawaii, by way of Southern California; world-ranked #9 in 1991. Thomas was born

Marty McClaurey in 1967 in Downey, California, began surfing at age four, and was runner-up in the menehune division of the 1980 United States Surfing Championships. The following year he moved to Hawaii, and in 1985 he changed his surname to Thomas, his mother's maiden name. He didn't win an event in his 11-year world tour pro career (1986 to 1997), but finished runner-up in five contests, including the 1987 O'Neill Cold Water Classic and the 1991 Op Pro. "Every turn is properly linked," a surf journalist said of Thomas's riding style in 1989, "and by the end of a normal ride a viewer has taken in a range of maneuvers that spell style and precision." Thomas is seen in *No Exit* (1992) and *Cyclone Fever* (1994), among other surf videos.

Thomopolous/Thompson, George   Confident regularfoot surfer from Durban, South Africa; men's division winner in the South African Championships in 1965, 1967, 1968, and 1969. George Thomopolous was born in 1947 in the landlocked Transvaal city of Springs, and moved with his family to Durban at age nine, where he began surfing. Aside from his national titles, the dark-haired Thomopolous was South Africa's team captain to the World Surfing Championships in 1966, 1968, and 1970; in the 1968 titles he placed seventh. (He used an Anglicized version of his name, George Thompson, during this period.) As South Africa's *Zigzag* magazine later recalled, Thomopolous was "the supreme contest rider, functional, smooth and unwilting under pressure." In 1967 he was the highest-polling South African surfer in *International Surfing* magazine's Hall of Fame Awards. From 1971 to 1973, Thomopolous hosted *High Wave,* a surfing radio program broadcast out of Durban, and from 1983 to 1985 he wrote a weekly column titled "Watersports" for the *Durban Daily News.*

Thorson, Mitch   Down-home power surfer from Western Australia; world-ranked #16 in 1986 and 1987. Thorson was born (1964) and raised on Rottnest Island—a gorgeous and sparsely inhabited seven-mile-long island located 12 miles off Perth—and his formative surfing years were spent riding big waves alone on the craggy Rottnest reefs. He was Western Australia's juniors division champ in 1980 and 1981, and was runner-up to world-beater Mark Occhilupo in the 1984 Pro Junior. "Not a glamour boy," as described by *Surfer* magazine, but Thorson became the insider's favorite when the surf turned big and nasty.

He was also known for his dry wit. "All part of the plan," he told surf journalist Derek Hynd, bruised and scraped while walking up the beach at Pipeline, in Hawaii, after a vicious early morning wipeout. "Take a battering early, and the rest is easy." Thorson appeared in a small number of surf movies and videos, including *Surf Into Summer* (1987) and *Gripping Stuff* (1987).

three-sixty   Flashy maneuver in which surfboard and rider, angling across a wave, both rotate 360 degrees. In the original version—known as the "sliding 360" and popularized by California surfer J Riddle in 1969—the surfer leaned forward, disengaged the fin, pushed down with the back foot, and slid the board around in a circle. The sliding 360 for the most part was dismissed as a trick, and with the exception of a few top surfers (Larry Bertlemann, Buttons Kaluhiokalani, Mike Purpus, Derek Hynd), it was left out of the progressive surfer's repertoire for years. The 360 was revived in the early '90s by the Kelly Slater–led New School group, who split it into a dozen or more variations—many of them airborne—including the roundhouse 360 (the cutback turn is extended into a same-rail off-the-lip move), the carving 360 (a bottom turn sustained into a single-turn loop), the floating 360 (a quick spin done at the end of a floater), and the backside air reverse (a complex aerial move that is in fact a 540).

Three-sixty; Hawaiian surfer Chava Greenley

Thruster Model name for the original tri-fin surfboard, designed and built by Australian surfer/shaper Simon Anderson in 1981. Anderson's board, made under his own Energy label, was soon being copied worldwide, and by late 1982 the tri-fin had replaced the traditional single-fin and the skittish twin-fin as the high-performance board of choice. Anderson claims the "Thruster" name was a nod to the multi-fin system's added thrust and drive, and wasn't intended to be a surfboard-as-phallus metaphor. Nectar Surfboards in California was the first to market the tri-fin design in America, licensing the name from Anderson and billing it as the "3-Fin Thruster." "Kids these days . . . they just slide around," Nectar owner Gary McNabb said in 1981, noting how the twin-fin design was producing a generation of soft-turning young surfers. "The Thruster is meant to go forward, not sideways." *See also* Simon Anderson, tri-fin.

tidal bore waves Tidal bore waves are formed in a small number of ocean-connected rivers worldwide, and take shape when a higher-than-average tide funnels through a rivermouth into a narrowing inland passage. The best-known surfing tidal bores are found in Britain's Severn River, the Amazon in Brazil, and the Dordogne River in France. Equinox tides generally produce the biggest bore surges, and a breaking bore wave will travel at two or three times the speed of the incoming tide. (The Severn wave moves at six to eight miles per hour; a 10-foot ocean wave generally travels at about 12 miles per hour when it breaks.) Bore waves are almost always larger near the riverbanks than at midstream, and the outer bank in a curve tends to produce an even bigger wave—occasionally up to eight foot or more. English surfer Rodney Sumpter introduced tidal bore surfing to the public with his 1968 *Surfer* magazine article "The World's Most Unusual Wave." Rides on the French Dordogne, through the scenic heart of Bordeaux wine country, last up to 10 minutes—short surfboards are occasionally used, but local river surfers prefer longboards, canoes, or surf-skis—and finish 60 miles from the nearest beach. The Pororoca, an Amazon River bore in northern Brazil was first surfed in 1997, has been featured in *Surfer* and the *Surfer's Journal,* and was the subject of a National Public Radio feature story. Bore waves are also found on the Shubenacadie River in Nova Scotia, the Turnagain in Alaska, the Hugli in India's West Bengal, and the Batang Lupar in Malaysia's Sarawak state. The largest recorded tidal bore wave swept up China's Qiangtaing River in 1993; it rose up to 20 feet in places, traveled 200 miles, and killed more than 100 people. *See also* Pororoca, Severn Bore.

tidal wave *See* tsunami.

tide The rhythmical rise and fall of the ocean's water levels, caused by the gravitational pull of the moon and sun; tide is one of the three main factors, along with oceangoing swell and nearshore wind, that determine surfing conditions at a given spot. The moon's gravitational pull creates a slight elliptical bulge in the ocean, directly in line with its position over the earth, with an offsetting bulge forming on the earth's opposite side. Coastlines in the bulge areas have a high tide, while the areas in between experience low tide. The sun has a lesser gravitational pull on earth, but nonetheless creates bulges of its own, which can either combine with or act against the moon's pull, depending on their respective positions. Spring tides—those having the greatest high-to-low range—occur when the sun and moon are either in alignment on one side of the earth, or on opposite sides of the earth. Low-ratio neap tides occur when the sun and moon form a 90-degree angle to the earth. Tides are measured in feet in America and by meters in most of the rest of the world; a "minus tide" occurs when the tide falls below a designated low-tide average for a given area.

While tides are one of nature's most predictable phenomena, knowable to the inch years in advance, tidal mechanics can be enormously complex in detail, with great variation from area to area, even along the same stretch of coast, mainly because of differences in underwater topography. Tropical islands in the Pacific generally have a tidal range of less than two feet. Tidal changes in western Europe, northern Brazil, Panama, and eastern Canada—all areas of convoluted underwater topography—are usually between 15 and 30 feet. The greatest tidal range is found in Nova Scotia's Bay of Fundy, where the levels change by as much as 50 feet. A tidal cycle consists of outgoing (ebb) and incoming (flow) phases, and takes roughly 12 and a half hours to go from high to low and back to high. Most coastlines either have two tide cycles per day (semidiurnal), while some vary between one and two daily cycles, and a rare few, such as Louisiana in the Gulf of Mexico and Mallorca in the Mediterranean Sea, receive only one tide per day (diurnal).

Avid surfers often keep a pocket-sized tide chart in their wallet or glove compartment; tide information is also available online, in all coast-serving newspapers, and even as a feature on some wristwatches. Generally speaking, higher tides produce easier-breaking wide-based waves, while lower tides create steeper, faster, tubing waves. During a large fast-moving ground swell, a high tide offers less resistance to the waves, which helps preserve their power as they strike the beach. Small surf is often better served by an outgoing tide, as the lowering water throws the reef, point, or sandbar into higher relief relative to the incoming wave. In places where the tidal range is extreme, such as England and northern Brazil, many surf breaks are only ridable for two or three hours at a time, before the reef, point, or sandbar is either drained of water from the outgoing tide or flooded by the incoming tide. (England and Brazil both feature telescoping coastal rivers that often produce a tidal bore surfing wave miles from the shore during particularly strong incoming tides.) In areas where the tidal range is less severe but still noticeable, such as California or the east coast of Australia—where the average tidal range is about four or five feet—tide often serves as a fine-tuning element for waves. Many surf breaks are known to be particularly tide-sensitive: Santa Barbara's Rincon is best on a low tide, while Kirra in Australia requires a high tide. The expression "tidal wave" is a misnomer, as the powerful and often-destructive waves—usually caused by an underwater landslide or earthquake—have nothing to do with tide.

tint   Highly concentrated translucent coloring agent; tints come in liquid form, and are mixed with resin, then brushed onto the surfboard during the fiberglass lamination process. Tints are used to color broad areas, usually the entire board, or the bottom and rails. Airbrushing began to replace tinting in the 1980s as a more popular and less-expensive coloring choice. *See also* airbrush, pigment.

Todd, Trudy   Spunky Australian pro surfer from Coolangatta, Queensland; winner of the 1999 Triple Crown. Todd was born (1974) and raised in Queensland, began surfing at 15, won six state amateur titles, and finished first on the Australian Championship Circuit pro tour in 1993, 1994, and 1996. An aggressive regularfooter, noted for her quick, sharp turns, and not overly concerned with surfing subtleties,

Todd marched steadily up the world tour ratings, finishing 20th in 1993, fifth in 1996, and third in 1998. Halfway through the 1999 season, while in contention for the title, the petite Todd (5′2″, 108 pounds) told Swell.com that the first thing she'd do upon winning the championships would be to "go Pamela Anderson all the way" and get a pair of extra-large breast implants. She won the prestigious Triple Crown in Hawaii, but again finished third in the final standings. The following season Todd was fined $1,200 for brawling with another competitor during a match; later in the year she had back surgery (unrelated to the fight), and was unable to hold her position on the world tour; she requalified in 2003. Todd has appeared in nearly a dozen surf videos, including *Peaches* (2000) and *Tropical Madness* (2001).

Todos Santos   Small, rocky, uninhabited island in northern Baja California, Mexico, eight miles off the mainland; home to Killers, a world-class big-wave break. Isla de Todos Santos (All Saints Island) was first ridden in 1963 or 1964 by visitors from Southern California, who surfed a left-breaking wave there called Thor's Hammer. By the early '80s, three breaks in Todos Santos had been charted, and empty 20-footers at the as-yet-unnamed Killers were featured in the 1983 surf movie *Ocean Fever*. California big-wave rider Marty Hoffman and a few others rode Killers occasionally during the mid-'80s, but it remained a largely unknown break until world tour pros Tom Curren and Dave Parmenter were photographed there for a 1987 *Surfing* magazine article titled "Big Time," with Parmenter writing that the 18-foot waves they came upon were "by far the largest I've ever ridden in North America." Waimea Bay in Hawaii had for decades been the undisputed big-wave capital of the world, but for a few years prior to the discovery of Maverick's in northern California and Jaws in Maui, the newly named Killers was the sport's runner-up big-wave break. ("Todos Santos," or just "Todos," is often used instead of "Killers" to describe the break itself, as well as the island. Todos Santos is also the name of a wave-fringed coastal town located just north of Cabo San Lucas, at the southern tip of Baja.)

Todos Santos breaks regularly from fall to early spring. It's positioned at the end of a wave-funneling underwater canyon that allows incoming swells to break at least twice as big as the surf found on the mainland. Unlike Waimea or Maverick's, both of which require a minimum wave height of 10 or 12

Todos Santos, with California's Taylor Knox

feet, Killers also produces worthwhile medium-small surf. From 15 to 35 feet, it offers a steep, thrilling take-off section that tapers quickly into a deep-water channel. Although Waimea and Maverick's are both thought to be slightly more powerful than Todos, the Mexican wave nonetheless remains one of the greatest big-wave challenges. Throughout the late '80s and '90s, San Clemente regularfooter Mike Parsons was regarded as Killers' dominant surfer. Visitors generally arrange to surf Todos Santos at least a day ahead of time, and charter day-rate fishing boats leaving out of Ensenada for the 45-minute ride to Killers. A pair of lighthouses are located on the island's northwest corner, not far from Killers, and a dirt track runs from east to west, but the flat scrub-covered Todos Santos is otherwise undeveloped.

The inaugural Reef Brazil Big-Wave World Championship, held at Killers in 20- to 35-foot surf in 1998, was won by Brazilian Carlos Burle. San Diego's Taylor Knox rode a giant wave in the semifinals that later earned him the $50,000 first-place check for the K2 Big-Wave Challenge, a first-of-its-kind event with contestants judged on photographs of their biggest successfully ridden wave. The 1999 Reef event at Todos took place in relatively small 12-foot waves, and was won by Australian Paul Paterson. Tow-in surfing—motoring into the wave from behind a personal watercraft—was introduced to Todos Santos in late 1999. Todos Santos has been featured in more than a dozen surf movies and videos, including *Gone Surfin'* (1987), *Overdrive* (1993), *Panama Red* (1994), and *The Reef at Todos* (1998). "Something Wicked This Way Comes," a feature article on Todos Santos written by Daniel Duane, was published in the May 1998 issue of *Outside* magazine. *See also* Baja California.

Tom Morey Invitational   Surfing's original prize-money competition, held in Ventura, California, on Fourth of July weekend, 1965; better known as the "Tom Morey Noseriding Contest." Surfboard manufacturer Tom Morey—who would later create the enormously popular Morey Boogie bodyboard—developed the Invitational as a way to promote his new factory-retail surf shop. The event was notable not just for its $1,500 purse (gathered for the most part by the $50 entry fee paid by each of the 24 competitors), but for its original scoring system. Instead of the traditional subjective method, with judges awarding a 1 to 10 score for each ride, surfers were clocked as they rode the nose, and ranked according to accumulated nose time. The noseriding craze was then at its zenith, the "sport within a sport," as described by *Surfer* magazine. Professional surfing had meanwhile been introduced two months before the Morey event, when prizes for the Laguna Sportswear Masters in Hermosa Beach, California, included an MG sedan, a Kawasaki motorcycle, a hi-fi set, and a new wardrobe.

Entrants in the Morey Invitational turned up on the first morning of competition with an array of customized boards (including brick-weighted tail sections, squared-off noses, and winged fins), all designed to improve noseriding. The front quarter of each board was spray-painted fluorescent red; surfers would be timed only while standing within the red area. The all-California field included David Nuuhiwa, Corky Carroll, Mickey Muñoz, Dewey Weber, Mike Doyle, Mike Hynson, Robert August, Skip Frye, John Fain, and Donald Takayama. The surf was an uninspiring two to three feet, and no more than 50 spectators were on hand at Fairgrounds, the rock-lined Ventura pointbreak picked by Morey as the contest site. The competition was exciting nonetheless, with Muñoz edging Hynson by seven-tenths of a second to pick up the $750 winner's check—although years later Morey announced that he'd just discovered a timer's error, and that Hynson should have won. Skip Frye finished third.

In 1966, the event was renamed the United States Professional Surfing Championships, the number of contestants was raised to 43 (and the per-surfer entry fee went to $125), and the purse was $5,000. For the first time ever, surf contest spectators were charged admission: $1. The waves were excellent for much of the contest, and local surfer Terry Jones won $2,000 for first place, followed by Skip Frye ($1,000) and Bob Purvey ($500). *See also* Tom Morey, noseriding, professional surfing.

Tomson, Ernie   Surf coach and contest organizer from Durban, South Africa; cofounder of the Gunston 500 competition in 1969; father of 1977 world champion Shaun Tomson. Ernie Tomson was born (1923) and raised in Durban, and was training for the Olympic swimming team in 1947 when he was attacked by a shark at Durban's South Beach and lost the bicep on his right arm. He went on to have a successful career in auto-body repair and real estate. Tomson became interested in surfing in the early '60s, along with his son Shaun; by the end of the decade Ernie was coaching Shaun, as well as other rising Durban-based surfers including Michael Tomson (Ernie's nephew), Mike Esposito, Bruce Jackson, Paul Naude, and later Mike Savage, Michael Burness, and Martin Potter. Tomson was a judge in the 1970 world championships, held in Victoria, Australia. The Gunston 500 (inaugurated as the Durban 500) was South Africa's first professional contest. While Tomson was very much a member of the South African business establishment, he took a stand in 1971 against his government's racist apartheid policies, inviting Eddie Aikau into his well-appointed beachfront apartment after the dark-skinned Hawaiian surfer arrived in South Africa for the Gunston 500 and was turned away from a whites-only Durban hotel. Tomson died of a heart attack in 1981 at age 57. *See also* sharks and surfing.

Tomson, Michael   Forceful, articulate pro surfer and surfwear entrepreneur, originally from Durban, South Africa; world-ranked #5 in 1976; the founder of Gotcha beachwear. Tomson was born (1954) and raised in Durban, and began surfing at age 10, along with his slightly younger cousin and future world champion Shaun Tomson. Both of the teenaged Tomsons competed in the 1970 World Surfing Championships in Australia, with Shaun advancing to the semifinals. Michael remained in Shaun's shadow more or less throughout his pro surfing career. In the Gunston 500—Durban's best-known international pro event—Michael placed fifth in 1973, fourth in 1974, and third in 1975, while Shaun won all three years. But it was the older cousin who came out ahead

on the debut world pro tour in 1976, as Michael finished #5 to Shaun's #6. He also placed runner-up in the 1977 World Cup in Hawaii, and won the 1978 Hang Ten in South Africa. As a surfer, the strong-jawed Tomson is best remembered for charging fearlessly into the tube at Pipeline during the winter of 1975–76, when he helped lead the "backside attack" that brought regularfooters into near parity with goofyfooters at the world's most famous break.

Tomson began moonlighting in the mid-'70s as a surf journalist. In 1976 he founded *Down the Line,* a short-lived newsprint surf magazine published out of Durban, and also became a contributor to *Surfing* magazine. (Tomson became an assistant editor at *Surfing,* and went on to publish nearly 75 columns and features in the American surf press between 1976 and 2000.) In 1978, when virtually everyone associated with professional surfing was eagerly looking forward to the sport being accepted and enriched by mainstream audiences, it was Tomson who shrewdly pointed out that spectators in "Ohio and Michigan want a blood-busting winner, one they can understand because they can *see* the bastard who gets from A to B first." Surfing, he noted, would never satisfy this kind of audience. Tomson emigrated to America in 1978, moving to Laguna Beach, California, where he founded Gotcha, the instantly popular surfwear company known for its hip designs and aggressive ad campaigns. Tomson had years earlier received a B.A. in business from the University of Durban, and by 1987 Gotcha's $65 million in surfwear sales was bested only by Ocean Pacific and Hobie; Quiksilver was a distant fourth, at $30 million.

Tomson appeared in nearly a dozen surf movies, including *Free Ride* (1977), *Tubular Swells* (1977), and *Fantasea* (1978); as CEO of Gotcha, he also produced *Waterborn* (1987) and *Surfers: The Movie* (1990). From 1990 to 1999, Tomson served as president of the Surf Industry Manufacturers Association. Tomson has been married once and has one child. *See also* backside attack, Gotcha.

Tomson, Shaun   Innovative and aristocratic regularfoot surfer from Durban, South Africa; 1977 world champion, and inventor of the climb-and-drop method of tuberiding; often described as "the ultimate pro." Tomson was born (1955) and raised in Durban, the son of Ernie Tomson, a wealthy property owner and surf contest organizer. Shaun Tomson began surfing at age 10, under his father's tutelage;

Shaun Tomson

two years later he won the boys' division of the South African National Championships, and at age 14 he was regarded as a longshot contender for the 1970 World Championships. Tomson utterly dominated the South African competition scene, and in 1973 won the first of six consecutive titles in the Durban-held Gunston 500, the biggest international pro event outside of America and Australia. (Tomson served his mandatory 18 months in the South African National Army in 1973 and 1974, but did so near his home and was allowed to surf often.) In early 1975, the dashingly handsome Durbanite won the Hang Ten Pro Championships in Hawaii, and over the course of the year earned just over $10,000 in prize money from various contests, more by far than any other pro that season.

Tomson made his biggest mark on surfing the following winter on the North Shore of Oahu. His win in the 1975 Pipeline Masters was in itself dramatic, but really just a signifier for the way he had, in just a few weeks, changed the look and the parameters of high-performance surfing. Tomson rode in a wide stance, and instead of making weight shifts over his board by moving his feet—the conventional method—he simply leaned backward or forward. He meanwhile kept his leading arm extended, letting it rise and drop as necessary while using it as a sight line to lead him out of tight spots. These basic but im-

portant changes in stance gave Tomson an unprecedented degree of balance and stability, which in turn encouraged him to draw exciting new up-and-down lines across the wave, even while behind the curl. Tomson (6′1″, 180 pounds) introduced his weaving tube style in late 1975 at Backdoor and Off the Wall in Hawaii, where he rode deeper than anybody, and with greater frequency and control, often exiting the tube with a joyous smile. He was just as groundbreaking with his backside approach at Pipeline, standing nearly straight up in the tube when circumstances allowed, or dropping to a crouch and bringing his right shoulder forward in a prototype of what would later be called the "pigdog" stance. Tomson's thrilling new moves were captured beautifully in the era-defining surf movie *Free Ride*. The following generation of surfers, especially Dane Kealoha and Tom Carroll, patterned their tuberiding on that of Tomson's, and present-day techniques are virtually all based on lines Tomson worked out in the mid-'70s. "I remember certain tubes," he later told *Tracks* magazine, "where I was so in control of my mind and body, that it actually felt as if I were controlling the wave itself."

Tomson was taking economics classes at the University of Durban in 1976 when the world pro circuit was formed; competing part-time, he finished the year rated sixth. Dedicating himself to the circuit in 1977, he moved into the ratings lead halfway through the season and held on to win the title. Tomson was a new kind of champion: articulate and neatly groomed (he worked briefly as a Calvin Klein model), with a distinctly patrician air. "In an era filled with rough-hewn Australians and street-wise Hawaiians," surf journalist Phil Jarratt later wrote, "Tomson strode in like the Great Gatsby." Surf magazine profiles noted that he had never camped out on a surf trip or fixed his own surfboard dings.

Tomson's performances suffered in the late '70s and early '80s when he switched to the twin-fin surfboard design, but he nonetheless remained near the top of the ratings, finishing fourth in 1978, sixth in 1979, third in 1980, fourth in 1982, and sixth in 1983. He meanwhile moved from Durban to Santa Barbara, California. In 1984, two years after switching to a tri-fin, the 29-year-old Tomson won three world tour events and finished runner-up in the ratings to Australian Tom Carroll; two years later he dropped out of the top 10 for the first time, and after the 1989 season—his 14th—he retired from competitive surfing. Tomson had 12 career world tour wins, including a victory in the 1986 Spur Steak Ranch Surfabout in South Africa, where the 31-year-old veteran became the first over-30 male surfer to win a world pro tour event.

Tomson founded Instinct surfwear and Shaun Tomson Surfboards in the late '70s (cousin Michael Tomson had meanwhile formed Gotcha surfwear), and in 1985 he opened Surfbeat surf shop in Santa Monica, California. Both businesses had failed by the time Tomson moved back to Durban in 1990 with his wife and newborn son; he returned to college and received a B.A. in business finance. In 1995, the Tomson family returned to California, where he worked in marketing and sales for Patagonia clothing, then O'Neill wetsuits. He founded Solitude surfwear, headquartered in Santa Barbara, in 1998.

Tomson was featured in more than 40 surf movies and videos, including *Tracks* (1970), *Playgrounds in Paradise* (1976), *Fantasea* (1978), *We Got Surf* (1981), *Wave Warriors* (1985), and *Surfers: The Movie* (1990). In 1985, he appeared on the *Merv Griffin Show* and *Good Morning America*. Tomson was profiled in *20th Century Surfers* (1998), an Outdoor Life Network documentary series, and received good notices later that year for his role as a surf journalist in TriStar's big-wave movie *In God's Hands*. He wrote more than a dozen surf magazine articles between 1979 and 1991, including 1980's "Everything You Always Wanted to Know about Pro Surfing But Didn't Know Who the Hell to Ask," a four-part series published by *Surfing* magazine; he also wrote the foreword for *Pure Stoke* (1982) and *Above the Roar: 50 Surfer Interviews* (1997). Tomson won the *Surfer* Magazine Readers Poll Award in 1978. He was inducted into the South African Sports Hall of Fame in 1978, the Jewish Sports Hall of Fame in 1995, and the Huntington Beach Surfing Walk of Fame in 1997. *Australia's Surfing Life* magazine named Tomson as the world's all-time best tuberider in 1991. He served as vice president of the Association of Surfing Professionals from 1990 to 1994; in 2002 he was appointed as chairman of the National Advisory Board for the Surfrider Foundation environmental group. *See also* backside attack, Durban, duck dive, Free Ride, Gunston 500, tuberiding.

Tonga   Kingdom in the tropical South Pacific Ocean, made up of roughly 150 volcanic islands and coral atolls, located 3,200 miles east of Australia. Tonga's surf is generally hollow, powerful, and well-formed, but rarely over six foot, and breaks over shallow coral-lined barrier reefs. May to September is usually the best time for surf, but waves can arrive during the rest of the year. Dozens of breaks have been charted here, and dozens more are as yet unmapped or kept secret. Ha'atafu Beach, a multifaceted break located on the west shore of Tongatapu, is the most popular surfing area. The weather is tropical, but drier and slightly cooler than Hawaii. Water temperatures range from 70 to 80 degrees. Most breaks in Tonga require a high tide, as the reefs are otherwise too shallow.

Bodysurfing was described in the journal of a British missionary visiting Tonga in 1796: "It is astonishing to see with what dexterity they will steer themselves on the wave, one hand being stretched out, as the prow, and the other guiding them like a rudder behind. Several hours are often spent at one time in this sport, in which the women are as skillful as the men. I never attempted this diversion myself, as the trial might have been fatal." Tonga, like Hawaii, was one of surfing's ancestral homes. But unlike Hawaii, the sport was slow to recover from its near extinction in the 19th century, even after Tongan King Taufa'ahau Tupou IV took to the water in the 1960s on a board given to him by Hawaiian surfing and swimming legend Duke Kahanamoku. Australian surfer Steve Burling founded a small surf camp in Tonga in 1979, but the island wasn't brought to the attention of the surf world at large until it was featured in the 1986 surf movie *Ticket to Ride*. Burling started the Tonga Surf Riders Association in 1994, with membership consisting mostly of native-born surfers, and in 1997 the TSRA entered a team in the Rip Curl Oceania Surfing Cup. In 2000, Tonga hosted (and won) its first international competition, the Tri-Nations Surf Challenge, a contest between Samoa, Fiji, and Tonga. There were about 75 resident surfers in Tonga in 2003.

toothpick   *See* hollow surfboard.

Torquay   Small, rugged, country-flavored holiday town known as "Surf City Australia," located 65 miles southwest of Melbourne on the west coast of Victoria. Torquay's rocky two-mile coastline is lined with a dozen surf breaks, including the celebrated Bells Beach and the long, beautifully tapered waves of Winkipop; the town itself is home to more than a dozen national or international surf-related businesses, including the domestic headquarters for Rip Curl and Quiksilver. "Torquay's evolution runs in such striking parallel with the development of surfing itself," surf journalist Tim Baker wrote in 1991, "that it almost seems like a fictitious town invented purely as a model for the sport's history." Torquay receives surf all year, and gets up to 15 feet between April and November. Winters here are often wet, windy, and cool; summers produce a fairly stable climate; spring and fall are marked by frequent and sometimes dramatic changes in weather. Torquay was first surfed in the mid-'40s; in 1946 it became home to Victoria's first surf lifesaving club; in 1958 the surfers'-only Bell's Boardriders Club was formed. The annual Bells Beach Easter Surf Contest was founded in 1962, and in 1973 Rip Curl put up the money to make Bells the nation's first pro surfing event; the Rip Curl Pro remains one of the most prestigious contests on the world circuit. Bells was also the site of the 1970 World Surfing Championships. Surfworld, the sport's biggest museum, opened in Torquay in 1994 and houses the Australian Surfing Hall of Fame.

Rip Curl Wetsuits was founded in Torquay in 1967, followed five years later by Quiksilver. Other name-brand companies who maintain corporate satellite offices in Torquay include Oakley, Reef, Piping Hot, and Dragon Optical. As of 2002, the Torquay surf industry employed more than 650 people (in a town of 10,000) and pumped more than $18 million into the local economy. International surf world figures from Torquay include shortboard revolution icon Wayne Lynch, five-time national champion Gail Couper, big-wave rider Tony Ray, surf explorer Peter Troy, Rip Curl founder Doug "Claw" Warbrick, and Quiksilver founder Alan Green. *See also* Bells Beach, Rip Curl, Rip Curl Pro, Quiksilver, Victoria.

Tostee, Pierre   Surf photographer and journalist from Durban, South Africa. Tostee was born (1966) and raised in Durban, began surfing at age 13, and competed on the world pro tour from 1986 to 1989. In Newcastle, Australia, in 1987, Tostee earned a distinction of sorts as the only surfer ever to be struck by lightning during a world pro tour competition. He recovered and continued riding the following day, and *Surfing* magazine noted the occurrence with a short article headlined "Toasty Tostee." After working through the '90s as a freelance surf journalist and photographer, Tostee was hired in 1999 as staff photographer for the Association of Surfing Professionals.

tow-in surfing   Motorized form of big-wave riding popularized in the early 1990s, in which the surfer, towed from behind a personal watercraft (PWC), is given a water-ski-style launch into the wave; tow-in

Tow-in surfing at Jaws, Maui

is widely regarded as the most significant breakthrough in big-wave surfing history. For decades paddle-in surfers were unable to overcome the rapid trough-to-crest flow of water on waves bigger than 25 or 30 feet; tow-in surfers, by getting a running start at the takeoff, broke the 30-foot barrier easily and continued riding ever-larger waves—up to 50 feet by 2001. "Tow-in surfing," surf journalist Sam George said, "has brought about the only real quantum leap in surfing's history."

The idea for power-assisted surfing dates back to at least 1963. "The surfer might be towed into the wave by a boat much like a water-skier," California's Mike Doyle wrote in *Surf Guide* magazine, wondering how a 35-foot wave might be mastered. Hawaii's Jim Neece tried using a speedboat-powered "water-ski takeoff" on smaller waves in 1974, with the idea of riding huge surf at Keana Point—a project he soon dropped. In 1987, California's Herbie Fletcher used his PWC to tow a group of surfers, including pro tour champions Martin Potter and Tom Carroll, in to 10-foot waves at Pipeline; in the fall of 1991, East Coast surfer Scott Bouchard was towed in to a half-dozen 12-footers at a Florida break called RC's.

But the invention of tow-in surfing is rightfully credited to Hawaiians Buzzy Kerbox, Laird Hamilton, and Darrick Doerner, who began by using Kerbox's inflatable Zodiac boat in late 1992 to tow each other in to 15-foot waves at Backyards, near Sunset Beach, on the North Shore of Oahu. The idea was simply to get a running start at the wave; the tow-rope was dropped as soon as the swell was caught, and the rider was then on his own. Hamilton and Kerbox moved to Maui a few months later, where they replaced the Zodiac with a PWC, and turned a nearby big-wave break called Jaws into their tow-in laboratory. The first surf magazine articles on tow-in surfing were published in 1993; *Endless Summer II,* released the following year, brought the spectacular new form of surfing to the big screen. With paddle speed no longer an issue (paddle-in big-wave "guns" are designed mainly to catch waves, and are about 10 feet long and 20 inches wide), the new tow-in boards were designed for riding only, and would soon be pared down to about 6′6″ by 15″. Footstraps were added to increase leverage and balance. Strapped into their new short boards, the tow-in surfers were able to do swooping turns and cutbacks, whereas paddle-in surfers—had they been able to catch the wave in the first place—could do little more than angle their oversize guns for deep water. PWCs also whisked the rider back to the lineup following each ride, kept him from getting caught inside while waiting for the next wave, and allowed him the chance to ride up to a dozen or more waves per hour. Paddle-in surfers often ride just one or two waves per session.

By 1994, Hamilton was leading a small group of Jaws-based surfers (included Dave Kalama and Pete Cabrinha) into waves measuring more than 35 feet, and riding in a high-performance style that would have been unimaginable just five years earlier. Critics said that tow-in was a blasphemy against the very nature of surfing—that drawing a bead on an incoming wave and paddling into a vertical drop was in fact the essence of big-wave riding, and that the sport in general derived its beauty in large part from its lack of mechanization. Most people, however, realized that the sport had in fact split in two. The vast majority of surfers would continue to paddle-surf. A small number of devotees—by 2003, the total number of hardcore tow-in surfers was thought to be fewer than 100—would use PWCs. The 155-horsepower Yamaha WaveRunner, with a top speed of 65 miles per hour, had become the tow-in surfer's vehicle of choice by the early '00s; tow-in accouterments include the flotation vest (to help the rider get to the surface after a wipeout), and a polyethylene foam rescue sled (at-

tached to the back of the PWC and used as a life raft during postwipeout drive-by pickups). Thirty feet of soft-braid water-ski line separates the rider from the PWC. Most surfers like to be towed in to the wave on a straight line; some prefer to run at the incoming swell and get "whipped" into position. Thanks to the added control of having a running start, tow-in surfers wipe out far less often than paddle-in big-wave surfers; mishaps, however, given the additional wave height, are especially violent. As of early 2003, there had been no tow-in surfing fatalities. Hawaii's Ken Bradshaw towing at Outside Log Cabins on the North Shore in 1998 became the first surfer to ride a 60-foot wave (as measured from trough to crest; using the prevalent "Hawaiian scale," the wave was said to be 40 foot); three years later, Mike Parsons of California matched Bradshaw's wave at a midocean break called Cortes Bank, off San Diego. Brazil's Carlos Burle hit the same mark later in 2001 at Maverick's.

Tow-in surfing was regularly practiced at Maverick's, California's premier big-wave break, by 1999; in the early '00s, surfers in Western Australia and South Africa were motoring into the biggest waves in their respective countries. Tow-in surfing had captured the attention of mainstream media outlets like nothing else in surfing, turning up in the *New York Times, National Geographic, Outside,* and *Vanity Fair,* plus Hollywood movies, IMAX movies, TV commercials, and network news shows. The long-simmering issue concerning the legality of tow-in surfing came to the surface in 2001, as environmentalists in California (supported by a small number of surfers, most notably San Francisco big-wave rider Mark Renneker) sought to have the noisy and polluting PWCs banned from the Monterey Bay National Marine Sanctuary, which covers 275 miles of central California coastline, including Maverick's. The issue was unresolved as of early 2003.

The Tow-In World Cup, held at Jaws in early 2002, was the first tow-in competition; winners Garrett McNamara of Hawaii and Brazil's Rodrigo Resende split the $70,000 first-place prize. The 2001 Swell XXL and the 2002 Nissan Xterra XXL Big Surf Awards, contests judged on photographs of surfers riding the year's biggest waves, were both won by tow-in surfers (Mike Parsons and Carlos Burle, respectively). A small number of tow-in-only surf videos had been made by early 2003, including *Condition Black* (1998), *Year of the Drag-In* (2000) and *Strapped: The Origins of Tow-In Surfing* (2002). In 1996, Sarah

Gerhardt of California became the first woman tow-in surfer, riding 15-footers on the North Shore of Oahu. World pro champion Layne Beachley, by 2002, was towing in to 25-footers. *See also* Biggest Wednesday, big-wave surfing, Darrick Doerner, Laird Hamilton, Jaws, Buzzy Kerbox, Maverick's, Outside Log Cabins, personal watercraft.

Townend, Peter   Smooth, deliberate, enterprising surfer from Coolangatta, Queensland, Australia; world champion in 1976, publisher of the *Surfing* magazine group since 2000, with adjunct work in coaching, board-building, marketing, and surf fashion. Townend was born (1953) and raised in Coolangatta, the son of a hotel manager, and began surfing in 1967. He had a remarkable run in the Australian National Titles, placing second in the juniors division in 1971, then moving up to the men's division to finish second in 1972, 1973, 1974, and 1976. He also placed third in the 1972 World Championships.

By the mid-'70s, two dozen surfers were traveling from Australia to Hawaii to South Africa, on what was later described as the "gypsy circuit," to compete in a loosely arrayed set of professional contests. In 1975, Townend helped found the Australian Professional Surfing Association, which formed a small domestic pro tour; in 1976 he was one of the leading voices for the creation of an standardized international pro circuit. Hawaiian organizers Fred Hemmings and Randy Rarick launched the International Surfing Professionals tour in October of that year, retroactively scoring nine events from earlier in the season, then running five events in Hawaii to come up with a 1976 world pro champion—Peter Townend. The 23-year-old Queenslander didn't win a contest in 1976, but was consistent throughout, making the finals in nearly half the events. His total prize money for the year was about $7,500; he worked between contests as a shaper for Gordon & Smith Surfboards in Australia.

Not a great natural talent, the diminutive Townend (5'7" 140 pounds) rode with consummate precision and intelligence, and his form was often compared to that of 1964 world champion Midget Farrelly, another exacting Australian. Townend had moments of flair, developing the full-body "soul arch" bottom turn, and riding aerodynamically inside the tube in big Hawaiian surf. He also paid careful attention to his surf world image and persona, as he filled his wardrobe with designer clothes, grew a pointy goatee, frequently danced on tabletops at

Peter Townend

postcontest banquets, and arrogantly declared that he favored hot pink surfboards and surf trunks because he didn't want to "look like the average kook on the beach." Townend and fellow Australian Ian Cairns cofounded the Bronzed Aussies promotional group in 1976, ostensibly to bring more glamour, wealth, and attention to the sport. But the two surfers were ridiculed after turning up at contest sites in matching Bronzed Aussie velour jumpsuits, and by the end of the decade the group was largely ignored.

Townend competed part-time in 1977, spending much of the year stunt-surfing for actor William Katt during the filming of *Big Wednesday,* and his world rating dropped to 14th. He rededicated himself to the world tour, finishing fifth in 1978 and 1979, then went into a long semiretirement. Townend's world tour winless streak was finally snapped in 1979, when he won the Hang Ten event in Durban, South Africa—his only major pro victory. Meanwhile, he'd become one of surfing's most prolific writers; in the '70s and early '80s he submitted dozens of feature articles to the American and Australian surf press; from 1975 to 1981 he wrote the "Surfing Today" column for the *Sydney Daily Mirror;* and from 1979 1980 wrote "Notes from the Pro Tour" for *Surfing* magazine.

Townend moved to California's Huntington Beach in 1979, and spent four years as the executive director and National Team coach for the National Scholastic Surfing Association, training Tom Curren, Mike Parsons, Brad Gerlach, and other young world tour-bound American surfers. In 1984 Townend began working for the *Surfing* magazine ad department; two years later he was named advertising director, and in 1989 he became associate publisher. Townend left *Surfing* in 1993 to work as the marketing director for Rusty surfwear, and in 1999 he was named as Rusty's global brand manager. (Townend himself had launched three short-lived beachwear lines: Soul-Arch Clothing, PT Designs, and Bronzed Aussies Sportswear.) He returned to print media in 2000 as the publisher of the Surfing Group of magazines, including *Surfing, Surfing Girl, Surfing Guide,* and *Bodyboarding.* Since 1987 he's moonlighted as a cable television broadcaster, covering surfing events for Prime Network and ESPN.

Townend appeared in more than two dozen surf movies, including *A Sea For Yourself* (1973), *Fluid Drive* (1974), *Super Session* (1975), *Free Ride* (1977), and *Fantasea* (1978), and was also featured in *Liquid Stage: The Lure of Surfing* (1995), a PBS documentary. He was inducted into the Huntington Beach Surfing Walk of Fame in 1998, the Gold Coast Sporting Hall of Fame in 1999, and the Australian Surfing Hall of Fame in 2001. Townend served as president of the Surf Industry Manufacturers Association in 1998 and 1999. He has been married once, and has three children. *See also* Australian Professional Surfing Association, Bronzed Aussies, Ian Cairns, the Gold Coast, International Professional Surfers, layback, National Scholastic Surfing Association, soul arch, Surfing America, Surfing magazine.

track, tracking   When a surfboard can't be maneuvered or adjusted in any way from the path its on, the result of either rider error or faulty board design, it is said to be "tracking." Tracking almost always happens at higher speeds, and is often the result of too much air and water turbulence around the board's fins, which renders the board unsteerable; it can also be caused by the surfer riding too far forward on the board. Tracking is more likely to occur on low-rockered boards (boards with less lift in the nose and tail sections), flat- or concave-bottom boards, or on smaller boards ridden in larger surf. "Track" is also used to describe the wake left by a surfboard as it moves across a wave.

Tracks magazine   Monthly surf magazine published out of Sydney, Australia; the national surf media flagship in the 1970s and early '80s. *Tracks* was founded in 1970 by editor David Elfick, surf journalist John Witzig, and surf moviemaker Alby Falzon as a counterculture alternative to magazines like *Surfer* and *Surfing World.* With its debut issue, *Tracks* made a clear break from the standard surf magazine format, publishing on black-and-white newsprint and using an oversize *Rolling Stone*–type format; the cover shot, instead of a high-voltage surf image, was of a smoke-belching beachfront refinery. Surfing was *Tracks'* primary focus, but the text-heavy issues in the early '70s were full of environmental features, anti-Vietnam articles, organic recipes, pull quotes from the Maharishi Mahesh Yogi, and editorials in defense of marijuana use and Aboriginal rights. Helping to define what would later be known as Australia's "country soul" period, *Tracks* published lifestyle photos of flowers, farmhouses, animals, and playing children, and for the most part denounced surfing competition. Wave-riding was viewed as something well beyond sport and recreation. "Just by going surfing," 1966 world champion and *Tracks* correspondent Nat Young wrote, not long after leaving Sydney for the bucolic fields of North Coast New South Wales, "we're supporting the revolution."

Tracks shifted tone in 1974 with the hiring of arch wit Phil Jarratt, one of surfing's finest and funniest writers. *Tracks* paid close attention to the rise of professional surfing, and jettisoned much of its nonsurfing editorial platform. Editor Jarratt wrote a kneeboard column titled "Cripple's Corner," and Queensland's soon-to-be world champion Wayne Bartholomew surfed in the nude for a 1976 *Tracks* cover. A new and hugely popular *Tracks* feature was Captain Good-vibes, a boorish surf-pig superhero. *Tracks'* circulation by mid-decade was 40,000, larger by far than any previous Australian surf publication. The magazine's reputation held steady under the editorial stewardship of Paul Holmes, followed by Nick Carroll (both of whom went on to edit American surf magazines). Articles continued in the Jarratt style: smart, funny, and more often than not snide. As Carroll later put it, *Tracks* "truly defined the Australian surf mag."

By the late '80s, *Tracks* was being challenged by 1985-founded *Australia's Surfing Life* and the 1987-founded *Waves,* both eager to probe the raunchier limits of sophomoric surf-related humor. The new material caught on; by the time *Tracks* editor Tim Baker left in 1991 to work for *Australia's Surfing Life,* the older magazine was a deflated, if not defeated, power. Publishing giant Emap bought *Tracks'* parent company in 1997, at which point the 28-year-old surf magazine was recast in standard magazine format; by 2002, circulation was back up to 40,000. *See also* David Elfick, Alby Falzon, surf magazines, John Witzig.

traction pad   Thin, porous, precut peel-and-stick rubber pad used on the deck of a surfboard for traction, as an alternative to surf wax; usually applied to just the board's tail area, below the rider's back foot. Commercially made nonwax alternatives date back to the mid-'60s. Slipcheck was introduced in 1966 by the Morey-Pope company in Ventura, California; a gritty, epoxy-based aerosol paint—available, as product marketers put it, in eight "mind-bending" colors—Slipcheck proved to be abrasive on skin and trunks. Surefoot, a messy mix-it-yourself product similar to Slipcheck but without the aerosol can, came and went in the late '60s. Suction-cup-soled booties (wetsuit socks) were an early '70s board-traction failure, as were Claws, a two-piece Velcro system made up of adhesive footstraps and a tail pad.

In late 1975, Orange County surfer Jim Van Vleck, while working for a urethane coating company, developed a spray-applied polyurethane deck coating that he began marketing in 1976 as Astrodeck. It weighed about six ounces more than a coat of wax, covered the surfboard's entire deck, was available in a variety of colors and textures, and cost $25. Van Vleck sold the product to Orange County surfer and surf entrepreneur Herbie Fletcher, who quickly developed a peel-and-stick version of Astrodeck; in 1981 Fletcher introduced a packaged set of 12 small geometric shapes—diamonds, squares, rectangles, and circles, each about three or four inches long—allowing surfers to create their own custom traction design. Larger Astrodeck tail and mid-deck patches (usually two or three pieces per set) were brought out in the mid-'80s, along with surfer-endorsed models, such as the Hans Hedemann Rash Relief Pad, the Archie Accelerator, and the Pottz Pro Model. Astrodeck was later joined by Trac-Top, Gorilla Grip, X-Trak, On a Mission, K-Grip, Hula Dek, and others. As of 2003, roughly 70 percent of shortboard surfers use a rear-foot traction pad (mid-deck pads were all but discontinued in the early '90s), along with about 15 percent of longboarders. "Deck grip," "deck pad," and "traction pad" are synonymous. *See also* surf wax.

Tracy, Terry "Tubesteak"   Avuncular regularfoot surfer from Los Angeles, California; Malibu trendsetter in the mid- and late 1950s; model for the "Kahuna" character in the book and movie versions of *Gidget.* Tracy was born (1935) and raised in southwest Los Angeles, and began surfing at age 15. In the summer of 1956, he lived in a palm-frond shack on the beach at Malibu where, as surf journalist Craig Stecyk recalled decades later, he "held court with humor and ruled with a velvet-shrouded iron hand." Tracy later claimed he was nicknamed "Tubesteak" because he worked at a Malibu restaurant called Tube's Steak and Lobster House. Surf lore holds that Mickey Dora owned the waves at Malibu, while Tracy owned the beach; the composite Malibu style, in turn, was exported up and down the California coast and across the surfing world. It was Tracy who looked at Kathy Kohner, a 16-year-old Malibu newcomer, and nicknamed her "Gidget," short for girl-midget. Teenage surfers flocked to Malibu in the late '50s—*Gidget* was published in 1957; the movie followed two years later—and Tracy, overwhelmed both by the crowds and the new Los Angeles County Lifeguard beach restrictions, dropped off the surf scene for 25 years. In 1985, encouraged by the longboard renaissance and a new interest in the sport's past, Tracy coproduced the Summer Reunion Longboard Classic, held at Malibu. Five years later he appeared in a nationally aired Nike ad, along with a few other late-middle-age surfers, all of whom were interviewed and photographed for "Endless Summer," a *Life* magazine feature. Tracy told *Life* that he hadn't surfed for years, but still lived by a surf-inspired code: "You can have a pressured Mercedes life, or you can get from A to B in an old Ford and die of natural causes." He appeared in the 1958 surf movie *Search for Surf,* and was featured in the 1987 documentary *The Legends of Malibu.* In the late '80s and '90s he wrote surfing articles for *H2O* and the *Surfer's Journal* under the pseudonym Bruce Savage. Tracy is married and has seven children. *See also* Gidget, Malibu.

TransWorld Surf magazine   Glossy teen-oriented surf magazine, founded in 1999, published 11 times a year out of Oceanside, California. *TransWorld Surf* clearly marked out its demographic turf from the beginning, with regular use of hip-hop vernacular (staff members are introduced in the debut issue under the headline "Players . . . Y'all Better Recognize") and surf slang updates ("'Instabro': Some dude who comes up and instantly thinks he's your bro"). The magazine also tweaked the standard surf tips column to acknowledge a younger, irony-raised audience: in "How to Shave with Jay Larson," readers learn that Pro Gel from Gillette is "one of the premium brands of shaving cream." But *TransWorld* has otherwise hewn closely to the traditional American surf magazine editorial formula, with lots of photo features, extended contest coverage from California and Hawaii, and surf star interviews. Circulation in 2002 was 58,000. The TransWorld Surf 2001 video game received good reviews and sold well. *TransWorld* was bought by Time Warner in 2000. *See also* surf magazines.

Treloar, David "Baddy"   Brawny Australian regularfooter from Angourie, New South Wales; pioneering shortboard surfer, and runner-up in the juniors division of the Australian National Titles in 1968 and 1969. Treloar was born (1951) and raised in Sydney, and began surfing at age seven, under the guidance of older brother and top Australian surfer Graeme Treloar. David (known since adolescence as "Baddy") invariably finished second to Victorian super-surfer Wayne Lynch in national events during the late '60s. In 1971, Treloar moved to Angourie, on the rural wave-rich North Coast of New South Wales; surf moviemaker Alby Falzon visited the North Coast that same year, filming for his new project *Morning of the Earth,* and captured Treloar's seemingly idyllic ocean-based existence—building surfboards in his vine- and plant-covered backyard, and running down a bucolic trail to ride the long, hollow, beautiful point waves at Angourie. Treloar appeared in a few other Australian-made surf movies, including *The Way We Like It* (1968), *Splashdown* (1969), and *Tracks* (1970). In 1993, he was named as the "Best Surfer at Angourie" by *Australia's Surfing Life* magazine.

Trent, Charles "Buzzy"   Hypermasculine big-wave surfer of the 1950s and '60s, from Honolulu, Hawaii. Trent was born (1929) in San Diego, California, the son of a mining engineer father and wealthy landholding mother, and raised in the Los Angeles County town of Santa Monica. He began surfing at age 12 at Malibu, and in his midteens was mentored by eccentric surfboard design genius Bob Simmons, 10 years Trent's senior. "They were a real pair," Malibu regular Dave Rochlen later recalled. "The mad scientist and his big, burly sidekick Igor." Few surfers in history have had Trent's measure for pure athletic skill. He was an all-state fullback in high school and ran the 100-yard dash in 10.1 seconds; as a freshman running

Buzzy Trent (right) with board-maker Dick Brewer

back for the University of Southern California, he broke his leg while playing against Ohio State, at which time he became a Golden Gloves boxer. According to fellow Santa Monica surfer and future big-wave rider Ricky Grigg, Trent once "hit an opponent so hard it killed him right there in the ring."

Trent moved to Honolulu in 1953, after seeing film footage of Makaha shot by Walter Hoffman of Laguna Beach. Hoffman was one of the original big-wave specialists, along with Hawaiian George Downing, but it was Trent who became the godfather and patron saint of adventure-seeking big-wave riders. He was a raw, no-frills surfer, using a functional straight-backed squat, and always seeking the highest possible line of attack. Once comfortable in Hawaii, he began searching for the biggest waves he could find, preferably 20-footers or larger at Point Surf Makaha. A 1953 Associated Press photo of Trent, Downing, and Woody Brown on a sparkling 12-foot wave at Makaha was published in newspapers across the country and encouraged a small but influential group of California surfers—including Peter Cole and Fred Van Dyke—to try their luck in the big Hawaiian surf.

Trent treated the surf media as a kind of theater in the late '50s and '60s. Asked to speak as a big-wave authority in a 1963 surf movie, the square-jawed Trent begins a lesson on riptides by calling for a blackboard, which is wheeled in by an attractive bikini-clad, lollipop-licking assistant. He also played the steely death-or-glory sportsman, as pictured in a 1965 Hobie Surfboards advertisement in which he stands bare-chested in a surfboard factory and stares coldly at a new big-wave board. Trent was the first to describe a big-wave surfboard as a "gun," and he coined one of the sport's most famous epigrams, saying that "big waves aren't measured in feet, but in increments of fear." The Buzzy Trent signature model big-wave board from Surfboards Hawaii, produced in 1964, was advertised as the ultimate surf vehicle and cost $250, more than double the price of a stock board. Trent was a judge for the 1965 Duke Kahanamoku Invitational, and in 1966 he was inducted into the *International Surfing* Magazine Hall of Fame. He appeared in about 10 surf films, including *Surf Crazy* (1959), *Surfing Hollow Days* (1962), and *Cavalcade of Surf* (1962). Trent quit surfing in 1976, age 47, because he "only enjoyed big waves," and felt he'd done all he could do in that field. He took up hang gliding, which he accurately described as "ten times more dangerous than surfing."

Trent worked as a lifeguard in the '40s and early '50s, as a fireman in the '50s and early '60, and as a construction worker until he retired in 1980. He's been married twice and has two children. Ivan Trent, Buzzy's son, rides big waves and was a Navy SEAL. *See also* big-wave surfing.

Trestles   Series of easy-to-ride, high-performance pointbreaks, located on the border between San Diego County and Orange County, about 75 miles south of Los Angeles. From north to south, the major surf spots at Trestles are: Cotton's Point, a shifty but predominantly left-breaking wave; Upper Trestles, an up-tempo right; Lower Trestles, the premier break in the area, a long and even-paced right matched with a shorter, quicker left; and Church, a tapering point divided into three separate breaks. Cotton's and Lowers break best during south or southwest swells (usually arriving between May and October); Uppers favors a west or northwest swell (November through March); the upper two takeoff areas at Church require southerly swells, while the inside break takes a northerly. All Trestles-area surf spots are lined with cobblestones. Trestles—named after a pair of wooden train trestles located at either end of the area—is sometimes described as America's most consistent wave zone, often producing small surf when the rest of the

coast is all but waveless, and bearing up well under the prevailing afternoon west winds. Rarely do any of the breaks here reach eight foot or bigger. Located at the northwest corner of the Camp Pendleton Marine Corps Base, a virtually undeveloped 125,000-acre tract of land used primarily as a military training ground, Trestles has long been an oasis in the middle of Southern California's otherwise prodigiously developed coastline. Estuaries and marshes are located just behind the beach at Church, Lowers, and Uppers; deer, bobcat, beavers, coyotes, mountain lions, and eagles live in the nearby foothills.

While a few of Orange County surfers rode Trestles as far back as the late 1930s, it was Mickey Dora and Phil Edwards, in their pre-surf-icon teenage years, who put the break on the map in the summer of 1951, walking one mile north from San Onofre to Lowers and riding by themselves day after day. By the end of the decade, Trestles was thought of as Orange County's answer to Malibu—except that while Malibu was the most public of surf breaks, the marine-patrolled Trestles was technically off-limits to all beachgoers, surfers included. Until 1971, when public access was allowed, the Trestles surfing experience was in large part a strategic and tactical engagement with the U.S. Marines. Entry and exit routes through the marshland reeds were plotted, surfboards were often hidden by their owners (and sometimes confiscated by the marines), and ammunition on occasion was fired over the heads of trespassing surfers. At one point, two platoons and a Coast Guard cutter were positioned on either side of the lineup at Lowers, just to remove two kneeboarders. "But Trestles," San Diego surfer Chuck Hasley once noted, "was the one beachhead the marines could never hold."

Trestles has been the home break to dozens of top California riders over the decades, including Bill Hamilton, Herbie and Christian Fletcher, Jericho Poppler, Dino Andino, Chris Ward, Cory and Shea Lopez, and Shane and Gavin Beschen. Overcrowding has been a problem at Trestles since the early '70s, and during a midsummer swell it's common to see as many as 100 surfers in the water at a time at Lowers.

The first annual All Military Surfing Championships, held at Church, took place in 1972; the first civilian event at Trestles was the $6,000 Sutherland Pro, held in 1977 and won by Hawaiian Michael Ho. Dozens of professional and amateur contests have been held at Trestles since the late 1980s. In 1990, world-champion-to-be Kelly Slater made his pro debut by winning the $100,000 Body Glove Surf Bout, held in perfect five-foot surf at Lowers. The world pro tour added a Trestles event to its schedule in 2001, with the Billabong Pro, held at Lowers, won by Andy Irons and Pauline Menczer. The National Scholastic Surfing Association has run its prestigious National Championships at Trestles since 1992.

Trestles has been featured in more than 50 surf movies and videos over the decades, including *Slippery When Wet* (1958), *Surfing Hollow Days* (1962), *Fluid Drive* (1974), *Ocean Fever* (1983), *Amazing Surf Stories* (1986), *Surfers: The Movie* (1990), *Momentum* (1992), *Bliss* (1996), and *Surf 365* (2000). Orange County surf band the Rhythm Rockers had a local hit in 1963 with the misspelled "Breakfast at Tressels."

tri-fin   Surfboard design used on virtually all shortboards and big-wave boards, and about half of all longboards; often described as the second most significant board-design advance, following the shortboard revolution. The tri-fin has three roughly equal-sized fins arranged in a triangular pattern: two matching side fins placed symmetrically just in from the rails, about 11 inches from the tail, and a rearward "trailing" fin about three inches from the tail. Australian surfer/board-maker Simon Anderson introduced his tri-fin Thruster model in 1981, and within two years the design gained near-universal acceptance among shortboard users, all but eliminating both the single- and twin-fin designs that preceded it.

Anderson, however, wasn't the first to experiment with the tri-fin concept. In 1970, Hawaiian master shaper Dick Brewer, along with surfer/shaper Reno Abellira, began making boards with a large single-fin set ahead of a pair of small half-moon trailing "finlets." (The following year saw the introduction of a do-it-yourself fin kit, featuring plastic peel-and-stick side fins.) In 1972, Malcolm and Duncan Campbell of Oxnard, California, unveiled their Bonzer design, a concave-bottomed board featuring a regular-sized single-fin set just behind a pair of long, low-profile keel fins. While Brewer's tri-fin and the Bonzer both received good reviews in the surf press, neither design caught on, and single-fin boards were used almost exclusively in the mid-'70s. In 1977, Australian pro surfer Mark Richards introduced his version of the twin-fin—a wide-backed board with a matching pair of six-inch-tall fins—which planed better and was easier turning than the single-fin. Richards used the twin-fin to win four consecutive world champi-

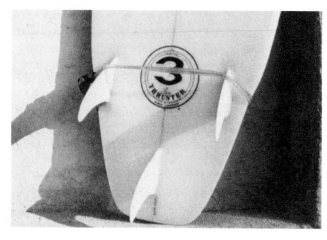

Simon Anderson's tri-fin Thruster, 1981

onships from 1979 to 1982, but many surfers found the boards skittish and hard to control in small surf and all but unridable in waves over six feet. Top surfers often used twin-fins in smaller surf, then switched to the stable riding single-fin when the waves got bigger.

Simon Anderson, world-ranked #3 in 1977 and frustrated with both the twin-fin and single-fin boards, began working on a tri-fin design in late 1980 after seeing Frank Williams—a surfer from Anderson's home break at Narrabeen in Sydney—riding a twin-fin board augmented with a half-moon fin located near the tail. "I was desperate," Anderson later said, noting that he was having trouble keeping up with the surfers who had adapted successfully to the twin-fins. The most noticeable feature of the prototype Thruster was that the three fins were roughly the same size, about four-and-a-half inches tall. The front fins angled in slightly toward the nose of the board, and were flat-foiled on the interior face and gently rounded on the exterior. Both sides of the rear fin, as with single-fins, were rounded. The Thruster also incorporated the reduced-forward-area "no-nose" design invented the year before by Australia's Geoff McCoy. Like the twin-fin, Anderson's tri-fin featured a wide tail, which gave the board improved planing speed compared to the single-fin. But whereas the twin-fin tended to lose traction and spin out, the Thruster, with its anchoring rear-set fin, remained firmly slotted on the wave. Anderson caused a stir in April 1981, when he rode his newly unveiled Thruster to victory in the Bells Beach world tour contest, held in 15-foot surf; he then won the Surfabout event in Sydney, and at the end of the year, again using a

Thruster, won the Pipeline Masters in Hawaii. By early 1983, virtually all small-wave board were tri-fins; big-wave boards and longboards were beginning to make the transition as well. Anderson's design has been continuously modified over the years—the modern version is narrower, thinner, and longer; the fins are now often removable instead of fixed to the board—but remains fundamentally true to the original. *See also* bonzer, Simon Anderson, fin, four-fin, single-fin, surfboard, Thruster, twin-fin.

tri-plane hull Multileveled surfboard bottom design. An early version of the tri-plane hull was introduced in 1968 by Hobie Surfboards as a variation on the vee-bottom concept; it was reintroduced nine years later by Los Angeles board-makers Jeff Ho and Mickey Fremont, then popularized in the late '70s and early '80s by Santa Barbara design-guru-in-the-making Al Merrick. As built by Ho and Fremont, the tri-plane featured a long, largely flat planing surface running down the center of the board, flanked on both sides by angled flat surfaces about three inches wide that ran out to the board's rails. This version was similar to the more sharply angled chine rail design introduced two years earlier. The tri-plane theory was that the board rode on the center plane while in a neutral (or "trimming") position, then, during a turn, transferred onto a side plane with less loss of speed compared to a conventional board. As built by Merrick, the center plane was reconfigured into side-by-side longitudinal concaves. Fifteen-year-old Tom Curren was one of the first to ride Merrick's tri-plane hull boards; the double-concave would later become one of the most popular shortboard bottom designs. *See also* concave, reverse vee.

trim Strictly defined as a basic angled path across the wave face; for beginning surfers who've learned to catch an unbroken wave, the next step is to get into trim. For the connoisseur, the word "trim" describes a fast, smooth, almost Zen-like progression, ideally just ahead of the curl, with the surfer in near-motionless standing repose. Trim, in this sense, denotes quiet mastery. Longboard surfers generally hold trim in higher esteem than shortboarders, and while young surfers often trim out of necessity, it has in fact lost nearly all of its cachet for those under 30. California surfer Mike Hynson trims along beautifully while riding Cape St. Francis, South Africa, in the 1966 classic surf movie *The Endless Summer*.

Triple Crown of Surfing Celebrated pro contest miniseries, founded in 1983, composed of three events held during the midwinter Association of Surfing Professionals (ASP) competition season on the North Shore of Oahu. Some Triple Crown events are part of the World Championship Tour circuit; some are on the second-tier World Qualifying Series circuit. The Triple Crown is the second most honored title in professional surfing, after the world championship. Because the world tour usually finishes in Hawaii, it's often the case that the winners for both the Triple Crown and the world championship are decided on the same day; occasionally the same surfer will take both titles.

The Triple Crown grew out of a pro tour schism in 1983, when ASP officials, unable to work out procedural differences with North Shore contest promoter Fred Hemmings, removed the North Shore events from the world tour schedule. Instead of canceling his contests, Hemmings consolidated the three events—the Pipeline Masters, the Duke Kahanamoku Classic, and the World Cup—into the Triple Crown, with the surfer tallying the most combined points declared as the series winner. The ASP warned that surfers who entered the 1983 Triple Crown contests would be stripped of their world tour ratings, and virtually all international pros remained on the sidelines. Some of the top Hawaiians, including Michael Ho and Dane Kealoha, ignored the ASP and entered the three events. In what would prove to be the most remarkable result in Triple Crown history, Kealoha won both the Duke and the Masters (although did poorly in the World Cup), but lost the Triple Crown title to Ho, who won the World Cup and placed well in the Duke and the Masters.

The Pipeline Masters and the World Cup have always formed two-thirds of the Triple Crown. The third event has been sponsored by a number of companies, including Billabong, Ocean Pacific, Wyland Galleries, and G-Shock. Pipeline, Sunset Beach, and Haleiwa usually make up the three Triple Crown surf sites. Umbrella sponsors for the Triple Crown include Red Dog, G-Shock, and Vans, among others. A Triple Crown women's division was added in 1997, using separate women's-only pro contests. Hawaiian contest organizer Randy Rarick has been head of the Triple Crown since its inception. Winners of the Triple Crown of Surfing are as follows:

    1983:   Michael Ho
    1984:   Derek Ho

1985:   Michael Ho
1986:   Derek Ho
1987:   Gary Elkerton
1988:   Derek Ho
1989:   Gary Elkerton
1990:   Derek Ho
1991:   Tom Carroll
1992:   Sunny Garcia
1993:   Sunny Garcia
1994:   Sunny Garcia
1995:   Kelly Slater
1996:   Kaipo Jaquias
1997:   Mike Rommelse, Layne Beachley
1998:   Kelly Slater, Layne Beachley
1999:   Sunny Garcia, Trudy Todd
2000:   Sunny Garcia, Heather Clark
2001:   Myles Padaca, (no women's division)
2002:   Andy Irons, Neridah Falconer

trough   As an oceanographic term, "trough" is used to describe either the low point between two waves or a deep-water trench in the ocean floor. As a surfing expression, it generally refers to the flat water immediately in front of the wave face. Bottom turns are performed in the trough.

Troy, Peter   Globe-trotting Australian surfer from Torquay, Victoria; cofounder in 1962 of the Bells Beach surf contest. Troy was born (1940) and raised in Torquay, and began surfing at age 10 on a 16-foot hollow paddleboard. He and four other members of the lifeguard-based Torquay Surf Club, using inflatable rubber rafts, became the first to ride the soon-to-be famous waves of Bells Beach in 1952. Four years later, at an international lifeguard competition held in conjunction with the 1956 Melbourne-held Olympic Games, Troy and the rest of the local surfers watched American surfer/lifeguards Greg Noll and Tommy Zahn, among others, ride their Malibu chips at Torquay Beach in ways that instantly made Australia's paddleboard "toothpicks" obsolete. Troy cofounded the Bells Beach Boardriders Club in 1958; in 1962 Troy and clubmate Vic Tantau planned and hosted the inaugural Bells Beach surfing contest, which evolved in 1973 into the Rip Curl Pro—Australia's first and longest-running professional surf contest.

Troy attended Geelong College, then worked as an accountant and screened American-made surf movies in Melbourne; in mid-1963 he set off on a

Peter Troy

four-year surfing sojourn that took him to Great Britain (where he introduced the sport to the English Channel Islands), Italy, Spain, Morocco, France (where he placed first in the debut European Surfing Championships), the Canary Islands, the Virgin Islands, mainland America, and Hawaii. Moving on to South America, he made the finals of the 1964 Peru International; later that year, after arriving in Brazil by train, Troy took a walk down the beach at Copacabana and spotted a brand-new surfboard lying on the sand next to what turned out to be the son of the French ambassador. Troy borrowed the board and gave an impromptu surfing demonstration that made national headlines, and earned him an introduction to the Brazilian president. Good luck followed the lanky blond-haired, blue-eyed Australian as he moved on to Argentina, where he was feted by the rich and beautiful, and flown from town to town in a government-provided DC3 plane. After returning to Peru to compete for the Australian team in the 1965 World Surfing Championships, Troy crossed the Panama Canal on a timber freighter, traversed the Atlantic and the Greenland Sea, and visited the Spitsbergen Islands, 600 miles from the North Pole. Dropping down through Europe into Africa, he passed through the Middle East (gaining a black "ejection" passport stamp in Syria on drug-smuggling charges), joined an anthropological expedition in Angola, walked 200 miles across the Kalahari Desert, and landed in South Africa in mid-1966, where he rode the newly discovered waves at Jeffreys Bay. Taking an arcing northeast route back to Australia, Troy visited Mauritius, without a surfboard, and watched flawless eight-foot waves pass by unridden at Tamarin Bay. Three years later, he returned to Tamarin with Torquay surfing phenomenon Wayne Lynch and filmmaker Paul Witzig to shoot footage for Witzig's 1971 movie *Sea of Joy*. In the mid-'70s, Troy spent much of his time in Bali and Java, and in 1975 he was one of the first surfers to ride the spectacular right-breaking tubes of Lagundri Bay, Nias.

In 1971, Troy briefly owned and operated a motel at Noosa Heads, Queensland; in 1974 he was co-owner of a Sydney theater that screened only surf movies; in the early '90s he owned a Queensland surf shop. In a 1987 *Surfing* magazine profile, Troy said that he'd visited 130 countries, including 38 in Africa alone. He was named one of "Australia's 50 Most Influential Surfers" by *Australia's Surfing Life* magazine in 1992; in 2002 he was inducted into the Australian Surfing Hall of Fame. In 2002, Troy and his wife were living near Noosa Heads. *See also* Bells Beach, Rip Curl Pro, surf travel.

tsunami   A fast-moving set of waves, sometimes hugely destructive, produced by an undersea earthquake, landslide, or volcanic eruption. Usually referred to as "tidal waves," a tsunami in fact has nothing to do with tides; "tsunami" means "harbor wave" in Japanese. An earthquake alone can create a tsunami, but the effect is thought to be greatly amplified when an earthquake is followed by an underwater landslide, as was the case on July 17, 1998, when a set of three tsunami waves out of the Bismarck Sea—one reported to be 30 foot high—suddenly roared into the northeast-facing coast of Papua New Guinea, killing more than 2,200. These "seismic sea waves" can move through deep water at 600 miles per hour, and are barely perceptible until they approach shore, at which point they can grow tremendously—up to 100 feet or more, by some accounts—as they slow down. Unlike storm-generated waves, tsunamis can retain their power for thousands of miles. In 1960, 5,000 Chileans were killed by a set of tsunami waves just minutes following an offshore earthquake; 14 hours later the waves reached Hawaii, killing 61 and causing millions in property damage; nine hours after

that the tsunami hit Japan and killed 150. "Whole buildings were driven directly through the ones behind, the way you'd close a telescope," reported Hawaii's *Hilo Tribune-Herald.* "Boulders weighing nearly a ton were picked up and set down hundreds of yards away." But destructive tsunamis are rare, and nobody has yet taken a photograph of a tsunami wave.

Surf lore contains at least two stories involving tsunamis. In the 1860s, surfer/farmer A'a Holaua is said to have been swept out to sea, along with his wooden house, as the first in a set of tsunami waves hit the northeast coast of the Hawaiian Islands. Ripping the door from his home, Holaua allegedly caught the following wave and rode back to the shore while standing on his makeshift surfboard.

A more credible story is told by 1965 world champion surfer Felipe Pomar, from Peru, who ventured into the water at a surf break near Lima with a friend on October 3, 1974, about one hour after a violent earthquake. Not long after they'd positioned themselves beyond the three-foot waves, Pomar and his friend were suddenly pulled more than a mile out to sea as the water drained away from the shore in a typical tsunami prologue. Both surfers then caught and rode separate 10-foot waves, one following the next, each pulling out a few hundred yards off the beach and watching as the waves exploded onto the shore, tossing a beached fishing boat into a building.

As California geologist Steven Ward reported in 2001, a big-enough submarine landslide in California's Monterey Bay could within minutes produce 50-foot waves in Santa Cruz and 85-foot waves in nearby Pacific Grove. "Sooner or later, tsunamis visit every coastline in the Pacific," warns the National Tsunami Hazard Mitigation Program Web site. "Never go down to the beach to watch for a tsunami. WHEN YOU CAN SEE THE WAVE YOU ARE TOO CLOSE TO ESCAPE." *See also* Felipe Pomar.

tube   Hollow interior formed as a wave crest arcs over and down to the trough. Tubes are generally formed at breaks where the incoming wave moves suddenly over a shallow area—a sandbar or a high spot in a reef or point. A land-to-sea offshore wind will help create a tube, as it lifts and supports the crest as it pitches forward. Most waves don't tube; of those that do, few are shaped properly to allow tube-riding. Thick, powerful tubes often will shoot out a horizontal tongue of vaporized water known as "spit." The tube has been described at various points in the sport's history as "tunnel," "barrel," "cylinder," "pit," "shack," "hole," "keg," "the womb," "the green room," and, as verbose Hawaiian surfer and pioneering tuberider Jock Sutherland phrased it in 1970, "the Pope's living room." *See also* spit, tuberiding.

tuberiding   Riding through the hollow area of the wave formed as the curl arcs out and down into the trough; regarded since the late 1950s as the ultimate surfing maneuver. Only a small percentage of waves are both hollow and well-shaped, and the infrequency of what are called "makable" tubes is one reason why tuberiding is among the most difficult surfing maneuvers; it's been estimated that less than 5 percent of surfers worldwide can consistently place themselves inside the tube. Most tuberides last less than three seconds; anything longer than five seconds is exceptional; rare tuberides at a select few surf breaks worldwide—Kirra in Australia, Grajagan in Indonesia, Restaurants in Fiji—last for as long as 15 seconds. Until the mid-'90s, tuberiding was rarely attempted in waves bigger than 15 feet.

Tuberiding is often thought of as separate from the rest of the sport, with its own constantly evolving set of strategies and techniques. In the most basic tuberiding scenario, the surfer, already angling on the wave face and having spotted a hollow section forming ahead, speeds up and crouches, arrives at the tube just as it's formed, gets encased, holds a line, and shoots out of the tube's mouth. ("Spit" is the lateral stream of mist blown out of the mouth of a thicker, harder-breaking tube.) Most tuberides, however, are set up with a stalling maneuver of some kind, with the surfer checking his forward movement in order to not outrun the tube. The tube stall is often done just after takeoff, usually by planting an arm in the wave face as a brake. The rider might also drop to the base of the wave and do a stalling "slow" turn while the tube forms overhead.

Tuberiding in the 1950s was a rare and frequently accidental event. Conrad Canha and Sammy Lee of Hawaii began riding the tube with some regularity in the early '60s at Ala Moana. California's Butch Van Artsdalen, however, often is cited as the first great tuberider, a distinction he earned at Pipeline, the funneling wave on the North Shore of Oahu that remains the iconic tuberiding break. Surf magazine publisher Steve Pezman was on the beach at Pipeline in late-November 1962 when Van Artsdalen made his

Tuberiding; Florida's CJ Hobgood

reputation. "The curtain threw out and over Butch," Pezman later recalled, "then erupted into a thundering explosion all around him, but through the falls we could still see the flash of his red trunks. Then he came flying out [and] we gasped in disbelief." Tuberides were nonetheless few and far between until the shortboard revolution of the late '60s, when boards went from 23-pound blunt-nosed 10-footers to spear-shaped seven-footers weighing as little as eight pounds. The new boards were often called "pocket rockets," as they were designed to perform in the curl-lined pocket of the wave, and tuberiding became the sport's highest calling. Hawaii's Jock Sutherland was the best tuberider in 1968 and 1969, and also strove mightily to capture the moment in words, describing the tube as a spinning field of "prismatic auras and shimmering spectrums," and viewing his approach to Pipeline as analogous to a caveman hunting and killing a Tyrannosaurus rex. Gerry Lopez, also from Hawaii, was the world's premier tuberider in the early and mid-'70s, transforming the act into a kind of Zen practice as he raced inside thundering Pipeline caverns in a relaxed crouch, with little or no expression on his mustachioed face. Other spots meanwhile gained notice as prime tuberiding breaks, including Kirra and Burleigh Heads in Queensland, Australia; Cave Rock and Bay of Plenty in Durban, South Africa; Big Rock in Southern California; and Mexico's Puerto Escondido. But Pipeline—including Backdoor and Off the Wall, two right-breaking waves adjacent to Pipeline—remained tuberiding's focal point. *Sports Illustrated* delved into tube-riding with a 1977 feature titled "All Aboard the Tunnel Express." South African Shaun Tomson had by that time reconfigured the tuberide by teaching himself how to maneuver his board from behind the curtain, which not only allowed him to ride deeper inside, but also greatly improve his rate of success. Tomson has often been described as the sport's most influential tuberider.

Tuberiding was at first thought of as something performed while riding frontside (facing the wave) rather than backside (back to the wave), as the latter demands a more difficult set of body position to avoid being hit by the falling curl. John Peck and Sam Hawk of California, along with Hawaii's Owl Chapman, developed rudimentary back-to-the-wall tube techniques at Pipeline in the '60s and early '70s, but backside tuberiding as it exists today took form in 1975, led by Shaun and Michael Tomson of South Africa and Wayne Bartholomew of Australia. The squatting rail-grab stance (with the surfer placing the trailing hand on the shoreward-facing edge of the board) gave way to the layback stance (back and shoulders planing on the water surface), which in turn led to the lay-forward, or "pigdog," stance (back knee lowered, trailing shoulder brought forward, chest atop front knee), out of which developed the self-explanatory backside stand-up tube. Frontside tuberiding remains the easier form for most surfers, but today's top pros—including Kelly Slater and Andy and Bruce Irons—ride with near-equal depth, length, and frequency in either direction.

Contests at Pipeline or Teahupoo in Tahiti are primarily tuberiding events. The only contest designated as such, however, was the Tavarua Tube Classic, held on Fiji's Tavarua Island in 1995 and 1996, with surfers judged solely on time spent behind the curtain. Big-wave tuberiding, meanwhile, was greatly advanced with the development of tow-in surfing in the '90s, as the personal watercraft-assisted running start, as well as the reduced-area tow-in boards, allowed the surfer to place himself in a more critical position on the wave, rather than just racing for deep water.

Dozens of synonyms for "tuberide" have been coined, used, and discarded over the decades, including "barreled," "slotted," "pitted," "piped," "shacked," and "kegged." *See also* closeout tube, dry tube, pigdog, Pipeline, stand-up tube.

Tubesteak   *See* Terry Tracy.

tucked-under edge   Surfboard rail design, likely invented by California-born surfer Anthony "Bunker" Spreckels in 1969, but developed and refined over the next three years by Hawaii's Dick Brewer and California's Mike Hynson, with Gordon Merchant doing similar work in Australia. In cutaway profile, the tucked-under edge is where the board's flat bottom meets the elliptical curve of the rail; the edge itself is generally set about a half inch in from the board's perimeter, although the distance changes depending on where the measurement is taken. Edge sharpness is also variable, but almost always most pronounced in the board's tail section, softer through the middle and nonexistent in the nose. As Australian surfboard shaper Bob McTavish wrote in the *Surfer's Journal* in 1995, the tucked-under edge "was a revelation. Nothing ever went as fast, and it ripped in small surf." The tucked-under edge is similar to what in the late '60s and '70s was called a "hard downrail." *See also* egg rail, rail.

Tucker, Cliff   Depression-era Southern California surfer and Palos Verdes Surf Club member who beat schoolmate Pete Peterson to win the 1940 Pacific Coast Surf Riding Championships. The contest was at San Onofre, and during the morning's preliminary rounds, held in windless conditions, Tucker rode his "ultralight"—a hollow, 50-pound plywood board. Later he switched to a 120-pound spruce board, partly to smooth his way through the wind-chopped afternoon waves, but also to put a little fear into his opponents. "If you were in a contest situation," Tucker recalled in 1982, "and a guy took off in front of you, it was your obligation to show no decency. You went right through him." In the final round of the Championships, with most surfers eliminated, Tucker went back to the lighter board and rode to victory.

Tudor, Joel   Supernaturally graceful longboarder from Del Mar, California; winner of the 1998 World Longboard Championships, and a model of surfing form and fluidity. Tudor was born (1976) and raised in San Diego, California, the son of a general contractor/father, and began surfing at age five; at 10 he quit riding shortboards to focus exclusively on longboards, and in his early and midteens he was mentored by '60s surf titans Nat Young and Donald Takayama. By 16 he was the pencil-thin Raphael of the longboard renaissance, and was earning $75,000 a year from sponsors, making him the era's best-paid longboarder,

Joel Tudor

with his income set to double over the next two years. Tudor had by that time mastered all aspects of longboarding, but was revered mainly as a stylist from the traditional school: quick but smooth, light-footed, able to hang ten for 15 seconds at a time, and possessed of a near-telepathic wave sense. Tudor could also do progressive shortboard-influenced turns and cutbacks, but believed that flow and under-statement were the cornerstones of longboarding. "This so-called 'modern' longboarding can go to hell," the high-voiced Tudor said in 1994, in one of many outspoken remarks that endeared him to long-board traditionalists of all ages. "It's so boring. If you want surf like that, get a 6'2" shortboard."

Tudor turned professional at 14, and won his first pro contest the following year. He was 16 when he finished runner-up in the 1992 World Longboard Championships, held in Biarritz, France, and it was assumed that Tudor would win championship titles at will for the next several years. He did in fact go on to win dozens of regional, national, and interna-tional pro contests, including the U.S. Open of Surf-ing (1995–2000, 2002), the Biarritz Surf Festival

(1991, 1993–99, 2001), and the Noosa Festival of Surf-ing (1999, 2000). But the world title proved elusive—he finished third in 1994, ninth in 1996, and fifth in 1997—until 1998, when he won the championship, held that year in the Canary Islands. He washed out early in the 1999 and 2001 titles, but finished runner-up in 2000 and third in 2001. In 1997 he became the first new-era longboarder to make the cover of *Surfer,* and in 2000—helped by his shrewdly developed role as surf world counterculture fashion trendsetter—he won the *Longboard* Magazine Readers Poll Award. The *Surfer's Journal* meanwhile described him as "the finest longboard surfer of all time." Tudor had by then broadened his surfboard quiver to include a number of shortboards, mostly copies of early-generation models from the late '60s and '70s.

Tudor (6'1", 150 pounds) is the primary subject of a number of surf videos, including *Adrift* (1996) and *Longer* (2001), and in 2001 he was featured on *Biographies,* an Outdoor Life Network cable TV series. He's appeared in more than 75 other surf movies and videos, including *On Surfari to Stay* (1992), *Long-boarding Is Not a Crime* (1995), *Super Slide* (1999), *The Seedling* (1999), and *Shelter* (2001). The Joel Tudor signature model, made by Donald Takayama Surf-boards—Tudor's longtime sponsor—was the best-selling board of its kind of the modern longboard era; Surfboards by Joel Tudor was founded in 2000. *See also* longboarding, World Longboard Tour.

turn turtle Method of pushing through a broken wave in which the surfer, paddling directly toward an oncoming line of whitewater, grips the rails of his board with both hands—sometimes wrapping his feet around the edges as well—flips upside down and holds on as the wave passes overhead. The idea is to present the lowest possible profile to the wave. Turn-ing turtle was probably developed in the 1920s or '30s, and was later used in waves up to eight or 10 feet. Surfers in the early shortboard era continued to use the technique, but two '70s developments—the duck dive and the surf leash—made turning turtle all but obsolete; the duck dive was a more efficient way to get through smaller waves, while the surf leash al-lowed the surfer to simply abandon ship, dive be-neath the whitewater, surface, and reel back his board. The launched longboard revival brought back the turtle maneuver in small waves.

Twain, Mark Revered American writer and wit, born Samuel Clemens (1835) in Florida, Missouri; author of *Tom Sawyer* (1876) and *Huckleberry Finn* (1884), and one of the first Americans, in 1866, to offer a published account of surfing—or "surf-bathing" as Twain called it. Twain, 30, was virtually unknown when he visited the Kona Coast on the Big Island of Hawaii as a $20-dollar-an-article travel correspondent for the *Sacramento Union* newspaper. While surfing took up just a single paragraph in one dispatch, Twain's portrayal of the sport was deft and funny. Although surfing had already been written about with a sense of interest and appreciation (Captain James Cook, after observing a canoe surfer in Tahiti, noted that the rider seemed to feel "the most supreme pleasure" as he shot toward the beach), most accounts prior to Twain's were disapproving, made by visiting missionaries to Hawaii, like Hiram Bingham of Vermont, who presented surfing as "being in opposition to the strict tenets of Calvinism [and] expressly against the laws of God."

Twain didn't seem to think so, and went so far as to give the sport a try himself.

> *In one place we came upon a large company of naked natives, of both sexes and all ages, amusing themselves with the national pastime of surf-bathing. Each heathen would paddle three or four hundred yards out to sea (taking a short board with him), then face the shore and wait for a particularly prodigious billow to come along; at the right moment he would fling his board upon its foamy crest and himself upon the board, and here he would come whizzing by like a bombshell! It did not seem that a lightning express train could shoot along at a more hair-lifting speed. I tried surf-bathing once, subsequently, but made a failure of it. I got the board placed right, and at the right moment, too; but missed the connection myself. The board struck the shore in three-quarters of a second, without any cargo, and I struck the bottom about the same time, with a couple of barrels of water in me. None but the natives ever master the art of surf-bathing thoroughly.*

Twain's articles for the *Sacramento Union* were collected for his 1872 travelogue *Roughing It.* The surfing portion of the book includes two small illustrations, one titled "Surf-Bathing—Success," in which three topless native women glide serenely along on their short wooden boards; the other, titled "Surf-Bathing—Failure," shows a mustachioed white man, legs in the air, imbedded in the crest and plunging headfirst for the bottom. Jack London, in 1907, was the next fa-

mous American writer to visit Hawaii and try his luck at surfing. *See also* books and surfing.

twin-fin While "twin-fin" can be used as a general description for any board with two fins, it usually refers to a particular type of stubby small-wave board popularized in the late 1970s by four-time world champion Mark Richards. In waves under six feet, the Richards-style twin-fin had great advantages over its single-fin predecessor: a wider planing surface meant increased speed, while reduced length helped open up maneuverability. The downside of the twin-fin was that it was jittery and slide-prone in all but the smallest waves, and unable to hold a sustained turn, making it hard to ride in midsize waves and worthless in large surf. With the introduction in 1981 of the tri-fin board—a design that worked in all size waves—the twin-fin was quickly rendered obsolete.

California board-design trailblazer Bob Simmons made a small number of twin-fins in the late '40s and early '50s, hoping to add stability to his wide-tailed balsa boards. Simmons himself favored what he called the "duel fin" design, and was riding one at San Diego's Windansea in 1954, when he drowned following a wipeout. In 1967, San Diego shaper Barry "Bear" Mirandon, working for La Jolla Surfboards,

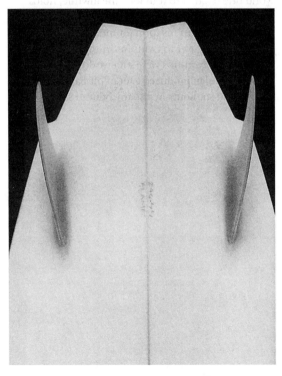

Twin-fin

developed and marketed the split-tailed, two-finned Twin-Pin model. Mirandon's board sold poorly, but led almost directly to the development of the Steve Lis–designed "fish"—another split-tailed twin-fin, adopted first by kneeboarders, then by stand-up surfers. At the 1972 World Surfing Championships in San Diego, Jim Blear and David Nuuhiwa finished first and second, respectively, while riding fish boards. Meanwhile, a thick, squat, square-backed version of the twin-fin, developed in large part by California shaper Mike Eaton and favored by 1970 world champion Rolf Aurness, also came and went in the early '70s. By 1973, few stand-up surfers were riding twin-fins of any kind.

Australian pro surfer Mark Richards began working on a twin-fin redesign in 1976, after watching Hawaiian surfer Reno Abellira use a 5'3" round-nose fish during the Australian pro competition season. By early 1977, Richards had developed his own 6'2" version—featuring a pair of six-inch-high fins set along the rails, about 11 inches from the tail—which he immediately described as "the ultimate small-wave board." Richards adapted better than anyone to the maneuverable but hard-to-control twin-fin design, pushing it into a series of tight arcs across the wave face, and riding it throughout his 1979–82 world title reign. (Pro tour lore, meanwhile, holds that 1977 world champion and single-fin advocate Shaun Tomson lost his form for more than five years after switching over to twin-fins in 1979.) Tens of thousands of twin-fins were sold worldwide, and while the design produced a lot of off-balance arm waving and spin-outs, it also introduced surfers to a new range of turning variables—all of which were better explored on the tri-fin, produced in 1981 by Simon Anderson, Richards's world tour peer and fellow Australian. Twin-fins have been manufactured in small numbers since the early '80s, mainly as kneeboards. The "twinzer," a variation on the twin-fin featuring an additional set of small side fins, was invented in 1988 by Huntington Beach shaper Will Jobson. *See also* fish, four-fin, Mark Richards, single-fin, tri-fin, twinzer.

twinzer   Four-fin surfboard design invented in 1988 by shaper Will Jobson of Huntington Beach, California. Jobson's idea was to revitalize the twin-fin, a speedy and maneuverable small-wave board popular in the late '70s and early '80s that had proven to be terminally skittish. The introduction of the tri-fin design in 1981 quickly rendered the twin-fin obsolete. With the twinzer, Jobson corrected many of the twin-fin's problems. The board's tail area was narrower than that found on the twin-fins, while the fins were pushed back a few inches and moved closer to the center of the board, behind a second set of smaller fins that were positioned closer to the rail. A shallow six-inch-wide channel was cut into the back few inches of the tail area. The result was a board that did indeed have more traction than the twin-fin, with just as much speed, and virtually no loss in maneuverability. While the twinzer made virtually no dent in the tri-fin's popularity, it did find a niche, and Jobson was still producing the board in small numbers in 2003. *See also* four-fin, twin-fin.

U

ugg boots   Thick, warm, blunt-toed boot, originally from Australia, made of fleece-lined sheepskin with hard rubber soles. Ugg—thought to be short for "ugly"—is both a brand and a generic name. Uggs were invented in the late 1960s by cold-footed surfers in Torquay, Victoria; the shin-high boots were a fashion hit with California surfers in the early and mid-'80s, only to become a much-ridiculed surf fashion cliché by the end of the decade, then slowly found their way into mainstream shoe stores and mail-order houses. Ugg boots are now produced by dozens of manufacturers, in dozens of styles. In 2001, *Surfer* magazine called the ugg a "tragic fashion *faux pas,*" while *Los Angeles* magazine described it as a "glorified house slipper, and the most superfluous Southern California fashion statement since mink." Thousands of surfers nonetheless keep a secret pair in the closet for cold winter mornings. *See also* fashion and surfing.

Uluwatu   Expansive left-breaking Balinese wave located on the southwest corner of Bukit Peninsula; the first in a near-endless chain of perfect Indonesian reef waves discovered by traveling surfers from the early '70s to present day. Pura Luhur Uluwatu ("Temple Above the Final Stone") is the name of the Balinese cliffside temple overlooking the break; Uluwatu breaks best from May to October, as Indian Ocean winter storms generate consistent four- to eight-foot swells—broken up by the occasional 10- to 12-footer—which are groomed as they reach shore by Bali's reliable southeast tradewinds. Uluwatu's sweeping, coral-covered lava reef has three main sections: 1) Outside Corner, a shifty wave located farthest out to sea, is best on lower tides, starts breaking at six foot, can hold form up to 15 foot, and sometimes produces rides up to 300 yards long. 2) The Peak (or Inside Corner) is the main surfing area, located just in front of a beach-access cave, and features an array of peaks when the swell is between three and six foot. 3) Racetrack, further inside, is Uluwatu's premium section; a long, fast, hollow wave that gets bigger as it coils and

spits down the reef. Racetrack requires a medium-sized swell and medium-to-high tide. Despite Uluwatu's broad playing field, 30 years of international fame have ensured that the lineup is almost always crowded, often with up to 100 visiting and local surfers at a time. (The Bali nightclub terror attacks in 2002, in nearby Kuta Beach, forced many would-be visiting surfers to reconsider their travel plans, and Uluwatu has seen a marked reduction in crowds.) Sharks and sea snakes have been spotted at Uluwatu, but the primary hazard here is a dangerously shallow reef at lower tides, particularly along the Racetrack section.

While Uluwatu was almost certainly ridden in the late '60s by visiting American and Australia GIs, its well-documented "discovery" took place in August 1971, when Aussie surf moviemaker Alby Falzon arrived with 14-year-old Steve Cooney of Sydney and former top-rated California surfer Rusty Miller; Falzon filmed the two riding perfect four- to eight-foot Peak and Racetrack waves for his seminal *Morning of the Earth* surf film. By the mid-'70s, local Balinese surfers including Ketut Menda, Made Kasim, and

Uluwatu

Gede Narmada were joining well-known visitors such as Gerry Lopez, Peter McCabe, and Jim Banks in Uluwatu's aquamarine lineup, and photos of the break were a regular feature in surf magazines. California surfer Bob Laverty drowned while surfing Uluwatu in 1972, just a few days after he led the first surfing expedition to Grajagan, on the neighboring island of Java. The 1980 OM Bali Pro, won by Terry Fitzgerald, was the first surf contest held at Uluwatu; the event returned the following two years. It continues to be the site of regional amateur and professional events.

Uluwatu has been featured in dozens of surf films and videos, including *Free Ride* (1977), *Bali High* (1981), *The Sons of Fun* (1993), and *Year of the Tiger* (1999); the wave at Uluwatu is detailed in a number of guidebooks, including *Indo Surf and Lingo* (1992), *Surfing Indonesia* (1999), and *The World Stormrider Guide* (2001). *Surfing* magazine in 1989 named Uluwatu as one of the "25 Best Waves in the World." *See also* Bali.

undergunned   Riding a board that is too small for prevailing wave conditions. "Gun" is shorthand for "big-wave gun" or "elephant gun"—a board used for larger surf. The undergunned surfer has a difficult time catching waves (guns are designed primarily for paddling speed) and, once up and riding, will struggle to maintain control and avoid "spinning out." When big waves arrive at locations generally known for small surf—along much of the eastern seaboard, for example—locals are often undergunned.

United Arab Emirates   *See* Persian Gulf.

United States Surfing Association (USSA)
Southern California–based organization, operating from 1961 to 1967; surfing's first nationwide association, launched as an advocacy group to improve the sport's image, then evolving into an administrative body for surf competition. American surfing in the early '60s was often presented in newspaper and magazine articles as filled with raucous bleach-blond hodads and gremmies; Southern California beach town city councils, meanwhile, were enacting regulations and restrictions against board-riding. The mission of the United States Surfing Association (USSA), founded by Laguna Beach surfer and liquor store owner Brennan "Hevs" McClelland, was to make the sport "more serious and respectable." (McClelland

was a curious choice to lead such a campaign; as surfing's beloved court jester he'd worn a wig and bikini for a surf movie skit, and sometimes drove his car down Laguna's shop-lined sidewalks for kicks.) The USSA elected a board of directors on June 3, 1961, and two days later selected pioneering California surfer Hoppy Swarts and surfboard magnate Hobie Alter as president and vice president, respectively. The organization was run out of McClelland's Laguna Beach home.

The USSA initially divided itself into seven districts: five in California, one in Hawaii and one on the East Coast. For a $3 to $10 joining fee, depending on the level chosen, members received a window decal, the USSA newsletter, and a promise that the group would "clean up and elevate surfing to its rightful position." The USSA formed a Committee for Legal Action on Surfing Legislation and spoke at a number of city council meetings at which surfing-related issues were debated. With limited funds and just 2,000 members in the group by 1964, however, its overall impact was slight. Meanwhile, the First Annual USSA National Surf Show, a trade show precursor to the Action Sports Retailer show, was held in Long Beach in 1963.

The USSA shifted its focus to surfing competition in 1965, after moving from Laguna to Redondo Beach. During the previous two years the group had sanctioned surfing events; now it imposed a standardized set of competition rules and regulations, created an aggregate contest-to-contest ratings system, required USSA membership of all competitors (immediately pushing membership up to just over 5,000), and made selections for America's three teams to the 1965 World Surfing Championships in Peru. The inaugural Duke Kahanamoku Invitational, also in 1965, was held under USSA rules. The following year, under new president Tom Morey, USSA contests were divided into three levels—A, AA, and AAA—with top-rated AAA surfers selected for the USSA-hosted 1966 World Championships in San Diego, California. (The elite AAAA division was added in 1968.) By that time, officials from the East Coast and Hawaii districts had lodged complaints saying their surfers were being overlooked in favor of West Coast surfers, and by the time a *Surfing* magazine "USSA Report" column in 1966 brought up the "many questions and misconceptions regarding the financial status of the USSA," the group's days were numbered. The USSA split into four regional groups following the 1967 season: the

Western Surfing Association, the Eastern Surfing Association, the Hawaiian Surfing Association, and the Gulf Coast Surfing Association. The United States Surfing Federation was formed 12 years later.

USSA year-end ratings leaders for men's, women's, juniors, and tandem divisions:

1965: Rusty Miller, Joyce Hoffman, David Nuuhiwa, Mike Doyle/Linda Merrill
1966: Corky Carroll, Joyce Hoffman, David Nuuhiwa, Pete Peterson/Barrie Algaw
1967: Corky Carroll, Joyce Hoffman, Dru Harrison, Wesley Thomas/Sally Reid

See also Brennan "Hevs" McClelland, politics and surfing, Lewis "Hoppy" Swarts.

United States Surfing Championships Sprawling annual competition for the country's top-ranked amateur surfers, usually held in late summer or early fall. The United States Surfing Championships (USSC) were held at Huntington Pier from 1964 to 1972, and regarded as the top event on the California competition calendar; since 1973 the contest has been held at rotating locations in Texas, Hawaii, California, and the East Coast.

The USSC grew out of the annual West Coast Surfing Championships, a weekend-long event founded in 1959, sponsored by the Huntington Beach Recreation Department and the local Chamber of Commerce. The name was changed in 1964 as the contest began to draw entrants from across the country. The number of spectators also grew steadily, and by the mid-'60s weekend crowds for the USSC often topped 10,000, with the loudest cheers often reserved for those surfers who shot the Huntington Pier on the biggest waves. (For insurance reasons, the city of Huntington demanded that competitors wear hard plastic safety helmets.)

The number of USSC age divisions and categories fluctuated in the '60s and early '70s, then grew steadily from the late '70s onward, along with the number of competitors: in 2002, just over 450 surfers competed in 30 categories, including eight longboard divisions, seven bodyboard divisions, and a prosthetic division. Surfers qualify for the USSC by competing in regional amateur circuits, including the Eastern Surfing Association, the Hawaiian Amateur Surfing Association, and the Pacific Region Surfing Association. Virtually immobilized by its enormity—and forced since the early 1980s to compete for a limited amount of surf world media interest and prestige with the National

Scholastic Surfing Association Nationals—the USSC is frequently held in subpar waves. Nonetheless, virtually every American surfer of note over the past 40 years has competed in the USSC, including Dewey Weber, Corky Carroll, David Nuuhiwa, Gerry Lopez, Dane Kealoha, Tom Curren, Kelly Slater, and Andy Irons. Senior surfer Les Williams of California was a 15-time USSC finalist and six-time victor from 1969 to 1997; senior surfer Bob Holland of Virginia was a 17-time finalist and six-time winner from 1967 to 2000.

Winners for the men's, women's, and juniors divisions of the West Coast Surfing Championships (1959–63) and the United States Surfing Championships are listed below. All events from 1959 to 1972 were held in Huntington Beach; the location for each of the remaining events is noted in parentheses.

1959: Jack Haley, Linda Benson, Louis Tarter
1960: Mike Haley, Linda Benson, Dave Willingham
1961: Ron Sizemore, Linda Benson, Butch Linden
1962: Ilima Kalama, Audie Wilke, Pete Kobsev
1963: LJ Richards, Candy Calhoun, Corky Carroll
1964: Jim Craig, Linda Benson, Rod Sumpter
1965: Mark Martinson, Joyce Hoffman, David Nuuhiwa
1966: Corky Carroll, Joyce Hoffman, David Nuuhiwa
1967: Corky Carroll, Joyce Hoffman, Dru Harrison
1968: David Nuuhiwa, Linda Benson, Brad McCaul
1969: Corky Carroll, Sharron Weber, Niles Osborn
1970: Brad McCaul, Jericho Poppler, Dane Sizzle
1971: David Nuuhiwa, Joyce Hoffman, Barry Amos
1972: Dale Dobson, Mary Setterholm, Lenny Foster
1973: Larry Bertlemann, Laura Powers, Jeff Smith (Malibu, California)
1974: Rick Rasmussen, Isabel McLaughlin, Mark Levy (Cape Hatteras, North Carolina)
1975: Aaron Wright, Grace Knowles, Timmy Carvalho (South Padre Island, Texas)
1976: Clippy Cabato, Laola Lake, Dane Kealoha (Ala Moana, Hawaii)

1977: Duane Wong, Karen McKay, Pat Mulhern (San Onofre, California)

1978: Tim Briers, Mary Ann Hayes, David Nuckles (Cape Hatteras, North Carolina)

1979: Brandon Hayes, Grace Knowles, Phil Treibel (South Padre Island, Texas)

1980: Denton Miyamura, Yolande Elliott, Robin Loo (North Shore of Oahu, Hawaii)

1981: Willy Morris, Lynn Garduque, Tom Curren (San Diego, California)

1982: Charlie Kuhn, Dorothy Dunn, Chris Frohoff (Cape Hatteras, North Carolina)

1983: John Thomas, Tippy Kelly, Chris Burke (South Padre Island, Texas)

1984: Joey Napoleon, Nikki Bockwinkle, Matt Archbold (Makaha, Oahu, Hawaii)

1985: Dan Miller, Dina Demeo, Jeff Booth (Ventura, California)

1986: Bill Johnson, Debra Swaney, Todd Holland (Sebastian Inlet, Florida)

1987: Walter Cerny, Melissa Proud, Scott Blake (North Padre Island, Texas)

1988: Scott Yoshizawa, Kim Briones, Heath Hemmings (Sandy Beach, Hawaii)

1989: Stephen Denham, Julie Whitegon, Jeff Deffenbaugh (North Jetty, Oceanside, California)

1990: Paul Reinecki, Julie Whitegon, Todd Morcom (Sebastian Inlet, Florida)

1991: Donnie Solomon, Connie Clark, Chad Delgado (Port Aransas, Texas)

1992: Jason Gantz, Lisa Wallace, Shea Lopez (Honolulu, Hawaii)

1993: Jason Harcharic, Kim Hamrock, Brian Hewitson (Oceanside, California)

1994: Fisher Bulberth, Kim Hamrock, Ben Bourgeois (Sebastian Inlet, Florida)

1995: Bryan Hewitson, Kim Hamrock, Kyle Garson (South Padre Island, Texas)

1996: Gavn Sutherland, Kim Hamrock, Andy Irons (Ala Moana, Hawaii)

1997: David Pinto, Sharon Polglase, Mikala Jones (Oceanside, California)

1998: Jody Davis, Sandy Chang, Fred Patachia (Oceanside, California)

1999: Ted Navaro, Julie Polansky, Joel Centeio (Oceanside, California)

2000: Travis Hashimoto, Sandy Chang, Joel Centeio (Honolulu, Hawaii)

2001: Justin McBride, Katie Whatley, Daniel Jones (Oceanside, California)

2002: Nathan Carroll, Katie Whatley, Josh Singh (Oceanside, California)

See also Huntington Beach, National Scholastic Surfing Association, surfing competition.

United States Surfing Federation (USSF) Umbrella group for American amateur surfing associations, founded in 1979 primarily by Colin Couture of Rhode Island, responsible for choosing America's team to the World Surfing Championships (and later the World Surfing Games); recognized by the International Olympic Committee as America's national governing body for surfing. Conceived as a unifying and organizing group for six existing organizations—the Western Surfing Association (WSA), Eastern Surfing Association (ESA), Hawaiian Surfing Association (HSA), Texas Gulf Surfing Association (TGSA), Women's International Surfing Association (WISA), and the National Scholastic Surfing Association (NSSA)—the United States Surfing Federation (USSF) was a product of the unstable and frequently petty world of American amateur surfing. Original USSF president Couture helped sort out some amateur surfing problems, but overall progress was minimal. "From the beginning," NSSA cofounder Chuck Allen recalled, "there was horrible mistrust between regional bodies, [and] the whole thing was just a bad scene."

Friction increased in 1985, the year after the NSSA filled nine of 10 positions for the country's World Championships team. The talent-rich NSSA argued that the national team should continue to be merit-based; the USSF—having taken on yet another group, the Christian Surfing Association (CSA)—wanted to distribute team slots equitably among its constituent groups. The USSF prevailed. In 1993, NSSA president Janice Aragon broke away her organization from the USSF, meaning that NSSA-only surfers were ineligible for the national World Championships team. (The NSSA Nationals had meanwhile eclipsed the USSF's United States Surfing Championships as America's premier amateur competition.) Thus divided, young competitors had to choose between the USSF-affiliated group in their region and the NSSA, or sign up for both organizations and somehow manage a double-duty contest schedule.

Hoping to streamline matters somewhat, the WSA and CSA disbanded in 1993 (WISA folded in

1991) to make way for the Western Region Surfing Association. The USSF fielded a plucky title-winning team for the 1996 World Surfing Games (replacement for the World Championships), but without the talented NSSA surfers, the Americans did poorly in the 1998 Worlds, finishing sixth, and even worse in 2000, placing 10th, prompting a *Surf News* magazine headline that read: "It's Official: America Sucks!"

In 2000, Surfing America, a just-formed amateur surfing group organized by the Surf Industry Manufacturers Association, made a failed bid to replace the USSF as the sport's national governing body; the USSF/NSSA chasm was still the main feature on the domestic amateur landscape in 2003, with no solution in sight. The USSF is funded by membership dues and corporate sponsorship, and in 2000 claimed 10,000 members among its seven component groups. *See also* Colin Couture, National Scholastic Surfing Association, Surfing America, World Surfing Championships, World Surfing Games.

urchin   *See* sea urchin.

Uruguay   Small and relatively affluent Spanish-speaking country on South America's Atlantic coast, between Argentina and Brazil; covered in gently rolling grasslands, and featuring a reasonable amount of soft, shapely, easy-to-ride surf. Uruguay's best waves are found along the central and northern portions of its 410-mile coast, especially around Punta del Este, a 50-mile stretch of shoreline containing at least 35 surf breaks. Incoming swells west of Punta del Este for the most part are blocked by Argentina.

While Uruguay has ridable waves all year, the spring and summer months (September to March) bring onshore winds and swarms of beachgoers. Fall and winter surf is bigger—sometimes up to six or eight foot—cleaner, and less crowded, although a broad continental shelf drains much of the power away from approaching swells. Most waves here are right-breaking, and form over sand-bottom beaches or rocky points. Midday coastal air and water temperatures both range from the mid-70s to the low 50s.

A visiting American missionary introduced surfing to Uruguay in 1961. Two years later, Omar Rossi, a lifeguard from Montevideo, built himself a wooden surfboard by following the instructions from an old *Popular Mechanics* article; two of Rossi's friends, Ariel Gonzalez (who later wrote a book on Uruguayan surfing history) and Jaime Mier, soon bought modern boards and also began riding waves. The first Uruguayan surf contest was held in 1969 at Manantiales beach in Punta del Este. The country hosted its first international surf contest 10 years later, also at Punta del Este. Film footage of the 1997 Reef Classic, Uruguay's first international professional contest, was broadcast across the country. By 2003, there were an estimated 2,750 native surfers in Uruguay, along with three surf camps, nearly 20 surf shops, and a small number of surf-related manufacturing outfits, including Flesh, one of South America's leading wetsuit manufacturers. *Mareas,* the country's only surf magazine, has been publishing since 1997. The 1993-founded Uruguay Surf Union had 950 members.

U.S. Open   *See* Op Pro Huntington Beach.

V

Valluzzi, Bruce Bright, impulsive, well-traveled surfer and writer from Cocoa Beach, Florida, who once described the sport as "three-dimensional free verse." Valluzzi began riding waves in 1963 at age 14; in 1966 he was the men's division runner-up in the East Coast Surfing Championships and competed in the World Championships; in 1967 he was invited to the Duke Kahanamoku Classic in Hawaii. He also published his first surf magazine article in 1967, and over the next two decades his byline appeared on more than 20 articles, most of them in *Surfer*. His best-known piece was 1982's "Morocco: Surf Madness and 1001 Moorish Days and Nightmares," a high-speed, liquor-soaked, first-person travelogue, clearly influenced by gonzo journalist Hunter S. Thompson, grouping Valluzzi with two-time Pipeline Masters winner Rory Russell (described as having "the grin of a convicted sex offender") and photographer Art Brewer ("large and fearless, easily given to thundering tantrums, who thinks Helmut Newton is a pussy-whipped choirboy"). The article was praised by *Surfer* readers, although one letter to the editor called Valluzzi's group "the original ugly Americans," and another cautioned Valluzzi against drinking and driving. But he never slowed down. "I'm really reckless," he said in a 1972 *Surfer* interview. "The faster I can go, the more dangerous it is, the more I like it." In 1987, at age 39, Valluzzi died in his Florida home of a drug overdose.

Van Artsdalen, Butch Gifted but self-destructive surfer from La Jolla, California, known as "Mr. Pipeline" for his breakthrough performances at Hawaii's most famous surf spot in the early and mid-1960s. Van Artsdalen was born (1941) and raised in Norfolk, Virginia, moved with his family to La Jolla at age 14, and began surfing the following year. A broad-shouldered natural athlete, he lettered in football, baseball, and track for three straight years at La Jolla High School; he meanwhile became a regular at Windansea, the area's best-known surf break, and was soon one of La Jolla's best surfers. Van Artsdalen was a drinker and a brawler, putting him in good stead with the always-rowdy local surfers who, in 1963, brought a kind of frat-house organization to their beach scene by forming the Windansea Surf Club—with the charismatic Van Artsdalen as a charter member. "Butch was a wild man," longtime Windansea local Carl Ekstrom recalled. "He never walked away from a fight or a party." During a group outing to the Plaza Monumental bullring in Tijuana, Mexico, Van Artsdalen heaved a tequila-soaked watermelon into the ring, covering the matador in red juice, seeds, and booze. He was arrested.

Van Artsdalen's had a nondescript first visit to Oahu's North Shore in 1961. On his return visit the following year, however, he seemed to click everywhere he rode, including Sunset Beach and Haleiwa; he was the first surfer to ride switchfoot at Waimea Bay, pivoting casually in midride from his natural right-foot-forward goofyfoot stance to a left-foot-forward regularfoot stance. At Pipeline he was on a separate and higher plane altogether. Hawaiians

Butch Van Artsdalen

Conrad Canha and Sammy Lee were among a small number of surfers who already had a basic understanding of how to ride inside the tube. But it was Van Artsdalen who became the first surfer to make tuberiding a repeatable step-by-step process. His best rides were seen on the big screen a few months later in surf movies like *Gun Ho!, Angry Sea,* and *Walk on the Wet Side,* and three years later he was featured in Bruce Brown's crossover hit *The Endless Summer.*

Van Artsdalen moved to the North Shore in 1966 and became a lifeguard. He made dozens of heroic rescues over the next few years, but was already losing ground to alcoholism. By 1969 he was a background figure in surfing, and in the mid-'70s was fired from his lifeguarding job for absenteeism. After fellow California big-wave transplant surfer Jose Angel died in what some felt was a suicidal deep-water dive in 1976, Van Artsdalen went into an alcoholic depression. He died of liver failure on July 17, 1979, at age 38. Fred Hemmings, 1968 world surfing champion, eulogized Van Artsdalen on the beach at Pipeline, then led a group of surfers into the water to scatter his ashes. Van Artsdalen was married twice and had two children. *See also* alcohol and surfing, Pipeline, switchstance, tuberiding, Windansea, the Windansea Surf Club.

Van Dyke, Fred   Friendly but outspoken big-wave rider from Haleiwa, Hawaii; one of the first surfers to emigrate from California to the North Shore of Oahu in the mid-1950s. Van Dyke was born (1929) in San Francisco, California, the son of a dentist, and learned to bodysurf as a teenager along the San Francisco–area beaches, but didn't ride stand-up until 1950, at age 20. He earned a double major B.A. in creative writing and physical education from San Francisco State in 1953, and later that year received a teaching credential. Van Dyke moved to Honolulu, Hawaii, in 1955, after seeing an Associated Press photo in a local newspaper of three surfers shooting across a 12-footer at Makaha; for 30 years he worked at the exclusive Punahou primary and secondary school, teaching math, science, English, and social studies, and coaching football, basketball, swimming, and diving. California surfers Rick Grigg and Peter Cole, among others, also moved to Hawaii in the mid-50s, and joined Van Dyke to form a loosely affiliated group of dedicated North Shore big-wave surfers.

Not a great natural surfing talent, Van Dyke compensated with extra hours spent in the water, and by

Fred Van Dyke

adhering to a strict health and fitness program. Personable, articulate, and ruggedly handsome, he was often called upon by mainstream magazines to speak on behalf of the sport. Eyebrows were raised among the big-wave fellowship after Van Dyke was interviewed in 1963 by *Life* magazine. "Many of us ride to supplement something lacking in our lives," Van Dyke said. "I'm sure the underlying reasons are concerned with a need for recognition." In "The Peril of the Surf: A Veteran Surfer Asks, Are Surfers Really Sick?," a cover story Van Dyke wrote for the Australian edition of *Life* in 1967, he went a step further in analyzing his peer group, infamously stating that many big-wave surfers were "latent homosexuals." Van Dyke explained that he wasn't talking so much about sexual preference, but merely stating that big-wave riders were like preadolescents, concerned only with impressing and interacting with male friends. But the nuances of his argument were lost, and he was soon being greeted along the North Shore with shouts of "faggot!" and "queer-boy!" Van Dyke says he also lost friends after he quit riding giant waves in the late '70s. "None of them would admit it," the soft-voiced surfer later recalled, "but I wasn't one of the big-wave gang any more. It hurt."

Van Dyke appeared in about 10 surf movies of the '50s and early '60s, including *Surf Crazy* (1959) and *Angry Sea* (1963). He was also featured in *Surfing for Life* (1999), a PBS-broadcast documentary on senior surfers. Between 1963 and 1988, Van Dyke authored about 25 features and columns for the surf press. He has also published five books, including *30 Years of Riding the World's Biggest Waves* (1989), *Surfing Huge Waves With Ease* (1993), and *Two Surf Stories for Children* (1994). *Once Upon Abundance,* Van Dyke's autobiography, was published in 2001. From 1965 to 1972, he was meet director for the annual Duke Kahanamoku Invitational, held at Sunset Beach. Van Dyke has been married three times, and has three children. His siblings—brothers Peter and Gene, and sister Gretchen—were all accomplished surfers.

Van Dyke, Peter   Candid regularfoot surfer from Santa Cruz, California; best known as the author of a 1965 *Surfer* magazine article "Big Wave Danger: A Hoax!" Peter Van Dyke, younger brother of big-wave surfing pioneer Fred Van Dyke, was born in San Francisco (1936), and began surfing at age 14 in Santa Cruz. He visited Hawaii in 1955, and again in the winter of 1956–57, and while his big-wave experience was limited, he was the debunking voice of confidence in "Hoax!," at a time when big-wave surfing was rarely presented as anything but heroic and death-defying. "Riding big waves," Van Dyke wrote, "isn't perilous, dangerous or as hairy as it's cracked up to be. I've ridden all kinds of surf and I've come much closer to being killed in small waves on a crowded day in California than I ever have in the Islands [Hawaii] in surf over 20 feet." Big-wave practitioners, Van Dyke said, generally trained on a diet of "cake, Kool-aid, ice cream, candy, and a pack of cigarettes a day." Wipeouts almost never lasted longer than 20 seconds, he continued, and big-wave danger wasn't in the same league as that found in Grand Prix racing, mountain climbing, or bullfighting. The *Surfer* audience wasn't convinced. "How about telling Van Dyke," responded a West Los Angeles reader, "that the real 'hoax' is screwball articles like his." Van Dyke appeared in *Surf Safari* (1959), *Gun Ho!* (1963), and other period surf movies.

Van Hamersveld, John   Illustrator and graphic designer from Los Angeles, California, best known to surfers as the creator of the Day-Glo poster for Bruce Brown's 1966 crossover hit movie *The Endless Summer.* After graduating from Art Center College of Design in Los Angeles in 1963, Van Hamersveld spent just over a year as the *Surfer* magazine graphic designer. In the mid-'60s he made handbills for rock acts like the Velvet Underground and the Who, then went on to design album covers for the Rolling Stones, Bob Dylan, Bonnie Raitt, and Kiss, among others. In 2000, copies of a limited-edition 35th-anniversary run of the *Endless Summer* poster, signed by Brown and Van Hamersveld, sold for $750 each. A lithographed copy of the original orange-pink-and-yellow poster is in the New York Museum of Modern Art's permanent collection. *See also* The Endless Summer, surf art.

Van Lennep, Chris   Athletic surf photographer from Durban, South Africa, best known for his intimate wide-angle images shot from inside the tube; a senior staff photographer at *Surfing* magazine beginning in 1989. Van Lennep was born (1959) and raised in Durban, and began surfing in 1974, the same year he started taking photographs. His first published shot was a 1984 center spread in the Durban-produced *Zigzag* surf magazine; in 1995 Van Lennep took four of his 12 *Surfing* covers, all of them close-up water shots, including an inside-the-tube-looking-out image at Pipeline, captioned as "the view we all desire." His work has been published in *Sports Illustrated* and *Outside,* and in surf magazines worldwide. In 2000, the *Surfer's Journal* published a 22-page text-free Van Lennep portfolio; he's also contributed to a number of illustrated surfing books, including *The Next Wave* (1991) and *The Perfect Day* (2001). Van Lennep is married and has two children.

Van Straalen, Dick   Understated Australian surfboard shaper from Queensland's Gold Coast; best known for the sleek single-fin boards he made throughout the 1970s, designed primarily for the racy pointbreak waves found at nearby Burleigh Heads and Kirra Point. Van Straalen was born (1944) and raised in The Hague, Netherlands, began surfing not long after moving with his family to the Sydney suburb of Avalon in 1951, and six years later began shaping boards. In the early and mid-'60s, he worked for Bill Wallace Surfboards and Dale Surfboards, both in Sydney; after he moved to Burleigh Heads in 1968, Van Straalen's fine-tuned boards were produced under a succession of short-lived backyard labels, including Country Spaceships, Spirit of the Sea, and Whitelight Projections. Van Straalen for the most part built streamlined pintails, similar to those made by Hawaiian master shaper Dick Brewer, to whom Van Straalen was often compared. Throughout the '70s, Van Straalen made boards for many of the world's best surfers, including Wayne Bartholomew, Peter Townend, Joe Engel, and Michael Ho. His heyday as a board-maker was brought to an abrupt end in 1979, when a factory fire destroyed most of his favorite board-pattern templates. He continued to shape, but drastically reduced his output; in the late '90s he began making high-end paddleboards. Van Straalen still lives and works on the Gold Coast.

Vancouver Island Heavily forested Canadian island located just north of the American-Canadian border; the largest Pacific Coast island in North America, with almost 300 miles of rugged, deeply fissured southwest-facing coastline; an area once known to sailors as the Graveyard of the Pacific. Jordan River, located deep inside the Juan de Fuca Strait, is Vancouver Island's most popular place to surf, as it's one of the very few places on Canada's west coast with beachfront access. At most other breaks, surfers park as close to the shore as possible, bundle up in thick wetsuits—hoods, gloves, and boots—then walk down forest trails and across log- and boulder-covered beaches to the waves. The island's few hundred surfers, often crowded into the few point-, reef-, and river-mouth breaks that are accessible, can be cranky or even hostile to outsiders—particularly at Jordan River. The rain-soaked Vancouver surf is best in fall, often huge and unruly in winter, and foggy during summer. Many of the breaks are set in areas of panoramic natural beauty. Midwinter air and water temperatures are generally in the low 40s; occasionally the beach will be covered in snowfall.

Canadian surfing originated at Vancouver's Wreck Bay (now Florencia Bay) in the mid-1960s, imported by nomadic American surfer/hippies. The first Canadian surf contest was held here in 1966, in the easygoing sand-bottom waves at Long Beach. Much of the surfing in *5mm,* the first all-Canadian surf video, takes place along Vancouver Island; *Numb* (2002) was also filmed there. *See also* Canada.

vee Convex surfboard bottom design that bisects the rear and/or middle area of the board into two longitudinal panels; introduced by Australian board-maker Bob McTavish in 1967. Vee makes the board easier to turn, as it tends to lean over on one panel or the other. Flat- or concave-bottom boards, however, are faster. While vee itself is a design feature, the "vee-bottom board" refers specifically to a type of board McTavish developed in 1967: the wide-backed, thick-tailed "plastic machine" that opened up the late-'60s shortboard revolution. "Spiral vee," popular in the '70s, is a slightly cone-shaped version of vee, with the point built into the area just below the surfer's back foot. "Reverse vee," invented in the early '90s and still in use, places an inversion, or concavity, in the middle section of the board, beneath the rider's front foot. Standard vee, as of 2002, was often so slight as to be nearly undetectable. *See also* belly, concave, reverse vee.

Velarde, Hector Dashingly handsome goofyfoot surfer from Lima, Peru; national champion in 1967. Velarde was born (1941) and raised in Lima, the son of a wealthy fishmeal-producing family, and began surfing in 1956. He proved to be not only a gifted rider in big and small waves, but a born entertainer, able to dazzle onlookers by gripping the rails of his surfboard and pressing up into a perfect toes-pointed handstand. Friendly and bright—a graduate of both Pennsylvania Military College and Clemson University—Velarde was popular with visiting surfers from California and Hawaii, and in 1963 became the first Latin American profiled in *Surfer* magazine. He was a consistent finalist throughout the '60s in the big-wave division of the Peru International. He also competed in the World Surfing Championships in 1964, 1965, 1966, and 1972. Carlos Velarde, Hector's older brother, was also a top Peruvian rider in the '60s.

Velzy, Dale Swaggering, innovative surfboard designer, builder, and retailer from Hermosa Beach, California, best known for creating the "pig" in 1955, a wide-hipped board that became a prototype for today's longboard. "Dale could out-drink, out-shoot, out-ride, out-shape, out-sell and out-finesse all comers," the *Surfer's Journal* magazine wrote in 1994. "And he made it all up as he went along." Velzy was born (1927) and raised in Hermosa Beach, the son of a mechanic and the grandson of a woodworker who built cabinets for Teddy Roosevelt. He began surfing in 1936, started shaping the following year, and was soon making balsa/redwood laminate surfboards for

Dale Velzy

himself and his friends beneath the Hermosa Pier. He's sometimes credited as the first surfer to hang ten. After working as a teenaged Merchant Marine during and just after World War II, Velzy began to shape boards commercially, first in Manhattan Beach (1949–50), where he opened Velzy Surfboards, regarded by some as the world's first surf shop; then Hawaii (1950–51) and Malibu (1953). Velzy teamed up with fellow board-maker Hap Jacobs in 1954 to open Velzy-Jacobs Surfboards in Venice Beach; four years later he opened a second Velzy-Jacobs shop in San Clemente, and before the decade was out he'd opened branches in San Diego, Newport Beach, Hermosa, and Honolulu.

Postwar shapers Bob Simmons, Joe Quigg, and Matt Kivlin, all from Southern California, had already made big improvements on the lumbering plank boards while Velzy was still a teenager—Simmons with his easy-to-ride "spoon" design, Quigg and Kivlin with the lighter Malibu chip boards. Velzy's balsa-constructed pig model—which dropped the board's wide point back toward the tail, further improving maneuverability—was another key step in surfboard design evolution. "It changed the sport," Quigg later said. "Suddenly you had thousands of

these kids out there riding pigs. There was a time when you couldn't even sell a board in California unless it looked like a Velzy." Other Velzy designs, including the Bump, the 7-11, the Banjo, and the Wedge, were valid to one degree or another, but brought little or no lasting change to the surfboard design field. His streamlined paddleboards were highly prized in the '80s and '90s.

Velzy was the undisputed king of surf retail in the mid- and late '50s. He had a skilled team of shapers assisting him in production and top-name surfers riding his boards, including Mickey Dora, Donald Takayama, Mike Doyle, Dewey Weber, and Mickey Muñoz. Velzy played the roll of surf world magnate, smoking enormous Cuban cigars and driving from shop to shop in a gull-wing Mercedes. In 1958 he bought a new camera for a young filmmaker named Bruce Brown, and paid his living and travel expenses for a year while he made his first surf film, *Slippery When Wet*; five years later Brown began shooting his surf classic *The Endless Summer*. Velzy's carefree accounting style caught up with him in 1959, however, and his shops were padlocked shut by the IRS. He opened Dale Surfboards in Newport Beach in 1962, but sold the business four years later and moved to Arizona. He returned to Southern California in 1970 and began freelance shaping, and was still going in 2003, primarily making collectible wooden boards and custom paddleboards.

Velzy was inducted into the *International Surfing* Magazine Hall of Fame in 1967 and the Huntington Beach Surfing Walk of Fame in 1997. Bear, the shop owner and board-making guru in Warner Brothers' 1978 surf movie *Big Wednesday,* is based on Velzy; Velzyland, a favorite high-performance wave on the North Shore of Oahu, is named in his honor. He lives in San Clemente, has been married twice, and has two children. *See also* chip, hang ten, Malibu board, paddleboarding, pig board, surfboard shop.

Velzyland   Small but feisty high-performance wave located at the far east end of the North Shore of Oahu in Hawaii; a two-way break, but generally known as a right. Velzyland requires a west swell, and breaks best from three to five foot. Bigger waves fold over on an outer reef, roll shoreward, and sometimes reform just prior to hitting the proper Velzyland reef. The rights are fairly short, but often wedge up in to create perfectly formed tubes, sometimes twice on the same wave; the lefts are longer but softer. Velzyland's jagged and notched reef is the sharpest of any break on the North Shore, and riders who fumble a tube section often surface with long red scratches and welts across their backs, shoulders, knees, elbows, hands, and feet. "For a hot-dog spot," as longboard ace Herbie Fletcher noted in 1974, "it's a wave with a lot of consequence." Velzyland has also been regarded since the late '60s as a hard-core locals break, and unwelcoming to visiting *haole* (white) surfers.

Velzyland was first ridden in late 1958, when surf moviemaker Bruce Brown and a small group of fellow Californians were in Hawaii shooting for *Slippery When Wet,* Brown's debut film. While out at Sunset Point one morning, they noticed a likely-looking peak to the east. Two weeks later, Brown filmed Dewey Weber and Kemp Aaberg dueling at the new break; Brown named it "Velzyland" in honor of California surfboard manufacturer and *Slippery When Wet* sponsor Dale Velzy. "Disneyland was the big new thing then," Weber later recalled. "And this place had much better rides than Disneyland, so we called it Velzyland."

Velzyland has been featured in more than a dozen surf movies and videos including *Walk on the Wet Side* (1963), *Cosmic Children* (1970), *Totally Committed* (1984), and *TV Dinners* (1995). The 1975 Lightning Bolt Pro, worth $5,000 and won by Australian Terry Fitzgerald, was the first and only professional contest held at Velzyland; fewer than a half-dozen amateur contests have been staged there since the mid-'80s. *See also* North Shore.

Venezuela   Oil-rich tropical country on the northern coast of South America, bordered by Colombia, Guyana, and Brazil. The majority of Venezuela's 1,750-mile coastline faces north into the Caribbean Sea, with some Atlantic waters to the east. While the country's biggest and most consistent surf is found along the Atlantic, most surf breaks in this lightly inhabited area remain uncharted. Venezuelan surfing is centered around the reefs and points near the capital city of Caracas; La Pulga, a fast, tubing Caracas beachbreak, is one of the country's most popular surf spots; Cuyagua and La Punta de Los Caracas are generally regarded as Venezuela's two best waves. There are also several breaks located on the small nearshore islands, including Margarita Island, a popular tourist destination. Venezuela's coastal climate is warm and humid all year, with air temperatures averaging 80 degrees and water temperatures generally in the upper 70s. The best waves arrive from December to April, although incoming swells from Atlantic nor'easters

lose power as they're filtered through the West Indies, and are slowed by Venezuela's continental shelf. Powerful hurricane swells occasionally hit between August and September; rarely, however, does the Venezuelan surf exceed eight foot.

Surfing was introduced to Venezuela in 1965, when central coast native Rodrigo Octavio began using a surfboard left behind by a visiting American cousin. Valencia resident Oswaldo Lebrum meanwhile began surfing on the northern beach of Patanemo, while Antonio Ruiz got things started near Caracas. The first Venezuelan Surfing Championships were held in 1967 in Caracas, organized by the just-formed Venezuelan Surfing Association, and the following year saw the opening of Surftique, the country's first surf shop. Venezuela surfers began competing in the World Amateur Surfing Championships in 1968; the country was a founding member of the 1993-formed Pan-American Surfing Association, and has twice been the host (in 1993 and 2002) of the biannual Pan-American Surfing Games. The Venezuela national team won the 2002 event. The Venezuelan Surfing Federation, founded in 1999, is currently the nationwide governing body for competitive surfing. Native surfer Augustin Cabrera competed in the 1998 Reef Big-Wave World Championships, held at Todos Santos, Mexico; other top pros include Pedro Rangel, Justin Mújica, and Magnum Martinez. As with South American country Peru, surfing in Venezuela is practiced for the most part by the upper class.

As of 2003, Venezuela was home to about 50 surf shops (many on the verge of closing due to nationwide economic woes), 25,000 surfers (up from 1,000 surfers in 1992), and three surf magazines (*Xtremo, Al Maximo,* and *Session*).

Ventures, The   Durable surf band from Tacoma, Washington; formed in 1959 by guitarists Bob Bogle and Don Wilson and described by *Rolling Stone* as the "first, best, most lasting, and influential of instrumental guitar-based rock combos." The original Ventures' demo, a twangy pre-surf-sound cover of jazz guitarist Johnny Smith's "Walk Don't Run," was a #2 hit in 1960, and was followed by a string of hot-selling albums and singles, including a surfed-up version of "Walk Don't Run" in 1964 and the theme to the hit TV show *Hawaii Five-O* in 1969. The group also released a first-of-its-kind instructional album, *Play Guitar with the Ventures,* which went to #9 in 1965. The Ventures have written more than 1,000 original songs, recorded more than 3,000 songs, and released over 250 albums. In their early '60s prime, the band made four to six albums a year, and at one point had five albums in the Billboard top 100. They were even bigger in Japan—as an instrumental band, they had no language barrier to overcome—where they sold 40 million of their career 90 million albums, and became the first foreign members of the Japan Conservatory of Music. The Ventures are the best-selling instrumental group in history. Nearly a dozen musicians have played in the Ventures over the years; as of 2002 the group was still performing live. *See also* surf music.

Victoria   Rugged Australian state located on the continent's southeast tip, with an 800-mile coastline flanked to the west by the Southern Ocean and to the east by the Tasman Sea; home to dozens of excellent cold-water surf breaks, including venerable Bells Beach, as well as the surf industry town of Torquay. Victoria can be divided into four main surfing areas: 1) The southeast coast, filled with dozens of broad and largely unpopulated beachbreaks, where the surf rarely gets over four foot, but is often well-shaped. 2) Phillip Island, the rocky and windswept island just south of state capital Melbourne, is home to the thumping right tubes of Express Point, and is often visited by day-tripping city surfers. 3) The Torquay area, southwest of the capital on the state-designated "Surf Coast," is filled with high-quality reefbreaks, including the long right walls of Bells Beach and Winkipop. 4) The southwest coast, from Cape Otway to the South Australian border, still regarded in 2003 as more or less a surfing outback, is home to some of the biggest ridable waves in the country, including the notorious right-breaking Easter Reef, which has been ridden at 20-foot-plus. Victoria's biggest and best surf arrives from March through October, in response to winter storms tracking across the fabled Roaring 40s region; driving wind and rain, however, frequently put the surf out of commission during this time. Average daytime air temperatures in Victoria range from the low 70s (summer) to the mid-50s (winter); water temperatures peak in the mid-60s and drop to the mid-50s. Surfing hazards include sharks, reefs, and cold water; isolation and lack of medical facilities can be a problem in the southwest.

Surfing was introduced to Victoria in 1919, when Geelong property developer Lou Whyte returned from a visit to Honolulu with four redwood surfboards, but the sport was slow to catch on. The year

Victoria reef surf

1946 brought the formation of the Torquay Surf Club, formed by locals Charles "China" Gilbert and Vic Tantau; the number of local surfers shot up after the introduction in 1956 of the easy-to-handle balsa-core Malibu board. Top Victoria riders by the end of the decade included world surf explorer Peter Troy and George "Ming" Smith, cofounders in 1958 of the Bells Boardriders Club. Torquay in the '50s and '60s was later described by Australian surf journalist Tim Baker as a "lawless town, where a crazy crew of young surfers could live and surf and do as they chose," but by 1969 it was already being reformed as a surf industry hub. Doug "Claw" Warbrick opened Victoria's first surf shop in 1963 in Torquay, and six years later formed Rip Curl Wetsuits; local surfers Alan Green and John Law formed the Torquay-based Quiksilver in 1973.

The first Victoria State Surfing Championships were held in 1964 at Bells. Victoria hosted the Australian National Titles in 1967, 1971, 1976, 1981, 1986, and 1992, as well as the 1970 World Championships. The 1963-founded Surfing Victoria meanwhile held regional and statewide contests; today the organization schedules more than 25 statewide pro and amateur events each year.

Despite an abundance of first-rate surf breaks and a healthy surf industry, Victoria is home to just a handful of internationally recognized surfers, including Wayne Lynch, the elastic goofyfooter who reinvented high-performance surfing during the late-'60s shortboard revolution, and five-time national champion Gail Couper. The Victorian surf (mainly Bells) has been featured in dozens of surf films and videos over the years, including *The Endless Summer* (1967), *Free Ride* (1977), and *Litmus* (1997). Victoria surf breaks are described in detail in *A Guide to the Surf Beaches of Victoria* (1987), *Surfing and Sailboarding Guide to Australia* (1993), *Surfinder Victoria* (1995), *Mark Warren's Atlas of Australian Surfing* (1998), *Surfing Australia* (1998), and *The World Stormrider Guide* (2001). As of 2003, there were roughly 100 surf shops and 20,000 surfers in Victoria. Surfworld, the world's biggest surfing museum, opened in Torquay in 1994, and is home to the Australian Surfing Hall of Fame. *See also* Bells Beach, Rip Curl Pro, Torquay.

Vietnam Vietnam extends in an S shape roughly 1,000 miles south from China to the Gulf of Thailand, and is bordered to the east by the South China Sea. While good surf is a rarity along most of Vietnam's tropical jungle-lined shore, the smaller continental shelf along the bulging central coast allows for bigger waves there than in the northern and southern portions of the country. The central Vietnamese coastline is filled with white-sand beaches, coral reefs, and rocky points, some of which produce well-shaped waves. The surf is often flat for weeks at a time, but the winter and summer monsoons often produce two-to-four-foot surf, and the typhoon season (particularly August and September) can create waves up to eight feet. Average daytime air temperatures in Vietnam range from 85 (summer) to 65 (winter); water temperatures range from the mid-70s to the low 80s.

Surfing was introduced to Vietnam in the mid-'60s by American and Australian troops serving in the Vietnam War. "The price for delivery on three boards was six cases of Chivas Scotch," an American serviceman later recalled, describing how he bribed a cargo pilot into shipping over a Weber Performer and two Jacobs noseriders. Soldiers created informal surf organizations (including the China Beach Surf Club and the Allied Surf Association of the South China Sea), ran small military surf contests, and even began making boards out of a military-subsidized plywood shack in Da Nang. Surfers on the coastal front lines allegedly made deals with local North Vietnamese soldiers: wave-riding privileges in exchange for a cease-fire during daylight hours. Tens of thousands of American surfers received Vietnam-related military draft notices in the '60s and early '70s; some served (big-wave rider Roger Erickson, for example), some

managed exemptions or permanent deferments (three-time Duke Kahanamoku Classic winner Jeff Hakman), and some left the country or went underground (U.S. champion Mark Martinson). Surfing during the Vietnam War was depicted in the 1979 movie *Apocalypse Now,* with a wave-crazed Robert Duvall, as Colonel Kilgore, ordering a napalm attack on a coastal village so that his troops could ride a nearby pointbreak. Told the area was held by "Charlie"— short for "Victor Charles," or Vietcong—Kilgore famously barked out, "Charlie don't surf!" Surfing was also shown on *China Beach,* the ABC war-drama series that ran from 1988 to 1991. *Surfing to Saigon,* a memoir by Santa Cruz surfer Pat Farley, is for the most part set in Vietnam.

A group of southern California teenage surfers visited Vietnam in 1993 on a goodwill expedition, and later that year a minor international pro contest was held at Non Nuc Beach, located a few miles south of China Beach. As of 2002, there were fewer than two dozen local wave-riders, all living in or around Da Nang. *See also* war and surfing.

violence and surfing Surfing has justly been described as meditative, even spiritual, but it also has a violent streak that goes back to the sport's very origins. Hawaiian legend tells of a handsome surfer at Waikiki who was nearly executed after riding the same wave as a high-ranking chieftess. In another incident, a prince whose board glanced off another rider during a surfing competition was later eviscerated on a stone alter as punishment. Surfing violence in modern times almost always has been the result of turf-protecting localism, overcrowding, or competition. (The mid-'60s beachside riots between "surfies" and "rockers" in Sydney, Australia, were a notable exception.) California surfers visiting Hawaii as far back as the 1940s were often challenged to fight. Californians in turn popularized localism in the late '60s as a way of keeping outsiders at bay; nonlocals were abused verbally and sometimes physically, but the most popular tactics were to smash visitors' car windows and/or puncture their tires. Localism-related violence made statewide headlines in the '90s and early '00s when surfers from Oxnard, Palos Verdes, and San Francisco were charged in separate incidences with beating up nonlocal surfers.

Intensely crowded lineups can also produce violent acts, particularly when one surfer interferes with another surfer's wave by "dropping in." Threats and

Violence and surfing; early 1970s California beach fight

shouting matches are common, but the aggrieved rider on occasion will paddle up to the drop-in surfer and simply begin punching. Even more dangerous, the trailing surfer might kick his board at the drop-in surfer.

Memorable acts of surfing violence are often associated with surfing competition. After boasting about his country's performance during the 1975–76 pro contest season on the North Shore of Oahu, Australian surfer and future world champion Wayne "Rabbit" Bartholomew returned to Hawaii in late 1976 and was immediately beaten up—losing two of his front teeth—at Sunset Beach. On the final day of the 1994 World Longboard Championships at Malibu, a noncompeting surfer who refused to leave the water area was assaulted by two men associated with the event; the noncompetitor was hospitalized with head trauma, facial cuts, and a separated shoulder, and felony charges were brought against the two attackers. Adding a gender twist to surf violence, pro surfer Lynette MacKenzie was fined and suspended from the world tour after a 1999 brawl with a fellow competitor.

Implied violence has meanwhile been used as a surf industry marketing tool, particularly in the '90s, as younger surfers brought inner-city street-style elements to the sport. In ads for Bad Boy Club beachwear, thuggish Hawaiian pro surfer Johnny-Boy Gomes was often featured scowling malevolently or raising a clenched fist. (Gomes earned a reputation as the sport's most violent high-profile surfer; he was fined in 1991 after punching a fellow competitor during a pro event, and in 1999 he was convicted of assault after breaking a surfer's nose during an argu-

ment in the water.) Surf-based fiction also has a penchant for violence—deadly at times—from Eugene Burdick's grim 1956 novel *The Ninth Wave* to Kem Nunn's 1997 noir thriller *The Dogs of Winter*.

Surfing's most infamous act of violence took place in March 2000, when 1966 world champion Nat Young of Australia was savagely beaten while surfing in front of his house at Angourie Point, New South Wales. Young got into a yelling match with an 18-year-old surfer, then hit him, at which point the teenager's father jumped Young, breaking both his eye sockets and his cheekbones, and damaging his sinuses. The incident provoked dozens of mainstream press articles on "surf rage," and prompted Young to write a book of the same title. Some felt the issue was being sensationalized. "We're not an inherently violent group," surf journalist Sam George wrote, "and that's what makes incidents like Nat's beating so notorious." *See also* the Hui, localism, Palos Verdes, surf rage.

Virginia   Virginia is held in slight regard as a surf destination, despite the fact that it's the birthplace of East Coast surfing and home to a full register of talented wave-riders, as well as the time-honored East Coast Surfing Championships. "The best spot in Virginia," as resident pro surfer and surf journalist Jason Borte wrote in 1996, "is the Outer Banks of North Carolina." Virginia's 112-mile coast is divided by the mouth of the Chesapeake Bay into two distinct regions. To the north is the island- and inlet-filled Accomack-Northhampton coast, for the most part undeveloped, accessible only by boat, and rarely surfed. While more than 15 breaks are mapped out from near the southern edge of the Chesapeake down to the North Carolina border, surfing in Virginia essentially begins and ends in the resort town of Virginia Beach, at First Street Jetty—a sandbar break in front of a hotel-crammed beachfront that for the most part offers soft and easy right-breaking waves. Virginia is the only state in the nation with a mandatory surf leash law, and board-surfing is prohibited during most daylight hours everywhere except at First Street, which often becomes, as *Surfer* magazine described it, "a two-block surfing insane asylum." The warm and dry months of late summer and early fall generally bring the best surf to Virginia, in response to hurricanes tracking up through the North Atlantic. Winter waves are stronger, but cold and usually less groomed; spring surf is cold and inconsistent; summer waves are small to flat. Daytime air temperatures in Virginia during winter can drop into the 20s, with water temperature in the low 40s. Summer air temperatures often hit 90 or higher, and while the water usually remains chilly until June, it warms to the mid-70s by August.

"Wave shooting" in dories and canoes was practiced in Virginia Beach as far back as 1910; two years later, Virginia Beach resident James Jordon returned from Hawaii with a nine-foot redwood surfboard, which he put to use immediately. Additional boards were imported during the 1910s and '20s; by the early '30s, local surfers (including John Smith, Dusty Hinnant, Babe Braithwaite, and Bob Holland Sr.) were given work as beachfront lifeguards, and later began making hollow surf-rescue paddleboards, which doubled as surfboards. When summer resort season was over, the Virginia Beach surfers would load up their boards and drive south to Miami, stopping frequently along the way to give surfing demonstrations. In 1935, the East Coast's first surfboard paddle race was held on a 14-mile south-to-north course across the mouth of the Chesapeake. In the mid- and late '50s, local surfer Scott Taylor imported a dozen balsa/fiberglass boards from California; in 1962, Bob Holland Jr. and Pete Smith opened Smith and Holland Surf Shop, the first shop of its kind in the state, on 19th Street in Virginia Beach. Holland would be a finalist in regional and national amateur surfing contests for the next five decades. Wave Riding Vehicles, founded by Virginia Beach surfer Bob White, opened in 1967 and went on to become one of the East Coast's leading board manufacturers.

The Virginia Beach Surfing Festival made its debut in 1964; the following year it was renamed the East Coast Surfing Championships, and the midsummer competition has run annually since then. Jimmy "Jimbo" Brothers was the first Virginia surfer to attract national surf world attention, when *Surfing* magazine in 1966 published a short profile on the 10-year-old up-and-comer. Virginia Beach surfer Wes Laine turned professional in 1979, was world-ranked #9 in 1983 and 1985, and has long been an East Coast surfing icon. Chris Culpen and Jason Borte are among the small number of Virginia surfers of the post-Laine era who performed well on the regional or domestic pro scene.

By 2003, there were nine surf shops in Virginia and roughly 12,000 surfers, most of whom frequently make the two-hour drive south to North Carolina's Outer Banks. Virginia has been featured in a tiny number of surf films and videos, including *Summer of '67* and *The Wrong Side* (2001). The Virginia Beach surf is detailed in *The Stormrider Guide North America* (2002).

Virostko, Darryl "Flea"   Hard-charging, rough-talking surfer from Santa Cruz, California; winner of the Quiksilver Men Who Ride Mountains big-wave contest at Maverick's in 1999 and 2000. Virostko was born (1971) and raised in Santa Cruz, the son of a landscaper father and a nurse/Jazzercise instructor mother, and began surfing at age four. The adolescent Virostko was nicknamed "Flea" for being small and feisty; he was also a bantering presence at Steamer Lane, Santa Cruz's best-known surf break, and by the early '90s he'd become a local sensation for his small-wave aerial maneuvers. He rode Maverick's for the first time—high on acid, he later said—in 1991.

A diehard member of Santa Cruz's loud and frequently vulgar West Side contingent, Virostko spoke about his hometown with fellow aerialist and big-wave surfer Shawn "Barney" Barron for a 1996 *Surfer* magazine article, talking disparagingly about "snippers" and "lip dodgers" (play-it-safe surfers), "trannies" (U.C. Santa Cruz surfers, primarily transplants from other areas), and "dirts" (Grateful Dead fans who hung out in the Steamer Lane parking lot; "When the northwest winds are blowing," Virostko noted, "the patchouli smell is so bad...").

Virostko showed up for the first Quiksilver/Maverick's contest in 1999 with his newly bleached hair covered in black polka dots; he successfully air-dropped a takeoff on one of the day's biggest waves—a 20-footer—was briefly tubed on the inside section, received an event-high score of 98, and took the $15,000 winner's check. The surf was bigger for the follow-up Quiksilver/Maverick's contest, and the small-framed (5'9", 150 pounds) and asthmatic Virostko was even sharper and more aggressive than he had been the year before, beating six-time world champion Kelly Slater in the final and earning $30,000. He meanwhile continued to feed colorful quotes to the surf press. Looking earnestly into the camera while taping a segment of *Great Waves,* an Outdoor Life Network cable TV series, Virostko noted that a recent fight to the surface after a long Maverick's wipeout was "like trying to do a sit-up with a fat chick sitting on my face." Some regarded him as a prime example of ongoing surf culture decay, while others cheered him as authentic and unfiltered, a "real" surfer, compared to the often-bland world tour pros. A 2002 *Vanity Fair* article on big-wave surfing described the unmarried Virostko as the "Tommy Lee of surfing—strangely magnetic, smelling of beer and utterly careless." Asked about his big-wave training regime, he said, "I beat off a lot."

Virostko has appeared in more than 20 surf videos, including *Cheap Thrills* (1994), *Monstrosity* (1999), and *The Year of the Drag-In* (2000). He placed third in the 2000 Madeira Big-Wave World Championships. *See also* big-wave surfing, Maverick's, Quik-silver Maverick's Men Who Ride Mountains, Santa Cruz, Steamer Lane.

volume A surfboard's bulk or mass. A board described as having "lots of volume" is generally wide and thick, while a "low volume" board is narrow and thin. Because added volume creates more buoyancy and stability, it's a design feature favored by both heavier and beginning surfers. "Defining the correct volume," says board-maker Dave Parmenter, "should be the single most important aspect of building a board for a new customer." *See also* foil, rocker.

W

Wahine magazine The first women's surf magazine, published out of Long Beach, California, from 1995 to 2001. *Wahine* was founded by Marilyn Edwards, former triathlete and director of the speech and hearing clinic of Long Beach City College, and newspaper journalist Elizabeth Glazner. Edwards sold her vintage Porsche to cover print costs for the first edition of *Wahine,* and just six issues total were published from 1995 to 1997, before it became a quarterly in 1998. Women have always been primarily represented in the male-owned-and-operated surf press as sexed-up bikini chicks, so female surfers were thrilled to see page after page of women-only contest, travel, and history features in *Wahine.* "Hooray!" an early letter to the editor began. "Finally a mag for the rest of us!" But at times *Wahine* seemed nearly as dedicated as other surf publications to the beach-babe ethic, filling a majority of pages, both advertising and editorial, with perfectly groomed nubile surfettes. Old school feminists meanwhile grimaced at *Wahine* columns such as "Beach Beauty," in which the editors pledged to "dig into the makeup bags of hardcore waterwomen to find out what beauty products they can't live without." *Wahine* circulation peaked at about 45,000 in 2001, but the magazine folded at the end of the year. Partly because of *Wahine*'s success, *Surfer* and *Surfing* soon began publishing ancillary women's surf magazines—*SurferGirl* and *Surfing Girl. See also* Elizabeth Glazner, surf magazines, women and surfing.

Waikiki Renowned beachfront area located on the south shore of Oahu, in the lee of Diamond Head, three miles southeast of downtown Honolulu; the sun-warmed birthplace of modern surfing, and the sport's most history-rich area. While maps define Waikiki Beach as a narrow strip of shoreline just a few hundred yards long, fronting an enormous wall of high-rise hotels, surfers generally think of Waikiki as extending over two miles from Diamond Head to the Ala Wai Yacht Harbor—an area containing more than 20 reefbreaks, including the churning left tubes at Ala Moana, the easy rollers at Canoes, and the high-performance rights at Queens. Waikiki (Hawaiian for "spouting water") breaks best from May to October, as Pacific Ocean storms to the south and southeast semiregularly produce three- to four-foot waves, and on occasion create surf up to eight foot or bigger, although in general the waves here are much smaller and less powerful than those that strike the North Shore of Oahu in winter. The tradewinds blow offshore at Waikiki so the waves are consistently smooth and well-groomed; the warm tropical air often carries a scent of plumeria, and the water temperature ranges from the mid- to upper-70s. Shallow reefs are a danger at a few breaks, but crowds are Waikiki's biggest surfing hazard.

Waikiki was second only to the Kona Coast on the Big Island of Hawaii as ancient Hawaii's most popular surfing area, and in centuries past a long ride at Kalehuawehe—Outside Castles—was thought of as the ultimate surfing experience. Romance was associated with Waikiki surfing from the beginning. Hawaiian legend tells of a handsome local surfer, enticed by a chiefess to ride alongside her at a Waikiki break reserved for royalty, who was nearly executed by the ruling chief, saving himself only after he was able to skewer 400 rats with a single arrow shot. Under the influence of visiting Calvinist missionaries, surfing in Hawaii was nearly extinguished during the 19th century. The sport's renaissance in the early decades of the 20th century was staged at Waikiki, led by Olympic gold medal swimmer and lifelong surfer Duke Kahanamoku, along with Irish-Hawaiian surfer George Freeth. Waikiki and surfing were almost synonymous prior to World War II: the gentle-rolling waves were perfectly suited to the era's heavy wooden surfboards, and Diamond Head made an ideal backdrop for the hundreds of black-and-white surfing photos used on postcards and published in general interest magazines including *Collier's, Sunset,* and *National Geographic.* Waikiki surfing also had a tireless

Waikiki; early 20th century

patron in Alexander Hume Ford, the South Carolina–born journalist/promoter who founded the Outrigger Canoe Club (surfing's first organized group), and convinced Jack London to write an article on the new sport. "That's what it is, a royal sport for the natural kings of earth," London wrote in his 1907 article for the *Woman's Home Companion,* after trying the Waikiki surf for himself, where the waves, he said in typically ornate style, were "bull-mouthed monsters . . . a mile long, with smoking crests."

Freeth left Waikiki and introduced Southern California to surfing in 1907; Kahanamoku, a few years later, became the sport's greatest emissary and representative, giving wave-riding demonstrations in California, New Jersey, New York, Australia, and New Zealand. Meanwhile, the rakish Waikiki beachboys—a group of natives loosely affiliated with the hotels, most of whom passed easily back and forth from surf instructor to entertainer to gigolo—were coming into their glory as Waikiki became America's first and most popular tropical vacation area. Waikiki was the home base for *haole* (white) surfers John Kelly and Wally Froiseth, who invented the streamlined "hot curl" board in 1937 and went on to become the first dedicated big-wave riders. Although Waikiki was no longer viewed as the center of the surfing universe by midcentury (Southern California was the sport's industrial hub; the North Shore of Oahu was the new high-performance arena), it remained the headwater of Hawaiian surfing talent from the '40s to the '70s, producing first-rate surfers like Albert "Rabbit" Kekai, George Downing, Conrad Canha, Paul Strauch, Fred

Hemmings, Joey Hamasaki, Joey Cabell, Reno Abellira, Gerry Lopez, Barry Kanaiaupuni, Larry Bertlemann, Dane Kealoha, Montgomery "Buttons" Kaluhiokalani, and Mark Foo. Favorite Waikiki breaks, along with those previously listed, include Number Threes, Kaisers, and Populars.

Hundreds of amateur surf contests have been held in Waikiki over the decades, including dozens of state titles, as well as the United States Championships in 1976, 1992, and 1996. A small number of regional and national pro meets have been held here as well. Surfing was filmed for the first time in 1906 at Waikiki; it was also featured in a small number of Hollywood features over the next four decades, including *Bird of Paradise* (1932) with Dolores Del Rio and *Waikiki Wedding* (1937) with Bing Crosby. *Hawaiian Surf Movies* (1954), the first surfing film, made by Californian Bud Browne, was shot almost exclusively at Waikiki; most surf movies of the '50s and early '60s included Waikiki footage. The area's waves, surfers, and history are looked at in detail in dozens of books, including *Hawaiian Surfriders* (1935), *Surfing Hawaii* (1972), *Surfing: The Ultimate Pleasure* (1984), and *Waikiki Beachboy* (1989). *See also* Ala Moana, beachboys, Hui Nalu Club, Duke Kahanamoku, Outrigger Canoe Club.

Waimea Bay   Hallowed big-wave break located on the North Shore of Oahu, Hawaii; big-wave surfing's main stage from the late 1950s to the early '90s. The Waimea season usually lasts from late fall to early spring, in response to swells produced by big North Pacific storms. Waves begin to fringe on the Waimea reef at about 10 or 12 feet, but regulars don't think of it as "real" until it's 15 feet, and some won't bother until it's at least 18 feet. Waves 30 feet or bigger are unridable as they closeout across the channel. (Pinballs, a mediocre right-breaking wave located inside of the regular Waimea takeoff area, is ridden from four to eight foot; the cataclysmic Waimea shorebreak closeouts are popular with bodysurfers and bodyboarders.) Waimea hits peak form between five and 10 times on an average season. The character of the wave changes slightly with the direction of the incoming surf—north swells create an easier takeoff and longer wave; west swells are steeper and shorter, but in general the ride is straightforward: a huge drop, often made at an angle, followed by a bottom turn, and a beeline race for the adjacent deep-water channel. Although Waimea has long been dismissed by some as "just a drop"—big-wave bulldog Buzzy Trent once described the break as "a mirage; now you see it, now you don't"—this near-vertical plunge from crest to trough is in fact one of the sport's greatest challenges, testing the surfer's equipment, wave judgment, physical fitness, and nerves. The drop will often "jack" (steepen and expand) without warning as the wave begins to curl, a phenomenon that can actually reverse the surfer's forward motion and send him back up toward the crest—and then to an annihilating wipeout. "On a 25-footer," Hawaii's Darrick Doerner said of Waimea in 1989, "it's a complete blur; you're going totally on instinct." Rides here usually last about 10 seconds.

Some historians believe that Waimea was surfed by ancient Hawaiians, but evidence is slight. Waimea made a disturbing entry onto the modern surf scene in 1943, as Honolulu surfers Woody Brown and Dickie Cross, after getting caught outside at nearby Sunset Beach on a fast-riding swell, were forced to paddle three miles down the coast to Waimea, where they hoped to come ashore through the channel. But the channel was closed out. Cross drowned in the still-rising 30-foot surf; Brown washed up on the beach unconscious. The incident helped keep surfers away from Waimea until 1957, when Greg Noll of California led a small group into the lineup on a 15-foot day, while surf moviemaker Bud Browne filmed from the shore. *The Big Surf,* released by Browne a few months later, introduced Waimea to thousands of American and Australian wave-riders, and for more than 10 years the break was a media sensation, featured in general interest magazine articles (including *Life* and the *Saturday Evening Post*), surf magazine covers, surf movies, and posters. Columbia Pictures' 1964 action-comedy *Ride the Wild Surf,* starring Fabian and Barbara Eden, finished with a Waimea Bay showdown. Top Waimea riders of the late '50s and '60s included Noll, Peter Cole, Pat Curren (maker of the finest Waimea gun boards), Buzzy Trent, and Ricky Grigg.

Although Waimea was overlooked somewhat during the '70s and early '80s, as tuberiding and high-performance small-wave surfing came to the fore, it nonetheless hosted a small number of professional surf contests, including the Duke Kahanamoku Classic in 1973, 1975, and 1980. The most spectacular Waimea event was the 1974 Smirnoff Pro, held in stunning 30-foot surf, and won by Hawaii's Reno Abellira. Hawaii's Eddie Aikau was then regarded as

Waimea Bay

Waimea's top performer; in 1977, James Jones became the first to ride inside the tube at Waimea. A mid-'80s resurgence in big-wave surfing was helped along by the Billabong Pro, held in part at Waimea in 1985 and 1986. The Quiksilver in Memory of Eddie Aikau made its Waimea debut in 1986—nine years after Aikau died in a boating accident—and was won by Clyde Aikau, Eddie's younger brother. The Quiksilver event returned in 1990, 1999, 2001, and 2002. Premier Waimea riders in the '80s and '90s included Mark Foo, Michael Ho, Darrick Doerner, Ken Bradshaw, Brock Little, Richard Schmidt, Ross Clarke-Jones, Shane Dorian, and Noah Johnson.

Waimea's big-wave dominance was undone in the early '90s, with the introduction of Maverick's in northern California (which broke more often than Waimea) and Jaws in Maui (where machine-aided tow-in surfing allowed riders access to waves bigger than anything available at Waimea). But if Waimea was no longer the last word in big-wave surfing, and was sometimes ridiculed for the crowds of neophyte big-wave riders it attracted, it was still respected and feared; its hoary reputation as a deadly break was justified in 1996 when 25-year-old semipro surfer Donnie Soloman of Ventura, California, drowned there after trying to paddle through a big set wave. "At Pipeline, it's white when you're underwater, and at Sunset it's gray," Hawaii's Dennis Pang said in 1990, comparing the terrifying Waimea wipeout to two other famous North Shore breaks. "Waimea is black."

"Waimea" means "reddish water"; the name comes from the combination of mud and silt that flows in from the nearby river valley during winter storms. Waimea has been featured in more than

75 surf movies and videos since the late '50s, including *The Big Surf* (1958), *Cavalcade of Surf* (1962), *The Endless Summer* (1966), *Golden Breed* (1968), *Going Surfin'* (1973), *Tales of the Seven Seas* (1981), *Amazing Surf Stories* (1986), *Surfers: The Movie* (1990), *Red Water* (1998), and *XXL* (2001). In 1998, Waimea was featured in *Great Waves,* an Outdoor Life Network documentary series; Waimea's surfing history is detailed in *Maverick's: The Story of Big-Wave Surfing* (2000). *See also* Eddie Aikau, big-wave surfing, North Shore, Quiksilver in Memory of Eddie Aikau, Smirnoff Pro.

wake surfing, wakeboarding Originally a surf world novelty in which a surfer rode the small but endless curling wave formed behind a moving boat; later an acrobatic hybrid sport blending freestyle waterskiing and snowboarding. Although wake surfing dates back to at least 1915, when pioneering surfer Duke Kahanamoku of Hawaii rode behind a boat in San Diego's Coronado Bay, it didn't really catch on until 1963, when Floridian Dick Pope began towing surfers behind his motorboat. The ride began with the surfer holding a shortened water-ski rope; after slotting into one of the two wake waves peeling off the stern, the rider dropped the rope, and "surfed" until done in by boredom, leg cramps, a misstep, or an empty gas tank. In 1965, California surfboard-manufacturing magnate Hobie Alter wake-surfed 30 miles from Long Beach to Catalina Island in just over one hour and 45 minutes. The surf industry had high hopes for wake surfing, envisioning, as one surf journalist put it, that "millions of people on lakes and rivers will soon discover the incomparable joy of surfing." A wakeboarding shot was used on the cover of *Petersen's Surfing* magazine in 1964; specialized wake-riding surfboards were designed and built; and Alter, in conjunction with Johnson Outboard Motors, toured the country in an attempt to sell the new sport to landlocked America. But wake surfing, also known as "freeboarding," never caught on.

In 1985, California surfer Tony Finn invented the Skurfer, a shorter, narrow version of a surfboard, with footstraps. Skurfers held the towrope continuously, carved turns off to either side of the boat like water-skiers, and utilized the wake primarily as a ramp for high-flying aerial maneuvers. In 1990, the first Skurfer championships were televised on ESPN. Washington water-ski manufacturer Herb O'Brien meanwhile began making his compression-molded Hyperlite model wakeboards (later versions had a

small fin on either end and could be ridden in either direction), while Texan Jimmy Redmon founded the World Wakeboarding Association. The first professional wakeboarding events were held in 1992, and *WakeBoarding* magazine was launched the following year. In 1996, when wakeboarding was included in the debut X-Games, the *New York Times* reported that more than 1.3 million wakeboards had been sold worldwide.

Wales Drizzly, wind-lashed peninsular region of the United Kingdom; bordered by England and the North Atlantic. The Welsh coastline is full of high cliffs, headlands, small sheltered coves, reefs, and sandy beaches, and can be divided into four main surf regions: 1) The industrialized Severn Estuary, separated from England by the Bristol Channel and dependent on the biggest winter swells for ridable waves. 2) The Gower Peninsula, Welsh surfing headquarters and home of most of the area's best waves and best surfers. 3) The remote and largely undeveloped Pembrokeshire area, full of empty point and reef surf. 4) The less-active northwest area, directly across St. George's Channel from Ireland. Surf in Wales is small to nonexistent during the mild summer months; from autumn to spring, Atlantic storms regularly send head-high waves into the Welsh coastline—not as big as those found on the premier beaches in England, Scotland, and Ireland, but well-shaped and with lots of variety. Winter surf is chilly, with air and water temperatures both usually in the upper 40s. Wave shape and form changes dramatically with the tide, which can climb or drop as much as 40 feet in six hours. The broad and beautiful Langland Bay, located near the city of Swansea, has long been the center of Welsh surfing.

Surfing was looked at as something of an oddity when it took root in Wales in the mid-'60s. "Among Welsh surfers," noted the *London Sunday Times* in 1966, "there are no T-shirts with surfboard slogans; no wild barbecues on the beach in the small hours; not a surfing song, even." The Welsh Surfing Federation was formed in 1973, and Crab Islands Surfboards, Wales' first surf shop, was founded two years later. Carwyn Williams, a gregarious and well-traveled surfer from the town of Mumbles, became the first Welshman to win a European surfing title, in 1983.

As of 2003, Wales was home to about a dozen surf shops and 1,500 surfers. Wales is featured in *Made in Britain,* a 2001 surf video; the Welsh surf is detailed in *The Stormrider Guide Europe* (1998) and *Surf U.K.* (2000).

walk the board   To walk across the deck of a surfboard; generally refers to a forward stroll using the cross-step method—one leg crossing the other with each set of steps; as compared to the crablike shuffle motion, with the surfer aiming to hang five or ten toes off the nose of the board. *See also* noseriding.

wall   A wave with little or no downward-sloping angle along the crest. Although a "walled up" or "walled off" wave is synonymous with a "closeout" and unsuitable for board-surfing, the expression "wall" can be used either as a designation for a closeout, or for a wave that appears to be a closeout, but in fact holds shape. Some of the world's best waves—including Laniakea, Rincon, and Jeffreys Bay—are described as having "long walls." *See also* closeout lined up.

war and surfing   Surfing was most directly affected by war during World War II. Six months after the bombing of Pearl Harbor in 1941, nearly all fighting-age surfers in America, Australia, and the territory of Hawaii had enlisted in the armed forces, "leaving the waves," as surf journalist John Grissim later wrote, "to a smattering of beachcombers, draft dodgers, kids, gentle vagabonds, and civilian locals who worked in defense-related jobs." Surfboard development came to a near standstill, and the 1928-founded Pacific Coast Surf Riding Championships, the sport's biggest competition, were canceled, never to return. Rationing forced those surfers who remained at home to pool their gas coupons in order to travel the coast in search of waves, while many beaches—including Malibu, Waikiki, and Bondi—were cordoned off with barbed wire as a defense against possible Japanese attack. Dozens of surfers (out of a global population of just a few thousand) were killed in battle.

Surfers returning from World War II immediately began constructing boards from new war-developed materials such as fiberglass and polyester resin; in the mid-'50s, board manufacturers began shaping boards from polyurethane foam, another war product. Surfers continued to enlist following World War II; filmmaker Bruce Brown (*The Endless Summer*), along with filmmaker/publisher John Severson (*Surfer* magazine) both launched their surf media careers while doing military service in Honolulu during the mid-'50s.

War and surfing, as depicted in 1979's *Apocalypse Now*

Surfers of the '60s and early '70s responded much differently to the Vietnam War than their predecessors had to World War II, with thousands dodging the draft and thousands more joining in Vietnam protest marches and rallies. The surf press had an antiwar slant in the late '60s, breaking from its long-standing political neutrality. A significant number of surfers, nonetheless, either volunteered or were drafted into military service (1967 Duke Kahanamoku Invitational winner Jock Sutherland was surfing's most conspicuous volunteer), and the American war effort, according to Hollywood film producer and screenwriter John Milius, was in large part shaped by "the forces of California culture," surfing included. Milius explored Vietnam's effect on surfers, and to a lesser degree the effect of surfers on Vietnam, in his screenplays for *Big Wednesday* (1978) and *Apocalypse Now* (1979). *Surfing to Saigon,* a memoir by Santa Cruz surfer Pat Farley, was published in 1994.

Surfing has often been described in tranquil phrases (*Surfer's Journal* publisher Steve Pezman has often referred to surfing as "a dance on a liquid stage"), but the sport's vernacular is in fact loaded with war metaphors: big-wave surfboards are commonly known as "guns"; surf magazine contest articles have titles like "The Day War Came to Malibu"; waves are often "charged," "attacked," and "destroyed"; extra big waves are "bombs," longboards are "tanks," and aggressive young wave-riders are "surf Nazis." Wayne Bartholomew of Australia, 1978 world champion, described himself as a "warrior" in his autobiography, viewed each world tour circuit as a "campaign," and during his annual season-finale plane flight from Sydney to Oahu liked to imagine himself as Hannibal crossing the Alps to destroy the Romans. Entering the water at Pipeline in Hawaii, Bartholomew said, was like "paddling into battle." *See also* Apocalypse Now, Vietnam.

Warbrick, Doug   Australian surf industrialist and cofounder, along with Brian Singer, of Torquay-based Rip Curl wetsuits. Warbrick began surfing in 1958 on Queensland's Gold Coast, and continued to ride when his family moved to the much colder state of Victoria the following year. In 1963 he opened Victoria's first surf shop. Rip Curl began in 1968 as a surfboard company; the wetsuit line followed in 1969. It was Warbrick, a confessed "surf contest junkie," who pushed hardest to get Rip Curl to sponsor the big annual Easter surfing contest at Bells Beach, and in 1973, with Rip Curl's backing, Bells became the country's first pro event. Warbrick was a judge during the 1970 World Surfing Championships, also held at Bells. He's been described as both garrulous and private. "Try to get him to talk about himself," surf journalist Derek Hynd wrote in 1994, "and he will talk about everything else." Warbrick was a finalist in the seniors division of the Australian National Titles in 1973, 1974, and 1976. *See also* Rip Curl, Rip Curl Pro, wetsuit.

Warren, Mark   Clean-cut, Australian pro surfer from Sydney's northern beaches; world-ranked #4 in 1976, and winner of the 1980 Duke Kahanamoku Classic. Warren was born (1952) in landlocked Gundagai, New South Wales, raised in the Narrabeen area, and began surfing at age 11. He was an Australian National Titles finalist in 1971, 1972, and 1974, before winning in 1976. A pro by then (few distinctions were made at the time between pro and amateur surfers), Warren also competed on the debut world circuit in 1976, winning the Smirnoff Pro in Hawaii, and finishing the year ranked fourth. He was an original member of the Bronzed Aussies, the strutting 1976-formed promotions troupe that included world champion Peter Townend and runner-up Ian Cairns; Warren left the group in 1978 claiming he was "just too much of an individual for a team concept." Always comfortable in bigger surf, Warren had some of his best pro results in the Duke contest, making the finals in 1977 and 1978, and winning in 1980,

when the event finished up at Waimea Bay. He never matched his first year-end world tour rating, finishing seventh in 1977, 24th in 1978, eighth in 1979, and 23rd in 1980.

Handsome, well-spoken, and often curt, Warren worked in other facets of the surf industry, both during and after his career as a touring pro: he produced and sold Mark Warren Surf Wax, wrote a column for the *Sunday Telegraph* newspaper, filed radio surf reports, and did network and local TV surf contest commentary, as well as on-site announcing at world tour events. His work as a commentator for the Australian version of *Wide World of Sports* took him to the 1988 Winter Olympics in Calgary, Canada. Warren also served as coach for the Australian national juniors team in the mid-'90s. Since 1997, he has worked in real estate.

Warren appeared in more than a dozen surf movies in the '70s and early '80s, including *Tracks* (1970), *A Sea for Yourself* (1973), *Fantasea* (1978), and *Wizards of the Water* (1982). His *Atlas of Australian Surfing* was published by HarperCollins in 1989, and revised in 1999. Warren is married and has two children, and lives in northeast Sydney's Avalon Beach. *See also* Bronzed Aussies, radio and surfing.

Washington   Washington's 230-mile rock-and-tree-lined coastline, often hit by forceful winter storms from the North Pacific, houses an assortment of temperamental surf breaks for a small, adventurous, insular surfing community. The state can be divided into two main surfing areas: 1) The weather-battered Pacific coast, with dozens of beachbreaks and rocky points, is best in fall and spring, and often overwhelmed by storms during winter. 2) The Strait of Juan de Fuca, a natural channel separating Washington and Canada's Vancouver Island, offers protected winter surf as huge swells filter down through the inland waterway. Because of the strait's narrow window to the Pacific, swells here are often short-lived. Washington is home to several Indian reservations and national parks, both of which can make access to several of the more remote breaks difficult and sometimes illegal. Westport, on Washington's south-central coast, is by far the state's most popular surfing area, and the south jetty at Westport's Westhaven State Park—a protected cove, easily accessed, with tubing sand-bottom peaks near a harbor jetty—is the area's best-known and most consistent surf break. Average daytime air temperatures in coastal Washington range from 65 in summer to 40 in winter; water temperatures range from the mid-60s to the low 40s. Heavy weather, sharks, and isolation are the primary Washington surf hazards. Washington surfers, meanwhile, tend to be closemouthed about their state, and can be cold, if rarely hostile, to outsiders.

Surfing came to Washington in the early '60s, as teenagers from Aberdeen and Olympia, during summer vacation gatherings, began riding the gentle waves at Point Grenville on the Quinault Indian Reservation. Ray Walters is often referred to as the "father of Washington surfing"; he prepared for his cold-water surf sessions with long-distance swims in Puget Sound. Other first-generation Washington surfers included Lee Evans and Tom McCobb from Aberdeen, and George South and Tom LeCompte from Westport. *Surfer* magazine introduced the Washington coast to its readers in 1969, describing "snow on the beach, 12 degree air temperatures, and big shaggy waves," and gloomily suggesting that the northwestern version of the sport might "inspire surfers preparing for the plague years." The Quinault tribe had meanwhile outlawed surfing at Point Grenville; by 1984 it was estimated there were only 30 surfers statewide. The Surf Shop opened in Westport in 1986, the first shop of its kind in Washington (not counting the Aberdeen sporting goods store that sold boards in the '60s), and the following year brought the debut Ricky Young Northwest Longboard Invitational, Washington's first and longest-running surf contest, held at Westport Jetty. The 2002-formed Cleanwater Classic, the first Washington pro-am surf contest, is also held at Westport Jetty. The Lost Coast Adventure Surf Camp, located on the Olympic Peninsula near the town of La Push, was founded in 2000.

Washington-born surfers include Hawaiian contest organizer Randy Rarick, surfboard manufacturer Dave Sweet, and pro surfer Conan Hayes; the Ventures, sometimes credited as the originators of surf music, formed in Seattle in the late '50s. The Washington surf was briefly featured in *Out of Control,* a 1961 surf movie. As of 2003, Washington was home to six surf shops and about 1,000 surfers; a few live on the coast, but most commute from inland towns and cities, including Seattle and Bellevue, and even east of the Cascade Range.

waterlogged   A state of oversaturation. The waterlogged surfboard is the result of one or more unfixed dings or cracks, allowing water into the polyurethane core, usually to board-terminating effect. The waterlogged surfer, having put in a well-above-average number of hours in the surf, is usually giddy and exhilarated, as well as tired, dehydrated, and prune-fingered. *Waterlogged* is the title of Bruce Brown's 1962 surf film.

waterman   Generally used to describe the surfer who is comfortable in a wide variety of ocean conditions and has a broad store of oceanic knowledge; more specifically applied to those who are accomplished at a particular set of surfing-related activities, including diving, swimming, sailing, bodysurfing, fishing, spearfishing, surf canoeing, and oceangoing rescue work. By the latter definition, virtually all watermen are Hawaiian. Surf journalist Dave Parmenter in 2000 described Makaha resident Brian Keaulana as "without a doubt the greatest all-around waterman alive, [someone who can] ride a shortboard or longboard at a world-class level, steer a four-man Hawaiian canoe through the Makaha bowl at 12 feet, and tow-in surf the local cloudbreak—all in a single afternoon." Big-wave rider Laird Hamilton is also regarded as a premier waterman.

Although "waterman" was likely introduced to the surf world lexicon in the 1950s, it was little used until the late '70s; the word appeared in a surf press headline for the first time in 1978, as *Surfer* magazine noted the death of lifeguard and big-wave rider Eddie Aikau with, "A Hawaiian Waterman's Final Return to the Sea." The expression quickly gained currency, and was eventually adopted for commercial use; the Waterman's Ball, a fund-raiser held by the Surf Industrial Manufacturers Association, has been an annual event since 1989. Australian surf journalist Nick Carroll, writing in 1989 about an imaginary University of Riding Waves, proposed a four-year Bachelor of Watermanship degree, with course work in oceanography and meteorology (to better understand wave formation), chemistry (surfboard and wetsuit construction), design and visual art (to better appreciate the sport's aesthetics), engineering (board-shaping machines), business, and literature (beginning with Homer's *Odyssey*). "Eventually," Carroll summarized, "you'd emerge as a full Waterman, the Total Surfer, somebody who doesn't just ride a wave, but understands it." While most surfers similarly admire the waterman ethic, and celebrate those who embody it, there have been dissenters. California surf icon Mickey Dora chose to live for most of his life away from the beach, and had as little to do with the water as possible during his nonsurfing hours. "When there's surf, I'm totally committed," Dora once said, asked about his relationship to the ocean. "When there's none, it doesn't exist." *See also* Laird Hamilton, Brian Keaulana.

Waterman's Ball   Annual black-tie-optional promotional event and fund-raiser, held in Orange County, California, organized and hosted by the Surf Industry Manufacturers Association (SIMA), a 1989-founded industry group. The first Waterman's Ball took place in 1990, at the Newport Beach Marriott, in a banquet room decorated with dozens of hanging papier-mâché seahorses, jellyfish, and barracudas. Four hundred people paid $100 a plate to attend. Donated items—framed surf art and photographs, surf instruction from former world champion Tom Carroll, Hawaiian vacations, surfboards from Al Merrick, Gary Linden, and Phil Becker—were raffled or auctioned, and about $30,000 in proceeds were divided between the United States Surfing Federation and the Surfrider Foundation environmental group. The Waterman Achievement Award, designed to honor a life's work in surfing, was added to the Waterman's Ball in 1993, and its presentation soon became the event highlight. Achievement Awards have gone to Hobie Alter (1993), Bruce Brown (1994), Walter Hoffman (1995), Rell Sunn (1996), John Severson (1997), Greg Noll (1998), Gerry Lopez (1999), Jack O'Neill (2000), Bud Browne (2001), and Fred Hemmings (2002). Nine hundred people at $175 a plate ($10 well drinks and valet parking not included) attended the 2000 Waterman's Ball, held at the Salt Creek Ritz-Carlton. At those prices, cheeky *Surf News* reporter Gina Makin noted, "You get a lot less surfers and a lot more accountants. I'd say if the Ritz-Carlton Ballroom suddenly filled with ten feet of water, half the guys here wouldn't be seen again." *See also* Surf Industry Manufacturers Association.

wave forecasting   *See* surf forecasting.

wave height and measurement   As a matter of science, wave weight is defined as the average distance between the trough and the crest of all open-ocean waves that pass by a stationary point over a given period of time—one hour for many Internet reports, for example. Open-ocean wave height is a primary indicator for surf size. Nearly as important is

wave "period" or "interval," roughly defined as the average amount of time between successive waves. Given equal wave height, a longer period translates into bigger surf. For example, an incoming swell with eight-foot wave height and a 20-second period might produce 10- to 15-foot surf; while an eight foot 12 second swell, in contrast, might produce six-foot surf.

There has traditionally been a gap between the actual trough-to-crest height of a breaking wave and the height as measured by surfers. In the early decades of the 20th century, surfers generally overestimated wave height. Southern California surfer George "Peanuts" Larson caught and rode a wave at a break called Church in 1939 that he later claimed to be 30 or 40 feet. Given that Larson was riding a finless wooden surfboard, that a photograph of the second-biggest ridden wave of the period (also surfed by him) shows a swell measuring about 12 feet from trough to crest, and that nobody has ever seen or photographed a wave measuring more than 15 feet at Church, Larson's estimate—accepted as gospel by surfers in the '40s and '50s—can be taken as a magnificent exaggeration.

Underestimating wave size got started in the late 1950s on the North Shore of Oahu, and the practice was widespread by the early '70s. While the degree of underestimation changes from area to area—in America, the differentiation is less on the East Coast, more pronounced on the West Coast, and greatest in Hawaii—surfers in general will judge a wave's size at about three-fifths of its true linear height. A wave measuring 10 foot from trough to crest, in other words, will be identified as six foot. Underestimating wave height may have originated from surfers trying to get a closer match between the breaking wave and its height as an open-ocean swell. Measuring from the back side of the wave, instead of the front (or "face"), so the old argument goes, gives a more accurate gauge of "real" wave height. Underestimation can also be viewed as a form of gamesmanship; the surfer offhandedly describing a 10-foot wave as six foot can look cool and superior. In what may be the sport's single most flagrantly underestimated wave, Hawaiian surfer Ken Bradshaw was towed in to a monster called Outside Log Cabins, on the North Shore of Oahu, that he at first labeled 35 feet. Video footage of the wave shows that it measured more than 60 feet from trough to crest. (For small- and medium-sized waves, surfers will often ignore numeric measurement altogether and instead use a body-height scale: waves are said to be waist-high, shoulder-high, or head-high, or double-overhead. Giant waves, as the old big-wave-riding adage goes, sidestepping the height issue entirely, are measured not in feet but in "increments of fear.")

California surf journalist Sam George has long been the sport's most vocal proponent of accuracy in measurement. "A wave's height, like that of a palm tree or an NBA center, is quantifiable," he wrote in 1998, signing off with the hope that the surf world would begin to "tell it like it is." Big-wave riders themselves continued to undervalue wave size, but judging panels for big-surf photo contests that require contestants submit photographs of themselves riding giant waves, set about making precise trough-to-crest measurements in order to pick a winner. Carlos Burle of Brazil won the 2002 Nissan Xterra XXL Big Surf Awards for a wave measured at 68 foot. Surfers from past generations likely would have called Burle's wave 35 or 40 feet.

wave-ski Buoyant surf craft vehicle ridden from a seated position, while holding a double-ended paddle. The wave ski was preceded by the Australian-invented surf ski: a 10- to 17-foot-long sit-down version of a hollow wooden paddleboard, developed by New South Wales lifeguards as far back as the late 1910s. Interest in surf skiing rose in the mid-'50s when pioneering Australian surfer Charles "Snow" McAlister retired his surfboard and began using a 12-foot surf ski. Nearly a decade later, California lifeguard Merv Larson, having already tried riding waves on a kayak, saw the Australians using their surf skis and modified his own paddleboard with a seat pocket, seat belt, and footstraps. California surf magazine publisher and filmmaker John Severson attended the 1969 Surf Ski and Kayak Championships at Santa Barbara's Rincon Point, was amazed by Larson's futuristic wave-riding repertoire—which included wraparound cutbacks and pinwheeling 360-degree turns—and subsequently used footage of Larson in his new film *Pacific Vibrations,* thus giving Americans their first look at this alternative form of surfing. A distinction between the surf ski and the wave ski was made in the early '70s, when Larson dropped the length of his skis down to as short as seven feet. Aussie lifeguard Michael Petrie and British-born Roger Shackleton both made significant design contributions to the wave ski. Australia held its first

Wave Ski National Championships in Sydney in 1980, the same year filmmaker Phil Sheppard released a documentary called *Wave Ski Titles.* The World Wave Ski Association was formed in 1981, and has hosted the Wave Ski World Championships since 1984. *The Fantastic Sport of Wave Ski Surfing,* an instructional film, was released three years later; *All About Wave Skis* was published in 1985.

Modern wave skis are made either from polyurethane foam and fiberglass, or molded plastic. Australian versions have fins (up to three), while American skis are often finless. Using the paddle as a rudder, a skilled wave ski rider can perform the same basic maneuvers as stand-up surfers. The self-righting "Eskimo roll" technique, originally developed by kayakers, is used to recover after a wipeout, and a few top performers incorporate the Eskimo roll during their rides.

Wave skiers have for decades been the object of scorn and derision from stand-up surfers, who complain that beginning ski-riders are particularly dangerous in a crowded surfing lineup, and that wave-hungry intermediate or advanced skiers—because of their huge advantage in paddling speed—often take more than their fair share of waves. In a 1991 *Australian Surfing Life* readers poll, 47 percent of respondents agreed with the statement that wave skiers are "middle-aged pot-bellied policemen and social rejects hated by even their own families." (Thirty-eight percent felt they were "a mild nuisance, but fun to drop in on.") A group of Santa Cruz surfers tried and failed in 2002 to get wave skis banned from Steamer Lane, the town's most popular surf break. Of the estimated 300,000 wave skiers worldwide, more than half live in Australia and a quarter in South Africa. Wave skiing is also popular in England, New Zealand, and Japan. *See also* canoe surfing, surf boat.

wavepools Just a tiny percentage of surfers have firsthand experience with mechanized wave-producing pools, but the machines have nonetheless always provoked strong reactions from within the sport. Some view them as a practical solution to over-crowded lineups, as the obvious way to increase the supply of "perfect" waves, and as a way to level the playing field for surfing competition. "As for the future of surfing," world tour competitor Richie Collins said in 1989, "all I gotta say is, why doesn't every country build an unreal wavepool?" But many surfers—almost certainly a majority—see wavepools as an

Wavepool in Irvine, California

automated perversion of a sport whose natural setting is its greatest attraction. "No matter how good technology gets at imitating Mother Nature," surf journalist Ben Marcus wrote in 1996, "riding waves in the chlorinated confines of a manmade tank will never compare to the raw experience of riding ocean waves over natural bottom contours."

The Wembley Swimming Pool, the world's first wavepool, opened in the summer of 1934 in London, England; it measured 200 feet by 60 feet, and had four electrically powered piston paddles in the deep end to rhythmically push forth mild swells that bubbled over in the shallows at the opposite end of the pool. The 1966-built Summerland wavepool near Tokyo, Japan—another piston-type indoor pool, nicknamed the "Surf-a-Torium"—was the first to be used by surfers. Each hour the pool was cleared of swimmers, and board-riders were given 15 minutes in the barely breaking waist-high waves. While the surf press described Summerland as "a forerunner of a fantastic era of artificial surfing," the Japanese pool—as with Wembley before it, and virtually all of the roughly 500 wavepools built since—was designed only to provide a safe and gently enhanced swimming experience for the general public; the inevitable result of bigger surf, wavepool owners understood, would be injuries and lawsuits. "Hard" surfboards (those with a hard fiberglass shell) are almost never allowed in a wavepool. Bigger waves, furthermore, also require bigger and prohibitively expensive pools and hydraulics.

Time magazine reported on the 1969 opening of Big Surf, the wavepool in Tempe, Arizona, funded by hair-coloring giant Clairol. Big Surf cost $2 million, and featured a 300-foot-by-400-foot pool set in a 20-acre Polynesian themed complex located in the middle of the desert. It produced chest-high waves by dropping millions of gallons of water down a vertical 40-foot-high concrete chute and refracting the flow into the pool through underwater metal gates. Groups of surfers alternated with groups of swimmers and rubber-raft riders. Featured in the surf press and in surf movies, visited by world surfing champion Fred Hemmings, U.S. champion Corky Carroll, and dozens of other top American riders, Big Surf represents a high point of sorts in the surfing/wavepool relationship.

Surfing competitions have occasionally been held in wavepools. World champion Tom Carroll won the 1985 World Professional Inland Surfing Championships, the first pro tour wavepool contest, at the Dorney Park Wildwater Kingdom in Allentown, Pennsylvania. At Disney World in Orlando, Florida, six-time world champion Kelly Slater won the 1997 Typhoon Lagoon wavepool contest, with Rob Machado taking the event the following year. Meanwhile, Australia's Matthew Pitts, a one-time world tour pro, spent nearly five years in the early and mid-'90s performing nightly as Sabu, the valiant sword-wielding surf prince, at the $100 million Ocean Dome wavepool in Miyazaki, Japan.

The oversized Sunway Bandar wavepool in Malaysia opened in 1997, and was able to produce a record-breaking wave of seven foot, from trough to crest. But by that time, the surf world's interest in artificially produced freshwater surf had for the most part turned to the stationary-wave FlowRider machines, developed in Southern California. *See also* FlowRider.

waves and wave formation   Differences from wave to wave are nearly infinite, but the basic principles of wave formation and travel are constant: storm winds blow across the ocean surface and create a transfer of energy into the water; the energy is parceled, stored, organized, and rhythmically broadcast into surrounding oceans and seas until reaching shallow water (usually a coastline, often thousands of miles distant from the storm source) and releasing the energy as breaking waves. Waves are captivating not just to surfers, sailors, and oceanographers, but to nearly anyone who has looked upon an incoming swell; waves have served as the muse to artists, writers, filmmakers, photographers, and poets. Lord Byron, the 19th-century British poet and rogue, bodysurfed off the Brighton coast, and later wrote about the experience in *Childe Harold's Pilgrimage*: "Once more upon the water! Yet once more! And the waves bound beneath me as a steed that knows his rider." Waves, it is often said, are what raise surfing above all other forms of sport. "When we surf," Australian surf journalist Nick Carroll wrote in 1989, "we are riding on pure energy, part of the roaring pulse that runs across the universe."

The wave-making process begins with solar heat, which creates uneven atmospheric pressure areas over the earth's surface, which in turn produces wind-driven storms. The initial wind from a young ocean-borne storm creates ripples, or capillary waves, on the water surface. As the wind gains purchase on the backs of the small and nearly inchoate capillary waves, they begin to merge, forming and reforming into ever-bigger waves, in a growth cycle that continues until the wind stops or gravity restricts further growth. Three factors determine initial wave size: wind strength, duration, and fetch (the distance over which the wind blows).

Discrete but linked waves now peel away from the storm front in a long, unbroken, corrugated "wave train," which, if strong enough, can move for thousands of miles with no further assist from the wind. (The aggregate waves from a given storm are called a "swell"; long-distance swells are often referred to as "ground swell.") Individual waves within a swell might be imagined, in cutaway, as rolling wheels of energy, most of which is efficiently submerged below the ocean surface. As the swell radiates out through the water—a large, organized swell will travel about 25 miles per hour—the waves begin to organize themselves into sets, with the fastest waves moving out in front and the slower waves grouping up behind them. Similar to a pack of bicyclists, slower waves conserve energy by drafting off the lead waves, which in turn slow down and relinquish the lead position to the next fastest wave. By this process, waves expend a minimal amount of energy as they travel. Swell size and character can be altered by crosshatching with another swell (or multiple swells) or by meeting up with another wind front. But if the swell is given a clear oceangoing run, two things will happen: 1) Individual waves within the swell will move further apart from one another, increasing the "period," which is the amount of time it takes succeeding wave crests to pass a stationary point; better wave quality is often directly linked to longer swell period. 2) The swell gradually but steadily will drop in size, losing one-third of its height for every doubling of the swell period.

Waves slow down as they approach land and begin making contact with the ocean floor. Some energy is lost to land-contact friction, but most is pushed up to create a larger, steepening wave. The wave breaks as the ground-dragging bottom portion of the wave is essentially overtaken by the cresting top portion, which spills over. Under neutral conditions—no wind, smooth swell, a gradually sloped bottom—a wave will break when the water depth is roughly one-third greater than the wave's height. If the ocean floor changes abruptly from deep to shallow (common to midocean island reefbreaks), the bottom of the wave will slow abruptly, causing the crest to pitch forward and make a tubing wave. Conversely, if the ocean floor is gradually angled (common to all nearshore zones featuring a continental shelf), the top of the waves will be slow in overtaking the bottom, resulting in rolling, easy-breaking waves. Depending on the bottom topography and the shape of the coastline itself, incoming swells often bend (refract), resulting in a swell line that, viewed from above, becomes either concave to convex to the shoreline. As virtually all coastlines are uneven and scalloped to one degree or another, refraction of some kind is nearly as common to wave formation as wind itself. The angle between a surf break and the incoming swell is crucial to wave shape and size at that particular break. Lower Trestles, a pointbreak in Southern California, responds best to swells angling in from the south or southwest, and is all but unridable during a northwest swell. Upper Trestles, just a few hundred yards away, is mediocre on a south swell, but first-rate on a west or northwest swell.

The mystery of wave formation, wave quality, and wave forecasting has become a specialized science involving swell vigor, swell direction, swell clarity (whether or not it's been crosscut by secondary swells), nearshore bathymetry (the topographic features of the ocean floor, including reefs, points, and sandbars), tide, and local wind conditions. As with all weather-related science, however, the contributing elements can be altered, skewed, amplified, or subordinated. Surf forecasting continues to improve year by year, but wave-related permutations as of 2003 remain incalculable, while the final outcome—a breaking wave—remains breathtaking.

Waves and Beaches (1964), by American oceanographer Willard Bascom, was the first book surfers read to gain a technical understanding of swell formation and wave/coastline interaction. *Surf Science: An Introduction to Waves for Surfing* was published in 2002.

Two surfer-designed photo books on the subject have also been published: *The Book of Waves* (1989) and *Visions of the Breaking Wave* (1999). *See* buoy reports, ground swell, low-pressure system, surf forecasting, swell period, wave height and measurement, wind waves.

Waves magazine   Colorful and mildly risqué Australian surf magazine, founded in 1980 by Geoff Greenwood and surf photographer Peter Crawford; published monthly out of Sydney, New South Wales. *Waves* gathered steam after a slow start (just two issues were released in the first year), and by the early '90s had set a prurient standard in surf publishing, with columns like "Gash of the Month," featuring reader-submitted photos of surfing injuries, and Mark Sutherland's popular Gonad Man cartoon strip. British publishing giant Emap bought *Waves* in 1998, and by 2002—after a visual overhaul by progressive graphic designer Campbell Milligan, and with the addition of staff writer Derek Rielly—it had become one of the sport's hippest magazines. *Waves* has a monthly circulation of 30,000. *See also* surf magazines.

wax   *See* surf wax.

wax comb   Thick-toothed plastic comb, three to five inches long, used to crosshatch the wax layer on the deck of a surfboard to increase traction. Wax combs were first manufactured in the early 1980s by Wax Research, a Southern California company; before that surfers occasionally used a standard plastic pocket comb to the same effect. The beveled edge often found on the flip side of a wax comb is used to scrape old wax from the board. *See also* surf wax.

wax rash   Skin irritation, generally on the inner thighs, stomach, or chest, brought on by prolonged rubbing against the wax-covered deck of a surfboard. Wax rash is a warm-water affliction, as surfers use trunks rather than wetsuits; "wetsuit rash" is a separate but similar problem. Knee-length surf trunks were introduced not long after World War II to prevent inner-thigh wax rash; the Lycra "rash guard" was developed in the mid-'80s to protect against wax rash on the torso. Also known as "board rash."

Way, Peter   Big, boisterous New Zealand surfing pioneer and surfboard manufacturer; winner of the inaugural New Zealand surfing championships in 1963.

Way was born (1939) and raised in Auckland, and began surfing at age 18 on a hollow plywood paddleboard. In the late '50s and early '60s, he made regular forays up and down the northeast coast of North Island and mapped out dozens of now-familiar surf breaks. After an hours-long rescue in heavy surf at North Piha beach in 1962, Way was given a New Zealand Royal Honours Silver Medal for bravery. Around the same time, as friend Chas Lake warmly recalls in *Gone Surfing: The Golden Years of Surfing in New Zealand,* the 6'3", 200-pound Way destroyed another surfer's hotel room for laughs. "He came across a parrot-shaped bottle filled with a green liquor," Lake noted, "smashed the top off on a table edge, and proceeded to skull the bottle in one go." The lantern-jawed Way competed in the 1968 World Surfing Championships. From 1964 to 1972 he owned and operated Peter Way Surfboards; he later formed Jackman-Way Surfboards with top Australian big-wave surfer Dave Jackman.

Weaver, Robert "Wingnut"   Neoclassic longboarder from Santa Cruz, California; best known as a costar in the 1994 surf movie *Endless Summer II.* Weaver was born (1965) in Cologne, Germany; moved with his family at age three to Newport Beach, California, began surfing in 1982 at age 16, and for reasons never made clear was dubbed "Wingnut" by a group of older Newport surfers. Alone among his teenage peers, Weaver was a longboard-only surfer from the beginning. He moved to Santa Cruz in 1986, four years later received a B.S. in economics from U.C. Santa Cruz, and spent most of 1992 and 1993 traveling around the world shooting *Endless Summer II* with filmmaker Bruce Brown (creator of the original *Endless Summer*) and shortboarding costar Pat O'Connell. In 1997, the always congenial Weaver became the director of the O'Neill Surf Academy in Europe, conducting instructional classes sponsored by industry giant O'Neill Wetsuits in England, Belgium, Spain, the Netherlands, and Italy.

Weaver is featured in three surf videos: *Wingnut's Search for Soul* (1997), *Wingnut's Art of Longboarding* (1997), and *Wingnut's Art of Longboarding II: The Traveler* (1999). He's also appeared in nearly three dozen other videos, including *On Surfari to Stay* (1992), *Powerglide* (1995), and *Super Slide* (1999). He did the voice-over narration for *50 Years of Surfing on Film* (1997), *Great Waves* (1998), and *Biographies,* all multipart cable TV series produced by the *Surfer's Journal* and Outdoor Life Network; Weaver himself is featured in an episode of *Biographies*.

Although not a dedicated competitor, Weaver won the Santa Cruz Surf-O-Rama longboard event, held at Pleasure Point, Santa Cruz, in 1989, 1990, 1991, and 1996. He was diagnosed with multiple sclerosis in 1997, but as of early 2003 the disease hadn't affected his balance or timing. Weaver is married and has one child.

Webb, Kylie   Tall, blond, leggy Australian regularfoot pro surfer from Kingscliff, New South Wales; world-ranked #4 in 1993, and described by *Surfing Girl* magazine as "one of the greatest natural talents in women's surfing." Webb was born in 1972, didn't begin surfing until age 15, and turned pro at 18. She was fluid and powerful in small- to medium-sized wave, won five pro circuit events in her career and spent four years in the top eight, but was a complete washout in bigger waves, partly due to asthma. Webb abruptly quit the tour in mid-1997, saying "I'm just sick of the traveling and the competition," and that "money fucks everything," but later admitting that she had "a pretty big problem with alcohol."

Weber, David "Dewey"   Flashy bleach-blond surfer and board manufacturer of the late '50s and '60s from Hermosa Beach, California; a hotdogging icon; founder and owner of surf industry powerhouse Dewey Weber Surfboards. Weber was born (1938) in Denver, Colorado, the son of a truck driver, moved with his family at age five to Manhattan Beach (just north of Hermosa), and began surfing four years later. He was already a minor celebrity, having been hired at age seven to dress up as the cartoon character Buster Brown in a national advertising campaign for Buster Brown Shoes. Early in his surfing life, Weber met and became friends with surfboard-maker Dale Velzy, 10 years his senior, and it was the new widebacked Velzy "pig" design, developed in the mid-'50s, that allowed Weber to develop his prototypical hotdog style. Soon he was the hottest thing on the coast. "In the late '50s," Malibu favorite Lance Carson later recalled, "on his best days, nobody could touch him." The tiny but well-muscled Weber (5'3", 130 pounds) rode in a bowlegged stance, and used jitterbugging foot speed to race up and down the deck of his board; he was soon nicknamed "the Little Man on Wheels." Weber also had a keen sense of leverage, and was able to turn with more power than his diminutive frame

Dewey Weber

would suggest. Best remembered for his small-wave performances, especially at Malibu, Weber also rode well in the bigger Hawaiian surf. He further stood out by accoutering himself with candy-apple red surfboards and surf trunks, and by peroxiding his already-blond hair to an incandescent platinum white. Weber was featured in nearly every surf movie of the late '50s and early '60s, including *Slippery When Wet* (1958), *Cat on a Hot Foam Board* (1959), and *Walk on the Wet Side* (1963). Following up on his early Buster Brown fame, meanwhile, Weber was a three-time national yo-yo champion by age 14, and performed on the Groucho Marx–hosted television program *You Bet Your Life.* In high school he was a three-time all-league wrestler, in junior college he was all-state, and in 1960 he made the finals of the Olympic wrestling team trials before dislocating an elbow.

Weber Surfboards opened in 1960 in Venice, and soon became the sport's second-most popular brand, following Hobie Surfboards. (*See* Weber Surfboards.) Weber meanwhile became a hard drinker in his off-hours who lived up to his media billing as "the surfing millionaire" by purchasing a gold Ford Thunderbird as a wedding gift for his new bride, and by walking barefoot into the local Porsche dealership and paying cash for a new bright yellow 911. He continued to be a force as a surfer, as he placed second in the 1964 United States Surfing Championships, earned a slot in the 1965 Duke Kahanamoku Invitational, made the finals of the 1965 and 1967 Malibu Invitational, and won the seniors division of the 1969 U.S. Championships. In 1966 he was inducted into the *International Surfing* Magazine Hall of Fame. After his company took a sharp dip in popularity following the shortboard revolution of the late '60s and early '70s, Weber built a two-man swordfishing boat, spent most of the daylight hours at sea, and drank heavily in the evenings. As a coda to his surfing career, Weber inaugurated the Peff Eick/Dewey Weber Invitational Longboard Classic at Manhattan Beach Pier in 1981, an event that has since been described as marking the beginning of the longboard renaissance.

Weber was married once and had three children. When he died of alcohol-related heart failure in 1993 at age 54, sleeping in tiny living quarters in the back of his surf shop, it was reported in the *Los Angeles Times* and the *Washington Post,* and on ABC, NBC, and CNN. *See also* alcohol and surfing, hotdogging, Malibu, pig board, Weber Surfboards.

Weber, Sharron   Triumphant but aggressively ignored goofyfoot surfer from Honolulu, Hawaii; winner of the World Surfing Championships in 1970 and 1972. Weber was 15 in 1963 when she moved with her family from Virginia to Oahu, and bought her first board from reigning U.S. champion Linda Benson. She won the first of six Hawaii state titles in 1965, was runner-up to Margo Godfrey in the 1968 World Surfing Championships, and won the 1969 United States Surfing Championships. Weber's first world title came in Victoria, Australia; the second in San Diego, California. She was never profiled or interviewed by *Surfer* or *Surfing* magazines. In 1973, Weber was about to fly to Durban, South Africa, to compete in a pro meet, but canceled upon learning that apartheid would bar her dark-skinned Hawaiian teammates from entering the contest. A few months later the 24-year-old Weber (no relation to California surfboard manufacturer Dewey Weber) opened a tire business in Kauai and retired from competitive surfing. "I only know two things," she said in a 2001 interview. "How to surf, and how to change a tire." Weber was the top female Hawaiian vote-getter in the 1967 *International Surfing* Magazine's Hall of Fame Awards, and finished second to Margo Godfrey in the 1969 *Surfer* Poll Awards. *See also* World Surfing Championships 1970, World Surfing Championships 1972.

Weber Surfboards   Southern California surfboard manufacturing and retail business, founded in 1960 by hotdog forefather Dewey Weber of Hermosa Beach; second in output only to Hobie Surfboards during the '60s. Weber, the small and nimble wrestler-turned-surfer known as "the Little Man on Wheels," opened the first Weber Surfboards in the same Venice, California, building that had for six years been the home of Velzy Surfboards. Weber had been Dale Velzy's protégé, and while details of the sudden turnover at the Venice location remain unclear, the two men never spoke again. Velzy told a surf journalist in 1996 that he'd "treated Dewey like a son," and that Weber had ended up "stabbing me in the back." The intense and driven Weber soon proved to be a gifted businessman: he hired top board-makers (particularly shaper Harold Iggy from Hawaii), and assembled a first-rate surf team (including David Nuuhiwa, Joey Hamasaki, Jackie Baxter, Mike Tabeling, and 1966 world champion Nat Young), which he dressed in matching red nylon jackets and trunks. Weber Surfboards also produced some of the industry's most eye-catching advertisements, and was the first surfing company to offer credit terms to customers. By 1966, Weber was producing up to 300 boards a week, with a majority shipped off to more than 35 distributors around the country. The brightly colored Weber Performer model, manufactured in 1966 and 1967, sold roughly 10,000 total units and is by far the best-selling model in surfing history; tens of thousands of Weber Surfboards logo T-shirts, meanwhile, sold annually. A second Weber factory/retail outlet opened in 1968 in Hermosa Beach; showroom-only outlets later opened briefly in San Diego, Honolulu, and Cocoa Beach, Florida.

The late-'60s shortboard revolution was disastrous for Weber Surfboards, as it was for all big-name surfboard manufacturers of the period, none of whom could keep up with the week-by-week changes in board design. Weber introduced the streamlined Ski model in 1969, designed by Australia's Nat Young, followed by the wide-backed Pig model in 1970, but the business never fully recovered, and by 1973 Weber Surfboards had been reduced to a single factory/retail outlet, in Hermosa Beach. Shea Weber, Dewey's son, opened a Weber Surfboards showroom in 1998 in San Clemente, California. *See also* Dewey Weber.

Webster, Dale   Sad-eyed monomaniacal surfer from Valley Ford, California, who as of 2003 hadn't missed a day of surfing for 28 years. Webster was born (1948) and raised in Alhambra, California, began mat-surfing in 1957, and stand-up surfing in 1961. He moved in 1973 to Sonoma County, just north of San Francisco, and two years later came up against a solid week of big surf. "I rode all seven days," Webster later recalled, "and then I thought, 'Let me see if I can keep this going.'" *Surfing* magazine reported in 1976 that Webster had surfed every day for an entire year, including 121 consecutive days in sub-55-degree water. A surf day, by Webster's own rules, requires at least three ridden waves, and the last wave must be surfed all the way to the beach.

In the years that followed, Webster's pursuit kept him from serious employment and from visiting inland relatives. He developed a near phobia about injuries, and was afraid to mow the lawn for fear that a rock might fly out of the rotors and strike him. Webster rode in near-hurricane winds, while sick with the flu, and while nursing sprains, cuts, and earaches. Nearly crippled by a kidney stone on one occasion, Webster had his wife carry his board to the water; he gingerly paddled out and rode his three waves, then crawled up the beach and went directly to the hospital. August 19, 2000, marked the 25th anniversary of Webster's daily wave riding ritual—9,132 consecutive days—and prompted a small burst of national media attention, including profiles in the *New York Times,* the *San Francisco Chronicle,* the *San Diego Union-Tribune,* and on CNN. The 51-year-old Webster was described by the *Times* as having "a broad back, long stringy blond hair, and piercing blue eyes that focus on the horizon when he speaks." In a slightly melancholy voice, Webster told the *Times* that he often thought about "all the things I'll have missed in life because of this. The only thing I'll have is the memory of riding all those waves." Webster is married, and has one daughter, Margo, who had perfect attendance from kindergarten through eighth grade.

wedge   A thick, hard-dumping, steep-shouldered wave or section of wave; frequently short in length, and often hooking in on itself as it breaks. Wedge waves can be formed as a swell refracts off a headland or jetty and angles across the following wave, with the wedge created at the point of intersection. Wedging waves are common at Florida's Sebastian Inlet and the aptly named Newport Beach Wedge in California. A wedge section is similar to a "bowl" section; both are good for tuberiding.

Wedge, The   Thick, punishing, highly specialized surf break adjacent to the west jetty of Newport Harbor, at the tip of Balboa peninsula in Orange County, California; ridden almost exclusively by bodysurfers,

The Wedge

bodyboarders, and kneeboarders. The Wedge is a classic "rebound" wave: each incoming swell pushes up against the jetty rocks and rolls back as a refractory wave, which then vectors against the following swell, effectively doubling the wave's height and power, and giving it a distinctive A-line "wedge" shape. Backwash from the steeply canted beach sometimes will add a third wave into the mix. The Wedge requires a swell from the south or southwest, and generally produces its biggest surf in late summer and early fall. While the Wedge peak can take shape more than 50 yards off the beach, the wave folds over much closer to shore, and terminates just a few yards from the wet sand. Rides here are short and invariably come to a brutal end; with the exception of Pipeline and Sandy Beach in Hawaii, the Wedge has injured more wave-riders than any break in the world. As of 2002, it was estimated that the Wedge had killed six people, paralyzed another 30, and sent thousands to the hospital with sprains, fractures, and dislocations. The Wedge thrill has nonetheless proven to be one of the most addictive in surfing; a devotee in 1971 described it as "the closet thing to the great trauma of being born."

One of dozens of man-made surf breaks in California, the Wedge was created in the late '20s when the Army Corps of Engineers built a 2,000-foot granite boulder jetty on the west side of the Newport Harbor. Surfers in the '40s and early '50s occasionally watched the explosive waves breaking in the nook formed by the jetty and the sandy beach, but not until the late '50s did bodysurfers ride the newly named Wedge consistently. Bellyboarders and kneeboarders joined the lineup in the early '60s, followed by bodyboarders in mid-'70s and skimboarders a few years later. Bodysurfer Fred Simpson, at his prime in the '60s and early '70s, invented the arm-extended "outrigger" position (also known as "the Fred"), rode with control through cyclonic Wedge tubes, and has long been the break's most revered figure. Other top Wedge bodysurfers through the decades include Jim Scanlon, John Forbes, Don Reddington, Kevin Egan, Terry "Sac" Wade, Mel Thoman, Mark "Big Daddy" McDonald, and Tom "Cashbox" Kennedy.

Ron Romanasky, a Wedge kneeboarding fixture since the mid-'60s, is also its top chronicler, writing more than a half-dozen surf press features on the Wedge since 1970, and photographing the break regularly. "It really is a freak show," Romanasky wrote in 1989, referring to the crowded Wedge lineup, full of "the competent, the clowns, the idiots, the showboaters and the wannabes." Other notable Wedge kneeboarders include John Ramuno, Rick Newcombe, Bill Sieler, and Bill Sharp. Stand-up surfers have been riding the Wedge on occasion since the late '60s, but the practice is for the most part looked down upon by Wedge regulars. Infighting among the various Wedge factions—bodysurfers, kneeboarders, bodyboarders—has been part of the Wedge scene for decades.

A staple in surf magazines and surf movies since 1960, the Wedge has periodically turned up in the mainstream media as well, hitting a peak in 1971 with a photo feature in *Life* magazine and a lengthy exposé in *Sports Illustrated.* While the city of Newport Beach has refused to legislate against riding the Wedge (and has successfully fended off dozens of personal injury cases), it has understandably never permitted any type of Wedge surfing competition. *See also* bodysurfing, injuries and surfing, Newport Beach, Sandy Beach.

West, Claude   Australian surfing pioneer from Sydney's Manly Beach; winner of the national surfing championship from 1919 to 1925. West was born (1898) in Sydney, raised in Manly, and began bodysurfing as a child. He was present when Hawaiian surfer and swimmer Duke Kahanamoku gave a wave-riding demonstration at nearby Freshwater Beach in 1914, using a nine-foot board he made himself from a slab of sugar pine; the 16-year-old West later not only coaxed the Hawaiian into giving him surfing lessons, but took possession of the board when Kahanamoku

left the country. West became a lifeguard and made headlines when he rescued Governor-General Sir Ronald Munro Ferguson from a heavy surf. As a young man, he was also an apprentice undertaker, and he applied the woodworking skills learned for making coffins toward crafting high-quality surfboards, beginning in the '20s. West himself rode Kahanamoku's board into the '50s; in 1957 he presented it to the Freshwater Life Saving Club. The 60-year-old West was seen displaying his Kahanamoku board and riding small waves at Manly Beach in Bud Browne's 1958 film *Surf Down Under.* When West died in May 1980, the Freshwater Life Saving Club scattered his remains just past the surf line. Although he was Australia's first celebrated surfer, the dignified and straight-backed West never captured the national surfing community's imagination as did fellow wave-riding original George "Snow" McAlister.

West Coast Surfing Championships   *See* United States Surfing Championships.

West Indies   Crescent-shaped chain of tropical and subtropical islands extending roughly 2,000 miles from near the southern tip of Florida to Venezuela's northern coast. The wave-lined West Indies—which at one time formed a volcanic mountain chain connecting North and South America—separate the Atlantic Ocean from the Caribbean Sea, and are made up of three island groups: the Bahamas to the north, the Greater Antilles (including Cuba, Jamaica, the Dominican Republic, and Puerto Rico), and the Lesser Antilles (including British Virgin Islands, Guadeloupe, St. Lucia, Barbados, Grenada, and Trinidad and Tobago) to the southeast. While pointbreaks and beachbreaks are occasionally located along the West Indies, the chain's premier surf spots are mostly located on outlying coral reefs and atolls. The August-to-October hurricane season brings the largest surf to the area, but wave consistency is better from October through April, with the Atlantic-facing coasts picking up ground swells at a fairly regular interval. Daytime air temperatures in the West Indies average about 75 to 80 degrees throughout the year, with water temperatures just a few degrees cooler.

Puerto Rico was the first place in the West Indies to be surfed, in the late '50s, and it soon became a popular warm-water getaway for surfers up and down the American eastern seaboard. While dozens, if not hundreds, of West Indies's surf spots remain either secret, rarely surfed, or undiscovered, many first-quality breaks have become well known over the years, including Gas Chambers in Puerto Rico, Soup Bowls in Barbados, Cane Garden Bay in Tortola, Garbonzo's in the Bahamas, and Le Moule in Guadeloupe. *See also* Bahamas, Barbados, Caribbean Sea, Cuba, and Puerto Rico.

Western Australia Arid and largely unpopulated rock-and-scrub-filled Australian state covering more than a million square miles; bordered to the north and west by the storm-lashed Indian Ocean, and to the south by the Southern Ocean. While the northern half of Western Australia is unsuitable for surfing, the state's southern portion is home to some of Australia's biggest, best, and most consistent waves. Western Australia can be broken into four main surfing areas: 1) The remote northwest desert, stretching 800 miles from the state capital of Perth to Exmouth, characterized by dusty hills and plateaus fringed by an aquamarine sea and a number of long, fast, hollow left-breaking reef waves, including Red Bluff and the fearsome tubes of Gnaraloo Station. 2) The Perth city area, filled mostly with beachbreak surf weakened by a swell-filtering offshore reef—although Rottnest Island, a 15-minute plane ride from Perth, has a small number of shapely reef waves. 3) The southwest coast, a temperate 50-mile-long area characterized by rolling hills, eucalyptus forests, and wineries, bordering a series of dazzling wave-filled bays and points, including the renowned Margaret River area. 4) The rugged and largely inaccessible south coast, studded with isolated reefs and empty beachbreaks, including the sand-bottomed right-breaking waves in Ocean Beach Denmark, seen in Bruce Brown's 1966 movie *The Endless Summer.* Western Australia produces good surf all year, with the southwest coast usually best from January to May, and the northwest coast best from April to November. Average daytime temperatures in the northwest range from 90 in summer to 72 in winter; the southwest is generally 10 to 15 degrees colder. Water temperatures range from the low 60s to the low 70s. The storm-filled Indian Ocean provides most of Western Australia's surf, which is frequently six foot and occasionally 15 foot or bigger. Surfing hazards include sharks, sea snakes, dangerously shallow reefs, powerful waves, and lack of emergency services along much of the coast.

Although Perth-area lifeguards began surfing in the 1930s, the sport didn't really catch on here until the late '50s, with the introduction of relatively lightweight balsa-core surfboards. Perth surfers Len Dibben, Peter Hawke, and Len Hawke became Western Australia's first native board-builders in 1957 and 1958. Several years later, in 1963, the City Beach Surfriders club was formed in Perth, as well as Surfing West Australia, a statewide association for amateur competitive surfing. Cordingley's Surfboards, the state's first surf shop, founded by brothers Rex and Colin Cordingley, opened in the Perth suburb of Subiaco in 1964; the debut Western Australian state titles were held that year as well, also in Perth. Margaret River first hosted the Australian National Titles in 1969, and the event returned to Margaret in 1973, 1978, 1988, and 1994. Margaret also hosted a world pro tour contest from 1985 to 1990 (with the exception of 1988), and winners included world champions Tom Carroll, Wendy Botha, Barton Lynch, and Mark Occhilupo. Gnaraloo—first surfed in 1975 by Western Australia surf explorers Craig Howe and Charlie Constantinides—was the site of the dramatic Billabong Challenge events in 1995 and 1996. Top Western Australian surfers over the years include world tour standouts Ian Cairns, Dave MacAulay, Jodie Cooper, Mitch Thorson, Jake and Paul Paterson, Taj Burrow, and Melanie Redman.

As of 2003, there were more than three dozen surf shops in Western Australia and roughly 75,000 surfers, the majority living in or near Perth. Dozens of regional and statewide amateur and pro contests are held in Western Australia annually, along with a minor international pro event at Margaret River. The Western Australian surf has been featured in more than two dozen surf movies and videos, including *Evolution* (1969), *Bunyip Dreaming* (1991), and *Sabotaj* (1999). *Surfing Wild Australia,* a lush 1985-published photo book, is centered around a surf trip to the northwest coast. Western Australian surf breaks are detailed in *The Surfing and Sailboarding Guide to Australia* (1993), *Surfing Australia* (1998), Mark Warren's *Atlas of Australian Surfing* (1998), and *The World Stormrider Guide* (2001). *See also* Margaret River.

Western Intercollegiate Surfing Council (WISC)
Surfing association formed in Los Angeles in 1966 to promote organized competition between college and university surf clubs; the first surf-based collegiate organization. The Western Intercollegiate Surfing Council (WISC) was conceived and developed by Jim Henry of Cal Western University (later renamed

United States International University), Bill Prothero of UCSD, and Rus Calisch of UCLA; charter member universities were UCLA, UCSB, UCSD, and Cal Western; in 1967 the Council expanded to include USC, San Diego State, U.C. Irvine, Los Angeles State College, and Long Beach State College; junior colleges were admitted in 1971. Each school fielded a 12-person team, and a series of meets over the school year concluded with a championship. UCLA won three of the first five WISC championships. Scandal visited WISC in 1970 when the group's four-foot-tall perpetual championship trophy vanished after being claimed the previous year by San Diego State—foul play by one of the other colleges was suspected, but never proven. WISC became part of the American Surfing Association in 1976; the ASA folded two years later. *See also* academia and surfing.

Western Sahara   Dry and foreboding desert area located on the northwest coast of Africa, between Morocco and Mauritania, and fronted by the Atlantic Ocean; claimed by Morocco, though many who live there—mostly nomadic Berbers and Arabs—dispute the claim. California surf adventurer Craig Peterson documented his 1975 journey down the coast of Western Sahara ("the road consisted of nothing more than driving the beach at low tide") in search of mythical pointbreaks described in second- and third-hand accounts by other wave-chasers. He found some shapely beachbreak waves, a rock point near an abandoned castle, and a rusted run-aground freighter producing a hypnotic but unridable tube amidships, but the trials of merely existing in Western Sahara's bleached and sun-baked environment persuaded Peterson to seek his oceanic fortune elsewhere. Temperatures along the 600-mile Western Sahara coast can range from 110 degrees in the daytime to near freezing at night, and there is virtually no natural shelter from the sun, wind, and pelting sand. Western Sahara is wide open to North Atlantic swells, and Peterson left convinced that perfect waves do exist here, "buried under mirages unseen."

Western Surfing Association (WSA)   California amateur competitive surfing association, based in Hermosa Beach, California, formed in 1968 after the United States Surfing Association (USSA) split into four regional groups. The Western Surfing Association (WSA) for the most part retained the USSA rules and bylaws, along with most of the USSA board of di-

rectors, with Lewis "Hoppy" Swarts serving as the last USSA president and the first WSA president. Swarts announced that the primary difference between the two groups would be that the WSA, unlike the USSA, would stay away from surf-related politics and legislation (e.g., beach access issues and beach city municipal surfing restrictions).

The WSA was originally divided into six districts from San Diego to Santa Cruz, and began the 1968 season with 1,700 registered competitors and a 50-event schedule of A-, AA-, or AAA-rated contests, along with an elite AAAA division for "professionally oriented surfers." From 1968 to 1970, and to a lesser degree from 1971 to 1975, America's best surfers—including Corky Carroll, Joyce Hoffman, Jock Sutherland, Mike Tabeling, Rolf Aurness, David Nuuhiwa, Skip Frye, Jeff Hakman, and Margo Godfrey—competed in the AAAA division. The WSA hosted the United States Surfing Championships from 1968 to 1973 and in 1977. Interest in surf contests was on the decline by 1970, and by the time the AAAA division was retired in 1975, the era's anticommercial, antiestablishment sentiments had rendered competitive surfing in California all but dormant. Any prestige the WSA retained was shot after the group hosted the wholly disorganized 1972 World Surfing Championships—a nadir not just for the WSA, but for competitive surfing in general.

Rival organizations to the WSA were founded in California one after the other over the next few years, including the Women's International Surfing Association, the American Surfing Association, the Christian Surfing Association, and, most significantly, the National Scholastic Surfing Association (NSSA). The introduction in 1979 of the United States Surfing Federation, designed to unify and organize the disparate American amateur groups, brought little relief; by the early '80s the NSSA had outgrown the rest and become amateur surfing's premier group. Many young surfers chose to compete in two or more of the amateur circuits in order to improve their chances at qualifying for the U.S. Championships or the American world contest team—an approach that was often confusing as well as tiring. "Every time I go to a contest," three-time U.S. amateur champion Sharon Wolfe said in 1990, "there's a different set of guidelines. The rules are so jumbled that you have to worry about not making mistakes, rather than just going out and surfing." In 1993, in a modest effort to reduce the chaos that had come to define Californian ama-

teur surfing, the WSA, along with the Christian Surfing Association, was decommissioned to make way
for the Western Region Surfing Association. *See also*
National Scholastic Surfing Association, surfing competition, Lewis "Hoppy" Swarts, United States Surfing
Association, United States Surfing Federation.

wetsuit   Warm, durable, flexible protection from
the elements has been the Holy Grail for cold-water
surfers since the sport was exported from sunny
Hawaii in the early 20th century. As a necessary piece
of surfing equipment, the wetsuit, for a vast majority
of surfers worldwide, is outranked only by the surfboard itself; and as stated in a famous wetsuit company slogan, with a well-made and properly fitted
suit, "It's always summer on the inside."
    The wetsuit was a result of World War II–funded
developments in plastics and rubber. In 1951, looking
to make underwater work more comfortable and pro-
ductive for U.S. Navy divers, U.C. Berkeley physicist
Hugh Bradner began testing prototype wetsuits constructed from various unicellular polymeric materials,
including neoprene. The navy declassified Bradner's
wetsuit designs the following year and encouraged
commercial production, a decision that would eventually bring relief to surfers who were then wearing
rubber caps and oil-steeped woolen sweaters as a defense against the cold. Bev Morgan, a surfer/diver
from Manhattan Beach, California, was given a copy
of Bradner's report on wetsuit design and construction in 1951, and immediately began making suits for
his diver friends. Morgan opened the Dive N' Surf
dive shop the following year, and soon brought in
fellow surfer/divers Bill and Bob Meistrell as partners;
the Meistrells founded Body Glove Wetsuits in 1965
as a Dive N' Surf offshoot. Meanwhile, surfer and
window salesman Jack O'Neill, inspired after seeing
neoprene foam carpeting along the aisle of a DC-3
passenger plane in 1952, began making and selling
wetsuit vests out of his just-opened beachfront surf
shop in San Francisco. O'Neill was the first to produce wetsuits specifically for surfers, and his company's technological innovations—particularly after
the business moved to Santa Cruz in 1959—have in
large part set the industry standard. Surfing wetsuits
didn't catch on until the late '50s, as the early models
were constricting and often abrasive to the skin, and
were also viewed by most wave-riders as sissified. The
first three wetsuit styles to gain popularity were the
tank-top, short john, the ankle-length long john, and

Wetsuit

the front-zip long- or short-sleeve jacket, or "surf
shirt"—also known as a "beaver tail," for the rear-
attached, wraparound codpiece flap that surfers generally left unsnapped and dangling. Other types of
wetsuits introduced over the years include the short-
leg/short- or long-armed springsuit, the long-leg/
long-arm fullsuit (the best-selling type of wetsuit, first
made by O'Neill in 1970; called a "steamer" in Australia), and the hooded fullsuit. Wetsuit accessories
such as gloves, hoods, and socklike booties are used
in colder climates.
    It's often said that wetsuits work by allowing in
a thin layer of water, which is then heated by the
surfer's skin. While it is true that the wetsuit isn't
watertight (unlike the tightly cuffed thin-rubber drysuit, developed during World War II and marketed to
surfers without much success in the 1970s), its main
objective is simply to provide a buffer zone between
the skin and the ambient air and water. Air-bubble-
filled neoprene rubber, lined on one or both sides

with a "jersey" of nylon, polyester, polypropylene, or spandex, is the material that best combines insulation with lightness, flexibility, comfort, and durability—wetsuit development over the decades has been nothing more than a series of improvements, singularly or in combination, in each of these categories. Increased warmth in large part has been a matter of better fit, which helps keep water from entering and pooling against the body. Comfort, flexibility, and lightness have been improved by advances in neoprene formulation and by combining neoprene thickness: the common "3/2" designation on a fullsuit, for example, means three-millimeter material is used primarily in the torso, with two-millimeter material used on the arms and lower legs; wetsuit thickness rarely goes above five millimeter or below one millimeter. Improved stitching, glued and taped seams, stress-equalizing patterns, and reinforced knees have all added to the wetsuit's durability. (Because saltwater is corrosive to rubber, a freshwater rinse after each use has always been the cardinal rule of wetsuit preservation. A full-time surfer in a moderate-to-cold region of the world can expect to get two seasons' wear out of a fullsuit.) Ease of use has also been a perennial concern of wetsuit makers, especially with fullsuits. The fullsuit zipper at various times has been placed vertically up the front, along the spin, horizontally across the upper back, across the upper chest, and from shoulder to neck in a matched set. Velcro-sealed zipperless wetsuits, an updated version of a design first introduced in 1989, became popular in 1997. Extra-thick wetsuits have allowed surfers to explore for waves in Norway, Iceland, Russia, Alaska, and even Antarctica.

Wetsuits have at times been used as a surfing fashion accessory, particularly in the '70s and '80s: Hawaiian surfer Larry Bertlemann wore a bell-bottom long john in 1976; Mark Richards of Australia, world champion from 1979 to 1982, emblazoned the front of his suits with a Superman-copied MR logo; and California trendsetter Danny Kwock has a neon-colored wetsuit wardrobe in 1980 that included a turquoise, cream, and magenta fullsuit. Santa Cruz aerialist Shawn "Barney" Barron took delivery on a custom-designed series of superhero wetsuits in the late '90s, but the vast majority of wetsuits produced by that time were black on black or black with dark blue accents. Wetsuits overtook surfboards in the early '70s as the second-largest division of the surf industry, behind surfwear. Quiksilver, the world's biggest surf-wear company, began making wetsuits in 1990, and Billabong soon followed. It was estimated that nearly 600,000 surfing wetsuits were sold worldwide in 2002, with retail cost on a 3/2 fullsuit ranging from $150 to $300. *See also* beavertail, booties, drysuit, fullsuit, long john, Meistrell brothers, Bev Morgan, Jack O'Neill, O'Neill Wetsuits, short john, springsuit.

wetsuit jacket   *See* beavertail.

wetsuit rash   Condition brought on by a poorly fitting wetsuit rubbing against the skin; most commonly found on the neck, armpits, and behind the knee; irritating in mild cases, unbearable in its most severe form. Saltwater increases the pain of a wetsuit rash, and on occasion can produce infection. The introduction of urine (unavoidable during a long surf session) can further aggravate a wetsuit rash. Pandemic in cold-water surfing areas during '60s and '70s, when wetsuits were made of less-flexible rubber, wetsuit rashes were generally treated by smearing Vaseline on the affected area before surfing. The thin nylon or polypropylene rash guard—a long- or short-sleeve undergarment, introduced in 1985—helped reduce the incidences of wetsuit rash. By the mid-'90s, softer neoprene material, along with improvements in wetsuit patterning and contouring, had all but eliminated wetsuit rash.

Wetteland, Max   Energetic surfer/board-maker/contest promoter from Durban, South Africa; a semifinalist in the 1964 World Surfing Championships, and cofounder of the Gunston 500 surfing contest. Wetteland was born (1938) and raised in Durban, began surfing at age 12, started building wooden surfboards at 15, and was the South African national paddleboard champion in 1958, 1959, and 1960. Because South Africa as of 1964 had yet to stage any kind of surfing competition, Wetteland was picked as his country's sole representative to that year's World Championships by an informal vote from his peers in Durban and Cape Town. He thus made his competition debut in what was then the sport's biggest-ever international event, and his semifinal placing came as a surprise to the rest of the field. He also competed in the 1965 World Championships, held in Lima, Peru, and was featured in the surf film classic *Endless Summer*. Wetteland and two Durban partners opened Surf Centre in 1965, South Africa's first surf shop, which sold Wetteland Surfboards. In 1969, Wetteland, along with Ian McDonald and Ernie Tomson (father of 1978 world champion Shaun Tomson), founded the Durban 500 pro surfing contest. Two years later the event was renamed the Gunston 500, and it later became a fixture on the world pro tour.

Wetteland moved with his family in 1975 to Vancouver, Canada, and developed a kind of prototype snowboard, which he patented as a "snow skate." He returned to Durban in 1982, abandoning the snowboard project, and began manufacturing polyurethane blanks for surfboards and sailboards. Wetteland won national seniors division longboard titles in 1991 and 1994.

whipturn Longboard maneuver performed almost exclusively in small waves, in which the surfer gets to his feet and immediately "whips" the board around into trim position. Usually the rider will add extra torque to the whipturn by paddling at an angle toward the "hook," or breaking section of the wave, before veering off into the opposite direction. Similar to a "left-go-right," "right-go-left," or "fade."

White, Bob Surfboard-maker and shop owner from Virginia Beach, Virginia; founder in 1968 of Wave Riding Vehicles, the East Coast's best-selling board company. White was born (1940) in Boston, Massachusetts, began surfing in 1963, founded Bob White Surfboards in Virginia Beach the following year, and changed the name of his company to Wave Riding Vehicles (WRV) in 1968. He marketed the new company with a series of simple, text-heavy black-and-white print ads that often featured line drawings of his latest model surfboards, each identified only by a number. (The double-ender Model No. 2, introduced in 1969, had a fin box on either end; all early WRV boards were stringerless and uncolored.) The company was helped by the fact that the WRV logo—five jumping dolphins arranged in an opened-ended circle—was one of the sport's best-designed marks. White made boards for some of the East Coast's best surfers, including Bruce Valluzzi and Jimbo Brothers; he was inducted into the East Coast Surfing Hall of Fame in 1996.

whitecaps Quickly dissipating whitewater fringe along the crest of open-ocean swells, created by a moderate to strong wind—the stronger the wind, the bigger and more powerful the whitecaps. A white-capped ocean means the surf is compromised or ru-

ined, unless the break is tucked in the wind-protected lee of a headland, point, cove, or breakwater. *See also* blown out, wind chop.

whitewater Roiling, bubbling, aerated water produced as a wave curls over and breaks. The force and power of whitewater varies tremendously, from playful and bubbly—beginning surfers almost always learn to surf on small inshore whitewater waves—to strong enough to break ships, bring down piers, and level beachfront homes. Surfers occasionally drown from being held under by whitewater. If the wave is especially powerful, whitewater can explode in kind of a geyser, sometimes up to double the height of the unbroken wave; during heavy surf, a fine mist rises off shoreward-bound whitewater like steam. In general, a line of whitewater will either dissipate as it moves into deeper water (as with virtually all barrier-reef surf breaks), rebound against a rocky shore or cliff, or gradually fizzle out as it moves toward a gently inclined shore. Whitewater can also re-form into an unbroken swell as it passes over a deep nearshore area, then break again. Whitewater is white because, unlike an unbroken wave or any relatively still body of water, its tiny-bubble texture isn't able to catch and reflect the color of the sky; incoming light instead is scattered and reflected back across the light spectrum, becoming white. Surfers often refer to whitewater as "foam"; prior to the 1970s it was also known as "soup." Soft-rolling whitewater is sometimes called "mush."

Whitman, Bill and Dudley Bill and Dudley Whitman, Florida's original surfers, were born in Miami Beach (1916 and 1921, respectively), and began riding homemade wooden bellyboards in 1932. The following year, after two Virginia Beach surfers visited Miami Beach with a redwood stand-up board, Bill Whitman quickly built a 10-foot, 87-pound copy out of sugar pine, and Dudley followed with a board of laminated spruce. The Whitman brothers became lifelong friends with California surf pioneer and board-maker Tom Blake after he visited Miami in 1934. The Whitmans at that point, along with nearly all of the small numbers of East Coast surfers, immediately switched over to the Blake-style hollow boards. A few years later, the Whitmans helped popularize surfing in Daytona Beach. In 1955, Bill met with West Coast surfboard manufacturer Hobie Alter, and a few years later he became the East Coast's first distributor for Hobie

Surfboards. The Whitmans were both still active surfers when they were inducted into the East Coast Surf Legends Hall of Fame in 1998.

Whitmore, John   Gruff and industrious surfer/ board-builder/organizer from Cape Town, South Africa; often described as the "father of South African surfing." Whitmore was born (1929) and raised in the beachfront suburb of Sea Point, near Cape Town, and began bodysurfing as a teenager. In 1949, the 19-year-old Whitmore, having seen photographs of surfers, began to make hollow plywood surfboards for himself and a few friends, and they started riding the breaks near his Sea Point home. Whitmore continued to build boards and search out new surf breaks along the Cape Town peninsula, as well as the coast between Cape Town and Durban. While driving west from Port Elizabeth in 1959, he pulled off the single-lane highway, looked to the ocean, and was captivated by a set of long right-breaking waves on a distant point; he later told a group of Cape Town surfers to look for the break near the township of Jeffreys Bay. Whitmore himself camped on a beach at Cape St. Francis in 1959, adjacent to the break made famous as "the perfect wave" in Bruce Brown's hit movie *The Endless Summer.*

John Whitmore

Whitmore began importing polyurethane surfboard blanks from Southern California's Clark Foam in 1958; four years later he licensed the Clark name and began making blanks in Cape Town. That same year he founded Whitmore Surfboards, became the Cape Town distributor for *Surfer* magazine, and played host and guide for Bruce Brown during the filming of *Endless Summer.* It was the goateed Whitmore who suggested to Brown that they look for waves at Cape St. Francis. In 1964, he was elected chairman of the Western Province Surfing Association, South Africa's first surfing organization; he also began touring the first surf films up and down the South African coast, from Capetown to East London. He started recording daily surf reports on Cape Town's Radio Good Hope, a service he provided for 18 years. Whitmore was elected president of the just-formed South Africa Surfing Association in 1965, a post he held for nine years. (Whitmore himself was the nation's top-ranked veterans division surfer in 1966, 1967, and 1969.) He managed South Africa's teams to the World Surfing Championships in 1966, 1970, and 1972.

Whitmore introduced South Africa to the Hobie Cat catamaran in 1971, and three years later became the first distributor in the country for the Morey Boogie bodyboard; he is seen riding a bodyboard at Eland's Bay (another break he discovered, northwest of Cape Town) in 1994's *Endless Summer II.* Whitmore died of lung cancer on Christmas Eve, 2001, at age 73. He was married and had three children. Jonathan Paarman, a world-ranked surfer in the mid-'70s, is Whitmore's nephew.

Wilkings, Steve   Versatile California-born photographer, heralded in the 1970s for his tight-angle water shots taken primarily on the North Shore of Oahu. Wilkings was born (1946) in Hollywood, California, raised in Hermosa Beach, began surfing in 1958 and taking photographs in 1964. Wilkings became a *Surfer* magazine staff photographer in 1971, after receiving a B.F.A. in photography from the Art Center College of Design in Pasadena and moving to Hawaii, and set out to bring the magazine audience closer than ever before to the powerful North Shore surf, doing so at times by floating up the wave just as the tube developed overhead. In 1976 he bolted a waterproof camera to the tail section of a surfboard, and by following the action from the beach and releasing the shutter with a remote control unit as the rider disappeared into the tube, Wilkings captured the first behind-the-surfer view of a tuberide. He was a senior staff photographer at *Surfer* until 1980; he continued living in Hawaii, working for the most part as a freelance watersports photographer. His photographs have appeared in *Time, Life, People, Playboy, Sports Illustrated,* and *Rolling Stone*; he's also contributed to more than a half-dozen illustrated surfing books, including *The History of Surfing* (1983), *Surfing: The Ultimate Pleasure* (1984), *SurfRiders* (1997), and *The Perfect Day* (2001). Wilkings is married and has one child.

Williams, Carwyn   Cheeky and disheveled pro surfer from Mumbles, Wales, United Kingdom; the European pro champion in 1985 and 1989. Williams was born (1965) in Llandovery, Wales, son of a pub owner and former Welsh national team rugby player; he moved with his family to the fishing and resort town of Mumbles at age three. He began surfing at 14, with only a pair of trunks and a rugby vest to guard against the Bristol Channel chill. In 1983 Williams simultaneously held the Welsh, British, and European juniors titles. He finished runner-up in the inaugural European pro circuit in 1984, won in 1985, then spent much of 1986 recovering from a broken wrist. For Williams, however, contests were always secondary to travel. He spent the first six months of 1987 driving the coast of New South Wales and Queensland, living out of a 1969 Morris Minor he'd bought for $300; in autumn he was in France and Spain, sleeping in a bat-

Carwyn Williams

tered 1979 BMW; that winter in Hawaii he lived in the backseat of a rusted 1976 Chevy Monte Carlo. "My father's really embarrassed," Williams said in a *Deep* magazine interview. "He's told me not to tell people I've slept in cars. You do that, and you live on sandwiches for weeks at a time, and people like my father just can't understand it." Williams meanwhile had no luck on the 1989 world pro circuit, his one and only full season, but regained the European pro circuit title.

Williams badly injured his right knee in a 1990 automobile accident in France, and doctors told him he'd never surf again. Eight months later he had reconstructive surgery, and two years after that he began surfing; by 1995, while still wearing a heavy knee brace, he was back in top form. He finished #5 on the European pro circuit in 1996 and 1997. Williams has appeared in a small number of surf movies and videos, including *All Down the Line* (1989) and *E2K* (2001).

Williams, John "Wheels"   Australian surfer and photographer. Williams was born (1940) and raised in Sydney, and began surfing at Bondi Beach at age 17. He was one of *Surfer* magazine's first Australian correspondents, and in 1963 it was his black-and-white photographs that gave American surf audiences their first look at the soon-to-be famous waves of Kirra and Byron Bay. Williams finished third in the 1965 European Championships.

Williams, Les   Pioneering high-performance surfer from Santa Monica, California; remembered for his banked turns at Malibu in the early 1950s, and as a senior competitive ace from the mid-'60s to the late '90s. Williams was born (1931) and raised in Utica, New York, moved with his family to Santa Monica in 1944, and began surfing the following year. In the summer of 1950, he borrowed a surfboard Joe Quigg had just built for his wife-to-be Aggie Bane—one of the "girl boards" made for a small group of pre-Gidget female Malibu surfers. Bane's nine-footer was not only smaller than those used by the men, but lighter, more streamlined, and "lifted" in the nose and tail, and the regularfooted Williams was able to push it up and down the wave rather than just angle across the face, as was the custom at the time. "He used to borrow that board and do circles around everyone," Bane later said. Williams's style of riding caught on, and the "girl boards" became the forerunners of the "Malibu chip," which in turn was the prototype for the longboard as it exists today.

Williams helped to develop the 1961-founded United States Surfing Association, and from 1962 to 1965 he was the United States Surfing Championships (USSC) head judge. In 1966, Williams himself began competing in the USSC, winning the seniors (age 35 to 50) in 1966, 1970, and 1971; the grandmasters (50 to 60) in 1977 and 1981; the senior grandmasters (60–65) in 1992, and the legends (65 and up) in 1997.

Williams, Ross Big, blond, regularfooter from Haleiwa, Hawaii. Williams was born (1973) in Toledo, Ohio, began surfing not long after moving with his family to Hawaii at age six, and won the boys' division of the 1988 United States Surfing Championships. A nine-year world circuit career saw Williams finish as high as 15th (in 1995, 1997, and 1999), before dropping off the Top 44 ratings sheet at the end of the 2000 season at age 28. If Williams's contest record was something of a disappointment—"After eight years on tour," the usually neutral *ASP Media Guide* said in 2000, "it is amazing that this surfer has never posted a win of any description"—Williams was nonetheless long regarded as one of the sport's best all-arounders, smooth and powerful in waves from two to 20-foot. He was featured on six cover shots between 1993 and 1996, three for *Surfer* and three for *Surfing,* and surf video king Taylor Steele gave Williams plenty of screen time in each of his annual productions, including *Momentum* (1992), *Loose Change* (1999), and *Hit and Run* (2000). Williams finished fourth in the 2001 Quiksilver/Eddie Aikau big-wave contest held at Waimea Bay, Hawaii.

Wills, Danny Quiet, even-keeled Australian pro surfer from Byron Bay, New South Wales; world-ranked #3 in 1998. Wills was born (1975) and raised in Byron Bay, began riding waves with his surfing father at age two, and at 13 was Tom Carroll's miniature sidekick in the popular surf movie *All Down the Line,* at which point he became a nationally recognized child surf star. In 1997, his debut year on the world tour, Wills finished #33. The following year he won back-to-back contests in Japan, led the ratings for more than four months, and was in second place going into the final event of the year at Hawaii's Pipeline, when he faltered. Two years later he dropped to #30; in 2001 he bounced back to finish ninth. Wills, meanwhile, distinguished himself as a pro surfer completely lacking in bluster and self-hype. "I was always just this young kid," he told *Aus-*

Danny Wills

tralia's Surfing Life magazine in 1998, "who had a really lucky life." He has appeared in more than two dozen surf videos, including *Oz on Fire* (1991), *The Theory* (1999), and *Performers III* (1999).

wind chop Short-lived ocean surface waves usually just a few inches high, produced by wind blowing either directly over the surf zone or in nearby offshore waters. The bumps, lumps, and ruffles that constitute chop make surfing more difficult and the surfer who "hits a chop" is either put off balance or thrown from the board altogether. Chop is generally the result of an onshore or sideshore breeze; chop from a land-to-sea offshore wind is rare, but not unheard of. In a sense, chop is the fundamental component for all waves, as individual chop waves combine and recombine during storms to create open-ocean swells. But surfers generally define chop only as it affects breaking surf. *See also* blown out.

wind waves, wind swell Tidal bores and tsunami waves excepted, all oceanic waves are created by storm-generated winds and might therefore be called "wind waves," just as all swells are wind swells. But as used by surfers, both phrases describe waves created either by strong local winds or winds in the not-too-distant offshore waters—up to a few hundred miles from the coast. Wind waves are tightly bunched as they move through the water (usually between four to 10 seconds apart), dissipate quickly as they travel, and are often ragged, bumpy, and not worth riding; wind swell surf is frequently described as "wind slop." But under the right conditions, at the right spots—particularly beachbreaks—wind swell can be groomed by a countervailing offshore breeze to produce virtually uninterrupted well-shaped waves. *See also* ground swell.

Windansea History-rich California surf break located in the affluent San Diego beach town of La Jolla. A wave-amplifying offshore canyon and a broad swell window both help to make Windansea one of America's most dependable surf breaks, ridable all year from two to 12 foot. Windansea breaks left and right over a flat rock reef, portions of which are often covered in sand; north swells create better rights, south swells produce long lefts; medium and low tides are preferred. The Windansea surf is often shifty, hard to read, thick-based, and sloped; hollow sections can pop up on occasion. Kelp beds located just beyond the break reduce the effect of the afternoon onshore wind. Consistency aside, however, Windansea itself isn't thought of as a great California surf break, like Malibu or Rincon. Adjacent surf breaks, just as mercurial as Windansea, include Big Rock, Simmons, and Bird Rock.

While nearby sand-bottom breaks like Mission Beach and La Jolla Shores were surfed as far back as the late 1920s, Windansea wasn't ridden until New York–born surf pioneer Woody Brown tried it out in 1937; La Jolla natives Don Okey and Townsend Cromwell followed the next day, and were soon joined by Woody Ekstrom, Dorian Paskowitz, John Elwell, and others. (Originally known as Neptune Beach, the break was renamed Windansea in the '40s after a nearby beachfront resort hotel.) A four-post palm-frond beach shack was erected on the sandstone cliffs in front of the break for the first time in 1946, and "the Shack" eventually became a surf world icon. By the mid-'50s, Windansea surfers had already earned a reputation for being fearless and talented in the water, bellicose and crudely funny on the beach. The Windansea surf meanwhile earned special notoriety in 1954, when board designer Bob Simmons died there during an eight-foot swell. Local surfers

long ago earned a reputation for being surly, even hostile, to visitors, and continued to push societal boundaries; as seen in Greg Noll's 1959 movie *Search for Surf,* a group of Windansea surfers wearing Third Reich army uniforms and carrying a Nazi flag sledded down an underground storm drain that let out on the beach just south of Windansea. By that time, a small number of locals were beginning to make their mark outside of the area, including surfboard shapers Pat Curren, Mike Diffenderfer, and Carl Ekstrom, ace switchfooter Butch Van Artsdalen, and future *Endless Summer* costar Mike Hynson. Early alumnus Buzzy Bent was preparing to cofound the Chart House restaurant chain.

Windansea's cultural magnetism was strongest in the 1960s; artist Andy Warhol filmed *San Diego Surf* here in 1967, one year after New Journalism proponent Tom Wolfe published his 7,000-word "Pump House Gang" essay, describing the local surf scene. Meanwhile, the 1963-formed Windansea Surf Club—with a membership that included surf world luminaries such as Hynson, Van Artsdalen, Joey Cabell, and Skip Frye—carried on the area's crass surfing tradition in a slightly more methodical manner, as they won contests and took high-profile road trips. Windansea surfers of the '70s seemed primarily interested in harassing nonlocals; freckle-faced Chris O'Rourke nonetheless emerged as a world-class talent, and part-time local Debbie Beacham went on to win the 1982 world pro tour title. Recent well-known surfers to emerge from the Windansea area include MTV personality and former pro surfer Peter King, *Longboard* magazine editor Devon Howard, and longboard world champion Joel Tudor. The San Diego Historical

Windansea

Site Board added the Windansea shack to its list of registered sites in 1998; a *Los Angeles Times* article noted that the shack had been used for surfer weddings, baptisms, christenings, and funerals.

The Windansea surf was featured in John "Doc" Ball's seminal photo book *California Surfriders* (1946), and in 2000 the break was the subject of a 36-page feature in the *Surfer's Journal.* Windansea has also been featured in more than a dozen surf movies and videos, including *Barefoot Adventure* (1960), *Cavalcade of Surf* (1962), *A Cool Wave of Color* (1964), *Blazing Longboards* (1994) ,and *Super Slide* (2000). *Malibu and Windansea: Parallel Surf Societies* was the title of a 1990 exhibit staged by the California Surf Museum in nearby Pacific Beach. *See also* localism, The Pump House Gang, Windansea Surf Club.

Windansea Surf Club   Rowdy but well-organized surf club from La Jolla, California, with a roster including many of the America's best surfers in the mid- and late 1960s. Former high school teacher Chuck Hasley re-formed the Windansea Surf Club in the summer of 1963 in order to field a team for the Malibu Invitational. (The long-disbanded Windansea Surf and Ski Club originated in 1947.) Joey Cabell, Butch Van Artsdalen, Rusty Miller, Skip Frye, and Mike Hynson were among the first recruits. For the Malibu contest, Hasley rented a bus, hired a generator-powered rock band, loaded in more than two dozen cases of beer, and picked up a cheer squad of friends and groupies. Wretchedly hungover by the time they arrived at Malibu, Windansea Surf Club members nonetheless took five of the six slots in the finals, and won the contest easily. "The attitude of Windansea," Hasley said years later, "was, 'We're going to win the contest; we're going to the dance and take all the girls; we're going to out-drink everybody. And if they don't like it, we're going to beat the shit out of them.'"

Windansea continued for another five years as a kind of talent-studded surfing frat house. It had few meetings, and the meetings it did have were almost always conducted without the club's best riders. Many club members rarely if ever surfed at Windansea, La Jolla's best-known break. But no other surfing group of the era, including the United States Surfing Association, had the pride or the high profile of the Windansea Surf Club. Members included Hobie Alter, Mickey Dora, Barry Kanaiaupuni, Linda Benson, Pat Curren, Ronald and Bobby Patterson, Phil Edwards, Mickey Muñoz, Donald Takayama, Joey Hamasaki,

Joyce Hoffman, Mike Purpus, Margo Godfrey, Corky Carroll, LJ Richards, and Mike Diffenderfer; all were issued matching T-shirts and nylon club jackets. Windansea won the team relay paddle race at the 1963 West Coast Surfing Championships; in 1964 and 1966 it again won the Malibu Invitational; in 1967 it won the Baja Surf Club Invitational. Public relations pro and club executive director Thor Svenson meanwhile arranged a number of well-publicized Windansea trips and events, including a November 1967 visit to Sydney, Australia; the journey was filmed for *The Fantastic Plastic Machine,* a 20th Century Fox movie, and written about in *The Fantastic Plastic Voyage,* a companion book. But this was Windansea's last hurrah, as the club arrived in Sydney to find that Australian board-makers had just developed the new short surfboard; the Windansea surfers were soundly beaten by a group of B-team Australians in a one-day surf contest. The club was dormant for more than a decade, then made a comeback of sorts beginning in the early '80s, during the longboard resurgence. *See also* Chuck Hasley, Malibu Invitational, surf clubs.

windsurfing   *See* sailboarding.

Wingnut   *See* Robert Weaver.

wings, winger   Surfboard rail design popular in the 1970s and '80s, in which the outline of the board was interrupted a few inches from the tail to form a bump-like "wing," then resumed. The wing itself, along with the narrower tail section, added extra "bite"—meaning the board was less likely to slide or skip during turns. While prototype versions of the wing were produced in the early and mid-'60s (the Dale Velzy Bump model and the 422 by Jacobs Surfboards), the design is generally credited to California surfer J Riddle, who invented in late 1972 what he called the "fangtail," so named because the cut line actually aimed upward and the wings looked like fangs on the rail line. The design was refined in 1973 by Hawaiian board-makers Dick Brewer and Jim Sidwell, along with Steve Walden in California, and renamed the "winger." Wings were placed between four to 10 inches from the tail, and the wing generally would connect a three-quarter-inch difference between the tail outline and the outline from the rest of the board. A narrow concave flute was often shaped into the underside of each wing parallel to the board's centerline. Double-wingers, even triplewingers, were made in the late '70s, with each set of wings separated by about six inches. Wings were increasingly blended to the rail line in the early and mid-'80s, and by 1990 the wing had all but disappeared. Australian and New Zealand surfers refer to wings as "bumps" or "flyers."

Winter, Russell Stocky regularfoot pro surfer from Newquay, England; the first British surfer to qualify for the world championship pro tour. Winter was born (1975) in London and raised in Newquay, the youngest of three surfing brothers. At the beginning of 1998, following a long competitive apprenticeship, he moved up to the championship tour; he failed to requalify in 1999, returned in 2000, then again dropped off following the 2002 season. Tropical surf breaks were a great pro tour perk, Winter said. When *Surfer* magazine called him at home in 1998 and asked about weather conditions at his local beach, he answered, "Well, it's freezing now and it snowed yesterday." The block-shaped Winter (5′6″, 155 pounds) is a precise, tight-cornering surfer; he's appeared in a small number of surf videos, including *Lost . . . On the Road with Spike* (1995) and *E2K* (2000).

Winton, Glen Enigmatic and good-natured goofyfoot pro surfer from Norah Head, New South Wales, Australia; world-ranked #5 in 1985. Winton was born (1960) in Melbourne, Victoria, and began surfing at age eight, five years after moving with his family to Norah Head. All the Wintons were accomplished and daring: Glen's mother had been the Victoria state cycling champion, his father a four-time national hydroplane champion, and his brother would become the international altitude record holder for ultralight planes, before dying in a flying accident. Glen Winton was the Australian Professional Surfriders Association champion in 1981 and 1982, and achieved notice for his odd multifinned surfboards. Asked in 1982 how he came up with his new four-fin design, Winton replied that he'd just simply knocked off two fins, leaving four. His style in the water was both innovative and ungainly; the tailslide maneuvers he invented in the early '80s were a blueprint for the Kelly Slater–led New School surfers in the early '90s. Winton won five world pro circuit events in his career, including the 1987 Gotcha Pro. While never standoffish, he kept some distance between himself and the surfing mainstream, and seemed to enjoy the air of mystery conferred upon

him by the surf media. He was called "Mr. X," although the anonymity was belied by his two *Surfer* magazine cover shots—and by Winton himself. "Everyone actually knows who I am," he said in 1987. "The thing is, everybody doesn't know that everyone else knows who I am." Winton finished runner-up in the 1993 Longboard World Championships, and retired from the shortboard pro circuit a few weeks later. He appeared in more than a dozen surf movies and videos, including *Gripping Stuff* (1987) and *Madmen, Saints and Sinners* (1992), and also made his own early '90s commercial surf videos, *Rad Movez I* and *Rad Movez II.*

"Wipe Out" The world's best-known surf song, containing the world's best-known drum solo, was recorded in December 1962 by the Surfaris, a four-month-old band from Glendora, California, made up of three 15-year-old guitarists and a 17-year-old drummer. The maniacal laugh that opens the song was supplied by the band's manager. The drum solo is said to have been copied directly from a roll used by a local high school marching band. The song was written as a throwaway: the Surfaris had rented $100 worth of studio time to record their single "Surfer Joe," and had some time left over at the end of the session; "Wipe Out" was composed in 15 minutes, and waxed on the second take. Released the following spring on Dot Records, it went to #2 nationally in June 1963 (and was named Record of the Year a few months later in Australia), and returned to the top 20 in 1966 as a reissue. "Wipe Out" was on the *Dirty Dancing* soundtrack in 1987, and was used in ad campaigns for Nissan, Wendy's, Pepsi, and Kodak. The Beach Boys and the Fat Boys (an early rap act) had a #12 hit in 1987 with their version of "Wipe Out." *See also* surf music, the Surfaris.

wipeout A ride-ending mishap that can assume any one of a dozen or more variations, from benign to deadly. Common forms of the wipeout include pearling (when the board's nose digs into the water), digging a rail (the board's edge catches), spinning out (the tail section loses traction), and free-fall (board and rider go airborne), along with poorly timed turns and cutbacks, and collisions with other surfers. Wipeouts often look worse than they are; just a tiny percentage of them are actually dangerous.

Of all surfing expressions, "wipeout" has penetrated furthest into common usage; the *Oxford English*

Wipeout by California's Shawn "Barney" Barron

Dictionary definition for "wipe-out" (the phrase is still occasionally hyphenated) reads: "a fall from one's surfboard, or from a wave. Now also more widely, a fall from a skateboard, bicycle, etc., especially while maneuvering at speed." "Wipeout," along with "stoke," is also one of the very few phrases surfers have used continuously through the decades. Surf lexicon synonyms for wipeout include "taking gas," "eating it," and a number of expressions starting with "getting": "getting worked," "lunched," "hammered," "pounded," "drilled," "nailed," "rooted," "stuffed," "tweaked," or "thrashed."

Surfing magazines over the decades have approached the wipeout from a number of angles: as a health and safety issue, with dozens of tips articles on how to make the best of a spill (the cardinal rule is to relax while underwater); as a wellspring for comedy (in articles like "TOADS: Take Off And Die Syndrome," "Altered States," and "Lunch Time!"); as a theme for fashion shoots ("Wipeout in Style"); as poetic muse ("Crisp water," surf publisher John Severson versified in 1965, "Clipping confident boardmen from their mounts"); and as celebrity showcases (each installment of "Wipeouts," a monthly column in *Australia's Surfing Life,* has a famous surfer recounting his or her worst wipeout). The cinematic wipeout sequence, usually a two- or three-minute montage of casualties, has long been a staple of the surf movie/video genre.

Some of the most famous wipeouts through the years include Tommy Lee's "cannonball" plunge at Waimea in 1962, Greg Noll's 1964 midface vault at Outer Reef Pipeline, Titus Kinimaka's femur-breaking wave at Waimea on Christmas morning, 1989, and Jay Moriarity's *New York Times*–published, over-the-falls shocker at Maverick's in 1994. Just as spectacular wipeouts often produce virtually no consequences (Moriarity broke his board during his Maverick's pileup but returned to the lineup on a backup board and rode for the rest of the morning), relatively harmless-looking wipeouts can be injurious or even fatal. After slipping from the back of his board while riding a six-foot wave during the 1983 Pipeline Masters, Florida-born surfer Steve Massfeller struck the reef headfirst and suffered a massive skull fracture over his right eye. On December 23, 1994, in what became the world's most famous wipeout, Hawaiian big-wave rider Mark Foo died after taking what appeared to be a routine spill midway down a 15-footer at Maverick's. As a rule, bad wipeouts generally occur at crowded breaks, as people run into each other, or in shallow-water reefbreaks like Hawaii's Pipeline or Teahupoo in Tahiti. While beginning surfers experience what appear to be mild wipeouts, they nonetheless tend to get hurt at a rate equal to or greater than intermediate and advanced surfers, as they haven't yet developed the habit of putting distance between themselves and their board, the bottom, and other surfers. *See also* closeout tube, dig a rail, freefall, injuries and surfing, logjam, over the falls, pearl, rail sandwich, spinout.

wired   To have mastery over a place, maneuver, or situation; a time-honored surfing expression that dates back to the mid-1950s. Kelly Slater, for example, has Backdoor Pipeline wired, just as Laird Hamilton has tow-in surfing wired. The expression comes from having everything—all the "wires"—properly connected and functioning. "Dialed" (or "dialed in") is synonymous with "wired."

Witzig, John   Intelligent and acerbic Australian surf journalist from Sydney, New South Wales; co-founder of *Tracks* magazine in 1970, but best known for "We're Tops Now," his 1967 *Surfer* magazine article that celebrated Australian surfers while bashing the Californians. Witzig was born (1944) in Sydney, raised near Palm Beach, began surfing in the late '50s, and started writing articles for Australia's *Surfing World* magazine in 1963. The following year he was a judge for the debut World Surfing Championships, held in Sydney, and two years later got his first taste of surf world controversy by writing much of the July/August "New Era" issue of *Surfing World,* in which the magazine seemed to dismiss 1964 world champion Midget Farrelly in favor of younger Australians Nat Young and Bob McTavish. When Young rode to victory in the 1966 World Championships—beating California favorite David Nuuhiwa and rendering the Nuuhiwa-led noseriding style of surfing obsolete—Witzig was justifiably upset at how the American surf press seemed to ignore the result. California surfers in particular, Witzig advised in his instantly notorious "We're Tops Now" article, needed to take off "the rose-colored spectacles" and come to grips with the fact that "everything the pedestal of California surfing is being built upon means nothing!" Witzig was shrill but correct: Young and the Australians had in fact changed the course of surfing. "We're on top," he summed up, "and will continue to dominate." Paul Witzig, John's older brother, would document the next phase of Australian surfing in his 1969 movie *Evolution.* John Witzig meanwhile went on to edit *Surf International* magazine from 1967 to 1969, then founded the counterculture surf tabloid *Tracks* in 1970, along with surf filmmaker Alby Falzon and editor David Elfrick. Witzig continued over the years to write articles for *Tracks, Surfer,* and other surf periodicals, but never again struck a nerve as he did with "We're Tops Now." *See also* Tracks.

Witzig, Paul Moonfaced Australian surf filmmaker from Sydney, Australia; best known for his rough-hewn 1969 film *Evolution,* which defined the opening phase of the shortboard revolution. Witzig was born (1940) and raised in Sydney, began surfing at Palm Beach at age 11, and got his first break as a filmmaker in 1962, when Californian Bruce Brown gave him a 16-millimeter camera and hired him to shoot Australian footage for Brown's upcoming movie *The Endless Summer.* Witzig later worked as Brown's Down Under liaison, screening the American's movies in New South Wales and Queensland. He also worked as a judge in the 1964 World Surfing Championships. Witzig became a full-time filmmaker after dropping out of architecture school in 1965 and released *A Life in the Sun* the following year, just a few months before surf journalist John Witzig, Paul's younger brother, angered American surf society with his infamous pro-Aussie "We're Tops Now" article, published in *Surfer* magazine. *Hot Generation* (1968), Witzig's second movie, includes the cinematic debut of the short surfboard, with Australians Bob McTavish and Nat

Paul Witzig

Young riding their stocky vee-bottom boards in flawless eight-foot surf at Hawaii's Honolulu Bay.

But it was Witzig's third film, *Evolution,* that really captured the spirit of the times. The movie costars Young, George Greenough, and Ted Spencer, but is for the most part a showcase for Wayne Lynch, the 17-year-old surfing sensation from Victoria. Lynch is credited as the first surfer to really bank off the crest of the wave, and his turns and cutbacks in *Evolution* can be seen as the dividing line between the longboard and shortboard eras. While reviews for *Evolution* were tepid ("Witzig's photography is uninspired," one notice said, "but he proves that if your subjects are creative and talented, you don't have to do anything but push the button . . ."), the film nonetheless became a period icon. Witzig produced or coproduced three more full-length surf movies: *Sea of Joy* (1971), *Islands* (1972), and *All Down the Line* (1989). He also worked on three short subjects: *Hawaii '68, Animals* (1971), and *Rolling Home* (1974). In 1986, he made *Blown Away!,* a feature-length sailboarding movie. Witzig received an M.A. in architecture from Columbia Pacific University in 1983, and began a career as an architect. In 1997 he was featured in *50 Years of Surfing on Film,* an Outdoor Life Network TV series. Witzig is married and has three children, and lives in Brooms Head, New South Wales. *See also Evolution,* surf movies.

Wolfe, Tom *See* the Pump House Gang.

Wolfson, Joe Energetic bodyboarder from Manhattan Beach, California; nicknamed "Dr. 360" for his devotion to the spinning 360-degree maneuver; unknown outside of the southern Los Angeles beach area until 1998 when, at age 48, he was diagnosed with inoperable lung cancer. Wolfson was born in

New York (1949), learned to bodysurf as a teenager after he moved with his family to Long Beach, California, and began riding a bodyboard in the late '70s. While he didn't in fact invent the bodyboarding 360 (as was later reported), he was nonetheless a competent and dedicated wave-rider, capable of staying in the water for five or six hours at a time. After his cancer diagnosis, Wolfson, a city park recreation director, withdrew $100,000 in savings and distributed it to friends and family, then gave away his car and other possessions. One evening in November, a despondent Wolfson wrote a brief suicide note, swallowed a handful of sleeping pills, put on his wetsuit, paddled 150 yards offshore, tied himself to a buoy, and blacked out. The next morning he was pulled from the water by a lifeguard and revived. Wolfson said he'd made a terrible mistake by trying to take his life, and spent many of the next 15 months telling his story, first to the local papers, then the *Los Angeles Times,* then on *20/20* and *Good Morning America,* and finally in his autobiography, *Full Circle.* In February 2000, when Wolfson died after his car unaccountably ran into a tree, *Time* magazine eulogized him as a "legendary surfer," the *New York Times* called him "an aquatic Peter Pan . . . the perennial California surfer," and the *Economist,* in a full-page obituary, compared him to James Dean and Buddy Holly, and called him a "national celebrity." *Surfer* magazine, respectful of a fallen comrade but amused at the sudden burst of interest by the mainstream media—for someone the editors had never heard of—titled its obit, "Joe, We Hardly Knew Ye."

women and surfing   Women surfers in ancient Hawaii rode alongside the men, had surf breaks named in their honor, were depicted in engravings, and even mythologized. An Oahu surfing chieftess was recalled in song and chant as a demigod with the power to transform into a gigantic lizard or huge shark; a 19th-century Hawaiian historian observed that "the gentler sex frequently carried off the highest honors" in surfing competitions. But when the sport was resurrected in the early 20th century after nearly disappearing during the previous few decades, it was practiced almost exclusively by men and boys, and gender imbalance was the rule as the sport was exported from Hawaii to America, Australia, Europe, and beyond. There were bright spots. Isabel Letham is known the "mother of Australian surfing" for riding tandem with Duke Kahanamoku during the Hawai-

ian's famous Sydney wave-riding demonstration in 1914; the thinner and lighter boards that in the early 1950s ushered in the turn/cutback style of high-performance surfing were made for women surfers at Malibu; and assertive teenager Kathy "Gidget" Kohner—a Malibu regular from 1956 to 1958—remains the world's most famous surfer. Each era, moreover, has produced exceptionally talented women surfers, from Mary Ann Hawkins in the '30s and '40s to Linda Benson in the '50s and '60s, on through Joyce Hoffman, Margo Oberg, Frieda Zamba, Wendy Botha, Pam Burridge, Lisa Andersen, and Layne Beachley. Nonetheless, women surfers by 2003 made up less than 15 percent of the surfing population worldwide, and the story of women's surfing is to a large degree told in terms of its generally uneasy relationship to the sport's male majority.

In the 1960s, the just-minted surf industry, including the surf media, was captained entirely by men, and attitudes toward women surfers ranged from benignly dismissive ("We finally gave in," *Surfer* magazine wrote in a caption for their self-described "groundbreaking" 1964 cover shot of Linda Merrill) to outright hostile ("Girls shouldn't surf," Australian Nat Young said after winning the 1966 World Championships, "they make fools of themselves"). The bikini girl was meanwhile endlessly celebrated; *Surfing Illustrated* had a monthly "Miss SI" feature, while zaftig blond Sherry Haley, twice profiled by American surf magazines in the '60s, was shown in a beachwear fashion spread being transported regally down the beach atop a board carried by six surfer/manservants. The result was that the overwhelming majority of coast-dwelling women stayed away from practicing what was often called "the sport of kings," while those few who undertook it were faced with equipment problems (bathing suits that wouldn't stay put during a wipeout, ill-fitting wetsuits) and a lack of local role models, as well as constant pressures about how surfing affected their looks and comportment. "Once a girl discontinues to express her femininity and becomes careless about grooming," reigning world champion Margo Godfrey wrote in 1969, "she loses a lot of respect." Godfrey went on to advise female surfers to apply a cream to knees each night to prevent unsightly "surf bumps."

The formation of a world pro surfing tour in the mid-'70s quantified women's second-rate status: the 1980 men's tour, for example, featured 11 contests worth an aggregate $239,000, while the women's tour consisted of two events worth a total of $10,000. Contest reporters in the '70s and '80s often ignored the women's events completely. "I can't remember who won the girls division," Australian surf journalist Phil Jarratt wrote in his coverage of the 1983 Rip Curl Pro at Bells Beach, "but I enjoyed meeting the sweet young things in the judging bus later on, and I thought South Africa's Wendy Botha and Australia's Helen Lambert were particularly foxy." Groups like the Women's International Surfing Association and the Australian Women Surfriders Association were formed in the mid- and late '70s in a partially successful bid for autonomy. (Top pro surfer Laura Blears of Hawaii meanwhile put a new spin on the bikini girl by posing and surfing nude in a 1975 *Playboy* spread; four-time world champion Wendy Botha of South Africa did the same in 1992.)

Women's surfing took a heavily publicized turn for the better in the mid-1990s, due in large part to the star power of Floridian Lisa Andersen, the blond-haired, blue-eyed single mom who rendered moot the "femininity" issue by being talented enough to win four consecutive world titles, and sexy enough to pose for a surf magazine portrait reclining in a bubble bath with a bottle of champagne. As noted in a 1996 cover story for *Outside* magazine, Andersen was responsible for "changing the way beach boys look at beach girls, [and for] bringing droves of young women to the sport." By the end of the decade there were three women's surfing magazines, dozens of women's surfwear lines, women-themed surf shops, women's surf wax, women-designed wetsuit lines, women's surfing documentaries, and women-only surf schools. A 2001 survey by the Labels Network market research firm showed that surfing was the sport women in North America most wanted to learn. *Blue Crush*—a teenage girls' coming-of-age movie, and at $35 million the most expensive Hollywood surf film ever made—was released in 2002, prompting another spike of women-surfing features in the mainstream media, with articles in *Time* and *Newsweek*. A few surfers resented the fact that marketing for what was being called the "girls surfing revolution" relied almost exclusively on young, beautiful models. "They all want cute little blonde surfie girls," pro surfer Pauline Menczer of Australia said in 1999. "I've been told, 'We won't sponsor you because you don't have the look we want.' I was world champion when they said that!" Women's wave-riding performance standards had meanwhile advanced by

decade's end, with Hawaiians Rochelle Ballard and Keala Kennelly becoming the first women to ride consistently inside the tube, while four-time world champion and big-wave rider Layne Beachley of Australia became the first woman to break the 20-foot barrier.

But in many respects gender inequities in 2003 were nearly as significant as they had been in the early '60s. Women have little or nothing to do with the surf industry decision-making process, and there are virtually no women surf photographers, videographers, or surfboard shapers. The men's division of the 2002 world pro circuit was worth just over $3 million, while the women's division total was $360,000. Australian surf journalist Tim Baker noted that while women's and girls' lines made up nearly 50 percent of total surfwear sales in 2001, just a tiny percentage of buyers actually surfed, and that the positive net gain for women's surfing in general had been greatly overstated. The number of female surfers was indeed going up, slowly but steadily, and their presence was a welcome one. But the revolution, Baker concluded, had been "in women's shopping, rather than women's surfing." *See also* Australian Women's Surfriders Association, Golden Girls, International Women's Surfers, Roxy, Wahine magazine, Women's International Surfing Association, Women's World Longboard Championships.

Women's International Surfing Association

First all-women's competitive surfing association, based in Huntington Beach, California; founded on March 8 (International Women's Day), 1975, by pro surfers Jericho Poppler and Mary Setterholm to help address the sport's gender inequities. "Surfing does not demand aggressive strength," Setterholm noted when she introduced the Women's International Surfing Association (WISA). "Waves treat everyone equally; men and women are on the same terms as far as nature is concerned." Launched during a low point in American commercial surfing, WISA nonetheless opened strongly with well-run amateur events at San Onofre, Huntington, and Newport Beach, followed by the $8,000 Hang Ten Women's International Professional Surfing Championships at Malibu. Included among the 24 Hang Ten entrants were women from Japan, Great Britain, and Australia; 1968 world champion Margo Oberg of Hawaii won the $1,500 first-place prize. Perfectly illustrating what Setterholm had earlier described as the "hustling, cussing, intimidating pressure" of the average surf lineup, dozens of male surfers refused to clear the water at Malibu, forcing the women competitors to swerve and dodge their way across the waves. WISA's California-based contest circuit was played for laughs as well as sisterhood and ratings points; the Newport Small Wave Regatta, for example, featured a surfing-and-hula-hoop division.

After being sexually assaulted by a group of surfers at a party, WISA president Setterholm moved to New York in 1976, and longtime California surfer Mary Lou Drummy became the organization's second and final president, assisted throughout by Poppler. When the 1976-founded International Professional Surfers world tour added a women's division in 1977, WISA had difficulty competing for surf industry prize money. The organization continued to hold events, but was plainly in decline by the early '80s. After a renewed burst of activity in 1990, when Drummy put together an eight-contest circuit for 100 active members, WISA was starved for sponsorship during the 1991 surf industry recession, and folded. Along with Oberg, top WISA competitors over the years included world champions Lynne Boyer, Debbie Beacham, and Kim Mearig, and Hawaiian surf style icon Rell Sunn. *See also* Jericho Poppler.

Women's Professional Surfers (WPS) Organization formed in 1981 by former Golden Girl and soon-to-be world champion Debbie Beacham from La Jolla, California. Membership in Women's Professional Surfing (WPS) included virtually all of the approximately two dozen female pros from America and Australia. WPS conducted women's-only surf clinics on the beach in La Jolla in 1982 and 1984, and a small number of pro-am contests were held under WPS's auspices. But the group never gained any real traction—top WPA surfers still competed on the Association of Surfing Professionals tour—and after a brief resurrection in 1986 the WPA quietly folded. *See also* Debbie Beacham, Women's International Surfing Association.

Women's World Longboard Championships
Midsummer women's professional longboard competition held annually since 1999 at Boca Barranca, Costa Rica. The world pro tour has named a men's longboard world champion since 1986, and the biannual amateur world championships (now the World Games) have produced a men's longboard winner

since 1988. The Women's World Longboard Championship is the first title of its kind for females. Organized by California events promoter Hank Raymond—moved to action in part by his competitive longboarder daughter Kirsten—along with Toes on the Nose beachwear founder Richard Allred, the first Women's World Longboard Championship (WWLC) was held as an adjunct to the seventh annual Rabbit Kekai Classic. Fifty-two women competed for a total prize purse of $4,000; the mud-brown rivermouth surf at Boca Barranca was small but perfectly shaped, with some rides lasting more than a minute, and the general atmosphere of the three-day event, in contrast to virtually all men's surf contests, was easygoing and playful. Hawaii-raised surfer/model Daize Shayne, 22, won the contest. WWLC prize money was doubled in 2000, and first place went to 1999 runner-up Cori Schumacher, from California, who competed with a mild concussion and stitches in both legs, the result of rolling her car on the freeway a week earlier. Schumacher repeated in 2001; California's Kim Hamrock won in 2002. A small number of professional women's longboarding contests had meanwhile taken place in America, France, Australia, and Brazil, and the women pros, as much as they enjoyed the WWLC, hoped to see the new events tied together into a world championship tour, similar to the Association of Surfing Professionals' shortboard circuit. Results of the Women's World Longboard Championships:

1999:	Daize Shayne
2000:	Cori Schumacher
2001:	Cori Schumacher
2002:	Kim Hamrock

Wong, Arne Cartoonist and animator from Los Angeles, California; creator of vibrant, humorous, mildly subversive short animated sequences used in surf movies from the early and mid-1970s, including *Cosmic Children* (1970), *A Sea for Yourself* (1973), and *Five Summer Stories Plus Two* (1975). Wong was born (1950) and raised in San Francisco, began surfing at 15, and became a self-taught animator during high school. In "Karma," a 70-second short backed by the Chantays' "Pipeline," a hulking local grabs a nearby surfer and squeezes him into a bar of wax, uses another surfer as a board, then suddenly gets sucked into a whirlpool—at which point Wong pulls back to reveal that the entire episode has taken place in a toilet. In "Acapulco Gold," the jaunty, psychedelic, sing-along short from *Five Summer Stories Plus Two,* President Richard M. Nixon resigns office and heads south with mistress Martha Mitchell (a Watergate-era figure) and Checkers the dog in search of Acapulco Gold, the era's premium-grade marijuana. Wong later worked on the animated movies *Heavy Metal* (1981) and *Tron* (1982).

Wood, Nicky   Enigmatic pro surfer from Newcastle, New South Wales, Australia; world-ranked #12 in 1990. Wood was born (1970) and raised in Newcastle, began surfing at age six, and seemed destined for greatness; he was godson to four-time world champion Mark Richards, and 1966 world champion Nat Young was a frequent Wood family houseguest. Wood was a two-time winner in the cadets division (under 16) of the National Titles, and was runner-up to the Australian Professional Surfing Association title at age 15. The following year, in his first outing on the world pro tour, he won the 1986 Rip Curl Pro at Bells Beach; he remains the youngest male surfer to win a world circuit event, and the only one to win in a debut effort. Wood's surfing was at times gangly and choppy, but just as often he was spectacular, throwing his lean frame into high-torque turns and cutbacks. He also earned a reputation for mystery; he was nicknamed the Phantom for being all but invisible on the world tour, turning up just prior to his matches and vanishing directly afterward. His pro career, meanwhile, began unraveling almost immediately. He grew more than 12 inches from age 15 to 17, and his stretched knee ligaments were a source of constant pain; in 1988 he was unable to surf except during competition. Wood drank frequently, and often heavily—"the first four times I met him," wife-to-be

Nicky Wood

Natalie Ayoub said in 1989, "I couldn't understand a word he said, 'cause he was so pissed"—and in early 1992 he was convicted and fined for marijuana possession. Wood failed to qualify for the 1994 world tour, and told *Australia's Surfing Life* magazine the following year that "if you take a lot of drugs it fuckin' disorganizes you. It dregged me out, pretty much." World champion Pam Burridge believed Wood was in part a victim of his own early success. "A classic case of too much too soon," she said. "He has scars from all those expectations, and it doesn't look as though he'll ever really recover." Wood appeared in a small number of surf movies and videos, including *Savage Cuts* (1988) and *Rad Movez* (1992). *See also* drugs and surfing.

Woods, Gordon   Fastidious pioneering Australian board manufacturer from Sydney's Manly Beach; founder in 1956 of Gordon Woods Surfboards, the first company of its kind in the nation, and an industry leader until the late 1960s. Woods was born (1925) and raised in Sydney, began riding waves using a canvas-topped canoe in 1939, and started to build surfboards commercially just after World War II. It was part-time work; Woods made about two boards a month, and sold them through Sydney-area lifeguard clubs. Australian surfers at the time all used hollow plywood "cigar boxes" at least 14 feet long. A turning point for Australian surfing—and Woods's career—came in 1956, when a team of visiting American surfer/lifeguards flew into Sydney with their 10-foot balsa Malibu boards, which were infinitely more maneuverable than the cigar boxes. Local surfers were amazed to see the Americans doing sharp turns and cutbacks; Woods quickly bought one of the Malibu boards, knowing that "everything we [in Australia] had done as surfers up to that point had just been made redundant," and set about trying to make copies to sell from his just-established surf shop in Bondi Beach. As balsa was unavailable, Woods and other Sydney board manufacturers were forced to improvise, and for the next two years made Malibu-like boards with timber frames and plywood covering.

The three biggest Sydney-based board-makers, with the energetic Woods leading the way, relocated in 1958 to Brookvale, a new industrial park in north Sydney; other surfboard companies soon followed. Two years later Woods began producing his own polyurethane foam blanks, which replaced balsa as the board's core material. His shop and his reputation continued to grow; Woods Surfboards' team riders in 1963 included soon-to-be world champions Midget Farrelly and Nat Young. Woods left the board-making business in 1974, and went on to build yachts.

Woodworth, David "Woody"   Photographer from Corona del Mar, California; described by *Surfer* magazine as "the surf world's supreme colorist." Woodworth was seven when he moved with his family in 1960 from West Virginia to Newport Beach, California. He became an avid bodysurfer, kneerider, and mat-rider, and in 1972 set out to take scrapbook photographs of surf breaks in and around his hometown. *Surfer* began publishing his photos the following year, and in 1975 he was awarded a masthead slot (which he still holds) as well as a five-page portfolio feature. He often focused on the thundering shorebreak surf at the Wedge, Newport's notorious bodysurfing spot, but soon began to capture the softer, subtler aspects of the sport—pelicans banking along a sun-tinged swell, a minuscule see-through wave folding onto the sand, a crystalline aerial view of the California coastline. Woodworth also wrote over a dozen surf magazine articles between 1975 and 2000.

woody   Nickname for a wood-paneled, station-wagon-style automobile, originally made by Ford, with versions introduced in the 1930s and '40s by every major American automaker; popular with American surfers in the '50s and early '60s because they were roomy and inexpensive; later restored, displayed, and sold for exorbitant prices by car collectors and a handful of wealthy nostalgia-struck surfers. "From beast of burden," surf journalist Brian Gillogly wrote in 1995, the woody was "transformed into a cultural icon." Because wood was cheaper than steel, Ford began using wood panels on the sides and rear hatch of its square-backed "station-wagon"—a name derived from the car's original use, which was to transport groups of passengers to and from the train station. As steel became more affordable in the early '50s, the woody was discontinued. Largely because the exterior wood paneling (usually oak, ash, maple, or mahogany) was prone to termite infestation, surfers in the '50s were able to buy partially decomposing woodys for as little as $75. Rear seats were often removed, so that 10-foot boards could be easily inserted through the raised rear window, and to create a sleeping area for overnight surf trips; on cold nights, wood paneling might be pried from the car

Woody

doors and used for firewood. Because surfers in general treated their cars poorly, and because inexpensive replacements were easy to find, a broken woody was often simply abandoned by the side of the road. Woody owners included big-wave rider Greg Noll, surfboard manufacturer Dewey Weber, and Hawaiian hotdog pioneer Rabbit Kekai.

Woody restoration began catching on in the early '60s; *Surf Guide* magazine began running a "Woody of the Month" feature in 1963, and in July of that year *Car Craft* magazine published a "Wild Woodies and Surf Wagons!" cover story. ("Woodie" is often used instead of "woody.") Surf bands meanwhile began referencing the woody in song lyrics. "Surf City," Jan and Dean's #1 hit from 1963, opens with "I've got a '34 wagon and we call it a woody." Later that year the Sunsets released "My Little Surfin' Woodie."

In 2002, the 1974-founded National Woodie Club, based in Lincoln, Nebraska, had more than 3,000 members and sponsored 15 woody shows across the country, including Wavecrest Woodie Meet at San Diego County's Moonlight Beach. A prime restored woody can sell for up to $150,000. The U.S. Postal Service issued a woody wagon stamp in 2001, featuring a rear view of a surfboard-carrying 1940 Ford wagon. Books on woodys include *American Woodys* (1998) and *Woodies and Wagons* (2000). *See also* cars and surfing.

World Cup   Professional men's and women's surf contest held annually since 1975 on the North Shore of Oahu, Hawaii; the season-ending event on the men's world pro circuit from 1975 to 1982, and again in 1991; the women's season ender in 1977, 1980–82, 1991–93, and 2001. Kentucky Fried Chicken, sponsor for the men's division of the inaugural World Cup, pulled out just days before the event got under way, forcing event organizer Fred Hemmings to put up the $6,500 in prize money himself. Early rounds were held at Haleiwa, with the finals moved to Sunset Beach; 18-year-old Australian Mark Richards won. Lancers wine, meanwhile, sponsored the women's portion of the World Cup, held at Haleiwa, and winner Margo Oberg of Hawaii earned $4,000 for her victory, the largest women's surfing cash prize up to that point. The world pro circuit debuted the following year, with the men's World Cup scheduled as the season's final event and broadcast on CBS-TV. The women's pro tour was formed the following year, with the World Cup wrapping up the tour. For the next few seasons the World Cup was usually held at Haleiwa. The finals for the 1979 men's World Cup, still regarded as one of the most exciting afternoons in pro surfing history, saw fourth-ranked Richards vault over three surfers to take his first pro tour championship.

The World Cup has been sponsored by nearly a dozen companies over the decades, including Hang Ten, Ocean Pacific, Hard Rock Cafe, and G-Shock. It became a men's-only event in 1994. Rip Curl began underwriting the contest in 1997, and in 2001 it was renamed the Rip Curl Cup and returned, for one year only, as the season finale. The $250,000 event was won by Hawaiian Myles Padaca, who earned $30,000 for the victory. Hawaii's Lynne Boyer is the only four-time World Cup winner; Michael Ho of Hawaii is the only three-time men's division winner.

World Cup winners are as follows. "Not rated" means the event wasn't included on that year's world tour schedule.

1975:	Mark Richards, Margo Oberg
1976:	Ian Cairns, Lynne Boyer
1977:	Shaun Tomson, Lynne Boyer
1978:	Buzzy Kerbox (no women's)
1979:	Mark Richards, Lynne Boyer
1980:	Ian Cairns, Margo Oberg
1981:	Dane Kealoha, Cheri Gross
1982:	Tom Carroll, Lynne Boyer
1983:	Michael Ho, Margo Oberg
1984:	Michael Ho, Lynne Boyer
1985:	Michael Ho, Jodie Cooper
1986:	Hans Hedemann (no women's)
1987:	Gary Elkerton (no women's)
1988:	Tom Carroll (no women's)
1989:	Hans Hedemann (no women's)
1990:	Derek Ho (no women's)
1991:	Fabio Gouveia, Pauline Menczer
1992:	Martin Potter (not rated), Jodie Cooper
1993:	Johnny-Boy Gomes (not rated), Jodie Cooper
1994:	Sunny Garcia (not rated)
1995:	Shane Powell (not rated), Pauline Menczer
1996:	Jake Paterson (not rated)
1997:	Michael Rommelse (not rated)
1998:	Shane Dorian (not rated)
1999:	Zane Harrison (not rated)
2000:	Sunny Garcia (not rated)
2001:	Myles Padaca
2002:	Joel Parkinson

World Longboard Tour   International circuit of professional longboard contests, inaugurated in 1986 and sanctioned by the Association of Professional Surfers (ASP). From 1986 to 1991, the longboard title was based on aggregate points over a circuit of events; from 1992 to 2000 it was decided solely by the Oxbow World Longboard Championship contest; in 2001 it returned to a circuit format. The World Longboard Tour (WLT) is for men only; a separate Women's World Longboard Championships event was started in 1999.

As longboarding grew in popularity in the late '70s and early '80s, the formation of a longboard world championship was inevitable. It came about in 1986 after a two-year lobbying effort by 1966 world champion Nat Young of Australia. The debut longboarding "world tour" consisted of two events in New South Wales, Australia, worth a cumulative $16,450; Young won the title easily. Brazil and France were added to the schedule before the decade was out; California was added in 1990. Young won three more titles during this period. The single-event Oxbow World Longboard Championship debuted in Biarritz, France, in 1992, with a field of 48 surfers and a $30,000 purse. The finals of the 1993 Oxbow Championships, held in rough surf at Haleiwa, Hawaii, highlighted the longboard schism between traditionalists and the progressives; two of the four finalists, Rusty Keaulana of Hawaii and Alex Salazar of Brazil, rode more or less in the traditional style, trimming often and walking the nose; Rob Bain and Glen

Winton of Australia, both former shortboard world title contenders, rode their nine-foot longboards as if they were six-foot tri-fins. Judges scored both approaches equally. Keaulana won, Winton was second, and over the next few years the traditionalists for the most part would set the longboard standard.

The 1994 Oxbow event at Malibu, California, is regarded as a low point in world longboarding competition, as the three Hawaiian finalists—Keaulana, Lance Hookano, and Bonga Perkins—ganged up to prevent sole California entrant Joel Tudor from catching any quality waves. Keaulana again won. In an unrelated event, Joe Tudor (Joel's father) and Lance Hookano beat up a 43-year-old Malibu regular who refused to leave the water on the final day of competition; the surfer was hospitalized.

A circuit-based world championship returned in 2001, with three events on the schedule worth a total of $170,000. World Longboard Tour champions, and sites for the 1992–2000 Oxbow Championships, are as follows:

1986:	Nat Young
1987:	Stuart Entwistle
1988:	Nat Young
1989:	Nat Young
1990:	Nat Young
1991:	Martin McMillan
1992:	Joey Hawkins (Biarritz, France)
1993:	Rusty Keaulana (Haleiwa, Hawaii)
1994:	Rusty Keaulana (Malibu, California)
1995:	Rusty Keaulana (St. Leu, Réunion Island)
1996:	Bonga Perkins (Guethary, France)
1997:	Dino Miranda (Makaha, Hawaii)
1998:	Joel Tudor (Fuerteventura, Canary Islands)
1999:	Colin McPhillips (One Mile Beach, Australia)
2000:	Beau Young (Praia do Rosa, Brazil)
2001:	Colin McPhillips
2002:	Colin McPhillips

World Surfing Championships Biannual surfing contest held at various locations around the world from 1964 and 1994; usually referred to as the World Contest. The World Surfing Championships were considered to be an amateurs-only event, although most of the top competitors from 1964 to 1972 were nominally professional. "It was obvious almost from the beginning," surf journalist Drew Kampion noted in 1984, "that a World Contest was an ambiguous

sort of thing; very unpredictable." The number of World Championships categories—gender and age divisions—ranged over the years from one to seven, and the competition format changed almost from event to event. Waves for the 1978 World Contest in South Africa were big and perfect, while finalists at the 1994 event in Brazil battled it out in two-foot dribblers. Some World Contest performances single-handedly changed the direction of surfing; most passed by virtually unnoticed. The World Championships can be divided into two distinct era: 1964 to 1972 and 1978 to 1994.

Before the world pro tour was created in 1976, the World Contest was the sport's biggest event, and six of these competitions were held during this period, in Sydney, Australia (1964), Lima, Peru (1965), San Diego, California (1966 and 1972), San Juan, Puerto Rico (1968), and Torquay, Victoria, Australia (1970). Each contest, except for the 1964 event, took place under the auspices of the International Surfing Federation (ISF). Amateur competitive surfing, after losing popularity in the late '60s, nearly went fallow in the early '70s, and the World Contest was tabled until 1978. (See following entries for detailed accounts of the first six World Championship events.)

The contest was officially called the World Amateur Surfing Championships from 1978 to 1994, in order to make a clear distinction from the 1976-founded world professional tour. Fourteen of the amateur-only contests were held, but the event was no longer the last word in competitive surfing. Hot young teenage surfers often viewed the World Contest as an important but hardly essential stop on the way to a pro tour career, while a huge majority of everyday surfers could no more name the reigning amateur world champions than they could the European heads of state. But the idea of holding a biannual international amateur contest was sound enough, and the overseeing International Surfing Association (ISA) was formed in 1976 as a replacement for the ISF, to provide a more or less consistent World Championships framework. The 1978 World Championships, held in South Africa, passed by virtually unnoticed: just 48 surfers from six countries competed in a sparsely attended one-day, men's-only contest, and apartheid politics prevented Australia from sending a team. But the contest grew in years to come, and by 1988 surfers were competing in men's, junior men's, women's, longboard, bodyboard, and kneeboard divisions, as well as for overall team points.

Tom Curren, Gary Elkerton, Damien Hardman, Lisa Andersen, Andy Irons, and dozens more future world tour stars competed in the World Championships before turning pro. Three hundred surfers from two dozen countries competed in the 1994 World Championships; host countries over the years included Japan, England, and Brazil. The World Amateur Surfing Championships were replaced in 1996 by the World Surfing Games.

Men's and women's division winners for the World Surfing Championships, along with the host country, are listed below. Tandem division winners included from 1972 and before; juniors division winners included from 1980 forward.

1964:   Midget Farrelly, Phyllis O'Donell (no tandem) (Sydney, Australia)
1965:   Felipe Pomar, Joyce Hoffman, Mike Doyle/Linda Merrill (Lima, Peru)
1966:   Nat Young, Joyce Hoffman, Pete Peterson/Barrie Algaw (San Diego, California)
1968:   Fred Hemmings, Margo Godfrey, Ron Ball/Debbie Gustavson (Rincon, Puerto Rico)
1970:   Rolf Aurness, Sharron Weber (no tandem) (Torquay, Australia)
1972:   Jim Blears, Sharron Weber, Steve and Barrie Boehne (San Diego, California)
1978:   Anthony Brodowicz (no women's) East London, South Africa)
1980:   Mark Scott, Alisa Schwarzstein, Tom Curren (Biarritz, France)
1982:   Tom Curren, Jenny Gill, Bryce Ellis (Gold Coast, Australia)
1984:   Scott Farnsworth, Janice Aragon, Damien Hardman (Huntington Beach, California)
1986:   Mark Sainsbury, Connie Nixon, Vetea David (Newquay, England)
1988:   Fabio Gouveia, Pauline Menczer, Chris Brown (Aquadilla, Puerto Rico)
1990:   Heifara Tahutini, Kathy Newman, Shane Beven (Niijima, Japan)
1992:   Grant Frost, Lynette MacKenzie, Chad Edser (Lacanau, France)
1994:   Sasha Stocker, Alessandra Vieira, Kalani Robb (Rio de Janeiro, Brazil)

See also competitive surfing, International Surfing Association, International Surfing Federation, World Surfing Games.

World Surfing Championships 1964   The annual Makaha International had long been regarded as the unofficial world title, but progressive surfers, by the early '60s, were beginning to think of the Makaha event as a relic from the wooden-board era. In 1963, Australian surf filmmaker and magazine publisher Bob Evans convinced Australian oil giant Ampol Petroleum Limited to sponsor the first official World Surfing Championships; the event was held the following year on May 16 and 17 at Sydney's Manly Beach. Australians Midget Farrelly and Phyllis O'Donell were the winners. A dozen overseas surfers attended the first World Championships, including Mike Doyle, Little John (LJ) Richards, and Linda Benson from California and 1963 Makaha winner Joey Cabell of Hawaii. Peru sent two surfers; England, South Africa, France, and New Zealand each sent one. The visitors were seeded directly into the quarterfinals, while the rest of the starting field—about 100 Australian men and women—were selected by state rankings. A juniors division event featured Australian surfers only.

The Manly event was the best-attended surf contest in history up to that point, as thousands of spectators filled the tree-lined beachfront promenade for the finals, while ABC-TV Australia filmed the action for the nightly news. Australia was in the middle of a short but intense "surf craze" period, and a cheerful mood prevailed among World Championship

Winners of the 1964 World Surfing Championships (left to right): Mike Doyle, Midget Farrelly, Joey Cabell

competitors, sponsors, organizers, and spectators. Linda Benson was favored going into the 50-minute women's final. But the predominantly right-breaking Manly surf meant that Benson, a goofyfoot, had to ride backside on all but one wave, and her wave selection throughout the match was off. Phyllis O'Donell, the newly crowned Australian champ and a regularfooter, caught better waves than Benson and rode with easy confidence, at one time speeding through a section with her heels together and her back arched. O'Donell won easily.

Australians Midget Farrelly, Bobby Brown, and Mick Dooley met Joey Cabell, Mike Doyle, and LJ Richards of America in the men's final. The general consensus was that Cabell outperformed the others, but a new "sportsmanship" rule, used for the first time, penalized competitors for "blatant drop-ins," and Cabell, after jamming his fellow finalists into the soup time and again, was docked accordingly and relegated to third place. Doyle, having caused a sensation just before the final by taking Linda Benson out for a tandem surfing display, finished second. Farrelly, the serious-minded 19-year-old, caught fewer waves than his competitors, but turned in a stylish and mistake-free performance—although he himself didn't think much of it. "I felt rotten," he later wrote in his biography. "I more or less took it easy and was probably a little lazy. When my name was announced as the winner I nearly fell through the sand." Farrelly was from the smooth, anti-hotdogging "functional" school, and attributed his victory in part to his surfboard, which weighed 10 pounds more than Cabell's.

Surfer magazine's prediction that the 1964 World Championships would help to get the sport "entered on the Olympic calendar" in the near future proved unfounded, but the event was nonetheless tightly organized, well-surfed, and upbeat. World Championship events in the future would have bigger and better waves and more contestants. But none would have the same sense of optimism and goodwill. The International Surfing Federation (ISF) was conceived during the 1964 titles, and founded shortly thereafter in Lima, Peru; the ISF's sole mission would be to stage future world contests. *See also* Bob Evans, Bernard "Midget" Farrelly, Phyllis O'Donell.

World Surfing Championships 1965   The first World Championships to be staged by the International Surfing Federation; held in Lima, Peru, on February 20 and 21, in shifty and difficult six- to 10-foot

Felipe Pomar, 1965 World Surfing Championships winner

surf. Peruvian Felipe Pomar and Joyce Hoffman of California were the winners. The 1965 event was the only World Championships held during an odd-numbered year. The English-speaking mainstream media ignored the 1965 titles entirely, and it was played down in the surf press. Twenty-two of the 54 total entrants were from California. Most of the remaining slots were filled by Hawaiians, Peruvians, and Australians, while South Africa, Ecuador, and France each sent a surfer. All competitors wore blazers and ties (or cocktail dresses) for a lavish opening reception hosted by populist Peruvian president Fernando Belaunde Terry, and local surfers would later talk some of the visitors into trying their hand at bullfighting. "The bulls had their horns trimmed," California competitor Mike Doyle remembered. "But several guys got flipped around, and it was lucky nobody got badly hurt."

The women's competition at Miraflores beach passed by virtually unnoticed (*Surfer* magazine didn't even bother to print the results), but it was a clean sweep for the Californians, with Joyce Hoffman, Nancy Nelson, and Candy Calhoun finishing first, second, and third, respectively. Hawaii's Paul Strauch won the small-wave hotdogging contest at Miraflores, held as an adjunct to the men's main event. In other specialty events, the California team won the relay paddle race, Nat Young of Australia won the four-mile paddle, Felipe Pomar won the 2,000-meter paddle, and Californians Mike Doyle and Linda Merrill won the tandem contest.

The men's division of the 1965 World Championships was held in big, gray, bumpy waves at Punta Rocas, a reefbreak located 30 miles south of Lima; three competitors in the preliminaries were unable to even make it out through the shorebreak. The 1964 titles, held just nine months earlier in Australia, had favored the sharp-turning, high-performance surfers. Here in Peru the advantage went to the big-wave experts, and the eight-man final for the most part consisted of surfers who'd earned reputations in the heavy surf of Oahu's North Shore, including Hemmings, Paul Strauch, and George Downing from Hawaii and California's Mike Doyle. Felipe Pomar was primed as well, having just returned to Lima following an 18-month stay in Hawaii. Seventeen-year-old Nat Young made up for a lack of big-wave experience with manic teenage energy, riding 22 waves in a one-hour semifinal heat. Defending Makaha International winner Hemmings was the early favorite in the 90-minute final in Peru, but had equipment problems. Downing, by far the oldest surfer in the final at age 35, lost his board early on and took a long swim to the beach, as did surprise finalist Ken Adler from Australia. In the end, just two points separated Pomar, Young, and Strauch, with the 21-year-old Peruvian getting the nod for his aggressive, driving attack. A "quiet, smiling Latin gentleman" on land, as *Surfer* reported, Pomar became "the Wild Bull of Punta Rocas" when he entered the water. Young placed second, and Strauch got third. *See also* Joyce Hoffman, Felipe Pomar.

World Surfing Championships 1966   The third and most memorable World Championships, held from September 29 to October 4 in San Diego, California; won by Australian Nat Young and California's Joyce Hoffman. The format used for the 1966 World Championships was different than the ones used in 1964 and 1965, as winners were determined by a cumulative point score over three consecutive but separate contests, instead of a single event. Furthermore, the contest was mobile, so organizers could move to the best surf location. President Lyndon Johnson sent the 76 World Championship competitors a letter of

Winners of the 1966 World Surfing Championships (left to right): Corky Carroll, Nat Young, Jock Sutherland

welcome; *Life, Newsweek,* and the *New York Times* reported from the beach, all of them giving the sport a pat on the head for apparently transcending its recent rowdy past. "Five or six years ago," *Newsweek* wrote, "the World Surfing Championships would have been about as welcome in a U.S. city as the Pot-Smoking Olympics." Dory races, tandem surfing, and other adjunct events further added to the color of the 1966 titles, and over 40,000 spectators gathered to watch the finals. Top-seeded Joyce Hoffman, 19, of Capistrano Beach, by winning the first two events of the week and placing runner-up in the third, took the women's division easily over California teammate Joey Hamasaki. Third place went to 14-year-old Mimi Munro from Florida. Hoffman, winner of the 1965 titles, became the sport's first two-time world champion. California ironman surfer Pete Peterson, along with partner Barrie Algaw, won the tandem division, while the American team (Rusty Miller, Mike Doyle, Steve Bigler, Corky Carroll) won the relay paddle race.

Although reigning U.S. champion Corky Carroll, along with 1964 world champion Midget Farrelly of Australia, were among a half-dozen contenders for the 1966 world title, the event was correctly billed a showdown between David Nuuhiwa and Nat Young. Nuuhiwa, 17, the silky-smooth Hawaiian-born goofy-footer from Huntington Beach, was the U.S. juniors division champ, and revered as the world's best nose-rider. Young, 18, the cocky Australian regularfooter from Sydney, was in the vanguard of the hard-turning "involvement" school of surfing. During the first round of competition, held in four-foot lefts at the Mission Beach Jetty, Nuuhiwa caught a wave, walked to the nose, and perched on the tip for 10 seconds, and from there cruised to victory for the day, with Young in second place. The curly-haired Australian roared back over the next five days to win the second and third rounds, both held in Ocean Beach in mainly right-breaking two- to four-foot waves. Nuuhiwa meanwhile lost early in round two, and the title was decided. Young gave much of the credit to Magic Sam, his 9'4" surfboard, which was lighter and thinner than the boards used by his competitors, and featured a long, swept-back, flexible fin that helped propel him through powerful turns and cutbacks. Switchfoot surfer Jock Sutherland of Hawaii finished runner-up; Corky Carroll placed third. Young dismissed Nuuhiwa in a postcontest interview—"Every wave, up front he walks, and stands there; I don't think this is good surfing"—then drove off in a brand-new Chevy Camero, his first-place prize. He left Magic Sam with a friend that afternoon and never saw it again, but it didn't matter, as the 1967-launched shortboard revolution would render Sam obsolete in a matter of months.

Not long after the contest, Australian surf journalist John Witzig wrote "We're Tops Now," a vitriolic article for *Surfer* magazine in which he described America's top surfers by and large as "run of the mill" and "ordinary." Young and his Aussie cohorts, Witzig continued, were "exciting and dynamic." It wasn't that simple. But Young's display in the 1966 titles was a preview for things to come, and the event itself was among the most exciting and dynamic surf competitions of the decade. *See also* Joyce Hoffman, Nat Young.

World Surfing Championships 1968   The fourth World Championship event was held in Rincon, Puerto Rico, from November 8 to the 14, and won by Hawaii's Fred Hemmings and Margo Godfrey of California. For six days the Puerto Rican surf was small and weak, if well-shaped, but the final day of competition brought perfect translucent-blue six-footers. Mexico, Brazil, Ireland, Japan, Panama, and India were among the 16 nations represented in the 1968 titles; the event was covered by ABC's *Wide World of Sports*. The competitors looked different than they had for the previous Championships, held two years earlier in San Diego, California. Crew cuts and competition-stripe T-shirts had been replaced by bushy sideburns and collar-length hair, beads, granny glasses, bell-bottoms, and paisley-print shirts. The shortboard revolution, meanwhile, was in full

swing, and the new boards were generally two feet shorter and five pounds lighter than those used in 1966. Surfers were now carving up and down the wave face, whereas two years earlier they'd been stalling, trimming, and noseriding.

Sixteen-year-old Wayne Lynch of Australia was the most progressive surfer in the 1968 World Championships, but poor wave selection knocked him out in the semifinals. U.S. men's champion David Nuuhiwa, another early favorite, also failed to place. Defending world champion Nat Young, 1964 world champion Midget Farrelly, and 1968 Australian champion Russell Hughes, all from Australia, qualified for the hour-long men's final, as did 1964 world title runner-up Mike Doyle from California, along with Hawaii's Fred Hemmings and Reno Abellira. The finals were held at a right-breaking reef called Domes. All six competitors had moments of brilliance, but Hemmings—just 21, yet defiantly old school, with the shortest hair and the longest board of any of the finalists—rode smoothly and consistently, and won by a fraction of a point over Farrelly. Hemmings was never a popular champion among surfing's tastemakers. "He won the world contest," surf journalist Drew Kampion wrote, "the same way Richard Nixon, a week earlier, won the presidential election: a triumph of the past over the future."

Fifteen-year-old Margo Godfrey of California easily won the women's division over Sharron Weber from Hawaii, with 1964 title winner Phyllis O'Donell of Australia placing third. Godfrey had dominated the California women's contest circuit in the months leading up to the world contest, so her win came as no surprise. Whereas women's title winners in the past were all but ignored, the surf press lauded Godfrey for her performance, and *Surfing* magazine invited her to submit a feature piece on the contest. "Pressure, pressure and more pressure mounted as I began to think about the championship," Godfrey wrote, sounding every bit the high school sophomore. "My stomach was turning, my legs were shaking and my mind was blowing." Godfrey went on to win three professional world titles.

Because surfing competition in general had begun to come under fire (the sport was now often referred to as an "art form"), and because event planning in Puerto Rico was nowhere near as tight as it had been in San Diego (bad food, poor communication between organizers and competitors, 30 surfboards stolen from visiting competitors over the course of the event), the World Championships met with criticism for the first time in its five-year history. "World Contest 1968 (Whatever That Means)" was the sardonic title of one surf magazine article. "Contestants met with every conceivable distraction, postponement and inconvenience," *Surfer* noted. But Puerto Rico's warm tropical setting was a big plus, and all agreed that the surfing on the final day had been first-rate. The World Championships would face bigger problems, and harsher denouncements, in 1970 and 1972. *See also* Fred Hemmings, Margo Oberg.

World Surfing Championships 1970   The fifth world contest was held in Victoria, Australia, between May 1 to May 14, amid wind, rain, hail, and at least a half-dozen miniature political firestorms. California's Rolf Aurness won the men's division, and Sharron Weber from Hawaii won the women's. Most of the event took place in sloppy four-foot waves at Bells Beach, and the poor conditions did nothing but magnify the anticontest sentiment that had been building in the surf world over the previous few years. Ted Spencer, 1970 Australian National Titles runner-up and a newly converted Hare Krishna, pulled out of the World Championships two days before the preliminaries began. David Nuuhiwa gave up his slot on the California team and flew back to Huntington Beach after his first heat. Runner-up U.S. champion Corky Carroll, interviewed at Bells during the early rounds of competition, called the event "a complete fiasco," and said the entire world title concept had been ruined by inept organizers and judging panels, and should be eliminated altogether. "Abolish the whole thing," Carroll said. "The world contest is wrong." A few days earlier he'd been temporarily suspended from the contest after starting a food fight in the local hotel bar. Carroll's California teammates then refused to march in the opening ceremonies, and threatened to boycott the contest. Event directors responded by preemptively throwing the California team out, but a meeting was held the following day, and the West Coasters—Carroll included—were reinstated. More drama followed, as state narcotics agents raided the competitors' rooms. One California surfer was found to have a small amount of marijuana, and another had a baggie of psilocybin mushrooms; neither was arrested. Surfers from the tropics, meanwhile, had a hard time adjusting to the chilly Australian autumn climate (air temperatures dropped into the low 40s; the water temperature was in the upper 50s), and many were laid up with a cold or the flu.

The women's final was moved from Bells to Skene's Creek, and held in poorly shaped left-breaking waves. Sharron Weber's victory over defending world champion Margo Godfrey was comprehensively ignored by the surf media, with *Surfer* devoting just two sentences to the women's final. The men's semifinals and finals were held at Johanna, 95 miles southwest of Bells, in beautiful peeling six-foot sandbar tubes. Rolf Aurness, the soft-voiced 18-year-old son of TV star James Arness, became the first California men's division world champion, and his unanimous victory seemed to be the only noncontroversial, nonpoliticized event of the competition. Aurness used a streamlined seven-foot board, while nearly all his rivals from Australia labored on stubby six-foot-or-under boards. Midget Farrelly, runner-up in the World Championships held in Puerto Rico two years earlier, again finished in second place. Peter Drouyn (Australia), Reno Abellira (Hawaii), Keone Downing (Hawaii), and Nat Young (Australia), in that order, rounded out the final. Three of the six finalists didn't bother to show up for the awards presentation.

This was the fourth World Championships event run by the International Surfing Federation, and surf journalist Drew Kampion went out of his way to praise ISF president Eduardo Arena, calling him a "hero" for acting as the event's "sole binding force." But after Australia there was little doubt that the World Championships event as an institution was in bad shape. "The Death of All Contests" was the title of a *Surfer* editorial related to the 1970 Championships. "Maybe they should abandon the idea of a world contest for awhile," *Surfing* magazine said. "At least until we all grow up." *See also* Rolf Aurness, Bells Beach, Sharron Weber.

World Surfing Championships 1972   The sixth and final amateur-era World Championships event; held in dismal waves in San Diego, California; won by Jim Blears and Sharron Weber, both of Hawaii; often recalled as competitive surfing's lowest point. Defending men's division world champion Rolf Aurness didn't enter the event, nor did the four previous men's champions—Midget Farrelly, Felipe Pomar, Nat Young, and Fred Hemmings. The 1968 women's champion, Margo Godfrey, also passed. Five weeks before the contest was scheduled to begin, California organizers confessed that they didn't have the required funds, and the contest was called off. Three weeks later, after a flurry of emergency meetings, the contest was back on. But the problems continued. Contest programs were held in boxes at the printers as the Championships got under way, because nobody could produce a cashier's check for payment. Competitors who billeted at a San Diego Travelodge motel broke the elevators, set off fire alarms, launched food fights, rang up enormous unpaid phone bills, and generally ran riot through the halls. A new Chevy sedan, on loan to Championship organizers from a local dealership, was stolen. Drug use was concealed, but barely. "There were even occasional snow flurries to break up the weather pattern in the hotel," *Surfing* magazine reported, with a broad wink and nudge.

Although the preliminary rounds of competition were held in reasonable head-high surf at Oceanside, competitors were justly upset because Newport, Trestles, and Malibu—all deemed off-limits to the Championships—were doing a far better job at picking up what turned out to be the year's best south swell. David Nuuhiwa of Huntington Beach was again favored to win the title, as he had been six years earlier during the first San Diego–staged World Championships. He surfed well in the preliminaries, even after his favorite board—a wide-backed, two-finned fish—was stolen. The board turned up on the final day of the event, broken in two and dangling by a rope from the Ocean Beach Pier, with GOOD LUCK DAVE spray-painted across the bottom. The fish design had been born in San Diego, and it was later reported that local surfers felt Nuuhiwa had ripped off "their" invention. Nuuhiwa went on to finish runner-up in the contest, and perhaps should have won. "Everyone rode well," surf journalist Drew Kampion reported, after commenting with dismay on the two-foot, windblown waves, "but Nuuhiwa surfed the best, while Jim Blears got the good waves toward the end when the judges tend to score higher." Future world champion Peter Townend finished third, Hawaii's Larry Bertlemann and Michael Ho—the contest's most progressive surfers—placed fourth and fifth, respectively. Sharron Weber successfully defended the title she'd won two years earlier in Australia, and did so virtually without notice by the surf press—no photos of her riding to victory; no postcontest interview, profile, or photographs. Steve and Barrie Boehne of California won the tandem event.

The unmitigated failure of the 1972 World Championships was a near death knell for American amateur surfing, and helped usher in a backward period for the entire California surf scene. "I want to get drunk and forget about it," Nuuhiwa said as he walked off the beach with the second-place trophy, and everyone else seemed to feel the same way. Six years passed before the next World Championships, and not until 1984 would the event return to California. Prize-money contests had meanwhile taken root, and a series of pro events on the North Shore of Oahu had replaced the World Championships as the new focal point for international competitive surfing. *See also* Jim Blears, Sharron Weber.

World Surfing Games   The World Surfing Games were founded in 1996 as a way to attract the attention of the International Olympic Committee, in hopes that surfing would be considered for inclusion in Olympic Games—not necessarily a popular goal among the sport's rank and file, but one that amateur contest organizers had dreamed about for decades. The World Games replaced the 1964-founded World Surfing Championships. Hoping for inclusion in the 2000 Olympics in Sydney, and copying the newly written Olympic rules that allowed professional athletes to compete with amateurs, a small number of pro surfers were invited to the debut World Surfing Games, organized primarily by Argentina-born beach sandal magnate Fernando Aguerre, and held amid much pomp and circumstance in Huntington Beach, California. San Diego surfer Taylor Knox lead Team USA to a win over Australia. But the Sydney Olympic dream proved futile, and by 2000 the upper echelon of pro surfers, almost without exception, had lost interest in competing in the World Games. The Games have since been held in Portugal (1998), Brazil (2000), and South Africa (2002); 600 surfers from 34 nations competed in the latter event. Surfers qualify for the World Games through national competition; the Games are held under the auspices of the International Surfing Association. Men's, women's, and juniors division winners of the World Surfing Games, and host country, are as follows:

1996:   Taylor Knox, Neridah Falconer, Ben Bourgeois (Huntington Beach, California)
1998:   Michael Campbell, Alcione Silva, Dean Morrison (Giuncho, Portugal)
2000:   Fabio Silva, Maria Tavares, Joel Centeio (Maracaipe, Brazil)
2002:   Travis Logie, Chelsea Georgeson, Warwick Wright (Durban, South Africa)

See also competitive surfing, International Surfing Association, Olympics and surfing, World Surfing Championships.

Wright, Allan "Bank"   Writer and book distributor from Los Angeles, California, best known for his 1973 guidebook *Surfing California.* Wright was born (1943) and raised in West Los Angeles, began surfing in 1953, and graduated with a B.S. in business from the University of Southern California in 1965. After living on Oahu for two years, Wright returned to California and published his *Surfing Hawaii* (1972), his first guidebook. *Surfing California,* similarly formatted but more detailed, came out the following year. California beaches at the time were mired in localism, and nonresident surfers in many areas were kept away through intimidation and sometimes violence. Wright's thorough and highly practical book—citing more than 400 breaks between south San Diego and Brookings, Oregon, illustrated with maps and photographs, and offering tips on access, optimum tide, and swell direction for each break—was therefore viewed by many California surfers as nothing less than heretical. When visiting new surf breaks, *Surfing* magazine advised in its review—"don't leave this book in full view inside your car."

Wright founded Mountain and Sea, a small Redondo Beach publishing/distributing business, in 1972. He later produced a series of poster-size maps charting the surf breaks in Baja California and the American East Coast. In 1979, Wright reprinted John "Doc" Ball's seminal photo book *California Surfriders*; in 1983 he reissued Tom Blake's 1935 book *Hawaiian Surfboard* (retitling it *Hawaiian Surfriders 1935*). At its peak in 1990, Mountain and Sea offered nearly 50 surf-related books, with a distribution network consisting almost entirely of surf shops. *See also* books and surfing.

Wright, Oscar "Ozzie"   Straw-haired aerial specialist from Narrabeen, Sydney, Australia. Wright was born (1976) in Sydney and raised in the suburb of Ingleside. He began surfing in 1986, at age 10; later that year he moved with his family to Narrabeen, one of the country's best-known surfing beaches. Wright developed into a fast, acrobatic rider, less concerned with form ("all flying elbows and knees," as surf journalist Matt George put it) as with testing the limits of aerial surfing. Doing so came at a cost: in 1997 he tore ligaments in his knee, was beached for three months, and immediately afterward suffered a knee injury that kept him out of the water of another six months. Wright also earned a reputation as a kind of anti-establishment professional; his quirky pen-and-ink sketches of thin, sad-eyed hipsters have been used in Volcom surfwear company ads, and Australia's *FHM* magazine named Wright the country's fifth best-dressed man in 2002 in an ironic nod to the shabby-chic trend he helped popularize. Wright has appeared in a number of surf videos, including *Computer Body* (2000), *The Decline* (2002), and *7873 Transworld Surf* (2003).

Y

Yater, Renolds Dignified surfer and board-builder from Santa Barbara, California; innovator and prime exemplar of a smooth, cool, central California surfing style; founder of Yater Surfboards. Yater was born (1932) in Los Angeles, the son of a shoe salesman, raised in Pasadena and Laguna Beach, began surfing at age 14, and started making his own boards at 21. Thin, hawk-nosed, and quiet, Yater apprenticed in the mid- and late '50s with the two biggest board-builders in the world, working as a laminator at Hobie Surfboards in Dana Point from 1955 to 1957, then as a shaper at Velzy Surfboards in San Clemente from 1957 to 1959. By the time Yater moved north and

Renolds Yater

opened Santa Barbara Surf Shop in 1959 (trademarking Yater Surfboards at the same time), he was renowned up and down the coast for a type of fast, finely tuned 10-foot board that performed best in long pointbreak surf—particularly Rincon, near Santa Barbara, and Malibu. Yater made boards for some of the best surfers of the period, including Mickey Dora and Joey Cabell. He was also the favorite board-maker among surf industry leaders, including *Endless Summer* producer Bruce Brown, *Surfer* magazine founder John Severson, and Clark Foam founder Gordon Clark. "He always reminded me of a Native American," California expatriate surfer/shaper Bob Cooper later recalled. "He's very efficient, everything minimal, yet he gets maximum usage out of time, equipment and conversation."

Where Hobie, Weber, Greg Noll, and other board-builders of the period entered the '60s surf market bent on expansion and conquest, Yater purposely kept his operation small. In 1964 he introduced the Yater Spoon, one of the era's thinnest, lightest, and most maneuverable boards, which sold well up and down the California coast, and were shipped in small numbers to Florida, New Jersey, Texas, and Hawaii.

Yater was a founder and the first president of the Santa Barbara Surf Club, formed in 1959 as a way for a small group of Santa Barbara surfers to gain access to the wave-rich and privately owned Hollister Ranch, located just north of town. Yater went virtually unnoticed by the surf magazines, but was featured in small number of surf movies of the late '50s and early '60s, including *Surf Crazy* (1959), *Big Wednesday* (1961), *Surfing Hollow Days* (1962), and *Walk on the Wet Side* (1963). As testimony to Yater's high rank among discriminating California surfers, Colonel Kilgore, the war- and surf-crazed character played by Robert Duvall in *Apocalypse Now,* wears an army-green Santa Barbara Surf Shop T-shirt while on duty, and has a Yater Spoon tucked among his personal effects. Yater is married and has two children. *See also* the Ranch, spoon.

Yerkes, Bill   Resilient surf filmmaker and entrepreneur, originally from New Jersey. Yerkes was born (1947) in Mount Holly, New Jersey, raised in Pemberton, and began surfing at Malibu in 1960, after his family moved briefly to Southern California. He founded a one-man film production company in the mid-'60s, and became the first East Coast surf moviemaker, with titles including *How the East Was Won* (1967) and *A Way of Life* (1968); he received a B.S. in film from New York's Ithaca College in 1969. In 1977 Yerkes became a licensee for Sundek beachwear—already known for its brightly colored nylon trunks and jackets—and during the late '70s and '80s he built the company into one of the largest in the surf world. In 1999, Yerkes opened the Balsa Bill Surf Shop in Satellite Beach, Florida. He was inducted into the East Coast Surf Legends Hall of Fame in 1998. Yerkes has lived on the central Florida coast since 1974.

You Should Have Been Here an Hour Ago
Wise, humorous, easy-rolling autobiography of Phil Edwards, revered California power surfer of the '50s and '60s, coauthored by *Sports Illustrated* staff writer Bob Ottum, and published by Harper & Row in 1967. *You Should Have Been Here an Hour Ago: The Stoked Side of Surfing, or How to Hang Ten Through Life and Stay Happy*—surfing's first full-length biography—grew out of an *SI* cover story Ottum wrote on Edwards in 1966, and is thought by many to be the finest book written on surfing. Edwards gives a chronological account of his life, from his early surfing years at Oceanside in the late '40s, to designing and manufacturing boards for Hobie Surfboards, to judging the 1964 World Championships in Australia. He also provides a detailed accounted of the morning he became the first surfer to ride the churning, inside-out waves at Pipeline on Oahu's North Shore. Throughout, Edwards's voice is simultaneously wise and laid-back. He said he had reservations, as a surfboard builder as well as a surfing icon, about inviting the rest of the world to further crowd the waves, but nonetheless felt it was the right thing to do. "The hackers of surfing are coming," he wrote. "Which is fine. Perhaps if we stoke a few people, life outside will calm down a little." *You Should Have Been Here an Hour Ago* is dedicated to "the Legions of the Unjazzed"—nonsurfers. *See also* books and surfing, Phil Edwards.

Young, Beau   Tall, broad-shouldered Australian regularfooter from Byron Bay, New South Wales; winner of the 2000 World Longboard Championships; oldest son of 1966 world champion Nat Young. Beau Young was born (1974) in the Byron-area town of Grafton, raised in Sydney, and began surfing at age six. For three years, beginning at age 18, he was a struggling minor league shortboard pro. At 21 he tried a longboard, "and for the first time," he later said, was actually feeling what riding a wave was all about, instead of trying to tear the thing to bits." Young's longboard style soon became polished and flowing, but would always reflect his shortboard upbringing, and he often rode a 10-foot single-fin as if it were a 6'6" tri-fin. In the 1998 World Longboard Championships, held in the Canary Islands, Young finished runner-up to Californian Joel Tudor. The 2000 championship event, held in Brazil, turned out to be a rematch between Tudor and Young, but this time the victory went to the Australian. Young placed third in the 2002 Championships. Beau and Nat Young are the first father-son team to hold longboard world titles; Nat had come out of a long semiretirement to win longboard championships in 1986, 1988, 1989, and 1990. Beau Young has been featured in a number of surf videos, including *Cruise Control* (1998), *Longboard Magic* (2001), and *Made in Britain* (2001).

Young, Robert "Nat"   Imposing regularfooter from Sydney, Australia; winner of the 1966 World Surfing Championships; in the vanguard of both the shortboard revolution and the longboard revival; winner of the Longboard World Championships in 1986, 1988, 1989, and 1990. Young was arguably the most influential surfer in the second half of the 20th century. "He was an overwhelming presence," surf journalist Paul Holmes wrote, "and accorded almost messianic awe." Young was born (1947) in Sydney, the son of a truck driver father and schoolteacher mother, raised in the beachfront suburb of Collaroy, and began surfing at age 10. Six years later, the gangly teenager won the open division of the 1963 Australian Invitational Surfing Championships, as well as the juniors division of the Australian National Titles, and was filmed for a sequence in Bruce Brown's crossover hit movie *The Endless Summer*. (He was then still known as "Gnat," a nickname picked up years earlier when he'd been the smallest surfer on the beach; "Nat" came after an adolescent growth spurt.) When fellow Sydney surfer Midget Farrelly won the first World Surfing Championships in 1964, he was

Nat Young

Young's friend, mentor, and surfboard-maker. The friendship became a lifetime rivalry the following year, as Young dropped out of high school, moved up to the men's division, placed runner-up to Farrelly in the Australian National Titles, then beat the older surfer to take second in the 1965 World Championships. (Still sniping at each other more than 30 years later, Farrelly described Young in a 1997 surf magazine article as a "ruthless megalomaniac," not long after Young called Farrelly a "whinging pom.")

Young made himself a board he called "Magic Sam" in 1966: a thin 9'4" squaretail with a swept-back fin designed by California kneerider George Greenough. Young rode Sam to a win in the Australian National Titles, then took it with him to San Diego, California, for the World Championships. Cat-footed David Nuuhiwa of Huntington Beach entered the contest as the American favorite; he was by far the sport's best noserider, able to perch on the tip for 10 seconds or more at a time. Young, along with Greenough and fellow Australian Bob McTavish, had meanwhile been working on what was called "involvement" surfing, based on powerful turns in and around the curl. Young was regarded as the heir to

original power surfers Phil Edwards and Mike Doyle, both from California; he rode in a medium-narrow stance, with a slightly hunched back, and used his well-muscled frame (6'3", 185 pounds) to leverage deep, well-defined turns. The power-storing crouch Young assumed while trimming across the wave's upper reaches was as beautiful as it was functional. He stumbled in the early rounds of the 1966 Championships, but quickly regained form and rode to the title virtually unchallenged. His natural confidence meanwhile began to shade at times into arrogance. When a *Newsweek* reporter at the 1966 World Championships relayed to him that Nuuhiwa had described good surfing as "blending" with the wave, Young curtly replied that he "didn't want to blend in with anything." Over the next few years, he had run-ins—some of them physical—with some of the sport's greatest figures, including big-wave pioneer George Downing and surfboard shaper Dick Brewer, both from Hawaii. "He was a terror in the lineup," surf journalist John Grissim later wrote, "stealing waves left and right, and pounding his board with his fist when things didn't go his way." Grissim said Young was "Australia's answer to Otto von Bismarck." But he was also charming when he wanted to be, honest and loquacious, with a probing mind.

Young and McTavish traveled to Hawaii in late 1967 with their wide-backed McTavish-designed "vee bottom boards," the first model in what was soon being called the "shortboard revolution." At Maui's Honolua Bay, the two Australians turned easily and repeatedly from trough to crest in a high-performance style that set a precedent for virtually all surfing that followed. *The Hot Generation,* an Australian-made surf film that closed with a sequence of Young and McTavish at Honolua, gave mainland American surfers their first look at the sport's future. (Young followed up by costarring with teenage phenomenon Wayne Lynch in 1969's landmark surf movie *Evolution.*) Young, nicknamed "the Animal," kept his hand in competition, winning the Australian Titles in 1967 and 1969 and the Bells Beach event in 1966 and 1970, as well as the 1970 Smirnoff Pro. He then quit competition and turned up the rhetoric against the "establishment," telling *Tracks* magazine in a typically well-crafted and theatrical comment that "just by going surfing we're supporting the revolution." He spent the early '70s farming, surfing, and getting stoned in the pastoral Byron Bay area of New South Wales; the era is beautifully captured in the marijuana-hazed surf film classic *Morning of the Earth.* Returning to competition in 1974, Young finished third in the Coca-Cola Surfabout in Sydney, and donated his $750 check to the Australian Labour Party. (A part-time environmental crusader, Young later ran unsuccessfully for a state parliament seat.) He began riding longboards regularly in the early '80s, and was all but unbeatable in the early years of professional longboarding, taking the world title in 1986, 1988, 1989, and 1990, and finishing second in 1987 and fourth in 1991 before making a second, and permanent, retirement from full-time competition. Twenty years earlier, Young's shortboard surfing had been a huge influence on the upcoming generation of Australian surfers, particularly Michael Peterson, Ian Cairns, and Simon Anderson. In the early '90s, he mentored California's adolescent longboard savant Joel Tudor.

Young by then had branched into surf media. A writer since the mid-'60s, when he had a weekly surfing column in the *Sunday Telegraph,* Young published *The Book of Surfing* in 1979, followed by *Surfing Australia's East Coast* (1980), *The History of Surfing* (1983; revised in 1994), *Surfing Fundamentals* (1985), and *The Surfing and Sailboard Guide to Australia* (1986). He also produced two documentaries: the short-subject *Fall Line* (1979), on surfing, skiing, and hang gliding; and the 90-minute *History of Australian Surfing* (1985). (Curly-haired and ruggedly handsome, Young also worked as a model in the '80s and '90s, appearing on the cover of *Men's Vogue* in 1989.) Young opened Nat's at the Point, a bed and breakfast at Angourie, New South Wales, in 1991.

One of surfing's most photogenic riders, he appeared in more than 75 surf movies, videos, and documentaries, including *Surfing the Southern Cross* (1963), *A Life in the Sun* (1966), *Fantastic Plastic Machine* (1969), *Waves of Change* (1970), *A Winter's Tale* (1974), *A Day in the Life of Wayne Lynch* (1978), *Surfers: The Movie* (1990), *Endless Summer II* (1994), *Adrift* (1996), *Biographies* (2000), and *Shelter* (2001). In 1967, Young starred in *Let's Go Surfing,* a 13-part instructional series airing on Australia's ABC-TV. *Nat's Nat and That's That: A Surfing Legend,* Young's modestly titled autobiography, was published in 1998. Two years later, the still-aggressive Young slapped a teenage surfer who had interfered with one of his rides while surfing at Angourie, and subsequently was beaten by the teenager's father. The eye sockets and cheekbones on both sides of his face were broken; the experience led him to write *Surf Rage: A Surfer's Guide to Turning Negatives into Positives* (2000), a book of essays on surfing violence.

In 1967, Young won the *Surfer* Magazine Readers Poll Award, and was the top Australian vote-getter in the International Surfing Hall of Fame Awards. He was inducted into the Australian Surfing Hall of Fame in 1986, the International Surfing Hall of Fame in 1991, and the Huntington Beach Walk of Fame in 1996. Young has been married twice and has three children; Beau Young, his oldest boy, won the 2000 World Longboard Championships. In 2001, Young and his family moved to Sun Valley, Idaho, but he returns often to New South Wales. *See also* power surfing, shortboard revolution, surf rage, violence and surfing, World Longboard Tour, World Surfing Championships 1966, World Surfing Championships 1968, World Surfing Championships 1970.

Z

Zahn, Tommy   Athletic and hyper-health-conscious surfer and paddleboard racer from Santa Monica, California; five-time winner of the Catalina-to–Manhattan Beach paddleboard race in the 1950s and early '60s. Zahn was born (1924) and raised in Santa Monica, began surfing at age eight, and became a lifeguard at 18, informally mentored by pioneering California surfer/lifeguard Pete Peterson. After high school, Zahn served in the U.S. Marines during the later years of World War II. He made his first extended visit to Hawaii in 1947, and returned often over the next decade, living and training with Wisconsin-born surf innovator Tom Blake. Earlier in 1947, Zahn began dating Darrylin Zanuck, daughter of Hollywood studio mogul Darryl Zanuck. When she expressed an interest in surfing, Zahn had Santa Monica board-maker Joe Quigg build her an all-balsa surfboard that was thinner and lighter (about 25 pounds) than anything on the beach. Zahn then commandeered the "Darrylin board," as it later came to be known, finding it to be quick and maneuverable, and by the following year all the top riders in Santa Monica and Malibu were riding similar boards—soon known as the "Malibu chip" design. After his relationship with Zanuck ended, the handsome blond-haired Zahn briefly dated Marilyn Monroe.

Along with Greg Noll, Mike Bright, and a few others, Zahn was a member of an American lifeguard team that visited Australia as an adjunct to the 1956 Olympic Games in Melbourne. Aussie surfers for the most part were riding straight for shore on long, narrow, outdated "toothpick" hollow boards; Zahn and the Americans, with their Malibu chips, gave informal wave-riding demonstrations in New South Wales and Victoria that brought about an instant modernization in Australian surfing.

Zahn was one of the first surfers to train regularly. He paddled or ran daily, didn't drink or smoke, and usually ate small meals of fruits, vegetables, and bread. In 1961, at age 36, the 5'11", 180-pound Zahn won the open division of the 32-mile Catalina-to–Manhattan Beach race (he also won in 1956, 1958,

and 1960); when he retired from lifeguarding at age 63, fitness tests placed him in the top half of all Los Angeles County guards.

Zahn died of cancer at age 67. He was married and had no children. "Swimming, surfing, paddling and a bit of rowing and outrigger canoeing was my thing," Zahn noted in a letter to a friend, not long before his death. "Everything else in life didn't interest me much." Some of the luster came off Zahn's legend when *H2O* magazine in 2001 reported that he "favored certain now-scientifically discredited and controversial beliefs regarding race and ethnicity." *See also* lifeguarding and surfing, paddleboarding.

Zamba, Frieda   Affable but resolute goofyfoot pro surfer from Flagler Beach, Florida; four-time world champion (1984, 1985, 1986, and 1988); a model of physical and mental fitness, with little interest in fame or recognition. Zamba was born (1964) and raised in Flagler Beach, and began surfing at age 12. She had no amateur competition record to speak of, and became a pro accidentally at 16, when she entered and won an event at nearby Cocoa Beach and cashed the $500 winner's check without knowing she'd lose her amateur status. The following year she won the 1982 Mazda Surfsport Pro, in Solana Beach, California, and at 17 became the youngest female world tour contest winner, a record she still owns. She finished the 1982 season ranked sixth, then placed second the following year, behind California's Kim Mearig. Zamba won five of the 10 events on the 1984 schedule (no other woman had more than a single win that year) to take the championship by an enormous margin. The 19-year-old was and remains the youngest surfer to win a pro tour season championship. Influenced primarily by loose-limbed, fast-turning Hawaiian surfer Larry Bertlemann, Zamba was something new in the sport: an aggressive female who knew where to find the speed and power in a wave. At 5'3", 110 pounds, she was lean and springy, rode out of a wide stance—her style improved steadily, even after her pro tour retirement—and didn't seem

Frieda Zamba

to lose momentum from one turn to the next. She performed best in small- to medium-sized waves.

Zamba had to come from behind in 1985 to take the title from Australians Pam Burridge and Jodie Cooper, winning the final two events of the season; her margin of victory was even smaller in 1986. She slumped in 1987, finishing third, then became the first woman pro surfer to take on a high-intensity fitness training program (going so far as to hire a sports psychologist), and came back to take the 1988 championship. "After that," Zamba later said, "I kind of lost the passion. It was all competition. Even in my free surfing, I found was doing it like competition. It took all the fun out of it." Zamba left the tour and opened Frieda's Surfline surf shop in Flagler Beach with her surfer husband Bill "Flea" Shaw. Ten years older than Zamba, Shaw had been her sponsor and board-maker since she was 15, and later became her on-tour coach; they were married in 1987. Zamba was even tempered and pleasant, but kept some distance between herself and the commercial surfing world, partly as a tactical effort to win events and partly out of a genuine disinterest in becoming a celebrity. "If she'd been a bit more of an ego-tripper," 1990 world champion Pam Burridge said, "she could have been a giant star. But she didn't pander to the surf industry much. She just liked to surf and win." If Zamba wasn't particularly interested in the spotlight, her dominance of the sport was enough to give her five consecutive *Surfer* Poll wins from 1985 to 1989, and she was featured in "Queen of the Surf," a 1987 *Sport's Illustrated* profile.

Zamba occasionally competed over the next few years, winning the 1990 O'Neill Classic in Santa Cruz, the 1991 Op Pro, and the 1994 Op Pro; over the length of her career she won a total of 18 world tour events. She was inducted into the Huntington Beach Surfing Walk of Fame in 1998. She appeared in more than a dozen surf movies, videos, and documentaries, including *Surfing's Super Series* (1985), *Atlantic Crossing* (1989), and *Surfer Girl* (1994).

zero break   General expression for any rarely seen big-wave break located well offshore, popular among pre-1970s Hawaiian surfers and virtually out of use today. "First break" is the place where medium to large swells normally crest; "second break" is the place where the same wave either re-forms and crests again, or where smaller waves initially break. Zero break waves are the biggest in any particular area, and are usually thought of as being dangerous and somewhat mysterious.

zinc oxide   Surfing's original sunscreen, used as a guard against sunburn and skin cancer. Chalk-colored zinc oxide products, with the shiny bluish-white zinc metal mixed into a wax- or petroleum-based ointment or cream, were first used in Europe in the early 20th century as a balm for irritated skin. In the late 1950s, lifeguards in Australia began rubbing ultraviolet-ray-blocking zinc oxide onto their lips, noses, and cheekbones in what looked like a kind of ritual tribal war painting; American lifeguards soon followed. Surfers of the period often did all they could to disassociate themselves from lifeguards, but this was one thing the two groups agreed on. Flesh-toned zinc oxide was introduced in 1970, and the mid-'80s saw a short-lived fad as the product was again reintroduced, this time in fluorescent greens, yellows, and pinks. Dozens of alternative sunblock products would follow, but many surfers have stuck with zinc oxide. "It's one of the most important things in a grommet's life," freckle-faced Australian pro surfer Shane Herring said in 1994. "If there wasn't zinc I'd be noseless by now. And earless." *See also* skin cancer, sunscreen.

Zog, Mr.   *See* Sex Wax.

APPENDIX 1

Selected Surfing Bibliography

Fiction titles listed below are generally set in the surfing world or feature a surfer as a main character. Nonfiction titles for the most part have surfing as the main subject; in those nonfiction works in which surfing makes up a small part of the larger work (Mark Twain's *Roughing It,* for example), the sport is given noteworthy treatment. There are hundreds of books not listed here with chapters or passages on surfing, most of them sports anthologies/collections or books on Hawaii.

Anthologies/Collections/Essays/Poetry

Adair, Virginia Hamilton. *Ants on the Melon.* New York: Random House, 1996.

Ahrens, Chris. *Good Things Love Water: A Collection of Surf Stories.* Cardiff-by-the-Sea, Calif.: Chubasco Publishing, 1994.

———. *Joyrides: Surf Stories, Volume Two.* Cardiff-by-the-Sea, Calif.: Chubasco, 1998.

———. *Kelea's Gift: Surf Stories.* Cardiff-by-the-Sea, Calif.: Chubasco, 2001.

Amadio, Nadine. *Pacifica: Myth, Magic and Traditional Wisdom From the South Sea Islands.* New York: HarperCollins, 1993.

Ambrose, Greg. *Shark Bites.* Honolulu: The Bell Press, 1996.

Appleman, Phillip. *Summer Love and Surf.* Nashville: Vanderbilt University Press, 1968.

Brisick, Jamie. *We Approach Our Martinis with Such High Expectations.* Los Angeles: Consafos Press, 2002.

Butt, Tony, and Paul Russell. *Surf Science: An Introduction to Waves for Surfing.* Penzance, Cornwall: Alison Hodge Publishers, 2002.

Curry, Steven. *Dancing the Waves and Other Poems.* Honolulu: Anoai Press, 1998.

Dixon, Peter L., ed. *Men and Waves: A Treasury of Surfing.* New York: Coward-McCann, 1966.

Dixon, Peter. *Men Who Ride Mountains: Incredible True Tales of Legendary Surfers.* New York: Bantam, 1969.

Drewe, Robert. *The Bodysurfers.* Darlinghurst, N.S.W., Aus.: J. Fraser, 1983.

Farber, Thomas. *On Water.* Hopewell, N.J.: Ecco Press, 1994.

Finlay, Jack. *Caught Inside: Surf Writings and Photographs.* Geelong, Vic., Aus.: Stormy Weather Publications, 1992.

Gardinier, Alain. *Surfeurs.* Boulogne-Billancourt, Fr.: Editions La Sirene, 1996.

———. *Surfeurs 2.* Boulogne-Billancourt, Fr.: Editions La Sirene, 1998.

Garner, Helen. *Postcards from Surfers.* Fitzroy, Vic., Aus.: McPhee Gribble, 1985.

George, Sam, ed. *The Perfect Day: 40 Years of Surfer Magazine.* San Francisco: Chronicle Books, 2001.

Gugelyk, Ted. *Mango Lady and Other Stories From Hawaii.* Honolulu: Anoai Press, 1997.

Higgins, Mike. *A Surfer's Guide.* San Diego: Windsor Associates, 1992.

Hollinger, Kimo. *Kimo: A Collection of Short Stories.* Honolulu: Anoai Press, 2002.

Jenkins, Bruce. *North Shore Chronicles: Big-Wave Surfing in Hawaii.* Berkeley, Calif.: North Atlantic Books, 1990.

Klein, H. Arthur, and M. C. Klein, eds. *Surf's Up!: An Anthology of Surfing.* Indianapolis, Ind.: Bobbs-Merrill, 1966.

Kuus, Arwo. *Shark Fin Soup.* Huntington Beach, Calif.: Red Dog Publishing, 1991.

Long, John, and Hai-Van K. Sponholz, eds. *The Big Drop: Classic Big Wave Surfing Stories.* Helena, Mont.: Falcon, 1999.

López, Jack. *Cholos & Surfers: A Latino Family Album.* Santa Barbara: Capra Press, 1998.

Marsh, Ari. *Smiling at the Sun: Ways of the Golden Path.* Leucadia, Calif.: Soul Rider Publications, 1993.

———. *The Soul Rider: A Surfer's Perspective of the World.* Leucadia, Calif.: Soul Rider Publications, 1993.

———. *The Soul Rider II: Neptune's Dream.* Leucadia, Calif.: Soul Rider Publications, 1995.

Opstedal, Kevin. *California Redemption Value.* San Francisco: Blue Press, 1998.

Penuelas, Bob. *Wilbur Kookmeyer and Friends.* Del Mar, Calif.: Yipes Publishing, 1985–90.

Pollard, Jack, comp. *The Australian Surfrider.* Sydney: K. G. Murray, 1963.

Severson, John, ed. *Great Surfing: Photos, Stories, Essays, Reminiscences, and Poems.* Garden City, N.Y.: Doubleday, 1967.

Thomas, G. Murray, and Gary Wright, eds. *Paper Shredders: An Anthology of Surf Writing.* San Clemente, Calif.: Orange Ocean Press, 1993.

Trachtenberg, Paul. *Making Waves.* Huntington Beach, Calif.: Cherry Valley Editions, 1985.

Twain, Mark. *Roughing It.* New York: Penguin Putnam, 1994.

Warshaw, Matt. *Above the Roar: 50 Surfer Interviews.* Santa Cruz, Calif.: Waterhouse, 1997.

White, John Wythe. *Short-Timers in Paradise.* Honolulu: Anoai Press, 2000.

Wolf, Don. *Sleeping in the Shorebreak and Other Hairy Surfing Stories.* Manhattan Beach, Calif.: Waverider Publications, 2000.

Wolfe, Tom. *The Pump House Gang.* New York: Farrar Straus & Giroux, 1968.

Young, Nat. *Surf Rage.* Sydney: Nymboida Press, 2000.

Biography/Autobiography/Memoir

Allen, James Lovic. *Locked In: Surfing for Life.* With photos by Dave Darling and others. South Brunswick, N.S.W., Aus.: A. S. Barnes and Co., 1970.

Allen, Michael A. *Tao of Surfing: Finding Depth at Low Tide.* Highland City, Fla.: Rainbow Books, Inc., 1997.

Bartholomew, Wayne, and Tim Baker. *Bustin' Down the Door.* Sydney: HarperSports, 1996.

Brennan, Joe. *Duke Kahanamoku: Hawaii's Golden Man.* Honolulu: Hogarth Press, 1974.

———. *Duke of Hawaii.* New York: Ballantine, 1968.

———. *Duke: The Life Story of Hawaii's Duke Kahanamoku.* Honolulu: Ku Pa'a Publishing, 1994.

Carroll, Corky. *Pier Pressure.* Huntington Beach, Calif.: Corky Carroll, 1999.

Carroll, Corky, with Joel Engel. *Surf-Dog Days and Bitchin' Nights.* Chicago: Contemporary Books, 1989.

Carroll, Tom, with Kirk Willcox. *Tom Carroll: The Wave Within.* Sydney: Pac Macmillan Australia Pty. Limited, 1994.

Cassidy, Graham, and Peter Crawford. *Greats of the Australian Surf.* Sydney: Lester-Townsend Publishing Pty., 1983.

Clark, Rosie Harrison. *Let's Go, Let's Go! The Biography of Lorrin "Whitey" Harrison: California's Legendary Surf Pioneer.* Choreau, Mont.: Harrison Clark, 1997.

Coleman, Stuart Holmes. *Eddie Would Go: The Story of Eddie Aikau, Hawaiian Hero.* Honolulu: MindRaising Press, 2002.

Doudt, Kenny. *Surfing With the Great White Shark.* Lihue, Hawaii: Shark-Bite Pub., 1992.

Doyle, Mike, with Steve Sorensen. *Morning Glass: The Adventures of Legendary Waterman Mike Doyle.* Redondo Beach, Calif.: Mountain & Sea, 1993.

Duane, Daniel. *Caught Inside: A Surfer's Year on the California Coast.* New York: North Point Press, 1996.

Edwards, Phil, and Bob Ottum. *You Should Have Been Here an Hour Ago: The Stoked Side of Surfing; or, How to Hang Ten Through Life and Stay Happy.* New York: Harper & Row, 1967.

Farley, Patrick. *Surfing to Saigon.* Santa Cruz, Calif.: Ranger Publications, 1994.

Farrelly, Midget, as told to Craig McGregor. *This Surfing Life.* Adelaide, Aus.: Rigby Limited, 1965. Republished as *How to Surf,* London: Sphere Books, 1968.

Grigg, Ricky. *Big Surf, Deep Dives, and The Islands: My Life in the Ocean.* Honolulu: Editions Limited, 1998.

Hall, Sandra Kimberley, and Greg Ambrose. *Memories of Duke: The Legend Comes to Life.* Honolulu: The Bess Press, 1995.

Hemmings, Fred. *The Soul of Surfing Is Hawaiian.* Maunawili, Hawaii: Sports Enterprises, 1997.

Jarratt, Phil. *Mr. Sunset: The Jeff Hakman Story.* London: General Publishing Group, 1997.

Knox, David. *Mark Richards: A Surfing Legend.* Pymble, N.S.W., Aus.: Collins/Angus & Robertson, 1992.

London, Charmain. *Our Hawaii.* New York: Macmillan, 1917.

Lorch, Carlos. *Lopez, The Classic Hawaiian Surfer.* Redondo Beach, Calif.: Mountain & Sea, 1981.

Lynch, Gary, et al. *Tom Blake: The Uncommon Journey of a Pioneer Waterman.* Corona del Mar, Calif.: The Croul Family Foundation, 2001.

McClelland, Gordon. *Rick Griffin.* San Francisco: Last Gasp, 2002.

Muirhead, Desmond. *Surfing in Hawaii: A Personal Memoir: With notes on California, Australia, Peru and Other Surfing Countries.* Flagstaff, Ariz.: Northland Press, 1962.

Noble, Valerie. *Hawaiian Prophet: Alexander Hume Ford.* Smithtown, N.Y.: Exposition Press, 1980.

Noll, Greg, and Andrea Gabbard. *Da Bull: Life Over the Edge.* Berkeley, Calif.: North Atlantic Books, 1989.

O'Brien, Frederick. *White Shadows in the South Seas.* Garden City, N.Y.: Garden City Publishing Co., 1919.

Occhilupo, Mark, with Paul Sargeant. *Occy: A Surfer's Year.* Sydney: HarperCollins, 2000.

Olney, Ross R., and Richard W. Graham. *Kings of the Surf.* New York: Putnam and Sons, 1969.

Philip, George Blackmore. *Sixty Years of Recollections of Swimming and Surfing in the Eastern Suburbs.* Sydney: George B. Philip & Son, 1939.

Sandman, The. *This Is My Surfboard.* Sydney: ABC Books, 1996.

Slater, Kelly. *Pipe Dreams: A Surfer's Dream.* New York: Regan Books, 2003.

Stell, Marion. *Pam Burridge.* Pymble, N.S.W., Aus.: Angus & Robertson, 1992.

Van Dyke, Fred. *Once Upon Abundance.* Honolulu: Anoai Press, 2001.

———. *Thirty Years Riding the World's Biggest Surf.* Santa Cruz, Calif.: Ocean Sports International Publishing Group, 1988.

Young, Nat. *Nat's Nat and That's That: A Surfing Legend.* Frenchs Forest, N.S.W., Aus.: Nymboida Press, 1998.

Ziolkowski, Thad. *On a Wave: A Surfer Boyhood.* New York: Atlantic Monthly Press, 2002.

Children (Fiction and Nonfiction)

Asato, Dennis. *A Dolphin Day in Hawaii.* Honolulu: Anoai Press, 1999.

Babcock, Chris. *No Moon, No Milk!* New York: Crown Publishers, Inc., 1993.

Bailey, Alice. *Kimo the Whistling Boy.* New York: The Wise-Parslow Company. 1928.

Berenstain, Stan, and Jan Berenstain. *The Bears' Vacation.* New York: Beginner Books, 1968.

Blake, Quentin. *Mrs. Armitage and the Big Wave.* New York: Harcourt, 1997.

Burton, Jane. *Surfer the Seal.* New York: Random House, 1989.

Collington, Peter. *The Coming of the Surfman.* New York: Alfred A. Knopf, 1994.

Collins, Terry. *Surf's Up! Rocket Power Adventures, #2.* New York: Simon Spotlight, 2001.

Cowan, Catherine, and Mark Beuhner. *My Life with the Wave.* New York: Lothrop, Lee and Shepard Books, 1997.

Foreman, Michael. *Seal Surfer.* New York: Harcourt, 1997.

Germain, Kerry, and Keoni Montes. *Surf's Up for Kimo.* Honolulu: Island Paradise Publishing, 2001.

Grabinsky, Marc. *Aqualusions.* Pacifica, Calif.: TruArt Publications, 1996.

Hale, Bruce. *Moki and the Magic Surfboard.* Honolulu: Words + Pictures Publishing, 1996.

———. *Surf Gecko to the Rescue!* Honolulu: Geckostuffs, 1991.

Harvey, Paul. *Surfer!* London: Penguin Group, 1996.

Hays, Scott. *Surfing.* Vero Beach, Fla.: Rourke Corporation, 1994.

Hinsley, Sandra. *Brain Gym Surfer.* Stuart, Fla.: Hinsley & Conley, 1989.

Jackson, Shelley. *The Old Woman and the Wave.* New York: DK Publishing, Inc., 1998.

Keast, Brett. *Tropicat.* South Laguna, Calif.: BK Publishing, 1996.

Laird, Donivee Martin. *The Three Little Hawaiian Pigs and the Magic Shark.* Honolulu: Barnaby Books, 1981.

Lappin, Jeff. *Simon Makes Waves!* Agoura Hills, Calif.: Endurance Publications, 2002.

Mammano, Julie. *Rhinos Who Surf.* San Francisco: Chronicle Books, 1996.

Marchand, Charlotte. *Goofy Foot.* Laguna Beach, Calif.: Goofy Foot Productions, 1989.

McCrady, Elizabeth. *Kala of Hawaii.* New York: Platt and Munk Co., 1936.

McKissick, Mitch. *Surf Lingo: A Complete Guide to Totally Rad Vocab!* Balboa, Calif.: Coastline Press, 1987.

Ormondroyd, Edward. *Broderick.* Berkeley, Calif.: Parnassus Press, 1969.

Quackenbush, Robert. *Surfboard to Peril.* Englewood, N.J.: Prentice-Hall Inc., 1986.

Radlauer, Ed. *Surfing.* Glendale, Calif.: Bowmar Publishing, 1968.

Raglus, Jeff. *Schnorky the Wave Puncher.* New York: Crown, 1996.

Rainger, Tim. *Surfing.* London: Franklin Watts, 1998.

Rogo, Thomas Paul. *The Surfrider: A Midwestern Odyssey.* Honolulu: The Bess Press, 1999.

Salisbury, Mike. *A Surfer's Coloring Book.* Orange, Calif.: Finicky Arts, 1963.

Saunders, Geoff and Richard. *Fun With Sport: Surfing.* Sydney: Lineup Publishing, n.d.

Smith, Don. *Surfing: The Big Wave.* Mahwah, N.J.: Troll Assoc., 1976.

Sorenson, Margo. *Kimo and the Secret Waves.* Logan, Iowa: Perfection Learning Corp., 1996.

Sperry, Armstrong. *One Day With Manu.* New York: E. M. Hale and Company, 1933.

Spurr, Elizabeth. *Surfer Dog.* New York: Dutton Children's Books, 2002.

Sunn, Rell, with Dave Parmenter. *Surf-A-Lele.* Honolulu: Menehune/Future Legends, 1997.

Sunn, Rell, with Dave Parmenter and Caroline Zimmerman. *Who Is a Surfer.* Honolulu: Menehune/Future Legends, 1995.

Sunn, Rell, with Dave Parmenter and Keith Woolsey. *The Waves You Ride.* Honolulu: Menehune/Future Legends, 1996.

Van Dyke, Fred. *Two Surf Stories for Children.* Taiwan: Mutual Publishing, 1994.

Fiction/Pulp Fiction

Aaberg, Dennis, and John Milius. *Big Wednesday.* New York: Bantam Books, 1978.

Adams, Lindly. *Surf Nurse.* Sydney: Calvert Publishing Co., n.d.

Barre, Richard. *The Ghosts of Morning.* New York: The Berkeley Publishing Group, 1998.

Beaver, Bruce. *Hot Sands.* Sydney: Horowitz, 1964.

Black, Douglas P. *The End of the Endless Summer: The Ron N. Scott Tapes and Papers.* Transcribed and edited by Dr. Christopher Dana Ryan. Laguna Beach, Calif.: Totally Bogus, 1994.

Blanding, Don. *Hula Moons.* New York: Dodd, Mead, 1930.

———. *Stowaways in Paradise: Two Boy Adventurers in Hawaii.* New York: Cosmopolitan Book Corporation, 1931.

Buck, Earl. *The Swapping Surfers.* Chatsworth, Calif.: Publisher's Consultants, 1974.

Bunn, A. G. *Water in the Blood.* Auckland: Heinemann Education, 1990.

Burdick, Eugene. *The Ninth Wave.* Boston: Houghton Mifflin, 1956.

Calisch, Rus. *Paumalu: A Story of Modern Hawaii.* San Clemente, Calif.: Paumalu Press, 1979.

Capp, Fiona. *Night Surfing.* St. Leonards, N.S.W., Aus.: Allen & Unwin Pty. Ltd., 1996.

Carey, Gabrielle, and Kathy Lette. *Puberty Blues.* Carlton, Vic., Aus.: McPhee Gribble, 1979.

Carr, Roger. *Surfie.* Sydney: Horowitz Publications, Inc., 1966.

Converse, Jane. *Surf Safari Nurse.* New York: Signet Books, 1966.

Crowe, Cameron. *Fast Times at Ridgemont High.* New York: Simon and Schuster, 1981.

David, Cliff. *A Surfer for Amanda.* New York: Carlyle Communications, 1974.

DeCure, John. *Reef Dance.* New York: Minotaur Books, 2001.

Dee, Douglas. *Queen of the Surf.* Fresno, Calif.: Saber-Tropic Books, 1967.

DeGregorio, Michael E. *Secret Spot.* Ben Lomond, Calif.: DeGregorio Productions, 1996.

———. *Thunder Bay.* Ben Lomond, Calif.: DeGregorio Productions, 1995.

Douglas, Diana. *Surfing Nurse.* New York: New American Library, 1971.

Foster, Alan Dean. *Dark Star*. New York: Ballantine Books, 1974.

Gilden, Mel. *Surfing Samurai Robots*. New York: Lynx, 1988.

———. *Tubular Android Superheroes*. New York: ROC, 1991.

Gillie, Bill. *Surfer Girl*. Canoga Park, Calif.: Brandon Books, 1977.

Golisch, Joy. *Surfing With Monkeys and Other Diversions*. Davenport, Iowa: Urban Legends Press, 1991.

Green, Bill. *Freud and the Nazis Go Surfing*. Sydney: Pan Books, 1986.

Hawkins, Christopher. *The Water's End*. Victoria, B.C., Can.: Trafford, 2001.

Houston, James D. *A Native Son of the Golden West*. New York: Dial Press, 1971.

Jekel, Pamela. *The Last of the California Girls*. New York: Kensington Pub. Corp., 1989.

Kohner, Frederick. *Cher Papa*. New York: Bantam Books, 1961.

———. *Gidget*. New York: Putnam, 1957.

———. *Gidget Goes Hawaiian*. New York: Bantam, 1961.

———. *Gidget Goes New York*. New York: Dell Publishing Co., 1968.

———. *Gidget Goes Parisienne*. New York: Dell Publishing Co., 1966.

———. *Gidget Goes to Rome*. New York: Bantam, 1963.

———. *Gidget in Love*. New York: Dell Publishing Co., 1965.

———. *The Affairs of Gidget*. New York: Dell Publishing Co., 1963.

———. *The Gremmie*. New York: New English Library, 1965.

Koontz, Dean. *Fear Nothing*. New York: Bantam Books, 1998.

———. *Seize the Night*. New York: Bantam Books, 1999.

Lee, Elsie. *Muscle Beach Party*. New York: Lancer Books, 1964.

Lingard, Tony. *Breaking Free*. Cornwall, U.K.: Ocean Press, 1987.

Lyon, Leslie and Charles. *Surf Clowns: Seven Mental Missions*. New York: Bad Cats Books, 2000.

Machado, Ed. *One Tree Island*. Encinitas, Calif.: Reef Publishing, 1994.

Maloney, Ray. *The Impact Zone*. New York: Delacorte Press, 1986.

McLean, John. *Island of the Gods*. Singapore: Winter Productions, 1990.

Morgan, Patrick. *Beach Queen Blowout*. New York: MacFadden-Bartell, 1971.

———. *Cute and Deadly Surf Twins*. New York: MacFadden-Bartell, 1970.

———. *Death Car Surfside*. New York: MacFadden-Bartell, 1972.

———. *Deadly Group Down Under*. New York: MacFadden-Bartell, 1970.

———. *The Girl in the Telltale Bikini*. New York: MacFadden-Bartell, 1971.

———. *Freaked Out Strangler*. New York: Manor Books, 1973.

———. *Hang Dead Hawaiian Style*. New York: MacFadden-Bartell, 1969.

———. *Scarlet Surf at Makaha*. New York: MacFadden-Bartell, 1970.

———. *Too Mini Murders*. New York: MacFadden-Bartell, 1969.

———. *Topless Dancer Hangup*. New York: MacFadden-Bartell, 1971.

Morris, Bill. *Stoked*. Half Moon Bay, Calif.: New Sun Publications, 1994.

Murray, William. *The Sweet Ride*. New York: New American Library, 1967.

Newton, Bez. *The Islander*. London: Mayflower, 1978.

———. *The Natural*. London: Mayflower, 1978.

Nicholson, Joy. *The Tribes of Palos Verdes*. New York: St. Martin's Press, 1997.

Novak, Walt. *The Haole Substitute*. Fort Bragg, Calif.: Cypress House, 1994.

Nunn, Kem. *The Dogs of Winter*. New York: Scribner's, 1997.

———. *Tapping the Source*. New York: Delacorte Press, 1984.

Parker, T. Jefferson. *Little Saigon*. New York: St. Martin's Press, 1988.

Pomeroy, Pete. *Wipeout!* New York: Four Winds Press, 1968.

Reiss, Fred. *Gidget Must Die: A Killer Surf Novel*. Santa Cruz, Calif.: Santa Cruz'n Press, 1995.

Rubel, Marc. *Flex*. New York: St. Martin's Press, 1983.

Spaulding, Michael. *Anything Under the Sun*. New York: Tower Publications Inc., 1964.

Train, Ray. *Surf Broad*. Detroit: Satan Press, 1965.

Twombly, Alexander S. *Kelea: The Surf-Rider: A Romance of Pagan Hawaii*. New York: Fords, Howard & Hulbert, 1900.

White-Prince, Terence. *What Happened to Sherlock Holmes: As Set to Rest in—The Legend of Wilson, the Amazing Athlete*. Marina del Rey, Calif.: Seagull Pub. Co., 1984.

Williams, J. X. *The Sex Surfers*. San Diego: Phoenix Publishers, 1968.

General Surf Interest/Surf History/Surf Reference

Alden, Holt R. *Surf Journal: Because You Surf*. Morro Bay, Calif.: 1995.

Anderson, Michael. *Southern California Beach and Surf Discriptionary*. Pacific Beach, Calif.: Pacific Beach Press, 1987.

Bascom, Willard. *Waves and Beaches*. New York: Anchor Books, 1964.

Bird, Isabella. *Six Months in the Sandwich Islands*. London: London and Edinburgh, 1875.

Blackburn, Mark. *Surf's Up: Collecting the Longboard Era*. Atglen, Pa.: Schiffer Publishing, 2001.

Blair, John. *The Illustrated Discography of Surf Music, 1959–1965*. Riverside, Calif.: J. Bee Productions, 1978.

Blake, Tom. *Hawaiian Surfboard*. Honolulu: Paradise of the Pacific Press, 1935. Reprinted as *Hawaiian Surfriding: The Ancient and Royal Pastime*. Flagstaff, Ariz.: Northland Press, 1961; and *Hawaiian Surfriders, 1935*, Redondo Beach, Calif.: Mountain & Sea, 1983.

Brawley, Sean. *Beach Beyond: A History of the Palm Beach Surf Club, 1921–1996.* Sydney: University of New South Wales Press, 1996.

Burt, Rob. *Surf City, Drag City.* New York: Blandford Press, 1986.

Bystrom, Chris. *The Glide: Longboarding and the Renaissance of Modern Surfing.* Brisbane, Qld., Aus.: Duranbah Press, 1998.

Cameron, Kirk, and Zack Hanle. *The Surfer's Handbook.* New York: Dell, 1968.

Campbell, Mark. *Surf Sports Down Under.* Sydney: Golden Press, 1982.

Carroll, Nick. *The Next Wave: The World of Surfing.* New York: Abbeville Press, 1991.

Cleary, William. *Surfing: All the Young Wave Hunters.* New York: New American Library, 1967.

Cohen, Stephane, and Sylvain Cazenave. *Surf.* France: Editions EPA, 1997.

Cook, Capt. James. *A Voyage to the Pacific Ocean.* London: Nicol & Cadell, 1784.

Cralle, Trevor, comp. and ed. *The Surfin'Ary: A Dictionary of Surfing Terms and Surfspeak.* Berkeley, Calif.: Ten Speed Press, 1991.

Curlewis, Jean, and Harold Cazneaux. *Sydney Surfing.* Sydney: Art in Australia Ltd., 1929.

Dalley, Robert. *Surfin' Guitars: Instrumental Surf Bands of the Sixties.* Los Angeles: Surf Publications, 1988.

De Soultrait, Gibus. *L'Homme Et La Vague.* Biarritz, Fr.: Surf Session, 1995.

Dixon, Peter L. *The Complete Book of Surfing.* New York: Coward-McCann, 1965.

Filosa, Gary. *The Surfer's Almanac: An International Surfing Guide.* New York: Dutton, 1977.

Finney, Ben R., and James D. Houston. *Surfing: The Sport of Hawaiian Kings.* Johannesburg: Hugh Keartland, 1966. Revised and retitled *Surfing: A History of the Ancient Hawaiian Sport,* 1996.

Gabbard, Andrea. *Girl in the Curl: A Century of Women in Surfing.* Seattle: Seal Press, 2000.

George, Sam. *Surfing: A Way of Life.* New York: Mallard Press, 1990.

Griffin, Rick. *A Cartoon History of Surfing.* Hermosa Beach, Calif.: Greg Noll Surfboards and Film Productions, 1962.

Grissim, John. *Pure Stoke.* New York: Harper, 1982.

Halacy, D. S., Jr. *The IN Sports.* Philadelphia: Macrae Smith, 1966.

Hemmings, Fred. *Surfing: Hawaii's Gift to the World of Sports.* Tokyo: Zokeisha Publications. Distributed in the U.S. by Grosset & Dunlap, 1977.

Hemmings, Fred, Randy Rarick, and Hideaki Ishi. *The Illustrated Encyclopedia of Surfing.* Hong Kong: HI Publications, Inc., 1982.

Hening, Glenn. *Groundswell Society Annual 1997.* Oxnard, Calif.: Glenn Hening, 1997.

Holmes, Paul. *Surfabout: The Complete Story of Professional Surfing and the World's Richest Contest.* Dalinghurst, N.S.W., Aus.: Soundtrack Publishing Co., 1980.

Holmes, Rod, and Doug Wilson. *You Should Have Been Here Yesterday—The Roots of British Surfing.* London: SeasEdge Publications, 1994.

Jarratt, Phil. *Surfing, The Dictionary.* South Melbourne, Vic., Aus.: SunBooks, 1985.

———. *The Wave Game.* Broadway, N.S.W., Aus.: Soundtracks Publishing, 1977.

Johnson, Barry. *Surf Fever.* Brisbane, Qld., Aus.: Jacaranda Press, 1963.

Kampion, Drew. *Stoked: A History of Surf Culture.* Los Angeles: General Publishing Group, 1997.

Kahanamoku, Duke, and Joe Brennan. *Duke Kahanamoku's World of Surfing.* New York: Grosset & Dunlap, 1968.

Kelly, John M., Jr. *Surf and Sea.* New York: A. S. Barnes, 1965.

Klein, H. Arthur. *Surf-Riding.* Philadelphia: Lippincott, 1972.

———. *Surfing.* Philadelphia: Lippincott, 1965.

Kuhns, Grant W. *On Surfing.* Rutland, Vt.: C. E. Tuttle, 1963.

Lencek, Lena, and Gideon Bosker. *The Beach.* New York: Viking Penguin, 1998.

Lockwood, Craig, ed. *The Whole Ocean Catalog.* Dana Point, Calif.: Surfer Publishing, 1986.

Lowe, A. M. *Surfing, Surf-Shooting and Surf-Life-Saving Pioneering.* Manly, N.S.W., Aus.: S. N., 1955.

Lueras, Leonard. *Surfing: The Ultimate Pleasure.* Honolulu: Emphasis International/Workman, 1984.

Margan, Frank, and Ben R. Finney. *A Pictorial History of Surfing.* Sydney: Hamlyn, 1970.

Martin, Andy. *Walking on Water.* London: John Murray Ltd., 1991.

McGuinness, Laurie, and Peter Crawford. *Wild Water: The Surfing Way of Life.* Sydney: Rigby Limited, 1977.

McParland, Stephen J. *Beach, Street and Strip: The Albums.* Sydney: Seagull Productions, 1983.

Morris, Vic, and Joe Nelson. *The Weather Surfer: A Guide to Oceanography and Meteorology for the World's Wave Hunters.* San Diego: Grossmont Press, 1977.

Orbelian, George. *Essential Surfing.* San Francisco: Orbelian Arts, 1982.

Patterson, O. B. *Surfriding: Its Thrills and Techniques.* Rutland, Vt.: C. E. Tuttle, 1960.

Pearson, Kent. *Surfing Subcultures of Australia and New Zealand.* St. Lucia, Qld., Aus.: University of Queensland Press, 1979.

Prytherch, Reginald. *Surfing: A Modern Guide.* London: Faber and Faber, 1972.

Rebeix, Maurice. *Hawai'i: Aloha, Surf & Tradition.* Biarritz, Fr.: Editions Surf Session, 1993.

Schiffer, Nancy. *Surfing.* Atglen, Pa.: Schiffer Publishing Ltd., 1998.

Spinner, Stephanie. *Water Skiing and Surfboarding.* New York: Golden Press, 1968.

Sunn, Rell, and Ken Suiso. *Guide to Beach Survival.* Honolulu: Honolulu Water Safety, 1986.

Thoms, Albie. *Surfmovies: The History of Surf Film in Australia.* Sydney: Shore Thing Publishing, 2000.

Timmons, Grady. *Waikiki Beachboy*. Honolulu: Editions Limited, 1989.

Van Dyke, Fred. *Surfing Huge Waves with Ease*. Honolulu: Mutual Publishing, 1992.

Wardlaw, Lee. *Cowabunga!: The Complete Book of Surfing*. New York: Avon Books, 1991.

Warshaw, Matt. *Maverick's: The Story of Big-Wave Surfing*. San Francisco: Chronicle Books, 2000.

——. *Surfriders: In Search of the Perfect Wave*. Del Mar, Calif.: Tehabi Books, 1997.

Williamson, Luke. *Gone Surfing: The Golden Years of Surfing in New Zealand, 1950–1970*. Auckland: Penguin Books, Ltd., 2000.

Wilson, Jack. *Australian Surfing and Surf Life Saving*. Adelaide, S.A., Aus.: Rigby, 1979.

Wood, Jack. *Surf City: The California Sound*. New York: Friedman/Fairfax Publishers, 1995.

Young, Nat, and Craig McGregor. *The History of Surfing*. Palm Beach, N.S.W., Aus.: Palm Beach Press, 1983.

Guidebook/Travel

Abbot, Rick. *A Surfer's Guide to North Devon*. North Devon, U.K.: Aycliffe Press, 1982.

Ahrens, Chris. *The Surfer's Travel Guide: A Handbook to Surf Paradise*. Cardiff-by-the-Sea, Calif.: Chubasco, 1995.

Alderson, Wayne. *Surf UK: The Definitive Guide to Surfing in Britain*. Arundel, U.K.: Fernhurst Books, 1994.

Ambrose, Greg. *Surfer's Guide to Hawaii: Hawaii Gets All the Breaks!* Honolulu: Bess Press, 1991.

Barnett, Cornel. *Hitting the Lip: Surfing in South Africa*. Johannesburg: Macmillan South Africa, 1974.

Bhana, Mike. *The New Zealand Surfing Guide*. Auckland: Heinemann Reed, 1988.

Carroll, Tom, with Nick Carroll, Derek Hynd, and Peter Wilson. *Tom Carroll's Surfing the World*. Paddington, N.S.W., Aus.: Lester-Townsend, 1990.

Carter, Jeff. *Surf Beaches of Australia's East Coast*. Sydney: Angus & Robertson, 1968.

City Council of Swansea. *Surfing and Windsurfing In and Around Swansea*. Swansea, Wales, U.K.: City of Swansea, 1995.

Colas, Antony, and Bruce Sutherland. *The World Stormrider Guide*. London: Low Pressure, 2001.

Dalton, Bill. *Bali Handbook*. Chico, Calif.: Moon Publications, 1997.

Demovic, Tony Roland. *Surfing Australia*. Marrickville, N.S.W., Aus.: Western Colour Print, 1980.

Dixon, Peter L. *Where the Surfers Are: A Guide to the World's Great Surfing Spots*. New York: Coward-McCann, 1968.

Dixon, Peter, with Sarah Dixon. *West Coast Beaches*. New York: E. P. Dutton, 1979.

Fitzjones, Ollie, with Dan Haylock, Tim Rainger, and Bruce Sutherland. *The Stormrider Guide Europe*. London: Low Pressure, 1992.

Gardinier, Alain. *Surf Guide to France*. Boulogne-Billancourt, Fr.: Editions La Sirene, 1992.

Grigg, Ricky, and Ron Church. *Surfer in Hawaii: A Guide to Surfing in the Hawaiian Islands*. Dana Point, Calif.: John Severson, 1963.

Haylock, Dan, with Drew Kampion, Mike Kew, and Bruce Sutherland. *The Stormrider Guide North America*. London: Low Pressure, 2002.

Jury, Mark. *Surfing in Southern Africa: Including Mauritius and Réunion*. Cape Town: Struik, 1989.

Kerdel, Rod. *Surfinder Victoria*. Black Rock, Vic., Aus.: Surfinder Australia Pty. Ltd., 1995.

London, Jack. *The Cruise of the Snark*. New York: Dover Publications, 2000.

Loveridge, Richard. *A Guide to the Surf Beaches of Victoria*. Melbourne, Vic., Aus.: Lothian, 1987.

Lueras, Leonard. *Fielding's Surfing Indonesia, A Guide to the World's Greatest Surfing*. Redondo Beach, Calif.: Fielding Worldwide, 1996.

Neely, Peter. *Indo Surf & Lingo: Hardcore Surf Explorer's Guide to Indonesian Surf Spots & Indonesian Language*. Noosa Heads, Qld., Aus.: Indo Surf & Lingo, 1990.

Parise, Mike. *The Surfer's Guide to Baja*. Los Angeles: Surf-Press Publishing, 2001.

——. *The Surfer's Guide to Costa Rica*. Los Angeles: Surf-Press Publishing, 1996.

Power, Chris. *The British Surfing Association Guide to Surfing in Britain*. Penzance, U.K.: British Surfing Association, 1993.

Pruett, Matt, and Chris Towery. *Wavescape: Portraits of the Planet's Best Surf Spots*. New York: Barron's Educational Series, 2002.

Rennie, Chris. *The Surfer's Travel Guide*. Doncaster, Vic., Aus.: Liquid Addictions, 1998.

Severson, John, ed. *Modern Surfing Around the World*. Garden City, N.Y.: Doubleday, 1964.

St. Pierre, Brian. *The Fantastic Plastic Voyage: Across the South Pacific With Surfers and a Camera*. New York: Coward-McCann, 1969.

Stern, David H., and William S. Cleary. *Surfing Guide to Southern California*. Malibu, Calif.: Fitzpatrick Co., 1963.

Strazz, P. L. *Surfing the Great Lakes: An Insider's Guide to Monster Waves Along North America's Fresh Coast*. Chicago: Big Lauter Tun Books, 2000.

Thompson, Carl. *Surfing in Great Britain*. London: Constable, 1972.

Thornley, Mark, and Dante Veda. *Surfing Australia*. Redondo Beach, Calif.: Periplus Editions, 1998.

Vansant, Amy. *The Surfer's Guide to Florida*. Sarasota, Fla.: Pineapple Press, 1995.

Warren, Mark. *Atlas of Australian Surfing*. North Ryde, N.S.W., Aus.: Angus & Robertson, 1988.

Warwick, Wayne. *A Guide to Surfriding in New Zealand*. Wellington, N.Z.: Viking Sevenseas, 1978.

Wegener, Tom, and Bill Burke. *Southern California's Best Surf: A Guide to Finding, Predicting, and Understanding the Surf of Southern California*. Redondo Beach, Calif.: Green Room Press, 1989.

Wilson, Gary. *Surfing in Hawaii*. Honolulu: World Wide Distributors, 1976.

Wright, Bank. *Surfing California: A Complete Guide to the California Coast.* Redondo Beach, Calif.: Maanana Pub., 1973.

———. *Surfing Hawaii.* Redondo Beach, Calif.: Mountain & Sea, 1985.

Young, Nat. *Surfing Australia's East Coast.* Cammeray, N.S.W., Aus.: Horwitz, 1980.

———. *Surfing & Sailboard Guide to Australia.* Palm Beach, N.S.W., Aus.: Palm Beach Press, 1986.

How-To/Instructional

Abbot, Rick. *The Science of Surfing.* Cardiff, Calif.: John Jones Cardiff Ltd., 1972.

———. *Start Surfing.* London: S. Paul, 1980.

———. *This Is Surfing.* Braunton, U.K.: Rick Abbot, 1982.

Abreu, R. E. *Inside and Out: A Surfing Improvement Handbook.* Huntington Beach, Calif.: R. Abreu Surfing Division, 1974.

Alderson, Wayne. *Surfing: A Beginner's Manual.* Arundel, U.K.: Fernhurst Books, 1996.

Atkins, Alan. *The Basics of Surfing.* Torquay, Vic., Aus.: Australian Surfing Association, 1986.

Bennett, Lorraine, ed. *Come'n Try Surfing. Come'n Try Sport.* Melbourne, Vic., Aus.: Life. Be In It, 1985.

Bloomfield, John. *Know How in the Surf.* London: Angus and Robertson, 1960.

Brimner, Larry Dane. *Surfing. A First Book.* New York: Franklin Watts, 1997.

Colendich, George. *The Ding Repair Scriptures.* Soquel, Calif.: Village Green Publishing, 1986.

Collins, Chris. *The Name of the Game Is Surfing.* Surry Hills, N.S.W., Aus.: Aussie Sports Books, 1991.

Conway, John. *Surfing.* Harrisburg, Pa.: Stackpole Press, 1988.

Cook, Joseph. *Better Surfing.* London: Kaye & Word Ltd., 1968.

Cook, Joseph, and William Romeika. *Better Surfing for Boys.* New York: Dodd, Mead and Company, 1967.

Dewey, Nelson. *How to Body Surf.* B.C., Can.: Saltaire Publishing Co., 1970

Dixon, Peter. *The Complete Guide to Surfing.* Guilford, Conn.: Lyons Press, 2001.

Drummond, Ronald Blake. *The Art of Wave Riding.* Hollywood, Calif.: The Cloister Press, 1931.

Farrelly, Midget, and Craig McGregor. *How to Surf.* London: Sphere Books Ltd., 1968.

Flynn, Frank. *Safe Surfing: A Guide to Safer Surfboard Riding.* Torquay, Vic., Aus.: Torquay Clinic, 1986.

Frediani, Paul, and Peter Peck. *Surf Flex: Flexibility, Yoga, and Conditioning Exercises for Surfers.* New York: Hatherleigh Press, 2001.

Freeman, Tony. *Beginning Surfing. Sport for Everyone.* Chicago: Children's Press, 1980.

Furnas, Craig. *Surfing Made Easy.* Corona del Mar, Calif.: CJF, 1997.

Gabrielson, Bruce. *The Complete Surfing Guide for Coaches.* Huntington Beach, Calif.: Faquar Publishing, 1975.

Gardener, Robert. *The Art of Body Surfing.* Philadelphia: Chilton, 1972.

Holden, Phil. *Wind and Surf: All Action.* Hove, S.A., Aus.: Wayland, 1991.

Jennar, Howard. *Making a Surfboard: The Complete Manual.* Darlinghurst, N.S.W., Aus.: Mason Stewart Publishing Pty., 1985.

Kinstle, James. *Surfboard Design and Construction.* Long Beach, Calif.: Natural High Express Publishing, 1975.

Lowdon, Brian and Margaret. *Competitive Surfing: A Dedicated Approach.* Redondo Beach, Calif.: Mountain and Sea, 1988.

MacLaren, James. *Learn to Surf.* New York: Lyons & Burford, 1997.

Madison, Arnold. *Surfing Basic Techniques.* New York: David McKay Company, Inc., 1979.

Masters, Ted. *Surfing Made Easy.* Van Nuys, Calif.: Masters-Graham Publications, 1962.

McGuinness, Laurie. *Surfing Fundamentals.* Sydney: A. H. & A. W. Reed Pty. Ltd., 1978.

Moriarty, Jay, and Chris Gallagher. *The Ultimate Guide to Surfing.* London: First Lyons Press, 2001.

Olney, Ross. *The Young Sportsman's Guide to Surfing.* New York: Nelson, 1965.

Paskowitz, Dorian. *Surfing and Health.* Honolulu: Paskowitz Press, 2001.

Pierce, Franklin. *Fiberglass Ding Repair.* Encinitas, Calif.: Prince's Principals, 1993.

Pollard, Jack, ed. *How to Ride a Surfboard.* Wollstonecraft, N.S.W., Aus.: Pollard Publishing, 1972. Reprinted as *Surfing Fundamentals,* Terrey Hills, N.S.W., Aus.: Reed, 1978.

Nelson, William Desmond. *Surfing: A Handbook.* Philadelphia: Auerbach, 1973.

Renneker, Mark, Kevin Starr, and Geoff Booth. *Sick Surfers Ask the Surf Docs & Dr. Geoff.* Palo Alto, Calif.: Bull Pub. Co., 1993.

Shaw, Stephen. *Surfboard: How to Build Surfboards and Related Watersport Equipment.* Honolulu: Stephen M. Shaw, 1994. Formerly titled *Surfboard Builder's Manual* and *Surfboard Builder's Yearbook.*

Snyder, Rocky. *Fit to Surf: Surfer's Guide to Strength Training and Conditioning.* New York: Emerson Publishing, 2001.

Spacek, Peter. *Wetiquette: Wave Riding Rules: How to Hang Ten and Not Step on Anyone's Toes.* Montauk, N.Y.: Ditch Ink Pub., 2002.

Sufrin, Mark. *Surfing: How to Improve Your Technique.* New York: Franklin Watts, Inc., 1973.

Telegraph, Brisbane, The. How to Swim and Surf: A Guide for Better Swimming, Surfing and Other Water Sports. Brisbane, Qld., Aus.: *The Telegraph,* 1961.

Wagenvoord, James, and Lynn Bailey. *How to Surf.* New York: Collier Books, 1968.

Walters, Bill. *Maui Boardbuilding & Repair.* Makawao, Hawaii: Sun Flare Maui, 1991.

Webber, L. A. *How to Surf for the Beginner.* Honolulu: South Sea Sales, 1964.

Werner, Doug. *Longboarder's Start-Up: A Guide to Longboard Surfing.* San Diego: Tracks Publishing, 1996.

———. *Surfer's Start-Up: A Beginner's Guide to Surfing.* Ventura, Calif.: Pathfinder Pub. of California, 1993.

White, Graham. *Surfing*. Sydney: Summit Books, 1977.
Wilson, Doug. *Learn to Surf*. Newquay, U.K.: European Surfing Co. Ltd., 1967.
Young, Nat. *Nat Young's Book of Surfing: The Fundamentals and Adventure of Board-Riding*. Terrey Hills, N.S.W., Aus.: Reed, 1979.
———. *Surfing Fundamentals*. Palm Beach, N.S.W., Aus.: Palm Beach Press, 1985.

Photo/Art

Adler, Tom. *1936–1942 San Onofre to Point Dume, Photographs by Don James*. Santa Barbara: Tom Adler Books, 1996.
———. *Surf Life: 32 to oz*. Santa Barbara, Calif.: T. Adler Books, 2002.
Adler, Tom, and Gary Lynch. *Tom Blake Surfing 1922–1932*. Santa Barbara: Tom Adler Books, 1999.
Ball, Doc. *California Surfriders: A Scrapbook of Surfriding and Beach Stuff*. Redondo Beach, Calif.: Mountain & Sea, 1979.
Blackburn, Mark. *Hula Girls & Surfer Boys, 1870–1940*. Atglen, Pa.: Schiffer Publishing, 2000.
Bolster, Warren. *Masters of Surf Photography #3: Warren Bolster*. San Clemente, Calif.: Journal Concepts, Inc., 2002.
Brewer, Art. *Masters of Surf Photography #2: Art Brewer*. San Clemente, Calif.: Journal Concepts, Inc., 2001.
Burgoyne, Patrick, and Jeremy Leslie. *Board: Surf/Skate/Snow Graphics*. New York: Watson-Guptill, 1998.
Cariou, Patrick. *Surfers: Photographs by Patrick Cariou*. New York: Powerhouse Books, 1997.
Carol, Fred. *Surfers Dompteurs De Vagues*. Boulogne, Fr.: La Sirene, 1995.
Carson, David, and Craig Stecyk. *Surf Culture: The Art History of Surfing*. Corte Madera, Calif.: Gingko Press, 2002.
Channon, Bruce, and Hugh McLeod. *Surfing the Chain of Fire*. Sydney: Australian Surfing World, 1986.
———. *Surfing Wild Australia*. Sydney: Australian Surfing World, 1984.
Colburn, Bolton. *Papa Moana: Craig Stecyk*. Laguna Beach, Calif.: Laguna Art Museum, 1989.
Divine, Jeff. *Masters of Surf Photography #1: Jeff Divine; Thirty Years, 1970–1999*. San Clemente, Calif.: Journal Concepts, 2000.
Golding, Wayne. *Still Life with Franchise*. Rashcutters Bay, N.S.W., Aus.: Mambo Graphics Pty., Ltd., 1998.
Grannis, Leroy. *Photo: Grannis; Surfing's Golden Age 1960–1969*. San Clemente, Calif.: Journal Concepts, Inc., 1998.
Gurrey, A. R. *The Surf Riders of Hawaii*. Honolulu: Bulletin Pub. Co. Ltd., 1915.
Kampion, Drew. *The Book of Waves*. Dana Point, Calif.: *Surfer* Magazine & Arpel Graphics, 1989.
King, Don, and Maurice Rebix. *Aloha Blue*. Guethary, Fr.: Editions Surf Sessions—Vente De Terre, 1997.
Lassen, Chris, and Drew Kampion. *The Art of Lassen*. Maui, Hawaii: Lassen International, 1993.
Levin, Wayne. *Through a Liquid Mirror: Photographs by Wayne Levin*. Honolulu: Editions Limited, 1997.

Max, Blue, with Charlie Lyon and Leslie Lyon. *Jaws Maui*. Hong Kong: Jaws Maui Ltd., 1997.
Severson, John. *Surf Fever: John Severson Surfer Photography*. San Clemente, Calif.: The Surfer's Journal, 2003.
Stecyk, Craig, and David Carson. *Surf Culture: The Art History of Surfing*. Corte Madera, Calif.: Gingko Press, 2002.
Towery, Chris, with Matt Pruett. *Wavescape: Portraits of the Planet's Best Surf Spots*. Hauppauge, N.Y.: Barrons, 2002.
Trefz, Patrick. *Santa Cruz: Visions of Surf City*. Santa Cruz, Calif.: Solid Publishing, 2002.
Visions of the Breaking Wave. Burleigh Heads, Qld., Aus.: Morrison Media Publications, 1999.

Young Adult (Fiction and Nonfiction)

Abbott, Tony. *Zombie Surf Commandos From Mars*. New York: Scholastic, 1996.
Adams, Andy. *Hawaiian Sea Hunt Mystery*. New York: Grosset & Dunlap, 1960.
Barretto, Larry, with Bryant Cooper. *Hawaiian Holiday*. New York: Dodd, Mead and Company, 1938.
Bateson, David. *The Boy With the Golden Surfboard*. London: Carousel Books, 1973.
Bennet, Cherie. *Sunset Surf*. New York: Berkeley Publishing Group, 1993.
Bowen, Robert Sidney. *Wipeout*. 1968. New York: Criterion Books, 1969.
Brady, Casey. *The Big Wipeout. Baywatch Jr. Lifeguard Books #4*. New York: Random House, 1996.
Brimner, Larry Dane. *Surfing*. New York: Franklin Watts, 1997.
Buehler, Stephanie. *There's No Surf in Cleveland*. New York: Clarion Books, 1993.
Bunting, Eve. *Surfing Country*. Chicago: Children's Press, 1974.
———. *A Sudden Silence*. New York: Harcourt Brace, 1988.
Caldwell, Claire. *Surf's Up for Laney. First Love #90*. New York: Silhouette Books, 1984.
Cargill, Linda. *The Surfer*. New York: Scholastic Inc., 1995.
Cavanna, Betty. *The Surfer and the City Girl*. Philadelphia: Westminster Press, 1981.
Ching, Patrick, and Jeff Pagay. *How Fo' Surf Wit' Palaka Joe*. Honolulu: Naturally Hawaiian, 1995.
Choyce, Lesley. *Wave Watch*. Halifax, Can.: Formac Publishing, 1990.
Clark, Margaret. *Hold My Hand—or Else!* Milsons Point, N.S.W., Aus.: Random House Australia, 1993.
Connor, James. *Surfing Summer*. New York: W. R. Scott, 1969.
Cosgrove, Marilyn. *The Surfing Kid*. Sydney: Hodder & Stoughton, 1987.
Couper, J. M. *Looking for a Wave*. Scarsdale, N.Y.: Bradbury Press, 1973.
Cruise, Beth. *Surf's Up (Saved by the Bell)*. New York: Aladdin Paperbacks, 1995.
Daniels, Lee. *Capsized! Surf City #5*. New York: Lynx, 1989.

———. *Hidden Reef. Surf City #4.* New York: Lynx, 1989.

———. *Riptide. Surf City #3.* New York: Lynx, 1988.

———. *Storm Warnings. Surf City #2.* New York: Lynx, 1988.

———. *Wipeout. Surf City #1.* New York: Lynx, 1988.

Davidson, Linda. *Treading Water. Endless Summer #1.* New York: Ballantine Books, 1988.

Dixon, Franklin W. *Fright Wave. The Hardy Boys #40.* New York: Pocket Books, 1990.

Dixon, Peter L. *Wipe Out. The Hardy Boys #96.* Glendale, Calif.: Bowmar, 1971.

Dubowski, Cathy East. *The Case of the Surfing Secret. New Adventures of Mary-Kate & Ashley, #12.* New York: HarperEntertainment, 1999.

Earls, Nick. *After January.* Qld., Aus.: University of Queensland Press, 1996.

Erskine, Helen. *Golden Girl. First Love #17.* New York: Silhouette Books, 1982.

Evans, Jeremy. *Surfing. Adventurers Series.* New York: Crestwood House, 1993.

Farber, Erica, and J. R. Sansevere. *Surf's Up: Mercer Mayer's LC & the Critter Kids.* Racine, Wis.: Western Pub. Co., 1994.

Filichia, Peter. *Girls Can't Do It.* New York: Avon Books, 1990.

Gleasner, Diana C. *Illustrated Swimming, Diving, and Surfing Dictionary for Young People.* New York: Harvey House, 1980.

Gutman, Bill. *Surfing.* Minneapolis: Capstone Press, 1995.

Halacy, D. S., Jr. *Surfer!* New York: Macmillan, 1965.

Harkin, Philip. *Young Skin Diver.* New York: Berkeley Books, 1956.

Harvey, Kevan Jane. *No Girls Allowed.* New York: Scholastic Book Services, 1972.

Keene, Carolyn. *The Phantom Surfer. The Dana Girls Mystery Stories #6.* New York: Grosset & Dunlap, 1968.

Laklan, Carli. *Surf With Me.* New York: McGraw-Hill, 1967.

Lantz, Francis Lin. *Surfer Girl. A Caprice Romance #28.* New York: Tempo Books, 1983.

Leibold, Jay. *Surf Monkeys. Choose Your Own Adventure #131.* New York: Bantam, 1993.

Martin, Ann M. *California Girls! Baby-Sitters Club Super Special #5.* New York: Scholastic, 1990.

———. *Dawn and the Surfer Ghost. Baby-Sitters Club Mystery #12.* New York: Scholastic, 1993.

Maybee, Bette Lou. *Barbie's Hawaiian Holiday.* New York: Random House, 1963.

Meillon, Claire. *The New Surf Club.* Sydney: Angus and Robertson, 1959.

Miner, Jane Claypool. *Malibu Summer.* New York: Scholastic Inc., 1995.

Mustapha, Gael. *Surfer Boy.* Aiea, Hawaii: Island Heritage Publishing, 1998.

Nentl, Jerolyn Ann. *Surfing. Funseeker Series.* Mankato, Minn.: Crestwood House, 1978.

O'Brien, John. *Endless Wave.* Gosford, N.S.W., Aus.: Ashton Scholastic, 1993.

———. *Impact Zone.* Rydalmere, N.S.W., Aus.: Starlight Publishers, 1995.

O'Conner, Patrick. *South Swell.* New York: Washburn, 1967.

Ogan, Margaret, and George Ogan. *Goofy Foot.* New York: Funk & Wagnalls, 1967.

Parry, Glyn. *LA Postcards.* Milsons Point, N.S.W., Aus.: Random House, 1994.

———. *Radical Take-Offs.* St. Leonards, N.S.W., Aus.: Allen & Unwin Publications, 1994.

———. *Stoked! Real Life, Real Surf.* St. Leonards, N.S.W., Aus.: Allen & Unwin Publications, 1994.

Pascal, Francine, *The New Elizabeth. Sweet Valley High #63.* New York: Bantam, 1990.

Quin-Harkin, Janet. *Surf's Up! Sugar & Spice #8.* New York: Ivy Books, 1987.

Richardson, Vivian. *Surf Shredder Breaking the Green.* London: Bloomsbury Publishing, 1966.

Roddy, Lee. *The Mystery of the Wild Surfer. A Ladd Family Adventure.* Pomona, Calif.: Focus on the Family Pub., 1990.

Sansevere, John R., and Erica Farber. *Over the Edge: The Surf and Skate Monster Unleashed.* Racine, Wis.: Western Pub. Co., 1993.

Sears, Jane L. *Surfboard Summer.* Racine, Wis.: Whitman, 1965.

Singer, A. L.. *Surf Ninjas.* New York: Bantam Books, 1993.

Stone, Hampton. *The Kid Was Last Seen Hanging Ten. An Inner Sanctum Mystery.* New York: Simon and Schuster, 1966.

Summers, James L. *The Cardiff Giants.* Philadelphia: Westminster Press, 1964.

Tomlinson, Theresa. *Riding the Waves.* New York: Atheneum, 1993.

Winton, Tim. *Lockie Leonard, Human Torpedo.* South Yarra, Vic., Aus.: McPhee Gribble, 1990.

———. *Lockie Leonard, Legend.* Sydney: Pan, 1997.

———. *Lockie Leonard, Scumbuster.* Chippendale, N.S.W., Aus.: Piper, 1993.

Zakarin, Debra. *Surf's Up! A Surf Style Handbook.* New York: Grosset and Dunlap, 2002.

Zindel, Paul. *The Surfing Corpse. P. C. Hawke Mysteries #2.* New York: Hyperion, 2001.

Select Surf Contest Results, 1954–2002

Results for the American and Australian national championships are included up until 1976, when the world pro tour debuted; only international events are listed from 1976 forward. World pro tour winners, along with Triple Crown champions, are listed in the shaded box below the contest results. A majority of events, starting in 1976, are world pro tour contests, but this appendix does not represent the full schedule of tour events, and the number of cited events in a given year has been capped at 10. Contests are listed alphabetically within each year, not chronologically. If an event has multiple divisions, only men's, women's, and juniors results, in that order, are noted.

1954   **MAKAHA INTERNATIONAL**
George Downing, Allen Gomes

1955   **MAKAHA INTERNATIONAL**
Rabbit Kekai, Ethel Kukea, Allen Gomes

1956   **MAKAHA INTERNATIONAL**
Conrad Canha, Ethel Kukea, J. Raydon

        PERU INTERNATIONAL
Eduardo Arena

1957   **MAKAHA INTERNATIONAL**
Jamma Kekai, Vicky Heldrich, Timmy Guard

        PERU INTERNATIONAL
Conrad Canha

1958   **MAKAHA INTERNATIONAL**
Peter Cole, Marge Calhoun, Joseph Napoleon

1959   **MAKAHA INTERNATIONAL**
Wally Froiseth, Linda Benson, Paul Strauch

        WEST COAST SURFING CHAMPIONSHIPS
Jack Haley, Linda Benson, Louis Tarter

1960   **MAKAHA INTERNATIONAL**
Buffalo Keaulana, Wendy Cameron, Erick Romancheck

        WEST COAST SURFING CHAMPIONSHIPS
Mike Haley, Linda Benson, Dave Willingham

1961   **MAKAHA INTERNATIONAL**
George Downing, Anona Naone, Fred Hemmings

        PERU INTERNATIONAL
John Severson

        WEST COAST SURFING CHAMPIONSHIPS
Ron Sizemore, Linda Benson, Butch Linden

1962   **BELLS BEACH**
Glen Ritchie

        MAKAHA INTERNATIONAL
Midget Farrelly, Nancy Nelson, Peter Kahapea

        MALIBU INVITATIONAL
Dave Rochlen

        PERU INTERNATIONAL
Felipe Pomar

        WEST COAST SURFING CHAMPIONSHIPS
Ilima Kalama, Audie Wilke, Pete Kobsev

1963   **AUSTRALIAN NATIONAL TITLES**
Doug Andrews, Pearl Turton, Nat Young

        BELLS BEACH
Doug Andrews, Glen Ritchie

        MAKAHA INTERNATIONAL
Joey Cabell, Nancy Nelson, Fred Hemmings

        MALIBU INVITATIONAL
Joey Cabell

        PERU INTERNATIONAL
Paul Strauch

        WEST COAST SURFING CHAMPIONSHIPS
LJ Richards, Candy Calhoun, Corky Carroll

1964   **AUSTRALIAN NATIONAL TITLES**
Midget Farrelly, Phyllis O'Donell, Robert Conneeley

        BELLS BEACH
Mick Dooley, Nat Young

        MAKAHA INTERNATIONAL
Fred Hemmings, Joyce Hoffman, Joey Gerard

        MALIBU INVITATIONAL
Bobby Patterson

        PERU INTERNATIONAL
Fred Hemmings

        UNITED STATES INVITATIONAL
Ricky Irons, Linda Benson, Mark Martinson

        UNITED STATES SURFING CHAMPIONSHIPS
Jim Craig, Linda Benson, Rod Sumpter

WORLD CHAMPIONSHIPS
Midget Farrelly, Phyllis O'Donell

1965   AUSTRALIAN NATIONAL TITLES
Midget Farrelly, Phyllis O'Donell, Peter Drouyn

BELLS BEACH
Robert Conneeley

DUKE KAHANAMOKU INVITATIONAL
Jeff Hakman

LAGUNA SWIMWEAR MASTERS
John Boozer, Joyce Hoffman, Corky Carroll

MAKAHA INTERNATIONAL
George Downing, Nancy Nelson, David
Nuuhiwa

MALIBU INVITATIONAL
Buzz Sutphin, Charline Tarusa

PERU INTERNATIONAL
Felipe Pomar, Joyce Hoffman

TOM MOREY INVITATIONAL
Mickey Muñoz

UNITED STATES SURFING CHAMPIONSHIPS
Mark Martinson, Joyce Hoffman, David
Nuuhiwa

WORLD CHAMPIONSHIPS
Felipe Pomar, Joyce Hoffman

1966   AUSTRALIAN NATIONAL TITLES
Nat Young, Gail Couper, Peter Drouyn

BELLS BEACH
Nat Young, Gail Couper, Wayne Lynch

DUKE KAHANAMOKU INVITATIONAL
Ricky Grigg

MAKAHA INTERNATIONAL
Fred Hemmings, Joyce Hoffman, Reno Abellira

MALIBU INVITATIONAL
Steve Bigler, Joey Hamasaki

PERU INTERNATIONAL
Felipe Pomar

SWAMI'S PRO-AM
Dru Harrison

**UNITED STATES PROFESSIONAL SURFING
CHAMPIONSHIPS**
Terry Jones

UNITED STATES SURFING CHAMPIONSHIPS
Corky Carroll, Joyce Hoffman, David Nuuhiwa

WORLD CHAMPIONSHIPS
Nat Young, Joyce Hoffman

1967   AUSTRALIAN NATIONAL TITLES
Nat Young, Gail Couper, Wayne Lynch

BAJA SURF CLUB INVITATIONAL
Mike Doyle

BELLS BEACH
Nat Young, Gail Couper, Wayne Lynch

DUKE KAHANAMOKU INVITATIONAL
Jock Sutherland

LAGUNA SWIMWEAR MASTERS
Skip Frye, Joyce Hoffman, Mike Tabeling

MAKAHA INTERNATIONAL
Joey Cabell, Martha Sunn, Reno Abellira

MALIBU INVITATIONAL
George Szegetti

PERU INTERNATIONAL
Corky Carroll

UNITED STATES SURFING CHAMPIONSHIPS
Corky Carroll, Joyce Hoffman, Dru Harrison

1968   AUSTRALIAN NATIONAL TITLES
Keith Paull, Judy Trim, Wayne Lynch

BAJA SURF CLUB INVITATIONAL
Skip Frye

BELLS BEACH
Ted Spencer, Gail Couper, Wayne Lynch

DUKE KAHANAMOKU INVITATIONAL
Mike Doyle

MAKAHA INTERNATIONAL
Joey Cabell, Margo Godfrey, Keone Downing

MALIBU INVITATIONAL
Angie Reno

PERU INTERNATIONAL
Joey Cabell

SANTA CRUZ PRO-AM
Corky Carroll, Joyce Hoffman

UNITED STATES SURFING CHAMPIONSHIPS
David Nuuhiwa, Linda Benson, Brad McCaul

WORLD CHAMPIONSHIPS
Fred Hemmings, Margo Godfrey

1969   AUSTRALIAN NATIONAL TITLES
Nat Young, Josette Lagardere, Wayne Lynch

BAJA SURF CLUB INVITATIONAL
Jeff Hakman

BELLS BEACH
Ted Spencer, Vivian Campbell, Wayne Lynch

DUKE KAHANAMOKU INVITATIONAL
Joey Cabell

GUNSTON 500
Gavin Rudolph

MAKAHA INTERNATIONAL
Paul Strauch, Martha Sunn, Keone Downing

PERU INTERNATIONAL
Mike Doyle

SMIRNOFF PRO-AM
Corky Carroll, Margo Godfrey

UNITED STATES SURFING CHAMPIONSHIPS
Corky Carroll, Sharron Weber, Niles Osborn

1970   **AUSTRALIAN NATIONAL TITLES**
Peter Drouyn, Judy Trim, Wayne Lynch

BELLS BEACH
Nat Young, Gail Couper, Michael Peterson

DUKE KAHANAMOKU INVITATIONAL
Jeff Hakman

GUNSTON 500
Midget Farrelly

MAKAHA INTERNATIONAL
Peter Drouyn, Craig Wilson, Martha Sunn

NEWCASTLE PRO
Peter Drouyn, Steve Butterworth

PERU INTERNATIONAL
Joey Cabell

SMIRNOFF PRO-AM
Nat Young

UNITED STATES SURFING CHAMPIONSHIPS
Brad McCaul, Jericho Poppler, Dane Sizzle

WORLD CHAMPIONSHIPS
Rolf Aurness, Sharron Weber

1971   **AUSTRALIAN NATIONAL TITLES**
Paul Neilsen, Gail Couper, Simon Anderson

BELLS BEACH
Paul Neilsen, Gail Couper, Simon Anderson

DUKE KAHANAMOKU INVITATIONAL
Jeff Hakman

GUNSTON 500
Brad McCaul

MAKAHA INTERNATIONAL
Mark Sedlack, Larry Bertlemann, Becky Benson

PERU INTERNATIONAL
Sergio Barreda

PIPELINE MASTERS
Jeff Hakman

SMIRNOFF PRO-AM
Gavin Rudolph

UNITED STATES SURFING CHAMPIONSHIPS
David Nuuhiwa, Joyce Hoffman, Barry Amos

1972   **AUSTRALIAN NATIONAL TITLES**
Michael Peterson, Gail Couper, Simon
Anderson

BELLS BEACH
Terry Fitzgerald, Gail Couper, Simon Anderson

DUKE KAHANAMOKU INVITATIONAL
James Jones

EASTERN SURFING ASSOCIATION PRO
Yancy Spencer, Barbie Belyea

GUNSTON 500
Jeff Hakman

HANG TEN AMERICAN PRO
Jeff Hakman

PIPELINE MASTERS
Gerry Lopez

SMIRNOFF PRO-AM
Paul Neilsen

UNITED STATES SURFING CHAMPIONSHIPS
Dale Dobson, Mary Setterholm, Lenny Foster

WORLD CHAMPIONSHIPS
Jim Blears, Sharron Weber

1973   **AUSTRALIAN NATIONAL TITLES**
Richard Harvey, Kim MacKenzie, Mark Richards

DUKE KAHANAMOKU INVITATIONAL
Clyde Aikau

GUNSTON 500
Shaun Tomson

HANG TEN AMERICAN PRO
Jeff Hakman

PA BENDALL
Richard Harvey

PERU INTERNATIONAL
Sergio Barreda

PIPELINE MASTERS
Gerry Lopez

RIP CURL PRO, BELLS BEACH
Michael Peterson, Gail Couper

SMIRNOFF PRO
Ian Cairns

UNITED STATES SURFING CHAMPIONSHIPS
Larry Bertlemann, Laura Powers, Jeff Smith

1974   **AUSTRALIAN NATIONAL TITLES**
Michael Peterson, Kim MacKenzie, Steve Jones

COKE CLASSIC
Michael Peterson

DUKE KAHANAMOKU INVITATIONAL
Larry Bertlemann

GUNSTON 500
Shaun Tomson

PA BENDALL
Michael Peterson

PERU INTERNATIONAL
Jeff Hakman

PIPELINE MASTERS
Jeff Crawford

RIP CURL PRO, BELLS BEACH
Michael Peterson, Gail Couper

SMIRNOFF PRO
Reno Abellira

UNITED STATES SURFING CHAMPIONSHIPS
Rick Rasmussen, Isabel McLaughlin, Mark Levy

1975   **AUSTRALIAN NATIONAL TITLES**
Terry Fitzgerald, Gail Couper, Steve Jones

COKE CLASSIC
Wayne Lynch

DUKE KAHANAMOKU INVITATIONAL
Ian Cairns

GUNSTON 500
Shaun Tomson

HANG TEN WOMEN'S INTERNATIONAL PRO CHAMPIONSHIPS
Margo Oberg

PIPELINE MASTERS
Shaun Tomson

RIP CURL PRO, BELLS BEACH
Michael Peterson, Gail Couper

SMIRNOFF PRO
Mark Richards

UNITED STATES SURFING CHAMPIONSHIPS
Aaron Wright, Grace Knowles, Timmy Carvalho

WORLD CUP
Mark Richards, Margo Oberg

1976   **COKE CLASSIC**
Mark Richards

DUKE KAHANAMOKU INVITATIONAL
James Jones

GUNSTON 500
Shaun Tomson

HANG TEN WOMEN'S INTERNATIONAL PRO CHAMPIONSHIPS
Lynne Boyer

LIGHTNING BOLT CHAMPIONSHIPS
Rory Russell

PIPELINE MASTERS
Rory Russell

PRO CLASS TRIALS
Barry Kanaiaupuni

RIP CURL PRO, BELLS BEACH
Jeff Hakman, Gail Couper

SMIRNOFF PRO
Mark Warren, Jericho Poppler

WORLD CUP
Ian Cairns, Lynn Boyer

WORLD PRO TOUR
Peter Townend (no women's division)

1977   **COKE CLASSIC**
Simon Anderson, Margo Oberg

DUKE KAHANAMOKU INVITATIONAL
Eddie Aikau

GUNSTON 500
Shaun Tomson

HANG TEN WOMEN'S INTERNATIONAL PRO CHAMPIONSHIPS
Lynne Boyer

PIPELINE MASTERS
Rory Russell

PRO CLASS TRIALS
Col Smith

RIP CURL PRO/BELLS BEACH
Simon Anderson, Margo Oberg

SMIRNOFF PRO
Reno Abellira, Jericho Poppler

STUBBIES SURF CLASSIC
Michael Peterson

WORLD CUP
Shaun Tomson, Lynne Boyer

WORLD PRO TOUR
Shaun Tomson, Margo Oberg

1978   **COKE CLASSIC**
Larry Blair, Lynne Boyer

DUKE KAHANAMOKU INVITATIONAL
Michael Ho

GROG'S SEASIDE PRO
Wayne Bartholomew

GUNSTON 500
Shaun Tomson

HANG TEN WOMEN'S INTERNATIONAL PRO CHAMPIONSHIPS
Brenda Scott-Rogers

PIPELINE MASTERS
Larry Blair

RIP CURL PRO, BELLS BEACH
Mark Richards, Margo Oberg

STUBBIES SURF CLASSIC
Wayne Bartholomew, Margo Oberg

WORLD AMATEUR CHAMPIONSHIPS
Anthony Brodowicz (no women's division)

WORLD CUP
Buzzy Kerbox (no women's division)

WORLD PRO TOUR
Wayne Bartholomew, Lynne Boyer

1979   **COKE CLASSIC**
Cheyne Horan

DUKE KAHANAMOKU INVITATIONAL
Mark Richards

GROG'S SEASIDE PRO
Dane Kealoha

GUNSTON 500
Dane Kealoha

JAPAN CUP
Wayne Bartholomew

OFFSHORE WOMEN'S MASTERS
Jericho Poppler

PIPELINE MASTERS
Larry Blair

RIP CURL PRO, BELLS BEACH
Mark Richards, Lynne Boyer

STUBBIES SURF CLASSIC
Mark Richards

WORLD CUP
Mark Richards, Lynne Boyer

WORLD PRO TOUR
Mark Richards, Lynne Boyer

1980   **COKE CLASSIC**
Buzzy Kerbox

DUKE KAHANAMOKU INVITATIONAL
Mark Warren

GUNSTON 500
Mark Richards

OM BALI PRO
Terry Fitzgerald

PIPELINE MASTERS
Mark Richards

PRO CLASS TRIALS
Bobby Owens

RIP CURL PRO, BELLS BEACH
Mark Richards, Margo Oberg

STUBBIES SURF CLASSIC
Peter Harris

WORLD AMATEUR CHAMPIONSHIPS
Mark Scott, Alisa Schwarzstein, Tom Curren

WORLD CUP
Ian Cairns, Margo Oberg

WORLD PRO TOUR
Mark Richards, Margo Oberg

1981   **COKE CLASSIC**
Simon Anderson

DUKE KAHANAMOKU INVITATIONAL
Michael Ho

GUNSTON 500
Cheyne Horan

OFFSHORE WOMEN'S MASTERS
Margo Oberg

OM BALI PRO
Jim Banks

PIPELINE MASTERS
Simon Anderson

RIP CURL PRO, BELLS BEACH
Simon Anderson, Linda Davoli

STUBBIES SURF CLASSIC
Mark Richards

WAIMEA 5000
Cheyne Horan

WORLD CUP
Dane Kealoha, Cheri Gross

WORLD PRO TOUR
Mark Richards, Margo Oberg

1982   **COKE CLASSIC**
Wayne Bartholomew

DUKE KAHANAMOKU INVITATIONAL
Ken Bradshaw

GUNSTON 500
Mark Richards

MAZDA WOMEN'S SURFSPORT CHAMPIONSHIPS
Frieda Zamba

OP PRO
Cheyne Horan, Becky Benson

PIPELINE MASTERS
Michael Ho

RIP CURL PRO, BELLS BEACH
Mark Richards, Debbie Beacham

STUBBIES SURF CLASSIC
Cheyne Horan

WORLD AMATEUR CHAMPIONSHIPS
Tom Curren, Jenny Gill, Bryce Ellis

WORLD CUP
Tom Carroll, Lynne Boyer

WORLD PRO TOUR
Mark Richards, Debbie Beacham

1983   **COKE CLASSIC**
Tom Carroll

DUKE KAHANAMOKU INVITATIONAL
Dane Kealoha

FOSTERS EURO PRO
Tom Carroll

GUNSTON 500
Hans Hedemann

MICHELOB CUP
Pam Burridge

OP PRO
Tom Curren, Kim Mearig

PIPELINE MASTERS
Dane Kealoha

RIP CURL PRO, BELLS BEACH
Joe Engel, Helen Lambert

STUBBIES SURF CLASSIC
Martin Potter

WORLD CUP
Michael Ho, Margo Oberg

WORLD PRO TOUR
Tom Carroll, Kim Mearig

TRIPLE CROWN
Michael Ho

1984   **DUKE KAHANAMOKU INVITATIONAL**
Derek Ho

GUNSTON 500
Tom Carroll

MARUI WORLD PRO
Tom Carroll, Kim Mearig

OP PRO
Tom Curren, Frieda Zamba

PIPELINE MASTERS
Joey Buran

RIP CURL PRO, BELLS BEACH
Cheyne Horan, Frieda Zamba

STUBBIES SURF CLASSIC
Tom Carroll

STUBBIES U.S. PRO
Shaun Tomson

WORLD AMATEUR CHAMPIONSHIPS
Scott Farnsworth, Janice Aragon, Damien
Hardman

WORLD CUP
Michael Ho, Lynne Boyer

WORLD PRO TOUR
Tom Carroll, Frieda Zamba

TRIPLE CROWN
Derek Ho

1985   **BEAUREPAIRES OPEN**
Mark Occhilupo, Frieda Zamba

BILLABONG PRO, NORTH SHORE
Mark Richards

GUNSTON 500
Mark Occhilupo

MARUI WORLD PRO
Tom Curren, Jolene Smith

OP PRO
Mark Occhilupo, Jodie Cooper

PIPELINE MASTERS
Mark Occhilupo

RIP CURL PRO, BELLS BEACH
Tom Curren, Frieda Zamba

STUBBIES SURF CLASSIC
Tom Curren, Liz Benavidez

STUBBIES U.S. PRO
Brad Gerlach, Pam Burridge

WORLD CUP
Michael Ho, Jodie Cooper

WORLD PRO TOUR
Tom Curren, Frieda Zamba

TRIPLE CROWN
Michael Ho

1986   **BILLABONG PRO, NORTH SHORE**
Mark Richards

COKE CLASSIC
Barton Lynch

GUNSTON 500
Gary Green

OP PRO
Mark Occhilupo, Frieda Zamba

PIPELINE MASTERS
Derek Ho

QUIKSILVER IN MEMORY OF EDDIE AIKAU
Clyde Aikau

RIP CURL PRO, BELLS BEACH
Tom Carroll, Frieda Zamba

STUBBIES SURF CLASSIC
Tom Curren, Wendy Botha

WORLD AMATEUR CHAMPIONSHIPS
Mark Sainsbury, Connie Nixon, Vetea David

WORLD CUP
Hans Hedemann

WORLD PRO TOUR
Tom Curren, Frieda Zamba

TRIPLE CROWN
Derek Ho

WORLD PRO TOUR LONGBOARD
Nat Young

1987   **BILLABONG PRO, NORTH SHORE**
Gary Elkerton

COKE CLASSIC
Tom Carroll, Frieda Zamba

GOTCHA PRO
Glen Winton

GUNSTON 500
Damien Hardman

MARUI WORLD PRO
Damien Hardman, Frieda Zamba

OP PRO
Barton Lynch, Wendy Botha

PIPELINE MASTERS
Tom Carroll

RIP CURL PRO, BELLS BEACH
Nick Wood, Jodie Cooper

STUBBIES U.S. PRO
Tom Curren, Wendy Botha

WORLD CUP
Gary Elkerton

> **WORLD PRO TOUR**
> Damien Hardman, Wendy Botha
>
> **TRIPLE CROWN**
> Gary Elkerton
>
> **WORLD PRO TOUR LONGBOARD**
> Stuart Entwistle

1988   **BILLABONG PRO, NORTH SHORE**
Barton Lynch

COKE CLASSIC
Damien Hardman, Toni Sawyer

GUNSTON 500
Bryce Ellis

O'NEILL COLDWATER CLASSIC
Richie Collins

OP PRO
Tom Curren, Jorja Smith

PIPELINE MASTERS
Robbie Page

RIP CURL PRO, BELLS BEACH
Damien Hardman, Kim Mearig

STUBBIES U.S. PRO
Tom Curren, Jorja Smith

WORLD AMATEUR CHAMPIONSHIPS
Fabio Gouveia, Pauline Menczer, Chris Brown

WORLD CUP
Tom Carroll

> **WORLD PRO TOUR**
> Barton Lynch, Frieda Zamba
>
> **TRIPLE CROWN**
> Derek Ho
>
> **WORLD PRO TOUR LONGBOARD**
> Nat Young

1989   **BILLABONG PRO, NORTH SHORE**
Cheyne Horan

COKE CLASSIC
Martin Potter, Wendy Botha

GOTCHA PRO
Derek Ho

GUNSTON 500
Brad Gerlach

MARUI WORLD PRO
Dave MacAulay, Wendy Botha

O'NEILL COLDWATER CLASSIC
Martin Potter

OP PRO
Richie Collins, Frieda Zamba

PIPELINE MASTERS
Gary Elkerton

RIP CURL PRO, BELLS BEACH
Martin Potter, Wendy Botha

WORLD CUP
Hans Hedemann

> **WORLD PRO TOUR**
> Martin Potter, Wendy Botha
>
> **TRIPLE CROWN**
> Gary Elkerton
>
> **WORLD PRO TOUR LONGBOARD**
> Nat Young

1990   **BILLABONG PRO, NORTH SHORE**
Nicky Wood

COKE CLASSIC
Rob Bain, Wendy Botha

GUNSTON 500
Damien Hardman

O'NEILL COLDWATER CLASSIC
Tom Curren, Frieda Zamba

OP PRO
Todd Holland, Frieda Zamba

PIPELINE MASTERS
Tom Carroll

QUIKSILVER IN MEMORY OF EDDIE AIKAU
Keone Downing

RIP CURL PRO, BELLS BEACH
Tom Curren, Lisa Andersen

WORLD AMATEUR CHAMPIONSHIPS
Heifara Tahutini, Kathy Newman, Shane Bevan

WORLD CUP
Derek Ho

> **WORLD PRO TOUR**
> Tom Curren, Pam Burridge
>
> **TRIPLE CROWN**
> Derek Ho
>
> **WORLD PRO TOUR LONGBOARD**
> Nat Young

1991   **ALTERNATIVA SURF INTERNATIONAL**
Flavio Padaratz

COKE CLASSIC
Brad Gerlach, Wendy Botha

GUNSTON 500
Brad Gerlach

MARUI WORLD PRO
Damien Hardman

OP PRO
Barton Lynch, Frieda Zamba

PIPELINE MASTERS
Tom Carroll

RIP CURL PRO, BELLS BEACH
Barton Lynch, Pauline Menczer

WORLD CUP
Fabio Gouveia, Pauline Menczer

WYLAND HAWAIIAN PRO
Tom Curren

YOPLAIT RÉUNION PRO
Jeff Booth

WORLD PRO TOUR
Damien Hardman, Wendy Botha

TRIPLE CROWN
Tom Carroll

WORLD PRO TOUR LONGBOARD
Marty McMillan

1992   **ALTERNATIVA SURF INTERNATIONAL**
Damien Hardman, Wendy Botha

COKE CLASSIC
Shane Herring, Pam Burridge

GUNSTON 500
Sunny Garcia, Neridah Falconer

MARUI WORLD PRO
Fabio Gouveia, Wendy Botha

PIPELINE MASTERS
Kelly Slater

RIP CURL PRO, BELLS BEACH
Richie Collins, Lisa Andersen

RIP CURL PRO, HOSSEGOR
Kelly Slater, Wendy Botha

WORLD AMATEUR CHAMPIONSHIPS
Grant Frost, Lynette MacKenzie, Chad Edser

WORLD CUP
Martin Potter, Jodie Cooper

YOPLAIT RÉUNION PRO
Richard Marsh, Anne-Gaelle Hoarau

WORLD PRO TOUR
Kelly Slater, Wendy Botha

TRIPLE CROWN
Sunny Garcia

WORLD PRO TOUR LONGBOARD
Joey Hawkins

1993   **COKE CLASSIC**
Todd Holland, Layne Beachley

GUNSTON 500
Gary Elkerton, Rochelle Ballard

LACANAU PRO
Martin Potter, Pauline Menczer

MARUI WORLD PRO
Kelly Slater, Pauline Menczer

OP PRO
Sunny Garcia, Kim Mearig

PIPELINE MASTERS
Derek Ho

QUIKSILVER SURFMASTERS
Shane Powell, Kylie Webb

RIP CURL PRO, BELLS BEACH
Damien Hardman, Pauline Menczer

RIP CURL PRO, HOSSEGOR
Damien Hardman, Kylie Webb

WORLD CUP
Johnny-Boy Gomes, Jodie Cooper

WORLD PRO TOUR
Derek Ho, Pauline Menczer

TRIPLE CROWN
Sunny Garcia

WORLD PRO TOUR LONGBOARD
Rusty Keaulana

1994   **COKE CLASSIC**
Shane Powell, Pauline Menczer

MARUI WORLD PRO
Rob Machado, Lynette MacKenzie

OP PRO
Rob Machado, Frieda Zamba

PIPELINE MASTERS
Kelly Slater

RÉUNION PRO
Sunny Garcia, Lisa Andersen

RIP CURL PRO, BELLS BEACH
Kelly Slater, Layne Beachley

RIP CURL PRO, HOSSEGOR
Flavio Padaratz, Lynette MacKenzie

U.S. OPEN
Shane Beschen, Lisa Andersen

WORLD AMATEUR CHAMPIONSHIPS
Sasha Stocker, Alessandra Vieira, Kalani Robb

WORLD CUP
Sunny Garcia

WORLD PRO TOUR
Kelly Slater, Lisa Andersen

TRIPLE CROWN
Sunny Garcia

WORLD PRO TOUR LONGBOARD
Rusty Keaulana

1995 **COKE CLASSIC**
Vetea David, Michelle Donoghoe

MARUI WORLD PRO
Rob Machado, Lynette MacKenzie

OP PRO
Sunny Garcia, Lisa Andersen

PIPELINE MASTERS
Kelly Slater

QUIKSILVER PRO, GRAJAGAN
Kelly Slater

REUNION PRO
Matt Hoy

RIP CURL PRO, BELLS BEACH
Sunny Garcia, Lisa Andersen

RIP CURL PRO, HOSSEGOR
Rob Machado, Layne Beachley

U.S. OPEN
Rob Machado, Neridah Falconer

WORLD CUP
Shane Powell, Pauline Menczer

WORLD PRO TOUR
Kelly Slater, Lisa Andersen

TRIPLE CROWN
Kelly Slater

WORLD PRO TOUR LONGBOARD
Rusty Keaulana

1996 **BILLABONG PRO, JEFFREYS BAY**
Kelly Slater, Lisa Andersen

BILLABONG PRO, QUEENSLAND
Kaipo Jaquias, Kylie Webb

COKE CLASSIC
Kelly Slater, Kylie Webb

PIPELINE MASTERS
Kelly Slater

QUIKSILVER PRO, GRAJAGAN
Shane Beschen

RIP CURL PRO, BELLS BEACH
Sunny Garcia, Pauline Menczer

RIP CURL PRO, HOSSEGOR
Kelly Slater, Serena Brooke

U.S. OPEN
Kelly Slater, Layne Beachley

WORLD CUP
Jake Paterson

WORLD SURFING GAMES
Taylor Knox, Neridah Falconer, Ben Bourgeois

WORLD PRO TOUR
Kelly Slater, Lisa Andersen

TRIPLE CROWN
Kaipo Jaquias

WORLD PRO TOUR LONGBOARD
Bonga Perkins

1997 **BILLABONG PRO, QUEENSLAND**
Kelly Slater, Rochelle Ballard

COKE CLASSIC
Kelly Slater, Kylie Webb

DA HUI BACKDOOR SHOOTOUT
Kalani Robb

MARUI WORLD PRO
Kelly Slater, Lisa Andersen

PIPELINE MASTERS
Johnny-Boy Gomes

QUIKSILVER PRO, GRAJAGAN
Luke Egan

RIP CURL PRO, BELLS BEACH
Matt Hoy, Neridah Falconer

RIP CURL PRO, HOSSEGOR
Rob Machado, Neridah Falconer

TAHITI PRO
Andy Irons

WORLD CUP
Michael Rommelse

WORLD PRO TOUR
Kelly Slater, Lisa Andersen

TRIPLE CROWN
Mike Rommelse, Layne Beachley

WORLD PRO TOUR LONGBOARD
Dino Miranda

1998 **BILLABONG PRO, JEFFREYS BAY**
Michael Barry, Trudy Todd

BILLABONG PRO, QUEENSLAND
Kelly Slater, Trudy Todd

COKE CLASSIC
Shane Beschen, Layne Beachley

OP PRO
Andy Irons, Layne Beachley

PIPELINE MASTERS
Jake Paterson

THE REEF BIG-WAVE TEAM WORLD CHAMPIONSHIPS
Carlos Burle

RIP CURL PRO, BELLS BEACH
Mark Occhilupo, Layne Beachley

TAHITI PRO
Kobi Aberton, Keala Kennelly

WORLD CUP
Shane Dorian

WORLD SURFING GAMES
Michael Campbell, Alcione Silva, Dean Morrison

WORLD PRO TOUR
Kelly Slater, Layne Beachley

TRIPLE CROWN
Kelly Slater, Layne Beachley

WORLD PRO TOUR LONGBOARD
Joel Tudor

WORLD PRO TOUR JUNIOR
Andy Irons

1999   **BILLABONG PRO, JEFFREYS BAY**
Joel Parkinson, Melanie Redman

BILLABONG PRO, QUEENSLAND
Beau Emerton, Serena Brooke

DA HUI BACKDOOR SHOOTOUT
Johnny-Boy Gomes

GOTCHA PRO
Neco Padaratz, Rochelle Ballard

PIPELINE MASTERS
Kelly Slater

QUIKSILVER IN MEMORY OF EDDIE AIKAU
Noah Johnson

QUIKSILVER PRO, FIJI
Mark Occhilupo

RIP CURL PRO, BELLS BEACH
Shane Dorian, Layne Beachley

TAHITI PRO
Mark Occhilupo, Kate Skarratt

WOMEN'S WORLD LONGBOARD CHAMPIONSHIPS
Daize Shayne

WORLD PRO TOUR
Mark Occhilupo, Layne Beachley

TRIPLE CROWN
Sunny Garcia, Trudy Todd

WORLD PRO TOUR LONGBOARD
Colin McPhillips

WORLD PRO TOUR JUNIOR
Joel Parkinson

2000   **BILLABONG PRO, JEFFREYS BAY**
Jake Paterson, Megan Abubo

BILLABONG PRO, QUEENSLAND
Sunny Garcia, Layne Beachley

BILLABONG PRO, TRESTLES
Andy Irons, Lynette MacKenzie

PIPELINE MASTERS
Rob Machado

QUIKSILVER PRO, FIJI
Luke Egan

RIP CURL PRO, BELLS BEACH
Sunny Garcia, Megan Abubo

TAHITI PRO
Kelly Slater, Keala Kennelly

WOMEN'S WORLD LONGBOARD CHAMPIONSHIPS
Cori Shumacher

WORLD CUP
Sunny Garcia

WORLD SURFING GAMES
Fabio Silva, Maria Tavares, Joel Centeio

WORLD PRO TOUR
Sunny Garcia, Layne Beachley

TRIPLE CROWN
Sunny Garcia, Heather Clark

WORLD PRO TOUR LONGBOARD
Beau Young

WORLD PRO TOUR JUNIOR
Pedro Henrique

2001   **BILLABONG PRO, JEFFREYS BAY**
Jake Paterson

HIC PIPELINE PRO
Bruce Irons

PIPELINE MASTERS
Bruce Irons

QUIKSILVER IN MEMORY OF EDDIE AIKAU
Ross Clarke-Jones

RIO SURF INTERNATIONAL
Trent Munro

RIP CURL PRO, BELLS BEACH
Mick Fanning, Neridah Falconer

RIP CURL WORLD CUP
Myles Padaca

ROXY SURF JAM
Megan Abubo

TAHITI PRO
Cory Lopez, Layne Beachley

WOMEN'S WORLD LONGBOARD CHAMPIONSHIPS
Cori Shumacher

WORLD PRO TOUR
CJ Hobgood, Layne Beachley

TRIPLE CROWN
Myles Padaca (no women's division)

WORLD PRO TOUR LONGBOARD
Colin McPhillips

WORLD PRO TOUR JUNIOR
Joel Parkinson

2002   **BILLABONG PRO, JEFFREYS BAY**
Mick Fanning

BOOST MOBILE PRO
Luke Egan

PIPELINE MASTERS
Andy Irons

QUIKSILVER IN MEMORY OF EDDIE AIKAU
Kelly Slater

QUIKSILVER PRO, QUEENSLAND
Joel Parkinson, Lynette MacKenzie

RIP CURL PRO, BELLS BEACH
Andy Irons

RIP CURL WORLD CUP
Joel Parkinson

TAHITI PRO
Andy Irons, Keala Kennelly

TOW-IN WORLD CUP
Garrett McNamara/Rodrigo Resende

WORLD SURFING GAMES
Travis Logie, Chelsea Georgeson, Warwick Wright

WORLD PRO TOUR
Andy Irons, Layne Beachley

TRIPLE CROWN
Andy Irons, Neridah Falconer

WORLD PRO TOUR LONGBOARD
Colin McPhillips

APPENDIX 3
Surf Movies, Videos, and DVDs

Surf movies, videos, and DVDs are generally defined as niche films made for surfers. About three-quarters of the titles under the "Surf Movie" category, and roughly one-third of the video titles, are no longer available in any form. In the case of a filmmaker uncredited for a surf movie or video, the production company is noted. Hollywood-made movies featuring surfing are found in the subsection titled "General Audience: Studio and Independent"; the production studio and the director are noted after the release year. All of these movies have surfing scenes, but less than a third feature surfing as the primary subject.

Surf Movies

Acapulco Gold (1977, Arnie Wong; animated short)
Adventures in Paradise (1982, Scott Dittrich)
All Down the Line (1989, Paul Witzig)
Always Another Wave (1964, Don Wolf)
Amazing Surf Stories (1986, Scott Dittrich)
Angry Sea (1963, John Severson)
Animals (1971, Paul Witzig, Tommy Taylor; short subject)
Another Wave (1966, Barry Mirandon)
Asian Paradise (1984, Hideaki Ishii)
Atlantic Crossing (1989, Paul Prewitt)
Aussies in the Islands (1974, Alan Rich; short subject)
Aw-oo! (1977, Warner Wacha)
Bali High (1981, Steve Spaulding)
Band on the Run (1981, Harry Hodge)
Barefoot Adventure (1960, Bruce Brown)
Barrels of Fun (1983, Joe Mickey, Dave Natal)
Beautiful Day (1972, Andy McAlpine, John Cassidy; short subject)
Better Days (1973, Jim Clark)
Big Surf, The (1957, Bud Browne)
Big Wave (1984, Hiro Furukawa)
Big Wednesday (1961, John Severson)
Blazing Boards (1983, Chris Bystrom)
Blue Cool (1972, John Bennett)
Boardriders (1966, Bill Fitzwater)
Bottoms Up (1961, J. Perkinson)
Call of the Surf, The (1964, Val Valentine)
Cat on a Hot Foam Board (1959, Bud Browne)
Children of the Sun (1968, Andy McAlpine)
Circumfusion (1975, Dennis McDonald)
City Slicker (1971, Fred Windisch)
Coastal Disturbance (1994, Andrew Forrester)
Cold Lines (1973, Greg Huglin, Paul Gillane)
Come Surf With Me (1967, Rod Sumpter)

Cool Wave of Color, A (1964, Greg MacGillivray)
Cosmic Children (1970, Hal Jepsen)
Crystal Eyes (1981, Yuri Farrant)
Crystal Voyager (1973, Alby Falzon, David Elfick, George Greenough)
Cycles of the Northern Sun (1976, Chris Klopf)
Day War Came to Malibu, The (1965, Greg MacGillivray; short subject)
Diary of a Surfing Film (1976, Greg DeSantis)
Directions (1972, Bruce Walker)
Dr. Strangesurf (1965, Walt Phillips)
Dynamite (1962, Buzz Bailey)
Echoes (1973, George Greenough; short subject)
Eclipse (1969, Chris Young)
End of the World, The (1972, Arnie Wong; animated short)
Endless Summer, The (1966, Bruce Brown)
Evolution (1969, Paul Witzig)
Family Free (1971, Bob Evans)
Fantasea (1978, Greg Huglin)
Fiberglass Jungle, The (1967, John Arnold; short subject)
Five Summer Stories (1972, Greg MacGillivray, Jim Freeman)
Flowing Free (1980, Joe Alber)
Fluid Drive (1974, Scott Dittrich, Skip Smith)
Fluid Journey, A (1969, Peter Clifton)
Follow Me (1968, Robert Peterson)
Follow that Surf (1963, Bill Singer)
Follow the Sun (1983, Scott Dittrich)
Follow the Surf (1963, Dennis Elton)
For Surfers Only (1964, Grant Rohloff)
Forgotten Island of Santosha (1974, Larry Yates)
Free and Easy (1967, Greg MacGillivray, Jim Freeman)
Free Ride (1977, Bill Delaney)
Free Ride: Final Edition (1983, Bill Delaney)
Free Rides (1976, Bruce Walker)
Freedom Riders (1972, Dennis McDonald)
Freeform (1970, Rod Sumpter)
Full Blast (1983, Curt Mastalka)
Give Us This Day Our Day in the Sun (1972, Bruce Usher, Phil and Russell Sheppard; short subject)
Glass Wall, The (1965, Jim Freeman)
Go For It (1981, Hal Jepsen)
Going My Wave (1962, John Severson)
Going Surfin' (1973, Bud Browne)
Golden Breed (1968, Dale Davis)
Gone Surfin' (1987, Scott Dittrich)
Gone with the Wave (1964, Bruce Anderson)
Great Wave, The (1982, Tony Gooley; animated short)
Gun Ho! (1963, Bud Browne)
Harmony Within (1976, Doug Swanson, Paul Dunaway)

Have Board, Will Travel (1963, Don Brown)
Hawaii '68 (1968, Paul Witzig; short subject)
Hawaii '81 (1981, Tim Bonython; short subject)
Hawaiian Holiday (1954, Bud Browne)
Hawaiian Magic (1980, John Fisher)
Hawaiian Safari (1977, Rodney Sumpter)
Hawaiian Surf Movies (1953, Bud Browne)
Hawaiian Surf Movies (1955, Bud Browne)
Hawaiian Thrill (1964, Bob Evans; short subject)
High on a Cool Wave (1967, Bob Evans)
Highway One (1977, Steve Otton)
Hot Dog on a Stick (1962, Bill Stromberg)
Hot Generation, The (1968, Paul Witzig)
Hot Lips and Inner Tubes (1975, Yuri Farrant)
Hot to Trot (1977, Tony Edwards; animated short)
How the East Was Won (1967, Bill Yerkes)
Huh? (1967, Grant Rohloff)
I Think We're All Bozos on These Boards (1976, Jim Plimpton)
In Natural Flow (1971, Steve Core)
In the Midst of Summer (1977, Rick Jorgensen, Gary Pennington)
Indo Express (1990, Chris Fowler, Ronnie Gorringe)
Innermost Limits of Pure Fun, The (1970, George Greenough)
Inside Out (1965, Dale Davis)
Inspiration (1973, Larry Bennett)
Invisible Tracks (1972, Bob Evans)
Island Magic (1972, John Hitchcock)
Islands (1972, Paul Witzig, Tommy Taylor)
Jeffreys Bay Dream (1977, Dick Hoole, Jack McCoy; short subject)
Just Cruisin' (1978, Alastair Waddell)
Karma (1973, Arnie Wong; animated short)
Karma II (1981, Arnie Wong; animated short)
Kong's Island (1983, Jack McCoy; short subject)
Last Ride, The (1976, Dennis MacDonald)
Last Wave, The (1965, Grant Rohloff)
Let There be Surf (1963, Jim Freeman)
Life in the Sun, A (1966, Paul Witzig)
Liquid Gold (1976, Harry Hodge)
Liquid Space (1973, Dale Davis)
Living Curl, The (1969, Jamie Budge)
Locked In (1964, Bud Browne)
Long Way 'Round, The (1966, Bob Evans)
Loose in the Juice (1979, Rimus Lokys; short subject)
Loser, The (1968, Greg MacGillivray, Jim Freeman; short subject)
Many Classic Moments (1978, Gary Capo)
Matter of Style, A (1975, Steve Soderberg)
Men Who Ride Mountains (1964, Grant Rohloff)
Midget Goes Hawaiian (1963, Bob Evans; short subject)
Moods of Surfing (1967, Greg MacGillivray, Jim Freeman; short subject)
Morning of the Earth (1972, Alby Falzon)
Moving Out (1972, Bob Evans; short subject)
Nas Ondas do Surf (1975, Livio Bruni, Rossini Maranhão)
Natural Art, The (1969, Fred Windisch)
New Blue Goose Rides Again, The (1963, John Arnold; short subject)

New Wave (1977, Rodney Sumpter)
New Wave (1980, Steve Otton)
Nirvanic Symphony (1972, Murray McIntosh)
Nomadic Surfer, The (1964, John Raymond)
Nomads, The (1968, Dennis Cuyler)
North Side Story (1964, Val Valentine)
North Swell (1963, Grant Rohloff)
Ocean Fever (1983, Steve Soderberg)
Ocean Motion (1978, Mike Moir)
Ocean Rhythms (1975, Steve Core)
Oceans (1972, Rodney Sumpter)
Off the Wall (1982, Joe Mickey)
On Any Morning (1974, David Sumpter)
Once Upon a Wave (1963, Walt Phillips)
Our Day in the Sun (1972, Phil Sheppard, Bruce Usher; short subject)
Out of Control (1961, Grant Rohloff)
Out of the Blue (1968, Tim Murdoch)
Out of the Blue (1976, Aaron Chang)
Outside the Third Dimension (1964, Jim Freeman)
Over Under Sideways Down (1970, Ken Anderson)
Pacific Dreams (1981, Chris Bystrom)
Pacific Vibrations (1970, John Severson)
Passing Images (1978, Grant Young; short subject)
Perfect Board, The (1966, Bob Evans; short subject)
Performers, The (1965, Greg MacGillivray)
Pipeline (1963, Bruce Gibson; short subject)
Pipeline (1964, Walt Phillips)
Place Called Malibu, A (1966, Dale Davis; short subject)
Playgrounds in Paradise (1976, Alan Rich)
Psyche Out (1962, Walt Phillips)
Red Hot Blue (1973, Curt Mastalka)
Reflections (1973, Rodney Sumpter)
Ride on the Wild Side (1964, Ed dePriest)
Rincon '71 (1971, George Greenough; short subject)
Rolling Home (1974, Paul Witzig, David Lourie; short subject)
Rolling Thunder (1991, Scott Dittrich)
Room to Move (1977, Chris Bystrom)
Room to Move 2 (1978, Chris Bystrom)
Rubber Duck Riders (1971, George Greenough; short subject)
Sacrifice Surf (1960, Bob Bagley)
Salt Water Wine (1973, Alan Rich)
Sea Dreams (1971, Peter French, Curt Mastalka)
Sea for Yourself, A (1973, Hal Jepsen)
Sea of Joy (1971, Paul Witzig)
Sea People, The (1975, Michael Aston; short subject)
Seaflight (1981, Bob and Ron Condon)
Search for Surf (1957, 1958, 1959, 1960, 1961, Greg Noll)
Seven Sundays (1970, Tim Murdoch)
Shock Waves (1987, Bob and Ron Condon)
Siestas and Olas (1997, Dan Wozniak)
Silver, Sun, Sand (1975, Dennis McDonland; short subject)
Slippery When Wet (1958, Bruce Brown)
Solid Glass Tube, The (1970, Dennis McDonald)
Some Like it Wet (1965, Ed dePriest)
Spinning Boards (1961, Bud Browne)
Splashdown (1969, Bob Evans)
Standing Room Only (1978, Allen Maine, Hugh Thomas)

Standing Room Only (1962, J. Perkinson)
Step Into Liquid (2003, Dana Brown)
Stop the Wave, I Want to Get Off (1965, Jim Wilhoite; short subject)
Storm Riders (1982, Dick Hoole, Jack McCoy)
Strictly Hot (1964, Dale Davis)
Style Masters (1978, Greg Weaver)
Summer Breeze (1973, Allen Maine)
Summer Search, The (1966, Hans Pomeranz)
Sun Seekers, The (1974, Bob Cording, Jerry Humphries)
Sun Waves (1982, Joe Alber)
Sundancer (1976, Curt Mastalka)
Sunset Surf Craze (1959, Walt Phillips)
Sunshine Sea (1971, Greg MacGillivray, Jim Freeman)
Super Session (1975, Hal Jepsen)
Surf (1958, John Severson)
Surf Attack (1982, Jack and Clark Poling)
Surf Crazy (1959, Bruce Brown)
Surf Down Under (1958, Bud Browne)
Surf Dreams (1971, David Lourie; short subject)
Surf Fever (1960, John Severson)
Surf Happy (1960, Bud Browne)
Surf Mania (1960, Walt Phillips)
Surf Safari (1959, John Severson)
Surf Scene (1966, Ron Taylor; short subject)
Surf Stomp (1963, Dennis Milne; short subject)
Surf Trek to Hawaii (1962, Bob Evans)
Surf Wars (1978, Steve Lomas; animated short)
Surf's Breed (1971, Al Benson, Bill Kaiwa)
Surf's Up (1961, Don Brown)
Surfabout '74 (1974, Alby Falzon; short subject)
Surfboards, Skateboards and Big Waves (1969, Homer Groening)
Surfers: The Movie (1990, Bill Delaney)
Surfin' Wild (1962, Grant Rohloff)
Surfing and Skateboarding (1966, Grant Rohloff; short subject)
Surfing Aussie (1964, Val Valentine; short subject)
Surfing Highlights (1958, Greg Noll; short subject)
Surfing Hollow Days (1962, Bruce Brown)
Surfing in Hawaii (1962, Clarence Maki)
Surfing in Solitude (1963, John Arnold)
Surfing Roundabout (1965, David Price; short subject)
Surfing the Southern Cross (1963, Bob Evans)
Surfing Years, The (1966, Peter Thompson)
Surfing's North Shore Magazine (1983, *Surfing* magazine; short subject)
Swell, The (1983, Tim Bonython)
Tales from the Tube (1975, Jerry Humphries, Bob Cording)
Tales of the Seven Seas (1981, Scott Dittrich)
Taste of Juice, A (1978, Curt Mastalka)
Thunder Down Under (1981, Chris Bystrom)
Ticket to Ride (1986, Steve Soderberg)
Tiger on a Hot Balsa Board (1961, Greg Noll)
Too Hot to Handle (1961, Grant Rohloff; short subject)
Total Involvement (1970, Bill Kaiwa)
Totally Committed (1984, Steve Spaulding)
Tracks (1970, Bob Evans)
Trek to Makaha (1956, Bud Browne)
Tubular Swells (1977, Dick Hoole, Jack McCoy)

200,000 Reasons (1973, Eric Fullilove; short subject)
Viva Las Olas! (1962, John Williams)
Walk on the Wet Side (1963, Dale Davis)
War at Malibu (1967, Dale Davis; short subject)
Wave Masters (1978, Grant Young)
Wave of the Future (1985, Chris Bystrom)
Waves (1975, Gene Bagley, Bill Gellantly)
Waves of Change (1970, Greg MacGillivray, Jim Freeman)
Waves Seen (1974, Paul Gross)
Waves, The (1964, Walt Phillips)
Way of Life, A (1968, Bill Yerkes)
Way We Like It, The (1968, Bob Evans)
We Got Surf (1981, Hal Jepsen)
Wet and Wild (1968, Grant Rohloff; short subject)
Wet Lips (1983, Jack and Clark Poling)
Wet Set, The (1965, Bruce Brown; short subject)
White Waves (1979, Rodney Sumpter; short subject)
Who's Best? (1969, Greg MacGillivray, Jim Freeman; short subject)
Wild Surf (1975, Grant Rohloff; short subject)
Winter's Tale, A (1974, Phil Sheppard, Bruce Usher)
With Surfing in Mind (1968, Rod Sumpter)
Wizards of the Water (1982, Alan Rich)
Wonderful World of Surfing (1960, Grant Rohloff)
World Champion Wavemen (1967, Bob Evans; short subject)
Young Wave Hunters, The (1964, Bob Evans)
Zypher (1972, Yuri Farrant)

Surf Videos and DVDs

Above and Beyond (1995, Tony Roberts)
Adrenaline Surf Series: Vol. 1 (1993, Herbie Fletcher)
Adrenaline Surf Series: Vol. 2 (1994, Herbie Fletcher)
Adrenaline Surf Series: Vol. 3 (1994, Herbie Fletcher)
Adrenaline Surf Series: Vol. 4 (1995, Herbie Fletcher)
Adrenaline Surf Series: Vol. 5 (1995, Herbie Fletcher)
Adrift (1996, J. Brother)
Aegis (2002, George Bryan)
African Sensimillia (1998, Neil Webster)
Aftermath, The (1996, Bill and George Bryan)
Ahead (2002, Electric Productions)
Alive We Ride (1993, Richard Woolcott)
All Aboard (2002, Bill Ballard)
All Tha Way Live (2000, Justin Purser)
All Things Glide (2001, Peter Ratcliff)
Alley Oop (1997, Jack McCoy)
Aloha Bowls (1994, Sonny Miller)
Aloha Bowls '95 (1996, Sonny Miller)
Aloha From Hell (2000, FAB)
Aloha Waves (1997, Denjiro Sato)
Animal, The: Peterson Rosa (2002, Rosaldo Cavalcanti)
Area 949 (1998, George Bryan)
Around the World in 80 Waves (1989, Chris Bystrom)
Awakening, The (2001, Travis Karian)
Baja Pacific (1995, Herbie Fletcher)
Because (2002, Bill Ballard)
Beyond Blazing Boards (1985, Chris Bystrom)
Beyond Monster Maverick's (1996, Chris Bystrom)
Beyond the Boundaries (1994, Sonny Miller)

Biggest Wednesday: Condition Black (1998, Tim Bonython)
Billabong Surf Into Summer (1987, Bob Hurley, Gordon Merchant)
BIO (1998, Tim Bonython)
BIO II (1999, Tim Bonython)
Blade Runners of Maconde, The (1994, Trevor Avedissian)
Blast-Off (1991, Chris Bystrom)
Blast-Off 2 (1992, Chris Bystrom)
Blast-Off 3 (1992, Chris Bystrom)
Blazing Longboards (1994, Chris Bystrom)
Bliss (1996, Josh Pomar)
Blowing Up: The Search 8 (1999, Peter Kirkhouse)
Blue Crush (1998, Bill Ballard)
Blue Horizon (1984, Glyn Morris)
Boardriders, The (2001, Pavilion)
Bomb 2000, The (1999, Liam McNamara)
Bomb, The (1995, 10th St. Bros.)
Bomb, The (1995, Bill and George Bryan)
Bomb, The (1998, Masato Kase)
Boost (2000, Boost)
Bottom Line, The (1998, Taylor Steele)
Bring It On (1995, Red Eye)
Brothers Neilsen Get the Feeling (1993, Brothers Neilsen)
Bruce Brown's The Endless Summer Revisited (2000, Dana Brown)
Bunyip Dreaming (1991, Jack McCoy)
Burnt Toast (1999, Richard Lehrer)
Busted (1997, Johnny D)
Bustin' Out (1990, Chris Klopf)
Calling, The (2001, George Mays)
Can't Step Twice on the Same Piece of Water (1992, Alby Falzon)
Captain Surf and the Tube Dudes (1989, Joe Mickey, Dave Natal)
Changes (2000, Edward Feuer and Bryan Jennings)
Changing Faces (2001, No Limit)
Channel One (2001, Matt Gye)
Cheap Thrills (1994, Josh Pomar)
Chocolate Barrels and Liquid Trips (1998, Peter Kirkhouse)
Classical Gas (1999, Chris Klopf)
Clean Surf (2002, One Eye)
Cold (1996, Peter Kirkhouse)
Cold Heaven (1995, Mark Matovich)
Computer Body (2000, Veeco)
Contagious (1995, Marty Calabrese)
Contours (2002, Longboard)
Cool and Stylish (2001, Herbie Fletcher)
Couch Tour (2002, Mike Nelson, Dave Juan, Brian Walsh)
Cruise Control (1998, Chris Bystrom)
Cruisin' (1998, Herbie Fletcher)
Cyclone Fever (1994, Chris Bystrom)
Damage, Inc. (2002, Alexis Usher, Jason Blanchard)
Decline, The: Lost Across America 2 (2002, Lost)
Decompression (1999, Illusory Movement)
Deep and Green (1998, Bernard Auriol)
Defiant, The (1996, Brett Rose)
Diffusion (2000, Fluid Films)
Digital Daze (1999, Rob Elseewi, Cyrus Navabapour)
Down the Line (1994, Herbie Fletcher)
Download (2001, Tim Bonython)

Drive Thru (2002, Taylor Steele)
Eat Sand (2001, Isle Groove)
Eight (1998, On a Mission)
80 Grit (1999, Josh Everson)
Electro Ember (2000, Fluid Films)
Elements (1996, Brad Teufel)
Empress (1999, Misty Productions)
End of Summer (1995, Herbie Fletcher)
ETR: Enjoy the Ride (1997, Matt Gye)
E2K (2001, Greg Martin, Konrad Begg)
Euro Trash (1995, Alexis Usher)
Evolve (2002, Bali Strickland)
Experience, The (1999, Bill Ballard)
Exploders, The (2000, Chris Klopf)
Eyes to the Sea: A North Shore Experience (2002, Todd Messick)
Faces (1997, Tim Curran Sr.)
Factory Seconds (1995, Taylor Steele, Jason Weatherly)
Fade (1999, Mick King)
Farsiders, The (2001, Greg Lewis)
Feeding Frenzy (2000, Jamie Mosberg)
Feral Kingdom (1995, Sonny Miller)
Fifth Symphony Document, The (2001, Chad Campbell)
Fightoony (2002, Daz)
Filthy Habits (1987, Billabong)
Finally the Endless Winter (1999, John Forse)
First Name Basis (2002, Mike Latronic, Larry Haynes)
5'5" x 19¼" (1997, Lost)
5mm Canada (2000, Aaron Jackson)
Fix, The (2002, Alastair McKevitt)
Flail (1996, Right Skool)
Fletcher's Los Cabos Classic: Blistering Hot (1991, Herbie Fletcher)
Flight Academy (2002, Josh Pomar)
Fluid Combustion (1995, Larry Haynes)
Fluid Combustion II (1995, Larry Haynes)
Fluid Combustion III: Live It (1997, Larry Haynes)
Fluid Combustion: Pits in Paradise (2001, Larry Haynes)
Focus (1994, Taylor Steele)
Follow the Leader (1998, Bryan Jennings)
For the Sea (1994, Sonny Miller)
Forbidden Wall (2002, Jamie Mosberg, Larry Haynes)
Forcing the Limits (2002, IGH)
Foundation Project, The (2001, Tight)
Frankenplasm (1999, Veeco)
Freeze Frame (1989, Chris Bystrom)
Friday the 17th (1997, Shane Barbara)
From This Day Forward (2002, Travis Karian)
Full Cycle (1994, Chris Bystrom)
Gen X (1990, Brian Bleak)
Gondwana (2002, Pancho Sullivan)
Good Times (1995, Taylor Steele)
Got Surf? (1998, Alexis Usher)
Got Surf? II (1999, Alexis Usher)
Got Surf? III (2001, Alexis Usher)
Gravity Sucks (1994, Chris Bystrom)
Green Iguana, The (1992, Jack McCoy)
Green Room, The (2000, One Eye)
Gripping Stuff (1987, Volatile)
Gripping Stuff 2: Fire and Water (1991, Volatile)

Groovin (1999, Herbie Fletcher)
Half Moon Bay (1998, John Mills, Curt Meyers)
Hard Road (1999, Arturs Innis)
Hatteras Surf-Fest (1991, Bryan Murray)
Hawaii Nine-0 (1990, Tim Bonython, Jason Muir)
Hawaii Nine-1 (1991, Tim Bonython, Jason Muir)
Hawaii Nine-2 (1992, Tim Bonython, Jason Muir)
Hawaii Nine-3 (1993, Tim Bonython, Jason Muir)
Hawaii Nine-4 (1994, Tim Bonython, Jason Muir)
Hawaii Nine-5 (1995, Tim Bonython, Jason Muir)
Hawaii Nine-6 (1996, Tim Bonython, Jason Muir)
Hawaiian Surf Stories (1998, Jimi Berlin)
Hawaiian Watermen (1999, Greg Huglin)
Heavy Water (1994, Curt Myers)
High Noon at Low Tide (1994, Eric Nelson)
High Volume (1993, Aaron Salas)
Hit and Run (2000, Taylor Steele)
Hole, The (1997, Don King, Jeff Hornbaker)
Horny For Surf (1999, Kona)
Imagine: Surfing as Sadhana (2000, Marshall Hattori)
In the Wind (1990, Jack McCoy)
Indo Express 2: Escape (1995, Chris Fowler, Ronnie Gorringe)
Insanity (1995, Bill Ballard)
Inspired (2000, Shane Beschen)
Intense (1991, Phil Sheppard)
Iratika (2001, Bill Ballard)
It's All Good (1999, Larry Haynes)
Jacked (1995, Tony Roberts)
Journey to the Impact Zone (1987, Jeff Neu)
Joyride (1998, Chris Bauman)
Just Surfing (1989, Rusty)
Kill, The (1994, Josh Pomar)
Kill 2, The (1995, Josh Pomar)
Kill 3, The (1997, Josh Pomar)
Kill 4, The (1999, Josh Pomar)
Kill 5, The (2001, Josh Pomar)
Kill 6, The (2002, Josh Pomar)
Killing the Pier (2000, Mira Mira)
Kinetic (2001, Carve)
La Bruja (1996, Aquatika)
La Scene: Surfing France (1994, Alex Usher)
Last Surf Movie, The (1988, Chris Bystrom)
Last Wave, The (2002, Herbie Fletcher)
Latitudes (2000, Aquavision)
LC-1 (1999, Chris Rodriguez)
Leisure Society (2001, Arturs Innis)
Let It Flow (1999, Super X)
Liptocious (2000, Conrad Perez)
Liptocious II (2001, Conrad Perez)
Liquid Nation (2000, A. C. Slade)
Liquid Supernova (1999, Isle Groove)
Liquid Thunder (1990, Richard Wargo)
Liquidate (1996, Carve)
Litmus (1997, Andrew Kidman, Jon Frank, Mark Sutherland)
Loaded (1999, Tim Bonython)
Living Long (1999, Luke Sorenson)
Locked-In (2000, Bill Ballard)
Longboard Magic (2001, Richard Lehrer)
Longboarder (1995, Hal Jepsen)

Longboardin' (1994, Golden Pictures)
Longboarding Aussie Style (1996, Michael Peterson)
Longboarding Is Not a Crime (1995, Chris Bystrom)
Longboards: The Rebirth of Cool (1993, Chris Bystrom)
Loose Change (1999, Taylor Steele)
Loose Lips: Longboarding in California (1999, Richard Lehrer)
Lost Across America (1999, Lost)
Lost at Sea (2000, Lost)
Lost in Costa Rica (1998, Mike Wohran)
Lost: On the Road with Spike (1995, Lost)
Low Profile (1995, Brad Teufel)
Lunar Road (2002, Chris Klopf)
Mad Dogs (1994, Johnny D.)
Mad Wax: The Surf Movie (1987, Grant Young)
Made in Britain (2001, Dreaming Fish)
Madmen '93: Changing of the Guard (1993, Chris Bystrom)
Madmen, Saints and Sinners (1992, Chris Bystrom)
Magic Carpet Ride, The (1999, Bill and George Bryan)
Magnaplasm (1998, Richard Woolcott, Troy Eckert)
Malibu Heaven (1994, James Pradella)
Marching Onward (1999, Josh Williams)
Maverick's: Know Fear (1999, Curt Meyer, Eric Nelson)
Maverick's: Condition Black (1998, Alexis Usher)
Mental Surfing (1993, Tony Roberts)
Mental Surfing, Vol. 2 (1993, Tony Roberts)
Mentawai (2001, Alain Gardinier)
Mirage (1994, Ian McLaughlin)
Misfits, The (2002, Art Brewer)
Modern Hawaiian Longboarding (1996, Mana Surf)
Moment, The (1998, Bill Ballard)
Momentum (1992, Taylor Steele)
Momentum 2 (1993, Taylor Steele)
Momentum: Under the Influence (2001, Taylor Steele)
Mondo X-treme X-periment, The (1992, Brian Bleak)
Monstrosity (1999, Eric Nelson)
M-10 Movie, The (1999, Josh Pomar)
M-10: Squared (2001, Wilson Prod.)
Multiple Personalities (2000, Richard Lehrer)
Native State (2000, Rick Doyle)
Newborn (1999, Lional Sarran)
Next in Line (1999, Chris Klopf)
Nine Lives (1999, Jack McCoy)
No Destination (1998, Don King, Jeff Hornbaker)
No Exit (1992, Chris Klopf)
No Limits (1988, Tony Roberts)
No Thrills for the Cautious (1994, Rusty)
Nomads (2000, Chris Klopf)
North Swell (2000, Gelo Prod.)
Nose Zone (1998, Un Productions)
Numb (2002, Bruhwiler Brothers)
Nuthin' But Nuts (1998, African Rose)
O-Zone (1990, Tony Roberts)
Off the Wall 2 (1982, Joe Mickey, Dave Natal)
Ombak, The (2002, Timmy Turner)
On Surfari to Stay (1992, Chris Ahrens)
On the Edge (1997 Larry Haynes)
On the Outside (1998, Ian McLaughlin)
156 Tricks (2001, Cowboy)
110/240 (1992, Brian Bleak)
Our Turn (2000, XX Prod.)

Outside In (1999, Rick Rifici)
Overdrive (1993, Rusty)
Overdrive: The Journey (1999, Underground Surf)
Oz on Fire, Vol. 1 (1991, Chris Bystrom)
Oz on Fire, Vol. 2 (1991, Chris Bystrom)
Palmetto Drive (1998, Jon Krizmanich)
Panama Red (1994, Jeff Neu)
Path, The (2000, Tony Roberts)
Peaches (2000, Bill Ballard)
Performers, The (1984, Jack McCoy, Harry Hodge)
Performers 2, The (1988, Michael Honensee, Grant Young)
Performers 3, The (1999, Tom Carroll, Bruce Raymond)
Pickled (2001, Jamie Mosberg)
Players (1995, Tony Roberts)
Playground (1995, Rusty)
Poetic Silence (2001, Bill Ballard)
Powerglide (1995, Opper)
Pressure Drop (2001, Costa Esmeralda)
Primal Urge (1993, Chris Bystrom)
Primo Days (1993, Video Hotshots)
Progression Sessions (1994, Tony Roberts)
Progression Video Magazine (1997, Lockdown)
Progression Video Magazine 2 (1998, Lockdown)
Progression Video Magazine 3 (1999, Lockdown)
Progression Video Magazine 4 (2000, Lockdown)
Progression Video Magazine 5 (2001, Lockdown)
Progression Video Magazine 6 (2001, Lockdown)
Progression Video Magazine 7 (2002, Lockdown)
Proj. X (1999, Matt Kechele, Justin Purser)
Project Earth (1990, Jeff Neu)
Proland (1999, Derek Hynd)
Puerto Underground (1995, Dave Ogle)
Puerto Underground Dos (1996, Dave Ogle)
Puerto Underground III: Con Huevos (1997, Dave Ogle)
Pulse (1996, Justin Gane)
Pump! (1990, Billabong)
Punk Rock Surfers (2000, Josh Pomar)
Pure Filth (1993, Adam Good)
Quik Trip (1996, Mark Warren)
Quiksilver Country (1996, Alby Falzon)
Rad Movez (1992, Glen Winton)
Rad Movez 2 (1994, Glen Winton)
Radical Attitude (1993, Envision)
Rail to Rail (1996, Envision)
Raw Energy (1994, Ian McLaughlin)
Raw Power (1991, Chris Klopf)
Red Tide (1999, Anthony Passerelli)
Red Water (1998, Rick Doyle, Dana Brown)
Reflection (2002, Dave Ogle)
Return of the Drag-In (2001, Frank Quirarte)
Revelation (2000, Bill Ballard)
Rhythm (2000, Herbie Fletcher)
Rhythm of the Sea (1994, Jack McCoy)
Ripping Down the Walls (1990, Chris Bystrom)
Ripple Effect (2000, Seth Silberfein)
Rise and Shine (1999, Bill Ballard)
Rise: Five North Swells Plus Four (2001, Monty Webber)
Rising, The (2002, Josh Williams)
Ritual, The (2000, Matt Gye)
Road, The (2001, Arballo Entertainment)
Rock Your Soul (1998, Neil Webster)

Rubber Soul (1989, Peter Kirkhouse)
Runman (1987, Ray Klienman)
Runman II (1988, Ray Klienman)
Runman '69 (1989, Ray Klienman)
Runmental (2002, Ray Klienman)
Salt Water High (1998, Emerge)
San Clemente Locals (1990, Jeff Neu)
Sand Crabs (1997, Bill and George Bryan)
Sarge's Scrapbook, Take 1 (1990, Paul Sargeant)
Sarge's Scrapbook, Take 2 (1991, Paul Sargeant)
Sarge's Scrapbook, Take 3 (1991, Paul Sargeant)
Sarge's Scrapbook, Take 4 (1992, Paul Sargeant)
Sarge's Scrapbook: Take 5 (1993, Paul Sargeant)
Sarge's Scrapbook, Take 6 (1993, Paul Sargeant)
Sarge's Scrapbook, Take 7 (1995, Paul Sargeant)
Sarge's Scrapbook, Take 8 (1995, Paul Sargeant)
Sarge's Scrapbook, Take 9 (2001, Paul Sargeant)
Satisfaction (1995, Herbie Fletcher)
Savage Beast (1992, Herbie Fletcher)
Savage Cuts (1987, Peter Kirkhouse)
Savage Cuts II (1988, Peter Kirkhouse)
Scavengers, The (2000, Brad Evers)
Search, The (1992, Sonny Miller)
Search II, The (1993, Sonny Miller)
Seasick (2000, Blanc)
Secret Spots on Celluloid (1989, Chris Bystrom)
See It to Believe It (1996, Mike Hunt)
Seedling, The (1999, Thomas Campbell)
September Sessions (2000, Jack Johnson)
Session Impossible (1991, Jeff Neu)
7 Girls (2002, Roxy)
Shelter (2002, Taylor Steele, Chris Malloy)
Short and Sweet (2000, John Joseph Lynch)
Show, The (1996, Taylor Steele)
Side B (1997, Bill Ballard)
Sik Joy (1995, Jack McCoy)
Skillz (2000, Tony Roberts)
Skinned (1997, Johnny D.)
Snuff (1999, Tim Bonython)
Snuff 2 (2000, Tim Bonython)
Snuff 3: Automatic (2001, Tim Bonython)
Son of the Last Surf Movie (1987, Chris Bystrom)
Son Riders (1988, Mark Hartman)
Sons of Fun, The (1993, Jack McCoy)
Soul Patrol (1997, Chris Bystrom)
Soulag (1994, Bill and George Bryan)
Speechless (1998, Marshall Hatori)
Spike Snaps: On the Road with Spike (1989, Lost)
Spit (1996, Mitch Kaufmann)
Spit 2 (1997, Mitch Kaufmann)
Spit 3 (1998, Mitch Kaufmann)
Spit 4 (1999, Mitch Kaufmann)
Spit 5 (2000, Mitch Kaufmann)
Spit 6 (2001, Mitch Kaufmann)
Stash (2002, Double Keg)
Static (2001, Hamish Mathieson)
Stomp (1997, Peter Baker)
Stoney Baloney (1995, Brian Bleak, Richard Woolcot)
Strange Desires (1990, Jeff Hornbaker)
Strangers in Paradise (1995, Toshiro Izawa)
Strike Force (1988, Tim Bonython, Rod Brooks)

Style Equals Shred Plus Soul (1994, Tom Boyle)
Style Masters (1998, Herbie Fletcher)
Sultans of Speed (1988, Phil Sheppard)
Sultans 2: The Force Strikes Back (1989, Phil Sheppard)
Sultans 4: Surf Nastys (1993, Paul Sargeant, Chris Stecyk)
Sultans 5: Smoke on Water (1994, Phil Sheppard)
Summer of '67 (1995, Bill Yerkes)
Summer Sessions (1998, Herbie Fletcher)
Super Computer (2000, Jon Frank)
Super Slide (1999, Ira Opper)
Surf Addicts (1997, Jeff Neu)
Surf Aliens (1997, Pete Hodgson)
Surf Assassins (1991, Chris Bystrom)
Surf Espetacular (1992, Massangana Prod.)
Surf Hits, Volume One: Jungle Jetset (1988, Jack McCoy)
Surf Michigan (2000, Vince Deur)
Surf Michigan 2 (2002, Vince Deur)
Surf NRG (1990, Kevin Welsh)
Surf NRG, Vol. 2: Island Energy (1991, Kevin Welsh)
Surf NRG, Vol. 3: Liquid Energy (1994, Kevin Welsh)
Surf NRG, Vol. 4: Nuclear Energy (1995, Kevin Welsh)
Surf NRG, Vol. 5: Blue Energy (1996, Kevin Welsh)
Surf NRG, Vol. 6: Positive Energy (1997, Kevin Welsh)
Surf NRG, Vol. 7: Pure Energy (1998, Kevin Welsh)
Surf NRG, Vol. 8: NRG 2000 (1999, Kevin Welsh)
Surf NRG, Vol. 9: Ocean Energy (2000, Kevin Welsh)
Surf NRG, Vol. 10: XS Energy (2001, Kevin Welsh)
Surf NRG, Vol. 11: Solar Energy (2002, Kevin Welsh)
Surf! Surf! Surf! (1996, Don James)
Surf 365 (2000, Stormproof)
Surfer Magazine: Aussie Aggronauts (1990, Surfer)
Surfer Magazine: Classic California (1990, Surfer)
Surfer Magazine: Hawaiian Island Magi (1990, Surfer)
Surfer Magazine: Hawaiian Pure Juice (1990, Surfer)
Surfer Magazine: Outrageous Contest Action (1990, Surfer)
Surfer Magazine: Oz and Beyond (1990, Surfer)
Surfer Magazine: Pacific Power Bases (1990, Surfer)
Surfer Magazine: South of the Border (1990, Surfer)
Surfer Magazine: South Seas Adventure (1990, Surfer)
Surfer Magazine: Surfing Legends (1990, Surfer)
Surfer Magazine: Viva Surf (1990, Surfer)
Surfers of Fortune (1994, Brian Bleak)
Surfing A to Z (1998, Peter King, Michael Bloom)
Surfun (1996, Kurt Shaefer)
Take a Trip (1999, Paul Barranco)
Tanker Re-Evolution (1995, Jim Berlin)
Tavarua: Pressure Drop (Costa Esmeralda Productions)
Taz Zero One (2002, Thomas Moore)
Teardevils (1996, Jesse Schluntz)
Teardevils II: Hellbound (1997, Jesse Schluntz)
Teardevils III: The Final Incineration (1998, Jesse Schluntz)
Technologies Thunderphuq (2001, Liquid Technologies)
10X (2002, Rip Curl)
These Are Better Days (1999, Bill Ballard)
Thicker Than Water (1999, Jack Johnson)
Three Fins Firing (1995, Matt Kechele)
Three Phase (2001, Andrew Chisholm)
Through the Eye (1999, John Lynch)
Thunder (1997, Johnny D)
Tip Time (1996, Lightwave)
Toes Across America (1996, Tom Wegener)

Tom Curren's Ocean Surf Aces (1992, Rip Curl)
Too Cold (1997, Peter Kirkhouse)
Trailer Trashed (2002, DWS Prod.)
TransWorld Surf 7873 (2000, *TransWorld*)
Trash (1993, Peter Kirkhouse)
Trick or Treat (2001, Rick Rifici)
Triple C (1996, Bill Ballard)
Tripping the Planet (1996, Sonny Miller)
Tropical Madness (2001, Lisa Ross)
TV Dinners (1996, Snapping Turtle)
Twelve Eleven (1999, Curt Meyer, Eric Nelson)
Twenty Feet Under (1998, Eric Neilson)
UK2K: A New Wave Rising (2001, Danny Wright)
Under Down Under (1998, Arturs Innis)
Under the Same Sun (1994, Peter Townend)
Untitled (2002, George Manzanilla)
Vaporware (1994, Ira Opper)
Ventura: The Surf Movie (1994, Scott Aichner)
Virtuality (1996, Rusty)
Voluptuous: The Big Movie (1996, Snapping Turtle)
Voluptuous 2: Double D (2000, Snapping Turtle)
Vortex Children (2001, Brad Evers)
Wake Up Call (1995, Dave Nash)
Walkin in Style (2002, Herbie Fletcher)
Wanderers (1998, Chris Klopf)
Wanted: High Volume II (1994, Aaron Salas)
Water and Power (1996, Johnny D.)
Water Slaughter (1988, Tim Bonython)
Waterborn (1987, Bill Delaney)
Wave of Life, A (1990, Brian Brodersen)
Wave Warriors (1985, Greg Weaver, Herbie Fletcher)
Wave Warriors 2 (1986, Herbie Fletcher)
Wave Warriors 3 (1988, Herbie Fletcher)
Wave Warriors 4: On the Loose (1989, Herbie Fletcher)
Waves of Adventure in the Red Triangle (1993, Gary Mederios)
Western Promise (1995, Jesse Schluntz)
Wet Cement (1995, Chris Klopf)
Wet Cement II (1997, Chris Klopf)
What!? (1994, Cosmo Prod.)
What Exit? (2001, Time Bomb)
What Next? (1996, Marshall Hattori)
What Now!? (1995, Marshall Hattori)
What's Really Goin' On (1995, Lost)
What's Really Goin' Wrong (1995, Lost)
Whipped!!! (2001, Eric Nelson, Curt Myers)
Wordz (2002, Opper)
Wrong Side, The (2001, Obscene Prod.)
Year of Surfing in France, A (1996, Tony Bernos)
Year of the Drag-In (2000, Curt Meyers, Frank Quirarte)
Year of the Tiger (1998, Gene Kreyd)
Year, The (1999, No Limit)
Youngbloods (1995, Pete Hodgson)
Youthful Energy (1999, Astrodeck)
Y2K: Surfing Without a Net (2000, Chris Gabriel)
Zagland (1999, Neil Webster)

General Audience: Studio and Independent

Adventures in Wild California (2000, MacGillivray-Freeman, Greg MacGillivray)

Apocalypse Now (1979, Zoetrope, Francis Ford Coppola)
Around the World in Eighty Minutes (1931, UA, Victor Fleming)
Back to the Beach (1987, Paramount, Lindy Hobbs)
Beach Ball (1965, Paramount, Lennie Weinrib)
Beach Blanket Bingo (1965, AIP, William Asher)
Beach Girls and the Monster, The (1965, Edward Janis, Jon Hall)
Beach Party (1963, AIP, William Asher)
Behold Hawaii (1983, MacGillivray-Freeman, Greg MacGillivray)
Big Wednesday (1978, Warner Bros., John Milius)
Bikini Beach (1964, AIP, William Asher)
Bird of Paradise (1932, RKO, King Vidor)
Black Rock (1996, Polygram, Steve Vidler)
Blue Crush (2002, Universal, John Stockwell)
Blue Hawaii (1961, Paramount, Norman Taurog)
Blue Juice (1995, Skreba Films, Carl Prechezer)
Breaking Loose (1988, Avalon, Rod Hay)
California Dreaming (1979, Cinema 77, John D. Hancock)
Catalina Caper (1967, Crown-International, Lee Sholem)
Chairman of the Board (1998, Trimark, Alex Zamm)
Dish Dogs (1998, 7.23 Productions, Robert Kubilos)
Don't Make Waves (1967, MGM, Alexander Mackendrick)
Dr. Goldfoot and the Bikini Machine (1966, AIP, Norman Taurog)
Dust off the Wings (1997, Bombshell, Lee Rogers)
Endless Summer 2 (1994, New Line, Bruce Brown)
Extreme (1999, Jon Long)
Fantastic Plastic Machine (1969, 20th Century Fox, Eric and Lowell Blum)
Fast Times at Ridgemont High (1982, Universal, Amy Heckerling)
For Those Who Think Young (1964, UA, Leslie H. Martinson)
Ghost in the Invisible Bikini (1966, AIP, Don Weis)
Gidget (1959, Columbia, Lewis J. Rachmil)
Gidget Goes Hawaiian (1961, Columbia, Jerry Bresler)
Girls on the Beach, The (1965, Paramount, William Witney)
Honolulu (1939, MGM, Edward Buzzell)
Horror of Beach Party (1964, Iselin-Tenney Productions, Del Tenney)
How to Stuff a Wild Bikini (1965, MGM, William Asher)
In God's Hands (1998, TriStar, Zalman King)
It's a Bikini World (1967, TransAmerica, Stephanie Rothman)
Kings of the Wild Waves (1964, Paramount, Ed dePriest; short subject)
Lilo and Stitch (2002, Disney, Clark Spencer)
Lively Set, The (1964, Universal, Jack Arnold)
Living Sea, The (1995, MacGillivray-Freeman, Greg MacGillivray)
Malibu Beach (1978, Marimark, Robert Rosenthal)
Meet the Deedles (1998, Disney, Steve Boyum)
Muscle Beach Party (1964, AIP, William Asher)
North Shore (1987, Universal, William Phelps)
Ocean Tribe (1997, SeaReel, Wil Geiger)
Out of Sight (1966, Universal, Lennie Weinrib)
Pajama Party (1964, AIP, Don Weis)
Palm Beach (1979, Albie Thoms Prod., Albie Thoms)

Point Break (1991, 20th Century Fox, Katherine Bigelow)
Popcorn (1969, United Screen Artists, Peter Clifton)
Psycho Beach Party (2000, New Oz/Red Horse, Robert Lee King)
Puberty Blues (1981, Limelight Productions, Bruce Beresford)
Rainbow Bridge (1972, Antahkarana, Chuck Wein)
Red Surf (1990, Arrowhead Films, Gordon Boos)
Ride the Wild Surf (1964, Columbia, Don Taylor)
Riding the Crest (1939, PictoReels, Frederic Ullman Jr.)
San Diego Surf (1968, Andy Warhol Films, Andy Warhol)
Scene at the Sea (1992, Takeshi Kitano)
Summer City (1977, Avalon Films, Christopher Fraser)
Surf II (1984, Surf's Up, Randall Badat)
Surf Nazis Must Die (1987, Troma Films, Peter George)
Surf Ninjas (1993, New Line Cinema, Neal Israel)
Surf Party (1963, 20th Century Fox, Maury Dexter)
Surfari (1967, American Sports Films, Don Brown)
Surfboard Rhythm (1947, MGM, Charles Trego; short subject)
Surfer, The (1988, Frontier Films, Frank Shields)
Sweet Ride, The (1968, 20th Century Fox, Harvey Hart)
Swinging Summer, A (1965, National Talent Consultants, Robert Sparr)
Trade Winds (1938, UA, Tay Garnett)
Waikiki Wedding (1937, Paramount, Frank Tuttle)
Where the Boys Are (1960, MGM, Henry Levin)
White Flower, The (1923, Paramount, Julia Crawford Ivers)
Wild on the Beach (1965, 20th Century Fox, Maury Dexter)
Wild Wild Winter (1966, Universal, Lennie Weinrib)
Young Einstein (1988, Warner Bros., Yahoo Serious)
Youth Takes a Fling (1938, Universal, Archie Mayo)

Documentary, Biography

Addiction: The Archy Story (1999, Alister McKevitt)
All For One: The Brothers Malloy (1997, Shane Barbara)
Arc: Taylor Knox (2002, Poor Speciman)
Ask an Australian About Surfing (1975, Alex Ezzard)
Australia (1998, Ira Opper, *Surfer's Journal Great Waves*)
Balinese Surfer (1978, Bill Leinback)
Blueprint, The: Based on the Life of Shane Dorian (2002, Chad Campbell)
Bondi (1979, Paul Winkler; short subject)
California (1998, Ira Opper, *Surfer's Journal Great Waves*)
Condition Black (2002, PBS)
Day in the Life of Wayne Lynch, A (1978, Jack McCoy, Dick Hoole, David Lourie; short subject)
Desert Surfers, The (1995, Heather Croall, Milo Hyde)
Doc Ball: Surfing's Legendary Lensman (1999, Carl Ackerman)
Dogtown and Z-Boyz (2001, Stacey Peralta)
Drifting: Rob Machado and Friends (1996, Shane Barbara)
Drouyn and Friends (1974, Bob Evans)
Duke Kahanamoku's World of Surfing (1968, Larry Lindburgh)
Ecstasy (1971, Colin Turner)
Fall Line (1979, Nat Young)
Fanning the Fire (2002, Rip Curl)
Far Shore, The (2002, Greg Schell)

50 Years of Surfing on Film: Browne/Severson/Noll (1996, Ira Opper, *Surfer's Journal*)
50 Years of Surfing on Film: Brown/MacGillivray/Greenough (1996, Ira Opper, *Surfer's Journal*)
50 Years of Surfing on Film: Dittrich/McCoy/Steele (1996, Ira Opper, *Surfer's Journal*)
50 Years of Surfing on Film: Witzig/Falzon/Jepsen/Delaney (1996, Ira Opper, *Surfer's Journal*)
Golden Pig, The (1996, SBS Films)
Greats of Women's Surfing (2000, Ira Opper, *Surfer's Journal Biographies*)
Hawaii (1998, Ira Opper, *Surfer's Journal Great Waves*)
Heart of the Sea (2002, Charlotte Lagarde)
History of Surfing (1965, Don Wolf)
In Search of Da Cat (1996, Ovidio Salazar)
Joel Tudor/Nat Young (2000, Ira Opper, *Surfer's Journal Biographies*)
Kelly Slater in Black and White (1991, Richard Woodcott)
Kelly Slater in Kolor (1997, Taylorvision)
Kelly Slater/Tom Curren (2000, Ira Opper, *Surfer's Journal Biographies*)
Laird (2001, Laird Hamilton)
Legend of Bells, The (1982, Colin Turner)
Legends: An Australian Surfing Perspective (1994, Darrell Rigby)
Legends of Malibu (1987, Ira Opper, Paul Holmes)
Liquid Stage: The Lure of Surfing (1995, Michael Bovee)
Longer (2002, J. Brother)
Mark Richards Tapes, The (1987, Buzz Sands, Jon Conte)
Maverick's (1998, Grant Washburn, Lili Schad)
Modern Legends in Hawaiian Surf: MR to KS (1995, Surfer's Video)
Montaj (2002, Matt Gye)
Nat Young's History of Australian Surfing (1985, Nat Young)
Occy: The Occumentary (1999, Jack McCoy)
Outposts (1998, Ira Opper, *Surfer's Journal Great Waves*)
Passing Images (1978, Grant Young, Phil Sheppard)
Psycho Ward (1999, Snapping Turtle)
Ratboy: Quality Time with Jason Collins (2001, Bill Ballard)
Raw Irons (1998, Snapping Turtle)
Robert August/Robert Weaver (2000, Ira Opper, *Surfer's Journal Biographies*)
Rusty's World: Trip You Out (1999, Surf Vision)
Sabotaj (1999, Jack McCoy)
Scream in Blue (1986, Grant Young)
Searching for Tom Curren (1996, Sonny Miller, Derek Hynd)
Shaun Tomson/Mark Richards (2000, Ira Opper, *Surfer's Journal Biographies*)
Source, The (1995, Georgina Corzine)
Sunny Dayz (2001, High Voltage)
Surf Adventures (2000, Arthur Fontes; short subject)
Surf Chronicles: Great Moments in the Sport of Surfing (1994, Ira Opper)
Surfavela (1996, Nuno Leonel, Joaquim Pinto)
Surfer Girl (1994, Donna Olson)
Surfing for Life (1999, David Brown)
Surfing in the '30s (1994, Don James)
Surfing Odyssey, A (1972, John Phillips; short subject)
Surfmovies (1981, Albie Thoms)

Swell (1996, Charlotte LaGarde)
Taming the Snake (1987, Chris Darling)
Terry Fitzgerald/Cheyne Horan (2000, Ira Opper, *Surfer's Journal Biographies*)
That's Surfing (1998, Graham McNeice, Paula Bycroft)
These Colors Taste Like Music (2002, Quiksilver)
Tim Curran: Here and Now (1996, Tim Curran, Sr.)
Travellin' Round (1975, CFU)
Twenty Years of Surfing (1984, *Surfing* magazine; short subject)
Wave Rock (1993, Wayne Murphy)
Waves to Freedom (1988, Mark Cunningham, Robert Pennybacker, Albert Rosen)
Wayne Lynch/Tom Carroll (2000, Ira Opper, *Surfer's Journal Biographies*)
Where's Wardo? (2001, Poor Speciman)
Wingnut's Search for Soul (1997, Dana Brown)
Women in the Surf (1986, Ingrid Hillman, Esta Hanfield)
Zuef (1998, Charlotte Lagarde)

Compilation

Best of Wave Warriors: Back and Bad (1992, Herbie Fletcher, Brian Bleak)
Cavalcade of Surf (1962, Bud Browne)
Decade: Ten Years of Great Longboarding (2002, Herbie Fletcher)
Last Decade, The (1998, Taylor Steele)
Ride a White Horse (1968, Bob Evans)
Search for Surf (1992, Greg Noll)
Surf Classics (1964, John Severson)
Surfin' Shorts (1990, Bruce Brown)
Surfing the '50s (1994, Bud Browne)
Ten Years After (2002, Ira Opper)
Water-Logged (1963, Bruce Brown)

How-To, Instructional

Airbrushing 101 (2002, Carl Ackerman)
Backyard Ding Repair (1996, Action Sport)
Surfing Techniques with Tim Curran: Beginner (2000, Anthony Curran)
Carve It Up (1996, Wayne Winchester)
Corky Carroll's Learn to Surf the Safe, Fast and Easy Way (1996, Corky Carroll)
Ding Repair for Beginners (2000, Gray Wall Films)
Fluid Power Yoga for Surfers (2002, Peggy Hall)
Glassing 10 (1998, Carl Ackerman)
Intermediate Surfing Techniques with Tim Curran (2000, Anthony Curran)
Learn to Surf and Ocean Safety with Richard Schmidt (1997, Richard Schmidt, Tony Roberts)
Learning to Surf with Surfer Joe #1: The Ocean, You, and Your Board (2001, Norlynne Coar)
Learning to Surf with Surfer Joe #2: Get Out, Get Up, and Go! (2002, Norlynne Coar)
Let's Go Surfing: The Basics (2002, Stewart Surfboards)
Master Shaping Series, The (2002, Damascus Productions)
Original Surfboard Repair Video, The (1995, Venture Video)
Roxy: Learn to Surf, Now (2002, Quiksilver)

Safe Surfing with Danger Woman (1996, Kim Hamrock)
Secrets of Power Surfing (1993, Martin Dunn)
Shaping 101 (1996, Carl Ackerman)
Surfer's Guide to Ding Repair (1996, Steven Spaulding)
Theory, The (1999, Matt Haymes)
Trick Tips (1995, Snapping Turtle)
Wingnut's Art of Longboarding (1997, George Cockle,
    Toshiro Izawa)
Wingnut's Art of Longboarding 2: The Traveller (1999,
    George Cockle, Toshiro Izawa)
Yoga for Surfers (2002, Peggy Hall)
Yoga for Surfing (2002, Kevin Wood)

Surf Contests

Atlantic Moon: The 1998 World Longboard Championships
    (1999, Ira Opper)
Backdoor Shootout (1998, Da Hui)
Bells '81 (1981, Tim Bonython)
Billabong Challenge (1995, Jack McCoy)
Billabong Challenge: Jeffreys Bay (1995, Jack McCoy)
Blue Shock: The 1997 World Longboard Championships
    (1998, Ira Opper)
Bu, The: Women Really Do Walk on Water (2001, Arballo
    Entertainment)
Chicken Skin (1999, Quiksilver)
Deep Jungle Open 2000 (2000, Greg Martin)
Expression Session (1971, MacGillivray Freeman)
Expression Session 2 (1972, Hal Jepsen)
Getting Back to Nothing (1970, Tim Burstall)
Holy Water (1999, Gotcha)
Hot Surf: The 1998 Oxbow World Masters Championships
    (1998, Ira Opper)
JJJ '83 Surfing Championships (1983, Tim Bonython)
Masters, The (1998, Ira Opper)
Metaphysical (1997, Alby Falzon)
1983 Bells Beach Championship (1983, Tim Bonython)
1983 Straight Talk Tyre Open (1983, Tim Bonython)
1987 Triple Crown of Surfing, The (1988, International
    Sports Productions)
1990 ASP World Tour (1990, DynoComm)
1990 Eddie Aikau/Quiksilver Contest (1990, Jack McCoy)

1991 ASP World Tour (1991, DynoComm)
1992 ASP World Tour (1992, DynoComm)
1993 ASP World Tour (1993, DynoComm)
1994 ASP World Tour (1994, DynoComm)
1997 Quiksilver Pro (1997, Tom Carroll)
1999 Hui O He'e Nalu Backdoor Shootout (1999, Da Hui)
82 Om-Bali Pro (1982, Steve Core; short subject)
Om-Bali Pro '82 (1982, Steve Core)
Psychedelic Desert Groove (1997, Jack McCoy)
Quiksilver Eddie Aikau Big Wave Invitational (1986, Jack
    McCoy)
Quiksilver G-Land Java (1997, Quiksilver)
Quiksilver G-Land Pro 1995 (1995, Doug Silva, Seth Elmer)
Quiksilver G-Land Pro 1996 (1996, Quiksilver)
Quiksilver G-Land Pro 1998: Not (1998, Tom Carroll)
Reef at Todos, The (1998, Poor Speciman)
Rusty C-5 Design Challenge (1999, Poor Speciman)
Sacred Water: '99 Gotcha Pro (1999, Gotcha)
Second Pan-American Surfing Championships (1995, Bruce
    Walker)
St. Leu: Réunion Island (1996, Herbie Fletcher)
Stubbies '77 (1977, Hoole McCoy)
Stubbies '78 (1978, Mike Williams)
Stubbies '79 (1979, Mike Williams)
Stubbies '81 (1981, George Muskens)
Stubbies '83 (1983, Tim Bonython)
Stubbies, The (1977, Mike Williams, Brian Rennie)
Surf Odyssey, A (1964, Frank Killian)
Surfabout '75 (1975, David Elfick)
Surfabout '78 (1978, Simon Dibbs)
Surfabout '79 (1979, David Hill)
Surfabout '80 (1980, John Fisher)
Surfabout '81 (1981, Tim Bonython)
Surfabout '82 (1982, Graham McNeice)
Surfabout '83 (1983, Graham McNeice)
Surfing's Super Series (1985, Jim Hayes)
Trinity Gotcha Pro Tahiti 2000 (2000, Alastair McKevitt)
25 Years of Pipeline Masters (1995, Chiemsee)
2001 Op Pro, The (2002, Jason Baffa)
World Contest '72 (1972, Hal Jepsen)
World Contest, The (1972, Bill Yerkes)
World Surfing Championships, The (1972, Tuzo Jerger)

APPENDIX 4
Surfing Magazines

Most of the publications listed below are surfing-only magazines; a small number combine a related subject— surfing and sailboarding, for example, or surfing and beach fashion. 'Zines and online magazine are not included. A general time period is cited in those cases where the exact publication launch or end dates are unavailable.

Argentina

Alborde (1999–)
Argentina Surf and Skate (1978–80)
MDQ Surf (1990s)
Rad (1996–99)
Surfista (1998–)

Australia

Aerial (1990s)
Australasian BoardRider (1964)
Australian Bodyboarder (1994–)
Australian Longboarder (1998–)
Australian Sport and Surfriding (1962–64)
Australian Surfer (1994–95)
Australian Surfer, The (1961)
Australia's Surfing Life (1985–)
Backdoor (1975–77)
Breakaway (1973–78)
Captain Goodvibes (1975–76)
Chick (1998–)
Coastal Tubes (1982–83)
Core (1999)
Country Surf (1985)
Crank (1993–)
Cross Over (1997–2000)
Deep (1985–2000)
Free Surf (1989–90)
Free Surf Press (1977)
Freesurf Australia (1991–97)
Get Wet News (1990–91)
Ground Swell (1992–93)
Ground Swell (1998–2001)
Howl (1990s)
Line Up (1981–89)
Locals Only (1997–98)
Longboarding (1998)
Mal Magic (1996–99)
Manly Surf Journal (2000)
Noserider (1991)
Ocean Express (1986–88)
Oceans (1973)

Pacific Longboarder (1997–)
Pro Surf (1983)
Pure Journey (1993–94)
Rag (2001–2002)
Riptide (1988–)
Rush (2000–)
Sea Notes (1977–78)
Shred Betty (1998)
Southern Flyer (1980–91)
Sunshine Fluid (1976)
Surf (1976–78)
Surf Adventures (1991–93)
Surf Adventures (1999–2000)
Surf Avenge (1993)
Surf International (1967–70)
Surf Rider Weekly (1992)
Surf Scene (1964)
Surf Superstars (1982–94)
Surfabout Australasian Surfer (1962–68)
Surfer's Journal (1998–2000)
Surfing World (1962–)
Surf's Up (1968)
Tracks (1970–)
Underground Surf (1994–)
Wave Talk (1986–88)
Wave Torque (1985–86)
Waverider (1992–98)
Waves (1985–)
West Coast Surfer (1980–83)
Wet Side (1992–94)
Womensurf (1998)

Brazil

Adrenalina News (1990–95)
Adrenow (1995–2000)
Alltas (1998–2000)
Alma Surf (2000–)
Aloha (1997–2000)
ASN (1987–91)
Aspgua (1999)
Backwash (1989–93)
Barra Surf (1995)
Beach (1992–2000)
Beach Break (1990–91)
Boards (1998–99)
Boardsport Observer (1999–2000)
Brazil Surf (1975–78)
Conexao (1993)
Costa Sul (1985–87)
Drop (1998–2001)

Espirito Surf (1999–2000)
Expresso (1992–2000)
Feserj (1989–91)
Fluir (1983–)
Fluir Girls (2001–)
Folha Do Surf (1993–96)
Greensurf (1991)
Hardcore (1989–)
Info Wave (2000)
Informar (1993–96)
Informe Surf (1996–98)
Inside (1983–97)
Inside Now (1998–2000)
Jornal Do Surf (1986)
Jornal Extra Surf (1996)
Jornal Paulista De Surf (1994–95)
Jornal Surf Informacao (1989)
Kssino (1991)
Line Up (1995–96)
Maneco (1998–)
Mundo Rad (2001–)
North Shore Surf Paulista (1995–99)
Now (1989–97)
Nuts (2002–)
Quebra-Mar (1978)
Quiver (1987–98)
Radical (1995–)
Resgate (1999–2000)
Revista Longboard (1999–2000)
Ride It (2000–)
Rio Surf (1998–2000)
Solto Na Vala (2000)
Sport Session (1996–2001)
Staff (1985–87)
Storm (1996–2001)
Surf (1986)
Surf City (1999–2000)
Surf Link (1997–2000)
Surf News (1984–85)
Surf Nordeste (1986)
Surf People (1989–90)
Surf Press (1992)
Surf Press, The (1991–)
Surf Sul (1978–79)
Surf Tres (1987)
Surf Week (1985)
Surfar (1998–99)
Surfboards (2001–)
Surfer Brazil (1987–91)
Top Surf (1999–2000)
Trip (mid-1990s)
Venice (1997–)
Vertical Surf News (1998)
Visual Esportive (1980–90)
Visual Surf (1985–96)
Wet Paper (1993–94)
X-pression (2002–)

Canada

Island Swell (1992–94)
Northern Swell (1994–95)

Canary Islands

Marejada (1990–91)
Radical Surf (1999–)
Rompelolas (1993–95)

Chile

Demolition (1998–)
La Tabla (1998–99)
La Quilla Loca (1987)
Marejada (1999–)
Nauta (1990–91)

Costa Rica

Global Surf (2000–)
Planet Surf (1997–)
Surf Guide (1998–)
Surfos (1997–)

Ecuador

Ola's de Mar (1999)

France

Bodyrider (1990s)
Free Surf (1997)
Plein Sud (1980s)
Radical Surf (1993)
Spot (1984–86)
Surf Atlantique (1964)
Surf Roll-Surf (1976)
Surf Saga (1993–98)
Surf Session (1986–)
Surf Session Girls (1999–)
Surf Time (1992–)
Surfer's Journal (1995–)
Trip Surf (1994–)

Germany

Blue (2000–)
Line Up (1996)
Surfers (1995–)
Wave (mid-1990s)
Wax (1993)

Great Britain

Asylum (1998–99)
Atlantic Surfer (1978–80)
British Sponger (1999–)
British Surfer (1969–70)
Carve (1994–)
Channel Views (1987–93)
Freeride (1998–99)
Groundswell (1983–93)
Line Up (1974–75)
Malibu (1999–2000)
Onboard Surf Magazine (1989–2002)

Pure Stoke (1994)
Ripple (1973-75)
Shorebreak (1974-75)
Source, The (2000-)
Surf (1974-78)
Surf Chat (1975)
Surf Insight (1972-73)
Surfer's Path (1997-)
Surfing Roots (1993)
Surf's Up (1989-95)
Surf Scene (1980-89)
SYM (1971-74)
ThreeSixty (1990s)
Tube News (1980-91)
Urf (1992-93)
Wavelength (1981-)

Indonesia

Surf Time (1999-)

Italy

King Surfer (1994-)
Revolt (1990s)
Surf (1992-94)
Surf Latino (1996-)
Surf News (1994-)
Surfando (1990s)

Japan

Flipper (1994-)
Flow (1995-)
Japan Surfer (1986-91)
Longboard, The (2002-)
Miss Surfer's (2002-)
Nalu (1995-)
On the Board (1997-)
Side Ways Stance (1997-2001)
Surf (1975-84)
Surf Patrol (1994-97)
Surf Stories (1980s)
Surf Times (1995)
Surf Trip (1987)
Surfaholic (1994-)
Surfer (1980s)
Surfing Classic (1980-84)
Surfing Life Japan (1980-)
Surfing World Japan (1976-)
Surftrip Journal (1995-99)
Take Off (1978-91)
TransWorld Surf Japan (2001-)

Mexico

La Ola Mexicana (1994)

Netherlands

Surf Sport and Style (1994-98)

New Zealand

Expressions (1977)
Freebird (1980-83)
Groundswell (1994-96)
Kiwi Surf (1990-)
New Zealand Longboarder (2000-01)
New Zealand Surf (1965-66)
New Zealand Surf (1970-71)
New Zealand Surfing (1985-)
NZ Tracks (1974-77)
Runt (1997)
Shredabout (1980s)
Surf NZ (1971-72)
Surfing New Zealand (1968-69)
Surfriding in New Zealand (1968)
Wai-Ngaru (1977-78)
Waves (1973)

Peru

Tabla (1982-84)
Tablista (1985-)
Tubos (1997)

Portugal

Nose Rider (2000-)
Portugal Radical (1996-97)
Surf (mid-1990s)
Surf Portugal (1987-)
Vert (2001-)

Puerto Rico

Caribbean Surf (1985-87)
Low Pressure (1999-)
Surfinrico (1997-99)

South Africa

Back Door (1998)
Down the Line (1976-77)
Moments (1986)
Offshore (1987-89)
Saltwater Girl (1999-)
Soul Surfer (1995-96)
South African Surfer (1965-68)
Southern Surfer (1971-77)
Surf Africa (1974-76)
Wet (1989-90)
Zigzag (1977-)

Spain

Surf Time (1999-)
Surfer Rule (1990-)
Tres60 (1987-)

Sweden

Edge (1995)

Tahiti

Tahiti Waves (2001–)

United States

Action Now (1981–82)
Atlantic Surfer (1993–94)
Atlantic Surfing (1965–68)
Automatic (1999–)
Beach Culture (1990–91)
Beach Happy (1989–; changed to *Happy* in 1998)
Beach'n Waves (1988–92)
Bodyboarder (1990s)
Bodyboarding (1985–)
Bodyboarding International (1994–96)
Breakout (1979–89)
California Surfers (1998)
California Wave (1995)
Carvin' (2000–)
Competition Surf (1966–67)
Corpus Christi Breaks (1993)
Cross Step (1993)
Cross Step (1993)
Eastern Surf (1992–)
Easter Waves (1974–75)
Electric Ink (1996–2001)
5 Star (1998)
Fla. Surf (1990)
Flat (1996)
Ground Swell (1989–91)
Gulf Coast Surf (2002–)
Hang Ten (1973)
Hapa (1995)
Hawaiian Line (1987)
High Surf Advisory (1999)
Hodads Beware (1962)
Hot Water (1980s)
H2O (1979–)
H3O (1989–98)
Inside Surf (2002–)
International Surf (1991–93)
Jacksonville Surfer (1983–85)
Juice, The (1996)
Kema (1988–92)
Locals (1996)
Longboard (1993–)
Longboarder (1992–93)
Maui Surfing (1989–98)
Modern Longboard Times (1993)
North Coast Surf Press (1999–2000)
Northeast Surf News (1999)
Pacific Lines (1977–78)
Peterson's Surfing Magazine (1963–64)
Peterson's Surfing Yearbook (1963–69)
Peterson's Surftoons (1965–69)
Pit, The (1996–2000)

Rare Breed (1996–97)
Reef Magazine (1960)
Shorebreak (1998)
Shred (1987–88)
So Cal Surf News (1963)
Soul Surf (1996)
South Bay Surfer (1982–83)
South Swell (1987–89)
Surf (1977–79)
Surf Crazed Comics (1991)
Surf Guide (1963–65)
Surf Humor (1963)
Surf News (1999–2001)
Surf Scene (1972–74)
Surfbeat (1993)
Surfer Girl (1998–2000)
Surfer magazine (1960–; called *The Surfer* from 1960 to 1962)
Surfer's Journal, The (1992–)
Surf'in East (1975)
Surfing (1964–; called *International Surfing* from 1964 to 1974)
Surfing Action Around the World (1968–70)
Surfing East (1965–67)
Surfing Girl (1997)
Surfing Hawaii (1965)
Surfing Illustrated (1962–67)
Surfing News (1960)
Surfing News (1965)
Surfing News (1967)
Surfing Siren (1998)
Surfing Times (1966)
Surfing Tracks (1973)
Surfing Wahine (1995)
Surfwriters Quarterly (1994)
Tiaregirl (2001–)
TransWorld Surf (1999–)
U.S. Surf (1983–84)
Wahine (1995–2001)
Water (2001–)
Wave Action (1993–2000)
Wave Rider (1975–82)
Wavelength (1986–87)
Waves (1992–94)

Uruguay

Mareas (1997–)

Venezuela

Al Maximo (1999–)
S&N (1993–)
Surf Carib (1993)
Surf Star (1998–)
Xtremo (1998–99)

APPENDIX 5
Selected Surf Music Discography

While a majority of artists listed below are made up of '60s instrumental groups, "surf music," as applied to this appendix, includes vocal groups, such as the Beach Boys, as well as albums and singles recorded by well-known surfers. As of 2003, there were more than 500 instrumental surf bands playing and recording worldwide, and a sampling of these groups is included here. (See Reverb Cental online for a comprehensive list of surf bands old and new.) In the cases of a band or artist who went beyond the surf music genre, the accompanying list of albums and singles for that act may be abbreviated. Singles are generally limited to A side song titles only, and where applicable, a song's highest Billboard chart ranking is included. Surf music compilations and tribute albums are listed at the end of the appendix. Finally, hot rod music was invented simultaneously with surf music—same musical structure; different lyrics and song titles—and most of the '60s-era groups listed here played both.

Aqua Velvets

Formed 1989, San Francisco, California (instrumental)

ALBUMS
The Aqua Velvets (1992, Heyday)
Surfmania (1995, Mesa)
Nomad (1996, Milan)
Guitar Noir (1997, Milan)
Radio Waves (2001, Milan)

SINGLES
"Raymond Chandler Evening" (1995)
"Martini Time" (1995)
"Martin Denny Esq." (1995)
"Mexican Rooftop Afternoon" (1995)
"Nomad" (1996)
"Mermaids After Midnight" (1997)
"Guitar Noir" (1997)

The Astronauts

Formed 1962, Boulder, Colorado (instrumental)

ALBUMS
Surfin' With The Astronauts (1963, RCA)
Everything Is A-OK (1964, RCA)
Competition Coupe (1964, RCA)
Astronauts Orbit Kampus (1964, RCA)
Go Go Go (1965, RCA)

For You From Us (1965, RCA)
Down the Line (1965, RCA)
The Astronauts: Rarities (1991, Bear Family)

SINGLES
"Baja" (1963, #94)
"Hot Doggin'" (1963)
"Surf Party" (1963)
"Competition Coupe" (1963)
"Go Fight For Her" (1964)
"Can't You See I Do?" (1964)
"Almost Grown" (1965)
"It Doesn't Matter Any More" (1965)
"Main Street" (1965)
"I Know You Ride" (1967)

The Atlantics

Formed 1961, Sydney, Australia (instrumental)

ALBUMS
Bombora (1963, CBS)
Now It's Stompin' Time (1963, CBS)
Greatest Hits (1963, CBS)
The Explosive Sound of the Atlantics (1963, CBS)
Great Surfin' Sounds of the Atlantics (1970, Music for Pleasure)
Flight of the Surf Guitar (2000, Atlantics Music)
The Next Generation (2002, Atlantics Music)

SINGLES
"Moon Man" (1963)
"Bombora" (1963, #1 in Australia)
"The Crusher" (1963)
"Rumble and Run" (1964)
"Boo Boo Stick Beat" (1964)
"Giant" (1965)
"Goldfinger" (1965)
"Theme from Peter Gunn" (1965)

The Avengers VI

Formed 1964, Anaheim, California (instrumental)

ALBUMS
Real Cool Hits (1964, Mark)
Mrs. Faruki's Sazuki (1964, Mark)

SINGLES
"Time Bomb" (1966)

Baymen

Formed 1961, Palos Verdes, California (instrumental)

SINGLES
"Bonzai" (1963)

The Beach Boys

Formed 1961, Hawthorne, California (vocal)

ALBUMS
Surfin' Safari (1962, Capitol)
Surfin' U.S.A. (1963, Capitol)
Surfer Girl (1963, Capitol)
Little Deuce Coupe (1963, Capitol)
All Summer Long (1964, Capitol)
Beach Boys' Christmas Album (1964, Capitol)
Beach Boys' Concert (1964, Capitol)
The Beach Boys Today! (1965, Capitol)
Summer Days (And Summer Nights!) (1965, Capitol)
Beach Boys' Party (1965, Capitol)
Pet Sounds (1966, Reprise)
Best of the Beach Boys (1966, Capitol)
Best of the Beach Boys, Vol. 2 (1967, Capitol)
Wild Honey (1967, Reprise)
Smiley Smile (1967, Reprise)
Friends (Reprise, 1968)
20/20 (1969, Reprise)
Close Up (1969, Capitol)
Beach Boys '69 (1969, Capitol)
Sunflower (1970, Reprise)
Surf's Up (1971, Reprise)
Dance Dance Dance/Fun Fun Fun (1971, Capitol)
Holland (1972, Reprise)
The Beach Boys in Concert (1973, Reprise)
Endless Summer (1974, Capitol)
Spirit of America (1975, Capitol)
Good Vibrations: Best of the Beach Boys (1975, Reprise)
Stack O' Tracks (1976, Capitol)
15 Big Ones (1976, Reprise)
Love You (1977, Reprise)
L.A. (Light Album) (1979, Caribou)
Keepin' the Summer Alive (1980, Caribou)
Ten Years of Harmony (1981, Capitol)
Sunshine Dream (1982, Capitol)
The *Beach Boys '85* (1985, Caribou)
Made in U.S.A. (1986, Capitol)
Still Cruisin (1989, Capitol)
Summer in Paradise (1992, Brother)
Good Vibrations: Thirty Years of the Beach Boys (1993, Capitol)
The "Smile" Era (1995, Capitol)
Stars and Stripes, Vol. I (1996, River North)
20 Good Vibrations: The Greatest Hits, Vol. I (1999, Capitol)
20 More Good Vibrations: The Greatest Hits, Vol. II (1999, Capitol)
Best of the Brother Years: Greatest Hits, Vol. III (1970–1986) (1999, Capitol)

The Beach Boys: Hawthorne, CA (2001, Capitol)

SINGLES
"Surfin'" (1961, #75)
"Surfin' Safari" (1962, #14)
"Surfin' U.S.A." (1963, #3)
"Surfer Girl" (1963, #7)
"Little Deuce Coupe" (1963, #15)
"Be True to Your School" (1963, #6)
"Don't Worry, Baby" (1964, #23)
"In My Room" (1963, #23)
"Fun, Fun, Fun" (1964, #5)
"I Get Around" (1964, #1)
"Dance, Dance, Dance" (1964, #8)
"California Girls" (1965, #3)
"Help Me, Rhonda" (1965, #1)
"Caroline, No" (1966, #23)
"Wouldn't It Be Nice" (1966, #38)
"God Only Knows" (1966, #39)
"Good Vibrations" (1966, #1)
"Heroes and Villains" (1967, #12)
"Wild Honey" (1967, #31)
"Darlin'" (1967, #19)
"Friends" (1968, #47)
"Do It Again" (1968, #20)
"I Can Hear Music" (1969, #24)
"Add Some Music to Your Day" (1970, #64)
"Long Promised Road" (1971, #89)
"Sail On Sailor" (1973, #49)
"California Saga" (1973, #84)
"It's O.K." (1976, #29)
"Come Go With Me" (1976, #18)
"Kokomo" (1988, #1)

The Bel-Airs

Formed 1960, Palos Verdes, California (instrumental)

ALBUMS
The Bel-Airs: Origins of Surf Music (1993, Gee Dee)
Volcanic Action! (2001, Sundazed)

SINGLES
"Mr. Moto" (1961)
"Baggies" (1963)
"Kamikaze" (1963)

The Blue Hawaiians

Formed 1994, Los Angeles, California (instrumental)

ALBUMS
Christmas on Big Island (1995, Restless)
Live at the Lava Lounge (1997, Pascal)
Sway (1998, Pascal)
Savage Nights (1999, Interscope)

SINGLES
"Glimpses of Savage Nights" (1999)

Corky Carroll

Orange County, California (vocal/instrumental)

ALBUMS
Laid Back: Corky Carroll and Friends (1971, Rural)
Tales from the Tube (1972, Rural)
A Surfer for President (1979, Casual Tuna)
Fretless (1980, Pacific Arts)
Wavesliders (1990, Waveslider)
Best of a Soul Surfer (1994, GFR)
Surf Dreams (1995, GFR)
Surf Dogs on the Range (1996, Gee Dee)
Tropical Undertone (1998, Little Moby)
Beachtown Rhapsody (1999, Little Moby)
Liquid Measures (2000, Little Moby)
California Boy (2001, Little Moby)
Born to Surf (2001, Polygram)

SINGLES
"Skateboard Bill" (1978)
"Tan Punks on Boards" (1979)

Al Casey

Phoenix, Arizona; Los Angeles, California (instrumental)

ALBUMS
Surfin' Hootenanny (1963, Stacy)

SINGLES
"Cookin'" (1962)
"Surfin' Hootenanny" (1963, #48)
"Guitars, Guitars, Guitars" (1963)
"What Are We Gonna Do in '64" (1963)

The Challengers

Formed 1962, Palos Verdes, California (instrumental)

ALBUMS
Surf Beat (1963, Vault)
Lloyd Thaxton Goes Surfing With The Challengers (1963, Vault)
Surfin' Around the World (1963, Vault)
K-39 (1964, Vault)
The Challengers Go Sidewalk Surfin' (1965, Triumph)
Surf's Up (1965, Vault)
Challengers at the Go-Go (1965, Vault)
Challengers' Greatest Hits (1965, Vault)
Challengers at the Teenage Fair (1965, GNP/Crescendo)
Man From U.N.C.L.E. (1966, GNP/Crescendo)
California Kicks (1966, GNP/Crescendo)
Wipe Out (1966, GNP/Crescendo)
25 Greatest Instrumental Hits (1967, GNP/Crescendo)
Where Were You in the Summer of '62 (1970, Fantasy)
Best of the Challengers (1982, Rhino)
Tidal Wave! (1995, Sundazed)

SINGLES
"Torquay" (1962)
"Moon Dawg" (1962)
"Foot Tapper" (1963)

"Hot Rod Hootennany" (1964)
"Hot Rod Show" (1964)
"Channel 9" (1965)
"Wipe Out" (1965)
"Mr. Moto '65" (1965)
"Pipeline" (1965)
"Rampage" (1965)
"Asphalt Wipe Out" (1965)
"The Man From U.N.C.L.E." (1966)
"Summer Night" (1966)
"North Beach" (1966)
"Milord" (1966)

The Chantays

Formed 1961, Santa Ana, California (instrumental)

ALBUMS
Pipeline (1963, Downey)
Two Sides of The Chantays (1964, Dot)
Next Set (1994, Chantays Productions)
Out of the Blue (1996, Chantays Productions)

SINGLES
"Pipeline" (1962, #4)
"Monsoon" (1963)
"Space Probe" (1963)
"Only If You Care" (1964)
"Beyond" (1964)

The Crossfires

Formed 1962, Westchester, California (instrumental)

ALBUMS
Out of Control (1981, Rhino)

SINGLES
"Fiberglass Jungle" (1963)
"One Potato, Two Potato" (1964)

Tom Curren's Ocean Surf Aces

Santa Barbara, California (instrumental)

ALBUMS
Ocean Surf Aces (1995, Surfside)

Dick Dale and His Del-Tones

Formed 1959, Newport Beach, California (instrumental)

ALBUMS
Surfer's Choice (1962, Deltone)
King of the Surf Guitar (1963, Capitol)
Checkered Flag (1963, Capitol)
Mr. Eliminator (1964, Capitol)
Summer Surf (1964, Capitol)
Rock Out With Dick Dale and His Del-Tones Live At Circo's (1965, Capitol)
Dick Dale's Greatest Hits (1975, GNP)
The Tigers Loose (1983, Balboa)
The Best of Dick Dale and His Del-Tones (1989, Rhino)

Tribal Thunder (1993, Hightone)
Unknown Territory (1994, Hightone)
Calling Up the Spirits (1996, Beggars Banquet)
Spatial Disorientation (2002, Dick Dale)

SINGLES
"Oh-Whee Marie" (1959)
"Stop Teasin'" (1959)
"Jessie Pearl" (1961)
"Let's Go Trippin'" (1961, #60)
"Jungle Fever" (1962)
"Misirlou" (1962)
"Surf Beat" (1962)
"Peppermint Man" (1962)
"A Run For Life" (1963)
"We'll Never Hear the End of It" (1963)
"Wild Ideas" (1963)
"The Wedge" (1963)
"Surfin' Secret Spot" (1963)
"Mr. Eliminator" (1963)
"King of the Surf Guitar" (1963)
"Wild Wild Mustang" (1964)
"Glory Wave" (1964)
"Who Can He Be" (1964)
"A Run for Life" (1965)
"Ramblin' Man" (1967)
"Taco Wagon" (1967)
"Don't Worry Baby" (1974)
"One Double One Oh!" (1986)

The Delltones

Formed 1959, Sydney, Australia (vocal)

ALBUMS
The Delltones (1962, Leedon)
Come a Little Bit Closer (1963, Leedon)
Surf 'n Stomp (1963, Leedon)
Best of the Delltones (1964, Leedon)
Dellies Burst Out (1965, Leedon)
20 Golden Greats (1978, Festival)
The Original Hits (1988, Festival)
The Delltones Live: The Ultimate Recollection (1993, Starseed)

SINGLES
"Hangin' Five" (1963)
"Out the Back" (1964)
"Walking Along" (1964)
"Hey Girl Don't Bother Me" (1964)
"Lonely Boy" (1965)
"Tonight We Love" (1965)
"Breaking Waves" (1995)

Johnny Devlin and the Devils

Formed 1958, Auckland, New Zealand (vocal)

ALBUMS
Surf Club Stomp (1963, Festival)

SINGLES
"Chi Chico Teek" (1963)

"Stomp the Tumbanumba" (1963)
"Do It Right" (1964)
"Blue Suede Shoes" (1964)
"Mod's Nod" (1964)
"You Won't Be My Baby" (1965)

Eddie and the Showmen

Formed 1963, Palos Verdes, California (instrumental)

ALBUMS
Surf Party (1980, Surfsville)
Squad Car (1996, AVI)

SINGLES
"Toes on the Nose" (1963)
"Squad Car" (1963)
"Mr. Rebel" (1963)
"Lanky Bones" (1964)
"We Are The Young" (1964)

Johnny Fortune

Los Angeles, California (instrumental)

ALBUMS
Soul Surfer (1963, Park Avenue)
Life Goes On (1999, Media)

SINGLES
"Soul Surfer" (1963)
"Soul Traveler" (1963)
"Surf Rider" (1963)
"Siboney" (1963)
"Surfer's Trip" (1963)
"What Do You Think About That" (1999)
"She Just Don't Care" (1999)
"I Got a Woman" (1999)

Frogmen

Formed 1961, Culver City, California (instrumental)

SINGLES
"Underwater" (1961)
"Beware Below" (1961)
"Seahorse Flats" (1961)

The Gamblers

Formed 1960, Los Angeles, California (instrumental)

SINGLES
"Moon Dawg" (1960)
"Teen Machine" (1961)

The Halibuts

Formed 1986, Los Angeles, California (instrumental)

ALBUMS
Gnarly (1987, Iloki)
Chumming (1994, Upstart)

Life on the Bottom (1996, Upstart)
Halibut Beach (1996, What?)

The Honeys

Formed 1963, Hawthorne, California (vocal)

ALBUMS
Ecstasy (1983, Rhino)
The Honeys Collector Series (1992, Capitol)
The Honey Collection (2001, Rhino)

SINGLES
"Shoot the Curl" (1963)
"Pray for Surf" (1963)
"The One You Can't Have" (1963)
"He's a Doll" (1964)

Honk

Formed 1971, Laguna Beach, California (vocal/
    instrumental)

ALBUMS
Soundtrack from Five Summer Stories (1972, GNP)
Honk (1973, 20th Century)
Honk (1975, Epic)
Coach House Live (1991, Restless)

SINGLES
"Pipeline Sequence" (1972)

The Impacts

Formed 1962, Morro Bay, California (instrumental/vocal)

ALBUMS
Wipeout (1963, Del-Fi)
Surf War (1963, Del-Fi)
Big Surf Hits (1964, Del-Fi)

The Invaders

Formed 1963, Montebello, California (instrumental)

SINGLES
"Blast Off" (1965)
"You'll Never Know" (1966)

Jan and Dean

Formed 1958, Los Angeles, California (vocal)

ALBUMS
Golden Hits (1962, Liberty)
Surf City (1963, Liberty)
Take Linda Surfing (1963, Liberty)
Drag City (1964, Liberty)
Ride the Wild Surf (1964, Liberty)
The Little Old Lady From Pasadena (1964, Liberty)
Command Performance/Live in Person (1965, Liberty)
Filet of Soul (1966, Liberty)
Popsicle (1966, Liberty)

Jan and Dean Anthology Album (1971, United Artists)
Gotta Take That One Last Ride (1974, United Artists)
One Summer Night/Live (1982, Rhino)
Teen Suite, 1958–1962 (1995, Varése Vintage)
Golden Summer Days (1996, Varése Vintage)
Jan and Dean Live (1998, Center Stage)

SINGLES
"Jennie Lee" (1958, #8)
"Baby Talk" (1959, #10)
"White Tennis Sneakers" (1960)
"Judy's an Angel" (1961)
"Surf City" (1963, #1)
"Heart and Soul" (1961, #25)
"Linda" (1963, #28)
"Honolulu Lulu" (1963, #11)
"Drag City" (1964, #10)
"Dead Man's Curve" (1964, #8)
"The Little Old Lady From Pasadena" (1964, #3)
"Ride the Wild Surf" (1964, #16)
Sidewalk Surfin'" (1964, #25)
"You Really Know How to Hurt a Guy" (1965, #27)
"I Found a Girl" (1965, #30)
"A Surfer's Dream" (1966)
"Popsicle" (1966, #21)

Jon and the Nightriders

Formed 1979, Riverside, California (instrumental)

ALBUMS
Surf Beat '80 (1980, Voxx)
Recorded Live at Hollywood's Famous Whiskey A-Go-Go
    (1981, Voxx)
Charge of the Nightriders (1984, Enigma)
Stampede (1990, Norton)
Banished to the Beach: An Anthology 1979–1986 (1994,
    NPR)
Fiberglass Rocket (1996, AVI)
Moving Target (1999, Gee Dee)
Raw & Alive at the Foothill Club (1999, Gee Dee)
Undercover (2000, Surf Waves)

SINGLES
"Rumble at Waikiki" (1979)
"California Fun" (1981)
"Splashback!" (1982)
"Thunder Over Rincon" (1998)

The Joy Boys

Formed 1957, Sydney, Australia (vocal/instrumental)

ALBUMS
Cookin' Up a Party (1963, Festival)
Surfin' Stompin' Joys (1964, Festival)

SINGLES
"Theme from Ant Hill" (1963)
"Bluebird" (1963)
"In the Mood" (1963)
"Murphy the Surfie" (1963)

"Boots, Saddle and Surfboard" (1964)
"Searchin'" (1964)
"Say One For Me" (1964)

The Lively Ones

Formed 1963, Los Angeles, California (instrumental)

ALBUMS
Surf Rider (1963, Del-Fi)
Surf Drums (1963, Del-Fi)
Surf City (1963, Del-Fi)
The Great Surf Hits (1963, Del-Fi)
Surfin' South of the Border (1964, Del-Fi)

SINGLES
"Guitarget" (1962)
"Surf Rider" (1963)
"Goofy Foot" (1963)
"Rik-A-Tik" (1963)
"Misirlou" (1963)
"High Tide" (1963)
"Telstar Surf" (1963)
"Night and Day" (1964)

Longboard Ranch

Formed 1999, Orange County, California (instrumental)

ALBUMS
Surfin' Out West (2002, Longboard Ranch)

The Marketts

Formed 1961, Hollywood, California (instrumental)

ALBUMS
Surfer's Stomp (1962, Liberty)
Take to Wheel (1963, Warner Bros.)
The Surfing Scene (1963, Liberty)
Out of Limits (1964, Liberty)
The Batman Theme (1966, Warner)
Surfin' and Stompin' (2001, ATM)
Summer Means Love (2002, Dore)

SINGLES
"Surfer's Stomp" (1962, #31)
"Beach Bum" (1962)
"Balboa Blue" (1962, #48)
"Stompin' Room Only" (1962)
"Woody Wagon" (1963)
"Out of Limits" (1964, #3)
"Batman Theme" (1966)

The Mermen

Formed 1988, San Francisco, California (instrumental)

ALBUMS
Krill Slippin' (1989, Mesa)
Food for Other Fish (1994, Mesa)
The Mermen at the Haunted House (1994, Mesa)
A Glorious Lethal Euphoria (1995, Atlantic)
Songs of the Cows (1996, Atlantic)

The Amazing California Health and Happiness Roadshow (2000, V2/Mesa)

Jim Messina and the Jesters

Formed 1963, Los Angeles, California (instrumental)

ALBUMS
The Dragsters (1964, Audio Fidelity)

SINGLES
"Breeze and I" (1964)
"Panther Pounce" (1964)
"Drag Race Boogie" (1964)

The Mighty Surf Lords

Formed 1995, Reno, Nevada (instrumental)

ALBUMS
Mental Surf (2002, Mighty Surf Lords)
Live at the Big Easy (2002, Mighty Surf Lords)

Dave Myers and the Surftones

Formed 1960, San Clemente, California (instrumental/vocal)

ALBUMS
Hanging Twenty (1963, Del-Fi)
Greatest Racing Themes (1965, Carol)

SINGLES
"Church Key" (1963)
"Moment of Truth" (1963)
"Gear" (1964)
"Come On Luv" (1965)

The New Dimensions

Formed 1962, Hollywood, California (instrumental)

ALBUMS
Deuces and Eights (1963, Sutton)
Surf'n Bongos (1963, Sutton)
Soul (1964, Sutton)
Best of the New Dimensions (1996, Sundazed)

Nobles

Formed 1960, El Monte, California (instrumental)

ALBUMS
Come Surf With Me (1963, Vee Jay)

SINGLES
"Body Surf" (1963)

The Original Surfaris

Formed 1962, Fullerton, California (instrumental)

ALBUMS
Wheels-Shorts-Hot Rods (1964, Diplomat)
Bombora (1995, Sundazed)

SINGLES
"Surfin'' '63" (1963)
"Moment of Truth" (1963)
"Bombora" (1963)
"Torchula" (1963)
"Midnight Surf" (1963)
"Gum-Dipped Slicks" (1964)

The Packards

Formed 1980, San Clemente, California (instrumental)

ALBUMS
Pray for Surf (1980, Surfside)
Guitar Heaven (1986, Frontline)
California (1987, Frontline)
The Packards (1997, Gee Dee)
High Energy (2001, Guitar Heaven)

The Phantom Surfers

Formed 1988, Santa Cruz, California (instrumental)

ALBUMS
Play the Music from the Big Screen (1992, Estrus)
18 Deadly Ones (1996, Norton)
Great Surf Crash of '97 (1996, Lookout)
The Exciting Sounds of Model Road Racing (1997, Lookout)
Skaterhater (1998, Lookout)
XXX Party (2000, Lookout)

SINGLES
"Single Whammy" (1996)
"Banzai Run" (1996)
"Great Surf Crash" (1996)
"Curb Job" (1998)
"Sidewalk City" (1998)

The Pyramids

Formed 1962, Long Beach, California (instrumental)

ALBUMS
The Original Penetration (1964, What?)
King of Kings (1974, Pyramid)
What Surf (1983, What?)
Penetration: Best of the Pyramids (1995, Sundazed)

SINGLES
"Cryin'" (1962)
"Pyramid's Stomp" (1962)
"Penetration" (1963, #18)
"Midnight Run" (1964)
"Contact" (1964)

Digger Revell's Denvermen

Formed 1960, Sydney, Australia (instrumental/vocal)

ALBUMS
Let's Go Surfside (1963, RCA)
To Whom It May Concern (1965, RCA)
My Prayer (1966, RCA)

SINGLES
"Outback" (1962)
"Surfside" (1963)
"Nightrider" (1962)
"Avalon Stomp" (1963)
"Mystery Wave" (1963)
"Hootenany Stomp" (1964)
"My Little Rocker's Turned Surfy" (1964)
"The Rebel" (1964)
"Surfer's Blues" (1964)

Revels

Formed 1960, San Luis Obispo, California (instrumental)

ALBUMS
On a Rampage (1964, Impact)
Intoxica! Best of the Revels (1994, Sundazed)

SINGLES
"Church Key" (1960)
"Intoxica" (1961)
"Comanche" (1962)
"It's Party Time" (1963)

The Rhythm Rockers

Formed 1960, Santa Ana, California (instrumental)

ALBUMS
Soul Surfin' (1963, Challenge)
Surfin' USA (1963, Challenge)

SINGLES
"Fanny Warble" (1962)
"Foot Cruising" (1962)
"Rendezvous Stomp" (1963)
"Pachoko Hop" (1963)

The Sandals

Formed 1962, San Clemente, California (instrumental)

ALBUMS
The Endless Summer (soundtrack) (1966, World Pacific)
The Last of the Ski Bums (soundtrack) (1969, World Pacific)
The Spirit of Surf: Music from Endless Summer II (1994, Tri-Surf)
Silvertone (2002, Tri-Surf)

SINGLES
"Theme from Endless Summer" (1964)
"Out Front" (1964)

The Sentinals

Formed 1961, San Luis Obispo, California (instrumental)

ALBUMS
Big Surf (1963, Del-Fi)
Surfer Girl (1964, Del-Fi)
Beach Party (1963, GSP)
Vegas Go-Go (1964, Sutton)

SINGLES

"Roughshod" (1961)
"Christmas Eve" (1962)
"Latin'ia" (1962)
"Big Surf" (1963)
"The Bee" (1964)
"Blue Booze" (1964)
"Hit the Road" (1964)
"Tell Me" (1964)

The Shadows

Formed 1958, London, England (instrumental)

ALBUMS

The Shadows (1962, Columbia)
Surfing With The Shadows (1963, Atlantic)
Greatest Hits (1963, Columbia)
More Hits (1965, Columbia)
Specs Appeal (1973, EMI)
Rarities (1976, EMI)
The Best of The Shadows (1977, EMI)
20 Golden Greats (1977, EMI)
Shadows Are Go! (1996, Scamp)

SINGLES

"Driftin'" (1959)
"Feelin'" Fine (1959)
"Apache" (1960)
"FBI" (1961)
"Kon Tiki" (1961)
"Atlantis" (1961)
"Frightened City" (1961)
"Shindig" (1963)
"Foot Tapper" (1963)
"Geronimo" (1963)
"Theme for Young Lovers" (1964)
"The Rise and Fall of Flingel Bunt" (1964)
"Don't Make My Baby Blue" (1965)

Slacktone

Formed 1995, Southern California (instrumental)

ALBUMS

Warning: Reverb Instrumentals (1997, Go Boy)
Into the Blue Sparkle (2000, Go Boy)
Surf Adventure Tour: Live in Prague (2002, Go Boy)

SINGLES

"Daytona Mona" (2001)

The Sunrays

Formed 1964, Los Angeles, California (vocal)

ALBUMS

Andrea (1966, Tower)
For Collectors Only: Vintage Rays (1996, Collectables)
The Tower Recordings (1999, Collectables)

SINGLES

"Outta Gas" (1964)

"I Live for the Sun" (1965)
"Andrea" (1965)
"Still" (1966)
"I Look, Baby, I Can't See" (1966)

The Superstocks (featuring Gary Usher)

Formed 1964, Los Angeles, California (vocal)

ALBUMS

School Is a Drag (1964, Capitol)
Surf Route 101 (1964, Capitol)
Thunder Road (1964, Capitol)

SINGLES

"Thunder Road" (1964)
"Midnight Run" (1964)

The Surfaris

Formed 1962, Glendora, California (instrumental)

ALBUMS

Wipe Out (1963, Dot)
The Surfaris Play (1963, Decca)
Hit City '64 (1964, Decca)
Fun City USA (1964, Decca)
Hit City '65 (1965, Decca)
It Ain't Me Babe (1965, Decca)
Surfaris Live (1983, Koinkidink)
Wipe Out! The Best of the Surfaris (1994, Varése Sarabande)
Surf Party! The Best of the Surfaris Live (1994, GNP/
    Crescendo)
Surfaris Stomp (1995, Varése Sarabande)

SINGLES

"Surfer's Christmas List" (1963)
"Scatter Shield" (1963)
"Wipe Out" (1963, #2)
"Point Panic" (1963, #49)
"Surfer Joe" (1963, #62)
"Murphy the Surfie" (1964)
"Boss Barracuda" (1964)
"Hot Rod High" (1964)
"Beat '65" (1965)
"Theme of the Battle Maiden" (1965)
"Catch a Wave With Me" (1965)

Surf Punks

Formed 1979, Los Angeles, California (vocal)

ALBUMS

Surf Punks (1979, Day-Glo)
My Beach (1980, Epic)
Locals Only (1982, Restless)
On No! Not Them Again (1988, Enigma)
Party Bomb (1988, Restless)

SINGLES

"My Beach" (1980)
"No Fat Chicks" (1980)
"Locals Only" (1981)

"Shark Attack" (1982)
"Surf's Up Medley" (1990)

The Surf Raiders

Formed 1980, Covina, California (instrumental)

ALBUMS
Raiders of the Lost Surf (1982, Surf Wax)
Surf Bound (1983, Surf Wax)
On the Beach (1984, Surf Wax)
Surfin' Fever (1991, Azra International)

SINGLES
"Waikiki Run" (1980)
"The Curl Rider" (1981)
"Surf'n '81" (1981)
"Point Conception '63" (1981)
"Gum Dipped Slicks" (1981)
"California Surf" (1982)
"Live at the Whiskey A-Go-Go" (1982)
"Steel Pier" (1982)
"Surf Busters" (1982)

The Surfers

Formed 1998, San Diego, California (vocal)

ALBUMS
Songs From the Pipe (1998, Epic)

Surfmen

Formed 1961, Los Angeles, California (instrumental)

SINGLES
"Ghost Hop" (1962)
"Paradise Cove" (1962)
"Malibu Run" (1962)
"Breakers" (1963)

The Temptations

Formed 1961, Garden Grove, California; renamed The
    Spats in 1964 (instrumental)

ALBUMS
Cooking with the Spats (1964, ABC Paramount)

SINGLES
"Egyptian Surf" (1963)
"Gator Tails and Monkey Ribs" (1964)
"Scoobee Doo" (1964)
"There's a Party in the Pad Below" (1964)

The Tornadoes

Formed 1962, London, England (instrumental)

ALBUMS
Away From It All (1963, Castle)
Telstar: The Original Sixties Hits of the Tornadoes (1994,
    Music Club)

SINGLES
"Telstar" (1963, #1)
"Ride the Wind" (1963)
"Globetrotter" (1963)
"Ice Cream Man" (1963)
"Robot" (1963)

The Tornadoes

Formed 1960, Redlands, California (instrumental)

ALBUMS
Bustin' Surfboards (1963, Josie)
Bustin' Surfboards '98 (1998, Garland)
Beyond the Surf (1999, Sundazed)

SINGLES
"Bustin' Surfboards" (1962)
"The Gremmie, Part 1" (1962)
"Moon Dawg" (1963)
"Phantom Surfer" (1963)

The Trashmen

Formed 1963, Minneapolis, Minnesota (vocal)

ALBUMS
Surfin' Bird (1964, Garrett)
The Tube City!: Best of the Trashmen (1992, Sundazed)
The Great Lost Trashmen Album (1994, Sundazed)
Bird Call! The Twin City Stomp of the Trashmen (1998,
    Sundazed)

SINGLES
"Surfin' Bird" (1963, #4)
"Bird Dance Beat" (1964, #30)

Gary Usher

Los Angeles, California (vocal)

ALBUMS
Gary Usher Greats: Vol. 1, The Kickstands vs. The Knights
    (1996, AVI)
*A Symphonic Tribute to a Great American Song Writer, Brian
    Wilson* (2001, Dreamsville)

SINGLES
"Tomorrow" (1962)
"Three Surfer Boys" (1963)
"The Beetle" (1964)
"Surfer's Holiday" (1964)
"Sacramento" (1964)
"Jody" (1965)

Bob Vaught and the Renegaids

Formed 1961, Los Angeles, California (instrumental)

ALBUMS
Surf Crazy (1963, GNP/Crescendo)

SINGLES
"Church Key Twist" (1962)

"Surfin' Tragedy" (1963)
"Surfin' in Paradise" (1963)

The Ventures

Formed 1959, Seattle, Washington (instrumental)

ALBUMS
Walk Don't Run (1960, Dolton)
Another Smash!! (1961, Dolton)
The Ventures (1961, Dolton)
The Colorful Ventures (1961, Dolton)
Twist with the Ventures (1962, Dolton)
The Ventures' Twist Party, Vol. 2 (1962, Dolton)
Mashed Potatoes and Gravy (1962, Dolton)
Going to the Ventures Dance Party (1962, Dolton)
The Ventures Play Telstar (1963, Dolton)
The Lonely Bull (1963, Dolton)
Surfing (1963, Dolton)
Let's Go! (1963, Dolton)
The Versatile Ventures (1963, Liberty)
Ventures in Space (1964, Dolton)
The Fabulous Ventures (1964, Dolton)
Walk, Don't Run, Vol. 2 (1964, Dolton)
The Ventures Knock Me Out! (1965, Dolton)
The Ventures on Stage (1965, Dolton)
The Ventures a Go-Go (1965, Dolton)
Play Guitar With the Ventures (1965, Dolton)
Christmas with the Ventures (1965, Dolton)
Where the Action Is (1966, Dolton)
The Ventures/Batman Theme (1966, Dolton)
Go With the Ventures (1966, Dolton)
Wild Things! (1966, Dolton)
Guitar Freakout (1967, Dolton)
Golden Greats by the Ventures (1967, Liberty)
Hawaii Five-O (1969, Liberty)
Swamp Rock (1969, Liberty)
More Golden Greats (1970, Liberty)
The Ventures Tenth Anniversary Album (1970, Liberty)
Theme From Shaft (1972, United Artists)
Joy/Ventures Play the Classics (1972, United Artists)
The Compact Ventures (1987, Garland)
Walk, Don't Run: The Best of the Ventures (1990, EMI)
Greatest Hits (1991, Curb/Cema)
Wild Again! (1997, GNP/Crescendo)
New Depths (1998, GNP/Crescendo)
The Ventures Play the Greatest Surfin' Hits of All-Time (2002, Varése Sarabande)

SINGLES
"Walk Don't Run" (1960, #2)
"Ghost Riders in the Sky" (1960)
"Perfidia" (1960)
"Lullaby of the Leaves" (1960, #69)
"2,000 Pound Bee" (1961)
"Lonely Bull" (1963)
"I Walk the Line" (1963)
"Journey to the Stars" (1964)
"Walk Don't Run '64" (1964, #8)
"Ten Seconds to Heaven" (1965)
"Diamond Head" (1965, #70)

"Penetration" (1965)
"Hawaii Five-O" (1969)
"Surfin' and Spyin'" (1981)

The Vibrants

Formed 1960, Manhattan Beach, California (instrumental)

SINGLES
"The Breeze and I" (1962)
"Fuel Injection" (1962)
"Scorpion" (1962)

The Vulcanes

Formed 1960, North Hollywood, California (instrumental)

SINGLES
"Stomp Sign" (1962)
"Cozimotto" (1963)
"Moon Probe" (1964)
"The Outrage" (1964)

Jim Waller and the Deltas

Formed 1961, Fresno, California (instrumental)

ALBUMS
Surfin' Wild (1962, Arvee)

SINGLES
"I've Been Blue" (1961)
"Church Key" (1962)
"Bells Are Ringing" (1963)
"Goodnight My Love" (1964)
"Surfin' Tragedy" (1964)

Surf Music Compilations and Tributes

American Surf Treasures, Vol. 1 (1998, AVI)
American Surf Treasures, Vol. 2 (1998, AVI)
Battle of the Bands (1964, Star)
Battle of the Beat (1964, California Recording Service)
Battle of the Surfing Bands (1963, Del-Fi)
Better Than Average Weekend (2001, Deep Eddy)
Big Surf (1991, Ace)
Big Surf Hits (1996, Del-Fi)
Big Surfing Sounds (1963, Capitol)
Big Surfing Sounds Are On Capitol (1964, Capitol)
Bustin' Surfboards (1982, GPN)
Cowabunga: The Surf Box (1996, Rhino)
Endless Summer II Soundtrack (1994, Warner Bros.)
Greatest Surf Guitar Classics (2001, Big Eye Music)
History of Surf Music, Vol. 1: Original Instrumental Hits 1961–1964 (1982, Rhino)
History of Surf Music, Vol. 2: Original Vocal Hits 1961–1964 (1982, Rhino)
History of Surf Music, Vol. 3: The Revival 1980–1982 (1982, Rhino)
Instrumental Fire (2001, MuSick)

Kamikaze Plunge (1999, Riptide)
Legends of Guitar, Volume 1: Surf (1991, Rhino)
MOM, Music For Our Mother Ocean (1996, Surf Dog)
MOM II, Music for Our Mother Ocean (1997, Surf Dog)
MOM III, Music for Our Mother Ocean (1998, Surf Dog)
Monster Summer Hits—Wild Surf (1991, Capitol)
Mustle Bustle: Classic Tracks From the Surf'N Drag Era
    (1994, Ace)
Oldies, Goodies and Woodies (1963, Vault)
Original Surfin' Hits (1963, GNP/Crescendo)
Planet Surf (1995, Tri-Surf)
Pulp Surfin' (1995, Donna)
Rare Surf, Vol. 5: The Capitol Masters (2001, ATM)
Rare West Coast Surf Instrumentals (2001, Ace)
Rock Don't Run (1996, Spin Out)
Rock Don't Run, Vol. 2 (1996, Spin Out)
Rock Don't Run, Vol. 3 (1998, Spin Out)
Rock Instrumental Classics, Volume 5: Surf (1994, Rhino)
Smells Like Surf Spirit (1997, Gee Dee)
Surf and Drag, Vol. 1 (1989, Sundazed)
Surf and Drag, Vol. 2 (1993, Sundazed)
Surf Battle (1963, GNP Crescendo)
Surf Battle at Redondo Beach (1996, Gee Dee)
Surf Christmas (2002, Heal the Bay)
Surf Crazy (1995, GNP)

Surf Creature (1992, Romulan)
Surf Creature, Vol. 2 (1993, Romulan)
Surf Creature, Vol. 3 (1994, Romulan)
Surf Legends and Rumors 1961–1964 (1995, Garland)
Surf Party (1964, 20th Century)
The Surf Set (1993, Sequel)
Surf War—Battle of the Surf Groups (1963, Shepherd)
Surf's Up at Bonzai Pipeline (1963, Reprise)
Surfin' Hits (1989, Rhino)
Surfing's Greatest Hits (1964, Capitol)
Swivlin' Wahine (2000, Skully)
Symphonic Sounds: Music of the Beach Boys (1998,
    Platinum Entertainment)
Takin' Out the Trash: A Tribute to the Trashmen (1999,
    Double Crown)
That's New Pussycat: A Surftribute to Burt Bacharach
    (2000, Omom)
Toes on the Nose: 32 Surf Instrumentals (1996, Ace)
Totally Tubular (2002, KFJC)
Waikiki Surf Battle, Vols. 1 and 2 (1963, Sounds of Hawaii)
War of the Surf Guitars (2000, Double Crown/Golly Gee)
Wax, Board, and Woodie (1996, Varése Sarabande)
Wild Surf! (1995, Del-Fi)
Wipe Out! (1998, Disky)

THANKS AND ACKNOWLEDGMENTS

This book would not have been possible without the generous help of Nick Carroll, Mark Fragale, and Al Hunt. Invaluable assistance was also provided by Greg Ambrose, Alan Atkins, Bernie Baker, Wayne Bartholomew, John Blair, Paul Botha, Antony Colas, Sean Collins, Gibus de Soultrait, Alex Dick-Reed, Sam George, Craig Jarvis, Daved Marsh, Dick Metz, Michael Mock, Steve Pezman, Kathy Phillips, Rusty Preisendorfer, Randy Rarick, Jose Schaffino, Bill Sharp, Craig Simms, Evan Slater, Ron Weeks, and Bill Wise. Thanks also to Tom Adler, Kirk Aeder, Greg Ambrose, Keith Anderson, Steve Barilotti, Harry Bold, Jason Borte, John Brasen, Jamie Brisick, Tony Butt, Alisa Cairns, Ian Cairns, Marge Calhoun, Rus Calisch, Graham Cassidy, Rosaldo Cavalcanti, Bruce Channon, John Dahl, Chris Dixon, Scott Eggars, Chris Evans, Ralph Fatello, Bob Fiegel, Ben Finney, Andrea Gabbard, Ross Garrett, Malcolm Gault-Williams, Jeff Hall, Dwayne Harris, Chuck Hasley, Steve Hawk, Dustin Hood, Scott Hulet, Derek Hynd, Drew Kampion, Tak Kawahara, Melissa Larsen, Mike Latronic, Peter Lee, Greg Loehr, Matias Lopez, Gary Lynch, Merlin Mann, Chris Mauro, Gordon McClelland, Dick Meseroll, Bob Mignona, Max Mills, Larry Moore, Mickey Muñoz, Chad Nelsen, Michael Novakov, Ira Opper, George Orbelian, Peter Pan, Dorian Paskowitz, Mike Perry, Mark Renneker, Derek Rielly, Roberto Salinas, Satoshi Sekino, John Severson, Jack Shipley, Luis Skeen, Bob Smith, Joel Smith, Michael Spence, Baron Stander, Taylor Steele, Shaun Tomson, Peter Townend, Peter Troy, Matt Walker, Robert Weaver, Paul West, Luke Williamson, Matt Wilson, and Nat Young.

Principal photography for *The Encyclopedia of Surfing* was supplied by Jeff Divine, Leroy Grannis, Tom Servais, and the *Surfer* magazine archive. Surf music discography appendix compiled with assistance from John Blair and Phil Dirt. Surf bibliography appendix complied with assistance from Daved Marsh. Surf magazine appendix complied with assistance from Al Hunt.

Matt Warshaw: Thanks first and foremost to Nathan Myers; this book in large part was built on his stamina, encouragement, and good cheer. Marcus Sanders's assistance and humor were also invaluable. Thanks also to Laura Putnam, Wendy Burton-Brouws, Kati Steele Hesford, and Liz Royles. My eternal gratitude to Mimi Kalland, Chris Warshaw, and Susan Warshaw for their love, support, patience, and benefaction, and special added megathanks to Michael Warshaw—a surfing encyclopedia was his idea.

Nathan Myers: Thanks to my parents, Jim and Marilyn Myers, and to Elaina Samaniego and Peter Lee for their vital presence throughout this project. Thanks also to Tom Gomes, Jacques Domerque, and Dru Danforth for giving me the ocean, and to Jason Gewehr, Luke Fisher, and Jeremy Webster for their assistance and friendship.

Marcus Sanders: Special thanks to Mom and Dad for the love and encouragement; to Paul Piscopo for couch use; and to Jamie Brisick, Matt Walker, and Evan Slater for phone counseling during much of this project; and to Sean Collins and Dave Gilovich for consistent support. Thanks also to Jade Hays and Marcos Cortez for their kind and consistent heckling.

ABOUT THE AUTHOR

Surf writer from San Francisco, California; editor of *Surfer* magazine in 1990; author or contributing writer to more than a half-dozen surfing books, including *SurfRiders* (1997) and *Maverick's: The Story of Big-Wave Surfing* (2000); described in a *San Diego Union-Tribune* profile as "tall, wiry and intense . . . the antithesis of a laid-back dude." Warshaw was born (1960) in Los Angeles, California, raised in Venice Beach and Manhattan Beach, and began surfing in 1969. He was the top-finishing amateur in the 1977 Katin contest in Huntington Beach, and surfed professionally in the early '80s. In 1984, he wrote articles and did graphic pasteup at *Breakout*, a regional surf magazine located in Carlsbad, California; he was hired as associate editor at *Surfer* in 1985, then became managing editor in 1988 and editor in 1990. Warshaw has published surfing articles in the *Wall Street Journal, Outside*, the *New York Times*, the *Los Angeles Times*, and *Men's Journal. SurfRiders*, his first book, was published in 1997, followed by *Above the Roar: 50 Surfer Interviews* (1997), *Maverick's* (2000), and *The Encyclopedia of Surfing* (2003); he wrote the forewords for *Surfers: Photographs by Patrick Cariou* (1997), *Masters of Surf Photography: Jeff Divine* (2000), and *The Perfect Day: 40 Years of Surfer Magazine* (2001); he also wrote and codirected the 1997 Outdoor Life Network documentary series *50 Years of Surfing on Film*, followed by the 1998 series *Great Waves*. Warshaw received a B.A. in history from U.C. Berkeley in 1992.

For the second edition of *The Encyclopedia of Surfing*, please send corrections, comments, and suggestions via e-mail to editor@encyclopediaofsurfing.com.

PHOTO CREDITS

Page 2: Jeff Divine; **5:** Tom Servais; **7:** Jeff Divine; **8:** Leroy Grannis; **11:** Bishop Museum; **13:** Leroy Grannis; **15:** Jock McDonald; **16:** Tom Servais; **17:** Jeff Divine; **21:** Tom Servais; **26:** Brad Barrett; **35:** *Surfer* Magazine Collection; **38:** John "Doc" Ball; **40:** Tom Servais; **41:** Tom Servais; **44:** Jeff Divine; **46:** Hulton Archive/Getty Images; **48:** Joanne Makalena Takatsugi; **50:** Tom Servais; **52:** Jeff Divine; **54:** Leroy Grannis; **55:** Jeff Divine; **57:** John Milius; **59:** Jeff Divine; **64:** Sandow Birk; **66:** John "Doc" Ball; **71:** Jeff Divine; **73:** *Surfer* Magazine Collection; **76:** Tom Servais; **78:** Jeff Divine; **79:** Steve Wilkings; **82:** Tom Servais; **83:** Drew Kampion; **85:** *Surfer* Magazine Collection; **87:** Bruce Brown; **91:** Jeff Divine; **93:** Tom Servais; **94:** Tom Servais; **97:** Leroy Grannis; **99:** Jeff Divine; **104:** Tom Servais; **107:** Jeff Divine; **109:** Ron Stoner photograph/courtesy *Surfer* Magazine Collection; **111:** Tom Servais; **113:** David Carson; **117:** Tom Servais; **118:** Drew Kampion; **123:** Jeff Divine; **125** (top): Jeff Divine; **125** (bottom): *Surfer* Magazine Collection; **128:** Jeff Divine; **132:** Tom Servais; **136:** Tom Servais; **140:** Jeff Divine; **141:** Tom Servais; **143:** Bud Browne; **144:** Tom Servais; **148:** *Surfer* Magazine Collection; **149:** Jeff Divine; **151:** *Surfer* Magazine Collection; **157:** Steve Wilkings; **159:** John "Doc" Ball; **160:** *Surfer* Magazine Collection; **163:** *Surfer* Magazine Collection; **166:** Leroy Grannis; **177:** *Surfer* Magazine Collection; **178:** Bruce Brown; **182:** Tom Servais; **183:** Bruce Brown; **188:** Tom Servais; **191:** Leroy Grannis; **192:** Tom Servais; **194:** *Surfer* Magazine Collection; **197:** Tom Servais; **200:** *Surfer* Magazine Collection; **201:** *Surfer* Magazine Collection; **202:** Jeff Divine; **204:** Tom Servais; **204:** Tom Servais; **206:** Tom Servais; **207:** Jeff Divine; **208:** Tom Servais; **209:** Tom Servais; **212:** Craig Peterson; **214:** Tom Servais; **215:** Witt Family Collection; **217:** *Surfer* Magazine Collection; **220:** Jeff Divine; **223:** Tom Servais; **228:** Jeff Divine; **230:** Jeff Divine; **231:** Jeff Divine; **235:** *Surfer* Magazine Collection; **237:** *Surfer* Magazine Collection; **238:** Jeff Divine; **240:** Tom Servais; **243:** Jeff Divine; **245:** Ron Stoner photograph/courtesy *Surfer* Magazine Collection; **246:** Tom Servais; **248:** Tom Servais; **250:** Tom Servais; **252:** Craig Stecyk/courtesy *The Surfer's Journal*; **257:** Jeff Divine; **258:** John "Doc" Ball; **259:** Leroy Grannis; **262:** Tom Servais; **263:** Tom Servais; **266:** Leroy Grannis; **268:** Jeff Divine; **270:** *Surfer* Magazine Collection; **272:** Jeff Divine; **273:** Jeff Divine; **274:** Matty Thomas; **278:** *Surfer* Magazine Collection; **284:** Tom Servais; **286:** Jeff Divine; **288:** Jeff Divine; **295:** Tom Servais; **297:** Alessandro Dini; **302:** Tom Servais; **303:** Jeff Divine; **307:** Jeff Divine; **308:** Hawaii State Archives/Used with permission of Malama Ponu, Ltd. **311:** Jeff Divine; **312:** Jeff Divine; **313:** Jeff Divine; **316:** Tom Servais; **317:** *Surfer* Magazine Collection; **319:** Tom Servais; **320:** Tom Servais; **323:** Tom Servais; **324** (top): Tom Servais; **324** (bottom): Jeff Divine; **326:** Jeff Divine; **328:** Bob Penuelas; **331:** Tom Servais; **334:** Jeff Divine; **336:** Craig Peterson; **337:** Jeff Divine; **339:** Tom Servais; **340:** Jeff Divine; **345:** Jeff Divine; **348:** Tom Servais; **354:** Tom Servais; **357:** Leroy Grannis; **360:** Leroy Grannis; **363:** Jeff Divine; **368:** Dan Gross; **370:** Patrick Trefz; **377:** Ron Stoner photograph/courtesy of *Surfer* Magazine Collection; **380:** Tom Servais; **382:** Matt George; **384:** Jeff Divine; **385:** John Milius; **388:** Leroy Grannis; **392:** *Surfer* Magazine Collection; **396:** Jeff Divine; **398:** Rick Griffin; **404:** Jeff Divine; **406:** Dick Meseroll; **409:** Rob Gilley;

413: *Surfer* Magazine Collection; **417:** Jeff Divine; **422:** *Surfer* Magazine Collection; **425:** Tom Servais; **427:** Jeff Divine; **429:** Tom Servais; **432:** Jeff Divine; **433:** Jeff Divine; **437:** Grant Ellis; **442:** Tom Servais; **443:** Jeff Divine; **445:** John "Doc" Ball; **448:** Tom Servais; **451:** Greg MacGillivray; **453:** Tom Servais; **461:** Jose Lavalle; **462:** Ron Perrott; **463:** Jeff Divine; **465:** Jeff Divine; **466:** Jack "Woody" Ekstrom; **470:** Peter French; **473:** Jeff Divine; **475:** Tom Servais; **477:** Rob Gilley; **480:** Leroy Grannis; **485:** *Surfer* Magazine Collection; **493:** Tom Servais; **497:** Jeff Divine; **498:** Tom Servais; **501:** Jeff Divine; **502:** Tom Servais; **503:** *Surfer* Magazine Collection; **504:** Jeff Divine; **507:** Jeff Divine; **510:** Tom Servais; **512:** Brad Barrett; **515:** Jeff Divine; **517:** Jeff Divine; **525:** Jeff Divine; **526:** Rob Gilley; **527:** Bruce Walker; **529:** Philippe Chvodian; **530:** *Surfer* Magazine Collection; **533:** Jeff Divine; **536:** *Surfer* Magazine Collection; **539:** Jeff Divine; **540:** The Silver Surfer TM & © 2003 Marvel Characters, Inc. Used with permission; **541:** John Larronde; **542:** *Surfer* Magazine Collection; **544:** Jeff Divine; **547:** Tom Servais; **550:** Tom Servais; **552:** Jeff Divine; **558:** Tom Servais; **559:** Jeff Divine; **564:** Jeff Divine; **565:** Leroy Grannis; **567:** Peter Crawford; **568:** Doug Wilson; **569:** Jeff Divine; **571:** James Cassimus; **573:** Jeff Divine; **574:** Mark Sutherland; **577:** Jeff Divine; **580:** Tom Servais; **587:** Tom Servais; **589:** Tony Roberts/Richard Schmidt surf school; **597:** Jeff Divine; **599:** *Surfer* Magazine Collection; **614:** Leroy Grannis; **616:** *Surfer* Magazine Collection; **617:** Leroy Grannis; **619:** Dutch Vandervoot; **624:** Brad Barrett; **627:** Tom Servais; **629:** *Surfer* Magazine Collection; **630:** Tom Servais; **631:** Tom Servais; **632:** Tom Servais; **636:** Jeff Divine; **639:** Jeff Divine; **641:** Jeff Divine; **643:** Tom Servais; **645:** Jeff Divine; **648:** *Surfer* Magazine Collection; **652:** Brad Barrett; **654:** Jeff Divine; **656:** Tom Servais; **659:** Jeff Divine; **664:** Bud Browne; **665:** *Surfer* Magazine Collection; **668:** Craig Stecyk/ courtesy *The Surfer's Journal;* **670:** Jeff Divine; **672:** *Surfer* Magazine Collection; **676:** *Surfer* Magazine Collection; **677:** Ron Church; **679:** Zoetrope Studios; **684:** Jeff Divine; **687:** Leroy Grannis; **689:** Jeff Divine; **693:** *Surfer* Magazine Collection; **696:** Dick Metz; **697:** Tom Servais; **698:** Jeff Divine; **699:** Jeff Divine; **702:** Tom Servais; **703:** *Surfer* Magazine Collection; **707:** Tom Servais; **708:** *Surfer* Magazine Collection; **712:** Greg Noll; **713:** Leroy Grannis; **718:** *Surfer* Magazine Collection; **720:** *Surfer* Magazine Collection; **723:** Jeff Divine.